Financial
Management
Principles and applications
6th edition

Financial
Management
Principles and applications
6th edition

Taking the 10 principles of finance one step further!

J WILLIAM PETTY • SHERIDAN TITMAN • ARTHUR J KEOWN • JOHN D MARTIN

PETER MARTIN • MICHAEL BURROW • HOA NGUYEN

Copyright © Pearson Australia (a division of Pearson Australia Group Pty Ltd) 2012

Pearson Australia
Unit 4, Level 3
14 Aquatic Drive
Frenchs Forest NSW 2086

www.pearson.com.au

Authorised adaptation from the United States edition entitled *Financial Management: Principles and Applications*, 11th edition, ISBN 0132340356 by Titman, Sheridan; Martin, Joh H.; Keown, Arthur J., published by Pearson Education, Inc., publishing as Prentice Hall, Copyright © 2011.

Sixth adaptation edition published by Pearson Australia Group Pty Ltd, Copyright © 2012

Senior Acquisitions Editor: Karen Hutchings
Senior Project Editor: Sandra Goodall
Development Editor: Nicola Poole
Editorial Coordinator: Aida Reyes
Production Controller: Barbara Honor
Copy Editor: Kathryn Lamberton
Proofreader: Nicole Le Grand
Indexer: Michael Ramsden
Cover and internal design by Liz Nicholson, design BITE
Cover photograph © Andrey Armyagov/Dreamstime
Typeset by Midland Typesetters, Australia

Printed in China (CTPS/05)

5 16 15 14

National Library of Australia
Cataloguing-in-Publication Data

Title:	Financial management : principles and applications / J. William Petty ... [et al.]
Edition:	6th ed.
ISBN:	9781442539174 (pbk.)
Notes:	Includes bibliographical references and index.
Subjects:	Corporations—Australia—Finance.
	Business enterprises—Australia—Finance.

Other Authors/Contributors: Petty, J. William, 1942–
Dewey Number: 658.150994

PEARSON AUSTRALIA
is a division of

Brief contents

Detailed Contents

Chapter 22: Mergers and acquisitions

(available online at: www.pearson.com.au/9781442539174)

APPENDIXES

The 10 basic principles of finance

The fundamental principles that drive the practice of corporate finance are presented in the form of 10 principles. These principles appear throughout the text in short inserts called 'Back to the principles' which serve to refocus the student's attention on the underlying principles behind what is being discussed. In effect, they serve to keep the student from becoming so wrapped up in specific calculations that the interrelationships and overall scheme are lost. A detailed description of each principle can be found in Chapter 1.

PRINCIPLE 1 The risk–return trade-off—we won't take on additional risk unless we expect to be compensated with additional return.

PRINCIPLE 2 The time value of money—a dollar received today is worth more than a dollar received in the future.

PRINCIPLE 3 Cash—not profits—is king.

PRINCIPLE 4 Incremental cash flows—it's only what changes that counts.

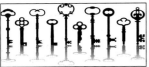

PRINCIPLE 5 The curse of competitive markets—why it's hard to find exceptionally profitable projects.

PRINCIPLE 6 Efficient capital markets—the markets are quick and the prices are right.

PRINCIPLE 7 The agency problem—managers won't work for owners unless it's in their best interest.

PRINCIPLE 8 Taxes bias business decisions.

PRINCIPLE 9 All risk is not equal—some risk can be diversified away, and some cannot.

PRINCIPLE 10 Ethical behaviour is doing the right thing, and ethical dilemmas are everywhere in finance.

These days it is all too easy for students to lose sight of the logic that drives finance and to focus instead on memorising formulae and procedures. As a result, students have a difficult time understanding the interrelationships between the topics covered in a textbook for a first course in finance. Moreover, later in life when the problems encountered do not fit neatly into the textbook presentation, the student may have problems abstracting from what was learnt. To overcome this problem, the opening chapter presents **10 basic principles of finance** that are woven throughout the book.

What results is a text tightly bound around these guiding principles. In essence, the student is presented with a cohesive, interrelated perspective from which future problems, as yet unknown, can be approached.

Teaching an introductory finance class while faced with an ever-expanding discipline puts additional pressures on the instructor. What to cover, what to omit, and how to make these decisions while maintaining a coherent presentation are inescapable questions. In dealing with these questions, the chapters have been presented in a stand-alone fashion so that they can easily be rearranged to fit almost any course structure and course length. Because the principles are woven into every chapter, the presentation of the text remains tight regardless of the order in which the chapters are used. Again, our goal is to facilitate an enduring understanding of the basic tools of finance and the fundamental principles on which finance is based. This will give a student beginning his or her studies in finance a strong base on which to build future studies and will give the student who takes only one finance class a lasting understanding of the basics of finance.

Although historical circumstances continue to serve as the driving force behind the development and practice of finance, the underlying principles that guide the discipline remain the same. With a focus on the big picture, we provide an introduction to financial decision making rooted in current financial theory and current world economic conditions. This focus can be seen in a number of ways, perhaps the most obvious being the attention paid to both valuation and the capital markets, and their influence on corporate financial decisions.

What results is an introductory treatment of a discipline rather than the treatment of a series of isolated finance problems. The goal of this text is to go beyond teaching the tools of a discipline or a trade and help students gain a complete understanding of the subject. This will give them the ability to apply what they have learnt to new and as yet unforeseen problems—in short, to educate students in finance.

New to this edition

In addition to updating and streamlining the material, the following major additions have been made to *Financial Management*:

- **NEW** *Regardless of your program* feature relates financial management content to other business majors and non-finance-related careers.
- **NEW** *Global Financial Crisis* feature examines the nature of the GFC and discusses the ongoing effects it has on the world today.
- **NEW** *Your Money* feature delivers a personal note on financial management and the many facets of life it may apply to.
- Chapter 9 includes expanded coverage of applying the capital asset pricing model to determining investors' required rates of return.
- Chapter 16 is revised and renamed to reflect capital-structure-policy decision making.

A note about the Tax Brackets included in this text

Due to the variable nature of the Australian Tax Brackets, examples included in this text may not be up to date with the current brackets. The brackets used in this text are intended as workable examples for the reader. To find the most recent tax brackets applicable please visit: **www.ato.gov.au/individuals/content.asp?doc=/content/12333.htm**.

Acknowledgements

We gratefully acknowledge the assistance, support and encouragement of our academic and administrative colleagues who have helped in the preparation of *Financial Management*. Particular thanks are owed to a number of users of the 5th edition who provided valuable feedback on the content and arrangement of the text and so influenced the writing of this new edition. Their names are listed on page xv.

We also sincerely thank the editorial and production staff at Pearson Australia, notably Karen Hutchings, Nicola Poole and Sandra Goodall, for their help and encouragement. Special thanks are also due to Kathryn Lamberton for her sterling efforts in editing the text and to Liz Nicholson of design BITE for her outstanding text design.

Peter Martin
Michael Burrow
Hoa Nguyen

Visual preface

The authors realise that each course in finance is unique, as is each student's learning style and experience. With this in mind, the 6th edition of *Financial Management* provides an approach to learning that is adaptable to specific needs, with the inclusion of a number of new features to assist both the teacher and the student.

LEARNING OBJECTIVES
These are stated at the beginning of each chapter, then revisited throughout. This provides an excellent revision tool for students.

REGARDLESS OF YOUR PROGRAM
This new feature illustrates the relevance of financial management and how it may apply to other areas of study and employment.

KEY TERMS
Definitions of key terms are provided in the margin close to the relevant text.

FYI
These short sections emphasise important concepts.

GFC
The so-called GFC (Global Financial Crisis) sent many of the world's financial markets tumbling in 2007–08, with repercussions still continuing four years later. Most chapters relate the GFC to the chapter material so that a comprehensive overview is provided of many of the GFC's different facets and implications for finance.

FINANCE AT WORK

To add relevance and immediacy to the conceptual coverage, 'Finance at Work' boxes are provided throughout the text, drawing attention to real-life applications of the principles discussed.

INTERNATIONAL SPOTLIGHT

Examples of international finance highlight the continued globalisation of world markets.

ONE STEP FURTHER

For the inquisitive student who wants to know more than the 'basics', the 'One Step Further' boxes extend the discussions.

YOUR MONEY

This new feature looks at practical situations students may come across during their everyday lives where knowing how to make the right financial decisions will be beneficial.

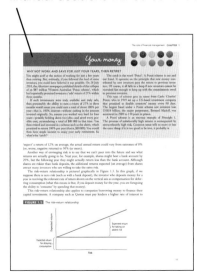

WEB WORKS

These end-of-chapter exercises introduce the student to useful information on the Internet, guiding them to information and data that make financial topics and concepts come alive.

Teaching tools for instructors

INSTRUCTOR'S MANUAL

This comprehensive teaching resource contains three key elements for each chapter:

1. A chapter orientation, which offers the instructor a simple statement of the authors' intent for the chapter.
2. A chapter outline for easy reference to key issues.
3. Answers to all end-of-chapter questions in the text.

COMPUTERISED TEST BANK

Each test-bank chapter contains a substantial number of true–false, multiple-choice, short-answer essay and matching questions. All questions have solutions, and the multiple-choice questions have been graded according to levels of difficulty.

POWERPOINT SLIDES

To facilitate classroom presentation, a full set of PowerPoint slides is available in Windows format. The slides have been completely revised and updated, and are available (along with all other instructor resources) online at **www.pearson. com.au/9781442539174**.

Learning tools for students

MYFINANCELAB
www.pearson.com.au/myfinancelab

MyFinanceLab is a fully integrated homework and tutorial system which solves one of the biggest teaching dilemmas in finance courses: students learn better when they practise by doing homework problems, but grading complex multi-part problems is time consuming for their lecturers. *MyFinanceLab* offers problems online, algorithmically generates values for extra practice, gives partial credit for sections of the questions students do get right, and includes an online grade book. Students can take pre-loaded Sample Tests for each chapter, and their test results will generate an individualised Study Plan. With the Study Plan, students learn to focus their energies on the topics they need to revise in order to be successful in class and in exams. Students who consistently make use of the Lab resource have reported increased grades and pass rates in their finance subjects.

MyFinanceLab author

The Australian adaptation of *MyFinanceLab* to accompany *Financial Management*, 6th edition, is authored by Tony Martin, La Trobe University. Tony holds a BSc in Computer Science from Monash University and an MFin from RMIT University. He has worked for many years on the development of online testing and the provision of online educational resources. His teaching focus is on introductory finance and financial institutions, and his research interests include equity markets, technical analysis and the use of generic algorithms in the creation of teaching strategies. Tony has previously authored *MyFinanceLab* content for Pearson to accompany first-year texts by Gitman, Berk & deMarzo and Frino, as well as the previous edition of Petty.

MyFinanceLab—for students

Instructors may choose to have the Petty *Financial Management* textbook packaged with access to *MyFinanceLab*, Pearson's online homework, testing and tutorial system. If their textbook came bundled with a *MyFinanceLab* access code, students may refer to the access card for registration instructions. If students are buying a second-hand copy of the text and/or their instructor did not choose to have the text and access card packaged together, access cards may be purchased online either as Lab and e-book access or Lab alone. Access codes may be purchased at: www.pearson.com. au/myfinancelab.

VitalSource

VitalSource is a downloadable e-book that can be used on computers and/or iPhone/iPad devices and is also accessible offline through the VitalSource Bookshelf. Students can search for key concepts, words and phrases; highlight and make notes as they study; share notes with friends; and print out five pages at a time from this digital version of the text. Upon purchasing a Pearson VitalSource eText access code, students will receive instructions on how to redeem this code and download the Pearson VitalSource eText. VitalSource text access codes can be purchased at: www. mypearsonstore.com.au/vitalsource.

Content consultants

The authors and publisher wish to acknowledge the work of Chris Deeley, Charles Sturt University, Toomas Truuvert, Macquarie University, and Kim Hawtrey, Hope College, in the developmental stages of the 6th edition of *Financial Management*. Their detailed feedback and suggestions have been invaluable in assisting the author team prepare this new edition.

Chris Deeley joined Charles Sturt University as a senior lecturer in accounting and finance in 1991. His research interests focus on capital structure theory, superannuation and accounting for income tax.

Toomas Truuvert has been a lecturer in finance at Macquarie University, Department of Accounting and Finance, since 2001. His special research interest is in corporate finance.

Kim Hawtrey is a Professor of Economics currently at Hope College, Holland, Michigan, USA. Kim is a Senior Fellow of the Financial Services Institute of Australia (FINSIA) and has received the international Pearson Finance Teacher Award, as well as the national Carrick Award from the Australian Federal Government.

Reviewers

Reviewers for this edition include:
Alex Proimos, Macquarie University
Dr Lalith Seelanatha, Victoria University
Larry O'Connor, La Trobe University
Dr Laurie Prather, Bond University
Marion Griffiths, Murdoch University
Phillip Minca, Central Queensland University
Associate Professor Sarath Depalchitra, Flinders University
Dr Sisira Colombage, Monash University
Tony Stanger, University of Tasmania
Dr Vijaya Thyil, Deakin University
Dr Lisa Barnes, The University of Newcastle
Brenton Price, University of Southern Queensland
Dr Jennifer Harrison, Southern Cross University
Peter Lennox, University of South Australia
Dr Kym Frawer, University of South Australia
Ben Jacobsen, James Cook University
Dr Mirela Malin, Griffith University
Stephen Sweeney, University of Ballarat
Dr Bulend Terzioglu, Australian Catholic University
Shagun Khemka, University of Ballarat
Dr Mary Dunkley, Swinburne University

About the Australian authors

Peter Martin is former head of the School of Economics and Finance at the University of South Australia. He teaches a number of postgraduate finance courses and has interests in risk management and the interface between finance and accounting for financial instruments.

Dr Michael Burrow is a senior lecturer in the School of Commerce at the University of South Australia. He teaches both undergraduate and postgraduate finance courses and his current research interest focuses on the financing and financial management of small and medium-sized businesses.

Dr Hoa Nguyen is a senior lecturer in the School of Accounting, Economics and Finance at Deakin University. She has extensive teaching experience in corporate finance and risk management. Her research interests include financial derivatives, corporate risk management and recently IPOs.

Photo credits

Scope and environment of financial management

1 The role of financial management

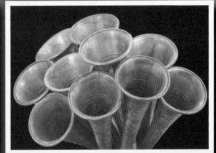

2 The tax environment

3 The financial markets

4 The time value of money

Learning objectives

After reading this chapter, you should be able to:

1 Describe what the subject of financial management is about and why it is studied.

2 Compare the three typical forms of business and explain why the company is the most logical choice for a firm that is large or growing.

3 Understand the goal of the financial manager.

4 Explain the 10 principles that form the basis for financial management.

5 Identify what has led to the era of the multinational corporation.

6 Appreciate some of the themes associated with the Global Financial Crisis and its aftermath.

For a complete eBook go to MyFinanceLab
www.pearson.com.au/myfinancelab

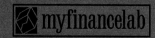

The role of financial management

chapter 1

CHAPTER PREVIEW

This chapter lays the foundation for the entire book. It explains what financial management is, and explains the key goal that guides financial decision making: the maximisation of shareholder wealth. The legal environment of financial decisions is examined, and then the golden thread that ties everything together is described: the 10 basic principles of finance. Finally, the chapter discusses the importance of looking beyond our geographic boundaries, including an outline of some facets of the Global Financial Crisis (GFC).

What is financial management?

OBJECTIVE 1

Describe what the subject of financial management is about and why it is studied.

Financial management is the study of how people and businesses evaluate investments and raise funds to finance them. Our interpretation of an investment is quite broad. When Apple first launched its iPhone, it was clearly making a long-term investment. The firm had to devote considerable expense to designing, producing and marketing the mobile phone with the hope that it would eventually pay off and make the investment worthwhile. In a completely different industry, the giant firm of BHP-Billiton also makes an investment decision whenever it starts up a new mining venture. But the scale of investment does not have to be as large as that—every time such a firm recruits a new graduate, it is making an investment, not only in recruitment and training costs but also knowing that it will be paying a salary for at least six months before the employee will have much to contribute.

Thus, there are three basic questions that are addressed by the study of financial management:

1. **What long-term investments should the firm undertake?** This area of finance is generally referred to as *capital budgeting*.
2. **How should the firm raise money to fund these investments?** The firm's funding choices are generally referred to as *capital structure* decisions.
3. **How can the firm best manage its cash flows as they arise in its day-to-day operations?** This area of finance is generally referred to as *working-capital management*.

We'll be looking at each of these three areas of business finance—capital budgeting, capital structure, and working-capital management—in the chapters ahead.

Why study financial management?

Even if you are not planning a career in financial management, a working knowledge of finance will take you far in both your personal and professional life. Accountants often span both finance and accounting and have a role to play in major financial decisions. In large organisations, there may be the scope for both finance specialists and accounting specialists, but in smaller and medium enterprises the roles become blurred and the accountant is often called upon to be the finance expert too.

Those interested in management will need to study topics such as strategic planning, which involves spending money today in the hope of generating more money in the future. For example, GMH (General Motors-Holden) made a strategic decision in 2010 to build the Holden Cruze, a four-cylinder motor car, in Australia. This recognised the falling demand for larger motor vehicles of the type that had been traditionally manufactured in this country. Around the same time, Toyota decided to produce a hybrid-technology Camry (part electric motor, part internal combustion engine), thus acknowledging the strategic imperative to 'go green'.

Similarly, marketing practitioners seek to understand and decide how aggressively to price products and how much to spend on advertising those products. This is important because aggressive marketing costs money today, but generates rewards in the future. Logistics and operations managers, too, need to understand how best to manage a firm's production and control its inventory and supply chain. These are all topics that involve risky choices that relate to the management of money over time, which is the central focus of finance.

A key component of finance is the management and interpretation of information. Indeed, if you pursue a career in management information systems or accounting, the finance managers are likely to be your most important clients.

For the student with entrepreneurial aspirations, an understanding of finance is essential— after all, if you can't manage your finances, you won't be in business very long.

Finally, an understanding of finance is important to you as an individual. The fact that you are reading this book indicates that you understand the importance of investing in yourself. By obtaining a university degree, you are clearly making an investment in your education in the expectation that it will bring benefits in the future, such as employability and career achievements. Some of you are relying on your own earnings and the earnings of your parents to finance your education, whereas others are 'borrowing' from the government via the HEC scheme or from the **financial markets** via institutions such as banks that facilitate financial transactions. Thus, financial decisions are everywhere, both in your personal life and in your career.

Although the primary focus of this book is on developing the corporate finance tools and techniques that are used in the business world, you will find that much of the logic and many of the tools we develop and explore along the way will also apply to decisions you will be making in your own personal life.

Regardless of your program

For the rest of your life, you will be both working and living in a world where you will be making choices that have financial consequences. Businesses make money by introducing new products, opening new sales outlets, hiring the best people and improving their productivity. All of these actions involve investing or spending money today with the hope of generating more money in the future. Regardless of your program, after graduation you are likely to be working for an organisation where your choices have uncertain costs and benefits, both then and in the future. This will be the case if you are working for a major company such as Telstra, starting your own firm, or working for a non-profit organisation such as a hospital. Moreover, you will be faced with a variety of personal choices—whether you can afford a new car or a house mortgage, or how much to begin investing in a retirement fund. These choices will require you to evaluate alternatives that involve uncertain future payoffs. Regardless of your program, there is simply no getting around the fact that you will be making financial choices throughout your life.

Three types of business organisation

The chapters ahead focus mainly on financial decisions for companies (corporations). Although the company is not the only legal form of business, it is the most logical choice for a firm that is large or growing. It is also the dominant business form in terms of numbers of business entities and sales turnover. This section explains why this is so.

There are three basic categories of business organisation: the sole proprietorship, the partnership and the company. To understand the basic differences between each form, each one needs to be defined and its advantages and disadvantages understood. As will be seen, as the firm grows, the advantages of the company form begin to dominate. As a result, most large firms take on this form.

Compare the three typical forms of business and explain why the company is the most logical choice for a firm that is large or growing.

SOLE PROPRIETORSHIP

A **sole proprietorship** is a business owned by a single individual. The owner maintains title to the assets and is personally responsible, generally without limitation, for the debts incurred. The proprietor is entitled to the profits from the business but must also absorb any losses. However, these organisations typically have limited access to outside sources of financing. The owners of a sole proprietorship typically raise money by investing their own funds and by borrowing from a bank. But, since there is no legal difference between the sole proprietor and the business he or she runs, there is no distinction between personal borrowing and business borrowing. In addition to banks, personal loans from friends and family are important sources of financing.

sole proprietorship
A business owned by a single individual.

This form of business is initiated merely by the proprietor starting business operations, particularly if the proprietor is conducting the business in his or her own name. If a special name is used, this name should be registered, and a small registration fee is required. The choice of name is restricted to one that is not misleading or offensive or could not be confused with an existing name. Once the name is accepted, a certificate, which is generally renewable every three years, is issued. Termination of the registered name occurs on the owner's death or by the owner's choice. Briefly stated, the sole proprietorship features, for all practical purposes, the absence of any formal *legal* business structure.

PARTNERSHIP

The primary difference between a partnership and a sole proprietorship is that the partnership has more than one owner. This means that the business may have access to more owners' funding than from a sole proprietorship and also a wider span of managerial and professional expertise than is possessed by one person. Often, therefore, partnerships are used by professional firms, such as accountants, lawyers, doctors, architects and engineers.

Legally, a **partnership** is an association of two or more persons carrying on a business in common for profit. In a partnership each partner is jointly and severally[1] responsible for the liabilities incurred by the partnership.[2] Also, if any partner is responsible for ill conduct, this renders the other partners liable too if the conduct appears to relate to the business. The relationship between partners is dictated entirely by the partnership agreement, which may be an oral commitment or a formal document.

partnership
An association of two or more individuals joining together as co-owners to operate a business for profit.

In the absence of a formal agreement between the partners, common law and state legislation specify the rights and obligations of the partners. Generally, the partners should draft a written agreement that explicitly sets forth the basic relationships within the firm. At a minimum, the agreement should include the nature and amount of capital to be invested by each partner, the authority of the individual partners, the means for determining how profits and losses are to be shared, the duration of the partnership, the procedures for admitting a new partner, and the method for terminating or reformulating the partnership in the event of a partner's death or withdrawal from the partnership. It is essential to include any important terms in the agreement in order to minimise later misunderstandings.

COMPANY

company
An entity that *legally* functions separately and apart from its owners.

The idea of a **company** is that it is a distinct and separate legal entity, created as an 'artificial being'. Thus, it can own assets and incur debts in its own name, independently of its owners (its shareholders). The creation of the legal concept of a company goes back about two centuries, an example of the idea: 'necessity is the mother of invention'. In this case, the 'necessity' was the industrial revolution and its aftermath, which gave rise to the need for funding that is beyond the scope of small businesses owned by sole proprietors or partners. In response, the 'invention' was a new legal entity that made it easier for the business to amass large amounts of funding and to grow. Thus, the company has been a significant factor in the economic development of countries such as Australia.

The legal innovation that distinguishes a company from other forms of ownership is that the entity functions separately and apart from its owners; that is, a company may operate a business in its own right. As such, the company can individually sue and be sued, and acquire assets and commit itself to liabilities. However, despite this legal separation, the company is composed of owners who dictate its direction and policies. The owners elect a board of directors, whose members in turn appoint individuals to serve as the corporate officers, including the CEO. Ownership is reflected by share certificates designating the number of shares owned by the holder. The number of shares owned relative to the total number of shares issued determines the shareholder's proportionate ownership in the company. Since the shares are generally transferable, ownership in a company may be changed by a shareholder simply remitting the shares to the new shareholder, following which the company's share register is updated.

The shareholder's liability is generally limited to the amount of his or her investment in the company, thereby preventing creditors from accessing the shareholder's personal assets in settlement of the company's debts. However, directors of a company are now personally liable if they allow a company to trade while it is insolvent or if they do not comply properly with their responsibilities as managers. Finally, the life of a company is not dependent on the status of the investors. The death or withdrawal of an investor does not affect the continuity of the company. In Australia all companies are subject to the statutory provisions of the Commonwealth *Corporations Act 2001*, enforced by the Australian Securities and Investments Commission (ASIC).

Within the above general description of companies, a distinction can be made between *limited* companies (which have the title Limited, abbreviated to Ltd, appended to the company name) and *proprietary limited* (Pty Ltd) companies. Limited companies are generally public companies whose shares may be listed on a stock exchange, ownership in such shares being transferable by public sale through the exchange. For listed companies, there is a ready measure of shareholder wealth, the current share price, which represents investors' views of the quality of performance of the firm and the quality of its decisions. In contrast, proprietary limited companies are basically private entities, as the shares can only be transferred privately; for this type of firm, shareholder wealth is not so readily measurable, being put to the test only when shares are sold or the firm[3] is sold as a going concern.[4]

COMPARISON OF ORGANISATIONAL FORMS

Business owners have some important decisions to make in choosing an organisational form. Whereas each business form has its merits, the company has major advantages as the firm grows and thus needs to attract additional funding, which can be accessed from external investors (or lenders) in the capital markets.

limited liability
Ordinarily, company shareholders are not liable for the debts of the company.

Because of **limited liability**, as well as the flexibility in dividing the shares (and the ease of transferring ownership through the sale of the shares), companies can pool the funds of large numbers of individual investors. Thus, the corporation is the ideal business entity in terms of attracting new capital, which makes it appealing to large and growing firms. In contrast, sole proprietors and partners generally have unlimited liability, which is a major deterrent to raising capital for those owners. Therefore, when developing decision models in later chapters, it will be assumed that we are dealing with the corporate form of ownership. Similarly, the emphasis will be on the tax treatment that applies to companies, in terms of the impact of taxation on financial decision making.

HOW DOES FINANCIAL MANAGEMENT FIT INTO THE FIRM'S ORGANISATION STRUCTURE?

The development of the company as the dominant type of business organisation for large firms goes hand in hand with the creation of the management profession. Large and medium-sized companies may have boards of directors who represent the firm's owners (shareholders) in terms of major policy decisions and strategies, but day-to-day operations necessitate the use of managers to take responsibility for running the firm. One such manager is the 'financial manager', the person who is appointed to manage and oversee the finance function in the firm.

Financial management is woven intimately into any aspect of the business that involves the payment or receipt of money. However, within the large firm the primary responsibility for the finance function lies with a manager who is often titled 'Chief Financial Officer' (CFO). Figure 1.1 presents a typical representation of how the finance area fits into a firm's structure. The CFO serves under the firm's Chief Executive Officer (CEO). The CFO is responsible for overseeing financial planning and corporate strategic planning, and controlling the firm's cash flow. Typically, a Treasurer and a Financial Controller serve under the CFO. In a smaller firm, the same person may fill both roles. The Treasurer generally handles the cash and credit management, making capital expenditure decisions, raising funds, financial planning, and managing any foreign currency. The Financial Controller is responsible for managing the firm's accounting duties, including producing financial statements, cost accounting, paying taxes, and gathering and monitoring the data necessary to oversee the firm's financial well-being. In this text, the focus is on the duties of the Treasurer.

FIGURE 1.1   How the finance area fits into a company structure

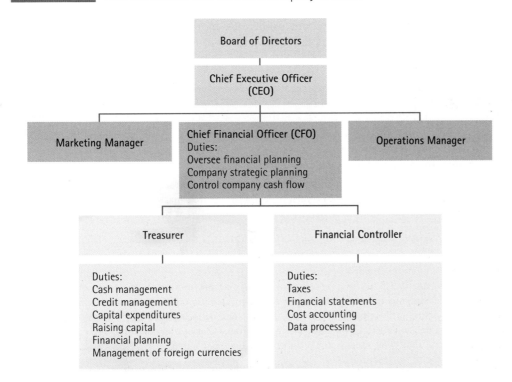

Concept check

1.1   What are the primary differences between a sole proprietorship, a partnership and a company?

1.2   Explain why large and growing firms tend to choose the company form of legal organisation.

1.3   What are the duties of the Treasurer? Of the Financial Controller?

For answers go to MyFinanceLab or
www.pearson.com.au/9781442539174

OBJECTIVE **3**

Understand the goal of the financial manager.

The goal of the financial manager

In 2001, in the USA, Tony Fadell turned to the Apple Corporation to develop his idea for a new MP3 player. Fadell's idea had already been rejected by his previous employer and another company, but the executives at Apple were enthusiastic about the idea of the new iPod MP3 player. They hired Fadell, and the rest is history. The successful sales of the iPod, coupled with efficient uses of financing and day-to-day funding, raised the firm's share price. This exemplifies how a management team (appointed by a company's board of directors) made an important investment decision that had a very positive effect on the value of the firm to its shareholders.

As mentioned previously, we can characterise the financial activities of a firm's management in terms of three important functions within a firm:

- *Making investment decisions (capital budgeting decisions):* The decision by Apple to introduce the iPod.
- *Making decisions on how to finance these investments (capital structure decisions):* How to finance the development and production of the iPod.
- *Managing funding for the company's day-to-day operations (working-capital management):* Apple's decision on, for example, how much inventory to hold.

In carrying out the above tasks, the financial managers must be aware that they are ultimately working for the firm's shareholders, who are the owners of the firm, and that the choices they make as financial managers will affect shareholders' wealth.

MAXIMISING SHAREHOLDER WEALTH

Although many firms talk generally about 'profits', it is more realistic to say that the goal of the firm is to maximise shareholder wealth. In effect, this means maximisation of the market value

FYI

CONFLICT BETWEEN THE FIRM'S GOAL AND THAT OF THE WIDER SOCIETY

One of the acknowledged problems of leaving firms to their own devices, free to maximise wealth, is that many of the harmful consequences of business decisions are not 'priced' within free markets. For example, if a firm causes pollution, the business does not pay the price unless sufferers can take successful legal action; this is often difficult because of the problem of proving cause and effect, not to mention the discrepancy between the funds at a large company's disposal to employ lawyers compared with those of an individual in the community. Thus, the social cost of an activity such as pollution is greater than the private cost. As a consequence, the goods produced are underpriced, in the sense that consumers do not pay the 'true' cost to society, and therefore resources may be allocated inefficiently, rather than efficiently, as theorists claim, in favour of free markets. Another aspect is that shareholders may gain wealth at the expense of others, because company profits are built on situations where the firm does not pay the true cost of the resources it consumes. It is the view of the authors of this text that the appropriate action to overcome this potential discrepancy between private cost and social cost is for governments to take action in the form of taxes and subsidies—taxes on activities that cause social harm, such as cigarette smoking, and subsidies that direct firms to use technologies and processes that are less harmful, such as subsidies for producing 'clean' electricity.

of the existing shareholders' ordinary shares. We will see, as this book unfolds, that all financial decisions can be incorporated into this goal. Investors react to poor investment decisions or poor financing decisions by causing the total value of the firm's shares to fall, and they react to good decisions by pushing up the price of the shares. In effect, under this goal, good decisions are those that create wealth for the shareholder.

The market price of the firm's shares reflects the value of the firm as seen by its owners and takes into account the complexities and complications of the real world. As we follow this goal throughout this book, we must keep in mind (just as the finance manager must keep in mind) that the shareholders are the legal owners of the firm.

INTERACTION BETWEEN THE COMPANY AND THE FINANCIAL MARKETS

Without question, the ease of raising capital is the major reason for the popularity of the company or corporation as the structure of choice for large firms. While the process of raising capital is looked at in more detail in Chapters 3, 18 and 19, let's spend a moment looking at the flow of capital through the financial markets, between the company, individuals and the government. Figure 1.2 examines these flows. (1) Initially, the company raises funds in the financial markets by selling securities such as shares and debt. The company receives cash in return for these securities. (2) The company then invests this cash in return-generating assets, such as new capital investment projects. (3) After paying the necessary taxes to the government, the remaining cash flow generated by those assets can be reinvested in the company (retained profits), given back to the investors in the form of dividends and interest payments, or used to repurchase shares.

An important distinction is the difference between primary and secondary markets. To begin with, a securities market is simply a place where you can buy or sell securities. (Securities are the 'instruments' used for borrowing or lending money, such as shares, loans and bonds.) These markets can take the form of anything from an actual building such as the headquarters of the ASX (Australian Securities Exchange) to an electronic hook-up among security dealers all over the world. Securities markets are divided into primary and secondary markets.

A **primary market** is a market in which new securities are traded. This is the only time that the issuing firm actually receives money for its shares. For example, if Telstra issues a new batch of shares, this issue would be considered a primary market transaction. In this case, Telstra

primary market
The segment of the financial markets in which securities are offered for sale for the first time.

FIGURE 1.2 Interaction between a firm and the financial markets

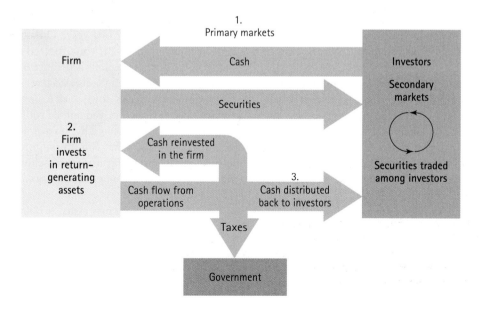

would issue new shares and receive money from investors. Actually, there are two different types of offerings in the primary markets: initial public offerings and seasoned new issues or primary offerings. An **initial public offering (IPO)** (also called a *share 'float'*) is the first time the company's shares are sold to the general public, whereas a **secondary issue** refers to stock offerings by companies that have been floated previously.

Securities that have previously been issued and bought are subsequently traded in the **secondary market**. For example, if you bought 100 shares in an IPO and then wanted to resell them, you would be reselling them in the secondary market. The proceeds from the sale of 100 BHP-Billiton shares in the secondary market go to the previous owner of the shares, not to BHP-Billiton. In other words, the only time BHP-Billiton ever receives money from the sale of one of its securities is in the primary market.

Ten principles that form the basis for financial management

At first glance, financial management can seem like a collection of unrelated decision rules. Nothing could be further from the truth. The logic behind the financial concepts and decisions covered in this book arise from 10 simple principles that can be understood without any prior knowledge of financial management. *However, while it is not necessary to understand finance in order to understand these principles, it is necessary to understand these principles in order to understand financial management.*

Principle 1

The risk–return trade-off—we won't take on additional risk unless we expect to be compensated with additional return.

If you have $10 000 to invest, you could deposit the money for a year in a bank account. Most of us would see this as a safe investment (as long as the bank is well regarded and managed and is monitored and regulated by an appropriate authority). Let's say you could earn 6% interest, so you would expect to get back a total of $10 600 after one year; that is, the return of your investment plus exactly $600 interest.

Alternatively, you could invest the $10 000 by buying the shares in a company listed on the stock exchange. But how much would your investment be worth after one year? On average, you would expect to get back more than on the bank account—after all, if you expected to get back less, you would be rather foolish to buy the shares in the first place. This is because experience tells you that the stock market is risky—for example, if the economy falls into a recession in the coming year, chances are that it will drag your company's shares down with it.

In fact, on average, investors in the Australian share market have received annual returns of about 12%, taken over a very long time. So, presumably this is the reason why, on average, an investor *expects* shares to offer a much greater return than a bank account. But, to reinforce the idea of shares being riskier, on average about one-fifth of the annual returns were below zero (in other words, the rate of return was *negative*), while at the other extreme, almost one-fifth of returns were above 30%.

This simple comparison is an example of Principle 1 at work: investors expect to be compensated with additional returns when they take on more risk. But note again that we are talking about *expected* return—as we have seen, this means that on average the return is higher when greater levels of risk are taken, but the very nature of this risk is that the returns can vary widely. Again returning to the bank versus share investment, the 6% return on the bank deposit is pretty much certain or risk-free. On the other hand, although history suggests that shares

initial public offering (IPO)
The first time the company's stock is sold to the public.

secondary issue
An issue of shares and/or debt by a company other than its first issue or flotation.

secondary market
The segment of the financial markets in which existing securities are bought and sold.

OBJECTIVE

Explain the 10 principles that form the basis for financial management.

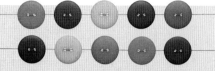

WHY NOT WORK AND SAVE FOR JUST FOUR YEARS, THEN RETIRE?

You might scoff at the notion of working for just a few years then retiring. But, evidently, if you followed the lead of some investors, you could have believed it was possible. On 28 July 2010, the *Advertiser* newspaper published details of the collapse of an $87 million Western Australian 'Ponzi scheme', which had reportedly promised investors a 'safe' return of 25% within three months.

If such investments were truly available and truly safe, then presumably the ability to earn a return of 25% in three months would mean you could earn a total of about 100% per year—that is, 100% interest—without cashing in the amount invested originally. So, assume you worked very hard for four years—possibly holding down two jobs—and saved every possible cent, accumulating a total of $80 000 in that time. You then retired and invested in a scheme such as the above, which promised to return 100% per year (that is, $80 000). You would then have ample income to enjoy your early retirement. So what's the 'catch'?

The catch is the word 'Ponzi'. A Ponzi scheme is out and out fraud. It operates on the principle that new money contributed by new investors pays the return to previous investors. Of course, it all falls in a heap if new investors cannot be recruited fast enough to keep up with the commitments owed to previous investors.

This type of scheme gets its name from Carlo 'Charles' Ponzi, who in 1919 set up a US-based investment company that promised to double investors' money every 90 days. The largest fraud under a Ponzi scheme saw investors lose US$18 billion; the major perpetrator, Bernard Madoff, was sentenced in 2009 to 150 years in prison.

A Ponzi scheme is an extreme example of Principle 1. The promise of unbelievably high returns is accompanied by extraordinarily high risk. Common sense tells us more or less the same thing: if it is too good to be true, it probably is.

'expect' a return of 12% on average, the actual annual return could vary from extremes of 0% (or, worse, negative returns) to 30% (or more).

Another way of envisaging risk is to say that we can't peer into the future and see what returns are actually going to be. Next year, for example, shares might beat a bank account by 20%, but the following year they might actually return less than the bank account. Although shares are riskier than bank deposits, the additional returns expected (on average) from shares attract many investors who are willing to take the extra risk.

The risk–return relationship is pictured graphically in Figure 1.3. In this graph, if we suppose there is zero risk (such as with a bank deposit), the investor who deposits money for a year is receiving the relevant rate of return shown on the vertical axis as compensation for deferring consumption (what this means is that, if you deposit money for the year, you are foregoing the ability to 'consume' by spending that money).

This risk–return relationship also applies to companies borrowing money to finance their capital investments. A company such as Qantas must pay lenders a higher rate of interest to

FIGURE 1.3 The risk–return relationship

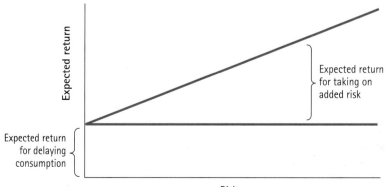

borrow debt than the Australian government pays. The additional interest rate convinces some lenders (or investors) to take on the added risk of lending money to Qantas.

Principle 1 is a key concept that recurs throughout this text when shares, bonds and proposed new projects are valued. Some time will also be spent determining *how* to measure risk. Interestingly, much of the work that led to the award of the 1990 Nobel Prize for Economics centred on the graph in Figure 1.3 and how to measure risk.

Principle 2

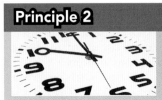

The time value of money—a dollar received today is worth more than a dollar received in the future.

A fundamental concept in finance is the time value of money (TVM), which states that money has a time value associated with it: a dollar received today is worth more than a dollar received a year from now. Because we can earn interest on money received today, it is better to receive money earlier rather than later.

The TVM concept also means that a dollar received in the future is not worth as much as a dollar today. So, if you were offered the choice between $10 000 today and a future sum, you might require the expectation of receiving $11 000 in a year's time to tempt you away from $10 000 today. In this instance, you require a return of 10% on the money, in order to defer its use for the year. The same idea applies to the development of a new car model; hundreds of millions of dollars are outlaid 'today', but it is necessary to achieve sales over a number of future years in order for the investment to be worthwhile. In total, more dollars have to be received in the future than were outlaid upfront because the car maker requires to earn a rate of return on the initial investment—this rate of return reflects the TVM.

Principle 3

Cash—not profits—is king.

When measuring wealth or value, cash flows, not accounting profits, will be used as our measurement tool. That is, we will be concerned with when the money hits our hand, when we can invest it and start earning interest on it, and when we can give it back to the shareholders in the form of dividends. Successful firms may be those that generate high profits, but profits are not the appropriate unit for measuring wealth. Looking at this from a different perspective, investing in new projects requires the company to outlay cash, and so it is logical that the same unit of measurement, cash, should be used to measure future benefits and costs.

Accounting profits, however, are the 'book' figures, not cash flows. Accountants recognise revenues and expenses when they occur rather than when the cash is actually received or paid. This can be seen by looking at Table 1.1, which shows an example of the difference between a period's cash flow and profit that arises because of depreciation expense. The cash outlaid when purchasing new equipment occurs 'upfront'. However, the depreciation expense associated with using this equipment occurs over several years, when the asset is producing income. As seen in Table 1.1, this results in a timing mismatch between cash flows and profits. Similar mismatches occur from accounting transactions such as accruals (revenue that is due but has not yet been received in cash) and prepayments (expenses that have been paid in cash before the due date).

TABLE 1.1 Example of the difference between profit and cash flow

	ACCOUNTING	CASH FLOW
Sales	$90 000	$90 000
Less: Cash expenses	40 000	40 000
Depreciation expense*	20 000	–
Profit	$30 000	
Cash flow		$50 000

* Depreciation expense is a book transfer that does not involve any flow of cash. If you have an accounting background, you will know that the relevant transaction is a debit to the Depreciation Expense account and a credit to Accumulated Depreciation.

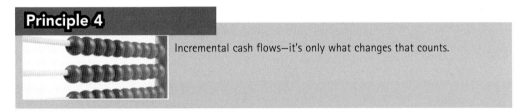

Principle 4

Incremental cash flows—it's only what changes that counts.

When Toyota introduced the latest model of its highly successful Corolla, a company representative announced that some of the buyers of this car would most probably purchase it instead of the larger Camry. In other words, some buyers would see these two cars as substitutes; some would-be Camry buyers would see the smaller, cheaper Corolla as a suitable alternative and switch purchases accordingly. Therefore, the value of the new Corolla to Toyota must take into account not only the benefit in the form of sales of the Corolla but also the 'cost' in the form of the Camry sales that are lost: if 10 sales of the Corolla include 1 buyer who would otherwise have bought a Camry, then the *change* in sales is only 9 cars, which represents the overall incremental benefit of the new model to Toyota.

So, the focus of the finance manager should be on the *incremental* or 'new' cash flows. In the case of the Corolla, only 9 in 10 sales are incremental. In other words, it is the *difference* between the revenues that the Corolla adds to Toyota's operations and the revenues lost by sales of the Camry being diverted to the other car.

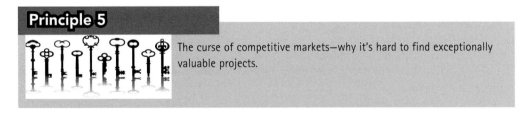

Principle 5

The curse of competitive markets—why it's hard to find exceptionally valuable projects.

The job of finance managers is to create wealth. It is easy when valuing a firm's investment projects to get tied up in the mechanics of identifying future cash flows and so lose sight of the process of creating wealth. This is particularly so when others in the decision-making team expect the finance manager to be expert at 'crunching numbers'.

However, why is it so hard to find projects and investments that are exceptionally beneficial? The answer to this question tells us a lot about how competitive markets operate and where to look for profitable projects. In reality, it is much easier doing the 'number crunching' than actually finding good investment opportunities. If an industry is generating large profits, new entrants are usually attracted. The additional competition and added capacity can result in profits being driven down. Conversely, if an industry is returning very low profits, some participants in the market drop out, reducing capacity and competition. In turn, prices are driven back up. This is precisely what happened in the video-cassette rental market in the mid-1980s. This market developed quickly and with it the opportunity for extremely large profits. Because there were no barriers to entry (no particular qualifications or legal requirements required of video-shop owners), the market was quickly flooded with new entrants. By the late 1980s the competition and price cutting produced losses for many firms in the industry, forcing them to flee the market. As the competition lessened, with firms moving out of the video-rental industry, profits again rose to the point where the business operators could earn a satisfactory return on their invested capital. (However, to highlight the risk of business operations, the rise of the DVD has brought sales of video rentals and VCR machines to a near halt.)

In competitive markets, extremely large profits simply cannot exist for very long. Given that somewhat bleak scenario, how can we find good projects—that is, projects that return more than their expected rate of return given their risk level (remember Principle 1). Because competition makes these projects difficult to find, we have to invest within markets that are not perfectly competitive. The two most common ways that firms can make markets less competitive are (1) to differentiate the product in some key way or (2) to achieve a cost advantage over competitors.

ONE STEP FURTHER

HOW TO ACHIEVE COMPETITIVE ADVANTAGE THROUGH DIFFERENTIATION AND COST

Product differentiation insulates a product from competition, thereby allowing a company to charge a premium price. If products are differentiated, consumer choice is no longer made on price alone. For example, many people are willing to pay a premium for Gloria Jean's coffee. They simply want Gloria Jean's and price is not important. In the pharmaceutical industry, patents create barriers to competitors. Schering-Plough's *Claritin*, an allergy-relief medicine, and Hoffman-La Roche's *Valium*, a tranquiliser, use patents to protect those drugs from direct competition. Other types of intellectual property, such as copyright on books, music and computer software, also help to legally protect profits. Trademarks (such as the McDonald's logo) and brand names (such as Coca-Cola) are protected from unauthorised use and thus can be immensely valuable to firms; as marketers say, 'people buy brands, not products'.

Quality and service are also used to differentiate products. For example, Levi's has long prided itself on the quality of its jeans. As a result, it has been able to maintain its market share. Similarly, much of Honda's brand loyalty is based on quality. Service can also create product differentiation, as shown by McDonald's fast service, cleanliness and consistency of product that brings customers back.

Product differentiation often comes from innovation, as witnessed by the success of the Apple iPhones. Whether product differentiation occurs because of advertising, patents, service or quality, the more the product is differentiated from competing products, the less competition it will face and the greater the possibility of large profits and cash flows and so the creation of value for the firm's owners.

Economies of scale and the ability to produce at a cost below that of competitors can also reduce competition by deterring new entrants to the market. IKEA, the Swedish furniture retailer, is one such case. For IKEA, the fixed costs are largely independent of the store's size. For example, the costs of rent, display stock, advertising expenses and managerial salaries are fixed and so are essentially the same for each store, regardless of how much is sold. Therefore, the more sales that can be generated, the lower the cost per item sold: if fixed costs are $2 million per year, selling 100 000 items results in average fixed costs of $20 per unit sold, but increasing sales to 200 000 decreases this fixed cost to $10 per unit.

Many global retail chains (such as IKEA, McDonald's, Borders and countless others) build further cost advantage by replication. Their outlets and management methods are 'cloned', so that each time they open a new outlet they do so more efficiently than the previous time, owing to learning from their prior experience. This gives them substantial advantage over competitors who have not had the benefit of riding the 'experience curve'.

Further cost advantages come from what economists and strategists call 'location advantage'—locating all or part of a company's activities in the most efficient place. This is why so many businesses are outsourcing production of consumer goods to China or production of software to India, where the costs are lower than in developed countries.

Regardless of how the cost advantage is created—by economies of scale or 'experience', or through location advantage—firms that can operate below the industry average cost deter new market entrants and have the potential for creating large profits and returning large cash flows.

Therefore, the key to identifying potential wealth-creating investment projects is to understand how and where they exist in competitive markets. Then the corporate philosophy must be aimed at creating or taking advantage of some imperfection in these markets, either through product differentiation or creation of a cost advantage. This may be more sensible than looking enviably at new markets or industries that *appear* to provide large profits. Any strongly competitive industry that looks too good to be true won't be good for long. It is necessary to understand this to know where to look for good projects and to accurately measure the project's cash flows. Finance managers can do this better if they recognise how wealth is created and how difficult it is to create it.

Principle 6

Efficient capital markets—the markets are quick and the prices are right.

The goal of financial managers is to create wealth for the firm's owners. How is shareholder wealth measured? It is the value of the shares that the shareholders hold. To understand what determines prices of securities, it is necessary to have an understanding of the concept of **efficient markets**. Whether a market is efficient or not has to do with the speed with which relevant information is absorbed into security prices. An efficient market is characterised by a large number of profit-driven individuals who act independently. In addition, new information regarding securities arrives in the market in a random manner. Given this setting, investors adjust to new information immediately and buy and sell the security until they feel the market price correctly reflects the new information. Under the efficient market hypothesis, information is reflected in security prices with such speed that there are no opportunities for investors to profit from publicly available information. Investors competing for profits ensure that security prices appropriately reflect the expected earnings and the risks involved and thus the true value of the firm.

What are the implications of efficient markets for finance managers? First, the price is right. Share prices reflect all publicly available information regarding the value of the company. This means that the goal of maximisation of shareholder wealth can be implemented by focusing on the effect each decision *should* have on the share price if everything else were held constant. That is, over time good decisions will result in higher share prices and bad ones will result in lower share prices. Second, earnings manipulations through 'cosmetic' changes will not result in benefits to shareholders. For example, 'bonus issues' of shares to existing shareholders are merely cosmetic changes: giving an investor one new share for each two held previously does

efficient market
A market in which the values of all assets and securities at any instant in time fully reflect all available information.

FYI

BEHAVIOURAL FINANCE

Although academics have long built finance theories on the assumption that markets are efficient and that investors are rational, recent research evidence has looked increasingly at how investors *actually* behave. This gives rise to what is generally called 'behavioural finance', which has found evidence of managerial behaviour that might be called irrational, such as having a 'herd mentality' (apparently believing that if everyone is doing something it must be the right thing to do) or buying shares merely because the price has been increasing rapidly (thus pushing the price to a level that may be unjustified by the intrinsic performance of the firm). Much contemporary research is therefore trying to reconcile the efficient market concept with the observed behaviour of investors and managers.

not add to the firm's cash flows or value, and thus any one investor's shareholding does not increase in value.

Market prices reflect expected cash flows available to shareholders. Thus, there is a justification in having a preoccupation with cash flows to measure the timing of the benefits. As will be seen, it is indeed reassuring that prices reflect value. It allows investors to look at prices and see value reflected in them. While it may make investing a bit less exciting, it makes corporate finance much less uncertain.

Principle 7

The agency problem—managers won't work for owners unless it's in their best interest.

Although the goal of the firm is the maximisation of shareholder wealth, in reality the agency problem may interfere with the implementation of this goal, particularly in large companies. The **agency problem** refers to the fact that a firm's managers will not work to maximise benefits to the firm's owners unless it is in the managers' interests to do so. This problem is the result of a separation of the management and the ownership of the firm. For example, a large firm may be run by professional managers who have little or no ownership position in the firm. As a result of this separation of the decision makers and the owners, managers may make decisions that are not in line with the goal of maximisation of shareholder wealth. They may approach work with little enthusiasm and attempt to benefit themselves in terms of salary and perquisites at the expense of shareholders. The exact significance of this problem is difficult to measure. However, although it might interfere with the implementation of the goal of maximisation of shareholder wealth in some firms, it does not affect the goal's validity. The costs associated with the agency problem are also difficult to measure, but occasionally the effect of this problem is seen in the marketplace. For example, if the market feels that the management of a firm is damaging shareholder wealth, there might be a positive reaction in the share price to the removal of that management. This gives rise to a definition of *agency costs* as the costs, such as a reduced share price, associated with potential conflict between managers and investors when these two groups are not the same.

If the management of the firm works for the owners, who are the shareholders, why doesn't the management get fired if it doesn't act in the shareholders' best interests? Although the shareholders are the legal owners of the company, typically they have little say in the day-to-day management. They rely on an elected board of directors to represent them. However, although *in theory* the shareholders choose the corporate board of directors, who in turn chooses the

agency problem
Problem resulting from conflicts of interest between the manager (the shareholder's agent) and the shareholders.

management, *in reality* the system frequently works the other way around. Existing directors may nominate for continuation of that role and may lobby major shareholders to support them. Also, management may in effect select the nominees and then distribute the voting papers. The end result is that the directors may have more allegiance to the managers than to the shareholders. This in turn sets up the potential for agency problems, with the board of directors not monitoring managers, on behalf of the shareholders, as thoroughly as they should.

Managerial performance can be monitored by auditing financial statements and managers' remuneration packages. The interests of managers and shareholders can be aligned by establishing management stock options, bonuses and perquisites that are directly tied to how closely their decisions coincide with the interest of shareholders. The agency problem will persist unless an incentive structure is set up that aligns the interests of managers and shareholders. In other words, what's good for shareholders must also be good for managers. If that is not the case, managers will make decisions in their best interests rather than emphasising the creation of shareholder wealth.

In order to lessen the agency problem, some companies have adopted practices such as issuing stock options (share options) to their executives. The idea is to provide the executives with a tangible incentive to work more closely towards the goal of maximising the value of the firm's shares, as the options take on value only if the share price rises above a specified level. However, this practice was a contributing factor in high-profile corporate scandals such as the collapse of the US-based Enron Corporation in 2001, with the loss of US$63 billion of shareholder value. Events such as the Enron scandal have led to much soul searching about standards of corporate governance and accountability, as well as reform in accounting standards for executive stock options.

Principle 8

Taxes bias business decisions.

Hardly any decision is made by the financial manager without considering the impact of taxes. When Principle 4 was introduced, it was said that only incremental cash flows should be considered in the evaluation process. One cash flow is the tax payable by the firm, notably the tax payable on company profits. If a decision made by the firm affects incremental taxes payable by the firm, then those incremental taxes must be taken into account. For example, incremental profits from sales of the new Toyota Corolla create an increment in taxes payable by the company.

Governments also realise that taxes can bias business decisions and so they use taxes to encourage spending in certain ways. If the government wanted to encourage spending on research and development (R&D) projects, it might offer a *tax rebate*. This would have the effect of reducing taxes on research and development projects, which would in turn increase the firm's after-tax cash flows from those projects. The increased cash flow would turn some otherwise unprofitable research and development projects into profitable projects. In effect, therefore, the government can use taxes as a tool to influence business investment in particular directions that accord with political goals.

Principle 9

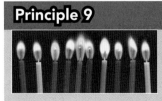

All risk is not equal—some risk can be diversified away, and some cannot.

Much of finance centres around *Principle 1: The risk–return trade-off*. But before we can fully use Principle 1, we must decide how to measure risk. As will be seen, risk is difficult to measure. Principle 9 introduces the process of diversification and demonstrates how it can reduce risk. This section also demonstrates how diversification makes it difficult to measure a project's or an asset's risk.

You are probably already familiar with the concept of diversification. There is an old saying, 'Don't put all of your eggs in one basket'. Diversification allows good and bad events to cancel each other out and thus reduce risk.

To see how diversification complicates the measurement of risk, let us look at the difficulty Santos Ltd has in determining the level of risk associated with a new project to drill for natural gas. Geologists estimate that a single well has only a 1 in 10 chance of success. If the well produces gas, the profits will be quite large, but if it comes up dry, the investment will be lost. Thus, with a 90% chance of losing everything, the project would be viewed as being extremely risky. However, what if Santos each year drills 100 wells? All wells have a 10% independent chance of success, so typically drilling 100 wells would produce 10 successes. Moreover, a bad year may result in only eight successful wells, and a good year may result in 12 successful wells. Looking at all the wells together, the extreme good and bad results tend to cancel each other out and the well-drilling projects taken together do not appear to have much risk or variability of possible outcome. Therefore, the amount of risk in a gas-well project depends on the perspective. Looking at one well standing alone, it looks quite risky; however, if the risk that each well contributes to the overall firm risk is considered, the risk is quite small. This is because much of the risk associated with each individual well is diversified away within the firm. The point is: a project can't be looked at in isolation. Later, it will be seen that some of this risk can be further diversified away within the shareholder's portfolio.

For now, we should realise that the process of diversification can reduce risk and, as a result, measuring a project's or an asset's risk is very difficult. A project's risk changes depending on whether it is measured standing alone or together with other projects the company may take on. Similarly, if shareholders are diversified, they can eliminate part of the risk associated with movements in a given company's share price.

Principle 10

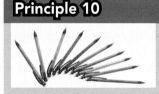

Ethical behaviour is doing the right thing, and ethical dilemmas are everywhere in finance.

Ethics in finance, or rather a lack of ethics, is a recurring theme in both fact and fiction. The American movie, *Wall Street*, featured the character Gordon Gekko (played by Michael Douglas) whose motto was 'Greed is good'. You might think that managers are tempted to do anything—enter into any 'shady deal'—whether legal or not, whether ethical or not, to maximise shareholder wealth. But *Principle 7: the agency problem* shows that managers like to do what suits them. Likewise, a company's directors might behave in a manner that puts their interests first. In other words, any problem of unethical behaviour can be attributed to misguided or unprincipled characters like Gordon Gekko, not to the ordinary shareholders.

Ethical behaviour means 'doing the right thing'. A difficulty arises, however, in attempting to define 'the right thing'. The problem is that each person has his or her own set of values, which forms the basis for their personal judgements about what is right and what is wrong. However, every society adopts a set of rules or laws that prescribe what 'doing the right thing' involves. In a sense, laws can be thought of as a set of rules that reflect the values of the society as a whole, as they have evolved. For the purposes of this text, it is recognised that individuals have a right to disagree about what constitutes 'doing the right thing', and the text will seldom venture beyond the basic notion that ethical conduct involves abiding by society's rules. However, some of the ethical dilemmas that have arisen in recent years will be pointed out with regard to the practice of financial management.

So, as you embark on your study of financial management and encounter ethical dilemmas, you are encouraged to consider the issues and to form your own opinions. Many students ask, 'Is ethics really relevant?' This is a good question and deserves an answer. First, although business errors can be forgiven, ethical errors tend to end careers and terminate future opportunities. Why? First, because unethical behaviour eliminates trust, and without trust, businesses cannot interact. Second, the most damaging event a business can experience is a loss of the public's confidence in its ethical standards. The ultimate problem for shareholders is that ethical errors are not forgiven in the business world. Companies may lose respect and support from consumers, investors and suppliers. Therefore, acting in an ethical manner is not only morally correct but it is also congruent with the goal of maximisation of shareholder wealth.

Beyond the question of ethics is the question of social responsibility. In general, corporate social responsibility means that a company has a responsibility to society beyond the maximisation of shareholder wealth. It asserts that a company answers to a broader constituency than to shareholders alone. As with most debates that centre on ethical and moral questions, there is no definitive answer. One opinion is that because financial managers are employees of the firm, and the firm is owned by the shareholders, financial managers should run the corporation in such a way that shareholder wealth is maximised and then allow the shareholders to decide if they would like to act in a socially responsible way by passing on some of the profits to deserving causes such as charities. Very few companies consistently act in this way. However, growing concerns about wider issues such as global warming have led to an increasing number of companies adopting energy-saving practices and other elements of a 'green' consciousness.

A FINAL NOTE ON THE 10 PRINCIPLES

These 10 principles are as much statements of common sense as they are theoretical statements. They provide the logic behind what is to follow in later chapters. The principles will be expanded and their implications for decision making will be highlighted. Keep in mind as you work through the book that, although the topics may change from chapter to chapter, the

Finance at work

LESSONS FROM VISY AND AMCOR

Suppose that your company and one competitor dominate your market. So, the two firms decide to fix prices; that is, you both decide that you will not compete with each other on the prices that you charge to customers. You thus avoid *Principle 5: the difficulty of making profits in competitive markets*. The result is higher profits, higher cash flows and increased shareholder wealth. Right? Not if you get caught.

This scenario is not a hypothetical one. In late 2007 the Australian packaging company, Visy, was fined a record $36 million for price fixing with its major rival, Amcor, which had previously blown the whistle on the arrangement between the two companies. The fine was imposed following action taken by the Australian Competition and Consumer Commission (ACCC) for illegal price fixing. The ACCC's chairman was reported as saying: 'Anyone who has in the past bought a chocolate bar or a piece of fruit packed in a box made by Visy or Amcor has probably been ripped off'.[5]

It could be argued that a $36 million fine is no more than a light slap on the wrist for a large company. But more significant is the loss of goodwill towards the companies. The extent of customer dissatisfaction is seen in the $700 million civil class action against the companies.[6] As Federal Court Judge Heerey commented: 'The whole point of price fixing is ... to obtain the benefit of prices greater than those which would be obtained in a competitive market ... Customers pay more ... and so suffer loss'.[7]

Thus, unethical or illegal behaviour that is intended to benefit the firm may ultimately be to its detriment. As well, business executives may be penalised monetarily (as happened to several of Visy's executives, who were fined large sums of money) or even by prison sentences in some countries.

logic driving the treatment of them is constant and is rooted in the 10 principles. See 'Finance at work', 'The entrepreneur and finance'.

Concept check

1.4   According to Principle 1, how do investors decide where to invest their money?
1.5   Why is it so hard to find extremely valuable projects?
1.6   Why is ethical behaviour relevant?

For answers go to MyFinanceLab or www.pearson.com.au/9781442539174

Finance at work

THE ENTREPRENEUR AND FINANCE

Do you ever think about some day owning your own business? Does being an entrepreneur have any appeal to you? Well, it does for a lot of people. During the past decade, setting up businesses has been the preferred career avenue for many people. In fact, while many of the large companies are reducing the number of employees, smaller companies are creating new jobs by the thousands. A lot of individuals have thought that there was greater security in working with a big company, only to be disillusioned in the end when they were informed that 'Friday is your last day'.

Defining an entrepreneur is not an easy thing to do. But we can say with some clarity what entrepreneurship is about. Entrepreneurship has been defined as a relentless pursuit of opportunity for the purpose of creating value, without concern for the resources owned.

To be successful, the entrepreneurial process requires that the entrepreneur be able to:

- Identify a good opportunity. Oftentimes people have a 'good idea', but it may not be a 'good opportunity'. Opportunities are market driven. There must be enough customers who want to buy their product or service at a price that covers their expenses and leaves an attractive profit—no matter how much they may like the idea.
- Gain access to the resources needed. For any venture, there are critical resources—human, financial and phys-

ical—that must be available. The entrepreneur usually does not have the capital to own all the resources that are needed. So they must have access to resources, but usually cannot afford to own them. The goal is to do more with less.

- Launch the venture. All the planning in the world is not enough. The entrepreneur must be action-oriented. It requires a 'can do' spirit.
- Grow the business. A business has to grow if it is to be successful. Frequently, the firm will not break even for several years, which means that the entrepreneur will be burning up cash each month. Being able to survive during the times when cash flows are negative is no easy task. If they grow too slow, they lose; but if they grow too fast, they may lose as well. During this time, additional capital will be needed, which requires that the entrepreneur knows how to value the firm and how to structure financing.
- Exit the business. If a venture has been successful, the entrepreneur will have created economic value that is locked up in the business. At some point in time, they will want to capture the value that has been created by the business. It will be time to harvest.

To be successful as an entrepreneur requires a good understanding of finance matters.

OBJECTIVE **5**

Identify what has led to the era of the multinational corporation.

Financial management and the new multinational firm

In the search for competitive advantage and increased profits, firms have been forced to look beyond their home country's borders. This movement has been spurred on by the acceptance of the free-market system in developing countries such as China and Vietnam, along with the collapse of communism and the liberalisation of markets in countries such as Russia and those in eastern Europe. All of this has taken place at a time when information technology has experienced a revolution brought on by the personal computer (PC) and communications have been liberated by the World Wide Web and email. Concurrently, many developed countries, including Australia and the United States, have undergone an unprecedented period of deregulation of their local markets and industries.

These changes have resulted in the opening of new international business opportunities, coupled with increased competition from new entrants to the deregulated local markets and from cheap imported products originating in the developing countries. The end result is that we see more evidence of globalisation in our own countries, such as the unavoidable 'Made in China' labels on a huge range of consumer goods, along with a proliferation of franchised outlets for global firms such as IKEA and McDonald's, and the ownership of local firms falling into foreign hands, such as Singtel's acquisition of Optus.

Increasing competition has led to many local firms looking offshore (notably to China) in order to remain competitive. For example, Australia once had a thriving textile manufacturing industry, but cheap imports have meant that local manufacturing has largely ceased and supplies are sourced from companies in China and elsewhere. Similarly, firms in service industries such as telecommunications and banking have taken their call centres and other so-called back-office work offshore to India, in order to save on costs and improve competitive advantage. Other firms have shifted production or marketing operations overseas to try and achieve growth by penetrating larger markets.

Today it is not easy to ascribe 'nationality' to a company in any meaningful way. We look at Toyota and think of a Japanese icon. But Toyota cars are increasingly being manufactured in countries other than Japan, such as Thailand, Australia and the United States. And Toyota sources more than 50 000 components from a vast array of suppliers in over 50 countries.

All of this means that just about all businesses, large and small, have some international dimension: sourcing of raw materials or supplies and components, international customers, out-sourcing of operations, or raising and investing funds in foreign markets and currencies. This makes financial management both more interesting and more complex. Today, the company treasurer may be juggling investment outlays, revenues and costs in a number of different currencies, all the time trying to manage risks such as those that arise from currency fluctuations, while the financial controller will be producing financial reports that consolidate profits earned in different countries and currencies.

Concept check

1.7 What events have increased globalisation and the international spread of corporations?

1.8 What are some of the complexities and risks of operating internationally?

For answers go to MyFinanceLab or www.pearson.com.au/9781442539174

GFC

OBJECTIVE **6**

The Global Financial Crisis (GFC) occupies a prominent place in the present edition of this book. It is a theme that emerges in Chapter 3 and resurfaces in a number of other chapters. In this way, a picture emerges of many of the GFC's various facets. Taking snapshot views of contemporary issues like the GFC is a feature of this book. These snapshots relate both to the practice of financial management as well as to its wider economic and social setting. However, this edition gives unprecedented coverage to the GFC. This is warranted for a number of reasons.

First, the huge scale and impact of the GFC justifies our taking more than a passing look at it. It is acknowledged to be the most significant worldwide economic catastrophe since the Great Depression of 1929. Prior to the GFC, the global economy had been growing at a steady 4% per annum for a number of years. During 2008, that growth rate dropped by 6% per annum to minus 2%, with even more prominent falls in stock markets. Directly or indirectly, the GFC has wiped trillions of dollars off global debt markets and share markets, it has seen millions

of people lose their houses, it has set back the retirement plans and aspirations of many millions of individuals, and it has caused anguish and hardship for many businesses, their managers and their employees. Moreover, actions to limit the damage have been funded largely by government programs, to the tune of many billions of dollars, which in effect means that taxpayers will ultimately bear the cost of these programs.

Second, arguably we need to understand the GFC in order to learn from it and avoid repeating its mistakes. Reforms have been proposed, such as limiting irresponsible lending practices, improving the transparency and liquidity of the markets, and enhancing the capability to absorb systemic 'shocks' such as the GFC's. In this regard, the US government has announced sweeping reforms to the regulation of financial markets and international banking regulations have been tightened.

Appreciate some of the themes associated with the Global Financial Crisis and its aftermath.

Third, the GFC is not merely a chapter of our past history. It continues to impact significantly in many areas of the economy and financial markets, such as housing markets, government fiscal management, banking practices and the business entities that depend on banks for funding, and the ways in which firms have had to adapt their financing programs.

Fourth, our discussion of the GFC leads the reader gently into the field of 'financial engineering', which was once a showpiece for modern financial practice but has now been tarnished through its association with the GFC. This association centres on a process known as *securitisation*, which before the GFC was a multi-trillion dollar activity that was supposed to benefit the financial sector by spreading lending risks (the rationale for this being the adage 'don't put all your eggs in one basket'). Instead, it shifted risks to investors who apparently did not understand the implications and, in the wake of the systemic failure of the US housing market, resulted in massive losses on 'engineered' securities, the fallout from which is at the heart of the GFC.

Finally, many of the in-chapter snapshots of the GFC provide further support for the relevance of the *10 principles of finance* that were introduced in this chapter as a unifying theme for the book. Some of this chapter content includes the following:

- *Chapter 3.* In the context of Chapter 3's overview of financial markets, we take a brief look at the economic situation in the US that led to the housing boom and then crash in the mid 2000s, along with the resultant 'sub-prime crisis' (SPC). The SPC describes a phenomenon whereby US housing prices virtually doubled from 2003 to 2006 in a speculative boom, only to bust even more spectacularly, falling just as much by early 2008. The SPC then spread beyond the US and evolved into the GFC, mainly through the process of securitisation, whereby the collapse of the housing market led to a collapse of the market for a class of securities known as MBS (mortgage-backed securities) whose value ultimately derived from the repayments on housing loans—a payment stream that virtually evaporated as the housing market collapsed and millions of borrowers were evicted from, or chose to quit, their houses.
- *Chapter 4.* The topic of term loans and their amortisation, part of this chapter on the time value of money, leads to a more detailed look at the role of such loans in housing finance and

the factors that contributed to the 'mortgage meltdown' associated with the sub-prime crisis.
- *Chapter 7.* The GFC brought about a credit squeeze that impacted adversely on many businesses that were otherwise soundly managed. This therefore created problems for their ability to manage working capital, which is one of the concerns of Chapter 7 and its companion chapters.
- *Chapter 9.* The adverse effects of the GFC were so widespread (or systemic) throughout global markets and industries that some critics claimed that the concept of diversification collapsed—the role of diversification being one of the cornerstones of portfolio theory, which is part of this chapter's coverage of risk and return.
- *Chapter 10.* Huge securities losses came about because of the collapse of the US housing market, which raised doubts about the value of mortgage-backed securities (MBS). These securities rapidly lost value, some of the reasons for which are briefly summarised in this chapter, which is about valuation concepts in finance.
- *Chapter 12.* Inflation is a topic of concern for financial managers, and is discussed in this chapter in the context of capital budgeting. However, in the fallout from the GFC there have been fears that the US and other economies could shift to an environment of *deflation*, or falling prices, which is just as worrying as rampant inflation.
- *Chapter 16.* This chapter discusses the firm's financial structure, which concerns matters such as the desired mix of debt and equity finance. In the aftermath of the GFC and its attendant credit squeeze, firms were forced, by circumstance, to raise cash by means that they otherwise may have chosen not to.
- *Chapter 18.* This chapter covers long-term debt finance, including conventional bonds. These bonds are contrasted with MBS, along with elaboration of how the latter have come into existence via securitisation.
- *Chapter 20.* The context of this chapter is international finance, which provides a springboard for a brief recap of some of the international dimensions of the GFC and, in its wake, moves for reform of financial markets.
- *Chapter 21.* This chapter refers to derivatives markets and how parallels may be drawn between them and the problems of the SPC and the GFC.

Overview of the book

This text focuses on the maintenance and creation of wealth. Although this will involve attention to decision-making techniques, the logic behind those techniques will be emphasised to ensure that you do not lose sight of the concepts driving finance and the creation of wealth. The text begins in this chapter by discussing the goal of maximisation of shareholder wealth, a goal that is to be used in financial decision making. The text outlines the legal environment, which highlights the advantages of the company or corporation as the most suitable legal form of ownership for large and growing businesses.

The chapter then presents the 10 guiding principles that provide the conceptual framework that ties together the various decision-making tools which are encountered in the following parts of the book. Chapters 2 and 3 discuss the tax environment that is so important to financial decisions and then the financial markets within which firms issue securities and in which shareholder wealth is attained. Chapter 4 provides basic tools for understanding the time value of money, which is fundamental to virtually all major financial decisions involving investing in assets and financing those assets.

Chapters 5 to 8 provide the basic financial tools to guide the financial manager in maintaining control over the firm and its ongoing operations and in making sound short-term financial decisions. Chapters 5 and 6 outline techniques that enable the financial manager to locate potential problem areas and plan for the future. Chapters 7 and 8 deal with *working-capital management*, the management of current assets and liabilities. Methods for determining the appropriate investment in cash, marketable securities, inventory and accounts receivable are discussed, as well as the risks associated with these investments and the control of these risks, along with the ways of financing the assets.

Chapters 9 to 14 form the core of the financial management curriculum: the valuation of long-term assets. This part of the book provides the tools and knowledge to value the firm and create shareholder wealth. Because investing is risky (and owning shares in a firm represents a risky investment for shareholders), Chapter 9 develops an understanding of the meaning and measurement of risk. Chapter 10 proceeds from there to look at the valuation of the long-term securities that are used to finance the firm, notably fixed income bonds, together with models that attempt to explain how different financial decisions affect the firm's share price. Extending the valuation principles just developed, Chapter 11 discusses capital-budgeting decisions, which involves the financial evaluation of investments; these decisions lie at the core of financial management, underlying the firm's choice of projects and assets that are acquired to implement the firm's strategies for creating shareholder wealth. Chapter 12 goes on to examine the identification and measurement of the cash flows that ultimately determine if a capital investment is worthwhile or not. Then, methods to incorporate risk in the analysis are outlined in Chapter 13. Finally, the topics on valuation close with Chapter 14, where the financing of the firm's chosen projects is examined, looking at what costs are associated with alternative ways of raising new funds.

Chapter 15 examines the firm's capital structure along with the impact of leverage on returns to the enterprise. Once these relationships between leverage and valuation are developed, Chapter 16 moves on to the process of planning the firm's financing mix. This is followed in Chapter 17 by a discussion of the issues that arise when deciding if the firm should pay dividends out of the profits or retain the profits in the business.

Chapters 18 and 19 build on the discussion of financial markets, first encountered in Chapter 3. Chapter 18 discusses the workings of securities used for long-term debt, notably term loans and bonds, while Chapter 19 looks at issuing shares and so-called 'hybrid' securities.

Chapter 20 presents a discussion of the use of futures, options and swaps by financial managers to reduce risk, and Chapter 21 deals with international financial management, focusing on how financial decisions are affected by the international environment. Chapter 22 provides an introduction to corporate restructuring, including mergers with, and acquisitions of, other firms.

Summary

OBJECTIVE 1

Finance is largely about investing to create wealth, financing that investment and managing the day-to-day cash resources of the firm. These three areas interact in the financial management of the firm and provide focal points for the following chapters of this book.

OBJECTIVE 2

The company is the most popular form of legal organisation for medium to large and growing firms. Companies, however, feature separation of ownership from control. Ownership legally resides with the shareholders, but control and running of the firm are carried out by directors and managers. One such manager is the finance manager, who is responsible for the treasury and accounting operations of the firm.

OBJECTIVE 3

The finance manager's role centres on the goal of creating wealth for the firm's ultimate owners or shareholders. This goal must be constantly borne in mind when making financial decisions such as investing, financing and managing working capital.

OBJECTIVE 4

In pursuit of the wealth-creation goal, the finance manager is guided by 10 principles that provide a unifying theme for the following chapters of this book. One or more of these principles will be paramount in just about every financial decision of any consequence.

- *Principle 1*: The risk–return trade-off—we won't take on additional risk unless we expect to be compensated with additional return.
- *Principle 2*: The time value of money—a dollar received today is worth more than a dollar received in the future.
- *Principle 3*: Cash—not profits—is king.
- *Principle 4*: Incremental cash flows—it's only what changes that counts.
- *Principle 5*: The curse of competitive markets—why it's hard to find exceptionally valuable projects.
- *Principle 6*: Efficient capital markets—the markets are quick and the prices are right.
- *Principle 7*: The agency problem—managers won't work for owners unless it's in their best interest.
- *Principle 8*: Taxes bias business decisions.
- *Principle 9*: All risk is not equal—some risk can be diversified away, and some cannot.
- *Principle 10*: Ethical behaviour is doing the right thing, and ethical dilemmas are everywhere in finance.

OBJECTIVE 5

Finance increasingly has an international dimension, which is just one aspect of why financial decisions cannot be divorced from the economic, social and political environment within which the firm operates.

OBJECTIVE 6

The so-called GFC (Global Financial Crisis) can be traced back to the collapse of the US housing market in 2006/07, known as the sub-prime crisis (SPC). This is linked, through a process known as *securitisation*, to the subsequent collapse of the market for mortgage-backed securities, which had adverse consequences for institutions and markets throughout the world. Various facets of the SPC and the GFC are outlined in a number of chapters of this book.

Key terms

For a complete flashcard glossary go to MyFinanceLab at www.pearson.com.au/myfinancelab

1-1 Apple's launch of the iPad is the result of interaction between the three main areas of finance. Discuss these areas in the context of Apple's decision.

1-2 What are the main reasons why the company is the dominant form of business organisation for large and growing businesses?

1-3 The finance manager has one particular goal in mind. What is this goal and why adopt it as the focal point for financial management? What are some of the difficulties, in achieving this goal, that were outlined in this chapter?

1-4 Principle 2 deals with the time value of money (TVM). Outline a financial decision that you have already made in your life (or one that you expect to make in the future) that involves this principle.

1-5 What does Principle 1 suggest about investing your money (or a firm's money)?

1-6 Assume that you were working full time for $30 000 per annum. Now you have reduced your working hours by one-third in order to study part time in the expectation that this will benefit your career and job promotion prospects. How can this situation be related to Principle 4?

1-7 Principle 5 is about the difficulty of finding very valuable projects. How can firms improve their competitive position and so make projects potentially more attractive?

1-8 Outline some of the challenges that globalisation poses for the finance manager.

1-9 Discuss any ways in which you or your family, or a particular sector of the community, or a business you are aware of, has been directly or indirectly impacted by the GFC.

You are in the final stage of the selection process for the job of assistant financial analyst at the Antipodes Mineral Resources company (AMR). This involves a test of your understanding of basic financial concepts. You are given the following memo and asked to respond to the questions. Whether or not you are offered a position at the company will depend on the quality of your responses.

To: Applicants for the position of assistant financial analyst
From: K. Abbott-Gill, CFO, Antipodes Mineral Resources Co. (AMR)
Re: A test of your understanding of basic financial concepts
Please respond in writing to the following questions:

1. What types of investment projects would you expect to find in a minerals company?
2. You will be working in the CFO's office if you obtain this job. What activities do you expect are undertaken in this office?
3. AMR is a public company, listed on the stock exchange. How does this fact have a bearing on the goal we should bear in mind when managing our finances?
4. Does or should AMR have any other accountabilities apart from responsibilities to the firm's owners?

1. This means that partners may be sued as individuals (severally) and collectively (jointly).
2. *Limited partnerships* are nowadays generally permitted. These enable partners to have some of the advantages of the company form, notably limited liability. However, their use is not widespread, as any business of significance will tend to adopt the company form of organisation.
3. For partnerships and sole proprietorships, too, the value of an ownership share is put to the test only in the event of the sale of all or part of a firm, but there is a direct link between the ongoing success of the firm and the owners' wealth in that the owners' drawings from the firm provide the main source of personal wealth.
4. Another special class of Australian company is called the *no liability* (NL) company. Its shareholders are not liable to meet calls on shares made by the company during its operations or in the event of being wound up. NL companies are rare nowadays, but they assumed some importance, historically, in the mining industry. This industry is by its nature speculative and companies in this industry were able to attract investors who could be secure in the knowledge that they would not be liable for calls if the mining venture proved unsuccessful.
5. Quoted in the *Advertiser* (Adelaide), 3 November 2007.
6. A class action is a combined lawsuit, where a group of plaintiffs takes collective legal action, thus spreading the legal costs that might otherwise be prohibitive for any one plaintiff.
7. *Weekend Australian*, 3–4 November 2007.

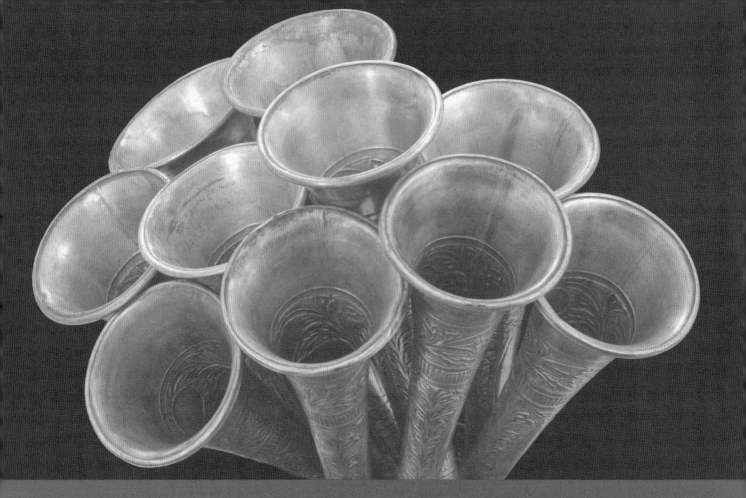

Learning objectives

After reading this chapter, you should be able to:

1 Calculate the taxable income and tax payable for Australian individual and company taxpayers.

2 Understand the basic components of the Australian dividend imputation system and the implications for the after-tax wealth of shareholders.

3 Appreciate some of the implications of the Australian taxation system for the financial decisions of Australian individuals and businesses.

4 Understand the basic elements of Australian capital-gains taxation.

5 Appreciate some of the implications of income tax and capital-gains tax on rates of return for shareholders.

For a complete eBook go to MyFinanceLab
www.pearson.com.au/myfinancelab

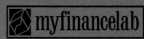

The tax environment

Chapter 2

CHAPTER PREVIEW

This chapter introduces some of the basics of the Australian taxation system to provide an example of how a country determines the income tax obligations of its individuals and businesses and to illustrate the impact of taxation on financial decision making.

At the simplest level, the requirement by individuals and businesses to pay tax to the government reduces the financial resources available to them. Although this is complicated by each country having its own taxation laws that prescribe the way in which amounts of tax are determined for its taxpayers, there are some general features of the taxation systems of most developed countries that are similar. For example, income tax is payable by a business on a net income amount that is determined by deducting from revenue earned for a period expenses such as cost of goods, wages, rent and interest.

What does tax have to do with financial management?

You may have heard the saying 'there are only two things certain in life—death and taxes'. So, one answer to the question of 'What does tax have to do with financial management?' is that individuals and businesses need to manage their finances to ensure they can pay their taxes.

Another answer to the question comes from Chapter 1, where it was proposed that a major focus of financial management is to assist business decision makers to make choices between investment and financing alternatives. It was also proposed that the criterion for choosing between alternatives should be the maximisation of the wealth of the business owners (who for a company are its shareholders). But what do we mean by wealth? A simple definition of wealth is 'the amount of goods and services that can be purchased'. So, if a business makes good investment and financing decisions, its owners will be able to purchase more goods and services in the future. However, for this to occur, the business owners have to receive cash from the business. In general, owners can receive cash from their business in two ways:

- the business paying the owners a salary and/or a share of profits
- the owners selling their ownership of the business (e.g. shares).

This seems fairly straightforward, but there is a significant complicating factor in determining the amount of cash (and therefore wealth) that owners can receive from their business. This complicating factor is tax. To exist in a modern economy, individuals and businesses are subject to taxation laws that require the payment of cash to the government. So, the financial management decision-making objective needs to be modified to the maximisation of the *after-tax* wealth of the owners of the business. To be able to put this objective into practice, we need to have an understanding of some of the major components of a country's taxation system, such as for Australia.

It is important to bear in mind as you read this chapter that its purpose is not to make you a taxation expert but to enhance your awareness of the impact of taxation on investment and financing decisions that are the focus of financial management.

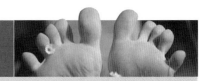

FYI

Why are tax considerations important in financial management? Basically, the answer is that taxation affects the amount of the firm's cash flows available to its owners (shareholders).

Regardless of your program

TAXATION MATTERS

In a modern society taxation is ever present and affects the financial lives of all individuals and businesses. As taxation is inescapable, regardless of your program you should have some knowledge and understanding of the major ways that governments raise tax and how it impacts your financial decisions. For example, will you be able to claim a tax deduction for the interest you pay on money you borrow to start a business, or what capital gains tax would you have to pay if you sold your business?

OBJECTIVE

Calculate the taxable income and tax payable for Australian individual and company taxpayers.

An introduction to income taxation

Why does every country have a taxation system? The main reason is the need for a country's government to generate funds for its expenditures, although it is now quite common for governments to implement important *social* and *economic* policies via the taxation system. Examples of socially oriented aspects of the tax laws include concessions on the amount of tax payable on the earnings of retirement funds, and by individuals with low incomes.

Similarly, government tax policy may be aimed at stimulating the level of business expenditure on a particular activity which in turn is expected to result in an increase in employment. An example is a tax system that allows a business to have its income-tax payments reduced if it spends money on certain technological research and development.

The government can also use its tax laws to stabilise the economy. For example, in a period of economic recession, individual income taxes may be reduced in order to increase the public's discretionary income, which if spent increases the demand for goods and services, which in turn is expected to stimulate employment.

In summary, three outcomes from a taxation system can be identified:

1. the provision of revenues to fund government expenditures
2. the achievement of socially desirable goals
3. business incentives and economic stabilisation.

TYPES OF TAXPAYERS

To understand how a tax system operates, we must first ask 'Who is the taxpayer?'. In the Australian taxation system, there are three main types of taxpayers (also known as tax entities): individuals, companies, and fiduciaries. *Individuals* include employees, self-employed persons running their own businesses, and members of a partnership. Income earned by these individuals is reported in their personal income tax returns.[1]

The *company*, as a legal entity separate from its owners (i.e. shareholders), reports income and expenses from the business it operates and pays income tax at company rates on its net income. The shareholders are then required to pay income tax at individual rates on any dividends that are paid to them from the company's net income.

Fiduciaries, such as trusts, are also regarded as a tax entity and therefore must file an income tax return reporting net income. Income tax is paid either by the trust itself or by the individual beneficiaries reporting their share of the trust income in their personal tax returns. The taxation of fiduciary income can be an important source of funds to the government, but it is unlikely to be especially relevant to the company financial manager.

As most businesses of any size are companies, the following material outlines the major components (at the time of writing) of the Australian system to tax the income and capital gains of companies and their owners (shareholders) and the major implications of this taxation system for company financial management. Although Australia has a goods and services tax (GST), which taxes the value-added of most goods and services, it is not discussed in this chapter because its impact on most investment and financing decisions is relatively minor.

It is important at this stage to introduce a caveat. As tax legislation is often complex and can change relatively quickly, some of the details provided in the following sections may be different by the time you are reading this. Although it can be true that 'a little knowledge is a dangerous thing', you will see as the chapter progresses that it is important for you to have some understanding of the major elements of the taxation system, as this will enable you to appreciate how tax has an impact on financial decision making.

COMPUTING TAXABLE INCOME

To determine the amount of income tax an entity has to pay to the federal government, the Australian income-tax law[2] specifies the rules to calculate a taxpayer's *taxable income* to which a *rate of tax* is applied. Taxable income is equal to *assessable income* minus *allowable deductions*.

Assessable income

Broadly, for Australian resident taxpayers *assessable income* means all income that they earn in Australia and overseas. For an individual this would include such items as salary and wages, income from a sole-trader business, share of net income from a partnership or a trust, interest, dividends and capital gains.

The assessable income of a business broadly equates to its accounting revenue. However, the tax law has its own rules to determine assessable income, so sometimes the accounting and tax measures of income can be different. For example, the tax law allowed for a proportion of the revenue from an Australian film to not be included as assessable income if the investment in the film occurred before 25 May 1988.[3] Conversely, it is possible for the tax law to require amounts to be included in the taxpayer's assessable income even though they may not be recognised as accounting revenue in that period.

Allowable deductions

The Australian income-tax law allows the taxpayer to deduct from assessable income amounts called *allowable deductions*. Again, the tax law has its own rules to determine what constitutes an allowable deduction, but basically it encompasses expenditure incurred by the taxpayer in order to earn assessable income in a particular tax year. For businesses, allowable deductions broadly equate to the operating expenses recorded in the firm's accounts to determine the profit or loss for the period.

However, the amount allowed by the tax law as a tax deduction may differ from the accounting expense. For example, a business may believe that the useful life of a piece of equipment is three years and recognise a straight-line depreciation expense in its accounts using a rate of 33.3% per annum. But the tax law might allow a rate of only 20% per annum to calculate the allowable depreciation deduction for this equipment. This difference will result in the business's taxable income exceeding its accounting income for the first three years and then the reverse in years 4 and 5 when the accounting income will exceed its taxable income.

Some examples of taxable income

To demonstrate how to compute taxable income, following are two examples—an individual salary or wage earner, and a business.

EXAMPLE 2.1   Calculation of taxable income: individual—Jane Piper

---

Jane Piper has been working as an apprentice plumber for J & S Plumbing. For the financial year just ended on 30 June she received gross wages of $45 000. During the year she purchased protective clothing and boots costing $250 and she spent $250 on replacing some of her plumbing tools that had been damaged. She can claim both of these expenditures as allowable deductions.

	$	$
Assessable income		
Gross wages		45 000
Less: Allowable deductions		
Protective clothing and boots	250	
Replacement of tools	250	500
Taxable income: Jane Piper		$44 500

EXAMPLE 2.2   Calculation of taxable income: business—J & S Plumbing

---

During the financial year just ended on 30 June, J & S Plumbing earned from the provision of plumbing services a gross income of $600 000. The cost of materials purchased during the year totalled $230 000 and other operating expenses were $100 000 (the break-down of these costs is shown below). The business has $125 000 in debt outstanding, at a 16% per annum interest rate, which resulted in $20 000 interest expense for the year (i.e. $125 000 × 0.16 = $20 000). The taxable income of J & S Plumbing is $250 000, as shown below.

	$	$	$
Assessable income			
Sales			600 000
Less: Allowable deductions			
Cost of materials used		230 000	
Operating expenses			
Apprentice wages	45 000		
Machinery and vehicle depreciation	15 000		
Other expenses	40 000	100 000	
Financing expenses			
Interest		20 000	350 000
Taxable income: J & S Plumbing			$250 000

COMPUTING THE INCOME TAX PAYABLE

Once a taxpayer's taxable income is known, the amount of income tax to be paid to the Australian government can be determined. The income tax to be paid by taxpayers will be based on three components:

- the amount of *taxable income* calculated in the way shown above
- the *type of taxpayer*—whether an individual, a company, etc.
- the *income tax rate* applicable for the type of taxpayer.

For Australian individual taxpayers, there is a range of income-tax rates, with the rate that is applied being dependent on the amount of taxable income.

Looking at the rates in Table 2.1, it can be seen that no tax is levied on the first $6000 of the individual taxpayer's taxable income. Each dollar of taxable income from $6001 to $37 000 is taxed at 15% (i.e. 15 cents for every dollar), and so on, with steps up to a maximum rate of 45% of each dollar of taxable income above $180 000.

These individual tax rates (and also the company tax rate) are *marginal tax rates*, as they are rates that are applied to the next (or incremental) dollar of income included in the taxpayer's taxable income. In financial decision making it is the marginal tax rate which is important because this is the rate that will be applicable for any changes in taxable income that result from the decision. Thus, *in making financial decisions that have tax consequences, always use the appropriate marginal tax rate in your calculations*.

Once the amount of total tax payable is determined for a given amount of taxable income, an *average tax rate* can be calculated. This is illustrated in Example 2.3. You will note that the stepped individual tax rates result in the average tax rate being different from the marginal tax rate.

EXAMPLE 2.3 **Calculation of income tax payable for an individual taxpayer: Jane Piper**

Jane Piper's taxable income (from Example 2.1) is $44 500. Assuming that this income was earned in the financial year for which the individual tax rates in Table 2.1 were applicable, her tax payable would be:

TAXABLE INCOME	TAX TO BE PAID ON $	TAX RATE %	TAX PAYABLE $	AFTER-TAX INCOME $
0–6000	6 000	0	Nil	
6001–37 000	31 000	15	4 650	
37 001–44 500	7 500	30	2 250	
Total	$44 500		($6 900)	$37 600

At her current level of taxable income, Jane's marginal tax rate is 30% (until her taxable income exceeds $80 000, when the marginal rate changes to 37%). At Jane's current marginal rate, if her taxable income increased to $44 600, the extra $100 would result in an additional $30 of tax being payable. The average tax rate on Jane's current taxable income is $6900/$44 500 = 15.51%.

The tax rate to be applied to the taxable income of a business depends on whether the business is conducted as a sole trader, a partnership, a trust or a company. Let us start by assuming

---

TABLE 2.1 Australian income-tax rates for resident taxpayers

EACH DOLLAR OF TAXABLE INCOME IN RANGE	TAXED AT
0–6000	0%
6001–37 000	15%
37 001–80 000	30%
80 001–180 000	37%
180 001 and above	45%

Note:
(a)   These rates are provided only for illustration of the material and examples in this chapter and should not be relied upon as the current Australian individual tax rates.
(b)   The rates do not include the Medicare levy which is a surcharge based on taxable income to partially fund the Australian health system.

that the business of J & S Plumbing is conducted as a partnership called J & S Plumbing. Under the partnership agreement there are two partners, with John Smith being entitled to 90% of the net income of the partnership and Sue Smith being entitled to 10%.

EXAMPLE 2.4 Calculation of income tax payable for a business partnership: J & S Plumbing

Under Australian tax law, income tax is not payable by the partnership itself but by each partner on their respective share of the partnership net income. So for J & S Plumbing for the financial year ended 30 June, John will include $225 000 (90% of $250 000) in his taxable income and Sue will include $25 000 (10% of $250 000) in her taxable income. Income tax is then payable by each partner at the respective individual income-tax rates.

Assuming that John and Sue received no other income, were not entitled to any deductions, and the individual income-tax rates in Table 2.1 were applicable, they would have to pay the following income tax.

John: Taxable income $225 000

TAXABLE INCOME	TAX TO BE PAID ON $	TAX RATE %	TAX PAYABLE $	AFTER-TAX INCOME $
0–180 000	180 000	various	54 550	
180 001–225 000	45 000	45	20 250	
Total	$225 000		($74 800)	$150 200

Sue: Taxable income $25 000

TAXABLE INCOME	TAX TO BE PAID ON $	TAX RATE %	TAX PAYABLE $	AFTER-TAX INCOME $
0–6000	6000	0	Nil	
6001–25 000	19 000	15	2 850	
Total	$25 000		($2 850)	$22 150

Now let's assume that, instead of the partnership, John and Sue Smith have established a company called J & S Plumbing Limited to conduct the same J & S Plumbing business. As illustrated in Example 2.5, the tax situation will now be quite different, because a company, being an entity that is legally separate from it owners (i.e. shareholders John and Sue Smith), is required to pay income tax at company rates.

EXAMPLE 2.5 Calculation of income tax payable for a company: J & S Plumbing Limited

In Australia, only one tax rate is applied to all of the taxable income of a company. At the time of writing this rate was 30%. So, applying this tax rate to the taxable income for J & S Plumbing Limited (which was calculated in Example 2.2 as $250 000), the amount of income tax payable by the company is $75 000 ($250 000 × 0.30 = $75 000).

	$
Taxable income:	250 000
– Company tax @ 30%	(75 000)
Net income after tax	$175 000

The above examples calculating the amount of income tax payable assume that all of the taxpayer's income was derived in Australia. However, the increasing internationalisation of Australian business means that some income may have originated in a foreign country. If this is the case, the Australian income-tax law will generally require the taxable income of an Australian resident taxpayer to include amounts earned from overseas so that Australian income tax is levied on the foreign income. However, if the taxpayer has already paid tax in another country on this foreign income, then they are entitled to a credit to offset the amount of the Australian tax levied on that income.

Concept check

2.1 Distinguish between sole traders, partnerships and companies in terms of how their income tax obligations are determined.

2.2 What is the difference between marginal tax rates and average tax rates?

2.3 Why do we use marginal tax rates instead of average tax rates when making financial decisions?

For answers go to MyFinanceLab or www.pearson.com.au/9781442539174

TIMING OF TAX PAYMENTS

In the above examples, each taxpayer's taxable income and income tax payable were calculated for a standard Australian income tax year, which is from 1 July to 30 June. Accordingly, one would expect that the actual *payment* of income tax would occur after the end of each tax year. In reality, the timing of tax payments to the Australian government is a bit more complicated because for most types of taxpayers the Australian tax system requires *instalments* of tax to be paid *during* the financial year in which the income is being earned.

After the end of the financial year, an accurate calculation of the taxable income for the financial year is able to be made, with the amount of tax payable being reduced by instalments paid during the year. If the instalments are insufficient to offset the tax payable, the taxpayer is required to make a final payment of the balance of tax owing. Conversely, if the instalments paid during the year are more than the tax payable, a refund of the excess tax is paid to the taxpayer. As you will see in later chapters, the accurate identification of the amount and timing of tax payments is important for cash budgeting (Chapter 6) and for capital budgeting (Chapter 12).

TAX SAVINGS

The major theme of this chapter is the need for financial managers to have some knowledge of the taxation system so that they can correctly include the impact of tax in their financial decisions. **Tax savings** are an illustration of this impact. As the name implies, a tax saving is a reduction in the amount of tax that is associated with a particular decision or action.

We will use the example of J & S Plumbing Limited to illustrate tax savings. The management of J & S Plumbing Limited is considering investing in a new pipe-making machine costing $100 000 and they can choose to buy the new machine in either this tax year or the next. Let us suppose that, as a one-off measure to encourage investment in plant and equipment, the federal government has included in the tax law an *investment allowance* which entitles business taxpayers to a special tax deduction equal to 10% of the cost of plant and equipment that must be purchased in the current tax year. This investment allowance tax deduction is in addition to the normal plant and equipment depreciation amounts that can be claimed as a tax deduction.

The management of J & S Plumbing Limited now face an investment decision that has clear tax implications. If they decide to buy the new machine in the current tax year, the company will be entitled to the investment allowance tax deduction of $10 000 ($100 000 × 10%), in addition to the amounts claimed in Example 2.2. This additional tax deduction will reduce the company's previously calculated taxable income of $250 000 to $240 000 and the income tax that would be payable by the company is now $72 000 ($240 000 × 30%) instead of $75 000. Therefore, by making the investment decision to spend $100 000 on the new machine in the

tax savings
A reduction in the amount of tax that is associated with a particular decision or action. A negative tax saving occurs when a particular decision or action results in an increase in the amount of tax.

current tax year instead of next year, the company will obtain a *tax saving* equal to $3000 ($75 000 – $72 000).

More directly, the tax saving[4] of $3000 is equal to the reduction in taxable income ($10 000) multiplied by the marginal tax rate (30%).

Tax saving = change in taxable income × marginal tax rate

It is also possible to have a *negative* 'tax saving'. For example, suppose that, as a result of purchasing the new machine, J & S Plumbing Limited will reduce its operating expenses by $2000 per annum. The effect of this change is that the company's taxable income will increase by $2000 and its tax payable will increase by $2000 × 0.30 = $600. In other words, we can say that another tax consequence of the company's decision to purchase the new machine is a negative tax saving of $600 per annum.

SALE OF PLANT AND EQUIPMENT

When an investment project involves the sale of plant and equipment for an amount that is different from its tax depreciated (written-down) value, any profit-on-sale will be taxed and any loss-on-sale will produce a tax saving. This is illustrated in the following example.

The new machine that J & S Plumbing Limited is considering purchasing for $100 000 will replace an existing machine that was purchased four years ago at a cost of $60 000. When the existing machine was purchased, it was estimated to have a useful life of six years with a salvage value of $0. Assuming that the company uses the straight-line method to calculate depreciation for tax purposes, the annual depreciation tax deduction for the existing machine is ($60 000 – $0)/6 = $10 000 (this has been included as part of the annual $15 000 depreciation amount in Example 2.2).

At the start of the fifth year of the existing machine's useful life, its tax written-down value is $20 000 (i.e. purchase cost $60 000 – depreciation for 4 years totalling $40 000). Also, the company has identified a potential buyer who is willing to pay $25 000 for the existing machine.

If the company decides to purchase the new machine and sell the existing machine for $25 000, it will have made a taxation profit-on-sale of the existing machine of $5000 (sale value $25 000 minus tax depreciated (written-down) value $20 000). As a consequence, the company will be required to pay income tax on this profit-on-sale of $5000 × 0.30 = $1500.

Another way to explain why the profit-on-sale of $5000 and the additional income tax of $1500 occurs is to compare the company's annual depreciation tax deductions. For the previous four years the company has claimed a depreciation tax deduction for the existing machine of $10 000 per year. However, if the company had known when it purchased the existing machine four years ago that it would sell the machine at the start of year 5 for $25 000, it should have claimed a depreciation tax deduction of only ($60 000 – $25 000)/4 = $8750 per year. If the company had claimed depreciation of only $8750 instead of $10 000 each year, it would have paid more income tax in each of the past four years than it actually has paid. But the company didn't have the benefit of hindsight to know when it purchased the existing machine that it would be able to sell it after four years for $25 000. It is only when the existing machine is sold that the profit-on-sale is identified and an adjustment for the previous underpayment of tax is required to be made.

What would happen in the above example if the existing machine was only able to be sold at the start of year 5 for $12 000 when its tax depreciated (written-down) value was $20 000? The company would incur a loss-on-sale of $8000 (i.e. $12 000 – $20 000 = –$8000) which it would claim as an additional tax deduction, producing a tax saving of $8000 × 0.30 = $2400. This tax saving has occurred because, with the benefit of hindsight, instead of the company claiming a tax deduction of $10 000 per year for depreciation of the existing machine, it should have claimed a larger tax deduction for depreciation of ($60 000 – $12 000)/4 = $12 000 per year. As a consequence, the company has paid a total of $2400 more income tax in the previous four years than it should have (i.e. $2000 × 0.30 = $600 per year × 4 years). It is only when the existing machine is sold for $12 000 that the company becomes entitled to a tax saving for this amount.

Income tax on companies and shareholders

Understand the basic mechanics of the Australian dividend imputation system and the implications for the after-tax wealth of shareholders.

In Example 2.4, where it was assumed that the business of J & S Plumbing was conducted as a partnership, the *after-tax income* of the owners of the business (the partners) was calculated at $150 200 for John Smith and $22 150 for Sue Smith. A total after-tax income from the business of $172 350. This means that total tax of $77 650 (i.e. 250 000 – 172 350) was payable on the business's net income of $250 000, which is an average tax rate of 77 650/250 000 = 31.06%.

However, if the same business of J & S Plumbing is conducted by a company, the impact of income tax on the after-tax wealth of the owners of the business (i.e. the shareholders) becomes more complex. This is because Australian law treats the company and its owners (shareholders) as separate legal and taxpayer entities. A major implication of this legal separation is that shareholders are not entitled to a direct share of the business's profits (as is the case for a sole trader or partners) and have to obtain after-tax wealth from their investment in the company by either:

- receiving a dividend paid to them by the company
- selling their shares in the company at prevailing market prices.

As a consequence, to determine the after-tax wealth of shareholders we need to be able to calculate the amount of income tax levied on:

- company net income
- dividends received by shareholders from the company
- capital gains earned by shareholders when they sell their shares in the company.

CLASSICAL TAX SYSTEM

A **classical tax system** applies a strict separation between a company that generates net income and its shareholders, which results in the double taxation of company net income. How does this occur?

- As it is regarded as a separate entity, the company is required to pay tax on its taxable income at the company tax rate. (For simplification, we will initially assume that the company's taxable income is the same as its accounting net income.)
- The company can then pay dividends to its shareholders from its net income after tax.
- For the financial year in which the shareholders receive dividends from the company, they are required to include the dividend amount in their taxable income, on which income tax is payable at individual tax rates.

The effect of a classical tax system is that every dollar of net income earned by the company is taxed twice when it is paid to shareholders as dividends—first at the company level and then at the shareholder level. This is illustrated in Example 2.6.

classical tax system
A tax system applying to companies and their shareholders, where the net income of the company is taxed twice, first at the company level and then again when dividends are received by the shareholders.

EXAMPLE 2.6   Income tax payable under a classical tax system

In Example 2.5, J & S Plumbing Limited had a net income after tax of $175 000 ($250 000 – $75 000) that could be paid out as dividends to the shareholders. It is assumed in this example that the company pays out all of its net income after tax to its two shareholders, John and Sue, in the following proportions and amounts:

John:	90%	$157 500	
Sue:	10%	$17 500	
Total	100%	$175 000	(= company net income after tax)

Also, it is assumed that John and Sue are residents of Australia, earned no other income and were entitled to no tax deductions. Applying the individual rates in Table 2.1, John and Sue would have to pay income tax on their dividend income as follows:

	JOHN	SUE	TOTAL
Dividend income	$157 500	$17 500	$175 000
Income tax[a]	($46 225)	($1 725)	($47 950)
After-tax income	$111 275	$15 775	$127 050

a   Calculated using the individual tax rates shown in Table 2.1.[5]

It can be seen from Example 2.6 that, on a net income of $250 000 earned by the company, total income tax of $122 950 is required to be paid—$75 000 by the company and $47 950 by the shareholders. This is an average tax rate of 49.18% (i.e. $122 950/$250 000), which means that John and Sue as the owners of the business received only 50.82% of the business net income after all income taxes had been paid. Compare this with Example 2.4, when the same business conducted as a partnership had an average tax rate of only 31.06%, which resulted in 68.94% of the business net income being available for the partner owners after all income taxes had been paid!

This comparison clearly shows that under a classical tax system there is a clear tax disadvantage for the owners to conduct their business as a company instead of as a partnership. Therefore, a decision to conduct a business as a company will be influenced by other factors such as the limitation of the liability of the owners in the event of the failure of the business and the ability of the company to claim tax deductions.

Under a classical tax system a company can increase the after-tax income of its shareholder owners by maximising its tax deductions and paying less company income tax. We can see this by returning to Example 2.6.

J & S Plumbing Limited, having decided to buy a new pipe-making machine costing $100 000, is entitled to claim in the current tax year an *investment allowance* tax deduction of $10 000, which results in a company tax saving of $10 000 × 0.30 = $3000. As the company's net income hasn't changed from $250 000, the $3000 reduction in company income tax increases the amount that the company can pay as dividends to its shareholders by $3000 to $178 000. Assuming, as previously, that the company pays out all of its after-tax net income as dividends, John and Sue would have to pay income tax on their dividend income as follows:

	JOHN	SUE	TOTAL
Dividend income	$160 200	$17 800	$178 000
Income tax[a]	($47 224)	($1 770)	($48 994)
After-tax income	$112 976	$16 030	$129 006

a   Calculated using the marginal tax rates shown in Table 2.1.[6]

In this example, the $3000 tax saving obtained by the company from the additional tax deduction increased the total after-tax income of its shareholders by $1956 (from $127 050 to $129 006). Therefore, we can conclude that under a classical tax system a company can increase the after-tax income and wealth of its shareholders by making investment (e.g. purchase of equipment) and financing decisions that *minimise* the income tax payable by the company.

DIVIDEND IMPUTATION SYSTEM

Prior to 1987 a classical system applied to the taxation of the income of Australian companies and shareholders. At the time, many investors argued that the double taxation of company net income was inequitable, particularly when a comparison was made with the income tax that was payable if the same business was conducted as a partnership. Another argument against the classical tax system was that it resulted in debt finance having a tax advantage over equity finance because the interest paid by a company to lenders for the use of debt finance was an allowable deduction for the company, whereas dividends paid by the company to shareholders for the use of equity finance were not an allowable deduction for the company. In response to these arguments against the classical tax system, the Australian federal government introduced the **dividend imputation system** in 1987.

The aim of the dividend imputation system is to ensure that the net income earned by the company when paid as a dividend to a shareholder is effectively taxed only once at the share-holder's marginal income-tax rate. Consequently, the outcome of the imputation system should be that, for the same amount of business net income, the after-tax income of the business's owners will be the same irrespective of whether the business is conducted as a company or as a partnership.

The way this is achieved is how the dividend imputation system gets it name. A company is required to pay company income tax on the net income it earns. When a shareholder receives a dividend from the company, the system *imputes* to the shareholder a share of the company's net income from which the dividend was derived. This imputed amount is included as assessable income of the shareholder and is taxed at the shareholder's marginal income-tax rate. To avoid double taxation of this income, each shareholder has imputed to them a share of the income tax paid by the company that can be credited against the income tax levied on the dividend amount imputed to the shareholder.

To appreciate how the imputation system works, let us continue with the example of J & S Plumbing Limited, starting at the point at which the company determines its taxable income and following the various stages to the after-tax income of its two shareholders, John and Sue Smith. Along the way, some of the names that the imputation system gives to various items will be introduced.

THE MECHANICS OF THE DIVIDEND IMPUTATION SYSTEM

Taxable income
In Example 2.5, J & S Plumbing Limited has a taxable income of $250 000, from which company tax of $75 000 (30% of taxable income) is payable. This leaves the company with $175 000 net income after tax, which can be paid to the shareholders as dividends that are *fully franked*.

Franked dividends
Under the dividend imputation system, dividends are called *franked dividends* because not only do shareholders receive a dividend amount but they also receive **franking** (also known as **imputation**) **credits**. The franking credit amount reflects the extent of income tax paid by the company on its net income from which the dividend was paid.

Accordingly, a dividend that is *fully franked* is paid from company net income on which the full amount of company income tax has been paid. Conversely, a dividend that is *unfranked* is paid from company net income on which no income tax has been paid by the company. The distinction between dividends that are fully franked, unfranked and also *partially franked* will become more apparent as this section progresses.

Returning to the example of J & S Plumbing Limited, shareholder John receives 90% of the dividends paid by the company and shareholder Sue receives 10%. As we are assuming that the company pays out as dividends all of its $175 000 net income after tax, each shareholder will receive a cheque for the following dividend amounts that are fully franked.

dividend imputation system
A tax system applying to companies and their shareholders, where the net income of the company is imputed to the shareholders and taxed at their marginal rate. Although company income is taxed twice—first at the company level and then again when dividends are received by the shareholders—the shareholders receive a credit for the income tax paid by the company.

franking (imputation) credits
An amount of income tax paid by the company that is credited to shareholders when they receive company dividends and which can be used by the shareholders to offset income tax levied on the grossed-up dividend amount imputed to them.

J & S PLUMBING LIMITED: FULLY FRANKED DIVIDEND PAYMENTS

John	$157 500	(i.e. $175 000 × 90%)
Sue	$ 17 500	(i.e. $175 000 × 10%)
Total	$175 000	(= company net income after tax)

Franking (imputation) credits

When John and Sue receive their respective dividend cheques, the tax law requires the company to advise them of the amount of the *franking credits* (also called *imputation credits*) that accompany the dividend. The amount of these credits represents each shareholder's proportion of the income tax ($75 000) paid by J & S Plumbing Limited on the company net income ($250 000) from which the dividends came, as shown below.

J & S PLUMBING LIMITED: IMPUTATION CREDITS

John	$67 500	(i.e. 90% of $75 000 company income tax)
Sue	$7 500	(i.e. 10% of $75 000 company income tax)
Total	$75 000	(= income tax paid by the company on its net income of $250 000)

When a shareholder receives a fully franked dividend, an alternative way of calculating the imputation credit is by using the following formula:

$$\text{Imputation credit} = \frac{\text{fully franked dividend} \times \text{company tax rate}}{1 - \text{company tax rate}} \qquad \textbf{(2-1)}$$

Applying this formula to the above examples:

$$\text{John's imputation credit} = \frac{157\,500 \times 0.30}{1 - 0.30} = \$67\,500$$

$$\text{Sue's imputation credit} = \frac{17\,500 \times 0.30}{1 - 0.30} = \$7500$$

The benefit to the shareholders of these imputation (franking) credits can be seen below.

Grossing-up of franked dividends

The ultimate objective of the imputation system is to ensure that, when shareholders receive dividends from a company, their after-tax income is the same as if they were in a partnership and received their share of the business's net income. This is achieved by the shareholders having imputed to them a *grossed-up* dividend amount. The grossed-up dividend amount can be calculated by either one of the following two methods:

1. Directly calculate each shareholder's share of the company's net income before tax from which the dividend was derived. In the current example, J & S Plumbing Limited's net income before tax (taxable income) from which the dividends came is $250 000. Using the same proportion as for the dividend payments, John's share of this net income is $225 000 (90% of $250 000) and Sue's is $25 000 (10% of $250 000).
2. For each shareholder, add the amount of the imputation credit to the amount of the dividend received:

Dividend + imputation credit = Grossed-up dividend amount   **(2-2)**

SHAREHOLDERS JOHN AND SUE: CALCULATION OF GROSSED-UP DIVIDEND AMOUNTS

	Dividend	+	Imputation credit	=	Grossed-up dividend amount
John	$157 500	+	$67 500	=	$225 000
Sue	$17 500	+	$7 500	=	$25 000
			Total (company net income before tax)		$250 000

Compare these grossed-up dividend amounts for each shareholder with each partner's share of the business net income in Example 2.4. They are the same! This is the aim of the imputation system.

If a shareholder receives a *fully franked dividend*, an alternative way of calculating the grossed-up dividend amount is to divide the amount of the fully franked dividend by 1 minus the company tax rate.

$$\text{Grossed-up fully franked dividend} = \frac{\text{fully franked dividend amount}}{1 - \text{company tax rate}} \qquad \textbf{(2-3)}$$

SHAREHOLDERS JOHN AND SUE: CALCULATION OF GROSSED-UP FULLY FRANKED DIVIDEND AMOUNTS

John	$157 500 fully franked dividend/(1 – 0.30)	=	$225 000
Sue	$17 500 fully franked dividend/(1 – 0.30)	=	$25 000
	Total (company net income before tax)		$250 000

TAX PAYABLE BY INDIVIDUAL SHAREHOLDERS

The next step of the imputation system requires each shareholder to include the grossed-up dividend amount in their taxable income. For individual shareholders, income tax is calculated on this amount at individual tax rates. However, the company has already paid income tax as reported by the imputation credit amounts.

So the final step of the imputation system, as shown in Example 2.7, allows shareholders to subtract the amount of their imputation credits from their tax liability. It is this last step that removes the double taxation of dividend income that occurs with a classical tax system.

EXAMPLE 2.7   Calculation of individual tax payable on fully franked dividends

	SHAREHOLDER JOHN		SHAREHOLDER SUE	
	TAX CALC.	INCOME	TAX CALC.	INCOME
Franked dividend received		$157 500		$17 500
Grossed-up franked dividend amount	$225 000		$25 000	
Taxable income	$225 000		$25 000	
Tax on taxable income[a]	($74 800)		($2 850)	
Less: Imputation credit	$67 500		$7 500	
Tax (payable)/refund		($7 300)		$4 650
After-tax income		$150 200		$22 150

a   Calculated using the marginal tax rates shown in Table 2.1.[7]

Compare the after-tax income of John and Sue in Example 2.7 with that calculated in Example 2.4 when they were taxed as partners in the business. They are exactly the same! The dividend imputation system has achieved its aim.

SURPLUS IMPUTATION (FRANKING) CREDITS

You will notice in Example 2.7 that Sue had an imputation credit ($7500) that exceeded the tax levied on her taxable income ($2850). The amount of this excess ($4650) is called a *surplus imputation (franking) credit* and in this example would be paid to Sue by the tax administration. The surplus credit arises because Sue's average tax rate of 11.4% (i.e. $2850/$25 000) on her $25 000 share of company net income is less than the 30% tax rate paid by the company on its net income.

Shareholders can also use surplus imputation credits to offset other income-tax obligations. For example, suppose during the year Sue had also earned wages income of $24 000. Her taxable income would now be $49 000 ($24 000 wages plus $25 000 grossed-up dividend). On a taxable income of $49 000, income tax of $8250 would be levied[8], but when the imputation credit of $7500 is deducted, only $750 tax would be payable by Sue.

This ability to use surplus imputation credits to reduce income tax levied on other income is important to people (like Sue) with low taxable incomes. For example, investors can plan their investment portfolios to include shares in companies that pay fully franked dividends so that surplus imputation credits can be used to offset the tax liability of other investment income such as interest.

UNFRANKED DIVIDENDS

Under Australian company law, companies are able to pay dividends to shareholders only up to the amount of current year accounting profits (i.e. net income) and revenue reserves (i.e. retained earnings). One of the complications of the Australian dividend imputation system is that quite often the accounting rules used to determine company net income can be different from the rules that the taxation law uses to determine company taxable income and tax payable. Such a situation has already been discussed (see just after Example 2.6), where the company obtained an additional tax deduction via an *investment allowance*. As this investment allowance is a creation of the tax law and is not an accounting expense, the company's taxable income was different from its accounting net income.

It is therefore possible for a company to report an accounting net income from which dividends are declared, but the tax law has not required the company to pay any income tax on that net income. If no income tax has been paid by the company on the net income from which the dividend was derived, the dividend is called an *unfranked dividend* as it has no imputation (franking) credits. This is illustrated in Example 2.8.

EXAMPLE 2.8 Unfranked dividend amounts

Returning to the example of J & S Plumbing Limited, the company's net income is still $250 000 but we will now assume that the company has purchased an expensive item of new equipment that entitles it to claim in the current tax year an investment allowance tax deduction of $250 000. As a result, the company's taxable income falls from the previous calculation of $250 000 to zero and no income tax is payable.

Therefore, the company's net income after tax will be $250 000, which can be paid out as unfranked dividends to shareholders, as follows:

J & S PLUMBING LIMITED

Previous taxable income (Example 2.2)	$250 000
– Investment allowance deduction	($250 000)
= Taxable income	0
Tax payable @ 30%	0
Company net income after tax	$250 000
Unfranked dividend paid to:	
John: 90%	$225 000
Sue: 10%	$25 000
Total	$250 000

As unfranked dividends are paid from company net income on which no tax has been paid by the company (and therefore there are no imputation credits), the grossed-up dividend amount to be included as a component of shareholders' taxable income is the same as the amount of the unfranked dividend. This is illustrated in Example 2.9.

EXAMPLE 2.9   **Calculation of individual tax payable on unfranked dividends**

Each shareholder of J & S Plumbing Limited receives unfranked dividends as detailed in Example 2.8. The value of the unfranked dividends is included in each shareholder's taxable income, and, as there are no imputation credits, each shareholder has income tax levied at their relevant marginal tax rate on the amount of the unfranked dividend:

	SHAREHOLDER JOHN		SHAREHOLDER SUE	
	TAX CALC.	INCOME	TAX CALC.	INCOME
Dividend received		$225 000		$25 000
Grossed-up franked dividend amount	$225 000		$25 000	
Taxable income	$225 000		$25 000	
Tax on taxable income[a]	($74 800)		($2 850)	
Less: Imputation credit	0		0	
Tax payable		($74 800)		($2 850)
After-tax income		$150 200		$22 150

a   Calculated using the marginal tax rates shown in Table 2.1.

PARTIALLY FRANKED DIVIDENDS

In Example 2.8, J & S Plumbing Limited was able to claim such a large investment allowance tax deduction amount that it paid no income tax on its net income of $250 000 and consequently dividends paid to shareholders are unfranked.

The third situation is between the fully franked and unfranked dividend examples. This occurs when a company has a taxable income that is somewhat less than its accounting net income and therefore any dividends paid to shareholders will be *partially franked*. Example 2.10 illustrates this situation.

EXAMPLE 2.10   **Partially franked dividend amounts**

J & S Plumbing Limited's net income (accounting profit) before tax is unchanged at $250 000 and the company is entitled to an investment allowance tax deduction, but this deduction is now only $100 000. As a consequence, the company's taxable income becomes $150 000, on which income tax of $45 000 (i.e. $150 000 \times 30\%$) is payable by the company. This leaves the company with net income after tax of $250 000 - $45 000 = $205 000, which can be paid out as dividends with imputation credits totalling $45 000. Applying the same shareholding percentages as before, each shareholder is entitled to the following dividend and imputation credits, with the grossed-up dividend amount being in the calculation of their taxable income.

	DIVIDEND	+	IMPUTATION CREDIT	=	GROSSED-UP DIVIDEND AMOUNT
John: 90%	$184 500	+	$40 500	=	$225 000
Sue: 10%	$20 500	+	$4 500	=	$25 000
Total	$205 000	+	$45 000	=	$250 000

It can be seen that the dividends in Example 2.10 are only partially franked by taking John as an example. If the $184 500 dividend had been fully franked, John would have received imputation credits of $79 071 (calculated using equation 2-1), whereas he received imputation credits of only $40 500. The effect of the lower imputation credit amount on the tax payable by each shareholder is illustrated in Example 2.11.

EXAMPLE 2.11 Calculation of individual tax payable on partially franked dividends

| | SHAREHOLDER JOHN | | SHAREHOLDER SUE | |
	TAX CALC.	INCOME	TAX CALC.	INCOME
Dividend received		$184 500		$20 500
Grossed-up franked dividend amount	$225 000		$25 000	
Taxable income	$225 000		$25 000	
– Individual tax levied[a]	($74 800)		($2 850)	
Less: Imputation credit	$40 500		$4 500	
Individual tax (payable)/refund		($34 300)		$1 650
After-tax income		$150 200		$22 150

a   Calculated using the marginal tax rates shown in Table 2.1.

Now that you are familiar with the major components of the dividend imputation system, the next section examines the extent to which the system achieves its primary aim of ensuring that the net income of a company is not taxed twice, as occurs under a classical tax system.

For answers go to MyFinanceLab or www.pearson.com.au/9781442539174

Concept check

2.4 Are there any differences in the tax deductibility of interest expense between a classical tax system and a dividend imputation system?

2.5 How does a classical tax system result in the double taxation of company net income paid to shareholders?

2.6 How does the Australian dividend imputation system ensure that company net income paid to shareholders is only taxed once at the shareholder's marginal tax rate?

INTEGRATION OF THE DIVIDEND IMPUTATION SYSTEM

The discussion and examples presented so far have been of a dividend imputation system with *full integration*. What does 'full integration' mean? Full integration occurs when the dividend imputation system produces the same amount of net income after tax for the owners of the business irrespective of whether the business is conducted as a partnership or as a company. In other words, the outcome of the dividend imputation system is as if the shareholders were integrated into their company as a single tax entity, as occurs with a partnership.

You can see full integration occurring in Table 2.2, where in each of the scenarios the net income after tax received by John from his 90% ownership of the J & S Plumbing business is the same amount of $150 200.

Another way you can see full integration in Table 2.2 is that John's 90% share of the $250 000 business net income determines the total amount of income tax of $74 800, and that any increase (or decrease) in the amount of income tax paid by the company automatically

TABLE 2.2   John Smith: summary of net income after tax

	PARTNERSHIP	FULLY FRANKED DIVIDEND	UNFRANKED DIVIDEND	PARTIALLY FRANKED DIVIDEND
J & S Plumbing business	(Example 2.4)	(Example 2.7)	(Example 2.9)	(Example 2.11)
Business net income	$250 000	$250 000	$250 000	$250 000
– Tax paid by business (company)	0	(75 000)	0	(45 000)
= Business net income after tax	250 000	175 000	250 000	205 000
John Smith				
Receives 90% share of business net income after tax	225 000	157 500	225 000	184 500
– Tax paid by John	(74 800)	(7 300)	(74 800)	(34 300)
Net income after tax	$150 200	$150 200	$150 200	$150 200

'flows through' via the amount of imputation credits to decrease (or increase) the amount of income tax payable by John. The result is that under each scenario the net income after tax that John receives is a constant amount of $150 200.

EXTENT OF FULL INTEGRATION OF THE DIVIDEND IMPUTATION SYSTEM IN AUSTRALIA

We have now detailed two tax systems that have significantly different impacts on the net income after tax that shareholders receive from a given amount of net income earned by their company (e.g. $250 000).

At one extreme is the dividend imputation system with full integration where a reduction in the amount of income tax paid by the company *does not* affect the after-tax net income of shareholders (see Table 2.2).

At the other extreme is the classical tax system where a reduction in the amount of income tax paid by the company *increases* the after-tax net income of shareholders (see Example 2.6). A classical tax system usually reflects the explicit tax policy and laws of a country where the net income of companies is taxed twice. It is also possible for the dividend imputation system to have *no integration*, with the effect that a particular company is taxed as if it were subject to a classical tax system. This occurs for non-Australian resident shareholders who are subject to the income tax laws of their home country and are not able to use Australian imputation credits to offset their home country tax. The result is that the net income of the Australian company that is the source of the dividend paid to the non-resident shareholder will be taxed twice— first by Australia as company income tax and then by the shareholder's home country as tax on dividend income.

In between the two extremes of full integration and no integration is *part integration* of the dividend imputation system where the amount of a shareholder's net income after tax is affected *to some extent* by the amount of income tax paid by the company. This can occur when an Australian company earns income from overseas and, although any income tax paid to the foreign government provides a tax credit to the company, it does not qualify as an imputation credit for shareholders. Consequently, the less foreign income tax the company pays, the more Australian income tax it pays, which will provide Australian shareholders with imputation credits.

What is the implication of integration of the dividend imputation system for the financial management of Australian companies? We can conclude that, for a given amount of company net income (e.g. $250 000) that is ultimately paid to shareholders as a dividend, the effect of financial decisions that increase or decrease the amount of income tax paid by the company on the amount of shareholder net income after tax and therefore shareholder wealth will *depend on the extent of integration of the dividend imputation system for the company.*

OBJECTIVE

Appreciate some of
the implications of the
Australian taxation system
for the financial decisions of
Australian individuals and
businesses.

Implications of dividend imputation for business decision making

The introduction of the dividend imputation system has generally resulted in Australian company shareholders being financially better off than was the case under the former classical tax system. For example, Chapter 17 details evidence that the managers of Australian companies have made decisions to increase dividend payout ratios so as to maximise the tax benefit that imputation credits provide to many of their shareholders.

However, dividend payout is not the only business decision in which taxation considerations figure prominently. It will be seen that taxes (income tax and capital-gains tax) are also important factors in the following chapters:

- Chapters 11 to 13, which deal with investment decisions by businesses
- Chapter 14, which details the calculation of the cost of capital that reflects decisions about the sources of finance the business uses to fund its investment projects
- Chapter 16, which identifies the factors that need to be considered in deciding the mix or proportions of debt and equity finance that the business should use
- Chapter 17, which examines dividend policy decisions
- Chapter 19, which outlines the factors that impact on the decision to use preference shares and convertible securities.

Underpinning each of these financial management decisions is the objective to *maximise the after-tax wealth of the owners of the business*. But, as the previous sections of this chapter have outlined, the impact of the tax system on the after-tax wealth of the owners of a business is not entirely straightforward. To assist the correct inclusion of the impact of tax in the analysis of investment and financing decisions, allocating an entity into one of the following three groups is recommended.

Taxation category 1
Companies with shareholders that are fully or substantially integrated by the dividend imputation system

Implications for financial management
- The amount of income tax paid by the company on its net income is largely *irrelevant* to the amount of net income after tax of its shareholders (see Table 2.2).
- Investment and financing decisions should focus on maximising the company's *pre-tax* net income and cash flows because reducing the amount of income tax paid by the company will not increase the net income after tax of shareholders. This same conclusion applies to organisations such as eligible cooperatives and educational and charitable institutions that do not pay income tax. Their financial decisions should be to maximise the amount of the entity's net income.

Taxation category 2
(a) Sole trader
(b) Partnerships
(c) Companies with shareholders that are not integrated by the dividend imputation system

Implications for financial management
- The amount of income tax paid on business net income is *relevant* to the amount of net income after tax of the owners of the business.
- Investment and financing decisions should focus on maximising the *after-tax* income and cash flows of the business because reducing the amount of income tax paid by the business/ company will increase the net income after tax of owners/shareholders.

Although the major focus of this book is on companies, many small businesses are conducted as a sole trader or as a partnership. The owners of these sole trader and partnership businesses pay income tax on their share(s) of the business's net income at individual tax rates. So, decisions that reduce the amount of tax payable on business net income will increase the after-tax income and wealth of the owners. For these non-company businesses, the major implication for their investment and financing decisions is clear. Minimise the amount of income tax so as to maximise the business's *after-tax* income and cash flows.

This same applies to Australian companies where there is no integration of the dividend imputation tax system as its shareholders are effectively subject to a classical tax system. A company would be in this category if most or all of its shareholders were resident overseas and unable to use any imputation (franking) credits to offset their home country tax liabilities.

The major implication for the investment and financing decisions of these Taxation category 2 companies is that the company should make decisions that reduce the amount of company income tax it is required to pay and thereby *maximise the after-tax net income* and cash flows that can be paid to the shareholders as a dividend.

Taxation category 3
The in-between case—companies with shareholders that are part integrated by the dividend imputation system

Implications for financial management
- The amount of income tax paid by the company *has some effect* on the after-tax wealth of its shareholders.
- Investment and financing decisions should focus on maximising business *after-effective-tax* income and cash flows.

The impact on shareholders of Taxation category 3 companies is that the amount of Australian income tax paid by the company can have some effect on their after-tax income and wealth. The question is: how much of an effect? One way of answering this question is to measure and use an effective company tax rate (T_{eff}) rather than the statutory company tax rate (T). The effective tax rate is discussed in the 'One Step Further' box below.

Identification of the entity's taxation category
For businesses that are not conducted as a company (e.g. sole trader, partnership) it is easy to identify that they fall into Taxation category 2 and the financial management decision-making focus should be on the after-tax cash flows of the business.

With companies, it is necessary to determine the level of integration that reflects the extent that shareholders are able to utilise imputation credits. In practice, this is often not easy to do, especially for Taxation category 3 companies, which require estimation of the proportion of the value of imputation credits that shareholders can utilise to credit against their own income tax. Accordingly, the analysis and examples in subsequent chapters will refer only to category 1 and 2 entities.

Concept check
2.7   What does integration of the dividend imputation system mean for companies and their shareholders?
2.8   Why is it recommended that before-tax values be used to evaluate the investment decisions of Taxation category 1 companies?
2.9   Why is it recommended that after-tax values be used to evaluate the investment decisions of Taxation category 2 companies?

For answers go to MyFinanceLab or www.pearson.com.au/9781442539174

ONE STEP FURTHER

THE EFFECTIVE RATE OF COMPANY TAX UNDER THE DIVIDEND IMPUTATION SYSTEM

The ultimate objective of the Australian dividend imputation system is for income tax to be levied at the shareholder's marginal tax rate on the net income earned by the company's business. By taxing shareholders on the grossed-up value of dividends and providing them with imputation credits for tax paid by the company, the imputation system aims to ensure that any income tax paid by the company is irrelevant to the amount of net income after tax of its shareholders.

An alternative way of explaining this outcome from the perspective of the after-tax wealth of shareholders is via an *effective* company tax rate that reflects the income tax levied on the company at the statutory company rate (T) and the extent to which shareholders are able to utilise the value of imputation (franking) credits.

As the shareholders of a Taxation category 1 company are able to fully utilise all the value of the income tax paid by the company via imputation credits, the *effective* company income tax rate (T_{eff}) is zero because this company has *effectively* paid no income tax.

However, factors such as foreign income earned by the company and foreign shareholders can reduce the value of imputation credits to some or all of the company's shareholders. If these factors are significant, the dividend imputation system will produce the same result as a classical tax system because business income will be taxed twice, first as income of the company and then as dividend income of the shareholders. As these Taxation category 2 companies pay income at the nominal or statutory company tax rate, T, and their shareholders get no benefit from the value imputation credits, the effective company tax rate (T_{eff}) is the same as the statutory company tax rate, T. Consequently, any reduction in the amount of income tax paid by the company will result in an increase in the net income after tax of shareholders.

Between the two extremes of Taxation category 1 and 2 companies are Taxation category 3 companies, whose shareholders can only *partly* benefit from the value of imputation credits. This means that there will be some double taxation of business income paid to shareholders and therefore the effective company tax rate (T_{eff}) for category 3 companies will be somewhere between the two extremes of zero and T.

More formally, the effective company tax rate (T_{eff}) can be defined as follows:

$$T_{eff} = T(1 - u) \tag{2-4}$$

Where T = the nominal or statutory company income tax rate

u = the proportion of the income tax paid by the company that shareholders are effectively able to use to offset their individual income-tax liabilities.

In this equation, u has a maximum value of 1 if all of the value of imputation credits is able to be fully utilised by all shareholders to offset their income-tax liability and a minimum value of 0 if none of the value of imputation credits is able to be utilised by any of the shareholders.

Therefore, equation (2-4) can be applied to the identification of Australian companies:

1. Taxation category 1—*effective company tax rate is zero*.
   Companies with Australian-derived income and Australian shareholders who can fully utilise the value of imputation credits. Thus $u = 1$ and $T_{eff} = T(1 - u) = T(1 - 1) = 0$.
2. Taxation category 2—*effective company tax rate is equal to the statutory company tax rate (T)*.
   Companies with shareholders who are not able to utilise the value of imputation credits. Thus $u = 0$ and $T_{eff} = T(1 - u) = T(1 - 0) = T$.

3. Taxation category 3—*effective company tax rate is between zero and the statutory company tax rate (T)*.

For these companies, the effective company tax rate varies from case to case. For example, if on average shareholders in IBC Ltd can utilise only 70% of imputation credits, u equals 0.7. Accordingly, with the statutory company income tax rate (T) = 30%, this company's effective tax rate is given by equation (2-4) as: $T_{eff} = T(1 - u) = 0.3(1 - 0.7) = 0.9$ (9%).

A 9% effective tax rate makes sense intuitively, because if IBC Ltd's shareholders are only able to utilise 70% of the value of imputation credits, the company is closer to being in category 1 than in category 2 and so the effective tax rate for the company would be expected to be closer to zero than to the statutory rate (T) of 30%.

What is the significance of the *effective* company tax rate (T_{eff})? It is an estimate of the extent to which the income tax paid by Australian companies is relevant to the net income after tax of shareholders and therefore to their after-tax wealth. Consequently, if a company determines that it has an effective company tax rate of, say, 6%, then this rate should be used in the evaluation of its investment and financing alternatives.

International spotlight

Shareholders subject to the tax law of a country with a *classical tax system* face double taxation of business income, first when earned by the company and second when paid to the shareholders as dividends. A classical tax system applied in Australia until 1987, when the dividend imputation system was introduced, and continues to apply in many other countries around the world.

Back to the principles

For a firm to correctly evaluate its investment projects it has to apply **Principle 4: Incremental cash flows—it's only what changes that counts.** One of the incremental project cash flows is income tax. However, the impact of incremental tax cash flows on the wealth of the owners of the business will depend on the tax system. Accordingly, some understanding of the tax system is necessary to correctly apply **Principle 8: Taxes bias business decisions.**

RETAINED EARNINGS/PROFITS

In the example of J & S Plumbing Limited, it was assumed that all of the company's after-tax income was paid out to the shareholders as dividends. This is unusual for large Australian companies, as their normal policy is to retain a proportion of after-tax income (profits) to fund future operations and growth. Under the dividend imputation system the amount of tax paid by the company on the income generating these retained profits provides imputation credits that are held by the company until dividends are paid to the shareholders.

Shareholders of companies that retain profits with imputation credits would hope that the company's ordinary share price would rise to reflect the value of the dividends and imputation credits that have not yet been paid. However, if the shareholders sell their shares at higher prices, they may incur *capital-gains tax* (see next section). Thus, when shareholders sell shares

Your money

To be a successful investor you do not need to know all the intricacies of complex tax law. But you do need to know how taxes impact on your income and wealth, particularly the taxation of dividends and capital gains. You also need to know when to call on the tax experts for specialised advice on complex tax situations.

in companies that retain some profits with imputation credits, there can be a form of double taxation, as income tax will have been paid by the company and the shareholder will be paying tax on any capital gains when the shares are sold.

These issues will be discussed in more detail in later chapters, particularly Chapter 17, which examines company dividend policy.

OBJECTIVE 4

Understand the basic elements of Australian capital-gains taxation.

An introduction to capital-gains taxation

Apart from levying income tax, many countries also levy capital-gains tax. A capital gain is the profit resulting from selling an asset at an amount higher than the sum for which it was purchased. In 1985 capital-gains tax was introduced to the Australian tax system, and this tax essentially requires taxpayers to include in their taxable income *capital gains* associated with an asset that has been sold in the year of income.

The Australian capital-gains tax law has the following main components:

1. The taxation of capital gains applies only to assets that have been purchased after 19 September 1985. Assets acquired before that date and sold for an amount greater than the purchase price are generally not subject to tax.

2. A **capital gain** is assessed as the difference between the *sale value* of the asset and its *purchase value*. For assets purchased prior to 21 September 1999, a modification of the previous system which indexed the cost base (purchase value) can be used to determine the assessable capital gain.

3. A **capital loss** occurs when the *sale value* of the asset is less than its *purchase value*. Capital losses can be used as offsets against assessable capital gains but not as offsets against other assessable income. Any surplus capital losses of a particular tax year may be carried forward indefinitely to offset assessable capital gains of future years.

4. A concessional discount is provided for certain taxpayers exempting a proportion of the net assessable capital gain (i.e. assessable capital gains minus capital losses from current and/or previous years) from inclusion in taxable income for the year. The amount of the exemption depends on the class of taxpayer: companies receive no exemption; qualifying superannuation funds receive an exemption of 33.3% of the value of assessable capital gains; individuals and trusts are entitled to an exemption of 50%.

Example 2.12 illustrates the basics of the Australian capital-gains tax system for an individual.

capital gain
A capital gain occurs when the sale price minus the purchase price is positive.

capital loss
A capital loss occurs when the sale price minus the purchase price is negative.

EXAMPLE 2.12 Calculation of capital-gains tax payable by an individual taxpayer

On 20 January of the current financial year John Smith sold his shares in Nova Bank Limited for $50 000. As these shares were purchased a little over 12 months previously for $30 000, their sale produces a capital gain of $20 000. Assuming that John has sold no other assets during the financial year and has no capital losses carried forward from previous years, the 50% concessional discount results, so that only $10 000 of the capital gain has to be included in his taxable income.

Assuming that John's other income during this financial year gives him a marginal tax rate at the top rate of 45%, all of the $10 000 taxable capital gain will be taxed at that rate and John will be required to pay tax of $4500 on this amount (i.e. $10 000 × 0.45).

Note that, because of the 50% discount concession, the average tax rate on the capital gain ($20 000) received by John is 22.5% ($4500/$20 000 = 22.5%).

Concept check

2.10 What is a capital gain?

2.11 What are the restrictions that the Australian tax system places on capital losses?

For answers go to MyFinanceLab or
www.pearson.com.au/9781442539174

Finance at work

TELSTRA'S SHARE BUYBACK SCHEME

In 2004 Telstra announced a $750 million share buyback that was the latest in its four-year program to return capital to shareholders. The buyback gave shareholders the opportunity to sell their shares back to the company at a price set by the company. For shareholders who participated in the buyback, the amount they received comprised two components—a capital return amount of $1.50 and a fully franked dividend amount equal to the difference between $1.50 and the buyback price.

As the company set the buyback price at an amount below the current share price in the market, what was the attraction of the buyback for shareholders? The answer is tax benefits. Specifically, the fully franked dividend component provided shareholders with imputation (franking) credits. For example, if the buyback price was $4.50, shareholders would receive not only $1.50 capital return and $3.00 dividend but also $1.29 imputation credits. This would give shareholders who sold their shares back to the company a theoretical total value per share of $5.79.

However, the value of imputation credits varies for different shareholders. For example, Telstra's Australian shareholders with low marginal tax rates (such as retirees, charities and superannuation funds) might have obtained surplus imputation credits that could have been used to offset taxes on their other income. On the other hand, high marginal tax rate shareholders could have used all the imputation credits to offset only some of the tax levied on the dividend component of the buyback. In the extreme case, the imputation credits would have had no value for overseas shareholders who participated in the buyback.

The buyback also provided an opportunity for shareholders who had purchased Telstra shares for amounts much higher than the current share price to realise the capital loss. For example, an investor who paid $7.40 to buy Telstra shares through the T2 float and sold his/her shares through the buyback could claim a capital loss of $5.90 per share (i.e. $7.40 – $1.50).

Source: Based on D. Koch, 'Own Telstra shares? It's crunch time', *Sydney Morning Herald*, 4 October, 2004.

Implications of income tax and capital-gains tax on rates of return for shareholders

OBJECTIVE 5

Appreciate some of the implications of income tax and capital-gains tax on rates of return for shareholders.

Investors who want to buy shares in a particular company will have to pay the current price for those shares. This will be either the *issue price* when new shares are offered by the company or the *quoted price* on the stock exchange for previously issued shares.

The discussion in the previous sections has highlighted that the return that shareholders may obtain from their share investment has two tax aspects:

- taxation of any dividend received
- taxation of any capital gain when the shares are sold.

The amount of tax payable on both these components will depend on the tax law applying to each shareholder. For example, Australian resident shareholders would need to know, among other things:

- the amount of the dividend they received
- the amount of the imputation credit (if any) associated with the dividend
- the amount of their other net income (if any)
- their marginal tax rate
- whether they had any capital losses available to offset any assessable capital gain.

After shareholders have determined the amount of tax payable on dividends and capital gains, they are able to calculate the after-tax *dollar* return from the share investment and the after-tax percentage *rate* of return from the investment. Example 2.13 illustrates some of these calculations.

EXAMPLE 2.13 Calculation of after-tax rates of return

Continuing with Example 2.12, John Smith has also received during the financial year fully franked dividends totalling $2000 from Nova Bank. Combined with the capital gain of $20000, his total dollar return during the year from these shares is $22000 and the after-tax return is calculated as follows:

	TAX CALC.	INCOME
Fully franked dividend received		$2000
Grossed-up franked dividend[a]	$2857	
Capital gain received		$20000
Assessable capital gain[b]	$10000	
Incremental taxable income	$12857	
Incremental individual tax levied[c]	($5786)	
Less: Imputation credit	$857	
Individual tax (payable)/refund		($4929)
After-tax return		$17071

a   Using equation (2-2), the grossed-up value of the fully franked dividend = dividend amount/(1 − company tax rate) = $2000 (1 − 0.30) = $2857. Imputation credit = $857.
b   Assessable capital gain = $20000 × 50% = $10000.
c   Assuming John's marginal tax rate is 45%.

On the original investment in shares of $30000, the after-tax rate of return = $17071/$30000 = 57% p.a.

This rate of return can be compared with the after-tax rate of return calculated for other investments (such as property and fixed-interest investments). However, to do this comparison correctly will require measurement of the risk of each investment, which is discussed in detail in Chapter 9.

In Australia there are three main types of taxpaying entities: the individual (which includes partnerships), the company and the fiduciary. The Australian income-tax system requires taxpayers to calculate their taxable income from their assessable income minus allowable deductions. Income tax is then levied on the taxable income at rates of tax applying to the taxpaying entity.

OBJECTIVE 1

Although the rules specified by the tax law to determine an entity's taxable income can be different from the rules accountants use to calculate an entity's net income, the taxable income for many businesses will often be equivalent to its accounting net income (profit) plus any assessable net capital gains.

Until 1987 Australian companies and shareholders were subject to a *classical tax system* whereby the company's net income paid to shareholders as dividends was taxed twice. First, income tax was paid by the company on the net income it had earned and, second, income tax was paid by the shareholders on dividends received from the company.

Since 1987 the *dividend imputation system* has applied in Australia to the taxation of the income of companies and their shareholders. The aim of this system is to remove the double taxation of company net income by giving shareholders a credit for the income tax paid by the company. The effective outcome of this system is that when the company's net income is distributed as dividends to shareholders it is taxed only once, at each shareholder's tax rates. As a consequence, the amount of income tax payable by a company on its net income will not change the after-tax wealth of its shareholders.

OBJECTIVE 2

A major implication of the Australian income taxation system is for the after-tax wealth of owners to vary depending on the type of business entity.

OBJECTIVE 3

For *Taxation category 1* companies, the amount of income tax paid by the company does not affect the after-tax wealth of shareholders.

For *Taxation category 2* companies—sole trader and partnership firms—the amount of income tax paid by the company/firm directly affects the after-tax wealth of shareholders/firm owners.

For *Taxation category 3* companies, the impact on shareholder after-tax wealth is between the two extremes of taxation categories 1 and 2.

In 1985 capital-gains tax was introduced into the Australian tax system. For Australian shareholders this system requires tax to be paid at income-tax rates on any capital gain that results from the shareholder selling company shares for a value that is higher than the purchase value.

OBJECTIVE 4

To be able to correctly compare alternative investments, investors need to determine the after-tax rate of returns. As many investments provide a return via income (e.g. interest, dividends) and via capital gains (changes in prices), it is important for investors to have some knowledge of the taxation of income and capital gains.

OBJECTIVE 5

Providing a brief outline of the major elements of Australian taxation of income and capital gains, the main aim of this chapter was to identify the major implications that taxation has on financial management decisions.

Key terms

capital gain	48	dividend imputation system	37
capital loss	48	franking (imputation) credits	37
classical tax system	35	tax savings	33

For a complete flashcard glossary go to MyFinanceLab at www.pearson.com.au/myfinancelab

Review questions

2-1 What is the difference between assessable income and taxable income?

2-2 Why is the taxable income of a business not always the same as its accounting net profit?

2-3 Why is the marginal tax rate the important rate for financial decisions?

2-4 Identify the components required to determine the tax payable for an individual taxpayer.

2-5 Does a partnership pay taxes on its net income? Explain.

2-6 What is the major implication of the classical tax system for companies?

2-7 What is the purpose of the dividend imputation system and how does it achieve its aim?

2-8 **(a)** What is the difference between a fully franked dividend, a partially franked dividend and an unfranked dividend?
(b) How should each be included in calculating a shareholder's taxable income?

2-9 What is an imputation credit and what is its purpose in the dividend imputation system?

2-10 What is the importance of identifying whether a fully integrated dividend imputation system applies to a company and its shareholders?

Self-test problems

For answers go to MyFinanceLab
www.pearson.com.au/myfinancelab

All the following problems apply the individual income-tax rates as detailed in Table 2.1 and a company income-tax rate of 30%.

ST-1 (*Individual income tax*) Mark Roscoe runs a truck-repair and spare-parts business as a sole trader. During the most recent year his business generated sales of $4 million, with a combined cost of goods sold and operating expenses of $3.2 million. Also, $600 000 in interest expense was paid during the year. Calculate Mark Roscoe's income-tax liability for the most recent year.

ST-2 (*Individual income tax, fully franked dividends*) When preparing his current year's tax return Mark Roscoe realised that he had forgotten about the fully franked dividend of $5000 which he had received from an investment in a company. Determine the impact of this dividend on the tax payable by Mark Roscoe.

ST-3 (*Individual income tax, fully franked dividend, capital loss*) Roger Cooper works as a part-time accountant and received a salary and wages income of $27 000 for the financial year just ended. Roger incurred expenses of $200 related to his work, which he can claim as an allowable deduction in his tax return. Roger also received interest income of $400 and fully franked dividends of $1500. In June of the financial year just ended he sold some shares in XYZ Ltd for $1600 which he had bought for $2000 two months earlier. Determine the amount of tax to be paid by Roger Cooper.

ST-4 (*Individual income tax, tax saving*) Roger Cooper realised after doing his tax calculations in question ST-3 that he had omitted to claim a tax deduction for $500 for travel expenses related to his work. Determine the effect of the additional allowable deduction on Roger's tax liability.

ST-5 (*Individual income tax, partially franked dividend, unfranked dividend*) Diana Drennan runs a photographic store that had sales of $600 000 during the past year. Her cost of goods sold was 70% of sales, and operating expenses, including depreciation, amounted to $140 000. During the past year Diana received an unfranked dividend of $2000 from MPQ Ltd and a partially franked dividend from STV Ltd of $1500 with an attached imputation credit of $150. Determine the tax payable for Diana Drennan for the past year.

ST-6 (*Company income tax, fully franked dividend*) Burgess Limited is an oil wholesaling company that had sales last year of $2.5 million with cost of goods sold of $700 000. The company paid interest of $200 000 and its cash operating expenses were $150 000. Its depreciation expense was $150 000.

(a) Determine Burgess Limited's taxable income and tax payable for the last year.
(b) Determine the total amount of (i) fully franked dividends and (ii) imputation credits that the company is able to declare from its past year's results.

ST-7 (*Company income tax, tax saving, partially franked dividends*) The tax accountant for Burgess Limited in question ST-6 forgot about the special depreciation concession that the federal government had granted to oil wholesalers for the past tax year. The special depreciation concession entitles taxpayers to claim a deduction for depreciation equal to 150% of the standard depreciation deduction.

(a) Determine the impact of the company claiming the depreciation concession in calculating its taxable income and tax payable.
(b) Determine the total amount of franked dividends and imputation credits that Burgess Limited is now able to declare.

Problems

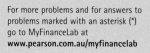

All the following problems apply the individual income-tax rates as detailed in Table 2.1 and a company tax rate of 30%.

2-1* (*Individual income tax*) Amy Chou operates her own business as a sole trader, which during the past financial year had sales of $340 000, with the cost of merchandise sold being 55% of sales. Her cash operating expenses were $50 000, depreciation expense was $10 000 and interest on bank loans used to finance the business was $25 000. Determine Amy's tax liability for the past financial year.

2-2 (*Individual income tax, tax saving*) Amy Chou in question 2-1 omitted to include in her tax calculations her entitlement to an allowable deduction for an investment allowance equal to 10% of the cost of a new computerised cash-register system that she had bought for $50 000. Determine the effect of this additional tax deduction on Amy's tax liability.

2-3* (*Individual income tax, tax saving*) After adjusting her tax calculations in question 2-2, Amy Chou realised that she had also omitted to include commission income of $45 000 which she had received in the past financial year. Determine the effect of this additional assessable income on Amy's tax liability calculated in question 2-2.

2-4 (*Individual income tax, capital gains*) Kate Menielle is the principal of a management consultancy business run as a sole trader. During the past financial year the business earned fees of $900 000 and incurred employee expenses equal to 70% of fees earned. Other operating expenses amounted to $85 000. Also during the period in question, Kate sold an investment asset for $160 000 which she had bought two years earlier at a cost of $115 000. Determine Kate Menielle's tax liability for the financial year just ended.

2-5* (*Individual income tax, fully franked dividends, unfranked dividends*) For the tax year just ended, sales for Phil Schubert & Co., which is a sole-trader business supplying statistical information to engineering companies, amounted to $120 000, with operating and depreciation expenses of $50 000 and $10 000 respectively. Also during the tax year just ended, Phil received fully franked dividends of $15 000 and unfranked dividends of $5000. Determine Phil Schubert's tax payable.

2-6 (*Individual income tax, fully franked dividends, unfranked dividends*) Phil Schubert in question 2-5 had got himself into a bit of a muddle in calculating his tax payable. He had classified $5000 as being an unfranked dividend, whereas on closer inspection of his records he realised that he had received a fully franked dividend of $3500 with imputation credits of $1500. Therefore, he should have included in his tax calculations the receipt of fully franked dividends totalling $18 500.

(a) Determine the effect of this change in dividend income on Phil's tax liability for the last tax year.

(b) Comment on the effect of this change on Phil's after-tax income.

2-7* (*Individual income tax, franked dividends, unfranked dividends*) Sam Marino is semi-retired and received wages from part-time work of $31 000 last year. He also received net income of $2000 from a rental property and the following dividend income from five companies:

COMPANY	DIVIDEND	IMPUTATION CREDIT
1	250	107
2	695	297
3	430	Nil
4	720	220
5	189	81
Total	$2284	$705

Determine Sam Marino's tax liability for the last tax year.

2-8 (*Individual income tax, fully franked dividends, unfranked dividends, capital gain*) Joan Johnson runs an electronics store as a sole trader and had sales in the last financial year of $690 000, cost of goods sold of $320 000 and operating expenses of $110 000. The business paid interest of $18 000 and had a depreciation expense of $25 000. In addition, Joan has an extensive portfolio of public company shares and during the last financial year she received $25 000 in fully franked dividends and $6500 in unfranked dividends. She also sold shares in two companies that she had held for more than 12 months:

For more problems and for answers to problems marked with an asterisk (*) go to MyFinanceLab at **www.pearson.com.au/myfinancelab**

| ABC Ltd Sale value | $25 000 | Purchase cost $17 000 |
| XYZ Ltd Sale value | $10 000 | Purchase cost $14 000 |

Determine Joan Johnson's tax liability for the last financial year.

2-9* (*Corporate income tax*) Sales for Sunlake Ltd during the last financial year amounted to $5 million. The company provides parts and supplies for oil exploration companies. Gross profits for the year were $2.5 million and operating expenses totalled $900 000. The company earned interest income of $15 000 and incurred interest expense on funds borrowed of $100 000. Determine the tax liability of Sunlake Ltd for the last financial year and identify the total amount of fully franked dividends that the company would be able to pay and the amount of imputation credits associated with the dividends.

2-10 (*Corporate income tax, tax saving, franked dividends*) Sunlake Ltd in question 2-9 has just realised that it is entitled to an investment allowance deduction which was not included in the calculation of its tax liability. The investment allowance deduction is equal to 10% of the cost of equipment that the company had purchased for $500 000. Determine the effect of claiming the investment allowance on Sunlake Ltd's tax liability and identify the type and amount of dividends the company is able to pay.

2-11*(*Corporate income tax, unfranked dividends*) Compstart Limited develops and sells computer software. The company's past year's sales were $4.5 million, with the cost of sales totalling $2.2 million. Other operating expenses were $175 000, depreciation expense was $130 000 and the company paid $150 000 interest on loans. In addition, during the past year the company spent $1.5 million on wages for contract programmers who were engaged to write a new accounting software program that the company intends to sell. Under the federal government's drive to encourage research and development, the company is entitled to a tax deduction equal to 150% of the wages cost incurred in developing the new computer program. Determine the tax liability for Compstart Limited and identify the type and amount of dividends the company is able to pay from last year's results.

2-12 (*Corporate income tax, individual income tax*) M&K Pty Ltd supplies wholesale industrial chemicals, and last year the company had sales of $6.5 million with cost of goods sold and operating expenses amounting to 90% of sales. Depreciation and interest expenses were $150 000 and $360 000 respectively. The company has two shareholders, with M. Utsumi holding 80% of the shares and K. Utsumi owning 20%. Assuming that the company pays out 100% of its net profit after tax as dividends and both shareholders earn no other assessable income and have no allowable deductions, determine the tax liability of M. Utsumi and K. Utsumi.

2-13 (*After-tax rate of return*) Wilson Change receives wages of $65 000 per year. A bit over 12 months ago he bought some shares in Amax Limited for $20 000 and has just sold them for $27 000. Also, during the year he received from Amax Limited a fully franked dividend of $1800. Determine the after-tax rate of return Wilson earned from his investment in Amax Limited.

2-14 (*Profit/loss on sale*) Jasper Limited is considering selling one of its old machines. The machine, purchased for $30 000 five years ago, had an expected life of 10 years and an expected salvage value of zero. As Jasper uses straight-line depreciation, depreciation of $3000 per year has been claimed as a tax deduction, with the income-tax rate being 28%.

(a) If Jasper could sell the old machine for $25 000, what would be the taxes associated with the sale?

(b) If the old machine were sold for $15 000, what would be the taxes associated with the sale?

(c) If the old machine were sold for $12 000, what would be the taxes associated with the sale?

2-15 (*Profit/loss on sale*) Jason Alexander makes cabinets and is considering replacing his existing hand-operated, wood-planing machine with a new fully automated machine. The existing machine when purchased five years ago at a cost of $50 000 was estimated to have a useful life of 10 years and zero salvage value. Due to technological obsolescence, Jason estimates that he could currently sell the existing machine for only $5000. If Jason's marginal tax rate is 30%, determine:

(a) the amount of annual depreciation and current written-down value of the existing machine

(b) the amount of any profit or loss on sale of the existing machine

(c) the amount of tax payable or saved from the sale of the existing machine.

2-16 (*Corporate income tax, capital gains, individual income tax*) Margot and Spence Pty Ltd is an electronics dealer and distributor. Sales for the last year were $690 000 and cost of goods sold and operating expenses totalled $430 000. The company also paid $70 000 in interest and its depreciation expense totalled $40 000. In addition, the company sold land for $147 000 which it had purchased two years ago for $37 000. The company has two shareholders, Margot Crisp and Spence Smith, who own 70% and 30% of the company's shares respectively. Both shareholders earned no other assessable income in the last year and had no allowable deductions. Determine the after-tax income for Margot Crisp and Spence Smith for the last year.

2-17 (*Effective tax rate*) Neoman Ltd has estimated that its shareholders on average can use only 60% of franking credits.

    (a) What is the company's effective tax rate and what are the implications of this rate if the company is entitled to a tax deduction equal to 125% of research and development expenditure totalling $100 000?

    (b) What would your answer to (a) be if the company and its shareholders were fully integrated by the imputation system?

    (c) What would your answer to (a) be if the company and its shareholders were not integrated by the imputation system?

2-18 (*Individual income tax*) Sam Wills runs a juice bar business as a sole trader. For the financial year just ended, he earned sales revenue of $146 000; paid operating costs of $87 000; and incurred depreciation expenses of $17 000. Determine Sam's tax liability for the past financial year.

2-19 (*Individual income tax, tax saving*) Sam Wills in question 2-18 omitted to include in his tax calculations $6500 interest and fees that he had paid on his bank overdraft. Determine the effect of this additional tax deduction on Sam's tax liability.

2-20 (*Indiviual income tax, capital gains*) Phoebe Snowden is paid extremely well as the finance director in a large Australian public company and has a marginal personal tax rate of 45 cents in the dollar. During the financial year just ended Phoebe sold, for $125 000, shares in a company that she had bought five years earlier for $68 000. Determine Phoebe's tax liability for the capital gain.

2-21 (*Individual income tax, fully franked dividends, unfranked dividends*) Lucy Campbell has been retired for a number of years and supports herself with the income earned from her share investment portfolio that is currently valued at $900 000. For the last financial year, Lucy received $14 480 fully franked dividends, $37 350 from partially franked dividends with imputation credits of $10 290, and unfranked dividends of $2150. Determine Lucy's tax liability.

2-22 (*After-tax rate of return*) Determine the after-tax rate of return Lucy Campbell in question 2-21 earned from her investments during the last financial year.

2-23 (*Corporate income tax*) During the last financial year Bargain Bits Retail Ltd generated sales revenue of $225 million. By sourcing a large proportion of its product from China the company was able to achieve a 60% gross profit margin. Operating expenses, mostly comprising rent and wages, totalled $90 000 000 and its depreciation expense was $10 000 000. The company also incurred interest expense on funds borrowed of $5 000 000. Determine the company's tax liability for the last financial year and identify the total amount of fully franked dividends that the company would be able to pay and the amount of imputation credits associated with the dividends.

2-24 (*Corporate income tax, tax saving, franked dividends*) The financial manager of Bargain Bits Retail Ltd in question 2-23 has discovered that the company is entitled to claim accelerated depreciation to determine its tax liability. The accelerated depreciation tax is a deduction equal to 175% of the standard depreciation amount. Determine the effect of claiming accelerated depreciation on the company's tax liability and identify the type and amount of dividends the company is able to pay.

2-25 (*Profit/loss on sale*) Jim Southby runs a sole-trader crash-repair business and he is considering selling one of his old machines. The machine, purchased for $235 000 six years ago, had an expected life of eight years and an expected salvage value of zero. Jim uses straight-line depreciation and has a marginal personal tax rate of 37%.

    (a) If Jim could sell the old machine for $70 000, what would be the taxes associated with the sale?

    (b) If the old machine were sold for $58 750, what would be the taxes associated with the sale?

    (c) If the old machine were sold for $40 000, what would be the taxes associated with the sale?

Case study

Currently, the business you work for as financial manager is organised as a partnership with three owners who share the profits from the business equally. In the early days of the business, each owner would reinvest in the business most of the after-tax amount of their share of the partnership income. However, now that the business is well established and generating a net income of about $900 000 annually, the owners want to explore the implications of converting to a company form of ownership with each partner holding an equal number of shares.

The partners are aware that under the imputation tax system dividends are no longer 'double taxed', and they feel that a suitable business structure must be established to underpin future growth as well as to minimise the amount of income tax that they will pay.

1. Outline the legal differences between a partnership structure and a company structure.
2. Using the current business net income, calculate the net income after tax for each partner.
3. Using the current business net income, calculate the net income after tax for each shareholder.
4. What conclusions can you make about the impact on the net income after tax of the owners by changing the business structure from a partnership to a company?

Notes

1. Partnerships report only the net income from the partnership and each partner's share of that net income. Each partner's share of the partnership net income is also reported by the partner in his/her personal tax return, from which the amount of tax calculated at individual rates to be paid by the partner will be determined.
2. *Income Tax Assessment Act 1936* as amended by *Income Tax Assessment Act 1997*.
3. Section 23H of the *Income Tax Assessment Act 1936* as amended.
4. As will be seen later, the dividend imputation system may have the effect that this investment allowance tax deduction and its saving of company tax may have no value to shareholders.
5. John:

Taxable income	=	$157 500
Tax on first $80 000	=	$17 550
Tax on remaining income	=	(157 500 − 80 000) × 37%
	=	28 675
Tax payable	=	$46 225

Sue: =

Taxable income	=	$17 500
Tax payable	=	(17 500 − 6000) × 15% = $1725*

* Does not include the low-income-tax offset.

6. John:

Taxable income	=	$160 200
Tax on first $80 000	=	$17 550
Tax on remaining income	=	(160 200 − 80 000) × 37%
	=	29 674
Tax payable	=	$47 224

Sue:

Taxable income	=	$17 800
Tax payable	=	(17 800 − 6000) × 15% = $1770*

* Does not include the low-income-tax offset.

7. John:

Taxable income	=	$225 000
Tax on first $180 000	=	$54 550
Tax on remaining income	=	$20 250
Tax payable	=	$74 800

Sue:

Taxable income	=	$25 000
Tax payable	=	(25 000 − 6000) × 15% = $2850*

* Does not include the low-income-tax offset.

8. Sue:

Taxable income	=	$49 000
Tax on first $37 000	=	$4 650
Tax on remaining income	=	(49 000 − 37 000) × 30%
	=	3 600
Tax payable	=	$8 250

Learning objectives

After reading this chapter, you should be able to:

1 Define financial markets.
2 Explain the role of financial markets in a developed economy.
3 Describe financial intermediaries in a developed financial market.
4 Discuss movement of funds to finance business activities.
5 Describe the various component market groups that make up the overall Australian financial markets.
6 Outline the main pattern of fund flows underlying the financing of businesses in Australia.

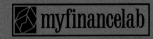

The financial markets

Chapter 3

CHAPTER PREVIEW

In this chapter the important concept of financial markets is introduced. As the term 'market' suggests, financial markets provide a 'market place' for buyers and sellers to get together to transact in a very special type of commodity—financial assets. There are many sub-financial markets depending on the type of financial assets being traded. For example, the share market is the financial market where shares, or stocks, in companies are bought and sold. Similarly, the corporate bond market is the market where corporate bonds are traded, while the government bond market provides facilities for transactions in government bonds. The purpose of this chapter is to provide an overview of financial markets, discuss their important functions in a modern economy, and describe financial institutions and different securities markets that are essential components of a modern financial market. By the end of this chapter, you should appreciate the richness of the financial market, the critical role that it plays in our lives and how corporations use financial markets to raise capital for their activities.

The content of this chapter shows that financial markets are organised to offer investors a wide range of investment opportunities that have different risks and different expected rates of return that reflect those risks. Accordingly, you will find *Principle 1: The risk return tradeoff—we won't take on additional risk unless we expect to be compensated with additional return* relevant throughout the chapter. The chapter is also closely linked to *Principle 6: Efficient capital markets—the markets are quick and the prices are right.*

What are financial markets?

'Financial markets' can be broadly defined as a complex of institutions, procedures and arrangements that facilitate a transfer of funds from one entity in the economy to another. A typical transaction in the financial market involves one party, the investor, transferring funds to another party, the net user of funds, and in exchange receiving a **financial asset** that entitles the investor to receive some cash flows in the future. You can relate this transaction in the financial market to other transactions that you undertake in your daily lives. You transfer $2000 to a computer seller and in exchange receive a computer for that amount of money. In the case of the investor in the financial market, he or she receives a financial asset in exchange for the transfer of funds. Other names that are used to describe a financial asset include 'financial claim', 'financial instrument' and 'financial security'.

'Financial markets' is a general term that describes many sub-markets, for example the *debt market*, where firms and individuals borrow and lend money, and the *share market*, or *stock market*, where firms and individuals buy and sell company shares. It is in financial markets that firms seek financing for their investments and where company shareholders achieve much of their wealth through the price of their shares on the share market. Also in these markets, many individual financial transactions occur, such as taking out a loan to purchase a home, putting money in a fixed-term deposit and taking out a life insurance policy. The debt market and the stock market are the two most popular sub-financial markets, but they are not the only ones. There are other financial assets that are being traded in the financial markets, which will be investigated in more detail in later sections.

OBJECTIVE **1**

Define financial markets.

financial asset
A non-tangible asset that entitles the holders to receive a set of cash flows in the future.

For answers go to MyFinanceLab or
www.pearson.com.au/9781442539174

> ## Concept check
> 3.1 Do financial markets refer to a physical marketplace where people can gather to trade financial assets?
> 3.2 What is the relationship between financial markets and the share market?

OBJECTIVE **2**

Explain the role of financial markets in a developed economy.

external funds
Funds raised from outside sources, such as from a bond issue or an equity issue.

internal funds
Funds generated within the company through retaining profits.

Role of financial markets

When you wish to invest in an asset, for example a computer, you will need to pay for that asset using money that you have already saved. Alternatively, if you are currently not in possession of the money required for payment, you will need to resort to **external funds**. From a corporate point of view, external finance is the funds obtained by means other than through retained earnings. Funds from retained earnings are commonly called **internal funds**. As far as you are concerned, external finance comes primarily in two forms. First, you can borrow money from your parents and promise to pay them back at some time in the future, preferably without interest payment. Or you can borrow money from a bank, when you will not be so lucky regarding interest. Second, you can give your brother the right to co-own the computer should he be willing to contribute towards the payment of it. In this case, your brother will have the same ownership right to the computer as you do. Of course, if he pays only 30% of the value of the computer, he will have the right to use the computer only 30% of the time. Both of these methods provide you with a source of finance necessary to pay for the computer that you desire. Corporate financing needs, while much more complicated and on a much larger scale, are not very different in principle from your financing need for a computer. When a firm wishes to make a capital investment, either to acquire new assets or to take over another company, it will need to either use retained earnings or raise external funds. Firms raise external funds by borrowing from or issuing shares to financial institutions, other corporations or individual investors. Financial markets provide a medium for firms to conduct these transactions.

The essential role of financial markets is to bring together the net users of funds in the economy with the net savers of funds. For example, an insurance company would be a net saver when the premium income from its insurance policies exceeds the claims made against those policies. It could use the financial markets to invest its surplus funds into, say, an interest-bearing account with Westpac, a commercial bank.

On the other hand, a large mining company with a major capital-investment project may not have sufficient funds of its own to undertake the project. It would therefore be a net user of funds and want to use the financial markets to obtain the funds it requires. It could do this, for example, by borrowing the funds it needs from Westpac. In this example, Westpac has facilitated the transfer of funds from the net saver (the insurance company) to the net user (the mining company). In terms of the earlier classification, Westpac is one of the financial institutions comprising the financial markets. Another name for an organisation like Westpac is a **financial intermediary**, an institution that assists the transfer of savings from economic units with excess savings to those with a shortage of savings. That is, it acts as an intermediary between saver and borrower.

Why do financial markets exist? Would the economy be worse off if there wasn't a complex system of financial markets? Some economic units, such as firms and governments, spend more on current consumption during a given period than they earn. On the other hand, other economic units spend less on current consumption than they earn and so have a surplus of funds. As a result, some mechanism is needed to facilitate the transfer of savings from those economic units with a surplus to those with a deficit. That is precisely the function of the financial markets. Financial markets exist in order to allocate the supply of savings in the economy to the demanders of those savings. The central characteristic of a financial market is that it provides the mechanisms through which the forces of demand for funds and supply of funds are brought together. For example, many transfers of funds are achieved through financial claims,

financial intermediary
An institution whose business is to bring together individuals and institutions with money to invest or lend with other firms or individuals that need money.

also known as financial assets, financial instruments or financial securities, such as corporate debentures or the issue of new shares. Providers of funds have a claim over recipients of funds for future cash flows, a return for committing funds.

Why would the economy suffer without a developed financial market system? The answer is simple. The wealth of the economy would be less without the financial markets. The rate of capital formation would not be as high if financial markets did not exist. Example 3.1 clearly illustrates this point.

EXAMPLE 3.1   Capital formation

Consider a simple economy in which the two main market participants are A and B. A has $50 000 savings that she does not need for her current consumption, while B needs $50 000 to finance an investment opportunity that can potentially generate a return of 8%. In the absence of the financial markets, A is not able to channel the savings to B and hence both A and B get a zero return. A developed financial market, on the other hand, would be able to facilitate a transfer of funds from A to B. Assuming that B pays A 3% as a reward for committing the money, A is $50 000 × 3% = $1500 better off. B is $50 000 × 5% = $2500 better off and society as a whole is $1500 + $2500 = $4000 better off.

When financial markets are not fully developed, as in the case of emerging markets, capital formation takes place at a lower rate. This means that the net additions during a specific period to the amount of (1) dwellings, (2) productive plant and equipment, (3) inventory, and (4) consumer durables would occur more slowly. Figure 3.1 helps clarify the rationale behind this assertion. The abbreviated balance sheets in the figure refer to firms or other types of economic units that operate in the private sector of the economy as opposed to the government sector. This means that such units cannot issue money to finance their own activities.

At Stage 1, only real assets exist in the hypothetical economy. **Real assets** are tangible assets such as houses, equipment and inventories. They are distinguished from financial assets or paper assets, which represent claims for future payment on other economic units. Ordinary shares and preference shares, debentures, bills and notes are all types of financial assets. If only real assets exist, then savings for a given economic unit, such as a firm, must be accumulated in the form of real assets. If the firm has a great idea for a new product, that new product can be developed, produced and distributed only out of company savings (retained earnings). Furthermore, all investment in the new product must occur simultaneously with the savings being generated. If you have the idea but we have the savings, there is no mechanism to transfer our savings to you. This is not an ideal situation.

At Stage 2, paper money comes into existence in the economy. Here, at least, you can *store* your own savings in the form of money. Thus, you can finance your great idea by drawing down your cash balances. This is an improvement over Stage 1, but there is still no effective mechanism to transfer our savings to you. You see, we will not just hand you our money. We will want a receipt.

The concept of a receipt, which represents the transfer of savings from one economic unit to another, is a monumental advance. The economic unit with excess savings can lend the savings to an economic unit that needs them. To the lending unit, these receipts are identified as 'other financial assets' in Stage 3 of Figure 3.1. These receipts are financial assets to the lending unit as they give the lenders the right to receive repayment of funds in the future plus some interest. To the borrowing unit, the issuance of financial claims (receipts) shows up as 'financial liabilities'—an amount that it has to pay back at some future date—on the Stage 3 balance sheet. The economic unit with surplus savings will earn a *rate of return* on those funds. The borrowing unit will pay that rate of return, but it also has been able to finance its great idea.

real assets
Tangible assets such as houses, equipment and inventories. Real assets are distinguished from financial assets.

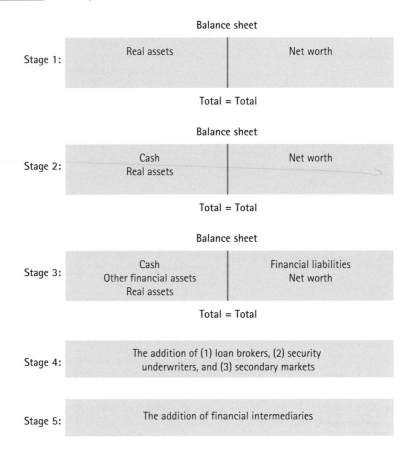

FIGURE 3.1 Development of a financial market system

In Stage 4, the financial market system moves further towards full development. Loan brokers come into existence. These brokers help locate pockets of excess savings and channel such savings to economic units needing the funds. Some economic units will actually purchase the financial claims of borrowing units and sell them at a higher price to other investors.

The progression towards a developed and complex system of financial markets ends with Stage 5. Here, financial intermediaries come into existence. The major financial institutions that most people deal with on a regular basis can be thought of as financial intermediaries. These include banks, building societies, credit unions, life insurance companies and trust funds. Financial intermediaries share a common characteristic: they offer their own financial claims, called *indirect securities*, to economic units with excess savings. When financial intermediaries sell financial claims, they are effectively borrowing money, as they receive money from investors in exchange for a promise to pay them back in the future with some interest payments. The proceeds from selling their indirect securities are then used to purchase the financial claims of—or invest in—other economic units. These latter claims can be called *direct securities*. Thus, a bank might sell fixed term deposits (their indirect security) and purchase the debentures (direct securities) of some major companies. Similarly, a life insurance company would sell life insurance policies and purchase a range of government and company debt instruments and company shares. Financial intermediaries thereby involve many small savers in the process of capital formation. Financial intermediaries add value by pooling small and short-term deposits from individual investors and transforming these deposits into larger and longer term loans. This process is referred to as asset transformation; the financial securities have been 'transformed' in terms of size and maturity.

Well-functioning financial markets are instrumental to a developed economy. An efficient financial market ensures that funds are allocated to the most productive entities. Financial markets also allow individuals and businesses to follow the spending patterns that they desire. Net savers can invest for future consumption, while net spenders can afford a consumption level that they would not otherwise be able to afford.

Concept check

3.3 What is the main role of financial markets?

3.4 How does the development of financial markets relate to economic development?

For answers go to MyFinanceLab or www.pearson.com.au/9781442539174

The discussion so far suggests that within the financial markets, there are three principal sets of players that interact:

1. *Borrowers.* Those who need money to finance their purchases. They include businesses who need money to finance their investments or expand their inventories as well as individuals who borrow money to purchase a new car or a new house.
2. *Lenders or investors.* Those who have money to invest. These are principally individuals who save money for a variety of reasons such as accumulating a deposit for a home. Firms can also save when they have excess cash.
3. *Financial intermediaries.* The financial institutions and markets that help bring borrowers and lenders together. The financial institution you are probably most familiar with is the commercial bank, a financial institution that accepts deposits and makes loans, such as the Commonwealth Bank of Australia or National Australia Bank, where you might have a savings account. However, there are many other types of financial institutions that bring together borrowers and investors, and these will be discussed in more detail in the next section.

Financial intermediaries

OBJECTIVE 3

Describe financial intermediaries in a developed financial market.

We hope it is clear from the previous discussion that the primary role of the financial markets is to facilitate the movement of money from savers who tend to be individuals to borrowers who tend to be businesses. Financial intermediaries are key players in the financial markets that fulfil this role. Commercial banks are the most popular financial intermediaries. However, financial intermediaries also extend to other financial institutions such as insurance companies and managed funds.

COMMERCIAL BANKS

Commercial banks are authorised by the Australian Prudential Regulation Authority (APRA) to take deposits from the public. The core business of commercial banks is to collect deposits mostly from individuals and then lend these pooled savings to other individuals, businesses and government. They make money by charging a rate of interest to borrowers that exceeds the rate they pay to depositors. Commercial banks play a very important role in the financing of businesses as bank loans constitute a major source of finance to the corporate sector. Apart from bank loans, commercial banks also provide funding to the corporate sector through the purchase of debt securities issued by companies such as corporate bonds. In recent years, commercial banks have shown signs of gradually moving away from the traditional realm of taking deposits and making loans. They are establishing themselves as major providers of financial services such as foreign-exchange and financial-derivative dealings.

commercial banks
Financial institutions that accept deposits, make loans and provide other financial services to the public.

The Australian commercial banking sector is dominated by the Australia and New Zealand Banking Corporation (ANZ), the Commonwealth Bank of Australia (CBA), National Australia Bank (NAB) and the Westpac Banking Corporation. Collectively, these banks, as shown in Table 3.1, are known as the Big 4. As of 30 June 2010, the Big 4 had 75.26% of all consumer deposits and 74.38% of the total assets of the banking sector in Australia.

TABLE 3.1	Four biggest commercial banks in Australia as of 30 June 2010	
INSTITUTION NAME	**TOTAL DEPOSITS ($m)**	**TOTAL ASSETS ($m)**
Westpac Banking Corporation	276 957	523 539
Commonwealth Bank of Australia	278 631	501 859
National Australia Bank	206 502	399 187
Australia and New Zealand Banking Corporation	190 748	360 569

Source: Australian Prudential Regulation Authority

NON-BANK AUTHORISED DEPOSIT-TAKING INSTITUTIONS

building societies and credit unions
Authorised deposit-taking institutions that provide banking services to their members.

Apart from commercial banks, **building societies** and **credit unions** are also authorised by APRA to take retail deposits. Despite their commonality with commercial banks in regard to deposit-taking and loan-making activities, building societies and credit unions are different to the extent that their ownership and hence services are restricted to members. These institutions are unlisted not-for-profit organisations and profits generated are used to improve the services provided to their members in the form of lower fees, cheaper loans and/or higher interest rates on members' savings. Since the deregulation of the financial system in Australia in 1983, the building societies sector has contracted significantly due to their inability to compete with commercial banks. In 2010, there were only 11 building societies operating in Australia.[1] Credit unions, on the other hand, appear to have a stronger presence in the Australian financial landscape. Members of credit unions usually identify with the institution via their employment or social group. For example, the Defence Force Credit Union comprises members who are employees of the Australian Department of Defence. Since building societies and credit unions provide only financial services to their members, they play a more important role in personal finance than in corporate finance.

INVESTMENT BANKS

Investment banks are specialised financial intermediaries that help companies and government raise money and provide advisory services to client firms. Their major source of revenue is fees for the financial services rendered. The main advisory services that investment banks provide include advice on equity and debt, mergers and acquisitions, and corporate restructurings. The Global Financial Crisis in 2008 caused a major shake-up of the investment banking industry, resulting in the demise of the stand-alone investment banking industry in the US. In the aftermath of the GFC, some of the biggest names in investment banking either failed (Lehman Brothers), were acquired by commercial banks (Bear Sterns and Merrill Lynch) or were converted into commercial banks (Morgan Stanley and Goldman Sachs). The investment banking sector in Australia, in contrast, was not as severely impacted by the GFC, partly due to their non-independent structure. Australian investment banks are usually owned by a holding company or a commercial bank. For example, the largest Australian-owned investment bank in Australia, the Macquarie Group, is the holding company which owns Macquarie Bank—an authorised deposit-taking commercial bank.

INSURANCE COMPANIES

Insurance companies are in the business of selling insurance to individuals and businesses to protect the value of their investments. They collect premiums and hold the premiums in reserves until there is an insured loss that calls for an insurance payout. In the course of collecting and holding premiums, the insurance companies build up huge pools of reserves which are invested in individual and business loans, company stocks and government securities. Due to the magnitude of the collected premiums, insurance companies are active players in the financial markets.

SUPERANNUATION FUNDS

superannuation fund
A retirement fund that helps individuals save and invest for their retirement.

A **superannuation fund** is a retirement fund that helps individuals save and invest for their retirement. Superannuation funds receive contributions from employers on behalf of their

GFC

THE GLOBAL FINANCIAL CRISIS EXPLAINED

In 2007–08, the world financial markets witnessed a number of extremely unpleasant events ranging from defaults and credit squeezes to stock-market freefall and institutional collapses that made the Great Depression of the 1930s seem like 'a walk in the park'. The series of events that unfolded during 2007 and 2008 are now commonly referred to as the Global Financial Crisis (GFC).

Just like the Great Depression, the GFC started in the US and soon spread worldwide. The underlying causes of the GFC are no doubt complex. However, in a nutshell, they can be summarised by two concepts—'sub-prime lending' and 'securitisation'.

The early years of the 21st century witnessed strong performance in the real estate market in the United States. The strength of the market was such that people were filled with a sense of over-optimism and home loans were offered to borrowers with low credit ratings. These sub-prime borrowers, as they are known, were not likely to be able to repay their loans but were offered the loans anyway as the lenders were optimistic that they could always recoup their money through the increasing value of the houses that was used as collateral for the mortgage loans. The growth of sub-prime lending led to the inevitable fallout in mid 2007 when defaults on the sub-prime loans put a massive supply of housing stock on the market. The law of supply and demand dictates that when there is an increase in supply without a matching increase in demand prices have to fall. That was exactly what happened—the housing market in the US collapsed and sub-prime borrowers systematically defaulted on their loan repayments.

What appeared to be a home-grown problem for the US quickly spread, however, to the rest of the world since sub-prime home loans had been repackaged into new financial assets by virtue of a financial innovation called 'securitisation' and those assets were sold all over the world. These repackaged financial assets were backed by mortgage repayments from sub-prime borrowers and were given a fancy name—mortgage-backed securities (MBS). Through the process of securitisation, financial institutions worldwide who had bought MBS were exposed to the risk imposed by sub-prime lending. At the height of the sub-prime fallout, financial institutions suffered massive losses on their MBS which, coupled with withdrawals from panicking investors, dried up their cash accounts. Faced with what appeared to be a systemic failure of the financial system, central banks quickly came to the rescue. By March 2008, central banks worldwide had injected more than US$1 trillion into the banking system to support its liquidity.[2]

In the meltdown of the global financial markets, thousands of people lost their jobs and commercial banks worldwide were forced to write off massive amounts of sub-prime related loans. The governments in many countries were put in a position where they needed to intervene to support their country's faltering financial system. These interventions took a number of forms: explicitly guaranteeing bank deposits to restore confidence in the banking system, buying toxic debt or recapitalising banks by buying shares in them.

Australia was by no means the hardest hit by the GFC. However, three weeks before the end of the 2009 calendar year, the local stock market recorded the largest annual fall ever of 45%.[3] Similar declines were experienced in other developed markets. Furthermore, the liquidity squeeze emanating from the cash-strapped banking system hit hard many otherwise successfully managed business enterprises, whose banks withdrew or failed to renew short-term loan arrangements. The Australian government helped to minimise this credit squeeze by guaranteeing the local banks' bonds so that they could continue to raise funds in overseas financial markets and so maintain at least part of their funding of local business firms.

To many, the GFC was a regulatory failure in lending practices. With the multi-billion dollar bailout bills that the governments of the US and other countries had to foot to avoid a systemic failure of the financial system, they have surely learned their lesson.

---

employees and from employees directly. By law, most Australian employers have an obligation to contribute at least 9% of their employees' incomes to their superannuation funds. This compulsory contribution is referred to as the **superannuation guarantee (SG)**. Employees can also choose to make additional contributions to their superannuation funds. For low-income earners, when they make personal contributions they may be eligible for a government co-contribution where the government matches the personal contribution up to a maximum of $1000. Investments in superannuation are long term as individuals do not have access to the money until they reach a certain age, known as the **preservation age**. As of 2010 the preservation age for people born after June 1964 is sixty. Superannuation is designed to help individuals save for their retirement and as such superannuation funds receive preferable tax treatment and other government benefits.

Due to the regular contributions, superannuation funds have a large amount of money to invest. Most of these monies are invested in the bond and share markets, both domestically and internationally. Through these investments superannuation funds help finance corporate

superannuation guarantee
The compulsory contribution that employers must make on behalf of their employees.

preservation age
The age at which individuals have access to their superannuation money.

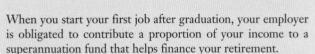

Regardless of your program

When you start your first job after graduation, your employer is obligated to contribute a proportion of your income to a superannuation fund that helps finance your retirement.

Traditionally, there were two superannuation options available to workers: a defined benefit fund and an accumulation fund. In a defined benefit fund, the final payout is defined by a formula based on the length of service, the level of income and the contribution history. The accumulation fund, on the other hand, works like a savings account where the final balance depends on contributions and investment performance. However, as of recently, defined benefit funds are no longer on offer to new members, possibly due to the excessive level of risk that superannuation funds had to take in order to guarantee the defined payments.

What this will mean for you when you start working is that your employer will make contributions into a fund of your choice, which reflects your general investment strategy.

Superannuation funds typically offer accumulation members a range of investment strategies that range from low risk to medium and high risk, with of course low expected return to medium and high expected return. Remember *Principle 1: The risk–return tradeoff—we won't take on additional risk unless we expect to be compensated with additional return.* Your investment choice is important as it will determine the amount of money that you have for your retirement. So it does not matter whether you are studying to be a finance manager, doctor, pharmacist, engineer or architect, you are going to be a superannuation fund manager.

---

capital expenditure and expansion. Also through these investments, most ordinary Australians have exposure to the bond and share markets, and fluctuations in these markets have an impact on how much they will have for retirement. An exception exists for individuals who have a **defined benefit fund**, the payout of which is determined by a fixed formula and does not depend on market performance.

INVESTMENT COMPANIES

Investment companies are financial institutions that pool the savings of individuals and invest the money, purely for investment purposes, in the securities issued by other companies. Perhaps the most widely known type of investment company is the **mutual fund**, a special type of intermediary through which individuals can invest in virtually all of the securities offered in the financial markets. When individuals invest in a mutual fund, they receive shares in a fund that is professionally managed according to a stated investment objective or goal—for example, investing only in international stocks. Shares in the mutual fund grant ownership claim to a proportion of the mutual fund's portfolio.

A share in a mutual fund is not really like a share, or stock, since you can only buy and sell shares in the mutual fund directly through the mutual fund itself. The price that you pay when you buy your shares and the price you receive when you sell your shares is called the mutual fund's **net asset value (NAV)**, which is calculated daily based on the total value of the fund divided by the number of mutual fund shares outstanding. In effect, as the value of the mutual fund investments go up, so does the price of the mutual fund's shares.

Some funds are traded on the stock exchanges, allowing shares in the funds to be traded in the same manner as company shares. These funds are known as **exchange-traded funds (or ETFs)**. Most ETFs track a stock index. In Australia, both Australian and international ETFs are available for trading. The Australian ETFs track the performances of the S&P/ASX 300 Index, S&P/ASX 200 Index and the S&P/ASX 50 Index.[4]

Mutual funds and ETFs provide a cost-effective way to diversify, which reduces risk—a great benefit for the small investor. If you only have $10 000 to invest, it is difficult to diversify by purchasing shares of individual companies, since you have to pay a brokerage commission for each individual stock you purchase. For example, buying 50 different stocks is likely to cost you $1500 or more in commissions, which would be 15% of the amount invested.[5] By buying a mutual fund or ETF you can indirectly purchase a portfolio of 50 or more stocks with just one transaction.

defined benefit fund
A superannuation fund that provides a retirement benefit determined by a formula, not by investment performance.

mutual fund
A professionally managed investment company that pools the investments of many individuals and invests them in financial assets such as stocks, bonds and other types of securities.

net asset value
The difference between the current market value of a fund's assets and the value of its liabilities.

exchange-traded fund (ETF)
An investment vehicle traded on stock exchanges much like a share or stock. The entity holds investments in assets that meet the investment objective of the entity.

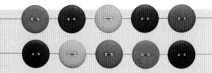

Your money

You probably find it strange thinking about retirement now when you are still at university. However, as you will learn in the next chapter, money has a time value, and the earlier you start investing for retirement, the more you will have when you eventually retire. In the 2009–2010 Federal Budget announced in May 2010, the Labor government proposed a number of changes to superannuation. Some of these proposed changes, if passed into law by Parliament, will have a direct impact on you and your superannuation when you join the workforce, as follows:

- *Increasing the superannuation guarantee (SG) rate to 12%.* The current superannuation guarantee rate is 9%. The government is proposing to change this to 12% by 2020 through progressive annual increments of 0.25% in 2013 and 2014 and 0.5% onwards until the superannuation guarantee reaches 12%. The government believes this measure will directly relieve the reliance on the social welfare system of our ageing population and boost private and national savings, bringing broader benefits to the community and the nation.
- *Introducing a government contribution for low-income earners.* The government proposes to make an annual contribution of up to $500 for individuals whose annual incomes are $37 000 or less. This proposal aims to provide low-income earners with additional tax benefits that the current tax system does not provide. In particular, all contributions to superannuation funds are currently taxed at a flat concession rate of 15%. As a result, a high-income earner in a

high tax bracket receives substantially more tax concessions than a low-income earner, whereas low-income earners on a marginal tax rate of 15% or less receive little or no concession at all.

Other proposed changes that are more relevant to older workers include:

- *Raising the superannuation guarantee age limit from 70 to 75.* Currently, the superannuation guarantee is only available to workers aged 70 or below. Under the proposed new system, workers aged between 70 and 75 who are still working will also be eligible to receive the superannuation guarantee.
- *Introducing a permanent concessional contribution cap.* The Labor government has proposed the introduction of a permanent concessional contribution cap of $50 000 for workers aged 50 or above. Under this measure, workers who are at least 50 years old are allowed to make annual non-compulsory contributions up to the value of $50 000 to their superannuation at the concessional tax rate of 15%. These contributions can be made before tax. By making contributions to superannuation, workers can effectively reduce the tax rate they pay on their incomes from their marginal level to 15%. This contribution cap, however, applies only to people with a superannuation balance of less than $500 000.

The rules and regulations surrounding superannuation may appear complex and they do vary over time. However, keep in mind that superannuation is your money and it pays to understand the rules!

A **hedge fund** is very much like a mutual fund, but hedge funds are more regulated and tend to take more risks. They also tend to more actively influence the managers of the corporations that they invest in. Because of the higher risk, hedge funds are open to a limited range of investors who are deemed to be sufficiently savvy. Only an accredited investor, which means an individual with a net worth exceeding $1 million, can invest in a hedge fund.

Management fees are also somewhat higher for hedge funds; they typically run at about 2% of assets and include an incentive fee, typically 20% of profits, based on the fund's overall performance.

hedge fund
An investment fund which is open to a limited range of investors and which can undertake a wider range of investment and trading activities than a mutual fund.

PRIVATE EQUITY FIRMS

A **private equity firm** is a financial intermediary that invests in private companies. These companies by definition are not traded on the public capital markets. In recent years, private equity firms have emerged as key players in the global financial landscape. They are responsible for a large number of mergers and acquisitions, debt raisings and initial public offering activities. Private equity firms are dominated by two main groups: venture capital firms and leveraged buyout (LBO) funds. **Venture capital firms** raise money from wealthy individuals and financial institutions which they use to provide finance for private start-up companies. Some globally well-known venture capital firms include Sevin Rosen Funds and Kleiner Perkins Caufield and Byers (KPCB). However, these firms are perhaps not as well known as the firms that they help to succeed, such as Google, Facebook, Microsoft and Apple. In Australia, venture capital firms had approximately A$2 billion under management in 2009 and they are behind the success

private equity firms
Financial intermediaries that invest in companies that are not traded on the public capital markets.

venture capital firms
Investment companies that raise money from accredited investors and use the proceeds to invest in new start-up companies.

stories of Cochlear, the global provider of hearing loss solutions, Compumedics, the developer and manufacturer of diagnostic technologies for sleep disorders, and Ausra, the designer and manufacturer of solar thermal energy systems.[6]

leveraged buyout funds
Private equity funds that raise capital from investors and use those funds, along with significant amounts of debt, to acquire controlling interests in operating companies.

The second major category of private equity firms is the **leveraged buyout fund**. These funds acquire established firms that typically have not been performing very well with the objective of making them profitable again and then selling them. LBO funds are distinctive in that they rely heavily on debt when acquiring companies and the acquired companies are taken privately subsequent to the buyout. LBO funds have been the subject of a number of movies, including *Barbarians at the Gate*, *Other People's Money* and *Wall Street*. In Australia, the most famous LBO in recent history was the acquisition of Myer, the nation's second largest retailer, in 2004 by TPG Capital (formerly Texas Pacific Group) and Blum Capital. Following the purchase, the LBO funds spent a substantial amount on renovating stores and updating logistics operations. In late October 2009, Myer was put on the market again through an initial public offering (IPO). The IPO raised approximately $2.4 billion, which represented a gross profit of $1 billion for the LBO funds on the purchase price of $1.4 billion.

Beyond the massive dollar investments, the importance of private equity firms needs to be recognised. Private equity funding is largely responsible for the birth of new businesses and the rebirth of old and faltering businesses.

Concept check

3.5 How do commercial banks differ from non-bank deposit-taking institutions?
3.6 Give some examples of investment companies.
3.7 What is a hedge fund and how does it differ from a mutual fund?
3.8 What are the two principal types of private equity firms?

For answers go to MyFinanceLab or www.pearson.com.au/9781442539174

OBJECTIVE 4

Movement of funds

Discuss movement of funds to finance business activities.

In a developed financial market system funds are transferred to businesses in need of cash in three ways: direct transfer of funds, indirect transfer using commercial banks, and indirect transfer using other financial intermediaries.

DIRECT TRANSFER OF FUNDS

In a direct transfer of funds, firms seeking cash sell their securities, for example shares or bonds, directly to investors who are willing to purchase them in the hope of earning a reasonable rate of return. Established businesses can raise new equity funds by selling their shares on the share market or raise new debt funds by selling their debt securities, such as bonds, directly to the public. In the direct transfer of funds, investors provide firms with the finance they need in

FYI

The movement of financial capital (funds) throughout the economy simply means the movement of savings to the ultimate users of those savings. Some sectors of the economy save more than other sectors. As a result, those savings are moved to a productive use—say, to manufacture that car you want to buy.

The price of using someone else's savings is expressed in terms of a rate of return on investment (yield); interest rates are

an example. The financial market system helps to move funds to the most productive end use. Those economic units with the most promising projects should be willing to bid the highest (in terms of rates of return) to obtain the savings.

The concepts of financing and moving savings from one economic unit to another are important underpinnings of modern finance theory and practice.

exchange for financial assets or financial securities issued by the firms. This process is illustrated in Figure 3.2.

INDIRECT TRANSFER USING COMMERCIAL BANKS

Banks perform the important function of collecting the savings of numerous individuals and businesses and providing those funds by way of loans to the individuals and businesses in the economy that need funds. In other words, banks issue financial claims to providers of funds, mostly individuals and households. The proceeds are then used to purchase financial claims issued by other economic units such as other financial institutions and companies. Note that, in an indirect transfer of funds, two types of financial securities are created, as opposed to one type in a direct transfer of funds. *Indirect securities* are issued by the bank and *direct securities* are issued by the institutions or corporations that the bank ultimately lends money to. There are inherent differences between these two types of financial securities. Indirect securities are characterised by small denominations, large volumes and short maturity, whereas direct securities are in larger denominations and smaller volumes and are of longer maturity. It is important to emphasise that banks not only bring lenders and borrowers together but also play an active role in transforming the characteristics of the fund flows. Figure 3.3 depicts an indirect transfer of funds involving banks.

INDIRECT TRANSFER USING OTHER FINANCIAL INTERMEDIARIES

This type of indirect fund transfer is essentially the same as before, except that the financial intermediary, instead of being a bank, is another type of financial institution, such as a credit union, a building society, an insurance company and so on. This is the part of the system within which life insurance companies and superannuation funds collect the savings of individuals and issue their own indirect securities in exchange for these savings. These intermediaries then use the funds collected from the individual savers to acquire as investments the business firm's direct securities, such as shares and bonds.

Everyone benefits from these three transfer mechanisms. Capital formation and economic wealth are greater than they would be in the absence of a system of financial markets.

FIGURE 3.2 The direct transfer of funds

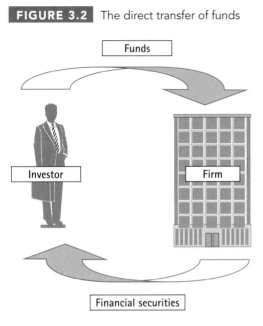

FIGURE 3.3 The indirect transfer of funds

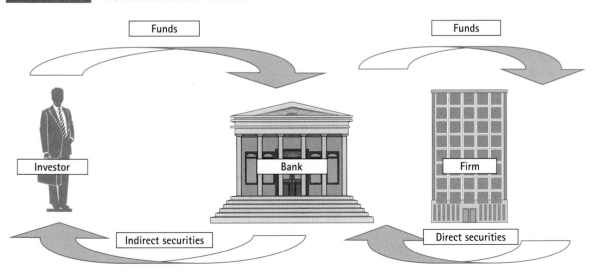

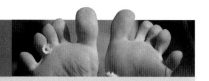

FYI

Recently there has been a shift in the pattern of funds flow in Australia whereby direct transfers of funds are increasingly taking over indirect transfers of funds as the predominant pattern. Half a century ago, individuals mostly stored their wealth in bank accounts and thus facilitated an indirect funds transfer. This is not the case anymore. The households sector is increasingly investing directly in the corporate sector. There are both demand and supply explanations for this phenomenon. On the demand side, advances in information technol-ogy enhance investors' understanding of financial markets and products and make investing directly in financial assets as easy as a mouse click. Furthermore, compulsory superannuation, which requires working Australians to invest for their retire-ment, is classified as a direct transfer of funds. On the supply side, many companies with good credit ratings find it more cost-effective to approach investors directly for their funding needs. This poses a question for the banking system: what do they have to do to gain an edge for the future?

Concept check

For answers go to MyFinanceLab or
www.pearson.com.au/9781442539174

3.9   In September 2005 the third instalment of Telstra shares was sold to the public in what was known as T3. Are Telstra shares sold under T3 considered direct securities or indirect securities? Why?

3.10   Describe the three main types of fund transfer in the financial market.

OBJECTIVE **5**

Describe the various component market groups that make up the overall Australian financial markets.

Components of Australian financial markets

Numerous approaches exist for grouping the financial markets and at times the array of groups can be confusing. Generally speaking, financial markets can be grouped along three main dimensions:

- By the type of financial asset being traded. This includes the stock market, the debt market, the foreign-exchange market and the derivative market. As can be deduced from the names of these markets, shares, bonds, foreign currencies and derivatives respectively are being traded in these markets.
- By the maturity of the financial asset. Financial assets can be partitioned into short term and long term. As a result, there is the capital market which encompasses transactions in long-term financial assets, while the money market captures transactions in short-term financial assets.
- By the way in which financial assets are created. This dimension of financial market classifi-cation underpins the market for initial public offerings and private placements as well as primary and secondary markets.

THE STOCK MARKET

The stock market provides a platform for stocks to be traded. Stocks are a form of equity that represents ownership of the corporation. There are two major types of equity securities: common stock, which is more widely traded, and preferred stock. When you buy stock or equity you are making an investment that you expect will generate a return. However, unlike debt, which provides a promised set of interest payments and a schedule for the repayment of principal, the returns earned from an equity security are less certain.

Common stock provides voting rights and entitles the holder to a share of the company's success in the form of dividends and any capital appreciation in the value of the security. Investors who purchase common stock are the residual owners of the firm. This means that the common stockholder's return is earned only after all other security holder claims like debt and preferred equity have been satisfied in full.

Preferred stock, like common stock, is an equity security. However, as the name implies, preferred stockholders take a preferred position relative to common shareholders. This means that preferred shareholders receive their dividends before any dividends are distributed to the common stockholders, who receive their dividends from whatever is left over. Note, however, that if the company does not earn enough to pay its interest expenses, neither preferred nor common stockholders will be paid a dividend. However, the dividends promised to the preferred stockholders will generally accrue and must be paid in full before common shareholders can receive any dividends. This feature is oftentimes referred to as the 'cumulative feature', and preferred stock with this feature is often referred to as 'cumulative preferred stock'. In addition, preferred stockholders have a preferred claim on the distribution of assets of the firm in the event that the firm should go bankrupt and sell or liquidate its assets. Very simply, the firm's creditors (bondholders) get paid first, followed by the preferred stockholders, and anything left goes to the common stockholders. Of interest is that not all firms issue preferred stock.

Preferred stock is sometimes referred to as a 'hybrid security' because it has many characteristics of both common stock and bonds. Preferred stock is similar to common stock in that (1) it has no fixed maturity date, (2) the non-payment of dividends does not bring on bankruptcy for the firm, and (3) the dividends paid on these securities are not deductible for tax purposes. Preferred stock is similar to corporate bonds in that (1) the dividends paid on the stock, like the interest payments made on bonds, are typically a fixed amount, and (2) it does not usually come with any voting rights.

preferred stock
An equity security that holds preference over common stock in terms of the right to the distribution of dividends and the right to the distribution of proceeds in the event of the liquidation and sale of the issuing firm.

THE BOND MARKET

Firms borrow money by selling debt securities in the debt market. If the debt must be repaid in less than a year, these securities are typically called notes and are sold in the short-term debt market, also referred to as the money market. If the debt has a maturity of longer than one year, then the debt security is called a bond and is sold in the capital market. The capital market refers to the market for long-term financial instruments.

International spotlight

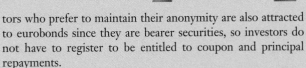

THE EUROBOND MARKET

Debuted in the 1960s, the eurobond is an example of how national borders have truly broken down in financial markets. Unlike any other bond, a eurobond is a debt instrument that is simultaneously issued to investors located in a number of countries. Usually denominated in a currency that is foreign to the issuer, the intended audience of a eurobond issue is the broad 'international' market.

The eurobond market provides an extremely important financing choice for borrowers whose funding needs are not met by the domestic capital market. The attractiveness of the eurobond market lies in its unique features. First, the eurobond market does not fall under the jurisdiction of any government and it is a somewhat self-regulated market. Second, the lack of capital adequacy requirement for institutional lenders means that a lower interest rate can usually be achieved in the eurobond market compared to the domestic market.[7] Despite the lack of government regulation, defaults in the eurobond market are relatively rare as the borrowers in the market, more often than not, carry the highest credit ratings. Third, investors who prefer to maintain their anonymity are also attracted to eurobonds since they are bearer securities, so investors do not have to register to be entitled to coupon and principal repayments.

In its early days, the major issuers of eurobonds were generally governments, financial institutions and international agencies. However, the corporate sector quickly entered the scene and by the 1990s had become the dominant player in the market. On the demand side, apart from corporate borrowers, international agencies such as the European Investment Bank and the International Bank for Reconstruction and Development make up approximately 10% of the market.[8]

The eurobond market is particularly well developed in Europe where integration measures implemented by the European Monetary Union (EMU) in recent years have meant that the boundary between EMU countries is now a nominal concept. The introduction of the euro currency in 2000 has also led to the downfall of the USD as the most popular currency of denomination in the eurobond market.[9]

The vast majority of these bonds pay a fixed interest rate, which means that the interest the owner of the bond receives never changes over its lifetime. Bonds are generally described using fairly exotic terminology. For example, we might say that a bond has a face or par value of $1000 and that it pays an 8% coupon rate, with two payments per year. What this means is that when the bond matures and the issuer (borrower) has to repay it, the owner of the bond (the lender) will receive a payment of $1000. In the meantime, the holder will receive an interest payment every six months equal to $40, or $80 per year, which is 8% of $1000.

FOREIGN EXCHANGE MARKET

The description of the components of financial markets described above has assumed that the transfer of funds between savers and users occurs in only one currency. However, in a modern global economy transfers occur between all currencies. This is where the foreign exchange market plays a part.

The foreign exchange market provides a mechanism for the transfer of purchasing power from one currency to another by facilitating the exchange of currencies. This market is not a physical entity but is an international network of foreign-exchange dealers and customers who transact with each other via electronic connections such as the telephone, fax, telex, email and financial data display screens. Most countries license foreign-exchange dealers to buy and sell foreign currencies. Licensed dealers are usually banks and other financial organisations.

The foreign exchange market operates simultaneously at two levels. At the first level, individuals and businesses can buy and sell foreign currencies through the foreign-exchange dealers. This is the retail and corporate segment of the foreign exchange market. At the second level, dealers buy and sell foreign currencies from other dealers in the same country or from dealers in foreign-exchange markets located in other countries. This is called the interbank or wholesale segment of the foreign exchange market. Wholesale transactions account for more than 90% of all transactions in the foreign exchange market.

Two types of transactions are carried out in the foreign exchange markets:

- *Spot transactions.* These are essentially conducted at the current or going price (spot price) of the currencies. In practice, settlement of the transaction occurs two working days after the transaction is agreed.
- *Forward transactions.* These transactions enable the buyer and seller of the currency to agree 'now' to a price for the exchange of the currency at some future (forward) date, this date being longer than two working days in the future. Thus, a forward transaction is a way of protecting against currency price movements between now and the future settlement date.

DERIVATIVES MARKETS

derivative
A financial instrument whose value is derived from or based on the value of an underlying asset.

In the past two decades there has been an explosion in derivative financial instruments, such as financial futures, options and swaps. They are called **derivatives** because their value is based on, or derived from, actual commodities or financial instruments. Derivative instruments such as futures contracts are useful in managing risk for investors and borrowers. They are also used by speculators aiming to make profits by speculating on price movements. While the use of financial derivatives for risk management purposes reduces risk, speculation involving financial derivatives exposes market participants to a very high level of risk.

exchange-traded instruments
Financial instruments that are bought and sold through an organised exchange.

over-the-counter instruments
Financial instruments that are privately arranged between two parties.

The financial manager needs to be aware of how derivatives can assist in managing many kinds of risk, such as from the firm's interest-bearing borrowings or investments, from foreign currency transactions, and from risks associated with fluctuations in the price of the key commodities in which the firm deals. A large firm may have a treasury division that uses **exchange-traded instruments**. That is, the derivatives can be bought and sold through an organised exchange. A smaller firm is likely to use a financial institution, such as its bank, to provide it with **over-the-counter instruments** that are tailor made for the firm and can help to manage its financial risks. Chapter 18 includes a brief outline of how firms use derivatives to protect against what is called 'interest rate risk'. The two major exchange-traded derivatives markets are for futures and options.

ONE STEP FURTHER

Financial derivatives currently constitute the fastest growing financial market in the world. Periodical statistics reported by the Bank for International Settlement show an unprecedented level of growth in the volume of derivative transactions. The principle of competitive markets predicts that the use of financial derivatives grows because there is a demand for them. Indeed, the prevalence of derivative usage has allowed corporations, including financial institutions, to effectively manage their business and financial risks at relatively low cost. As a result, from a risk management point of view, financial derivatives should be seen as socially desirable. Nevertheless, has the financial market gone too far in designing complex derivative structures? This concern, shared by many market commentators and regulators, is fuelled by the collapse of American International Group (AIG) in 2008 and its controversial bailout that to date has cost US taxpayers $182 billion.

AIG's problems are rooted in a financial product known as credit default swap (CDS). The CDS is like an insurance policy against default risk. Essentially when you buy a CDS, you will get a payout if there is a default in your bond portfolio. AIG, however, are on the selling side of the CDS. Through a subsidiary, it sold CDSs to the value of US$447 billion to a consortium of financial institutions including Goldman Sachs, Merrill Lynch and Deutsche

Bank. The CDSs, or insurance policies, that AIG sold are no ordinary policies; they are policies on financial assets whose cash flows and value depend on a pool of assets like residential and commercial mortgages. In theory, AIG should have collected insurance premiums from these CDSs that were commensurate to the level of risk that they entailed. The problem is AIG underestimated the risk exposure these CDSs would put the company under. When it sold them, it simply did not see the sub-prime mortgage crisis and the subsequent Global Financial Crisis coming. As the sub-prime mortgage crisis hit in 2007, many mortgagees defaulted on their mortgage repayments, requiring AIG to put up collateral for the losses they were suffering from their CDSs. The losses to AIG grew larger as the value of mortgage-backed securities continued to fall and this required a substantial cash infusion that AIG simply did not have. The company collapsed in September 2008.

It is one thing that US taxpayers have had to put their hard-earned money towards the rescue of AIG. But the more fundamental question that needs to be asked is: how did AIG get it so wrong? The answer may lie in the fact that many financial products that AIG sold CDS on, such as Collateralised Debt Obligations, are just too hard to value, making the task of accurately valuing a CDS on these products a near impossibility.

Concept check

3.11 Briefly describe the structure of financial markets in a developed economy.

3.12 How are over-the-counter (OTC) transactions different from exchange-traded transactions?

For answers go to MyFinanceLab or www.pearson.com.au/9781442539174

Futures markets

Futures markets are where futures contracts are traded. A **futures contract** is a legally binding agreement to buy or sell a stated commodity or financial instrument, at a specified price, at some future specified time called the settlement date. When the price of the underlying commodity changes, the market value of the futures contract also changes. On the settlement date, most participants simply settle the profit or loss on the contract. That is, they do not take delivery of the underlying commodity or contract. A profit or loss can arise because the actual or 'physical' market price on settlement date is likely to differ from the price that had been agreed to previously as part of the futures contract.

futures contract
Legally binding agreement to buy or sell a stated commodity or financial instrument at a specified price at some future specified time.

Options markets

Options markets are where options are traded. An **option**, or option contract, gives its owner the *right* (but not the *obligation*) to buy or sell a commodity at a specified price over some time

option
Agreement that gives the holder the right (but not the obligation) to buy (or sell) a commodity or financial instrument at a specified price on or before a specified date.

call option

Option to buy a specified asset at a specified price on or before a specified date.

put option

Option to sell a specified asset at a specified price on or before a specified date.

For answers go to MyFinanceLab or www.pearson.com.au/9781442539174

money market

All institutions and procedures that facilitate transactions in short-term financial instruments.

capital market

All institutions and procedures that facilitate transactions in long-term financial instruments.

public offering

Offer of new securities to the public.

period. In contrast, a futures contract obliges the parties to settle the transaction. There are two basic types of options. A **call option** gives the owner the right to *buy* an asset at a specified price over a given period of time, and a **put option** gives its owner the right to *sell* an asset at a specified price over a given period of time.

Concept check

3.13 What is a financial derivative?

3.14 What are the two major uses of financial derivatives?

MONEY MARKET AND CAPITAL MARKET

The key feature that distinguishes the money market from the capital market is the maturity period of the securities issued and traded. The **money market** refers to all institutions and procedures that provide for transactions in short-term debt instruments, generally issued by borrowers with very high credit ratings. By financial convention, 'short-term' means maturity periods of one year or less. Note that shares, long-term debt and convertible securities are not traded in the money market because they have maturities of more than 12 months. The major instruments issued and traded in the money market are treasury notes, certificates of deposit, commercial bills and promissory notes. Descriptions of these instruments as elements of the firm's short-term financing and current asset management are given in Chapters 7 and 8.

Keep in mind that the money market, just like financial markets, is an intangible market. You do not walk into a building that has the words 'Money Market' etched in stone over its arches. Rather, the money market is primarily an electronic market, and trading does not occur at any specific location. Transactions to buy and sell money-market instruments are conducted over the phone and electronically.

The **capital market** refers to all institutions and procedures that provide for transactions in long-term financial instruments. In this context, 'long-term' means having maturity periods that extend beyond one year. In the broad sense this encompasses long-term debt instruments such as debentures, notes and bonds, term loans and financial leases, and other corporate instruments such as shares and convertible securities. All of these long-term financing modes are introduced in later chapters.

These long-term financing mechanisms available in the capital markets can be characterised further by identifying how they transfer funds from the lender to the borrower. A distinction can be made between two groups of funds-transfer mechanisms. The first group involves devices such as term loans and financial leases, where the borrower obtains the finance through a financial intermediary such as a bank. For example, if a business needs to obtain funds to invest in new equipment, it can approach its bank and borrow the required funds via a term loan or a lease. This financing arrangement is therefore solely between the bank and its customer and is often called intermediated finance. The second group comprises long-term debt securities such as debentures, notes and bonds, equity instruments such as ordinary shares and preference shares, and 'hybrid' securities such as convertible notes. These securities are sold or issued directly by the firm to investors, either via a public offering through the share market or by a private placement. As seen earlier, this direct sale or issue of securities is classified as a primary-market transaction. Once these securities have been issued, they can then be resold through the share market, thus being classified as a secondary-market transaction.

PUBLIC OFFERINGS AND PRIVATE PLACEMENTS

When a company decides to raise external capital, the funds can be obtained by making a public offering or a private placement of the company's securities. These securities can be in the form of equity via shares, or in the form of debt, for example via *debentures* or bonds. In a **public offering** both individual and institutional investors have the opportunity to purchase the securities. The securities are usually made available to the public at large by a stockbroking firm

Finance at work

HOUSING FUTURES

For years, financial futures have been used by corporations and individuals to hedge against fluctuation in the price of financial securities. An anticipated fall in the price of a particular financial asset can be managed by selling a futures contract on that financial asset. Nevertheless, until recently there was little that US home-owners could do to hedge against a much feared housing price slump, as the US housing market moved into a correction period. In May 2006 the Chicago Mercantile Exchange introduced for the very first time futures contracts based on a housing price index. The housing price index, called S&P Case Shiller Index, is a broad index that measures changes in house prices in 20 US metropolitan areas. This index was developed by two economists, Robert Shiller and Karl Case. Robert Shiller is an economics professor from Yale University who for years has been voicing his concern about a housing bubble in the United States. He is also the author of *Irrational Exuberance* (Princeton University Press, 2005) and a founder of New Jersey-based MacroMarkets, the co-publisher of the Case-Shiller Index. Karl Case is an economics profes-

sor from Wellesley College and a founding member of Fiserv Case Shiller Weiss, Inc., the other company responsible for the publishing of the Case-Shiller Index.

The way these housing futures work is simple. If you own a house in cosmopolitan Chicago and want to hedge against the risk that your house may be worth less than its current value in the future, you can sell housing futures that you will benefit from in the case of a fall in the housing price as indicated by the Case-Shiller Index. Nevertheless, like other financial futures, these housing contracts are not just for hedging against a falling housing price; those with a positive outlook for the housing market can indeed buy these contracts and effectively benefit if housing prices go up.

Despite a short trading history, housing futures contracts have the potential to become big. The housing market in the United States alone is estimated to be worth approximately US$22 trillion, which is bigger than the US$16 trillion equity market and is not far away from the US$26 trillion debt market. Only time will tell.

or a syndicate of firms. The company selling its securities does not meet the ultimate purchasers of the securities in the public offering. The public market is an impersonal market.

In a **private placement**, the securities are offered and sold to a limited number of investors, who are often the current major investors in the business. The firm will usually hammer out with a broker and the prospective buyers the details of the offering. The private placement market is a more personal market than its public counterpart.

private placement
The offer of financial securities directly to selected potential purchasers, in contrast to a public offering.

PRIMARY MARKETS AND SECONDARY MARKETS

A **primary market** is the name given to the component of the financial markets in which securities are offered for the first time to potential investors. A new issue of ordinary shares by a company listed on the stock exchange is a primary-market transaction. This type of transaction increases the total number of financial assets in the economy. Similarly, a new issue of debentures by a finance company is a primary market transaction.

primary market
The segment of the financial markets in which securities are offered for sale for the first time.

The **secondary market** represents transactions in currently issued securities. For example, if the first buyer of a newly issued share subsequently sells it, he or she does so in what is called the secondary market. Therefore, all transactions after the initial issue of the security take place in the secondary market. The sale of these securities does not affect the total number of financial assets that exist in the economy. Both the money market and the capital market, described above, have primary-market and secondary-market aspects.

secondary market
The segment of the financial markets in which existing securities are bought and sold.

THE AUSTRALIAN SECURITIES EXCHANGE (ASX)

The Australian Securities Exchange (ASX) is the major primary and secondary market for equity securities such as ordinary shares, and a secondary market for debentures, notes and bonds that have initially been issued to the public directly by the borrower or issued through a broker. In July 2006 the ASX merged with the Sydney Futures Exchange (SFE), and now also provides a platform for some derivatives to be traded. As the ASX is a major component of the Australian capital markets, financial managers need to understand its operations.

The Australian Securities Exchange Limited is a publicly listed company that provides a market for investors to buy and sell securities. Historically, each of the six states had a separate stock exchange, but in 1987 they merged to form the Australian Stock Exchange and create a nationally integrated market, later becoming the Australian Securities Exchange. In 1998 the ASX became a public company and was itself listed on the Australian Securities Exchange. Under the *Corporations Act 2001*, the ASX has the principal role of providing efficient, fair, honest, competitive and informed markets for trading Australian and overseas financial securities.

It is important to note that of the many thousands of companies operating in Australia there were only 2198 listed on the ASX at the end of June 2009.[10] Together, these companies have a market capitalisation of $1.1 trillion, which is more than the size of the Australian economy (GDP). Nevertheless, this market capitalisation figure represents a 21.43% decrease on the market capitalisation in June 2008. Since June 2007, the market capitalisation of listed Australian equities has fallen by 31.29%. This significant loss in shareholder wealth reflects the market turmoil in 2008 and 2009 as a result of the Global Financial Crisis.

To have its shares listed on the ASX, a company must satisfy the listing requirements imposed by the ASX. These requirements, which are discussed in more detail in Chapter 19, specify such items as minimum paid-up capital, minimum number of shareholders, minimum operating profit over the previous three years, and minimum level of net tangible assets that the company must have before it can be listed. In addition, the company must agree to provide regular information to the market, including periodic financial statements.

The most important benefit that a company gets out of listing its shares on a stock exchange is 'liquidity enhancement' which allows the shares to be readily converted into cash via exchange-based transactions at market-determined prices. The stock exchange provides a very active secondary market for the trading of listed shares, which enables listed companies to raise new equity capital by selling its shares by public offering to the market. In 2009–2010, in the aftermath of the Global Financial Crisis, the number of new listings fell dramatically to 45 from a record high of 284 in 2007. Despite the low value of initial capital raised, listed firms had a strong demand for funds with $88 billion secondary capital raised.[11] Being listed on the ASX also adds to a company's image and reputation. In return for these benefits, companies pay the stock exchange ongoing listing fees.

The ASX also provides a market for interest rate instruments such as debentures and for options and warrants on shares.

OBJECTIVE

Outline the main pattern of fund flows underlying the financing of businesses in Australia.

Pattern of fund flows in Australia's financial markets

Australia's financial markets are made up of the sub-markets discussed above. Contemporary statistics for the various financial market components, detailing factors such as the value and volume of transactions, are available from publications produced regularly by the Australian Bureau of Statistics and the Reserve Bank of Australia.

Figure 3.4 details the financial claims that the major sectors of the Australian economy had outstanding at the end of March 2010. As can be seen from this figure, business firms in the non-financial corporate sector of the Australian economy rely heavily on the nation's financial market system for funding. At the end of March 2010, the amount of financial claims on the sector totalled $1415.9 billion. Of this total, $761.3 billion was outstanding to financial corporations, $123.2 billion to Australian households, $76.9 billion to general government and $454.5 billion to the rest of the world. The most obvious trend in the pattern of corporate financing to emerge in the 2007–10 period was the increasing reliance of Australian companies on international sources of finance. In this three-year period, the amount of financial claims that the rest of the world had on the Australian corporate sector increased by approximately 27% from $358.6 billion in March 2007 to $454.5 billion in March 2010. While the amount of

FIGURE 3.4 Financial claims in Australia at the end of March 2010 (A$ billion)

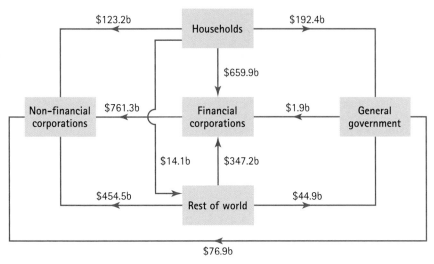

© Commonwealth of Australia, Australian Bureau of Statistics, cat. no. 5232.0, Australian National Accounts, March 2010 quarter.

financing provided by financial corporations has remained stable, the households and government sectors have become less important providers of funds for Australian businesses.

The Australian households sector has historically been a net saver of funds. The investing of these savings in bank accounts, shares, and superannuation and other funds has resulted in the households sector having at 31 March 2010 net claims on non-financial corporations totalling $123.2 billion, $659.9 billion on financial corporations, $192.4 billion on general government and $14.1 billion on the rest of the world.

One important aspect apparent from the data in Figure 3.4 is the role played by financial corporations in transferring funds from the surplus segments of the economy to the deficit segments. It can be seen that financial corporations financed claims on the non-financial corporations sector ($761.3 billion) from net claims by the Australian households sector ($659.9 billion), the general government ($1.9 billion) and the rest of the world ($347.2 billion).

A further factor evident from the data in Figure 3.4 is the significant source of finance provided to various sectors of the Australian economy by funds from overseas. Does this matter? In 1980–81 Australia's net foreign debt was around 5% of GDP. At 31 March 2010, Australia had $654.3 billion of net foreign debt outstanding, which is equivalent to approximately 59% of the nation's estimated GDP for 2010. Whether these levels of foreign debt are of concern can be viewed as being dependent on the ability of the economy to (1) reduce the current-account deficit by increasing exports and/or reducing dependence on imports, (2) reduce government budget deficits, and (3) ensure that businesses productively use the money borrowed from overseas to enable them to be internationally competitive.[12]

Summary

The chapter focused on the market environment, known as financial markets, in which funds are transferred between different market participants.

OBJECTIVE 1

The economic role of financial markets is to allocate savings efficiently to the ultimate demanders or users of the savings. This can be achieved by financial intermediaries channelling funds from savers to users via loans, or by markets trading financial instruments. Without a fully developed financial market system, the wealth of an economy would not be as great as it could be.

OBJECTIVE 2

Financial intermediaries play an important role in facilitating the transfer of funds between market participants. Commercial banks are the traditional financial institutions that play this conduit role by taking deposits from the public and making loans. However, there are non-bank financial institutions such as building societies, credit unions, insurance companies, superannuation funds, investment companies and private equity firms which also facilitate fund transfers.

Fund transfers from investors to users of funds can be broadly categorised into (1) direct transfer, (2) indirect transfer using banks, and (3) indirect transfer using other financial intermediaries. In a direct transfer of funds, investors provide direct funding to the net user of the funds and receive a financial security in exchange. In an indirect transfer of funds, investors invest money in a financial intermediary which subsequently undertakes a range of investments in the corporate sector.

There are many sub-financial markets. The stock market, debt market, foreign-exchange market and derivatives market are so named because of the type of financial assets that are transacted in these markets. In contrast, the money market and the capital market are distinguished by financial assets with different maturities. The way in which financial assets are created or traded also plays a role in the portioning of financial markets. Public offerings create financial securities that are sold to the public at large, while private placements are aimed at a particular group of investors. The primary market is the market for new issues, whereas the secondary market represents transactions in previously issued securities. In Australia, the Australian Securities Exchange (ASX) is the largest organised exchange, providing a platform for the trading of stocks, bonds and derivatives.

Households and overseas investors are the major net suppliers of funds to Australian financial markets. These markets channel funds to the non-financial business sector, which is a net user of funds. The corporate sector in Australia has a strong reliance on overseas funding for their operations.

Key terms

For a complete flashcard glossary go to MyFinanceLab at www.pearson.com.au/myfinancelab

building societies and credit unions	64	mutual fund	66
call option	74	net asset value	66
capital market	74	option	73
commercial banks	63	over-the-counter instruments	72
defined benefit fund	66	preferred stock	71
derivative	72	preservation age	65
exchange-traded fund (ETF)	66	primary market	75
exchange-traded instruments	72	private equity firms	67
external funds	60	private placement	75
financial asset	59	public offering	74
financial intermediary	60	put option	74
futures contract	73	real assets	61
hedge fund	67	secondary market	75
internal funds	60	superannuation fund	64
leveraged buyout funds	68	superannuation guarantee	65
money market	74	venture capital firms	67

Web works

Go to the Australian Bureau of Statistics website, **www.abs.gov.au**, and select 'National Accounts' on the left-hand menu. Locate Catalogue 5232 which details the most up-to-date financial claims in Australia. How have these claims changed from Figure 3.4, which was correct as at March 2010?

Review questions

3-1 What are financial markets? What function do they perform? How would an economy be worse off without them?

3-2 Which are the three major groups of players that interact in the financial markets? Briefly describe them.

3-3 Define in a technical sense what is meant by a 'financial intermediary'. Give an example.

3-4 What are the main activities of an investment bank? How do investment banks differ from commercial banks?

3-5 How does a venture capital firm raise funds and how does it invest the funds?

3-6 Distinguish between an indirect financial security and a direct financial security. Give an example of each.

3-7 Compare and contrast ordinary stocks and preferred stocks.

3-8 Distinguish between the money market and the capital market.

3-9 What major benefits do you think companies and individuals enjoy because of the existence of an organised stock exchange?

3-10 What aspects of a company do you think the stock exchange would want to examine to determine whether its securities should be listed?

3-11 Why do you think a large company might want to raise long-term debenture finance through a private placement rather than through a public offering?

3-12 In the last decade there has been a shift towards the direct transfer of funds from investors to the corporate sector. Examine some of the reasons for this trend.

3-13 What are the two major market-traded forms of financial derivatives? Outline the main features of these contracts.

3-14 Outline the major fund flows in the Australian financial economy. In your answer, clearly identify the sectors that are net savers and the sectors that are net users of funds.

3-15 What is an option? What is the major difference between a call option and a put option?

Case study

Troy Dexter is an affluent venture capitalist based in Sydney. In 2009 Troy founded a hedge fund called Northwest Capital Management. A hedge fund is an investment fund whose aim is to deliver positive returns on money invested while minimising risk. A hedge fund can be thought of as a company whose main activity is to invest in a range of financial assets. Troy's hedge fund adopts a macro investment strategy that aims to profit from significant shifts in the economy. Apart from his own money which he uses to invest in a range of financial assets, the fund is also open to investors who can participate in the fund for an annual management fee. Although hedge funds aim at reducing risk by employing different hedging techniques, there is still a certain element of risk as there are periods where the returns on investments are negative. Troy's vision of the future is that the strong growth in the Australian housing market will come to an end, economic growth will stall and the price of oil will escalate. Thus, Troy is currently buying treasury bonds in the debt market and energy stocks in the share market.

1. From the point of view of Northwest Capital Management, are treasury bonds and energy stocks direct or indirect securities?
2. Consider an investor who invests money in Northwest Capital Management. The money ends up being invested in treasury bonds and energy stocks. From the perspective of the investor, does she hold direct securities by investing in Northwest Capital Management? Explain.

Notes

1. Data sourced from the Australian Prudential Regulation Authority.
2. T. Valentine, *Finance in focus: the Global Financial Crisis*, Pearson Australia, Frenchs Forest, NSW, 2010.
3. A. Carswell, 'Global Financial Crisis worse than Great Depression—analyst', *The Advertiser*, 11 December 2009.
4. See the Australian Securities Exchange website <www.asx.com.au> for more detail.
5. It is probably not comforting for you to know that brokerage fees in Australia are among the highest in the world.
6. Data sourced from The Australian Private Equity and Venture Capital Association Ltd website <www.avcal.com.au>.
7. However, some commentators have noted that benefits to Eurobond issuers from lower interest rates may be offset by higher underwriting costs compared to a domestic bond issue. For more detail, see R. Ardalan, 'Eurobond issue and firm value', *Journal of Business and Economics Research*, 6, 2008, pp. 63–70.
8. A. Melnik and D. Nissim, 'Issue costs in the Eurobond market: the effects of market integration', *Journal of Banking and Finance*, 30, 2006, pp. 157–77.
9. According to data published by the European Central Bank. See <www.ecb.int> for more information.
10. Australian Securities Exchange Limited, *Report to Shareholders, 2009/10*.
11. ibid.
12. Data sourced from the Reserve Bank of Australia website <www.rba.gov.au>.

Learning objectives

After reading this chapter, you should be able to:

1. Explain the mechanics of compounding: how money grows over time when it is invested.
2. Determine the future or present value of a sum of money.
3. Discuss the relationship between compounding (future value) and bringing money back to the present (present value).
4. Calculate the effective annual rate of interest and then explain how it differs from the nominal or stated interest rate.
5. Define an ordinary annuity and calculate its future value and present value.
6. Apply the annuity present value model to the process of loan amortisation.
7. Understand the notion of a general annuity and the concept of equivalent interest rates.
8. Determine the present value of an annuity due.
9. Understand how perpetuities work.
10. Deal with complex cash flows and deferred annuities.
11. Determine how bond values change in response to changing interest rates.
12. Interpolate values within financial tables.
13. Formulate multi-part and non-standard problems.

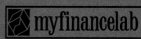

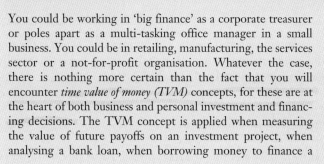

The time value of money

Chapter 4

CHAPTER PREVIEW

Much of this book focuses on determining the value of the firm and the value of investment proposals. A key concept that underlies this material is the *time value of money (TVM)*. The TVM principle is that a dollar today is worth more than a dollar received at a future date. This is because a dollar today can be invested and earn interest, so it is worth *more than* one dollar at a future date.

Different investment proposals produce different sets of cash flows over different time periods. Likewise, borrowing money often involves repayments over a series of future dates. How does the manager compare these? We will see that the concept of the time value of money will let us do this. Thus, knowledge of the TVM concept is essential in just about every facet of financial management and so this chapter develops the tools to incorporate *Principle 2: The time value of money—a dollar received today is worth more than a dollar received in the future* into a host of financial calculations.

Regardless of your program

You could be working in 'big finance' as a corporate treasurer or poles apart as a multi-tasking office manager in a small business. You could be in retailing, manufacturing, the services sector or a not-for-profit organisation. Whatever the case, there is nothing more certain than the fact that you will encounter *time value of money (TVM)* concepts, for these are at the heart of both business and personal investment and financing decisions. The TVM concept is applied when measuring the value of future payoffs on an investment project, when analysing a bank loan, when borrowing money to finance a house or apartment, when investing for retirement ... the list goes on and on. Engineers often work on evaluating major projects, where the technical feasibility sits side by side with the financial feasibility; likewise for marketing analysts working on new product proposals. Human resource managers may encounter the TVM through responsibility for administering aspects of superannuation or pension schemes. Even if you don't encounter TVM in your working life, you can be sure of encountering it in life's major monetary decisions.

Compound interest concepts

OBJECTIVE 1

Most people encounter the concept of **compound interest** at an early age. Anyone who has ever had a savings account has received compound interest. Compound interest also applies to many other ways of investing or borrowing money. But, before proceeding further, it is necessary to explain the notation used to portray compound interest.

Explain the mechanics of compounding: how money grows over time when it is invested.

SPECIFICATION OF COMPOUND INTEREST RATES

The annual rate of compound interest is often known as the *nominal annual rate*, sometimes identified by the symbol j. This rate is also called the *APR* (annual percentage rate). Given

compound interest
The situation in which interest paid on the investment during the first period is added to the principal, and during the second period interest is earned on the original principal plus the interest earned during the first period.

the nominal annual rate, the periodic rate of compound interest (symbol i) is defined by equation (4-1), where m is the number of times that interest is compounded each year.

$$i = j/m \qquad \textbf{(4-1)}$$

The use of equation (4-1) is demonstrated in Example 4.1.

EXAMPLE 4.1 Compound interest rates

If interest is compounded twice per year at a nominal annual rate of 12% per annum, what is the half-yearly rate of compound interest?

Substituting in equation (4-1), j = 12% compounded m = 2 times per annum, so the half-yearly rate i is 6%:

$$i = j/m = 12\%/2 = 6\%$$

As will be seen later, the reason that knowing the rate per period, i, is important is that this rate is used for actual compound interest computations. Another point that needs to be understood is that, if interest is compounded m times per year for t years, the total number of compounding periods, n, is given by equation (4-2):

$$n = m \times t \qquad \textbf{(4-2)}$$

Concept check

4.1   If interest is compounded at 6% every half-year for three years, what is:
   (a)   the *APR*?
   (b)   *j*?
   (c)   the total number of compounding periods, *n*?

For answers go to MyFinanceLab or www.pearson.com.au/9781442539174

OBJECTIVE **2**

Determine the future or present value of a sum of money.

Future value

Saving or accumulating money at compound interest results in a future value, which is the sum of money received in the future after adding compound interest to the amount invested initially. This application of compound interest is introduced in Example 4.2.

EXAMPLE 4.2 Future value at compound interest

Table 4.1 shows the accumulation, period-by-period, of $1000 invested at compound interest of 12% per annum, compounded half-yearly, for three years. This means, in effect, that interest is compounded at a rate i = 6% every half-year for n = six half-years. Table 4.1 shows that the amount of $1000 accumulates to $1418.52 by the end of that time.

As shown in Table 4.1, in half-year number 1, $60 interest is paid, which represents 6% of the $1000 principal that was invested initially. Therefore, adding the interest to the initial principal, the accumulated sum of the investment is $1060 at the end of the first half-year. This sum of $1060 then receives 6% interest in half-year 2, an amount of $63.60, which adds to the beginning amount of $1060 so that the accumulated sum at the end of half-year number 2 (the first year) is $1123.60. This process continues in the way shown in Table 4.1 until the end of half-year number 6 (end of year 3), at which time the accumulated sum has grown to $1418.52.

Looking at the second line of Table 4.1, the second period's interest of $63.60 includes an amount of $3.60, which represents interest at 6% of the first period's $60 interest. This shows the key characteristic of compound interest, which is that interest is paid on interest.

TABLE 4.1 Accumulation schedule

$1000 invested at 12% p.a. compounded half-yearly for 3 years

HALF-YEAR	OPENING BALANCE	INTEREST AT 6%	CLOSING BALANCE
1	$1000.00	$60.00	$1060.00
2	1060.00	63.60	1123.60
3	1123.60	67.42	1191.02
4	1191.02	71.46	1262.48
5	1262.48	75.75	1338.23
6	1338.23	80.29	1418.52

TIMELINES, PRESENT VALUE AND FUTURE VALUE

In Example 4.2, the sum of money invested originally ($1000) represents a present value, symbol PV. A *present value* is an amount of money exchanged (borrowed/invested) 'today'—that is, in the present. This PV of $1000 grows to $1418.52 at the end of three years (six half-years). The accumulated amount is known as a future value. A *future value* is money exchanged (received/paid) at a specified future time. The relationship between a present value and its future value can be portrayed on a timeline.

A timeline uses a horizontal line to represent the passage of time, with cash inflows being shown above the timeline and cash outflows below the timeline. For example, if you invest $1000 'today', this represents a cash outflow, and if the investment accumulates to $1418.52 after three years, the sum received at that future date is a cash inflow, as shown in Figure 4.1.

However, if you *borrow* $1000 'today' at 12% per annum compounded half-yearly for three years, the sum of $1000 represents a cash inflow and the relevant timeline (Figure 4.2) is a mirror image of Figure 4.1

FIGURE 4.1 Timeline showing $1000 invested at 12% p.a., compounded twice per year for 3 years

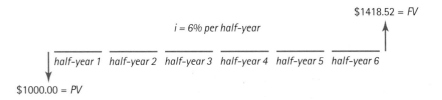

FIGURE 4.2 Timeline showing $1000 borrowed at 12% p.a., compounded twice per year for 3 years

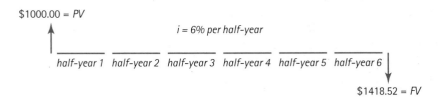

The timeline helps to identify a point that is significant when it comes to computing present values and future values; when financial calculators or spreadsheets are used as a computational aid, cash inflows must be input as positive amounts and cash outflows must be input as negative amounts.

COMPUTING THE FUTURE VALUE

Fortunately, it is not necessary to draw up a schedule like Table 4.1 every time money is accumulated. Instead, the *FV* can be determined by using equation (4-3). This equation is derived in the Appendix to this chapter, and in this equation FV_n means the future value at the end of the *n*th period:

$$FV_n = PV(1 + i)^n \qquad \textbf{(4-3)}$$

Future values can also be computed by means of a financial calculator, by use of financial tables and by use of spreadsheets.

Important note

Throughout this text, the symbol is used to identify solutions that use the relevant equation, ⟋ is used to identify financial calculator solutions, and ⊞ is used to identify solutions that use financial tables. Your lecturer may specify that you need to know only one or two of these methods, in which case these symbols will quickly guide you to the appropriate part of each computation.

EXAMPLE 4.3 Computing the future value at compound interest

This example demonstrates three different ways of computing the future value of the problem that was first identified in Example 4.2, namely the future value after three years of $1000 at 12% per annum compounded half-yearly.

Substituting in equation (4-3), *PV* = $1000, *i* = 6% (per half-year) and *n* = 6 (half-years), and so we have:

$$FV_6 = PV(1 + i)^n = \$1000(1.06)^6 = \$1000(1.41852) = \$1418.52$$

Note that all mathematical equations require the interest rate to be expressed as a decimal number; in this case, 6% represents .06 as a decimal.

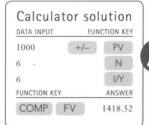

Calculator solution

DATA INPUT		FUNCTION KEY
1000	+/–	PV
6 .		N
6		I/Y
FUNCTION KEY		ANSWER
COMP FV		1418.52

Note the use of the +/– key to enter $1000 as a negative amount, because it is a cash outflow (an amount that is invested).

The section 'Moving money through time with the aid of a financial calculator' (below) shows how to set up the Sharp EL-738 (or EL-735S) calculator. (If you have a different calculator model, consult your calculator handbook.) After following the set-up instructions, the three given variables are input by entering the relevant numbers followed by the corresponding function key. Then, the answer is computed by selecting the COMP key, followed by the desired variable (in this case, the *FV*), as shown in the solution panel in the page margin.

future value interest factor
The factor $FVIF_{i,n}$ that converts $1 to its future value in *n* periods time at *i*% compound interest per period. To determine the future value of, say, $100, the factor is multiplied by 100.

We have seen from the above use of equation (4-3) that $1418.52 = $1000(1.41852). In that solution, 1.41852 represents the future value of an amount of $1 for *n* = 6 periods at *i* = 6% per period. More generally, the future value of $1 for *n* periods at *i*% is represented by the symbol $FVIF_{i,n}$ which is known as the **future value interest factor** (that is, $FVIF_{i,n}$ is the future value of $1 compounded at *i*% for *n* periods). Therefore, if $*PV* is invested or borrowed 'today', its future value is given by multiplying PV by the relevant future value interest factor. This gives rise to equation (4-4):

$$FV_n = PV(FVIF_{i,n})$$ **(4-4)**

To solve the Example 4.2 problem, we therefore have:

$$FV_6 = 1000(FVIF_{6\%,6})$$

The value of $FVIF_{6\%,6}$ can be found in Appendix A at the back of this book, where it is seen that, for an interest rate of 6% and $n = 6$, the future value of $1 is approximately 1.419. Thus, the FV of $1000 ≈ $1000(1.419) ≈ $1419. This answer alerts us immediately to two fundamental problems with using financial tables:

1. Table values are rounded and so answers may be only approximate.
2. Tables are limited to a specific set of values (e.g. there is no value for $i = 6.2\%$; nor for $n = 240$).

Concept check

4.2 If $1000 is invested at 12% p.a. compounded half-yearly, what is the accumulated sum after two years?

For answers go to MyFinanceLab or www.pearson.com.au/9781442539174

Figure 4.3 extends Table 4.1 by showing how an investment of $1000 continues to grow for 10 periods at a compound interest rate of 6% per period. In addition, Figure 4.3 shows the FV of the investment at rates of 0% and 10% per period, respectively. It can be seen that the future value increases with n, the number of periods, and with i, the interest rate per period. The same conclusion can also be drawn by looking at equation (4-3); increasing the exponent n in turn increases the FV, or increasing the value of i in turn increases the FV.

The graphs in Figure 4.3 exhibit what mathematicians call *exponential behaviour*. This means that money invested at compound interest (except for a zero interest rate) accumulates *at an increasing rate*, period by period. This characteristic of exponential behaviour can also be seen in Table 4.1, where interest is $60.00 in period 1, $63.60 in period 2, $67.42 in period 3, and so on. That is, each period's interest is greater than the previous period's interest, and the amount of the increase each period is also growing.

FIGURE 4.3 Future value of $1000 deposited initially, at 0%, 6% and 10% compound interest per period

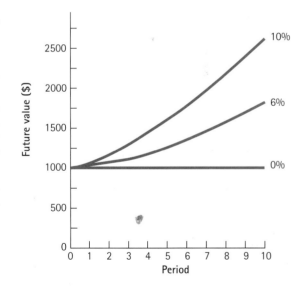

FYI

If, instead of investing, you borrow $1000 for three years at 12% per annum compounded half-yearly, the debt could be repaid by a single future payment (FV) of $1418.52. This shows that borrowing is the mirror image of investing. Put another way, if you *borrow* $1000, someone else is *investing* that amount (by lending it to you).

MOVING MONEY THROUGH TIME WITH THE AID OF A FINANCIAL CALCULATOR

Time-value-of-money calculations can be simplified greatly with the aid of a financial calculator. In solving time-value-of-money problems with a financial calculator, you will often be given three of four variables and will have to solve for the fourth. Before examining any solutions using a financial calculator, let us look at the calculator's five most common keys. (In any particular time-value-of-money problem, only four of these keys are generally used.) For the Sharp EL-738 or -735S calculator, these keys are:

MENU KEY	DESCRIPTION
N	Stores (or calculates) the total number of compounding periods (or payments).
I/Y	Stores (or calculates) the interest or discount rate, expressed as a percentage.
PV	Stores (or calculates) the present value of a future cash flow (or a series of cash flows).
FV	Stores (or calculates) the future value; that is, the compound value of a single initial cash flow (the present value) or a series of cash flows. FV also stands for the final cash flow.
PMT	Stores (or calculates) the dollar amount of each annuity payment deposited or repaid at the end of each period. (This key will not be used until later in this chapter.)

One thing you must keep in mind when using a financial calculator is that cash outflows normally have to be entered as negative numbers. In general, each problem will have cash flows with two signs: *outflows* with a negative value and *inflows* with a positive value.

Before you can use your calculator, it is necessary to set it up for TVM computations.

Setting up your calculator for financial problems

You will want your calculator to be in the *financial* (or *normal*) *mode*. For the Sharp EL-738/735S calculator, this is accomplished as follows:

- Press the MODE key. The number '0' should flash on the display under the displayed heading 'NORMAL'.
- Press = to confirm that this is the mode you want.

Next, you may wish to select the number of decimal places displayed. To do so:

- Press the SET UP key. The number '0' should flash under the displayed heading 'DSP'.
- Press = to confirm that this is the function that you want.
- The number '0' should flash under the displayed heading 'TAB'.
- Press = to confirm that this is the function that you want.
- The calculator will then display 'DIG (0≈9)', which refers to the number of decimal places from 0 to 9. For instance, to select 2 places (e.g. dollars and cents) merely enter the number: 2 .

Clearing the calculator between different problems

It is good practice to clear the calculator between successive, different problems so that old values stored in the calculator's memory do not find their way into a new problem.

This is accomplished by entering 2ndF then the key with CA written above (note, the 2ndF key is used generally to access all functions written above the keys).

Most of your computations will use at least four of the five compound interest functions identified by the symbols N I/Y PV PMT and FV . However, when switching to other types of computations, such as 'CASH' (unequal cash flow computations), it is necessary to reset the calculator by putting it back in NORMAL mode as shown above. Whenever a particular problem seems to give nonsense answers, reset the calculator in this way and try again.

Other useful procedures include:

- To clear the current display, press ON/C .

- To correct a wrong number, scroll back to the invalid number (using the [◄] key) until the cursor is positioned over the wrong number, then press [DEL] to delete it.

USING SPREADSHEETS FOR TIME-VALUE-OF-MONEY PROBLEMS

Setting up a spreadsheet to solve most of these problems is somewhat like using a sledge-hammer to crack a walnut. All the same, if you have some basic experience in using spread-sheets you will readily be able to use the spreadsheet functions for solving compound interest problems.

There are several competing spreadsheets, the most popular one being Microsoft Excel. Just as with the keystroke calculations on a financial calculator, a spreadsheet can make easy work of most common financial calculations. Following are some of the functions used with Excel when moving money through time:

CALCULATION	FORMULA
Present value	= PV (rate, number of periods, payment, future value, type)
Future value	= FV (rate, number of periods, payment, present value, type)
Payment	= PMT (rate, number of periods, present value, future value, type)
Number of periods	= NPER (rate, payment, present value, future value, type)
Interest rate	= RATE (number of periods, payment, present value, future value, type, guess)

where:

Rate	= i, the interest rate or discount rate per period
Number of periods	= n, the number of periods
Payment	= PMT, the annuity payment deposited or received each period
Future value	= FV, the future value of the investment at the end of n periods
Present value	= PV, the present value of the future sum of money or the future stream of payments
Type	= when the payment is made (0 if omitted)
	0 = at end of period
	1 = at beginning of period
Guess	= a starting point when calculating the interest rate; if omitted, the calculations begin with a value of 0.1, or 10%

Just as with a financial calculator, the outflows have to be entered as negative numbers. In general, each problem will have at least two cash flows, at least one positive and at least one negative. The idea is that you deposit money at some point in time (an outflow or negative value) and at some point later in time you withdraw your money (an inflow or positive value).

	A	B	C	D	E	F	G	H	I
1									
2		Spreadsheets and the time value of money							
3									
4	If we invest $500 in a bank where it will earn 8% compounded								
5	annually, how much will it be worth at the end of 7 years?								
6									
7			rate (i) =	8%					
8		number of periods (n) =		7					
9			payment (PMT) =	$0					
10			present value (PV) =	−$500					
11		type (0 = at end of period) =		0					
12									
13			Future value =	$856.91					
14									
15	Excel formula: =FV (rate,number of periods,payment,present value,type)								
16									
17	Entered value in cell D13: =FV (D7,D8,D9,D10,D11)								
18	Notice that present value ($500) took on a negative value.								
19									

Sheet1 / Sheet2 / Sheet3 /

	A	B	C	D	E	F	G	H	I
1									
2									
3			**Spreadsheets: Solving for _i_**						
4									
5	In 10 years you'd like to have $20 000 to buy a new Jeep, but you only								
6	have $11 167. At what rate must your $11 167 be compounded								
7	annually for it to grow to $20 000 in 10 years?								
8									
9		number of periods (_n_) =		10					
10		payment (_PMT_) =		$0					
11		present value (_PV_) =		–$11 167					
12		future value (_FV_) =		$20 000					
13		type (0 = at end of period) =		0					
14									
15									
16			_i_ =	6.00%					
17									
18	Excel formula: =RATE(number of periods,payment,present value,future value,type,guess)								
19									
20	Entered value in cell D16: =RATE(D9,D10,D11,D12,D13)								
21									
22	Notice that present value ($11 167) took on a negative value.								
23									

Sheet1 / Sheet2 / Sheet3 /

OBJECTIVE 3

Discuss the relationship between compounding (future value) and bringing money back to the present (present value).

discount rate
The interest rate that converts a future value to the present value.

discounting
The process of converting a future value to its present value.

discount factor
The quantity that converts a particular future sum of money to its present value.

Present value

Going back to Figure 4.1, it can be seen that $1000 is the present value of $1418.52 receivable in three years time at 12% per annum compounded half-yearly. A _present value_ is defined as a sum of money exchanged in the present that is mathematically equivalent to a future value. Present values are computed by starting from a given _FV_, along with _i_ and _n_, and solving for _PV_ as the unknown. (In contrast, previous examples started with the investment of _PV_ 'today' and solved for the unknown _FV_.)

When computing present values, some particular terminology is often used. The **discount rate** is the rate of compound interest when it is used to convert a future value to its present value. And **discounting** is the process of converting a future value to its present value. Furthermore, in equation (4-5a) below, it will be seen that multiplying a _FV_ by the quantity $1/(1 + i)^n$ converts that _FV_ to its _present value_; in this process, $1/(1 + i)^n$ is known as the discount factor; that is, the **discount factor** is the quantity that converts a particular future sum of money to its present value.

Some potential interpretations of present-value computations, based on the timelines in Figures 4.1 and 4.2 respectively, are as follows:

- What amount needs to be deposited today in order to accumulate $1418.52 after three years, if the interest rate is 12% per annum compounded half-yearly? (_Answer:_ $1000)
- What amount was borrowed 'today' if the debt was repaid by a lump sum of $1418.52 in three years time, given that the interest rate is 12% per annum compounded half-yearly? (_Answer:_ $1000)

COMPUTING THE PRESENT VALUE

By rearrangement of equation (4-3), we have equation (4-5) or its equivalent (4-5a):

$$PV = FV_n / (1 + i)^n \qquad \textbf{(4-5)}$$

$$= FV_n (1 + i)^{-n} \qquad \textbf{(4-5a)}$$

This equation is used in Example 4.4 to solve for unknown _PV_, along with other computational methods.

EXAMPLE 4.4 Solving for the present value (including calculator solution)

Suppose you intend to reach a savings target of $3000 after two years at 8% per annum compounded quarterly. How much would you have to invest today? It is clear that the answer is equal to *PV* of the $3000 *FV*, as shown in the following timeline:

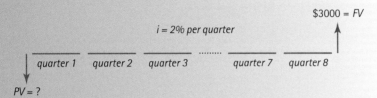

Three different computational methods are now outlined, each of which shows that $2560.47 must be deposited 'today' (a present value).

Substituting in equation (4-5), we have FV_n = $3000, i = 2% per quarter (or .02 as a decimal), and n = 8 quarters (2 years):

$PV = FV_n / (1 + i)^n = \$3000 / (1.02)^8 = \$3000 / 1.17166 = \$2560.47$

Before solving this problem, it is a good idea to get into the habit of clearing the old values from the calculator's memories, which is accomplished by entering: [2ndF] [CA]

Note that the calculator solution (which is shown in the margin) outputs a negative amount for the *PV*. This is because it is necessary to invest $2560.47 today, which requires a cash outflow (a negative cash flow).

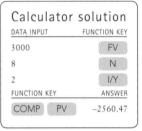

Calculator solution

DATA INPUT	FUNCTION KEY
3000	FV
8	N
2	I/Y
FUNCTION KEY	ANSWER
COMP PV	−2560.47

Equation (4-5) can be re-expressed as:

$PV = FV_n \times [1/(1 + i)^n]$ **(4-5b)**

In this expression, the quantity $[1/(1 + i)^n]$ is known as the **present value interest factor**, $PVIF_{i,n}$. It represents the *PV* of $1 receivable in *n* periods time at *i* per period compound interest. Therefore, the *PV* of a future sum of money, FV_n, is equal to the future value multiplied by the relevant present value interest factor, as shown in equation (4-6):

$PV = FV_n (PVIF_{i,n})$ **(4-6)**

In order to solve Example 4.4, we can formulate the problem as follows:

$PV = \$3000 (PVIF_{2\%,8})$

Selected values of $PVIF_{i,n}$ are found in Appendix B at the back of this book. For example, the present value of $1 in eight periods' time at 2% is approximately 0.853. Thus,

$PV \approx \$3000 (0.853) \approx \$2559.$

present value interest factor
The factor $PVIF_{i,n}$ that converts (discounts) a future value to its present value, at a discount rate of *i* per period compound interest for *n* periods. For example, the present value of $200 is equal to the $PVIF_{i,n}$ factor multiplied by 200.

Concept check
4.3 If there is an increase in the interest rate (or discount rate) *i*, is it true that the *PV* increases also?

For answers go to MyFinanceLab or www.pearson.com.au/9781442539174

SOLVING FOR THE NUMBER OF PERIODS, *n*

By rearrangement of equation (4-3), we have:

$$n = \log(FV/PV) \,/\, \log(1 + i)$$

(4-7)

This equation is now used to solve the problem outlined in Example 4.5.

EXAMPLE 4.5 **Solving for the number of periods**

How many months did it take to repay a loan of $300 if the sum repaid was $358.84 at an interest rate of 12% per annum compounded monthly? This means that interest is compounded at a rate of 1% per month, so a timeline representing this situation would be as follows:

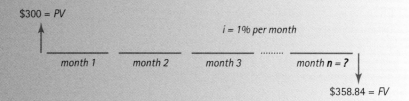

$300 = PV

$i = 1\%$ per month

month 1   month 2   month 3   ....   month **n = ?**

$358.84 = FV

Substituting in equation (4-7) we have:

$$n = \log(358.84/300) \,/\, \log 1.01$$
$$= \log 1.19613 \,/\, \log 1.01 = .07778 \,/\, .00432 = 18 \text{ (months)}$$

Note that the calculator will not give an answer unless the *FV* is input as a negative amount, as shown in the margin computation; this is because the *FV* represents a cash outflow (the amount repaid on the loan).

Substituting in equation (4-4), we have $358.84 = 300\,(FVIF_{1\%,n})$. That is,

$$358.84/300 = 1.196 = FVIF_{1\%,n}$$

Examining Appendix A at the back of the book, it is necessary to look in the 1% column for the table value 1.196. This value corresponds with $n = 18$.

Calculator solution

DATA INPUT		FUNCTION KEY
300		PV
358.84	+/−	FV
1		I/Y
FUNCTION KEY		ANSWER
COMP N		18

SOLVING FOR THE INTEREST RATE, *i*

By rearrangement of equation (4-3), we have:

$$i = (FV/PV)^{1/n} - 1$$

(4-8)

This equation is now used to solve the problem outlined in Example 4.6.

EXAMPLE 4.6 **Solving for the interest rate**

Assume that two years ago you made an investment of $10 000. This investment has grown to a sum of $12 668. The interest was compounded quarterly. Have you achieved your goal of earning at least 12% per annum on your investment? The relevant timeline is:

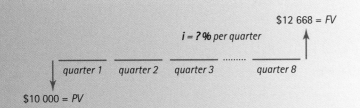

Before continuing, note that this problem must initially be formulated in periods of *quarters*. This is because all solution methods implicitly solve for the interest rate per compounding period and in this case the compounding frequency is quarterly.

Substituting in equation (4-8) we have:

$$i = (12\,668/10\,000)^{1/8} - 1$$
$$= (1.2668)^{.125} - 1 = 1.03 - 1$$
$$= .03, \text{ or } 3\% \text{ per quarter, which represents a nominal rate (or } APR) \text{ of } 12\% \text{ p.a.}$$

This is confirmed by use of equation (4-1), which reminds us that the nominal rate j is equal to $m \times i$, where m represents the number of compounding periods per year. In this case, therefore, $j = 4 \times 3\%$.

The solution panel in the margin computes $i = 3\%$ and, once again, since this is a quarterly rate it represents 12% p.a. nominal, or *APR*.

Substituting in equation (4-4), we have $12\,668 = 10\,000\,(FVIF_{?\%,8})$. That is,

$$1.2668 \approx 1.267 = FVIF_{?\%,8}$$

In Appendix A at the back of the book, it is necessary to look in the row for $n = 8$ periods, where the table value of 1.267 corresponds to a rate of 3% (per quarter), which represents 12% p.a. nominal.

Calculator solution

DATA INPUT		FUNCTION KEY
10 000	+/−	PV
8		N
12 668		FV
FUNCTION KEY		ANSWER
COMP I/Y		3.00%

OBJECTIVE 4

Calculate the effective annual rate of interest and then explain how it differs from the nominal or stated interest rate.

Making interest rates comparable

At the beginning of this chapter, reference was made to the **nominal annual rate of interest**, j, also known as the *APR*. This rate is used to specify *how* interest is computed; in general, if a rate j is compounded m times per annum, it means that interest is compounded at a rate i per period (where $i = jm$). In other words, the per-period rate i is the relevant rate for computational purposes. All of the examples so far in this chapter have employed this property of compound interest. However, that is not the end of the interest-rate story.

nominal annual rate of interest
The nominal annual rate j is a way of representing how interest is paid (or charged). If the rate j is paid m times per annum, the periodic rate paid is j/m. Alternatively, if a periodic rate i is compounded m times per annum, the nominal annual rate is j. A nominal rate is sometimes known as the annual percentage rate (*APR*).

THE EFFECTIVE ANNUAL INTEREST RATE

Returning to Example 4.2, it can be seen that $1000 invested 'today' grows to a sum of $1123.60 after one year, if the interest rate is 12% per annum compounded half-yearly. This means that, effectively, interest of $123.60 has been earned on the principal of $1000, for a period of one year. This represents a rate of 12.36%:

$$\frac{\$123.60 \text{ interest}}{\$1000 \text{ principal}} = .1236 = 12.36\%$$

Thus, the stated nominal rate of 12% per annum disguises the fact that the effective rate earned in this case is 12.36% per annum with half-yearly compounding. In fact, whenever a periodic rate i is compounded m times per annum, the effective annual rate, EAR, is given by equation (4-9), which is derived in the Appendix to this chapter:

$$EAR = (1 + i)^m - 1 \qquad\qquad \textbf{(4-9)}$$

We know from equation (4-1) that $i = j/m$, so equation (4-9) can be rewritten:

$$EAR = (1 + j/m)^m - 1 \qquad\qquad \textbf{(4-9a)}$$

Example 4.7 applies this equation.

EXAMPLE 4.7 Determining the effective annual interest rate

What is the effective annual rate if 12% per annum is compounded twice per year? Here, the given nominal rate of $j = 12\%$ (which represents .12 as a decimal) is compounded $m = 2$ times per annum. Substituting in equation (4-9a) we have:

$$EAR = (1 + .12/2)^2 - 1 = (1.06)^2 - 1 = 1.1236 - 1 = .1236, \text{ or } 12.36\%$$

Example 4.7 draws attention to the fact that the nominal annual rate generally understates the 'true' or effective rate, the EAR. This is shown in Table 4.2, which portrays the relationship between the number of compounding periods per year, m, and a nominal interest rate of 12%, for selected values of m ranging from 1 to infinity (∞). As indicated in Table 4.2, the only case in which the nominal rate equals the EAR is when interest is compounded once per year. This can be established by substituting appropriately in equation (4-9a): if interest is compounded $m = 1$ time per year, then:

$$EAR = (1 + j/1)^1 - 1 = 1 + j - 1 = j$$

In Table 4.2, the symbol $m = \infty$ refers to the notion of compounding an infinite number of times per annum or compounding continuously, which is explained in 'One step further', 'The concept of continuous compounding'.

THE RATE OF SIMPLE INTEREST

Long-term investing and borrowing decisions invariably are based on compound interest. However, it is the custom in financial markets to use simple interest as the basis for short-term borrowing/investing, examples of which are given in Chapter 7. In the meantime, a brief mention of simple interest will suffice.

Simple interest is *not* compounded. Instead, interest is paid only on the original amount borrowed or invested (the principal, P). Therefore, interest is in direct proportion to the time of the investment; for instance, interest for three years is three times as much as interest for one year. This is shown in the following simple interest equation, where t represents the number of years and r represents the annual rate of simple interest:

$$\text{Interest} = P \times r \times t$$

TABLE 4.2 The effective annual interest rate if 12% p.a. is compounded m times p.a.

m	EFFECTIVE ANNUAL INTEREST RATE	m	EFFECTIVE ANNUAL INTEREST RATE
1	12.000%	12	12.683%
2	12.360%	365	12.747%
4	12.551%	∞	12.750%
6	12.616%		

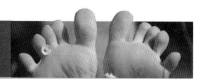

FYI

The main role of the effective interest rate, the *EAR*, is to make interest rates comparable—in other words, to measure rates on a suitable common scale. Suppose that you see two quoted interest rates. One says: '12% p.a. compounded once per year'. The other says: '12% p.a. compounded four times per year'. These quoted rates of 12% appear to be identical. However, because the rates are not compounded the same number of times per year, they are in fact not comparable. Table 4.2 shows that, effectively, there is a difference of 0.551% per annum between those rates. Therefore, to make interest rates comparable, it is necessary to convert them to a common basis, namely an *effective* annual interest rate, the *EAR*. This is analogous to measuring distance; a distance measured in kilometres cannot be compared with a distance measured in miles unless the two are converted to a common scale.

Applying this equation to the circumstances of Example 4.3, if a $1000 investment accumulates simple interest at $r = 12\%$ per annum for three years (t), total interest is $360:

Interest = $1000 \times .12 \times 3 = \$360$

In contrast, if interest is compounded twice per year at 12% per annum, it is clear from Example 4.3 that total interest is $418.52 (which is the difference between the accumulated sum, $1418.52, and the amount invested, $1000).

Concept check

4.4   If $1000 is invested at 8% per annum compounded quarterly, is this better than investing at 8.2% compounded once per year?

For answers go to MyFinanceLab or www.pearson.com.au/9781442539174

ONE STEP FURTHER

THE CONCEPT OF CONTINUOUS COMPOUNDING

In the case of *continuous compounding*, a nominal rate j compounds an infinite number of times per year; that is, m approaches infinity (∞). The future value equation for continuous compounding is:

$$FV_t = PVe^{jt} \tag{4-10}$$

where FV_t = the future value of the investment at the end of t years
  $e \approx 2.71828$ (e is known as 'e exponential')
  t = the number of years during which compounding occurs
  j = the nominal annual interest rate or *APR* (compounded continuously)
  PV = the present value

Continuous compounding may appear complicated, but it is a valuable theoretical concept. The following is an example of a computation using equation (4-10).

How much money will be accumulated at the end of 20 years if $1000 is deposited in a savings account that pays 10% interest per annum compounded continuously? Substituting $t = 20$, $j = 10\%$ (.1) and $PV = \$1000$ into equation (4-10) yields:

$$FV_{20} = \$1000 (2.71828)^{0.10 \times 20} = \$1000 (2.71828)^2 = \$1000 (7.38905) = \$7389.05$$

Equation (4-10) can also be adapted to determine the effective annual rate with continuous compounding. Every $1 invested for $t = 1$ year at rate j per annum compounded continuously will accumulate to:

$$FV_1 = \$1e^j$$

Thus, analogous to the derivation of equation (4-9) in the Appendix to this chapter, the effective rate earned is equal to $[\$1e^j - \$1] / \$1 = e^j - 1$.

For example, if $j = 12\%$ (.12), the $EAR = e^{.12} - 1 = 1.1275 - 1 = .1275$, or 12.75%, which confirms the relevant entry in Table 4.2.

OBJECTIVE **5**

Define an ordinary annuity and calculate its present and future value.

annuity
A series of equal dollar payments for a specified number of periods.

Annuities

An **annuity** is a series of equal dollar payments for a specified number of periods. Annuities are encountered frequently in everyday life, for example as payments on a housing loan or as pension receipts from a superannuation (pension) fund. In business, too, annuities feature prominently, such as payments of interest on bonds.

It is possible to find the overall future value or present value of an annuity by finding the FV or PV of each individual payment and adding them together. However, doing so is cumbersome and time-consuming, especially for annuity payments that occur over a large number of periods. Thus, the following annuity formulae have been simplified so that the payment amount appears only once in the relevant equation.

Future value of an ordinary annuity

Suppose you can invest $100 at the end of each quarter for a year and a half, with interest paid at a rate (APR) of 8% per annum compounded quarterly. This series of six quarterly payments therefore forms an annuity. It is an example of an **ordinary annuity**, which has payments at the end of each period.

ordinary annuity
An annuity whose payments are made at the end of each period.

From the previous discussion, it will be recalled that the APR of 8% means in this case that interest is compounded at a rate $i = 2\%$ per quarter for $n = 6$ quarters. The timeline for this annuity highlights the fact that the FV occurs at the end of the sixth quarter, the same time as the final annuity payment (investment) is made:

	i = 2% per quarter					FV
quarter 1	quarter 2	quarter 3	quarter 4	quarter 5	quarter 6	
$100	$100	$100	$100	$100	$100	

The FV of this annuity is found in Table 4.3. If you follow carefully the construction of this table, you will see that the accumulated value of the annuity increases period by period as interest is added and as additional payments are invested. Note that, in the first quarter, there is no interest, because the first payment is not invested until the *end* of that period. Subsequently, each quarter's interest is computed at 2% of the relevant quarter's opening balance.

Determining the FV by means of a schedule such as Table 4.3 is informative, in that it shows us exactly how an annuity accumulates over time. However, a less cumbersome shortcut is provided via equation (4-11), which is derived in the Appendix at the back of this chapter:

$$FV_n = PMT \frac{[(1 + i)^n - 1]}{i} \qquad \textbf{(4-11)}$$

TABLE 4.3 Schedule showing the future value of an annuity of $100 per quarter at the end of each of 6 quarters, at an interest rate of 2% per quarter

QUARTER	OPENING BALANCE	INTEREST AT 2%	ANNUITY PAYMENT	CLOSING BALANCE
1	0	0	$100.00	$100.00
2	$100.00	$2.00	100.00	202.00
3	202.00	4.04	100.00	306.04
4	306.04	6.12	100.00	412.16
5	412.16	8.24	100.00	520.40
6	520.40	10.41	100.00	630.81

The only new symbol in this equation is *PMT*, which represents the periodic annuity payment. Example 4.8 shows the use of this equation to determine the *FV* of an annuity and also shows the other computational methods.

EXAMPLE 4.8   Determining the future value of an ordinary annuity

What is the *FV* of an annuity of $100 per quarter for one and a half years if the interest rate is 8% per annum compounded quarterly? As remarked in relation to Table 4.3, this means the annuity has the following features: *PMT* = $100 per quarter, *n* = 6 quarters, and *i* = 2% per quarter (.02 as a decimal).

Substituting in equation (4-11) we have:

$$FV_6 = \$100 \frac{[(1.02)^6 - 1]}{.02} = \$100 \frac{[1.1261624 - 1]}{.02} = \$630.81$$

In the margin panel, the symbol for an annuity payment (*PMT*) is used for the first time; in this case, it is represented as a negative cash flow because the money is being deposited by the saver and is thus a cash outflow. Apart from that, the calculator symbols are consistent with their previous uses in this chapter.

Looking again at equation (4-11), it should be clear that the quantity $[(1 + i)^n - 1]/i$ represents the *FV* of an annuity with a payment of $1 per period. This quantity is known as the **future value interest factor for an annuity**, symbol $\textbf{FVIFA}_{i,n}$. That is, $FVIFA_{i,n}$ represents the *FV* of an annuity payment of $1 per period for *n* periods at an interest rate of *i* per period. Therefore, the *FV* of a payment of *PMT* per period is given by equation (4-12):

$$FV_n = PMT(FVIFA_{i,n}) \qquad \qquad \textbf{(4-12)}$$

For example, looking at Appendix C at the back of this book, it can be seen that the *FV* of $1 per period for *n* = 6 periods at a rate *i* = 2%, that is $FVIFA_{2\%,6}$, is approximately 6.308. Therefore, the *FV* of a payment of $100 per period is:

$$FV_6 = \$100(FVIFA_{2\%,6}) \approx \$100(6.308) \approx \$630.80$$

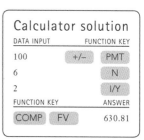

Calculator solution

DATA INPUT		FUNCTION KEY
100	+/−	PMT
6		N
2		I/Y
FUNCTION KEY		ANSWER
COMP FV		630.81

future value interest factor for an annuity
The factor $FVIFA_{i,n}$ that converts a payment of $1 per period (at the end of the period) to its future value in *n* periods of time at *i*% compound interest per period. To determine the future value of a payment of, say, $100, the factor is multiplied by 100.

Concept check

4.5 Suppose you want to save towards a future target and you plan to put aside $1200 per year. Would you be better off saving $100 at the end of each month or $1200 at the end of the year, assuming that interest is compounded monthly?

SOLVING FOR THE ANNUITY PAYMENT AMOUNT

If the annuity's future value is known, along with i and n, what is the periodic payment? This question is answered in Example 4.9.

EXAMPLE 4.9 Determining the payment amount of an annuity

Assume that you wish to accumulate a sum of $630.81 in a year and a half, at an interest rate of 2% per quarter (.02). What is the necessary payment at the end of each quarter?

Rearrangement of equation (4-11) gives:

$$PMT = \frac{i(FV_n)}{(1+i)^n - 1} \qquad (4\text{-}13)$$

Substituting in this equation:

$$PMT = \frac{.02(\$630.81)}{(1.02)^6 - 1} = \frac{.02(\$630.81)}{1.12616 - 1} = \$100.00$$

Calculator solution

DATA INPUT	FUNCTION KEY
630.81	FV
6	N
2	I/Y
FUNCTION KEY	ANSWER
COMP PMT	−100.00

The financial calculator solution is shown in the margin. Note that the answer is negative, indicating that the payment is a cash outflow (the payment that needs to be made each period to achieve the savings target of $630.81, which is a cash inflow).

Rearranging equation (4-12):

$$PMT = \frac{FV_n}{FVIFA_{i,n}} = \frac{FV_6}{FVIFA_{2\%,6}} = \frac{\$630.81}{6.308} = \$100.00$$

SOLVING FOR THE NUMBER OF ANNUITY PERIODS (PAYMENTS)

Sometimes, the number of periods is the unknown, for example the time period that is required to achieve a savings target. Example 4.10 examines this problem.

EXAMPLE 4.10 Determining the number of annuity periods

Assume that you wish to accumulate a sum of $630.81 at an interest rate of 2% per quarter (.02). What is the necessary number of $100 payments made at the end of each quarter?

Rearrangement of equation (4-11) gives:

$$n = \log[\{FV.i/PMT\} + 1] / \log(1 + i) \qquad (4\text{-}14)$$

Substituting in this equation yields:

$$n = \log[\{630.81 \times .02/100.00\} + 1] / \log(1.02)$$
$$= \log 1.12616 / \log 1.02 = .0516 / .00860 = 6 \text{ periods}$$

The margin solution clearly identifies the necessity to input the payment as a negative amount, because it is a cash outflow (the savings deposited each period), whereas the future value must be input as a positive cash flow.

Rearranging equation (4-12):

$$FVIFA_{2\%,n} = \frac{FV_n}{PMT} = \frac{FV_6}{PMT} = \frac{\$630.81}{\$100.00} = 6.308$$

Looking in Appendix C at the back of this book, for $i = 2\%$ the table value of 6.308 corresponds to $n = 6$; that is, 6 periods.

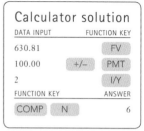

Calculator solution

DATA INPUT		FUNCTION KEY
630.81		FV
100.00	+/–	PMT
2		I/Y
FUNCTION KEY		**ANSWER**
COMP	N	6

SOLVING FOR THE ANNUITY INTEREST RATE

An investor might, for example, wish to know the interest rate earned on an investment. Example 4.11 examines the issue of determining an unknown interest rate.

EXAMPLE 4.11 Determining the annuity interest rate

We already know that the interest rate is 2% per quarter (or 8% per annum nominal) if you deposit $100 per quarter for a year and a half and the accumulated sum (*FV*) is $630.81. However, what if the interest rate is not known?

In equation (4-11), the interest rate i appears twice on the right-hand side. Therefore it is impossible to solve for i by rearrangement. This means that i can be found accurately only by trial and error (although there are some approximation algorithms that are not discussed herein). Thus, it is necessary to use one of the other methods shown below.

The financial calculator is programmed to solve for i by trial and error. In effect, it finds the rate i that makes the left-hand side of equation (4-11) equal to the right-hand side, resulting in the solution shown in the margin.

Calculator solution

DATA INPUT		FUNCTION KEY
630.81		FV
100.00	+/–	PMT
6		N
FUNCTION KEY		**ANSWER**
COMP	I/Y	2 (%)

Rearranging equation (4-12):

$$FVIFA_{i,n} = \frac{FV_n}{PMT} = \frac{FV_6}{PMT} = \frac{\$630.81}{\$100.00} = 6.308$$

Looking in Appendix C at the back of the book, for $n = 6$ the table value of 6.308 corresponds to $i = 2\%$.

Present value of an ordinary annuity

Suppose that you borrow a loan that has repayments of $100 at the end of each quarter for one and half years, at a rate of 8% per annum compound interest. As discussed above, this means that interest is compounded for $n = 6$ quarters at a rate $i = 2\%$ per quarter. It should be clear that the amount borrowed represents the PV of the future annuity payments, as shown on the following timeline:

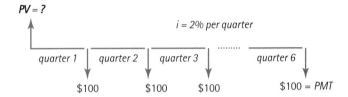

At this point we do not know the value of PV. However, equation (4-15), which is derived in the Appendix to this chapter, shows that the PV of an annuity with equal payments of amount PMT at the end of each period for n periods, at interest rate i, is given by:

$$PV = PMT \frac{[1 - (1 + i)^{-n}]}{i} \tag{4-15}$$

Example 4.12 demonstrates the use of this equation, together with other ways of computing the PV.

EXAMPLE 4.12 Determining the present value of an ordinary annuity

What is the PV of an annuity of $100 per quarter for one and a half years if the interest rate is 8% per annum compounded quarterly?

This means the annuity has the following features: $PMT = \$100$ per quarter, $n = 6$ quarters, and $i = 2\%$ per quarter (.02 as a decimal).

Substituting in equation (4-15) we have:

$$PV = \$100 \frac{[1 - (1.02)^{-6}]}{.02} = \$100 \frac{[1 - .8879714]}{.02} = \frac{100[.1120286]}{.02} = \$560.14$$

The fact that this PV amount is correct is demonstrated in Table 4.4.

The margin panel confirms that the PV is $560.14. Note that the PMT is input as a negative amount because it represents the periodic repayment on the loan, a cash outflow, while the computed PV is a positive cash flow (from the perspective of the borrower) because it represents the amount borrowed initially.

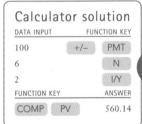

Calculator solution

DATA INPUT	FUNCTION KEY
100	+/− PMT
6	N
2	I/Y
FUNCTION KEY	ANSWER
COMP PV	560.14

present value interest factor for an annuity
The factor $PVIFA_{i,n}$ that converts an annuity payment of $1 per period for n periods to its present value, at $i\%$ compound interest per period. For example, the present value of an annuity of $160 per period is equal to the factor multiplied by 160.

In equation (4-15), it should be clear that the quantity $[1 - (1 + i)^{-n}]/i$ represents the PV of an annuity payment of $1 per period. This quantity is known as the **present value interest factor for an annuity**, $PVIFA_{i,n}$; that is, it represents the PV of an annuity of $1 at the end of each period for n periods at rate i per period. Therefore, the PV of a payment of PMT per period is given by equation (4-16):

$$PV = PMT(PVIFA_{i,n})$$ **(4-16)**

For instance, looking at Appendix D at the back of the book, it can be seen that the *PV* of $1 per period for $n = 6$ periods at a rate $i = 2\%$, that is, $PVIFA_{2\%,6}$, is approximately 5.601. Therefore, the *PV* of a payment of $100 per period is:

$$FV = \$100(PVIFA_{2\%,6}) \approx \$100(5.601) \approx \$560.10$$

Paying off (amortising) a term loan

OBJECTIVE 6

Apply the annuity present value model to the process of loan amortisation.

Paying off a debt means paying interest at the required rate plus the original principal borrowed, so that the balance of the debt is reduced to zero after the specified number of periods (payments). This process is called *loan amortisation*. Example 4.12 suggests that a loan of $560.14 can be fully repaid (that is, *amortised*) by six equal $100 instalments, if interest is at 2% per period. Admittedly a loan of $560.14 is an unusual amount to borrow, but if you approached a lender and said, 'I can afford to repay $100 per quarter for six quarters', the lender would tell you that you could borrow $560.14.

Loans that are amortised in this way are often called *term loans*, the 'term' being the specified number of periods required to amortise the debt. Term loans are the basis for widespread forms of borrowing by households and individuals, for purposes such as housing finance and consumer finance. Term loans are also a widespread form of business finance, commonly used to acquire assets such as land and buildings, equipment and vehicles. Chapter 18 provides further discussion on term loans.

HOW MUCH CAN YOU BORROW?

Along with planning for retirement through avenues such as investing in superannuation, buying a home is the biggest financial decision made by most individuals. Many of us need to borrow a significant sum of money—a few hundred thousand dollars or more—to achieve the goal of home ownership. Typically, we need to borrow for a long period, often as much as 20 to 30 years; the reason for the long term is that longer terms mean smaller payments (other things being equal), which in turn means more borrowing power.

Term loans—loans that are fully repaid (amortised) over a specific number of periods (the 'term')—are used as the primary model for long-term housing loans, which are provided predominantly by banks. The providers of housing finance base their lending decisions on a number of factors, notably the borrower's income. Sometimes, the lenders look in detail at the borrower's financial commitments in order to ascertain how much spare cash will be available to service loan repayments. In other cases, they use a rule of thumb, such as allowing maximum loan repayments of 30% of the borrower's gross income (which means income before tax is taken out of the salary). For instance, suppose you have a gross income of $60 000 per annum. If the lender will allow you to commit to loan repayments of up to 30% of that income, you will be permitted maximum repayments of $18 000 per annum. This represents $1500 per month, which typically is the frequency of loan repayments. If the loan interest rate is 9% *APR*, this represents a rate i of 0.75% per month.

If you take the loan over 20 years, or 240 months (*n*), you should be able to determine that you can borrow a maximum of about $166 700—this amount is the *PV* of an annuity with a payment (*PMT*) of $1500 per month for $n = 240$ months at $i = 0.75\%$ (the various ways of computing an annuity's present value are outlined generally in Example 4.12). Extending the loan term to 35 years (usually the maximum period that lenders will permit) would result in a maximum loan of about $191 300.

Based on the previous analysis, you should be able to see that the ways of increasing borrowing power (other things being equal) are to:
- have a greater income, permitting increased repayments and so a larger *PV*
- borrow at a lower interest rate, resulting in a larger *PV*
- take a longer term, giving a larger *PV*.

In order to establish that the $100 payment amount is just right to repay the debt in full, Table 4.4 presents an *amortisation schedule* for the loan from Example 4.12. This schedule shows the relationship between the payments, interest charges and the remaining balance of the debt, period by period. It is worth noting, when you study this schedule, that interest is charged for the entire period on the period's opening balance (because the relevant payment does not occur until the end of the period).

As can be seen in Table 4.4, the present value of an annuity is a valuable tool, because it 'models' the behaviour of loans whose payments are designed to fully amortise a debt.

FINDING THE ANNUITY PAYMENT AMOUNT

Example 4.13 addresses the problem of finding the amount of the annuity payment when the annuity's present value is known, along with i and n.

EXAMPLE 4.13   Finding the payment amount of an annuity

Assume that you borrowed a sum of $560.14, repayable by six equal quarterly instalments (loan repayments) at an interest rate of 2% per quarter (.02). What is the necessary loan payment at the end of each quarter?

Rearrangement of equation (4-15) gives:

$$PMT = \frac{i(PV)}{1 - (1 + i)^{-n}}$$
(4-17)

Substituting in this equation gives:

$$PMT = \frac{.02(\$560.14)}{1 - (1.02)^{-6}} = \frac{.02(\$560.14)}{1 - .88797} = \$100.00$$

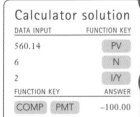

Calculator solution

DATA INPUT	FUNCTION KEY
560.14	PV
6	N
2	I/Y
FUNCTION KEY	ANSWER
COMP PMT	−100.00

With the *PV* representing the sum borrowed, this sum is a cash inflow to the borrower and thus the calculator's output shows a negative payment amount (the loan repayments made by the borrower).

Rearranging equation (4-16) and using Appendix D to find the relevant value of $PVIFA_{i,n}$:

$$PMT = \frac{PV}{PVIFA_{i,n}} = \frac{PV}{PVIFA_{2\%,6}} = \frac{\$560.14}{5.601} = \$100.00$$

TABLE 4.4   Amortisation schedule for the loan in Example 4.12

PERIOD	OPENING BALANCE	+ INTEREST AT 2%	− LOAN PAYMENT	CLOSING BALANCE
1	$560.14	$11.20	$100.00	$471.34
2	471.34	9.43	100.00	380.77
3	380.77	7.62	100.00	288.39
4	288.39	5.77	100.00	194.16
5	194.16	3.88	100.00	98.04
6	98.04	1.96	100.00	0

FINDING THE NUMBER OF ANNUITY PERIODS (PAYMENTS)

Suppose the *PV* and the *PMT* amounts are known, along with the interest rate. Example 4.14 looks at the question of determining the unknown number of periods.

EXAMPLE 4.14   Finding the number of annuity periods

Assume that you have borrowed $560.14, repayable by equal $100 payments at the end of each period, with an interest rate of 2% per period (.02). What is the number of payments necessary to fully repay the debt (the amount borrowed)?

Rearrangement of equation (4-15) gives:

$$n = -\log[1 - (PV.i/\text{PMT})] / \log(1 + i) \qquad \textbf{(4-18)}$$

Substituting in this equation gives:

$$n = -\log[1 - (560.14 \times .02/100)] / \log(1.02)$$
$$= -\log[1 - .11203] / \log(1.02) = -(-.0516) / .0086 = 6 \text{ periods}$$

The margin solution clearly identifies the necessity to input the loan payment as a negative amount, from the borrower's viewpoint.

Rearranging equation (4-16):

$$PVIFA_{2\%,n} = \frac{PV}{PMT} = \frac{\$560.14}{\$100} = 5.601$$

Looking in Appendix D at the back of this book, for $i = 2\%$ the table value of 5.601 corresponds to $n = 6$.

Calculator solution

DATA INPUT		FUNCTION KEY
560.14		PV
100.00	+/–	PMT
2		I/Y
FUNCTION KEY		ANSWER
COMP	N	6

FINDING THE ANNUITY INTEREST RATE

A borrower is very likely to be interested in knowing the loan interest rate, since a suitable interest rate is the scale used for comparing the costs of different borrowing alternatives. Example 4.15 looks at this problem.

EXAMPLE 4.15   Determining the annuity interest rate

What interest rate are you paying on your loan if you borrow $56 014 payable by instalments of $10 000 at the end of each of six quarters?

Because *i* appears twice in the right-hand side of equation (4-15), it is impossible to rearrange the equation to solve for unknown *i*. Therefore, it is necessary to use one of the other methods.

As discussed in Example 4.11, the financial calculator is programmed to solve by trial and error for the unknown annuity interest rate *i*. In the margin solution, note that *i* is the rate per quarter.

Calculator solution

DATA INPUT	FUNCTION KEY
56 014	PV
10 000 +/−	PMT
6	N
FUNCTION KEY	ANSWER
COMP I/Y	2 (%)

Rearranging equation (4-16):

$$PVIFA_{i,6} = \frac{PV}{PMT} = \frac{\$56\,014}{\$10\,000} = 5.601$$

Looking in Appendix D at the back of this book, for *n* = 6 the table value of 5.601 corresponds to *i* = 2%.

Concept check

4.6 If 2% per quarter is the interest rate on the loan in Example 4.15, what interest rate should you use for comparing this loan with others?

For answers go to MyFinanceLab or www.pearson.com.au/9781442539174

GFC

TERM LOANS AND THE GFC

How does the topic of term loans find its way into a discussion of the GFC? The answer lies in the fact that the GFC was sparked by the sub-prime crisis (SPC), which was very much tied up with term loans—specifically, term loans used for housing finance.

Until the past decade or so, it was normal for lenders such as banks to restrict housing finance to well-qualified borrowers who met criteria such as a good credit history, stable employment, low (or well-affordable) debt levels, and so on. These 'good' borrowers are known as *prime* borrowers. In contrast, *sub-prime* borrowers typically fail to meet some or all of these lending criteria. Ordinarily, sub-prime applicants would not be graced with a bank loan.

However, in the early to mid 2000s, US banks and other lenders increasingly began to make loans to sub-prime customers. Partly this was in response to a mandate from the US government to make loans more accessible and so make home ownership an attainable goal for people who normally would be barred from home ownership.

But the reality was that many of these sub-prime loans were doomed to failure. In some cases, borrowers had been given below-market 'teaser' (or 'honeymoon') interest rates for a year or two. This, combined with market rates that were themselves relatively low, enabled the sub-prime borrowers to afford their repayments for a short period. But when the rates 'reset' to the higher normal market levels after the honeymoon period, many borrowers lacked the capacity to continue making their payments and so defaulted on their debts. The number of annual defaults was in the order of several million after the SPC erupted and, several years later in 2010, the number of defaults was still estimated to be as high as four million per year.[1]

Were the banks crazy in making such loans, which reached a peak of about 20% of US housing finance in 2006, just before the SPC began to grab hold of the US economy? In retrospect, perhaps they were crazy, but there are a number of factors that help to explain the apparently reckless attitude of the lenders. First, the US housing price boom (which was outlined briefly in Chapter 3) may have led lenders to believe that, in the event of default, borrowers' houses could be repossessed and sold at a price that would cover the debt. Second, many loans were arranged with borrowers via agents (mortgage brokers) whose main concern was to sell finance packages, with little concern for the *quality* of such loans (although it must be acknowledged that the lenders could have been more judicious in scrutinising these agents).

A third factor is that, through the early and mid 2000s, trillions of dollars of housing loans[2] were, in effect, sold by the original lenders via a process known as *securitisation* (which is discussed in more detail in Chapter 18). A characteristic of securitisation is that the risks attached to the loans (notably, the risk of borrowers defaulting) are *passed through* to the buyer of the loans. Therefore, the lenders may have acted as if loan quality no longer mattered— it was someone else's problem.[3] In contrast, it is likely that the lenders would have had a far more conservative attitude to their lending practices if the exposure to loan losses had remained with them.

Colloquially, sub-prime loans were known by names such as *NINJA* (No Income, No Job or Assets) or *LIAR* (alluding to the fact that lenders or their agents allowed borrowers to make unsubstantiated claims about factors such as their credit history, income and employment).[4] However, it would be wrong to assume that the default problem was confined to the low-quality sub-prime loans. As outlined in Chapter 3, the dizzying boom in US housing prices, which peaked in 2006, was equally the outcome of speculation by middle-class borrowers. These people had invested in housing in the belief that buying a house was as good as having a 'goldmine in their backyards'.[5] A factor contributing further to the high default rate is that, in the US, borrowers can walk away from a property by handing the keys back to the lender, who has no further recourse. This gives borrowers an incentive to default if the value of the house falls below the mortgage balance, particularly if the house has been bought as a speculative investment rather than as the main place of residence.

Some appreciation of the consequences of the collapse of the US housing market can be seen from the data relating to sales of newly constructed houses. Sales fell 75% from 8 million homes per year, prior to the SPC, to as low as 2 million by 2010. It is not difficult to comprehend why this happened. With millions of people being displaced from their houses through foreclosure by lenders, or by voluntarily walking away from their houses and mortgages, construction of *new* homes ground to a halt (after all, builders could not make a profit from selling new houses at a price that was competitive with the millions of established houses that had become vacant in the fallout from the SPC). In turn, this collapse of the housing construction industry had multiplier effects throughout the economy, leading to decreased demand for building supplies (bricks, cement, timber, steel, insulation and the like) as well as fittings and fixtures (such as bathroom and kitchen fittings, floor coverings, window furnishings, light fittings and so on), along with furniture, appliances and the many other items that new home owners usually purchase. These widespread effects are major contributors to the persistent economic slowdown of the US economy, which continued into the new decade.

FYI

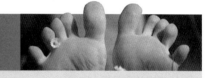

The annuity present value model has applications other than amortising a loan (Examples 4.12 to 4.15). For instance, the *PV* could represent the amount of money that you need to invest 'today' if you want to receive future payments of *PMT* at the end of each period. Or, turning the problem around, you could determine the future payments that you would receive if you deposited *PV* dollars 'today'.

ONE STEP FURTHER

GENERAL ANNUITIES AND THE CONCEPT OF EQUIVALENT INTEREST RATES

So far in this chapter, all the annuities have been examples of ordinary annuities. An *ordinary annuity* has payments at the end of each period. In contrast, an *annuity due* has payments at the beginning of each period. Both ordinary annuities and annuities due are called *simple annuities* if the interest rate is compounded with the same frequency as the payment frequency (which is the case so far—for instance, in Example 4.12 the rate is compounded quarterly and payments are also quarterly). On the other hand, a **general annuity** features an annuity payment frequency that differs from the interest-compounding frequency.

To give an example of a general annuity, in Example 4.12 we might have been told that interest was to be compounded at a rate of 4.04% per *half-year*, thus making it a general annuity (because the payments were *quarterly*). However, all of the solution methods shown in this chapter require the interest frequency to be the same as the payment frequency. To overcome this problem, the simplest procedure is to convert the given interest rate to a frequency that is identical to the payment frequency. Doing so introduces the concept of **equivalent interest rates**.

OBJECTIVE 7

Understand the notion of a general annuity and the concept of equivalent interest rates.

general annuity
An annuity that features a payment frequency that differs from the interest-compounding frequency.

equivalent interest rates
Interest rates that have the same effective annual rate.

Two interest rates are equivalent if they have the same effective annual rate. The Appendix to this chapter uses this relationship to derive equation (4-19):

$$i = (1 + i')^{p/m} - 1 \qquad \text{(4-19)}$$

where: i = the (unknown) interest rate, compounded m times p.a.

i' = the given interest rate, compounded p times p.a.

For instance, if an interest rate is stated as 4.04% (or .0404) compounded every half-year, but payments are quarterly, then equation (4-19) can be used to convert the given rate i' = 4.04% compounded p = 2 times per annum to the rate i compounded m = 4 times per annum, as follows:*

$$i = (1 + .0404)^{2/4} - 1 = (1.0404)^{.5} - 1 = 1.02 - 1 = .02, \text{ or } 2\%$$

The quarterly rate of i = 2% can then be used to solve problems involving quarterly annuity payments in the normal way. That is, the general annuity is changed to an ordinary annuity by converting the given interest rate to the same frequency as the payment frequency.

* Note that this formula is inapplicable in situations where $m < p$.

Determine the present value of an annuity due.

annuity due
An annuity where payments are made at the beginning of each period.

Annuity due

An **annuity due** has cash-flow payments that occur at the beginning of each period. This type of annuity is quite common; for example, most financial arrangements for leasing or renting assets (such as motor vehicles, computing equipment, office premises, etc.) require payments to be made at the beginning of each period. In effect, this means that an annuity due is like an ordinary annuity except that the first payment is shifted back one period, from the end of period 1 to its beginning; and there is no payment at the *end* of the final period, as it occurs at its beginning. This can be seen most readily if we compare the timelines in Figure 4.4.

The main use of the annuity due concept in this book occurs in Chapter 18. In the meantime, some annuity due problems are presented below.

PRESENT VALUE OF AN ANNUITY DUE

Comparing the two timelines in Figure 4.4, it can be seen that the annuity due has payments at the *end* of each of periods 1 to $n - 1$, plus an 'upfront' payment at the beginning of period 1, that is, in the present. Therefore, the *PV* of an n-period annuity due is equivalent to the *PV* of an ordinary annuity of $n - 1$ periods, *plus* the amount of one initial payment, *PMT*. Adapting equation (4-15) accordingly:

$$PV_{due} = PMT + PMT \, \frac{[1 - (1 + i)^{-(n-1)}]}{i}$$

Rearranging:

$$PV_{due} = PMT \left\{ 1 + \frac{[1 - (1 + i)^{-(n-1)}]}{i} \right\} \qquad \text{(4-20)}$$

FIGURE 4.4   Timelines for payments* of (a) an ordinary annuity and (b) an annuity due

(a) *Ordinary annuity*

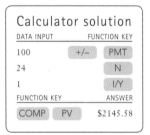

(b) *Annuity due**

*   It should not be inferred that the payment amount for an ordinary annuity is the same as the payment amount for an annuity due that has the same *PV*, *n* and *i* as the ordinary annuity; owing to the effect of the time value of money, these payment amounts will differ.

EXAMPLE 4.16   Finding the present value of an annuity due

Assume that you want to 'rent-purchase' a computer system from a computer supplies company. The arrangement is that payments are made at the beginning of each month for 24 months, at an interest rate of 12% per year compounded monthly. These payments will be called rentals, but if you make the entire 24 payments the computer's ownership will be transferred to you (thus the name 'rent-purchase'). The first payment is, in effect, a deposit; it is payable at the same time as you take delivery of the computer. If you are required to pay $100 per month, what is the maximum price of the computer system?

The price represents the *PV* of the subsequent payments. Substituting in equation (4-20), *PMT* = $100, *n* = 24 months, *i* = 1% (.01) per month:

$$PV_{due} = \$100\left\{1 + \frac{[1-(1.01)^{-23}]}{.01}\right\} = \$100\left\{1 + \frac{.204558}{.01}\right\} = \$100\{21.4558\}$$

$$= \$2145.58$$

The annuity due mode on the EL-738/735S calculator is accessed by pressing [2ndF] then [BGN], which results in the symbol 'BGN' appearing on the calculator's display. Then, data are input in the normal way as shown in the margin.

This book does not have appendix tables for annuity due computations. However, as stated previously, the *PV* of an *n*-period annuity due is equivalent to the *PV* of an ordinary annuity of *n* − 1 periods, plus the amount of one payment, *PMT*. This means that ordinary annuity tables can be adapted for some annuity due problems. Adapting equation (4-16) accordingly, $PV = PMT + PMT(PVIFA_{i,n-1})$, or:

$$PV_{due} = PMT(1 + PVIFA_{i,n-1}) \tag{4-21}$$

Substituting for *n* = 24, *i* = 1% and *PMT* = $100 and using Appendix D:

$$PV_{due} = \$100(1 + PVIFA_{1\%,23}) \approx \$100(1 + 20.456) \approx \$2145.60$$

Calculator solution

DATA INPUT		FUNCTION KEY
100	+/−	PMT
24		N
1		I/Y
FUNCTION KEY		**ANSWER**
COMP PV		$2145.58

Concept check

4.7   Other things being equal, will an annuity due have a present value that is less than an ordinary annuity with the same payment amount and number of periods?

For answers go to MyFinanceLab or www.pearson.com.au/9781442539174

OBJECTIVE 9

Understand how
perpetuities work.

perpetuity
An annuity with an infinite life.

Perpetuity

A **perpetuity** is an annuity that continues forever; it has an infinite life. That is, every year from its establishment this investment pays the same dollar amount. An example of a perpetuity is the dividend stream on preference shares; this type of share can yield a constant dollar dividend indefinitely.

Clearly, a perpetuity does not have a *FV* because the payments continue forever! However, determining the present value of a perpetuity is delightfully simple; it is merely necessary to divide the constant payment by the discount rate. For example, the present value of a $100 perpetuity discounted back to the present at 5% is $100/0.05 = $2000. Thus, the equation representing the present value of a perpetuity is:

$$PV = PMT/i \qquad\qquad \textbf{(4-22)}$$

where *PV* = the present value of the perpetuity
PMT = the constant (perpetual) periodic payment provided by the perpetuity
i = the discount (or interest) rate

EXAMPLE 4.17 Present value of a perpetuity

What is the present value of a $500 annual perpetuity at the end of each year, discounted back to the present at 8%? Substituting *PMT* = $500 and i = 0.08 in equation (4-22), we find:

PV = $500/0.08 = $6250

The numbers in this example make a lot of sense. If you have $6250 invested at 8% and you receive a dividend payment of $500 at the end of each year, this payment represents 8% of the amount invested, so the principal amount of $6250 will be left intact and it can therefore go on paying interest forever.

Finance at work

THE AUSTRALIAN GOVERNMENT ESTABLISHES A PERPETUITY TO FUND UNIVERSITY RESEARCH

In the 2007 Federal Budget the Australian government announced the establishment of a multi-billion-dollar endowment fund to finance future research programs at Australian universities. An endowment fund is a type of perpetuity. The idea is that the annual earnings on the fund can be withdrawn and allocated to finance particular research projects, leaving the principal intact and thus able to be reused to generate future payments indefinitely. For example, if a $5 billion fund is assumed to earn 10% per annum, $500 million can be withdrawn at the end of each year (that is, paid as research grants), leaving the $5 billion fund intact, to finance future research grants. Realistically, the annual rate of return earned by the fund is not likely to be constant and so the payment in a particular year is limited by that year's rate of return. For example, if the rate in a particular year is 8%, only $400 million can be paid out, in order to leave the principal intact.

OBJECTIVE 10

Deal with complex cash
flows and deferred
annuities.

Complex cash flows

When an organisation invests in a 'project', such as an expansion of the product line, there is the expectation that the investment will generate cash flows in the future. Typically, these future cash flows will vary from year to year. For example, during the first few years the cash flow from sales of a new product might grow as market acceptance is attained, and then they might start to taper off as competitors begin to take away market share or as the product becomes outdated. As will be seen in Chapters 11 and 12, one measure of the worth of an investment project is the present value of its future cash flows. Suppose, for example, that we have the cash-flow stream shown in Table 4.5.

PRESENT VALUE OF IRREGULAR FUTURE CASH FLOWS

The present value of the Table 4.5 cash-flow stream will now be determined, at a discount rate of 6% per annum, by a number of methods, shown in Example 4.18. This example shows that the investment's future cash flows are estimated to be worth a total of about $3083 in today's dollars (present value). By the way, this is not the same as saying that the investment is worthwhile. If the investment cost $2000 at the outset, you will be $1083 ahead. But if the investment cost $4000, you would not be interested in it.

TABLE 4.5 Cash flows expected from an investment

END OF YEAR (t)	CASH FLOW ($)
1	500
2	700
3	1000
4	800
5	500
6	200

EXAMPLE 4.18 Present value of irregular cash flows

There is no single equation for the *PV* of a series of unequal future cash flows. Therefore, the total *PV* of the cash flows in Table 4.5 must be determined by adding up the present values of the individual cash flows. If each future cash flow occurring at the end of year *t* is denoted CF_t, then the use of equation (4-5a) means that the *PV* of that cash flow is equal to $CF_t (1 + i)^{-t}$.

END OF YEAR, t	CASH FLOW, CF_t	PRESENT VALUE, $CF_t (1 + i)^{-t}$		
1	$500	$500(1.06)^{-1}$	=	$471.70
2	700	$700(1.06)^{-2}$	=	623.00
3	1000	$1000(1.06)^{-3}$	=	839.62
4	800	$800(1.06)^{-4}$	=	633.67
5	500	$500(1.06)^{-5}$	=	373.63
6	200	$200(1.06)^{-6}$	=	140.99
				$3082.61

Finding the present value of an uneven cash flow stream is relatively straightforward when using a suitably programmed financial calculator. For the EL-738/735S calculator, successive cash flows are entered using the CASH function and the (ENT) key as shown below, in order to compute the Net Present Value or NPV, which for the time being can be regarded as identical to the *PV*.

Calculator solution

DATA INPUT	FUNCTION KEY
0	ENT
500	ENT
700	ENT
1000	ENT
800	ENT
500	ENT
200	ENT
2ndF	CASH
RATE (I/Y) = 6	ENT
	▼

FUNCTION KEY	ANSWER
NET_PV = COMP	3082.61

Step 1 Set-up and clear the calculator

To begin, it is necessary to reset the calculator MODE to NORMAL as shown on p. 86. Then, clear the calculator by entering successively CFi 2ndF CA.

Step 2 Enter the cash flows and interest rate, then solve for NPV

The cash flows are input in succession via the ENT key. Note that the calculator assumes always that there is a cash flow at the beginning of period 1, that is, at time period '0'. In our case, the first cash flow is at the *end* of period 1, so we start by entering a cash flow of zero dollars at time '0'. The keystroke sequence for inputting the successive, uneven cash flows is therefore:

0 ENT 500 ENT 700 ENT 1000 ENT 800 ENT 500 ENT 200 ENT

Next, the CASH function is selected by entering 2ndF CASH. The display then prompts you to enter the interest rate (I/Y), in response to which you need to input the number 6 then ENT. Next, scroll down using the ▼ key, which will result in the display showing 'NET_PV = 0'.

Then, to compute NPV, simply enter COMP which gives the answer 3082.61.

The present value of each individual payment can be determined by multiplying it by the relevant present-value interest factor ($PVIF_{i,n}$) from Appendix B at the back of the book. These amounts are then summed to obtain the total present value.

END OF YEAR (t)	CASH FLOW	$PVIF_{6\%,t}$	PRESENT VALUE ($)
1	$500	0.943	$471.50
2	700	0.890	623.00
3	1000	0.840	840.00
4	800	0.792	633.60
5	500	0.747	373.50
6	200	0.705	141.00
			$3082.60

FINDING THE INTEREST RATE

Suppose that you have invested $3083, which is expected to generate the future cash flows shown in Table 4.5. You want to know what rate of return this investment's cash flows have earned for you. This rate is known as the internal rate of return (*IRR*). Essentially it means the same as the rate of compound interest per period. Example 4.19 shows how to determine this rate by several methods.

EXAMPLE 4.19   Rate of return on a series of future, irregular cash flows

---

There is no way of solving algebraically for the interest rate of a series of future irregular cash flows and therefore trial and error must be used.

First, reset to NORMAL (MODE) and clear, as shown in Step 1 on p. 108, then follow the key-stroke sequence shown in the margin.

There is no way of using financial tables to solve for the interest rate of a series of future irregular cash flows, except by trial and error.

FUTURE VALUE OF UNEQUAL CASH FLOWS

The overall *FV* of a series of unequal cash flows can be determined by summing the future values of all the individual cash flows, similarly to the case with the *PV* in Example 4.18. However, instead of doing so, a financial mathematics principle will be introduced and this will enable a shortcut to be taken.

The principle is: *the future value of a series of future cash flows is equal to the future value of their present value.* Therefore, the total future value of the Table 4.5 cash flows is simply found by determining the *FV* of the *PV*. The overall *PV* of $3083 has already been computed in Example 4.18. Any of the various solution methods could equally be used to determine this *FV*; the solution here uses equation (4-3):

$$FV = PV(1 + i)^n = \$3083(1.06)^6 = \$3083(1.41852) = \$4373$$

ONE STEP FURTHER

THE CONCEPT OF A DEFERRED ANNUITY AND THE PRESENT VALUE 'NOW', PV_0

Beginning students of finance often find it difficult to grasp that a 'present' value can exist at different points on a timeline. Consider the following:

This annuity is *deferred* three periods. That is, the first payment occurs three months from 'now' (time 0). If you compute the *PV* of the above annuity at the specified interest rate of $i = 2\%$, you will obtain a figure of $288.39. However, whatever computational method you use, the *PV* of an annuity is *automatically* at the beginning of the *first* payment period. That is, the annuity *PV* formula (and the calculator and spreadsheet routines that are derived from that formula) is mathematically based on determining the *PV* as at the beginning of the first period in which payments start. Therefore, the appropriate place to enter this $288.39 present value is at the *beginning* of month 3:

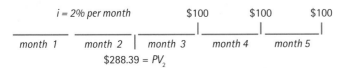

The beginning of month 3 is mathematically identical to the end of month 2. Thus, on the preceding timeline, $288.39 is denoted PV_2, meaning 'present value as at the end of period 2'.

However, what if we want to know the present value 'today', which is denoted PV_0 (that is, at the *beginning* of month 1)? To find PV_0, it is necessary to discount back the amount of $288.39 to two periods earlier:

$$PV_0 = \frac{\$288.39}{(1+i)^2} = \frac{\$288.39}{(1.02)^2} = \frac{\$288.39}{1.0404} = \$277.19$$

i = 2% per month $100 $100 $100

month 1   month 2 | month 3   month 4   month 5

$277.19 = PV_0 ⟵ $288.39 = PV_2

A practical interpretation of this example is: 'How much would you have to invest today to provide you with an income of $100 per month for three months, the first payment starting at the end of month 3?' The validity of this answer can be seen by studying Table 4.6, which is a *payment schedule* (a schedule that shows the payments that can be made from a sum invested).

Generalising from this example, if the first annuity payment occurs in period q (e.g. period 3), the present value 'today' can be found by discounting the annuity's PV back a further $q - 1$ periods (e.g. 2 periods).

TABLE 4.6 'Payment schedule' showing the payments that can be made monthly, starting 3 periods in the future, if a sum of $277.19 is invested 'today' at 2% per month

	OPENING BALANCE	+ INTEREST AT 2%	– ANNUITY PAYMENT	CLOSING BALANCE
1	$277.19[1]	$5.54	0	$282.73
2	282.73	5.65	0	288.38[2]
3	288.38	5.77	–100.00	194.15
4	194.15	3.88	–100.00	98.03
5	98.03	1.97[3]	–100.00	.00

Notes
1 $277.19 = PV_0
2 $288.38 = PV_2
3 rounded upwards

Combining the present value of an annuity with a single future value: the case of bond valuation

Determine how bond values change in response to changing interest rates.

bond
A long-term debt security issued by the borrower, promising to pay the owner of the security a predetermined amount of interest each year and a principal amount at maturity.

The term '**bond**' refers to a particular type of financial instrument (*financial instruments* are the vehicles used for borrowing and lending money). Formally, a bond may be defined as a long-term debt security issued by the borrower, promising to pay the owner of the security a predetermined amount of interest each year. Usually the interest rate is fixed for the life of the bond and only interest payments (known as 'coupons') are paid during the term of the bond. The principal is repaid at maturity, and is known as the *maturity* or *redemption value*, or par value. Australian examples of bonds are company debentures and notes, corporate bonds, Australian government treasury bonds and savings bonds. They are explained in more detail in Chapters 10 and 18.

The workings of a bond combine simultaneous use of the present value of an annuity with a single, lump-sum future payment. This is outlined in Figure 4.5.

FIGURE 4.5 Timeline showing the amount of funds raised via a bond issue (*PV*), together with the future coupon interest payments (*PMT*) and the principal repaid at maturity (*FV*) after *n* periods

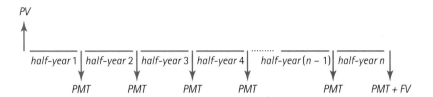

In Figure 4.5, the sum of money raised by the borrower ('issuer'), through selling (issuing) the bond, is shown as a cash inflow, the initial *PV*. Subsequently, the borrower (the bond issuer) makes a series of annuity payments, which represent the 'coupon' interest, *PMT*, for *n* periods (the maturity of the issue). Finally, at maturity, the maturity (redemption) value is repaid, that is mathematically the future value *FV*, which represents the principal owing to investors. Almost invariably, bonds pay half-yearly interest, as suggested by Figure 4.5.

Looking at the situation from the viewpoint of the investor who purchases a bond for a present sum of money (the *PV*), the investor/bond owner is entitled to receive two things: (1) future interest payments (*PMT*), and (2) repayment at maturity of the full principal (*FV*). Thus, the investor's timeline is essentially a mirror image of Figure 4.5, except that the investor's *PV* is a cash outflow and the *PMT* amounts and *FV* are cash inflows.

BOND PRICE FOR THE ORIGINAL INVESTOR WHO REQUIRES AN INTEREST RATE OF 10%

The main concern of this chapter is to show how bond prices change in response to interest-rate changes in the financial markets, as shown in Figure 4.6 and Example 4.20.

EXAMPLE 4.20 **Price of a bond at the time of acquisition**

Suppose you can invest in a $1000 face-value (*FV*) bond that pays $45 interest half-yearly (*PMT*) for 10 years. At the time you buy the bond, market interest rates on comparable 10-year bonds are 10% per annum, so you demand the same rate of return on your investment. This rate is known as the investor's *yield* and is used as the discount rate to determine the price (*PV*) that you will be willing to pay for the bond. Your timeline is shown in Figure 4.6. The timeline highlights the fact that the relevant term is actually 20 half-years, because interest payments are made half-yearly for 10 years.

The bond price is the *PV* of all the future cash flows that accrue to the investor, discounted at the investor's required rate of return or yield, which we have seen is 10% per annum (nominal), that is, 5% (.05) per half-year. Therefore, there are two present value components:

FIGURE 4.6 Investor's timeline for a bond that pays half-yearly coupon interest payments of $45 for 10 years, plus $1000 maturity value (face value)

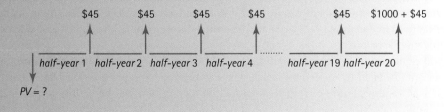

1. *Present value of the coupon interest payments*
   The coupon interest payments form an annuity of $45 per half-year for 20 periods.
2. *Present value of the maturity value*
   The maturity value is a single *FV*, payable 20 half-years in the future.

The computation of the bond price is now shown.

The present value of the interest-payment annuity is given by substitution in equation (4-15) and the present value of the maturity value is given by substitution in equation (4-5), so that the total *PV* or bond price is given by equation (4-23):

$$PV = PMT \frac{[1-(1+i)^{-n)}]}{i} + \frac{FV_n}{(1+i)^n} \tag{4-23}$$

$$= \$45 \frac{[1-(1.05)^{-20}]}{.05} + \frac{\$1000}{(1.05)^{20}} = \$560.80 + \$376.89 = \$937.69$$

In other words, the *PV* of the coupon interest payments is $560.80 and the *PV* of the maturity value is $376.89, so the bond price is $937.69.

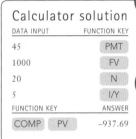

Calculator solution

DATA INPUT	FUNCTION KEY
45	PMT
1000	FV
20	N
5	I/Y
FUNCTION KEY	ANSWER
COMP PV	–937.69

As indicated in the margin solution, the *PMT* and *FV* amounts can be input in combination. Therefore, only one present-value computation is required. From the investor's viewpoint, the price paid is a cash outflow and so the calculator shows the *PV* as a negative amount.

The present value of the interest-payment annuity is given by equation (4-16) as $PMT(PVIFA_{i,n})$, and the present value of the maturity value is given by equation (4-6) as $FV_n (PVIF_{i,n})$, so the combined *PV* or price is:

$$PV = PMT (PVIFA_{i,n}) + FV_n (PVIF_{i,n})$$
$$= \$45 (PVIFA_{5\%,20}) + \$1000 (PVIF_{5\%,20})$$

Using Appendixes D and B respectively, this gives:

$$PV \approx \$45 (12.462) + \$1000 (.377) \approx \$560.79 + \$377 \approx \$937.79$$

As can be seen, use of three-decimal-place tables is not quite accurate for bond pricing purposes.

PRICE OF THE BOND IF THE YIELD IS 12%

Suppose that the investor's yield (required rate of return) has increased to 12% rather than the rate of 10% as in Example 4.20. The effect of the higher yield is that the price is lower. The reason for this is that the future cash flows are fixed (the coupon payments and the maturity value) and the period to maturity is the same, so if the yield increases only the price can change. The price moves downwards in response to a rate increase because the effect of an increased discount rate (*i*) in equation (4-23) is to increase the denominator of the right-hand side, which decreases the *PV* or price.

If you replicate the computational methods shown in Example 4.20, but this time using a 12% per annum yield (6% per half-year), you will find that the price is $827.95. That is, an investor who requires a rate of return equal to 12% per annum will be willing to pay $827.95 for this bond.

International spotlight

THE GREEK BOND CRISIS

In 2010, a highly publicised problem emerged in Europe, known by names such as the 'Greek bond crisis' or, more widely, the 'Mediterranean debt crisis' or 'European debt crisis'.

Governments typically sell (issue) bonds to finance long-term capital projects and other spending programs. When a bond reaches maturity, sometimes the old bond is repaid by issuing new bonds. However, in early 2010, global investors came to the collective judgement that lending more funds to the Greek government (by buying its bonds) was looking very risky. As a result, there was fear that the government might be forced to default on its maturing bonds because of the inability to refinance the sums repayable to investors. One sign of this perceived risk was that yields on the Greek bonds rose to approximately 10%, compared, say, to Germany's 2%.[6] (This is an instance of *Principle 1: The risk return trade-off—we won't take on additional risk unless we expect to be compensated with additional return*.)

There were two major sources of this risk. First, the Greek national budget was running at a significant deficit, over 10%[7]—in other words, the government's annual expenditure was about 110 euros for every 100 euros of income. Second, the Greek government already had large levels of debt relative to other countries—debts in excess of 300 billion euros[8] (roughly $500 billion)—with an average maturity of around 8 years, amounting in total to almost 120% of annual government revenues.[9] In part, these high levels of debt stemmed from prior budget deficits—the Greek government had adopted the practice of borrowing to finance its previous shortfalls of annual income.[10]

In order to try and put a brake on the spiralling cost of Greek government debt[11], as well as to forestall spillover problems for other EU countries with budgetary situations similar to those of Greece (such as Spain and Portugal), EU member countries proposed various schemes to remove investors' concerns. However, the first such proposals were greeted with scepticism, largely because many EU member countries had themselves embarked on substantial programs of borrowing in order to finance GFC bailouts and economic stimulus packages, which raised the spectre that their guarantees were of limited virtue (this goes to show that the GFC and its aftermath are likely to hang around for a number of years into the new decade). Then, in mid 2010, a more acceptable plan was evolved by the EU, together with the IMF (International Monetary Fund)—a 110 billion euro loan plan aimed at giving Greece three years to reform its unsustainable budgetary practices.

To put the previous paragraphs in perspective, imagine the reception your bank-loan application would receive if you spent more each year than you earned. Then, on top of that, imagine that you already had very high levels of debt! Drawing parallels with the Greek fiscal situation, if the bank was willing to lend to you at all, it would require a high interest rate to compensate for the risk, along with the requirement for you to restructure your finances and quite likely an arrangement for others to guarantee your debts.

PRICE OF THE BOND IF THE YIELD IS 8%

Now suppose that the investor's yield is lower, this time 8%. The mathematical effect of the lower yield is to decrease the denominator of the right-hand side in equation (4-23), which increases the *PV* or price. Again, replicating the computational methods shown in Example 4.20, but this time using an 8% per annum yield (4% per half-year), you will find that the price is $1067.95.

Interpolation within financial tables: finding missing table values

OBJECTIVE 12

Interpolate values within financial tables.

Note: This is unnecessary if you do not use financial tables.

As a matter of practicality, financial tables cannot contain all possible values. For example, assume that you want to find the present value of an annuity of $1000 at the end of each half-year for three years, at an interest rate of 5% per annum. First, there is no problem switching from annual cash flows; this example simply means there are six periods (each of a half-year's duration), with interest at 2.5% per half-year. The problem is that if we look at the tables there is no column for 2.5%. To overcome this, we can *interpolate* between known values, to estimate the unknown. Looking in Appendix D at the back of the book, we know that 2.5% lies halfway between the table values of 2% and 3%, so we can assume that the relevant *PVIFA* value in the body of the table also lies halfway between the surrounding values. For this example, reading across the row $n = 6$, we assume that the relevant table value is half-way between 5.601 and 5.417; that is, we assume that $PVIFA_{2.5\%,6}$ is equal to 5.509. Accordingly, we *interpolate* that the relevant present value is:

$$PV = \$1000 \,(PVIFA_{2.5\%,6})$$
$$= \$1000 \,(5.509)$$
$$= \$5509$$

The exact answer is 5508.13, so in this case the interpolation is quite reasonable.

The problem with interpolation is that it assumes straight-line behaviour (thus the full name 'linear interpolation'), which is not true of compound interest. Rather, compound interest exhibits what mathematicians call *exponential behaviour*, as shown in Figure 4.3. For example, if you look at Appendix D, you will see that for $n = 15$ the *PVIFA* value for 9% (namely 8.061) does *not* lie halfway ('straight line') between the value for 8% (8.560) and the value for 10% (7.606).

Solving more complex interpolation problems can be assisted by drawing up an *interpolation table*. For example, suppose we want to know the interest rate per month on a loan of $1000 repayable by instalments of $100 at the end of each month for one year. The problem is formulated as follows:

$$\$1000 = \$100 \,(PVIFA_{?\%,12\text{months}})$$
$$\$1000/\$100 = PVIFA_{?\%,12}$$
$$PVIFA_{?\%,12} = 10.000$$

If we look at the row $n = 12$ in Appendix D, we see that the value 10.000 is not shown, but it lies between the values 10.575 and 9.954, which are in the columns for $i = 2\%$ and $i = 3\%$ respectively. Thus, our unknown interest rate, ?%, must be between 2% and 3%. An interpolation table can be formulated to assist in evaluating the interest rate.

It can be seen from the table in the margin that, if the distance between 2% and ?% is denoted d_1, the unknown rate is equal to 2% plus d_1. So, how do we find the value of d_1? We simply assume that the relative distances between all the values in the table are the same; that is, the ratio d_1 to d_2 equals the ratio d_3 to d_4, or $d_1/d_2 = d_3/d_4$. Therefore, by rearrangement:

$$d_1 = d_2(d_3/d_4)$$

We can measure from the table that d_2 equals the difference between 2% and 3%, that is, 1%. Similarly, d_3 equals 10.575 minus 10.000, that is, 0.575; and d_4 equals 10.575 minus 9.954, that is, 0.621. Therefore, substituting to find d_1:

$$d_1 = d_2(d_3/d_4) = 1\%(0.575/0.621) = 0.926\%$$

Consequently, the unknown interest rate ?% is equal to 2% plus 0.926%, that is, 2.926%. It is more valid to say that the value obtained is approximately correct, because interpolation is inexact for the reasons explained above. To determine how accurate this answer is, it can be compared with the calculator solution of 2.923%.

INTERPOLATION TABLE

	i	$PVIFA_{i,n}$
	2%	10.575
d_2	?%	10.000
	3%	9.954

d_1 d_3 d_4

OBJECTIVE 13

Formulate multi-part and non-standard problems.

Solving multi-part and non-standard problems

This chapter has provided the *tools* for solving elementary financial mathematics problems. Problems such as 'find the present value of the following annuity ...' merely involve using the present-value formulae and tables (or a financial calculator or spreadsheet program) and substituting the appropriate numbers. However, many students do not know where to begin when confronted with non-standard or 'real world' questions. What do you do when confronted with problems that are apparently unstructured? There are a number of steps you can follow:

1. *Draw a timeline.* This will identify what you know and will help to highlight what you need to know. It will also help you to determine if the solution requires more than one part.

2. *Determine what unknown the problem involves.* To solve any problem, at least three variables need to be known to solve for the unknown. So, one way or another you will find that you are given the necessary three or four known values. Identifying these known values usually spotlights the unknown whose value has to be found. Remember that, for most compound interest problems, there are a limited number of variables: *i, n, PV, FV, PMT*, so if you are given three of these the unknown is almost self-identifying.

3. *Identify the class of problem.* Is it compounding of a single sum of money, or is it discounting? Is it an annuity, with regular payments? Is it a perpetuity? Does it involve an uneven stream of cash flows? As well, it is often necessary to know if it is a present-value or a future-value problem. This identifies what type of equation or computational procedure is necessary to formulate the problem.

4. *Be careful to recognise any 'traps' in the problem.* A common example is where you are told that a problem is for a number of years, but payments are non-annual (or the interest rate is non-annual). To solve any time-value-of-money problem, there must be equality between the unit of time and the payment/compounding frequency. (For example, if a 20-year housing loan is repaid monthly, you need to know the monthly interest rate, and that the relevant term is 240 months.)

5. *Formulate the problem.* This involves setting up the relevant equation (or calculator/spreadsheet routine) that relates the known and unknown variables. If using financial tables, you may need to interpolate if the tables do not contain the exact values you want (for example, an interest rate that involves a half percent).

Before looking at some of the more complex end-of-chapter problems where these five steps might need to be applied, consider Example 4.21.

EXAMPLE 4.21   Solving a multi-part financial mathematics problem

Suppose you are working as a financial adviser. A client is planning for future retirement and wants to know how much money must be invested 'today' at 8% per annum in order to pay a monthly annuity of $2000 for 20 years, starting one month after retirement date in 15 years time, assuming that the interest rate after retirement is 6% *APR*.

Step 1: Draw a timeline, entering the known variables and highlighting the unknown
The timeline starts with PV_0, the unknown amount that must be invested today. This accumulates to FV_{15}, the future value of the initial investment after 15 years. That amount of FV_{15} forms an investment fund from which an annuity of $2000 per month needs to be paid for a further 20 years/240 months:

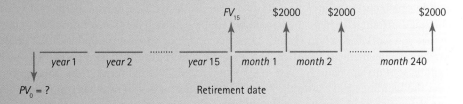

Step 2: Determine what unknown(s) the problem involves
We can see from the time diagram that this is a two-part problem. First, it is necessary to find the sum of money that is needed at the beginning of the *retirement period*, which begins 15 years from 'now'. Second, that sum must be converted back to the initial investment, PV_0.

Step 3: Identify the class of problem

The first part of the problem involves finding the *PV* of an *annuity* (whose payments start at the end of the first month after retirement), with payments of $2000 per month for 240 months, at 0.5% per month (6% *APR*). This is shown in the following partial timeline:

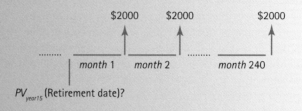

Step 4: Any traps?

Because the interest compounding frequency corresponds to the unit of time in each case, there are no such traps in this problem.

Step 5: Formulate the problem

First, the *PV* of the after-retirement annuity (as at the beginning of the annuity period, 15 years from now) is $279 162. This can be confirmed by several of the computational methods (the answer is outside the scope of the book's financial tables); only the financial calculator routine is shown here.

The second part of the problem is to treat $279 162 as a single future value amount in 15 years time, and then to find its present value 'today', PV_0. This initial investment is therefore the *PV* of $279 162 that is receivable in 15 years time at 8% per annum. Thus, PV_0 is $88 004, which can be confirmed by any of the three computational methods; the financial calculator solution is shown in the margin.

To sum up this problem, the following timeline shows the complete series of cash flows:

Calculator solution

DATA INPUT	FUNCTION KEY
2000	PMT
240	N
0.5	I/Y
FUNCTION KEY	ANSWER
COMP PV	−279 162

Calculator solution

DATA INPUT	FUNCTION KEY
279 162	FV
15	N
8	I/Y
FUNCTION KEY	ANSWER
COMP PV	−88 004

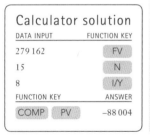

How financial managers use this material

Almost all business decisions involve cash flows that occur in different time periods. The tools and techniques introduced in this chapter enable you to compare these cash flows. For example, suppose that you work for Hilton Hotels. You have to decide whether to build a hotel or alternatively a block of apartments, some of which will be rented out ('managed apartments') while others will be sold off the plan. In each case money has to be outlaid right now to acquire the land, erect the buildings and fit out the rooms. However, the cash flows that you expect to get back from the initial outlays occur at different times; the cash will be received early in the future from the apartments that are sold off the plan, but will be spread out over a number of years—in the form of room occupancy charges—in relation to hotel rooms or apartments that are not sold off the plan. Because a dollar today is not worth the same as a dollar in a year's time, these cash flows that occur at different times have to be valued in such a way that they are comparable. In fact, every time you are evaluating a new product or service the same problem occurs; you have to outlay money now with the expectation of getting a return on that money in the future, so the time value of money comes into play. In short, there isn't any other business tool that is more essential to making good decisions.

The time value of money plays a central role too in valuing securities, not only bonds as seen in this chapter but also shares. When an investment consortium bid (without success) to take control of Qantas airlines in the late 2000s, an understanding of the time value of money enabled investors to work out how much they were willing to pay to purchase the shares necessary to take control of the company. In this case, the price the investor was willing to pay at that time depended on the expected future cash receipts from owning the share.

The time value of money underlies not only business financial decisions but also personal decisions. Borrowing money to finance the purchase of a house or apartment, investing in superannuation or saving money to pay for your children's education are just a few of the areas that involve the time value of money.

Summary

To make decisions, financial managers must compare the costs and benefits of alternatives that do not occur during the same time period. Whether to make profitable investments or to take advantage of favourable interest rates, financial decision making requires an understanding of the time value of money. Managers who use the time value of money in all of their financial calculations assure themselves of more logical decisions. The time-value process makes all dollar values comparable; since money has a time value, this process moves all dollar flows either back to the present or out to a common future date. All time-value formulae presented in this chapter actually stem from the single compounding formula $FV_n = PV(1 + i)^n$. The formulae are used to deal simply with common financial situations, for example discounting single flows, compounding annuities and discounting annuities. Table 4.7 provides a summary of these calculations.

TABLE 4.7 Summary of time-value-of-money calculations

CALCULATION	EQUATION	
Future value of a single amount	$FV_n = PV(1 + i)^n = PV(FVIF_{i,n})$	OBJECTIVE **1**
		OBJECTIVE **2**
Present value of a single amount	$PV = FV_n/(1 + i)^n = FV_n(PVIF_{i,n})$	OBJECTIVE **3**
Effective annual interest rate	$EAR = (1 + j/m)^m - 1 = (1 + i)^m - 1$	OBJECTIVE **4**

Notation:
FV_n = the future value of the investment at the end of period n
n = the number of periods until payment will be received or during which compounding occurs
i = the periodic interest or discount rate
PV = the present value of the future sum of money
m = the number of times compounding occurs during the year
PMT = the annuity payment deposited or received at the end of each period, or the constant dollar payment provided by the perpetuity

CALCULATION	EQUATION	
Future value of an ordinary annuity	$FV_n = PMT \dfrac{[(1 + i)^n - 1]}{i} = PMT(FVIFA_{i,n})$	OBJECTIVE **5**
Present value of an ordinary annuity	$PV = PMT \dfrac{[1 - (1 + i)^{-n}]}{i} = PMT(PVIFA_{i,n})$	
Present value of a perpetuity	$PV = PMT/i$	OBJECTIVE **9**

OBJECTIVE 6 In addition to calculations based on these formulae, the chapter discussed:
The application of the annuity present value model to the process of loan amortisation

OBJECTIVE 7 The concept of equivalent interest rates that can be used to formulate solutions to general annuity problems

OBJECTIVE 8 How to determine the present value of an annuity due

OBJECTIVE 10 How to handle complex cash flows such as unequal payment streams

OBJECTIVE 11 The relationship between bond prices and interest rates

OBJECTIVE 12 How to find missing table values

OBJECTIVE 13 Tips on solving problems in financial mathematics

Key terms

For a complete flashcard glossary go to MyFinanceLab at www.pearson.com.au/myfinancelab

annuity	94	future value interest factor for an annuity	95
annuity due	104	general annuity	103
bond	110	nominal annual rate of interest	91
compound interest	81	ordinary annuity	94
discount factor	88	perpetuity	106
discounting	88	present value interest factor	89
discount rate	88	present value interest factor for an annuity	98
equivalent interest rates	103		
future value interest factor	84		

Web works

1. How fast will your money grow? Use a *financial calculator* to determine how long it will take $50 000 to grow to $90 000 if it earns 10% interest. Again using a *financial calculator*, if you start with $50 000 and invest an additional $250 per month every month, how long will it take to grow to $90 000 if it earns 10% interest?

2. How much money will you need to start with if you make no additional investments? You want to have $90 000 in six years and your investment will grow at 10%. Use a *financial calculator* to determine how much money you will need to start with.

Review questions

4-1 What is the time value of money? Why is it so important?

4-2 The processes of discounting and compounding are related. Explain this relationship.

4-3 How would an increase in the interest rate (i) or a decrease in the holding period (n) affect the future value (FV_n) of a sum of money? Explain why.

4-4 Suppose you were considering depositing your savings in one of three banks, all of which pay 5% interest; bank A compounds annually, bank B compounds semi-annually, and bank C compounds continuously. Which bank would you choose? Why?

4-5 What is an annuity? Give some examples of annuities. Distinguish between an ordinary annuity and an annuity due. Distinguish between an ordinary annuity and a perpetuity.

4-6 What does continuous compounding mean?

4-7 'In order to compare two or more interest rates, they must be expressed on a suitable common scale.' Explain the meaning of this quotation and give a few numerical examples to illustrate.

4-8 What is a *term loan*? What is meant by *amortisation* of such a loan?

4-9 In what way do bond values change in response to changing interest rates?

Self-test problems

ST-1 You place $25 000 in a savings account paying annual compound interest of 8% for three years and then move it into a savings account that pays 10% interest compounded annually. How much will your money have grown at the end of six years?

For answers go to MyFinanceLab
www.pearson.com.au/myfinancelab

ST-2 What is the answer to the preceding problem if interest is compounded half-yearly?

ST-3 You purchase a boat for $35 000 and pay a $5000 deposit and agree to pay the rest over the next 10 years in 10 equal annual payments that include principal payments plus 13% compound interest on the unpaid balance. What will be the amount of each payment?

ST-4 For an investment to grow eight times in nine years, at what rate would it have to grow?

ST-5 You have the opportunity to buy a bond for $1000 that will pay no interest during its 10-year life and have a value of $3106 at maturity. What rate of return or yield does this bond pay?

Problems

4-1* (*Future value*) To what amount will the following investments accumulate?

For more problems and for answers to problems marked with an asterisk (*) go to MyFinanceLab at
www.pearson.com.au/myfinancelab

    (a) $5000 invested for 10 years at 10% compounded annually
    (b) $8000 invested for seven years at 8% compounded annually
    (c) $775 invested for 12 periods at 12% compounded annually
    (d) $21 000 invested for two and half years at 10% p.a. compounded half-yearly

4-2 (*Future value solving for* n) How many years will the following take?

    (a) $500 to grow to $1039.50 if invested at 5% compounded annually
    (b) $35 to grow to $53.87 if invested at 18% compounded half-yearly
    (c) $100 to grow to $298.60 if invested at 20% compounded annually
    (d) $53 to grow to $78.76 if invested at 2% compounded annually

4-3* (*Future value solving for* i) At what annual rate would the following have to be invested?

    (a) $500 to grow to $1948.00 in 12 years
    (b) $300 to grow to $422.10 in seven years
    (c) $50 to grow to $280.20 in 20 quarters
    (d) $200 to grow to $497.60 in five years

4-4 (*Present value*) What is the present value of the following future amounts?

    (a) $800 to be received 10 years from now discounted back to the present at 10%
    (b) $300 to be received five years from now discounted back to the present at 5%
    (c) $1000 to be received eight years from now discounted back to the present at 3%
    (d) $1000 to be received eight years from now discounted back to the present at 20%

4-5 (*Future value*) Calculate the amount of money that will be in each of the following accounts at the end of the given deposit period:

ACCOUNT	AMOUNT DEPOSITED ($)	ANNUAL INTEREST RATE (%)	COMPOUNDING PERIOD (EVERY – MONTHS)	DEPOSIT PERIOD (YEARS)
Mike Rabbitt	1 000	10	12	10
Arthur Coles	95 000	12	1	1
Sue Elliott	8 000	12	2	2
Mai Nguyen	120 000	8	6	4
Peter Rossini	30 000	10	3	3
Matthew Lock	15 000	12	6	3

4-6* (*Future value*) Brian Mosman, who recently sold his Porsche, placed $10 000 in a savings account paying annual compound interest of 6%.

   (a) Calculate the amount of money that will have accrued if he leaves the money in the bank for one, five and 15 years.
   (b) If he moves his money into an account that pays 8% or one that pays 10%, rework part **(a)** using these new interest rates.
   (c) What conclusions can you draw about the relationship between interest rates, time and future sums from the calculations you have done in **(a)** and **(b)**?

4-7* (*Future value*)

   (a) Calculate the future sum of $5000, given that it will be held in the bank for five years at an annual interest rate of 6%.
   (b) Recalculate part **(a)** using a compounding period that is (1) half-yearly, and (2) bi-monthly.
   (c) Recalculate parts **(a)** and **(b)** for a 12% annual interest rate.
   (d) Recalculate part **(a)** using a time horizon of 12 years (annual interest rate is still 6%).

4-8* (*Future value*) Sales of a new finance book were 15 000 copies this year and they were expected to increase by 20% per year. What are the expected sales during each of the next three years? Graph this sales trend and explain.

4-9* (*Solving for* i *in compound interest*) If you were offered $1079.50 ten years from now in return for an investment of $500 currently, what annual rate of interest would you earn if you took up the offer?

4-10 (*Solving for* i *in compound interest*) You lend a friend $10 000, for which your friend will repay you $27 027 at the end of five years. What interest rate are you charging your 'friend'?

4-11* (*Future value solving for* n) About how many years would it take for your investment to grow fourfold if it were invested at 16% compounded semi-annually?

4-12* (*Solving for* i *in compound interest*) In September 1963 the first issue of the comic book *X-MEN* was issued. The original price for that issue was 12 cents. By September 1992, 29 years later, the value of this comic book had risen to $990. What annual rate of interest would you have earned if you had bought the comic in 1963 and sold it in 1992?

4-13 (*Present value*) Sarah Wiggum would like to make a single investment and have $2 million at the time of her retirement in 35 years. She has found an investment fund that will pay interest at 4% annually. How much will Sarah need to invest today? What if Sarah were studying finance and learned how to earn a 14% annual return? How soon could she then retire?

4-14 (*Present value*) What is the present value of the following future amounts?

   (a) $800 to be received 10 years from now discounted back to the present at 10%.
   (b) $300 to be received five years from now discounted back to the present at 5%.
   (c) $1000 to be received eight years from now discounted back to the present at 3%.
   (d) $1000 to be received eight years from now discounted back to the present at 20%.

4-15 (*Compound interest: solving for* n) Approximately how many years would it take for an investment to grow fourfold if it were invested at 16% p.a. compounded semi-annually?

4-16 (*Present-value comparison*) You are offered $1000 today, $10 000 in 12 years, or $25 000 in 25 years. Assuming that you can earn 11% on your money, which should you choose?

4-17 (*Calculating an EAR*) Your grandmother asks for your help in choosing a deposit account from a bank. The deposit has a one-year maturity and a fixed interest rate. The first deposit pays 4.95% *APR* compounded daily, while the second deposit pays 5.0% *APR* compounded monthly. What is the effective annual rate (the *EAR*) of each desposit, and which account would you recommend to your grandmother?

4-18 (*Calculating an EAR*) Based on effective interest rates, would you prefer to deposit your money into Homer Bank, which pays 8.0% interest compounded annually, or into Bart Bank, which pays 7.8% compounded monthly?

4-19 (*Future value and effective interest rate*) After examining the various personal loan rates available to you, you find that you can borrow $10 000 for a year from a finance company at 12% compounded monthly or from a bank at 13% compounded annually. Which alternative is the most attractive? (Compute this answer in several different ways, including the use of the effective annual interest rate.)

4-20 (*Continuous compounding*) What is the value of $500 after five years if it is invested at 10% p.a. compounded continuously? (If you don't have a calculator capable of solving this problem, simply formulate the problem without solving it.)

4-21 (*Continuous compounding*) You want to have $2000 in two years time. If interest is compounded continuously at 6% p.a., how much do you need to invest today? (If you don't have a calculator capable of solving this problem, simply formulate the problem without solving it.)

4-22* (*Future value of an ordinary annuity*) What is the accumulated sum of each of the following streams of ordinary annuity payments?

(a) $500 a year for 10 years compounded annually at 5%
(b) $100 a year for five years compounded annually at 10%
(c) $35 per half-year for three and a half years at 14% p.a. compounded half-yearly
(d) $25 a year for three years compounded annually at 2%

4-23* (*Annuity future value*) The Aggarwal Company needs to save $10 million to discharge a $10 million mortgage loan (a kind of term loan) that matures on 31 December 2017. To discharge this mortgage, the company plans to put a fixed amount into an account at the end of each year for 10 years, with the first payment occurring on 31 December 2008. The Aggarwal Company expects to earn 9% annually on the money in this account. What equal annual contribution must it make to this account to accumulate the $10 million by 31 December 2017?

4-24 (*Solving for* i *in annuities*) Nicki Johnson, a first-year mechanical engineering student, receives a call from an insurance agent, who believes that Nicki is an older woman ready to retire from teaching. He talks to her about several annuities that she could buy that would guarantee her an annual fixed income. The annuities are as follows:

ANNUITY	INITIAL PAYMENT INTO ANNUITY (AT $T = 0$) ($)	AMOUNT OF MONEY RECEIVED PER YEAR ($)	DURATION OF ANNUITY (YEARS)
A	50 000	8 500	12
B	60 000	7 000	25
C	70 000	8 000	20

If Nicki could earn 11% on her money by placing it in a savings account, should she place it instead in any of the annuities? Which ones, if any? Why?

4-25* (*Solving for PMT in an annuity*) To pay for your child's education you wish to have accumulated $15 000 at the end of 15 years. To do this you plan on depositing an equal amount into the bank at the end of each year. If the bank is willing to pay 6% compounded annually, how much must you deposit each year to obtain your goal?

4-26* (*Future value of annuity*) You plan on buying some property in Queensland five years from today. To do this you estimate that you will need $20 000 at that time for the purchase. You would like to accumulate these funds by making equal annual deposits in your savings account, which pays 12% annually. If you make your first deposit at the end of this year and you would like your account to reach $20 000 when the final deposit is made, what would be the amount of each deposit?

4-27 (*Future value and effective interest rate*) Here are three ways of investing your money for five years:

(1) $10 000 invested at an *APR* of 12% compounded half-yearly
(2) $10 000 that matures as a single amount of $17 623

(3) $2000 invested at the end of each year, with a future value of $12 706.

    (a) Which investment is best?

    (b) If you were borrowing money, which would you prefer?

4-28 (*Future value of an annuity*) Upon graduating in accounting 35 years ago, Nick Leung was already planning for his retirement. Since then, he has made $300 deposits into a retirement fund on a quarterly basis. Nick has just completed his final payment and is at last ready to retire. His retirement fund has earned 9% p.a. compounded quarterly.

    (a) How much has Nick accumulated in his retirement account?

    (b) In addition to all this, 15 years ago Nick received an inheritance cheque for $20 000 from his beloved uncle. He decided to deposit the entire amount into his retirement fund. What is his current balance in the fund?

4-29 (*Present value of an ordinary annuity*) What is the present value of the following ordinary annuities?

    (a) $2500 a year for 10 years discounted back to the present at 7%

    (b) $70 a year for three years discounted back to the present at 3%

    (c) $280 a year for seven years discounted back to the present at 6%

    (d) $500 a period for 10 periods discounted back to the present at 10% per period

    (e) Compute the effective annual interest rate for parts **(a)** and **(b)** above, and explain how this rate relates to the dollar amount of the future sum.

4-30* (*Annuity present value: solving for* i) You lend a friend $30 000, which your friend will repay in five equal annual payments of $10 000, with the first payment to be received one year from now. What rate of return does your loan receive?

4-31 (*Present value and future value of an annuity*) In 10 years you are planning to retire and buy a house in Noosa, Queensland. The house you are looking at currently costs $1 000 000 and is expected to increase in value each year at a rate of 5%. Assuming that you can earn 10% annually on your investments, how much must you invest at the end of each of the next 10 years to be able to buy your dream home when you retire?

4-32 (*Present value*) You would like to have $75 000 in 15 years. To accumulate this amount you plan to deposit, each year, an equal sum in the bank, which will earn 8% interest compounded annually. Your first payment will be made at the end of the year.

    (a) How much must you deposit annually to accumulate this amount?

    (b) If you decided to make a large lump-sum deposit today instead of the annual deposits, how large should this lump-sum deposit be? (Assume you can earn 8% on this deposit.)

    (c) At the end of five years you will receive $20 000 and deposit this in the bank towards your goal of $75 000 at the end of 15 years. In addition to this deposit, how much must you deposit in equal annual payments to reach your goal? (Assume you can earn 8% on this payment.)

4-33* (*Annuity payment and term loan*) Bill and Sue Preston purchased an old run-down house in a small country town for the bargain price of $80 000. They paid a $20 000 deposit and agreed to pay the rest over the next 25 years in 25 equal annual payments that included principal payments plus 9% compound interest on the unpaid balance. What would these equal payments be?

4-34 (*Annuity payment and term loan*) On 31 December Liz Klemkosky bought a yacht for $50 000, paying a deposit of $10 000 and agreeing to pay the balance in 10 equal annual instalments that would include both the principal and 10% interest. How big would the annual payments be?

4-35* (*Annuity payment and term loan*) A firm borrows $25 000 from the bank at 12% compounded annually to purchase some new machinery. This loan is to be repaid in equal annual instalments at the end of each year over the next five years. How much will each annual payment be?

4-36* (*Loan amortisation*) TLC Company wants to borrow $50 million to finance its expansion into a chain of new Pamper Health & Beauty Spas. TLC's bank charges interest at 12% *APR* for loans of this type, with payments at the end of each month.

    (a) If TLC borrowed for 10 years, what would be the monthly payments?

    (b) Prepare an amortisation schedule for the first six months.

    (c) How much does TLC owe at the very end of the sixth month?

(d) Sometimes term loans have a fixed interest rate, and at other times the rate can be varied during the life of the loan by the lender. If interest rates increased by 1% p.a. at the end of the sixth month, can you figure out what would happen to the repayment, assuming that the bank has the right to increase the interest rate? (Assume also that the loan's term does not change.)

4-37 (*General annuity*) You have borrowed $10 000, repayable by equal half-yearly instalments for five years. If interest is compounded at i = .9759% per month, what will be your half-yearly payments?

4-38 (*General annuity*) You are planning to save, for two years, a regular sum at the end of each month in order to build up an accumulated sum of $70 000 to pay for an Audi Quattro motor car. Your savings account compounds interest daily at 10% p.a. How much must you deposit each month to reach your savings target of $70 000?

4-39 (*Annuity due present value*) Your firm recently financed a new computer system through a type of loan that has equal monthly payments starting at the beginning of each month, for one year. If your firm's repayments are $2000 per month and interest is at an *APR* of 9%, how much finance did your firm raise?

4-40 (*Annuity due present value*) The new Sunday night X-Lotto draw has a prize of $1 million to be paid over 19 years in $50 000 amounts. The first $50 000 payment is made immediately and the 19 remaining $50 000 payments occur at the end of each of the next 19 years. If 10% is the appropriate discount rate, what is the present value of this stream of cash flows? If 20% is the appropriate discount rate, what is the present value of the cash flows?

4-41* (*Perpetuities*) What is the present value of the following?

(a) A $300 perpetuity discounted back to the present at 8%
(b) A $1000 perpetuity discounted back to the present at 12%
(c) A $100 perpetuity discounted back to the present at 9%
(d) A $95 perpetuity discounted back to the present at 5%

4-42 (*Perpetuity: payment amount*) If your grandfather had deposited $50 000 in your family's 'perpetual education fund' before he died recently, how much could be taken from the fund at the end of each year without reducing the sum invested. Interest is at 6% p.a.

4-43 (*Perpetuity: interest rate*) Some companies borrow money by using 'income bonds'. These pay the investor a perpetual stream of interest payments, and they never mature. If $100 000 is invested and the payment is $7000 at the end of each year, what rate of interest is being earned?

4-44* (*Present value of a complex stream of payments*) You are given three investment alternatives to analyse. The cash flows from these three investments are as follows:

END OF YEAR	INVESTMENT ($)		
	A	B	C
1	10 000		10 000
2	10 000		
3	10 000		
4	10 000		
5	10 000	10 000	
6		10 000	50 000
7		10 000	
8		10 000	
9		10 000	
10		10 000	10 000

Assuming a 20% discount rate, find the present value of each investment.

4-45 (*Complex stream of payments: interest rate—financial calculator or spreadsheet solution only*) What annual interest rate is being earned on each of the three investments in problem 4-44 if the amount invested is $40 000 in each case, invested at the beginning of year 1?

4-46 (*Present value of an uneven stream of payments*) You are given three investment alternatives to analyse. The cash inflows (outflows) from these three investments are as follows:

END OF YEAR	INVESTMENT ($)		
	A	B	C
1	2000	2000	5000
2	3000	2000	5000
3	4000	2000	(5000)
4	(5000)	2000	(5000)
5	5000	5000	15000

What is the present value of each of these three investments if the appropriate discount rate is 10%?

4-47 (*Deferred annuity*) You have just borrowed $10000. You are required to repay equal amounts at the end of each of seven years, with the first payment starting in four years time. Your interest rate is 8% p.a. How much will be the amount of each payment?

4-48* (*Deferred annuity*) How much do you have to deposit today so that, beginning 11 years from now, you can withdraw $10000 a year for the next five years (periods 11 to 15) plus an additional amount of $20000 in the last year (period 15)? Assume an interest rate of 6%.

4-49 (*Bond values*) In early 2010 you held a Greek government bond with 100000 euros maturity value that pays coupon interest of 2000 euros per half-year. Assume that suddenly, in mid 2010, interest rates (yields) on Greek government debt doubled from 4% p.a. to 8% p.a. What would be the value of your bond **(a)** before the rate rise, **(b)** after the rate rise?

4-50 (*Bond values*) You are examining three bonds, each with a maturity value of $1000 and you are concerned with what would happen to their market value if interest rates (the market discount rate) changed. The three bonds are:

1. A bond with three years left to maturity that pays a $50 interest coupon at the end of every half-year.
2. A bond with seven years left to maturity that pays a $50 interest coupon at the end of every half-year.
3. A bond with 20 years left to maturity that also pays a $50 interest coupon at the end of every half-year.

What would be the value of these bonds if the market discount rates were:

(a) 10% per year compounded semi-annually?
(b) 4% per year compounded semi-annually?
(c) 16% per year compounded semi-annually?

What observations can you make about these results?

4-51* (*Multi-part problem*) Your employer is DIE Corporation. Having just reached age 30, you have obtained a senior management position and have qualified to join the company's pension scheme. You are paid $60000 per year, and at the end of each year the company contributes 10% of your salary to the scheme.

(a) How much money will be in your fund at age 60 (your projected retirement age), if the fund expects to earn an average rate of 11% p.a.?
(b) After retiring at age 60, you want to use your cash payout (from answer a) to buy a monthly annuity payable at the end of each month (that is, to buy a monthly pension payment from a superannuation company). The fund will invest your money safely and so will earn a relatively low expected rate of return, namely 6% *APR* compounded monthly. Actuarial statistics project that you will live until age 83 if you are a male or 86 if you are a female. How much can you expect to receive as your monthly pension (payable at the end of each month)?

4-52* (*Comprehensive multi-part problem*) You are trying to plan for retirement in 10 years, and currently you have $100000 in a savings account and $300000 in shares. In addition, you plan on adding to your savings by depositing $10000 per year in your savings account at the end of each of the next five years and then $20000 per year at the end of each year for the final five years until retirement.

(a) Assuming your savings account returns 7% compounded annually, while your investment in shares will return 12% compounded annually, how much will you have at the end of 10 years? (Ignore taxes.)

(b) If you expect to live for 20 years after you retire, and at retirement you deposit all of your savings in a bank account paying 10% interest, how much can you withdraw each year after retirement (20 equal withdrawals beginning one year after you retire) to end up with a zero balance at death?

4-53 (*Comprehensive*) You have just inherited a large sum of money and you are trying to determine how much you should save for retirement and how much you can spend now. For retirement you will deposit today (1 January 2011) a lump sum in a bank account paying 10% compounded annually. You don't plan on touching this deposit until you retire in five years (1 January 2016), and you plan on living for 20 additional years and then dropping dead on 31 December 2035. During your retirement you would like to receive income of $50 000 per year, to be received on the first day of each year, with the first payment on 1 January 2016 and the last payment on 1 January 2035. Complicating this objective is your desire to have one final three-year fling during which time you intend to track down all the original cast members of your favourite TV show and get their autographs. To finance this, you want to receive $250 000 on 1 January 2031, and *nothing* on 1 January 2032 and 1 January 2033, as you will be on the road. In addition, the day after you pass away (on 1 January 2036), you would like to have a total of $100 000 to leave to your children.

(a) How much must you deposit in the bank at 10% on 1 January 2036 to achieve your goal? (Use a timeline to answer this question.)

(b) What kinds of problems are associated with this analysis and its assumptions?

Case study

You have just obtained your first job after graduating, as a media research analyst. Your new employer, *Bizweek Online Services*, has asked you to prepare some background material for a series of news articles that are scheduled to appear in the next edition.

1. The government is rumoured to be proposing a new superannuation policy, aimed at giving all current full-time workers a $10 000 'handout' to boost their retirement savings. The average recipient is 44 years old and the average expected retirement age is 64. How much money would the handout grow to at the average person's retirement age if the money earned 6% p.a. in a special bank savings account established for retirement savings?

2. As an alternative to scenario 1, above, what would be the expected payoff from putting the money into the sharemarket if it had a projected average return of 12% p.a. in the long run?

3. What are some of the advantages and disadvantages of investing as outlined in 1, above, as opposed to 2, above?

4. If the government's plan is to spread the handout over five years (that is, $2000 p.a. at the end of each year, starting at age 44) what would this be worth to the average worker at retirement?

5. Australia has some of the most expensive housing in the world, relative to rental income and annual incomes. If the average house price is $500 000, and if the current mortgage interest rate is 9% *APR*, compounded and repayable monthly, how much would a borrower need to earn per month (and year) to buy an average house if the lender allowed the borrower to commit 40% of gross income to loan repayments, assuming the borrower had saved a $200 000 deposit and would pay the loan over a term of 30 years?

6. The recent 'Greek bond crisis' still surfaces from time to time as commentators speculate about the long-term fate of the Greek government's ability to repay its maturing bonds. If an investor held Greek bonds with 10 000 000 euros maturity value, paying 200 000 euros coupon interest per half-year, and with four years till maturity, how much would these bonds be worth if the yield on Greek government bonds was 8% p.a.?

Notes

1. *The Economist*, 3 April 2010.
2. Globally, securitisation grew from about 0.5 trillion dollars p.a. in 2000 to a peak of 2.5 trillion in 2006, the cumulative total for the eight-year period 2000–2007 being about $8 trillion. The US accounted for the major part of this activity.
3. A feature of securitisation is that the original lender (known as the *originator*) continues to service the administrative relationship with the individual mortgage borrowers. But the loan repayments receivable by the originator are 'passed through' to investors. This is treated as a 'sale' of the loans, which in effect shifts them 'off balance sheet' so that they no longer appear in the originator's financial statements (the same applies to any default losses, being also 'passed through' to investors).
4. In Australia, these were called 'low doc' loans, referring to the lack of supporting documentation to confirm employment and income. However, in Australia, such 'low doc' loans were never more than a minor part of the lending scene. Furthermore, Australian banks and other lenders did not give free rein to mortgage brokers—instead, the lenders typically subjected loan applications to further scrutiny before saying 'yes' or 'no'. Accordingly, Australia did not suffer a US-style crisis.
5. A similar phrase was aired in the ABC television documentary, 'Mortgage Meltdown', *Four Corners*, 17 September 2007.
6. *The Economist*, 17 July 2010.
7. *The Economist*, 6 February 2010.
8. *The Weekend Australian*, 1–2 May 2010.
9. *The Australian Financial Review*, 1–2 May 2010.
10. One of the problems of paying high interest rates is that, if the interest rate is greater than the growth rate of the economy, the future ability to service the debt tends to diminish.
11. *The Australian Financial Review*, 8–9 May 2010.
12. We are grateful to an anonymous reviewer for clarifying this point.

Origins of formulae

DERIVATION OF EQUATION (4-3)

Suppose we place PV dollars in a savings account that pays $i\%$ per period, compound interest. At the end of the first period we will have earned interest of $PV \times i$ on our initial deposit, giving us a total accumulated sum or future value of $PV + PVi$ in the savings account, which simplifies to the amount of $PV(1 + i)$

The mathematical formula illustrating this phenomenon is:

$$FV_1 = PV(1 + i) \qquad \textbf{(a)}$$

where FV_1 = the future value of the investment at the end of 1 period

i = the interest rate

PV = the present value, or original amount invested at the beginning of the first period

Carrying these calculations one period further, in the second period we now earn $i\%$ interest on a sum of $PV(1 + i)$, which means that we earn interest of $PV(1 + i)i$ during the second period. Therefore, the total amount accumulated by the end of the second period is given by:

$$FV_2 = PV(1 + i) + PV(1 + i)i = PV(1 + i)[1 + i] = PV(1 + i)^2 \qquad \textbf{(b)}$$

Taking these calculations into a third period, in that period we now earn $i\%$ interest on a sum of $PV(1 + i)^2$, which means that we earn interest of $PV(1 + i)^2 i$ during the third period. Therefore, the total amount accumulated by the end of the third period is given by:

$$FV_3 = PV(1 + i)^2 + PV(1 + i)^2 i = PV(1 + i)^2 [1 + i] = PV(1 + i)^3 \qquad \textbf{(c)}$$

Comparing equations (a), (b) and (c) we can see a pattern beginning to emerge, namely: the subscript of FV is equal to the exponent of $(1 + i)$. Generalising, we have equation (4-3) from earlier in the chapter:

$$FV_n = PV(1 + i)^n$$

where FV_n = the future value of the investment at the end of n periods

n = the number of periods during which compounding occurs

i = the periodic interest rate

PV = the present value or original amount invested at the beginning of the first period

DERIVATION OF EQUATION (4-9)

If \$1 is invested at a nominal rate i per period, compounded m times per annum, for a period of one year, it grows or compounds to $\$1(1 + i)^m$. Thus the dollar *amount* of interest earned on one dollar is equal to this compound sum minus the invested dollar; that is, the amount of interest is equal to:

$$\$1(1 + i)^m - \$1$$

To represent this amount of interest as an interest *rate*, it is necessary to divide it by the original dollar invested. Thus, the exact or effective rate earned per annum is equal to:

(\$ interest paid on \$1)/\$1 = [\$1(1 + i)^m - \$1]/\$1, which simplifies to equation (4-9):

$$EAR = (1 + i)^m - 1$$

DERIVATION OF EQUATION (4-11)

Assume that an annuity at the end of each of n periods accumulates interest at rate i per period compound interest. The following timeline shows the payments and the future value:

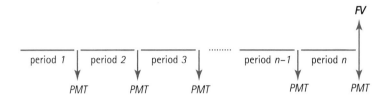

It can be seen that the first payment, being made at the end of the first period, accumulates interest for one less than n periods, so its future value is $PMT(1 + i)^{n-1}$. Similarly, the second payment accumulates interest for $n - 2$ periods so its future value is $PMT(1 + i)^{n-2}$, and the third payment accumulates interest for $n - 3$ periods, so its future value is $PMT(1 + i)^{n-3}$. Moving on to the second-last payment, this accumulates interest for 1 period, so its future value is simply $PMT(1 + i)$ which can be written $PMT(1 + i)^1$. The final payment accumulates interest for zero periods so its future value is simply PMT, which can be written $PMT(1 + i)^0$.

In order to obtain the overall future value, the accumulated sums of all of the annuity payments are added together, and this sum can be written:

$$FV_n = PMT(1 + i)^{n-1} + PMT(1 + i)^{n-2} + PMT(1 + i)^{n-3} \ldots + PMT(1 + i)^1 + PMT(1 + i)^0$$

This can in turn be factored as follows:

$$FV_n = PMT[(1 + i)^{n-1} + (1 + i)^{n-2} + (1 + i)^{n-3} + \ldots + (1 + i)^1 + 1] \qquad \textbf{(d)}$$

Multiplying both sides by $(1 + i)$ gives:

$$FV_n (1 + i) = PMT[(1 + i)^n + (1 + i)^{n-1} + (1 + i)^{n-2} + \ldots + (1 + i)^2 + (1 + i)] \qquad \textbf{(e)}$$

Subtracting (d) from (e) gives:

$$FV_n (1 + i) - FV_n = PMT[(1 + i)^n - 1]$$

Rearranged, this becomes:

$$i.FV_n = PMT[(1 + i)^n - 1]$$

Which leads to equation (4-11):

$$FV_n = PMT \frac{[(1 + i)^n - 1]}{i}$$

Returning to the above expression (d) for the future value:

$$FV_n = PMT[(1 + i)^{n-1} + (1 + i)^{n-2} + (1 + i)^{n-3} + \ldots + (1 + i)^1 + 1]$$

This can be written, using summation notation as equation (4a-1):

$$FV_n = PMT \left[\sum_{t=0}^{n-1} (1 + i)^t \right] \qquad \textbf{(4a-1)}$$

The summation notation (sigma, Σ) means that we are summing the factors $(1 + i)^t$ from $t = 0$ (associated with the last payment) to $t = n - 1$.

In essence, equation (4a-1) tells us that, to find the future value of an annuity, you can find the future value of each individual payment, then sum all of those individual future values to find the total future value of the annuity. However, doing so is rather tedious, which is why it is preferable to use equation (4-11).

DERIVATION OF EQUATION (4-15)

Here is a timeline representing the present value of an annuity with payments at the end of each period, for n periods:

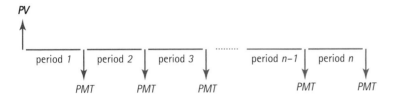

The present value of this annuity can be obtained by summing the present values of each individual annuity payment. This gives:

$$PV = PMT(1 + i)^{-1} + PMT(1 + i)^{-2} + PMT(1 + i)^{-3} \ldots + PMT(1 + i)^{-(n-1)} + PMT(1 + i)^{-n}$$

$$= PMT[(1 + i)^{-1} + (1 + i)^{-2} + (1 + i)^{-3} \ldots + (1 + i)^{-(n-1)} + (1 + i)^{-n}]$$

Multiplying and dividing the right-hand side by $(1 + i)^n$ gives:

$$PV = \frac{PMT}{(1 + i)^n} [(1 + i)^{n-1} + (1 + i)^{n-2} + (1 + i)^{n-3} \ldots + (1 + i) + 1]$$

In this equation, the square brackets contain a series that represents the future value of an annuity, as in equation (e) above, so this series can be replaced by $\{(1 + i)^n - 1\}/i$, which gives:

$$PV = \frac{PMT}{(1 + i)^n} \frac{[(1 + i)^n - 1]}{i}$$

Next, dividing the numerator and denominator of the right-hand side by $(1 + i)^n$ gives equation (4-15):

$$PV = PMT \frac{[1 - (1 + i)^{-n}]}{i}$$

Similarly to the case with the FV of an annuity, the annuity present value can be represented by summation notation, that is the sum of the present values of each individual payment, as follows:

$$PV = PMT \left[\sum_{t=1}^{n} (1/(1 + i)^t) \right]$$ **(4a-2)**

DERIVATION OF EQUATION (4-19)

In order to derive equation (4-19) it is necessary to start with the proposition that two interest rates are *identical* if they yield the same effective annual interest rate, EAR. If one rate is denoted i, compounded m times per annum, its effective rate is given by:

$$EAR = (1 + i)^m - 1$$ **(f)**

If the other rate is denoted i', compounded p times per annum, its effective rate is given by:

$$EAR = (1 + i')^p - 1$$ **(g)**

Therefore, if the two effective rates are identical:

$$(1 + i)^m = (1 + i')^p$$ **(h)**

Rearranging gives equation (4-19):

$$i = (1 + i')^{p/m} - 1$$

Note: In practical situations, this equation works successfully only where the number of contracted payments per year (p) is greater than the number of contracted compounding periods per year (m).[12]

Financial planning and analysis and working-capital management

Part **2**

Learning objectives

After reading this chapter, you should be able to:

1   Prepare and use a funds statement.
2   Prepare and use a cash-flow statement.
3   Calculate a comprehensive set of financial ratios and use them to evaluate the financial health of a company.
4   Understand the DuPont method of financial analysis.
5   Explain the limitations of ratio analysis.

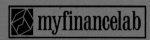

Evaluating a firm's financial performance

Chapter 5

CHAPTER PREVIEW

In this chapter the world of finance is viewed primarily as an accountant sees it. To begin, there is a review of the two basic financial statements that are used to understand how a firm is doing financially—the income statement, or what is sometimes called the profit and loss statement, and the balance sheet. A significant amount of time is also spent discussing how to measure and interpret a company's funds flows and cash flows, and how to use that information to answer important questions about a firm's financial resources and how they are being used.

Subsequently, financial statements are restated in relative terms to gain a more complete understanding about a firm's financial performance. Specifically, key financial relationships in the form of ratios are discussed. The specific relationships considered are:

- the risk that a firm will not have the needed cash to meet debt payments as they come due
- whether management is generating an attractive rate of return on the capital that has been entrusted to them
- how management chooses to finance the company
- whether the shareholders are receiving an acceptable rate of return on their investment.

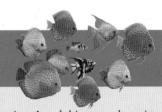

Regardless of your program

You will come across financial statements in your place of employment as well as in the financial media when company performance is discussed and analysed. Although your studies prepare you at a technical level, it is important not to lose sight of the big picture. A firm's financial statements provide a visual representation of the firm, which is used to describe the business to investors and others outside the firm as well as to the firm's employees.

Consequently, we can think of a firm's financial statements and the various terms used to describe the firm and its operations as the *language* of business. As such, everyone who becomes a manager, no matter what their area of expertise, needs to know how to 'speak business', and this means knowing how to read and interpret financial statements. For example, when the firm communicates with its banker or the investment analysts who follow the firm's share performance, financial statement results provide the common language. When the firm's top management is determining the bonuses to pay at year-end they look to the firm's financial performance as reflected in the financial statements. Moreover, progressing up the ranks of the firm's management team requires that you develop a broader understanding of the firm and how each of its components fit together. The firm's financial statements provide the key to gaining this knowledge.

Basic financial statements

Just about every financial manager spends time reviewing the firm's financial statements on a regular basis. This might seem surprising, given that finance is concerned with forward-looking decision making. However, the fact is that evaluating past performance can help to improve the firm's future profitability and efficiency, which is in line with the firm's objective of creating wealth for the owners or shareholders. This chapter shows how to 'dissect' the financial statements in a number of ways, to give more useful information than appears to be there at first glance. For example, funds-flow and cash-flow information enables managers to answer many important questions, such as how the new assets were financed, what happened to the loans that were borrowed during the year, and how the dividend payment was financed. Financial statement information can also be expressed in the form of ratios that enable managers to make useful judgements about the strength of the firm's financial structure or the efficiency of operations; for example, profit figures are more meaningful when expressed as a 'rate' of profitability (such as 10% of sales), which helps to assess trends in profitability over time and to make comparisons with rival firms.

Therefore, let's begin this chapter by reviewing the fundamental financial statements that are most familiar—the income (or profit and loss) statement and the balance sheet. These two reports are shown in Tables 5.1 and 5.2 for Jimco Ltd.

TABLE 5.1 Jimco Ltd, Balance Sheet, 30 June 20X3 ($'000)

		ASSETS	
Current assets			
Cash		$1 400	
Marketable securities—at cost			
(market value $320)		300	
Accounts receivable		10 000	
Inventories		12 000	
Prepaid expenses		300	
Total current assets			$24 000
Non-current assets			
Land		2 000	
Plant and equipment	$12 300		
Less: Accumulated depreciation	7 300		
		5 000	
Total fixed assets			7 000
Total assets			$31 000
Represented by:			
Current liabilities			
Accounts payable		$3 000	
Notes payable, 9%, due 1 September 20X3		3 400	
Accrued salaries, wages and other expenses		3 100	
Current portion of long-term debt		500	
Total current liabilities			$10 000
Deferred liabilities			
Deferred income taxes		1 500	
Mortgage, 7%, due 1 July 20X5		6 300	
Term loans, 8½%, due 31 December 20X7		2 900	
Total deferred liabilities			10 700
Total liabilities			$20 700
Shareholders' equity			
Share capital		2 100	
Retained earnings		8 200	
			$10 300
			$31 000

Back to the principles

Principle 7 warns us that there may be conflict between management and owners, especially in large firms where managers and owners have different incentives. That is, **managers won't work for owners unless it's in their best interest to do so.** Although the management is an agent of the owners, experience suggests that managers do not always act in the best interest of the owners. Thus, the firm's shareholders, as well as other providers of capital (such as bankers), have a need for information that can be used to monitor the managers' actions. Because the ordinary shareholders of large companies do not have access to internal information about the firm's operations, they must rely on public information from all sources. One of the main sources of such information is the company's financial statements, which are provided by the firm's accountants. Although this information is by no means perfect, it is an important source used by outsiders to assess a company's activities. This chapter demonstrates how to use data from the firm's public financial statements to monitor management's actions.

TABLE 5.2 Jimco Ltd, Income Statement for year ending 30 June 20X3 ($'000 except per-share data)

Net sales		$51000
Cost of goods sold		(38000)
Gross profit		13000
Operating expenses		
Selling expenses	$3100	
Depreciation expense	500	
General and administrative expense	5400	(9000)
Net operating income (NOI)		$4000
Interest expense		(1000)
Earnings before taxes (EBT)		$3000
Income taxes[a]		(900)
Net income (NI)		$2100
Disposition of net income		
Ordinary dividends		$600
Change in retained earnings		1500
Per-share data (dollars)		
Number of shares		100000 shares
Earnings per share ($2100000 ÷ 100000 shares)		$21
Dividends per share ($600000 ÷ 100000 shares)		$6

a A tax rate of 30% on all income is assumed.

Corporate and non-corporate business enterprises are required under Australian corporations law to report their financial performance and position through the use of the income statement and balance sheet as well as the statement of cash flows[1] (which will be examined in a subsequent section). These enterprises may also report a funds statement, although they are not obliged to do so by corporate law or accounting standards. However, the funds statement is a useful tool for financial analysis, so some time will be spent discussing its preparation and uses. It is prepared from information contained in the income statement and balance sheet.

Your money

YOUR PERSONAL FINANCIAL STATEMENTS

A personal balance sheet is a snapshot of your financial status at a particular point in time. It lists the assets you own and the debts, or liabilities, you owe. Your personal net worth is analogous to equity; it is equal to the difference between your assets and your liabilities. A sample balance-sheet worksheet is provided below. As you can see, it looks a lot like a business's balance sheet. A personal balance sheet is sometimes used by lenders when reviewing your loan application: the prospective lender wants to know your net worth and how it arises in order to evaluate what security you can offer, both in general and in terms of specific assets, as well as your existing debts.

Once you've prepared your personal balance sheet and identified your net worth, the next step is to trace where your money comes from and how it is spent. To do this, we put together a personal income statement that looks at both the money you take in and the money you spend. What's left over

(if anything) is like a firm's profit, the amount you have available for savings or investment, or for repaying new debt. If you're spending too much, your income statement will show you exactly where your money is going so that you can spot these problem areas quickly. With a good income statement, you'll never end another month wondering where your money went. A sample income-statement worksheet is provided below. This kind of information is, once again, used by lenders to assess how much 'spare' income you have to afford loan repayments. You, too, can use it to check your ability to save and invest to build your wealth.

YOUR PERSONAL BALANCE SHEET

ASSETS (WHAT YOU OWN)

A.	Monetary assets (bank account, etc.)	
B.	Investments	+
C.	Retirement plan investments	+
D.	Housing (market value)	+
E.	Automobiles	+
F.	Personal property	+
G.	Other assets	+
H.	Your total assets (add lines A–G)	=

LIABILITIES OR DEBT (WHAT YOU OWE)

Current Debt

I.	Current bills	
J.	Credit card debt	+

Long-term Debt

K.	Housing	
L.	Automobile loans	+
M.	Other debt	+
N.	Your total debt (add lines I–M)	=

YOUR NET WORTH

H.	Total assets	+
N.	Less: Total debt	–
O.	Equals: Your net worth	=

YOUR PERSONAL INCOME STATEMENT

YOUR TAKE-HOME PAY

A.	Total income	
B.	Total income taxes	–
C.	After-tax income available for living expenditures or take-home pay) (line A minus line B)	=

YOUR LIVING EXPENSES

D.	Total housing expenditures	
E.	Total food expenditures	+
F.	Total clothing and personal care expenditures	+
G.	Total transportation expenditures	+
H.	Total recreation expenditures	+
I.	Total medical expenditures	+
J.	Total insurance expenditures	+
K.	Total other expenditures	+
L.	Total living expenditures (add lines D–K)	=

TOTAL AVAILABLE FOR SAVINGS AND INVESTMENTS

C.	After-tax income available for living expenditures or take-home pay	
L.	Total living expenditures	–
M.	Income available for savings and investment (line C minus line L)	=

Preparing and using a funds statement

OBJECTIVE

Prepare and use a funds statement.

Although companies are not legally obliged to prepare a funds statement, they may choose to do so. If they do not do so, a funds statement can in any case be prepared by a financial analyst from the information contained in the income statement and the balance sheet.

USING FUNDS-FLOW INFORMATION

The purpose of a funds statement is to show the resources allocated to an enterprise during a specific period and the uses or applications of those resources. Specifically, the funds statement provides the basis for answering such questions as the following:

- Where did the profits go?
- Why were the dividends not larger?
- Why was money borrowed during the period?
- How was expansion in plant and equipment financed?
- How was repayment of debt accomplished?
- What became of the proceeds of the debt issue?

The funds statement is a tool of **financial analysis** because it contains useful information. Its preparation can take a number of different approaches depending on the definition adopted for 'funds'. This text uses the **'total resources' concept** of funds, meaning cash and cash equivalents (credit or barter) arising from or used in a firm's transactions with external parties. The key words are 'external parties': the firm's internal or book entries are excluded because they do not involve third parties. This concept of funds is a broad one, because it results in the disclosure of information relating to all of a firm's investing and financing activities during a period. For example, the purchase of an asset such as land may be financed by cash, by credit or by an issue of shares, and an increase in a firm's cash balance may result from increased sales, from a reduction in accounts receivable or from a new term loan. A funds statement summarises such fund flows—how funds were provided (where they came from) and how those funds were used or applied.

financial analysis
The assessment of a firm's financial condition or well-being. Its objectives are to determine the firm's financial strengths and to identify its weaknesses. The primary tool of financial analysis is the financial ratio.

'total resources' concept
A concept of funds, meaning cash and cash equivalents (credit or barter), arising from or used in a firm's transactions with external parties.

SOURCES OF FUNDS

The firm can obtain funds from one of four principal sources:

1. From its operations (commonly referred to as 'funds provided by operations')
2. By borrowing
3. By the sale of assets
4. By issuing shares

The firm's sources of funds (with the exception of funds provided by operations) and uses of funds can be identified by observing changes in the balance sheet between the beginning and the end of the relevant period, as follows:

SOURCES OF FUNDS	USES OF FUNDS
decrease in asset	increase in asset
increase in liability	decrease in liability
increase in equity	decrease in equity

For example, a decrease in the asset 'accounts receivable' over the period signals that the firm collected more dollars from its debtors than it created through new credit sales; hence, this is an overall source of funds. In general, a decrease in an asset balance denotes a source of funds. On the other hand, an increase in a liability account signals that new net additional borrowing took place during the period, thus providing a source of funds to the firm. An increase in the firm's equity (share capital) also indicates a source of funds to the firm.

FUNDS FROM OPERATIONS

Although the changes in assets, liabilities and equity can be analysed by comparing successive balance sheets, *funds from operations* are determined by analysing the income statement. The starting point is net income for the period, which represents a source of funds. However, under accrual accounting principles, some expenses (and maybe some revenue items) do not actually involve any cash flows—they are just book entries—and so they are called *non-cash expenses*. An example is depreciation expense, which is just the outcome of a book entry in the firm's records. (For those familiar with double-entry bookkeeping, there is a debit to the depreciation expense account and a corresponding credit to the accumulated depreciation account.) Therefore, depreciation expense does not involve any funds flow; it is just an internal book entry—there is no external party involved in the transaction. Example 5.1 clarifies the computation of funds from operations by adjusting net income for non-cash expenses such as depreciation.

EXAMPLE 5.1 Determining funds from operations by adjusting net income for non-cash expenses

Companies A and B have the following income statements:

	COMPANY A	COMPANY B
Cash sales	$100000	$100000
Less: Cost of sales (cash)	$60000	$60000
Less: Cash expenses	$10000	$22000
Less: Depreciation expense	$12000	—
Net income	$18000	$18000

For Company B, the net income of $18000 is the same as the net cash flow (or funds flow) from operations. This is because all revenues and expenses are in cash. However, in the case of Company A, net income is $18000, whereas cash (or funds) from operations is $30000. This is because the final expense item, depreciation $12000, is a book entry and so does not involve any cash flow.

Another way of determining funds from operations, for firms like Company A, is to *add back* to net income the non-cash expenses such as depreciation:

	COMPANY A
Cash sales	$100000
Less: Cost of sales (cash)	$60000
Less: Cash expenses	$10000
Less: Depreciation expense	$12000
Net income	$18000
Add back non-cash expense (depreciation)	$12000
Funds from operations	$30000

In other words, starting with a firm's reported net income, funds from operations can be determined by adding-back to net income the non-cash expenses such as depreciation.

USES OF FUNDS

A firm uses funds to purchase assets, to repay loans, to repurchase shares and to pay cash dividends to shareholders. Thus, uses of funds are just the opposite of the sources discussed earlier.

For example, raising debt is a source of funds, whereas repaying a debt is a use. Example 5.2 illustrates the computation of sources and uses of funds for Jimco Ltd.

EXAMPLE 5.2 Preparation of the funds statement for Jimco Ltd

TABLE 5.3 Jimco Ltd, Comparative Balance Sheets, 30 June 20X2 and 20X3 ($'000)

	ASSETS		
	20X2	20X3	CHANGES
Current assets			
Cash	$1 500	$1 400	$(100)
Marketable securities	300	300	—
Accounts receivable	8 500	10 000	1 500
Inventories	11 300	12 000	700
Prepaid expenses	200	300	100
Total current assets	$21 800	$24 000	$2 200
Non-current assets			
Land	$2 000	$2 000	$ —
Plant and equipment	11 200	12 300	1 100
Less: Accumulated depreciation	(6 800)	(7 300)	(500)
Net plant and equipment	4 400	5 000	600
Total non-current assets	6 400	7 000	600
Total assets	$28 200	$31 000	$2 800
Current liabilities			
Accounts payable	$3 200	$3 000	$(200)
Notes payable	900	3 400	2 500
Accrued salaries, wages and other expenses	3 800	3 100	(700)
Current portion of long-term debt	500	500	—
Total current liabilities	$8 400	$10 000	$1 600
Deferred liabilities			
Deferred income taxes	$1 400	$1 500	$100
Mortgage	6 600	6 300	(300)
Term loans	3 000	2 900	(100)
Total deferred liabilities	$11 000	$10 700	$(300)
Owner's equity			
Share capital	$2 100	$2 100	—
Retained earnings	6 700	8 200	1 500
Total equity	$8 800	$10 300	$1 500
Total liabilities and equity	$28 200	$31 000	$2 800

Jimco's comparative balance sheets for 20X2 and 20X3 are given in Table 5.3. These statements, along with Jimco's 20X3 income statement (Table 5.2), provide all the information needed to prepare the firm's funds statement for the year ended 30 June 20X3. The column entitled 'changes' in Table 5.3 provides the basis for determining Jimco's sources and uses of funds; in this column, any item that decreased between 20X2 and 20X3 is shown in brackets. Looking first at the assets, we can see that cash decreased by $100 000 during the year, which represents a use of funds. Marketable securities did not change; thus no source or use of funds was provided. The accounts receivable balance increased by $1 500 000, indicating that more credit sales were made during the period than were collected. Hence, the firm used funds to invest in accounts receivable. Inventories and prepaid expenses increased by $700 000 and $100 000 respectively, also indicating uses of funds. In addition, Jimco increased plant and equipment by $1 100 000, which constitutes still another use of funds.[2] Note that the $500000 increase in accumulated depreciation represents net depreciation expense for the period, which is considered later when the firm's income statement is analysed.

Looking next at the changes in the firm's liabilities, it can be seen that accounts payable decreased by $200000. This indicates that the firm paid off more accounts payable than it created during the year. This constitutes a use of funds. Notes payable increased by $2500000, signalling a source of funds from short-term borrowing. The accrued salaries, wages and other expense accounts decreased by $700000 during the period, which indicates a use of funds. Deferred income taxes increased by $100000 (source). Both the loan on the mortgage and the term loans decreased for the period, by $300000 and $100000 respectively. Both decreases constitute uses of funds for the period. The share capital account did not change for the period, indicating that no new shares were issued. However, Jimco's retained earnings increased by $1500000. This represents the net income for 20X3 of $2100000, less ordinary share dividends of $600000. The dividend payment is counted as a use of funds. But the net income is included as a source of funds within *funds provided by operations*.

To summarise, sources and uses of funds are determined by analysing the changes in the balance sheet accounts between two points in time (e.g. between 30 June 20X2 and 30 June 20X3). However, the change in retained earnings is not included directly in the statement. Because the change in retained earnings equals net income less dividends paid, these latter items are instead listed separately.

Table 5.4 contains Jimco's funds statement for the year ended 30 June 20X3. Note that the change in accumulated depreciation is disregarded in the balance sheet; rather, the net depreciation expense for the year is shown as an adjustment when determining funds from operations. Also, as noted above, the change in retained earnings is not included directly in the funds statement; instead, net income and dividends paid are shown separately.

Further analysis of Jimco's funds statement reveals that the main sources of funds were from operations (49%) and notes payable (47%). The firm's main uses of funds related to the purchase of plant and equipment (21%), increases in accounts receivable (28%) and inventories (13%), and accrued expenses (13%). Thus, the funds statement provides the analyst with a useful tool for determining *where the firm obtained funds* during a prior period and *how the funds were spent*.

TABLE 5.4 Jimco Ltd, Funds Statement for the year ended 30 June 20X3 ($'000)

Sources of funds			
Funds provided by operations:			
Net income	$2 100		
Depreciation	500	$2 600	49%
Increase in deferred income taxes		100	2
Increase in notes payable		2 500	47
Decrease in cash balance		100	2
Total funds provided		$5 300	100%
Uses of funds			
Dividends		$600	11%
Purchase of plant and equipment		1 100	21
Increase in accounts receivable		1 500	28
Increase in inventories		700	13
Increase in prepaid expenses		100	2
Decrease in accounts payable		200	4
Decrease in accrued salaries, wages and other expenses		700	13
Decrease in mortgage		300	6
Decrease in term loans		100	2
Total use of funds		$5 300	100%

Concept check

5.1   How does determination of *funds from operations* differ from determination of other sources and uses of funds?

5.2   If the balance sheet item 'plant and machinery' increased during the year, is this a source or a use of funds?

5.3   If the balance of the 'mortgage loan' account increased by $50 000, is this a source or a use of funds?

For answers go to MyFinanceLab or
www.pearson.com.au/9781442539174

ONE STEP FURTHER

THE 'HEDGING PRINCIPLE'

The time-matching or **hedging principle** basically states that, ideally, short-term uses of funds should be financed from short-term sources of funds, and long-term uses of funds should be financed from long-term sources of funds. For example, trade credit should be used to finance inventory, but the purchase of plant and equipment should be funded from long-term sources and not from a short-term source such as trade credit or a bank overdraft. The misuse of short-term funds can be a cause of a firm's difficulties, especially for small and medium-size enterprises. According to accountants: 'Time after time we see short-term funds used for the acquisition of long-term assets—it's incredible.'

Owing to the usefulness of the hedging principle for analysis of whether or not funds flows are time matched, it is useful to rearrange the funds statement into a format that shows changes in current assets and current liabilities in a column for short-term sources and uses of funds. Changes in all other assets and liabilities and funds from operations are placed in a column for long-term sources and uses. This is done here for Jimco's funds statement.

hedging principle
A working-capital management policy which states that the cash-flow-generating characteristics of a firm's investments should be matched with the cash-flow requirements of the firm's sources of financing. Very simply, short-lived assets should be financed with short-term sources of financing, while long-lived assets should be financed with long-term sources of financing.

	SHORT-TERM ('000)	LONG-TERM ('000)	TOTAL ('000)
Sources of funds			
Funds provided by operations		$2 600	$2 600
Increase in deferred taxes		100	100
Increase in notes payable	$2 500		2 500
Decrease in cash balance	100		100
	$2 600	$2 700	$5 300
Uses of funds			
Dividends		$600	$600
Purchase of plant and equipment		1 100	1 100
Increase in accounts receivable	$1 500		1 500
Incease in inventories	700		700
Increase in prepaid expenses	100		100
Decrease in accounts payable	200		200
Decrease in accrued salaries, wages and other expenses	700		700
Decrease in mortgage		300	300
Decrease in term loans		100	100
	$3 200	$2 100	$5 300
Excess of short-term uses	$600		
Excess of long-term sources		$600	

A funds statement using the all-resources concept of funds should always balance; total sources should equal uses for a given period. However, often this will not be the case in the short-term and long-term columns. It can be seen for Jimco that, on the long-term side, sources have exceeded uses by $600 000, whereas short-term uses exceed short-term sources by $600 000. The excess long-term funds have been used to finance an increase in working capital (current assets less current liabilities) of $600 000. Whether or not this is a wise course of action requires more information and analysis. For example, the major increase in working capital is $1 500 000 in accounts receivable. On the other hand, accounts payable have decreased by $200 000. If the firm's sales are increasing, it would be expected that accounts receivable would rise, but so should the spontaneous funding from accounts payable. The overall liquidity and profitability of Jimco will be evaluated later when ratio analysis is considered.

The hedging principle will be discussed in more detail in Chapter 7.

International spotlight

HARMONISING INTERNATIONAL FINANCIAL REPORTING

What happens when a global company is trying to determine its overall financial position and profitability? You might think the company's accountants just add together the profits of the various divisions around the globe. Unfortunately, it's not that simple. First, the financial data from different countries have to be converted into a common currency. For example, if a US company has a division in Australia, the Australian income statement and balance sheet data have to be converted into US dollars so that the US head office can meaningfully add together the dollars of the two different countries. So, if the relevant exchange rate is 1 Australian dollar equals 0.9 US dollar, a profit of A$10 million earned in Australia would represent US$9 million.

There is a second problem, one that is more significant and might surprise the non-accountant: if the Australian profits had been measured using US accounting principles, the Australian profit figure would most likely have been something other than A$10 million. The reason for this is that, for many years, different countries' accounting bodies have adopted different guidelines (called *accounting standards*) for measuring profits, assets and liabilities. The problem of different accounting standards is so acute that it has been estimated that Vodafone's 2004 net loss of £9 billion would have been the equivalent of a profit of £6 billion under US standards.[3]

This type of problem is of concern to both the investor and the financial analyst. How can a financial analyst meaningfully compare firms in different countries if their financial reports are prepared according to different standards? Fortunately, some sort of resolution is on the horizon. The International Accounting Standards Board (IASB), which is supported by the accounting professions of more than 100 countries (including Australia and members of the European Union (EU)), introduced uniform standards on 1 January 2005. These standards are known as International Accounting Standards (IAS). However, financial reporting in the United States is governed by the Financial Accounting Standards Board (FASB), which so far has gone its own way. Recently, however, the IASB and the FASB have taken steps towards working together with the intention of creating a common set of accounting standards.

But, even if the world's accounting professions can agree on common standards, political interference might mean that moves to uniformity will be thwarted when it comes to making the standards legally binding. For example, in October 2004 the EU watered down the IASB's proposal for IAS 39 (which deals with the accounting treatment of financial derivatives). In response, the regulators in some individual countries stated that they would follow the original recommendations of the IASB rather than the EU's version. Similarly, in the United States regulators had intervened to weaken the FASB's recommended accounting treatment for employee stock options, a high-profile area following the collapse of Enron Corporation. Furthermore, in 2010, both the FASB and the IASB had disagreements among professions in many member countries over accounting for financial instruments, which became a prominent issue after the GFC (when criticism was levelled at 'fair value accounting' that compelled organisations to report the decline in value of securities as a loss, a situation that would have been avoided (or, at least postponed) under historic cost accounting).

The statement of cash flows

OBJECTIVE **2**

Prepare and use a cash-flow statement.

Back to the principles

Principle 3 tells us that **Cash—not profits—is king**. In many respects, cash is more important than profits. Thus, this section of the chapter spends some time discussing how to measure cash flows.

The *statement of cash flows* reports the cash inflows and outflows during a specific period. It provides more details of cash flows than the funds statement. *Cash* means cash on hand and cash equivalents.[4] As with the funds statement, the flows result from transactions that are external to the firm.

USES OF CASH-FLOW INFORMATION

Cash-flow information may assist in assessing the ability of a firm to:

- generate cash flows in the future
- meet its financial commitments as they fall due, including the servicing of debt and the payment of dividends
- finance changes in the scope and nature of its operations
- obtain external finance where necessary.

CLASSIFICATION OF CASH FLOWS

It is useful to classify the statement of cash flows into operating activities, investing activities and financing activities. *Operating activities* relate to the provision of goods and services, such as payments to suppliers and receipts from customers. *Investing activities* relate to transactions involving non-current assets and financial investments (excluding investments regarded as part of *cash*). *Financing activities* relate to transactions that change the size and composition of the financial or debt structure, and the payment of the costs of finance (dividends, debt interest and principal payments).

A statement of cash flows for Jimco is shown in Table 5.5 using the classification discussed. A review of the statement indicates that the firm realised an $800 000 surplus cash flow from

TABLE 5.5   Jimco Ltd, Statement of Cash Flows for year ended 30 June 20X3 ('000)

Cash flows from operating activities		
Receipts from customers	$49 500	
Payments to suppliers	(38 900)	
Expenses paid	(9 300)	
Income taxes paid	(800)	
Net cash provided by operating activities		$500
Cash flows from investing activities		
Payment for plant and equipment	(1 100)	
Net cash from investing activities		(1 100)
Cash flows from financing activities		
Increase in notes payable	2 500	
Decrease in mortgage	(300)	
Decrease in term loans	(100)	
Dividends paid	(600)	
Interest paid	(1 000)	
Net cash provided by financing activities		500
Net increase (decrease) in cash held		(100)
Cash at 1 July 20X2		1 500
Cash balance at 30 June 20X3		$1 400

its financing activities, and $200000 from operations, which in total was $100000 less than the cash outflow for the investment in plant and equipment ($1 100000).

The method used to prepare Table 5.5 is called the *direct method*, which obtains the cash-flow information from the accounts of Jimco. It is also possible to use the *indirect method* to complete a statement of cash flows. This method begins with net income and then adds back all expenses that do not result in cash flows for the period. If you have access to the cash records of a firm, there is no need to use the indirect method. However, an external analyst can use the indirect approach from data in the income statement and balance sheet, in much the same way as the funds statement was prepared. This method is illustrated below for Jimco Ltd.

	$'000	
Net income (from the statement of income)[a]		$2 100
Add (deduct) to reconcile net income to net cash flow		
Increase in accounts receivable	$(1 500)	
Increase in inventories	(700)	
Increase in prepaid expenses	(100)	
Depreciation expense	500	
Decrease in accounts payable	(200)	
Decrease in accrued wages	(700)	
Increase in deferred income taxes	100	(2 600)
Net cash flow provided by operations		(500)
Add (deduct) non-operating cash items		
Purchase of plant and equipment	(1 100)	
Increase in notes payable	2 500	
Decrease in mortgage	(300)	
Decrease in term loans	(100)	
Dividends paid	(600)	400
Net increase (decrease) in cash held		(100)
Cash at 1 July 20X2		1 500
Cash balance at 30 June 20X3		$1 400

a The net cash from operating activities under the direct method (Table 5.5) was $500000, and $1000000 for interest paid was shown as a financing activity. Under the indirect method the interest is not shown as a separate item, but has reduced net income to $2100000. Thus the amount of cash derived from operations under the indirect method is $500000 ($1000000 interest less $500000 cash from operations).

The following additional information should be provided with a statement of cash flows:

1. A reconciliation of cash flows from operating activities with reported operating income after income tax
2. Details of the acquisition and disposal of entities
3. Details of external non-cash financing and investing activities
4. Details of credit standby facilities, and used and unused loan facilities.

The addition of this information means that the user can extract information which otherwise would have been available in a funds statement. Nevertheless, the preparation of a funds statement by an analyst is still useful because all relevant funds information is presented in one overview, rather than in the statement of cash flows and additional notes. Also, the time-matching concept can be applied to the funds statement.

Concept check

5.4 Why is cash flow during a period not necessarily the same as net income for that period?
5.5 If you only have access to the published financial statements of a firm, what method must you use to estimate cash flows for the period?

For answers go to MyFinanceLab or
www.pearson.com.au/9781442539174

Evaluating financial performance through ratio analysis

OBJECTIVE 3

Financial ratios join the funds statement as a useful way of analysing the performance and stability of a firm. In particular, financial ratios give the analyst a way of making meaningful comparisons of a firm's financial data at different points in time. For example, the firm can see if its management of accounts receivables appears to be getting better or worse over successive periods. Ratios can also be used to make comparisons with other firms. For example, although the inventories for a firm with $10 million in annual sales would be expected to be larger than those for a comparable firm with sales of only $5 million, the *ratio* of sales to inventory might be similar for the two firms. Thus, this ratio is used to *standardise* the inventories data in a way that enables meaningful comparisons to be made.

Calculate a comprehensive set of financial ratios and use them to evaluate the financial health of a company.

USING FINANCIAL RATIOS

Financial ratios provide useful tools for analysis when compared against a standard or norm. Two such norms are commonly used. The first consists of similar ratios for the same firm, from previous financial statements. In other words, ratios computed from the most recent financial statements are compared with previous ratios. An analysis based on comparisons of this type is commonly referred to as a **trend analysis**. A second norm comes from the ratios of other firms that are considered comparable in their general characteristics with the subject firm, for example firms in the same industry and of comparable size. The firm's ratios are compared with the industry-average ratios in order to form an opinion about how well the firm is faring relative to its competitors.

trend analysis
An analysis of a firm's financial ratios over time.

For this discussion let us assume that Jimco Ltd manufactures and sells light-duty agricultural equipment. The firm has been in business for more than 20 years and is considered by its competitors to be well managed. Later in this chapter a set of financial ratios will be computed for Jimco, using the 20X2–20X3 financial statements (Jimco's balance sheet and income statement were presented in Tables 5.1 and 5.2).[5] Jimco's ratios will then be compared with the published, standard ratios for the farm machinery and equipment manufacturing industry, which are presented in Table 5.6.[6]

Table 5.6 presents balance sheet and income statement data, classified by firm size to provide the basis for more meaningful comparisons. Thus, a firm with total assets of less than $500 000 would not be compared with firms having a much larger asset base. These **financial statements** are presented on a **common-size** basis: the common-size balance sheet simply represents each asset, liability and owner's equity account as a percentage of total assets, whereas each entry in the common-size income statement is given as a percentage of sales. Common-sizing normalises the data so that firms of different sizes can be compared; for example, if company A's gross profit ratio is 28%, and company B's ratio is 20%, we can reasonably conclude that A is performing better than B, a conclusion that could not be drawn validly if A's gross profit of $1 million was compared with B's gross profit of $2 million.

common-size financial statements
Financial statements that have been converted to a percentage of either sales in the case of the income statement or total assets in the case of the balance sheet. The information within the common-size statements is standardised and consequently can be used to compare firms of very different sizes.

Table 5.6 also presents 16 key ratios. These ratios are drawn from the entries in the balance sheet and income statement. Furthermore, three levels are reported for each of the key ratios. These refer to the first, second and third quartiles. Thus, the analyst is given some idea of how much variation exists within the industry in regard to each ratio.

Financial ratios provide the basis for answering four important questions concerning the financial well-being of the firm.

1. How liquid is the firm?
2. Is management generating sufficient operating profits on the firm's assets?
3. How is the firm financing its investments?
4. Are the owners (shareholders) receiving an adequate return on their investment?

Let's look at each of these questions in turn.

| **TABLE 5.6** | Hypothetical industry-average ratios |

	MANUFACTURERS' FARM MACHINERY & EQUIPMENT			
ASSET SIZE	0–500M[a]	500M–2MM	2–10MM	10–50MM
NUMBER OF STATEMENTS[b]	14	28	41	21
Assets	%	%	%	%
Cash and equivalents	8.5	6.0	4.4	6.4
Trade receivables (net)	22.5	17.4	19.0	30.3
Inventory	44.4	48.2	44.4	34.9
All other current	0.2	2.1	1.6	1.6
Total current	75.5	73.7	69.4	73.2
Fixed assets (net)	22.9	21.3	22.9	17.7
Intangibles (net)	0.9	0.5	0.7	1.0
All other non-current	0.7	4.5	7.0	8.1
Total assets	100.0	100.0	100.0	100.0
Liabilities				
Notes payable—short term	11.1	14.0	14.5	13.8
Current maturity—LTD	2.8	4.0	3.3	3.0
Trade payables	20.7	14.7	11.5	9.1
Income taxes payable	1.0	0.5	1.0	0.4
All other current	8.2	8.9	8.2	0.6
Total current	44.0	42.2	38.4	36.9
Long-term debt	17.8	15.4	17.9	14.4
Deferred taxes	0.0	0.1	0.9	0.8
All other non-current	4.8	3.0	2.1	2.8
Net worth	33.4	39.3	40.7	45.1
Total liabilities and net worth	100.0	100.0	100.0	100.0
Income data				
Net sales	100.0	100.0	100.0	100.0
Gross profit	29.2	31.1	28.9	26.7
Operating expenses	24.7	24.8	22.0	17.9
Operating profit	4.5	6.3	6.9	8.9
All other expenses (net)	1.6	2.7	2.6	2.0
Profit before taxes	2.9	3.6	4.3	6.9
RATIOS[c]				

RATIOS[c]								
Current		2.3		2.8		2.5		3.2
		1.7		2.0		1.8		2.0
		1.6		1.1		1.4		1.7
Quick		0.9		1.0		1.1		1.6
		0.6		0.5		0.5		1.1
		0.4		0.3		0.4		0.6
Sales/Receivables[d]	13	27.2	12	30.3	24	15.1	41	8.8
	26	13.9	22	16.4	37	10.0	63	5.8
	35	10.5	43	8.5	49	7.5	111	3.3
Cost of sales/Inventory[e]	47	7.7	73	5.0	76	4.8	69	5.3
	61	6.0	126	2.9	126	2.9	101	3.6
	96	3.8	174	2.1	183	2.0	159	2.3
Cost of sales/Payables	6	56.5	11	33.2	17	21.7	20	18.5
	27	13.3	24	15.3	26	13.9	28	12.9
	62	5.9	51	7.1	46	7.9	37	10.0
Sales/Working capital		5.4		4.5		3.7		2.4
		9.6		7.6		6.1		4.6
		16.2		67.4		9.6		7.0

ASSET SIZE		0–500M[a]		500M–2MM		2–10MM		10–50MM
NUMBER OF STATEMENTS[b]		14		28		41		21
EBIT/Interest[f]	(13)	7.5 3.8 1.4	(26)	5.0 3.0 1.5	(40)	4.3 2.3 1.3	(20)	9.5 2.4 1.7
Net profit + depreciation, depletion, amortisation/Currently maturing long-term debt			(16)	5.1 1.9 0.7	(34)	3.6 2.5 1.0	(13)	49.0 4.4 1.8
Fixed/Worth		0.3 0.5 1.5		0.2 0.6 1.1		0.3 0.6 0.9		0.2 0.3 0.6
Debt/Worth		1.0 1.7 3.5		0.7 1.8 4.0		0.8 1.5 2.8		0.7 1.0 3.6
% Profit before taxes/Tangible net worth	(13)	55.6 33.1 8.1	(27)	50.7 21.2 8.3	(40)	30.7 17.5 3.6		34.5 21.0 10.5
% Profit before taxes/Total assets		22.4 7.2 3.3		15.3 9.2 1.9		11.7 7.7 1.4		15.3 8.7 3.9
Sales/Net fixed assets		43.2 14.1 6.9		28.4 10.7 6.6		16.0 9.4 5.0		19.6 9.8 7.1
Sales/Total assets		4.4 3.4 1.8		2.7 2.2 1.6		2.4 1.6 1.3		2.0 1.4 1.1
% Depreciation, depletion, amortisation/Sales	(12)	1.1 1.6 3.1	(26)	0.9 1.3 3.1	(40)	0.9 1.7 2.6	(20)	1.0 1.6 2.6
% Officers' compensation/Sales			(13)	1.3 5.9 11.9				
Net sales ($)		12032M		66780M		347880M		809740M
Total assets ($)		4235M		30715M		189788M		517151M

a   M = $ thousand; MM = $ million.

b   When there are fewer than 10 financial statements for a particular size category, the composite data are not shown in that category because such a small sample is usually not representative and could be misleading.

c   Three ratio values are reported. The middle value is the median and represents the ratio falling halfway between the strongest ratio and the weakest ratio. The figure that falls halfway between the median and the strongest ratio is the upper quartile and the figure that falls halfway between the median and the weakest ratio is the lower quartile.

d   The columns in bold type are 'days' receivables' or average collection period.

e   The columns in bold type are 'days' inventory' or the average number of days that a dollar is held in inventory.

f   Numbers in brackets refer to the number of firms for which the relevant rates are computed.

FYI

Mathematically a financial ratio is nothing more than a ratio whose numerator and denominator are comprised of financial data. The objective in using a ratio when analysing financial information is simply to standardise the information being analysed so that comparisons can be made between ratios of different firms or the same firm at different points in time.

So keep this in mind as you read through the discussion of financial ratios.

All we are doing is trying to standardise financial data so that we can make comparisons with industry norms or other standards.

QUESTION 1: HOW LIQUID IS THE FIRM?

Liquidity ratios provide the basis for answering two questions: *Does the firm have sufficient cash and near-cash assets to pay its bills on time? How quickly does the firm convert its liquid assets (accounts receivable and inventory) into cash?*

Current liabilities represent the firm's financial obligations that will be maturing in the short term (within the coming year). The firm's ability to repay these obligations when due depends largely on whether it has sufficient cash, together with other assets, that can be converted into cash before the current liabilities mature. The firm's current assets are the primary sources of funds needed to repay current and maturing financial obligations. Thus, the current ratio is a logical measure of liquidity.

Current ratio

The **current ratio** is computed for Jimco as follows:

$$\text{Current ratio} = \frac{\text{current assets}}{\text{current liabilities}} \qquad (5\text{-}1)$$

$$= \frac{\$24\,000\,000}{\$10\,000\,000} = 2.40 \text{ times}$$

Industry average = 2.0 times

For the year ended 30 June 20X3, Jimco's current assets were 2.40 times larger than its current liabilities. Although no firm plans deliberately to liquidate a major portion of its current assets to meet its matching current liabilities, this ratio does indicate the margin of safety (the liquidity) of the firm.

Using the industry norms provided in Table 5.6, note that Jimco has between $10 million and $50 million in total assets; thus the fourth-column figures are appropriate. Jimco's current ratio is higher than the median industry ratio of 2. In addition, Jimco's 2.40 current ratio falls well within the range of the first and third quartile of 1.7 to 3.2 observed for its industry. Thus, Jimco's current ratio is *not out of line* with the current ratios of many of the firms in its industry.

Acid-test or quick ratio

Because inventories are generally the least liquid of the firm's assets, a more precise assessment of liquidity may be obtained by excluding inventories from the numerator of the current ratio. For Jimco, the 20X3 **acid-test ratio** is computed as follows:

$$\text{Acid-test ratio} = \frac{\text{current assets} - \text{inventories}}{\text{current liabilities}} \qquad (5\text{-}2)$$

$$= \frac{\$12\,000\,000}{\$10\,000\,000}$$

$$= 1.20 \text{ times}$$

Industry average = 1.1 times

Jimco's acid-test ratio is again higher than the median ratio for its industry of 1.1. Thus, on the basis of its current and acid-test ratios, Jimco offers no visible evidence of a liquidity problem.

In essence, comparing current assets and current liabilities measures solvency (i.e. the excess of the value of the assets of a firm over its liabilities).[7] This approach has long been used by financial analysts.

An additional insight about liquidity is gained by ascertaining how quickly a firm can convert its accounts receivable and inventory into cash. The ratios used in this approach are now shown; they can be called 'efficiency' ratios, because they provide a basis for assessing how effectively a firm is using its resources in generating sales.

Average collection period

The **average-collection-period ratio** serves as the basis for determining how rapidly the firm's credit accounts (receivables) are being collected. The lower this number, other things being the same, the more efficient the firm is in managing its investment in accounts receivable, as a low number indicates that receivables are being collected promptly. The average collection period is obtained by dividing the accounts receivable balance by the firm's average daily credit sales. Computing the ratio for Jimco, we find:

average-collection-period ratio
Provides a basis for determining how rapidly the firm's accounts are being collected; alternatively, the 'accounts receivable turnover ratio'.

$$\text{Average collection period} = \frac{\text{accounts receivable}}{\text{annual credit sales}/365} \qquad \textbf{(5-3)}$$

$$= \frac{\$10\,000\,000}{\$51\,000\,000/365}$$

$$= 70.6$$

Industry average = 63 days

On average, Jimco collects its credit sales every 71 days.

Accounts-receivable-turnover ratio

This ratio is based on the same information and is therefore interchangeable with the average-collection-period ratio. For Jimco this ratio is:

$$\text{Accounts receivable turnover} = \frac{\text{credit sales}}{\text{accounts receivable}} \qquad \textbf{(5-4)}$$

$$= \frac{\$51\,000\,000}{\$10\,000\,000}$$

$$= 5.10 \text{ times}$$

Industry average = 5.8 times

Thus, Jimco is turning its accounts receivable over at a rate of 5.10 times per year, which translates into an average collection period of 71 days. That is, if Jimco's receivables turnover is 5.10 times in a 365-day year, then its average collection period must be 365/5.10 = 71.6 days.

The industry norm for the receivables turnover ratio is 5.8 times, which translates into an average collection period of 365/5.8 = 63 days. Jimco's ratios are well within the first and third quartiles for its industry, so there is no evidence of slow-paying accounts, the existence of which would call for added analysis.[8]

Inventory turnover

Other things being the same, a firm is regarded as being more efficient in its use of inventories if it turns its stock over on a frequent basis. The importance of this is obvious for a business that sells, say, fresh food. But the same principle applies for most firms. For example, if a furniture retailer can sell 12 sofas a year that are the same as the display model held on the showroom floor, the firm is likely to be more profitable than a competitor that sells only three per year.

The way in which inventory turnover is determined is as follows:

$$\text{Inventory turnover} = \frac{\text{cost of goods sold}}{\text{inventories}} \qquad \text{(5-5)}$$

$$= \frac{\$38\,000\,000}{\$12\,000\,000}$$

$$= 3.17 \text{ times}$$

$$\text{Industry average} = 3.6 \text{ times}$$

Thus, Jimco turns over its inventories 3.17 times per year. Note that cost-of-sales figures are used in the numerator so as to measure the amount of the sales made at cost price; they are therefore in the same units as inventory (which is also carried in the accounts at cost price).[9]

Jimco's **inventory-turnover ratio** of 3.17 compares quite well with the industry norm of 3.6 times, although Jimco's lower ratio means that it invests slightly more in inventories per dollar of sales than does the average firm in its industry.

To summarise, Jimco's liquidity situation is not substantially out of line with the industry norms. Its current ratio and acid-test ratio are greater than those for the industry, although its average collection period for accounts receivable is eight days longer and its inventory turnover is somewhat slower.

Using financial ratio analysis to improve a firm's cash management

If financial ratios are out of step with industry norms or are showing unsatisfactory trends, the firm's managers are alerted to the need for corrective action. Often, weaknesses in one or a number of ratios will signal weaknesses in other financial data. For example, a firm's cash position is dependent on a number of factors, including profitability and efficiency in managing working capital. A firm's cash position might be strained if its inventory turnover and accounts receivable management are poorly controlled, as signalled by adverse movements in the relevant ratios. It follows that improvements in such ratios might ease the cash position.

Consider the *inventory-turnover ratio*. This is a critical performance indicator for firms like wholesalers and retailers, because these firms earn profits by acquiring inventories and reselling them at a profit. For example, suppose you are working for a large chain of retail department stores such as David Jones or Target. You see that inventory turnover in the just-released financial statements has declined from last year's figure of 5.5 times to 5.0 times. The latest ratio is based on the following figures:

$$\text{Inventory turnover} = \frac{\text{cost of goods sold}}{\text{inventories}} = \frac{\$400\,000\,000}{\$80\,000\,000} = 5.0 \text{ times}$$

Now suppose that the firm can implement a series of strategies to boost turnover to the previous level of 5.5. Rearranging this ratio:

$$\text{Inventories} = \frac{\text{cost of goods sold}}{\text{inventory turnover}} = \frac{\$400\,000\,000}{5.5} = \$72\,727\,000$$

Such a reduction in inventories, from $80 000 000 to $72 727 000, would decrease the amount of financing needed to carry these inventories. In effect, this liberates about $7 million in funds for use elsewhere and takes pressure away from the firm's strained cash position.

QUESTION 2: IS MANAGEMENT GENERATING SUFFICIENT OPERATING PROFITS?

Financial ratios should also be used to assess the effectiveness of the firm's management of its resources to produce profits. A firm generates profits from its operating decisions and also from

inventory-turnover ratio
Cost of goods sold divided by inventory; a ratio that measures the number of times a firm's inventories are sold and replaced during the year. This ratio reflects the relative liquidity of inventories.

its financing decisions. This section considers operating profitability (i.e. before the company's financing costs have been deducted from income).

For discussion purposes, operating profit ratios will be divided into two groups: operating profitability in relation to sales, and operating profitability in relation to investment in assets.

Operating profitability in relation to sales

These ratios can be used to assess the ability of the firm's management to control the various expenses involved in generating sales. Profit ratios discussed here are commonly referred to as **profit margins** and include the gross profit margin and the operating profit margin.

The **gross profit margin** is calculated as follows:

$$\text{Gross profit margin} = \frac{\text{gross profit}}{\text{net sales}} \qquad \textbf{(5-6)}$$

$$= \frac{\$13\,000\,000}{\$51\,000\,000}$$

$$= 0.255, \text{ or } 25.5\%$$

Industry average = 26.7%

Thus, Jimco's gross profit constitutes 25.5% of sales. This margin reflects the firm's markup on its cost of goods sold as well as the ability of management to minimise the firm's cost of goods sold in relation to sales. The common-size income statement found in Table 5.6 provides an industry norm of 26.7%. Thus, Jimco's gross profit margin does not appear to be out of line.

Moving down Jimco's income statement, the next profit figure encountered is net operating income, NOI (sometimes known as EBIT, 'earnings before interest and taxes'). This profit figure serves as the basis for computing the **operating profit margin**. For Jimco this profit margin is found as follows:

$$\text{Operating profit margin} = \frac{\text{net operating income}}{\text{sales}} \qquad \textbf{(5-7)}$$

$$= \frac{\$4\,000\,000}{\$51\,000\,000}$$

$$= 0.0784, \text{ or } 7.84\%$$

Industry average = 8.9%

The operating profit margin reflects the firm's operating expenses as well as its cost of goods sold. Therefore, this ratio serves as an overall measure of operating effectiveness. Again, the industry norm is obtained from the common-size income statement in Table 5.6. Jimco's operating profit margin is slightly lower than the industry norm of 8.9%. Thus, Jimco's operating expenses per dollar of sales were slightly higher than the industry norm.

Operating profitability in relation to investment

This category of profitability ratios attempts to measure the firm's profits in relation to the invested funds used to generate those profits. Thus, these ratios are very useful in assessing the overall effectiveness of the firm's management of its assets.

The **operating income return on investment** reflects the rate of return (before interest and taxes) on the firm's total investment. For Jimco this return measure is computed as follows:

profit margins
Financial ratios (sometimes referred to simply as margins) that reflect the level of a firm's profits relative to sales. Examples include the gross profit margin (gross profit divided by sales), operating profit margin (operating earnings divided by sales), and the net profit margin (net profit divided by sales).

gross profit margin
Gross profit divided by net sales; a ratio denoting the gross profit of the firm as a percentage of net sales.

operating profit margin
Net operating income divided by sales. This ratio serves as an overall measure of operating effectiveness.

operating income return on investment
Ratio that reflects the rate of return on the firm's total investment before interest and taxes.

$$\begin{matrix} \text{Operating income} \\ \text{return on investment} \end{matrix} = \frac{\text{net operating income}}{\text{total assets}} \qquad \textbf{(5-8)}$$

$$= \frac{\$4\,000\,000}{\$31\,000\,000}$$

$$= 0.129, \text{ or } 12.9\%$$

Industry average = 12.5% (see explanation surrounding equation (5-9))

Jimco's management produced a 12.9% return on its total assets before interest and taxes were taken into account.[10] This rate of return is therefore useful in assessing the operating effectiveness of the firm's management, because it excludes the influence of the firm's use of 'financial leverage' (which involves the use of debt funds, on which interest expense is paid).[11] The exclusion of the effects of leverage can be seen from the relevant computations: neither the numerator (operating income) nor the denominator (total assets) is affected by the way in which the firm has financed its assets. Thus it provides a measure of management's effectiveness in making operating decisions as opposed to financing decisions.

Note that an industry norm for this ratio is not readily apparent in Table 5.6. However, one can be calculated using the information given there. Sales divided by total assets equals 1.4, and the operating profit margin is 8.9% of sales for the industry. Using the relationship below, an industry norm of 12.5% can therefore be derived. Thus, Jimco's 12.9% operating rate of return compares favourably with the industry norm.

$$\frac{\text{Operating income}}{\text{sales}} \times \frac{\text{sales}}{\text{total assets}} = \frac{\text{operating income}}{\text{total assets}} \qquad \textbf{(5-9)}$$

$$0.089 \quad \times \quad 1.4 \quad = \quad 0.125, \text{ or } 12.5\%$$

Total asset turnover

total-asset turnover ratio
Sales divided by total tangible assets; an overall measure of the relation between the firm's tangible assets and the sales they generate.

The **total-asset turnover ratio** indicates how many dollars in sales the firm squeezes out of each dollar it has invested in assets. For Jimco, this ratio is calculated as follows:

$$\text{Total asset turnover} = \frac{\text{sales}}{\text{total assets}} \qquad \textbf{(5-10)}$$

$$= \frac{\$51\,000\,000}{\$31\,000\,000}$$

$$= 1.645 \text{ times}$$

Industry average = 1.4 times

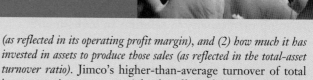

FYI

In deriving the industry norm for the *operating return on investment ratio* (equation (5-9)), a very useful relationship has been identified between operating profit margin and the ratio of sales divided by total assets. This latter ratio is called *total asset turnover*. That is, *a firm's operating rate of return on investment is a function of (1) how much profit it squeezes out of each dollar of sales* (as reflected in its operating profit margin), and (2) how much it has invested in assets to produce those sales (as reflected in the total-asset turnover ratio). Jimco's higher-than-average turnover of total investment in assets outweighs the effect of the below-average operating profit margin, so, in total, the firm's operating income return on investment is above the industry norm.

Jimco's total-asset turnover ratio compares favourably with the industry norm of 1.4. This ratio indicates that, compared with other firms in its industry, Jimco's management has efficiently used its resources in generating sales.

Non-current asset turnover

In addition to total asset turnover, the efficiency with which the firm uses its investment in non-current assets can be calculated as follows:

$$\text{Non-current assets turnover} = \frac{\text{sales}}{\text{non-current assets}} \qquad \textbf{(5-11)}$$

$$= \frac{\$51\,000\,000}{\$7\,000\,000}$$

$$= 7.286 \text{ times}$$

Industry average = 9.8 times

Thus, Jimco has a larger investment in non-current assets relative to its sales volume than is the case for the industry norm. Because Jimco's total-asset turnover ratio (see above) was higher than the industry norm, the below-average **non-current-asset turnover ratio** indicates that Jimco's investment in current assets must be smaller, in relation to sales, than the industry norm.

To summarise, Jimco's operating profit margins are close to those of the industry. However, by obtaining higher-than-average sales per dollar of assets, it has generated a better-than-average operating return on investment.

non-current-asset turnover ratio
Sales divided by non-current assets; a ratio indicating how effectively a firm is using its non-current assets to generate sales.

QUESTION 3: HOW DOES THE FIRM'S MANAGEMENT FINANCE ITS INVESTMENTS?

Leverage ratios (see below) are used to provide the basis for answering two questions about financial leverage: *How has the firm financed its assets? And can the firm afford the level of fixed charges associated with its use of debt interest instead of owner-supplied funds?* The first question is answered through the use of balance-sheet leverage ratios, the second by using income-statement-based ratios, or simply 'coverage' ratios.

It will be useful at this point to review the concept of financial leverage.[12] Financial leverage results when a firm obtains financing for its investments from sources other than the firm's owners. For a company, this means funds from any source other than the ordinary shareholders. Thus, **financial leverage** is leverage that results from the firm's use of debt financing, financial leases and preference shares. These sources of financing share a common characteristic: they all require a fixed cash payment or return for their use. That is, debt requires contractually set interest and principal payments, leases require fixed rental payments, and preference shares usually require a fixed cash dividend. This requirement to pay interest and similar charges provides the basis for the word 'leverage' in this context. If the firm earns a return on leverage funds greater than the rate required by the suppliers of those funds, then the excess goes to the ordinary shareholders. However, should the return earned fall below the required return, then these shareholders must make up the difference out of the returns on their invested funds. This, in a nutshell, is the concept of financial leverage.

leverage ratios
Ratios that provide a basis for determining how a firm financed its assets and the ability of the firm to pay for the non-owner-supplied funds.

financial leverage
The use of securities that pay a fixed rate of return to finance a portion of the firm's assets. Financial leverage can arise from the use of either debt or preference-share financing. The use of financial leverage exposes the firm to financial risk.

Balance-sheet leverage ratios

These ratios provide the basis for answering the question: *where did the firm obtain the financing for its investments?* The label **balance-sheet leverage ratios** is used to indicate that these ratios are computed using information from the balance sheet alone.

balance-sheet leverage ratios
Financial ratios used to measure the extent of a firm's use of borrowed funds, calculated using information found in the firm's balance sheet.

debt ratio
Total liabilities divided by total assets; a ratio that measures the extent to which a firm has been financed with debt.

The **debt ratio** measures the extent to which the total assets of the firm have been financed using borrowed funds. For Jimco the ratio is computed as follows:

$$\text{Debt ratio} = \frac{\text{total liabilities}}{\text{total assets}} \text{ or } \frac{\text{current liabilities} + \text{non-current liabilities}}{\text{total assets}} \quad \textbf{(5-12)}$$

$$= \frac{\$10\,000\,000 + \$10\,700\,000}{\$31\,000\,000}$$

$$= 0.668, \text{ or } 66.8\%$$

Industry average = 54.9%

Thus, Jimco has financed approximately 67% of its assets with borrowed funds. This compares with only 54.9% for the industry. Jimco has relied on the use of non-owner financing to a far greater extent than the average firm in its industry. This, in turn, means that Jimco may have difficulty trying to borrow additional funds in the future. (Note that the industry ratio is found by using the common-size balance sheet in Table 5.6: simply sum the percentages of total assets financed respectively by current liabilities, by long-term debt and by all other non-current liabilities.)

long-term debt to total capitalisation ratio
Long-term liabilities divided by the sum of all the permanent sources of finance used by a firm; indicates the extent to which a firm has used long-term debt in its permanent financing.

The **long-term debt to total capitalisation ratio** indicates the extent to which the firm has used long-term debt in its permanent financing. Total capitalisation represents the sum of all the permanent sources of financing used by the firm, notably long-term debt (including finance leases[13]), preference shares and ordinary equity. For Jimco the ratio is computed as follows:

$$\frac{\text{Long-term debt to}}{\text{total capitalisation}} = \frac{\text{long-term (non-current) liabilities}}{\text{long-term debt} + \text{preference shares} + \text{equity}} \quad \textbf{(5-13)}$$

$$= \frac{\$10\,700\,000}{\$10\,700\,000 + \$10\,300\,000}$$

$$= 0.509, \text{ or } 50.9\%$$

Industry average = 22.8%

Therefore, Jimco has obtained slightly more than half its permanent financing from debt sources, far more than is characteristic of its industry. (Once again referring to the common-size balance sheet in Table 5.6 for an industry norm, note that current liabilities account for 36.9% of total assets; thus, permanent financing is equal to 100% minus 36.9%, or 63.1% of total assets. Furthermore, long-term debt accounts for 14.4% of total assets; thus, it accounts for 14.4/63.1 = 22.8% of the firm's total capitalisation.)

Coverage ratios

These ratios are a second category of leverage ratios, and they are used to measure the firm's ability to cover the finance charges associated with the use of financial leverage. They provide the basis for answering the question of whether the firm has used too much financial leverage.

times-interest-earned ratio
Earnings before interest and taxes (EBIT) divided by interest expense; a ratio that measures the firm's ability to meet its interest payments from its annual operating earnings.

The **times-interest-earned ratio** indicates the firm's ability to meet its interest payments out of its annual operating earnings. The ratio measures the number of times that the firm's operating income is covering its interest. Jimco's ratio is computed as follows:[14]

$$\text{Times interest earned} = \frac{\text{net operating income (NOI) or}}{\text{earnings before interest and taxes (EBIT)}}{\text{annual interest expense}}$$ **(5-14)**

$$= \frac{\$4\,000\,000}{\$1\,000\,000}$$

$$= 4.00 \text{ times}$$

Industry average = 2.4 times

It appears from the above ratio that Jimco's earnings of $4 million before interest and tax are such that it can reasonably *afford* the higher use of financial leverage. (It is important to remember, however, that interest is not paid with income but with cash. Also, the firm may be required to repay some of its debt principal as well as interest. It follows that the times interest earned is only a crude measure of a firm's capacity to service its debt.) This ratio is much higher than the industry norm of 2.4 times, which is somewhat surprising in light of Jimco's higher-than-average use of financial leverage.

Summarising the results of Jimco's leverage ratios, two basic observations can be made: first, Jimco has used more non-owner financing than is characteristic of its industry; and, second, Jimco's earnings are such that it can apparently afford the higher use of financial leverage.

QUESTION 4: ARE THE ORDINARY SHAREHOLDERS RECEIVING SUFFICIENT RETURNS ON THEIR INVESTMENT?

The net income, or 'bottom line', is the result of both the operating and financing (leverage) policies of the firm, which have been analysed already. The net income can be assessed in relation to sales and then in relation to the investment in assets.

Net profitability in relation to sales
Net profit margin. The net profit margin expresses the net after-tax profits of the firm as a percentage of sales. For Jimco the **net profit margin** is computed as follows:

$$\text{Net profit margin} = \frac{\text{net income}}{\text{sales}}$$ **(5-15)**

$$= \frac{\$2\,100\,000}{\$51\,000\,000}$$

$$= 0.0412, \text{ or } 4.12\%$$

Industry average = 4.83%

net profit margin
Net income divided by sales; a ratio that measures the net income of the firm as a percentage of sales.

Therefore, $0.0412 of each sales dollar is converted into profits, after taxes. Note that this profit margin reflects the firm's cost of goods sold, operating expenses, borrowing costs and taxes. For the industry, profits before taxes are 6.9% of sales. Assuming that firms on the average pay approximately 30% of their taxable earnings in taxes, as does Jimco, this produces a net profit margin of 0.069 (1 − 0.30) = 0.0483, or 4.83%. Hence, Jimco's net profit margin is slightly below par for its industry.

Net profitability in relation to investment
Return on total assets. The **return-on-total-assets ratio** or *return-on-investment ratio* relates after-tax net income to the firm's total investment in assets. For Jimco this ratio is found as follows:

return-on-total-assets ratio
Net income divided by total assets. This ratio determines the yield on the firm's assets by relating net income to total assets; also called 'return-on-investment ratio'.

$$\text{Return on total assets} = \frac{\text{net income}}{\text{total assets}} \tag{5-16}$$

$$= \frac{\$2\,100\,000}{\$31\,000\,000}$$

$$= 0.0677, \text{ or } 6.77\%$$

$$\text{Industry average} = 6.76\%$$

The industry norm has been obtained by manipulation of several other ratios found in Table 5.6:

$$\text{Return on total assets} = \frac{\text{net income}}{\text{sales}} \times \frac{\text{sales}}{\text{total assets}} \tag{5-17}$$

The net-income-to-sales ratio for the industry was previously estimated to be 4.83%. Combining this with the industry's sales-to-total-assets ratio of 1.4 produces an industry measure of return on total assets of $0.0483 \times 1.4 = 0.0676$, or 6.76%. Thus, Jimco provides the same return on its total investment as the average for other firms in its industry.

return-on-equity ratio
Net income available to the ordinary shareholders; a ratio relating income to the ordinary shareholder's investment.

Return on ordinary equity. The **return-on-equity ratio (*ROE*)** expresses the return in relation to the funds invested by the ordinary shareholders. Jimco earned the following rate of return for its ordinary shareholders:

$$\text{Return on equity} = \frac{\text{net income}}{\text{equity}} \tag{5-18}$$

$$= \frac{\$2\,100\,000}{\$10\,300\,000}$$

$$= 0.2039, \text{ or } 20.39\%$$

$$\text{Industry average} = 9.32\%$$

To summarise, Jimco has slightly below-average profits in relation to its sales; however, the firm has an above-average return on equity. This factor results from the firm's above-average asset turnover and the fact that Jimco used more leverage than the norm for its industry.

TREND ANALYSIS

It was noted earlier that a firm's financial ratios can be compared with two types of norms or standards: industry norms, as discussed above, and *trends*, which show the changes in the firm's ratios over time. For example, Figure 5.1 graphs Jimco's current ratio, acid-test ratio, debt ratio and return-on-total-asset ratio for recent years.

Surveying the trend in Jimco's liquidity ratios reveals a gradual deterioration. This deterioration in liquidity does not, at least for the present, appear to represent a problem, as Jimco's current and acid-test ratios compare very favourably with their respective industry norms. However, any increase or continuation of the trend could pose a problem for Jimco and the trend should be monitored closely.

Jimco's debt ratio appears to have declined slightly over the past four years, with moderate interim fluctuations. However, no material change in the ratio appears to have occurred over the period. But, in light of Jimco's relatively high current use of leverage, any further increases in this ratio may be unwarranted.

FIGURE 5.1   Trend analysis illustration

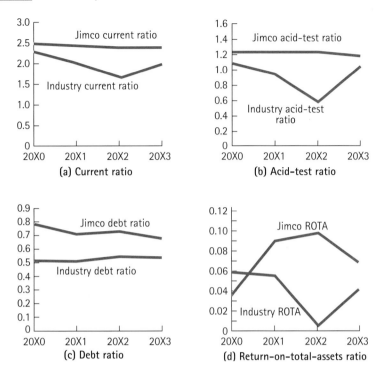

(a) Current ratio

(b) Acid-test ratio

(c) Debt ratio

(d) Return-on-total-assets ratio

Finally, the return-on-total-assets ratio for the past four years depicts the relatively volatile nature of Jimco's business, with returns ranging from 4% in 20X0 to 10% in 20X2. However, based on Jimco's return-on-total-assets ratio for 20X3 and that of the industry, it would appear that Jimco has done as well as or better than the median for its industry.

SUMMARY OF JIMCO'S FINANCIAL RATIOS

Table 5.7 (see over) summarises Jimco's financial ratios, as well as the corresponding industry norms. Each ratio is evaluated in relation to the appropriate norm. Briefly, the results of those comparisons are as follows:

1. Jimco's liquidity position is very closely in line with the industry.
2. Jimco's operating profit margins are approximately equal to the respective norms; however, the firm has been able to convert these profit margins into a better-than-average rate of return on investment. This resulted from a higher-than-average sales per dollar invested in assets.
3. Jimco has made extensive use of financial leverage. The firm has financed 67% of its assets with non-owner debt.
4. The firm can apparently afford its higher use of financial leverage, as indicated by the times-interest-earned ratio.
5. Finally, Jimco has benefited from the favourable use of financial leverage. The firm earned a very favourable 20.39% return on the investment of its shareholders, compared with 9.32% for the industry.

Concept check

5.6   How can financial ratios be used to make useful comparisons?

5.7   What four important questions can be answered using the financial ratios outlined in this chapter?

5.8   Which number in the income statement should be used to measure profitability relative to total assets, and why?

5.9   What is the relationship between the use of debt and the return on equity for shareholders?

For answers go to MyFinanceLab or www.pearson.com.au/9781442539174

TABLE 5.7   Summary of ratios for Jimco Ltd

	RATIO	FORMULA	CALCULATION	INDUSTRY AVERAGE	EVALUATION
1.	Current ratio	Current assets/current liabilities	$24 000 000/10 000 000 = 2.40 times	2.0 times	Good
2.	Acid-test ratio	(Current assets – inventories)/ current liabilities	$12 000 000/10 000 000 = 1.20 times	1.1 times	Good
3.	Average collection period	Average accounts receivable/ (annual credit sales/365)	$10 000 000/(51 000 000/365) = 71.6 days	63 days	Satisfactory
4.	Inventory turnover	Cost of goods sold/ending inventory	$38 000 000/12 000 000 = 3.17 times	3.6 times	Satisfactory
5.	Gross profit margin	Gross profit/sales	$13 000 000/51 000 000 = 25.5%	26.7%	Satisfactory
6.	Operating profit margin	Net operating income/sales	$4 000 000/51 000 000 = 7.84%	8.9%	Satisfactory
7.	Operating income return on investment	Net operating income/total assets	$4 000 000/31 000 000 = 12.9%	12.5%	Satisfactory
8.	Total-asset turnover	Sales/total assets	$51 000 000/31 000 000 = 1.645 times	1.4 times	Good
9.	Non-current asset turnover	Sales/non-current assets	$51 000 000/7 000 000 = 7.286 times	9.8 times	Poor
10.	Debt ratio	Total liabilities/total assets	$20 700 000/31 000 000 = 66.8%	54.9%	Poor
11.	Long-term debt to total capitalisation	Long-term debt/total capitalisation	$10 700 000/21 000 000 = 50.9%	22.8%	Poor
12.	Times-interest-earned	Net operating income/annual interest expense	$4 000 000/1 000 000 = 4.00 times	2.4 times	Excellent
13.	Net profit margin	Net income/sales	$2 100 000/51 000 000 = 4.12%	4.83%	Satisfactory
14.	Return on total assets	Net income/total assets	$2 100 000/31 000 000 = 6.77%	6.76%	Satisfactory
15.	Return on equity	Net income/equity	$2 100 000/10 300 000 = 20.39%	9.32%	Excellent

Back to the principles

Principle 5 tells us that **competitive markets make it hard to find exceptionally profitable projects.** Some financial ratios can help us better know if management is finding exceptional investments, or if the investments are in fact just the opposite—exceptionally bad. For example, the summary of Jimco's ratios shows that the firm is earning an average profit margin, which suggests that its business activities are not presently exceptional in any way.

Principle 1 also is at work in this part of the chapter; that is, **the risk–return trade-off—we won't take on additional risk unless we expect to be compensated with additional return.** As seen in Jimco's summary, management has chosen to finance the business with relatively high levels of debt (which could potentially be risky) but this has resulted in a higher-than-average return on investment.

ONE STEP FURTHER

OBJECTIVE **4**

Understand the DuPont method of financial analysis.

THE DUPONT ANALYSIS: AN INTEGRATED APPROACH TO RATIO ANALYSIS

There is an alternative format for analysing financial ratios. This approach focuses on the firm's earning power as measured by two of the firm's profitability ratios: the operating income return on investment and the return on equity. This methodology is particularly well suited to internal analyses carried out by the firm's management. The reason is that the analysis focuses directly on firm profitability, which in turn reflects how well the firm is being managed. In addition, the

Evaluating a firm's financial performance **CHAPTER 5**

analysis of earning power is a valuable guide to analysing a firm's financial management from the ordinary shareholder's perspective.

The analysis of a firm's earning power involves a two-stage procedure designed to answer two basic questions:

- *Stage 1:* How effective has the firm's management been in generating sales using the total assets of the firm and converting those sales into operating profits?
- *Stage 2:* How effective has the firm's management been in forming a financial structure that increases the returns to the ordinary shareholders? To answer this question, analysis focuses on the effect of the firm's financing decisions (i.e. the mixture of debt and owner financing used by the firm) on the rate of return earned on the ordinary shareholder's investment.

Figure 5.2 provides a template for carrying out the first stage of the analysis of Jimco's earning power. Note first that the focus of this stage is on the operating income return on

FIGURE 5.2 Analysing earning power: Stage 1 (analysing the operating income return on investment)

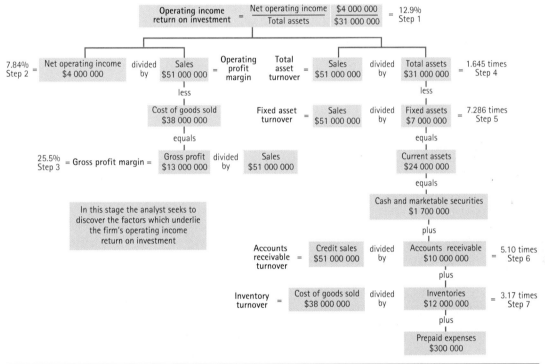

Step	Ratio	Formula	Calculation	Industry[a]	Evaluation
1	Operating income return on investment	$\dfrac{\text{Net operating income}}{\text{Total assets}}$	$\dfrac{\$4\,000\,000}{\$31\,000\,000} = 12.9\%$	12.5%	Satisfactory
2	Operating profit margin	$\dfrac{\text{Net operating income}}{\text{Sales}}$	$\dfrac{\$4\,000\,000}{\$51\,000\,000} = 7.84\%$	8.9%	Satisfactory
3	Gross profit margin	$\dfrac{\text{Gross profit}}{\text{Sales}}$	$\dfrac{\$13\,000\,000}{\$51\,000\,000} = 25.5\%$	26.7%	Satisfactory
4	Total asset turnover	$\dfrac{\text{Sales}}{\text{Total assets}}$	$\dfrac{\$51\,000\,000}{\$31\,000\,000} = 1.645\text{ times}$	1.4 times	Good
5	Fixed asset turnover	$\dfrac{\text{Sales}}{\text{Fixed assets}}$	$\dfrac{\$51\,000\,000}{\$7\,000\,000} = 7.286\text{ times}$	9.8 times	Poor
6	Accounts receivable turnover	$\dfrac{\text{Credit sales}}{\text{Accounts receivable}}$	$\dfrac{\$51\,000\,000}{\$10\,000\,000} = 5.10\text{ times}$	5.8 times	Satisfactory
7	Inventory turnover	$\dfrac{\text{Cost of goods sold}}{\text{Inventories}}$	$\dfrac{\$38\,000\,000}{\$12\,000\,000} = 3.17\text{ times}$	3.6 times	Satisfactory

a Based on figures from Table 5.6.

investment. This ratio reflects the return earned on the firm's investment in assets from operations, before giving any consideration to how the firm's investments were financed. Note that the operating income return on investment can be broken down into the product of two ratios:

Operating income return on investment = operating profit margin × total asset turnover

or

$$\frac{\text{operating income}}{\text{sales}} \times \frac{\text{sales}}{\text{total assets}} = \frac{\text{operating income}}{\text{total assets}}$$

Figure 5.2 simply lays out the relationships that underlie the operating profit margin and total-asset turnover ratios. The left-hand branch of Figure 5.2 shows the determinants of the operating profit margin, and the right-hand branch details the determinants of the total-asset turnover ratio.

Seven ratios are calculated in the first stage of the analysis of Jimco's earning power. The first is the operating income return on investment (Step 1). Step 2 involves calculating the operating profit margin which, along with the total asset turnover (in Step 4), determines the operating income return on investment. Step 3 involves calculation of the gross profit margin, which provides the basis for assessing the impact of cost of goods sold on the operating profit margin calculated in Step 2. Steps 5 to 7 involve the calculation of the fixed (or non-current) asset turnover, accounts-receivable turnover and inventory-turnover ratios, which provide the basis for a detailed analysis of the determinants of the total-asset turnover ratio (calculated in Step 4).

Note that by following the steps in Figure 5.2 the analyst is led through a detailed analysis of the determinants of the operating income return on investment. Each successive step provides the basis for understanding more about the determinants of this rate of return. For example, the total-asset turnover ratio is one of the two basic determinants of the operating income return on investment (the other is the operating profit margin). By analysing the fixed (or non-current) asset turnover ratio in conjunction with the total-asset turnover, the analyst can determine whether fixed or current assets caused the total-asset turnover ratio to deviate from the industry average. Furthermore, the accounts-receivable turnover and inventory-turnover ratios can be analysed to determine the effect of the level of investment in these assets on total asset turnover and, consequently, the observed operating income return on investment.

Figure 5.3 provides a template for use in analysing the effect of the firm's financing decisions on the return earned on the ordinary shareholder's investment. The analysis presented in Figure 5.3 depends on the following basic relationship:

$$\text{Return on equity} = \frac{\text{net income}}{\text{equity}}$$

The figure leads us through an analysis of the determinants of this ratio. Note that the analysis begins with the operating income return on investment ratio, which was the subject of the analysis in Figure 5.2. Next, Step 9 involves calculation of the return on total assets. This ratio is then adjusted for the influence of the firm's use of financial leverage in order to calculate the return on ordinary equity. In Step 10 the rate of return earned on the ordinary shareholder's investment in the firm is measured, which reflects both the firm's operating decisions and its financing decisions.

The 10-step procedure outlined in Figures 5.2 and 5.3 connects the return earned on ordinary equity to the firm's use of financial leverage and operating profitability. The operating rate of return ratio was shown to be determined by the firm's profit margins on sales (Steps 2 and 3) and the sales-to-assets relationship (Steps 4 to 7). The real value of this approach to financial analysis is its ability to demonstrate the interrelationships between the return earned on the

FIGURE 5.3   Analysing earning power: Stage 2 (analysing the return on equity)

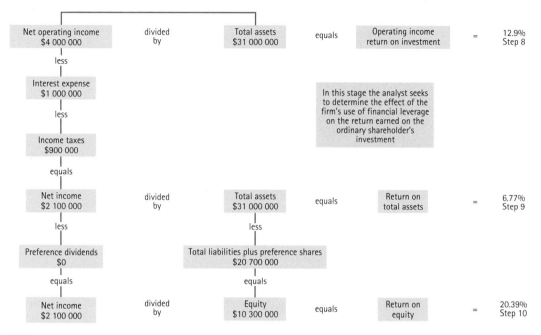

Step	Ratio	Formula	Calculation	Industry[a]	Evaluation
8	Operating income return on investment	Net operating income / Total assets	$4 000 000 / $31 000 000 = 12.9%	12.5%	Satisfactory
9	Return on total assets	Net income / Total assets	$2 100 000 / $31 000 000 = 6.77%	6.76%	Satisfactory
10	Return on equity	Net income / Equity	$2 100 000 / $10 300 000 = 20.39%	9.32%	Excellent

a Based on figures from Table 5.6.

owners' investment in the firm and a wide variety of financial attributes of the firm. The analyst is provided with a 'road-map' to follow in determining how successful the firm's management has been in managing its resources to maximise the return earned on the owners' investment. In addition, the analyst can determine why that particular return was earned.

Concept check
5.10 What two ratios are the key to the DuPont method?

For answers go to MyFinanceLab or www.pearson.com.au/9781442539174

Limitations of ratio analysis

OBJECTIVE 5

Explain the limitations of ratio analysis.

The analyst who works with financial ratios must be aware of the limitations involved in their use. The following list includes some of the more important pitfalls that may be encountered in computing and interpreting financial ratios.

- It is sometimes difficult to identify the industry category to which a firm belongs when the firm engages in multiple lines of business.

- Published industry averages are approximations only and provide the user with *general guidelines* rather than scientifically determined averages of the ratios of all (or even a representative sample) of the firms within the industry.
- Accounting practices differ widely between firms and can lead to differences in computed ratios. For example, firms may choose different methods of depreciating their fixed assets. Historical cost accounting too may result in different firms reporting different written-down values for assets that perform the same service in earning income but which were acquired at different times.
- Financial ratios can appear favourable (or unfavourable) but in fact may be too high or too low. For example, a current ratio that exceeds the industry norm may signal the presence of excess liquidity which results in a lowering of overall profits in relation to the firm's investment in assets. On the other hand, a current ratio that falls below the norm indicates the possibility that the firm has inadequate liquidity and may at some future date be unable to pay its bills on time. Furthermore, the greater the difference in the upper and lower quartiles, the less meaningful is the industry average in terms of its ability to represent that ratio for the industry.
- Many firms experience seasonality in their operations. Thus, balance-sheet entries and their corresponding ratios will vary with the time of year when the statements are prepared. To avoid this problem, an average account balance should ideally be used (for several months or quarters during the year) rather than the year-end total. For example, an average of the month-end inventory balance might be used to compute a firm's inventory-turnover ratio when the firm is subject to a significant seasonality in its sales (and correspondingly in its investment in inventories). The problem is that the external analyst may not have access to monthly or quarterly data.

Despite their limitations, financial ratios provide the analyst with a very useful tool for assessing a firm's financial condition. The analyst should, however, be aware of these potential weaknesses when performing a ratio analysis. In many cases the real value derived from analysing financial ratios is that they tell us what questions to ask.

Concept check

5.11 Why is it difficult to create industry categories, especially among larger companies?

5.12 What differences in accounting practices create problems in using financial ratios?

5.13 Why should a firm be careful when making comparisons with industry norms?

For answers go to MyFinanceLab or www.pearson.com.au/9781442539174

Summary

OBJECTIVE 1

Evaluation of financial performance takes place through two main avenues. First, it is done through reformatting standard financial information (from the income statement and balance sheet) so that the sources and uses of funds and cash flows can be determined. Funds-flow information can be used to answer important questions about how the firm is financed and what those funds are being used for. Similarly, cash-flow information enables us to focus on the key determinants of liquidity, which is critical to the firm's continued well-being.

OBJECTIVE 2

The other main avenue of evaluation involves financial ratios, which are the principal tools of financial analysis. Sometimes referred to simply as benchmarks, ratios standardise financial information so that comparisons can be made between firms of varying sizes. Two groups find financial ratios useful. The first consists of managers who use them to measure and track company performance over time. The focus of their analysis is frequently related to various measures of profitability used to evaluate the performance of the firm from the perspective of the owners. The second group includes analysts external to the firm who, for one reason or another, have an interest in the firm's economic well-being. An example of this group would be a loan officer of a commercial bank who wishes to determine the creditworthiness of a loan applicant. Here the focus of the analysis is on the firm's previous use of financial leverage and its ability to pay the interest and principal associated with the loan request.

Financial ratios may be used to answer at least four questions: (1) How liquid is the company? (2) Is management effective at generating operating profits from the firm's assets? (3) How is the firm financed? (4) Are the returns earned by the common stockholders adequate? Two methods may be used in analysing financial ratios. The first involves trend analysis for the firm over time; the second involves making ratio comparisons with a selected peer group of similar firms. In this chapter a peer group was chosen for analysing the financial position of Jimco.

OBJECTIVE 3

Another approach frequently used to evaluate a firm's profitability and the return on equity is the DuPont analysis. This analysis follows a two-stage, ten-step process that dissects the drivers of the operating income return on investment ratio and then links that ratio to the return on total assets and the return on equity, respectively.

OBJECTIVE 4

The following limitations may be encountered in computing and interpreting financial ratios:
- It is sometimes difficult to identify an appropriate industry category.
- Published industry averages are only approximations rather than scientifically determined averages.
- Accounting practices differ widely between firms and can lead to differences in computed ratios.
- An industry average may not provide a desirable target ratio or norm.
- Many firms experience seasonality in their operations. Thus, ratios will vary with the time of year when the statements are prepared.

In spite of their limitations, financial ratios are very useful tools to use when assessing a firm's financial performance.

OBJECTIVE 5

Key terms

For a complete flashcard glossary go to MyFinanceLab at www.pearson.com.au/myfinancelab

Web works

Browse the websites of Connect4 **www.connect4.com.au** and the ASX **www.asx.com.au**. Summarise the information available for subscribers to these sites from the perspective of an external analyst of a listed company.

Review questions

5-1 What annual financial reports of a company are required under Australian corporations law? What information do they report and what purpose do they fulfil?

5-2 What is a funds statement? How does its function differ from the reports in 5-1?

5-3 What is meant by applying the hedging principle (time-matching concept) to a funds statement, and why might this be done?

5-4 Why can the shareholders' equity section of the balance sheet change from year to year regardless of whether new ordinary shares are issued?

5-5 Discuss reasons why cash flow during a period is not necessarily the same as net income during that period.

5-6 Explain the basis for classifying financial ratios into four groups, as illustrated in this chapter for Jimco.

5-7 What are some of the main limitations of ratio analysis?

5-8 Briefly outline some of the issues faced by the international financial analyst when comparing companies from different countries.

5-9 Discuss briefly the two broad types of standards or norms that can be used in performing ratio analyses. What are the limitations of such data?

Self-test problems

For answers go to MyFinanceLab
www.pearson.com.au/myfinancelab

ST-1 (*Ratio analysis and short-term liquidity*) The Mining Supply Company (MSC) has been expanding its level of operations for the past two years. The firm's sales have grown rapidly as a result of the expansion in the Australian economy. However, MSC's only source of available funds is a line of overdraft credit with the firm's bank. The company needs to expand its inventories to meet the needs of its growing customer base, but also wishes to maintain a current ratio of at least 3 to 1. If MSC's current assets are $6 000 000, and its current ratio is now 4 to 1, how much can it expand its inventories (financing the expansion with its line of credit) before the target current ratio is violated?

ST-2 (*Ratio analysis of loan request*) On 3 February 20X3 Ms Jenny Simmons, chief financial officer for JS Traders, contacted the firm's bank regarding a term loan. The loan was to be used to repay bills payable and to finance current assets. Jenny wanted to repay the loan plus interest in one year. On receiving the loan request, the bank asked that the firm supply it with complete financial statements for the past two years. These statements are presented below:

JS Traders: Balance Sheets at end of calendar year

	20X1	20X2
Cash	$9 000	$500
Accounts receivable	12 500	16 000
Inventories	29 000	45 500
Total current assets	$50 000	$62 000
Land	20 000	26 000
Building and equipment	70 000	100 000
Less: Accumulated depreciation	(28 000)	(38 000)
Total fixed assets	$62 000	$88 000
	$112 500	$150 000
Accounts payable	$10 500	$22 000
Bank bills	17 000	47 000
Total current liabilities	$27 500	$69 000
Long-term debt	28 750	22 950
Share capital	31 500	31 500
Retained earnings	24 750	26 550
	$112 500	$150 000

JS Traders: Income Statements at end of calendar year

	20X1	20X2
Sales	$125 000	$160 000
Cost of goods sold	75 000	96 000
Gross profit	$50 000	$64 000
Operating expense		
Fixed cash operating expense	21 000	21 000
Variable operating expense	12 500	16 000
Depreciation	4 500	10 000
Total operating expense	$38 000	$47 000
Earnings before interest and taxes	12 000	17 000
Interest	3 000	6 100
Earnings before taxes	9 000	10 900
Taxes	4 500	5 450
Net income	$4 500	$5 450

(a) Based on the preceding financial statements, complete the following table:

JS Traders: ratio analysis

	INDUSTRY AVERAGES	ACTUAL 20X1	ACTUAL 20X2
Current ratio	1.80		
Acid-test ratio	0.70		
Average collection period[a]	37 days		
Inventory turnover[a]	2.50 times		
Debt to total assets	58%		
Long-term debt to total capitalisation	33%		
Times interest earned	3.8 times		
Gross profit margin	38%		
Operating profit margin	10%		
Net profit margin	3.5%		
Total asset turnover	1.14 times		
Fixed asset turnover	1.40 times		
Operating income return on investment	11.4%		
Return on total assets	4.0%		
Return on ordinary equity	9.5%		

a Based on a 365-day year and on end-of-year figures.

(b) Analyse Jenny Simmons's loan request. Would you grant the loan? Explain.

ST-3 *(Funds statement and statement of cash flows)*

(a) For JS Traders, prepare a funds statement for the year 20X2 (all-resources concept) using the time-matching format, and a statement of cash flows (indirect method), using information given in ST-2.

(b) How do these statements supplement your ratio analysis from ST-1? Explain.

Problems

For more problems and for answers to problems marked with an asterisk (*) go to MyFinanceLab at www.pearson.com.au/myfinancelab

5-1   (*Review of financial statements*) Prepare a balance sheet as at 30 June 20X6 for the Mixto Company from the scrambled list of account balances below.

Machinery and equipment	$1 000 000	Accounts receivable	250 000
Accumulated depreciation	300 000	Accounts payable	120 000
Short-term note payable	90 000	Long-term debt	360 000
Inventory	190 000	Cash	40 000

5-2   (*Review of financial statements*) Prepare a balance sheet and income statement at 31 December 20X4 for the Sabine Manufacturing Company from the scrambled list of items below. Ignore income taxes and interest expense.

Accounts receivable	$150 000	Cost of goods sold	550 000
Machinery and equipment*	464 000	Operating expenses	280 000
Notes payable—current	90 000	Share capital	320 000
Net sales	900 000	Cash	90 000
Inventory	110 000	Retained earnings—prior year	?
Accounts payable	90 000	Retained earnings—current year	?
Long-term debt	160 000		

* Machinery and equipment is shown as a net amount, that is, after deducting accumulated depreciation (which is $236 000).

5-3   (*Review of financial statements*) A scrambled list of accounts from the income statement and balance sheet of Belmond, Inc. is found below:

Inventory	$6 500	Accounts payable	4 800
Share capital	45 000	Long-term debt	55 000
Cash	16 550	Cost of goods sold	5 750
Operating expenses	1 350	Buildings and equipment	122 000
Short-term notes payable	600	Accumulated depreciation	34 000
Interest expense	900	Taxes	1 440
Depreciation expense	500	General and administrative expense	850
Sales	12 800	Retained earnings	?
Accounts receivable	9 600		

(a) How much is the firm's net working capital?

(b) Complete an income statement and a balance sheet for Belmond.

(c) If you were asked to complete parts (a) and (b) as part of a training exercise, what could you tell your boss about the company's financial condition based on your answers?

5-4   (*Preparing the funds statement and statement of cash flows*) Comparative balance sheets for 31 December 20X5 and 31 December 20X6 for ABC Company are:

	20X5	20X6
Cash	$200 000	$178 000
Accounts receivable	140 000	128 000
Inventory	200 000	224 000
Prepaid expenses	20 000	20 000
Plant and equipment	622 000	476 000
Accumulated depreciation	−132 000	−80 000
	$1 050 000	$946 000
Accounts payable	$180 000	$170 000
Accrued liabilities	126 000	136 000
Mortgage payable		140 000

Preference share capital	240 000	
Ordinary share capital	410 000	410 000
Retained earnings	94 000	90 000
	$1 050 000	$946 000

ABC's 20X6 profit and loss statement is:

Sales	$368 000
Cost of sales	300 000
Gross profit	68 000
Operating expenses	20 000
Net income	$48 000

Additional information

1. The only entry in the accumulated depreciation account is for 20X6 depreciation.
2. The firm paid $44 000 in dividends during 20X6.

Prepare a 20X6 funds statement and statement of cash flows for ABC.

5-5 (*Statement of cash flows*) Comparative balance sheets for 31 December 20X5 and 31 December 20X6 for Barron Manufacturing Company are found below:

	20X6	20X5
Cash	$70 000	$89 000
Accounts receivable	70 000	64 000
Inventory	80 000	102 000
Prepaid expenses	10 000	10 000
Plant and equipment	301 000	238 000
Accumulated depreciation	(66 000)	(40 000)
Total assets	$465 000	$463 000
Accounts payable	$80 000	$85 000
Accrued liabilities	63 000	68 000
Mortgage payable		60 000
Preference share capital	70 000	
Ordinary share capital	205 000	205 000
Retained earnings	47 000	45 000
Total liabilities and equity	$465 000	$463 000

ABC's 20X6 profit and loss statement is:

Sales	$204 000
Cost of sales	160 000
Gross profit	44 000
Operating expenses	10 000
Net income	$34 000

Additional information

1. The only change in the accumulated depreciation account is for 20X6 depreciation.
2. The firm paid $32 000 in dividends during 20X6.

Prepare a 20X6 cash-flow statement for Barron Manufacturing Company using the indirect method.

5-6* (*Funds statement and cash-flow statement*) The following information has been provided in the year 20X3 for Waterhouse Co.

	20X2	20X3
Cash	$75 000	$82 500
Receivables	102 000	90 000
Inventory	168 000	165 000
Prepaid expenses	12 000	13 500
Non-current assets	325 500	468 000
Accumulated depreciation	94 500	129 000
Patents	61 500	52 500
	$649 500	$742 500
Accounts payable	$124 500	$112 500
Taxes payable	97 500	105 000
Mortgage payable	150 000	–
Preference share capital	–	231 000
Ordinary share capital	225 000	225 000
Retained earnings	52 500	69 000
	$649 500	$742 500

Additional information

1. The only change in the accumulated depreciation account is the depreciation expense for 20X3.
2. The only entries in the retained earnings account are for dividends paid in the amount of $18 000 and for the net income for the year.
3. The income statement for 20X3 is as follows:

Sales	$187 500
Cost of sales[a]	141 000
Gross profit	46 500
Operating expenses	12 000
Net income	$34 500

a Includes depreciation expense of $34 500.

(a) Prepare a funds statement (all-resources concept) with the time-matching format. What were the primary sources and applications of funds?

(b) Use the indirect method to prepare a statement of cash flows. Explain whether or not this provides additional information to the funds statement.

5-7 (*Analysing the statement of cash flows*) Identify any financial weaknesses revealed in the statement of cash flows (indirect method) for the Westlake Manufacturing Co.

Westlake Manufacturing Co. Statement of Cash Flow for current year

Cash flow from operating activities		
Net income		$540 000
Add (deduct) to reconcile net income to net cash flow		
Decrease in accounts receivable	40 000	
Increase in inventories	(240 000)	
Increase in prepaid expenses	(10 000)	
Depreciation expense	60 000	
Decrease in accrued wages	(50 000)	
Net cash flow from operating activities		$340 000
Cash flow from investing activities		
Sale (purchase) of plant and equipment		2 400 000

Cash flow from financing activities		
New term loan		1 000 000
Repayment of short-term debt	(3 000 000)	
Payment of long-term debt	(500 000)	
Payment of dividends	(1 000 000)	
Net cash from financing activities		(3 500 000)
Net increase (decrease) in cash for the period		(760 000)

5-8 (*Ratio analysis-efficiency*) Baryla Pty Ltd manufactures high-quality decorator lighting in a factory located in Sydney. Last year the firm had sales of $100 million and a gross profit margin of 40%.

  (a) How much inventory can Baryla hold if it maintains an inventory turnover ratio of at least 6.0 times?

  (b) Currently, some of Baryla's inventory includes $2 million of outdated and damaged goods that simply remain in inventory and are not saleable. What inventory turnover ratio must the good inventory have, in order to achieve an overall turnover ratio of at least 6.0 (including the unsaleable items)?

5-9 (*Ratio analysis-efficiency*) ALei Industries has credit sales of $150 million a year. ALei's management reviewed its credit policy and decided that it wanted to maintain an average collection period of 40 days.

  (a) What is the maximum level of accounts receivable that ALei can carry so as to have a 40-day average collection period?

  (b) If ALei's current accounts receivable collection period is 50 days, how much would it have to reduce its level of accounts receivable in order to achieve its goal of 40 days?

5-10 (*Ratio analysis*) The balance sheet and income statement for the J. P. Robards Manufacturing Company are as follows:

Balance Sheet ($'000)

Cash	$500
Accounts receivable	2 000
Inventories	1 000
Current assets	$3 500
Net non-current assets	4 500
Total assets	$8 000
Accounts payable	$1 100
Accrued expenses	600
Short-term notes payable	300
Current liabilities	$2 000
Long-term debt	2 000
Owners' equity	4 000
Total liabilities and owners' equity	$8 000

Income Statement ($'000)

Net sales (all credit)	$8 000
Cost of goods sold	(3 300)
Gross profit	$4 700
Operating expenses[a]	(3 000)
Operating income	$1 700
Interest expense	(367)
Earnings before taxes	$1 333
Income taxes (40%)	(533)
Net income	$ 800

a Includes depreciation expense of $500 for the year.

Calculate the following ratios:

Current ratio	Gross profit margin
Debt ratio	Operating profit margin
Times interest-earned	Average collection period
Operating return on investment	Non-current-asset turnover
Inventory-turnover	Total-asset turnover
Return on equity	

5-11 (*Ratio analysis*) The financial statements for the Destchild Music Company include the following information:

Selected balance sheet items ($'000)	
Cash	$800
Accounts receivable	1 200
Accounts payable	700
Accrued expenses	500
Inventories	1 400
Non-current assets	6 000
30-day note payable	300
Current liabilities	1 500
Accumulated depreciation	1 700
Long-term debt	2 400

Selected income statement items ($'000)	
Net sales (all on credit)	$8 000
Cost of goods sold	3 300
Operating expenses[a]	2 900
Interest expense	412

a Including depreciation expense of $500 for the year.

Income tax is payable at 40%.

Calculate the following ratios:

Current ratio	Gross profit margin
Debt ratio	Operating profit margin
Times interest earned	Net profit margin
Average collection period	Operating return on investment
Inventory turnover	Return on total assets
Non-current-asset turnover	Return on equity
Total-asset turnover	

5-12* (*Ratio analysis*) The Mitcham Marble Company has a target current ratio of 2 but has experienced some difficulties financing its expanding sales in the past few months. At present the current ratio of 2.5 is based on current assets of $2.5 million. If Mitcham expands its receivables and inventories using its short-term lines of credit (bills and overdraft), how much additional funding can it borrow before its current ratio standard is reached?

5-13* (*Analysing profitability*) The R. M. Smithers Corporation earned a net profit margin of 5% based on sales of $10 million and total assets of $5 million last year.

(a) What was Smithers' rate of return on total assets?

(b) During the coming year the general manager has set a goal of attaining a 12% return on total assets. How much must sales rise, other things being the same, for the goal to be achieved? (State your answer as an annual growth rate in sales.)

(c) If Smithers financed 30% of its assets by borrowing, what was its return on ordinary equity for last year? What will it be next year if the return-on-total-asset goal is achieved?

5-14 (*Using financial ratios*) Brenda Smith Pty Ltd had a gross profit margin of 25% and sales of $9.75 million last year. Of the firm's sales, 75% were on credit and the remainder were cash sales. The company's current assets equal $1 550 000, its current liabilities equal $300 000, and it has $150 000 in cash plus marketable securities.

(a) If Smith's accounts receivable were $562 500, what is its average collection period?

(b) If Smith reduces its average collection period to 20 days, what will be its new level of accounts receivable?

(c) Smith's inventory-turnover ratio is eight times. What is the level of the firm's inventories?

5-15 (*Ratio analysis*) TC Company earned an operating profit margin of 10% based on sales of $10 million and total assets of $5 million last year.

(a) What was TC's *total-asset-turnover ratio*?

(b) During the coming year, the CEO has set a goal of attaining a total-asset turnover of 3.5. How much must sales rise, other things being the same, for the goal to be achieved? (State your answer in both dollars and percentage increase in sales.)

(c) What was TC's *operating income return on investment* last year? Assuming that the firm's operating profit margin remains the same, what will be the operating income return on investment next year if the total-asset-turnover goal is achieved?

5-16 (*Ratio analysis*) HiTech's income statement for 20X9 and the balance sheet for 31 December 20X9 follow. Compute the financial ratios for HiTech for 20X9 and, using the industry norms, evaluate the firm in the following areas:

(a) liquidity
(b) operating profitability
(c) financing policies
(d) return on the shareholders' investment

HiTech Income Statement for year ended 20X9

	20X9
Sales	$29 389 000
Cost of goods sold	9 061 000
Gross profit	$20 328 000
Selling, general and administrative expense	6 983 000
Depreciation	3 186 000
Operating profit	$10 159 000
Interest expense	41 000
Non-operating income (expense)	1 110 000
Pretax income	$11 228 000
Total income taxes	3 914 000
Net income	$7 314 000

HiTech Balance Sheet, for 31 December 20X9

	20X9
ASSETS	
Cash and equivalents	$11 788 000
Accounts receivable	3 700 000
Inventories	1 478 000
Other current assets	853 000
Total current assets	$17 819 000
Gross plant, property and equipment	24 360 000
Accumulated depreciation	(12 645 000)
Net plant, property and equipment	$11 715 000
Other investments	7 911 000
Intangibles	4 322 000
Other assets	2 082 000
Total assets	$43 849 000
LIABILITIES	
Notes payable	$230 000
Accounts payable	1 370 000
Taxes payable	1 695 000
Accrued expenses	3 195 000
Other current liabilities	609 000
Total current liabilities	$7 099 000
Long-term debt	955 000
Deferred taxes	3 130 000
Total liabilities	$11 184 000

EQUITY	
Preferred stock	$130000
Ordinary shares	3334
Capital surplus	7312666
Retained earnings	25219000
Common equity	$32535000
Total equity	32665000
Total liabilities and equity	$43849000

INDUSTRY NORMS	

FIRM LIQUIDITY	
Current ratio	2.01
Acid-test ratio	1.66
Average collection period	72.64
Accounts receivable turnover	5.02
Inventory turnover	4.42

OPERATING PROFITABILITY	
Operating income return on investment	9%
Operating profit margin	13%
Total asset turnover	0.69
Accounts receivable turnover	5.02
Inventory turnover	4.42
Fixed asset turnover	2.27

FINANCING DECISIONS	
Debt ratio	0.44
Times interest earned	8.87

RETURN ON EQUITY	
Return on equity	12%

5-17* (*Financial ratios—investment analysis*) The annual sales for Salco Ltd were $4.5 million last year. The firm's end-of-year balance sheet appeared as follows:

Current assets	$500000	Liabilities	$1000000
Net non-current assets	1500000	Owners' equity	1000000
	$2000000		$2000000

The firm's profit and loss statement for the year was as follows:

Sales	$4500000
Less: Cost of goods sold	(3500000)
Gross profit	1000000
Less: Operating expenses	(500000)
Net operating income	500000
Less: Interest expense	(100000)
Earnings before taxes	400000
Less: Taxes	(200000)
Net income	$200000

(a) Calculate Salco's total-asset turnover, operating profit margin and operating income return on investment.

(b) Salco plans to renovate one of its plants, which will require an added investment in plant and equipment of $1 million. The firm will maintain its present debt ratio of 0.5 when financing the new investment, and it expects sales to remain constant, while the operating profit margin will rise to 13%. What will be the new operating income return on investment for Salco after the plant renovation?

(c) Given that the plant renovation in part (b) takes place and that Salco's interest expense rises by $50 000 per year, what will be the return earned on the ordinary shareholders' investment? Compare this rate of return with that earned before the renovation.

5-18* (*Ratio analysis of loan request*) Pamplin Ltd has recently applied for a loan from the Southern Bank to be used to expand the firm's inventory of soil pipe used in construction and agriculture. This expansion is based on expanded sales predicted for the coming year. Pamplin's financial statements for the two most recent years are as follows:

Pamplin Ltd, Balance Sheet at 31/12/20X1 and 31/12/20X2 ('000)

ASSETS	20X1	20X2
Cash	$200	$150
Accounts receivable	450	425
Inventory	550	625
Current assets	1 200	1 200
Plant and equipment	2 200	2 600
Less: Accumulated depreciation	(1 000)	(1 200)
Net plant and equipment	1 200	1 400
Total assets	$2 400	$2 600

LIABILITIES AND OWNERS' EQUITY	20X1	20X2
Accounts payable	$200	$150
Notes payable—current (9%)	0	150
Current liabilities	200	300
Bonds	600	600
Owners' equity		
Share capital	900	900
Retained earnings	700	800
Total owners' equity	1 600	1 700
Total liabilities and owners' equity	$2 400	$2 600

PROFIT AND LOSS STATEMENT	20X1	20X2
Sales	$1 200	$1 450
Cost of goods sold	700	850
Gross profit	$500	$600
Operating expenses	30	40
Depreciation	220	200
Net operating income	$250	$360
Interest expense	50	60
Net income before taxes	$200	$300
Taxes (40%)	80	120
Net income	$120	$180

(a) Compute the following ratios for Pamplin Ltd from the financial statements provided above:

	20X1	20X2	INDUSTRY NORM
Current ratio			5.0
Acid-test (quick) ratio			3.0
Inventory turnover			2.2
Average collection period			90 days
Debt ratio			0.33
Times interest earned			7.0
Total asset turnover			0.75
Non-current asset turnover			1.0
Operating profit margin			0.20
Net profit margin			0.12
Return on total assets			0.09

(b) Based on your answer in part **(a)** above, what are Pamplin's financial strengths and weaknesses?

(c) Would you make the loan? Why or why not?

5-19 (*Cash-flow statement*) Prepare a statement of cash flows (indirect method) for Pamplin Ltd for the year ended 31 December 20X2 (problem 5-18). Does this reinforce or add to your knowledge of Pamplin? Explain.

5-20 (*Comprehensive financial analysis*) RIP Pty Ltd is a manufacturer and retailer of high-quality sleepwear. Since its inception the firm has been profitable, with last year's sales being $700 000 and assets in excess of $400 000. The firm now finds that its growing sales are outstripping its ability to finance its inventory needs. The firm estimates that it will need temporary finance of $100 000 during the coming year. To finance this funding requirement, management plans to seek an overdraft from its bank. The firm's most recent financial statements were provided to its bank as support for the firm's loan request, and the bank's financial analyst has been asked to compute and evaluate the relevant ratios.

RIP Pty Ltd Balance Sheets for 31/12/X5 and 31/12/X6

	20X5	20X6
Assets:		
Cash	$16 000	$17 000
Marketable securities	7 000	7 200
Accounts receivable	42 000	38 000
Inventory	50 000	93 000
Prepaid rent	1 200	1 100
Total current assets	$116 200	$156 300
Net plant and equipment	286 000	290 000
Total assets	$402 200	$446 300

Liabilities and shareholders' equity:

	20X5	20X6
Accounts payable	$48 000	$55 000
Notes payable	16 000	13 000
Accruals	6 000	5 000
Total current liabilities	$70 000	$73 000
Long-term debt	$160 000	$150 000
Shareholders' funds	$172 200	$223 300
Total liabilities and equity	$402 200	$446 300

RIP Pty Ltd Income Statement for year ended 31/12/X6

Sales		$700 000
Less: Cost of goods sold		500 000
Gross profit		$200 000
Less: Expenses		
General and administrative	$50 000	
Interest	10 000	
Depreciation	30 000	
Total		90 000
Profit before tax		$110 000
Less: Tax		27 100
Profits after tax		$82 900
Less: Dividends		31 800
To retained earnings		$51 100

(a) Calculate the financial ratios for 20X6 corresponding to the industry norms provided below and write a brief evaluation of each ratio.

	INDUSTRY NORM	RIP'S RATIO	EVALUATION
Current ratio	1.8 times		
Acid-test ratio	.9 times		
Debt ratio	.5		
Long-term debt to total capitalisation	.7		
Times interest earned	10 times		
Average collection period	20 days		
Inventory turnover (based on COGS)	7 times		
Return on total assets	8.4%		
Gross profit margin	25%		
Net profit margin	7%		
Operating return on investment	16.8%		
Operating profit margin	14%		
Total asset turnover	1.2 times		
Fixed asset turnover	1.8 times		

(b) What strengths and weaknesses are apparent from your analysis of RIP's financial ratios?

Case study

You are applying for a job as a financial analyst at Analco, a US-based firm that is in the process of setting up operations in Australia. Analco's business is to provide investment analysis data to portfolio managers and other investment professionals. As one part of the job-selection process, the American interviewer has put you in front of a computer terminal and asked you to go to **http://finance.yahoo. com** and locate current financial statements for Starbucks Corp. (SBUX) and McDonald's Corp. (MCD). With this information, the interviewer has requested you to:

1. Compute the financial ratios for both firms for the most recent year, and evaluate the relative performance of the two firms in the following areas:
   (a) Liquidity
   (b) Profitability/asset-management efficiency
   (c) Financing practices
   (d) Returns on shareholders' investment.
2. Based on your analysis, what is your personal assessment of the two firms' recent performance?

Notes

1. Under Australian Accounting Standards, from the year ended 30 June 2001, the first two of these three statements were named the Statement of Financial Performance and the Statement of Financial Position respectively. However, since then the names have been changed back to Income Statement and Balance Sheet respectively.
2. The use of funds attributed to the purchase of plant and equipment can also be obtained from an analysis of the change in the net plant and equipment account. For Jimco Ltd, this can be accomplished as follows: Net plant and equipment (20X3) $5000 plus depreciation expense for the period $500 equals $5500, deduct net plant and equipment (20X2) $4400, giving net purchase of plant and equipment $1100.
3. See *The Wall Street Journal Online*, 9 December 2004.
4. 'Cash equivalents' means highly liquid investments with short maturity periods, readily convertible into cash (at the option of the holder) and subject to insignificant risk of valuation change (these usually include cash at bank and investments in money-market investments with up to a three-month maturity), and borrowings integral to a term facility (bank overdrafts normally satisfy this definition).
5. Note that although the focus is on 20X2–20X3 for Jimco, the comparative data being used may be from 20X1–20X2. The analyst will often find that published industry averages are a year behind, owing to the time required to collect and publish them.
6. This data is hypothetical and should not be assumed to relate to an actual industry.
7. See T. S. Maness and J. T. Zietlow, *Short-Term Financial Management*, Dryden Press, New York, 1997, chapter 2.
8. Although it will not be discussed here, one tool for further assessing the liquidity of a firm's receivables is an ageing of the accounts receivable schedule. Such a schedule identifies the number and dollar value of accounts outstanding for various periods. For example, accounts that are less than 30 days old, 31 to 45 days, and so forth might be examined. Still another way to construct the schedule is to analyse the length of time to eventual collection of accounts over a past period. For example, how many accounts were outstanding for less than 30 days when collected, between 30 and 45 days, and so forth.
9. When monthly or quarterly inventory data are available, their average should be used as a more representative measure of annual inventory holdings, particularly in order to eliminate the effect of seasonality.
10. Intangible assets are often subtracted from total assets in an effort to measure the firm's return on invested capital. The lack of physical qualities of intangible assets makes evidence of their existence elusive, their value often difficult to estimate, and their useful lives indeterminable. However, because Jimco has no intangible assets, no adjustment is necessary.
11. Refer to Chapter 15 where the concept of leverage is more fully developed.
12. Refer to Chapter 15.
13. The Appendix to Chapter 18 discusses lease accounting further.
14. The interchangeable use of EBIT and NOI presumes there was no 'other' income earned by the firm. If the presence of other non-operating income is thought to be transitory, then NOI should be used; if not, then EBIT is appropriate.

After reading this chapter, you should be able to:

1 Understand the process of forecasting the firm's financial needs.
2 Use the percent-of-sales method of financial forecasting.
3 Describe the limitations of the percent-of-sales method.
4 Understand how to prepare budgets, particularly the cash budget.
5 Prepare pro-forma financial statements.

For a complete eBook go to MyFinanceLab
www.pearson.com.au/myfinancelab

Financial forecasting, planning and budgeting

CHAPTER PREVIEW

Chapter 6 has two main themes. First, the financial manager's role in financial forecasting is outlined. Firms go through an annual planning and budgeting exercise in which the financial manager is asked to develop a forecast of the firm's cash flow, by working with other divisions of the firm to produce revenue and expense forecasts along with estimates of other costs and outlays. This cash flow forecast then becomes the basis for estimating the firm's financing requirements. Second, the pro-forma (planned) income statement, the pro-forma balance sheet and the cash budget are reviewed. These statements constitute the principal elements of the firm's financial forecast and serve as a benchmark against which future performance can be compared.

The chapter emphasises two principles:

- *Principle 3: Cash—not profits—is king.* Firms pay bills and dividends with cash and borrowers make mortgage payments using cash, not profits.
- *Principle 7: The agency problem—managers won't work for owners unless it's in their best interest.* Financial planning entails the construction of detailed budgets that can be used as an oversight tool for monitoring the activities of the firm's employees.

Regardless of your program

Businesses require planning, and planning requires the cooperation of everyone in the organisation. This is true regardless of your program and your specific role in the organisation.

Consider the basic steps involved in developing an annual financial plan for a firm that manufactures a line of dental care products. Step 1: Gather historical data on sales and expenses for each product spanning the last six to twelve months. The logical place to start this process is with the firm's accountants, who maintain cost and revenue information by product. Step 2: Analyse the historical data to identify any trends that might be useful in predicting future levels. This analysis would probably fall on the firm's financial analysts, who are developing the financial plan. Step 3: Make adjustments to projections of revenues by product line to reflect the firm's current marketing plans. This analysis logically comes from the firm's marketing staff, who develop sales plans and forecasts as well as advertising campaigns. The marketing group will also be very familiar with the latest information on competitors and any new product offerings that might impact on the sales forecast. Step 4: Revise estimates of per-unit costs and expense estimates to reflect any changes that might be planned for the firm's operations. The firm's operations staff will be the keepers of this information which, when analysed by the firm's cost accountants, can be used to revise cost per unit estimates across all the firm's product lines. Step 5: Forecast the company's after-tax cash flows, which will in turn be used to help the firm decide on its future financing needs.

Forecasting financial needs

Forecasting in financial management is used to estimate a firm's future financial requirements. If the financial manager has not attempted to anticipate the firm's future financing needs, then a crisis occurs every time the firm's cash inflows fall below its cash outflows. Proper planning means anticipating and preparing for those times in the firm's future when it will need to obtain additional financing and, on the other hand, when it will have an excess of cash. For example, the financing requirements of growth firms frequently outstrip the firm's ability to generate cash. Planning for growth means that the financial manager can anticipate the firm's financing requirements and develop a strategy to meet those requirements well in advance of need. Advance planning means that the financial manager can explore more alternatives and obtain the most favourable set of financing terms available.

The basic steps involved in predicting those financing needs are as follows:

Step 1: Project the firm's sales revenues and expenses over the planning period.

Step 2: Estimate the levels of investment in current and fixed assets that are necessary to support the projected sales.

Step 3: Determine the firm's financing needs throughout the planning period.

SALES FORECAST

The key ingredient in the firm's planning process is the *sales forecast*. This projection will generally be derived using information from a number of sources. At a minimum, the sales forecast for the coming year will reflect (1) any past trend in sales that is expected to carry through into the new year, and (2) the influence of any events that might materially affect that sales trend.[1] An example of the latter would be the initiation of a major advertising campaign or a change in the firm's pricing policy.

FORECASTING FINANCIAL VARIABLES

Traditional financial forecasting takes the sales forecast as a given or starting point. The level of sales then enables projections to be made of the firm's various expenses, assets and liabilities. The most commonly used method for making these projections is the percent-of-sales method.

THE PERCENT-OF-SALES METHOD OF FINANCIAL FORECASTING

The **percent-of-sales method** of forecasting involves estimating the level of an expense, an asset or a liability for a future period as a percentage of that period's sales forecast. For example, cost of sales might be projected as 60% of sales, which means in turn that gross profit will be estimated as 40%. Or inventories might have averaged 20% of sales, so this figure could be used in the coming period's forecast.

The percentage used can come from the most recent financial statement item, as a percentage of current sales. Alternatively, it can come from an average computed over several previous years, from the judgement of the analyst, or from some combination of these sources.

Table 6.1 outlines the use of the percent-of-sales method of financial forecasting. It presents a firm's actual financial data for the most recent reporting year, 20X3. In the firm's 20X3

Back to the principles

Financial decisions are made today in light of our expectations of an uncertain future. Financial forecasting involves making estimates of the future financing requirements of the firm. **Principle 3: Cash—not profits—is king** speaks directly to this problem. Remember that effective financial management requires that consideration be given to cash flow and when it is received or disbursed.

Finance at work

ALCOA ADOPTS REAL-TIME MANUFACTURING SYSTEMS TO REPLACE FORECASTS[2]

Alcoa is a global aluminium producer, whose Australian holdings include a refinery (production plant) in Tasmania and a bauxite mine in north Queensland. During the past decade or so, the firm has generated savings of hundreds of millions of dollars by implementing the Alcoa Business System. This is an adaptation of Toyota's production methods that focuses on managing the business in real time. Managing in real time requires accurate, live information in order to produce an actual demand rather than relying on forecasts. It also means the use of many other modern manufacturing techniques like just-in-time inventory control, small-batch production, flexible production lines, quick machine-tool changes and minimal waste of materials.

This all sounds great, but how was it made to work? The key to Alcoa's success has been moving production decisions to the workers. A worker who has a problem with equipment or product defect summons a leader who is charged with fixing the problem on the spot. The manufacturing process is a 'pull' system in which workers in upstream processes respond to demand requests from workers downstream. Workers often negotiate with co-workers to buy their inputs from, and sell their outputs to, others in the process.

Results of the change in the manufacturing process have increased inventory turnover in Brazil to 60 times per year, and in Mississippi, USA. the customer delivery time has been reduced from three weeks to just two days. At its Massena, New York, plant, the speed of production increased fourfold while work-in process inventories were reduced by 85%. Across the USA, Alcoa was able to reduce inventories by more than $250 million while increasing sales to just under $1 billion. Furthermore, Alcoa believes it can multiply these savings when suppliers and customers are integrated into the system. Integrating supplier and customer systems requires trust and impeccable reliability from all parties. By focusing on reducing costs and improving responsiveness, Alcoa will continue to revolutionise its manufacturing process and be a leader in the aluminium industry.

TABLE 6.1 Using the percent-of-sales method to forecast future financing requirements

ASSETS	PRESENT (20X3)	PERCENT OF SALES (20X3 SALES = $10M)	PROJECTED (BASED ON 20X4 SALES = $12M)	
Current assets	$2m	$\frac{\$2m}{\$10m} = 20\%$	$0.2 \times \$12m =$	$2.4m
Net non-current assets	$4m	$\frac{\$4m}{\$10m} = 40\%$	$0.4 \times \$12m =$	$4.8m
Total	$6m			$7.2m

LIABILITIES AND OWNERS' EQUITY				
Accounts payable	$1.0m	$\frac{\$1m}{\$10m} = 10\%$	$0.10 \times \$12m =$	$1.2m
Accrued expenses	$1.0m	$\frac{\$1m}{\$10m} = 10\%$	$0.10 \times \$12m =$	$1.2m
Notes payable	0.5m	na[a]	no change	0.5m
Long-term debt	2.0m	na[a]	no change	2.0m
Total liabilities	$4.5m			$4.9m
Share capital	0.3m	na[a]		0.3m
Retained earnings	1.2m		$1.2m + [.05 \times \$12m \times (1 - 0.5)]=$	1.5m[b]
Equity	$1.5m			$1.8m
Total	$6.0m		Total financing provided	$6.7m
			Discretionary financing needed	0.5m[c]
			Total	$7.2m

a   Not applicable. These account balances are assumed not to vary with sales.
b   Projected retained earnings equals the beginning level ($1.2m) plus projected net income less any dividends paid. In this case net income is projected to equal 5% of sales, and dividends are projected to equal half of net income: $0.05 \times \$12m \times (1 - 0.5) = \$300\,000$.
c   Discretionary financing needed equals projected total assets ($7.2m) less projected total liabilities ($4.9m) less projected equity ($1.8m), or $7.2m - $4.9m - $1.8m = $500\,000$.

balance sheet, each item that varies with sales is converted to a percentage of that year's sales. Then, in order to forecast ahead to the coming year, 20X4, the new balance for each item is calculated by multiplying this percentage by $12 million, which is the sales figure projected for 20X4. This method of forecasting future financing is not as precise or detailed as the method using a cash budget, which is presented later; however, it offers a relatively low-cost and easy-to-use first approximation of the firm's financing needs for a future period.

Table 6.1 highlights items that are assumed to vary directly in line with changes in sales. It might seem surprising that this includes non-current assets (such as plant and equipment). The reason for this is that the firm believes in this instance that it does not have sufficient productive capacity (in the form of 'fixed' assets) to absorb a projected increase in sales. Thus, the firm assumes that if sales were to rise by $1, non-current assets would rise by $0.40, or 40% of the projected increase in sales. (However, in different circumstances, if the firm's non-current assets had sufficient capacity to support the projected level of new sales, these assets should not be allowed to vary with sales. If this were the case, then non-current assets would not be converted to a percent of sales and would be projected to remain unchanged for the period being forecast.)

Also, note that accounts payable and accrued expenses are the only liabilities allowed to vary with sales. Both these accounts might reasonably be expected to rise and fall with the level of sales—hence the use of the percent-of-sales forecast. Because these two categories of current liabilities normally vary directly with the level of sales, they are often referred to as **spontaneous sources of financing**. Chapter 7, which discusses working-capital management, has more to say about these forms of financing. Notes payable, long-term debt, ordinary shares and paid-up capital are not assumed to vary directly with the level of sales. These sources of financing are termed **discretionary**, in that the firm's management must make a conscious decision to seek additional financing using any one of them. Finally, note that the level of retained earnings *does* vary with estimated sales. The predicted change in the level of retained earnings equals the difference between estimated after-tax profits (projected net income) of $600 000 and ordinary share dividends of $300 000.

Thus, using the example from Table 6.1, it is estimated that sales will increase from $10 million to $12 million, which will cause a need for the firm's total assets to rise to $7.2 million. These assets will then be financed as follows:

- $4.9 million in existing liabilities plus spontaneous liabilities
- $1.8 million in owners' funds, including $300 000 in retained earnings from next year's sales
- $500 000 in discretionary financing, which can be raised by using a bank overdraft, by issuing notes payable or other debt, by issuing shares, or through some combination of these sources.

In summary, the firm's need for discretionary financing can be estimated, using the percent-of-sales method of financial forecasting, by following a four-step procedure (using, by way of illustration, the figures from Table 6.1):[3]

Step 1: Convert each asset and liability account that varies directly with sales to a percent of the current year's sales. For example:

$$\frac{\text{current assets}}{\text{sales}} = \frac{\$2\text{m}}{\$10\text{m}} = 0.2, \text{ or } 20\%$$

Step 2: Project the level of each asset and liability account in the forecast balance sheet using its percent of sales multiplied by projected sales or by leaving the account balance unchanged where the account does not vary with the level of sales. For example:

$$\text{Projected current assets} = \text{projected sales} \times \frac{\text{current assets}}{\text{sales}}$$

$$= \$12\text{m} \times 0.2 = \$2.4\text{m}$$

---

spontaneous sources of financing
The trade credit and other accounts payable that arise 'spontaneously' in the firm's day-to-day operations.

discretionary sources of financing
The sources of financing that require an explicit decision on the part of the firm's management every time funds are raised.

Step 3: Project the level of new retained earnings available to help finance the firm's operations. This equals projected net income for the period less planned ordinary share dividends. For example:

Projected addition to retained earnings

$$= \text{projected sales} \times \frac{\text{net income}}{\text{sales}} \times \left(1 - \frac{\text{cash dividends}}{\text{net income}}\right)$$

$$= \$12\text{m} \times 0.05 \times (1 - 0.5) = \$300\,000$$

Step 4: Project the firm's need for discretionary financing as the projected level of total assets less projected liabilities and owners' equity. For example:

$$\text{Discretionary financing needed} = \text{projected total assets} - \text{projected total liabilities} - \text{projected owners' equity}$$

$$= \$7.2\text{m} - \$4.9\text{m} - \$1.8\text{m} = \$500\,000$$

Concept check

6.1 If we cannot predict the future perfectly, then why do firms engage in financial forecasting?
6.2 Why are sales forecasts so important to developing a firm's financial forecast?
6.3 What is the percent-of-sales method of financial forecasting?
6.4 What are some examples of spontaneous and discretionary sources of financing?

For answers go to MyFinanceLab or www.pearson.com.au/9781442539174

Limitations of the percent-of-sales method of financial forecasting

OBJECTIVE **3**

Describe the limitations of the percent-of-sales method.

As noted earlier, the main virtue of the percent-of-sales method of financial forecasting is its simplicity. But this method assumes that we can accurately forecast future financial items (such as assets) as a given percentage of sales. In other words, a straight-line relationship is assumed between sales and asset costs. This may be a valid assumption for inventory levels that rise and fall in direct proportion to sales volumes. However, depending on the type of operations of the firm and the types of assets used, this one-to-one relationship may not hold.

Non-current assets such as large-scale equipment may need to be purchased or built well in advance of the use of their full capacity to generate sales. Because there is excess capacity until a full sales volume is reached, there is not a direct relationship between regular sales and the cost of the equipment. Also, although some firms purchase finished goods inventories daily on demand, other firms need to have a constant level on hand and then to increase this according to sales demands. Although the purchase of inventory then varies with sales, there is not a straight-line relationship between the overall inventory levels and sales levels.[4]

To obtain a more precise estimate of the amount and timing of the firm's future financing needs, a cash budget is required. For many firms, or divisions of firms, the percent-of-sales method of financial forecasting may provide a useful low-cost forerunner to the development of the more detailed cash budget, which the firm will ultimately use to estimate its financing needs. The budget will reflect the simple percent-of-sales method if this is appropriate; otherwise, it will use the more complex relationships between sales and financial variables.

Concept check

6.5 Why is it that the percent-of-sales method may not be applicable, in particular, to non-current (fixed) assets?

For answers go to MyFinanceLab or www.pearson.com.au/9781442539174

FYI

During the past few decades, computers have made a dramatic impact on the practice of financial forecasting, planning and budgeting. Proprietary spreadsheet programs such as Excel have allowed financial analysts to formulate budgets on the computer. These can then be modified readily to reflect any number of possible scenarios. This type of 'what if' analysis has greatly enhanced analysts' decision-making capability, by allowing them to assess quickly and easily the importance of the projections and assumptions that go into any financial plan.

Vast amounts of data can be captured and stored on databases, analysed under different scenarios on spreadsheets and then reported via the Internet or intranet.

But, before these computer capabilities can be accessed, the financial analyst needs to thoroughly understand the essential elements that underlie the practice of financial forecasting, planning and budgeting, the topics that are covered in this chapter.

Financial planning, budgets and the cash forecast

Back to the principles

Elaborate cash budgets are needed so that firms can avoid a cash crisis when anticipated cash inflows fall below cash outflows. This is a direct reflection of **Principle 3: Cash—not profits—is king**. It is cash flow and not accounting profits that pay the firm's bills. In addition, budgets are the critical tool of managerial control. **Principle 7: The agency problem—managers won't work for owners unless it's in their best interest** speaks to the root source of the problem, and budgets provide one tool for attempting to deal with it. Specifically, budgets provide management with a tool for evaluating performance and consequently maintaining a degree of control over employee actions.

Financial forecasts are the basis for constructing financial plans. These plans culminate in the preparation of a cash budget and a set of pro-forma statements for a future period in the firm's operations.

BUDGET FUNCTIONS

budget
A written forecast of future events designed as an aid to planning and controlling operations and/or financial management.

A **budget** is simply a forecast of future events. For example, students preparing for final exams make use of time budgets, which help them allocate their limited preparation time to their various courses. Students also must budget their financial resources, dividing them among competing uses such as books, tuition, food, rent, clothes and extracurricular activities.

Budgets perform three basic functions for a firm. First, they indicate the amount and timing of the firm's needs for future financing. Second, they provide the basis for taking corrective action in the event that actual performance figures do not match the previously budgeted figures. Third, budgets provide the basis for performance evaluation. Plans are carried out by people, and budgets provide benchmarks that management can use to evaluate the performance of those responsible for carrying out those plans and, in turn, control their actions. Thus, budgets are valuable aids in both the planning and control aspects of the firm's financial management.

In the pages that follow, a budgetary system for a hypothetical wholesaling firm will be developed. The primary emphasis will be on the cash budget and pro-forma financial statements. These statements provide the information needed for a detailed estimate of the firm's future financing requirements.

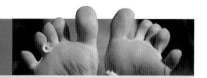

A characteristic of a wholesaler is that it buys substantially on credit from manufacturers or other suppliers and resells them on credit to retailers. Thus, it has a significant investment in accounts receivable (trade debtors) as well as significant 'spontaneous' financing from payables (creditors).

In this respect, budgeting is similar to a manufacturer, who typically sources materials and components from debtors and sells on credit to wholesalers or retailers. In contrast, retailers are more likely to sell for cash so there is not such a heavy investment in accounts receivable.

THE BUDGETARY SYSTEM

Although our interest in financial planning focuses on the cash budget, a number of other budgets provide the basis for its preparation. In general, a business will use four types of budgets: physical budgets, cost budgets, profit budgets and cash budgets. This system of budgets allows planning for each source of cash flow, both inflow and outflow, that will affect the firm throughout the planning period. Figure 6.1 presents an overview of the budgetary system.

Physical budgets include budgets for physical, as opposed to financial, items. Examples include budgets for unit sales, number of personnel, unit production, inventory amounts and physical facilities. These budgets are used as the basis for generating cost, cash and profit budgets. **Cost budgets** are prepared for every major expense category of the firm. For example, a manufacturing firm would prepare cost budgets for manufacturing or production costs, selling costs, administrative costs, financing costs, and research and development costs. These cost budgets along with the sales budget provide the basis for preparing a **profit budget**. Finally,

physical budgets
Budgets for unit sales, personnel, unit production, inventories and physical facilities. These budgets are used as the basis for generating cost and profit budgets.

cost budgets
Budgets prepared for every major expense category of the firm, such as production cost, selling cost, administrative cost, financing cost, and research and development cost.

profit budget
A budget of forecasted profits based on information gleaned from the cost and sales budgets.

FIGURE 6.1 The budget system

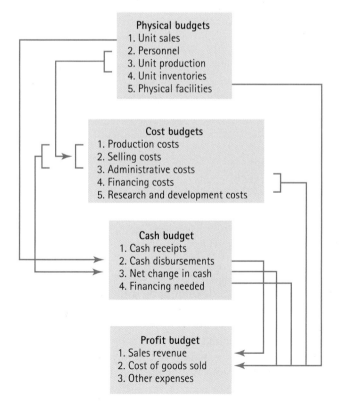

converting all the budget information to a cash basis provides the information required to prepare the cash budget.

THE CASH BUDGET

cash budget
A detailed plan of future cash flows. This budget is composed of four elements: cash receipts, cash disbursements, net change in cash for the period, and new financing needed.

The **cash budget** represents a detailed plan of future cash flows and is composed of four elements: cash receipts, cash disbursements (payments), net change in cash for the period, and new financing needed. Example 6.1 demonstrates the construction and use of a cash budget.

EXAMPLE 6.1 Preparation of a cash budget

Furnco is a regional wholesaler of household furniture. Furnco's sales are highly seasonal, peaking in the months of March to May. Roughly 30% of Furnco's sales are collected one month after the sale, 50% two months after the sale, and the remainder during the third month following the sale.

Furnco attempts to pace its purchases in line with its forecast of future sales. Purchases generally equal 75% of sales and are made two months in advance of anticipated sales. Payments are made in the month following purchases. For example, June sales are estimated at $100 000, thus April purchases are 0.75 × $100 000 = $75 000. Correspondingly, May payments equal $75 000 for April purchases. Wages, salaries, rent and other cash expenses are recorded in Table 6.2, which gives Furnco's cash budget for the six-month period ended June 20X3. Additional expenditures recorded in the cash budget are the $14 000 purchase of equipment during February and the repayment of a $12 000 loan in May. In June, Furnco will pay $7500 interest (covering the six-month period of January–June 20X3) on its $150 000 long-term debt. Interest of $600 is payable in May (covering the period January to May) on the $12 000 short-term note repaid in May.

Furnco presently has a cash balance of $20 000 and wants to maintain a minimum balance of $10 000. Additional borrowing necessary to maintain that minimum balance is estimated in the final section of Table 6.2. Borrowing takes place at the beginning of the month in which the funds are needed. Interest on borrowed funds equals 12% per annum, or 1% per month, and is paid in the month following the one in which the funds are borrowed. Thus, interest on funds borrowed in February will be paid in March, equal to 1% of the loan amount outstanding during February.

The financing-needed line on Furnco's cash budget indicates that the firm will need to borrow $36 350 in February, $29 524 in March, $20 759 in April, and $10 966 in May. Only in June will the firm be able to reduce its cumulative borrowing to $79 875. Note that the cash budget indicates not only the amount of financing needed during the period but also when the funds will be needed.

FIXED VERSUS FLEXIBLE BUDGETS

fixed budget
Future budget estimates based on a single level of production or sales/revenue.

flexible budget
Various future budget estimates based on a range of levels of production or sales/revenue.

The cash budget given in Table 6.2 for Furnco is an example of a **fixed budget**. Cash-flow estimates are based on a single set of monthly sales estimates. Thus, the estimates of expenses and new financing needed are meaningful only for the level of sales for which they were computed. To avoid this limitation, several budget scenarios can be prepared, each corresponding to a different set of sales estimates. Such a **flexible budget** fulfils two basic functions: first, it gives information regarding the range of the firm's possible financing needs, and, second, it provides a standard against which to measure the performance of employees who are responsible for the various cost and revenue items contained in the budget.

This second function deserves some additional comment. The obvious problem is that costs vary with the actual level of sales experienced by the firm. Thus, if the budget is to be used as a standard for performance evaluation or control, it must be constructed to match realised sales

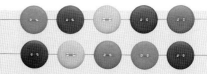

Your money

YOUR PERSONAL BUDGET

To many people, the term 'budget' brings to mind the idea of a financial straitjacket, something that takes all the spontaneity out of life. In reality, a budget is simply a tool that can be used to help you reach your personal goals. A budget (or cash flow plan) helps you to use restraint, to think about what you spend your money on and to avoid living beyond your means. For example, if you've already spent this month's budgeted amount on eating at fast-food joints, the budget will indicate that you will be eating at home the rest of the month or you'll have to free up money from another area of your budget.

Self-restraint is tough—especially when you are being bombarded by TV, Internet, radio, newspaper and magazine advertisers, all with their sights on your money.

Here's how to go about preparing a personal budget.

Step one is to document how you are spending your money. You will need to carefully track your expenses for a month. You'll find a number of budgeting worksheets on the Internet which you can download free. An immediate benefit of preparing a budget is that the very act of documenting how you are spending your money will help you identify expenses you can eliminate.

Step two is to prepare a personal cash budget, the key tool for helping you control your cash inflows and outflows. The cash budget will include projections of your future income and when it will be received, as well as your planned expenditures. Once prepared, the cash budget becomes a tool for controlling your spending habits. By comparing actual expenditures with planned or budgeted expenditures you can gauge how much money you will have left over and what can be saved for future use. Instead of the negative idea of a financial straightjacket, most people find that having a personal cash budget gives them a feeling of control and security.

TABLE 6.2 Furnco: Cash budget for the six months ended 30 June 20X3

WORKSHEET	OCT	NOV	DEC	JAN	FEB	MAR	APR	MAY	JUNE	JULY	AUG
Sales	$55000	$62000	$50000	$60000	$75000	$88000	$100000	$110000	$100000	$80000	$75000
Collections:											
One month ago (30%)				15000	18000	22500	26400	30000	33000		
Two months ago (50%)				31000	25000	30000	37500	44000	50000		
Three months ago (20%)				11000	12400	10000	12000	15000	17600		
Total				$57000	55400	62500	75900	89000	100600		
Purchases			$56250	66000	75000	82500	75000	60000	56250		
Payments (one-month lag)				56250	66000	75000	82500	75000	60000		
Cash receipts:											
Collections				$57000	55400	62500	75900	89000	100600		
Cash disbursements:											
Purchases				$56250	66000	75000	82500	75000	60000		
Wages and salaries				3000	10000	7000	8000	6000	4000		
Rent				4000	4000	4000	4000	4000	4000		
Other expenses				1000	500	1200	1500	1500	1200		
Interest expense on existing debt ($12000 note and $150000 in long-term debt)								600	7500		
Taxes					4460				5200		
Purchase of equipment				14000							
Loan repayment ($12000 note due in May)								12000			
Total disbursements				$64250	94500	91660	96000	99100	81900		
Net monthly change				$(7250)	(39100)	(29160)	(20100)	(10100)	18700		
Plus: Beginning cash balance				20000	12750	10000	10000	10000	10000		
Less: Interest on short-term borrowing				—	—	(364)	(659)	(866)	(976)		
Equals: Ending cash balance—no borrowing				12750	(26350)	(19524)	(10759)	(966)	27724		
Financing needed[a]				—	36350	29524	20759	10966	(17724)[b]		
Ending cash balance				$12750	10000	10000	10000	10000	10000		
Cumulative borrowing				—	36350	65874	86633	97599	79875		

a The amount of financing that is required to raise the firm's ending cash balance up to its $10000 desired cash balance.

b Negative financing needed simply means the firm has excess cash that can be used to retire a part of its short-term borrowing from prior months.

and production figures. This can involve much more than simply 'adjusting cost figures up or down in proportion to the deviation of actual from planned sales'; that is, costs may not vary in strict proportion to sales, just as inventory levels may not vary as a constant percentage of sales. Thus, preparation of a flexible budget involves re-estimating all the cash expenses that would be incurred at each of several possible sales levels. This process might use a variant of the percent-of-sales method discussed earlier.

BUDGET PERIOD

There are no strict rules for determining the length of the budget period. However, as a general rule it should be long enough to show the effect of management policies yet short enough so that estimates can be made with reasonable accuracy. Applying this rule of thumb to the Furnco example in Table 6.2, it appears that the six-month budget period is too short. This is because it is not known if the cash deficit of the first six months will be reversed during the following period. If the cash situation is not remedied, then a re-evaluation of the firm's plans and policies will clearly be needed. In this respect, firms with seasonal sales patterns, such as Furnco, typically have cash flow deficits during each month when they build up stocks of inventory, followed by cash flow surpluses in months when peak sales occur. Thus, financing raised during the cash-deficit months can possibly be repaid during the following cash-surplus months.

capital-expenditure budget
Detailed plans by a firm for acquiring plant and equipment over a five-year, 10-year or even longer period. See also **budget**.

Longer range budgets are also prepared in the form of a **capital-expenditure budget**. This budget details the firm's plans for acquiring plant and equipment over a five-year, 10-year or even longer period. Furthermore, firms often develop comprehensive long-range plans extending up to 10 years into the future. These plans are generally not as detailed as the annual cash budget, but they do consider such major components as sales, capital expenditures, new-product development, capital funds acquisition and employment needs.

Concept check

6.6   What is a firm's cash budget and how is it used in financial planning?
6.7   How long should the firm's budget period be?

For answers go to MyFinanceLab or
www.pearson.com.au/9781442539174

Finance at work

FORECASTING PROBLEMS AT DREAMWORKS

The difficulty of forecasting sales, along with the central role played by the sales forecast in budgeting for profits, is illustrated by the problems encountered by DreamWorks media company in the mid 2000s. DreamWorks had listed on the stock exchange after a successful run of animated movies such as *Shrek*. However, the company soon encountered problems with lower than expected sales of DVDs such as *Shrek 2*. This in turn led to excessive inventory levels of that movie and others. In part, the problem was attributed to a flood of DVD releases that forced retailers to return DVDs that were not selling rapidly, in order to clear space on the shelves for the influx of new titles.

Previously, retailers had found that movies had a shelf-life of six months, but this decreased rapidly when the proliferation of titles gave consumers a much wider choice. High sales of one title over a long time period had been replaced by low sales per title over a short time period. Thus, it seems that DreamWorks suffered from two main factors. First, it had pinned its budget excessively on the expected high sales performance of 'blockbusters' such as *Shrek 2*. Second, there had been rapid change in the dynamics of DVD retailing, exemplified by the flood of new titles.

Pro-forma financial statements

OBJECTIVE **5**

Prepare pro-forma financial statements.

pro-forma financial statements
Statements of planned profit or loss, balance-sheet items or cash-flow items.

The final stage in the budgeting process involves construction of a set of **pro-forma financial statements** depicting the outcome of the planning period's operations. Financial information for Furnco is used to demonstrate the construction of the pro-forma income statement and balance sheet. To do this, we need Furnco's cash budget (found in Table 6.2) and its beginning balance sheet at 31 December 20X2, which depicts the financial condition of the firm at the start of the planning period (see Table 6.3).

THE PRO-FORMA INCOME STATEMENT

The pro-forma income statement represents a statement of planned profit or loss for a future period. For Furnco a six-month pro-forma income statement is constructed in Table 6.4.

TABLE 6.3   Furnco, Balance Sheet, 31 December 20X2

ASSETS		
Current assets		
Cash	$20 000	
Accounts receivable	104 400	
Inventories	101 250	
Total current assets		$225 650
Non-current assets		
Net plant and equipment		180 000
Total assets		$405 650

LIABILITIES AND OWNERS' EQUITY		
Current liabilities		
Accounts payable	$56 250	
Notes payable	12 000	
Taxes payable	4 460	
Total current liabilities		$72 710
Non-current liabilities		
Long-term debt		150 000
Shareholders' equity		
Contributed capital	70 000	
Retained earnings	112 940	
Total equity		182 940
Total liabilities and equity		$405 650

EXAMPLE 6.2   Preparation of a pro-forma income statement

Furnco's final pro-forma income statement is presented in Table 6.4.

In Table 6.4, sales total $533 000, found by summing the six-monthly sales projections (January to June) from Table 6.2. Cost of goods sold, $399 750, is computed as 75% of sales. (This figure could also have been found by summing purchases for November to April, which represent items sold from January to June. Recall that purchases are made two months in advance, so items sold in January to June were purchased in November to April.)

Depreciation expense cannot be obtained from the cash budget, since it does not constitute a cash flow. Thus, this expense must be determined from the depreciation schedules of Furnco's plant and equipment. On its existing fixed assets, Furnco has an annual depreciation expense of $17 200. In addition, the $14 000 piece of equipment purchased at the end of February will

TABLE 6.4	Furnco: Pro-forma income statement for the six-month period ended 30 June 20X3		
Sales	(from cash budget, Table 6.2)		$533 000
Cost of goods sold	(75% of sales)		(399 750)
Gross profit	(calculation)		$133 250
Operating expenses			
Depreciation	[($17 200 ÷ 2) + $230]	$8 830	
Wages and salaries	(from cash budget, Table 6.2)	38 000	
Rent	(from cash budget, Table 6.2)	24 000	
Other expenses	(from cash budget, Table 6.2)	6 900	(77 730)
Net operating income	(calculation)		$55 520
Interest expense	(calculation)		(11 764)
Earnings before taxes	(calculation)		$43 756
Income taxes payable	(40%)		(17 502)
Net income	(calculation)		$26 254

be depreciated over a 15-year life towards a $3650 salvage value. Using straight-line depreciation and depreciating the asset for four months of the budget period, we find that this amounts to roughly $230. Thus, total depreciation expense for the period is $8830 (or [$17 200/2] + $230).

Wages and salaries, rent and other expenses are found by summing the relevant cash-flow items from the cash budget for the months of January to June. This assumes, of course, that all these expenses are paid at the end of the month in which they are incurred, that rent is not paid in advance, and that all other expenses are paid on a monthly basis except interest on short-term borrowing, which is paid in the month following its incurrence. Wages and salaries total $38 000, rent expense equals $24 000, and other expenses are expected to be $6900.

Subtracting the above operating expenses from gross profit leaves a net operating income of $55 520. Interest expense[5] of $11 764 is then deducted from net operating income to obtain earnings before taxes of $43 756. Income taxes payable are found using an assumed 40% income-tax rate. For Furnco this equals a tax expense for the period of $17 502. Finally, subtracting the estimated taxes from earnings before taxes indicates net income for the period of $26 254.

THE PRO-FORMA BALANCE SHEET

The pro-forma balance sheet for Furnco can be constructed by using information from the cash budget (Table 6.2), the 31 December 20X2 balance sheet (Table 6.3), and the pro-forma

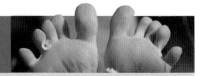

FYI

NET CASH FLOW VERSUS NET INCOME

The difference in the cash and accrual bases of accounting for corporate income is vividly demonstrated in the cash budget and pro-forma income statement over the period shown for Furnco. On a cash-flow basis the firm has a substantial negative net cash flow, while on an accrual basis the firm earned a profit of $26 254. The difference, of course, relates to when revenues and expenses are accounted for or recognised in the two statements. In the cash budget, revenues and expenses are included in the months in which cash is actually received or disbursed. In the income statement, which is prepared on an accrual basis, revenues and expenses are included in the month in which the corresponding sale took place, which is often not the same month in which cash is received.

income statement (Table 6.4). Furnco's pro-forma balance sheet for 30 June 20X3 is presented in Example 6.3.

EXAMPLE 6.3   Preparation of a pro-forma balance sheet

Furnco's pro-forma balance sheet is shown in Table 6.5. Estimates of the individual balance-sheet entries are provided after the table.

TABLE 6.5	Furnco: Pro-forma balance sheet, 30 June 20X3		
ASSETS			
Current assets			
Cash		$10000	
Accounts receivable		197000	
Inventories		116250	
Total current assets			$323250
Non-current assets			
Net plant and equipment			185170
Total assets			$508420
LIABILITIES AND OWNERS' EQUITY			
Current liabilities			
Accounts payable		$56250	
Interest payable		799	
Notes payable[a]		79875	
Taxes payable		12302	
Total current liabilities			$149226
Non-current liabilities			
Long-term debt			150000
Shareholders' equity			
Contributed capital		70000	
Retained earnings		139194	
Total equity			209194
Total liabilities and equity			$508420

a Cumulative borrowing for the period was assumed to take the form of notes payable. This figure is taken from the cumulative-borrowing row of the cash budget contained in Table 6.2.

Asset accounts in the balance sheet
Ending cash of $10000 is taken from the cash budget, and it becomes the corresponding cash entry in Furnco's pro-forma balance sheet.

Accounts receivable balance is determined from the following items: the beginning balance is taken from the 31 December 20X2 balance sheet (Table 6.3), and credit sales and collections are obtained by summing across the relevant monthly totals in the Table 6.2 cash budget:

Accounts receivable, 31/12/X2 (from Table 6.3)	$104 400
+ Credit sales (from Table 6.2)	533000
– Collections (from Table 6.2)	(440 400)
Accounts receivable, 30/6/20X3 (calculation)	$197000

Inventories are determined in a similar manner:

Inventories, 31/12/X2 (from Table 6.3)	$101 250
+ Purchases (from Table 6.2)	414 750
– Cost of goods sold (from Table 6.4)	(399 750)
Inventories, 30/6/20X3 (calculation)	$116 250

Purchases were found by summing relevant monthly figures from the cash budget (Table 6.2) for all six months of the budget period, and cost of goods sold was taken from the pro-forma income statement in Table 6.4.

Plant and equipment figures are found as follows:

Net plant and equipment, 31/12/X2 (from Table 6.3)	$180 000
+ Purchases of plant and equipment (from Table 6.2)	14 000
– Depreciation expense (from Table 6.4)	(8 830)
Net plant and equipment, 30/6/20X3 (calculation)	$185 170

Purchases of plant and equipment are reflected in the cash budget, and depreciation expense is taken from the pro-forma income statement. The only changes that took place during the period involved the $14 000 asset purchase, along with depreciation expense of $8830, leaving a net balance of $185 170. Total assets for Furnco are therefore expected to be $508 420.

Liability accounts in the balance sheet

The liability accounts are estimated using the same basic methodology as that used in finding the asset balances.

Accounts payable is found as follows, with purchases and payments being taken from the cash budget for each of the six months of the budget period:

Accounts payable, 31/12/X2 (from Table 6.3)	$56 250
+ Purchases (from Table 6.2)	414 750
– Payments (from Table 6.2)	(414 750)
Accounts payable, 30/6/20X3 (calculation)	$56 250

Interest payable's ending balance can be analysed as follows: during June the firm had total borrowings of $77 875, on which it owes $799 in interest. However, since interest is not paid in the month in which the expense is incurred, this interest liability still exists at the end of June:

Interest payable, 31/12/X2	$0
+ Interest expense	11 764
– Interest paid	10 965
Interest payable, 30/6/20X3 (calculation)	$799

Notes payable can be determined after it is assumed that the total new financing needed during the period ($79 875) would be raised through notes payable. (Furnco's use of short-term financing may or may not be desirable, as we will see in Chapter 7 when working-capital management is discussed.)

Notes payable, 31/12/X2 (from Table 6.3)	$12 000
+ Borrowings needed, 30/6/20X3 (from Table 6.2)	79 875
– Repayments (from Table 6.2)	(12 000)
Notes payable, 30/6/20X3 (calculation)	$79 875

Accrued interest expense is created by the $799 interest expense that was incurred during June on the short-term borrowing that will not be paid until July, as discussed above.

Taxes payable are computed as follows:

Taxes payable, 31/12/X2 (from Table 6.3)	$4 460
+ Tax liability for the period (from Table 6.4)	17 502
– Tax payments made during the period (from Table 6.2)	(9 660)
Taxes payable, 30/6/20X3 (calculation)	$12 302

Long-term debt remains unchanged for the period.

Equity accounts in the balance sheet
Contributed capital remains unchanged for the period. However, the *retained earnings* balance is found as follows:

Retained earnings, 31/12/X2 (from Table 6.3)	$112 940
+ Net income for the period (from Table 6.4)	26 254
– Cash dividends (from Table 6.2)	0
Retained earnings, 30/6/20X3 (calculation)	$139 194

Financial monitoring and control

The pro-forma statements just prepared can be used to *monitor* or control the firm's financial performance. One approach involves preparing pro-forma statements for each month during the planning period. Actual operating results for each month's operations can then be compared with the projected or pro-forma figures. This type of analysis provides an early-warning system to detect financial problems as they develop. In particular, by comparing actual monthly (or even weekly) operating results with projected revenue and expense items (from pro-forma income statements), the financial manager can maintain a very close watch on the firm's overall profitability and take an active role in determining the firm's overall performance for the planning period.

Financial planning and budgeting: closing comments

Two aspects of pro-forma statements should be emphasised. First, these figures represent single-point estimates of each of the items in the entire system of budgets and the resulting pro-forma statements. Although these might be the *best* estimates of what the future will hold for Furnco, drawing up at least two additional sets of estimates is desirable, corresponding to the very worst set of circumstances that the firm might face and the very best. These extremes provide the necessary input for formulating contingency financing plans should a deviation from the expected figures occur. Second, notes payable was used as a *plug* figure for additional financing needed. The actual source of financing selected will depend on a number of factors, including (1) the length of the period for which the financing will be needed, (2) the cost of alternative sources of funds, and (3) the preferences of the firm's management regarding the use of debt versus equity. These factors will be further investigated in Chapter 7, when short-term financing is discussed.

Concept check
6.8   How is the pro-forma income statement linked to the pro-forma balance sheet?
6.9   What is the link between the cash budget and the pro-forma balance sheet?

For answers go to MyFinanceLab or www.pearson.com.au/9781442539174

International spotlight

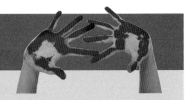

PLANNING TAX PAYMENTS IN GLOBAL COMPANIES

Part of the planning process in global firms is *tax planning*. This involves planning ahead to legally minimise tax payments. Global companies or multinational enterprises (MNEs) have the potential to minimise their overall tax liability by 'juggling' various payments between different subsidiary companies or divisions located in different countries. This arises from the fact that governments levy income tax (or tax on profits) at different rates in different countries, and so it is in the interests of the MNE to pay tax in countries where its divisions are taxed at low rates. The amount of tax payable can be influenced by means such as royalties and transfer payments. *Royalties* are ongoing fees payable for the use of technology or intangible property such as copyright, trademarks, designs, formulae and so on. *Transfer payments* are the prices paid for the sale of things like components or raw materials between different divisions of the MNE.

For example, Division A might be in a high-tax country and Division B might be in a low-tax country. Suppose that Division A is licensed by Division B to use some intangible property such as a manufacturing process developed by B. In return, A makes an annual royalty payment to B. It would thus be in the MNE's overall interests to set a high royalty payment.

In this way, A's expenses would be increased and so its taxable income would be decreased, a significant factor if A is located in a high-tax country. B's income would increase proportionately, but this would be taxed at a lower rate than if the income were earned in A's country. Thus, the overall amount of tax payable by the MNE would be less than if a lower royalty amount were payable.

Similar considerations apply to *transfer payments*. For example, Division X might sell components that are used in Division Y's manufacturing operations in another country. The price paid for such materials can be set in such a way that it minimises taxable income in a high-tax country and increases taxable income in a low-tax country. However, the MNE needs to centralise control over such transfer payments and royalties, because a local division's managers might otherwise resist steps to reduce their apparent income. In addition, the MNE's central management needs to take account of anticipated exchange-rate movements that might otherwise counteract the benefits of transfer payments and the like. Furthermore, the MNE's ability to manipulate its internal transfer payments and the like may be limited by taxation laws, with many countries' tax authorities paying close attention to payments that are not at 'arm's length'.

Summary

OBJECTIVE 1 This chapter develops the role of forecasting within the context of the firm's financial planning processes. Forecasts of the firm's sales revenues and related expenses provide the basis for projecting *future financing needs*.

OBJECTIVE 2 A useful first approximation method for forecasting financial variables is the percent-of-sales method. However, users of the percent-of-sales method need to be aware of the limitations of the method.

OBJECTIVE 3

OBJECTIVE 4

OBJECTIVE 5 Forecasts of sales and expenses are used to develop the cash budget for the planning period, which is then used to estimate the firm's future financing needs. The cash budget is integral to preparing pro-forma financial statements, which are forecasts of the income statement and the balance sheet. Pro-forma financial statements provide the user with a basis for:
- evaluating the results of the firm's financial plans
- controlling the firm's operations during the planning period.

In this chapter, it was assumed that all discretionary financing needs are met through short-term notes. However, Chapters 7, 18 and 19 will look more closely at sources of financing. Chapter 7 deals with the choice between current or short-term financing and long-term financing, Chapter 18 covers medium-term and long-term debt, and Chapter 19 deals with ordinary shares, preference shares and convertible securities.

budget	184	flexible budget	186
capital-expenditure budget	188	percent-of-sales method	180
cash budget	186	physical budgets	185
cost budgets	185	profit budget	185
discretionary sources of financing	182	pro-forma financial statements	189
fixed budget	186	spontaneous sources of financing	182

For a complete flashcard glossary go to MyFinanceLab at www.pearson.com.au/myfinancelab

Web works

You can find financial information for Myer at **www.myer.com.au**. Look in 'Investors' and determine the company's projected sales. Why are sales forecasts so important to developing a firm's financial forecast?

Review questions

6-1 One of the objectives of financial forecasting is, ultimately, to determine how much finance the firm will need to raise in the planning period. Explain what steps are involved in this process.

6-2 A simplified way of financial forecasting is the percent-of-sales method. Discuss the limitations of this method.

6-3 Explain how a fixed cash budget differs from a variable (or flexible) cash budget.

6-4 What two basic needs does a flexible (variable) cash budget serve?

6-5 What would be the probable effect on a firm's cash position of the following events?

(a) A blowout in collection of receivables
(b) A delay in the payment of payables
(c) Rapidly rising sales
(d) Holding larger inventories

6-6 Is it fair to say that all budgets should be for a 12-month period?

6-7 A cash budget is usually thought of as a way of determining the need for finance in future periods. Why would a cash budget also be important for a firm that has excess cash on hand?

6-8 Explain why a cash budget would be of particular importance to a firm that experiences seasonal fluctuations in its sales.

6-9 Outline briefly some of the differences in the budgetary processes for a typical manufacturer, wholesaler and retailer, respectively.

6-10 Is there a difference between estimated net profit after taxes for a period and the estimated net addition to the cash balance? Explain.

6-11 Briefly explain how, in planning their international operations, multinational corporations might be able to use methods such as transfer payments to minimise their total tax bill.

Self-test problems

ST-1 (*Financial forecasting*) Use the percent-of-sales method to prepare a pro-forma income statement for Calico Sales Co. Projected sales for next year equal $4 million. Cost of goods sold equals 70% of sales, administrative expense equals $500 000 and depreciation expense is $300 000. Interest expense equals $50 000 and income is taxed at a rate of 40%. The firm plans to spend $200 000 during the period to renovate its office facility and will retire $150 000 in notes payable. Finally, selling expense equals 5% of sales.

For answers go to MyFinanceLab www.pearson.com.au/myfinancelab

ST-2 (*Cash budget*) Stauffer Ltd has estimated sales and purchase requirements for the last half of the coming year. Past experience indicates that it will collect 20% of its sales in the month of the sale, 50% of the remainder one month after the sale, and the balance in the second month following the sale. Stauffer prefers to pay for half its purchases in the month of the purchase and the other half the following month. Labour expense for each month is expected to equal 5% of that month's sales, with cash payment being made in the month in which the expense is incurred. Depreciation expense is $5000 per month; miscellaneous cash expenses are $4000 per month and are paid in the month incurred. General and administrative expenses of $50000 are recognised and paid monthly. A $60000 truck is to be purchased in August and is to be depreciated on a straight-line basis over 10 years with no expected salvage value. The company also plans to pay a $9000 cash dividend to shareholders in July. The company feels that a minimum cash balance of $30000 should be maintained. Any borrowing will cost 12% annually, with interest paid in the month following the month in which the funds are borrowed. Borrowing takes place at the beginning of the month in which the need for funds arises. For example, if during the month of July the firm should need to borrow $24000 to maintain its $30000 desired minimum balance, then $24000 will be taken out on 1 July with interest owed for the entire month of July. Interest for the month of July would then be paid on 1 August. Sales and purchase estimates are shown below. Prepare a cash budget for the months of July and August. (Cash on hand 30/6 was $30000, while sales for May and June were $100000 and purchases were $60000 for each of these months.)

MONTH	SALES	PURCHASES
July	$120000	$50000
August	150000	40000
September	110000	30000

ST-3 (*Pro-forma statements and liquidity analysis*) The balance sheet for Odom Manufacturing Company on 31 December 20X3 is shown below. The treasurer of Odom Manufacturing wishes to borrow $500000, the funds from which would be applied in the following manner:

1. $100000 to reduce accounts payable
2. $75000 to retire current notes payable
3. $175000 to expand existing plant facilities
4. $80000 to increase inventories
5. $70000 to increase cash on hand

Odom Manufacturing Company, Balance Sheet, 31 December 20X3

Cash	$250000	Accounts payable	$850000
Accounts receivable	760000	Notes payable	550000
Inventory	860000	Current liabilities	$1 400000
Current assets	$1 870000	Long-term debt	800000
Property, plant and equipment	1 730000	Share capital	600000
		Retained earnings	800000
Total assets	$3 600000	Total liabilities and equity	$3 600000

Repayment of the $500000 will be in 20 years with interest paid annually.

(a) Assuming that the loan is obtained, prepare a pro-forma balance sheet for Odom Manufacturing that reflects the use of the loan proceeds.

(b) Did the firm's liquidity improve after the loan was obtained and the proceeds dispensed in the above manner? Why or why not?

6-1 (*Percent-of-sales forecasting*) Which of the following accounts would probably vary directly with the level of the firm's sales? Discuss each briefly.

For more problems and for answers to problems marked with an asterisk (*) go to MyFinanceLab at www.pearson.com.au/myfinancelab

	YES	NO
Cash	____	____
Marketable securities	____	____
Accounts payable	____	____
Notes payable	____	____
Plant and equipment	____	____
Inventories	____	____

6-2* (*Financial forecasting*) Farsight Company Ltd projects its sales next year to be $4 million and expects to earn 5% of that amount after taxes. The firm is currently in the process of projecting its financing needs and has made the following assumptions (projections):

1. Current assets will equal 20% of sales, while fixed assets will remain at their current level of $1 million.
2. Ordinary equity is presently $0.8 million, and the firm pays out half of its after-tax earnings in dividends.
3. The firm has short-term payables and trade credit that normally equal 10% of sales, and has no long-term debt outstanding.

What are Farsight's financing needs for the coming year?

6-3 (*Financial forecasting—percent of sales*) Futuro Sales Ltd has current-year sales of $36 million, with a 5% profit margin and $1 200 000 paid as dividends. Fixed assets are $12 million and the firm's current assets are $14 million. On the other side of the balance sheet, accounts payable equal $3 million, and there is $4 million of long-term debt; equity totals $19 million (including $8 million in retained earnings). The company is in the middle of its annual planning exercise. The finance director estimates that next year's sales will be $50 million, that current assets will equal the same proportion of sales as this year, and that fixed assets will increase by $200 000.

(a) What is your estimate of Futuro's total financing needs (i.e. total assets) for the coming year?
(b) Given the firm's projections and assuming the same dividend payment, what are the firm's discretionary financing needs?
(c) Based on the projections given and assuming that the $200 000 increase in fixed assets will occur, what is the largest increase in sales the firm can support without having to resort to the use of discretionary sources of financing?

6-4* (*Financial forecasting—percent of sales*) The balance sheet of the Quickspress Delivery Company follows:

Quickspress Delivery Company, Balance Sheet, 31 December 20X5 ($ million)

Current assets	$10	Accounts payable	$5
Net fixed assets	15	Notes payable	0
		Debt	10
		Equity	10
Total	$25		$25

Quickspress had sales for the year ended 31/12/20X5 of $50 million. The firm follows a policy of paying out all net earnings to its ordinary shareholders in cash dividends. Thus, the company generates no funds from its earnings that can be used to expand its operations. (Assume that depreciation expense is just equal to the cost of replacing worn-out assets.)

(a) If Quickspress anticipates sales of $80 million during the coming year, develop a pro-forma balance sheet for the firm for 31/12/20X6. Assume that current assets vary as a percentage of sales, net fixed assets remain unchanged, and accounts payable vary as a percentage of sales. Use notes payable as a balancing entry.

(b) How much 'new' financing will the company need next year?

(c) What limitations does the percent-of-sales forecast method suffer from? Discuss briefly.

6-5 (*Financial forecasting—percent of sales*) Tulley Appliances Ltd projects next year's sales to be $20 million. Current sales are at $15 million, based on current assets of $5 million and non-current assets of $5 million. The firm's net profit margin is 5% after taxes. Tulley forecasts that current assets will rise in direct proportion to the increase in sales, but fixed assets will increase by only $100000. Currently, Tulley has $1.5 million in accounts payable (which varies directly with sales), $2 million in long-term debt (due in 10 years), and ordinary equity (including $4 million in retained earnings) totalling $6.5 million. Tulley plans to pay $500000 in share dividends next year.

(a) What are Tulley's total financing needs (that is, total assets) for the coming year?

(b) Given the firm's projections and dividend payment plans, what are its discretionary financing needs?

(c) Based on your projections, and assuming that the $100000 expansion in fixed assets will occur, what is the largest increase in sales the firm can support without having to resort to the use of discretionary sources of financing?

6-6 (*Estimating collections from accounts receivable*) On 31 March 20X3, the Sylvia Gift Shop had outstanding accounts receivable of $20000. Sylvia's sales are roughly evenly split between credit and cash sales, with half the credit sales collected in the month after the sale and the remainder two months after the sale. Historical and projected sales for the gift shop are:

MONTH	SALES	MONTH	SALES
January	$15000	March	$30000
February	20000	April (projected)	40000

(a) Under these circumstances, what should the balance in accounts receivable be at the end of April?

(b) How much cash did Sylvia realise during April from sales and collections?

6-7 (*Estimating collections from accounts receivable*) On 31 March 20X4, the Floydata Food Distribution Company had outstanding accounts receivable of $52000. Sales are roughly 40% credit and 60% cash, with half of the credit sales collected in the month after the sale and the remainder two months after the sale. Historical and projected sales for Floydata follow:

MONTH	SALES
January	$100000
February	100000
March	80000
April (projected)	60000

(a) Under these circumstances, what should the balance in accounts receivable be at the end of April?

(b) How much cash did Floydata realise during April from sales and collections?

6-8   (*Pro-forma balance sheet construction*) Use the following industry average ratios to construct a pro-forma balance sheet for CM Company.

Total asset turnover		2 times
Average collection period (assume a 365-day year)		9 days
Fixed asset turnover		5 times
Inventory turnover (based on cost of goods sold)		3 times
Current ratio		2 times
Sales (all on credit)		$4 million
Cost of goods sold		75% of sales
Debt ratio		50%
Cash	_____	Current liabilities _____
Inventory	_____	Long-term debt _____
Accounts receivable	_____	Share capital *plus* _____
Net fixed assets	_____	retained earnings _____
Total	$ _____	Total $ _____

6-9   (*Financial forecasting—pro-forma balance sheet*) Use the following industry-average ratios to construct a pro-forma balance sheet for the V. M. Willet Co.

Total asset turnover		2.5 times
Average collection period (assume a 360-day year)		10 days
Fixed asset turnover		6 times
Inventory turnover (based on cost of goods sold)		4 times
Current ratio		3 times
Sales (all on credit)		$5 million
Cost of goods sold		80% of sales
Debt ratio		60%
Cash	$ _____	Current liabilities $ _____
Accounts receivable	$ _____	Long-term debt $ _____
Inventories	$ _____	Share capital *plus* $ _____
Net fixed assets	$ _____	retained earnings $ _____
Total	$ _____	Total $ _____

6-10*   (*Financial forecasting—changing credit policy*) Island Resorts has $400 000 invested in receivables throughout much of the year. It has annual credit sales of $3 600 000 and a gross profit margin of 80%.

> **(a)** What is Island Resorts' average collection period? (Hint: Recall that average collection period = accounts receivable/(credit sales/365).)
>
> **(b)** How much 'cash' would Island Resorts free up by reducing its accounts receivable if it were to change its credit policies in a way that reduced its average collection period to 30 days without affecting annual credit sales?

6-11   (*Forecasting discretionary financing needs*) Software Sales and Development Co. Ltd estimates that it invests 40 cents in assets for each dollar of new sales. However, 6 cents in profits are produced by each dollar of additional sales, of which 1 cent can be reinvested in the firm. If sales rise from their present level of $10 million by $1 million next year, and the ratio of spontaneous liabilities to sales is 0.15, what will be the firm's need for discretionary financing? (Hint: In this situation you do not know what the firm's existing level of assets is, nor do you know how those assets have been financed. Thus, you must estimate the change in financing needs and match this change with the expected changes in spontaneous liabilities, retained earnings and other sources of discretionary financing.)

6-12 (*Forecasting discretionary financing needs*) The most recent balance sheet for the Armadillo Dog Biscuit Co. is shown in the following table. The company is about to embark on an advertising campaign, which is expected to raise sales from the current level of $5 million to $7 million by the end of next year. The firm is currently operating at full capacity and will have to increase its investment in both current and fixed assets to support the projected level of new sales. In fact, the firm estimates that both categories of assets will rise in direct proportion to the projected increase in sales.

Armadillo Dog Biscuit Co. ($ million)

	PRESENT LEVEL	PERCENT OF SALES	PROJECTED LEVEL
Current assets	$2.0		
Net fixed assets	3.0		
Total	$5.0		
Accounts payable	$0.5		
Accrued expenses	0.5		
Notes payable	–		
Current liabilities	$1.0		
Long-term debt	$2.0		
Share capital	0.5		
Retained earnings	1.5		
Equity	$2.0		
Total	$5.0		

The firm's net profits were 6% of current year's sales but are expected to rise to 7% of next year's sales. To help support its anticipated growth in asset needs next year, the firm has suspended plans to pay cash dividends to its shareholders. In past years, a $1.50 per-share dividend has been paid annually.

Armadillo's payables and accrued expenses are expected to vary directly with sales. In addition, notes payable will be used to supply the funds that are needed to finance next year's operations and that are not forthcoming from other sources.

    (a) Fill in the table and project the firm's needs for discretionary financing. Use notes payable as the balancing entry for future discretionary financing needed.

    (b) Compare Armadillo's current ratio and debt ratio (total liabilities/total assets) before the growth in sales and after. What was the effect of the expanded sales on these two dimensions of Armadillo's financial condition?

    (c) What difference, if any, would have resulted if Armadillo's sales had risen to $6 million in one year and $7 million after only two years? Discuss only; no calculations are required.

6-13 (*Forecasting discretionary financing needs*) Symbolic Logic Company (SLC) is a leader in the application of surface mount technology in the manufacture of printed circuit boards used in the personal computer industry. The firm has recently patented an advanced version of its original path-breaking technology and expects sales to grow from their present level of $5 million to $8 million by the end of the coming year. Since the firm is at present operating at full capacity, it expects to have to increase its investment in both current and fixed assets in proportion to the predicted increase in sales.

The firm's net profits were 7% of current year's sales but are expected to rise to 8% of next year's sales. To help support its anticipated growth in asset needs next year, the firm has suspended plans to pay cash dividends to its shareholders. In years past a $1.25 per-share dividend has been paid annually.

Symbolic Logic Company ($ million)

	PRESENT LEVEL	PERCENT OF SALES	PROJECTED LEVEL
Current assets	$2.5		
Net fixed assets	3.0		
Total	$5.5		
Accounts payable	$1.0		
Accrued expenses	0.5		
Notes payable	–		
Current liabilities	$1.5		
Long-term debt	$2.0		
Share capital	0.5		
Retained earnings	1.5		
Equity	$2.0		
Total	$5.5		

SLC's payables and accrued expenses are expected to vary directly with sales. In addition, notes payable will be used to supply the funds needed to finance next year's operations and those that are not forthcoming from other sources.

(a) Fill in the table and project the firm's needs for discretionary financing. Use notes payable as the balancing entry for future discretionary financing needed.

(b) Compare SLC's current ratio and debt ratio (total liabilities/total assets) before the growth in sales and after. What was the effect of the expanded sales on these two dimensions of SLC's financial condition?

(c) What difference, if any, would have resulted if SLC's sales had risen to $6 million in one year and $8 million after only two years? (Discuss only; no calculations are required.)

6-14 (*Cash budget*) The Halitos Dental Company's projected sales of mouthwash for the first eight months of 20X5 are as follows:

January	$100000	May	$275000
February	110000	June	250000
March	130000	July	235000
April	250000	August	160000

Of Halitos's sales, 20% are for cash, another 60% are collected in the month following sale, and 20% are collected in the second month following sale. November and December sales for 20X4 were $220000 and $175000 respectively.

Halitos purchases its raw materials two months in advance of its sales for a cost equal to 70% of the final sales price. The supplier is paid one month after it makes delivery. For example, purchases for April sales are made in February and payment is made in March.

In addition, Halitos pays $10000 per month for rent and $20000 each month for other expenditures. Tax prepayments of $23000 are made each quarter, beginning in March.

The company's cash balance at 31 December 20X4 was $22000; a minimum balance of $20000 must be maintained at all times. Assume that any short-term financing needed to maintain the cash balance would be paid off in the month following the month of financing if sufficient funds are available. Interest on short-term loans (12%) is paid monthly. Borrowing to meet estimated monthly cash needs takes place at the beginning of the month. Thus, if in the month of April the firm expects to have a need for an additional $60500, these funds would be borrowed at the beginning of April with interest of $605 ($0.12 \times 1/12 \times 60500) owed for April and paid at the beginning of May.

(a) Prepare a cash budget for Halitos covering the first seven months of 20X5.

(b) Halitos has a bank loan of $250000 due in July that must be repaid or renegotiated for an extension. Will the firm have ample cash to repay the loan?

6-15* (*Preparation of a cash budget*) Harrison Printing has projected its sales for the first eight months of 20X6 as follows:

January	$100000	May	$275000
February	120000	June	200000
March	150000	July	200000
April	300000	August	180000

Harrison collects 20% of its sales in the month of the sale, 50% in the month following the sale, and the remaining 30% two months following the sale. During November and December of 20X5 Harrison's sales were $220000 and $175000 respectively.

Harrison purchases raw materials two months in advance of its sales at a cost equal to 65% of its final sales. The supplier is paid one month after delivery. Thus, purchases for April sales are made in February and payment is made in March.

In addition, Harrison pays $10000 per month for rent and $20000 each month for other expenditures. Tax prepayments of $22500 are made each quarter beginning in March. The company's cash balance at 31 December 20X5 was $22000; a minimum balance of $20000 must be maintained at all times to satisfy the firm's bank's line-of-credit agreement. Harrison has arranged with its bank for short-term credit at an interest rate of 12% p.a. (1% per month) to be paid monthly. Borrowing to meet estimated monthly cash needs takes place at the beginning of the month, but interest is not paid until the end of the following month. Consequently, if the firm were to need to borrow $50000 during the month of April, it would pay $500 (= 0.01 × $50000) in interest during May. Finally, Harrison follows a policy of repaying any outstanding short-term debt in any month in which its cash balance exceeds the minimum desired balance of $20000.

(a) Harrison needs to know what its cash requirements will be for January to June so that it can renegotiate the terms of its short-term credit agreement with its bank, if necessary. Prepare a cash budget for Harrison for January–June, and use it to evaluate the firm's cash needs.

(b) Harrison has a $200000 note due in June. Will the firm have sufficient cash to repay the loan?

6-16 (*Preparation of a cash budget*) Halsey Enterprises has projected its sales for the first eight months of 20X4 as follows:

January	$120000	May	$225000
February	160000	June	250000
March	140000	July	210000
April	190000	August	220000

Halsey collects 30% of its sales in the month of the sale, 30% in the month following the sale, and the remaining 40% two months following the sale. During November and December of 2003, Halsey's sales were $230000 and $225000, respectively.

Halsey purchases raw materials two months in advance of its sales equal to 75% of its final sales. The supplier is paid in the month after delivery. Thus, purchases for April sales are made in February and payment is made in March.

In addition, Halsey pays $12000 per month for rent and $20000 each month for other expenditures. Tax prepayments of $26500 are made each quarter beginning in March. The company's cash balance as of 31 December 20X3 was $28000; a minimum balance of $25000 must be maintained at all times to satisfy the firm's bank line of credit agreement. Halsey has arranged with its bank for short-term credit at an interest rate of 12% p.a. (1% per month) to be paid monthly. Borrowing to meet estimated monthly cash needs takes place at the beginning of the month, but interest is not paid until the end of the following month. Consequently, if the firm were to need to borrow $50000 during the month of April, then it would pay $500 (= .01 × $50000) in interest during May. Finally, Halsey follows a policy of repaying any outstanding short-term debt in any month in which its cash balance exceeds the minimum desired balance of $25000.

(a) Halsey needs to know what its cash requirements will be for the next six months so that it can renegotiate the terms of its short-term credit agreement with its bank, if necessary. To evaluate this problem, the firm plans to assess the impact of a 20% variation in its monthly sales efforts. Prepare a six-month cash budget for Halsey and use it to evaluate the firm's cash needs.

(b) Halsey has a $200 000 note due in July. Will the firm have sufficient cash to repay the loan?

6-17* (*Financial forecasting—pro-forma statements*) The Dingling Mobile Phone Company has been engaged in the process of forecasting its financing needs over the next quarter and has made the following forecasts of planned cash receipts and disbursements.

1. Historical and predicted sales:

	HISTORICAL		PREDICTED	
April	$80 000	July		$130 000
May	100 000	August		130 000
June	120 000	September		120 000
		October		100 000

2. The firm incurs and pays a monthly rent expense of $3000.
3. Wages and salaries for the coming months are estimated as follows (with payments coinciding with the month in which the expense is incurred):

July	$18 000
August	18 000
September	16 000

4. Of the firm's sales, 40% is collected in the month of sale, 30% one month after sale, and the remaining 30% two months after sale.
5. Merchandise is purchased one month before the sales month and is paid for in the month it is sold. Purchases equal 80% of sales.
6. Tax prepayments are made on the calendar quarter, with a prepayment of $1000 in July based on earnings for the quarter ended 30 June.
7. Utilities (power, water, etc.) for the firm average 2% of sales and are paid in the month of their incurrence.
8. Depreciation expense is $12 000 annually.
9. Interest on a $40 000 bank note (due in November) is payable at an 8% annual rate in September for the three-month period just ended.
10. The firm follows a policy of paying no cash dividends.

Based on the above, supply the following items:

(a) Prepare a monthly cash budget for the three-month period ended 30 September 20X3.
(b) If the firm's beginning cash balance for the budget period is $5000, and this is its minimum desired balance, determine when and how much the firm will need to borrow during the budget period. The firm has an $80 000 line of credit with its bank, with interest (12% annual rate) paid monthly (e.g. for a loan taken out at the end of December, interest would be paid at the end of January and every month thereafter as long as the loan was outstanding).
(c) Prepare a pro-forma income statement for Dingling covering the three-month period ended 30 September 20X3. Use a 40% tax rate.
(d) Given the following balance sheet dated 30 June 20X3, and the pro-forma income statement from part (c), prepare a pro-forma balance sheet for 30 September 20X3.

Dingling Mobile Phone Company, Balance Sheet, 30 June 20X3

Cash	$5 000	Accounts payable	$104 000
Accounts receivable	102 000	Bank notes (8%)	40 000
Inventories	114 000	Accrued taxes	1 000
Current assets	221 000	Current liabilities	145 000
Net fixed assets	120 000	Ordinary shares	100 000
		Share capital	28 400
		Retained earnings	67 600
		Total liabilities	
Total assets	$341 000	and capital	$341 000

Case study

In November of each year, the CFO of Duggitt Mining Co. begins the financial forecasting process to determine the firm's projected needs for new financing during the coming year. The CFO begins the process with the most recent year's income statement, then projects sales growth for the coming year, then estimates net income, and finally estimates the additional earnings that can be expected for retaining and reinvesting in the firm. The firm's income statement for 20X1 follows:

Income Statement, year ended 31 December 20X1
(This statement and all following figures are in $ millions)

Sales	$1 500
Cost of goods sold	(1 050)
Gross profit	$450
Operating costs	(225)
Depreciation expense	(50)
Net operating profit	$175
Interest expense	(10)
Earnings before taxes	$165
Taxes	(58)
Net income	$107
Dividends	$20
Addition to retained earnings	$87

Duggitt's mining business has been growing rapidly over the past few years on the back of demand from China, and the CFO estimates that sales will expand by 20% in the next year. Depreciation expense will equal $50 000 and interest expense is estimated to be $10 000. In addition, the CFO estimates the following relationships next year between each of the income statement expense items and sales:

COGS/sales	70%
Operating expenses/sales	15%
Tax rate	35%*

1. Estimate Duggitt's net income for 20X2, and the addition to retained earnings, under the assumption that the firm leaves 20X2 dividends at the 20X1 level. (Note that for the coming year both depreciation expense and interest expense are projected to remain the same as in 20X1).
2. Re-evaluate Duggitt's net income and addition to retained earnings if sales, instead, grow at 40% over the coming year. (This scenario requires the addition of new plant and equipment in the amount of $100 000, which increases annual depreciation to $58 000 per year, and interest expense rises to $15 000.)

* This is the expected effective tax rate under the new tax rules for mining companies.

Notes

1. A complete discussion of forecast methodologies is outside the scope of this book. The interested reader will find the following references helpful: F. Gerard Adams, *The Business Forecasting Revolution*, Oxford University Press, Oxford, 1986; C. W. J. Granger, *Forecasting in Business and Economics*, 2nd edn, Academic Press, Boston, MA, 1989; and Paul Newbold and Theodore Bos, *Introductory Business Forecasting*, Southwestern, Cincinnati, OH, 1990.
2. Adapted from Thomas A. Stewart, 'How Cisco and Alcoa make real time work', *Fortune*, 29 May 2000.
3. An alternative to this approach is to use a DFN (discretionary financing needed) model. Refer to A. Keown, J. D. Martin, J. W. Petty and D. F. Scott, *Basic Financial Management*, 9th edn, Prentice Hall, New York, NY, 2002, chapter 4.
4. Other useful references regarding financial planning include S. C. Myers and G. A. Pogue, 'A programming approach to corporate financial management', *Journal of Finance*, 29, May 1974; J. C. Francis and D. R. Rowell, 'A simultaneous equation model of the firm for financial analysis and planning', *Financial Management*, 7, Spring 1978; R. C. Higgins, 'Sustainable growth under inflation', *Financial Management*, 10, Autumn 1981; C. F. Lee, *Financial Analysis and Planning: Theory and Application*, Addison-Wesley, Reading, MA., 1985.
5. Total interest expense incurred (but not necessarily paid) during the period equals $7500 on long-term debt plus $600 on the $12 000 note repaid in May, plus the sum of all interest incurred during the budget period on short-term borrowing. Note that $364 is included for February, $659 for March, and so forth, plus $799 for June, which was incurred but not paid until July.

After reading this chapter, you should be able to:

Learning objectives

After reading this chapter, you should be able to:

1. Understand the nature and importance of working capital.
2. Appreciate the nature of the risk–return trade-off in managing current assets and current liabilities.
3. Explain the hedging principle and the factors that determine the appropriate level of working capital for a firm.
4. Understand how to determine the cost of short-term finance.
5. Describe the typical sources of short-term finance used by the firm.

For a complete eBook go to MyFinanceLab
www.pearson.com.au/myfinancelab

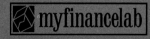

Working-capital management and short-term financing

CHAPTER PREVIEW

Chapter 7 is the first of two chapters that address working capital decisions, which concern short-term financing and short-term asset management. These decisions relate to the management of current assets (which, by definition, are converted into cash within a period of one year or less) and current liabilities (which must be repaid in one year or less). Short-term financing issues include such things as making sure that the firm has sufficient cash to pay its bills on time, managing the firm's collection of accounts receivable (trade debtors), extending credit to the firm's customers, and determining the proper amount and mix of short-term borrowing. This chapter provides the framework for analysing how much short-term financing the firm should use and what specific sources of short-term financing it should use. Chapter 8 discusses the management of current assets, notably cash, marketable securities, accounts receivable and inventories.

This chapter emphasises *Principle 1: The risk–return trade-off—we won't take on additional risk unless we expect to be compensated with additional return; Principle 2: The time value of money—a dollar received today is worth more than a dollar received in the future; Principle 3: Cash—not profits—is king;* and *Principle 4: Incremental cash flows—it's only what changes that counts.*

Regardless of your program

Working capital might not be a topic that finds its way into the daily work schedule of most professionals. But, regardless of your program, there's quite a good chance that you will have worked part time in a retail sales position during your university studies. So, you know that to make a sale you need to have inventory on hand. Otherwise, the customer may walk away and buy elsewhere. This is not good for your employer—there is a saying that a lost sale is lost forever. So, if your boss has his or her way, the firm will carry plenty of inventory. But this may put the sales team in conflict with the finance team, who know that carrying inventories is costly. Apart from the fact that inventories need to be

financed, there are storage and display expenses, to mention just a few of the other costs.

Similar conflicts apply in many other fields where graduates are employed, in wholesaling and manufacturing, construction and fabrication. Just like sales staff, engineers, production managers and logistics managers don't want to wait for critical parts or components. But, as much as *they* want stock on hand, there are organisational forces pushing in the other direction to reduce costs. Thus, creating a satisfactory working-capital policy is a difficult task, one in which the people concerned may benefit by understanding the trade-offs involved between having too little and too much inventory.

Understand the nature and importance of working capital.

working capital
A concept traditionally defined as a firm's investment in current assets.

current assets
All the assets the firm expects to convert into cash within 12 months.

current liabilities
All the liabilities the firm expects to pay within 12 months.

net working capital
The difference between the firm's current assets and its current liabilities.

liquidity
A firm's ability to pay its bills on time. Liquidity is related to the ease and quickness with which a firm can convert its non-cash assets into cash, as well as the size of the firm's investment in non-cash assets vis-a-vis its short-term liabilities.

Working capital

Working capital is made up of a firm's *current assets* and *current liabilities*. **Current assets** comprise all assets that the firm expects to convert into cash within the coming year, including cash, marketable securities, accounts receivable and inventories. *Cash* includes balances of bank accounts as well as cash on hand in the business (such as 'floats' held in cash registers). *Marketable securities* include bonds, notes and other financial instruments that can be readily sold in order to generate cash. *Accounts receivable* include short-term debts owing to the firm, notably trade debtors (debts that arise when the firm advances credit to its customers, such as happens when goods or services are sold on account). *Inventories* comprise primarily stocks of goods that are held for resale, a prominent asset for retailers, wholesalers and manufacturers (manufacturers also hold stocks of raw materials and partly completed goods).

Current liabilities comprise all liabilities that the firm must meet or pay within the coming year, including accounts payable, notes payable, bank overdrafts, and other forms of short-term finance. *Accounts payable* are the converse of accounts receivable, comprising mainly the firm's debts that arise from trade credit that creditors have advanced to the firm. *Notes payable* are short-term sources of finance that are payable on a specific (maturity) date, including promissory notes and bills of exchange. A *bank overdraft* is a form of 'revolving credit' whereby the firm may owe its bank a debt whose amount can vary from day to day up to a maximum called the 'overdraft limit'. The firm's current account goes into overdraft when cheques are drawn, or funds are withdrawn, that exceed the credit balance of the account. (In some ways, therefore, an overdraft is analogous to a personal credit card).

NET WORKING CAPITAL AND LIQUIDITY

Managing the firm's working capital revolves around the concept of **net working capital**, which refers to the difference between the firm's current assets and its current liabilities:

Net working capital = current assets – current liabilities   **(7-1)**

Because net working capital measures the difference between cash receivable in the coming year and cash payable during that time, working capital management emphasises the firm's liquidity. In essence, **liquidity** refers to the ability to have sufficient cash (from current assets) to pay current liabilities when they fall due.

Finance at work

DELL COMPUTES BIG SAVINGS ON WORKING CAPITAL

For manufacturers such as Dell (Dell Computer Corporation), working capital management is critical to the firm's profitability. Inventories are often the biggest single asset for a manufacturer. These inventories need to be financed, and holding them is also costly in terms of storage and handling expenses. So, Dell convinced its suppliers to leave truckloads of inventory at the back door of Dell's factories, with Dell not taking ownership until the items were needed in the plant, at which time they would be moved inside. This way, Dell made use of components exactly when needed, without carrying large inventory amounts in its books.

At the same time, Dell stretched the payment for the goods as long as possible, meaning in effect that the component suppliers were financing Dell's (already reduced) inventory holdings. Furthermore, Dell at the time was making most of its sales by credit card, so it was not carrying trade debtors (which accountants call *accounts receivable*). In effect, Dell was able to eliminate its net investment in working capital, with the result that profits soared and the share price rose dramatically.

Current assets may be up to half of the total assets of a typical manufacturer, wholesaler or retailer. Thus, minimising the need to raise additional funds to finance those assets is not only a profitable move but also decreases reliance on lenders, which can be critical to the firm's survival in times when credit is tight, such as it was in the aftermath of the sub-prime crisis.

Therefore, managing liquidity entails managing two related aspects of the firm's operations:

- the amount of investment in current assets
- the amount of short-term finance (current liabilities).

Managing current assets and liabilities

OBJECTIVE **2**

Appreciate the nature of the risk–return trade-off in managing current assets and current liabilities.

Other things remaining the same, the greater the firm's investment in current assets, the greater its liquidity. In order to increase its liquidity, the firm may choose to invest additional surplus funds in cash or marketable securities. Doing so, however, involves a trade-off, since cash earns a zero rate of return while marketable securities generally earn a relatively small return. The firm thus finds that it can reduce its risk of illiquidity only by reducing its overall return on invested funds, and vice versa.

THE RISK–RETURN TRADE-OFF FROM INVESTING IN CURRENT ASSETS

The *risk–return trade-off* that arises in managing the firm's liquidity is illustrated in Example 7.1.

EXAMPLE 7.1   Risk–return trade-off in managing liquidity

Assume that Companies A and B are identical in every respect but one: Company B has invested $10 000 in marketable securities that earn interest of 6% per annum. These marketable securities have been financed with equity. That is, Company B sold shares in order to raise the $10 000 needed to buy the short-term securities and thus boost its liquidity. The balance sheets and net income positions of the two companies are shown in Table 7.1.

From Table 7.1 it can be seen that Company A earns 10% on its total assets, whereas Company B earns only 9.75%. This arises because of Company B's larger investment in marketable securities (which earn a return of only 6% before taxes). B's larger investment in marketable securities is reflected in its greater liquidity: its current ratio is 3 and its net working capital is $40 000, whereas Company A has a current ratio of 2.5 (which reflects its net working capital of $30 000).

TABLE 7.1   Effects of investing in current assets on liquidity and profitability

	BALANCE SHEETS	
	COMPANY A	COMPANY B
Cash	$1 000	$1 000
Marketable securities		10 000
Accounts receivable	19 000	19 000
Inventories	30 000	30 000
Current assets	$50 000	$60 000
Net non-current assets	100 000	100 000
Total assets	$150 000	$160 000
Current liabilities	$20 000	$20 000
Long-term debt	30 000	30 000

continues

	BALANCE SHEETS	
	COMPANY A	COMPANY B
Equity	100 000	110 000
Total liabilities and equity	$150 000	$160 000
Before-tax net income	$15 000	$15 600[a]

Current ratio = [current assets/current liabilities]
Company A: $50 000/$20 000 = 2.5 times
Company B: $60 000/$20 000 = 3.0 times
Net working capital = [current assets – current liabilities]
Company A: = $30 000
Company B: = $40 000
Before-tax return on total assets = [net income before tax/total assets]
Company A: $15 000/$150 000 = 10%
Company B: $15 600/$160 000 = 9.75%

a During the year Company B held $10 000 in marketable securities, which earned a 6% return or $600 for the year.

Generalising from Example 7.1, investing in current assets—and, in particular, in marketable securities—does have a favourable effect on liquidity, but it also has an unfavourable effect on the firm's rate of return earned on invested funds. That is, there is a risk–return trade-off in the form of added liquidity/reduced profitability versus reduced liquidity/added profitability.

THE RISK–RETURN TRADE-OFF IN MANAGING CURRENT LIABILITIES

The second determinant of the firm's net working capital relates to its use of current liabilities. Here, too, the firm faces a risk–return trade-off between the use of short-term debt versus long-term debt: *other things remaining the same, the greater the firm's reliance on short-term debt or current liabilities in financing its assets, the lower will be its liquidity.*

The risk–return trade-off from using short-term debt versus long-term debt is illustrated in Example 7.2.

EXAMPLE 7.2   Risk–return trade-off from using current liabilities

Table 7.2 shows balance sheets and income statements for Company X and Company Y.

Both companies had the same seasonal needs for financing throughout the past year. In December they each required $40 000 to finance a seasonal expansion in accounts receivable. In addition, during the four-month period beginning in August and extending to November both companies needed $20 000 to support a seasonal build-up in inventories. Company X financed its seasonal financing requirements using $40 000 in long-term debt carrying an annual interest rate of 10%. Company Y, on the other hand, satisfied its seasonal financing needs using short-term borrowing on which it paid 9% interest. Since Company Y borrowed only when it needed the funds and did so at the lower rate of interest on short-term debt, its interest expense for the year was only $900, whereas Company X incurred $4000 in annual interest expense (calculations are found in the footnotes to Table 7.2).

The end result of the two companies' financing policies is evidenced in their current ratio, net working capital and return on total assets, which appear at the bottom of Table 7.2. Company X, using long-term rather than short-term debt, has a current ratio of 3, along with $40 000 in net working capital, whereas Company Y's current ratio is only 1, which represents zero net working capital. However, owing to its lower interest expense, Company Y was able to earn 21.55% on its invested funds, whereas Company X produced a 20% return. Generalising from the example, a firm can reduce its risk of illiquidity through the use of long-term debt, but this occurs at the expense of a reduction in its return on invested funds. Once again it is seen that the risk–return trade-off involves an increased risk of illiquidity versus increased profitability.

TABLE 7.2 Effect of current versus long-term debt on company liquidity and profitability

	BALANCE SHEETS	
	COMPANY X	COMPANY Y
Current assets	$60000	$60000
Net non-current assets	140000	140000
Total assets	$200000	$200000
Accounts payable	20000	20000
Short-term finance	–	40000
Current liabilities	$20000	$60000
Long-term debt	40000	–
Equity	140000	140000
Total liabilities and equity	$200000	$200000
INCOME STATEMENTS		
Net operating income	$44000	$44000
Less: Interest expense	4000[a]	900[b]
Net income before taxes	$40000	$43100

Current ratio = [current assets/current liabilities]
Company X: $60000/$20000 = 3 times
Company Y: $60000/$60000 = 1 time
Net working capital = [current assets – current liabilities]
Company X: = $40000
Company Y: = $0
Before-tax return on total assets = [net income before tax/total assets]
Company X: $40000/$200000 = 20%
Company Y: $43100/$200000 = 21.55%

a Company X paid interest during the entire year on $40000 in long-term debt at a rate of 10%. Its interest expense for the year was $40000 × 0.10 = $4000.
b Company Y paid interest on $40000 for one month and on $20000 for four months at 9% interest during the year. Thus, Company Y's interest expense for the year equals ($40000 × 0.09 × 1/12) + ($20000 × 0.09 × 4/12), or $300 + $600 = $900.

The risk–return trade-off in managing a firm's net working capital is illustrated in Figure 7.1.

FIGURE 7.1 The risk–return trade-off in managing net working capital

	Firm profitability	Firm liquidity
Investing in additional marketable securities and inventories	Lower	Higher
Increasing the use of short- versus long-term sources of financing	Higher	Lower

Concept check

7.2 How does investing more in net working capital decrease both returns and risk?

For answers go to MyFinanceLab or www.pearson.com.au/9781442539174

Back to the principles

Working-capital decisions provide a classic example of the risk–return nature of financial decision making. Decreasing the firm's net working capital (current assets less current liabilities) increases the risk that the firm will not be able to pay its bills on time (i.e. increases the risk of illiquidity) but at the same time it increases the overall profitability of the firm. Thus, working-capital decisions involve **Principle 1: The risk–return trade-off—we won't take on additional risk unless we expect to be compensated with additional return**.

OBJECTIVE **3**

Explain the hedging principle and the factors that determine the appropriate level of working capital for a firm.

The hedging principle and the appropriate level of working capital

Managing the firm's net working capital (its liquidity) has been shown to involve simultaneous and interrelated decisions regarding investment in current assets and use of current liabilities. Fortunately, a guiding principle exists that can be used as a benchmark for the firm's working-capital policies: the *hedging principle*, also known as the *principle of self-liquidating debt*. This principle provides a guide to the maintenance of a level of liquidity sufficient for the firm to meet its maturing obligations on time.[1]

HEDGING PRINCIPLE

Put simply, the hedging principle involves *matching* the cash-flow-generating characteristics of an asset with the maturity of the source of financing used to acquire the asset. For example, a seasonal expansion in inventories, according to the hedging principle, should be financed with a short-term loan or current liability. The rationale underlying the hedging rule is straightforward: funds are needed for a limited period of time and, when that time has passed, the cash needed to repay the loan will be generated by the sale of the extra inventory items. Obtaining the needed funds from a long-term source (longer than one year) would mean that the firm would still have the funds after the sale of the inventories that were financed by those funds. In this case the firm would have 'excess' liquidity, which it either holds in cash or invests in low-yield marketable securities until the seasonal increase in inventories occurs again and the funds are needed. This would result in an overall lowering of profits, as seen earlier in Example 7.2.

Consider a contrasting example in which a firm purchases a long-life asset such as a new conveyor belt, which is expected to produce cash savings to the firm by eliminating the need for two employees and consequently their salaries. Suppose that this amounts to an annual saving of $50 000, while the conveyor belt costs $450 000 to install and will last 20 years. If the firm chooses to finance this asset with a one-year note, it will not be able to repay the loan from the cash flow generated by the asset. In accordance with the hedging principle, the firm should finance the asset with a source of financing that more nearly matches the expected life and cash-flow-generating characteristics of the asset. In this case, a 15- to 20-year loan would be more appropriate.

PERMANENT AND TEMPORARY ASSETS

The notion of *maturity matching* in the hedging principle can be most easily understood when we think in terms of the distinction between **permanent** and **temporary investments in assets** as opposed to the more traditional non-current and current asset categories used by accountants when classifying the balance sheet.

A permanent investment in an asset is an investment that the firm expects to hold for a period longer than one year. Note that this refers to the period of time the firm plans to hold an investment, not the useful life of the asset. For example, on average a firm's inventories

permanent investments in assets
These assets will not be liquidated or replaced within 12 months; in other words, they will be held for more than one year. Contrast with **temporary investments in assets**.

temporary investments in assets
Investments in assets that the firm plans to sell (liquidate) within a period no longer than one year. Although temporary investments can be made in fixed assets, this is not the usual case. Temporary investments generally are made in inventories and receivables.

GFC

LIQUIDITY PROBLEMS IN THE GFC

In the aftermath of the sub-prime crisis (SPC), a credit squeeze enveloped the global financial system. Banks and other financial institutions faced severe pressure on their liquidity positions. There were fears regarding the degree of exposure to the sub-prime crisis, so the banks were reluctant to lend to one another. The consequent lack of liquidity in credit markets meant that funding that had been plentiful dried up almost overnight and interest rates increased. This led to problems for large numbers of businesses in the 'real economy', many of which were quite well managed and profitable.

The problem was particularly acute for businesses that had been overlooking the *hedging principle*. Among other things, this principle suggests that long-term assets should be financed with long-term liabilities. However, prior to the sub-prime crisis, short-term financing had been plentiful and relatively cheap. So, many businesses were in a 'comfort zone' of rolling over their short-term debt from month to month. The textbooks warn of two main problems with this policy and both of these happened. First, when the debt matures and 'rollover' is due, the cost may increase if the level of interest rates has risen in the financial markets. Second, lenders may be unwilling to re-finance the debt.

This problem confronted Centro Properties Group (ASX code CNP) in mid-December 2007, when lenders refused to re-finance

maturing loans. Virtually overnight, Centro's share price dropped by 76%, from $5.70 to $1.36, and the total market value of the company fell from $4.82 billion to $1.15 billion.

Centro's problems were accentuated by the fact that the sub-prime crisis had led to financial institutions becoming very conservative in their attitude to anything to do with real estate assets. In this regard, Centro operated more than 800 shopping centres in Australia and the United States, having expanded into the US market through high levels of debt borrowing ('high gearing').

Centro turned to the banks for finance after the SPC-induced collapse of the *securitisation* market (see Chapter 18). Prior to that, the company had been relying heavily on funds from securitisation to finance its activities. In the fallout from the sub-prime crisis, this form of financing evaporated and left Centro little choice but to switch to bank finance. However, with Centro's high degree of leverage, the prospect of increased interest rates would lead to a decreased profit outlook. Coupled with tight liquidity conditions, this seems to explain the banks' refusal to rollover Centro's credit, with the consequent drop in investor support for Centro's shares. This situation has continued in the several years after the SPC, during which time Centro has been compelled to restructure both its business operations and its financing arrangements. In early 2011, Centro's share price was down to 14 cents.

---

may never fall below $100 000, so this represents a 'permanent' investment in that type of asset. However, at a particular time of the year, inventories may rise to a seasonal maximum of $140 000, of which $40 000 therefore represents a temporary (seasonal) investment. These temporary asset investments are composed of current assets that will be liquidated and *not* replaced within the current year.

Thus, some part of the firm's current assets is permanent and the remainder is temporary. As shown, a seasonal increase in the level of inventories is a temporary investment; the build-up in inventories will be eliminated when it is no longer needed.

SPONTANEOUS, TEMPORARY AND PERMANENT SOURCES OF FINANCING

Previously in this chapter, a distinction was made between temporary assets and permanent assets. Similarly, it is possible to distinguish between temporary and permanent finance, along with a category that can be called 'spontaneous finance'.

Spontaneous sources of financing are those that occur 'automatically' in line with the firm's ongoing operations. An example is accounts payable, which increase in line with the acquisition of inventories that have been bought on credit from a trade supplier. Therefore, in the firm's balance sheet, the size of the accounts-payable balance varies directly with the firm's purchases of inventory items. In addition to trade credit, other valuable sources of spontaneous financing include wages and salaries payable, accrued interest and accrued taxes. These expenses accrue throughout the period until they are paid. For example, if a firm pays its employees at the end of each month and has a wage expense of $10 000 a week, its employees effectively provide financing equal to $10 000 by the end of the first week following the previous payday, $20 000 by the end of the second week, and so forth. Since these accrued expenses generally arise in line with the firm's ongoing operations, they too are referred to as spontaneous.

Temporary sources of financing consist of non-spontaneous current liabilities, such as bank overdrafts, bills of exchange, promissory notes, and loans that are secured by accounts receivable and inventories. These sources of finance must be raised deliberately by the firm, otherwise they will not happen. They do not arise spontaneously: in the words of Chapter 6, these types of finance are *discretionary*.

Permanent sources of financing include long-term debt finance such as bonds, term loans and leases (discussed in Chapter 18), and equity finance such as ordinary shares and hybrid securities (discussed in Chapter 19).

HEDGING PRINCIPLE: GRAPHIC ILLUSTRATION

It follows from the preceding discussion that total assets must always equal the sum of spontaneous, temporary and permanent sources of financing. The hedging approach provides the financial manager with the basis for determining the appropriate mix of these sources of financing. Put succinctly, *asset needs of the firm that are not financed spontaneously should be financed in accordance with this rule: permanent asset investments are financed with permanent sources, and temporary investments are financed with temporary sources.*

The hedging principle is depicted in Figure 7.2. Total assets are broken down into temporary and permanent asset categories. The firm's permanent investment in assets is financed by the use of permanent sources of financing (intermediate- and long-term debt, preference shares and ordinary equity) or spontaneous sources (trade credit and other accounts payable).[2] Its temporary investment in assets is financed with temporary (short-term) debt.

FIGURE 7.2 Hedging financing strategy

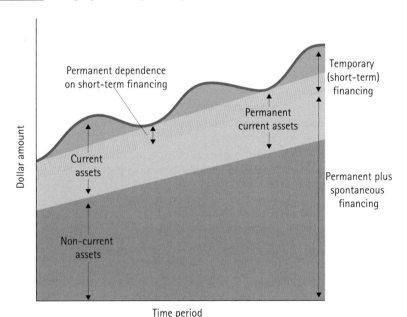

Concept check

7.3 What does the *hedging principle* mean?

7.4 What are some examples of temporary and permanent investments in current assets?

7.5 Is trade credit a permanent, temporary or spontaneous source of finance?

For answers go to MyFinanceLab or
www.pearson.com.au/9781442539174

Short-term financing and its cost

Although current liabilities provide financing for periods of less than one year, the time value of money is still relevant and should be incorporated into our estimation of their cost. Thus, estimating the cost of short-term credit provides yet another case where we rely on **Principle 2: The time value of money—a dollar received today is worth more than a dollar received in the future**.

OBJECTIVE **4**

Understand how to determine the cost of short-term financial management.

The firm's short-term financing needs are met with what accountants call current liabilities—that is, liabilities that mature within the coming year. Two key issues are involved in managing the firm's use of short-term financing:

1. How much short-term financing should the firm use?
2. What specific sources of short-term financing should the firm select?

HOW MUCH SHORT-TERM FINANCE?

The answer to this question comes from the earlier sections of this chapter where the *hedging principle* of working-capital management was discussed. That is, the firm should match its temporary need for funds with short-term sources of financing, and match the permanent needs with long-term sources of financing.

HOW TO SELECT SPECIFIC SOURCES OF SHORT-TERM FINANCE

In general, three basic factors should be considered in choosing between alternative sources of short-term finance (credit):

* the effective cost of credit
* the availability of credit in the amount needed and for the period when financing is required
* the influence of the use of a particular credit source on the cost and availability of other sources of financing.

The general procedure for estimating the cost of short-term credit will be discussed next. This general procedure will be followed later in this chapter with examples of the cost of credit for particular types of short-term financing.

ESTIMATION OF THE COST OF SHORT-TERM CREDIT

If the objective of the firm is to maximise the wealth of the owners, the firm should aim to minimise the cost of finance—including the cost of short-term finance. Estimating the cost of short-term credit is relatively straightforward, as detailed below.

Approximate cost of credit: the nominal annual interest rate

It will be recalled from Chapter 4 that interest rates are often disclosed in the form of a nominal annual interest rate, symbol *j*, which is alternately known as the *APR* (annual percentage rate). If the nominal annual interest rate is labelled 'RATE' for the purposes of this chapter, the procedure for estimating the cost of short-term credit is very simple and relies on the basic simple-interest equation:

$$\text{Interest} = \text{principal} \times \text{rate} \times \text{time} \qquad \textbf{(7-2)}$$

where *interest* is the dollar amount of interest on a *principal* that is borrowed at some nominal annual *rate* for a fraction of a year (represented by *time*). For example, a $1000 loan at 8% annual interest for six months (a ½ year) would require an interest payment of $40:

215

Interest = $1000 × 0.08 × ½ = $40

Alternatively, if $5000 is borrowed at 7% for 60 days, the interest expense will be $5000 × 0.07 × 60/365 = $57.53.

This basic relationship can be rearranged to solve for the nominal annual rate. Using an interest rate as a measuring stick is more useful than using the dollar cost for comparing alternative sources of finance, because it standardises for the effect of different amounts borrowed for different time periods. Rearranging equation (7-2) gives:

$$\text{RATE} = \frac{\text{interest}}{\text{principal} \times \text{time}} \qquad \textbf{(7-3)}$$

or

$$\text{RATE} = \frac{\text{interest}}{\text{principal}} \times \frac{1}{\text{time}}$$

This equation, called the RATE calculation, is clarified in Example 7.3.

EXAMPLE 7.3 **Computation of the nominal annual interest rate**

The SKC Company plans to borrow $1000 for a 90-day period (thus, *time* = 90/365). At maturity the firm will repay the $1000 principal amount plus $30 interest. The nominal annual rate of interest for this loan can be estimated using the RATE equation, as follows:

$$\text{RATE} = \frac{\$30}{\$1000} \times \frac{1}{90/365} = 0.1216, \text{ or } 12.16\% \text{ p.a.}$$

The nominal annual interest rate that the firm will pay on the loan funds is therefore 12.16% p.a.

Effective interest rate formula

As outlined in Chapter 4, the nominal annual interest rate does not allow for the effect of compounding within the year: according to the nominal rate, 12% per annum compounded quarterly is identical to 12% per annum compounded annually, but we saw in Chapter 4 that the *effective* interest rate (symbol *EAR*) is 12.55% in the first case and 12% in the second case. To account for the influence of compounding, Chapter 4 derived equation (4-9a), which is relabelled as (7-4) for the purposes of this chapter:

$$EAR = (1 + j/m)^m - 1 \qquad \textbf{(7-4)}$$

where *EAR* is the effective annual percentage rate, *j* is the nominal rate of interest per year (or *APR*), and *m* is the number of compounding periods within a year. Example 7.4 computes the effective interest rate on the credit for SKC Company, for which the nominal annual rate was computed in Example 7.3.

EXAMPLE 7.4 **Computation of the effective annual interest rate**

To compute the effective rate of interest for the SKC Company, we have the following:

- *j* = nominal annual interest rate or *EAR* = 12.16% (0.1216 as a decimal), from Example 7.3
- *m* = number of compounding periods in a year: since the loan is for 90 days, interest is compounded 365/90 times in a year. Note that, since *m* = 365/90, *m* can also be represented as 1/TIME, that is 1/[90/365].

Thus, substituting in equation (7-4):

$$EAR = (1 + .1216/[365/90])^{365/90} - 1 = (1 + .1216/4.0556)^{4.0556} - 1$$
$$= (1 + .03)^{4.0556} - 1 = .1274 \ (12.74\%)$$

Subsequent computations in this chapter will, for simplicity, use the annual nominal RATE, but this rate can be converted readily to an effective annual rate using the procedure shown in Example 7.4.

Concept check

7.6   What three factors influence a firm's choice between alternative sources of short-term finance?

7.7   Why is the *EAR* preferable to the nominal annual rate as a measure of the cost of finance?

For answers go to MyFinanceLab or
www.pearson.com.au/9781442539174

International spotlight

MANAGING WORKING CAPITAL IN MULTINATIONAL FIRMS

Multinational enterprises (MNEs) have a spread of international operations that adds many complexities to the management of working capital. In particular, an MNE receives and spends money in a number of different currencies. This poses concerns about fluctuations in exchange rates.

The head office of an MNE is located in what is called its home country. Assets held overseas will decline in value if the foreign currency depreciates relative to the home currency. This fall may be offset by a decline in the value of liabilities that are denominated in that foreign currency. A firm has a *net asset (long) position* if it holds an excess of assets over liabilities in a particular currency. In contrast, a *net liability (short) position* indicates an excess of liabilities over assets in a particular currency.

A firm with a long position has an adverse exposure to depreciation of the relevant foreign currency, and so the firm should speed up the disposal of assets before there is further currency depreciation. Speeding up the disposal of assets and converting them into a stronger currency is known as *leading*. Conversely, *lagging* is the process of delaying payment of a bill that is denominated in a depreciating currency until the currency has weakened. Leading is particularly suited to current assets such as cash, receivables and inventories, as these assets are relatively liquid. Similarly, lagging is suited to short-term liabilities such as accounts payable.

Management of actions such as leading and lagging needs to be coordinated centrally by the MNE. This is because a central or overall view of the firm's exposures is essential, and this view is not necessarily the same as that of an individual division or subsidiary company of the MNE.

Sources of short-term finance

OBJECTIVE 5

Describe the typical sources of short-term finance used by the firm.

From a legal perspective, short-term sources of finance can be classified into two basic groups: unsecured and secured. *Unsecured* sources include all those sources that rely solely on the promise of the borrower to repay the debt when due. There are three major sources of unsecured short-term credit: trade credit, promissory notes and bills of exchange. *Secured* loans, on the other hand, involve the pledge of assets as collateral in the event that the borrower defaults on the payment of the principal or interest. Banks, finance companies and factors are the primary suppliers of secured credit. The sources of security can include specifically identified assets or property such as accounts receivable or inventories, or a general charge over the assets of the borrower.

Remaining sections of this chapter discuss specific sources of short-term finance, with an emphasis on the computation of the relevant cost of credit.

ACCRUED WAGES AND TAXES

As outlined previously, most firms accrue a wages-payable account that is, in essence, a loan from their employees for the time interval between the employees providing their services and the employer actually paying their salaries. For example, if the wage expense for the Appleton Manufacturing Company is $450 000 per week and it pays its employees fortnightly, then by the end of a two-week period the firm will owe its employees $900 000 in wages for services they have already performed during the period. Consequently, the employees finance their own efforts through waiting a full fortnight for payment.

Similarly, firms typically accrue various types of taxes payable. As discussed in Chapter 2, many businesses make periodic income-tax payments during the year: for example, if a tax liability is incurred on 1 July and is paid at the end of September, the firm has had 'free' use of funds for three months. In addition to income taxes and payroll taxes (taxes on employee earnings), many firms incur a liability to pay the GST (goods and services tax), but there is a delay between collection of the funds from customers (who pay the GST as part of the cost of goods and services supplied) and ultimate payment to the taxation authorities. The longer the period that the firm withholds or accrues the tax payments, the greater the amount of financing that is provided.

Note that these sources of financing typically *rise and fall spontaneously* with the level of the firm's sales. That is, as the firm's sales increase, so do its labour expense and resultant payroll tax, and its GST liability. To the extent that taxable profits rise in line with sales, income taxes too increase with sales. Consequently, these accrued expense items provide the firm with automatic or spontaneous sources of financing.

TRADE CREDIT

trade credit
Credit made available by a firm's suppliers in connection with the acquisition of materials. Trade credit appears on the balance sheet as accounts payable.

Trade credit provides one of the most flexible sources of short-term financing available to the firm. Earlier in this chapter it was noted that trade credit is a significant source of spontaneous, or on-demand, financing. That is, trade credit arises spontaneously with the firm's credit purchases. To arrange for credit the firm need only place an order with one of its suppliers. The supplier checks the firm's credit rating and, if it is good, sends the merchandise. The purchasing firm then pays for the goods in accordance with the supplier's credit terms.

'Cost' of credit terms and cash discounts

Sometimes, the credit terms offered to the purchaser involve a cash discount in return for early payment. For example, a supplier might offer terms specified as '2/5, net 30'. This means that a 2% discount is offered for payment within 5 days, otherwise the full amount of the debt is due in 30 days. If this discount is ignored by the purchaser, there is an *opportunity cost* which can be represented in the form of an interest rate, as shown in Example 7.5.

EXAMPLE 7.5 Cost of forgoing a cash discount

Assume that OCD Company is offered credit terms of '2/10, net 30'. This means that, if OCD does not pay within 10 days, it will presumably delay payment for a further 20 days (from the 10th day, after which the discount can no longer be claimed, till the 30th day when the full debt is otherwise payable). But by delaying payment in this way, OCD forgoes the 2% discount. In other words, OCD suffers a 2% penalty for *not* paying within 10 days. The percentage annual cost of forgoing the cash discount can be quite severe. Using an arbitrary $1 invoice amount, the nominal annual percentage cost of passing-up a discount of 2/10, net 30 can be estimated by adaptation of equation (7-3):

$$\text{RATE} = \frac{\$0.02}{\$0.98} \times \frac{1}{20/365} = 0.3724, \text{ or } 37.24\% \text{ p.a.}$$

In this computation:

- $0.02 represents 2% per $1 invoice amount; that is, $0.02 is the amount of interest-saving that is forgone by not accepting the discount.
- $0.98 is the amount of the debt actually payable, per $1 of the invoice, if the discount of $0.02 is taken.
- 20/365 represents TIME; that is, not accepting the discount delays payment of the account by 20 days.

As Example 7.5 demonstrates, the annual cost of passing-up a trade discount can be quite substantial. Table 7.3 lists the annual cost of a number of alternative credit terms. Because the cost of giving trade discounts can be quite substantial from the viewpoint of the supplier, their use has become less prevalent.

'Stretching' on trade credit

Some firms that use trade credit engage in a practice called *stretching* of trade accounts. This practice involves delaying payments beyond the prescribed credit period. For example, a firm might purchase materials under credit terms of 3/10, net 60; however, when faced with a shortage of cash, the firm might delay payment to the 80th day. Continued violation of trade terms can eventually lead to a loss of credit. However, for short periods, and at infrequent intervals, stretching offers the firm an emergency source of short-term credit. Stretching tends to be more prominent during 'tough' economic conditions, as more and more firms have difficulty paying their debts.

Advantages of trade credit

As a source of short-term financing, trade credit has a number of advantages. First, trade credit is conveniently obtained as a normal part of the firm's operations. Second, no formal agreements are generally involved in extending credit. Furthermore, the amount of credit extended expands and contracts with the needs of the firm; this is why it is classified as a spontaneous, or on-demand, source of financing.

BANK OVERDRAFTS

In Australia, most business firms—whether very small or very large—make extensive use of a **bank overdraft** account as a key component of working-capital management. In the year ended 30 June 2010, for example, overdraft lending by Australian banks amounted to almost $100 billion.[3] The main reason for the widespread access to this type of credit is that an overdraft operates in conjunction with a firm's current account (or cheque account) at the bank, with just about every business having such a cheque account. The current account changes automatically, from an account for depositing money to a form of credit, by becoming overdrawn.

The account becomes *overdrawn* when the customer makes withdrawals or payments (by cheque or electronic transfer) in excess of the funds deposited. From the bank's viewpoint, when the customer goes into *overdraft* (that is, becomes overdrawn), this represents a shift from a credit balance in the customer's account to a debit balance and thus the amount overdrawn

bank overdraft
A form of bank lending where the bank allows a customer to borrow money by making payments in excess of the amount that the customer has on deposit in the account.

TABLE 7.3 Annual rates of interest on selected trade credit terms

CREDIT TERMS	ANNUAL RATE (%)
2/10, net 60	14.90
2/10, net 90	9.31
3/20, net 60	28.22
6/10, net 90	29.12

overdraft limit
The maximum amount that a customer can borrow with a bank overdraft facility.

represents an asset in the form of a debt owing to the bank. The maximum amount of this debit balance is called the **overdraft limit**. The account remains overdrawn until the customer places sufficient funds in the account to return it to a credit balance. If the customer attempts to draw a cheque or make a transfer in excess of the overdraft limit, the bank has the right to refuse to 'honour' the cheque or transfer.

This type of account gives a great deal of flexibility in managing short-term cash needs. The reason for this is that the firm can borrow (up to the pre-agreed overdraft limit) at any time without notice, then can repay all or part of the overdraft and subsequently re-borrow (redraw) again and again. Thus, a bank overdraft facility provides a form of *revolving credit*. This is analogous to a personal credit card, whereby the balance outstanding can vary from day to day up to the credit limit. However, unlike a credit card, no specific repayments are required as long as the account balance is currently less than the overdraft limit. Many firms use overdrafts to finance seasonal asset purchases, such as a build-up of inventories that will subsequently be sold and so allow the overdrawn balance to be repaid.

In common with other ways that banks advance money, the bank may desire that the debt (whose maximum amount is the overdraft limit) be secured.

ONE STEP FURTHER

BANK CREDIT: SECURED OR CASH-FLOW BASIS?
Banks use two basic approaches in determining the total amount of money that they will advance on bank overdrafts together with any other loans. These two approaches are often termed *secured lending* and *cash-flow lending* respectively.

Secured lending
Secured lending involves the bank lending a maximum of some specified percentage of the value of the assets that the customer pledges as security (collateral). To be acceptable as security, an asset must have three basic attributes:

1. *It must have a value at least as much as the amount of the loan.* Because the value of any asset is not always known with certainty over the term of the loan, the percentage of the value of the security that banks will lend depends on the type of asset used as security. For example, if the borrower has a portfolio of Australian government securities that it wants to use as collateral, the bank might advance a loan of up to 90% of the face value of these securities, whereas it might loan as little as 20% against the estimated cost of the firm's work-in-progress inventories, as such inventories have little value in their unfinished condition.
2. *It must be relatively easy for the bank to take possession of the asset.* Consequently, an asset such as real estate is often accepted as security because it is not mobile and so it cannot readily be removed out of the bank's reach.
3. *The asset must be easily identified.* This requirement is actually an important element of item (2) above. For example, although banks do make loans secured by the overall pool of a firm's assets, or a portion of the assets (e.g. inventories), they sometimes prefer not to do so because it is more difficult to determine just what specific assets they hold claim to in the event of default. Thus, clearly identifiable assets such as land and buildings are preferable as a form of security.

Cash-flow lending
Banks also engage in cash-flow lending, whereby the amount that the bank will lend is based on the borrower's perceived ability to service the debt. Specifically, the bank is interested in the

ability of the borrower to generate future cash flows, as these cash flows provide the means to service the debt. To lend on this basis the bank needs a good estimate of the borrower's normal 'free' cash flow. *Free cash flow* can be assessed as the amount of the firm's net profit after tax, plus depreciation expense and interest charges. That is, free cash flow is the amount of cash the borrower should have available to meet the periodic principal and interest payments. An appropriate *coverage ratio* (such as the ratio of the firm's free cash flow to the firm's interest and principal payments) can also be used to measure the ability to service a loan. This type of ratio gives a quick indication of the firm's ability to pay its borrowing obligations. What constitutes an acceptable coverage ratio will vary with the nature of the firm's business: riskier businesses are required to have higher coverage ratios.

Often banks assess lending limits by taking into account both cash-flow projections and security offered. In other words, they want the borrower to be able to afford the loan but, in the event that the borrower does default, they want security as back-up. Cash-flow lending alone is more common in the case of businesses that do not have substantial tangible assets (for example where premises and equipment are rented or leased rather than owned by the borrower).

Interest calculation and account charges

The cost of using a bank overdraft represents a mix of interest charges and non-interest fees. Interest is charged on the daily balance of the overdrawn amount. The rate applying to the bank's 'best' customers is known as the *prime rate* or *indicator rate*. Other customers with lower credit ratings may be charged a higher rate. Additionally, non-interest fees and charges are levied by banks for the establishment and service of overdraft accounts. One of these fees is the *unused-limit fee*. This fee is justified, according to the banks, by the practice of customers arranging large overdraft credit limits but not using them (which is claimed to present problems for cash planning within the banks, as customers may overdraw their accounts at any time, up to the agreed limit, without having to give the bank prior notification). The fee therefore acts as a disincentive to customers to seek unnecessarily large overdraft limits, as well as compensation to the banks for the risk associated with the unpredictable cash flows that arise from customer behaviour.

The cost of overdraft credit

The cost of overdraft credit is determined by a combination of the interest rate charged on funds overdrawn, the unused-limit fee charged on funds not drawn, and other fees and charges associated with operating the account. Ignoring the other fees and charges for simplicity, equation (7-5) computes the cost of an overdraft account as an 'all-up' interest rate that reflects the interplay between the bank's interest rate and the unused-limit fee:

$$\text{RATE} = \frac{u}{b}\left[L + b\left(\frac{i}{u} - 1\right)\right] \tag{7-5}$$

where: RATE = 'all-up' cost of using the overdraft account, expressed as a nominal annual interest rate

b = balance of the overdraft (i.e. the amount actually overdrawn)

i = interest rate per annum charged by the bank on the overdrawn balance

L = overdraft limit

u = percentage rate per annum charged on the unused limit

Clearly, Example 7.6 is highly simplified in assuming that there is a constant overdraft balance (and thus a constant unused limit). However, it serves to highlight that the interest rate is only one part of the total cost of operating an overdraft facility. In order to more accurately model an overdraft account, it is necessary to set up a spreadsheet that replicates the bank statement, which records transactions on a day-to-day basis. That way, any fees and charges can be incorporated into the account balance, as and when they arise. The spreadsheet can be set up to highlight cash flows into and out of the account, enabling the spreadsheet to solve for the daily interest rate, which can then be annualised.

Back to the principles

In order to estimate the cost of credit, we focus on cash received and paid, an application of **Principle 3: Cash—not profits—is king**. This is clear from Example 7.8, later, where it is seen that we need to know the cash flows in order to work out the cost of finance. This example also shows that we need to consider all the cash-flow consequences of the use of a particular source of short-term credit. In particular, we are interested in all the incremental cash inflows and outflows associated with the financing source. This reflects the use of **Principle 4: Incremental cash flows—it's only what changes that counts.**

PROMISSORY NOTES

Whereas a bank overdraft provides a form of revolving credit, some other forms of short-term finance involve borrowing a specific amount of principal that is repayable after a specific period of time. A promissory note is one such source of credit. A **promissory note** is a financial instrument whereby the borrower (also called the 'issuer' or 'drawer') promises to pay a sum of money to the investor or lender (also called the 'holder' or 'bearer') at a specified future date. Usually, no added security is offered and so the debt is only as good as the borrower's promise—thus the name. Because no one except the borrower has any obligation to repay the debt, promissory notes are often known as **one-name paper**; they are also called **commercial paper**.

The investor or lender can sometimes sell the debt to another person who then 'holds' the debt that is payable by the borrower. Thus, the current *holder* (or *bearer*) of the promissory note may be the original lender or may be a subsequent buyer of the debt.

The investor or bearer outlays a sum of money, the principal P, for a period of n days. The future sum of money repayable by the borrower, after n days, can be labelled V (which represents the maturity value or face value). The amount V is greater than P and thus includes an interest element. This amount of interest is conventionally called the discount, D. In other words, the face value V is 'discounted' by D to give the principal P. That is:

$$D = V - P = \text{interest}$$

promissory note
A short-term financial instrument whereby the borrower (drawer) promises to repay the face value, at maturity, to the holder. Also known as **one-name paper** or, in some countries, **commercial paper**.

(This concept of 'discount' has lent its name to a family of *discount-type* financial instruments: those where the amount of interest represents the maturity value minus the principal and where there are no intervening cash flows between the date when the principal is invested/borrowed and the date of maturity.)

Because promissory notes usually rely solely on the borrower's promise to repay the debt, their use is confined to 'prime' borrowers with very good credit ratings, such as leading public companies and semi-government authorities. The term (maturity) of promissory notes is typically between 30 and 180 days, and they are normally issued in multiples of $100 000. They are generally *negotiable*, which means that they can be sold by the holder (investor) prior to maturity.

Since promissory note issues are frequently for large sums of money, a bank or merchant bank is often involved in managing the issue on behalf of the borrower. The issue too is sometimes *underwritten*, which means that there is an underwriter (such as the bank or merchant bank) who agrees to make good any funds that are not contributed by investors. The underwriter is paid a fee for this service.

Legally speaking, the promissory note is evidenced by a document that contains the following details:

* The *borrower* (also called the *drawer*), the entity who 'draws up' the note and promises to make the payment at the maturity date.
* The *lender*, who originally provides the money and is to be repaid on maturity. (Alternatively, the term *bearer* may be substituted on the note for 'lender'. This enables the original lender to sell the promissory note to another party, who as the 'bearer' of the note may present it to the borrower for payment on the due date.)
* The *principal* of the note (P), which will be stated along with the *face value*—the maturity value (V). The face value may be in 'units' (e.g. multiples of $100 000) to aid standardisation and marketability.
* The *maturity date* and *issue date*.
* *Security* or collateral offered, although this is unusual as most issues are unsecured.

Cost of promissory note finance

As stated, the amount of *interest* or *discount*, D, is equal to the maturity or face value (V) minus the sum borrowed or *principal* (P). In equation (7-6), the RATE formula given by equation (7-3) is adapted to calculate the annual interest rate for a discount-type instrument such as a promissory note:

$$\text{RATE} = \frac{V - P}{P} \times \frac{1}{n/365} \tag{7-6}$$

This equation can be rearranged to give:

$$\text{RATE} = \frac{365}{n} \times \left(\frac{V}{P} - 1\right) \tag{7-7}$$

This equation can again be rearranged to determine the 'price' (P) of a short-term discount instrument given its face value (V), annual interest rate (RATE) and term to maturity (n days):

$$P = \frac{365V}{365 + \text{RATE}\,(n)} \tag{7-8}$$

Example 7.7 illustrates how these equations can be used.

EXAMPLE 7.7 Promissory note computations

PN Company draws a promissory note with a face value of $100 000. It is issued on 1 July and matures on 31 July.

1. What is the interest rate if the drawer receives $99 023?

$$\text{RATE} = \frac{(\$100\,000 - \$99\,023)}{\$99\,023} \times \frac{1}{30/365} = 0.12 = 12\% \text{ p.a.}$$

or

$$\text{RATE} = \frac{365}{30}\left(\frac{100\,000}{99\,023} - 1\right) = 0.12 = 12\% \text{ p.a.}$$

2. Confirm the sum obtained by the drawer (borrower) if the interest rate is 12% p.a.

$$P = \frac{365\,(100\,000)}{365 + 0.12\,(30)} = \$99\,023$$

In addition to the interest rate of the note, the borrower may have to pay management or underwriting fees, which have the effect of reducing the funds obtained (P) via the note, thereby increasing the RATE or cost of funds obtained.

With promissory notes being unsecured, the ability to obtain finance is significantly enhanced if the borrower has a suitable credit rating. In this regard, organisations called *ratings agencies* (see Chapter 18 for further discussion) may provide assessments of the short-term or long-term creditworthiness of companies and government entities. Investors use these ratings to assess the relative risk of lending funds to the borrower: the higher the rating, the lower the risk, and so the lower the interest rate, other things being equal. Table 7.4 summarises the different categories of short-term ratings employed by one of the major ratings agencies, Standard & Poor's (S&P).

TABLE 7.4 Standard & Poor's short-term credit ratings

A-1	A short-term obligation rated 'A-1' is rated in the highest category by Standard & Poor's. The obligor's capacity to meet its financial commitment on the obligation is strong. Within this category, certain obligations are designated with a plus sign (+). This indicates that the obligor's capacity to meet its financial commitment on these obligations is extremely strong.
A-2	A short-term obligation rated 'A-2' is somewhat more susceptible to the adverse effects of changes in circumstances and economic conditions than obligations in higher rating categories. However, the obligor's capacity to meet its financial commitment on the obligation is satisfactory.
A-3	A short-term obligation rated 'A-3' exhibits adequate protection parameters. However, adverse economic conditions or changing circumstances are more likely to lead to a weakened capacity of the obligor to meet its financial commitment on the obligation.
B	A short-term obligation rated 'B' is regarded as having significant speculative characteristics. Ratings of 'B-1', 'B-2' and 'B-3' may be assigned to indicate finer distinctions within the 'B' category. The obligor currently has the capacity to meet its financial commitment on the obligation; however, it faces major ongoing uncertainties which could lead to the obligor's inadequate capacity to meet its financial commitment on the obligation.
B-1	A short-term obligation rated 'B-1' is regarded as having significant speculative characteristics, but the obligor has a relatively stronger capacity to meet its financial commitments over the short-term compared to other speculative-grade obligors.
B-2	A short-term obligation rated 'B-2' is regarded as having significant speculative characteristics, and the obligor has an average speculative-grade capacity to meet its financial commitments over the short-term compared to other speculative-grade obligors.
B-3	A short-term obligation rated 'B-3' is regarded as having significant speculative characteristics, and the obligor has a relatively weaker capacity to meet its financial commitments over the short-term compared to other speculative-grade obligors.
C	A short-term obligation rated 'C' is currently vulnerable to non-payment and is dependent upon favourable business, financial and economic conditions for the obligor to meet its financial commitment on the obligation.
D	A short-term obligation rated 'D' is in payment default.

BILLS OF EXCHANGE

A bill of exchange (also known as a *commercial bill*) is another member of the family of discount-type financial instruments. However, whereas a promissory note contains a promise by the borrower to repay the debt at maturity, a **bill of exchange** is a written order that *requires* payment to be made, either on demand or at a specified time. Typically, bills have maturity values of $100 000 or $500 000.

Bills had their origins as instruments to facilitate trade, providing a means whereby a creditor could use the bill to formalise the requirement for payment by a debtor to whom goods or services had been provided. However, once the basic structure of bills of exchange had evolved, it was realised that they could be used solely as a means of raising finance, without any underlying transaction for the provision of goods and services. A bill that is used as a form of financing is called an *accommodation bill* and Example 7.8 looks at how a business can use this type of bill to obtain short-term finance.

bill of exchange
A short-term financial instrument requiring the face value to be repaid on demand or at a specified date.

EXAMPLE 7.8 Using a bill to raise short-term finance

Suppose that Company A wishes to raise approximately $100 000 for 90 days via a bill, to finance its seasonal stock build-up for Christmas time. A is known as the drawer of the bill, which is a document containing details of the parties involved and the maturity date when the face value (V) has to be paid. In this example, maturity is in 90 days time and the bill has a face value of $100 000.

The mechanism of an accommodation bill requires that A must find an acceptor of the bill. The acceptor B provides an independent guarantee of payment of the bill's face value to the party who holds the bill on the maturity date. In turn, the acceptor will not 'accept' the bill unless it is satisfied that A is likely to have the capacity to repay the face value of the bill to the acceptor, on maturity. If the bill is accepted by a bank, it is called a **bank bill**. Bank bills are an important part of short-term business finance; in the year ended 30 June 2010, bank bill lending averaged in excess of $140 billion per month. Bank bills are potentially more expensive than promissory notes because notes involve direct borrowing from investors. However, such notes are typically restricted to companies with a suitable credit rating (see above), whereas firms have much wider potential to access bill finance via their banks.

bank bill
A commercial bill that has been either accepted or endorsed by a bank.

Although B 'accepts' the responsibility for payment of the debt at maturity, B is not necessarily the financier. Instead, the financier is called the discounter. The discounter, C, buys the bill from A for a price (P) that is less than the face value of the bill. The difference between this price and the face value (V) is known as the discount or interest on the bill, that is: interest = discount = V – P. For example, if C purchases the bill for $98 000, A will obtain $98 000 now, in exchange for having to pay $100 000 in 90 days time. Therefore, on maturity C will receive interest of $2000 (i.e. $100 000 – $98 000), while conversely A will have paid $2000 in interest.

Because the bill is a negotiable instrument, C is potentially able to sell it via the money market. This means that the bill could be bought and sold by investors a number of times before its maturity date. On the maturity date the final holder of the bill has a legally enforceable entitlement to receive $100 000 on presentation of the bill to the acceptor, B.

Obtaining a bank as an acceptor significantly improves its marketability because of the high creditworthiness of banks. In this regard, if the acceptor (such as a bank) has a formal credit rating (as in Table 7.1), that rating is likely to 'attach' to the bill and thus it provides an indicator of the relative interest rate demanded by the lender (the discounter). As part of establishing the bill finance facility, the acceptor B has a separate agreement that requires the drawer of the bill, A, to repay to B the face value of the bill on the maturity date.

The cash flows associated with this bill can be outlined as follows:

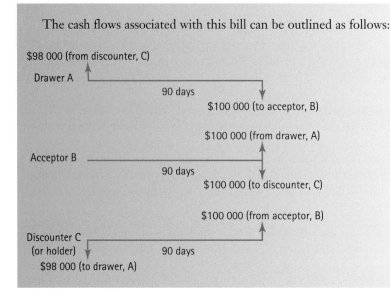

It might seem pertinent to ask, in relation to Example 7.8, why Company A cannot simply borrow directly from C via a promissory note. Why enter into such a convoluted arrangement as the bill in order to raise short-term finance? There are several reasons for using bills. First, only 'prime' organisations have a credit rating high enough to issue promissory notes. To attract investors, other borrowers may need the additional stature that is provided by an acceptor with a higher credit rating (such as a bank). Another reason is that borrower companies may not be sufficiently prominent in the money market to arrange the issue of a bill themselves, so they may remunerate a bank or a merchant bank (via establishment or facility fees) for arranging an acceptor and a discounter. (Note that the acceptor may itself act as the discounter.) Simpler bill mechanisms can also be used. For example, the borrower (if of sufficient credit rating) could act as its own acceptor, and the discounter could draw up the bill; so on maturity the borrower/acceptor would simply repay the drawer/discounter.

Cost of bill finance

The drawer may face a number of non-interest charges associated with a bill of the kind outlined above. There may be *establishment* or *facility* fees payable to the bank or other institution that arranges the issue, as well as ongoing *maintenance* or *activity* fees. In addition, there will be an *acceptance* fee payable to the acceptor. These non-interest costs may be incorporated into the cash flows of the borrower to enable an all-up percentage cost of finance to be calculated, as detailed in Example 7.9 below.

Accommodation bills are usually in standard 'units', to facilitate marketability, and are for a short-term period (e.g. 90 or 180 days). However, a chain of successive bills can be arranged (on a *rollover* basis) to extend the term. Typically, such rollovers are arranged between the drawer and a bank. The bank will arrange for a discounter and will pass on the cost of interest, as well as other charges such as the accommodation fee, to the drawer.

At any given time, bank bills of a given maturity have a 'going' (market) interest rate. Thus, the interest rate will tend to vary each time a rollover occurs. That is, from the viewpoint of the drawer, rolling over bills constitutes a form of floating-rate financing. Sometimes, however, the 'true' cost of such borrowing may not be clear to the borrower, as it is made up of an amalgam of interest and other fees. Example 7.9 illustrates how it is possible to calculate an all-up percentage cost of bill finance.

EXAMPLE 7.9 Cost of a bill (incorporating a rollover)

Suppose that a company wishes to raise around $1 million for about six months. The company's bank is unwilling to provide a fixed interest rate for this period, but it is willing to help arrange an accommodation bill with a face value of $1 million on the basis that the bill will be 'rolled over' after 90 days for a further 90 days. The bank also advises that it will levy an accommodation fee of 1% of the face value of each bill plus an initial establishment fee of $5000. Also, an activity fee of 10% of interest charges will be levied on the first bill, at the time rollover occurs. What is the 'all-up' cost of the finance, given interest rates of 16.5% per annum for the first bill and 16.8% for the second?

The 'all-up' cost is found in three steps, as follows.

Step 1: Tabulate the cash flows from the viewpoint of the borrower:

Day 0

Cash inflow	$960 905	(price of first bill)[a]
Cash outflows	–10 000	(accommodation fee, 1% of face value of first bill)
	–5 000	(establishment fee)
Net cash flow	+$945 905	

Day 90

Cash outflow	–$1 000 000	(maturity of first bill)
Cash outflow	–3 909	(activity fee, 10% of $39 095 interest on first bill)
Cash outflow	–10 000	(accommodation fee, 1% of face value of second bill)
Cash inflow	960 223	(price of second bill)[b]
Net cash flow	–$53 686	

Day 180

Cash outflow	–$1 000 000	(maturity of second bill)
Net cash flow	–$1 000 000	

Step 2: Summarise the cash flows on a timeline:[c]

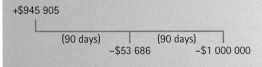

Step 3: Determine the implicit rate of compound interest—that is, the internal rate of return (IRR).[d]
From the timeline above, it is seen that the transaction has been split into two 90-day periods. Therefore, the *IRR* can be determined on a 90-day basis:

- *Using the irregular cash-flow routine on a financial calculator* (see 'Complex cash flows' in Chapter 4). This gives an answer of 5.6966% per 90-day period. Annualised, this represents a nominal annual rate of 23.1%.

$$\text{RATE} = 5.6966\% \times \frac{1}{90/365} = 23.10\% \text{ p.a.}$$

- *Using financial tables.* The per-period interest rate is the rate that satisfies the following equation:

$$945\,905 = 53\,686 PVIF_{i\%,1} + 1\,000\,000 PVIF_{i\%,2}$$

By trial and error, using interpolation (see Chapter 4), the interest rate is approximately 5.7% per period, which is about 23.1% p.a.

a	The price of bill $P = 365V/[365 + \text{RATE}(n)]$.
	Issue price of first bill = $365(1\,000\,000)/[365 + 0.165(90)] = \$960\,905$.
	Amount of discount (interest) on first bill = $1\,000\,000 - 960\,905 = \$39\,095$.
b	Issue price of second bill = $365(1\,000\,000)/[365 + 0.168(90)] = \$960\,223$.
	Amount of discount (interest) on second bill = $1\,000\,000 - 960\,223 = \$39\,777$.
c	Note that any statutory charges can be incorporated into the cash-flow schedule in a similar manner to the above non-interest charges.
d	With all calculator cash-flow functions, the periodicity of the cash flows defines the frequency of the interest rate calculated. In this case, a 90-day cash-flow sequence generates a 90-day interest rate.

Your money

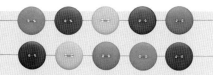

PERSONAL CREDIT RATINGS

Just as companies and government bodies may have a credit rating, you will typically acquire a personal credit rating too. This rating is usually expressed as a number—a *credit score*. Your credit score has an enormous effect on your financial life, influencing everything from the size of your credit card limit to the interest rate on credit cards, personal loans and housing loans. The score even influences the amount of junk mail you receive asking you to take on another credit card! In short, when it comes to lending money, you'll be evaluated by your credit score.

Credit reports and scores are compiled by professional *credit agencies* (such as Dun & Bradstreet, D&B, and Veda Advantage). These agencies collect credit data on both businesses and individuals, from which they compile both credit reports and scores. Then, lenders may pay for access to the agency's database, information from which plays a significant role in the lending decision.

Different credit agencies use different numerical scales for their scoring systems. Some lending institutions run their own scoring models, too. Outside the US, credit agencies typically do not publish their scoring systems. However, in the US, the well-known 'FICO' scoring system (named after its founder, Fair Isaac Corporation), ranges from a low of 300 to a high of 850, with a cut-off around 500 normally being necessary to obtain a loan. To give some notion of the significance of the score, one source[4] suggests that the 2009 interest rate on a 3-year automobile loan could vary from a low of 6% per annum for an individual scoring 760 or above to about 16% per annum for an individual scoring between 500 and 579. The FICO score takes into account the following five factors:

1. *The individual's payment history (35% of the score)*. Since a lender is considering extending credit, it only makes sense that they want to know how the applicant has handled credit payments in the past.
2. *The amount owed and the available credit (30% of the score)*. The amounts that the individual owes on credit cards, mortgage, car loan, and any other outstanding debts are factored into the score, along with whether or not the person is close to (or at) their credit limit.
3. *Length of credit history (15% of the score)*. The longer that the individual's credit accounts have been open and the longer he or she has had accounts with the same creditors, the higher the credit score will be.
4. *Types of credit used (10% of the score)*. If the individual has several different types of credit outstanding (for example, credit cards, retail accounts, automobile loans and a mortgage loan), this is taken as an indicator that the person knows how to manage his or her finances.
5. *New credit (10% of the score)*. Applying for lots of new credit is generally a bad sign. This is because individuals who are moving towards bankruptcy generally take one last grasp at credit, hoping it will keep them afloat. This will lower the score.

From the first time we borrow money, credit agencies may collect information about our personal circumstances and build a picture of our credit histories. Under Australian privacy legislation, credit agencies are required to offer individuals access to a copy of their personal credit reports (which does not include the score).

ACCOUNTS RECEIVABLE LOANS

Some common sources of short-term credit use particular assets of the firm as security (collateral) for the loan. In the event of default on the loan agreement, the lender has first claim to the 'pledged' assets, in addition to any claim as a general creditor of the firm. Hence, the secured credit agreement offers an added margin of safety to the lender.

Generally, a firm's accounts receivable are among its most liquid assets. For this reason they are considered by many lenders to be prime collateral for a secured loan. Two basic procedures can be used in arranging for financing based on receivables: *pledging* and *factoring*.

Pledging of accounts receivable

Under the **pledging** arrangement, the borrower simply uses accounts receivable as security for a loan obtained from either a bank or a finance company. The amount of the loan is stated as a percentage of the face value of the receivables pledged. If the firm provides the lender with a *general line* on its receivables, then all of the borrower's accounts receivables are pledged as security for the loan. This method of pledging is simple and inexpensive. However, because the lender has no control over the quality of the receivables being pledged, it will set the maximum loan at a relatively low percentage of the total face value of the accounts (generally ranging downwards from a maximum of around 75%).

Another approach to pledging involves the borrower presenting specific invoices to the lender as security for a loan. This method is somewhat more expensive in that the lender must assess the creditworthiness of each individual account pledged. However, given this added knowledge, the lender may be willing to increase the loan as a percentage of the face value of the invoices. In this case the loan might reach as high as 85% or 90% of the face value of the pledged receivables.

Accounts-receivable loans generally carry an interest rate several percent higher than the bank's prime lending rate. Finance companies, which are the main sources of accounts-receivable loans, charge an even higher rate.

The primary advantage of pledging as a source of short-term credit is the flexibility it provides the borrower. Financing is available on a continuous basis. The accounts receivable created through new credit sales provide the collateral for the financing of new business. Furthermore, the lender may provide credit management and monitoring services that eliminate (or at least reduce) the need for similar services within the firm. The primary disadvantage associated with this method of financing is the relatively low amount of finance obtained in relation to the value of the receivables pledged.

Factoring of accounts receivable

Factoring accounts receivable involves the outright sale of a firm's accounts receivable to a financial institution called a *factor*, which is often a finance company. The factor, for a fee, bears the risk of collection of the firm's accounts receivable and may also administer these accounts for the firm. The fee is stated as a percentage of the face value of all receivables factored (usually from 2.5% to 5%).

Alternatively, under a *maturity factoring* arrangement the factor does *not* make payment for factored accounts until the accounts have been collected or the credit terms have been met. For example, for a fee of 1% to 2% of the firm's receivables the factor will guarantee to pay to the firm the value of its accounts receivable 30 days after the invoices have been issued to the firm's customers.

The annual cost of factoring can be quite high, as illustrated in Example 7.10. However, the firm may offset part of this credit cost through savings in bad debts and through savings in administrative costs.

> **pledging**
> A loan that uses the firm's accounts receivable as collateral.

> **factoring accounts receivable**
> The outright sale of a firm's accounts receivable to another party (the factor) who in turn bears the risk of collection.

EXAMPLE 7.10   Cost of accounts-receivable factoring

ARF Company's credit sales average $100 000 per month, with payment terms of net 30 days. The firm factors all of its accounts receivable in return for payment of a fee equal to 5% of the value of the accounts.

Face amount of receivables factored	$100 000
Less: Fee (0.05 × $100 000)	(5 000)
Funds obtained by the firm each month	$95 000

$$\text{RATE} = \frac{\$5\,000}{\$95\,000} \times \frac{1}{30/365} = 0.64 = 64\% \text{ p.a.}$$

INVENTORY LOANS

inventory loans
Loans secured by inventory.

Inventory provides another specific source of collateral for short-term secured credit. The maximum amount of the **inventory loan** depends on both the marketability and the perishability of the inventory. Some raw materials (such as grains, oil, timber and chemicals) are excellent sources of security, because they can easily be sold. Other items, such as work-in-process inventories, provide very poor security because of their lack of marketability. Finance companies are the main sources of inventory loans. However, for these lenders, keeping track of the security can be a difficult task, as evidenced in the salad-oil scandal in the United States in the 1960s. Fifty-one banks loaned nearly $200 million to the Allied Crude Vegetable Oil Refining Company, based on warehouse receipts. The alleged vegetable oil that was used as security turned out to be mostly sea water and sludge.

To counter this problem, collateral management companies have been set up. They provide services such as field warehousing where the inventories used as collateral for a loan are physically separated from the firm's other inventories. For example, a refinery might use part of its inventory of fuel oil to secure a short-term bank loan. Under a field warehousing agreement, the oil reserves would be set aside in specific storage tanks which would be controlled (monitored) by the collateral management company. This means that the borrower is no longer allowed to use or sell the inventory items without the consent of the lender.

The costs of inventory loans can be quite high and comprise not only the finance company's normal interest rate but also the fees for the collateral management company's services, as illustrated in Example 7.11.

EXAMPLE 7.11   Cost of an inventory loan

The ILC Company follows a practice of obtaining short-term credit based on its seasonal finished-goods inventory. The firm builds up its inventories of outdoor furniture throughout the winter months for sale in spring and summer. Thus, for the two-month period ended 30 September it uses its autumn and winter production of furniture as collateral for a short-term loan. The finance company advances inventory loans at 14% interest, plus a fixed fee of $2000 to cover the costs of a field warehousing arrangement. During this period, the firm usually has about $200 000 in inventories, against which it borrows the maximum 70% that the financier will permit. The dollar cost of this credit therefore consists of two components:

- two months interest: $140 000 × 0.14 × 60/365 = $3222
- the field warehousing fee of $2000.

The overall percentage cost of the short-term credit is therefore given by:

$$\text{RATE} = \frac{\$3\,222 + \$2\,000}{\$140\,000} \times \frac{1}{60/365} = 0.2269 = 22.69\% \text{ p.a.}$$

Concept check

7.8 Which of the sources of short-term finance are 'spontaneous'? Discretionary?

7.9 Why are bank overdrafts found in just about every business, large or small?

7.10 What is the main difference between a promissory note and a bill?

For answers go to MyFinanceLab or www.pearson.com.au/9781442539174

This chapter discussed the determinants of a firm's investment in working capital and the factors underlying the firm's choice between various sources of short-term financing. Working capital represents a significant component of most firms' total investment, and thus efforts to manage working capital can have a substantial impact on the firm's overall profitability. *Net working capital* is the difference between the firm's current assets and its current liabilities. Investments in current assets are largely determined by the nature of the firm's business (such as whether it is a manufacturing firm or a retail establishment) and how efficiently the firm is managed. A firm's use of current liabilities is a function of the availability of short-term sources of financing to the firm and management's willingness to expose itself to the risks of insolvency posed by the use of short-term as opposed to long-term or permanent sources of financing.

OBJECTIVE 1

Managing working capital can thus be thought of as managing the firm's liquidity, with a risk–return trade-off arising from the fact that increased investment in net current assets reduces the risk of illiquidity but at the expense of profitability.

OBJECTIVE 2

The hedging principle provides a benchmark for managing a firm's net working capital position. Very simply, the principle involves matching the cash-flow-generating characteristics of an asset with the cash-flow requirements of the financing source chosen. Temporary asset investment should be financed with correspondingly short-term sources of funds, whereas long-term asset investment should be financed with long-term funds.

OBJECTIVE 3

In deciding between alternative sources of short-term finance, the cost of short-term credit can be approximated by using the nominal annual percentage rate (symbol *j* or *APR*), which is identified as RATE in equation (7-3):

OBJECTIVE 4

$$\text{RATE} = \frac{\text{interest}}{\text{principal} \times \text{time}}$$

More accurately, the cost of funds can be determined by the effective annual interest rate or *EAR*, given by equation (7-4)

$$EAR = (1 + j/m)^m - 1$$

Short-term credit can be obtained from a variety of sources and in a wide array of forms. In countries such as Australia, a bank overdraft is found in just about every business, large or small. This type of finance has the advantage of flexibility: the company can draw funds up to the overdraft limit at any time without reference to the bank and likewise can reduce the balance whenever desired. Thus an overdraft provides a form of revolving credit that is an ideal form of temporary finance.

OBJECTIVE 5

Overdrafts are generally secured by the use of suitable assets as collateral. Other sources of short-term finance are often unsecured (the repayment is assured only by the pledge of the borrower to pay). These include accounts that arise spontaneously (in the normal course of business), such as accounts payable and accrued expenses (notably wages and taxes). Discretionary unsecured short-term finance includes promissory notes (known also as notes payable) and bills.

Key terms

For a complete flashcard glossary go to MyFinanceLab at www.pearson.com.au/myfinancelab

Review questions

7-1 What is the difference between working capital and net working capital?

7-2 Discuss the risk–return relationship that relates to working-capital management.

7-3 Explain what is meant by the statement: 'The use of current liabilities as opposed to long-term debt subjects the firm to a greater risk of illiquidity.'

7-4 Define the hedging principle. How can this principle be used in the management of working capital?

7-5 Define the following terms:

(a) Permanent asset investments
(b) Temporary asset investments
(c) Permanent sources of financing
(d) Temporary sources of financing
(e) Spontaneous sources of financing

7-6 What distinguishes short-term, intermediate-term and long-term debt?

7-7 Discuss the different considerations that should be used in selecting a source of short-term credit?

7-8 What is meant by the following trade credit terms: 2/10, net 30? 4/20, net 60? 3/15, net 45?

7-9 Define the following:

(a) Overdraft   (d) Bank bill
(b) Promissory note   (e) Overdraft limit
(c) Prime rate

7-10 Explain the meaning of the following terms with reference to discount-type financial instruments:

(a) Promissory note   (d) Acceptor of a bill
(b) Bank bill   (e) Discounter of a bill
(c) Drawer of a bill

7-11 Outline briefly the purpose of leading and lagging in multinational firms.

7-12 Distinguish between cash-flow lending and secured lending by institutions such as banks.

7-13 With reference to a bank overdraft, explain the following:

(a) Overdraft limit
(b) Unused limit fee
(c) What it means when the account is 'in credit'
(d) Revolving credit

7-14 Discuss the benefits of a bank overdraft account for managing a firm's cash position.

Self-test problems

For answers go to MyFinanceLab
www.pearson.com.au/myfinancelab

ST-1 (*Using marketable securities to increase liquidity*) The balance sheet for Simplex Manufacturing Ltd follows for the year ended 31 December 20X1:

Simplex Manufacturing Ltd, Balance Sheet, 31 December 20X1

Cash	$10 000	
Accounts receivable	50 000	
Inventories	40 000	
Total current assets	$100 000	
Net non-current assets	100 000	
Total		$200 000
Current liabilities	$60 000	
Long-term liabilities	40 000	
Equity	100 000	
Total		$200 000

During 20X1 the firm earned net income after taxes of $20000, based on net sales of $400000.

(a) Calculate Simplex's current ratio, net working-capital position and return-on-total-assets ratio (net income/total assets), using the above information.

(b) The financial controller at Simplex is considering a plan for enhancing the firm's liquidity. The plan involves raising $20000 in equity and investing in marketable securities that will earn 8% before taxes and 5.6% after taxes. Calculate Simplex's current ratio, net working capital and return-on-total-assets ratio after the plan has been implemented. (Hint: Net income will now become $20000, plus 0.056 × $20000, or $21 120.)

(c) Will the plan proposed in part **(b)** enhance liquidity? Explain.

(d) What effect does the plan proposed in part **(b)** have on profitability? Explain.

ST-2 (*Using long-term debt to increase liquidity*) On 30 April 20X2 the Jamax Sales Company had the following balance sheet and partial income statement for the year just ended:

Jamax Sales Company, Balance Sheet, 30 April 20X2

Current assets	$100000	
Net non-current assets	200000	
Total		$300000
Accounts payable	$30000	
Notes payable (14%)[a]	40000	
Total	$70000	
Long-term debt (10%)	100000	
Equity	130000	
Total		$300000

Partial Income Statement for the year ended 30 April 20X2

Net operating income	$72800
Less: Interest expense[b]	(12800)
Earnings before taxes	$60000
Less: Taxes (36%)	(21600)
Net income	$38400

a The short-term notes are outstanding during the latter half of the firm's fiscal year in response to the firm's seasonal need for funds.

b Total interest expense for the year consists of 14% interest on the firm's $40000 note for a six-month period (0.14 × $40000 × 1/2), $2800, plus 10% for the firm's $100000 long-term note for a full year (0.10 × $100000), or $10000. Thus, total interest expense for the year is $2800 plus $10000, or $12800.

(a) Calculate Jamax's current ratio, net working capital and return on total assets.

(b) The treasurer of Jamax was recently advised by the firm's investment banker that its current ratio was considered below par. In fact, a current ratio of 2 was considered to be a sign of a healthy liquidity position. In response to this news, the treasurer devised a plan whereby the firm would issue $40000 in 13% long-term debt and pay off its short-term notes payable. This long-term note would be outstanding all year long, and when the funds were not needed to finance the firm's seasonal asset needs they would be invested in marketable securities earning 8% before taxes. If the plan had been in effect last year, other things being the same, what would have been the firm's current ratio, net working capital and return-on-total-assets ratio? (Hint: With the change, the firm's net income after tax would have been $41440.)

(c) With implementation of the plan put forth in part **(b)**, did Jamax's liquidity improve to the desired level (based on a desired current ratio of 2)?

(d) How was the firm's profitability in relation to total investment affected by the change in financial policy?

ST-3 (*Analysing the cost of a promissory note offering*) The Marilyn Sales Company is a wholesale machine-tool broker which has gone through a recent expansion of its activities resulting in a doubling of its sales. The company has determined that it needs an additional $200 million in short-term funds to finance peak-season sales during roughly six months of the year. Marilyn's treasurer has recommended that the firm use a promissory note offering to raise the needed funds. Specifically, it has been

determined that a $200 million offering would require 2000 notes with a face value of $100 000 each to be issued at a discount of $4931.51 per note plus a $125 000 placement fee payable upfront. The notes would carry a six-month (180-day) maturity. What is the annual percentage cost of this credit?

ST-4 (*Analysing the cost of short-term credit*) The Samples Manufacturing Co. provides specialty steel products to the oil industry. Although the firm's business is highly correlated with the cyclical swings in oil exploration activity, it also experiences some significant seasonality. The firm currently is concerned with this seasonality in its need for funds. The firm needs $500 000 for the two-month July–August period each year, and as a result is considering the following two sources of financing:

(a) Forgo its trade discounts over the two months of July and August when the funding will be needed. The firm's discount terms are 3/15, net 30, and the firm averages $500 000 in trade credit purchases during July and August.

(b) Enter into a pledging arrangement with a local finance company. The finance company has agreed to extend Samples the needed $500 000 if it pledges $750 000 in receivables. The finance company has offered to advance the $500 000, with 12% annual interest payable at the end of the two-month loan term. In addition, the finance company will charge a 0.5% fee based on pledged receivables to cover the cost of processing the company's accounts (this fee is paid at the end of the loan period).

Analyse each of the sources of credit and select the least costly. Note that a total of $500 000 will be needed for a two-month period (July–August) each year.

ST-5 (*Analysing the cost of a bill rollover facility*) On 21 April, Concrete Pty Ltd ordered a load of sand costing $50 000 to be delivered on 30 April. If the account is paid by bank cheque on delivery, the company can receive a 6.4% cash discount. It is company policy to take all cash discounts, so the financial manager originally decided to draw up a 90-day bill in order to raise the funds to pay for the sand. The company's bank has confirmed that it will accept the bill and that it can find a discounter who requires a return of 10.4% per annum.

After preparing a cash budget for the next six months, the financial manager realises that the bill will have to be rolled over for a further 90 days. The bank has advised that the charges for this bill facility will be an acceptance fee of 0.85% on the face value of the first bill, payable upfront on the first bill, plus an activity fee of 8% of the interest charges levied on the first bill and a rollover fee of 0.5% of the face value of the second bill, both payable at the time of the rollover. It is expected that the 90-day bill rate in three months time will be 12.5% per annum. What is the expected percentage cost per annum of the bill finance raised by the company?

Problems

For more problems and for answers to problems marked with an asterisk (*) go to MyFinanceLab at www.pearson.com.au/myfinancelab

7-1* (*Investing in current assets and the return on equity*) The managers of Tharp's Tarps Ltd are considering a possible change in their working-capital management policy. Specifically, they are concerned with the effect of their investment in current assets on the return earned on ordinary shareholders' equity. They expect sales of $7 000 000 next year and project that non-current assets will total $2 000 000. The firm pays 11% interest on both short- and long-term debt (which is managed by the firm so as to equal a target of 30% of assets) and faces a 30% tax rate. Finally, the firm projects its earnings before interest and taxes to be 15% of sales.

(a) If management follows a working-capital strategy calling for current assets equal to 50% of sales, what will be the firm's return on equity?

(b) Answer part (a) for a current-asset-to-sales ratio of 40%.

(c) Is it reasonable to assume, as has been done, that the rate of return earned by the firm on sales is independent of its investment in current assets?

7-2 (*Managing liquidity*) As of 30 June 20X6, the balance sheet and income statement of Hardwear Paint Ltd appeared as follows:

Hardwear Paint Ltd, Balance Sheet, 30 June 20X6

Current assets	$1 250 000
Non-current assets	800 000
Total	$2 050 000
Accounts payable	$250 000
Bank bill (12%)[a]	800 000
Total	$1 050 000
Long-term debt (10%)	200 000
Ordinary equity	800 000
Total	$2 050 000

a Short-term bills are used to finance a three-month seasonal expansion in Hardwear's asset needs. This period is the same for every year and extends from April to June, with the bill being due on 1 July.

Hardwear Paint Ltd, Income Statement for year ended 30 June 20X6

Net operating income	$401 332
Less: Interest expense[a]	(44 000)
Earnings before taxes	$357 332
Less: Taxes (30%)	(107 200)
Net income	$250 132

a Interest expense was calculated as follows:
Bank bill (0.12 × $800 000 × 1/4 year)   = $24 000
Long-term debt (0.10 × $200 000 × 1 year) = $20 000
Total   = $44 000

(a) Calculate the current ratio, net working capital, return-on-total-assets ratio and return-on-equity ratio for Hardwear Paint Ltd.

(b) Assume that you have just been hired as the financial manager of Hardwear Paint Ltd. One of your first duties is to assess the firm's liquidity. Based on your analysis, you plan to issue $800 000 in ordinary shares and use the proceeds to repay the firm's bank bill. Recalculate the ratios from part (a) and assess the change in the firm's liquidity.

(c) Given your actions in part (b), assume that in the future you will finance your three-month seasonal need for $800 000 using a long-term loan that will carry an interest cost of 10%. (Note: During the time the funds are needed your current assets increase by $800 000 because of increased inventories and receivables.) In addition, you estimate that during the nine months you do not need the funds they can be invested in marketable securities to earn a rate of 6%. Recalculate the financial ratios from part (a) for 20X7, assuming that all revenues and non-finance expenses are expected to be the same as in 20X6. Analyse the results of your plan.

7-3* (*Managing firm liquidity*) Re-analyse part (c) of problem 7-2 assuming that a three-month bank bill is used instead of the long-term loan. The bill carries a rate of 10% p.a.

7-4 (*The hedging principle*) The Canoob Wax Company Ltd estimates that its current assets are about 25% of sales. The firm's current balance sheet is presented here:

Canoob Wax Ltd, Balance Sheet, 31 December 20X6 ($ million)

Current assets	$6.0	
Net non-current assets	8.4	
Total		$14.4
Accounts payable	$2.4	
Long-term debt	3.0	
Equity	9.0	
Total		$14.4

Canoob pays out all its net income in cash dividends to its shareholders. Trade credit and accounts payable equal 10% of the firm's sales.

(a) Based on the following five-year sales forecast, prepare five end-of-year pro-forma balance sheets (see methods discussed in Chapter 6) that indicate 'additional financing needed' for each year as a balancing account. Non-current assets are expected to increase by $0.6 million each year.

YEAR	PREDICTED SALES ($ MILLION)
20X7	30
20X8	33
20X9	39
2X10	42
2X11	45

(b) Using your answer to part (a) above, develop a financing policy for Canoob that is consistent with the following goals:
(i) A minimum current ratio of 2 and a maximum of 3.
(ii) A debt-to-total-assets ratio of 35 to 45%. You may issue new ordinary shares to raise equity funds.

7-5* (*Cost of trade credit*) Calculate the cost of the following trade credit terms where payment is made on the net due date.

(a) 2/10, net 30
(b) 3/15, net 30
(c) 3/15, net 45
(d) 2/15, net 60

7-6 (*Effective interest rate*) Compute the effective cost of the trade credit terms in problem 7-5, using the effective interest rate.

7-7 (*Cost of bank overdraft*) Your business has a bank overdraft with a limit of $100 000 (on which there is an unused limit fee of 1% p.a.). The interest rate is 10% p.a.

(a) What is the approximate cost of this overdraft account if your average overdrawn balance is $60 000?
(b) Re-compute the answer in (a) assuming the balance averages (i) $80 000 (ii) $40 000.
(c) What general conclusions can you draw from your preceding answers?

7-8 (*Cost of bank overdraft*) STN Company is reviewing its banking arrangements. Its existing bank, ABN, currently allows STN an overdraft limit of $6 000 000, with an unused limit fee of 0.5% p.a. STN's analysis shows that the average account balance is $2 400 000 and the interest rate is 9% p.a. ABC bank, a competitor of STN, is trying to win STN's business and is offering the 'same deal' except that the firm can have a higher overdraft limit, namely $10 000 000.

(a) Analyse the cost of the two alternatives.
(b) What other factors would have a bearing on STN's decision?

7-9 (*Cost of promissory note*) XYZ Childcare Centre Ltd has adopted the practice of financing its balance sheet by use of promissory notes. The company has an A-3 credit rating from S&P, which differs by 1.5% p.a. from yields on A-1 rating securities. XYZ wants to issue a new 180-day note, with $50 million face value, when its present note expires.

(a) What interest rate will XYZ pay if 180-day A-1 securities are yielding 6% p.a. on the date of maturity of the old note?
(b) What will be the principal of the new note?
(c) Assume XYZ's notes are sold by a dealer who charges a fee of 0.3% of the face value. What effect will this have on the cost of the new note?
(d) Critically evaluate XYZ's financing practice in relation to the 'hedging principle'.

7-10 (*Cost of bill financing*) You are planning to borrow $1 000 000 short-term finance that is needed for 90 days. Your bank has offered to arrange a bill with a face value of $1 million at an interest rate of 10% p.a.

(a) How much money will you obtain?

(b) If the bank charges an upfront arrangement fee of 0.25% of the face value, what will be the cost to you of this bill?

7-11 (*Cost of short-term financing*) The Bildup Construction Company needs to borrow $100 000 to help finance a new $150 000 hydraulic crane used in the firm's commercial construction business. The crane will pay for itself in one year. The firm is considering the following alternatives for financing its purchase:

Alternative A: The firm's bank has agreed to lend the $100 000 at a rate of 14% by arranging a bill for one year.

Alternative B: The equipment dealer has agreed to finance the equipment with a one-year loan. The $100 000 loan would require payment of principal and interest totalling $116 300 at year-end.

    (a) Determine the face value of the bill.
    (b) Which alternative should Bildup select?
    (c) What would be your answer if the bank charged a $2000 arrangement fee for the bill?

7-12* (*Cost of secured short-term credit*) The S-J Import Co. (S-J) needs $500 000 for the three-month period ending 30 September 200X. The firm has explored two possible sources of credit:

- S-J has arranged with its bank for a $500 000 loan secured by accounts receivable. The bank has agreed to advance S-J up to 80% of the value of its pledged receivables at a rate of 11% plus a 1% fee based on all receivables pledged. S-J's receivables average a total of $1 million year-round.
- An insurance company has agreed to lend the $500 000 at a rate of 9% p.a., using a loan secured by S-J's inventory of salad oil. A field warehouse agreement would be used, which would cost S-J $2000 a month.

Which source of credit should S-J select? Explain.

7-13 (*Cost of promissory notes*) On 3 February 200X, the Burlington Western Company plans a promissory note issue of $20 million. The firm has never used promissory notes before but has been assured by the firm placing the issue that it will have no difficulty raising the funds. The notes will carry a 270-day maturity and investors will require interest at a rate of 11% p.a. In addition, the firm will have to pay fees totalling $200 000 in order to bring the issue to market and place it. What is the annual percentage cost of the promissory note issue to Burlington Western?

7-14* (*Cost of bill rollover*) Pearl Jam Ltd has arranged a bill rollover facility with a total face value of $200 000 to raise funds for about nine months. The company's finance director has arranged with the bank to provide the facility via 90-day accommodation bills having a face value of $50 000 each. The bank has advised the company that the following charges will apply:

- establishment fee of 0.4% of the face value of the bills, payable at the start of the facility
- stamp duty of 0.05% of the face value of the bills, payable at the start of the facility and at each rollover date.

What is the annual interest cost of the finance obtained by Pearl Jam given interest rates of 15% for the first bill, 15.5% at the first rollover date (day 90) and 13.75% for the bill rollover in 180 days time?

7-15 (*Cost of bill rollover*) JBHF Company has arranged a bill rollover facility with a total face value of $100 000 to raise funds for about six months. The company's finance director has arranged with the bank to provide the facility via two 90-day accommodation bills having a face value of $50 000 each. The bank has advised the company that the following charges will apply:

- an establishment fee of 0.3% of the face value of the bills, payable at the start of the facility
- an activity fee of 0.1% of the face value of the bills, payable at the start of the facility and at each rollover date.

What is the nominal annual interest rate of the finance obtained by JBHF Company given annual interest rates of 12% for the first bill and 10.8% at the rollover date (day 90)? What is the effective annual rate?

7-16 (*Cost of accounts receivable*) Johnson Enterprises Ltd is involved in the manufacture and sale of electronic components used in mobile telephones. The firm needs $300 000 to finance an anticipated expansion in receivables due to increased sales. Johnson's credit terms are net 60, and its average monthly credit sales are $200 000. In general, the firm's customers pay within the credit period; thus, the firm's average accounts-receivable balance is $400 000.

Charles Idol, Johnson's financial manager, approached the firm's bank with a request for a loan for the $300 000, using the firm's accounts receivable as collateral. The bank offered to make the loan at a rate of 2% over prime, plus a 1% processing charge on all receivables pledged ($200 000 per month). Furthermore, the bank agreed to lend up to 75% of the face value of the receivables pledged.

Estimate the cost of the receivables loan to Johnson. The prime rate is currently 11%.

7-17* (*Cost of factoring*) MDM Ltd is considering factoring its receivables. The firm has credit sales of $400 000 per month and an average receivables balance of $800 000 with 60-day credit terms. The factor has offered to purchase and manage the receivables for a fee of 6% of the receivables' face value. If MDM decides to factor its receivables, it will sell them all so that it can reduce its credit department costs by $1500 a month.

(a) What is the annual percentage cost of the credit available to MDM through the factoring agreement?

(b) What considerations other than cost should be accounted for by MDM in determining whether or not to enter the factoring agreement?

7-18 (*Cost of secured short-term credit*) DST, a producer of inflatable river rafts, needs $400 000 over the three-month summer season. The firm has explored two possible sources of credit:

(a) DST has arranged with its bank for a $400 000 loan secured by accounts receivable. The bank has agreed to advance DST 80% of the value of its pledged receivables at a rate of 11% plus a 1% fee based on all receivables pledged. DST's receivables average a total of $1 million year-round.

(b) An insurance company has agreed to lend the $400 000 at a rate of 9% p.a., using a loan secured by DST's inventory. A field warehouse agreement would be used, which would cost DST $2000 a month.

Which source of credit would DST select? Explain.

7-19 (*Inventory financing*) In December of each year the Arlyle Publishing Company starts to build up its inventories for the next year's sales. The company has explored the possibility of a field warehouse security agreement as collateral for an inventory loan from its bank during the three summer months. During these months inventories average $400 000. The field warehouse arrangement will cost Arlyle a flat fee of $2000 a month on all its inventory regardless of the amount the firm borrows. The bank has agreed to lend up to 70% of the value of the inventory at a rate of 14%.

(a) If Arlyle borrows $200 000 using the inventory loan for December to February, what will be the annual cost of credit?

(b) What is the annual cost of borrowing $280 000 for the December to February period?

7-20 (*Opportunity cost of decreasing wages payable*) In June of this year AMB Manufacturing Company negotiated a new union contract with its employees. One of the provisions of the new contract involved increasing the frequency of its wages payments from once a month to once every two weeks. AMB's bi-weekly payroll averages $250 000 and the firm's opportunity cost of funds is 12% p.a.

(a) What is the annual dollar cost of this new wages payment scheme to AMB?

(b) What is the maximum percentage increase in wages that AMB would have been willing to accept in lieu of the increased frequency of wages payments?

7-21 (*Analysing cost of alternative sources of finance*) JoBlo Clothing Ltd manufactures men's fashion summer clothing and accessories. Although the firm's business is highly correlated with the general state of the economy, it also experiences significant seasonality in its cash flow. The firm's financial manager is concerned that the firm needs finance of $250 000 for the four-month May–August period each year when it is manufacturing and supplying garments for the southern hemisphere summer season. As a result, the financial manager is considering the following two sources of financing:

(a) Forgo its trade discounts over the four months of May to August when the funding will be needed. The firm's discount terms are 2/10, net 30, and the firm averages $250 000 in trade credit purchases during these months.

(b) Enter into a pledging arrangement with a local finance company. The finance company has agreed to extend the needed $250 000 if JoBlo pledges $500 000 in receivables. The finance company has offered to advance the $250 000, with 8.5% annual interest payable at the end of the four-month loan term. In addition, the finance company will charge a 0.75%

fee based on pledged receivables to cover the cost of processing the company's accounts (this fee is paid at the end of the loan period).

Analyse the cost of each of the alternative sources of credit and select the best one. Note that a total of $250 000 will be needed for a four-month period (May–August) each year.

In your job as a researcher for ACB TV's *BizNews*, a one-hour weekly program, you have been asked by the program's producer and lead presenter to prepare some briefing notes that will be used in a forthcoming segment about working-capital management, aimed at bringing managers of Small and Medium Enterprises (SMEs) up to date on available ways of financing current assets. The producer's idea is to discuss this in the context of a business whose balance sheet includes the following components of working capital:

Inventories	$2.1 million
Accounts receivable	$1.5 million
Accounts payable	$1.6 million
Net working capital	$2.0 million

The presenter plans to illustrate how payables are a spontaneous source of funding, helping to finance inventory as a natural part of business operations, and tending to grow as the business grows. Then, the presenter wants to discuss the main discretionary sources of short-term finance. Accordingly, the program's producer has asked you to prepare a brief note that looks at some of the available alternatives for short-term finance that are accessible to SMEs (promissory notes, for example, are just about ruled out, because they are limited to large companies with a suitable credit rating).

In this regard, the producer suggests that you prepare a table that compares and contrasts these funding sources in a format as follows, with the rows showing each type of finance and the columns headed:

COST	FLEXIBILITY	SUITABLE FOR
Interest rate	Ease of arranging?	Unforeseen/emergency cash needs?
Other fees	Ability to keep up with the business's growth?	Seasonal financing?

You can also add other comments, such as whether or not it is likely that the business or its owners would have to offer security or collateral for the loan, and whether the business might benefit from a suitable *mix* of the funding types.

After you have prepared the table, the producer and presenter will hold further talks with you to add detail as necessary to build the program content.

1. A value-maximising approach to the management of the firm's liquidity involves assessing the value of the benefits derived from increasing the firm's investment in liquid assets and weighing them against the added costs to the firm's owners resulting from investing in low-yield current assets. Unfortunately, the benefits derived from increased liquidity relate to the expected costs of bankruptcy to the firm's owners, and these costs are 'unmeasurable' by existing technology. Thus, a 'valuation' approach to liquidity management exists only in the theoretical realm.
2. For illustration purposes, spontaneous sources of financing are treated as if their amount were fixed. In practice, of course, spontaneous sources of financing fluctuate with the firm's purchases and its expenditures for wages, salaries, taxes and other items that are paid on a delayed basis.
3. This amount is an approximation for several reasons. First, ABS data specify that this amount represents increases in limits together with new limits, rather than funds actually drawn. Second, the nature of overdraft lending is that it represents a form of revolving credit and so amounts may be drawn, then repaid, and redrawn a number of times in any time interval.
4. Sheridan Titman, Arthur J. Keown and John D. Martin, *Financial Management*, 11th edn, Prentice Hall, Boston, 2011, p. 608.

After reading this chapter, you should be able to:

1 Appreciate the importance of cash and marketable securities as a component of the firm's working capital.
2 Understand the motives for holding cash.
3 Understand the objectives of cash management and the associated risks.
4 Use the appropriate techniques to improve the collection and disbursement of cash.
5 Understand the principles for managing the marketable securities portfolio.
6 Describe the different types of marketable securities in which firms can invest.
7 Apply a range of techniques for managing accounts receivable.
8 Understand how to manage inventory.

For a complete eBook go to MyFinanceLab
www.pearson.com.au/myfinancelab

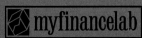

Current asset management

chapter 8

CHAPTER PREVIEW

Chapter 7 introduced the concept of working-capital management as well as the liabilities side of the balance sheet. This chapter will look at the assets side of the firm's working capital in some detail. It focuses on the formulation of financial policies for management of cash and marketable securities as well as accounts receivable and inventories.

In relation to cash and marketable securities, three major areas are explored: (1) improving cash receipts and disbursements patterns, (2) sensible investment possibilities that enable the company to productively employ excess cash balances, and (3) deciding how much cash to hold. These areas relate partly to *Principle 1: The risk–return trade-off—we won't take on additional risk unless we expect to be compensated with additional return* and partly to *Principle 2: The time value of money—a dollar received today is worth more than a dollar received in the future.*

In relation to accounts receivable and inventories, emphasis too is on *Principle 1*, specifically in understanding the trade-off between a 'tight' credit policy and an 'easy' policy, and the trade-off between holding too much inventory and holding too little.

Regardless of your program

'Cash' will be a preoccupation of both your business life and your personal life. Many people would be surprised to learn that being profitable is no guarantee that a business can pay its way. Accounting students know that profits are not the same as cash flow, but even they might be surprised to learn that cash is probably the more critical of the two. A business can sometimes trade at a loss for a year or as long as it has sufficient cash to pay suppliers, to pay employees and to pay creditors.

Starting a new business is sometimes the aspiration of a new graduate, and watching cash is particularly critical in such a case; sales could be slow for a new business but the bills still have to be paid! Furthermore, the new business often finds it hard to obtain external finance, such as bank loans, because it does not have a proven track record. Something like 90% of new restaurants fail in their first year, not necessarily because the business is in any way bad, but as often as not because insufficient funding has been secured to tide the business over the start-up period when cash inflow is slow.

OBJECTIVE **1**

Appreciate the importance of cash and marketable securities as a component of the firm's working capital.

The importance of cash in managing the firm

First, it will be helpful to understand some key terms. **Cash** is the currency and coin the firm has on hand, mainly in cash registers (tills) or in cheque or deposit accounts at the various banks where its accounts are maintained. **Marketable securities** are those investments in securities

cash
The currency and coin the firm has on hand in petty cash, cash registers or cheque accounts.

marketable securities
Security investments that the firm can quickly convert into cash balances.

that the firm can quickly convert into cash balances. Many firms hold marketable securities with maturity periods of less than one year. No law, of course, dictates that instruments with longer terms to maturity must be avoided. Rather, the decision to keep the average maturity quite short is based on sound business reasoning, which will be discussed later. Marketable securities are also referred to as 'near-cash' or 'near-cash assets' because they can be turned into cash in a short period of time. Taken together, cash and near-cash are known as **liquid assets**.

liquid assets
Cash and marketable securities.

A thorough understanding of why and how a firm holds cash requires an accurate conception of how cash flows into and through the enterprise. Figure 8.1 depicts the process of cash generation and disposition in a typical manufacturing setting. The arrows designate the direction of the flow into or out of the firm—that is, whether the cash balance increases or decreases.

THE CASH-FLOW PROCESS

Some cash inflows arise from the firm's financing activities. These activities tend to occur irregularly; for example, the firm might need funds to launch a new product, buy some new assets or expand a plant so as to increase production capacity. To raise this cash, the firm may sell (issue) securities such as bonds or shares, or it may raise a bank loan. These funds are raised from external sources.

Whereas cash inflows from external sources are irregular, the internal cash flows (from operations) occur on a more regular basis. For many businesses, the largest cash receipts come from accounts receivable collections and to a lesser extent from direct cash sales. Also, at various times non-current assets such as plant and machinery may be sold, thereby generating further cash inflows. This is not a large source of funds except in unusual situations, for instance when a complete plant renovation is taking place.

As *excess* cash becomes available temporarily, through the above kinds of external financing activities or through normal internal business operations, the excess cash may be invested by purchasing marketable securities (a form of near-cash). Then when cash is in short supply a portion of the marketable securities portfolio can be liquidated. Alternatively, a firm that operates a bank overdraft may allow the overdrawn balance to increase during periods when cash is in short supply, and then repay (reduce) the overdrawn balance when excess cash becomes available. In most organisations a financial officer such as the treasurer is responsible for cash

FIGURE 8.1 The cash generation and disposition process

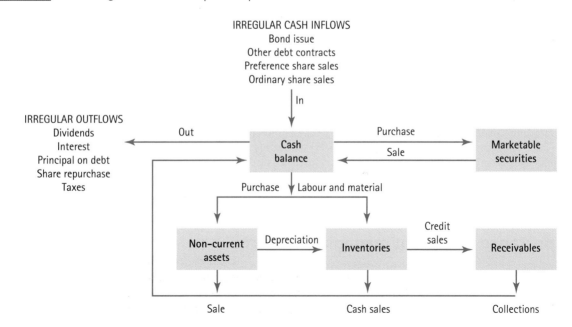

management and also controls the transactions that affect the firm's investment in marketable securities.

Apart from the investment of excess cash in near-cash assets, the cash balance may decrease for three main reasons:

1. To make irregular payments, such as:
   • paying interest on debt contracts (such as bonds or loans)
   • repaying the principal borrowed on debt contracts
   • paying cash dividends on preference shares or ordinary shares
   • paying tax bills.
   (These payments are mostly *irregular* in the sense that they do not occur on a daily basis or on a frequent schedule, although some of them are at regular time intervals.)
2. To pay for the firm's capital expenditure program, which budgets for acquisition of fixed assets at various intervals.
3. To purchase inventories on a regular basis in order to ensure their availability to meet the flow of goods for sale. Note that, in Figure 8.1, the arrow linking the investment in non-current assets with the inventory account is labelled *depreciation*. This indicates that a portion of the capital cost of plant and equipment is recovered (as depreciation expense) from sales revenue created through the sale of inventory.

Concept check

8.1   Describe the cash-flow process for a typical firm.

For answers go to MyFinanceLab or www.pearson.com.au/9781442539174

Motives for holding cash

OBJECTIVE 2

Understand the motives for holding cash.

The variety of influences that affect the cash balance held by the firm can also be analysed in terms of the motives for holding cash, as identified in the literature of economic theory. In a classic treatise, John Maynard Keynes segmented the demand for cash into three categories: (1) the transactions motive, (2) the precautionary motive, and (3) the speculative motive.[1]

TRANSACTIONS MOTIVE

Balances held for transaction purposes allow the firm to dispense with cash needs that arise in the ordinary course of doing business, because cash inflows from sales revenues can satisfy a portion of outflows. Thus, in Figure 8.1, transactions balances would be used to meet the irregular outflows as well as planned capital expenditures and acquisition of inventories.

The amount of transactions cash held by a firm is significantly affected by the industry in which the firm operates. If revenues can be forecast to fall within a tight band of outcomes, then the ratio of cash and near-cash to total assets will be less for the firm than if the prospective cash inflows might be expected to vary over a wide range. It is well known, for example, that public utilities (such as electricity, gas and water authorities) can forecast cash receipts quite accurately, because of stable demand for their services. This enables the organisation to stagger its billings throughout the month and to time them to coincide with planned expenditures. Inflows and outflows of cash are thus synchronised. The cash holdings of public utilities (relative to sales or assets) would therefore be expected to be less than those associated with a major retail chain that sells groceries.

THE PRECAUTIONARY MOTIVE

Precautionary balances provide a 'buffer' stock of liquid assets. This motive for holding cash relates to the maintenance of balances to be used to satisfy possible, but as yet indefinite, needs.

In the discussion of transactions balances it was seen that cash-flow predictability could affect a firm's cash holdings through synchronisation of receipts and disbursements. Cash-flow predictability also has a material influence on the firm's demand for cash through the precautionary motive. The airline industry provides a typical illustration. Airlines are plagued by a high degree of cash-flow uncertainty: when they try to forecast ahead, they face uncertainty about passenger bookings as well as costs such as fuel prices, and they are subject to global events such as terrorism and disease epidemics. The upshot of this problem is that, because of all the things that *might* happen, an airline's management tends to desire relatively large minimum cash balances.

The precautionary motive for holding cash is also affected by access to external funds. Especially important are cash sources that can be tapped at short notice. Good banking relationships and established access to credit (such as bank overdraft facilities) can reduce the need to keep cash on hand. This unused borrowing power reduces somewhat the need to invest in precautionary balances.

In actual business practice, the precautionary motive is met to a large extent by the holding of a portfolio of *liquid assets*, not just cash. Notice in Figure 8.1 the two-way flow of funds between the company's holdings of cash and marketable securities. In large corporate organisations, funds may flow either into or out of the marketable securities portfolio on a daily basis. Because some actual rate of return can be earned on the near-cash assets, compared with a zero rate of return on cash holdings, it is logical that holding marketable securities will meet, in part, the firm's precautionary needs.

THE SPECULATIVE MOTIVE

Cash is held for speculative purposes in order to take advantage of potential profit-making situations. For example, construction firms that build private dwellings may accumulate cash in anticipation of a significant drop in timber costs. If the price of building supplies does drop, the companies that have built up their cash balances stand to profit by being able to purchase materials in large quantities. This will reduce their cost of goods sold and increase their net profit margin. Generally, the speculative motive is the least important component of a firm's preference for liquidity. The transactions and precautionary motives account for most of the reasons that a company holds cash balances.

Concept check

For answers go to MyFinanceLab or
www.pearson.com.au/9781442539174

8.2 What are the three primary motives for holding cash?

Your money

PERSONAL REASONS FOR HOLDING CASH

We all need funds to meet day-to-day and month-to-month *transactions*. Similarly, if we are prudent, we will keep some *precautionary* cash in reserve to tide us through periods of illness or unemployment, or to meet unforeseen expenses. Funds, too, might be held for *speculative* purposes, for example in anticipation of the end-of-calendar-year automobile sales period, in the hope that your dream car will be discounted by the dealer before the calendar rolls over to a new year and makes the car, all of a sudden, 'last year's model'.

Managing cash is made easier by having a personal cash budget, which helps you to identify exactly when income is coming in and outgoings have to be met. And, just like a business overdraft, managing your cash is made much more flexible by access to a line of credit such as a credit card, which enables you to pay bills or make purchases even if cash is not to hand. However, credit cards can be a very expensive form of credit. They are best used in such a way that the full balance is repaid before expiry of the interest-free days rather than as a form of ongoing financing. In this regard, the *hedging principle* applies equally to personal finances; after all, who would finance a house purchase via a credit card? Such a card should be used to finance periods of temporary cash shortages, whereas long-term assets should be financed with long-term loans.

Cash-management objectives and risks

OBJECTIVE **3**

Understand the objectives of cash management and the associated risks.

THE RISK–RETURN TRADE-OFF

One of the major objectives of a firm's overall cash-management program is to minimise the risk of **insolvency**. In the context of cash management, the term 'insolvency' describes the situation in which the firm is unable to pay its maturing liabilities on time: the firm is *technically insolvent* when it lacks the necessary liquidity to make prompt payment on its current debt obligations. This problem could be avoided by carrying large cash balances in order to pay the bills that come due. After all, if the firm were continually late in paying suppliers (or failed entirely to pay), production would soon come to a halt as suppliers would cut off further shipments. In fact, fear of irritating a key supplier does cause some financial managers to invest in too much liquidity.

insolvency
The situation in which a firm is unable to meet its maturing liabilities on time.

The management of the company's cash position, however, is one of those problem areas where managers are criticised if they don't and criticised if they do. On the one hand, the firm's operations will eventually grind to a halt should too little cash be available to pay the bills. But, on the other hand, if excessive cash balances are carried, the value of the enterprise in the financial marketplace will be suppressed because of the large opportunity cost of income forgone as a result of the zero return on cash balances.

The financial manager must strike an acceptable balance between holding too much cash and holding too little cash. This is the focal point of the risk–return trade-off. A large cash investment minimises the chances of insolvency but penalises company profitability. A small cash investment frees excess balances for investment in both marketable securities and longer lived assets; this enhances company profitability and the value of the firm's ordinary shares but increases the chances of running out of cash.

THE OBJECTIVES

The risk–return trade-off can be reduced to two prime objectives for the firm's cash-management system:

- Enough cash must be on hand to meet the disbursal needs that arise in the course of doing business.
- Investment in idle cash balances must be reduced to a minimum.

Evaluation of these operational objectives, and a conscious attempt on the part of management to meet them, gives rise to the need for some typical cash-management decisions.

THE DECISIONS

Two conditions would allow the firm to operate for extended periods with cash balances near or at a level of zero: (1) a completely accurate forecast of net cash flows over the planning horizon, and (2) perfect synchronisation of cash receipts and disbursements.

Cash-flow forecasting is the initial step in any effective cash-management program. The *cash budget* is a device used to forecast the cash flows over the planning period. (Cash-budgeting procedures were explained in Chapter 6.) This budget is usually prepared by the finance division of the firm, which evaluates sales estimates supplied by the marketing division, along with cost-of-sales forecasts. It must be emphasised that a totally accurate cash-flow projection is an ideal, not a reality; the net cash flows pinpointed in the cash budget are only estimates, subject to considerable variation.

The discussion of the cash-flow process depicted in Figure 8.1 showed that inflows and outflows are not synchronised. Some inflows and outflows are irregular; others are more continual. Some finished goods are sold directly for cash, but it is more likely that the sales will be on account. The receivables, then, will have to be collected before a cash inflow is realised. Raw materials have to be purchased, but several suppliers are probably used, and each may have its own payment date. Further, no 'law' of doing business fixes receivable collections to coincide with the payment dates for supplies. So the second criterion that would permit operation of the firm with extremely low cash balances is also not met in actual practice.

Given that the firm will, as a matter of necessity, invest in some cash balances, certain types of decisions related to the size of those balances dominate the cash-management process. These include decisions that answer the following questions:

- What can be done to speed up cash collections and slow down, or better control, cash disbursements (outflows)?
- What should be the composition of a marketable securities portfolio?

Concept check

8.3 Describe the risk–return trade-off in managing cash.

8.4 What are the fundamental decisions that the financial manager must make with respect to cash management?

For answers go to MyFinanceLab or
www.pearson.com.au/9781442539174

Back to the principles

The dilemma faced by the financial manager is a clear example of the application of **Principle 1: The risk–return trade-off—we won't take on additional risk unless we expect to be compensated with additional return.** To accept the risk of not having sufficient cash on hand, the firm must be compensated with a return on the cash that is invested. Moreover, the greater the risk of the investment into which the cash is placed, the greater the return that the firm demands.

OBJECTIVE **4**

Use the appropriate techniques to improve the collection and disbursement of cash.

Improving collection and disbursement of cash

The efficiency of the firm's cash-management program can be enhanced by (1) accelerating cash receipts, and (2) improving the methods used to disburse cash. The greater opportunity for profit improvement lies with the cash receipts side of the funds flow process.

MANAGING THE CASH INFLOW

For virtually every business the balance of the cash-at-bank account recorded in its books will be different from the amount of cash available in its bank account. For example, the business may receive a cheque for $100 000 which it records in its books. That cheque has to be deposited with its bank and cleared before funds are available in the bank account. The cheque-clearing process can take a number of business days. The difference at any point in time between the business's account for cash and the balance in its bank account is called *float*.

A major source of float is the time it takes for a payment due from a customer to be received and processed and thus provide funds in the business's bank account.

The reduction of float lies at the centre of the many approaches employed to speed up cash receipts. Float has four elements, as follows:

1. *Mail float* is caused by the time lapse from the moment a customer mails a remittance cheque until the firm begins to process it.
2. *Processing float* is caused by the time required for the firm to process remittance cheques before they can be deposited in the bank.
3. *Transit float* is caused by the time necessary for a deposited cheque to clear through the banking system and become usable funds to the company. For example, in Australia value for a cheque deposited may be delayed for five or more business days while the cheque is cleared through the cheque-clearing system.

4. *Disbursing float* derives from the time that funds remain in the company's bank account until the company's payment cheque has cleared through the banking system. Typically, funds available in the firm's bank account exceed the balances indicated in its own records. Thus, the effect of disbursing float is opposite to items 1, 2 and 3 above.

The term 'float' will be used to refer to the total of the four elements just described. Float reduction can yield considerable payoffs in terms of usable funds that are released for the firm's benefit and the returns produced on such freed-up balances. As an example, during 2009 the resources group BHP-Billiton reported revenues of about $50 billion. This represented average daily sales of about $137 million. Thus, if float could be reduced by one day, about $137 million would be released. Not only would this ease liquidity pressure for the firm, but if this could be invested at, say, 6% per annum, the annual value of this one-day float reduction would be about $8 million.

It is clear, therefore, that effective cash management can yield impressive opportunities for profit improvement. The most effective way that organisations can reduce total float is to replace their receipts that would otherwise be made by cheque with receipts processed via electronic funds transfer (EFT). For example, there are many situations in which businesses that receive regular payments from their customers (e.g. health insurance subscriptions) can reduce processing float by arranging for the employers of their customers to deduct the regular payments from the customers' wages and make a direct-to-account transfer (via EFT).

ELECTRONIC FUNDS TRANSFER

Float is really a measure of the inefficiency of the financial system in an economy. It is a 'friction' of the business environment that stems from the fact that all information arising from business transactions cannot be transferred instantaneously from, and to, the parties involved. In the purest economic sense, 'total' float should equal zero dollars, as in a frictionless payments system there should be no delay from the time when a client makes a payment to the time when those funds are available in the business's bank account.

Today, the use of electronic funds transfer (EFT) is serving to significantly reduce float. The central concept of EFT is simple. If firm A pays money to firm B, the funds from firm A's bank account are electronically transferred to the bank account of firm B and at the same time firm B is advised that the payment has been made. Importantly, under the EFT system the transaction does not proceed unless firm A has sufficient funds in its account. Therefore, this instantaneous transfer of funds will eliminate float. In addition, it has the benefit of removing the uncertainty about whether a payer who presents a cheque has sufficient funds in the bank account so that the cheque is not dishonoured by the payer's bank. The process of EFT should therefore provide for a more efficient economy. Funds previously tied up in accounts receivable, for example, will be released for more productive uses.

Automated teller machines (ATMs) and electronic funds transfer at point-of-sale (EFTPOS) terminals are now familiar devices to consumers. Also familiar are automatic payments systems, whereby regular bills can be deducted automatically from a bank account or credit card account and transferred directly via the payments system to the recipient's bank account. Behind the scenes, businesses are also using even more advanced systems, such as terminal-based electronic transfers, to move funds within their cash-management systems and to transfer funds to other organisations. Many banks offer cash-management services to their clients, for example automatic funds transfers from zero-interest accounts (such as cheque accounts) to accounts that earn interest, or (for firms with a multiplicity of bank accounts) from an account with excess cash to an account that has an overdrawn balance. They also offer allied services, such as integrated EFTPOS and inventory-control systems: the rationale for integrating these systems is that sales of inventory are recorded automatically at EFTPOS terminals in many businesses, so if inventory purchases are also recorded on the same database, current inventory levels are able to be readily determined.

> **Concept check**
> 8.5 Define *float* and its origins in the cash management process.
> 8.6 Describe the role of EFT in reducing float.

Back to the principles

All of these collection and disbursement procedures are an illustration of what is meant by **Principle 2: The time value of money—a dollar received today is worth more than a dollar received in the future.** The faster the firm can take possession of the money to which it is entitled, the sooner the firm is able to put the money to work generating a return.

OBJECTIVE 5

Understand the principles for managing the marketable securities portfolio.

The composition of the marketable securities portfolio

Once the design of the firm's cash receipts and payments system has been determined, the financial manager faces the task of selecting appropriate financial assets for inclusion in the firm's marketable securities portfolio.

GENERAL SELECTION CRITERIA

Certain criteria can provide the financial manager with a useful framework for selecting a proper mix of marketable securities. These considerations include evaluation of (1) financial risk, (2) interest-rate risk, (3) liquidity, (4) tax liability, and (5) yields among different financial assets. These criteria will be briefly delineated from the investor's viewpoint.

Financial risk or default risk

Financial risk here refers to uncertainty associated with the expected returns from a security. There is some possibility that the security issuer (borrower) may default on future payments of interest and/or principal, arising from possible changes in the financial capacity of the borrower to make those payments to the lender/investor (the owner or holder of the security). If the chance of default on the terms of the instrument is high (low), then the financial risk is said to be high (low). Chapter 18 (and also Chapter 7) discuss the process of *debt rating*, whereby independent agencies endeavour to rank the quality of the various issuers of debt. It ought to be clear, for example, that the financial risk associated with holding commercial paper, which is nothing more than a corporate IOU, exceeds the risk of holding securities issued by the government.

Because the marketable securities portfolio is designed to provide a return on funds that would otherwise be tied up in idle cash held for transactions or precautionary purposes, the financial officer is not usually willing to assume much financial risk in the hope of greater return. Therefore yields on the safest instruments, such as Australian Treasury notes (short-term, government-issued promissory notes) are weighed up against yields of higher risk securities such as corporate promissory notes and bank bills. In some cases (primarily debt issued by government bodies and large corporations), debt ratings are available to provide guidance as to the relative risks of the alternative securities, as outlined (for short-term securities) in Chapter 7.

Interest-rate risk

Interest-rate risk refers to the uncertainty of expected returns from a financial instrument because of the possibility of changes in interest rates. Among other things, changes in interest rates affect the price of a security, which means that a holder cannot be sure what the price of the security will be when it is sold at some future time. In Chapter 4, for example, it was shown that bond prices can change significantly in response to changes in market interest rates. Of particular concern to the corporate financial manager is the fact that the price volatility of long-maturity securities tends to be greater than the volatility of securities with short terms to maturity. Example 8.1 helps to clarify this point.

EXAMPLE 8.1   Interest-rate risk of a long-term bond and a short-term bond

Suppose that the firm's treasurer is weighing the merits of investing temporarily available excess cash in two different government bonds. One matures in three years, the other in 20 years. The purchase price of both the three-year bond and the 20-year bond is currently $1000, which also represents the maturity value. Both securities have a coupon rate (stated interest rate) of 7%, payable annually, which means that interest coupon payments are $70 per year.

If, one year after the date of purchase, the prevailing market interest rate rises to 9%, the market prices of these bonds will fall. But the significant point is that the price of the 20-year instrument will decline by a greater dollar amount than that of the three-year instrument. The procedures for determining changes in bond prices are outlined in Chapter 4.

One year after the date of purchase, the price obtainable in the marketplace for the original 20-year bond (which now has 19 years to go to maturity) can be found by computing P as follows, which shows that the rise in interest rates has forced the market price of the bond down to $821.01:

$$P = \sum_{t=1}^{19} \frac{\$70}{(1 + 0.09)^t} + \frac{\$1000}{(1 + 0.09)^{19}}$$

$$= \$70(PVIFA_{9\%,19}) + \$1000(PVIF_{9\%,19})$$

$$= \$821.01$$

(In this computation, t is the year in which the particular return, either interest or principal amount, is received; $70 is the annual interest payment; and $1000 is the contractual maturity value of the bond.)

Now, what will happen to the price of the original three-year bond that has two years remaining to maturity? In a similar manner, its price, P, can be computed:

$$P = \sum_{t=1}^{2} \frac{\$70}{(1 + 0.09)^t} + \frac{\$1000}{(1 + 0.09)^2}$$

$$= \$70(PVIFA_{9\%,2}) + \$1000(PVIF_{9\%,2})$$

$$= \$964.84$$

The market price of the shorter term bond will decline to $964.84.

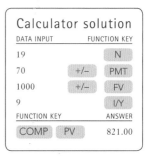

Calculator solution

DATA INPUT		FUNCTION KEY
19		N
70	+/−	PMT
1000	+/−	FV
9		I/Y
FUNCTION KEY		ANSWER
COMP PV		821.00

Calculator solution

DATA INPUT		FUNCTION KEY
2		N
70	+/−	PMT
1000	+/−	FV
9		I/Y
FUNCTION KEY		ANSWER
COMP PV		964.82

By way of summary, Table 8.1 highlights the fact that the market value of the shorter term security in Example 8.1 was penalised much less by the given rise in the general level of interest rates.[2]

If the conclusion from Example 8.1 is extended, it would be seen that, in terms of market price, a one-year security would be affected less than a two-year security, a 90-day security less than a 180-day security, and so on. Therefore, unless more active means are used to hedge against interest-rate risk, the firm's marketable securities portfolio will tend to be composed of instruments that mature over short periods.

TABLE 8.1 Market price effect of 2% rise in interest rates		
	THREE-YEAR INSTRUMENT	20-YEAR INSTRUMENT
Original price	$1 000.00	$1 000.00
Price after one year	$964.84	$821.01
Decline in price	$35.16	$178.99

Liquidity

liquidity
Liquidity is related to the ease and quickness with which a firm can convert its marketable securities.

In the present context of managing the marketable securities portfolio, **liquidity** refers to the ability to transform a security into cash. Should an unforeseen event require that a significant amount of cash be available immediately, a sizeable portion of the portfolio might have to be sold. The financial manager will want the cash quickly and will not want to accept a large *price concession* in order to convert the securities to cash. Thus, in the formulation of preferences for the inclusion of particular instruments in the portfolio, the treasurer must consider (1) the time taken to arrange the sale of the security, and (2) the likelihood that the security can be sold at or near its prevailing market price. This means that a treasurer will tend to avoid holding securities for which the market is 'thin'—that is, securities in which relatively few transactions take place or where trades are accomplished only with large price changes between transactions.

Tax liability

The tax treatment of the income a firm receives from its security investments does not affect the ultimate mix of the marketable securities portfolio as much as the criteria mentioned earlier. This is because both the interest income and the capital gains from most instruments suitable for inclusion in the portfolio are likely to be subject to income tax. However, as seen in Chapter 2, in the Australian environment only a proportion of a capital gain may be assessable (depending on the type of taxpayer), which means that capital gains are, in effect, taxed at a lower rate than interest income.

Under these circumstances, bonds selling at a discount below their face value may be attractive investments to some taxpaying firms. If a high level of interest rates currently prevails, then the market prices will be depressed on debt issues that were issued in the past at low coupon rates. This price reduction has the effect of bringing the yield to maturity up to that obtainable on a new issue. Part of the yield to maturity on a bond selling at a discount is therefore the source of a *capital gain*—that is, the amount by which the maturity value exceeds the purchase price. Therefore, the favourable tax treatment of the capital gain (provided the firm has held the fixed-income security for more than 12 months) means that the after-tax return could be higher than the return on a comparable issue that carries a higher coupon but sells at par. (We say *could* be higher, as the marketplace is relatively efficient and recognises this taxation advantage of discount bonds; consequently, discount bonds will tend to sell at lower yields than issues which have similar risk characteristics but larger coupons. For short periods, however, a firm *might* find a favourable yield advantage by purchasing discount bonds.)

Yields

The final selection criterion is a significant one—the yields that are available on the different financial assets suitable for inclusion in the near-cash portfolio. As outlined in Chapter 7 (with additional discussion in Chapter 9, later), there is a term structure of interest rates: often, longer term securities carry greater yields than short-maturity securities. The relative yields may therefore influence the period of time for which the treasurer will invest excess cash. However, for a given maturity it is quite probable that differences in yield merely reflect differences in risk—other things being equal, the greater the financial risk, or the greater the interest-rate risk, or the greater the liquidity risk, the higher will be the yield to compensate for the relevant risk. Therefore, in efficient markets the treasurer needs to weigh up the benefits of greater yields against the greater risks.

Figure 8.2 summarises the overall framework for designing the firm's marketable securities portfolio. The four basic considerations are shown to influence the yields available on securities. The financial manager must focus on the risk–return trade-offs identified through suitable analysis of these considerations. Coming to grips with these trade-offs will enable the financial manager to determine the proper marketable securities mix for the company. Let us look now at how and where firms can obtain marketable securities for their near-cash portfolios.

FIGURE 8.2 Designing the marketable securities portfolio

CONSIDERATIONS ⟶ INFLUENCE ⟶ FOCUS ON ⟶ DETERMINE

- Financial risk
- Interest-rate risk
- Liquidity
- Tax liability

Yields

Risk vs return
preferences

Marketable
securities mix

Concept check

8.7 What are *financial risk* and *interest rate* risk?

For answers go to MyFinanceLab or
www.pearson.com.au/9781442539174

International spotlight

CASH AND MARKETABLE SECURITIES IN THE MULTINATIONAL FIRM

In terms of principles, not much changes for a multinational firm as opposed to a domestic firm. However, just as with other basic financial principles, everything becomes a bit more complicated. No longer can a firm simply look at the operations of its different divisions and allow those divisions to make corporate decisions. In fact, more often than not, the global or centralised financial decisions that a firm makes tend to be superior to decisions made by the different subsidiaries.

As outlined in Chapter 7, when cash management enters the international arena the firm may benefit by delaying collections when the currency being collected is strong, or by converting cash into a relatively stronger currency. The bottom line here is that when multiple currencies are introduced the process of cash management is greatly complicated. A finance manager's job may be to manage collections from several countries and to make sure that those collections are maintained in as strong a currency as possible, which means that the emphasis of the job is on transferring funds from country to country rather than on the location where cash is collected in the first place.

Representative instruments for the marketable securities portfolio

Businesses can buy and sell securities for their near-cash portfolios via the **money market**. Other participants in this market include the money-market dealers who facilitate the trade of the securities, other financial institutions, and the country's central bank. In Australia, many money-market organisations are also referred to as merchant (or investment) banks.

Representative securities traded in the money market are detailed below, based on current usage in Australia. You may find that similar instruments have different names in other countries.

TREASURY NOTES

Treasury notes (T notes) are issued by the Australian government for the purpose of short-term monetary management. Typically they have terms to maturity of 5, 13 or 26 weeks. They are *discount-type instruments* (like promissory notes and bills, discussed in Chapter 7), which means

OBJECTIVE 6

Describe the different types of marketable securities in which firms can invest.

money market
All institutions and procedures that facilitate transactions in short-term financial instruments.

that they are sold at a price less than the face value. The investor could buy an existing T note issue in the open market or could subscribe at the date of a new issue. The price at issue date is determined by competitive tendering and is based on the yields prevailing in the market for similar risk/maturity instruments.

SHORT-DATED TREASURY BONDS

Treasury bonds (T bonds) are medium- to long-term fundraising instruments issued by the Australian government. They are issued in multiples of $1000 face value, and pay half-yearly coupon interest. New issues are offered on a tender basis and, once issued, are able to be bought and sold openly by any investor. T bonds are sold with remaining maturities varying from a few days to many years; the ones that are called 'short-dated' usually have less than 12 months remaining until their maturity.

STATE GOVERNMENT, LOCAL GOVERNMENT AND SEMI-GOVERNMENT SECURITIES

The state and local governments of Australia, as well as semi-government authorities, raise funds by issuing medium- to long-term bonds. These instruments are like treasury bonds and are able to be bought and sold on the money market once they have been issued.

COMMERCIAL BILLS

Commercial bills are another name for bills of exchange. As outlined in Chapter 7, bills are generally issued by companies to raise short-term finance. However, they are *negotiable instruments*, which means that, once they have been issued, they can be bought and sold for near-cash portfolios. The way in which this can be achieved on the money market is quite simple: the bills can be bought from the current holder by a purchaser, who pays a price that is determined by the current market yield and the time to maturity of the bill. The bill can subsequently be re-sold prior to its maturity or held to maturity.

Bills are discount-type instruments (like treasury notes). Typically, at the date of issue they have maturities of 90, 120 or 180 days, with standard face values of $100 000 or $500 000. Commercial bills are of two main types: (1) *bank bills*, which have been *accepted* or *endorsed* by a bank and so are highly marketable because of the creditworthiness of the bank that attaches its name to the bill, and (2) *non-bank bills*, which are those accepted or endorsed by non-bank organisations and whose marketability is dependent on the creditworthiness of the acceptor/endorser.

PROMISSORY NOTES

Promissory notes, too, were outlined in Chapter 7 in the context of their use for fundraising by firms and other organisations that have relatively high financial standing. Like commercial bills, they are discount-type instruments and are issued with terms of 90, 120 or 180 days. Once issued, promissory notes can be bought and sold on the money market in the same way as commercial bills.

NEGOTIABLE CERTIFICATES OF DEPOSIT

A negotiable certificate of deposit (NCD) is a discount-type instrument issued mostly by banks to fund their operations. They are usually issued in amounts of $50 000 or more with maturities generally of three months up to two years. Once issued, they can be bought and sold like the other instruments via the money market.

YIELD STRUCTURE OF A MARKETABLE SECURITIES PORTFOLIO

What type of return can the financial manager expect on a marketable securities portfolio? This is a reasonable question. Some insight can be obtained by looking at what has happened in the past, although it must be realised that future returns are not guided by past experience. It is also useful to have some understanding of how the returns on one type of instrument stack up against another. Some generalisations of the behaviour of yields on short-term debt instruments can be made:

1. The returns from different short-term instruments tend to be highly correlated in a positive direction over time. That is, the yields tend to rise and fall together.
2. Yields can be quite volatile over time, which means that the financial manager cannot plan on any given level of returns to prevail over a long time period.
3. The yields on high credit-risk instruments will be greater than for less risky instruments.

Concept check

8.8   Describe treasury notes, treasury bonds, commercial bills and promissory notes.

8.9   What is meant by the yield structure of marketable securities?

For answers go to MyFinanceLab or
www.pearson.com.au/9781442539174

Accounts receivable management

OBJECTIVE 7

Apply a range of techniques for managing accounts receivable.

Business firms, by their very nature, are involved in selling either goods or services. Although some of these sales will be for cash, a large portion will involve credit. Whenever a sale is made on credit, it increases the firm's accounts receivable. Thus, the importance of how a firm manages its accounts receivable depends on the degree to which the firm sells on credit.

SIZE OF INVESTMENT IN ACCOUNTS RECEIVABLE

The major advantage of selling on credit is that a company will generate more sales, because it is easier for customers to purchase on credit. These credit sales spontaneously create accounts receivable. The total size of the investment in accounts receivable is determined by three main factors:

1. *The percentage of credit sales to total sales.* This factor is generally not within the control of the financial manager. Rather, the nature of the business tends to determine the blend of credit sales and cash sales. A supermarket, for example, tends to sell largely on a cash basis, whereas most construction supply firms make their sales primarily with credit.
2. *The total level of sales.* Very simply, the more sales, the greater the accounts receivable. As the firm experiences seasonal and permanent growth in sales, the level of investment in accounts receivable will naturally increase. Thus, although the level of sales affects the size of the investment in accounts receivable, it is not a decision variable for the financial manager.
3. *The firm's credit and collection policies.* These policies involve the terms of sale, the quality of customer and the collection efforts. The terms of sale influence the level of accounts receivable by specifying both the time period during which the customer must pay and the terms (such as penalties for late payments or discounts for early payments). The quality of customer (or credit policy) also affects the level of investment in accounts receivable; for example, the acceptance of poorer credit risks and their subsequent delinquent payments may lead to an increase in accounts receivable. The strength and timing of the collection efforts can affect the period for which overdue accounts remain delinquent, which in turn affects the level of accounts receivable. These credit and collection policy decisions may further affect the level of investment in accounts receivable by causing changes in the sales level and the ratio of credit sales to total sales. However, the three credit and collection policy variables are the only true decision variables under the control of the financial manager. Figure 8.3 shows where a financial manager can—and cannot—make a difference.

While the major emphasis in this section is on the cost of trade credit, it should also be noted that some firms actually make money by carrying accounts receivable. That is, if the firm charges interest on the outstanding accounts receivable, credit sales can be more profitable than cash sales. A good example of this is the firm Ford Credit, which finances loans to Ford dealers for the purchase of their stock.

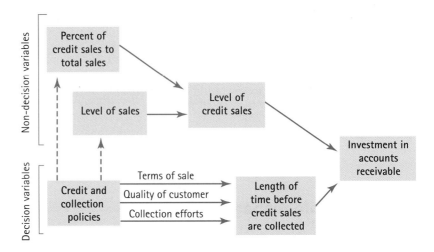

FIGURE 8.3 Determinants of investment in accounts receivable

Terms of sale—decision variable

The **terms of sale** identify the discount granted to the debtor for early payment, the discount period, and the total credit period. As explained in Chapter 7, trade credit terms of 2/10, net 30, for example, indicate that a 2% discount can be taken if the account is paid within 10 days; otherwise the full amount must be paid within 30 days. What if the customer decides to forgo the discount and not pay until the final payment date? If such a decision is made, the customer has the use of the money for the time period between the discount date and the final payment date. However, failure to take the discount represents a cost to the customer. For instance, if the terms are 2/10, net 30, Example 7.5 showed that the annualised opportunity cost of passing up this 2% discount, in order to withhold payment for an additional 20 days, is 37.24%.

The terms of sale can be generalised as 'a/b, net c', where a = percentage discount (2% in the above computation) that the customer can take if the account is paid within b days (10 days in the above computation); otherwise the account must be paid in c days (30 days in the above example).

This type of computation can be generalised through equation (8-1) as follows:

$$\text{Annualised opportunity cost of forgoing the discount} = \frac{a}{(1-a)} \times \frac{365}{(c-b)} \tag{8-1}$$

Applying this equation to the above example, we get .3724, which, when multiplied by 100, yields 37.24%:

$$37.24\% = \frac{0.02}{(1-0.02)} \times \frac{365}{(30-10)} \times 100$$

Because the cost of offering a discount can be very high to the firm (as reflected in the debtor's opportunity cost of not taking the discount), managers must carefully weigh up the benefits against the costs. The main benefit is that offering a discount for prompt payment reduces the likelihood that debtors will be excessively late in making payment. Also, offering more generous terms of sale can attract business away from competitors. However, although the terms of sale vary from industry to industry, they tend to remain relatively uniform within any particular industry. Moreover, the terms tend to remain relatively constant over time, and thus they do not appear to be used frequently as a decision variable.

Quality of customer—decision variable

This decision variable involves determining the *quality of customer* who is to qualify for trade credit. Several costs are associated with extending credit to less creditworthy customers

Finance at work

USING CREDIT AGENCIES TO APPRAISE CREDIT RISK OF CUSTOMERS

Some businesses have relatively simple credit-granting rules. For example, new customers typically are accepted readily without formal checks and are granted a modest credit limit. This limit may be reviewed after some time and, if customer performance has been satisfactory, the credit limit may be increased.

Other businesses, however, make use of *credit agencies* (or *credit bureaux*) to conduct more extensive credit checks. These agencies, such as Dun & Bradstreet, provide a number of services in return for paying the appropriate fee. The information provided includes 'basic' data on a firm's existence through

to comprehensive analysis of financial information and credit history. Information is available globally as well as locally.

The objective of using an agency is to minimise the risk of making poor credit decisions that could result in delays in receiving payments (which strains the firm's liquidity and profitability) and increased bad debts. Thus, although agency services are not free of charge, they can pay for themselves through better customer-quality choices. Furthermore, in the event that a customer's payment performance does become unsatisfactory, the agencies provide professional debt collection services.

(high-risk firms or individuals), including credit investigation costs, default costs and collection costs.

Credit investigation costs are incurred in assessing the credit history and financial standing of prospective customers. The aim is to identify which of the possible new customers would be a poor risk. As more time tends to be spent investigating the less creditworthy customer, the costs of credit investigation increase accordingly.

Default costs also vary directly with the quality of the customer. As the customer's credit rating declines, the chance that the account will not be paid on time increases. In the extreme case, payment never occurs. Thus, taking on less creditworthy customers results in increases in default costs.

Collection costs also increase as the quality of the customer declines. The firm has to spend more time and money collecting delinquent accounts.

Overall, therefore, the decline in customer quality results in increased costs of credit investigation, default and collection.

In determining whether or not to grant credit to an individual customer, the financial manager is primarily interested in the customer's (debtor's) short-run financial circumstances. Thus, the customer's liquidity ratios, other financial obligations and overall profitability become the focal point in this analysis. Credit services such as Dun & Bradstreet (D&B) provide information on the financial status, operations and payment history for most firms. Other possible sources of information include trade associations, chambers of commerce, competitors, bank references, public financial statements and, of course, the customer's past relationship with the firm.

One way in which both individuals and firms can be evaluated as credit risks is through the use of credit scoring. **Credit scoring** involves an applicant receiving a score based on his or her answers to a simple set of questions. This score is then evaluated according to a predetermined standard to determine whether or not credit should be extended. The major advantage of credit scoring is that it is inexpensive and easy to perform. For example, once the standards are set, a computer or clerical worker without any specialised training could easily evaluate any applicant. Credit scoring was also discussed (in the context of obtaining credit and personal finance) in Chapter 7.

credit scoring
The numerical evaluation of credit applicants, where the score is evaluated relative to a predetermined standard.

Some benefits associated with the use of credit-scoring models include (1) consistency in credit-granting decisions, (2) quicker decisions, (3) less training time for staff, (4) quantification of risk, and (5) identification of credit-risk predictor variables.

Back to the principles

The decision to grant (or not grant) credit is another application of **Principle 1: The risk–return trade-off—we won't take on additional risk unless we expect to be compensated with additional return**. The risk is the chance of non-payment, whereas the return stems from additional sales. Although it may be tempting to look at the credit decision as a yes or no decision based on some 'black-box' formula, keep in mind that simply looking at the immediate future in making a credit decision may be a mistake. If extending credit means that the new customer may become a regular customer in the future, it may be appropriate to take a risk that otherwise would not be prudent. In effect, our goal is to ensure that all cash flows affected by the decision at hand are considered, not simply the most immediate cash flows.

Collection efforts—decision variable

The key to maintaining control over collection of accounts receivable is the fact that the probability of default increases with the age of the account. Thus, control of accounts receivable focuses on the control and elimination of overdue (past-due) receivables. One common way of evaluating the current situation is ratio analysis. The financial manager can determine whether or not accounts receivables are under control by examining a number of indicators, notably the average collection period, the ratio of receivables to assets, the ratio of credit sales to receivables (called the accounts-receivable turnover ratio) and the amount of bad debts relative to sales over time. When analysing the collection period and other ratios, the manager must be familiar with industry norms in order to ascertain if the firm's performance is out of line. (For example, in 2009, the average collection period had blown out to almost 60 days for Australian firms. This indicated that debtors were paying their bills almost a month late, reflecting the 'tight' state of liquidity in the wake of the GFC.) In addition, the manager can perform what is called an ageing of accounts receivable in order to provide a break-down in both dollars and percentages of the proportion of receivables that are past due. Comparing the current ageing of receivables with past data offers even more control. An example of an *ageing account* or *schedule* appears in Table 8.2.

Once the delinquent accounts have been identified, the firm's accounts receivable department makes an effort to collect them; the employee given this task is usually called the 'collections manager' or a similar title. (Legal requirements may require the firm to proceed in a specific fashion in the collection process, such as giving proper notification and the like.) For example, a past-due letter is sent if payment is not received on time, followed by an additional letter in a more serious tone if the account becomes three weeks past due, followed after six weeks by a telephone call. Finally, if the account becomes 12 weeks past due, it might be turned over to a collection agency. Again, a direct trade-off exists between collection expenses and lost goodwill on the one hand and non-collection of accounts on the other.

TABLE 8.2 Ageing account

AGE OF ACCOUNTS RECEIVABLE (DAYS)	DOLLAR VALUE	% OF TOTAL
0–30	$234 000	39
31–60	150 000	25
61–90	102 000	17
91–120	72 000	12
Over 120	42 000	7
Total	$600 000	100

CREDIT POLICY CHANGES

Changes in credit policy involve direct trade-offs between costs and benefits. When credit policies are eased, sales and gross profits from customers increase. However, easing credit policies can also involve an increase in bad debts, additional funds being tied up in accounts receivable and inventory, and additional costs from customers taking a cash discount. Given these costs, when is it appropriate for a firm to change its credit policy? The answer is when the increased sales generate enough in the way of new gross profit to more than offset the increased costs associated with the change.

Concept check

8.10 What factors influence the size of a firm's investment in accounts receivable? Which of these factors can the financial manager control?

8.11 What costs are associated with extending credit to high-risk firms or individuals?

8.12 How can a firm evaluate the credit risk of its customers?

For answers go to MyFinanceLab or www.pearson.com.au/9781442539174

Finance at work

THE TQM PHILOSOPHY

TQM (or 'total quality management') is an approach to managing many aspects of the firm's operations. It is so influential that firms often will not deal with a supplier unless that supplier adheres to TQM principles and is accredited by relevant bodies such as the ISO (International Standards Organisation).

Prior to the development of TQM concepts, the traditional view relating to acquiring supplies (which then become inventories) was to minimise costs, which recognised that some defects were permissible as long as that allowed the average cost to be kept at a minimum level. In contrast, the TQM view argues that the traditional analysis is flawed because it ignores the fact that better quality products result in increased sales and market share, which will more than offset the higher costs associated with increased quality. Furthermore, the benefits from quality improvement programs seem to have spill-over effects resulting in increased worker motivation, higher productivity and improved employee relations, not to mention improved customer relations and buyer satisfaction.

In defiance of the traditional view about cost versus quality, when Xerox Corporation introduced TQM it experienced a decline of 90% in defective items and a 20% drop in manufacturing costs. Furthermore, high quality ultimately becomes a source of competitive advantage—one firm's products are differentiated from another's by higher quality and thus buyers will pay prices that permit greater profits and cash flows.

Back to the principles

The benefits of TQM are a way of overcoming **Principle 5: The curse of competitive markets—why it's hard to find exceptionally profitable projects.** Product differentiation can be used as a means of insulating a product from competition, thereby allowing prices to stay sufficiently high to support large profits. Producing a quality product is one of the ways of differentiating products. This strategy has been used effectively by Caterpillar Tractors and Honda Motors in recent years.

Managing inventories

Inventory management involves the control of the assets that are used in the production process or are produced or purchased for sale in the normal course of the firm's operations. The general categories of inventory for a manufacturer include raw materials inventory, work-in-process

OBJECTIVE 8

Understand how to manage inventory.

inventory and finished goods inventory. The importance of inventory management to the firm depends on the extent of the inventory investment, which also varies widely from industry to industry. For example, inventory management is much more important to a retailer, where inventories are a significant proportion of total assets, than to the hotel business, where the average investment in inventory is only around 2% of total assets. In 2010, Australian business firms held approximately $140 billion in inventories; of this amount, about a third was held by both manufacturers and wholesalers, with about a quarter held by retailers; together, these three categories of business account for about 90% of inventory holdings.

PURPOSES AND TYPES OF INVENTORIES

The purpose of carrying inventories is to uncouple the operations of the firm—that is, to make each function of the business independent of every other function—so that delays or shutdowns in one area do not affect the production and sale of the final product. Because production shutdowns result in increased costs, and because delays in delivery can lose customers, the management and control of inventory are important duties of the financial manager.

To illustrate the uncoupling function that inventories perform, let us look at several general types of inventories.

Raw materials inventory

Raw materials inventory consists of basic materials purchased from other firms to be used in the firm's production operations. These goods may include steel, timber or petroleum, or manufactured items such as wire, ball bearings and tyres, or components such as electric motors, microchips, engines and so on. Essentially, raw materials consist of all supplies that the firm does not produce itself. Regardless of the specific form of the raw materials inventory, all manufacturing firms by definition maintain a raw materials inventory. The purpose of holding inventory is to uncouple the production function from the purchasing function—that is, to make these two functions independent of each other, so that delays in shipments of raw materials do not cause production delays. In the event of a delay in shipment, the firm can satisfy its need for raw materials by using part of its inventory.

Work-in-process inventory

Work-in-process inventory consists of partially finished goods that require additional work before they become finished goods. The more complex and lengthy the production process, the larger the investment in work-in-process inventory. The purpose of work-in-process inventory is to uncouple the various operations in the production process so that machine failures and work stoppages in one operation will not affect the other operations. Assume, for example, that there are 10 different production operations, each one involving further operations on the piece of work produced in the previous operation. If the machine performing the first production operation breaks down, a firm with no work-in-process inventory will have to shut down all 10 production operations. However, if a firm has the requisite inventory, the remaining nine operations can continue by taking the input for the second operation from inventory rather than directly from the output of the first operation.

Finished-goods inventory

Finished-goods inventory consists of goods on which the production has been completed but which have not yet been sold. The purpose of finished-goods inventory is to uncouple the production and sales functions so that it is not necessary to produce the good specifically so that a sale can occur—instead, sales can be made out of inventory. In the motor-vehicle industry, for example, people might not buy from a dealer who makes them wait weeks or months, when another dealer could fill the order immediately.

Stock of cash

Although cash management was discussed at some length earlier, it is worthwhile to mention cash again in the light of inventory management. This is because the *stock of cash* carried by a firm is simply a special type of inventory. In terms of uncoupling the various operations of the firm, the purpose of holding a stock of cash is to make the payment of bills independent of the collection of accounts due. When cash is kept on hand, bills can be paid without prior collection of accounts.

INVENTORY-MANAGEMENT TECHNIQUES

An optimal inventory policy is very individual and firm-specific. This is much like the optimal capital-structure decision that is discussed in Chapter 16.

Decision making in relation to the investment in inventory involves a basic trade-off between risk and return. The risk is that if the level of inventory is too low the various functions of the business are unable to operate independently and delays in production and customer delivery can result. The return from low inventory results from the fact that reduced inventory investment saves money. On the other hand, increases in the level of inventory reduce the risk of running out of stock, but inventory expenses rise. This is because a high level of inventory increases storage and handling costs, as well as the cost for the use of the capital that is invested in inventory.

Inventory carrying costs vary widely from company to company. For example, in the high-fashion clothing business, carrying costs are quite large, largely due to the costs of obsolescence associated with style changes. On the other hand, a tailor who makes clothing to order may have an inventory that is limited to samples of fabrics, so inventory is very low.

The importance of effective inventory management is directly related to the size of the investment in inventory. Effective management of the assets is essential to the goal of shareholder wealth maximisation in firms such as retailers, wholesalers and manufacturers. To control the investment in inventory, management must solve two problems: the *order-quantity problem* (which involves the question of how much to order each time an order is placed to replenish inventory) and the *order-point problem* (when orders should be placed).

Economic-order-quantity problem

The *economic-order-quantity problem* involves determining the optimal order size for an inventory item. This is a function of its expected usage, its carrying costs and its ordering costs. The economic-order-quantity (EOQ) model attempts to determine the order size that will minimise total inventory costs. It assumes that:

Total inventory costs = total carrying costs + total ordering costs   **(8-2)**

Carrying costs

In equation (8-2), the inventory *carrying costs* include warehouse or storage costs (such as rent, insurance, utilities and so on), wages for those who operate the warehouse, and costs associated with inventory shrinkage (such as obsolescence, damage or theft). In addition, there is a 'cost' for the funds or capital tied up in inventory, which depends on the required rate of return on these funds. Thus, total carrying costs include both cash outlays and the opportunity costs associated with having funds tied up in inventory. Some carrying costs are fixed. (For example, up to maximum capacity, warehouse rental expense is the same whether there is one item of inventory stored or one thousand items.) Other carrying costs are variable, such as the insurance premium, which is a function of the value of inventory on hand.

Since the total carrying cost depends to some extent on the amount of inventory carried, it is necessary to have some idea of this amount. If it is assumed that each order is for Q items and that inventory is allowed to diminish to zero before being replenished, then clearly the average amount of inventory carried is equal to $Q/2$. This is shown graphically in Figure 8.4, where the average amount of inventory on hand is represented by the dotted horizontal line. (The assumption of inventory being allowed to drop to zero will be relaxed below.)

As mentioned, some of the carrying costs are fixed, but others are variable and will depend on the number of orders placed. Given that the average level of inventory is equal

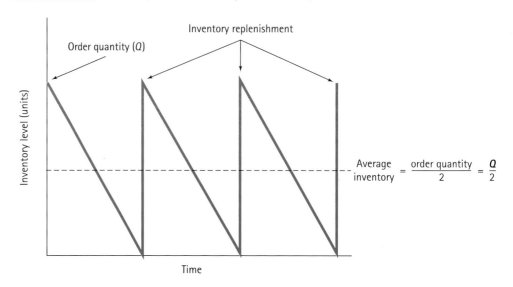

FIGURE 8.4 Inventory level and the replenishment cycle

to $Q/2$, if the carrying cost per unit is denoted C, total carrying costs can be represented by equation (8-3):

$$\text{Total carrying costs} = (\text{average inventory}) \times (\text{carrying cost per unit}) \qquad \textbf{(8-3)}$$
$$= (Q/2) \times C$$

Ordering costs

Ordering costs include costs for placing the order, production set-up, shipping, handling, and quantity or 'bulk buying' discounts (which are benefits—that is, negative costs). Some ordering costs are fixed and others are variable, but it is not always obvious whether a particular cost is fixed or variable. Although the salary of the employee responsible for ordering inventory may be fixed, an increase in orders beyond a certain point may result in the need for an additional employee or a need for more office space. Note that, to simplify the discussion, this chapter focuses on ordering costs for items produced outside the firm; if the order is produced within the firm, 'order costs' are the production set-up costs (e.g. in the motor vehicle industry, the set-up costs associated with resetting stamping machines that produce work-in-process inventory).

The total ordering costs incurred in a period are equal to the ordering costs per order times the number of orders. If we assume that total demand over the planning period is S and we order in lot sizes of Q, then S/Q represents the number of orders over the planning period. If the ordering cost per order is O, then:

$$\text{Total ordering costs} = (\text{number of orders}) \times (\text{ordering cost per order}) \qquad \textbf{(8-4)}$$
$$= (S/Q) \times O$$

Total inventory costs

Combining equations (8-3) and (8-4), total inventory costs become:

$$\text{Total costs} = ((Q/2) \times C) + (S/Q \times O)) \qquad \textbf{(8-5)}$$

Figure 8.5 illustrates this equation graphically. As can be seen, as the order size increases, so do the carrying costs, because the firm is holding more inventory. Eventually, the increased carrying costs outweigh the savings in ordering costs from not placing so many orders. At this point, total costs are minimised. In Figure 8.5, the minimum costs are shown at the point EOQ, which therefore represents the economic order quantity. This quantity can be found

FIGURE 8.5 Total cost and EOQ determination

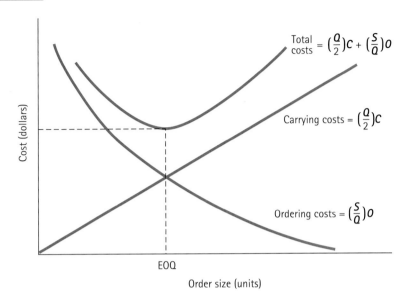

mathematically using differential calculus to ascertain the order size Q^* that minimises the value of the function shown in equation (8-5); the resultant equation that identifies the optimum order quantity is equation (8-6):[3]

$$\text{EOQ} = Q^* = \sqrt{\frac{2SO}{C}}$$ **(8-6)**

The use of the EOQ model is illustrated through Example 8.2.

EXAMPLE 8.2 Using the economic order quantity model

Suppose a firm expects total demand (S) for its product over the planning period to be 5000 units, the ordering cost per order (O) is $200, and the carrying cost per unit (C) is $2. Substituting these values into equation (8-6) yields:

$$Q^* = \sqrt{\frac{2 \times 5000 \times 200}{2}}$$

$$= \sqrt{1\,000\,000}$$

$$= 1000 \text{ units}$$

Thus, if this firm orders in 1000-unit lot sizes, it will minimise its total inventory costs.

If demand doubles, what is Q^*? Answer: 1414 units. Notice that Q^* does not double but increases with the square root.

ORDER-POINT PROBLEM

The two most limiting assumptions of the EOQ problem are those of *constant* or *uniform demand* and *instantaneous delivery*. The first problem is dealt with through the inclusion of safety stock, which is mentioned under the EOQ assumption under point 1 in 'One Step Further' below, while the second of these problems is discussed under point 5.

ONE STEP FURTHER

EXAMINATION OF EOQ ASSUMPTIONS

Despite the fact that the EOQ model tends to yield quite good results, there are weaknesses in the model associated with several of its assumptions. When its assumptions have been dramatically violated, the EOQ model can generally be modified to accommodate the situation. The model's assumptions are as follows.

1. *Constant or uniform demand.* Although the EOQ model assumes constant demand, demand may vary from day to day. If demand is stochastic—that is, not known in advance—the model must be modified through the inclusion of a safety stock which in turn adds to total costs. The question of a safety stock is discussed further below.
2. *Constant unit price.* If the firm receives a quantity discount, this means that there is an incentive to place bigger orders and that unit prices vary accordingly. The resultant variable prices can be handled quite easily through a modification of the original EOQ model, redefining total costs and re-solving for the optimum order quantity.
3. *Constant carrying costs.* Unit carrying costs may vary substantially as the size of the inventory rises, perhaps decreasing because of economies of scale or storage efficiency or increasing as storage space runs out and new warehouses have to be rented. This situation can be handled through a modification in the original model similar to the one used for variable unit price.
4. *Constant order cost.* Although this assumption is generally valid, its violation can be accommodated by modifying the original EOQ model in a manner similar to the one used for variable unit price.
5. *Instantaneous delivery.* It is usually the case that delivery is not instantaneous. Therefore, the original EOQ model must be modified through the inclusion of a delivery time stock, the need for which is discussed further below.
6. *Independent orders.* If multiple orders result in cost savings by reducing paperwork and transportation cost, the original EOQ model must be further modified. Although this modification is somewhat complicated, special EOQ models have been developed to deal with it.

These assumptions illustrate the limitations of the basic EOQ model and the ways in which it can be modified to compensate for them. An understanding of the limitations and assumptions of the EOQ model provides the financial manager with a sounder basis for making inventory decisions.

safety stock
The inventory held to accommodate any unusually large and unexpected usage during delivery time.

Safety stock is held in order to cover any unusually large and unexpected usage during the delivery time. The necessity to hold an amount of safety stock clearly adds to total inventory costs, putting them above what they were without a safety stock. In other words, demand and delivery uncertainties create an explicit additional cost to the firm. However, if safety stock is not held, there will be various opportunity costs, such as lost sales due to stock-outs, costs associated with production stoppages owing to stock-outs, and lost future sales as customers find new sources for the item during stock-out periods and perhaps cease to do additional business with the firm. The decision about how much safety stock to hold is generally referred to as the *order-point problem*; that is, how low should inventory be depleted before it is reordered?

Back to the principles

The decision about how much inventory to keep on hand is a direct application of **Principle 1: The risk–return trade-off—we won't take on additional risk unless we expect to be compensated with additional return.** The risk is that if the level of inventory is too low, the various functions of business do not operate independently and delays in production and customer delivery can result. The return results because reduced inventory investment saves money. As the size of inventory increases, there is a consequent increase in storage and handling costs as well as the required return on capital invested in inventory. Therefore, as the level of inventory increases, the risk of running out of inventory is lessened, but inventory expenses rise.

Delivery-time stock is the amount of inventory held to cover usage during the time between placement of an order and when that order will be filled, along with stock held to cover possible delivery delays. As with safety stock, there is an explicit cost associated with holding this amount of inventory, but there are opportunity costs in not holding it.

Overall, therefore, two factors go into the determination of the appropriate order point: (1) the safety stock desired, and (2) the delivery-time or procurement stock. Figure 8.6 graphs the process involved in order-point determination.

As shown in Figure 8.6, the order point is reached when inventory falls to a level equal to the delivery-time stock plus the safety stock.

$$\text{Inventory order point} = (\text{delivery-time stock}) + (\text{safety stock}) \qquad \textbf{(8-7)}$$

delivery-time stock
The inventory needed between the order date and the receipt of the inventory ordered.

Effects of carrying extra safety stock

As a result of the extra amount of safety stock, the average level of inventory increases. When we previously computed the EOQ, the average level of inventory was equal to EOQ/2, but now it is given by equation (8-8):

$$\text{Average inventory} = \frac{\text{EOQ}}{2} + \text{safety stock} \qquad \textbf{(8-8)}$$

FIGURE 8.6 Order-point determination

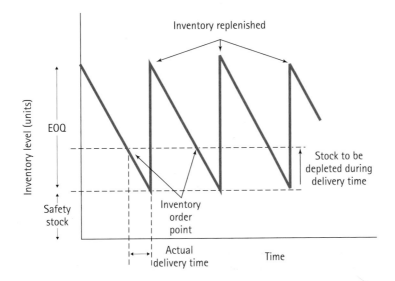

The amount of safety stock and delivery-time stock that needs to be held depends on a number of factors. First, an efficient replenishment system reduces the need for delivery-time stock. Another factor is the uncertainty surrounding both the delivery time and the demand for the product—the more certain the patterns of these inflows and outflows of inventory, the less safety stock required. (In effect, if these inflows and outflows are highly predictable, there is little chance of any stock-out occurring. However, if they are unpredictable, it becomes necessary to carry additional safety stock to prevent unexpected stock-outs.) A third factor is the desired safety margin. If it is a costly experience to run out of inventory, the safety stock held will be larger than it would be otherwise. A final factor is the cost of carrying additional inventory, in terms of both the handling and storage costs and the opportunity cost associated with the investment in additional inventory—very simply, the greater the costs, the smaller the safety stock.

The determination of the level of safety stock therefore involves a basic trade-off between the risk of a stock-out, resulting in possible customer dissatisfaction and lost sales, and the increased costs associated with carrying additional inventory.

INFLATION AND EOQ

Inflation affects the EOQ model in two major ways. First, although the EOQ model can be modified to assume constant price increases, often major price increases occur only once or twice a year and are announced ahead of time. If this is the case, the EOQ model may lose some of its applicability and may be replaced with *anticipatory buying*—that is, buying in anticipation of a price increase to secure the goods at a lower cost. Of course, as with most decisions, there are trade-offs. The costs are the added carrying costs associated with the extra inventory that is bought to beat the price rise. The benefits, of course, come from buying at a lower price. The second way inflation affects the EOQ model is through increased carrying costs. As inflation pushes up interest rates, the cost of carrying inventory increases. In the EOQ model this means that C increases, which results in a decline in Q^*, the optimal economic order quantity:

$$\downarrow Q^* = \sqrt{\frac{2SO}{C\uparrow}} \qquad\qquad (8\text{-}9)$$

Reluctance to stock large inventories because of high carrying costs became particularly prevalent during the late 1970s and early 1980s when inflation and interest rates were at high levels. This led to the implementation by many firms of just-in-time inventory control.

Just-in-time inventory control

The *just-in-time inventory control system* is more than just an inventory control system: it is a production and management system. Not only is inventory cut down to a minimum but the time and physical distance between the various production operations are also reduced. In addition, management is willing to trade off the costs of developing close relationships with suppliers (and thus promote speedy replenishment of inventory) in return for the ability to hold less safety stock.

The just-in-time inventory control system was originally developed in Japan by Taiichi Okno, a vice-president of Toyota. Originally the system was called the *kanban* system, named after the cards that were placed in the parts bins and used to order new supplies. The idea behind the system is that the firm should keep a minimum level of inventory on hand, relying on suppliers to furnish parts 'just in time' for them to be assembled. This is in direct contrast to the traditional inventory philosophy of non-Japanese firms, which is sometimes referred to as a 'just-in-case' system, which keeps healthy levels of safety stocks to ensure that production will not be interrupted. Large inventories may not be a bad idea when interest rates are low, but when interest rates are high they become very costly.

Although the just-in-time inventory system is intuitively appealing, it has not proved easy to implement. Long distances from suppliers, and plants constructed with too much space for storage and not enough access (doors and loading docks) to receive inventory, have limited its successful implementation. Many firms have been forced to change the relationships with their suppliers. Because firms rely on suppliers to deliver high-quality parts and materials immediately, they must have a close long-term relationship with them. But despite the difficulties of implementation, many firms are committed to moving towards a just-in-time system. Dell Computer's former inventory management practices (outlined at the beginning of Chapter 7) are a classic example, as the firm avoided taking ownership of raw materials and components until the time when they were needed for production, while at the same time Dell did not carry any work-in-process or finished-goods inventory because it did not assemble computers until they were ordered.

Although the just-in-time system does not at first appear to bear much of a relationship to the EOQ model, it simply alters some of the assumptions of the model with respect to delivery time and ordering costs, and draws out the implications. Actually, it is just a new approach to the EOQ model that tries to produce the lowest average level of inventory possible. If we look at the average level of inventory as defined by the EOQ model, we find it to be:

$$\text{Average inventory} = \dfrac{\sqrt{\dfrac{2SO\downarrow}{C}}}{2} + \text{safety stock} \downarrow$$

The just-in-time system attacks this equation in two places. First, the ordering cost O is reduced by placing inventory supplies in convenient locations, laying out plants in such a way that it is inexpensive and easy to unload new inventory shipments, and computerising the inventory order system. Second, *safety stock* is reduced by developing a strong relationship with suppliers located in the same geographical area and setting up restocking strategies that cut time. The philosophy behind the just-in-time inventory system is that the benefits associated with reducing inventory and delivery time to a bare minimum through adjustment in the EOQ model will more than offset the costs associated with the increased possibility of stock-outs. However, if there is a breakdown in the supply of inventory to the system (e.g. due to a strike), the results can be severe, with workers being laid off and the firm losing sales revenue. Firms can overcome this problem by dealing with more than one supplier for any particular raw material.

Concept check

8.13 Describe the types of inventory a firm holds and the purpose of each type.

8.14 What is the objective of the economic order quantity model?

8.15 What is meant by the order-point problem?

8.16 Explain the just-in-time inventory system.

For answers go to MyFinanceLab or www.pearson.com.au/9781442539174

Summary

OBJECTIVE 1

Liquid assets are the total of cash and marketable securities. Cash is the currency and coin the firm has on hand in cash drawers, cash registers or bank accounts. Cash balances earn no return. Near-cash assets, also known as marketable securities, are security investments that earn a rate of return and that the firm can quickly convert into cash balances.

OBJECTIVE 2

OBJECTIVE 3

OBJECTIVE 4

Firms hold cash for liquidity to satisfy transactions, precautionary and speculative needs. Of these, the transactions and precautionary motives are the most important. In the firm's overall cash-management program, the financial manager must make sure that enough cash is on hand to meet the payment needs that arise in the course of doing business, and attempt to reduce the firm's idle cash balances to a minimum. The firm can significantly reduce its total float by encouraging customers to use electronic funds transfer (EFT) instead of cheques.

OBJECTIVE 5

Because cash balances provide no direct return, marketable securities are used to satisfy the precautionary motive for holding 'cash'. The factors that affect the yields available on the marketable securities are:

- financial risk
- interest-rate risk
- liquidity
- taxation liability.

By considering these four factors simultaneously with returns desired from the portfolio, the financial manager can design the mix of near-cash assets most suitable for the firm.

OBJECTIVE 6

Extremely safe marketable securities that can be used for the near-cash portfolio include treasury notes, near-dated treasury bonds, and state government, local government and semi-government instruments. Negotiable certificates of deposit issued by banks and bank bills that are accepted or endorsed by banks would generally be considered safe investments. Non-bank bills and promissory notes, which rely solely on the creditworthiness of the issuing organisation, expose the holder to a higher risk of default and therefore should provide the highest return to compensate for this risk.

OBJECTIVE 7

The size of the investment in accounts receivable depends on three factors:

- the percentage of credit sales to total sales
- the level of sales
- the credit and collection policies.

However, only the credit and collection policies are decision variables open to the financial manager. The policies that the financial manager has control over include the terms of sale, the quality of the customer, and the collection efforts.

OBJECTIVE 8

Inventory management and control is another important function of the financial manager. The purpose of holding inventory is to make each function of the business independent of the other functions—that is, to uncouple the firm's different operations. Inventory-management techniques primarily involve questions of how much inventory should be ordered and when the order should be placed. The answers directly determine the average level of investment in inventory. The EOQ model can be used to answer the first of these questions, that is, 'how much'. This model attempts to calculate the order size that minimises the sum of the inventory carrying and ordering costs. The order-point problem attempts to determine how low inventory can drop before it needs to be reordered. The order point is reached when the inventory falls to a level equal to the delivery-time stock plus the safety stock. Determining the level of safety stock involves a direct trade-off between the risk of running out of inventory and the increased costs associated with carrying additional inventory.

The just-in-time inventory control system lowers inventory by reducing the time and distance between the various production functions. The idea behind the system is that the firm should keep a minimum level of inventory on hand and rely on suppliers to furnish parts 'just in time' for them to be assembled.

For a complete flashcard glossary
go to MyFinanceLab at
www.pearson.com.au/myfinancelab

Review questions

8-1   What is meant by the cash-flow process?

8-2   Identify the principal motives for holding cash and near-cash assets. Explain the purpose of each motive.

8-3   What are the two major objectives of the firm's cash-management system?

8-4   What three decisions dominate the cash-management process?

8-5   Within the context of cash management, what are the key elements of (total) float? Briefly define each element.

8-6   Distinguish between *financial risk* and *interest-rate risk* as these terms are commonly used in discussions of cash management.

8-7   What is meant when we say: 'A money-market instrument is highly liquid'?

8-8   What factors determine the size of the investment a firm makes in accounts receivable? Which of these factors are under the control of the financial manager?

8-9   What do the following trade credit terms mean?

    (a) 1/20, net 50

    (b) 2/30, net 60

    (c) net 30

    (d) 2/10, 1/30, net 60

8-10   What is the purpose of the use of an ageing account in the control of accounts receivable? Can this same function be performed through ratio analysis? Why or why not?

8-11   If a credit manager experienced no bad-debt losses during the past year, would this be an indication of proper credit management? Why or why not?

8-12   What is the purpose of credit scoring?

8-13   What are some of the advantages of using a credit agency or bureau?

8-14   What are the risk–return trade-offs associated with adopting a more liberal trade credit policy?

8-15   What is the purpose of holding inventory? Name several types of inventory and describe the use to which they are put.

8-16   Can cash be considered a special type of inventory? If so, what functions does it attempt to uncouple?

8-17   To control investment in inventory effectively, what two questions must be answered?

8-18   What are the major assumptions made by the EOQ model?

8-19   What are the risk–return trade-offs associated with inventory management?

8-20   How might inflation affect the EOQ model?

8-21   What benefits flow from improving quality in a firm's operations? How does a TQM approach contribute to this?

8-22   What are the benefits and costs of a just-in-time inventory management system?

Self-test problems

For answers go to MyFinanceLab
www.pearson.com.au/myfinancelab

ST-1 (*Buying and selling marketable securities*) Mountaineer Outfitters has $2 million in excess cash that it might invest in marketable securities. In order to buy and sell the securities, however, the firm must pay a transactions fee of $45 000.

    (a) Would you recommend purchasing the securities if they yield 12% annually and are held for:
        (i) One month?
        (ii) Two months?
        (iii) Three months?
        (iv) Six months?
        (v) One year?
    (b) What minimum required yield would the securities have to return for the firm to hold them for three months? (That is, what is the break-even yield for a three-month holding period?)

ST-2 (*EOQ calculations*) A local gift shop is attempting to determine how many sets of wine glasses to order. The store feels it will sell approximately 800 sets in the next year at a price of $18 per set. The wholesale price that the store pays per set is $12. Costs for carrying one set of wine glasses are estimated at $1.50 per year, and ordering costs are estimated at $25.

    (a) What is the economic order quantity for the sets of wine glasses?
    (b) What are the annual inventory costs for the firm if it orders in this quantity? (Assume constant demand and instantaneous delivery and thus no safety stock is carried.)

ST-3 (*EOQ calculations*) The following inventory information is given for the F. Beamer Company:

1. Orders can be placed only in multiples of 100 units.
2. Annual unit usage is 300 000. (Assume a 50-week year in your calculations.)
3. The carrying cost is 30% of the purchase price of the goods.
4. The purchase price is $10 per unit.
5. The ordering cost is $50 per order.
6. The desired safety stock is 1000 units. (This does not include delivery-time stock.)
7. Delivery time is two weeks.

Given the above information:

    (a) What is the optimal EOQ level?
    (b) How many orders will be placed annually?
    (c) At what inventory level should a reorder be made?

Problems

For more problems and for answers to problems marked with an asterisk (*) go to MyFinanceLab at
www.pearson.com.au/myfinancelab

8-1 (*Marketable securities portfolio*) Mac's Tennis Racquet Manufacturing Company currently pays its employees on a weekly basis. The weekly wages bill is $675 000. This means that on average over the week the firm has accrued wages payable of ($675 000 + $0)/2 = $337 500.

    Roger Federror works as the firm's senior financial analyst and reports directly to his uncle, who owns all of the firm's ordinary shares. Roger wants to move to a monthly wage payment system. Employees would be paid at the end of every fourth week. Roger is aware that the union representing the company's workers will not permit the monthly payments system to take effect unless the workers are given some type of fringe-benefit compensation.

    A plan has been worked out whereby the firm will make a contribution to the cost of life insurance coverage for each employee. This will cost the firm $50 775 annually. Roger expects the firm to earn 8.5% annually on its marketable securities portfolio.

    (a) Based on the projected information, should Mac's Tennis Racquet Manufacturing Company move to the monthly wage payment system?
    (b) What annual rate of return on the marketable securities portfolio would enable the firm to break even on this proposal?

8-2* (*Buying and selling marketable securities*) Morialta Dice & Card Company has generated $800 000 in excess cash that it could invest in marketable securities. In order to buy and sell the securities, the firm will pay total transactions fees of $20 000.

    (a) Would you recommend purchasing the securities if they yield 10.5% annually and are held for:

        (i) One month?
        (ii) Two months?
        (iii) Three months?
        (iv) Six months?
        (v) One year?

    (b) What minimum required yield would the securities have to return for the firm to hold them for two months? (What is the break-even yield for a two-month holding period?)

8-3 (*Marketable securities portfolio*) Western Photo Company has $1 million in excess cash that it might invest in marketable securities. In order to buy and sell the securities, however, the firm must pay a transactions fee of $25 000 plus government stamp duties of $10 000.

    (a) Would you recommend purchasing the securities if they yield 10% annually and are held for:

        (i) One month?
        (ii) Two months?
        (iii) Three months?
        (iv) Six months?
        (v) One year?

    (b) What minimum required yield would the securities have to return for the firm to hold them for three months? (What is the break-even yield for a three-month holding period?)

8-4 (*Valuing float reduction*) Griffey Manufacturing Company is forecasting that next year's gross revenues from sales will be $890 million. The senior treasury analyst for the firm expects the marketable securities portfolio to earn 9.60% over this same time period. A 365-day year is used in all the firm's financial procedures. What is the value to the company of one day's float reduction?

8-5 (*Valuing float reduction*) Sprightly Step Company produces a line of walking shoes that has become extremely popular with ageing baby boomers. The company's recent rapid growth to $80 million in annual credit sales to shoe stores around the country has made consideration of a more advanced billing and collection system worthwhile. Sprightly's bank has proposed a banking system to Sprightly's CFO, Roberto Dylan, that would save the company three days in mail float, two days in processing float, and $50 000 in annual clerical costs. The bank would charge a flat fee per year of $80 000 to operate the system for Sprightly. Roberto believes that the funds freed by such an arrangement could be invested in the money market and could earn an annual rate of return of 5.5%.

    By comparing the costs with the benefits, advise if Roberto should accept the bank's proposal. (Make your computations for a one-year period.)

8-6* (*Interest rate risk*) Your company holds a bond at its par value of $1000, with 15 years to maturity. The coupon rate on this security is 6%. Interest payments are made to bondholders once a year. Currently, bonds of this particular risk class are yielding investors 9%. A cash shortage has forced you to instruct the company's treasurer to liquidate this bond.

    (a) At what price will your bond be sold? Assume annual compounding.
    (b) What will be the amount of your gain or loss over the original purchase price?
    (c) What would be the amount of your gain or loss if you instead held a bond with one year to maturity? (Assume all characteristics of the bonds are identical except their maturity periods.)
    (d) What do we call the type of risk that is illustrated by the previous analysis?

8-7 (*Interest rate risk*) Two years ago, your company treasurer purchased for the firm a 20-year bond at its par value of $1000. The coupon rate on this security is 8%. Interest payments are made to bondholders once a year. Currently, bonds of this particular risk class are yielding investors 9%. A cash shortage has forced you to instruct your treasurer to liquidate his bond.

    (a) At what price will your bond be sold? Assume annual compounding.
    (b) What will be the amount of your gain or loss over the original purchase price?

(c) What would be the amount of your gain or loss had the treasurer originally purchased a bond with a four-year rather than a 20-year maturity? (Assume all characteristics of the bonds are identical except their maturity periods.)

8-8 (*Interest-rate risk*) Five years ago your firm purchased a 15-year maturity bond at its par value of $100 000. The coupon rate on this security is 6%. Coupon payments are made once a year. The firm also purchased, at the same time, a $100 000 eight-year bond with the same risk class as the 15-year bond and a coupon rate, payable annually, of 5%. Currently, the term structure of interest rates for bonds of this particular risk class is as follows:

MATURITY	YIELD
1 year	8%
2 years	8%
3 years	8%
4 years	9%
5 years	9%
10 years	10%
15 years	11%

As a consequence of a cash shortage, your firm must sell one of the bonds.

(a) Which bond do you recommend should be sold? Explain why. (Use relevant supporting computations.)

(b) What principle is illustrated by the computations in part (a)?

8-9 (*Trade credit discounts*) Your firm offers trade credit terms of 2/10, net 50. If your customer pays on the last day that qualifies for the discount, what is the cost to your firm?

8-10 (*Trade credit discounts*) If credit customers are offered trade credit terms of 2/20, net 60, and they pay on the last day that qualifies for the discount, what is the cost to your firm?

8-11* (*Trade credit discounts*) Determine the effective annualised cost of forgoing the trade credit discount on the following terms:

(a) 1/5, net 20
(b) 2/20, net 90
(c) 1/20, net 100
(d) 4/10, net 50
(e) 5/20, net 100
(f) 5/30, net 50

8-12* (*Accounts payable policy and cash management*) Meadowbrook Paving Company is suffering from a prolonged decline in new development in its sales area. In an attempt to improve its cash position, the firm is considering changes in its accounts payable policy. After careful study it has determined that the only alternative available is to slow disbursements. Purchases for the coming year are expected to be $40 million. Sales will be $65 million, which represents about a 15% drop from the current year. Currently, Meadowbrook discounts approximately 25% of its payments at 3%, 10 days, net 30, and the rest of the accounts are paid in 30 days. If Meadowbrook adopts a policy of payment in 45 days or 60 days, how much can the firm gain if the interest rate is 11%? What will be the result if this action causes Meadowbrook Paving suppliers to increase their prices to the company by 0.5% to compensate for the 60-day extended term of payment? In your calculations use a 365-day year and ignore any compounding effects related to expected returns.

8-13* (*Marketable securities portfolio*) Red Raider Feedlots has $4 million in excess cash to invest in a marketable securities portfolio. Its broker will charge $10 000 to invest the entire $4 million. The president of Red Raider wants at least half of the $4 million invested at a maturity period of three months or less; the remainder can be invested in securities with maturities that do not exceed six months. The relevant term structure of short-term yields is as follows:

MATURITY	AVAILABLE YIELD (ANNUAL)
1 month	6.2%
2 months	6.4%
3 months	6.5%
4 months	6.7%
5 months	6.9%
6 months	7.0%

(a) What maturity periods of the securities purchased with the excess $4 million would maximise the before-tax income from the added investment? What would be the amount of the income from such an investment?

(b) Suppose that the president of Red Raider relaxes his constraint on the maturity structure of the added investment. What would be your profit-maximising investment recommendation?

(c) If one-sixth of the excess cash is invested in each of the maturity categories shown above, what would be the before-tax income generated from such an action?

8-14* (*Inventory ratio analysis*) Assuming a 360-day year, calculate what the average investment in inventory would be for a firm, given the following information in each case:

(a) The firm has sales of $600 000, a gross profit margin of 10%, and an inventory-turnover ratio of 6.

(b) The firm has a cost of goods sold figure of $480 000 and an average age of inventory of 40 days.

(c) The firm has a cost of goods sold figure of $1 150 000 and an inventory-turnover ratio of 5.

(d) The firm has a sales figure of $25 million, a gross profit margin of 14%, and an average age of inventory of 45 days.

8-15 (*Inventory ratio analysis*) Assuming a 360-day year, calculate what the average investment in inventory would be for a firm, given the following information in each case:

(a) The firm has sales of $550 000, a gross profit margin of 10%, and an inventory-turnover ratio of 5.

(b) The firm has a cost of goods sold figure of $480 000 and an average age of inventory of 35 days.

(c) The firm has a cost of goods sold figure of $1 250 000 and an inventory-turnover ratio of 6.

(d) The firm has a sales figure of $25 million, a gross profit margin of 15%, and an average age of inventory of 50 days.

8-16* (*EOQ calculations*) A bookstore is trying to determine the optimal order quantity for a popular novel just printed in paperback. The store feels that the book will sell at four times its hardback figures. It would therefore sell approximately 3500 copies in the next year at a price of $1.50. The store buys the book at a wholesale figure of $1. Costs for carrying the book are estimated at $0.20 a copy per year, and it costs $9 to place an order for more books.

(a) Determine the EOQ.

(b) What would be the total costs for ordering the books 1, 4, 5, 10 and 15 times a year?

(c) What questionable assumptions are being made by the EOQ model?

8-17 (*EOQ calculations*) The local burger fast-food restaurant purchases 20 000 boxes of bread rolls every month. Order costs are $50 an order, and it costs 25 cents a box for storage.

(a) What is the optimal order quantity of rolls for this restaurant?

(b) What questionable assumptions are being made by the EOQ model?

8-18* (*EOQ calculations*) A local car-manufacturing plant has a $75 per-unit per-year carrying cost on a certain item in inventory. This item is used at a rate of 50 000 per year. Ordering costs are $500 per order.

(a) What is the EOQ for this item?

(b) What are the annual inventory costs for this firm if it orders in this quantity? (Assume constant demand and instantaneous delivery.)

8-19 (*EOQ calculations*) Leisurewear Industries Ltd sells 100 000 items per year and has inventory-associated expenses totalling $15 per unit, covering insurance, financing costs, storage and related costs. Costs of placing an order are $1200. What are the annual inventory costs for this firm? (Assume constant demand and instantaneous delivery.)

8-20 (*EOQ calculations*) Swank Products is involved in the production of camera parts and has the following inventory, carrying and storage costs:

1. Orders must be placed in round lots of 200 units.
2. Annual unit usage is 500 000. (Assume a 50-week year in your calculations.)
3. The carrying cost is 20% of the purchase price.
4. The purchase price is $2 per unit.
5. The ordering cost is $90 per order.
6. The desired safety stock is 15 000 units. (This does not include delivery-time stock.)
7. The delivery time is one week.

Given the above information:

(a) Determine the optimal EOQ level.
(b) How many orders will be placed annually?
(c) What is the inventory order point? (That is, at what level of inventory should a new order be placed?)
(d) What is the average inventory level?

8-21* (*EOQ calculations*) Toledo Distributors has determined the following inventory information:

1. Orders can be placed only in multiples of 200 units.
2. Annual unit usage is 500 000 units. (Assume a 50-week year in your calculations.)
3. The carrying cost is 10% of the purchase price of the goods.
4. The purchase price is $5 per unit.
5. The ordering cost is $100 per order.
6. The desired safety stock is 5000 units. (This does not include delivery-time stock.)
7. Delivery time is four weeks.

Given the above information:

(a) What is the EOQ level?
(b) How many orders will be placed annually?
(c) At what inventory level should a reorder be made?
(d) Now assume that the carrying costs are 50% of the purchase price of the goods and recalculate parts **(a)**, **(b)** and **(c)**. Are these the results you anticipated?

8-22 (*Analysing change in credit policy*) Hyndlee Street Enterprises is considering relaxing its current credit policy. Currently the firm has annual sales (all credit) of $6 million and an average collection period of 40 days (assume a 360-day year). Under the proposed change, the trade credit terms would be changed from net 40 days to net 90 days and credit would be extended to a riskier class of customer. It is assumed that bad debt losses on current customers will remain at their current level. Under this change, it is expected that sales will increase to $7 million. Given the following information, should the firm adopt the new policy?

New sales level (all credit)	$7 000 000
Original sales level (all credit)	$6 000 000
Contribution margin	20%
Percent bad debt losses on new sales	8%
New average collection period	90 days
Original average collection period	40 days
Additional investment in inventory	$40 000
Pre-tax required rate of return	15%

8-23 (*Analysing change in credit policy*) Hoapfool Ltd is considering a major change in credit policy. Managers are considering extending credit to a riskier class of customer and extending their credit period from net 10 days to net 30 days. They do not expect the bad debt losses on their current customers to change. Given the following information, should they go ahead with the change in credit

272

policy? The dollar amount of cash sales is expected to remain the same after the extension of credit terms.

Original sales level (20% cash sales)	$20 000 000
New sales level	$24 000 000
Contribution margin	25%
Percent bad debt losses on new sales	8%
New average collection period on credit sales	30 days
Original average collection period on credit sales	10 days
Additional investment in inventory	$100 000
Pre-tax required rate of return	12%

Case study

You have begun work as a cost analyst for AERE Ltd, a company that has been awarded the contract to supply about half of the airbags needed by General Motors-Holden (GMH) for the new 4-cylinder *Cruze* motor car. The company's factory closes for two weeks annually, during the Christmas/New Year period. AERE's main inventory item is a prefabricated sensor and gas-release unit that is the critical component for making the airbags. AERE expects to use 80 000 of these items per year, at a unit cost of $70, and the overseas supplier requires orders to be in multiples of 200, which is the standard way that they are packaged. Preliminary estimates suggest that insurance, storage, financing costs and other carrying costs will total $560 000 per year. The desired safety stock represents five weeks' usage (which does not include delivery-time stock, delivery time also being five weeks). You have estimated also that ordering costs will total $2600 per order.

On the basis of the above estimates, the company's production manager and CFO have asked for a brief report that will be used in formulating an inventory policy for the sensor/gas-release units. To assist with this task, your boss has asked you to determine the following:

(a) The optimal EOQ level for this item.
(b) The number of orders that will be placed annually.
(c) The inventory order point.
(d) The average inventory level.
(e) What would happen to the EOQ if the company gets the entire contract for the airbags and so annual unit sales double (all other unit costs and safety stocks remaining constant)?

Notes

1. John Maynard Keynes, *The General Theory of Employment, Interest, and Money*, Harcourt Brace Jovanovich, New York, 1936.
2. Example 8.1 implies a flat yield curve and that the long-term bond and the short-term bond are subject to the same amount of increase in interest rates, which assumes parallel shifts in yield curves.
3. This result can be obtained through calculus:

total cost $(TC) = [(Q/2) \times C] + [(S/Q) \times O]$

The first derivative with respect to Q defines the slope of the total-cost curve. Setting the derivative equal to zero specifies the minimum point (zero slope) on the curve. Thus:

$$(dTC/dQ) = C/2 - SO/Q^2 = 0$$
$$Q^2 = (2SO)/C$$

$$Q^* = \sqrt{\frac{2SO}{C}}$$

To verify that a minimum point is being found, rather than a maximum point where the slope would also equal zero, we check for a positive second derivative:

$$d^2TC/dQ^2 = (2SO)/Q^3 = 0$$

The second derivative must be positive, because SO and Q can only take on positive values; hence, this is a minimum point.

Valuation and management of long-term investment

Part **3**

9 Risk and rates of return

10 Valuation of bonds and shares

11 Capital budgeting: concepts and methods

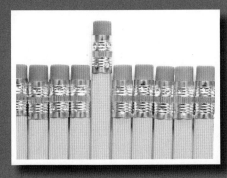

12 Capital budgeting: cash-flow identification and project ranking conflicts

13 Risk in capital budgeting

14 Cost of capital

Learning objectives

After reading this chapter, you should be able to:

1 Describe the relationship between investors' average returns and the riskiness of those returns.

2 Explain the effect of inflation on rates of return.

3 Describe the *term structure of interest rates*.

4 Define and measure the expected rate of return of an individual investment.

5 Define and measure the riskiness of an individual investment.

6 Explain how diversifying investments affects the riskiness and expected rate of return of a portfolio of assets.

7 Measure the market risk of an individual asset.

8 Calculate the market risk of a portfolio.

9 Calculate the expected return and risk of a two-asset portfolio.

10 Explain the relationship between an investor's required rate of return on an investment and the risk of the investment.

11 Understand the fundamental principles of portfolio theory.

12 Explain the notion of efficient markets and its importance to share prices.

For a complete eBook go to MyFinanceLab
www.pearson.com.au/myfinancelab

Risk and rates of return

Chapter 9

CHAPTER PREVIEW

Taken over the very long term, Australian share investors have received average annual returns of about 7% above the returns received by investors in Australian government bonds. So, why do people bother to invest in these bonds; why not buy shares only? The answer is that investors know that buying bonds tends to be much less risky than buying shares and some investors prefer the certainty of bonds. The extra return on shares reflects the workings of *Principle 1: The risk–return trade-off—we won't take on additional risk unless we expect to be compensated with additional return.*

Why are bonds less risky than shares? As we saw in Chapter 4, bonds return a specified amount of cash to the investor, consisting of the periodic interest payments (the 'coupons') followed by the return of the principal at maturity. In the case of bonds issued by the Australian government, these amounts are more or less 'guaranteed'. In contrast, if you buy shares, their prices can vary considerably (both upwards and downwards) over time—returns on shares tend to be far more volatile than those on bonds. You may get back more cash than you invested, or less cash. However, on average, share markets do bring greater returns than bonds, over the long term, which is consistent with Principle 1.

In this chapter, we approach risk largely from the viewpoint of shareholders who fund the firm's investment projects. Share investors require a minimum rate of return on their funds, which contributes to the discount rate that is used when computing the present value of the future cash flows on a project. These projects, too, differ in risk. To give an example, let's consider Apple Corporation. It seems intuitively obvious that a project to launch a new model of the iPhone—a tried and tested success—will be less risky than launching a phone with brand new technology that has just been developed by the company's R&D (Research and Development) division. However, the rewards from the new technology might be potentially large, particularly if competitors are not in the race. This raises the question: how are different *project* risks taken into account? And how are these risks reflected in the investor's required rate of return? These are questions that are addressed in later chapters, notably Chapters 13 and 14.

This chapter focuses on *Principle 1: The risk–return trade-off—we won't take on additional risk unless we expect to be compensated with additional return.* In addition, three other basic principles play a prominent role in this chapter:

- *Principle 3: Cash—not profits—is king.* Investors outlay cash and the subsequent returns take the form of cash.
- *Principle 6: Efficient capital markets—the markets are quick and the prices are right.* This principle holds that we can rely on market prices as the best estimate of the true worth of a security.
- *Principle 9: All risk is not equal—some risk can be diversified away, and some cannot.* Some investors 'diversify' by spreading their risk across multiple investments, which has implications for how risk is assessed in diversified portfolios.

Rates of return in financial markets

OBJECTIVE **1**

Chapter 3 introduced the concept of *financial markets*, in which firms seek financing for their investments and from which shareholders of a company achieve much of their wealth through share price movements. However, involvement with financial markets is risky. When we invest in a security, such as a company's shares, there is always some degree of risk, because we cannot be certain what the price of the share will be in the future and how much we will get back on the investment. That is, we face uncertainty in trying to assess the payoffs in financial markets. However, the degree of risk varies from one financial security to another. For example, when you invest in Qantas shares, you are less certain about the end value of your investment than

Describe the relationship between investors' average returns and the riskiness of those returns.

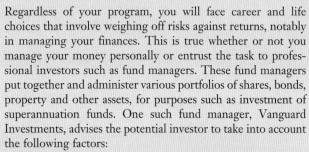

Regardless of your program

Regardless of your program, you will face career and life choices that involve weighing off risks against returns, notably in managing your finances. This is true whether or not you manage your money personally or entrust the task to professional investors such as fund managers. These fund managers put together and administer various portfolios of shares, bonds, property and other assets, for purposes such as investment of superannuation funds. One such fund manager, Vanguard Investments, advises the potential investor to take into account the following factors:

1. *Investment type and risk.* All investments carry some level of risk. The type and degree of risk will vary depending on the investments you choose—usually the higher the risk, the higher the potential return.
2. *Diversification.* Spreading your money across a range of investments is one of the best ways to reduce your exposure to market risk. This way you are not relying on the returns of a single investment. With a diversified portfolio of investments, returns from better performing investments can help offset those that underperform.

3. *Asset allocation.* Research confirms that how you allocate your assets to each asset class (such as shares, property, interest-bearing securities) is more important to long-term performance than the individual stocks you choose.
4. *Your own investment profile.* Before choosing your asset allocation, you need to look at:
    * the time-frame (are you investing short term, medium term, or for the long haul?)
    * your attitude to risk
    * your current circumstances and constraints and your future prospects.

To give an example, a recent retiree would typically want a low-risk investment, so that retirement income is not threatened in the short to medium term. In contrast, a recent graduate, looking a long way ahead to future retirement, would probably want to maximise long-term returns and would typically be willing to accept some risk along the way.

when you invest in a government bond that pays 6% per annum. The share investment is obviously riskier. However, on your Qantas shares you are expecting to get a return of greater than 6%. If you did not expect the share investment to generate a return *greater than* 6%, would you not be better off investing in government bonds? This example again illustrates the relationship between risk and return: investors won't take on an additional risk unless they expect to be compensated with additional returns.

THE RELATIONSHIP BETWEEN RISK AND RATES OF RETURN

History can tell us about returns that investors have earned in the Australian financial markets. Based on data from July 1984 to July 2010, Table 9.1 displays the annual rates of return that have been calculated for:

* The share market accumulation index (which represents a large portfolio of shares and thus approximates the behaviour of the stock market as a whole; this index incorporates dividends as well as changes in share prices)
* five-year government bonds
* ten-year government bonds.

Share prices and dividends are highly variable. Thus, returns rise and fall, over time, in an apparently random manner. The extent of this variability is indicated by a statistical measure known as *standard deviation*, which is also reported in Table 9.1. Not surprisingly, this measure indicates that stock-market returns have been much more variable than the returns on bonds and so standard deviation is used as one measure of investment **risk**. Its computation is elaborated on later in the chapter.

As stated previously, we would expect Australian government bonds to provide a relatively 'safe' return. Safe, in this respect, refers largely to freedom from **default risk**, the possibility that the borrower will not repay a debt in the future. However, bond returns do vary over time, partly because bond prices change in response to changes in market interest rates, as noted in Chapter 4 (in this respect, longer term bond prices tend to be more volatile than shorter term

risk
The potential variability in future cash flows. It may be measured by the standard deviation of the expected return.

default risk
The possibility that the borrower will not repay a debt in the future.

TABLE 9.1 Average Australian annual rates of return and standard deviation 1984–2010

SECURITIES	NOMINAL AVERAGE ANNUAL RETURNS*	STANDARD DEVIATION OF RETURNS	REAL AVERAGE ANNUAL RETURN**
Five-year government bonds	8.2%	3.4%	4.4%
Ten-year government bonds	8.3%	3.2%	4.5%
Shares	10.1%	14.3%	6.3%

Source: Copyright © Reserve Bank of Australia, 2001–2010. All rights reserved.

* It is worthwhile mentioning that these relatively high returns on government bonds are partly attributable to the high interest rates in the 1980s and early 1990s which saw interest rates in the region of 12–15% per annum.

** Real average return equals approximately the nominal return less the average inflation rate (3.8%).

bonds). However, looking at the first two rows of Table 9.1, during the selected period there is not much difference between the five-year and ten-year bond returns, nor is there much difference in variability as assessed by standard deviation.

Finally, the third row of Table 9.1 indicates that the share market provided an average return of about 2% above that of bonds; this extra return is the **risk premium** for taking on the average risk of the stock market. In this case, the risk is indicated in the second column of Table 9.1 by the fact that the share investment's variability (standard deviation) is much larger than that of the bonds. Although the risk premium is not large during the period studied in Table 9.1, it is worth noting that the average premium taken over the past 120 years is about 7% per annum.

risk premium
The additional return expected for taking on additional risk.

The effect of inflation on rates of return—the Fisher effect

OBJECTIVE **2**

Explain the effects of inflation on rates of return.

Looking again at Table 9.1, the third column reports the *real* average return to investors. For now, the *real return* can be viewed as the return achieved in the absence of inflation. During the period 1984 to 2010 the average rate of inflation was about 3.8% per annum, which enabled the following real returns to be reported in Table 9.1:

	FIVE-YEAR BONDS	TEN-YEAR BONDS	SHARES
Nominal return	8.2%	8.3%	10.1%
less Inflation	3.8%	3.8%	3.8%
Real return	4.4%	4.5%	6.3%

When an interest rate is observed and quoted in financial markets, the rate is generally expressed as a nominal rate. The *real* rate of interest, in contrast, represents the rate of increase in actual purchasing power after adjusting for inflation. For example, if you have $1000 today and deposit it for one year at a nominal rate of interest of 5%, you will receive a total of $1050 in one year (comprising $1000 principal plus $50 interest). But, if prices of goods and services rose by 3% during the year, it would require $1030 (i.e. $1000 × 1.03) at the end of the year to purchase the same amount of goods and services that $1000 purchased at the beginning of the year.

What would be the increase in your purchasing power over the year resulting from your $1000 investment? The quick and easy answer appears to be 2%, found by subtracting the inflation rate from the nominal rate (that is, 5% – 3% = 2%). But this is not exactly correct. To be precise, let the nominal rate of interest be represented by i, the anticipated rate of inflation by r and the real rate of interest by R. Using these notations, the relationship between the nominal interest rate, the rate of inflation and the real rate of interest can be expressed as follows:

$$1 + i = (1 + R)(1 + r) \qquad \textbf{(9-1)}$$

or

$$i = R + r + rR$$

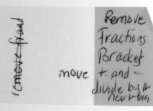

FYI

The reasoning behind the Fisher effect can be seen in this example: if you have $1000 at the beginning of the year and anticipated inflation is 3%, you will need $1030 at the end of the year just to compensate for inflation. To earn 2% 'real' on top of this, you will need $20.60 real interest (2% of $1030). So, in total, you need a return of $1050.60 at the end of the year, representing a nominal rate of 5.06% on the $1000 invested.

According to this equation, to gain a real rate of 2% per annum if the rate of inflation is 3%, you would need to earn a nominal rate of 5.06% (.0506 = .02 + .03 + (.02 × .03)).

This relationship between nominal rates, real rates and the rate of inflation is known as the *Fisher effect*.[1]

To further illustrate the concept of nominal versus real return using the data in Table 9.1, the 3.8% average annual inflation rate represents an *inflation-risk premium*. This means that an investor who earns only the rate of inflation from an investment has earned no *real* return. The real return is the amount by which the nominal return earned from an investment exceeds the rate of increase in the general price level for goods and services in the economy, as measured by the inflation rate.

Thus, the **nominal interest rate** is the actual interest rate paid or earned and the **real interest rate** is approximately equal to the nominal interest rate less the rate of inflation. (The exact relationship between nominal interest rate and real interest rate is given above in equation (9-1)).

In summary, the return from an investment can be viewed as coming from two major sources. The first is compensation to the investor for forgoing the use of his or her money over the period of the investment. This is known as the *opportunity cost* of investing, meaning that, by committing to a particular investment, the investor forgoes the opportunity to spend (and thus consume) 'now'. The second is the *risk premium*, representing the compensation to the investor for accepting a degree of uncertainty (risk) surrounding the investment's ability in the future to pay the return and to repay the funds invested.

Using these concepts, Table 9.1's return on shares can be decomposed as follows:

Nominal rate of return on ordinary shares	10.1%
– *Inflation rate*	3.8%
= *Real rate of return* on ordinary shares	6.3%
– *Opportunity cost* of funds (based on five-year bonds' real return)	4.4%
= *Risk premium* on shares	1.9%

nominal interest rate
The interest rate paid on debt securities without an adjustment for loss in purchasing power.

real interest rate
The nominal rate of interest less any loss in purchasing power during the time of the investment.

EXAMPLE 9.1   The real rate of return

What is the real rate of return if the nominal return is 10% per annum and inflation is 3% per annum?

Substituting in Equation (9-1), the real interest rate R can be calculated as follows:

$$1 + i = (1 + R)(1 + r)$$

$$1 + 0.1 = (1 + R)(1 + 0.03)$$

$$1 + R = \frac{1.1}{1.03}$$

$$R = 0.068, \text{ or } 6.8\% \text{ p.a.}$$

For answers go to MyFinanceLab or
www.pearson.com.au/9781442539174

The term structure of interest rates

OBJECTIVE 3

Describe the *term structure of interest rates.*

The preceding section showed that investors' returns depend on risk. In addition, the return on a debt security is influenced by the security's time to maturity. The relationship between the maturities and the returns of debt securities belonging to the same risk class is known as the **term structure of interest rates**. The graphical representation of the term structure of interest rates is known as the **yield curve**.

The rate of return on a debt security (such as a bond) is often called the rate of interest. However, another name for the rate of return on a debt security is the *yield*. The **yield to maturity** is the rate of return (expressed as an APR or nominal percentage rate per annum) that investors will earn if they hold the debt security until maturity. For the relationship to be meaningful to us, all factors other than the time to maturity—such as the chance of the borrower defaulting (i.e. not paying in the future)—must be held constant. Thus, at a particular moment in time, the term structure of interest rates represents *the relationship between observed rates of return (yields) and the length of time until maturity, on similar-risk debt securities.*

Figure 9.1 shows an example of the term structure of interest rates. In this case, the yield curve is upward sloping, indicating that at that point in time debt securities with longer terms to maturity have higher rates of return (yields). From this hypothetical yield curve, it can be identified that the rate of interest on a five-year note or bond is 11.5%, whereas the comparable rate on a 20-year bond is 13%. An upward-sloping yield curve is the most typically encountered type of yield curve and is commonly referred to as the *normal yield curve*. Sometimes the yield curve is downward sloping, resulting in an *inverse yield curve*. When the yield curve is inverse, the shorter term debt securities have higher yields than their longer term counterparts. If short-term and long-term debt securities have approximately the same rates of return, the so-called *flat yield curve* is observed. Occasionally, the term structure rises then falls, resulting in a 'humpbacked' yield curve.[2]

term structure of interest rates
The relationship between interest rates and the term to maturity, where the risk of default is held constant.

yield curve
A graphical representation of the term structure of interest rates.

yield to maturity
The annual rate of return the investor will earn if a bond is held to maturity.

FIGURE 9.1   The term structure of interest rates

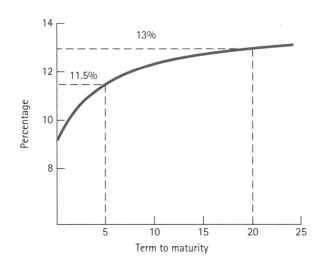

OBSERVING THE HISTORICAL TERM STRUCTURE OF INTEREST RATES

As might be expected, the term structure of interest rates changes over time as the economic environment changes. The term structure observed today may be quite different from the term structure a month ago and different still from the term structure one month from now.[3] A striking example of the changing term structure, or yield curve, was witnessed following the event known as '9/11' (the September 11, 2001 attack on the twin towers of the World Trade Center in New York). In a matter of days, short-term interest rates increased markedly as investors developed fears about the prospect of increased inflation.

Table 9.2 details the term structure, at different points in time, for Australian government securities with a maturity of 90 days, 180 days, two years, five years and ten years. Figure 9.2 subsequently shows the graph of these yield curves. In the early 1990s, the yield curve was inverse, suggesting that shorter debt securities attracted higher interest rates. The general level of interest rates in the early 1990s was also relatively high. One explanation of high interest rates was the booming economy at the time, which had led to Reserve Bank of Australia (RBA) intervention to depress demand and counter rapidly rising inflation. Then, low inflation and the global recession of the early 2000s saw a characteristic rate fall due to reduced demand for funds from business and individuals. The yield curve in 2004 shows a reduction in interest rates from the 2000 level, with a slightly inverse-humpbacked curve. An inverse yield curve is observable in June 2007, while the 2010 yield curve mirrors the shape of the 2004 curve except that the level of rates were lower in 2010, in part reflecting global recessionary forces in the wake of the GFC.

Having introduced some historical data for risk and return, let us now look in more detail at the question of how risk and return are *measured*, not only for individual assets but also for a portfolio of assets.

TABLE 9.2 Returns on government securities with different time horizons, at selected dates

	90-DAY	180-DAY	2-YEAR	5-YEAR	10-YEAR
June 1990	14.75%	14.63%	14.06%	13.8%	13.4%
June 2000	5.84%	5.87%	5.89%	6.05%	6.16%
June 2004	5.5%	5.57%	5.34%	5.67%	5.87%
June 2007	6.36%	6.46%	6.27%	6.17%	6.04%
June 2010	4.89%	5.00%	4.57%	4.97%	5.33%

FIGURE 9.2 Australian yield curves at selected times

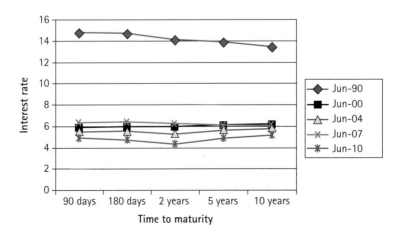

Measuring return

OBJECTIVE 4

Define and measure the expected rate of return of an individual investment.

historical return
The observed return earned on an investment in the past.

Earlier in the chapter, we saw some data on observed rates of return for shares and government bonds. These rates of return are referred to as **historical returns** because the returns have already happened—they are said to have been 'realised'. But investors' current decisions about where to place their investment funds are made on the basis of the *expected returns* or future payoffs on alternative investments—that is, on the basis of what they expect to get back from an investment.

The expected benefits or returns come in the form of cash flows, and therefore *cash flows*, not accounting profits, are the relevant variable that the financial manager should use to measure returns. This is consistent with *Principle 3: Cash—not profits—is king*. This notion holds true regardless of the type of security, whether it is a debt instrument, a preference share, an ordinary share or any mixture of these. The only difference is in the form in which the investor receives the cash flow (e.g. interest for debt, dividends and capital gains (hopefully!) for shares).

It is important to understand the distinction between these two concepts of return. Historical return is a backward-looking measure, while expected return is a forward-looking measure. In other words, historical return is the answer to the question: 'What *have* I earned on my investment?' while expected return is the answer to the question: 'What do I *expect* to earn from my investment?'.

EXPECTED RETURN

In our uncertain world, it is not easy for an investor to make an accurate assessment of future cash flows. The uncertainty associated with investment is apparent any time you buy shares and watch the price of the shares fluctuate up and down. At the corporate level, uncertainty comes into play in almost any decision made, but particularly when investing in new product lines or entering a new geographical market.

To illustrate the concept of uncertainty and expected return, let us assume that you are considering a share investment of $10 000. The future cash flows from owning the security depend to a large extent on the future state of the economy—this is a reasonable point of view given that the macro factors which 'drive' the overall share market are common to many firms, so that most firms benefit from a boom but suffer from a bust. Table 9.3 gives an estimate of what these cash flows might be for an economy that is alternately assumed to go into recession, show moderate growth, or 'boom' (showing strong economic growth). The probabilities assigned to these three possible states of the economic environment have to be determined subjectively, which requires management to have a thorough understanding of both the outlook for the general economy and the implications for the cash flows earned from the investment.

Table 9.3 shows that, in the next year, the investment could earn any of three possible cash flows depending on the state of the economy at that time. But from this information, how can a single rate of return expected from this investment be measured? One approach is to calculate an *expected* cash flow, which is simply the weighted average of the *possible* cash-flow outcomes (with the weights being the probabilities of the occurrence of the various states of the economy).

TABLE 9.3 Estimated returns on a $10 000 investment

STATE OF THE ECONOMY	PROBABILITY OF THE STATE	CASH FLOWS EARNED FROM THE $10 000 INVESTMENT	% RETURNS (CASH FLOW ÷ INVESTMENT COST × 100)
Recession	.2	$1 000	10% [($1 000 ÷ $10 000) × 100]
Moderate growth	.3	$1 200	12% [($1 200 ÷ $10 000) × 100]
Strong growth	.5	$1 400	14% [($1 400 ÷ $10 000) × 100]

The cash flows can be represented by letting X_1 designate the first possible cash flow, X_2 designate the second possible cash flow and so on, with X_n reflecting the final possible cash flow (and thus n is the number of possible states of the economy). Similarly, $P(X_1)$ indicates the probability that the first cash flow or state of the economy will occur, $P(X_2)$ the probability that the second cash flow or state of the economy will occur, and $P(X_n)$ the probability of the nth and final cash flow.

Next, the *expected* cash flow, X^*, may be calculated as the probability-weighted average of cash flows 1 to n, as follows in equation (9-2):

$$X^* = X_1 P(X_1) + X_2 P(X_2) + ... + X_n P(X_n) \tag{9-2}$$

So for the example in Table 9.3, where $n = 3$:

$$X^* = (0.5)(\$1400) + (0.3)(\$1200) + (0.2)(\$1000) = \$1260$$

As an alternative to computing an expected dollar return from an investment, we can also calculate an expected percentage rate of return earned on the $10 000 investment. As the last column in Table 9.3 shows, assuming strong economic growth the $1400 cash inflow earned on an investment of $10 000 represents a 14% return [($1400/$10 000) × 100]. Similarly, the $1200 and $1000 cash flows result in 12% and 10% rates of return respectively. Using these percentage rates of return in place of the dollar amounts, the expected rate of return, R^*, may be expressed as follows:

$$R^* = R_1 P(R_1) + R_2 P(R_2) + ... + R_n P(R_n) \tag{9-3}$$

In our example:

$$R^* = (0.5)(14\%) + (0.3)(12\%) + (0.2)(10\%) = 12.6\%$$

The above example illustrates that, although it is difficult to accurately predict the return on an investment, we can make predictions about the range of returns that we are likely to get, the probability that a particular return will eventuate, and hence the return that we can *expect* to get.

expected rate of return
The arithmetic mean or average of all possible outcomes where each outcome is weighted by its probability.

The **expected rate of return** may therefore be defined as the average of all possible outcomes, where those outcomes are weighted by the probability that each will occur. While return can be expressed in terms of an absolute dollar amount or a percentage, it is more common to use a percentage as the measure of return. The reason a percentage is used is to allow comparisons to be made between different investment opportunities requiring different outlays. For example, if you consider two investments paying 12% per annum and 14% per annum respectively, you know that the one that returns 14% is a better investment. On the other hand, a project that returns $150 000 is not necessarily a better project than one that returns $100 000, as we do not know the initial amounts invested in these projects (that is, we do not know the scale of the investments).

Share has a lower standard deviation = good & higher expected return

EXAMPLE 9.2 Calculating the expected rate of return

You are interested in investing in Qantas shares. Your friend who works as a financial analyst provides you with the following estimates regarding possible returns on Qantas for next year:

PROBABILITY $P(R_i)$	RETURN (R_i)
.2	25%
.5	15%
.3	5%

What is the expected return if you invest in Qantas?

According to equation (9-3), your expected rate of return is:

$$R^* = R_1 P(R_1) + R_2 P(R_2) + R_3 P(R_3)$$
$$= 0.2 \times 25\% + 0.5 \times 15\% + 0.3 \times 5\% = 14\%$$

Back to the principles

In the above example, we were interested in cash flows, not earnings, in computing the investment's rate of return. This is an important distinction, as noted in **Principle 3: Cash—not profits—is king**. Since we spend cash to make an investment it is natural for us to want cash in return. In this sense, it is cash that matters.

Concept check

9.2   When we speak of the 'benefits' from investing in an asset, what do we mean?

9.3   Why is it difficult to measure future cash flows?

9.4   Define 'expected rate of return'.

For answers go to MyFinanceLab or www.pearson.com.au/9781442539174

HISTORICAL RETURN

Unlike expected return, historical return is a measure of the return earned on a previous investment. As a result, the calculation of historical return is more straightforward and relies on historical data rather than requiring estimation of the probability of occurrence. The historical return over a particular period of time is calculated as follows:

$$R_t = \frac{P_t}{P_{t-1}} - 1 \tag{9-4}$$

where R_t is the historical return over the period beginning at time $t-1$ and ending at t

   P_t is the price of the investment at time t

   P_{t-1} is the price of the investment at time $t-1$

This historical return calculated as above is also known as holding-period return (see Examples 9.3 and 9.4). Intuitively, this is the return that is earned on an investment over a specific period of time.

EXAMPLE 9.3   Calculating holding-period return

Two years ago you bought 1000 shares in Foster's Brewery for \$12 each. Foster's shares are currently selling for \$15.50 per share. What is your holding-period return? Your holding-period return can be calculated using equation (9-4) above:

$$R = \frac{15.5}{12} - 1 = 0.2917 = 29.17\%$$

Note that this return is over a two-year period that you held Foster's shares. If you want to work out your return on a yearly basis you have to annualise the return. The simplest (non-compounded) method to annualise your return is to divide your holding period return by the number of years you hold the investment, as below:

$$R = \frac{\text{Holding-period return}}{\text{Number of years}} \qquad \text{(9-5)}$$

$$R = \frac{0.2917}{2} = 0.14585 = 14.585\%$$

With many securities investments the main source of return is the increase in the price of the investment. However, some investments also provide a regular stream of income. For example, an investment in shares may come with dividend payments. Alternatively, a rental property provides regular rental income. When you receive income from your investment, these incomes should also be accounted for in your return calculation. As a result, equation (9-4) can be generalised as:

$$R_t = \frac{P_t + CF_t}{P_{t-1}} - 1 \qquad \text{(9-6)}$$

where R_t is the holding-period return over the period beginning at time $t-1$ and ending at time t

P_t is the price of the investment at time t

P_{t-1} is the price of the investment at time $t-1$

CF_t is the income received from the investment over the period $t-1$ to t

EXAMPLE 9.4   Calculating holding-period return

You bought an investment property last year for $350\,000. This year the value of the property has gone up to $400\,000. You also received $12\,000 in rental income for the year. What is your holding period return on the investment?

The return is comprised of both the price appreciation and the rental income, and is calculated as:

$$R_t = \frac{400\,000 + 12\,000}{350\,000} - 1 = 0.1771 = 17.71\%$$

Concept check

9.5   What is the difference between expected return and holding-period return?

9.6   You bought CSR shares last year for $4.50 per share. CSR share prices are now $5.50 per share. You also received a dividend of $0.60. What is your holding-period return?

For answers go to MyFinanceLab or www.pearson.com.au/9781442539174

OBJECTIVE 5

Define and measure the riskiness of an individual investment.

Measuring risk

Because we live in a world of uncertainty, how we see risk is vitally important in almost all dimensions of our life and thus risk means different things to different people, depending on the context and on how they feel about taking chances. For the student, risk is the possibility

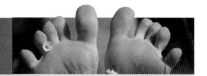

The first Chinese symbol represents danger, the second stands for opportunity. The Chinese define risk as the combination of danger and opportunity. Greater risk, according to the Chinese, means we have greater opportunity to do well, but also greater danger of doing badly.

of failing an exam or of not making his or her best grades. For the coal-miner or the oil-field worker, risk is the chance of an explosion in the mine or at the well site. For the retired person, risk means the possibility of not being able to live comfortably on a fixed income. For the entrepreneur, risk is the chance that a new venture will fail. In a financial context, managers want to understand risk so that they can assess the level of risk inherent in an investment.

To gain a basic understanding of investment risk, we might ask: 'What is risk and how is it measured?' To begin, let us examine the risk inherent in a single investment.

RISK AND A SINGLE INVESTMENT

To help us grasp the fundamental meaning of risk, consider two possible investments:

1. The first investment is an Australian government treasury bond that matures in one year and promises to pay an annual return of 8%. If we purchase and hold this security for a year, we are virtually assured of receiving no more and no less than 8%. For all practical purposes, the risk of loss is non-existent.
2. The second investment involves the purchase of shares in a local bank. Looking at the past returns on the firm's shares, the following estimates of the annual returns from the investment have been made:

CHANCE OF OCCURRENCE	RATE OF RETURN ON INVESTMENT
1 chance in 10 (10% or 0.1)	0%
2 chances in 10 (20% or 0.2)	5%
4 chances in 10 (40% or 0.4)	15%
2 chances in 10 (20% or 0.2)	25%
1 chance in 10 (10% or 0.1)	30%

Investing in the bank shares could conceivably provide a return as high as 30% if all goes well or no return (0%) in the worst case. However, in future years, both good and bad, we could *expect* a 15% rate of return on average, based on equation (9-3):

$$R^* = (0.10)(0\%) + (0.20)(5\%) + (0.40)(15\%) + (0.20)(25\%) + (0.10)(30\%) = 15\% \text{ p.a.}$$

Comparing the treasury bond investment with the bank investment, it can be seen that the treasury bonds offer an expected 8% rate of return while the bank has an expected rate of return of 15%. However, the investment in the bank is clearly more 'risky'—that is, there is greater uncertainty about the final outcome or which state of nature will eventuate. Stated somewhat differently, the bank investment has a greater variation or dispersion of possible returns, which in turn implies greater risk. Figure 9.3 shows these differences graphically in the form of discrete probability distributions. Remember that the *expected return* is just the weighted average of the possible returns from investing in the bank's shares.

Although the return from investing in the bank is clearly uncertain in contrast to the return from the treasury bonds, quantitative measures of risk are useful when the difference between two investments is not so evident. The standard deviation (σ) is such a measure. The standard deviation is basically a way of indicating the weighted average of the deviations of the returns

FIGURE 9.3 Probability distribution of returns for (a) treasury bonds, and (b) bank shares

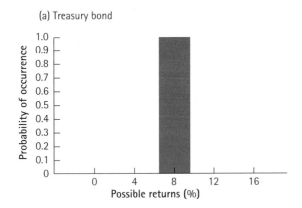

(a) Treasury bond

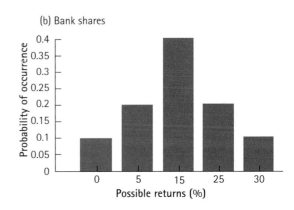

(b) Bank shares

from the mean (expected) value. If you look at Figure 9.3(b) you will see that some of the possible returns deviate either side of the expected (average) return of 15%, and the size and probability of these deviations indicates the degree of risk. Mathematically, standard deviation σ is simply *the square root of the average squared deviation of each possible return from the expected return*, as indicated in equation (9-7):

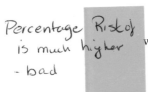

$$\sigma = \sqrt{\sum_{i=1}^{n} (R_i - R^*)^2 \, P(R_i)} \qquad\qquad (9\text{-}7)$$

where n = the number of possible outcomes or different rates of return on the investment

R_i = the value of the ith possible rate of return

R^* = the expected return

$P(R_i)$ = the chance or probability that the ith outcome or return will occur

For the bank, the standard deviation is 9.22%, computed as follows:

$$\sigma = \sqrt{\begin{array}{l}(0\% - 15\%)^2(0.10) + (5\% - 15\%)^2(0.20) + (15\% - 15\%)^2(0.40) + \\ (25\% - 15\%)^2(0.20) + (30\% - 15\%)^2(0.10)\end{array}}$$

$$= \sqrt{85\%} = 9.22\%$$

Although the standard deviation of returns provides a measure of an asset's riskiness, how should the result be interpreted? What does it mean? Is the 9.22% standard deviation for the bank investment good or bad? First, we should remember that statisticians tell us that an event will fall within one standard deviation of the expected value about two-thirds of the time (assuming that the returns are distributed 'normally'; that is, the distribution is shaped like a bell, being symmetrical and thus having 50% of values above the mean and 50% below).

Thus, for the bank investment with a 15% mean (or expected) return and a standard deviation (s.d.) of about 9%, we may reasonably anticipate that about two-thirds of the time the actual returns will fall between approximately one s.d. above the mean and one s.d. below the mean. In other words, about two-thirds of the values will lie between 6% and 24% (that is, the mean of 15% minus 1 s.d. of 9%, and 15% plus 1 s.d. of 9%). Thus, there is clearly quite a degree of uncertainty with this investment's return.

What about the treasury bond? It is essentially regarded as risk-free, and as Figure 9.3(a) shows, there is no deviation around the expected (average) return of 8%. There is only one expected outcome, so the standard deviation is zero.

A second way of answering the question about the meaning of a standard deviation figure is by comparing the investment in the bank against other investments. The attractiveness of a security with respect to its return and risk cannot be determined in isolation. Only by

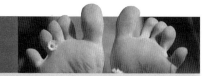

FYI

HUMAN BEHAVIOUR AND FINANCE: ATTITUDES TO RISK FOR DIFFERENT PROFESSIONS

In the wake of the GFC, many firms are putting more effort into assessing the various risks that confront the organisation. However, research suggests that different professions view risks differently, and thus the organisation's conduct, when facing uncertainty, might be influenced by the backgrounds and behaviours of different groups of staff. According to Incept Labs, finance professionals are likely to fall into six distinct groups, and examples of differences between professions include: *actuaries*, who are highly risk averse and believe that uncertainty can be 'tamed' by analysis of past data and models;

auditors, who believe that there are clear-cut 'right and wrong ways to do things'; *compliance officers* (staff who are responsible for ensuring the organisation adheres to its own risk policies), who have a low tolerance to risk, which they 'see almost entirely in terms of threat'; and *structured finance professionals* (whose work includes the process of securitisation), who have a 'win at all costs' attitude and a 'willingness to gamble'.

Source: 'Complex culture defines risk management', *The Australian Financial Review*, 21–22 August 2010.

examining other available alternatives can a conclusion be reached about the significance of a particular investment's risk. For example, if another investment, say an investment in a firm that owns a local radio station, has the same expected return as the bank (15%) but with a standard deviation of 7%, we would consider the risk associated with the bank (9.22%) to be excessive. In the technical jargon of modern portfolio theory (see later in this chapter), the radio company investment is said to 'dominate' the bank investment. This means that the radio company investment has the same expected return (15%) as the bank investment, but as it is less risky it will dominate in attracting funds from investors.

What if we compare the investment in the bank with one in a pizza bar franchise, an investment in which the expected rate of return is 24% but in which the standard deviation is estimated at 13%? Now what should we do? Clearly, the pizza franchise has a higher expected rate of return, but it also has a higher risk as measured by its larger standard deviation. With this example, we see that the real challenge in selecting the better investment comes when one investment has a higher expected rate of return but also exhibits greater risk. *Here the final choice is determined by our attitude towards risk, and thus there is no single correct answer.* One person might select the bank, while another might choose the franchise investment, and neither would be wrong. They would simply be expressing their tastes and preferences about risk and return.

Concept check

9.7 Define 'risk'.
9.8 How does the standard deviation help us to measure the riskiness of an investment?
9.9 Does greater risk imply a bad investment?

For answers go to MyFinanceLab or www.pearson.com.au/9781442539174

Risk and diversification

OBJECTIVE 6

Explain how diversifying investments affects the riskiness and expected rate of return of a portfolio of assets.

From the preceding discussion, risk can be defined as the variability of anticipated (expected) returns, and it can be measured by the standard deviation. Let's consider how risk is affected when an individual or a firm holds more than one asset. Table 9.4 shows annual standard deviation and return figures for some selected stocks that were listed on the Australian Securities Exchange during the period from January 1996 to August 2010.

According to the figures, Dominion Mining's stocks appear to be the most risky, with a standard deviation of 53.52% per annum, while an investment in Foster's would be the least risky. Remember, when making these statements, that we are presently associating the degree of risk with a stock's standard deviation. Hence, Foster's is 'safest' to the extent that its stock

TABLE 9.4 Annual returns and standard deviations of selected Australian listed shares and the All Ordinaries Index, January 1996 to August 2010

	ANNUAL STANDARD DEVIATION (%)	AVERAGE ANNUAL RETURN (%)
Amcor	18.38	0.10
David Jones	34.81	12.90
Dominion Mining	53.52	16.83
News Corporation	48.06	14.07
Coca-Cola Amatil Australia	22.04	5.78
Santos	27.05	12.71
Consolidated Media Holdings	25.50	12.42
Foster's Group	17.58	8.11
Woodside Petroleum	27.14	15.95
All Ordinaries Index	13.34	5.46

prices are the least volatile. It does not mean that by investing in Foster's stocks you are insured against losses.

What is more intriguing, however, is the standard deviation of the All Ordinaries Index, which is also presented in Table 9.4. This market index captures the average of the price movements of all the above companies as well as many other stocks that are listed on the Australian Securities Exchange. As a result, we might expect the standard deviation of the market index to be an average of the standard deviations of the component stocks. What we observe here provides a striking contrast. The standard deviation of the return on the market index is significantly lower than that of almost all of the individual stocks. It seems that by holding a collection of many stocks you can achieve a lower degree of variability in the combined returns than by holding just a single one. Although we have not figured out the secret to wealth creation, we have figured out a way to reduce risk. And the secret is 'diversification'—always invest in more than one financial asset. The benefit of diversification is encapsulated in the common saying: 'Don't put all your eggs in one basket.'

WHAT RISK HAS BEEN DIVERSIFIED AWAY?

To understand how risk can be reduced by holding a variety of securities, let's assume you were reading *The Australian Financial Review* (*AFR*) on 20 August 2010, and you saw that one of your shares—Billabong Ltd—had fallen 13% on the day. Analysts stated that this was due to factors such as an 11% drop in annual profit, together with a significant fall in forward orders for the company's products. You were hardly over the pain of your Billabong wipe-out when your eye caught the headlines relating to Perseus Mining—the other stock that you hold—which rose 4% on the same day, following positive results in one of its exploration programs.

Clearly, if you had owned only shares in Billabong you would have suffered from the large decline in its share price. Thankfully, your investment in Perseus helped to reduce the extent of your loss. This is an example of the benefits of being diversified—good performance of one stock can offset the bad performance of another.

It is therefore apparent that if we diversify our investments across different securities, rather than invest in only one share, the variability of returns of our portfolio should decline. This reduction in risk will occur if the returns from the investments do not move precisely together over time—that is, if they are not perfectly correlated. In other words, some of the volatility in returns of a particular share is unique to that share, as illustrated by Billabong's price change being due to factors that had nothing to do with Perseus's price change.

However, being *sensibly* diversified requires a little bit of thought and common sense. Shares belonging to the same industry tend to move together and, as a result, investing in four banks (for example, ANZ, NAB, Westpac and the Commonwealth) would provide little risk reduction. In contrast, if the objective is to reduce risk in a portfolio of shares, it would be more sensible to spread investments across different industries, for instance ANZ (a bank), Coca-Cola (a soft drinks manufacturer/distributor), Santos (a resources company) and David Jones (a retail department store). Doing this would most likely have a greater impact on reducing the volatility of the portfolio.

To be even more effective at reducing risk, you could invest in various large and small firms in different industries as well as in foreign companies. However, despite such widespread diversification, you would not be able to remove all the variation in return. Figure 9.4 shows graphically what might be expected to happen to the variability of returns as additional investments are added to the portfolio. It shows that a portfolio needs about 20 sensibly diversified investments to get most of the potential risk reduction, but it also shows that there is a limit to the risk-reduction effects of diversification—there is some risk that can't be removed.

The risk that cannot be removed is represented by the straight line that divides the shaded regions in Figure 9.4. Looking at the horizontal axis of Figure 9.4, it can be seen that the straight line represents the level of risk as *n* increases to the maximum number possible (*n* is the number of shares in the portfolio). Therefore, it represents the level of risk that on average is common to the market as a whole, since the entire market is as big as a portfolio can become!

This raises the question: why can't that level of risk be further reduced by more diversification? Looking at this from an economic perspective, there are various 'macro' factors whose effects are very widespread and so are more or less common to all stocks, which means that these factors cannot be removed. Two such factors are: (1) the general state of the economy (when an economy is booming, for example, most companies and their shares benefit); (2) interest rates (a rate rise is detrimental to most firms, directly through the cost of funds and indirectly because increased interest rates reduce consumers' discretionary incomes—a bigger proportion of their incomes is needed to pay debts such as house mortgages—thus reducing the ability to buy other goods and services).

In contrast to the risk that is, on average, common to the market as a whole, the risk that can be removed by diversification (that is, *diversifiable risk*) is the risk that is unique to each individual company. The opening example showed that one company's (Billabong's) unique circumstances led to a share-price fall on the same day as another company's (Perseus Mining's) shares increased in value. Statistically, these share-price movements are said to be *uncorrelated*. However, when shares tend to move in unison, the movements are said to be *correlated*. Thus, correlation is a key factor in assessing the opportunity to reduce risk through diversification, a point that will be addressed in more detail later in this chapter.

Summarising the picture portrayed in Figure 9.4, the total risk of a portfolio investment can be thought of as comprising two types of risk: (1) *firm-specific* or *company-unique risk*, and (2) *market-related risk*. **Company-unique risk** can also be called *diversifiable (unsystematic) risk*, since it can be diversified away. The underlying level of **market risk** is *non-diversifiable*

company-unique risk
The risk component that can be eliminated by diversification. Company-unique risk is also known as 'firm-specific' or 'diversifiable' risk, or 'unsystematic' risk.

market risk
The risk component that cannot be diversified away by holding more than one security in the portfolio. Market risk is also known as systematic risk or non-diversifiable risk and is measured by a factor labelled as *beta*.

FIGURE 9.4 Variability of returns compared with size of portfolio

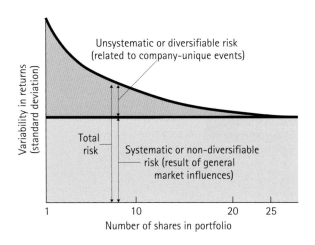

Finance at work

THE SUB-PRIME MORTGAGE CRISIS, THE GFC AND SYSTEMATIC RISK

Earlier chapters outlined the sub-prime crisis (SPC), which was the major trigger of the GFC. By August 2007, the sub-prime crisis had started to affect Australia. On 10 August 2007 the Australian share market fell 3.8%, the biggest one-day fall since '9/11' 2001. A subsequent series of large falls were experienced in the second half of 2008, and again after that year, as the implications of the GFC were absorbed by stock markets such as Australia's.

The SPC and GFC are examples of systematic or market risk, which tends to affect all stocks in the market. But this commonality is only true on average, and not all stocks are affected to the same extent. Macquarie Bank, for example, suffered one of the largest losses, with a fall of 7% on 10 August 2007, whereas most other stocks fell by a much smaller extent. The SPC and GFC provide real-life illustrations of the fact that, no matter how much you diversify, there are some risk factors that will cause volatility in your portfolio.

(systematic) risk, as it cannot be eliminated no matter how much an investor diversifies a portfolio of risky assets such as company shares. Figure 9.4 graphically shows these two types of risk. Total risk declines until there are approximately 20 securities, and then the decline becomes very slight.[4] The remaining risk, which would typically be about 40% of the total risk, is the portfolio's market risk. At this point, when the portfolio has at least 20 securities, its return is highly correlated with the average return on all securities in the marketplace.

WHAT RISK MEASURE IS RELEVANT AFTER SOME OF A PORTFOLIO'S STANDARD DEVIATION HAS BEEN DIVERSIFIED AWAY?

Principle 1 suggests that the higher the risk the higher the expected return. However, when it comes to a share that is part of a well-diversified portfolio, we know that part of the share's *unique* variability (standard deviation) can be offset by the variability of other stocks. Therefore, why should an investor be rewarded with a higher return for an individual stock merely on the basis of that stock's unique variability? When any single asset is combined in a well-diversified portfolio, standard deviation is no longer the relevant measure of risk for that asset. Instead, the relevant risk measure is *market risk*, as this is the only type of risk that investors cannot remove from a portfolio of risky assets.

Market risk can be measured as the responsiveness of a stock or portfolio to changes in a *market portfolio*. A market portfolio theoretically holds all the stocks available in the market. However, for practical purposes a market index is used to calculate the return on a market portfolio. It is also important to note that the market risk of a security is relative to the market to which it belongs. For example, to calculate the market risk of a stock that is traded on the New York Stock Exchange, you will use either the Dow Jones Index or the S&P 500 Index. The Straits Times Index will be used to calculate the market risk of a Singapore stock, for example Singapore Airlines. In Australia, the market index that is commonly used is the All Ordinaries Index.

Back to the principles

We have just explained **Principle 9: All risk is not equal—some risk can be diversified away, and some cannot.** As we diversify our portfolio, we reduce the effects of company-unique risk, but non-diversifiable risk or market risk remains, no matter how much we diversify.

Concept check

9.10 What risk is diversified away when an investor holds more than one asset in a portfolio?

9.11 Does it matter which assets are chosen to construct a portfolio to achieve a reduction in risk?

For answers go to MyFinanceLab or
www.pearson.com.au/9781442539174

International spotlight

WHY ARE INVESTORS HEADING OVERSEAS?

Improved international equity returns and diversification are the underlying reasons for adopting an overseas investing strategy. Diversification is an important motive for Australian investors, as the Australian share market accounts for only 2% of the world equity value. Although Australian investors are reputedly the keenest share owners in the world, with about half the population owning shares, the Australian share market is highly concentrated, dominated by a number of companies and sectors that account for the lion's share of market capitalisation. Thus, Australians who invest solely in the domestic share market are not sufficiently diversified. From the 1990s, institutional investors have considered international shares as a portfolio diversifier rather than as a source of extra income.

Investors should, however, be aware of what is meant by 'international shares'. By the new millennium, the index used to measure the performance of international shares, the Morgan Stanley Capital International (MSCI), comprised more than 50% US stocks. Specifically, these were 'large-cap' US stocks (that is, stocks with high *market capitalisation*, which is the multiple of the share price and the number of shares on issue). Therefore, investors might get less diversification with 'international' shares than they expect.

Nevertheless, given the weighting attached to US stocks in the MSCI, the benefits of investing in international shares

will depend on how well the US market performs. During six out of eight US bear markets between 1973 and 2003, a 20% allocation to stocks in Australia, Europe and the Far East provided a 2.3% greater return and 0.59% lower volatility on average than a portfolio of just US stocks. However, during US bull markets between 1973 and 2003, a 20% international equity allocation provided a 1.12% lower return and 1.18% lower volatility on average.[5] The bottom line is: international diversification results in lower volatility of return but not necessarily higher returns, depending on how the local markets fare.

The quest to 'go global' gained increasing support in the late 2000s from the low capital gains experienced by developed countries' share markets, with some prominent investment managers signalling increased allocations to the growth tigers of Asia, such as China and India. It is, however, important to consider the correlation between domestic market returns and the stock returns of developed economies. *Pensions and Investment* journal suggested in the mid-2000s that the correlation among developed markets is about 50%[6], which according to some criteria implies that a 30% weight should be allocated to international stocks. But this percentage of international stocks will have to be adjusted over time as the correlation changes.

Measuring market risk

OBJECTIVE **7**

Measure the market risk of an individual asset.

To help clarify the idea of market or systematic risk, let's examine the relationship between the returns on ordinary shares of the Australian and New Zealand Banking Group (ANZ) and the returns of the **All Ordinaries Index** (All Ords). The All Ords represents the general price movement of stocks that are listed on the Australian Securities Exchange (ASX). The change in the All Ords is therefore commonly referred to as the return on the market; that is, if you hold all stocks that are listed on the ASX you will effectively get a return that is equal to the return on the All Ords. All stock exchanges around the world have their own market indices and changes in these index values are widely quoted in the press as representing the direction of share prices for that market. Some examples are the Dow Jones Index for the New York Stock Exchange, the FTSE (pronounced 'footsie') for the London Stock Exchange, the Hang Seng Index for the Hong Kong Stock Exchange, the Straits Times Index for the Singapore Stock Exchange and the Nikkei for the Tokyo Stock Exchange.

The monthly returns for ANZ and the All Ords for 60 months from July 2005 to June 2010 are listed in Table 9.5 and compared graphically in Figure 9.5. It can be seen that in many

All Ordinaries Index
An index number representing the average value of shares on the Australian Securities Exchange. The change in the index number between two dates represents the average rate of return during that time interval (excluding dividends, the effect of which is incorporated into the All Ordinaries Accumulation Index).

TABLE 9.5 Monthly holding-period returns[a]: ANZ and the All Ordinaries Index, July 2005 to June 2010

MONTH AND YEAR	ANZ		ALL ORDINARIES INDEX	
	PRICE (A$)	RETURNS (%)	PRICE	RETURNS (%)
2005				
July	20.92	–	4346.7	–
August	21.61	3.30	4413.5	1.54
September	23.4	8.28	4592.6	4.06
October	22.96	−1.88	4412.7	−3.92
November	23.91	4.14	4583.6	3.87
December	23.95	0.17	4708.8	2.73
2006				
January	24.9	3.97	4880.2	3.64
February	25.72	3.29	4878.4	−0.04
March	26.5	3.03	5087.2	4.28
April	27.95	5.47	5207	2.35
May	26.45	−5.37	4972.3	−4.51
June	26.59	0.53	5034	1.24
July	25.25	−5.04	4957.1	−1.53
August	27.25	7.92	5079.8	2.48
September	26.86	−1.43	5113	0.65
October	29.04	8.12	5352.9	4.69
November	28.45	−2.03	5461.6	2.03
December	28.21	-0.84	5644.3	3.35
2007				
January	29.11	3.19	5757.7	2.01
February	29.3	0.65	5816.5	1.02
March	29.7	1.37	5978.8	2.79
April	30.6	3.03	6158.3	3.00
May	28.84	−5.75	6341.8	2.98
June	28.99	0.52	6363.4	0.34
July	28.3	−2.38	6187.5	−2.76
August	28.99	2.44	6248.3	0.98
September	29.7	2.45	6315.7	1.08
October	30.1	1.35	6779.1	7.34
November	28.16	−6.45	6593.6	−2.74
December	27.46	−2.49	6421	−2.62
2008				
January	26.01	−5.28	5697	−11.28
February	22	−15.42	5674.7	−0.39
March	22.55	2.50	5409.7	−4.67
April	21.9	−2.88	5657	4.57
May	21.68	−1.00	5773.9	2.07
June	18.72	−13.65	5332.9	−7.64
July	16.25	−13.19	5052.6	−5.26
August	16.61	2.22	5215.5	3.22
September	18.75	12.88	4631.3	−11.20
October	17.36	−7.41	3982.7	−14.00
November	14.8	−14.75	3672.7	−7.78
December	15.29	3.31	3659.3	−0.36
2009				
January	13.27	−13.21	3478.1	−4.95
February	13.31	0.30	3296.9	−5.21
March	15.75	18.33	3532.3	7.14
April	15.9	0.95	3744.7	6.01

MONTH AND YEAR	PRICE (A$)	RETURNS (%)	PRICE	RETURNS (%)
May	15.9	0.00	3813.3	1.83
June	16.49	3.71	3947.8	3.53
July	18.53	12.37	4249.5	7.64
August	21.29	14.89	4484.1	5.52
September	24.39	14.56	4739.3	5.69
October	23.06	–5.45	4646.9	–1.95
November	22.15	–3.95	4715.5	1.48
December	22.88	3.30	4882.7	3.55
2010				
January	21.73	–5.03	4596.9	–5.85
February	23.14	6.49	4651.1	1.18
March	25.36	9.59	4893.1	5.20
April	24.2	–4.57	4833.9	–1.21
May	22.31	–7.81	4453.6	–7.87
June	21.61	–3.14	4324.8	–2.89
Average monthly return		0.31		0.11
Monthly standard deviation		6.27		4.83

a For computational simplicity, dividends and any franking credits have been excluded from the calculation of monthly returns for ANZ. Likewise, the All Ords Index excludes dividends on its constituent companies.

FIGURE 9.5 Monthly holding-period returns: ANZ and the All Ordinaries Index, July 2005 to June 2010

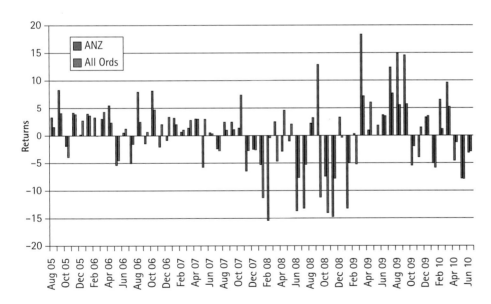

months the company return is positive when the market return is also positive. These monthly returns are computed using the concept of the **holding-period return**, equation (9-4).

For instance, the monthly return of ANZ and the All Ords for the month ending October 2005 is calculated as follows:

$$R_{ANZ,Oct05} = \frac{P_{ANZ,Oct05}}{P_{ANZ,Sep05}} - 1 = \frac{22.96}{23.40} - 1 = -0.0188 \text{ or } -1.88\%$$

$$R_{AllOrds,Oct05} = \frac{P_{AllOrds,Oct05}}{P_{AllOrds,Sep05}} - 1 = \frac{4412.7}{4592.6} - 1 = -0.0392 \text{ or } -3.92\%$$

holding-period return
The return an investor would receive from holding a security for a designated period of time. For example, a monthly holding-period return would be the return for holding a security during a particular month.

At the bottom of Table 9.5 the averages of the returns for the 60 months have also been computed, for both ANZ and the All Ords, as have the standard deviation for these returns. Because historical data are being used, it is implicit that each observation has an equal probability of occurrence. Thus the average return, R^*, is found by summing the returns and dividing by the number of months; that is:

$$\text{Average return} = \frac{\sum_{t=1}^{n} \text{return in month } t}{\text{number of months}} = \frac{\sum_{t=1}^{n} R_t}{n} \qquad (9\text{-}8)$$

and the standard deviation is computed as:

$$SD = \sqrt{\frac{\sum_{t=1}^{n}(\text{return in month } t - \text{average return})^2}{\text{number of months} - 1}} \qquad (9\text{-}9)$$

$$= \sqrt{\frac{\sum_{t=1}^{n}(R_t - R^*)^2}{n-1}}$$

An examination of Table 9.5 and Figure 9.5 suggests the following:

- The average monthly return for ANZ is greater than the average return on the All Ords: 0.31% compared with 0.11%.
- ANZ has experienced greater volatility of returns than the All Ords, with a monthly standard deviation of 6.27% compared with 4.83% for the index. It seems that over this 60-month period, ANZ has outperformed the market on one score (return) but has been outperformed by the market on the other score (risk). The lower risk of the All Ords is indicative of the fact that, as explained earlier, the unique risk of individual investments, such as ANZ, can

FYI

MEASURING RATES OF RETURN, DIVIDENDS AND THE IMPUTATION TAX SYSTEM

When equation (9-4) was applied to the computation of the holding-period returns on ANZ's shares, for simplicity no account was taken of the fact that periodic dividends may be received, thus adding to the return in the period when received. For example, consider the month ending March 2010. During that period, the share price increased by $2.22, from $23.14 to $25.36, representing a return of 9.59% as shown in Table 9.5. If a dividend of $1.00 had also been received in March, the total return would therefore have been $3.22. Thus, the rate of return in that month would have been $3.22/$23.14, or 13.92%, rather than 9.59%.

The situation is made more complex for some companies by the dividend imputation tax system. As seen in Chapter 2, some Australian companies pay franked dividends. The resulting franking credits may benefit some shareholders by reducing personal tax payable. For example, suppose that the March 2010 dividend carried tax credits worth 30 cents. If the simplifying assumption is made that these credits are received at the same time as the dividend, the dividend is 'worth' $1.30

to the shareholder and so the total rate of return for the period becomes $3.52/$23.14, or 15.21%.

The same principles apply to the computation of returns on the market index. Again for simplicity it has been assumed thus far that returns on the index exclude dividends. However, a measure called the *All Ordinaries Accumulation Index* incorporates the average value of dividends received by the companies included in the index. So, in practice, the Accumulation Index provides a more inclusive measure of average market returns than the All Ords. The complication is that some companies in the index will have dividends that carry franking credits, so ideally the value of these credits should be added to the return that is computed from the periodic changes in the index. This introduces two additional estimation problems: first, estimating the amount of the credits attributable to companies that are incorporated in the index; second, estimating the value of the credits to recipients (which depends on the average extent to which they can be used effectively in reducing personal tax payable).

be neutralised by diversifying the portfolio, in this case by notionally owning all the shares that are included in computation of the All Ords index.

- ANZ's stock price tends to increase (decrease) as the value of the All Ords increases (decreases). In 45 of the 60 months, ANZ's returns were positive (negative) when the All Ords returns were positive (negative). Obviously, there is a positive, although not perfect, relationship between ANZ's stock returns and the All Ords returns.

The market risk of a stock is the risk that a market movement will carry the stock with it. Market risk is therefore defined as the sensitivity of a stock's return to fluctuations in the return of the market. The relevant measure of market risk is **beta** (symbol β), which measures the average relationship between a stock's returns and the overall market returns. The market as a whole has a beta of 1. *Defensive stocks* have betas of less than 1 and are on average less risky than the market, while *offensive stocks* have betas greater than 1 and are on average more risky than the market.

To determine the market risk or beta of ANZ in our example, it is helpful to plot ANZ's returns against the All Ords' returns, which is done in Figure 9.6.

When a line of 'best fit', also known as the **characteristic line**, is drawn through the plotted points, the slope of the line is the *beta* of the stock.[7] Statistically, beta can be portrayed by the following equation, which is a way of representing the slope of the characteristic line:

$$\beta_j = \rho_{jm} \times \frac{\sigma_j}{\sigma_m} \tag{9-10}$$

where β_j = beta of security j

$\rho_{j,m}$ = correlation coefficient between returns on security j and market m returns

σ_j = the standard deviation of returns on security j

σ_m = the standard deviation of market returns.

ANZ's beta has been calculated to be 0.86 from the data in Table 9.5 (the appendix to this chapter details some of the principles involved in measuring a share's beta).

Beta shows the average movement in the stock price of ANZ *in response to* the movement in the general market (as captured by the return on a market index). Therefore, a way of interpreting this beta figure of 0.86 is to say that, on average, every 1% increase (or decrease) in the market induces a 0.86% increase (or decrease) in ANZ. So, a 10% increase in the market would,

beta, β
The relationship between an investment's returns and the market returns. This is a relative measure of the investment's non-diversifiable or market risk.

characteristic line
The line of 'best fit' through a series of returns for a firm's shares relative to the market returns. The slope of the line, frequently called beta, represents the average movement of the firm's share returns in response to a movement in the market's returns.

FIGURE 9.6 Monthly holding-period returns: ANZ and the All Ordinaries Index, July 2005 to June 2010

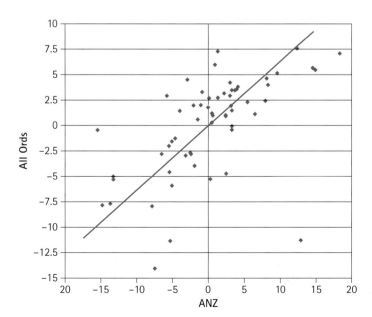

on average, be associated with an 8.6% increase in ANZ. (This same idea can be used to show that the market as a whole has a beta of exactly 1.0, because it is self-evident that a 1% increase in the market is associated with a 1% increase in itself!)

Beta is accordingly a measure of a firm's market risk or systematic risk, which is the risk that remains even after a portfolio has been diversified. It is this risk—and only this risk—that matters for any investors who have broadly diversified portfolios. So, if beta is a measure of a stock's systematic risk, how should we interpret a specific beta? For instance, when is a beta considered low and when is it considered high? If a share has a beta of 1.1, it means that on average the share price increases (decreases) 1.1% if the market increases (decreases) 1%. Additionally, a stock with a beta of zero has no systematic risk; a stock with a beta of 1 has systematic risk equal to the average for the market as a whole; and a stock with a beta exceeding 1 has more market risk than the typical stock. Most stocks have betas between 0.6 and 1.60. Debt securities, on the other hand, always have betas of zero, as their returns are independent of the returns of a market portfolio as measured by the returns on a market index.

Calculating beta is not an exact science. The final estimate of a firm's beta is heavily dependent on the chosen methodology. For instance, it matters whether you use 24 months in your measurement or 60 months (as most professional investment companies do). This chapter's computation using 60 specific months of price data suggests that the beta of ANZ is 0.86. However, a computation for the 24-month period July 2005 to June 2007 provides a figure of 0.98, which highlights the fact that beta depends on the time period used to calculate it and that it varies through time. However, although an individual stock's beta tends to be unstable— that is, varies over time—the beta of a portfolio tends to be more stable, a point to which we now turn.

Concept check

9.12 What is the measure of a market portfolio? Is the risk of this portfolio systematic, unsystematic or a combination of both?

9.13 What is the measure of market risk? What does that measure represent?

For answers go to MyFinanceLab or www.pearson.com.au/9781442539174

OBJECTIVE

Calculate the market risk of a portfolio.

Measuring a portfolio's beta

From Figure 9.6 it can be seen that the share price of ANZ on average moves a bit less than one-for-one with the market. At the same time there is also a lot of fluctuation around this characteristic line—the line that shows the *average* relationship of how the shares of ANZ move in response to the market as a whole. However, if the investor's portfolio was to be diversified and to consist of 20 shares with betas of about 1, like that of ANZ, and a new graph of the portfolio return and the market was drawn, the variation around the line could essentially be eliminated. The new graph would look something like the one shown in Figure 9.7. That is, almost all the volatility in returns has been removed, except for that caused by the general market, represented by the slope of the line. This is consistent with Figure 9.4, which shows that most of the unique risk has been removed in a sensibly diversified portfolio of about 20 stocks, so that the remaining risk is virtually identical to the average level of market risk.

One remaining question needs to be addressed. Assume that the portfolio is to be diversified, as has been suggested, but instead of acquiring shares with the same beta as ANZ, eight shares with betas of 1 and 12 shares with betas of 1.5 are bought. What would the beta of the portfolio become? As it works out, the *portfolio beta* is merely the weighted average of the individual securities' betas, with the weights being equal to the proportion of the portfolio invested in each security. Thus, the beta (β) of a portfolio consisting of n shares is equal to:

$$\beta_{portfolio} = \sum_{j=1}^{n} (\text{percentage invested in stock } j) \times (\beta \text{ of stock } j) \qquad \textbf{(9-11)}$$

So, assuming that equal amounts are spent on each share in the new 20-share portfolio, the beta would simply be 1.3, calculated as follows:

$$\beta_{portfolio} = \left(\frac{8}{20} \times 1.0\right) + \left(\frac{12}{20} \times 1.5\right)$$

$$= 1.3$$

Thus, whenever the general market increases or decreases 1%, the new portfolio's returns would on average change 1.3%, which says that the new portfolio has more systematic or market risk than has the market as a whole.

It can be thus concluded that the beta of a portfolio is determined by the betas of the individual shares. If a portfolio consists of shares with high betas, the portfolio will have a high beta. The reverse is true as well. Figure 9.8 presents these situations graphically for a portfolio with a high beta (1.5) and another with a low beta (0.5).

In a world where investors can create portfolios and get the risk-reduction benefits of diversification, the relevant measure of risk is no longer merely the standard deviation of a stock. Instead it is the stock's beta. In this respect, equation (9-10) shows that beta is made-up of *three* variables; first, the stock's own standard deviation σ_i; second, the average standard deviation of the market as a whole σ_m; and third, the correlation $\rho_{i,m}$ between returns on the stock i and the market m.

The concept and measurement of beta is useful when attempting to specify what the relationship *should be* between an investor's required rate of return and a share's risk or a portfolio's risk—that is, the higher the market risk, the higher the required return, which is a point that is discussed further towards the end of this chapter.

FIGURE 9.7	Holding-period returns: hypothetical portfolio and the market index

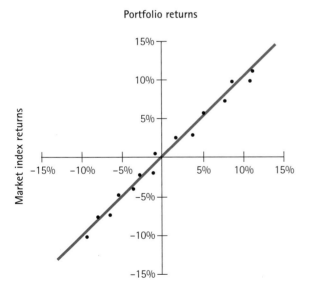

FIGURE 9.8	Holding-period returns: high- and low-beta portfolios and the market index

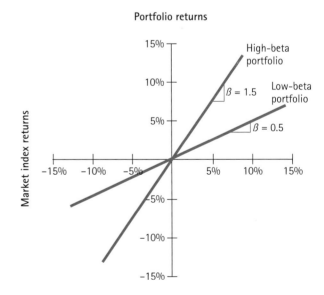

EXAMPLE 9.5   Calculating portfolio beta

Nigel Fang is a portfolio manager at Fifth Dimensional Pty Ltd. He is currently in charge of a portfolio that consists of a number of investments in both stocks and bonds. The following table provides information about the composition of Nigel's portfolio.

SECURITIES	PROPORTION (WEIGHT) OF PORTFOLIO	ESTIMATED BETA
Ten-year T-bonds	.05	0.00
Telstra debentures	.15	0.00
Qantas stocks	.20	1.13
Karoon stocks	.25	1.50
Venus Resources stocks	.35	1.25

What is the beta of this portfolio?

Applying equation (9-11), the beta of Nigel's portfolio can be calculated as:

$$\beta_{portfolio} = 0.05 \times 0.00 + 0.15 \times 0.00 + 0.2 \times 1.13 + 0.25 \times 1.50 + 0.35 \times 1.25$$

$$= 1.0385$$

Recalling the concept of weighted average introduced earlier in the calculation of expected return, you will see that a portfolio's beta is essentially a weighted average of the individual assets' betas, where the weights are determined by the percentage of the overall portfolio that is invested in each individual asset.

OBJECTIVE 9

The expected rate of return and risk of a two-asset portfolio

Calculate the expected return and risk of a two-asset portfolio.

The concept of diversification suggests that a rational investor would always hold a sensibly diversified portfolio of assets rather than an individual asset. As a result, while it is important to be able to compute the expected return and standard deviation of a single asset, as illustrated in earlier sections, it is of equal importance to be able to calculate the expected return and standard deviation of a portfolio of assets. Obviously, the complexity of these computations escalates as you increase the number of assets in a portfolio. When the number of assets becomes sufficiently large, computer programs are usually employed to help in the computational process. However, the simplest portfolio—a portfolio that consists of two assets—is adequate to illustrate many of the important technical aspects of portfolios and diversification.

EXPECTED RETURN OF A TWO-ASSET PORTFOLIO

Let's revisit Table 9.4, which provides the average annual return of some selected Australian stocks. If you had decided to invest in a portfolio made up of Dominion Mining and News Corporation, your return would obviously be higher than if you had invested in Foster's and Amcor. So, let's assume you put your funds into News Corp. and Dominion. If most of your money goes into Dominion, then your portfolio return will lean towards the return on that stock; that is, if most of the money is being invested in the higher return stock, the overall portfolio return would be higher than if you invested most of the money in the lower return stock.

From this introductory example, it can be seen that, when two assets are combined into a portfolio, the expected return of the portfolio will depend on two factors:

- the expected return of each of the assets
- the amount (proportion) of money invested in each of the assets.

Generalising, the expected return on a portfolio is simply the weighted average of the returns on the individual investments in that portfolio, as indicated in equation (9-12):

$$R_p = \sum_{i=1}^{n} w_i R_i \qquad\qquad \textbf{(9-12)}$$

where R_p is the expected return on the portfolio

w_i is the proportion of money being invested in asset i, also known as the *weight* of asset i

R_i is the expected return of asset i

For a two-asset portfolio, which is the focus of our discussion, equation (9-12) reduces to:

$$R_p = w_1 R_1 + w_2 R_2 \qquad\qquad \textbf{(9-13)}$$

where R_p is the expected return on the two-asset portfolio

w_1 is the weight of the first asset

w_2 is the weight of the second asset

R_1 is the expected return of the first asset

R_2 is the expected return of the second asset

EXAMPLE 9.6   Expected return of a two-asset portfolio

Alex has decided to withdraw $10 000 from his savings account in order to make his first investment in the share market. Following his father's advice, he invests $3000 in SkyCity Ltd and $7000 in IT World Ltd. The expected return on SkyCity is 8% per annum, while the expected return on IT World is 20% per annum. What is the expected rate of return on Alex's portfolio?

As Alex invests $3000 in SkyCity, the weight of this investment is:

$$w_1 = \frac{\$3\,000}{\$10\,000} = 0.3$$

And the weight of the investment in IT World is:

$$w_2 = \frac{\$7\,000}{\$10\,000} = 0.7.$$

Hence the expected return on Alex's portfolio is:

$$(0.3 \times 0.08) + (0.7 \times 0.2) = 0.164 \text{ or } 16.4\%$$

RISK OF A TWO-ASSET PORTFOLIO

The overall variability or risk of a portfolio can be measured by the standard deviation of its returns. However, unlike the expected portfolio return, the standard deviation of a portfolio is *not* simply the weighted-average of the standard deviations of the individual assets that make up the portfolio.

The standard deviation of a portfolio depends partly on the standard deviation of each asset in the portfolio. For example, if your portfolio was made up entirely of high variability stocks, then other things being equal the portfolio would have a high standard deviation. Furthermore, the standard deviation of a portfolio depends on the weights or proportions of funds invested in each asset. For example, if you invested most of your money in low standard deviation stocks, then other things being equal the portfolio would have a low standard deviation.

However, there is an additional ingredient that determines the standard deviation of a portfolio. This ingredient is the *correlation* between the returns of the assets in the portfolio. The role of correlation was introduced previously when we discussed market risk. To reinforce the role played by correlation in determining portfolio risk, Figure 9.9 shows a two-asset portfolio made up of investments A and C, with *half* of the funds invested in each. Therefore, from equation (9-12), the portfolio return is *half-way* between the returns on A and C.

It can be seen in Figure 9.9 that assets A and C move together in unison; when one is going up (down), so is the other in exact harmony. This is an example of *perfect positive correlation*. Figure 9.9 also shows that the variability (or standard deviation) of the A, C portfolio is exactly the same as that of A and C individually.

In general, the co-movement between two assets *i* and *j* is called the *correlation*, represented by a number called the *correlation coefficient*, symbol $\rho_{i,j}$ (ρ is the Greek letter 'rho'). When the correlation is perfectly positive (that is, the two assets move in perfect unison, as is the case with A and C), ρ takes on a value of +1.

In contrast, perfect *negative* correlation is indicated in Figure 9.10, where funds are equally divided between two different assets, E and F, so that, again, the portfolio return lies half-way between their individual returns. However, in this case, the two assets' returns are completely out of step (one goes up exactly as the other goes down), which is called *perfect negative correlation*, such that ρ takes on a value of –1. Figure 9.10 shows, in this extreme case, that there is no variability in the returns on the portfolio. This is because the portfolio return (half-way between E's and F's returns) forms a straight horizontal line.

Two generalisations about portfolio risk and correlation are supported intuitively by comparing Figures 9.9 and 9.10.

- The variability (standard deviation) of a portfolio depends on the correlation between the assets in the portfolio.
- The standard deviation of a portfolio decreases as the correlation decreases.

Therefore, as emphasised in earlier sections, the key to successful diversification is to select assets whose returns do *not* move in unison (are not highly positively correlated). Ideally, assets with returns that are negatively correlated would provide most risk reduction.

Correlation coefficient is in fact a standardised measure of what is called **covariance**. The covariance measure can be calculated as the product of the correlation coefficient and the standard deviations of the two assets, as indicated in equation (9-14). While covariance can theoretically take on any value, the correlation coefficient takes on values between +1 and –1. As seen, you can maximise your diversification benefit if you can identify perfectly negatively correlated pairs of stocks. Unfortunately, high negative-correlation stocks are hard to come by and the correlation coefficient tends to change over time. As a result, your two stocks might be negatively correlated today but six months down the track they may not be.

correlation coefficient
A standardised measure of covariance. While covariance can theoretically take on any value, the correlation coefficient takes on values between –1 and 1.

covariance
The statistical measure of the degree of co-movement between two asset returns. It essentially measures the tendency of the two stocks to 'co-vary'. A positive covariance between two stock returns suggests that as one return goes up the other tends to go up as well, and vice versa.

FIGURE 9.9 Variability of returns on assets A, C and a two-asset portfolio, with perfect positive correlation between the assets

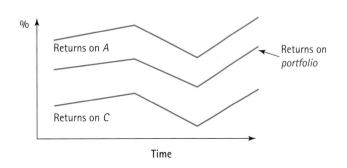

FIGURE 9.10 Variability of returns on assets E, F and a two-asset portfolio, with perfect negative correlation between the assets

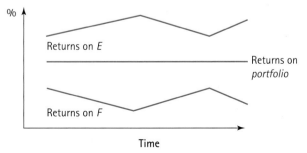

Your money

DIVERSIFYING YOUR INVESTMENTS, EASIER SAID THAN DONE?

Looking ahead to life after graduation, you may well be planning to apply the principles of this chapter. In particular, the significance of diversification has been stressed. In a sense, diversification is like getting something for nothing: you can reduce risk without a commensurate reduction in average returns.

Some degree of diversification arises naturally for many of us. We buy a residence and other personal assets. We hold at least some minimum amount of superannuation, given that legal requirements oblige employees to contribute a proportion of their incomes to superannuation. Maybe we add extra superannuation to this legal minimum. At stages in life when we have surplus cash, we may buy shares and other securities, or 'lifestyle' investments such as collectible motor cars or works of art.

But, to diversify requires more than a little bit of effort, even if you understand the notion of *sensible* diversification. Unless you have a lot of money at your disposal your personal portfolio will tend to be small and so selection of investments is relatively important (after all, you will not want a big proportion of your funds to disappear through the failure of one of your small number of stocks or other assets).

If you don't have much time or expertise, you may entrust your surplus investment cash to a *managed fund*. One problem here is that the funds charge fees for their efforts, so your potential returns are reduced accordingly. On the other hand, these funds tend to build diversified portfolios and so you might judge that they can spread the risk more effectively than you can.

However, the fact is that some funds perform better than others, but not necessarily consistently so: fund A might outperform fund B this year, but the tables might be turned next year; or a calamity such as the GFC might hurt one fund more than another. In this respect, investing in a single managed fund is analogous to investing in a single stock—all your eggs are in one (managed) basket. Thus, risk-averse investors who want others to do the work for them should consider spreading investments across a *range* of managed funds, so that the well-performing fund can counterbalance the poor performer. Of course, ultimately, diversifying in this way means that you will finish with average performance, the average of the managed funds. If the funds are diversified globally, you will obtain average global investment performance.

If you are not risk averse, you could choose just one managed fund and hope that it proves to be a good performer. Or, at this point, you could forget altogether about entrusting your money to others and back your own judgement in the casino or at the racetrack! But, in favour of diversification, Haggstrom and Raffle see it in behavioural terms as a defence against irrational behaviour (such as the herd mentality of everyone chasing a good thing and so pushing the price too high): '… investors are generally greedy. They see one asset moving up more than another and they want to get a piece of the action. Diversification is … a systematic way of counteracting this basic human emotion.'[8]

The relationship between covariance and correlation is:

$$\sigma_{1,2} = \rho_{1,2} \times \sigma_1 \times \sigma_2 \qquad \text{(9-14)}$$

where $\sigma_{1,2}$ is the covariance between asset 1 and asset 2

$\rho_{1,2}$ is the correlation coefficient between asset 1 and asset 2

σ_1 is the standard deviation of asset 1

σ_2 is the standard deviation of asset 2

COMPUTING THE STANDARD DEVIATION OF A TWO-ASSET PORTFOLIO

The previous section enabled us to conclude that the standard deviation (variability) of a portfolio depends on three factors:

1. the *standard deviation* of each individual asset in the portfolio
2. the *weight* (proportion) of portfolio funds invested in each asset
3. the *correlation* between the returns on the assets (or, alternatively, the *covariance* between the assets)

These three factors are found in the equation for σ_p, the standard deviation of a two-asset portfolio:

$$\sigma_p = \sqrt{w_1^2\sigma_1^2 + w_2^2\sigma_2^2 + 2\sigma_{1,2}w_1w_2} \qquad \text{(9-15)}$$

Substituting the right-hand side of equation (9-14) for $\sigma_{1,2}$, equation (9-15) can be expressed as:

$$\sigma_p = \sqrt{w_1^2\sigma_1^2 + w_2^2\sigma_2^2 + 2\rho_{1,2}\sigma_1\sigma_2 w_1 w_2} \qquad \textbf{(9-16)}$$

Equations (9-15) and (9-16) suggest that the standard deviation of a two-asset portfolio can be calculated using either the covariance ($\sigma_{1,2}$) or the correlation coefficient ($\rho_{1,2}$). Examining the relationship between these two measures, equation (9-14) shows that $\rho_{1,2}$ assesses merely whether or not two assets move in unison, whereas $\sigma_{1,2}$ assesses the *size* of the co-movement (as represented by the product of σ_1 and σ_2). Further, it can also be seen from equations (9-15) and (9-16) that a negative covariance (or correlation) between the two assets will make negative the third term in the right-hand side of the equation, hence having a significant effect on reducing the overall standard deviation of the portfolio.

EXAMPLE 9.7   Standard deviation of a two-asset portfolio

Further to the calculation of expected return for this portfolio in Example 9.6, Alex also wants to evaluate the risk of his portfolio by calculating its standard deviation. The standard deviation of SkyCity Ltd is estimated to be 15% per annum, while the standard deviation of IT World Ltd is 28% per annum. The returns of these two stocks have a correlation coefficient of 0.2. What is the standard deviation of Alex's portfolio?

From Example 9.6, we know that $w_1 = 0.3$ and $w_2 = 0.7$. The information above further indicates that $\sigma_1 = 0.15$, $\sigma_2 = 0.28$ and $\rho_{1,2} = 0.2$. Since we have data for the correlation coefficient rather than the covariance, we will apply equation (9-16).

$$\sigma_p = \sqrt{w_1^2\sigma_1^2 + w_2^2\sigma_2^2 + 2\rho_{1,2}\sigma_1\sigma_2 w_1 w_2}$$

$$= \sqrt{0.3^2 \times 0.15^2 + 0.7^2 \times 0.28^2 + 2 \times 0.2 \times 0.15 \times 0.28 \times 0.3 \times 0.7}$$

$$= \sqrt{0.044}$$

$$= 0.2097, \text{ or } 20.97\% \text{ p.a.}$$

Observe in this computation that the standard deviation of the portfolio (20.97%) is less than the weighted average of the standard deviations of the individual investments, which is 24.13% (that is, $0.3 \times 15\% + 0.7 \times 28\%$). This is another way of indicating the risk-reducing benefits of diversification and the role played by low correlation values. (To make the point even more convincing, compute the standard deviation for a correlation of +1.0.)

When the number of securities held in the portfolio increases, the calculation of the standard deviation of the portfolio becomes more complicated. Nevertheless, the underlying factors that determine this standard deviation remain the same. The standard deviation of an *n*-asset portfolio depends on the standard deviations of the assets constituting the portfolio, the proportion of investment in each of the assets and, most importantly, the correlation of the returns of the assets in the portfolio.

OBJECTIVE 10

Explain the relationship between an investor's required rate of return on an investment and the risk of the investment.

The investor's required rate of return

In a preceding section, beta was developed as the measure of the *market risk* of an investment, as this is the risk that investors cannot remove by diversification. This section examines the concept of the investor's required rate of return and shows how this can be related to the beta measure of market risk. That is, the section develops a *relationship* between market risk and the required rate of return, a critical step in the progress of financial management.

GFC

DID PORTFOLIO THEORY 'COLLAPSE' DURING THE GFC?

One of the most striking features of the GFC was that stock markets appeared to collapse just about across the board, along with other markets such as property. As has often been remarked, the GFC's effects were *systemic*, that is spread across much of the global economic landscape. The nature of a truly systemic collapse is that different markets and sectors suffer more or less simultaneously. This implies that those sectors' returns become aligned or, in the terminology of this chapter, *highly correlated*. As a consequence, there may be a temptation to claim that portfolio theory has collapsed, too, because being diversified did not necessarily save investors from the downside impacts of the GFC.

However, we believe, to the contrary, that a GFC-type systemic collapse is not at all inconsistent with portfolio theory. After all, the theory is quite clear in showing that, if sectors become aligned or move in unison (correlations increase), the benefits of diversification are lessened. Perhaps the problem with critics of portfolio theory is one of perspective. For practising portfolio managers to rely on portfolio theory, they are implicitly assuming that investment sectors are not highly correlated. So, when the GFC came, it was their assumptions that were at fault, not the theory as such. Portfolio theory is relatively modern, dating back only a few decades, during which there had not been a massive system-wide shock until the GFC came about, and so onlookers had never before experienced such a calamitous event. Therefore, they may never have questioned the universality of

their assumption that today's low correlations will be tomorrow's correlations, under all economic conditions.

Furthermore, it is an oversimplification to claim that all market/investment sectors collapsed simultaneously. For instance, bond portfolio returns have been high in the post-GFC era, as a result of low interest rates pushing up bond prices and returns.[9] PIMCO, the world's biggest manager of bond funds, has posted consistently high returns during the several years since the subprime crisis.[10] Furthermore, developing countries such as China and India were not set back much at all by the GFC, with their economies rebounding swiftly.

The old adage 'Don't put all your eggs in one basket' has been around a lot longer than portfolio theory, but it too would have been challenged by the events surrounding the GFC. In a sense, however, there is nothing wrong with the adage, it is more a case that the GFC restricted the number of 'baskets' available. However, now that professional investment managers have taken a hit from the GFC, they will no doubt learn from the experience. In particular, they will more actively look for warning signs of other potential systemic shocks. And they will be more critical in their reliance on correlations—they will think more constructively about which asset sectors tend to escape the systemic net. This may mean that the primacy of *asset allocation* over *asset selection* will be reversed to some extent.

Back to the principles

The point should be increasingly clear—in the words of **Principle 9: All risk is not equal—some risk can be diversified away, and some cannot**. As we diversify our portfolio, we reduce the effects of company-specific risk but non-diversifiable risk, or market risk, still remains. It is therefore the market risk that we must be concerned about. Beta is the measure of this risk and is represented by the slope of the characteristic line. The slope of the characteristic line indicates the average response of a stock's returns to the change in the market as a whole.

THE REQUIRED RATE OF RETURN CONCEPT

An investor's **required rate of return (RRR)** can be defined as the minimum rate of return that is necessary to attract that investor to purchase or hold a particular security. How can it be determined what the minimum return should be? One way is to determine the investor's opportunity cost of making an investment; in other words, if that investment is made, the investor must forgo the opportunity to earn the return available from the next best investment. This forgone return is the opportunity cost of undertaking the investment and consequently is the investor's required rate of return. In other words, investors choose a particular investment with the intention of achieving a rate of return that is sufficient to warrant making that investment.

required rate of return (RRR)
The minimum rate of return necessary to attract an investor to purchase or hold a security. (It is also the discount rate that equates the present value of the cash flows with the value of the security).

For instance, if a share with a particular level of risk is providing a rate of return of 14%, an investor should require at least 14% on an alternative investment with the same level of risk.

There is also a link between the required rate of return and the price of an investment. An investment will be made only if its purchase price is low enough relative to its expected future cash flows so that it provides a rate of return greater than or equal to the required rate of return. To illustrate: your required rate of return is 14%, and if the investment is expected to provide cash flows of $114 in a year's time, you would be willing to pay no more than $100 today for the investment. This is because paying that price will return you $14 on $100, or 14%.

To better understand the nature of an investor's required rate of return, the rate of return can be separated into its basic components: the *risk-free rate of return* plus a *risk premium*. This can be expressed as an equation:

$$R = R_f + RP \tag{9-17}$$

where R = the investor's required rate of return
R_f = the risk-free rate of return
RP = the risk premium

The risk-free rate of return rewards investors for deferring consumption but provides no return for accepting risk. That is, the risk-free return can be viewed as the base compensation for the fact that investors invest today so that they can consume more later. By itself, the risk-free rate should be used as the required rate of return (also known as the discount rate) only for *riskless* investments. Arguably, the measure for the risk-free rate is the rate of return on short-term government securities such as Australian treasury notes (these have effectively zero default risk as well as little likelihood of significant market-price movement within a short time-frame).

The risk premium, RP, is the additional return investors should expect to receive for accepting risk. As the level of risk increases, investors will demand additional expected returns. Even though they may not actually receive this incremental return for risk, they must have a reason to *expect* it; otherwise, why would they expose themselves to the chance of losing all or part of their money?

THE CAPITAL ASSET PRICING MODEL (CAPM)

We have seen that (1) for diversified investors, systematic (market) risk, as represented by beta, is the only relevant risk—the rest can be diversified away—and (2) the required rate of return, R, equals the risk-free rate, R_f, plus a risk premium, RP. Let us now examine how investors' required rates of return are actually estimated. Looking at equation (9-17), it can be seen that the really tough task is how to estimate the risk premium.

The finance profession has had difficulty in developing a practical approach to measuring risk premiums and thus investors' required rates of return, but financial managers most often use a method called the **capital asset pricing model (CAPM)**. Despite its critics, the CAPM provides an intuitive approach for determining the return that an investor should require on an investment, given the asset's systematic (market) risk.

capital asset pricing model (CAPM)
An equation stating that the expected rate of return on an investment is a function of (1) the risk-free rate, (2) the investment's systematic risk, and (3) the expected risk premium in the market.

Equation (9-17) provides the natural starting point for measuring the investor's required rate of return and sets us up for using the CAPM. Rearranging this equation to solve for the risk premium (RP), we have:

$$RP = R - R_f \tag{9-18}$$

which simply says that the risk premium for a security, RP, equals the security's expected return, R, less the risk-free rate existing in the market, R_f. For example, if the expected return for a security is 15% and the risk-free rate is 7%, the risk premium is 8%. Also, if the average expected return for the market, R_m, is 12%, and the risk-free rate, R_f, is 7%, the risk premium for the general market would be 5%. This 5% risk premium would apply to any security having systematic risk equivalent to the general market, whose beta is 1.

In this same market, a security with a beta of 2 should provide a risk premium of 10%, or twice the 5% risk premium existing for the market as a whole. Hence, in general, the appropriate required rate of return for the *j*th security, R_j, should be determined by:

$$R_j = R_f + \beta_j (R_m - R_f) \qquad \qquad \textbf{(9-19)}$$

Equation (9-19) is the CAPM. Thus, the capital asset pricing model is an equation showing that the expected rate of return on some investment *j* is a function of:

- the risk-free rate of return, R_f
- the investment's systematic (market) risk, β_j
- the expected risk premium in the market, $R_m - R_f$

This equation designates the risk–return trade-off existing in the market, where risk is measured by beta.

Figure 9.11 graphs the CAPM as the **security market line**, which is simply a graphical presentation of the CAPM.

As presented in this figure, securities with betas equal to 0, 1 and 2 should have required rates of return as follows:

if $\beta_j = 0$: $R_j = 7\% + 0(12\% - 7\%) = 7\%$
if $\beta_j = 1$: $R_j = 7\% + 1(12\% - 7\%) = 12\%$
if $\beta_j = 2$: $R_j = 7\% + 2(12\% - 7\%) = 17\%$

where the risk-free rate, R_f, is 7% and the expected market return, R_m, is 12%.

The first case ($\beta = 0$) simply reaffirms that the required rate of return on a risk-free investment, one with a beta of 0, is equal to the risk-free rate, 7%. The second case confirms that the market as a whole, or any other security or portfolio with the same level of systematic risk ($\beta = 1$), would have a risk premium of 5% and thus a required rate of return equal to 12%. The final case features an investment with a level of systematic risk twice that of the market, so $\beta = 2$, and therefore there is twice the risk premium at 10% and thus a required return of 17%.

security market line
A graph of the capital asset pricing model; the return line that reflects the attitudes of investors regarding the minimal acceptable return for a given level of systematic risk (beta).

FIGURE 9.11   Security market line (graph of the CAPM)

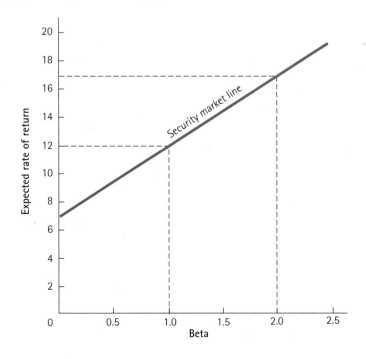

EXAMPLE 9.8 Measuring a share's required rate of return

To illustrate the use of beta in estimating a fair rate of return for a given stock, let us suppose a financial analyst is endeavouring, in 2010, to determine a fair rate of return on Telstra's ordinary shares ('fair' return meaning expected rate of return in accordance with the CAPM). As indicated above, to use the CAPM requires three inputs into the right-hand side of equation (9-19), namely (1) the expected risk-free rate of return, R_f; (2) the stock's expected beta β; and (3) the expected market risk premium, $R_m - R_f$.

1. The expected risk-free rate of return, R_f
   Customarily, analysts use the current yield on government bonds as a proxy for the (expected) risk-free rate of return. In this respect, today's bond yield is forward looking rather than historical in nature—it reflects investors' expectations about returns over the coming period. Sometimes it is argued that short-term government securities are the closest thing to 'risk-free', because imminent default is improbable and also the price volatility of short-term securities is low compared to that of long-term bonds. However, in a recent paper, Officer and Bishop argue that the current yield on long-term government bonds should be used as the estimator of the expected risk-free rate. Their main argument is that—in a context such as capital budgeting—the investor has a long-term horizon rather than a short-term outlook.[11]

   Based on this reasoning, Table 9.2 suggests that a rate of about 5.3% per annum (the 2010 yield on 10-year government bonds) should be used as the estimate of R_f.

2. Telstra's expected beta, $β_{Telstra}$
   Using methods explained earlier in this chapter, Telstra's historic beta (looking back from 2010) is estimated to be about 1.05. However, historic betas are somewhat unstable over time, so this figure may not be a particularly good predictor of the forthcoming or expected beta. In this regard, just as the beta of a portfolio is more stable than that of an individual stock, the average industry beta tends to be more stable over time than an individual company's stock, the industry beta being 0.95 for the telecommunications industry.

   Accordingly, in equation (9-19) the analyst would use 0.95 as the estimate of $β_{Telstra}$.

3. The expected market risk premium, $R_m - R_f$
   Based on an analysis of theoretical reasoning, along with conventions adopted by practitioners and comparisons with other developed countries, Officer and Bishop argue that the long-term historical risk premium is the most satisfactory predictor of the *expected* risk premium. One reason for this is that a long-term measure avoids giving undue influence to 'one-off' events such as the Australian stock market's fall of 42% in 2008: 'Looking at the longest time period provides a weighting of events in accordance with their "likelihood" of occurrence'.[12] Accordingly, they have calculated Australia's market risk premium as about 7% for the period 1883 to 2008 (including an estimate of the value of franking credits under the dividend imputation tax system that was introduced in 1987). Thus, the analyst would adopt the figure of 7% for the expected market risk premium, $R_m - R_f$.

   Overall, therefore, by substitution in the CAPM, the analyst would estimate the expected rate of return on Telstra's ordinary shares to be about 12%:

$$R_{Telstra} = R_f + β_{Telstra}\,(R_m - R_f)$$
$$= 5.3\% + 0.95(7\%)$$
$$= 12\%$$

Before concluding this section, let's recap the notion of the market risk premium (MRP) and its role in the CAPM.

The market return R_m represents the average return that the investor receives for spreading the investment across the market as a whole, that is across a fully diversified portfolio (thus, this return is estimated by measuring the average return on a suitable stock index). Therefore, the MRP, $R_m - R_f$, is the average percentage return by which the market beats a risk-free investment (the return on a risk-free investment being estimated by the return on government bonds).

Next, the beta of the market as a whole is 1, so (according to the CAPM) an investor who invests in an individual stock or portfolio whose beta is 1 expects also to receive the MRP. And, since beta is an indicator of the systematic or market risk of a security, a security with a beta of 0.9 will command a risk-premium that is 0.9 of the MRP, or a security with a beta of 1.5 will require a risk-premium of 1.5 times the MRP.

Criticisms of CAPM

Example 9.8 directs our attention to a number of problems with using the capital asset pricing model (CAPM) to estimate the expected return on a security (some commentators also use the term 'fair return'). The basic problem is that we only have historic data for a stock's beta, the risk-free rate and the market-risk premium, whereas the model is endeavouring to estimate the *expected* return. Choosing suitable estimates is therefore, invariably, somewhat subjective.

For a number of years, the CAPM was touted as the new investment technology and received the blessing of the vast majority of professional investors and finance academics. The CAPM was attractive largely because of its ability to present important theoretical insights (which academics loved) in simple and practical terms that could be applied in practice (which professional investors loved). In more recent years, however, researchers have questioned whether the model really works.

The CAPM, like any abstract theory, has weaknesses. For example, it might be questioned whether the risk of an asset can be totally captured in the single dimension of sensitivity to the market, as the CAPM proposes. There is some evidence that such things as the firm's size and various accounting ratios may affect risk–return relationships. Also, financial managers could become discouraged in their efforts to measure a security's beta if they found that different computation methods and different periods of measurement gave noticeably different results. An even more basic issue is the ability to test the model empirically. Some argue that the accuracy of the model cannot be verified because it cannot be known with certainty that the 'true market portfolio' is being used in comparing systematic risk and returns.

Although critics of the CAPM have been vocal, the model is still widely used. Only one alternative theory has been offered as a complement to, and even as a substitute for, the CAPM. This newer theory, the *arbitrage pricing theory (APT)*, considers multiple economic factors when explaining required rates of return, rather than looking at systematic risk or general market returns as the single determinant of an investor's required rate of return. However, despite having some desirable features and potential for the future, the arbitrage pricing model has yet to be of much practical use.

Whichever model is used, one key point remains. To formulate a complete concept or understanding of security valuation, the topic of the next chapter, the nature of the investor's required rate of return, must be understood. The required rate of return, which serves as the discount rate in the valuation process, is the investor's minimum acceptable return that would induce him or her to purchase or hold a security.

Back to the principles

The conclusion of the matter is that **Principle 1: The risk-return trade-off—we won't take on additional risk unless we expect to be compensated with additional return**, is truly alive and well.

For answers go to MyFinanceLab or
www.pearson.com.au/9781442539174

Finance at work

NEGATIVE BETAS?

Although portfolio betas tend to be stable, individual betas are not always either stable or particularly meaningful. A classic example of how individual stock betas can sometimes be misleading is described by Burton G. Malkiel in his book, *A Random Walk Down Wall Street*.[13] Malkiel describes how Meade Johnson, following its takeover by Bristol–Myers, had a negative beta in the 1960s. Apparently, Meade Johnson introduced a product called 'Metrecal', a dietary supplement that Meade Johnson sold to consumers, who drank this instead of eating their normal lunches. In any case, the public loved it, and Meade Johnson's stock shot up in price just as the market sank into a deep slump. As the market rebounded in 1963 and 1964, the Metrecal fad died and Meade Johnson dropped in price, again moving in an opposite direction from the market. Later in the 1960s, just as the market began to drop, Meade Johnson reintroduced the same product, renamed 'Nutrament', advertising it as a drink to add to the normal diet in order to put on weight. Once again, Meade Johnson's stock price went up as the market went down. The result of all this was that Meade Johnson had a negative beta. Needless to say, it would be unfortunate if capital-budgeting decisions were made using Meade Johnson's beta as the yardstick, for using the CAPM might imply shareholders would accept a negative return! The point here is that betas for individual stocks are not always reliable. In fact, typically only about 30% of the variation in returns of a stock can be statistically related to the market portfolio, and sometimes it is as low as 5%.

ONE STEP FURTHER

Understand the fundamental principles of portfolio theory.

AN OVERVIEW OF PORTFOLIO THEORY

By now you will have developed an appreciation of the importance of diversification. Diversification can eliminate firm-specific risk, leaving systematic risk the only source of risk for a well-diversified portfolio. However, how do we go about choosing assets for a portfolio? General principles regarding portfolio construction were documented by Harry Markowitz in 1952 in his seminal article entitled 'Portfolio selection'. Markowitz's work has provided a foundation for a substantial amount of academic material and practical applications.

Stock selection

To construct a portfolio of stocks there are at least two questions that you need to ask:

1. What stocks should I choose?
2. How should I allocate my funds among these stocks?

In relation to the first question, the guiding principle is that diversification works best when stock returns do not move precisely together. As a result, you should be looking for stocks that do not have a tendency to move in the same direction at the same time. You want pairs of stocks that are likely to move in opposite directions. As indicated earlier, stocks that belong to different industries, have different sizes and have different growth potentials are best for diversification purposes. Stocks that belong to the same industry and are similar in size and growing potential tend to move together and produce very little diversification benefit.

Once you have identified the stocks to be included in your portfolio, it is time to answer the question of how to divide your money between the stocks. Naturally, as you change the amount of money invested in each of the stocks, the risk and return parameters of the portfolio, as measured by standard deviation and expected return, will change. If you work with a portfolio that consists of 20 stocks, you will end up with hundreds of combinations of risk and return. Some of these combinations will be clearly superior to others in terms of the risk–return trade-off. 'Superior' portfolios will have a higher level of return for the same level of risk, or a lower level of risk for the same level of return. Markovitz termed these portfolios '**efficient portfolios**'. You need to allocate your money between your selected stocks in such a way that you end up with an efficient portfolio. There is never only one efficient portfolio with the same risk–return characteristics and therefore the final decision depends on your tolerance for risk. If you are a risk-taker, you may want to consider an efficient portfolio that has relatively high levels of risk and return. On the contrary, if you want to lead a more peaceful life, a portfolio with lower levels of risk and return may be the one for you.

efficient portfolios
Portfolios with a higher level of return for the same level of risk, or a lower level of risk for the same level of return.

Asset allocation

Having a portfolio of stocks that is 'efficient' means that you have reduced your overall risk without having had to compromise too much return. Nevertheless, it might occur to you one day that apart from stocks there are other financial securities in the market that you can also invest in, such as bonds, to further diversify your portfolio. Diversifying with different kinds of assets (such as stocks, bonds and real estate), as opposed to diversifying within one asset class, is called **asset allocation**. Markowitz showed that by combining a stock portfolio with an investment in bonds investors can achieve an even better portfolio. Therefore, there is no reason for investors to hold a stock portfolio in isolation. In order to come up with the most superior portfolio, the stock portfolio should be combined with an investment in a risk-free asset. Empirical evidence confirms the benefit of asset allocation. Analysts report that over 91% of the differences in pension fund returns in the United States can be accounted for by the asset allocation decision, while only 4.6% of the difference is attributable to the decision of selecting specific securities.[14]

asset allocation
Identifying and selecting the asset classes appropriate for a specific investment portfolio and determining the proportions of these assets within the given portfolio.

FYI

Investors who diversify sensibly can get a higher return for a given level of risk, or can have less risk for a given level of return. Portfolio managers who diversify internationally may benefit from a relatively low correlation between their home securities markets and foreign markets, thus giving further potential to reduce risk below the level that would be obtained if the investment portfolio was confined to the home market. However, there is a need for the investor to understand that, by investing overseas, the portfolio is exposed to a new kind of risk—foreign-exchange (or currency) risk.

For example, suppose the exchange rate was A$1 to US$0.50 and at that time an Australian portfolio manager spent A$100 million to purchase US securities worth US$50 million.

Then, during the following year, suppose that the Australian market returned an average of 5% while the US market returned 10%. Thus, the investment in the United States will have grown to US$55 million (US$50m × 1.1) as opposed to A$105 million (A$100m × 1.05) if the funds had been kept in the Australian market. On the face of it, the portfolio manager has benefited more from the US investment with the higher rate of return. But what if the exchange rate has varied and A$1 now buys US$0.55 at the end of that year? In that case, the investment now worth US$55 million is valued at only A$100 million (A$55m/0.55), which represents a return of 0% when measured in Australian dollars.

OBJECTIVE

What determines share prices?

Explain the notion of efficient markets and its importance to share prices.

Our earlier review of financial market history tells us that stock returns are subject to substantial fluctuations. As an investor, how should you use this information to form your portfolio? Should you invest all of your retirement funds in stocks, since historically stocks have performed very well? Or, should you be timing the market, buying stocks when the returns look good and buying bonds when the stock market is looking rather weak?

To answer these questions, we must first understand what causes stock prices to move from month to month. In short, stock prices tend to go up when there is good news about future profits, and they go down when there is bad news about future profits. This, in part, explains the mainly favourable returns of Australian stocks, on average, during much of the past century or so, and it also explains the very bad GFC-related returns of 2008 and 2009.

One might be tempted to use the above logic and invest more in stocks when the economy is doing well and less in stocks when the economy is doing poorly. Indeed, one might think that it is possible to do even better by picking the individual stocks of companies whose profits are likely to increase. For example, one might want to buy oil stocks when oil prices are increasing and at the same time sell airline stocks, since the profits of these latter firms will be hurt by the increased cost of jet fuel.

Unfortunately, according to the *efficient markets hypothesis (EMH)*, a strategy of shifting one's portfolio in response to public information, such as changes in oil prices, will not result in higher expected returns. This is because in an efficient market, stock prices are forward looking and reflect all available public information about future profitability. Strategies that are based on such information can generate higher expected returns only if they expose the investor to higher risk. This theory underlies much of the study of financial markets and is the foundation for the rest of this chapter and Chapter 10.

THE EFFICIENT MARKETS HYPOTHESIS

efficient markets hypothesis (EMH)
The EMH states that securities prices accurately reflect future expected cash flows and are based on all information available to investors.

The concept that *all* trading opportunities are fairly priced is referred to as the **efficient markets hypothesis (EMH)**, which is the basis of *Principle 6: The markets are quick and the prices are right.* The efficient markets hypothesis states that securities prices accurately reflect future expected cash flows and are based on all information available to investors.

efficient market
A market in which the values of all assets and securities at any instant in time fully reflect all available information.

An **efficient market** is a market in which all the available information is *fully* incorporated into securities prices, and the returns investors will earn on their investments cannot be predicted. Taking this concept a step further, we can distinguish between *weak-form efficient markets*, *semi-strong form efficient markets* and *strong-form efficient markets*, depending on the degree of efficiency:

1. The **weak-form (WF) efficient market hypothesis** asserts that all past security market information is fully reflected in securities prices. This means that all price and volume information is already reflected in a security's price. And so there is no point in studying past price trends.
2. The **semi-strong form (SSF) efficient market hypothesis** asserts that all publicly available information is fully reflected in securities prices. This is a stronger statement because it isn't limited to price and volume information, but includes all public information. Thus, the firm's financial statements, news and announcements about the economy, industry, company, analysts' estimates on future earnings, or any other publicly available information is already reflected in the security's price. As a result, studying an investments course won't be of any value to you in picking a winner. In general terms, equities markets tend to be SSF efficient.
3. The **strong-form (SF) efficient market hypothesis** asserts that all information, regardless of whether this information is public or private, is fully reflected in securities prices. This form of the efficient market hypothesis encompasses both the weak-form and semi-strong form efficient market hypotheses. It asserts that there isn't any information

that isn't already embedded into the prices of all securities. In other words, even insider information—that is, material information that isn't available to any other investor—is of no use.

DO WE EXPECT FINANCIAL MARKETS TO BE PERFECTLY EFFICIENT?

A famous quote from the late US economist Milton Friedman says that 'there is no such thing as a free lunch'. In other words, everything that has benefits also has costs. The efficient markets hypothesis can be viewed as a special case of Milton Friedman's notion of 'no free lunch'. The basic idea is that, if someone is offering free lunches, the demand for those lunches will explode, and thus be impossible to satisfy.

Similarly, if there was a simple trading strategy that made money without subjecting investors to risk, then every investor would want to invest using that strategy. However, this is clearly impossible, since for every stock that is bought, there must be someone selling. In other words, the stock market can offer you a free lunch (in this case, an underpriced stock) only when other investors exist who are willing to provide millions of free lunches—to both you and all the other investors who would be very pleased to buy underpriced stocks and sell overpriced stocks. Individuals generally like to think that when they buy and sell stock they are trading with an impersonal 'market'. In reality, when you buy or sell a stock, in most cases you are trading with professional investors representing the various managed funds.

What this means is that when you buy a stock because you think it is underpriced, you are likely to be buying it from someone who thinks the same stock is overpriced! The above argument suggests that one should not expect to find profitable investment strategies based on publicly available information. In other words, markets should be at least weak-form and semi-strong form efficient. If there did exist simple profitable strategies, then they would attract the attention of investors who, by implementing those strategies, would compete away their profits. For example, suppose that it became known that well-managed firms were, on average, underpriced. This would encourage investors to increase their holdings of well-managed companies, thereby increasing the stock prices of these firms to the point where their stocks would be no better or worse long-term investments than the stocks of poorly managed firms.

What about investment strategies that require private information, or that are complicated and require quite a bit of work to figure out? If the market were so efficient that investment strategies, no matter how complex, earned no profits, then no one would bother to take the time and effort to understand the intricacies of security pricing. Indeed, it is hard to imagine how security markets could be efficient if no one put in the time and effort to study them. For this reason, we would not expect financial markets to be strong-form efficient. We expect the market to partially, but not perfectly, reflect information that is privately collected and thus to be SSF efficient much of the time.

To understand this concept, let's think about how biotech stock prices are likely to respond when a promising new drug receives TGA approval (TGA, the Therapeutic Goods Administration, is the Australian body responsible for approving pharmaceutical drugs and other health remedies), thus signalling a likely improvement in profitability. If almost all market investors ignored information about drug approvals, the market might respond very little. This would allow those investors who collected and interpreted information about new drugs to be able to exploit the information to earn significant trading profits. However, if those profits are very high, then we might expect more investors to become interested in collecting information of this type, which would in turn make the market more efficiently incorporate this type of information into market prices. However, if there were absolutely no profits to be made from collecting this type of information, then the incentive to collect the information would be eliminated. For this reason, we expect markets to be just inefficient enough to provide some investors with an opportunity to recoup their costs of obtaining information, but not so inefficient that there is easy money to be made in the stock market.

A behavioural view

Milton Friedman's 'no free lunch' view of markets assumes that investors, as a group, are pretty rational. This was the view taken by most economists until very recently. Financial economists have since started to study the implications of the fact that individuals are not strictly rational. This new approach to the study of finance has gained a strong following and even resulted in a Nobel Prize for US psychologist Daniel Kahneman in 2002.

If we believe that investors do not rationally process information, then market prices may not accurately reflect even public information. As an example, economists have suggested that overconfident investors tend to underreact when a company's management announces earnings or makes other statements that are relevant to the value of the firm's stock. This is because investors have too much confidence in their own views of the company's true value and tend to place too little weight on new information provided by management. As a result, this new information, even though it is publicly and freely available, is not completely reflected in share prices.

MARKET EFFICIENCY: WHAT DOES THE EVIDENCE SHOW?

The extent to which financial markets are efficient is an important question with broad implications. As a result, this question has generated thousands of empirical studies. While this is a topic that has prompted considerable debate and disagreement, our interpretation of the matter is that, historically, there has been some evidence of inefficiencies in the financial markets.

Most of the evidence of market inefficiency can be summarised by three observations found in Table 9.6. Note that evidence that the equity market is inefficient is tantamount to saying that investors can earn returns—greater than their investment's risks would warrant—by engaging in a trading strategy designed to take advantage of the mispricing.

We should stress that, although the evidence relating to the preceding return patterns is quite strong in studies that examine returns over the past 25 years, more recent evidence suggests that these patterns largely disappeared after 2000. Why do we think the more recent time period is different? Following the publication of the academic research that documents this evidence of market inefficiency, institutional investors started what are known as quantitative hedge funds to exploit these return patterns. By trading aggressively on these patterns, the hedge funds have largely eliminated the inefficiencies. This suggests that, looking forward, one should probably assume that the financial markets are efficient much of the time, at least in the semi-strong form. In other words, we expect that market prices reflect public information.

TABLE 9.6 Summarising the evidence of anomalies to the efficient market hypothesis

ANOMALY	DESCRIPTION
#1. Value stocks outperform growth stocks	*Value stocks, which are stocks with tangible assets that generate current earnings, have tended to outperform growth stocks, which are stocks with low current earnings that are expected to grow in the future.* More specifically, stocks with low price-earnings ratios, low price-to-cash flow, and low price-to-book value ratios tend to outperform the market.
#2. Momentum in stock returns	Stocks that have performed well in the past six to twelve months tend to continue to outperform other stocks.
#3. Over- and under-reaction to corporate announcements	*The market has tended to under-react to many corporate events.* For example, stock prices react favourably on dates when firms announce favourable earnings news, which is exactly what we would expect in an efficient market. However, on the days after favourable earnings news, stock returns continue to be positive on average. This is known as post-earnings announcement drift. Similarly, there is evidence of some degree of predictability in stock returns following other major announcements, such as the issuance of shares or bonds.

Concept check

9.16 Distinguish between asset selection and asset allocation.

9.17 What is an 'efficient' market?

9.18 What are the three categories of information that are commonly used in tests of the efficient markets hypothesis?

This chapter began with an examination of the historical relationship between risk and rates of return. The variability of returns is the factor that defines risk for investors and financial managers. There is no simple way to measure risk, and individuals' attitudes towards risk taking vary.

OBJECTIVE 1

The rate of inflation has an effect on the nominal rate of return that an investor receives on an investment. That is, part of the return on an investment is to keep an investor from losing purchasing power from holding an investment.

OBJECTIVE 2

The term structure of interest rates compares the rates of return of similar securities with their respective times to maturity. For instance, if long-term government bonds offer a higher rate of return than short-term government securities, then the yield curve is upward sloping. But if the treasury bill is paying a higher rate of interest than its long-term counterparts, then the yield curve is downward sloping.

OBJECTIVE 3

In a world of uncertainty, we cannot make forecasts with certainty. Thus, we must speak in terms of *expected* events. The expected return on an investment may therefore be stated as the arithmetic mean or average of all possible outcomes where those outcomes are weighted by the probability that each will occur. Historical return, on the other hand, is a measure of realised return on a past investment. Unlike expected return, historical return can be calculated with certainty based on prices that have realised.

OBJECTIVE 4

Risk, for our purposes in this chapter, refers to the variability of investment returns. It may be measured by the standard deviation, which is an indicator of the degree of variability or dispersion around the mean (or expected) return. (Many people think of risk only in terms of adverse outcomes, but risk can go either way, *upside* or *downside*.)

OBJECTIVE 5

An important distinction was made between non-diversifiable risk and diversifiable risk. It was concluded that the only relevant risk given the opportunity to diversify a portfolio is a security's non-diversifiable risk, which is called by two other names: 'systematic risk' and 'market risk'.

OBJECTIVE 6

A security's market risk is represented by beta, the slope of the characteristic line. Beta measures the average responsiveness of a security's returns to the movement of the general market. If beta is 1, the security's returns move one-to-one with the market returns; if beta is 1.5, the security's returns move up and down 1.5% for every 1% change in the market's returns.

OBJECTIVE 7

A portfolio's beta is simply a weighted average of the individual stocks' betas, where the weights are the percentage of funds invested in each stock. The portfolio beta measures the average responsiveness of the portfolio's returns to the movement of the general market.

OBJECTIVE 8

The expected return of a two-asset portfolio is a weighted average of the assets' individual returns, while the standard deviation of a two-asset portfolio depends on three factors: the standard deviation of each asset, the weight of each asset, and the extent to which the assets co-vary (measured by the covariance or the correlation coefficient between the two returns).

OBJECTIVE 9

The capital asset pricing model (CAPM), even with its weaknesses, provides an intuitive framework for understanding the investors' required rate of return. The CAPM suggests that investors determine an appropriate required rate of return, depending upon the amount of systematic risk inherent in a security. This minimum acceptable rate of return is equal to the risk-free rate plus a return premium for accepting risk.

OBJECTIVE 10

Portfolio theory, as developed by Harry Markowitz, suggests that security selection within an asset class is important in reducing risk. However, diversification across different asset classes, or asset allocation, is even more important in achieving a well-diversified portfolio.

OBJECTIVE 11

The concept of efficient markets describes the extent to which information is incorporated into security prices. In an efficient market, security prices reflect *all* available information at *all* times; and, because of this, it is impossible for an investor to consistently earn high rates of return without taking substantial risk.

OBJECTIVE 12

Market efficiency is a relative concept. We do not expect financial markets to reflect 100% of the available information, but we also do not expect to see very many easy profit opportunities. In general, we expect financial markets to be *weak-form efficient*, which means that information about past prices and volumes of trading is fully reflected in current prices. For the most part we also expect financial markets to be *semi-strong form efficient*, which means that market prices fully reflect all publicly available information (that is, information from the firm's publicly released financial statements, information revealed in the financial press, and so forth). Finally, to a lesser extent, finance markets are *strong-form efficient*, meaning that prices fully reflect privately held information that has not been released to the general public.

Key terms

Web works

Go to **www.moneychimp.com**. Select the link 'Volatility' and complete the retirement planning calculator, making the assumptions that you believe are appropriate for you. Then go to the Monte Carlo simulation calculator. Assume that you invest in large-company ordinary shares during your working life and then invest in long-term company bonds during retirement. Use the average annual returns and standard deviations shown in Table 9.4 (p. 290). What did you learn?

Review questions

9-1   What would you say to your uncle, who is approaching retirement, about the four factors that he should take into account when deciding how to invest his superannuation payout?

9-2   Over the last 25 years we have had the opportunity to observe the rates of return and the variability of these returns for several different types of securities. Do these observations tend to support Principle 1?

9-3   Explain the impact of inflation on the investor's required rate of return.

9-4   Define the 'term structure of interest rates'. If the *yield curve* is sloping downwards, what does that tell you about the relationship between long-term rates and short-term rates?

9-5   In the mid-2000s the National Australia Bank (NAB) lost approximately A$180 million in unauthorised options trading. NAB's share price subsequently fell by 1.5%. The Australian All Ordinaries Index also finished the month 0.76% lower. Was this fall in NAB's share price an example of systematic or firm-specific risk? Why?

9-6 **(a)** What is meant by the investor's required rate of return?

(b) How do we measure the riskiness of a security such as a company share?

(c) How should **(b)**'s proposed measurement of risk be interpreted?

9-7 What is (a) unsystematic risk and (b) systematic risk? Is the sub-prime crisis an example of (a) or (b)? Give another example for each type of risk.

9-8 What is the meaning of beta? How is it used to calculate R, the investor's required rate of return?

9-9 Define the security market line. What does it represent?

9-10 How do we measure the beta for a portfolio?

9-11 Contrast standard deviation and beta as two measures of risk. Under which circumstances is standard deviation the appropriate measure of risk? When is beta the appropriate measure of risk?

9-12 **(a)** What would you say is the key measure underpinning successful diversification? Use this measure to explain why Australian investment managers are looking overseas to further diversify their portfolios.

(b) If you decide that all of your spare cash will be invested in *managed funds*, why might it be prudent to spread your investments across a number of such funds?

9-13 What is a share price index? If the All Ordinaries Index jumped 17.98% in a year, would this mean that all Australian listed stocks would increase 17.98% in value?

9-14 Compare and contrast covariance and the correlation coefficient as the two measures of the degree of co-movement between asset returns. To illustrate your answer, show two diagrams where: (a) two assets are perfectly positively correlated and have small standard deviations; and (b) two assets are perfectly positively correlated and have large standard deviations.

9-15 In the context of a two-asset portfolio, what are the factors that determine the expected return of the portfolio? What factors determine the standard deviation of the portfolio?

9-16 What does the CAPM allow you to calculate? Does it imply that a stock with a beta of zero will offer a zero expected rate of return? If so, why?

9-17 If we were to graph the returns of a share against the returns of the All Ordinaries Index and the points did not follow a very ordered pattern, what could we say about that share? If the share's returns tracked the Index returns very closely, what could we say?

9-18 Due to mismanagement, Oregon Ltd's share price has experienced increased volatility in the first half of 2011. Your friend suggests that Oregon is a good buy as it would provide a high return to compensate investors for bearing a high risk. Is your friend's argument valid? Why or why not?

9-19 Distinguish between *selection* and *allocation* in the context of portfolio management.

9-20 Do you agree with the contention that the GFC caused the collapse of portfolio theory?

9-21 What is the efficient markets hypothesis? Explain this concept in your own words.

9–22 Compare and contrast the notions of weak-form, semi-strong form and strong-form market efficiency.

9-23 Do you think that the capital markets are completely efficient, efficient most of the time or completely inefficient? Support your position as if you were talking to your favourite nephew or niece, who is only 10 years old.

Self-test problems

ST-1 (*Real interest rates*) If the expected inflation rate is 4% and the nominal interest rate is 10.24%, what is the real interest rate?

For answers go to MyFinanceLab
www.pearson.com.au/myfinancelab

ST-2 (*Expected return and risk*) Universal Company is planning to invest in a security that has several possible rates of return. Given the following probability distribution of returns, what is the expected rate of return on the investment? Also compute the standard deviation of the returns. What do the resulting numbers represent?

PROBABILITY	RETURN
0.10	–10%
0.20	5%
0.30	10%
0.40	25%

ST-3 (*Capital asset pricing model*) Using the CAPM, estimate the appropriate required rate of return for the three shares listed below, given that the risk-free rate is 5% and the expected return for the market is 17%.

SHARE	BETA
A	0.75
B	0.90
C	1.40

ST-4 (*Expected return and risk*) Given the holding-period returns shown below, calculate the average returns and the standard deviations for Kaifu Company and for the market.

MONTH	KAIFU COMPANY	MARKET
1	4%	2%
2	6%	3%
3	0%	1%
4	2%	–1%

ST-5 (*Holding-period returns*) From the price data that follow, compute the holding-period returns.

TIME	SHARE PRICE
1	$10
2	$13
3	$11
4	$15

ST-6 (*Security market line*)

(a) Determine the expected return and beta for the following portfolio:

SHARE	PERCENTAGE OF PORTFOLIO	BETA	EXPECTED RETURN (%)
1	40	1.00	12
2	25	0.75	11
3	35	1.30	15

(b) Given the information above, draw the security market line and show where the securities fit on the graph. Assume that the risk-free rate is 8% and that the expected return on the market portfolio is 12%. How would you interpret these findings?

Problems

9-1 (*Relationship between risk and return*) During a past 20-year period, ordinary shares provided an average annual return of 12.6% and their real rate of return was 8.7%, while the yield on government bonds averaged 4.6%. Based on these figures, what is:

(a) the average annual rate of inflation
(b) the risk-premium on ordinary shares?

For more problems and for answers to problems marked with an asterisk (*) go to MyFinanceLab at www.pearson.com.au/myfinancelab

9-2* (*Inflation and interest rates*) What would you expect the nominal rate of interest to be if the real rate was 4% and you expected inflation to be 7%?

9-3 (*Inflation and interest rates*) Assume that the current expected inflation rate is 2.5%. If the current real rate of interest is 6%, what would the nominal rate be?

9-4* (*Inflation and interest rates*) Assume that the expected inflation rate is 5%. If the current real rate of interest is 6%, what should the nominal rate of interest be?

9-5 (*Holding-period return*) The ordinary shares of Plaza Paving Company had a market price of $12 on the day you purchased it just one year ago. During the past year the stock has paid a $1 dividend and closed at a price of $14. What rate of return did you earn on your investment in these shares?

9-6 (*Holding-period return*) In 2008, the GFC began to really impact on the Australian stock market. At the beginning of the year, the All Ords Index had a value of 6421. At the end of the year, the index value was 3659. What was the average return on the market during that year?

9-7 (*Estimating expected return*) Christopher Lee is considering making an investment in David Jones Ltd (DJ). He has done some research and is happy about the fundamentals of the company. Nevertheless, he is totally unsure of what the annual return on his investment is going to be. Luckily, a friend of his father who works in a brokerage firm has provided him with the following estimates about the different possible outcomes of DJ's shares in the coming year.

PROBABILITY	RETURN (%)
0.15	25
0.20	22
0.30	15
0.25	10
0.10	–5

What is Christopher's expected rate of return if he invests in DJ shares?

9-8* (*Expected rate of return and risk*) Visual Enterprises is evaluating a security. No treasury notes are currently on issue but two-year treasury bonds pay 5.1%. Calculate the investment's expected return and its standard deviation. Should Visual Enterprises invest in this security?

PROBABILITY	RETURN
0.15	–2%
0.30	5%
0.40	7%
0.15	10%

9-9 (*Expected rate of return and risk*) Syntex Ltd is considering an investment in one of two shares. Given the information that follows, which investment is better, based on risk (as measured by the standard deviation) and return?

SHARE C		SHARE D	
PROBABILITY	RETURN	PROBABILITY	RETURN
0.2	–2%	0.2	–5%
0.5	18%	0.3	6%
0.3	27%	0.3	14%
		0.2	22%

319

9-10* (*Expected rate of return and risk*) Friedman Manufacturing Ltd has prepared the following information regarding two investments under consideration. Which investment should be accepted?

SHARE A		SHARE B	
PROBABILITY	RETURN	PROBABILITY	RETURN
0.3	11%	0.1	4%
0.4	15%	0.3	6%
0.3	19%	0.4	10%
		0.2	15%

9-11 (*Expected rate of return and risk premium*) Yun Fat Ltd is considering investing in an infrastructure project in northern China. Initial estimates of the returns on the project have revealed the following figures:

PROBABILITY	RETURN
0.15	–10%
0.25	18%
0.40	25%
0.2	40%

The current risk-free rate of return in the market is 6.25%. Yun Fat's board of directors has decided that infrastructure projects are risky in general and as such a risk premium of 20% is required. Should Yun Fat invest in this particular project? Why or why not?

9-12 (*Expected return and standard deviation of a two-asset portfolio*) Achieva Ltd and Asia Silk Holdings Ltd are two companies that are listed on the Singapore Stock Exchange. Your preliminary research into the two companies reveals the following:

COMPANY	ANNUAL RETURN (%)	ANNUAL STANDARD DEVIATION (%)
Achieva	8	12
Asia Silk Holdings	15	18

The correlation between these two companies has been estimated to be –0.2.

(a) If you decide to put 30% of your money into Achieva and the remaining in Asia Silk Holdings, what is your portfolio's expected return and standard deviation?

(b) If you decide to split your money equally between these two stocks, what is your portfolio's expected return and standard deviation?

9-13 (*Required rate of return using CAPM*)

(a) Compute the investor's required rate of return for Intel Ltd ordinary shares, which have a 1.2 beta. The risk-free rate is 6% and the market portfolio (All Ordinaries Index) has an expected return of 16%.

(b) Why is the rate you computed a 'fair' rate?

9-14* (*Capital asset pricing model*) OP-IM Trust is considering several investments. The rate on government bonds is currently 6.75%, and the expected return for the market is 18% p.a. Using the CAPM, what should be the required rates of return for each investment?

SECURITY	BETA
A	1.60
B	0.75
C	0.85
D	1.25

9-15 (*Capital asset pricing model and security market line*) Assume that the risk-free rate of return is 5% and the market risk premium is 11%. Security A has a beta of 0.75 and Security B has a beta of 1.2.

   (a) What are the required rates of return for Security A and Security B?
   (b) Draw the security market line. What does it represent?
   (c) Suppose that Security C has a risk–return characteristic such that it lies above the security market line. Is Security C a desirable investment? Why or why not?
   (d) What conclusions can you make with regard to securities that lie above the security market line and those that lie below it?

9-16* (*Capital asset pricing model*) CSB Ltd has a beta of 0.765. If the expected market return is 11.5% and the risk-free rate is 7.5%, what is the appropriate required return of CSB (using the CAPM)?

9-17 (*Capital asset pricing model*) The expected return for the general market is 12.8%, and the risk premium in the market is 4.3%. Tasaco, LBM and Exxos have betas of 0.864, 0.693 and 0.575 respectively. What are the corresponding required rates of return for the three securities?

9-18 (*Capital asset pricing model*) Investors in Longman Ltd require an 18% return on the stock. The market return is estimated to be 12% p.a. and the risk-free rate of return is 6% p.a. What is the implied beta for Longman Ltd?

9-19 (*Average return, standard deviation and market risk*) The following table details the end-of-month prices for Commonwealth Bank (CBA) stock and the S&P ASX 200 Industrials, another common market index in Australia.

TIME	CBA $	S&P ASX 200 INDUSTRIALS
January 20X6	44.65	5418.4
February 20X6	44.85	5412.3
March 20X6	45.3	5530.8
April 20X6	47	5517.9
May 20X6	43.18	5330.8
June 20X6	44.41	5309.8
July 20X6	44.8	5294.6
August 20X6	45.72	5383.8
September 20X6	45.75	5626.4
October 20X6	47.7	5768.4
November 20X6	47.43	6043.3
December 20X6	49.48	6273.1
January 20X7	48.74	6464.1

   (a) Using the above data, calculate the holding-period return for each month for CBA and the S&P index.
   (b) Calculate the average monthly return and standard deviation of these returns for both CBA and the S&P index.
   (c) Draw a graph similar to Figure 9.6 that shows the relationship between CBA stock returns and the returns on the S&P index.
   (d) From your graph, describe the nature of the relationship between CBA returns and the returns for the S&P index.

9-20 (*Beta*) Beta can be measured in Excel using the function SLOPE if you have a range of data consisting of returns for a particular stock and the market. The function takes the following form: *SLOPE(range of stock returns, range of market returns)*. Using the holding-period return data in problem 9-19, use Excel to estimate the beta of CBA.

9-21 (*CAPM and the required return*) Assume the beta computed for CBA in problem 9-20 was estimated in 2010. What is your estimate of the share investor's required rate of return? (If you did not do problem 9-20, assume a beta value of 1.1.)

9-22 (*Risk and the rate of return*)

   (a) Given the holding-period returns shown below, compute the average returns and the standard deviations for Sugita Trading and for the market.

MONTH	SUGITA	MARKET
1	1.8%	1.5%
2	−0.5	1.0
3	2.0	0.0
4	−2.0	−2.0
5	5.0	4.0
6	5.0	3.0

(b) If Sugita's beta is 1.18 and the risk-free rate is 8% p.a., what would be an appropriate required return for an investor owning Sugita? (Note: Because the above returns are based on monthly data, you will need to annualise the returns to make them compatible with the risk-free rate. For simplicity, you can convert from monthly to yearly returns by multiplying the average monthly returns by 12.)

(c) How does Sugita's historical average return compare with the return you believe to be a fair return, given the firm's systematic risk?

9-23 (*Portfolio beta and security market line*) You own a portfolio consisting of the following shares:

SHARE	PERCENTAGE OF PORTFOLIO	BETA	EXPECTED RETURN
1	20%	1.00	16%
2	30%	0.85	14%
3	15%	1.20	20%
4	25%	0.60	12%
5	10%	1.60	24%

The risk-free rate is 7%. Also, the expected return on the market portfolio is 15.5%.

(a) Calculate the expected return of your portfolio. (Hint: The expected return of a portfolio equals the weighted average of the individual shares' expected returns, where the weights are the percentage invested in each share.)

(b) Calculate the portfolio beta.

(c) Given the information above, plot the security market line on paper. Plot the shares from your portfolio on the graph.

(d) From your plot in part (c), which shares appear to be the winners and which ones appear to be the losers?

(e) Why should you consider your conclusion in part (d) to be less than certain?

Case study

Trang Nguyen is a Vietnamese-born, Australian-educated client-relationship manager who works for DIP funds management in Melbourne. Trang is responsible for managing the investment accounts of a small number of very wealthy investors in the DIP #2 Fund, which is diversified internationally across stocks and property as well as bonds. She also oversees a small team of client advisers and plays a role in the company's wider educational activities.

Trang and her staff had spent a number of years explaining the benefits of diversification to her risk-averse clients, including concepts of international diversification and principles of asset alloca-tion. However, despite this, the DIP #2 Fund fell about 25% in 2008 and has not recovered all of this ground since then. Quite a few of DIP's clients were very upset at this fall, saying to her and her fellow workers things like: 'We followed your advice but look where it has got us. What benefit is there in being diversified? We might as well have stayed in the Australian share market.' Other clients have sug-gested pulling their money out of the #2 Fund and investing in bonds, citing EQT PIMCO's successful performance from 2008 to 2010.

You recently joined DIP as a graduate trainee and you have been assigned to work the next three months with Trang, as part of your initial job-rotation schedule. Trang's first task for you is to prepare a brief memo that can be circulated to all client advisers and which can be used to respond to clients who are upset. The memo should include suitable data to support the following points:

1. Would investors have benefited from staying with the Australian share market through 2008 instead of being in the DIP #2 Fund?
2. Should clients transfer their money to a Bond Fund at this point in time?
3. Does international diversification still make sense in the post-GFC era?
4. What is the fundamental risk exposure of a global investment fund?

Notes

1. This relationship was named after Irving Fisher who had analysed it many years ago. A more detailed discussion of the Fisher effect can be found in Peter N. Ireland, 'Long-term interest rates and inflation: A Fisherian approach', Federal Reserve Bank of Richmond, *Economic Quarterly*, 82, Winter 1996, pp. 22–26.
2. Various theories have been developed to explain the shape of the yield curves. Interested readers can refer to Richard Roll, *The Behaviour of Interest Rates: An Application of the Efficient Market Model to US Treasury Bills*, Basic Books, New York, 1970; J. R. Hicks, *Value and Capital*, Oxford University Press, London, 1946; and F. A. Lutz and V. C. Lutz, *The Theory of Investment in the Firm*, Princeton University Press, Princeton, NJ, 1951.
3. For a discussion of the problems involved in actually estimating the term structure at any point in time, see Willard T. Carleton and Ian A. Cooper, 'Estimation and uses of the term structure of interest rates', *Journal of Finance*, 31, September 1976, pp. 1067–84.
4. A number of studies have noted that portfolios consisting of approximately 20 randomly selected ordinary shares have virtually no company-unique or diversifiable risk. See Robert C. Klemkosky and John D. Martin, 'The effect of market risk on portfolio diversification', *Journal of Finance*, March 1975, pp. 147–54.
5. 'Chasing global returns—why investors are heading overseas', *The Australian*, 22 September 2004.
6. 'Vanguard report: Buy international stocks but watch correlations', *Pensions and Investments*, 14 June 2004.
7. Linear regression is the statistical technique used to determine the slope of the line of best fit. An example of its application to measuring beta is in the appendix to this chapter.
8. 'Diversification is investor's best friend', *The Australian Financial Review*, 26–27 June 2010.
9. Recall from Chapter 4 that falling interest rates increase bond prices. These price increases in turn lead to higher holding-period returns (HPRs), since a bond's HPR depends on price changes plus interest-coupon income.
10. For example, in 2010, EQT PIMCO's Australian Bond Fund reported three-year returns of about 10% per annum, during a period in which the stock market's overall performance was rather static.
11. Bob Officer and Stephen Bishop, *Market Risk Premium: A Review*, Value Advisor Associates, Melbourne, 2008, www.ena.asn.au/udocs/24092008aersub/Appendix%20G%20-%20Market%20Risk%20Premium%20Report%20-%20Officer%20and%20Bishop.pdf (accessed 8 September 2010).
12. Bob Officer and Stephen Bishop, *Market Risk Premium: Further Comments*, Value Advisor Associates, Melbourne, 2009, www.aer.gov.au/content/item.phtml?itemId=726694&nodeId=3094b9b4f42503b7151a5c678a8d61e7&fn=JIA+Appendix+J+-+Officer+and+Bishop+-+Market+risk+premium-Further+comments.pdf (accessed 8 September 2010).
13. Burton G. Malkiel, *A Random Walk Down Wall Street*, W. W. Norton, New York, 1996.
14. These findings are reported in G. Brinson, B. Singer and G. Beebower, 'Determinants of portfolio performance', *Financial Analysts Journal*, May–June 1991.

Appendix

Measuring a share's return and risk using a calculator

The capital asset pricing model (CAPM) draws heavily on the ability to measure a share's return statistics, such as its market risk as measured by beta. An accurate beta must be determined because an estimate of the appropriate required rate of return using the CAPM is only as accurate as the data used to achieve it.

As noted earlier, there are some real difficulties in using the CAPM, most of which relate to empirical problems. Specifically, from where is the data drawn in making the estimates? In order to use the model correctly, investor *expectations* about future returns must be known. However, only *historical* rates of return are available. Nevertheless, the best hope of seeing the future is by looking at the past. Essentially, the historical return data can be used in the hope that the past will fairly reflect investor expectations about future returns. Thus, when the beta for a share or a portfolio was computed, as was done with ANZ Ltd's shares in the chapter, historical returns of the share and the All Ordinaries Index were used. A dilemma for statisticians revolves around the need to have sufficient historical observations to ensure that the determination of beta by this method is statistically significant. To do so, one may need to go back some years into the past, but the danger then is that the company's performance relative to the market may have changed in more recent times, so that the past pattern of return behaviour is no longer relevant.

As seen briefly in the chapter, beta is the slope of the line in which returns on the share (such as ANZ's in Figure 9.6) are plotted on the vertical axis against returns on the market as a whole (as represented by the All Ords), plotted on the horizontal axis. The slope of that line shows how, on average, the share's returns vary in response to the market. For example, if the slope is 0.86, it means that, if the market goes up (or down) 10%, on average the return on the ANZ shares goes up (or down) 0.86 times as much, that is, 8.6%.

In everyday language, it can be seen that the slope of 0.86 is equal to 'opposite' over 'adjacent', looking from the zero intercept where the axes meet—that is, 8.6% over 10% = 0.86. Other words used to describe the same concepts are a 'rise' of 8.6% in response to a 'run' of 10%.

To compute the return statistics, professional analysts typically use five years of monthly return data, or 60 months, and make certain adjustments in their computations. For instance, we know that betas over time tend to move towards a value of 1. If the beta is at present substantially greater than 1, it will gradually decline over time, and betas that are substantially below 1 will tend to increase in future periods. So forecasters adjust for this observed tendency.

In order to calculate the beta for asset j, be it a share or a portfolio, its returns are regressed with the market portfolio returns. The regression equation is as follows:

$$R_{jt} = a_j + \beta_j(R_{mt}) + e_{jt} \qquad \text{(9-20)}$$

where R_{jt} = the monthly holding-period return on security j for month t
    a_j = the alpha value for security j, the point where the regression line intercepts the vertical axis
    β_j = the beta for security j, the slope of the regression line
    R_{mt} = the return on the market portfolio in month t
    e_{jt} = the error term; the difference between the actual return and the expected return given the market's return—that is, the distance the actual return lies from the regression line.

The objective with linear regression is to find the alpha and beta values that minimise the sum of the squares of the error terms. To do this, we have to find the line that best fits the data—that is, the line that best describes the average relationship between security j's returns and the market's returns. There are three ways of determining alpha and beta:

1. We can plot the return data on graph paper and then 'eyeball' the regression line, trying to get what appears to be the best fit to the data. The point where the line crosses the vertical axis indicates our estimate for the alpha value (note that, in the above example, ANZ has an alpha of zero). We would then estimate the beta using the approach mentioned above for ANZ by measuring how steeply the line increases vertically (asset *j*'s return) relative to a change on the horizontal axis (the market's return); that is, we would find that the slope (and beta) is equal to:

$$\beta = \frac{\text{rise}}{\text{run}} = \frac{\Delta R_{jt}}{\Delta R_{mt}} \qquad\qquad \textbf{(9-21)}$$

The obvious limitation with this approach is its potential for error; accuracy depends in part on the sharpness of the eye. Your estimate would probably be somewhat different from another person's, especially if the data did not have a tight fit.

2. We can use a statistical package or a computer spreadsheet (as mentioned in problem 9-20) to determine alpha and beta. This option is preferred, because of the easy calculations and the option to view the original return data to check for accuracy in data entry. Also, we can quickly plot the data along with the fitted regression line.

3. We can use a calculator for the computation. To demonstrate the use of the calculator in measuring the return statistics for a share, let us use CC Ltd's historical returns for the 12 months ending November 20X5. These returns, along with the corresponding returns for the Market Index, are shown in Table 9.A1. The Sharp EL-738/735S calculator will be used to make the calculations.

TABLE 9.A1   Monthly holding-period returns for CC Ltd and the market index

MONTH AND YEAR	MONTHLY RETURNS ON MARKET INDEX (%)	MONTHLY RETURNS ON CC LTD (%)
December 20X4	2.02	0.54
January 20X5	2.24	4.84
February 20X5	8.80	7.44
March 20X5	0.50	3.58
April 20X5	3.14	–2.76
May 20X5	2.85	8.53
June 20X5	–4.79	–4.80
July 20X5	2.63	10.32
August 20X5	3.81	9.36
September 20X5	–1.91	–1.90
October 20X5	–0.94	3.29
November 20X5	–1.99	4.13

(a) Set up the calculator

The EL-738/735S must be placed in 'Stat 1' mode for linear regression. To do this, press MODE then use ▶ to scroll so that '1' flashes under the heading 'Stat'. Press = to select this mode, then scroll ▶ so that '1' flashes under the heading 'LINE'. Press = to select this 'LINE' (that is, linear regression) function.

(b) Enter the data

Financial calculators generally assume a linear regression equation of the form $y = a + b.x$, in which y is the dependent variable and corresponds to the values of the returns on the share (CC Ltd), x is the independent variable and corresponds to the values of the returns on the market index, a represents the vertical axis intercept (thus corresponding with α_j), and b represents the slope of the regression line (thus corresponding with beta, β_j).

Data have to be entered in the calculators as pairs, starting with the x value and then its associated y value. So, from Table 9.A1, we must enter the first pair of data, namely x equals 2.02(%) and then y equals 0.54(%), followed by the next pair, and so on.

The EL-738/735S: First clear any previous data by pressing (2ndF) (CA). Then, after each *x* value is input, the (x,y) key is pressed, and after each *y* value is input, the (ENT) key is pressed.

Following this procedure, the keystrokes required to input the data from Table 9.A1 are now shown (do not forget to use the (+/–) key to make a number negative for a negative return before it is input; e.g. the number –2.76 would be specified as 2.76 (+/–) followed by the next relevant key to enter the number):

EL-735 CALCULATOR	
2.02 (x,y)	0.54 (ENT)
2.24 (x,y)	4.84 (ENT)
8.80 (x,y)	7.44 (ENT)
0.50 (x,y)	3.58 (ENT)
3.14 (x,y)	–2.76 (ENT)
2.85 (x,y)	8.53 (ENT)
–4.79 (x,y)	–4.80 (ENT)
2.63 (x,y)	10.32 (ENT)
3.81 (x,y)	9.36 (ENT)
–1.91 (x,y)	–1.90 (ENT)
–0.94 (x,y)	3.29 (ENT)
–1.99 (x,y)	4.13 (ENT)

(c) Compute the alpha and beta values for the regression (characteristic) line

Having entered the data, to obtain the alpha or *a* value enter (RCL) (a), giving 2.39; then, to obtain the beta or *b* value enter (RCL) (b), giving 0.85.*

Interpreting the value of 0.85 for beta, the slope of the regression or characteristic line, it means that on average a 1% change in the market index brings about a 0.85% change in the returns on CC Ltd. And, interpreting the alpha value of 2.39, if we were to draw a graph plotting returns on CC Ltd against the share-market returns, alpha would represent the intercept on the vertical axis.

* Note: The character (a) is located above the (÷) key, while (b) is located above the (DEL) key.

Learning objectives

After reading this chapter, you should be able to:

1 Explain why we need to understand valuation.
2 Give various definitions for the term 'value'.
3 Explain the process of valuing an asset.
4 Understand how to value bonds, preference shares and ordinary shares.
5 Appreciate the concept of an investor's expected rate of return and be able to compute the expected rate of return on bonds, preference shares and ordinary shares.
6 Understand the relationship between a company's earnings and the value of its ordinary shares (see Appendix, page 355).

For a complete eBook go to MyFinanceLab
www.pearson.com.au/myfinancelab

Valuation of bonds and shares

Chapter 10

CHAPTER PREVIEW

A major focus of this book is how to use the objective of the maximisation of the wealth (after-tax) of the firm's owners to decide between investment and financing alternatives. For ordinary shareholders, the major source of their wealth as owners of the company is from the value (market price) of the company's shares. Therefore, to maximise shareholder wealth, company financial managers must select investment and financing alternatives that will maximise the company's share price. To do this requires an understanding of the determinants of a company's share price and the application of simple models to estimate the value of a company's preference and ordinary shares.

Before examining the valuation of shares, the first part of the chapter identifies some general valuation principles and then examines the valuation of bond-type debt instruments as the sale of these instruments in the financial markets is a major source of debt finance for governments and large companies.

Regardless of your program

'BORROW NOW, PAY LATER'

Are you interested in starting your own business? If you are, then one of the major challenges will be obtaining the finance. Borrowing money makes it possible to make purchases today in return for assuming a debt obligation that has to be repaid at a future date. You will have the opportunity to choose between many varieties of debt. Should you get a loan that is repaid over four or five years? Should you get a mortgage that fixes the interest rate and monthly payments for a period, or one where the monthly payments change if interest rates change? The only real difference between how individuals and companies borrow money is that large companies can issue bonds while individuals cannot and are restricted to borrowing from a bank and using their own (equity) money.

If you start a company that becomes a success and you want to sell some or all of your equity ownership interest, you will want to know how to determine the value of your shares in the company.

Why we need to understand valuation

Valuation is an area of finance that raises many questions. What determines the value of assets like shares and bonds, land or capital goods? Why did the price of shares in ABC Limited rise from $4.90 to $6.75 in two months? Why did the price of shares in XYZ Limited fall from $12.50 to $7.95 in just one week? Why is the value of a commercial property likely to be higher if it has a secure long-term tenant than if the property is vacant? Why does something seemingly intangible, like a legal right to exclusively manufacture a pharmaceutical drug, have value despite the fact that the right is only a bundle of legal paper?

OBJECTIVE 1

Explain why we need to understand valuation.

These examples highlight both the difficulty and the importance of the valuation of assets, and particularly the need in financial management to predict future values. The *Maxims* of the French writer La Rochefoucauld, written over three centuries ago, still speak to us: 'The greatest of all gifts is the power to estimate things at their true worth.'

The study of valuation brings together the concepts from earlier chapters of risk, return and the time value of money. This chapter examines the principles of and procedures for valuing assets, especially *financial assets* such as bonds, preference shares and ordinary shares.[1] Note that the terms *financial assets*, *securities* and *instruments* are simply different names that are commonly used for the same thing and this chapter uses them interchangeably so that you become familiar with them.

Given that the objective of maximising shareholder wealth requires financial managers to make decisions that will maximise the company's share price, it is important to understand how to value financial securities such as ordinary shares.

In addition, the discount rate needed to make capital budgeting decisions using NPV (net present value) or IRR (internal rate of return) (see Chapters 11, 12 and 13) comes from the cost of capital (discussed in detail in Chapter 14). At this point we can identify that the cost of capital is computed from the required rates of returns of investors, which are often estimated by using a valuation model and the observed value of the company's securities in the financial markets. A simple example will illustrate this process. An investor is willing to pay $100 in the financial markets for a company security that promises to pay $114 to the investor in a year's time. We can use financial mathematics as a valuation model linking the present value of $100 with a future value of $114 to determine that for this security the investor expects a rate of return from the security of 14% per annum (i.e. 100 +/– *PV*, 114 *FV*, 1 *n*, *COMP i* = 14%). From the perspective of the company, if it wants to raise funds by selling similar securities to investors, this rate of 14% per annum reflects the current 'cost' to the company to obtain this capital.

Definitions of value

OBJECTIVE **2**

Give various definitions for the term 'value'.

book value
The value of an item in a firm's balance sheet.

The word *value* is often used in different contexts, depending on its application. Examples of different uses include book value, liquidation value, going-concern value, market value and intrinsic value. This section looks briefly at what each of these terms means.

Book value is the value of an item as shown in a firm's balance sheet. It often represents an historical value rather than a measure of the current worth. Also, some assets are depreciated, so the *net* book value represents the depreciated historical cost. Thus, from an accounting perspective, the net book value of the whole company is equal to the depreciated value of all the company's assets less its outstanding liabilities and represents the amount of owners' equity in the company.

Usually the equity of a company is reported in its balance sheet as the sum total of amounts identified by names such as 'contributed or issued equity', 'retained profits' and other 'reserves'. The *contributed equity* is equal to the amount the company has received from the issue of shares to investors. *Reserves* arise from bookkeeping entries that are placed in the equity section so the balance sheet will balance (e.g. an 'asset revaluation reserve' arises when a company's assets are revalued above historic cost). *Retained profits* are the amount of net profit retained within the company after any payment of dividends to shareholders. As you will see in later chapters, the retention of profits is an indirect way for the shareholders to invest more money in the company.

The book value *per ordinary share* can be found by simply dividing the total book value of the ordinary shares by the number of shares outstanding. For example, the book value on 30 June for each share of CDF Limited is $4.06, computed as follows:

Contributed (issued) equity	$1 610 800 000
+ Retained profits	726 400 000
+ Reserves	232 500 000
= Total book value	$2 569 700 000
÷ Number of ordinary shares issued	633 423 000
= Book value per share	$4.06

Liquidation or **disposal value** is the dollar amount that could be realised if an asset were sold individually and not as a part of the whole business as a going concern. For example, if a product line is discontinued, the machinery used in its production might be sold. This disposal sale price would be different from the value that the machinery would have if it were part of the sale of the whole business to a new owner who believed they could put the machinery to productive use.

Similarly, if the firm's operations were discontinued, *all* its assets could be sold as separate items and the proceeds used to repay the firm's liabilities. The total net amount remaining represents the firm's liquidation value.

In contrast to the liquidation value, the **going-concern value** is the amount realised if the entire firm is sold as a going concern rather than on the basis of liquidating its assets. This value will be different because the buyer is willing to pay a price on the basis of synergy benefits from the firm's future profits and cash flows from keeping the firm intact.

The **market value** of an asset is the observed value of the asset in the marketplace. This value is determined by supply and demand forces working together in the marketplace, where buyers and sellers negotiate a mutually acceptable price for the asset. For instance, if the market price of each CDF Ltd ordinary share on 30 June is $6.62, this is the price reached by a large number of buyers and sellers trading through the stock exchange. In theory, a market price exists for all assets; however, many assets have no readily observable market price because trading seldom occurs. For instance, the market price of the ordinary shares of a proprietary limited company (a private company that is not able to offer its shares to the public) is much more difficult to establish than the price of a public company share listed on the stock exchange.

The **intrinsic value** of an asset is the present value of the asset's expected future cash flows. This present-value amount is also called the *fair value* and represents how much an investor is willing to pay given his or her perception of the amount, timing and riskiness of the asset's future cash flows. An investor can then compare this intrinsic (fair) value with the asset's market value (price). If the intrinsic value is greater than the market value, then in the eyes of the investor the asset is undervalued and would be good to buy. On the other hand, if the market value exceeds the investor's intrinsic value, the asset is overvalued and should not be purchased, or if the investor already owns the asset it should be sold.

liquidation or **disposal value**
The amount that could be realised if an asset were sold independently of the going concern.

going-concern value
The amount realised if the entire firm is sold as a going concern rather than on the basis of liquidating its assets.

market value
The value observed in the marketplace, where buyers and sellers negotiate a mutually acceptable price for the asset.

intrinsic value
The present value of the investment's expected future cash flows, discounted at the investor's required rate of return.

Back to the principles

The fact that investors have difficulty identifying securities that are undervalued relates to **Principle 6: Efficient capital markets—the markets are quick and the prices are right**. In an efficient market, the price reflects all available public information about the security, and therefore it is priced fairly.

Market—book –ratio
market $ per share
──────────────
book value per share.
> 1

Concept check

10.1 When should the market value equal the intrinsic value?

10.2 How does risk play a role in asset valuation?

For answers go to **MyFinanceLab** or
www.pearson.com.au/9781442539174

ONE STEP FURTHER

MARKET EFFICIENCY AND BEHAVIOURAL FINANCE

When the securities market is working efficiently, the market value and the intrinsic value of a security will be equal. This is because whenever a security's intrinsic value differs from its current market price, investors aiming to make a profit will either buy or sell the security. The result of these supply and demand forces will be to drive the security's market price back into equilibrium with its intrinsic value.

efficient market
A market in which the values of all assets and securities at any instant in time fully reflect all available information.

Another outcome of an **efficient market** is that the market values of all securities at any instant in time will fully reflect all available information. This will occur because investors who are assumed to act rationally will use the information to determine the intrinsic value of the security. Their actions to buy or sell the security will result in the market value (price) of the security changing to be the same as the intrinsic value. When this occurs, it would not be feasible for an investor to consistently make extra profits by being able to repeatedly predict asset market prices that are different from intrinsic values.

This conjecture of market efficiency has been the source of much disagreement between academics and professional investors. For example, some finance academics have contended that, because markets are efficient, investors could select their investments by throwing darts at a list of securities and make as much profit as professional money managers who believe they can consistently identify undervalued and overvalued securities.

Many market practitioners, on the other hand, retort that the academic view of market efficiency and investors acting rationally is too divorced from reality and that some investors do indeed possess superior ability to analyse information available about securities and consistently pick undervalued or overvalued securities and thereby make super-normal profits.

Intellectually, this view has received a boost in recent years from the discipline of Behavioural Finance which has emerged to challenge the doctrine of efficient markets. The basis of behavioural finance theory is that markets are not efficient and market prices do not always accurately reflect all available information. Consequently, there is the potential for past prices to be used to predict future prices and for investors to improve the returns they receive by analysing price trends and data in financial reports. An explanation for why this occurs is that the behaviour of investors in buying and selling shares may not always be rational. For example, if during certain periods investors are gripped by emotions such as greed or fear, their buying/selling actions will have an identifiable effect on market prices that other investors may be able to profit from.

Supporters of behavioural finance believe that investors often make judgement errors that are both systematic and predictable. For example, overconfidence can result in investment errors being made, such as insufficient diversification of investments, trading too frequently and relying too heavily on the recent past to forecast future market prices.

price–earnings ratio (PE)
The price that the market places on $1 of a firm's earnings. For example, if a company has earnings per share of $2 and a share price of $30, its PE ratio is $30 ÷ $2 = 15.

The experience of the United States share market since the late 1990s provides some evidence to support behavioural finance theory. During the early part of this period the share prices of many companies increased significantly. As a result, there were many companies that had historically very high **price–earnings ratios**, and there were even companies that had rising share prices although they were consistently reporting losses. There was a perception by many investors that past increases in share prices would continue into the future. As a counter-argument, the proponents of efficient markets explain this period as evidence that the high demand and prices for shares reflected the response of investors to the positive information that was available at that time. Proponents of behavioural finance argue that some of the precipitous fall of share prices around the world in 2008 was due to an irrational fear and panic response of investors to the Global Financial Crisis.

Although behavioural finance theory proposes that the irrational behaviour of investors in the market can have an effect on share prices, it is generally considered that an individual investor who tries to consistently profit by outguessing the behaviour of market participants will usually fail.

Moreover, efficient market proponents consider that not all players need to be rational for the market to be efficient; all it takes is that there are some rational investors who can identify and exploit market inefficiencies and drive prices back to their intrinsic value. Although such players may generate excess returns from their investment decisions in the process, these will disappear once price anomalies have been eliminated.

Both behavioural finance and efficient market supporters agree that investors can be successful by considering factors that are under their control, such as being properly diversified, minimising transaction costs and investing in index funds that purchase a broad range of shares that comprise a particular market index.[2]

Valuation: the process

OBJECTIVE 3

Explain the process of valuing an asset.

The basis for valuing an asset is its *intrinsic value* which is calculated by the *present value of the asset's expected future cash flows discounted at the investor's required rate of return*.

As depicted in Figure 10.1, the basic process to determine the value of an asset involves:

- assessing the asset's characteristics, which include the amount and timing of the expected cash flows and the riskiness of these cash flows
- determining the investor's required rate of return, which embodies the investor's attitude about assuming risk and his/her perception of the riskiness of the asset
- discounting the expected cash flows back to the present, using the investor's required rate of return as the discount rate.

To put the valuation process into practice requires determining the investor's required rate of return (R). As discussed in Chapter 9, R can be calculated using the CAPM and will be equal to the amount of the risk-free rate of interest plus the risk premium that the investor feels is necessary to compensate for the market risk of the asset.

FIGURE 10.1 Basic factors determining an asset's value

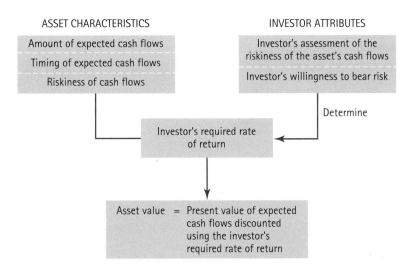

Once *R* has been determined, the basic valuation model can be defined mathematically as:

$$V = C_1/(1+R)^1 + C_2/(1+R)^2 + \ldots + C_n/(1+R)^n$$

or

$$V = \sum_{t=1}^{n} \frac{C_t}{(1+R)^t} \tag{10-1}$$

where V = the intrinsic value of an asset = present value of expected future cash flows, C_t, in years 1 to n

C_t = cash flow to be received in year t

R = the investor's required rate of return

Equation (10-1), which measures the present value of future cash flows, is the basis of the valuation process. It is the most important equation in this chapter, because all the remaining equations are merely a reformulation of this one equation. If you are not familiar with this equation, review the material in Chapter 4, especially the sections on the present value of an annuity and the present value of an uneven stream.

There are three key steps to using equation (10-1) to determine the value of an asset:

- *Step 1: Estimate the amount and timing of the future cash flows that an investor can expect to receive.*
  C_t in equation (10-1).
- *Step 2: Determine the investor's required rate of return by evaluating the riskiness of the expected future cash flows.*
  This may involve using the CAPM (Chapter 9) to determine the investor's required rate of return, R. First, obtain a measure of the risk-free rate (R_f) from, for example, the current rate of interest on 90-day treasury notes. Second, obtain a measure of the systematic risk of the asset's future cash flows (e.g. β). Third, estimate an appropriate market return measure (R_M) and calculate the asset's risk premium value ($R_M - R_f$)β. Fourth, add together the risk-free rate and the risk premium to give the required rate of return, R.
- *Step 3: Calculate the intrinsic value equal to the present value of the expected future cash flows discounted at the investor's required rate of return.*
  V is the present value of expected future cash flows (C_t) discounted at the investor's required rate of return (R).

To give a brief example of the application of these steps and Figure 10.1, we can use a security that is expected to return $114 at the end of a year. We know the *amount of the expected cash flows* ($114) and their *timing* (end of one year).

Back to the principles

Determining the intrinsic value of an asset always relies on these three principles:

Principle 1: The risk–return trade-off—we won't take on additional risk unless we expect to be compensated with additional return.

Principle 2: The time value of money—a dollar received today is worth more than a dollar received in the future.

Principle 3: Cash—not profits—is king.

Without these principles we would have no basis for explaining and measuring value. With them, we know that the amount and timing of cash, not earnings, drive value. Also, investors must be rewarded for taking risk; otherwise they will not invest.

What about the riskiness of the expected cash flow? The investor, in *assessing risk*, needs to consider whether the security is essentially risk-free (issued by the government) or risky. Having identified the riskiness and deciding to bear this risk, the investor has to determine a *required rate of return*. Assuming that this rate is 14%, the *asset value* is found by discounting $114 back one year at 14%, giving a present value of $100 (i.e. 114 *FV, 1 n, 14 i COMP PV* = −100).

With these brief but important principles of valuation as a foundation, let us now apply them to valuing three types of financial securities—bonds, preference shares and ordinary shares.

Concept check

10.3 What are the three important elements in determining the intrinsic value of an asset?

For answers go to MyFinanceLab or
www.pearson.com.au/9781442539174

Bond valuation

OBJECTIVE 4

Understand how to value bonds, preference shares and ordinary shares.

At the end of Chapter 4 there was an illustration of how to use financial mathematics to determine the valuation of bonds. The same process will be followed here, together with some of the terminology and institutional characteristics of bonds.

The name *bond* is used to refer to a family of debt securities, which includes government bonds such as Australian treasury bonds and savings bonds, and company-issued debentures, unsecured notes and corporate bonds. In this section the emphasis is on the common characteristics that are essential to an understanding of the valuation process of bond-type securities issued by a company. Chapter 18 provides further details of the contractual and institutional provisions of bonds.

TERMINOLOGY

There are a number of different ways in which large companies are able to obtain long-term finance and one way is through bonds. A **bond** is a debt financial instrument, issued by the borrower, who promises to pay whoever owns the bond a predetermined and fixed amount of interest each year as well as the principal amount of the bond when the bond matures. Although a bond issue might contain a number of complex contractual terms and conditions between the borrower and the lender (investor), there are only three items of the bond contract that *directly* affect the bond cash flows. They are: the bond's *par value*, the *maturity date*, and the *coupon rate* of interest.

bond
A long-term debt security issued by the borrower, promising to pay the owner of the security a predetermined amount of interest each year and a principal amount at maturity. Examples include debentures and unsecured notes.

Par value

When a company creates a bond to raise finance it has to specify the amount it will pay to the holder of the bond on the maturity date. This amount cannot be altered after the bond has been issued, and can be referred to by a number of different names, such as *par value, face value, principal amount* or *maturity value*. Typically, the par value of a bond is set at multiples of $100 or $1000.

Maturity date

A bond normally has a maturity date, which is the day the company specifies when it issues the bond that it will pay the par value to the owner of the bond on the maturity date.

Coupon interest rate

Besides paying the owner of the bond the par value at the maturity date, the issuing company promises to regularly pay to the owner a specified amount of interest. For a bond this amount of interest does not change once the bond is issued and is called the *coupon*. Sometimes the coupon value is stated directly, such as $9, or the **coupon interest rate** as a percentage of the par value is provided (e.g. 9%) from which the coupon amount can be calculated (e.g. 9% × $100 = $9). The coupon interest rate is often just called the *coupon rate* and should not be confused with the required rate of return, which will become clearer below.

coupon interest rate
The cash flow to be regularly paid to the bondholder as coupon interest payments, expressed as a percentage of par value.

BOND VALUATION PROCEDURE

The valuation process for a bond, as depicted in Figure 10.2, requires three essential elements to be identified:

1. maturity date of the bond
2. amount and timing of the bond cash flows, consisting of the periodic coupon amounts and the par value at the maturity date
3. investor's required rate of return.

Given these elements, the value of the bond is equal to the present value of the bond's future cash flows.

FIGURE 10.2 Data requirements for a bond valuation

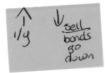

Inverse relationship between market interest rates & bond price

↑ i/y ↓ sell bonds go down

(1) Cash-flow information

Periodic coupon interest payments
For example $10.75 per year

Principal amount or par value
For example $100

(2) Term to maturity

For example 5 years

(3) Investor's required rate of return

For example 10%

EXAMPLE 10.1 Valuation of annual coupon bond

You have some money to invest and you are considering purchasing unsecured notes[3], which are a bond-type instrument that have been issued by St Marks Ltd. The notes mature in five years time and have a coupon rate of 10.75%, with coupons paid annually. What price (value) would you be prepared to pay for the notes if your required rate of return is 10% per annum?

Step 1: Estimate the amount and timing of the expected future cash flows.
If you buy the notes, you will be legally entitled to receive the following cash flows:

(a) Annual coupon interest amounts, equal to the coupon rate multiplied by the face (par) value of the note: $(0.1075 \times \$100) = \$10.75$. Assuming that a coupon amount has just been paid, there will be five more annual coupon amounts of $10.75 to be received (years 1 to 5 inclusive) before the note matures.
(b) The face (par) value of the note, $100, to be paid on the maturity date in five years time.

We can summarise the future cash flows you will receive from each note, using the following timeline:

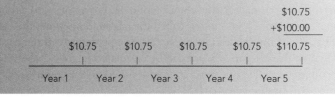

	$10.75
	+$100.00
$10.75 $10.75 $10.75 $10.75	$110.75
Year 1 Year 2 Year 3 Year 4	Year 5

Step 2: Determine the investor's required rate of return by evaluating the riskiness of the expected future cash flows.

For the purposes of this example, the 10% per annum required rate of return reflects the risk faced by St Marks note-holders. The major source of this risk is St Marks defaulting on payment of the coupon and face-value amounts.

Step 3: Calculate the intrinsic value equal to the present value of the expected future cash flows discounted at the investor's required rate of return.

The present value of St Marks notes is calculated as follows:

$$V_b = \sum_{t=1}^{5} \frac{\$I}{(1 + R_b)^t} + \frac{\$M}{(1 + R_b)^n} \qquad \textbf{(10-2)}$$

where *I* represents the coupon interest payment in year *t*

  M represents the maturity (or par) value

  R_b is equal to the note- (bond-) holder's required rate of return.

Since the coupon interest payments *I* comprise an annuity for *n* years, and the maturity value is a once-only amount in year *n*, the present-value factors in Appendices B ($PVIF_{i,n}$) and D ($PVIFA_{i,n}$) can be used to solve for the present value:

$$V_b = \$I(PVIFA_{i,n}) + \$M(PVIF_{i,n}) \qquad \textbf{(10-2a)}$$

$$\begin{aligned} V_b &= \$I(PVIFA_{10\%,5}) + \$M(PVIF_{10\%,5}) \\ &= \$10.75(3.791) + \$100(0.621) \\ &= \$40.75 + \$62.10 = \$102.85 \end{aligned}$$

Thus, if you consider 10% to be an appropriate required rate of return in view of the risk level associated with St Marks notes, you would be prepared to pay a price of $102.85 for each note.

To show this solution graphically, a present value of $102.85 can be attached at the beginning of the relevant timeline:

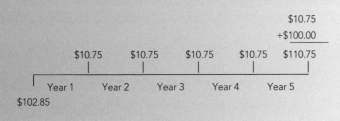

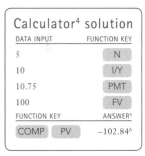

Calculator[4] solution

DATA INPUT	FUNCTION KEY
5	N
10	I/Y
10.75	PMT
100	FV
FUNCTION KEY	ANSWER[5]
COMP PV	−102.84[6]

SEMI-ANNUAL INTEREST PAYMENTS

In Example 10.1 the coupon (interest) amounts were paid annually. However, companies and other bond issuers, such as governments, typically issue bonds that pay coupon amounts half-yearly. When this occurs, the bond valuation process is essentially the same as above except that the different amount and timing of the coupon payments needs to be recognised, as illustrated below and in Example 10.2.

Rather than paying an annual coupon interest amount (*I*), suppose St Marks decided to issue the notes with a coupon rate of 10.75% paid semi-annually. This would mean that each coupon amount would be half of $10.75 (*I/2*) = $5.375, paid at the end of each six-month period. The note-holder could not be paid fractions of cents, but this would not be an issue as most investors would hold multiples of $100. For example, an investor who holds notes with a total par value of $1000 would receive $53.75 each half-year.

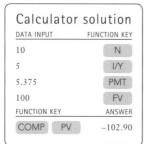

To adapt equation (10-2) for semi-annual interest payments[7], it is necessary to think in terms of *coupon payment periods* rather than years. This is because a bond-type instrument with a term of n years paying coupon interest semi-annually has $2 \times n$ coupon payment periods. So, a note with a term of five years ($n = 5$) that pays semi-annual coupons will have $2 \times 5 = 10$ coupon payment periods. Also, the annual percentage required rate of return (R_b) has to be halved to provide a rate per coupon period ($R_b/2$). Therefore, R_b is now $R_b/2$ and I becomes $I/2$:

$$V_b = \sum_{t=1}^{2n} \frac{\$I/2}{(1 + R_b/2)^t} + \frac{\$M}{(1 + R_b/2)^{2n}}$$ (10-3)

However, if the present-value tables are used, V_b is calculated as:

$$V_b = \frac{\$I}{2}(PVIFA_{R_b/2,2n}) + \$M(PVIF_{R_b/2,2n})$$ (10-3a)

EXAMPLE 10.2   Valuation of a semi-annual coupon bond

To see the effect of semi-annual interest amounts, let us look again at the five-year notes issued by St Marks Ltd. Assuming a coupon rate of 10.75% per annum paid semi-annually, there will be 10 coupon payments until maturity, each of $5.37(5) per $100 par value. As investors have a required rate of return of 10% per annum, the discount rate becomes 5% per half-year. The price per $100 par value is given by:

$$V_b = \sum_{t=1}^{10} \frac{\$5.375}{(1 + 0.05)^t} + \frac{\$100}{(1 + 0.05)^{10}}$$

$$= \$5.375(PVIFA_{5\%,10}) + \$100(PVIF_{5\%,10})$$
$$= \$5.375(7.722) + \$100(0.614)$$
$$= \$41.51 + \$61.40 = \$102.91$$

Thus, the present value of a $100 par-value bond-type instrument paying coupons of $5.37(5) per half-year for five years, if the investor's required rate of return is 10% per annum, is $102.91.[8]

Calculator solution

DATA INPUT	FUNCTION KEY
10	N
5	I/Y
5.375	PMT
100	FV
FUNCTION KEY	**ANSWER**
COMP PV	−102.90

Concept check

10.4 What are some of the important features of a bond? Which features determine the cash flows of a bond?

10.5 How is the rate of return required by bond investors used to calculate the present value of the bond's cash flows?

10.6 Given the convention of quoting coupon rates and required rates of return as 'percent per annum', what adjustments need to be made for semi-annual coupon payments?

For answers go to MyFinanceLab or www.pearson.com.au/9781442539174

International spotlight

EUROBONDS

To raise large amounts of debt finance as cheaply as possible, a bond issue needs to be offered to as many investors as possible. One way of doing this is to issue bonds to investors in different countries, but this imposes the additional complexity of foreign currency. The issuer of the bond has to decide on not only the bond term and the coupon rate but also the currency that the coupons and par value will be paid in. When a bond is issued in a country that is different from the currency of the bond, it is called a eurobond. The term can be a bit misleading, because it doesn't refer only to bonds issued in Europe. For example, the bonds of Australian businesses that are denominated in Australian dollars and issued in Singapore are still called 'eurobonds'.

Preference share valuation

Bond-type instruments are a major way for companies to raise large amounts of long-term debt finance, with ordinary shares being the major instrument to raise equity finance. Before examining ordinary shares we will look at the valuation of preference shares which give the preference shareholder the preferential right to be paid a constant dividend amount from company profits before any dividend is paid to ordinary shareholders.

Before a company can offer new preference shares to investors it has to make three decisions. First, it has to specify the fixed amount of preference dividend that will be paid in the future. Sometimes a percentage of a notional par value is specified, from which the preference dividend amount can be determined. For example, an 11.5% preference share with a $10 par value will pay a dividend of 11.5 cents per share.

The second decision is whether the preference share dividends are cumulative or non-cumulative. As Australian corporate law specifies that a company can only pay dividends from profits, if a company does not have sufficient profits in a particular year, it cannot pay the fixed preference dividend amount for that year. If this occurs, the holders of *cumulative* preference shares will be entitled to receive the cumulative value of any missed dividends once the company earns sufficient profits. The holders of *non-cumulative* preference shares, on the other hand, are not entitled to be paid any missed dividends.

The third decision is whether the preference shares are to be redeemable or irredeemable. With *redeemable* preference shares, companies pay a constant dividend amount only for a period of time until the date when the shares are redeemed by the company. As redeemable preference shares have a finite life, their valuation is analogous to the valuation of bonds.

Usually, preference shares are *irredeemable*, which makes them like ordinary shares, because the constant dividend amount (assuming sufficient profits) is theoretically paid forever (unless the company is liquidated). The constant preference dividend stream can therefore be modelled as a **perpetuity**, which makes finding the value of a preference share (Vp) relatively easy.

perpetuity
An annuity with an infinite life.

EXAMPLE 10.3   Valuation of a preference share

To illustrate the valuation of an irredeemable preference share, a three-step valuation procedure is used.

Step 1: Estimate the amount and timing of the future cash flows that an investor can expect to receive.
For this example, each preference shareholder can expect to receive an annual dividend of 15 cents per share at the end of the year. As the preference shares do not have a maturity date, these dividend amounts comprise a perpetuity.

Step 2: Determine the investor's required rate of return by evaluating the riskiness of the expected future cash flows.
The riskiness reflects the uncertainty that the company will make sufficient profits in the future to be able to pay the constant preference dividend amount. As this risk is higher than the risk to bond investors, the preference share investor's required rate of return is assumed in this example to be equal to 12% per annum.

Step 3: Calculate the intrinsic value equal to the present value of the expected future cash flows discounted at the investor's required rate of return.
The valuation model for a preference share, Vp, is defined as follows:

$$V_p = \sum_{t=1}^{\infty} \frac{D_t}{(1 + R_p)^t} \qquad \text{(10-4)}$$

Since the preference share dividends in each period are equal, equation (10-4) can be reduced to the following:

$$V_p = \frac{\text{annual dividend}}{\text{required rate of return}} = \frac{D}{R_p} \qquad (10\text{-}5)$$

Equation (10-5) represents the present value of a perpetuity as the cash flows are the same each year and they begin in a year's time from now.

The value of each preference share can be determined using equation (10-5) as follows:

$$V_p = \frac{D}{R_p} = \frac{\$0.15}{0.12} = \$1.25$$

Concept check

10.7 What features of preference shares are different from those of bonds?

10.8 Which preference share cash flows are included in the valuation model?

10.9 What is the benefit to investors of cumulative preference shares?

For answers go to MyFinanceLab or www.pearson.com.au/9781442539174

Valuation of ordinary shares

The third and last security to be valued in this chapter is the ordinary share. *Like both bonds and preference shares, the intrinsic value of an ordinary share is equal to the present value of all future cash flows expected to be received by the investor.*

In contrast to bonds and preference shares that pay investors fixed cash-flow amounts, the dividend amount received by the owners of ordinary shares can vary from period to period. In addition to the legal constraint that dividends can be paid only from profits, the amount of an ordinary share dividend is determined each year by the company's board of directors. As a consequence, the future amounts of ordinary share dividends are more uncertain (risky) than the cash flows from bonds and preference shares. To try and reduce some of this uncertainty we will be using a valuation model that specifies a constant growth rate to future ordinary dividend amounts if they are expected to increase with an anticipated growth in corporate earnings.

THE GROWTH FACTOR IN VALUING ORDINARY SHARES

What is meant by the term *growth* when used in the context of valuing ordinary shares? A major way a company can grow is to invest in new projects that are financed by borrowing money and/or issuing new shares. Although management can say that the company has grown, the original shareholders may or may not benefit from this growth. This is because, even though the company's size may have increased, unless the original ordinary shareholders increase their investment in the company they will end up owning a smaller portion of the expanded business.[9]

Another way a company can grow is to retain some or all of its profits for reinvestment in the business. This internal growth is evidenced by an increase in the company's future earnings and a rise in the value (price) of its ordinary shares, as illustrated in Example 10.4.

EXAMPLE 10.4 Internal growth and share prices

Assume that the return on equity for PCP Ltd is 16%.[10] If PCP's management decided to pay all of its profits in dividends to its shareholders, the company would have no retained earnings for reinvestment and internal growth. The only way the company could grow would be to raise money by borrowing or by issuing new shares.

If, on the other hand, PCP retained all its profits, the shareholders' investment in the company would grow by the return on equity rate assumed in this example to be 16% per annum. In other words, each dollar of profits that is retained and reinvested would generate an extra $0.16 per annum for the shareholders.

If, however, management retained only 50% of the profits for reinvestment, with 50% paid out as ordinary dividends, the ordinary shareholders' investment would increase by only half of the 16% return on equity, or by 8%. Generalising this relationship, we have:

$$g = ROE \times r \qquad \textbf{(10-6)}$$

where g = the growth rate of future earnings and the growth in the ordinary shareholders' investment in the firm

ROE = the return on equity (net income/equity at book value)

r = the percentage of company profits retained, called the *profit retention rate*[11]

Similarly, if only 25% of the profits were retained by PCP Ltd, we would expect the ordinary shareholders' investment in the company and the value of the share price to increase or grow by only 4%, because:

$$g = 16\% \times 0.25 = 4\%$$

Example 10.4 shows that, when a company retains a portion of current year profits for reinvestment, future profits and dividends should grow. Provided that the rate of return on the equity funds reinvested exceeds the investor's required rate of return, this growth should be reflected in an increase in the future in the market price of the company's shares.

This relationship will now be used to examine how an investor might value an ordinary share that is to be held for only one year.

ORDINARY SHARE VALUATION—SINGLE HOLDING PERIOD

For an investor holding an ordinary share for only one year, the current value of the share should be equal to the total of the present values of both the expected dividend to be received at the end of the year, D_1, and the anticipated market price of the share at year end, P_1. Given that we know the rate of return that investors require from investing in the company's ordinary shares (R_E) the value of the share, V_E, would be:

$$V_E = \text{present value of dividend } (D_1) + \text{present value of expected market price } (P_1)$$

$$= \frac{D_1}{(1 + R_E)} + \frac{P_1}{(1 + R_E)}$$

EXAMPLE 10.5 Calculation of ordinary share value—single holding period

Suppose that an investor is contemplating at the beginning of the year the purchase of RMI Ltd ordinary shares and has gathered the following data. At the end of the year RMI is expected to pay an ordinary share dividend of $1.64 and the market price for each share at the end of the year is projected to be $22. The rate of return required by the company's ordinary shareholders is 18%.

To determine the intrinsic value of RMI ordinary shares at the beginning of the year, use the same three-step process as that used to value bonds and preference shares.

> *Step 1: Estimate the amount and timing of the future cash flows that an investor can expect to receive.*
> At the end of the year: $1.64 dividend amount and a $22 expected share price.
>
> *Step 2: Determine the investor's required rate of return by evaluating the riskiness of the expected future cash flows.*
> In this example the required rate of return is given as 18%.
>
> *Step 3: Calculate the intrinsic value equal to the present value of the expected future cash flows discounted at the investor's required rate of return.*
>
> $$V_E = \frac{\$1.64}{(1 + 0.18)} + \frac{\$22}{(1 + 0.18)}$$
>
> $$= \$20.03$$

ORDINARY SHARE VALUATION—MULTIPLE HOLDING PERIODS

Since an ordinary share is frequently held by an investor for more than one year, a *multiple-holding-period valuation model* is needed. Also, as ordinary shares have no maturity date, the current shareholder is theoretically entitled to receive dividends forever. Even when the current shareholder dies, this entitlement is transferred to the shareholder's heirs, and so on. Therefore, we can define a general model for the valuation of an ordinary share as follows:

D_1 = dividend a year from now

$$V_E = \frac{D_1}{(1 + R_E)^1} + \frac{D_2}{(1 + R_E)^2} + \dots + \frac{D_n}{(1 + R_E)^n} + \dots + \frac{D_\infty}{(1 + R_E)^\infty} \tag{10-7}$$

Equation (10-7) states that the value of an ordinary share of equity (V_E) is equal to the present value of a perpetual stream of dividend amounts starting with the dividend at the end of the first year (D_1).

A problem with putting equation (10-7) into practice is that you might be able to get a reasonable estimate of the dividend amounts to be paid in one or two years time, but what about getting estimates of dividend amounts further into the future (and theoretically, infinity)?

One way around this problem is to make an assumption that the ordinary share dividend amounts will grow at a constant rate each year into the future. The resultant *constant-dividend-growth* ordinary-share valuation model is defined in words by equation (10-8) and symbols by equation (10-9).[12]

$$\text{Ordinary share price} = \frac{\text{dividend in year 1}}{\text{required rate of return} - \text{growth rate}} \tag{10-8}$$

$$V_E = \frac{D_1}{R_E - g} \tag{10-9}$$

Although the interpretation of equation (10-9) may not be intuitively obvious, it should be remembered that it calculates the present value of the infinite future dividend stream that grows at a rate, g, assuming that R_E is greater than g.

EXAMPLE 10.6   Calculation of ordinary share value—constant-dividend-growth model

Absco Ltd has just paid a $2 dividend to its ordinary shareholders and is expected to continue paying dividends every year from now to infinity, with the dividend amount forecast to grow at a rate of 10% per annum. Based on an assessment of the risk characteristics of Absco Ltd, the rate of return required by ordinary share investors is estimated to be 15%. Using this information and the constant-dividend-growth valuation model, the intrinsic value of the ordinary share is computed by the following three steps:

Step 1: Estimate the amount and timing of the future cash flows that an investor can expect to receive.
Since the $2 dividend has just been paid (D_0), we need to estimate the dividend amount to be received at the end of the first period (D_1). With a 10% per annum growth rate (g) of dividends, D_1 is expected to be 10% more than the previous dividend amount of D_0:

to determine the dividend price in life
← next dividend

$$D_1 = D_0(1 + g)$$
$$= \$2(1 + 0.10) = \$2.20$$

Step 2: Determine the investor's required rate of return by evaluating the riskiness of the expected future cash flows.
In this example the required rate of return is given as 15%.

Step 3: Calculate the intrinsic value equal to the present value of the expected future cash flows discounted at the investor's required rate of return.
Using equation (10-9):

$$V_E = \frac{D_1}{R_E - g}$$

$$= \frac{\$2.20}{0.15 - 0.10}$$

$$= \$44$$

What would happen to the intrinsic value of Absco Ltd's ordinary shares if the dividend growth rate (g) was greater than 10% per annum? We would expect investors to value the share more highly. For example, a 12% per annum growth rate would give a share value of $2.00(1.12)/(0.15 − 0.12) = $74.67.

An important constraint with the constant-dividend-growth model is that the dividend growth rate (g) cannot be greater than the required rate of return (R_E). For example, an 18% dividend growth rate would give a negative share value $2.00(1.18)/(0.15 − 0.18) = minus $78.66!

Another deficiency of the constant-dividend-growth valuation model is that its calculation of ordinary share value is dependent on a constant future dividend growth rate and being able to estimate the rate of return required by ordinary share investors. Even though the model is a simplification of reality, it helps to identify the major factors influencing ordinary share valuation, especially as managers frequently state that the *explicit* goal of the company is to annually increase its earnings and the amount of dividends that it pays per share.

In the sections above, the value of an ordinary share has been calculated as being equal to the present value of all future dividends. In practice, however, managers, along with many security analysts, often talk about the relationship between share value and earnings, rather than the relationship between share value and dividends. The appendix to this chapter provides some insights into the rationale and propriety of using earnings rather than dividends to value a company's shares. However, you should be cautious in using earnings to value a share, even though it may be a popular practice. This is because rational investors do not focus so much on reported earnings but on the cash flows generated by the company, with the present value of the future cash flows being the major determinant of a company's intrinsic value.

Finance at work

A COMPANY SPLIT INTO TWO

Publishing and Broadcasting Limited (PBL), established in the early 1990s through the merger of the Nine Television Network and Australian Consolidated Press, had grown from a diversified media organisation into a company with substantial gaming interests in Australia (Crown casino) and overseas.

In December 2007 Publishing and Broadcasting was split into two new companies: Consolidated Media Holdings (CMH) and Crown. Just prior to the split, the price of a PBL share on the Australian Securities Exchange was $20.80, which gave PBL a market value of more than $14 billion. At that time, the media business (to become CMH) was estimated to comprise about 20% of the value of PBL and the gaming business (to become Crown) comprised 80%.

The question challenging stock-market analysts prior to the PBL split was what the value of the shares of the two new companies would be when they listed on the stock exchange.

One way to estimate the new share prices is to apply the 20%–80% split to the last PBL price of $20.80, which gives an estimate for CMH shares of $4.16 and an estimate for Crown of $16.64.

This is a very crude share valuation method and is likely to be a poor estimate of the prices for the new shares. What method could be better?

Using the principles of valuation developed in this chapter, the focus should be on determining the present value of the cash flows that each of the new companies is expected to generate in the future.

Unfortunately, putting these valuation principles into practice is not so easy and requires answers to difficult questions, such as:

- What is the future earnings growth rate for the business of each company?
- What is the variability (risk) of these future earnings and what should be the discount rate used to calculate the present value?
- Should there be a 'holding company' premium or discount to the share price? For example, some analysts argue that the share price for a company like CMH, which has partial ownership of a number of different businesses, should be discounted.

Given these uncertainties, it is not surprising that investors encounter a range of share values from different analysts, such as predictions for the CMH share price ranging from $3.50 to $5.00 per share. Which of these valuations is correct can only be determined once the new shares trade on the share market.

Concept check

10.10 What features of ordinary shares are different from those of preference shares or bonds?

10.11 How does internal growth versus the growth from the infusion of new capital affect the original shareholders?

10.12 If a company decides to retain its earnings (profits), when would the value of the ordinary shares decrease?

10.13 What is the three-step process for ordinary share valuation? Explain the differences in the equations for a single holding period and multiple holding periods?

For answers go to MyFinanceLab or www.pearson.com.au/9781442539174

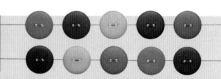

Your money

If you are thinking of buying or selling shares, what price should you be prepared to pay or receive? It can be confusing when the book value of a company's share is different from the share's market value. Being the outcome of the accounting process, which is largely based on historical costs, the book

(balance sheet) value of a share reflects the past. By contrast, the share's market value reflects the present value of the company's future earnings and dividends. As an uncertain future is of major concern to investors, the focus for investment decisions is on market values and not book values.

GFC

BOND AND SHARE VALUES

One of the major responses of governments to the Global Financial Crisis of 2008 was to significantly reduce official interest rates. If everything else had stayed constant, the expectation from the bond valuation formula would have been that, as bond yields fell in line with the fall in official interest rates, the price (value) of bonds would rise. Similarly, from the dividend-growth-valuation formula the expectation would have been that as the return required by shareholders fell in line with the fall in official interest rates, the price (value) of shares would rise.

However, one of the important lessons from the GFC was that everything else did not stay constant. In particular, the risk that some governments and companies could default on their bond obligations increased significantly so that the yield required by bond investors increased significantly, causing the prices of some bonds to fall. Similarly, the increased risk of shareholders receiving lower or nil dividend amounts had a significant downward effect on share prices.

Let us now turn to the last issue in bond and share valuation, that of the investor's expected returns, a matter of key importance to the financial manager.

Expected rates of return

OBJECTIVE 5

Appreciate the concept of an investor's expected rate of return and be able to compute the expected rate of return on bonds, preference shares and ordinary shares.

The chapter so far has discussed how investors can calculate the value (price) they are willing to pay or receive for an asset (security, instrument), by calculating the present value of the asset's future cash flows given the rate of return the investors require.

In Chapter 14, which deals with the cost of capital, this valuation process will be turned around by using the prices (value) of the company's debt and equity securities that are observed in the financial markets to infer the rates of return that debt and equity investors currently require. Even though, theoretically, individual investors determine the rate of return they require for each security, the market price of the security will be used to infer a consensus rate of return for all investors in that security.

To illustrate this process, suppose that Alpha Company has a bond maturing in one year with a face (par) value of $1000 and paying coupon interest of $100 per year. If the current market price of the bond is $1000, we can use the valuation model for a bond with a one-year term to solve for the rate of return the investor expects to receive (R_b):

$$V_b = \frac{\$I_1}{(1 + R_b)^1} + \frac{\$M}{(1 + R_b)^1}$$ **(10-10)**

$$\$1000 = \frac{\$100}{(1 + R_b)^1} + \frac{\$1000}{(1 + R_b)^1}$$

Solving for R_b gives 10% per annum. This answer means that for investors at the margin, the $1000 market price implies they have a required rate of return of 10% per annum. Investors at the margin are those who are willing to purchase the bond for $1000 but will not pay a higher price. For these investors, the rate of return they require (10%) is the same as the rate of return they can expect to receive (10%) if they pay the bond's current market price ($1000).[13]

BONDHOLDERS' EXPECTED RATE OF RETURN (YIELD TO MATURITY)

As illustrated in the example above, the **expected rate of return** on a bond-type instrument is given by the discount rate that equates the present value of the bond's future cash flows with the current market price of the bond.[14]

For a bond, the expected rate of return is also the rate of return the investor will earn if the bond is held to maturity, which is usually called the **yield to maturity**. Thus, when referring to bonds, you may often find the terminology of *expected rate of return*, *required rate of return*,

expected rate of return
The discount rate that equates the present value of the future cash flows with the current market price.

yield to maturity
The rate of return the investor will earn if a bond is held to maturity.

yield to maturity and *discount rate* used interchangeably. The symbol R_b will be used to represent the expected/required rate of return and the symbol *ytm* will be used for yield to maturity; however, these symbols too can be used interchangeably.

To determine the expected rate of return of a bond (R_b), we need to observe the current market price of the bond. Knowing that price, we can then solve for R_b by using equation (10-2) or (10-2a) for annual coupon payments, or equation (10-3) or (10-3a) for semi-annual payments.

EXAMPLE 10.7 Calculation of the expected rate of return on a bond

In Example 10.2 the investors' required rate of return was given as 10% per annum and we used the bond valuation model to calculate the value of St Marks 10.75% coupon notes with semi-annual payments that mature in five years time. Now we are going to observe in the financial markets the current price of these notes and use the bond valuation model to solve for the expected rate of return (yield to maturity).

Six months have passed since we did the valuation calculation in Example 10.2 and we have identified that the 10.75% per annum semi-annual St Marks coupon notes with four and a half years remaining until maturity (i.e. nine half-yearly coupon payments) are currently trading at a price of $118.49. The current expected rate of return (yield to maturity) for these notes is found by solving for $R_b / 2$ in equation (10-3) or (10-3a):

$$V_b = \sum_{t=1}^{9} \frac{\$5.375}{(1 + R^b/2)^t} + \frac{\$100}{(1 + R^b/2)^9}$$

$$\$118.49 = \$5.375(PVIFA_{i,9}) + \$100(PVIF_{i,9})$$

Without a financial calculator we have to use trial and error to solve for $R^b = i$. For example, if we try $i = 3\%$ (per half-year), $PVIFA_{3\%,9}$ (Appendix D) = 7.7861 and $PVIF_{3\%,9}$ (Appendix B) = 0.7664 produces an answer that is very close to the required present value of $118.49:

$$\$5.375 (7.7861) + \$100 (0.7664) = \$41.85 + \$76.64 = \$118.49$$

We can now conclude that the St Marks 10.75% per annum semi-annual coupon notes with a par/face/maturity value of $100, with four and a half years remaining until maturity and currently trading at a price of $118.49, have an expected rate of return of 3% per half-year coupon period. This is equal to a nominal yield to maturity rate of $2 \times 3\% = 6\%$ per annum.

What does this expected rate mean? An investor who buys a St Marks note for $118.49 can expect to receive a 6% per annum return on this investment that will be paid via the nine remaining $5.375 semi-annual coupon amounts and the $100 par value at maturity. Similarly, given these remaining cash-flow amounts of the note, an investor who requires a rate of return of 6% per annum would be prepared to pay $118.49 for the St Marks note.

Calculator solution

DATA INPUT		FUNCTION KEY
9		N
118.49	+/−	PV
5.375		PMT
100		FV
FUNCTION KEY		ANSWER
COMP I/Y		3.00%

Concept check

10.14 What does it mean if an investor's required rate of return for investing in a bond is different from the expected rate of return implied by the current market price of the bond?

10.15 How do semi-annual coupon payments affect the bond valuation process?

For answers go to MyFinanceLab or www.pearson.com.au/9781442539174

PREFERENCE SHAREHOLDERS' EXPECTED RATE OF RETURN

Computing the expected rate of return for non-redeemable preference shares is quite straightforward, as it only requires the rearrangement of the valuation equation (10-5) to solve for R_p:

$$R_p = \frac{D}{P}$$ **(10-11)**

Equation (10-11) states that the expected rate of return of a preference share (R_p) (also called the **dividend yield**) is equal to the perpetual constant preference dividend amount divided by the current preference share price.

For example, a preference share paying a constant \$0.52 annual dividend and with a present market price of \$4 has an expected rate of return (dividend yield) equal to:

$$R_p = \frac{D}{P} = \frac{\$0.52}{\$4} = 0.13, \text{ or } 13\% \text{ p.a.}$$

dividend yield
The dividend per share divided by the price of the security.

Therefore, investors at the margin who pay \$4 for a preference share that is paying \$0.52 in annual dividends can expect to receive a 15% per annum rate of return on their preference share investment.

Normally, the expected rate of return on preference shares is higher than the expected rate of return on bonds because the dividend cash flows from preference shares are likely to be more risky than the coupon interest and par value cash flows from bonds. A major cause of this difference in risk is that preference shareholders rank lower than bond investors in priority of payment if the company gets into financial difficulties.

The investor's expected rate of return is also affected by taxation considerations. For example, a preference dividend may be franked whereas interest income is not. As discussed in Chapter 2, preference shareholders are able to use franking (imputation) credits to offset their personal income tax liability on preference dividend income received. Thus, an investor may earn a higher after-tax rate of return from preference shares when compared with alternative investments that do not have franking credits or other tax benefits.

If preference dividends are franked, this has implications for the cost to the company of issuing new preference shares, especially on a pre-company-tax basis.[15]

ORDINARY SHAREHOLDERS' EXPECTED RATE OF RETURN

In an earlier section, equation (10-7) provided the valuation model of an ordinary share assuming that we could identify all the dividend amounts into infinity. Due to the obvious difficulty of applying this model in reality, a simplification is to assume that all future dividend amounts (D_t) increase at a constant annual compound growth rate of g so that the value of an ordinary share (V_E) can be estimated by the constant-dividend-growth model of equation (10-9).[16]

As was the case with bonds and preference shares, we can observe in the financial markets the current price for an ordinary share and rearrange equation (10-9) to solve for the expected rate of return (R_E) that is implied by the current market price:

$$R_E = \frac{D_1}{V_E} + g$$ **(10-12)**

$$\uparrow \qquad\qquad\qquad \uparrow$$

dividend yield   annual growth rate

Equation (10-12) states that the ordinary shareholder's expected rate of return is equal to the *dividend yield* plus the *dividend growth rate* (g). Although the growth rate, g, applies to the expected growth in the company's dividends in the future, the share's value may also be expected to increase at the same rate, given our assumptions. For this reason, g represents the annual percentage growth in the share value. In other words, the ordinary share investor's required rate of return is satisfied by receiving dividends and capital gains, as reflected by the expected percentage growth rate in the share price.

EXAMPLE 10.8 Calculation of the expected rate of return on an ordinary share

The ordinary share dividend expected to be paid by Violan Ltd at the end of the current year is $2.20 and the company's future earnings and dividends are expected to grow at a constant 10% annual rate. As the current price of Violan's ordinary shares is $44, the expected rate of return for investors in Violan Ltd's ordinary shares is:

$$R_E = \frac{D_1}{V_E} + g = \frac{\$2.20}{\$44} + 10\% = 5\% + 10\% = 15\% \text{ p.a.}$$

Note that the investor's expected rate of return of 15% per annum is equal to the dividend yield of 5% per annum plus the dividend growth factor of 10% per annum.

Concept check

10.16 In computing the expected rate of return, why should the growth factor be added to the dividend yield?

10.17 How does an efficient market affect the required and expected rates of return?

For answers go to MyFinanceLab or
www.pearson.com.au/9781442539174

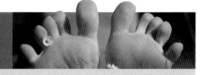

FYI

The current expected rate of return (yield to maturity) on a bond can be determined with a high degree of accuracy. This is because the bond's future cash flows, comprising coupon interest amounts and the maturity (par, face) value amount, are specified before the bond is issued and the current market price of the bond is observable from the financial market.

Similarly, the current expected rate of return on a preference share can be determined with a high degree of accuracy, because the fixed dividend amount is specified before the preference share is issued and the current market price of the preference share is observable from the financial market.

However, in the case of an ordinary share the investor's required rate of return is little more than an educated guess. This stems from the fact that, although the current market price of the share is observable from the financial market, the future dividend amounts of an ordinary share are not known with certainty. The best we can do is to make estimates of dividend amounts in the near future and assumptions about the future growth rate of dividends.

In summary, the expected rate of return implied by a given market price is the rate of return that investors at the margin require. These investors are willing to pay the current market price for a security because the rate of return they expect to receive is just equal to the rate of return they require to compensate them for the risk of investing in the security. The required rate of return of these investors is of particular significance to the financial manager, because it represents the amount the firm will have to pay (cost) to raise new finance by selling similar securities. This is the focus of Chapter 14, 'Cost of Capital'.

An understanding of the concepts and calculations regarding the valuation of securities is essential for sound financial decision making. This is especially the case in the context of the objective of maximising shareholder wealth, because this wealth is reflected by the *value* (price) of the company's ordinary shares.

OBJECTIVE 1

Valuation is an important component of financial management because it underlies the price that investors are prepared to pay to buy an asset or accept to sell an asset, including financial instruments such as bonds and shares.

OBJECTIVE 2

Although there are various definitions that can be used for the term *value*, the focus in this text is on the *intrinsic value of an asset which is equal to the present value of the future cash flows expected to be received from the asset, discounted at the investor's required rate of return.*

OBJECTIVE 3

Given this definition, the value of a financial security is a function of:
- *the amount and timing of the expected cash flows*
- the *riskiness* of the cash flows
- the investor's *required rate of return.*

OBJECTIVE 4

Although the valuation of any financial security entails the same basic principles, the components used in each situation vary. For example, valuing a bond-type instrument with a finite stream of cash flows involves computing the present value of the individual coupon interest amounts for each period and the par value amount on maturity. On the other hand, for securities such as irredeemable preference shares and ordinary shares that theoretically have an *infinite* dividend cash-flow stream, valuation involves calculating the present value of a perpetuity. For preference shares, the present value equals the amount of the annual dividend divided by the investor's required rate of return, whereas the value of ordinary shares, where the future dividends are expected to increase at a constant growth rate, is equal to the dividend yield plus the expected dividend growth rate.

OBJECTIVE 5

The *expected rate of return* on a security will be the required rate of return for investors who are willing to pay the current market price for the security. This rate is reached at the point where the present value of future cash flows to be received by the investor is just equal to the current market price of the security.

Key terms

bond	335	going-concern value	331	For a complete flashcard glossary go to MyFinanceLab at **www.pearson.com.au/myfinancelab**
book value	330	intrinsic value	331	
coupon interest rate	335	liquidation or disposal value	331	
dividend yield	347	market value	331	
earnings per share (EPS)	355	perpetuity	339	
efficient market	332	price–earnings ratio (PE)	332	
expected rate of return	345	yield to maturity	345	

Web works

Find the web page of an Australian retail company that interests you. Find the link that takes you to investor information. What types of information does the firm provide to its shareholders?

Review questions

10-1   What are the basic differences between book value, liquidation (disposal) value, going-concern value, market value and intrinsic value?

10-2   Explain the three factors that determine the value of an asset.

10-3   Explain the relationship between an investor's required rate of return and the value of a security.

10-4   What is a general definition of the intrinsic value of a security?

10-5   **(a)** How does a bond's par value differ from its market value?
(b) Explain the difference between the coupon interest rate and a bondholder's required rate.

10-6   Holders of ordinary shares receive two types of return from their investment. What are they?

10-7   State how the investor's required rate of return is computed.

10-8   Define the investor's expected rate of return.

10-9   Some practising financial analysts focus on earnings per share (EPS) as a major determinant of the firm's share price.

(a) Explain the link between EPS and the share price.
(b) What are the limitations of this approach to share valuation?

Self-test problems

For answers go to MyFinanceLab
www.pearson.com.au/myfinancelab

ST-1   (*Bond valuation*) Trico Ltd's debentures have a coupon rate of 8%, a par value of $1000, and they will mature in 20 years. If you require a return of 7%, what price would you be willing to pay for the debenture? What happens if you pay more for the debenture? What happens if you pay less? Assume that interest is paid annually.

ST-2   (*Bond valuation*) Sunn Ltd has corporate bonds, maturing in seven years, paying 8% interest on a $1000 face value. However, interest is paid semi-annually. If your required rate of return is 10% p.a., what is the value of the bond? How would your answer change if the interest were paid annually?

ST-3   (*Bondholder's expected rate of return*) Sharp Ltd's debentures are selling in the market for $1045. These 15-year debentures pay 7% interest annually on a $1000 par value. If they are purchased at the market price, what is the expected rate of return?

ST-4   (*Preference share valuation*) The non-redeemable preference shares of Armlo pay a $2.75 dividend per share. What is the value of a share if your required return is 9%?

ST-5   (*Share valuation*) Crosby Company Ltd has ordinary shares that paid $1.32 in dividends last year and this is expected to grow indefinitely at an annual 7% rate. What is the value of the shares if you require an 11% return?

Problems

For more problems and for answers to
problems marked with an asterisk (*)
go to MyFinanceLab at
www.pearson.com.au/myfinancelab

10-1*   (*Bond valuation*) Calculate the value of a bond that will mature in 12 years time and has a $1000 face value. The coupon interest rate is 8% p.a. paid annually and the bond investors' required rate of return is 12% p.a.

10-2   (*Preference share valuation*) What is the value of an irredeemable preference share that has a dividend rate of 14% on a $100 par value? The appropriate discount rate given the risk level for the preference shares is 12%.

10-3*   (*Bond valuation*) Enterprise Ltd has issued debentures with a par value of $1000 and a 9% p.a. coupon rate. The coupon interest amounts are paid semi-annually and the debentures mature in 8 years. If your required rate of return to invest in these debentures is 8% p.a., what is your valuation of the debenture? What would your valuation be if the debenture paid the coupon interest amount annually?

10-4 (*Bondholder expected return*) You are willing to pay $900 for a 10-year semi-annual coupon bond with $1000 par value and a coupon interest rate of 8% p.a. What is your expected rate of return?

10-5* (*Expected return on preference shares*) Minerva Ltd's preference shares are selling for $13 and paying $1.95 in dividends. What is your expected rate of return if you purchase this security at the current market price?

10-6 (*Expected return on preference shares*) You own 200 irredeemable preference shares issued by Irinic Resources Ltd, which currently sell for $30 per share and pay annual dividends of $3.40 per share.

   (a) What is your expected return?
   (b) Given the current preference share price and your requirement for a 10% p.a. return given your recent assessment of the risk associated with Irinic Resources Ltd preference shares, should you sell or buy more of the company's preference shares?

10-7* (*Ordinary share valuation*) It is January and you are considering purchasing Marigo Ltd's ordinary shares at the current price of $50 per share and then selling them at the end of December just after the annual dividend expected to be $6 is paid. How much will the company's ordinary share price have to appreciate by the end of December for you to earn your required rate of return of 15% p.a.?

10-8 (*Expected return on ordinary shares*) Made Ltd's ordinary shares currently sell for $22.50 each. The company's executives anticipate a constant dividend growth rate of 10% p.a. with $2 per share being the expected amount of the next dividend to be paid at the end of the year.

   (a) If you are considering purchasing Made Ltd's ordinary shares, what rate of return can you expect to earn?
   (b) If you require a 17% return, should you purchase the shares?

10-9* (*Ordinary share valuation*) Header Motors Ltd paid a $3.50 ordinary share dividend last year. If the company's ordinary share dividends are expected to have a growth rate of 5% p.a., what is the value of each ordinary share if ordinary share investors require a 20% rate of return?

10-10 (*Measuring growth*) Given that a company's return on equity is 18% p.a. and management plans to retain 40% of earnings for investment purposes, what will be the company's growth rate of future earnings?

10-11* (*Capital asset pricing model and share valuation*) You are considering the purchase of 100 ordinary shares of Main Ltd. The beta on the security is 1.65, and the current market premium is 5.6%.

   (a) If the riskless rate of interest is currently 12%, what will your required rate of return be? (The solution requires you to use what you learned in Chapter 9.)
   (b) Given the rate of return computed in part **(a)**, and an expected ordinary share dividend at the end of the next period of $8.50 which is assumed to grow at 5% p.a. thereafter, estimate the value of an ordinary share in this company.

10-12 (*Shareholder expected return*) Morris Ltd shares are currently selling for $3.38 and the company recently paid a dividend to ordinary shareholders of 30 cents per share and has projected its future growth at a rate of 8.5% p.a. If you purchase shares in the company at the market price, what is your expected rate of return?

10-13* (*Ordinary share valuation*) The next dividend that Hexaon Ltd is expected to pay to its ordinary shareholders in 12 months time is $1.85 and at that time the market price of the shares is projected to be $42.50. If the ordinary share investor's required rate of return is 11%, estimate the current value of each ordinary share.

10-14 (*Expected return on shares*) The current market price for Hobart Ltd's ordinary shares is $43 and analysts have estimated that in one year's time an ordinary share dividend of $2.84 can be expected to be paid and the price for each share at that time to be $48. Determine the rate of return that can be expected to be earned by investing today in the ordinary shares of Hobart Ltd.

10-15* (*Bondholder expected return*) ANX Ltd's corporate bonds with 20 years to maturity pay 9% coupon interest annually on a $1000 par value. If you buy the bonds at $945, what is your expected rate of return?

10-16 (*Bondholder expected return*) Hoyden Corporation's $1000 bonds mature in 15 years and pay 8% coupon interest annually. If you purchase the bonds for $1175, what is your expected rate of return?

10-17*(*Bond valuation*) An issue of Australian treasury bonds with par of $1000 matures in 15 years and pays 8% coupon interest annually. The market price of the bonds is $1085, and your required rate of return is 10% p.a.

    (a) Compute the bond's expected rate of return (yield to maturity).

    (b) Determine the value of the bond to you, given your required rate of return.

    (c) Should you purchase the bond?

10-18 (*Preference share valuation*) Gree Limited's preference shares are selling for $3.50 in the market and pay a 40 cent dividend.

    (a) What is the expected rate of return on the preference shares?

    (b) If a preference share investor has a required rate of return of 10% p.a., what is the value of the share for that investor?

    (c) Should that investor acquire the shares?

10-19*(*Ordinary share valuation*) The ordinary shares of NCP Ltd paid a dividend of $1.32 last year and dividends are expected to grow at an 8% annual rate for an indefinite number of years.

    (a) If NCP's current market price is $23.50, calculate the expected rate of return.

    (b) If your required rate of return is 10.5% p.a., calculate the value of a share for you.

    (c) Should you make an investment in NCP Ltd ordinary shares?

10-20 (*Bond valuation*) You own a bond with a par value of $1000 that pays a $100 annual coupon. The bond matures in 15 years. Your required rate of return is 12% p.a.

    (a) Calculate the value of the bond.

    (b) How does the value of the bond change if your required rate of return (i) increases to 15% p.a., or (ii) decreases to 8% p.a.?

    (c) Assume that the bond matures in 5 years instead of 15 years. Recompute your answers in part **(b)**.

10-21*(*Bondholder's expected rate of return*) Abner Corporation's bonds mature in 15 years and pay 9% annual coupons. If you purchased the bonds today for $1250, what is your expected rate of return?

10-22 (*Ordinary share valuation*) Wayne Co.'s outstanding ordinary shares are currently selling in the market for $33, paid a dividend of $2.30 per share last year, and the company expects annual earnings and dividend growth to be 5% p.a.

    (a) Given that you require a 15% p.a. rate of return, what is the value of an ordinary share to you?

    (b) Determine the return that you can expect to earn from purchasing an ordinary share in Wayne Co.

    (c) Should you purchase Wayne Co. ordinary shares?

10-23*(*Preference share valuation*) Pioneer Ltd's preference shares are selling for $33 each and pay a $3.60 annual dividend.

    (a) What is the expected rate of return on a preference share?

    (b) If a preference share investor's required rate of return is 10% p.a., what is the value of the preference share for the investor?

    (c) Should the investor purchase Pioneer Ltd's preference shares?

10-24 (*Ordinary shareholder expected return*) Michaels Ltd has just paid ordinary shareholders an annual dividend amount of $1.75 per share and management has announced that it expects future dividends to grow at 4% p.a. The company's ordinary shares are currently selling in the market for $29.50.

    (a) What is the expected rate of return from the company's ordinary shares?

    (b) Should you purchase the company's ordinary shares if your required rate of return is 14% p.a.?

10-25*(*Measuring growth*) Vitex Corporation's return on equity is 17% and management has plans to retain 30% of earnings for reinvestment in the company's business.

    (a) What is the company's growth rate?

    (b) How would the company's growth rate change if management **(i)** increased retained earnings to 40%, or **(ii)** decreased the retention of profits to 25%?

10-26 (*Integrative problem*) You are considering three investments. The first is a bond that is selling in the market at $1100. The bond has a $1000 par value, pays coupon interest annually at 13%, and is scheduled to mature in 15 years. For bonds of this risk class, you believe that a 14% p.a. rate of return should be required. The second investment that you are analysing is an irredeemable preference share ($100 par value) that pays an annual dividend of $13 and currently sells for $90. Your required rate of return to invest in this preference share security is 15% p.a. The third investment is the ordinary shares of a company that recently paid a $2 dividend. Over the last 10-year period the company's earnings per share have increased from $3 to $6, which analysts consider to be a reasonable reflection of the expected growth in the company's dividend amount per ordinary share for the indefinite future. These shares are currently selling for $20, and you think a reasonable required rate of return to compensate for risk is 20% p.a.

    (a) Calculate the value of each security based on your required rate of return.

    (b) Which investment(s) should you accept as an investment? Why?

    (c) (i) If the general level of interest rates fell so that your required rates of return changed to 12% p.a. for the bond, 14% p.a. for the preference share and 18% p.a. for the ordinary share, how would your answers change to parts **(a)** and **(b)**?

        (ii) Assuming again that your required rate of return for the ordinary shares is 20% p.a. but the anticipated growth rate changes to 12% p.a., would your answers to parts **(a)** and **(b)** be different?

10-27 (*Integrative problem*) You have a substantial amount of money invested in three different unlisted financial securities. As these investments are not traded on the financial markets, they do not have an observable market price but you have ascertained the following information:

- Company bonds: $1000 face (par) value with 6 years to maturity, paying 11% p.a. semi-annual coupons. Currently the yield on 6-year government bonds is 6% p.a. and you think that a risk premium of 4% p.a. is appropriate for these company bonds.
- Preference shares: Irredeemable, paying 8% annually on $10 par value, and your estimate of the risk premium for these shares is 7% p.a.
- Ordinary shares: Five years ago the annual dividend paid by the company was 12 cents per share and given this year's dividend of 18.5 cents per share you expect future dividends to grow at the same annual compound rate. From your analysis of the variability of the company's earnings over the last five years, you deem a reasonable estimate of the company's market risk (beta) to be 1.7. Also, you know that the long-term historical average return from a market portfolio investment is 13% p.a.

On the basis of this information, estimate the current value of each security.

Case study

Panteco Ltd is a diversified company that owns more than 20 subsidiary companies spanning many sectors of the economy. It is considering buying all the issued ordinary shares of a competitor company. The problem for Panteco Ltd is that, as the takeover target does not have its shares listed on the stock exchange, it is not possible to obtain from the market a price for the target's ordinary shares. The board of directors of Panteco Ltd has given you the task of providing an estimate of the intrinsic value of the target company's ordinary shares.

    1. What model would you recommend using to determine the intrinsic value of the target company's shares?

    2. What data does the model require you to determine?

    3. How could you estimate the dividend growth rate?

    4. How could you estimate the required rate of return?

Notes

1. The attributes of bond-type instruments are described in more detail in Chapter 18 and the attributes of preference shares and ordinary shares in Chapter 19.
2. Adapted from Justin Fox, 'Is the market rational?', *Fortune*, 3 December 2002.
3. Unsecured notes are classified as bond-type instruments (as are debentures) because they have similar characteristics to those of bonds. The main reason for these different names is what happens if the issuer defaults. A debenture is the name that has traditionally been given in Australia to instruments issued by companies that provide investors with some security (e.g. by a charge over the firm's assets) if default occurs. An unsecured note is the name given to instruments issued by companies that do not provide investors with a prior claim on the company's assets. Investors in unsecured notes will demand a higher rate of return, because their investment is unsecured and therefore riskier than the same company's debentures.
4. You may want to return to Chapter 4 to review the explanation of financial calculator solutions.
5. The calculator solution often results in a slightly different answer from the formula solution because of small rounding errors that occur when using the interest factors from the present-value tables. The more accurate calculator solutions would be used in practice to compute prices.
6. Recall from Chapter 4 that this answer is negative because the payments and future value were input as positive cash-flow amounts. The sign of these cash flows corresponds with a situation where a buyer would have to pay (cash outflow) a price of $102.84 to obtain future cash inflows in the form of the coupon payments and the maturity (par) value.
7. The logic for having to adapt equation (10-2) to recalculate the value of a semi-annual bond-type instrument is similar to that discussed in Chapter 4, where the effect of compounding within a year was examined. That is, 10% per annum compounded annually is not the same as 10% per annum compounded semi-annually. This is demonstrated by the effective rate, where 10% per annum compounded annually has an effective rate of 10% per annum, whereas 10% compounded semi-annually has an effective rate of 10.25% per annum. The rate of return on bond-type instruments (called the *yield*) is usually quoted as a nominal rate percent per annum (also known as the annual percentage rate, APR), with the number of compounding periods per annum corresponding to the number of coupons paid per annum. For example, quarterly coupons would imply quarterly compounding. So, if St Marks Ltd note issue does have half-yearly payments at a quoted yield of 10% per annum, the effective yield would be 10.25% per annum.
8. Due to rounding in the tables, this value is slightly different from the calculator solution value.
9. It is not being argued that the existing ordinary shareholders never benefit from the use of new external financing; however, this benefit is more evasive when there are efficient capital markets.
10. The return on equity is the percentage return on the ordinary shareholders' investment in the company and can be computed as:

$$\text{Return on equity} = \frac{\text{net profit}}{\text{book value of shareholders' funds}}$$

11. The retention rate is also equal to (1 – the percentage of profits paid out as dividends). The percentage of profits paid out as dividends is often called the dividend-payout ratio (see Chapter 17).
12. Where ordinary-share dividends grow at a constant rate of g every year, the dividend at the end of year 1 (D_1) can be estimated from the dividend that was actually paid at the end of the current year (D_0): $D_1 = D_0(1 + g)$. This principle can be applied to estimate the dividend at the end of any (t) year as $D_0(1 + g)^t$. This enables the multiple-period ordinary-share valuation equation (10-7) to be rewritten:

$$V_E = \frac{D_0(1 + g)^1}{(1 + R_E)^1} + \frac{D_0(1 + g)^2}{(1 + R_E)^2} + \dots + \frac{D_0(1 + g)^n}{(1 + R_E)^n} + \dots + \frac{D_0(1 + g)^\infty}{(1 + R_E)^\infty}$$

If both sides are multiplied by $(1 + R_E)/(1 + g)$, and then subtracted from the product, the result is:

$$\frac{V_E(1 + R_E)}{(1 + g)} - V_E = D_0 - \frac{D_0(1 + g)^\infty}{(1 + R_E)^\infty}$$

If $R_E > g$, which should normally hold, $[D_0(1 + g)/(1 + R_E)]$ approaches zero. As a result:

$$\frac{V_E(1 + R_E)}{(1 + g)} - V_E = D_0$$

$$V_E \frac{V_E(1 + R_E)}{(1 + g)} - V_E \frac{(1 + g)}{(1 + g)} = D_0$$

$$V_E \frac{V_E(1 + R_E) - (1 + g)}{(1 + g)} = D_0$$

$$V_E(R_E - g) = D_0(1 + g)$$

Thus, as stated in the chapter as equation (10-9):

$$V_E = \frac{D_1}{R_E - g}$$

13. In Chapter 14, this 10% required rate of return for the investor at the margin will be used to measure the cost of new debt capital to the firm. This is because, when the firm sells for $1000 a bond that requires it to pay $1000 plus $100 interest one year later, the cost to the firm to borrow $1000 for one year is 10% per annum.
14. When the text speaks of *computing* an expected rate of return, it is not describing the situation very accurately. This is because an *expected* rate of return is an *ex ante* (that is, *before the fact*) value based on 'expected future cash flows'. As a consequence, expected rates of return cannot be observed directly and therefore can only be 'estimated'.
15. Chapter 14 outlines the procedure to determine the before-tax cost of preference shares issued by a taxation category 1 company.
16. In some examples and problems the expected dividend at the end of year one (D_1) is not given. Instead the dividend amount that has been paid in the current year (D_0) is provided. If so, equation (10-9) must be restated as follows:

$$V_E = \frac{D_1}{R_E - g} = \frac{D_0(1 + g)}{R_E - g}$$

Appendix

The relationship between earnings and value

In understanding the relationship between a company's earnings and the value (price) of its ordinary shares, it is helpful to look at the relationship for a non-growth company and then for a growth company.

THE RELATIONSHIP BETWEEN EARNINGS AND VALUE FOR A NON-GROWTH COMPANY

When we speak of a non-growth company, we mean one that pays out all of its net profits (earnings per share) as dividends and therefore has no retained earnings for reinvestment. In this situation, the only investment the company makes is the amount of the depreciation on long-lived assets to maintain the status quo so that the company does not lose its current earnings capacity.

As the company is paying all of its earnings as dividends, the total dividend amount in year t equals the total earnings amount in year t. Also, because there is no growth, the company earns a constant annual amount of earnings and pays out a constant dividend annual amount to its ordinary shareholders. For the ordinary shareholders, a constant dividend stream is essentially no different from owning an irredeemable preference share. We can therefore use the formula for the valuation of a preference share to determine the value of the non-growth ordinary share, NG:

$$\text{Value of non-growth firm's share} = \frac{\text{earnings per share}_1}{\text{required rate of return}} \qquad \textbf{(10-13)}$$

$$= \frac{\text{dividends per share}_1}{\text{required rate of return}} \qquad \textbf{(10-14)}$$

$$V_{E,NG} = \frac{EPS_1}{R_E} = \frac{D_1}{R_E}$$

> **EXAMPLE 10.9 Value of non-growth firm's share**
>
> The Reeves Company expects its earnings per share this year to be $12, all of which is to be paid out as dividends to the investors. If the investors have a required rate of return of 14% per annum, the value of the non-growth ordinary share would be $85.71:
>
> $$V_{E,NG} = \frac{\$12}{0.14} = \$85.71$$

In this example, the relationship between **earnings per share (EPS)** and the value of an ordinary share is direct and unmistakable. For example, if due to inflation the company's earnings per share were to increase by 10% to $13.20, then the value of an ordinary share should also increase by 10% to $94.28 ($13.20/0.14 = $94.28). As a consequence, the ratio of share value (price) to earnings will be a constant (e.g. $85.71:$12 = 7.1425, $94.28:$13.20 = 7.1425), as will the ratio of earnings to price ($12:$85.71= 0.14, $13.20:$94.28 = 0.14).

A departure from these constant relationships would occur only if the investors changed their required rate of return, owing to a change in their perception about such things as risk or anticipated inflation. However, in the absence of a change in the required rate of return, there

earnings per share (EPS)
Earnings per share is equal to net profit (after tax) divided by the number of ordinary shares issued.

OBJECTIVE **6**

Understand the relationship between a company's earnings and the value of its ordinary shares.

is good reason to assume, for the non-growth company, that the ratio between next year's earnings and next year's share price will be the same as for this year.

THE RELATIONSHIP BETWEEN EARNINGS AND VALUE FOR A GROWTH COMPANY

We can now turn our attention to a growth company. This is a company that reinvests some of its profits back into the business and as a consequence its future earnings and dividend payouts should be able to grow. Note that this growth is in addition to increases in earnings and dividends which can occur due to factors such as inflation. If earnings and dividends are expected to increase at a constant growth rate, we can use the dividend growth valuation model to estimate the value of an ordinary share:

$$\text{Ordinary share price} = \frac{\text{dividend in year 1}}{\text{required rate of return} - \text{growth rate}} \qquad \textbf{(10-8)}$$

$$V_E = \frac{D_1}{R_E - g} \qquad \textbf{(10-9)}$$

Equations (10-8) and (10-9) are the conventional ways of estimating the value of an ordinary share for a growth company; however, they are not the only ways.

The value of an ordinary share could also be described by equation (10-15) as the present value of the earnings stream provided from the company's existing assets plus the present value of any future growth in ordinary share dividends resulting from the reinvestment of future earnings:

$$V_E = \frac{EPS_1}{R_E} + PVDG \qquad \textbf{(10-15)}$$

where EPS_1/R_E = the present value of the cash-flow stream provided by the existing assets
$PVDG$ = the net present value of any dividend growth resulting from the reinvestment of future earnings

The first term, EPS_1/R_E, is immediately understandable given the earlier discussion about non-growth shares, as it is the present value of a non-growth cash-flow stream.

The second term, the present value of future dividend growth, $PVDG$, needs some clarification.

First, we need to identify the fraction of the company's earnings that are retained in the business (r). From the earnings generated in year 1 (EPS_1), the amount the company reinvests will be equal, $r \times EPS_1$. This implies that the amount of earnings not retained and paid as a dividend in year 1 (D_1) will be equal to $(1 - r) \times EPS_1$.

Second, any earnings that are reinvested should be expected to yield a rate of return which we will assume is equal to the company's historical rate of return on equity (ROE). The company should therefore expect to receive an increased cash flow in all future years, which will come from the return generated by the investment of year one retained earnings, equal to $ROE \times (r \times EPS_1)$. As this return on year one investment cash flows continues in perpetuity, we can calculate the net present value from reinvesting a part of the company's year one earnings (NPV_1) as being equal to the present value of the perpetual return on year one investment cash flows less the cost of the investment (the amount retained in year one):

$$NPV_1 = \underset{\substack{\uparrow \\ \text{present value of} \\ \text{increased cash flows}}}{\frac{r \times EPS_1 \times ROE}{R_E}} - \underset{\substack{\uparrow \\ \text{amount of cash} \\ \text{retained and reinvested}}}{r \times EPS_1} \qquad \textbf{(10-16)}$$

If the company continued to reinvest a fixed percentage of earnings (r) each year after year one and earned a constant *ROE* on these investments, there would also be a net present value of the earnings from each year's reinvestment in all the following years. That is, we would have NPV_2, NPV_3, $NPV_4 \ldots NPV\infty$.

As we are assuming that r and *ROE* are both constant, this series of future *NPV*s will increase at a constant growth rate (g) equal to $r \times ROE$. We can therefore use a modification of the *constant-dividend-growth valuation model* to value *PVDG*, as follows:

$$PVDG = \frac{NPV_1}{R_E - g} \qquad \text{(10-17)}$$

Now we can determine the value of an ordinary share as being equal to the sum of:

(1) the present value of a constant stream of earnings generated from the company's existing assets, and

(2) the present value of an increasing dividend stream coming from earnings that are retained and reinvested in new assets:

$$V_E = \frac{EPS_1}{R_E} = \frac{NPV_1}{R_E - g} \qquad \text{(10-18)}$$

EXAMPLE 10.10   Value of growth firm's share

The Upp Company is expected to have earnings per share of $8 this year. Of these earnings, 40% will be retained (r) for reinvestment and 60% will be paid out as dividends to ordinary shareholders. The company's management expects to earn an 18% return on any funds retained (*ROE*) and the company's ordinary share investors have a 12% required rate of return (R_E).

We can use both the constant-dividend-growth model and the *PVDG* model to estimate the value of Upp Company's ordinary shares. However, it is important to be aware that these models assume that the company's *ROE* will be constant and that management will consistently retain the same percentage of earnings each year to be used for new investments

Constant-dividend-growth model
Given the company's retention ratio $r = 40\%$ and *ROE* = 18%, the company's ordinary dividend amount should increase by $r \times ROE = (0.4)(18\%) = 7.2\%$ each year = g.

On the basis of expected earnings for the current year of $8 per share, the ordinary share dividend amount to be paid at the end of this year (D_1) would be equal to the dividend-payout ratio $(1 - r) \times$ expected earnings per share (EPS_1): $0.60 \times \$8 = \$4.80$.

Given a 12% required rate of return (R_E) for the investors, the value of each ordinary share will be equal to:

$$V_E = \frac{D_1}{R_E - g} \qquad \text{(10-9)}$$

$$= \frac{\$4.80}{0.12 - 0.072}$$

$$= \$100$$

PVDG **model**
The *PVDG* model involves separately computing (1) the present value of the non-growth earnings stream, and (2) the present value of the earnings stream generated by reinvestment in future growth opportunities.

1. Solving for the value assuming non-growth [equation (10-19) is equivalent to equation (10-13)]:

$$V_{E,NG} = \frac{EPS_1}{R} \qquad \text{(10-19)}$$

$$= \frac{\$8}{0.12} = \$66.67$$

2. Value of the future growth opportunities coming from reinvesting company profits (earnings) each year:

$$PVDG = \frac{NPV_1}{R_E - g} \qquad \text{(10-17)}$$

Although we know R_E to be 12% and the earnings (dividend) growth rate to be 7.2%, we need to determine NPV_1:

$$NPV_1 = \frac{r \times EPS_1 \times ROE}{R_E} - r \times EPS_1 \qquad \text{(10-16)}$$

$$= \frac{(0.4)(\$8)(0.18)}{0.12} - (0.4)(\$8)$$

$$= \$4.80 - \$3.20$$

$$= \$1.60$$

The *PVDG* may now be computed using equation (10-17):

$$PVDG = \frac{\$1.60}{0.12 - 0.072}$$

$$= \$33.33$$

3. The value of the combined streams $V_E = \$66.67 + \$33.33 = \$100$

From Example 10.10 we see that the value of the growth opportunities represents a significant portion of the total ordinary share value—33%, to be exact. Furthermore, in looking at the *PVDG* model we can observe that the following factors influence the value of an ordinary share:

- the size of the company's beginning earnings per share (EPS_1)
- the percentage of profits retained (r)
- the spread between the return generated on new investments (ROE) and the ordinary share investor's required rate of return (R_E).

The first factor relates to company size and the second to management's decision about the company's retention rate of earnings (profits).

Although the first two factors are significant, the last one is the key to wealth creation by management. This is because wealth is not necessarily created for shareholders simply because management retains profits. Increases in wealth occur only if the return on equity from the investments (ROE) is greater than the ordinary share investor's required rate of return (R_E). Thus, we should expect the market to assign value not only to the reported earnings per share for the current year but also to the anticipated growth opportunities that have a marginal rate of return that exceeds the required rate of return of investors in the company's ordinary shares.

Appendix problems

A-1 (*Ordinary share valuation—PVDG model*) The Burgon Co. Ltd management expects the company's earning per share to be $5 this year. The company's policy is to pay out 35% of its earnings as dividend to ordinary shareholders. In looking at the investment opportunities available to the company, the return on equity is estimated to be 20% p.a. for the foreseeable future. Use the *PVDG* model to find the value of the company's ordinary shares. Ordinary shareholders' required rate of return is 16% p.a. Verify your results with the constant-dividend-growth model.

A-2 (*Ordinary share valuation—PVDG model*) You want to know the impact of changing the proportion of your company's earnings that are retained on the value of its ordinary shares. By the end of this current year the earnings per share on existing assets is estimated to be $7. Given the information below, calculate the value of an ordinary share under the different scenarios.

(a) No growth: zero retention and ordinary shareholder required rate of return of 18% p.a.

(b) You are considering three earnings-retention policies on a long-term basis:

(i) retain no earnings, instead distributing all earnings to shareholders in the form of dividends

(ii) retain 30% of earnings

(iii) retain 60% of earnings.

The return on equity may be as low as 16% or as high as 24%, with an expected return on equity of 18%.

Using the *PVDG model* estimate the ordinary share price for each scenario.

	RETENTION RATE		
POSSIBLE ROE	0%	30%	60%
16%			
18%			
24%			

(c) What do your answers show about the impact of different ROEs and retention rates on valuation of the company's ordinary shares?

For more problems go to MyFinanceLab at www.pearson.com.au/myfinancelab

359

Learning objectives

After reading this chapter, you should be able to:

1 Understand how to identify the sources and types of profitable investment opportunities.
2 Understand the general principles in selecting capital-budgeting criteria.
3 Evaluate projects using discounted-cash-flow criteria.
4 Evaluate projects using non-discounted-cash-flow criteria.
5 Understand the effects of taxation in capital budgeting.
6 Explain the importance of ethical considerations in capital-budgeting decisions.
7 Understand current business practice with respect to the use of capital-budgeting criteria.

For a complete eBook go to MyFinanceLab
www.pearson.com.au/myfinancelab

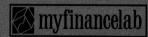

Capital budgeting: concepts and methods

CHAPTER PREVIEW

Every time a firm starts up, expands its facilities or operations, or just replaces its assets as they wear out or become obsolete, a capital-budgeting decision has to be made. **Capital budgeting** is the process by which the firm renews and reinvents itself, adapting old projects to the times and finding new ones. The success or failure of a major capital-investment project may carry the success of the firm along with it. The capital-budgeting process relies heavily on comparing cash inflows from the project, which may spread over many years, with cash outflows incurred by the firm, which typically occur close to the present. A number of capital-budgeting techniques exist to assist financial managers to determine the acceptability of investment proposals. In general, a *good investment is one that is worth more than it costs to make*. This observation is a good one to file away and come back to over and over again as we go through the rest of this chapter. Keep in mind during all this that what we are developing is a framework for decision making.

As we will illustrate in this chapter, the valuation of investment opportunities relies on a number of our basic principles. First, the value of a project largely depends on its expected cash flows, which is consistent with *Principle 3: Cash—not profits—is king*. Second, the cash inflows and outflows of an investment opportunity typically spread out over a number of years. As a result, managers rely on *Principle 2: The time value of money—a dollar received today is worth more than a dollar received in the future* to make cash flows that occur at different time periods comparable. Third, different projects carry different levels of risk which need to be accounted for in the capital-budgeting process. *Principle 1: The risk–return trade-off—we won't take on additional risk unless we expect to be compensated with additional return*, therefore, underpins a large part of the material covered in this chapter. We open the chapter with an overview of the capital-budgeting process, which is directly relevant to *Principle 5: The curse of competitive markets—why it's hard to find exceptionally profitable projects*.

capital budgeting
The decision-making process with respect to investment in fixed assets.

Regardless of your program

MAKING PERSONAL INVESTMENT DECISIONS

Over your career you will be faced with investment opportunities that require some type of evaluation and analysis. Whether the decision is to purchase a piece of property that you hope to develop and resell or to start and run a business, capital-budgeting analysis will help you make the right decision. Investment in real estate often requires substantial outlay in the form of the purchasing price and related purchasing costs such as stamp duty and legal fees. Many properties also require additional investment to improve their conditions. Having completed the renovation, you might consider at least two alternatives: selling the property to someone else to rent and manage, or keeping the property and managing the rentals yourself. The tools we develop in this chapter will help you evaluate the initial property investment as well as the decision of whether or not to keep and manage the property.

OBJECTIVE 1

Understand how to identify the sources and types of profitable investment opportunities.

The sources and types of profitable investment projects

In 1955 the Walt Disney Company was largely a movie studio, but that all changed when Disney decided to invest $17.5 million to build Disneyland Park in Anaheim, California. The decision to build the park was a major capital-budgeting decision for Disney and was so successful that Disney later decided to open theme parks in Orlando, Tokyo, Paris and Hong Kong. In retrospect, how important was this investment? Today, parks and resorts account for over 30% of Disney's revenue. There are three important lessons from the Disney theme park story:

Lesson 1: *Capital-budgeting decisions are critical in defining a company's business.* Had Disney not embarked on its theme park strategy, it would be a very different company today.

Lesson 2: *Very large investments are frequently the result of many smaller investment decisions that define a business strategy.* Disney did not launch its theme parks in 1955 with a plan to invest $3.5 billion some 50 years later to build the Hong Kong site. Rather, the $3.5 billion investment in Hong Kong Disneyland was the result of a series of smaller investments that led to the eventual decision to expand the franchise into Asia.

Lesson 3: *Successful investment choices lead to the development of managerial expertise and capabilities that influence the firm's choice of future investments.* Disney's early success with its theme park in California provided its managers with the expertise and confidence to replicate the theme park in Orlando and then internationally. This storehouse of talent and experience gave Disney a competitive edge on would-be competitors who might seek to enter the theme park business.

THE SOURCES OF PROFITABLE PROJECTS

How did the Walt Disney Company come up with the idea to invest in the theme park? Without question, it is much easier to *evaluate* profitable projects than to *find* them. In competitive markets, generating ideas for profitable projects is extremely difficult. If an industry is generating large profits, then new entrants are attracted to it, and the additional competition and added capacity can result in profits being driven down. As a result, in competitive markets extremely large profits and net cash flows simply cannot exist for very long. Given that somewhat bleak scenario, how can a firm find profitable projects? The answer is that as long as the markets are competitive they will be difficult to find, so what the firm has to do is to try to make its markets less prone to the rigours of perfect competition. The two most common ways of making the market less competitive are to *differentiate the product* in some key way and to *achieve a cost advantage* that competitors cannot match, which in turn discourages new entrants into the market. Sometimes, a successful project might not be developing a new product but *introducing an existing product in a new market.*

Product differentiation

Product differentiation insulates a product from competition, thereby allowing a company to charge a premium price. If products are differentiated, consumer choice is no longer made by

Back to the principles

The fact that profitable projects are difficult to find relates directly to **Principle 5: The curse of competitive markets—why it's hard to find exceptionally profitable projects**. When that principle was introduced, it was stated that successful investments involve the reduction of competition by creating barriers to entry, through either product differentiation or cost advantages. The key to locating profitable projects is to understand how and where they exist.

price alone. For example, many people are willing to pay a premium for Gloria Jean's coffee. They simply want Gloria Jean's and price is not important. In the pharmaceutical industry, patents create barriers to competitors. Schering-Plough's *Claritin*, an allergy-relief medicine, and Hoffman-La Roche's *Valium*, a tranquiliser, use patents to protect those drugs from direct competition. Other types of intellectual property, such as copyright on books, music and computer software, also help to legally protect profits. Trademarks (such as the McDonald's logo) and brand names (such as Coca-Cola) are protected from unauthorised use and thus can be immensely valuable to firms; as marketers say, 'people buy brands, not products'.

Quality and service are also used to differentiate products. For example, Levi's has long prided itself on the quality of its jeans. As a result, it has been able to maintain its market share. Similarly, much of Honda's brand loyalty is based on quality. Service can also create product differentiation, as shown by McDonald's fast service, cleanliness and consistency of product that bring customers back. Product differentiation often comes from innovation, as witnessed by the success of the Apple iPhones. Whether product differentiation occurs because of advertising, patents, service or quality, the more the product is differentiated from competing products, the less competition it will face and the greater the possibility of large profits and cash flows, and so the creation of value for the firm's owners.

Cost advantage

Taking advantage of economies of scale, and producing a product at a cost below a competitor's, is another way to effectively deter new entrants from entering the market and thereby reduce competition. **Economies of scale** arise from spreading fixed costs over a larger volume of output, thus reducing the average fixed cost per unit. For IKEA, for example, as described in Chapter 1, the fixed costs are largely independent of the store's size—the costs of rent, display stock, advertising expenses and managerial salaries are fixed and so are essentially the same for each store, regardless of how much is sold. Therefore, the more sales that can be generated, the lower the cost per item sold: if fixed costs are $2 million per year, selling 100 000 items results in average fixed costs of $20 per unit sold, but increasing sales to 200 000 decreases this fixed cost to $10 per unit. Regardless of how the cost advantage is created—by economies of scale, proprietary technology or monopolistic control of raw materials—it keeps new entrants out of the market while allowing production at below-industry cost. Thus, investments aimed at creating a significant cost advantage have the potential to be accompanied by large profits.

economies of scale
Economies achieved by spreading fixed costs over a larger volume of output, thus reducing the average cost per unit.

ONE STEP FURTHER

ECONOMIES OF SCOPE

The concept of economies of scale has been extended nowadays to the idea of economies of scope. The term, *economies of scope*, refers to widening the range or scope of services or products that an organisation can market profitably to the same customer base. The potential to achieve economies of scope has been given great impetus by the development of modern information technology, notably comprehensive customer databases. For example, when you apply to a bank or other financial institution for a loan, the firm will collect comprehensive information about you. It might learn that you do not have a car, or do not have life insurance, or do not have a credit card. So, it can selectively market other products and services to you. This practice is known as *cross-selling*. The point is that it is more economical for the firm to sell new products to existing customers than it is to attract entirely new customers.

Introducing existing product in a new market

New capital-budgeting projects don't necessarily mean coming up with a new product. It may be taking an existing product and applying it to a new market. That's certainly been the direction that McDonald's has taken. Today, McDonald's operates in over 118 countries with more than 60 000 restaurants. One of the biggest is a 700-seat McDonald's in Moscow. Was this an expensive venture? It certainly was. In fact, the food plant that McDonald's built to supply burgers, buns, fries and everything else sold there cost over $60 million. In addition to cost, the outlet in Moscow differed from a standard outlet in a number of ways. First, in order to keep the quality of what McDonald's sells identical to what is served at any McDonald's anywhere in the world, the company spent six years putting together a supply chain that would provide the necessary raw materials at the quality level the company demanded. On top of that, there were the risks associated with the Russian economy and its currency. However, since it opened, the Moscow outlet has proved to be an enormous success. It goes to show that not all capital-budgeting projects have to be new products; they can also be existing products in new markets.

Concept check

For answers go to MyFinanceLab or www.pearson.com.au/9781442539174

11.1 Why is it so difficult to find an exceptionally profitable project?

11.2 Why is the search for new profitable projects so important?

TYPES OF CAPITAL INVESTMENT PROJECTS

Revenue enhancing projects

Investments that lead to higher revenues often involve the expansion of existing businesses or the introduction of new products, such as the Cochlear Nucleus 5 implant system that was launched in 2009. The Nucleus 5 is a hearing aid system that helps people with moderate to severe hearing loss to lead a normal life by delivering superior hearing performance and user comfort. The strong demand for the Nucleus 5, market leader in the hearing aid market, delivered a 12% increase in sales and a 19% increase in net profit after tax for Cochlear (ASX code: COH) for the financial year ending 30 June 2010. Products like Nucleus 5 are invariably the result of collaborative work from personnel in research and development (R&D), executives, sales personnel and sometimes customers. The most common new investment projects, however, involve taking an existing product and selling it to a new market. That was the strategy that IKEA has successfully implemented. In 2010, the retailing giant announced plans to spend $600 million on opening six new stores in Australia including a 37 000-square-metre store in Tempe, to the south-west of Sydney, and a 34 000-square-metre store in Springvale, to the south-east of Melbourne. Both of these stores are due to open in late 2011.

Cost-reduction projects

The majority of a firm's capital expenditure proposals are aimed at reducing the cost of doing business. Telstra (ASX code: TLS) notoriously relocated many of their call centres to the Philippines to take advantage of the lower labour costs. The relocation of the call centres is part of a broader cost-cutting strategy that Telstra has been embarking on in the last couple of years.[1] Other types of cost-reducing investments arise when equipment either wears out or becomes obsolete due to the development of new and improved equipment.

Mandated investment projects

Companies frequently find that they must make capital investments to meet safety and environmental regulations. These investments are not revenue producing or cost reducing but are required for the company to continue doing business. An example would be the scrubbers that are installed on the smoke stacks of coal-fired power plants. The scrubbers reduce airborne emissions in order to meet government pollution guidelines.

Although the capital-budgeting process can be long and complicated at many major corporations, we can sum up the typical capital-budgeting process at any firm in terms of two basic phases:

Phase 1: *The firm's management identifies promising investment opportunities.* These opportunities generally arise from ideas generated by the management and employees of the firm. Employees who work closely with the firm's customers, generally the marketing department and the production management department, are often the idea generators.

Phase 2: *Once an investment opportunity has been identified, its value-creating potential is thoroughly evaluated.* It is at this stage that financial analysts enter the picture and aim to identify how the project is going to create value and how that value can be evaluated.

The logic of the two-phase process is very simple: identify promising investment opportunities and select those that offer an opportunity to create value for the firm's common stockholders.

But not all investments have sufficient potential for value creation to be undertaken, so we need some analytical tools or criteria to help us identify the most promising investments. In the sections that follow, we consider the most commonly used criteria or techniques for determining the desirability of alternative investment proposals.

Principles for selecting capital-budgeting criteria

OBJECTIVE **2**

Understand the general principles in selecting capital-budgeting criteria.

There are four main guiding principles by which financial managers should assess the pros and cons of the various capital-budgeting criteria:

1. Rely on cash flows rather than accounting profits to measure a project's costs and benefits.
2. Be consistent with the goal of maximising shareholders' wealth.
3. Allow for the time value of money.
4. Be able to account for the risks of projects.

USE OF CASH FLOWS RATHER THAN ACCOUNTING PROFITS TO MEASURE A PROJECT'S COSTS AND BENEFITS

The use of cash flows as a measurement tool, rather than accounting profits, is logical. When a firm invests in assets or projects, it outlays cash, so it is logical that the future costs and benefits should also be measured in units of cash. The firm receives and is able to reinvest cash flows, whereas accounting profits are shown when they are earned rather than when the money is actually in hand. Some people might say that profits are merely 'figures on paper', whereas cash flows represent real resource flows. Unfortunately, a firm's accounting profits and cash flows may not be timed to occur together, due to factors such as depreciation and credit sales. Accordingly, the use of accounting profits will not truly reflect the costs and benefits associated with a project.

Back to the principles

The use of cash flows, rather than accounting profits, in measuring a project's costs and benefits is consistent with **Principle 3: Cash—not profits—is king**. It is actual cash that is received by the firm that allows for reinvestment. As a result, cash flow is the focus of the capital-budgeting process.

Depreciation

Annual **depreciation** expense represents the portion of the original cost of the asset that is deemed to be 'used up' in the earning of revenue during the relevant year. Depreciation is treated as an expense that reduces reported accounting profits; however, it is a non-cash-flow

depreciation
The means by which an asset's cost is expensed over its useful life.

expense because it doesn't represent a cash outflow. In other words, depreciation expense is an allocation of a *previous* cash outlay (the acquisition of a depreciable asset) but is not in itself a cash flow. Therefore, when calculating cash flows, depreciation needs to be added back to accounting earnings. A simple example will clarify this point.

EXAMPLE 11.1 Operating cash flows in the presence of depreciation

Suppose that a firm invests in an asset costing $1 million. The asset is expected to generate cash revenues of $500 000 per year for four years. The firm expects that there will be cash expenses of $100 000 per year. The firm's accountant has ascertained that the asset will be used equally in each of the four years and that it will have no residual value at the end of those four years.

Thus the asset will be depreciated at the rate of $1 000 000/4 = $250 000 per year. In other words, there will be a *depreciation expense* of $250 000 each year. With this in mind, the expected profit for each of the four years can be compared with the expected cash flow every year, as follows:

EXPECTED ACCOUNTING PROFIT		EXPECTED CASH FLOW	
Years 1 to 4		Years 1 to 4	
Cash revenues	$500 000	Cash revenues	$500 000
Less: Cash expenses	$100 000	Less: Cash expenses	100 000
Depreciation	250 000		
Net profit	$150 000	Net cash flows	$400 000

Interest expenses

When a company decides to take on an investment project, it will undoubtedly involve a cash outlay. This cash outlay has to be raised somehow, either via retained profits from previous years or via a loan or a new issue of stock. No matter how the firm raises funds, they come at a cost. Later on you will learn that the cost of funds is known as the 'cost of capital' and it will be used as the discount rate when you discount future cash flows back to the present. The cost of capital represents the minimum rate of return that the company needs to earn on the project to make it acceptable. If after-tax accounting profit is used as a measure of a project's benefits, it will underestimate the true cash flows, as interest expenses have been *subtracted* from accounting profit. As you can see, if you subtract interest expense from the cash flows and also discount the cash flows back to the present using a discount rate that incorporates interest expense, you will double-count this item. For this reason, remember that interest expenses should never be subtracted from the cash flows when you are doing cash-flow projections; interest has already been accounted for in the discount rate.

Changes in net working capital

Many projects require an increase in working capital. Working capital is the firm's investment in current assets such as inventory, accounts receivable, and so on. However, some of this increased working capital can be financed by an increase in accounts payable; for example, you increase your inventory level by buying it on credit. As these potential changes are changes in assets and liabilities, accounting income is not affected, while in terms of cash-flow analysis any increase in working capital represents a cash outflow. An increase in working capital therefore represents a cash outflow that the use of accounting profit cannot capture.

Changes in capital spending

From an accounting perspective, the cash flow associated with the purchase of a fixed asset is not an expense. That means that when Marriott spends $50 million building a new hotel resort there is a significant cash outflow without any accompanying expense. Instead, the $50 million is recorded as an asset in the accounting books, which creates an annual depreciation expense over the life of the hotel. It is essential that any changes in capital spending are included in cash-flow calculations.

CONSISTENCY WITH THE GOAL OF WEALTH MAXIMISATION

The ultimate measuring stick for a firm's investment (capital-budgeting) decisions should be the effect on shareholders' wealth. Let us now look at a highly simplified example of a capital-budgeting decision and see how this might impact on shareholder wealth.

EXAMPLE 11.2 Capital budgeting and wealth maximisation

Organic Kitchen has decided to expand and diversify its operations by venturing into the fast-food market. It needs to outlay various costs totalling $2 million in order to develop an outlet. The firm's expectation is that careful site selection and the achievement of high sales perform-ance from the outset will enable it to recoup net cash flows of about $150 000 in the first year, after which it may then sell the outlet for $2.45 million. The firm knows that the venture is risky and it has assessed 20% as the required rate of return.

To appraise the impact on shareholder wealth, let us calculate the present value of the expected cash returns that will total $2.6 million ($0.15 million + $2.45 million) in a year's time.

$$PV = \frac{\$2\,600\,000}{1 + 0.2} = \$2\,167\,000$$

Discounted at 20%, the present value is $2 167 000. This compares with an outlay, already in present-value dollars, of $2 000 000. Thus, there is a present-value surplus of $167 000 which is called the **net present value (NPV)**. NPV is equal to the present value of the future cash flows returned by a project, minus the initial investment. NPV is an assessment of the expected addition to shareholder wealth[2], so it is used to decide if an investment is (a) worthwhile and (b) better than alternative investments.

net present value (NPV)
The present value of a project's annual net cash flows less the project's initial outlay.

ALLOWING FOR THE TIME VALUE OF MONEY

From Chapter 4, we know that a dollar today is not worth the same as a dollar in the future. If shareholders of a firm are offered $200 000 now as opposed to $200 000 in a year's time, it is reasonable to expect that they will choose $200 000 now. In fact, at a required rate of return of 20% per year, it has just been demonstrated in Example 11.2 that $200 000 in a year's time is worth only $167 000 in today's dollars.

An alternative way of looking at the above investment is this: $2 million of shareholders' funds are being invested at a required rate of 20%. Thus, in a year's time a total return of $2.4 million would satisfy this requirement by returning the outlay of $2 million plus an additional 20%. The project in question has an expected return of $2.6 million a year from now, so the expected surplus or benefit in a year's time is $200 000; the present value of that surplus is $200 000/(1.20), or $167 000.

Converting the benefit to present-value dollars makes sense because we want to know the expected benefit to shareholders 'today', when the decision is being made. This helps com-parison with alternative projects—the NPV of the alternatives provides a yardstick for their assessment on a common scale, in present-value dollars. For example, the firm might decide to evaluate the investment of $2 million in a supermarket instead of the fast-food outlet. If the supermarket project is assessed as having an NPV of $123 000, we would expect the firm to prefer the fast-food project because it has a greater NPV. Without converting these cash flows to a common-time benchmark, which is today, it is very difficult to compare projects. There may come a time, for example, when you have to choose between two projects with equal outlays, where one generates a positive cash flow of $150 000 in year 2 and the other one $250 000 in year 5. By recognising the time value of money and discounting cash flows to present value, this exercise should be a straightforward one.

ACCOUNTING FOR PROJECT RISKS

In the above discussion, it was emphasised that cash flows are *expected*, which means that they are the decision maker's best estimate of the amount of the future cash flows. However, investing is a risky business and there is no guarantee that the expected payoff will occur. The capital-budgeting criteria have to be devised to account for differing levels of project risk, as more risky projects are certainly expected to generate a higher return in order for them to be accepted. Risk in capital budgeting is dealt with in more detail in Chapter 13.

Back to the principles

The importance of accounting for project risks is a manifestation of **Principle 1: The risk–return trade-off—we won't take on additional risk unless we expect to be compensated with additional return**. A common way to account for a riskier project is to discount the expected cash flows by a higher discount rate to reflect the fact that the higher level of return is required for the project to be acceptable.

The four principles just discussed should look familiar. If you go back to Chapter 10, you will see that these ideas underlie Figure 10.1: Basic factors determining an asset's value. In Chapter 10 these ideas were applied to the valuation of securities such as bonds and shares. Now these ideas are being extended to the valuation of a firm's investment projects.

Your money

INVESTING IN A UNIVERSITY DEGREE

If you are aged 18 and looking for an investment with a rate of return far better than the share market or the real estate market can provide, invest in a university degree. That is the result shown by a research paper released by the Australian Bureau of Statistics (ABS) in August 2010. Using a quarter of a century of census data from 1986 to 2006, the study revealed extraordinary internal rates of return (IRR) for an investment in a four-year university degree, especially if you are a woman.

As is shown in Figure 11.1, for a man graduating in 1981 the resulting higher lifetime income was likely to produce a return on investment of 13% per annum. A woman could expect 18%. By 2001 a fresh graduate could expect even more—a lifetime rate of return of 20% per annum for a man;

19% for a woman. And then the return turned down. By 2006 the return had fallen back to 15% for men, 17% for women, most likely due to improved labour market conditions that made it easier for individuals without tertiary education to have access to well-paid jobs. The impact of the improved labour market conditions was more pronounced for men who possibly took advantage of job opportunities created by the resources boom.

It is obvious from these figures that education pays. That is not to mention the fact that a university education can and should enrich your life in ways that no monetary amount can capture. So if your parents or grandparents want to put aside some money as an investment for your future—a university degree is the way to go.

FIGURE 11.1 Internal rate of return on a bachelor degree

Private rates of return to a bachelor degree for persons in Australia: 1981–2006 (%)

	1981	1986	1991	1996	2001	2006
Male						
Prospective	13.1	17.5	17.6	18.4	19.6	15.3
Realised	17.4	19.9	19.7			
Female						
Prospective	18.0	20.3	18.7	19.3	19.0	17.3
Realised	20.0	20.1	20.5			

Notes: These estimates are for an 18-year-old group based on combined income flows of 47 years lifespan, which consist of 15 years observed and 32 years expected income flows. As the time period between 1996 and 2006 is less than 15 years, no ex-post returns are estimated for 1996 onwards.

Source: Copyright © Commonwealth of Australia, Australian Bureau of Statistics, *Measuring Economic Returns to Post-school Education in Australia*, cat. no. 1351.0.55.032, p. 10.

Discounted-cash-flow capital-budgeting criteria

OBJECTIVE 3

Evaluate projects using discounted-cash-flow criteria.

discounted-cash-flow criteria
Capital-budgeting decision-making criteria that are based on the time value of money.

Having identified the principles that underlie capital-budgeting criteria, we now turn our attention to those criteria that allow us to determine whether a certain project is worth undertaking and whether one project is better than another. The first three capital-budgeting criteria that will be examined base decisions on the investment's cash flows after adjusting for the time value of money. Because they incorporate the time value of money, they are called **discounted-cash-flow criteria**. For the time being, the problem of incorporating risk into the capital-budgeting decision is ignored and it will also be assumed that the appropriate discount rate is given. The three capital-budgeting techniques are net present value, profitability index, and internal rate of return.

NET PRESENT VALUE

The net present value (NPV) of an investment proposal is equal to the present value of its annual net cash flows less the investment's initial outlay. We saw a simple example of the calculation of NPV for the fast-food project in Example 11.2. In the most general form, the NPV can be expressed as follows:

$$NPV = \sum_{t=1}^{n} \frac{ACF_t}{(1+k)^t} - IO \qquad \textbf{(11-1)}$$

where ACF_t = expected annual cash flow in year t
k = the appropriate discount rate or required rate of return
IO = the initial outlay or the investment amount
n = the project's expected life

This equation discounts each year's cash flow back to the present, then deducts the initial investment, thus giving a *net value* to the investment in today's dollars. The annual cash flows may be expressed on a pre-tax basis or an after-tax basis as appropriate, depending on the nature and tax status of the firm that is making the decision, a point that will be elaborated on later in this chapter.

Because all cash flows are discounted back to the present, comparing the difference between the present value of the annual cash flows and the initial investment outlay satisfies the time-value-of-money principle. The difference between the present value of the annual cash flows and the initial outlay determines the net value of accepting the investment proposal in terms of today's dollars. The NPV shows the dollar-value addition to shareholders' wealth. As a result, whenever a project's NPV is greater than zero, the project will be accepted; and whenever the project returns a negative NPV, it will be rejected. If the project's NPV is zero, it returns the required rate of return and should be accepted. This accept–reject criterion is illustrated below:

NPV ⩾ 0 Accept the project
NPV < 0 Reject the project

Calculations of net present value are shown in Examples 11.3 and 11.4.

EXAMPLE 11.3 Calculating net present value

A firm is considering a $40 000 investment in new equipment, for which the expected cash flows are as follows:

	CASH FLOW
Initial outlay	–$40 000
Year 1	$15 000
Year 2	$14 000
Year 3	$13 000
Year 4	$12 000
Year 5	$11 000

If the firm has a 12% required rate of return, should the project be accepted?

Substituting in equation (11-1), the net present value of the project can be calculated as:

$$NPV = \frac{15\,000}{1 + 0.12} + \frac{14\,000}{(1 + 0.12)^2} + \frac{13\,000}{(1 + 0.12)^3} + \frac{12\,000}{(1 + 0.12)^4} + \frac{11\,000}{(1 + 0.12)^5} - 40\,000$$

$$= 13\,393 + 11\,161 + 9\,253 + 7\,626 + 6\,242 - 40\,000$$

$$= 47\,675 - 40\,000$$

$$= 7\,675$$

See the calculator solution in the margin.

The NPV of the project can also be worked out using the financial tables (Appendix B) as follows:

$$NPV = 15\,000 \times PVIF_{12\%,1} + 14\,000 \times PVIF_{12\%,2} + 13\,000 \times PVIF_{12\%,3} + 12\,000 \times PVIF_{12\%,4}$$
$$+ 11\,000 \times PVIF_{12\%,5} - 40\,000$$

$$= 15\,000 \times 0.893 + 14\,000 \times 0.797 + 13\,000 \times 0.712 + 12\,000 \times 0.636 +$$
$$11\,000 \times 0.567 - 40\,000$$

$$= 7\,678$$

Note that there is a slight difference between the answer obtained from using the financial tables as there are rounding errors in the present-value factors. As a result, the answer obtained using the formula and the financial calculator is more accurate.

Calculator solution

Reset NORMAL mode

DATA INPUT		FUNCTION KEY
CFi	2ndF	CA
40 000	+/–	ENT
15 000		ENT
14 000		ENT
13 000		ENT
12 000		ENT
11 000		ENT
	2ndF	CASH
RATE (I/Y) = 12		ENT
		▼

FUNCTION KEY	ANSWER
COMP	NET_PV = 7 675

Since the NPV of this project is greater than zero, the net present value criterion indicates that the project should be accepted.

In assessing the NPV criterion against the four principles discussed previously, it is found that it shapes up very well. First of all, it deals with cash flows rather than accounting profits. In this regard it is sensitive to the true timing of the benefits resulting from the project. Second, because projects are accepted only if a positive net present value is associated with them, the acceptance of a project using this criterion will increase the value of the firm, which is consistent with the goal of maximising the shareholders' or owners' wealth. Third, by discounting future cash flows back to the present, the NPV criterion recognises the time value of money and allows for comparison of the benefits and costs in a logical manner. Finally, the NPV criterion can incorporate risk into the assessment of a project, either by adjusting the expected cash flows or by adjusting the discount rate. These methods of incorporating risk into the NPV process will be discussed in Chapter 13. Because of these highly desirable characteristics of the NPV method, it is considered to be the golden method for evaluating new investment opportunities. It is the most theoretically correct criterion used in project evaluation.

EXAMPLE 11.4 Calculating net present value

A firm is considering the purchase of a new computer system, which will cost $30 000 initially, to aid in invoicing and inventory management. The benefits of this investment take the form of savings in future costs, such as reducing paperwork and the amount of labour. The future cash inflows resulting from this project are $15 000 annually for three years. The required rate of return demanded by the firm is 10%. What is the project's NPV? Should it be accepted?

Using equation (11-1), the NPV of the project is:

$$NPV = \frac{15\,000}{1.1} + \frac{15\,000}{1.1^2} + \frac{15\,000}{1.1^3} - 30\,000$$

$$= 13\,636 + 12\,397 + 11\,270 - 30\,000$$

$$= 7\,303$$

See the calculator solution in the margin.

Since the cash flows from year 1 to year 3 are identical, this particular stream of cash flow resembles an annuity. Hence we can use Appendix D to work out the NPV of the project:

$$NPV = 15\,000 \times PVIFA_{12\%,3} - 30\,000$$

$$= 15\,000 \times 2\,487 - 30\,000$$

$$= 7\,305$$

The NPV of this project is positive, so it should be accepted.

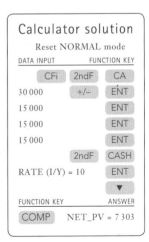

Calculator solution
Reset NORMAL mode

DATA INPUT			FUNCTION KEY
	CFi	2ndF	CA
30 000		+/–	ENT
15 000			ENT
15 000			ENT
15 000			ENT
		2ndF	CASH
RATE (I/Y) = 10			ENT
			▼

FUNCTION KEY	ANSWER
COMP	NET_PV = 7 303

Determining the appropriate time span over which to evaluate projects is extremely difficult because projects rarely have well-defined lives. For example, the new plant that must be constructed to produce a new product will eventually have to be replaced or remodelled and the product may well outlive the plant. Alternatively, for some projects the plant would have an expected life well beyond that of the product for which it was built. Thus, the calculation of the terminal cash flow is in general quite complicated, as it should provide an estimate of the true economic terminal value, including the value of the product when the plant's life is over or the future cash flows resulting from the plant when the product's life is over, rather than simply the salvage value.

Concept check

For answers go to MyFinanceLab or
www.pearson.com.au/9781442539174

11.3 Provide an intuitive definition of the net present value of a project.

11.4 Suppose a project has an NPV of $10 million. What does that mean?

PROFITABILITY INDEX

profitability index (PI)
A capital-budgeting criterion defined as the ratio of the present value of the future net cash flows to the initial outlay.

The **profitability index (PI)** is a cost-benefit ratio equal to the present value of the future net cash flows to the initial outlay. The NPV investment criterion gives a measure of the absolute dollar desirability of a project, whereas the profitability index provides a relative measure of an investment proposal's desirability—that is, the ratio of the present value of its future net benefits to its initial cost—in other words, the number of dollars of benefits per dollar of outlays. The profitability index can be expressed as follows:

$$PI = \frac{\sum_{t=1}^{n} \dfrac{ACF_t}{(1+k)^t}}{IO} \tag{11-2}$$

where ACF_t = expected annual cash flow in year t

k = the appropriate discount rate or required rate of return

IO = the initial outlay or the investment amount

n = the project's expected life

It is clear from this equation that the numerator is the present value of the benefits and the denominator is the initial outlay. The decision criterion with respect to the profitability index is to accept the project if the PI is greater than or equal to 1, and to reject the project if the PI is less than 1.

$PI \geq 1$ Accept

$PI < 1$ Reject

Looking closely at this criterion, it can be seen that it gives the same accept–reject decision as does the net-present-value criterion. Whenever the present value of the project's net cash flows is greater than its initial cash outlay, the project's net present value will be positive, signalling a decision to accept. When this is true, the project's profitability index will also be greater than 1, as the present value of the net cash flows (the PI's numerator) is greater than its initial outlay (the PI's denominator). Although these two decision criteria will yield the same decision, they will not necessarily rank acceptable projects in the same order. This problem of conflicting ranking will be dealt with at a later point.

Because the net-present-value and profitability-index criteria are essentially the same, the PI criterion has the same advantages and disadvantages as discussed above. However, the NPV criterion is relatively superior to the PI method, as it gives a dollar amount that represents the value increment as a result of undertaking the project, whereas the PI does not.

EXAMPLE 11.5 **Calculating the profitability index**

Using data from Example 11.3, calculate the profitability index (PI) for the project.

From Example 11.3, the present value of the future cash flows has been calculated as 47 675. Hence, the PI of the project is:

$$PI = \frac{47\,675}{40\,000} = 1.19$$

The PI is greater than 1, suggesting the acceptability of the project, which is consistent with the acceptance decision using the NPV criterion.

Concept check

11.5 Provide an intuitive definition of the profitability index of a project.

11.6 Suppose a project has a profitability index of 0.94. What does that mean?

11.7 Why do the net present value and profitability index always give the same accept or reject decision for any project?

For answers go to MyFinanceLab or
www.pearson.com.au/9781442539174

INTERNAL RATE OF RETURN

The **internal rate of return (IRR)** attempts to answer the question 'What rate of return does this project earn?' For computational purposes, the internal rate of return is defined as *the discount rate that equates the present value of the project's future net cash flows with the project's initial cash outlay.* In other words, IRR is the rate of return that makes the NPV equal to zero. Mathematically, the internal rate of return is defined as the value *IRR* in the following equation:

$$IO = \sum_{t=1}^{n} \frac{ACF_t}{(1 + IRR)^t} \qquad \textbf{(11-3)}$$

internal rate of return (IRR)
A capital-budgeting technique that reflects the rate of return a project earns. Mathematically it is the discount rate that equates the present value of the inflows with the present value of the outflows.

where ACF_t = expected annual cash flow in year t
  IO = the initial outlay or the investment amount
  n = the project's expected life
  IRR = the project's internal rate of return

What this equation tells us is that, given the initial outlay, *IO*, the annual cash flows, *ACF_t*, and the life of the project, *n*, we have to solve for *IRR* as the unknown that makes the present value of the future cash flows equal the initial outlay. In effect, the *IRR* is analogous to the concept of yield to maturity for bonds, which was examined in Chapter 10. In other words, a project's internal rate of return is simply the rate of return that the project earns, expressed on a compound-interest basis. It is also called the *implicit interest rate*, because it is the rate implied by a given series of cash flows.

The decision criterion associated with the internal rate of return is to accept the project if the internal rate of return is greater than or equal to the required rate of return. The project is rejected if its internal rate of return is less than this required rate of return. This accept–reject criterion is illustrated below:

IRR ⩾ required rate of return: Accept
IRR < required rate of return: Reject

If the internal rate of return on a project is equal to the investors' required rate of return, the project should be accepted. This is because the firm is earning the rate that satisfies its investors. However, the acceptance of a project with an internal rate of return below the investors' required rate of return will, in theory, decrease the firm's value.

If the NPV is positive, then the IRR must be greater than the required rate of return. Thus, all the discounted-cash-flow criteria are consistent and will give similar accept–reject decisions for a single project. However, as we will see later, these may give conflicting rankings when choosing between alternative projects. In addition, because the internal rate of return is another discounted-cash-flow criterion, it exhibits the same general advantages and disadvantages as both the net present value and the profitability index, and has an additional disadvantage of being tedious to calculate if a financial calculator or suitable computer package is not available.

An additional disadvantage of the IRR relative to the NPV involves the implied reinvestment rate assumptions made by the two methods. The NPV method implicitly assumes that cash flows received over the life of the project are reinvested back in projects that earn the required rate of return. That is, if we have a mining project with a 10-year expected life that produces a $100 000 cash flow at the end of the second year, the NPV technique assumes that this $100 000 is reinvested over the period year 3 to year 10 at the required rate of return. The use of the IRR, however, implies that the cash flows over the life of the project can be reinvested at the IRR. Thus, if the mining project has a 40% IRR, the use of the IRR implies that the $100 000 received at the end of year 2 could be reinvested at 40% over the remaining life of the project. In effect, the NPV method implicitly assumes that cash flows over the life of the project can be reinvested at the project's required rate of return, whereas the use of the IRR method implies that cash flows could be reinvested at the IRR. The better assumption is the one made by NPV because these cash flows will either be (1) returned in the form of dividends to shareholders who demanded the required rate of return on the project, or (2) reinvested in a

Finance at work

THE RESOURCE SUPER PROFITS TAX

In the May 2010 Federal Budget, the Australian government, led by the then Prime Minister Kevin Rudd, proposed a special tax targeted at the Australian resources sector known as the Resource Super Profits Tax (RSPT). This proposed scheme aimed to impose an additional level of tax on the super profits earned by approximately 2500 resources companies. This is how the proposed RSPT scheme would work. The profits earned by resources firms would be given a tax-free allowance of 6%; the remaining profit would be taxed at the 40% super profits tax rate. After super profits tax, profit would then be subject to the standard corporate tax rate, which is currently 30% per annum. Although there were many controversies surrounding the RSPT scheme, which was largely responsible for the downfall of Kevin Rudd just a few months after the scheme was announced, our main point of interest here is how the 6% allowance would be determined.

Essentially, the 6% allowance was based on the current yield on long-term government bonds. By applying the 6% tax-free allowance to resources companies, the government was effectively suggesting that the 'normal' return that these resources companies earned on their investments was equal to the risk-free rate, and any further return would represent 'super profits' and would be subject to the RSPT. In other words, the required rate of return for resources investment projects would be determined by the government to be 6% per annum. To understand how inadequate this allowance would have been, put yourself in the shoes of an investor who holds shares in a resources company. If the CEO of that company announced that the company's investment projects would earn the long-term government bond rate, how would you react? The obvious reaction would be to sell your shares immediately to invest in long-term government bonds, as that would be a much surer way to get the 6% return.

In July 2010, to address the many inadequacies of the RSPT, Prime Minister Julia Gillard, Kevin Rudd's successor, made a number of revisions to the RSPT, which was renamed the Minerals Resource Rent Tax (MRRT). The MRRT would apply to a smaller number of firms and raise the tax-free allowance to the government bond rate plus 7%. Given the risky nature of resources companies' investments, 13% does sound like a much more reasonable required rate of return.

new investment project. If these cash flows are invested in a new project, then they are simply substituting for external financing on which the required rate of return is demanded. Thus, the opportunity cost of these funds is the required rate of return. The bottom line is that the NPV method makes the best reinvestment rate assumption and, as such, is superior to the IRR method.

Computing the IRR with a financial calculator

With today's calculators, the determination of an internal rate of return is merely a matter of a few keystrokes. In Chapter 4, whenever we were solving time-value-of-money problems for *i*, we were really solving for the internal rate of return. Thus, with financial calculators we need only input the initial outlay, the cash flows and their timing, and then operate the function key I/Y to calculate the internal rate of return.

Computing the IRR for even cash flows

In Examples 11.6 and 11.7, the calculators are put aside and the mathematical process of calculating internal rates of return is examined in order to obtain a better understanding of the IRR.

EXAMPLE 11.6 Computing IRR for even cash flows

Nacho Ltd is considering a project that involves an initial outlay of $45 555. If the investment is taken up, the cash flows are expected to be $15 000 per annum over the project's four-year life. Nacho has a 10% required rate of return on investment. What is the IRR for this project?

In this case, the internal rate of return is equal to *IRR* in the following equation:

$$\$45\,555 = \frac{\$15\,000}{(1 + IRR)^1} + \frac{\$15\,000}{(1 + IRR)^2} + \frac{\$15\,000}{(1 + IRR)^3} + \frac{\$15\,000}{(1 + IRR)^4}$$

From the discussion of the present value of an annuity in Chapter 4, we know that this equation can be reduced to:

$$\$45\,555 = \$15\,000 PVIFA_{IRR,4}$$

Rearranging this equation gives:

$$PVIFA_{IRR,4} = \$45\,555/\$15\,000 = 3.037$$

An examination of Appendix D for $PVIFA_{i,4}$ shows that, in the $n = 4$ column of the table, the value 3.037 occurs when *i* equals 12%, which means that 12% is the internal rate of return or implicit interest rate for this investment. Since this IRR is greater than the required return of 10%, the project is acceptable.

EXAMPLE 11.7 Computing IRR for even cash flows

A firm with a required rate of return of 20% is considering two investment proposals, A and B. The cash flows for these projects are provided below:

	PROJECT A	PROJECT B
Initial outlay	$3817	$3817
Year 1	0	1784
Year 2	0	1784
Year 3	6271	1784

Management plans to calculate the internal rate of return for each project and determine which project should be accepted.

Project A's pay-off is a single amount in three years time, so its IRR can be found by the use of the $PVIF_{i,n}$ table in Appendix B. We know the present value $3817 and the future value $6271, as well as the term, $n = 3$ years. So the relationship between these variables is given by:

$$\$3817 = \$6271(PVIF_{i,3})$$

$$PVIF_{i,3} = \$3817/\$6271 = 0.609$$

Looking at the $n = 3$ row in Appendix B, we find that a table value of 0.609 corresponds with a value of i equal to 18%. In other words, project B has an IRR of 18% and, since this is less than the required rate of 20%, the project should be rejected.

Project B's cash inflows represent an annuity of $1784 per annum. The relationship between this annuity and its present value of $3817 is given by:

$$\$3817 = \$1784(PVIFA_{i,3})$$

$$PVIFA_{i,3} = \$3817/\$1784 = 2.140$$

Examining the three-period row of Appendix D, we find that a table value of 2.140 corresponds to an interest rate, i, equal to 19%; this is project B's IRR, which is less than the required rate of 20%, so this project should not be accepted.

Computing the IRR for uneven cash flows

Unfortunately, while solving for the IRR is quite easy when using a financial calculator or spreadsheet, it can be solved directly in the tables only when the future net cash flows are in the form of an annuity or a single payment. With a calculator, the process is simple. You will only need to key in the initial cash outlay, the cash flows and their timing, and press the COMP key. The process is illustrated in the calculator solution box.

When a financial calculator is not available and these flows are in the form of an uneven series of flows, a trial-and-error approach is necessary. To do this, the present value of the future net cash flows is determined using an arbitrary discount rate. If the present value of the future cash flows at this discount rate is larger than the initial outlay, the rate should increase (because a greater discount rate produces a smaller present value); if the present value is smaller than the initial outlay, the discount rate is lowered. Then the process begins again. This search routine is continued until the present value of the future cash flows is equal to the initial outlay. The interest rate that creates this situation is the internal rate of return. This is the same basic iterative process that a financial calculator uses to calculate an IRR.

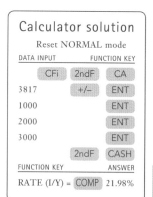

Calculator solution

Reset NORMAL mode

DATA INPUT		FUNCTION KEY
CFi	2ndF	CA
3817	+/–	ENT
1000		ENT
2000		ENT
3000		ENT
	2ndF	CASH

FUNCTION KEY	ANSWER
RATE (I/Y) = COMP	21.98%

EXAMPLE 11.8 Computing IRR for uneven cash flows

Consider an investment proposal that requires an initial outlay of $3817 and returns $1000 at the end of year 1, $2000 at the end of year 2 and $3000 at the end of year 3. In this case, the internal rate of return must be determined using trial and error.

Step 1: Pick an arbitrary rate, and use it to determine the present value of the outflows.
Try $i = 15\%$:

	NET CASH FLOW	PRESENT-VALUE FACTOR AT 15%	PRESENT VALUE
Inflow year 1	$1000	0.870	$870
Inflow year 2	2000	0.756	1512
Inflow year 3	3000	0.658	1974
Present value of inflows			4356
Initial outlay			(3817)

Step 2: Compare the above present value of the inflows with the initial outlay; if they are not
equal, pick another possible interest rate.
Since the previous PV of inflows is greater than the initial outlay, we must try a greater interest
rate so as to lower the PV.
Try $i = 20\%$:

	NET CASH FLOW	PRESENT-VALUE FACTOR AT 20%	PRESENT VALUE
Inflow year 1	$1000	0.833	$833
Inflow year 2	2000	0.694	1388
Inflow year 3	3000	0.579	1737
Present value of inflows			3958
Initial outlay			(3817)

Step 3: Again compare the present value with the outlay and repeat step 2.
Since the previous PV of inflows is still greater than the initial outlay, we must try an interest rate
that is greater again.
Try $i = 23\%$:

	NET CASH FLOW	PRESENT-VALUE FACTOR AT 23%	PRESENT VALUE
Inflow year 1	$1000	0.813	$813
Inflow year 2	2000	0.661	1322
Inflow year 3	3000	0.537	1611
Present value of inflows			3746
Initial outlay			(3817)

Step 4: Again compare the present value with the outlay and repeat step 2.
This time the PV is less than the initial outlay, meaning that the IRR is less than 23%. If it is
necessary to carry out further iterations, this should proceed. However, in our example we are
now reasonably close and we know that the IRR lies between 20% and 23%. We can therefore
use interpolation, as introduced in Chapter 4, to move towards a solution. Setting up the interpolation table, we have:

	I (IRR)	PV
	20%	$3958
$d_1 = ?$	i%	3817 $d_3 = \$141$
$d_2 = 3\%$	23%	3746 $d_4 = \$212$

By inspection of the interpolation table, we can see that the unknown IRR, i%, is equal to 20% plus the distance d_1. From Chapter 4, d_1 is equal to $d_2 \times d_3/d_4$; that is, $d_1 = 1.995\%$, or (3%) ($141/$212). This implies that the unknown i is about 22%, or 20% plus 1.995%. Indeed, if we try 22% in the above present-value computations, it yields the desired $3817 present value of inflows.

Complications with IRR: multiple rates of return

Although any project can have only one NPV and one PI, a single project under certain circumstances can have *multiple* IRRs. The reason for this can be traced to the calculations involved in determining the IRR. Equation (11-3) states that the IRR is the discount rate that equates the present value of the project's future net cash flows with the project's initial outlay:

$$IO = \sum_{t=1}^{n} \frac{ACF_t}{(1 + IRR)^t}$$

(11-3)

However, in mathematical terms equation (11-3) is a polynomial of degree n; this means that it has powers 1 to n and as a result there are n solutions—that is, there are n possible values of the IRR that will satisfy the equation. Now, if the initial outlay (IO) is the only negative cash flow and all the annual cash flows (ACF_t) are positive, then all but one of these n solutions is either a negative or an imaginary number and there is no problem. But complications occur when there are sign reversals in the cash-flow stream; in fact, there can be as many positive solutions as there are sign reversals. Thus, a normal cash-flow pattern, with a negative initial outlay followed by positive annual cash flows (–, +, +, + … +), has only one sign reversal, hence only one positive IRR. However, a pattern with more than one sign reversal can have more than one IRR. Consider the following pattern of cash flows:[3]

	CASH FLOW
Initial outlay	–$1600
Year 1	+$10000
Year 2	–$10000

In this pattern of cash flows there are two sign reversals, from –$1600 to +$10000 and then from +$10000 to –$10000, so there can be as many as two positive IRRs that will make the present value of the future cash flows equal to the initial outlay. In fact, two IRRs solve this problem, 25% and 400%.[4] Graphically, what we are solving for is the discount rate that makes the project's NPV equal to zero[5]; as Figure 11.2 illustrates, this occurs twice.

Which solution is correct? The answer is that neither solution is valid. Although each fits the definition of IRR, neither provides any insight into the true project returns. In summary,

FIGURE 11.2 Multiple IRRs

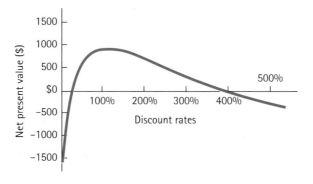

when there is more than one sign reversal in the cash-flow stream, the possibility of multiple IRRs exists, and the normal interpretation of the IRR loses its meaning.[6]

Concept check

11.8 What is the IRR of a project?

11.9 What are some of the drawbacks of the IRR method as a project evaluation technique?

For answers go to MyFinanceLab or www.pearson.com.au/9781442539174

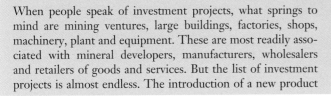

FYI

When people speak of investment projects, what springs to mind are mining ventures, large buildings, factories, shops, machinery, plant and equipment. These are most readily associated with mineral developers, manufacturers, wholesalers and retailers of goods and services. But the list of investment projects is almost endless. The introduction of a new product by a bank is an investment project, as funds are outlaid to develop the concept, reconfigure computer systems, train staff, and advertise and promote the product. The expected payoff comes in the form of profits from the margin on the funds raised or loaned via the new bank product.

ONE STEP FURTHER

MODIFIED INTERNAL RATE OF RETURN

Modified internal rate of return (MIRR) is the fourth capital budgeting measure that specifically recognises the time value of money when evaluating a project's cash flows. It has the merit of negating the three disadvantages of the IRR measure: (1) the IRR's assumption that a project's future cash inflows are reinvested at the IRR; (2) the prospect of multiple IRRs when future cash flows switch between positive and negative; and (3) the difficulty of calculating a project's IRR without the aid of a financial calculator or spreadsheet software.

The MIRR overcomes those disadvantages by assuming that future cash *inflows* will be reinvested at a required rate of return, and that future cash *outflows* will be financed out of funds notionally set aside for that purpose at the time of the project's initial outlay. Future cash inflows are therefore compounded at a project's required rate of return to determine its *terminal value*, while future cash outflows (if any) are discounted at the cost of finance in order to determine what funds will be required to finance a project in addition to the initial outlay. (In most situations the cost of finance will be the same as the required rate of return.) A project's MIRR is given by the following equation:

$$MIRR = \left(\frac{\text{terminal value}}{\text{PV of cash outflows}} \right)^{1/n} - 1$$

where n = project life in years.

To illustrate the application of the modified IRR, consider a project that has an initial outlay of $6000 followed by cash inflows of $2000, $3000 and $4000 at the end of the next three years respectively. If the required rate of return is 10%, the project's terminal value will be $9720 and its MIRR 17.446%, calculated as follows:

$$MIRR = \left(\frac{\$9.720}{\$6000}\right)^{1/3} - 1 = 0.17446 = 17.446\%$$

This example demonstrates how an MIRR can be calculated without the use of a financial calculator or spreadsheet software.

Using a project's MIRR, the decision criteria are as follows:

$MIRR \geq$ required rate of return: Accept
$MIRR <$ required rate of return: Reject

Back to the principles

The three capital-budgeting criteria presented above all incorporate **Principle 2: The time value of money—a dollar received today is worth more than a dollar received in the future** in their calculations. In order to make rational business decisions, we must recognise that money has a time value. In examining the following capital-budgeting techniques, you will notice that this principle is the driving force behind each of them.

OBJECTIVE 4

Evaluate projects using non-discounted-cash-flow criteria.

Non-discounted-cash-flow capital-budgeting criteria

You now have some idea about the use of discounted-cash-flow (DCF) techniques for selecting desirable investment projects. In addition to these DCF criteria, there are a number of others that are encountered in practice. This book does not advocate the use of these other non-discounted-cash-flow techniques in preference to DCF methods. However, because these techniques are used in practice it is sensible to take a brief look at them. The two non-DCF techniques that are examined are the *payback period* method and the *accounting rate of return* method.

PAYBACK PERIOD

payback period
A capital-budgeting criterion defined as the number of years required to recover the initial cash investment.

The **payback period** is the number of years needed to recover the initial cash outlay. As this criterion measures how quickly the project will return its original investment, it deals with cash flows rather than accounting profits. However, it ignores the time value of money and does not discount these cash flows back to the present. A project is accepted if its payback period is less than or equal to the firm's maximum desired payback period and it is rejected otherwise. For example, if a firm's maximum desired payback period is three years and an investment proposal requires an initial cash outlay of $10 000 and yields the set of annual cash flows shown in Table 11.1, what is its payback period? Should the project be accepted?

In this case, after three years the firm will have recaptured $9000 on an initial investment of $10 000, leaving $1000 of the initial investment to be recouped. During the fourth year a total of $3000 will be returned from this investment and, assuming that it will flow into the firm at a constant rate over the year, it will take one-third of the year ($1000/$3000) to recapture the remaining $1000. Thus, the payback period on this project is 3⅓ years, which is longer than the desired payback period. Using the payback-period criterion, the firm would reject this project.

Although the payback period is used frequently, it does have some rather obvious drawbacks, which can best be demonstrated through the use of an example. Consider two investment

TABLE 11.1	Cash flows for payback method calculation

YEAR	CASH FLOW ($)
1	2000
2	4000
3	3000
4	3000
5	3000

projects, A and B, which involve an initial cash outlay of $10 000 each and produce the annual cash flows shown in Table 11.2.

Both projects have a payback period of two years; therefore, in terms of the payback-period criterion, both are equally acceptable. However, if investors had a choice, it is clear that they would select A over B for at least two reasons. First, regardless of what happens after the payback period, project A returns the initial investment earlier within the payback period. Put another way, the payback period weights cash inflows equally regardless of when they occur, but the time value of money means that earlier cash flows are actually more valuable. Second, all cash flows that occur after the payback period are ignored. This violates the principle that investors desire more in the way of benefits rather than less—a principle that is difficult to deny, especially when talking about money.

This example illustrates three fundamental limitations associated with the use of the payback period as the sole criterion for evaluating projects:

• The payback period calculation ignores the time value of money. Cash flows at different points in time are treated equally.
• The payback period ignores cash flows that are generated by the project beyond the end of the payback period.
• There is no clear-cut way to define the cut-off criterion for the payback period that is tied to the value-creation potential of the investment.

DISCOUNTED PAYBACK PERIOD

To overcome the drawbacks of the payback period method, some firms use the discounted payback period approach. The discounted payback period method is similar to the traditional method except that it uses discounted cash flows rather than actual undiscounted cash flows in calculating the payback period. The **discounted payback period** is defined as the number of years needed to recover the initial cash outlay from the discounted cash flows. The accept–reject decision is made by comparing the discounted payback period with the desired payback period. Using the assumption that the required rate of return on projects A and B, illustrated in Table 11.2, is 17%, the discounted cash flows from these projects are given in Table 11.3. The discounted payback period for project A is calculated as follows:

Discounted payback period A = 3.0 + $74/$1068 = 3.07 years

discounted payback period An estimate of the time required for the discounted future cash flows of a project to recoup the initial outlay.

TABLE 11.2	Payback period example projects

	A	B
Initial cash outlay	–$10 000	–$10 000
Annual net cash inflows:		
Year 1	6000	5000
Year 2	4000	5000
Year 3	3000	0
Year 4	2000	0
Year 5	1000	0

TABLE 11.3   Discounted payback period

PROJECT A

YEAR	UNDISCOUNTED CASH FLOWS	DISCOUNT FACTOR (17%)	DISCOUNTED CASH FLOWS	CUMULATIVE DISCOUNTED CASH FLOWS
0	–$10 000	1	–$10 000	–$10 000
1	6 000	0.855	5 130	–4 870
2	4 000	0.731	2 924	–1 946
3	3 000	0.624	1 872	74
4	2 000	0.534	1 068	994
5	1 000	0.456	456	1 450

PROJECT B

YEAR	UNDISCOUNTED CASH FLOWS	DISCOUNT FACTOR (17%)	DISCOUNTED CASH FLOWS	CUMULATIVE DISCOUNTED CASH FLOWS
0	–$10 000	1	–$10 000	–$10 000
1	5 000	0.855	4 275	–5 725
2	5 000	0.731	3 655	–2 070
3	0	0.624	0	–2 070
4	0	0.534	0	–2 070
5	0	0.456	0	–2 070

If project A's discounted payback period was less than the firm's maximum desired discounted payback period, it would be accepted. Project A, however, does not have a discounted payback period because it never fully recovers the project's initial cash outlay and thus should be rejected. The major problem with the discounted payback period is setting the firm's maximum desired discounted payback period. This is an arbitrary decision that affects which projects are accepted and which ones are rejected. Therefore, although the discounted payback period takes into account the concept of time value in its calculations, its use is limited by the subjective process used to select the maximum discounted payback period. As it is now becoming clear, the net present value criterion is theoretically superior and not much more difficult to calculate.

Although these deficiencies limit the value of the payback period and the discounted payback period as tools for investment evaluation, they do have several positive features:

- They deal with cash flows, as opposed to accounting profits, and therefore focus on the true measure of the project's benefits and costs, even though these cash flows are not adjusted for the time value of money in the traditional payback period method.
- For many individuals, they are more intuitive and easier to understand than other decision criteria such as NPV.
- The discounted payback period method can be used as a supplemental analytical tool in instances where risk factors such as obsolescence or politics are of concern. In these instances, they are often used as a rough screening device to eliminate projects whose returns will not materialise until later years. This method emphasises the earliest returns, which in all likelihood are less uncertain and provide for the liquidity needs of the firm. Managers often find payback useful when capital is being rationed and they want to know how long the company's capital will be tied up in the project.

accounting rate of return (AROR)
A capital-budgeting criterion that relates the returns generated by the project, as measured by average accounting profits, to the average dollar size of the investment required.

ACCOUNTING RATE OF RETURN

The **accounting rate of return (AROR)** compares the average profits with the average dollar size of the investment. The *average-profits* figure is determined by adding up the profits generated by the investment over its life and dividing by the number of years. Profits can be expressed on a pre-tax basis or an after-tax basis as required. The *average investment* is determined by adding the initial outlay and the project's expected salvage value and dividing by two.

(This computation attempts to calculate the average book value of an investment by simply averaging the initial and liquidation values.) Thus, the accounting rate of return for an investment with an expected life of n years can be calculated as follows:

$$AROR = \frac{\dfrac{\sum\limits_{t=1}^{n} AP_t}{n}}{\dfrac{IO + SV}{2}} \qquad \textbf{(11-4)}$$

where AP_t = accounting profit in year t
IO = the initial outlay
SV = the expected salvage value of the project
n = the expected life of the project

The accept–reject criterion associated with the accounting rate of return compares the calculated return with a minimum acceptable AROR level. If the AROR is greater than this minimum acceptable level, the project is accepted; otherwise it is rejected.

EXAMPLE 11.9   Calculating accounting rate of return

Consider an investment in new machinery that requires an initial outlay of $20 000 and has an expected salvage value of zero after five years. Assume that this machine, if acquired, will produce profits of $800 each year for five years.

The accounting rate of return for the project can be calculated by applying equation (11-4):

$$AROR = \frac{\dfrac{(800 \times 5)}{5}}{\dfrac{(20\,000 + 0)}{2}}$$

$$= \frac{800}{10\,000} = 0.08, \text{ or } 8\%$$

This technique seems straightforward enough, but its limitations detract significantly from its value as a discriminating capital-budgeting criterion. To examine these limitations, let us first determine the AROR of three proposals, A, B and C, each with an expected life of five years. Assume that the initial outlay associated with each project is $10 000 and that each will have an expected salvage value of zero in five years. The minimum acceptable AROR for this firm is 8%, and the annual accounting profits from the three proposals are given in Table 11.4. In each case, the average annual accounting profit is $500, and the average investment is $5000—that is, ($10 000 + 0)/2. Therefore, the AROR is 10% for each project, which indicates that the AROR method does not do an adequate job of discriminating between these projects.

A casual examination leads to the conclusion that project B is the best, as it yields its returns earlier than either project A or project C. However, the AROR technique gives equal weight to all returns within the project's life without any regard for the time value of money. The second major disadvantage associated with the AROR method is that it deals with accounting profit figures rather than cash flows. For this reason it does not truly reflect the proper timing of the benefits.

TABLE 11.4 Annual accounting profits

YEAR	A	B	C
1	$0	$500	$0
2	1000	500	0
3	500	500	0
4	500	500	0
5	500	500	2500

Despite the criticisms, the accounting rate of return has been a relatively popular tool for capital-budgeting analysis, primarily because it involves familiar terms that are easily accessible. It is also easily understood. The AROR provides a measure of accounting profits per average dollar invested, and the intuitive appeal of this measurement has kept the method alive over the years. It is sometimes used as a method of comparing the performance of divisions within a company or group on the basis of actual performance. For the purpose of investment decision making, the AROR is inadequate, as it does not treat cash flows and does not take into account the time value of money.

Figure 11.3 summarises all capital budgeting techniques that are discussed in this chapter.

FIGURE 11.3 Summary of capital-budgeting criteria

Discounted cash–flow methods

1. *Net present value = present value of the* ~~initial outlay:~~

$$NPV = \sum_{t=1}^{n} \frac{ACF_t}{(1 + k)^t} - IO$$

$$-inv + pmt \left(\frac{1 - \frac{1}{1.0I^n}}{I}\right)$$

$$PI = \frac{}{inv}$$

(11-1)

where ACF_t = the annual cash flow in y~~ear t~~ ~~(could be ne~~gative)
k = the appropriate discount ~~rate~~
IO = the initial outlay of cash,
n = the project's expected lif~~e~~

Accept if $NPV \geq 0$
Advantages:
(a) Uses cash flows.
(b) Recognises the time value of money.
(c) Is consistent with the firm's goal of wealth maximisation.

(a) Requires detailed long-term forecasts of the incremental benefits and costs.

2. *Profitability index = the ratio of the present value of the future cash flows to the initial outlay:*

$$PI = \frac{\sum_{t=1}^{n} \frac{ACF_t}{(1 + k)^t}}{IO}$$

(11-2)

where ACF_t = the annual incremental cash flow in year t
k = the appropriate discount rate
IO = the initial outlay
n = the project's expected life

Accept if $PI \geq 1$
Advantages:
(a) Uses cash flows.
(b) Recognises the time value of money.
(c) Is consistent with the firm's goal of wealth maximisation.

Reject if $PI < 1$
Disadvantages:
(a) Requires detailed, long-term forecasts of the incremental benefits and costs.

3.   *Internal rate of return = the discount rate that equates the present value of the project's future cash flows with the initial outlay; it is the rate of compound interest returned by the project.*

The internal rate of return is found by solving for IRR in the following equation:

$$IO = \sum_{t=1}^{n} \frac{ACF_t}{(1 + IRR)^t} \qquad\qquad (11\text{--}3)$$

where ACF_t = the annual incremental cash flow in year t
IO = the initial cash outlay
n = the project's expected life
IRR = the project's internal rate of return

Accept if $IRR \geq$ required rate of return

Advantages:
(a)   Uses cash flows.
(b)   Recognises the time value of money.
(c)   Is consistent with the firm's goal of wealth maximisation.

Reject if $IRR <$ required rate of return

Disadvantages:
(a)   Requires detailed long-term forecasts of the incremental benefits and costs.
(b)   Can involve tedious calculations.
(c)   Possibility of multiple IRRs.

Non-discounted-cash-flow methods

1.   *Payback period = number of years to recapture the initial investment.*

Accept if payback ≤ maximum acceptable payback period
Reject if payback > maximum acceptable payback period

Advantages:
(a)   Uses cash flows.
(b)   Is easy to calculate and understand.
(c)   May be used as a rough screening device.

Disadvantages:
(a)   Ignores the time value of money.
(b)   Ignores cash flows occurring after the payback period.

2.   *Accounting rate of return (AROR) is defined as:*

$$AROR = \frac{\dfrac{\sum_{t=1}^{n} (\text{accounting profit in year } t)}{n}}{\dfrac{(\text{initial outlay} + \text{expected salvage value})}{2}} \qquad\qquad (11\text{--}4)$$

where n = project's life
Accept if $AROR \geq$ minimum acceptable rate of return; reject if $AROR <$ minimum acceptable rate of return

Advantages:
(a)   Involves familiar, easily accessible terms.
(b)   Is easy to calculate and understand.

Disadvantages:
(a)   Ignores the time value of money.
(b)   Uses accounting profits rather than cash flows.

Concept check

11.10   Why do you think the payback period is used as frequently as it is?
11.11   What is the main difference between the payback period and the discounted payback period?
11.12   What is the main problem with the AROR as a capital-budgeting technique?

For answers go to MyFinanceLab or www.pearson.com.au/9781442539174

The role of taxation in capital budgeting

OBJECTIVE **5**

Understand the effects of taxation in capital budgeting.

When it comes to determining the net cash flows in capital-budgeting decisions, a choice has to be made as to whether the cash flows should be pre-tax or after-tax amounts. The appropriate basis depends on the nature of the organisation making the decision. For some firms, evaluation should be based on pre-tax cash flows, for others on after-tax cash flows. Towards the end of Chapter 2, a number of conclusions were made about Australia's taxation system as it applies to financial management and a distinction was made between three taxation categories of firms. The relevant part of Chapter 2 should be re-read for a more complete understanding of the basis for the three categories discussed below.[7]

TAXATION CATEGORY 1: FIRMS THAT ARE WELL INTEGRATED WITH THE IMPUTATION TAX SYSTEM

This category consists mainly of companies which pay franked dividends and whose shareholders are able to use effectively the resultant franking credits. Such firms are said to be *well integrated* with the imputation system because any company tax paid is a kind of withholding payment (in the form of pre-paid personal taxes) that generates franking credits. These franking credits offset personal income tax payable by shareholders when dividends are received. So any decisions by financial managers that increase allowable tax deductions, and thus reduce the income tax payable by the company, result in fewer franking credits for shareholders. Consequently, shareholder wealth is best served by decisions that maximise the company's pre-tax income and cash flows and do not maximise company tax deductions. Therefore, for firms in taxation category 1, capital-budgeting decisions should be based on the company's pre-tax cash flows.

The same conclusion applies to the cash flows used in capital budgeting by non-taxpaying organisations, such as charities, educational institutions, eligible cooperatives, and so on. These organisations do not pay tax and so only 'raw' cash flows are relevant.

TAXATION CATEGORY 2: NON-COMPANY FIRMS AND COMPANIES THAT ARE NOT INTEGRATED WITH THE DIVIDEND IMPUTATION SYSTEM

This category applies to the many thousands of profit-making firms that are organised not as companies but as sole traders and partnerships. The owners of these firms pay personal tax on the firm's taxable income, so if the firm's tax deductions can be increased, the owners pay less tax. This means that decisions that increase the firm's tax deductions have value to the owners, and thus owners' wealth is best served by basing decisions on the after-tax income and cash flows of the business. Therefore, for firms in taxation category 2, capital-budgeting decisions should be based on a project's after-tax cash flows, with the relevant tax rate being the owner(s) personal tax rate(s).

This category also applies to Australian firms whose shareholders are unable to use any franking credits. Such companies are said to be *not integrated* with the dividend imputation tax system. Because their shareholders are unable to use franking credits, there is no relief from 'double taxation' of company income. This is because shareholders pay taxes on dividends in addition to the tax paid by the company on its profits. In effect, the classical tax system still applies to such companies because shareholders pay personal taxes on dividends that are paid from the *after-tax* profits of the company. Therefore, if the company can make decisions that increase its tax deductions and thereby reduce its income tax payable, company after-tax profits will increase. This means that larger dividends can be paid from the increased company after-tax profits, which leads to increased shareholder earnings after personal taxes and therefore increased shareholder wealth. Companies that fit this category effectively pay tax on their taxable income at the tax rate prescribed in the tax law, known as the *nominal* or *statutory* company tax rate (T). The conclusion that can be drawn for capital budgeting for taxation category 2 companies is that decisions should be based on the project's after-tax cash flows, with the amount of company income tax being based on the nominal or statutory rate of company income tax.

TAXATION CATEGORY 3: THE IN-BETWEEN CASE: COMPANIES THAT ARE PARTIALLY INTEGRATED WITH THE IMPUTATION TAX SYSTEM

Chapter 2 discussed the case of companies whose shareholders are able to make only partial use of franking credits. These companies fall between taxation categories 1 and 2. For taxation category 3 companies, the *effective corporate tax rate* (T_{eff}) depends on the proportion of franking credits that can be effectively used by the company's shareholders (u). Equation (2-4) in Chapter 2 defined the effective company tax rate as $T_{eff} = T(1 - u)$, where T is the statutory company tax rate. The conclusion that can be drawn for capital budgeting for taxation category 3 companies is that a project should be assessed on the basis of the project's after-tax cash flows, with the amounts of company income tax computed at the *effective* company tax rate. This contrasts with companies in category 2, where company income-tax cash flows are calculated at the nominal or statutory company tax rate.

TAX SAVINGS AND TAX PAYMENTS—AMOUNT AND TIMING

The payment of income tax by a firm constitutes a cash outflow. Therefore, if a firm in taxation category 2 or 3 has to pay *extra* income tax as a result of accepting a project, then that additional amount of tax must enter the capital-budgeting process in the form of a cash outflow. On the other hand, because tax deductions have value for firms in category 2 or 3, any additional tax deductions that occur from accepting a project will reduce the income tax payable by the firm. These *tax savings* will be included in the capital-budgeting process as a reduction in the project's tax cash outflows.

Note the emphasis on the extra income tax that stems from accepting a project—if a project generates extra accounting profits (or, more precisely, taxable income), extra tax will be payable. Conversely, if a project generates extra tax deductions for the firm, extra tax savings arise.

Because money has a time value, the time when tax is paid, or saved, is also relevant. In general, if a firm pays $10 000 tax 'now', it is less advantageous than paying that amount in a year's time. If a firm can defer the payment of tax, it benefits because money has a positive time value. Or, if the firm can bring forward the time of a tax deduction and the resultant tax saving, it also benefits. The timing of tax payments was introduced in Chapter 2, where it was seen that for many firms tax is payable in instalments during the year (based on the firm's estimate of its likely profits) rather than after the end of the year when the profit has been determined. In the following cases and problems, a simplifying assumption will generally be stated about when tax is payable.

THE NEED FOR CONSISTENCY

If a project is being evaluated for a firm that is in taxation category 1, only pre-tax cash flows are relevant, so no calculation is required of the company's after-tax cash flow. However, for consistency, the cost of capital that is used as the rate to discount the pre-tax cash flows back to a present value must also be determined on a pre-tax basis. Failure to do this would be like comparing apples with oranges. Similarly, if a company in category 2 is evaluating a capital-budgeting decision, after-tax cash flows are relevant. So it will be necessary to calculate the company's after-tax cash flow using the company's nominal or statutory tax rate. For consistency, the cost of capital must also be determined on an after-tax basis, using the same tax rate. If the category 2 firm is a sole trader or partnership, the relevant tax rate is the owner(s) personal tax rate(s). Finally, if the firm evaluating a project is in category 3, it should compute cash flows on an after-tax basis, using the *effective* company tax rate to determine the after-effective-tax cash flow, and the cost of capital should be computed using that same *effective* tax rate.

DEPRECIATION AND TAXATION

Earlier in this chapter it was shown that a depreciation amount is not a cash flow—it is an accounting expense that allocates the past cost of a long-lived asset over its useful or productive life. However, depreciation amounts may have taxation consequences. Specifically, if a project results in a change in a firm's depreciation amount then, because depreciation is an allowable deduction, the firm's income tax payable will also change. For taxation category 2 and 3 firms, depreciation amounts will need to be indirectly included in capital budgeting because of their effect on the firm's tax payable, which *is* a cash flow.

Australian tax law acknowledges two depreciation methods: the *prime cost* or straight-line method and the *diminishing balance* method. For ease of calculation, in this book it is often assumed that the prime cost method is used, because this method results in an equal depreciation expense each year. However, because the diminishing balance method gives greater deductions in earlier years, it will be preferred by firms that benefit from tax deductions. This stems from the fact that larger deductions mean smaller tax payments and, since tax payments have a time value, getting tax benefits 'now' is preferable to getting them later.

Table 11.5 demonstrates the difference between the two depreciation methods by showing the first three years depreciation expenses associated with an asset costing $35 000, assuming that the tax law allows a rate of 20% based on the prime cost or 30% based on the diminishing balance.

For answers go to MyFinanceLab or
www.pearson.com.au/9781442539174

TABLE 11.5 Calculation of depreciation for a new machine, first three years

	OPENING BALANCE		DEPRECIATION EXPENSE	
YEAR	PRIME COST	DIMINISHING BALANCE	PRIME COST	DIMINISHING BALANCE
1	$35 000	$35 000	$7 000	$10 500
2	28 000	24 500	7 000	7 350
3	21 000	17 150	7 000	5 145

OBJECTIVE **6**

Explain the importance of ethical considerations in capital-budgeting decisions.

Ethics in capital budgeting

What are the ethics of continuing to use refrigerants that damage the ozone layer, knowing full well the issues involved? Some firms have voluntarily replaced ozone-depleting chemicals with safer alternatives. Perhaps they figured that the short-term costs of switching to alternatives would be compensated by the long-term gains from getting in on the ground floor and obtaining a competitive advantage over other firms. It may have been done in anticipation of regulations that would make the use of the chemicals illegal; developed countries such as Australia undertook to phase out the harmful refrigerants by the late 1990s.

Would managers knowingly act unethically in their firms' investment activities? Unfortunately, the answer seems to be yes. The problem is that, even if people are well intentioned, they may see loyalty to shareholders and the wealth-creation goal as overriding other considerations such as social responsibility. As an example, manufacturers in the mid-1990s were still distributing in Australia some chemicals that are effective in treating termite infestation, despite the fact that the chemicals had long been banned in countries such as the United States. The decision makers of such a firm obviously judged the risk of expansion as being manageable, despite the impending threat of regulation or widespread public backlash against the firm. However, by continuing to produce and distribute the chemicals in those countries where it is not strictly illegal, ethical issues are raised. Some of the ethical issues in investment are value judgements, with the firm's managers having a responsibility to their shareholders but also to the wider society. In other cases, unethical behaviour may be clearly illegal.

Unethical behaviour can backfire on the firm, causing loss of public support or, in extreme cases, fines and other penalties. Therefore, although it may not seem obvious, ethics has a role to play in capital budgeting; even the most recalcitrant manager should realise that unethical behaviour may be bad for net present values.

International spotlight

THE EAST IS RED: CHINA CONTINUES TO BE THE TOP FOREIGN INVESTMENT DESTINATION

As the world economy is slowly recovering from the Global Financial Crisis, China once again is establishing itself as a major economic powerhouse. According to the Chinese National Bureau of Statistics (NBS), the crisis slowed the growth rate of the country a little, to 9% in 2008 and 8.7% in 2009. Since then, China appears to have shrugged off the bad memories of the financial crisis and quickened the rate of growth to 11.9% in the first quarter of 2010. Poised to overtake Japan as the world's second largest economy, China replaced the US as the world's largest auto market in 2009. It has taken little time for the world to realise that, with a low manufacturing cost structure and a huge consumer market, China is where they are likely to find positive NPV projects.

China currently ranks as the most attractive foreign investment destination. In 2008, $108.3 billion of foreign money poured into the country, accounting for approximately 2.2% of the national GDP. China has also been leading the foreign direct investment (FDI) confidence index since the index was first established by consultancy firm A.T. Kearney in 2002.

In November 2009, Novartis, the Swiss pharmaceutical giant, announced its plans to invest $1.25 billion in a pair of Chinese research and development (R&D) centres over the next five years. The company will put $250 million into a new R&D centre and manufacturing facility in Changshu, a city near Shanghai, and another $1 billion to the employment of 1000 additional researchers at an existing centre in Shanghai. The move is part of Novartis's overall strategic direction to tap one of the world's fastest growing major healthcare markets. Also attempting to share in the world's largest consumer market is Tesco Plc, the UK retailer. The company has committed $3.9 billion to opening 80 new Tesco stores in China over the next five years.

While concerns regarding an 'overheated' economy and its associated level of risks remain, the 'China phenomenon' is undoubtedly the critical factor that corporate policy makers need to take into account when devising their strategic plans for the future.[8]

A glance at actual capital-budgeting practices

OBJECTIVE **7**

Understand current business practice with respect to the use of capital-budgeting criteria.

During the past 50 years the popularity of each of the capital-budgeting methods has shifted rather dramatically. In the 1950s the payback period and AROR methods dominated capital budgeting, but through the 1960s and 1970s the discounted-cash-flow techniques slowly displaced the non-discounted methods. Interestingly, although many firms use the NPV and IRR as their primary techniques, they also use the payback period as a secondary decision method for capital budgeting. In a sense they are using the payback period to control for risk. The logic behind this is that because the payback period dramatically emphasises early cash flows, which are presumably more certain (i.e. have less risk) than cash flows that occur later in a project's life, its use will lead to projects with more certain cash flows.

A survey conducted in 2004 into the capital-budgeting practice of non-financial Australian companies confirmed the dominance of NPV in corporate investment decision making. The survey showed that the NPV technique was used by 94% of all respondents. Interestingly, the payback method was the second most popular capital-budgeting technique, being used by 91% of all companies, while IRR ranked third. Not only was the NPV method widely used, it was

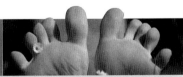

FYI

Surveys show that firms often look at more than one capital-budgeting criterion in selecting a particular project. In a sense, they are trying to have a bet each way, perhaps choosing the project that scores well in all criteria over a project that has a

greater NPV. This indicates the complexity of decision making in a world where decisions are made by groups such as management committees, whose members might have different aims and motives.

also considered to be the most important capital-budgeting technique. Ninety-five percent of responding firms perceived the NPV technique to be at least moderately important and 84% of respondents considered the payback period to be important. However, the majority of surveyed firms relied on more than one capital-budgeting method. Approximately 81% of the companies employed between three and six capital-budgeting techniques in evaluating their investment proposals. The survey confirmed the importance of NPV as a capital-budgeting technique and highlighted the popularity of the payback period as a secondary method of project evaluation. Figure 11.4 summarises the different techniques employed by companies in their capital budgeting.

Concept check

11.15 What capital-budgeting criteria seem to be used most frequently in the real world? Why do you think this is so?

For answers go to MyFinanceLab or
www.pearson.com.au/9781442539174

FIGURE 11.4 Capital budgeting in practice

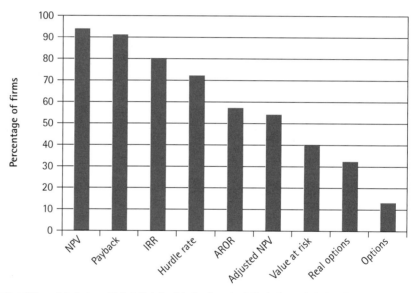

Source: Adapted from G. Truong, G. Partington and M. Peat, 'Cost of capital estimation and capital-budgeting practice in Australia', *Australian Journal of Management*, 33, 2008, pp. 95–122.

Before a profitable project can be adopted; it must be identified or found. Unfortunately, coming up with ideas for new products, for ways to improve existing products or for ways to make existing products more profitable is extremely difficult. In general, the best source of ideas for new, potentially profitable products is found within the firm. Those projects that do succeed commonly have a competitive edge through product differentiation or cost advantage.

OBJECTIVE 1

To determine the acceptability of projects, managers use a number of project-evaluation techniques to assist them in making the decisions. Good capital-budgeting techniques have to satisfy the following criteria: (1) Rely on cash flows rather than accounting profits; (2) Be consistent with the goal of maximising shareholders' wealth; (3) Allow for the time value of money; and (4) Be able to account for project risks.

OBJECTIVE 2

Some capital-budgeting methods account for the time value of money by discounting cash flows to the present. These methods are referred to as discounted-cash-flow (DCF) methods. Three DCF capital-budgeting methods are net present value, profitability index and internal rate of return. These methods are summarised in Figure 11.3.

OBJECTIVE 3

Non-discounted-cash-flow capital-budgeting methods do not take into account the time value of money and as such they are not ideal capital-budgeting techniques. However, these techniques, including payback period and accounting rate of return, are used frequently in practice due to their simplicity. These methods are also summarised in Figure 11.3.

OBJECTIVE 4

For non-company businesses, such as sole traders and partnerships, capital budgeting should be carried out on the basis of the project's after-tax cash flows, the relevant tax rate being the personal marginal tax rate(s) of the owner(s). For companies, capital budgeting can be carried out on the basis of pre-tax cash flows (which is appropriate for taxation category 1 firms), on an after-company-tax basis (which is appropriate for taxation category 2 firms), or on an after-*effective*-tax basis (which is appropriate for taxation category 3 firms). In all cases it is important to be consistent and to ensure that the discount rate is on the same pre-tax or after-tax basis as the cash flows.

OBJECTIVE 5

Ethics and ethical decisions crop up in capital budgeting. Just as with all other areas of finance, violating ethical considerations results in a loss of public confidence, which can have a significant negative effect on shareholder wealth.

OBJECTIVE 6

Over the past 50 years, the discounted-capital-budgeting decision criteria have continued to gain in popularity and today dominate in the decision-making process, although many firms also use the payback method. Most firms, however, use multiple investment criteria and often use payback as a secondary measure to reflect project risk considerations.

OBJECTIVE 7

Key terms

For a complete flashcard glossary go to MyFinanceLab at www.pearson.com.au/myfinancelab

Review questions

11-1 What is capital budgeting? What are the main issues that capital budgeting aims to address?

11-2 Why is the capital-budgeting decision such an important process? Why are capital-budgeting errors so costly?

11-3 How is the presence or absence of competition related to NPV? What are the types of barriers to market entry that tend to preserve positive NPVs?

11-4 (a) In what way can a product's brand name help to provide product differentiation? How might this also help achieve cost advantages?
(b) In what way can product differentiation or cost advantages help a firm achieve positive NPV projects?

11-5 What principles suggest that discounted-cash-flow criteria are the most appropriate to use for capital budgeting?

11-6 Why is NPV considered to be the best method for capital budgeting? What does the NPV tell you?

11-7 Why do we focus on cash flows rather than accounting profits in making our capital-budgeting decisions?

11-8 What are the differences between the straight-line and the diminishing-balance methods of depreciation? Which depreciation method would give the project a more favourable outcome? In other words, which depreciation method would make a particular project more likely to be accepted? Explain.

11-9 Briefly compare and contrast the three discounted-cash-flow criteria (NPV, PI and IRR). What are the advantages and disadvantages of the use of each of these methods?

11-10 What is the internal rate of return? Is it true that when the IRR method is used in project evaluation the discount rate will not need to be estimated?

11-11 (a) What are the limitations of the payback period as a capital-budgeting technique?
(b) What are its advantages? Why is it so frequently used?
(c) Does the discounted payback method overcome the problems associated with the traditional payback method? Why or why not?
(d) Under what conditions would the payback and discounted payback methods produce identical results?

11-12 If a project's payback period is less than the maximum acceptable payback period that the firm will accept, does this mean that the project's NPV will also be positive? Explain.

11-13 In some countries, expropriation of foreign investments has been a common practice from time to time. This means that the ruling government takes over ownership of a foreign owner's assets. If you were considering an investment in one of those countries, would the use of the payback-period criterion seem more reasonable than it otherwise might? Why?

11-14 Why can't the accounting rate of return be used as a reliable capital-budgeting technique? What are its advantages?

11-15 'It is convenient to think of firms as falling into three taxation categories for capital-budgeting purposes.' Explain.

11-16 Why can capital budgeting for taxation category 1 firms be conducted on a before-tax basis? Explain.

11-17 Why is it important for companies to consider ethics in their capital budgeting? Give an example of an ethical consideration in the capital-budgeting process.

Self-test problem

ST-1 In 2010, Caltec Enterprises was considering the acquisition of a new conveyor belt system for one of its plants. The system required an initial outlay of $54 200 in Year 0 and had an expected life of five years. The conveyor belt system was expected to reduce the firm's material handling costs by $20 608 at the end of each year over its five-year life. In addition to the $20 608 cash flow from operations during the fifth and final year, there will be an additional cash flow of $13 200 at the end of the fifth year associated with the salvage value of the system, making the cash flow in year 5 equal to $33 808. Thus, the cash flows associated with this project can be summarised as follows:

YEAR	CASH FLOW
0	–$54 200
1	20 608
2	20 608
3	20 608
4	20 608
5	33 808

Given a required rate of return of 15%, calculate the following:

    (a) Payback period
    (b) Discounted payback period
    (c) Net present value
    (d) Profitability index
    (e) Internal rate of return

Should this project be accepted?

Problems

11-1 (*NPV, PI and IRR calculations*) Oil Search is considering a major investment in a new oil field in Western Australia. According to initial estimates, the investment outlay would be $2 500 000 and the project would generate incremental pre-tax cash flows of $500 000 per year for eight years. The appropriate required rate of return is 8% p.a. and the project should be evaluated on a pre-tax basis.

For more problems and for answers to problems marked with an asterisk (*) go to MyFinanceLab at www.pearson.com.au/myfinancelab

    (a) Calculate the net present value.
    (b) Calculate the profitability index.
    (c) Calculate the internal rate of return.
    (d) Should this project be accepted?

11-2 (*NPV with varying required rates of return*) Specialty Foods Group is a leading manufacturer of non-dairy powdered coffee creamers. Recently, a proposal has been put forward to senior management regarding the purchase of a new labelling machine. The proposal indicates that the labelling machine costs $850 000 but would generate a cost saving of $150 000 p.a. It is expected that the machine will last for 10 years.

    (a) What is the project's NPV if the required rate of return is 8%?
    (b) What is the project's NPV if the required rate of return is 12%?
    (c) Would the project be accepted under part **(a)** or **(b)**?
    (d) What is this project's internal rate of return?

11-3 (*NPV, PI and IRR calculations*) Brambles Industry is considering a major expansion of its product line and has estimated the following cash flows associated with such an expansion. The initial outlay associated with the expansion would be $4 500 000 and the project would generate incremental cash flows of $750 000 per year for the first four years and $500 000 per year for the remaining six years of the project's life. The appropriate required rate of return is 12% and projects should be evaluated on a pre-tax basis.

    (a) Calculate the net present value.
    (b) Calculate the profitability index.
    (c) Calculate the internal rate of return.
    (d) Should this project be accepted?

11-4 (*NPV calculation*) Manly Sports is considering building a new factory to produce thermal diving gear. The cost of building the factory is estimated to be $5 000 000. Once completed, it will produce a net cash flow of $1 000 000 per year for eight years. Calculate the NPV for the project, given:

    (a) A required rate of return of 9%
    (b) A required rate of return of 11%
    (c) A required rate of return of 13%
    (d) A required rate of return of 15%

11-5* (*IRR calculation*) Determine the internal rate of return on the following projects:

    (a) An initial outlay of $10 000 resulting in a single cash flow of $17 182 after eight years
    (b) An initial outlay of $10 000 resulting in a single cash flow of $48 077 after 10 years
    (c) An initial outlay of $10 000 resulting in a single cash flow of $114 943 after 20 years
    (d) An initial outlay of $10 000 resulting in a single cash flow of $13 680 after three years

11-6* (*IRR calculation*) Determine the internal rate of return to the nearest % on the following projects:

    (a) An initial outlay of $10 000 resulting in a cash flow of $2000 at the end of year 1, $5000 at the end of year 2, and $8000 at the end of year 3
    (b) An initial outlay of $10 000 resulting in a cash flow of $8000 at the end of year 1, $5000 at the end of year 2, and $2000 at the end of year 3
    (c) An initial outlay of $10 000 resulting in a cash flow of $2000 at the end of years 1 to 5 and $5000 at the end of year 6

11-7* (*IRR calculation*) Given the following cash flows, determine the internal rate of return for projects A, B and C.

	PROJECT A	PROJECT B	PROJECT C
Initial investment	$50 000	$100 000	$450 000
Cash inflows:			
Year 1	$10 000	$25 000	$200 000
Year 2	15 000	25 000	200 000
Year 3	20 000	25 000	200 000
Year 4	25 000	25 000	–
Year 5	30 000	25 000	–

11-8 (*AROR calculation*) A business for which tax deductions are of benefit is currently evaluating two mutually exclusive projects using the accounting rate of return method. Project A has an initial cost of $50 000 and a salvage value of $5000 after six years, while project B has an initial cost of $35 000 and a salvage value of $7000 after six years. The following information is given.

Annual after-tax accounting profits

YEAR	PROJECT A	PROJECT B
1	$4 500	$8 500
2	4 500	8 500
3	4 500	8 500
4	12 000	7 000
5	12 000	7 000
6	12 000	7 000

    (a) Determine each project's AROR.
    (b) Which project should be selected, using this criterion? Would you support that recommendation? Why or why not?

11-9 (*Payback period calculations*) Taylor Lee runs a removal company and he is considering investing in a new fleet of trucks. The new fleet of trucks is estimated to cost the company $550000, but the new fleet will bring in additional cash flows of $100000 annually for three years and $80000 a year for the next three years.

    (a) What is the payback period for the project?

    (b) What is the discounted payback period for the project?

    (c) It is company policy to reject projects with a payback period of longer than four years. Should the company go ahead with the new truck purchase?

11-10 (*Payback period calculations*) Star Industries is considering three independent projects, A, B and C with the following estimated cash flows. The company does not want to make any investment that requires more than three years to recover the firm's initial investment.

YEAR	PROJECT A	PROJECT B	PROJECT C
0	–$900	–$9000	–$7000
1	600	5000	2000
2	300	3000	2000
3	200	3000	2000
4	100	3000	2000
5	500	3000	2000

    (a) Given Star Industries' three-year payback period, which of the projects qualify for acceptance?

    (b) Rank the three projects using their payback period. Which project looks the best using this criterion? Do you agree with this ranking? Why or why not?

    (c) If Star Industries uses a 10% discount rate to analyse projects, what is the discounted payback period for each of the three projects? If the firm still maintains its three-year payback policy for the discounted payback, which projects should the firm undertake?

11-11 (*NPV and IRR calculations*) Outdoors Venture Ltd is considering the purchase of a machine that makes caravan spare parts. The executive officer has to choose between two machines: the Doozy Model, which is the more expensive of the two but also the more efficient, and the Coozy Model (cheaper and less efficient). The company has a required rate of return of 9%. Estimated cash flows associated with the two models are as follows.

YEAR	1	2	3	4
Doozy ('000)	–$4000	1250	2000	2000
Coozy ('000)	–$2000	750	1000	1000

    (a) Calculate the IRR for each model.

    (b) Based on the calculations in part **(a)**, the chief executive officer decided to purchase the Coozy model. Do you support her decision? Calculate the NPV for the two models to validate your argument.

11-12 (*Payback period and NPV calculations*) Plato Energy is an oil and gas exploration and development company located in Perth, Western Australia. The company drills shallow wells in the hope of finding significant oil and gas deposits. The firm is considering two different drilling opportunities that have very different production potential. The first is in the Coral Bay region, north of Perth, and the other is in Albany, south of Perth. The Coral Bay project requires a much larger initial investment but will provide cash flows (if successful) over a much longer period of time than the Albany opportunity. In addition, the longer life of the Coral Bay project would also result in additional expenditures in year 3 of the project to enhance production throughout the project's 10-year expected life. This expenditure involves pumping either water or CO_2 down into the wells in order to increase the flow of oil and gas from the structure. The expected cash flows for the two projects are:

YEAR	CORAL BAY	ALBANY
0	–$5 000 000	–$1 500 000
1	2 000 000	800 000
2	2 000 000	800 000
3	–1 000 000	400 000
4	2 000 000	100 000
5	1 500 000	
6	1 500 000	
7	1 500 000	
8	800 000	
9	500 000	
10	100 000	

(a) What is the payback period for each of the two projects?

(b) Based on the payback periods calculated above, which of the two projects appears to be the best alternative? What are the limitations of the payback period ranking? That is, what does the payback period not consider important in determining the value creation potential of these two projects?

(c) If Plato's management uses a 20% discount rate to evaluate the present values of its energy investment projects, what is the NPV of the two proposed investments?

(d) What is your estimate of the value that will be created for Plato by the acceptance of each of these two investments?

11-13 (*Complex capital-budgeting calculations*) Noodles Plus is a chain of restaurants selling Chinese fast food. The owner of the chain wants to rejuvenate the four existing restaurants at a cost of $150 000 per store. The stores will have a new image and a new 'Noodles Plus' logo, accompanied by a colour scheme featuring cool hues and a clean, functional look. This re-imaging will be accompanied by intensive advertising and promotion, which is expected to cost a total of $40 000 for all four restaurants and to increase annual sales by $140 000 per restaurant in the next five years.

(a) What is the payback period of this rejuvenation project?

(b) Calculate the NPV and the PI for the project.

(c) Based on your calculation in part **(b)**, advise the owner of Noodles Plus on an appropriate course of action.

11-14 (*Complex capital-budgeting calculations*) Garmen Technologies Inc. operates a small chain of specialty retail stores throughout Australia and the Asia Pacific. The stores market technology-based consumer products both in their stores and on the Internet with sales split roughly equally between the two channels of distribution. The company's products range from radar detection devices and GPS mapping systems used in automobiles to home-based weather-monitoring stations. The company recently began investigating the possible acquisition of a regional warehousing facility that could be used both to stock its retail shops and to make direct shipments to the firm's online customers. The warehouse facility would require an expenditure of $250 000 for a rented space in Sydney and would provide a source of cash flow spanning the next 10 years. The estimated cash flows are found below:

YEAR	CASH FLOW
0	–$250 000
1	60 000
2	60 000
3	60 000
4	60 000
5	–45 000
6	65 000
7	65 000
8	65 000
9	65 000
10	90 000

The negative cash flow in year 5 reflects the cost of a planned renovation and expansion of the facility. Finally, in year 10 Garmen estimates some recovery of its investment at the close of the lease and, consequently, a higher than usual cash flow. Garmen uses a 12% discount rate in evaluating its investments.

(a) As a preliminary step in analysing the new investment, Garmen's management has decided to evaluate the project's anticipated payback period. What is the project's expected payback period? Jim Garmen, CEO, questioned the analyst performing the analysis about the meaning of the payback period since it seemed to ignore the fact that the project would provide cash flows over many years beyond the end of the payback period. Specifically, he wanted to know what useful information the payback provided. If you were the analyst, how would you respond to Mr Garmen?

(b) In the past, Garmen's management has relied almost exclusively on the IRR to make its investment choices. However, in this instance, the lead financial analyst on the project suggested that there may be a problem with the IRR since the sign on the cash flows changes three times over its life. Calculate the IRR for the project.

(c) Evaluate the NPV profile of the project for discount rates of 0%, 20%, 50% and 100%. Does there appear to be a problem of multiple IRRs in this range of discount rates?

(d) Calculate the project's NPV. What does the NPV indicate about the potential value created by the project? Describe to Mr Garmen what NPV means, recognising that he was trained as an engineer and has no formal business education.

Case study

RWE Enterprises: Expansion Project Analysis

RWE Enterprises, Inc. (RWE) is a small manufacturing firm located in the hills just outside Adelaide, South Australia. The firm is engaged in the manufacture and sale of feed supplements used by cattle raisers. The product has a molasses base but is supplemented with minerals and vitamins that are generally thought to be essential to the health and growth of beef cattle. The final product is put in 50-kg or 90-kg tubs that are then made available for the cattle to lick as desired. The material in the tub becomes very hard, which limits the animals' consumption.

The firm has been running a single production line for the past five years and is considering the addition of a new line. The addition would expand the firm's capacity by almost 120% since the new equipment requires a shorter down time between batches. After each production run, the boiler used to prepare the molasses for the addition of minerals and vitamins must be heated to 85° C and then must be cooled down before beginning the next batch. The total production run entails about four hours and the cool-down period is two hours (during which time the whole process comes to a halt). Using two production lines would increase the overall efficiency of the operation since workers from the line that is cooling down could be moved to the other line to support the 'canning' process involved in filling the feed tubs.

The second production line equipment would cost $3 million to purchase and install and would have an estimated life of 10 years at which time it could be sold for an estimated after-tax scrap value of $200 000. Furthermore, at the end of five years the production line would have to be refurbished at an estimated cost of $2 million. RWE's management estimates that the new production line would add $700 000 per year in after-tax cash flow to the firm. The 10-year cash flows for the line are as follows:

YEAR	CASH FLOW
0	–$3 000 000
1	700 000
2	700 000
3	700 000
4	700 000
5	–1 300 000
6	700 000
7	700 000
8	700 000
9	700 000
10	900 000

(a) If RWE uses a 10% discount rate to evaluate investments of this type, what is the net present value of the project? What does this NPV indicate about the potential value RWE might create by purchasing the new production line?

(b) Calculate the internal rate of return and profitability index for the proposed investment. What do these two measures tell you about the project's viability?

(c) Calculate the payback and discounted payback for the proposed investment. Interpret your findings.

Notes

1. These cost-cutting measures undertaken by Telstra have faced significant customer backlash. It is believed cost-cutting strategies have resulted in poorer service quality.
2. In an efficient market, the NPV would be translated into an increase in the value of shareholders' funds. Some of the conditions for market efficiency were touched on in Chapters 1 and 10.
3. This example is taken from James H. Lorie and Leonard J. Savage, 'Three problems in rationing capital', *Journal of Business*, 28, October 1955, pp. 229–39.
4. The fact that the rates 25% and 400% both yield the correct present value can be seen by substitution. The equation relating the future cash flows to the present value is:

$$\$1600 = \frac{\$10\,000}{(1 + IRR)^1} - \frac{\$10\,000}{(1 + IRR)^2}$$

If we substitute 25% for the *IRR* in the right-hand side, we have:

$$\frac{\$10\,000}{(1 + 0.25)^1} - \frac{\$10\,000}{(1 + 0.25)^2} = \frac{\$10\,000}{1.25} - \frac{\$10\,000}{1.5625}$$

$$= \$8000 - \$6400 = \$1600$$

For a rate of 400%, the equation becomes:

$$\frac{\$10\,000}{(1 + 4)^1} - \frac{\$10\,000}{(1 + 4)^2} = \frac{\$10\,000}{5} - \frac{\$10\,000}{25}$$

$$= \$2000 - \$400 = \$1600$$

5. As shown in Figure 11.1, the *IRR* is the rate that makes the NPV equal to zero. This concept has not been encountered previously, but if you look at the equation in note 4, you will see that the NPV is $1600, given by:

$$NPV = \$1600 = \frac{\$10\,000}{(1 + IRR)^1} - \frac{\$10\,000}{(1 + IRR)^2}$$

Now, if $1600 is subtracted from both sides, we have:

$$NPV = 0 = \frac{\$10\,000}{(1 + IRR)^1} - \frac{\$10\,000}{(1 + IRR)^2} - \$1600$$

In other words, the *IRR* will solve this equation such that the NPV is equal to zero. A numerical example is provided by the computations in note 4. For an *IRR* of 25%, it was seen that the present value of the future cash flows is $1600; this is equal to the initial outlay, so the NPV is zero.

6. Looking back at the *IRR* figures, would you be swayed by them to invest in a project that requires you to outlay $1000 now, will pay you $10 000 a year later, after which you will have to outlay another $10 000?
7. As mentioned in Chapter 2, it is difficult to be sure how many Australian companies are represented in each of these three taxation categories.
8. The following references were used in the writing of the International Spotlight article: 'Ambitious Tesco ready to risk expansion where others fear to trade', *The Telegraph*, 15 September 2010; 'Top 25 countries for overseas investment', *Bloomberg Businessweek*, 5 March 2010; 'Novartis unveiled $1.25 billion China investment', *Bloomberg Businessweek*, 3 November 2009.

Learning objectives

After reading this chapter, you should be able to:

1 Identify the guidelines by which cash flows are measured.
2 Explain how a project's benefits and costs—that is, its incremental cash flows—are calculated.
3 Apply discounted-cash-flow techniques in a typical 'asset-replacement' project.
4 Apply discounted-cash-flow techniques in a typical 'revenue-generating' project.
5 Understand how the capital-budgeting process changes when there is capital rationing or there are mutually exclusive projects.

For a complete eBook go to MyFinanceLab
www.pearson.com.au/myfinancelab

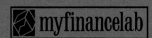

Capital budgeting: cash-flow identification and project ranking conflicts

chapter 12

CHAPTER PREVIEW

This chapter continues the discussion of decision rules for deciding whether to invest in new projects. Chapter 11 introduced different capital-budgeting techniques that assist financial managers in making long-term investment decisions. In that chapter it was assumed that cash flows arising from investment projects are easily identified, whereas in practice the process is much more complicated. This chapter details the guidelines to determine whether a particular cash flow is relevant to be included in the evaluation of a project and how to correctly identify and calculate the relevant cash flow amounts. This will be followed by a discussion of how to deal with the problems that occur when only one of a number of competing projects can be accepted or the total budget available for investment is limited.

The chapter relies on *Principle 3: Cash—not profits—is king, Principle 4: Incremental cash flows—it's only what changes that counts* and *Principle 5: The curse of competitive markets—why it's hard to find exceptionally profitable projects.* Be on the lookout for these important concepts.

Guidelines for identifying a project's incremental costs and benefits

 OBJECTIVE 1

Identify the guidelines by which cash flows are measured.

The key to the capital-budgeting evaluation process being useful for decision making is forecasting with accuracy the amount and timing of the project's cash flows. As a firm's day-to-day operations involve multiple sources of cash in and out flows, it is extremely important for investment decision making to correctly identify which cash flows are relevant to be included in the evaluation of the investment project. To do this requires implementation of the following guidelines.

USE CASH FLOWS RATHER THAN ACCOUNTING PROFITS

As highlighted in the previous chapter, cash flows—not accounting profits—are used as the measurement tool for project evaluation. This is because it is cash flows that the firm receives and is able to reinvest whereas the accounting process records accounting profits when they are earned rather than when the money is actually in hand. Accordingly, the timing of a firm's accounting profits and cash flows are not likely to occur together, and it is cash flows

Back to the principles

Principle 3: Cash—not profits—is king says that if we are to make intelligent capital-budgeting decisions, we must accurately measure the amount and timing of the investment project's cash benefits and costs. Remember, it is cash inflows that can be reinvested and cash outflows that involve paying out money.

Regardless of your program

'THE INTERNET ON AIRLINE FLIGHTS'

Cash-flow forecasting involves more than just the finance specialists in the firm. In practice, teams of technical, marketing, accounting and other specialists often work together to develop cash-flow forecasts for large investments. For example, some major airlines are beginning to provide Internet access on their flights. The idea is that, for a fee of say $10 per flight, a customer can buy wireless access to the Internet while in flight. However, the airline must overcome a number of hurdles to offer this service. There are technical issues related to both the hardware that must be installed on the aircraft and the infrastructure required to support access to the Internet—and all of this costs money. Then there is the question of how much revenue the airline can receive from this service. Consequently, for the airline to analyse the decision to include in-flight Internet access, it needs a team that includes technical staff, such as engineers, to determine the cost of installing and maintaining the service, marketing personnel to estimate customer acceptance rates and revenues, and a financial analyst to combine the various cost and revenue estimates into a project evaluation.

that correctly reflect the amount and timing of when the money is received, when it can be reinvested and when it must be paid out.

THINK INCREMENTALLY

incremental cash flows
The cash flows that occur only from the acceptance of a capital-budgeting project. The test to determine if a cash flow is not incremental is that it will exist both if a project goes ahead and if it does not go ahead (the 'with/without test').

To correctly evaluate a capital budgeting project the critical question is 'what *additional* cash flows will the firm receive or pay as a result of making the decision to undertake the project?'. As these additional or **incremental cash flows** are only those amounts that specifically relate to the project being evaluated, the key test of whether a cash flow is incremental is the 'with or without' question. If a cash-flow amount will occur if the project is accepted ('with') and will also occur if the project is not accepted ('without'), then the cash flow is *not* incremental and is *not* included in the evaluation of the project.

Conversely, if a cash-flow amount will only occur if the project is accepted ('with') and will *not* occur if the project is not accepted ('without'), then the cash flow is incremental and must be included in the evaluation of the project. Also remember that incremental cash flows can be negative (incremental costs) or positive (incremental benefits).

Back to the principles

In order to measure the true effects of capital-budgeting decisions, the benefits and costs of projects must be analysed on an incremental basis, which relates directly to **Principle 4: Incremental cash flows— it's only what changes that counts**. In effect, we have to determine what the cash flows will be if the project is accepted versus what they will be if the project is not taken on.

BEWARE OF CASH FLOWS DIVERTED FROM EXISTING PRODUCTS

Normally, the cash flows from the firm's existing business are not included as cash flows in the evaluation of a project because they are not affected by the decision to accept the project. That is, they are not incremental because they will occur with the project and will occur without the project.

However, it is possible that some cash-flow amounts from the firm's existing business need to be included as relevant incremental cash flows of the project. For example, the managers of a firm are evaluating a new product that, if introduced, is likely to compete with and reduce the sales of one of its existing products. In this situation, the incremental sales generated from the new product minus the incremental reduction in sales of the existing product need to be included as cash flow amounts to evaluate the project to introduce the proposed new product.

On the other hand, if the introduction of the new product is expected to have *no* impact on the sales of existing products, then there will be no incremental cash-flow amount from existing products to be included in the evaluation of the new product project. This is confirmed by the with/without test. If the new product is implemented ('with') there is no impact on existing product cash flows and if the new product project is not implemented ('without') there is also no impact on existing product cash flows.

Remember that we are interested in incremental cash flows to the firm only if a particular project is accepted, because we want to be able to determine whether the project in its own right will add value (e.g. positive NPV) to the firm's owners.

LOOK FOR INCIDENTAL OR SYNERGISTIC EFFECTS

Although in some cases the implementation of a new project may take sales away from a firm's existing products, in other cases a new project may have an incidental, or *synergistic*, effect by bringing new sales to the firm's existing products. The incremental cash flows that are relevant to be included in the evaluation of this type of project will comprise both the incremental sales from the new project plus the incremental sales from the existing products.

INCORPORATE ALLOWANCE FOR WORKING-CAPITAL REQUIREMENTS

In addition to an initial investment outlay and incremental sales and costs, sometimes a new project requires additional investment in working capital. *Working capital* is equal to a firm's current assets, such as cash, inventories and accounts receivable, minus its current liabilities, most notably accounts payable. The investment in working capital for a new project may take the following typical forms:

- Initial and subsequent expenditure on inventory to have products for sale when the new project starts. For example, a new retail outlet has to have stock on the shelves available for sale from day one. Subsequently, as sales increase/decrease, an additional investment/reduction in inventory to support the level of sales will be required to be included in the evaluation of the project.
- Increase/reduction in accounts receivable. If customers are given time to pay, then any increase/decrease in sales generated by the project will involve an increase/reduction in accounts receivable that affects the timing of receipt of sales cash flows. For example, a new project that provides customers with 30-day credit terms and has sales in January totalling $100000 will at the end of January have an accounts receivable balance of $100000. The financial implication for the evaluation of the project is that the $100000 cash flow from January sales will not be received in January but will be delayed until February or even later.
- Increased investment outlay to provide the cash 'float' for cash registers.
- Increase/decrease in project purchases. If suppliers to the project give it time to pay, then any increase/decrease in the project's purchases will involve an increase/reduction in accounts payable that affects the timing of the project's cash outflows. For example, a new project that is given 30-day credit terms and has purchases in January totalling $50000 will at the end of January have an accounts payable balance of $50000. The financial implication for the evaluation of the project is that the $50000 cash outflow for items purchased in January will not occur in January but will be delayed until February or even later.

Incremental working-capital amounts are relevant cash flows for project evaluation even though they do not leave the firm. How can the amount of investment in inventory be considered a relevant project cash outflow when the goods are still in the store? Because the money spent to purchase inventory cannot be used by the firm for other investments.

Generally, working-capital requirements are tied up over the life of the project and when the project terminates there is usually an offsetting cash inflow as the working capital is recovered. For example, if the average level of investment in working capital is $70 000, the firm would receive a cash inflow for this amount at the end of the project, as inventories are either run down or sold to a new purchaser of the business, accounts receivable balances are collected without more being created, and accounts payable balances are paid without more being created.

Why, then do the amounts for the investment in working capital need to be included in the evaluation of a project if these working-capital amounts are recovered at the end of the life of the project? The answer is simple—a dollar today does not have the same present value as a dollar in a year's time (Principle 2, Chapters 4, 7, 8 and 11). For example, the recovery in a year's time of a $100 000 investment in inventory is worth only $83 333 in today's dollars, if the discount rate is 20%.

This leads to a very important point that you need to remember for future capital-budgeting problems: when a project requires an increase in working capital, this increased amount needs to be included in the project evaluation as a cash outflow at that time. However, since the firm can sell these additional short-term assets in the future when the project winds up, the return or recapture of this amount at the end of the project needs to be included in the project evaluation as a cash inflow at the end of the final year. By doing this, the firm does not lose the cash flows associated with working capital but includes the impact of the time value of the money.

BE ON THE LOOKOUT FOR INCREMENTAL EXPENSES, NOT JUST BENEFITS

Just as the cash inflows from the sales generated by a new project are measured on an incremental basis, the cash inflows from the project's expenses (costs) need to be measured on an incremental basis. For example, if a project to introduce a new product requires expenditure to train sales staff, the amount spent for the training must be included as an incremental cash outflow in the project evaluation. Similarly, if the acceptance of a new project requires an existing production facility to be re-engineered, the expenditure associated with that capital investment is a relevant cash outflow of the project as it satisfies the with/without incremental rule. 'With' the project, the expenditure will be incurred; 'without' the project, the expenditure will not be incurred.

REMEMBER THAT 'SUNK COSTS' ARE NOT INCREMENTAL CASH FLOWS

Sometimes you will encounter people who argue that because a cash-flow amount is associated with a project it must be included in the project evaluation. For example, a firm may have spent $10 000 to do some test marketing of a proposed new product before the new product project is evaluated. In this case it is easy to think that the $10 000 should be included as a relevant cash outflow in the NPV evaluation of the new product project.

However, you now know that only incremental cash-flow amounts are included in the evaluation of a capital-budgeting project and that two questions need to be asked: (1) Will this cash flow occur if the project is accepted? (2) Will this cash flow occur if the project is rejected? If the answers are *yes* to the first question and *yes* to the second then the cash flow is *not* incremental.

sunk cost
A past cash outflow or cost that is not incremental to a particular project.

In this example, the amount spent on the test marketing is a **sunk cost** as it is not incremental. It is a *past* cash outflow that the firm has already paid, regardless of whether it accepts the project 'with' or rejects the project 'without'. Accordingly, it is not a relevant cash flow to be included in the evaluation of the new product project.

Another example of a sunk cost is a mining company that spent $1 million a year ago on a test drill and is now evaluating whether or not to develop the site. The $1 million is literally a sunk cost as it has already occurred and exists with or without the decision to develop the site.

To determine if a cash flow is a sunk cost, ask yourself this question: 'Can we save this cash flow by not doing this project?'. If the answer is 'No, we cannot, because this cost has already been incurred', then it is a sunk cost and should not be included as a cash-flow amount in the project evaluation.

ACCOUNT FOR OPPORTUNITY COSTS

An opportunity cost is an amount that is forgone when a particular course of action is taken. In the evaluation of capital-budgeting projects the course of action is the acceptance of the project, and any incremental opportunity-cost amounts are included as relevant project cash flows.

A good example of an opportunity cost is a project that will involve building a factory on vacant land that has been owned by the firm for many years. A current valuation of the vacant land if it was put on the market for sale is $1 million. Assuming that the firm was willing to sell the vacant land, but then decides to accept the project to build the factory on the land, it will have forgone the opportunity to sell the land for $1 million.

Accordingly, the $1 million opportunity cost should be included as a relevant initial cash outflow in the evaluation of the factory project because it satisfies the incremental with/without test. 'With' the project the firm forgoes selling the land for $1 million; 'without' the project the firm can sell the land for $1 million.

Although the $1 million opportunity cost being included as a cash-flow amount is not obvious, the key point is that opportunity-cost cash flows should reflect net cash flows that would have been received if the project under consideration had been rejected.

DECIDE IF OVERHEAD COSTS ARE TRULY INCREMENTAL CASH FLOWS

To correctly evaluate a capital-budgeting project, overhead expenses such as utilities (power, gas and water) and salaries need to be included, but it is important to make sure that they are incremental amounts. Many overhead expenses such as air-conditioning, lighting and rent are incurred whether or not a given project is accepted or rejected and there is often not a single specific project to which these expenses can be allocated.

Thus, the question is not whether or not the project benefits from overhead items but whether the overhead costs are incremental cash flows associated with the project and should be included in capital-budgeting evaluation. For example, the company management accountant may want to allocate 20% of $300 000 head-office salaries to the cost of operating a new project. If these salaries are already being paid by the company, even if some of the time of existing staff is spent on the new project, then none of the $300 000 amount spent on head-office salaries is an incremental cash flow amount to be included in the project's evaluation.

BE CONSISTENT IN THE TREATMENT OF FACTORS SUCH AS 'INFLATION'

To do an NPV or IRR evaluation of a capital-budgeting project it is necessary to estimate the amount and timing of the project's future incremental cash flows. This raises the question of whether future 'inflation' should be included in the estimates. For example, even if the future sales *volume* of the project is not expected to increase, the *dollar value* of sales may increase year by year as prices increase in line with the rate of inflation. This inflation effect also applies to estimates for future cash outflows such as operating costs.

Consistency in the relationship between how both the cash flows and the discount rate are estimated is the answer to the 'inflation' question. If the estimates of future incremental cash flows are *nominal* amounts because they include expected inflation, then to be consistent, a *nominal* discount rate that includes expected inflation must be used for the project evaluation (i.e. via NPV or IRR).

On the other hand, if the project's future incremental cash flows are estimated as *real* amounts because they do not include inflation (perhaps because managers lack the confidence to try to predict future inflation), then to be consistent a *real* discount rate that also excludes inflation must be used for the project evaluation.

As discount rates are usually *nominal* because they are obtained from the observation of *nominal* rates of return, if the project evaluation has estimated *real* cash-flow amounts it is necessary to convert the *nominal* discount rate to a *real* discount rate, by deducting expected inflation (see Chapter 9).

IGNORE INTEREST PAYMENTS AND FINANCING FLOWS

An important principle underlying the evaluation of a capital-budgeting project is to *include as cash flows* all the incremental amounts related to the investment decision (i.e. accept or reject the project) and to *exclude as cash flows* all the incremental amounts related to the financing decision (e.g. interest on debt to fund the initial outlay). The reason for this principle is to enable the investment decision to be separated from the financing decision of the proportion of debt and equity. As detailed in Chapter 14, the costs for the use of debt and equity finance to fund the project will be included in the evaluation of the project via the weighted average cost of capital being used as the discount rate.

Therefore, if a project uses debt finance and the incremental interest amounts are included as a project cash-flow amount and the cost of debt is also included in the discount rate to calculate the project's NPV or IRR, then this would be double counting of this financing cost.

> ## Concept check
>
> 12.1 What is an incremental cash flow?
>
> 12.2 Provide an example of a sunk cost.
>
> 12.3 If a car manufacturer introduces a new motor-vehicle model and some of the cash flows from the new car are diverted from those of the company's other existing models, how would you deal with this?

For answers go to MyFinanceLab or www.pearson.com.au/9781442539174

OBJECTIVE **2**

Explain how a project's benefits and costs—that is, its incremental cash flows—are calculated.

Calculation of a project's incremental cash flows

The implementation of discounted-cash-flow techniques in capital budgeting essentially involves the following steps:

*   estimating the amount and timing of relevant incremental cash flows
*   estimating the discount rate that reflects the risk of the project
*   calculating NPV, PI and/or IRR.

Of these three steps, estimating the amount and timing of relevant incremental cash flows can be a challenging task. For the capital-budgeting examples and problems in this chapter we will take the discount rate as given. In Chapter 14 the process of estimating the discount rate will be discussed in detail. The final step, calculating the NPV, PI and IRR, is a relatively straightforward process of using your financial calculator or a spreadsheet program.

To facilitate the evaluation process, we will group a project's incremental cash flows into the following categories:

*   initial outlay—any cash-flow amount that occurs at or very near to the start of the first period of the project. (As it is common for an annual period to be used for project evaluation the initial outlay will be at the start of the first year.)
*   periodic incremental cash flow—the net cash-flow amount timed at the end of each period (e.g. year) during the life of the project
*   terminal cash flow—any cash-flow amount that only occurs at or very near to the final period of the project.

Below, we briefly examine each of these cash-flow categories.

INITIAL OUTLAY

initial outlay
Any cash-flow amount that occurs at or very near to the start of the first period of the project.

The **initial outlay** comprises cash flows that occur at or near to the start of the first period of the project. Although it is possible for a project to have cash inflows at its start, most of the cash flows at this time are outflows, for expenditures of money. For example, the total initial outlay for the purchase of a new machine to replace an old machine would comprise the cash outflow to purchase the new machine plus/minus any other cash flows that occur at that time.

These other initial cash-flow components could be for items like the outflow for shipping and installation costs, the outflow for the initial retraining of machine operating staff and the inflow from the sale of the old machine, including any tax cash-flow effects from its sale. The total initial outlay amount may also comprise the incremental cash flows associated with any net investment in working capital from inventory, accounts receivable and accounts payable.

Although it was discussed in Chapter 2, it is worthwhile at this point reviewing the tax cash-flow consequences of selling an old asset. Whether the sale of an old asset will result in an incremental tax cash flow (in or out) at the start of the project depends on the amount to be received when the old asset is sold or salvaged compared to its book (written-down) value.

The book value of an asset is the amount of its cost minus accumulated depreciation that is recorded in the firm's accounts. For example, if an asset was bought some time ago for $100 000 and the firm had claimed tax deductions for depreciation of the asset totalling $60 000, then the book (written-down) value of the asset would be $100 000 – $60 000 = $40 000. The following details the three possible tax cash-flow consequences when the asset is sold:

1. If the asset's sale/salvage value (SV) is greater than its book value (BV), the asset is sold at a profit to the firm equal to SV – BV. The extra tax payable by the firm at the time of sale is (SV – BV) × T, where T is the marginal tax rate.
2. If the asset is sold at a price equal to its book value (SV = BV), there is no tax consequence from the sale as there is neither a profit nor a loss.
3. If the asset's salvage value is less than its book value, the asset is sold at a loss to the firm of BV – SV and the firm's tax liability is reduced by (BV – SV) × T. As the firm was able to 'save' this amount in tax that would otherwise be payable, the tax-saving amount is included as an initial cash inflow.

The tax saving or tax payable resulting from the sale of an old asset is further illustrated in Table 12.1.

In summary, the initial outlay typically includes the following items:

- installed cost of an asset
- additional non-expense outlay incurred (e.g. working-capital investments)
- additional expenses on an after-tax basis (e.g. training expense)
- in an asset-replacement decision, the after-tax cash flow associated with the sale of the old asset.

PERIODIC INCREMENTAL CASH FLOWS

The periodic incremental cash flows come from items that normally occur during each period (e.g. year) of the life of the project such as operating revenues and expenses, income tax, changes in working capital and any periodic capital expenditures.

Although depreciation is not a cash flow as it is only an accounting value, it reduces the firm's taxable income, which in turn lowers the amount of income tax the firm has to pay on its profits for the period. Accordingly, it is important to include in the project evaluation the periodic incremental cash flow arising from the *depreciation tax shield*.

Similarly, the amount of any change in the net working capital from one period to the next should be included in the project evaluation as a cash in/outflow for the period.

TABLE 12.1 Tax effects from the sale of an old asset

SALE/SALVAGE VALUE	BOOK VALUE	GAIN/(LOSS) ON SALE	TAX SAVING/(TAX PAYABLE*)
$55 000	$40 000	$15 000	15 000 × 0.3 = ($4500)
$30 000	$40 000	($10 000)	10 000 × 0.3 = $3000
$40 000	$40 000	–	–

* Assumes entity selling the old asset is a company subject to company tax rate of 30%.

TERMINAL CASH FLOWS

terminal cash flow
Any cash flow amount that occurs only at or very near to the final period of the project.

Terminal cash flows occur at or near to the end of the last period of the project, for example, the sale or salvage value of the project's assets plus or minus any taxable gains or losses associated with the sale. Sometimes there can be significant cash flows that are associated only with the termination of the project, such as significant expenditures to rehabilitate a mine site once it ceases revenue-generating operations.

Finally, any increases in net working capital that have been included as cash outflows at the outset and during the life of a project are likely to be recovered and produce a cash inflow at the project's termination.

Table 12.2 provides a list of the typical cash-flow items that are likely to be included in the capital budget. You will recall from previous chapters that the evaluation of a project using pre-tax cash flows is appropriate for a taxation category 1 Australian company. This is because, as a result of the Australian dividend imputation system, the amount of income tax paid by the company does not affect the after-tax wealth of the company's shareholders. Consequently, any incremental tax cash flows associated with a new project are not relevant when evaluating the project in accordance with the objective of maximising shareholder wealth.

On the other hand, for taxation category 2 entities comprising sole traders, partnerships and companies that are effectively subject to a classical tax system, any incremental tax cash flows associated with a new project directly affect the wealth of the firm's owners. Accordingly, after-tax cash-flow amounts are relevant for the evaluation of the capital-budgeting projects of these entities.

> ## Concept check
> 12.4 In general, a project's cash flows will fall into one of three categories. What are these categories?
> 12.5 What is depreciation? How is depreciation calculated?

For answers go to MyFinanceLab or www.pearson.com.au/9781442539174

TABLE 12.2 Checklist of typical items underlying the calculation of periodic incremental cash flows

ITEM	PRE-TAX BASIS	AFTER-TAX BASIS
A. Initial outlay		
Installed cost of asset	✓	✓
Additional non-expense outlays incurred (e.g. working-capital investments)	✓	✓
Additional expenses (e.g. training expenses)	✓	✓
Tax deductions from additional expenses	✗	✓
In a replacement decision, the cash flow associated with the sale of the old asset	✓	✓
Tax effects arising from profit or loss on disposal of the old asset	✗	✓
B. Differential cash flows over the project's life		
Added revenue from incremental sales	✓	✓
Extra expenses (excluding depreciation)[a]	✓	✓
Labour and material savings	✓	✓
Increases in overhead incurred	✓	✓
Increased taxes payable on incremental profits[b]	✗	✓
C. Terminal cash flows		
Salvage or disposal value of the project	✓	✓
Tax payable or deductible from gain or loss on disposal	✗	✓
Cash outlays to wind up the project	✓	✓
Recovery of non-expense outlays incurred at the project's start (e.g. investment in working capital)	✓	✓

a Depreciation expense is not a cash flow. However, it has an effect on the entity's tax cash flow (see note b).
b Incremental profits are based on increased accounting revenues less accounting expenses, including depreciation expense. Although the depreciation expense is not a cash flow, it affects the amount of the entity's tax cash flow. Whether this effect on the entity's tax cash flow is included as a relevant project cash flow depends on whether the evaluation is conducted on a pre- or an after-tax basis.

Finance at work

THE AUSTRALIAN WINE INDUSTRY'S INVESTMENT IN INTERNATIONAL SALES

In the early 1990s international sales of Australian wines were around $100 million per year and the Australian wine industry had a goal of $1 billion annual exports by 2000. By the beginning of 1999, well in advance of the target, annual export sales had attained the billion-dollar goal and a figure of $2 billion had been achieved by mid 2002.

Within the Australian wine market, which has not been renowned historically for its profitability, the successful firms have been those that have differentiated their products and achieved economies of scale. On the marketing front, large international sales volumes have been achieved by building successful brand names that have in turn carried other entrants successfully into the market. As brand names have the potential to be readily recognised by consumers, they achieve a form of product differentiation.

Other economies have been realised through rationalisation of production facilities and channels of distribution. For some companies, their product range is promoted on the basis of an acknowledged quality product that is recognised internationally, and some small winemakers have been able to reach niche markets by having their product distributed through exclusive stores.

The push into the international market has been made by the Australian wine industry as a whole as well as independently by large brands. The international thrust has been largely based on quality and value for money, carried on the back of frequent success in international wine shows, and by producing wines that consumers enjoy.

It is important to remember that even though past investment and performance may have been good, new capital investment is risky. For the Australian wine industry, maintaining and increasing its share of the international wine market will require significant investment in marketing campaigns, vineyards and production facilities.

The wine industry is notorious for the long lead time before a return is earned on investment. Not only does it take a number of years for a vineyard to become productive but it can take several more years of maturation before a red wine can be released to the market.

Care must also be taken to ensure that grape varieties are planted in the right regions so that the wine styles produced meet not only current international taste but also future demand. Then there is the threat from competitor countries such as Chile and South Africa, whose large wine production with its cost and distribution advantages has the potential, with the right investment in quality, to be very competitive in international markets.

Capital budgeting: an asset-replacement project

OBJECTIVE **3**

Apply discounted-cash-flow techniques in a typical 'asset-replacement' project.

Many investment projects involve evaluating the incremental cash flows expected from the replacement of an old asset with a new asset. For example, buying a new machine might have the potential to reduce labour costs, wastage rates, energy consumption and maintenance costs. Also, the new machine might have greater output capacity and/or quicker processing time, which is expected to have a positive impact on the firm's future revenues.

The evaluation of an asset-replacement capital-budgeting project involves determining if the present value of the incremental revenues/cost savings of the new asset compared to that of the old asset outweighs the cost of investment in the new asset.

Example 12.1 applies what we have learned to a comprehensive example of a machine replacement decision for an electronic components manufacturing firm.

EXAMPLE 12.1   An asset-replacement project

Beta Electronics is a firm specialising in manufacturing electronic components. The firm's management is considering replacing an old hand-operated assembly machine with a fully automated assembly machine.

For illustration purposes, the capital-budgeting evaluation of this machine is provided for the two main taxation categories. The first uses pre-tax cash-flow amounts if the firm is a taxation category 1 Australian company, while the second uses after-tax cash-flow amounts (company tax rate 30%) if the firm is a taxation category 2 Australian company. It is also assumed that the pre-tax required rate of return for the project for the tax category 1 company has been estimated as 19% per annum and the after-tax required rate of return for the project for the tax category 2 company has been estimated as 15% per annum.[1]

Financial estimates related to the existing machine and the proposed new machine are presented in part (a) of Table 12.3. Based on this information, and applying the with (purchase

---

TABLE 12.3 Comprehensive capital-budgeting example for new machine

(a) Information on which to base the decision

Existing machine:

One part-time operator—annual salary $12000, plus
    fringe benefits $1000 per year
Variable operator overtime—$1000 per year
Cost of defects—$6000 per year
Current book value—$10000
Expected, original life—15 years; current age 10 years
Expected salvage value at end, 15 years—$0
Annual depreciation—$2000
Current salvage value of old machine—$12000
Annual maintenance—$0

Proposed machine:

Fully automated operation—no operator necessary
Cost of machine—$50000
Shipping fee—$1000
Installation costs—$5000
Expected economic life—5 years
Depreciation method—straight-line (prime-cost) over
    5 years
Salvage value after 5 years—$0
Annual maintenance—$1000
Cost of defects—$1000 per year

(b) Initial outlay on new machine

	PRE-TAX	AFTER-TAX
Outflows:		
Cost of new machine	$50000	$50000
Shipping fee	1000	1000
Installation cost	5000	5000
Increased taxes on profit from sale of old machine ($12000 – $10000) (0.30)		600
Inflows:		
Salvage value—old machine	12000	12000
Net initial outlay	$44000	$44600

(c) Differential (incremental) annual cash flows

	BOOK PROFIT	CASH FLOW
Savings if accept project:		
Reduced salary	$12000	$12000
Reduced variable overtime	1000	1000
Reduced fringe benefits	1000	1000
Reduced defects ($6000 – $1000)	5000	5000
Costs if accept project:		
Increased maintenance expense	–1000	–1000
Increased depreciation expense ($11200 – $2000)	–9200	
Net pre-tax cash flow (category 1 firm)		$18000
Net profit before tax	$8800	
Taxes (30%)	–2640 →	–2640
Net after-tax cash flow (category 2 firm)		$15360

new machine)/without (don't purchase new machine) test, the relevant incremental cash flows for the project are identified and computed in parts (b) and (c) of the table. You will see that part (b) separately details the initial outlay and part (c) details the relevant annual cash flows over the life of the new machine.

The following provides further detail of the calculations:

1. *Initial outlay.* The only item that is not readily apparent stems from the treatment of the taxation consequences of selling the existing machine. If the new machine is purchased, the existing machine will be salvaged, generating a $12 000 cash inflow. But as the existing machine has a book value of $10 000 there will be a $2000 profit on disposal, which at a 30% tax rate will increase the company's tax cash outflow by $2000 × 30% = $600. However, to correctly evaluate the project, the question is: what is the impact of this extra $600 tax payable by the company if the project is accepted on the after-tax wealth of the company's shareholders?

   If the firm is a taxation category 1 company, its shareholders are able to utilise the full value of imputation (franking) credits from the company. As this $600 increase in company income tax will provide shareholders with an extra $600 of imputation credits to offset income tax payable on dividends from the company, it has no effect on the after-tax wealth of the company's shareholders. Accordingly, the $600 tax cash-outflow amount is not included as a relevant cash flow for the pre-tax basis evaluation of the project and the initial outlay on a pre-tax basis is $44 000.

   Conversely, if the firm is a taxation category 2 company, it is effectively subject to a classical tax system and this $600 increase in tax payable by the company does affect the after-tax wealth of the company's shareholders. Consequently, the $600 tax cash-outflow amount must be included as a relevant cash flow for the after-tax evaluation of the project, which is why the initial outlay amount on an after-tax basis is $44 600.

2. *Periodic incremental cash flows.* Part (c) shows that the periodic incremental (differential) cash flows that will occur from the decision to purchase the new machine are expected to be $18 000 before tax, or $15 360 after tax.

   Depreciation expense generates a tax deduction that must be included to determine after-tax cash-flow amounts. For an asset-replacement project it is necessary to determine the incremental tax cash-flow amount that results from any *change* in the depreciation expense from accepting the project.

   Since the current book value of the existing machine is $10 000 and it has a remaining life of five years, the firm's current depreciation expense for the existing machine is $10 000/5 = $2000 per year.

   The annual depreciation expense for the proposed new machine will be based on its depreciable value, which is equal to the cost of the new machine ($50 000) plus any outlays necessary to get the new machine in operating order (shipping fee of $1000 plus the installation fee of $5000). This depreciable amount totalling $56 000, divided by five years, gives an annual depreciation expense for the new machine of $11 200.

   If the firm makes the decision to replace the existing machine with the new machine, its annual depreciation expense will increase from $2000 to $11 200. This *incremental* (differential) increase in depreciation expense of $9200 per year is not a cash flow but for an after-tax evaluation reduces the firm's annual taxable income from $18 000 to $8800.

3. *Terminal cash flow.* For this project there are no terminal cash-flow amounts because at the end of the proposed new machine's five-year life it is expected to have a zero salvage value.

The overall cash flows over the life of the project are summarised as timelines in Figure 12.1. The top timeline shows the cash flows on a pre-tax basis, while the bottom timeline shows the cash flows on an after-tax basis, assuming that the relevant statutory tax rate (T) is 30%.

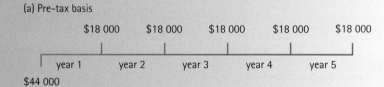

FIGURE 12.1   Net cash timeline for new machine

(a) Pre-tax basis

(b) After-tax basis

Capital-budgeting evaluation for a taxation category 1 company (conducted on a pre-tax basis)

If the electronics firm is a taxation category 1 company because it is fully integrated with the Australian dividend imputation system, the amount of tax paid by the company on the project's net income does not affect the after-tax wealth of the company's shareholders. Accordingly, the capital investment project should be evaluated on a pre-tax basis using the pre-tax cash-flow amounts with the given 19% per annum pre-tax discount rate.

- *Net present value.* Applying equation (11-1) the project's net present value (NPV) is calculated as follows:

$$NPV = \sum_{t=1}^{n} \frac{ACF_t}{(1+k)^t} - IO$$

$$= \sum_{t=1}^{5} \frac{18\,000}{(1+0.19)^t} - 44\,000$$

Since the cash flows from year 1 to year 5 are identical, this stream of cash flow represents an annuity. As a result, the present value of this stream can be found by applying equation (4-15):

$$NPV = \$18\,000 \times \left(\frac{1 - (1+0.19)^{-5}}{0.19} \right) - \$44\,000$$

$$= \$55\,037 - \$44\,000$$

$$= \$11\,037$$

$$NPV = \sum_{t=1}^{n} \frac{ACF_t}{(1+k)^t} - IO$$

$$= \sum_{t=1}^{5} \frac{18\,000}{(1+0.19)^t} - 44\,000$$

$$= \$18\,000(PVIFA_{19\%,5}) - \$44\,000$$

$$= \$18\,000 \times 3.058 - \$44\,000$$

$$= \$11\,044$$

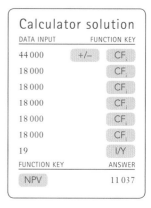

Calculator solution

DATA INPUT		FUNCTION KEY
44 000	+/−	CF$_i$
18 000		CF$_i$
18 000		CF$_i$
18 000		CF$_i$
18 000		CF$_i$
18 000		CF$_i$
19		I/Y
FUNCTION KEY		**ANSWER**
NPV		11 037

Note that due to the rounding errors the result from using financial tables is slightly different from that of a financial calculator.

Since this NPV is positive, the asset-replacement project should be accepted.

- *Profitability index.* The profitability index (PI) is calculated by applying equation (11-2) as follows:

$$PI = \frac{\sum_{t=1}^{n} \frac{ACF_t}{(1+k)^t}}{IO}$$

$$= \frac{\$55\,037}{\$44\,000} = 1.25$$

Since this PI is greater than 1, the asset-replacement project should be accepted.

- *Internal rate of return.* The project's internal rate of return can be found by solving the following equation (11-3) for IRR:

$$IO = \sum_{t=1}^{n} \frac{ACF_t}{(1+IRR)^t}$$

Because the example's future cash flows are an annuity, this equation can be formulated as follows:

$$\$44\,000 = \$18\,000(PVIFA_{i,5})$$

$$PVIFA_{i,5} = \$44\,000/\$18\,000 = 2.444$$

Looking in the five-year row in Appendix D, the table value of 2.444 corresponds to an interest rate of about 30%. This rate can be refined by interpolation. Using the financial calculator, an annuity of five years (*5 N*), having an initial outlay value of $44 000 (*44 000 +/− PV*) and annual inflows of $18 000 per year (*18 000 PMT*), to solve for *i* (*COMP I/Y*) gives 28.81% per annum.

Since the project's IRR of approximately 30% is in excess of the pre-tax required rate of return of 19% per annum the asset-replacement project should be accepted.

Capital-budgeting evaluation for a taxation category 2 company (conducted on an after-tax basis)

If the electronics firm is a taxation category 2 company, and thus effectively subject to a classical tax system, the amount of tax paid by the company on the project's net income does affect the after-tax wealth of the company's shareholders. Accordingly, the capital investment project should be evaluated on an after-tax basis using the after-tax cash-flow amounts with the given 15% per annum after-tax discount rate.

- *Net present value.* The NPV calculation uses the same formulae as detailed above except with after-tax cash-flow amounts and the after-tax discount rate.

$$NPV = \sum_{t=1}^{n} \frac{ACF_t}{(1+k)^t} - IO$$

$$= \sum_{t=1}^{5} \frac{15\,360}{(1+0.15)^t} - 44\,600$$

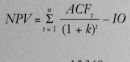

$$= \$15\,360 \times \left(\frac{1 - (1+0.15)^{-5}}{0.15} \right) - \$44\,600$$

$$= \$51\,489 - \$44\,600$$

$$= \$6889$$

See the calculator solution in the margin.

$$NPV = \sum_{t=1}^{n} \frac{ACF_t}{(1+k)^t} - IO$$

$$= \sum_{t=1}^{5} \frac{15\,360}{(1+0.19)^t} - 44\,600$$

$$= \$15\,360(PVIFA_{15\%,5}) - \$44\,600$$

$$= \$15\,360 \times 3.352 - \$44\,600$$

$$= \$6887$$

Calculator solution

DATA INPUT		FUNCTION KEY
44 600	+/–	CF$_i$
15 360		CF$_i$
15 360		CF$_i$
15 360		CF$_i$
15 360		CF$_i$
15 360		CF$_i$
15		I/Y
FUNCTION KEY		**ANSWER**
NPV		6 889

Since this NPV is positive, the asset-replacement project should be accepted.

- *Profitability index.* The profitability index is:

PI = \$51 489/\$44 600 = 1.15

Since this PI is greater than 1, the asset-replacement project should be accepted.

- *Internal rate of return.* As the annual after-tax cash flow amounts comprise an annuity, the internal rate of return is found by solving for i (the IRR) in:

$$\$44\,600 = \$15\,360(PVIFA_{i,5})$$

$$PVIFA_{i,5} = \$44\,600/\$15\,360 = 2.904$$

Looking in the five-year row in Appendix D, the table value of 2.904 corresponds to an interest rate of about 21%. This rate can be refined by interpolation. Using the financial calculator, an annuity of five years (*5 N*), having an initial outlay value of \$44 600 (*44 600 +/– PV*) and annual inflows of \$15 360 per year (*15 360 PMT*) to solve for i (*COMP I/Y*) gives 21.35% per annum.

Since the project's IRR of approximately 21% is in excess of the after-tax required rate of return of 15% per annum the asset-replacement project should be accepted.

If the firm considering this asset-replacement project had been a non-company organisation such as a sole trader or partnership, the evaluation would have been similar to the above, except that the company tax rate (30%) would have been replaced by the marginal tax rate of the business owner(s).

Capital-budgeting evaluation for a taxation category 3 company (conducted on an after-effective-tax basis)

As detailed in Chapter 2, a taxation category 3 company is an Australian company with shareholders that can only partially utilise the value of imputation (franking) credits. The investment projects of these companies should be evaluated on an after-effective-tax basis to correctly include the reduced impact of company income-tax payments and savings on shareholder wealth.

Equation (2-4) defined the effective tax rate as $T_{eff} = T(1 - u)$, where T is the nominal or statutory company tax rate and u is the proportion of income tax paid by the company that shareholders are effectively able to use to offset their income-tax liabilities.

To be consistent, a capital investment project evaluated (NPV, PI, IRR) on an after-effective-tax basis requires calculation of after-effective-tax cash-flow amounts and an after-effective-tax discount rate.

Suppose that the electronics firm is an Australian company with shareholders that can use only 60% of the value of imputation (franking) credits received from the company. As the company is in taxation category 3, its effective corporate tax rate is: $T_{eff} = T(1 - u) = 0.30(1 - 0.6) = 0.12$ (12%). This 12% rate should then be used instead of the statutory tax rate of 30% for all the tax computations in Table 12.3 and for the estimation of the project's after-effective-tax discount rate.

You may have noticed from Example 12.1 that most of the financial benefits from an asset-replacement project are generated via *cost savings*. However, for many other investment projects the objective is to generate incremental revenues by developing a new product or by increasing the sales or production capacity of an existing product. Whatever the nature of the investment project, you can see from the revenue-generating project in Example 12.2 that the evaluation process is the same:

1. Determine the amount and timing of the project's incremental cash flows.
2. Determine the discount rate to reflect the time value of money.
3. Calculate one or more of the recommended evaluation measures—NPV, PI, IRR.

International spotlight

CAPITAL BUDGETING FOR INTERNATIONAL PROJECTS

Calculating the NPV is the recommended method to evaluate capital-budgeting projects. This requires identification and estimation of the incremental cash flows that are expected to occur as a direct result of the acceptance of the project, for example, initial outlays, synergistic effects, working-capital requirements, additions to overhead costs and expenses, cost reductions, additions to revenues, opportunity costs and potential tax effects.

For an international capital-budgeting project, not only is it necessary to determine which cash-flow items need to be included in the evaluation but also whether they should be measured in a foreign currency or in the base (home) currency of the parent company. To ensure consistency, the same currency should be used to determine the company's costs of capital and to calculate its weighted average cost of capital (WACC).

As a general rule, foreign-currency cash-flow amounts should be converted to the company's base currency, and evaluated with a discount rate that reflects the base currency denominated market values and costs of the company's debt and equity.

OBJECTIVE 4

Apply discounted-cash-flow techniques in a typical 'revenue-generating' project.

Capital budgeting: a revenue-generating project

Although the evaluation process is the same, a revenue-generating project will have some cash-flow items that are not relevant for an asset-replacement project. For example:

- *Initial outlay*. If a new revenue-generating project does not involve the replacement of old equipment, there will be no initial cash-flow amount for the sale/salvage of an old machine. Although, there may be some incremental cash flows associated with existing plant if the revenue-generating project is to expand production capacity.
- *Periodic incremental cash flows*. The major annual cash-flow amounts will be from incremental sales and cost of sales of the product or service that the project aims to produce. Additional items include cash flows diverted from existing products, synergistic effects, working-capital requirements, and opportunity costs. The firm's budgeted revenue statement for the project is often the starting point to estimate the amount and timing of cash flows, with adjustments to include relevant opportunity costs and other incremental effects.
- *Terminal cash flow*. Likely terminal cash flows are recovery of prior investment in working capital and the sale of plant or equipment (or alternative uses for them).

EXAMPLE 12.2   A revenue-generating project

Joe and Maria Serano are equal partners in a very successful pizza business in their suburb and are considering a project to establish a new gourmet pizza restaurant in a nearby suburb. They have estimated it will cost $1.6 million to acquire and develop the site, including the erection of buildings, plus cost an additional $400000 to purchase plant and equipment that can be depreciated for tax purposes on a straight-line basis for five years.

Sales from the new restaurant are expected to be $600000 in the first year, and to increase to an annual average of $700000 in the second and subsequent years. They estimate that cost of goods sold for the restaurant will be similar to their existing pizza business at an average of 40% of sales revenue. Other costs such as salaries, training, light and power, advertising, promotion and cleaning are budgeted to cost $150000 annually. Additionally, from their experience, a net investment in working capital will be required, mainly in accounts receivable and inventories of 10% of annual sales.

Joe and Maria's intention is to develop and operate the new restaurant for three years and then to sell it as a going concern to their two sons who will then be old enough to obtain in their own right the finance needed for the purchase. A land and business agent has estimated that a successful business of this kind should be able to be sold in three years for a net price of approximately 20% more than its original cost to develop. Given the significant amount of their time that they will have to spend to establish the new restaurant, Joe and Maria expect that during its first year the annual sales from their existing pizza business will decline by about $70000.

Assume that Joe and Maria are subject to a marginal tax rate of 47% and their after-tax required rate of return is estimated to be 15% per annum.

The business is in taxation category 2 because it is conducted as a partnership. Accordingly, the evaluation of the new restaurant project should be on an after-tax basis and the relevant after-tax cash flows are detailed in Table 12.4.

You will notice that some new features have been introduced in Table 12.4. First, a column has been introduced for year 0, which represents the start of year 1 when the initial outlays occur. The Year 1 column records the amount of cash flows occurring throughout the year that are timed at the end of year 1. Second, the data have been presented as they would appear in an accounting profit and loss statement to determine a net profit after-tax amount. Third, the net profit after tax is then converted to a cash flow by adding back depreciation. This is to recognise

TABLE 12.4   Cash-flow estimates for new restaurant

	YEAR 0	YEAR 1	YEAR 2	YEAR 3
Operating cash flows				
1. Sales		$530000[a]	$700000	$700000
2. Less: Cost of sales[b]		212000	280000	280000
3. Gross profit		318000	420000	420000
4. Less: Operating costs		150000	150000	150000
5. Depreciation[c]		80000	80000	80000
6. Net profit before tax		88000	190000	190000
7. Less: Tax[d]		41360	89300	89300
8. Net profit after tax		46640	100700	100700
9. Add back: Depreciation[e]		80000	80000	80000
10. Operating cash flow after tax		126640	180700	180700
Other cash flows				
11. Initial development costs	−$2000000			
12. Proceeds of sale[f]				$2400000
13. Incremental working capital	−$53000[g]	−$17000[h]		
14. Recovery of working capital				$70000
Net cash flow, after tax	−$2053000	$109640	$180700	$2650700

a. Year 1 incremental sales are $600000 less sales of $70000 forgone from the existing pizza business.
b. Cost of sales is 40% of sales. Year 1 = 40% × $530000 = $212000. This reflects the increase in cost of sales from the new restaurant
    (40% × $600000 = $240000) less the reduction in cost of sales due to the lost sales from the existing business = 40% × $70000 = $28000.
c. Depreciation expense is $400000/5 = $80000 annually.
d. Marginal tax rate of the business proprietors is 47%.
e. Although depreciation is a non-cash-flow expense item, it has been included for its effect on net profit and the tax cash flow. However, it must
    be added back to the net profit to arrive at the underlying after-tax cash flow from the project. The validity of this adjustment can be checked
    by summing lines 1 and 2, subtracting lines 4 and 7, and arriving at the amount in line 10.
f. Initial development cost $1.6 million + $400000. Proceeds of sale at end of year 3 are estimated to be 20% greater than the $2 million initial
    development costs.
g. At the beginning of year 1 (i.e. period 0), the initial investment in inventories and accounts receivable will be 10% of incremental annual sales
    (line 1) of $530000 = $53000.
h. In year 2, incremental sales will be $170000 greater than in year 1, so net working capital will have to increase by 10% × $170000 = $17000.

the fact that depreciation is not a cash-flow item but its impact on the tax cash-flow amount needs to be included for an evaluation on an after-tax basis. By initially including depreciation in the schedule and then adding it back accounting values can easily be converted to after-tax cash-flow amounts.

Based on the cash-flow estimates presented in Table 12.4, the NPV of the project for a taxation category 2 firm is calculated as below:

$$NPV = \sum_{t=1}^{n} \frac{ACF_t}{(1+k)^t} - IO$$

$$= \frac{109640}{1+0.15} + \frac{180700}{(1+0.15)^2} + \frac{2650700}{(1+0.15)^3} - 2053000$$

$$= -78147$$

Calculator solution

DATA INPUT		FUNCTION KEY
2 053 000	+/–	CF₀
109 640		CFⱼ
180 700		CFⱼ
2 650 700		CFⱼ
15		i
FUNCTION KEY		**ANSWER**
NPV		–78 147

$$NPV = \sum_{t=1}^{n} \frac{ACF_t}{(1+k)^t} - IO$$

$$= 109\,640 \times PVIF_{15\%,1} + 180\,700 \times PVIF_{15\%,2} + 2\,650\,700 \times PVIF_{1r\%,3} - 2\,053\,000$$

$$\approx 109\,640 \times 0.870 + 180\,700 \times 0.756 + 2\,650\,700 \times 0.658 - 2\,053\,000$$

$$\approx -77\,304$$

As the NPV is negative the new restaurant project should be rejected.

If you examine Table 12.4, you will see that it relies on quite a few of the guidelines discussed earlier in the chapter. First, it accounts for an *opportunity cost* in the form of sales expected to be diverted from the existing business. Also, it allows for the need to invest in working capital at the start of the project as well as a year later when sales increase, and so the needed working capital increases, and then there is recovery of this working capital when the project is assumed to come to an end after three years.

Your money

EVALUATING ALTERNATIVE INVESTMENTS

You may think that NPV and IRR calculations are only applicable to businesses and don't apply to you. However, the principles we have developed to evaluate a capital-budgeting project for a business can be helpful in choosing your own personal investments. Suppose that your recently deceased uncle has left you a bequest of $500 000 and you have decided that you want to invest this money. One of the alternatives you are considering is to purchase a residential property in your neighbourhood which you will rent out for five years and then sell. Another alternative is to purchase a portfolio of listed shares that you also intend to sell after five years. How do you decide whether it is better to buy the property or the shares?

First, it is not unreasonable to assume that your decision-making objective is to choose the alternative that will maximise your wealth. Second, the cost (initial outlay) of the two alternatives will be the same—$500 000. The third component

requires you to compare the financial benefits you can expect from the rental property and from the share portfolio. As you know that the time value of money is important, you will need to estimate the amount and timing of the net cash flows that you can expect from the two alternatives over the next five years. The last component is to estimate the rate of return that you require from your investments. At the very least, you require a return equal to the interest rate you could earn by depositing the $500 000 in the bank, plus some extra return to compensate for the additional risk involved with property and share investment.

Now you can calculate the NPV of each alternative. You know that any alternative that has a negative NPV should be rejected, and if both alternatives are acceptable, you can identify which has the highest positive NPV.

OBJECTIVE 5

Understand how the capital-budgeting process changes when there is capital rationing or there are mutually exclusive projects.

Complications in capital budgeting

CAPITAL RATIONING

In Chapter 11 the focus was on deciding whether a *single* project was acceptable to be implemented. However, what happens if the firm has more than one acceptable project? If the firm has unlimited funds available, there is no problem and all positive NPV projects can be implemented. However, a firm may place a limit on the amount of money for its capital budget, which is called **capital rationing**. The following examination of how to deal with capital rationing demonstrates the superiority of the NPV method over the IRR method of evaluating capital-budgeting projects.

Suppose that a firm is using the internal rate of return (IRR) as its decision rule and will accept all projects with an IRR greater than the firm's required rate of return (RRR). This is illustrated in Figure 12.2, where projects A to E would be chosen (A to D exceed the required rate of return, while E just satisfies the required rate). However, when capital rationing is imposed, the amount of the firm's total investment is limited by the budget constraint of $X, which totally precludes the implementation of acceptable project E. Furthermore, you can see that the budget constraint of $X cuts in part-way through project D. If project D is *indivisible* because it is not possible to implement only a part of the project, then due to the capital rationing the acceptable project D would also not be able to be implemented.

The reason for capital rationing

In general, there are three principal reasons given by management for using capital rationing to impose a constraint on the acceptance and implementation of capital-budgeting projects. First, management may think that market conditions are temporarily adverse to raising finance, such as interest rates being high or share prices being depressed. Second, there may be a shortage of qualified managers to implement new projects, especially when projects are of a highly technical nature. Third, there may be intangible factors affecting the firm's decision making, such as having a fear of the use of debt and wishing to avoid interest payments at any cost.

As capital rationing is applied in many firms, what is its effect on the firm? In general, the effect of capital rationing is negative in the short run because it causes the rejection of some projects that have the potential to increase shareholder wealth. However, the degree of the negative impact depends on the extent and duration of the capital rationing relative to the opportunities and risks available in the economy. If the capital rationing is minor and short-lived, then few wealth-creating projects will be rejected and a company's expansion share price should not suffer to any great extent. This is positive while the economy is supportive, but may have negative consequences in a business-cycle downturn. On the other hand, if the capital rationing dramatically limits the number of new projects a firm implements over a long period, the firm's future growth rate can be expected to decline, having a significant negative impact on the firm's share price in a strong economy, but also providing a degree of prudential protection in a weak economy.

Capital rationing and project selection

If the firm decides to impose a capital constraint on investment projects, the appropriate decision criterion is to select the set of acceptable projects that produce the highest profitability index for the amount of constrained capital. The profitability index provides a measure of the amount of present value per dollar of the capital available for investment.

capital rationing
The placing of a limit by the firm on the amount of money for its capital budget, or the tightening of restrictions on the capital budget of the firm by placing limits on the amount of money for investment or by raising the required hurdle rate of return.

FIGURE 12.2 Projects ranked by IRR under capital rationing

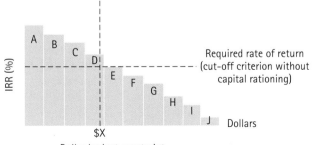

To illustrate this procedure, consider a firm with a capital budget constraint of $1 million and five indivisible projects, as given in Table 12.5. All of the projects are acceptable, but due to the capital constraint all cannot be implemented. If the highest PI-ranked projects A and B were implemented, there would not be enough capital left to implement project C, but there would be sufficient to implement projects D and E. However, the combination of projects A and C produces a higher total net present value per dollar invested and should be selected from the set of projects available.

TABLE 12.5 Capital-rationing example of five indivisible projects

PROJECT	INITIAL OUTLAY	PROFITABILITY INDEX	NET PRESENT VALUE
A	$200 000	2.4	$280 000
B	200 000	2.3	260 000
C	800 000	1.7	560 000
D	300 000	1.3	90 000
E	300 000	1.2	60 000

FYI

Capital rationing may be at odds with the goal of shareholder wealth maximisation because acceptable projects with positive net present values are not able to be implemented. For many companies capital rationing is a real constraint that managers must deal with. In addition, a company that imposes capital-budgeting constraints may also be signalling to the market that it does not have the managerial capacity or ability to obtain the finance and implement all wealth-generating projects.

PROJECT RANKING CONFLICTS

When there is no capital rationing, the decision rule is that all projects that satisfy one of the following evaluation criteria—a positive net present value, a profitability index greater than 1.0, or an internal rate of return that is greater than the required rate of return—should be implemented. However, this decision rule is not appropriate for acceptable projects that are *mutually exclusive*. **Mutually exclusive projects** are projects where the acceptance of one alternative project automatically precludes the acceptance of another alternative project. For example, a company considering the installation of a computer system evaluates four alternative systems from different manufacturers. All of these alternative projects have a positive net present value. However, because the company can only implement one computer system, the acceptance of the system from one manufacturer will automatically mean rejection of the other alternatives.

mutually exclusive projects
A menu of projects that perform essentially the same task, so that acceptance of one necessarily means rejection of the others.

Projects are also considered mutually exclusive when they will use the same unique resource. For example, a company owns a piece of land that can be used to build either a hotel or an office building. As it is impossible to build a hotel and an office building on the same piece of land, the acceptance of one project necessitates the rejection of the other project. To decide between such mutually exclusive projects, the net present value method is preferred to using the profitability index or the IRR. This is because the NPV provides a ranking of projects that is consistent with the objective of maximising shareholder wealth, whereas sometimes there are inconsistent rankings with the other two methods.

There are three situations—size disparity, time disparity and unequal lives—that can cause inconsistent rankings between the different methods (NPV, PI, IRR) of evaluating mutually exclusive projects.

Size disparity

The **size-disparity problem** occurs when the different project evaluation methods (NPV, PI and IRR) produce inconsistent rankings when mutually exclusive projects of unequal size are evaluated. This problem is illustrated in Example 12.3.

size-disparity problem
Occurs when mutually exclusive projects of equal cash-flow timing patterns over the lives of the projects, but of unequal size, are evaluated.

EXAMPLE 12.3 The size-disparity problem

A firm with a required rate of return of 10% per annum is considering two mutually exclusive projects, A and B. Project A requires a $200 initial outlay and produces a cash inflow of $300 at the end of one year, whereas project B requires an initial outlay of $1500 and produces a cash inflow of $1900 at the end of one year. As Table 12.6 details, each of the projects is acceptable when evaluated by the net present value, profitability index and internal rate of return.

However, ranking the two projects, to select which should be implemented, results in inconsistent rankings between the different methods. Under the net-present-value method, project B is ranked first and should be chosen because it has the higher NPV measure. However, under the rankings using the profitability-index method and the internal rate of return, project A with the highest PI and IRR would be ranked first and should be chosen. The question now becomes: which evaluation method should be used in ranking and choosing the project to be implemented? The general answer is the NPV method. If there is no capital rationing, project B should be chosen because, by having a larger net present value, it provides the largest increase in shareholder wealth.

If there is capital rationing, the focus changes to what can be done with the additional $1300 that is freed up if project A, with an initial outlay of $200, is chosen instead of project B, which has an initial outlay of $1500. If the firm can earn more from choosing project A *plus* what it can earn from investing the additional $1300 than it can earn on project B, then project A and the additional (marginal) investment project should be accepted. For example, if the marginal project has a net present value greater than $154.40 ($227.10 − $72.70), then selecting it *plus* project A whose net present value is $72.70, would provide a net present value greater than the $227.10 net present value from project B.

TABLE 12.6 Size-disparity ranking problem

PROJECT A		PROJECT B	
NPV	= $72.70	NPV	= $227.10
PI	= 1.36	PI	= 1.15
IRR	= 50%	IRR	= 27%

In summary, whenever the size-disparity problem results in conflicting rankings between the different methods of evaluating mutually exclusive projects, the net present value should be used and the project (or projects) producing the largest NPV should be selected.

Time disparity

The **time-disparity problem** arises when the different evaluation methods produce inconsistent rankings for mutually exclusive projects that are of equal size but have significantly different cash-flow patterns over their lives. For example, a project that generates the majority of its cash inflows early in its life and another that generates most of its cash flows in later periods will be ranked differently by the NPV and IRR methods. This is due to the reinvestment assumptions underlying each of the evaluation methods. The NPV criterion implicitly assumes that cash flows over the life of a project can be reinvested at the required rate of return or cost of capital, whereas the IRR criterion implicitly assumes that the cash flows over the life of a project can be reinvested at the internal rate of return. This is illustrated in Example 12.4.

time-disparity problem
Arises when two projects of equal size have significantly different cash-flow timing patterns over their lives.

EXAMPLE 12.4 **The time-disparity problem**

Suppose that a firm with a required rate of return of 10% per annum and no capital constraint is considering the two mutually exclusive projects illustrated in Table 12.7.

As can be seen from the time diagrams, the majority of project E's cash inflows occur at the end of the project, whereas project F's cash inflows are evenly spread during its life. The net present value and profitability index rank project E as the better of the two, whereas the internal rate of return ranks project F as the better.

This is because implicit in the calculation of an IRR is the assumption that cash flows are reinvested at the IRR rate, whereas implicit in the calculation of the NPV and PI is the assumption that cash flows are reinvested at the RRR rate. Consequently, the IRR ranking favours project F with its larger early cash inflows, whereas the NPV/PI ranking favours project E with its larger cash flows in later periods.

The decision about which evaluation method should be used to rank this type of mutually exclusive project depends on whether the RRR or IRR best reflects the reinvestment rate of project cash flows. Usually, the net-present-value ranking is preferred to the IRR ranking because it reflects the conservative assumption that the required rate of return is the reinvestment rate.

TABLE 12.7 Time-disparity ranking problem

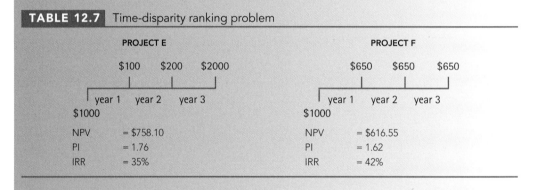

PROJECT E		PROJECT F	
NPV	= $758.10	NPV	= $616.55
PI	= 1.76	PI	= 1.62
IRR	= 35%	IRR	= 42%

Unequal lives

The final ranking problem centres on correctly evaluating mutually exclusive projects with different life spans. This is illustrated in Example 12.5.

EXAMPLE 12.5 **The unequal-lives problem**

Suppose that a firm with a 10% per annum required rate of return needs to replace an ageing machine and is considering two alternative replacement machines, one with a three-year life and one with a six-year life. The relevant cash-flow information for each of these new machine projects is given in Table 12.8.

Examining the discounted-cash-flow criteria that are summarised in Table 12.8, there appears to be a ranking inconsistency because the net-present-value and profitability-index criteria rank project K as the better project, whereas the internal rate of return ranks project J as the better. However, there is a more fundamental problem because, due to the different life spans, these initial measures of NPV, PI and IRR have not evaluated each project on a comparable basis.

It is not surprising that project K with cash inflows over six years has a larger NPV than project J, which only has cash inflows over three years. Accordingly, this problem of

TABLE 12.8 Unequal-lives ranking problem

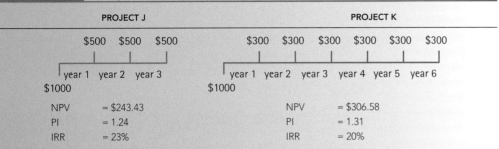

| | PROJECT J | | | | PROJECT K | | | | | |

NPV	= $243.43	NPV	= $306.58
PI	= 1.24	PI	= 1.31
IRR	= 23%	IRR	= 20%

incomparability of projects with different lives occurs because any future cash flows that the shorter project could generate if it were replaced at the end of its life are not included in the analysis.

If project J with the shorter life were chosen, then in three years time the firm could replace it with another machine and receive additional cash flows for another three years, which would then be comparable with the cash flows over six years if project K were accepted.

Therefore, to validly compare mutually exclusive projects with different lives is to project the reinvestment opportunity for the shorter life project (such as project J) into the future until each investment alternative has the same life. The simplest practicable method for doing this is the *replacement chain approach*, which assumes reinvestment opportunities in the future will be similar to those of the current project. For example, if it is assumed that project J can be replaced in three years with a new project with a similar pattern of cash flows for a further three years, then the lives of the two mutually exclusive alternative projects are equalised to six years and the cash flows for each project are able to be validly evaluated using NPV, PI or IRR.

Replacement chain approach

Under the replacement chain approach, project J would now be assumed to comprise the cash flows of *two* successive three-year J projects occurring back to back, as illustrated in Figure 12.3. As project J now has a total life of six years, which is the same as project K, the projects can be validly compared. The net present value of the six-year project J, comprising a replacement chain of two three-year J projects, is $426.32. As this NPV is greater than the six-year project K's net present value of $306.58, project J should be accepted.

You will notice that in calculating project J's replacement chain *total* present value of $426.32, Figure 12.3 shows that the $243.43 net present value at the start of the *second* J project three years into the future was discounted back to the present giving an amount in present-value

FIGURE 12.3 Replacement chain illustration: two J projects

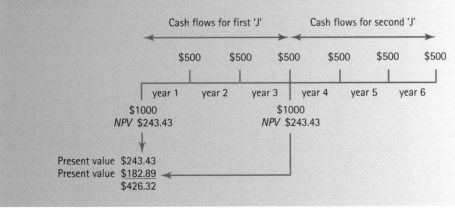

dollars of $182.89. This amount was then added to the first project J's present value of $243.43, giving a total of NPV for the six-year project J of $426.32.

Equivalent annual annuity (EAA) approach

One problem with using the replacement chain method is that, depending on the life of each mutually exclusive project, it can be quite difficult to come up with equivalent lives. For example, if the two projects had 7-year and 13-year lives respectively, many replacement chains would be needed for each project to establish equivalent lives of 91 years.

equivalent annual annuity (EAA)
An annual annuity amount that yields the same present value as the project's NPV. The annual annuity amount is calculated by dividing the project's NPV by the appropriate $PVIFA_{i\%, n}$ or by solving for PMT.

An alternative and often easier way to validly evaluate and compare mutually exclusive projects with different lives is to calculate each project's **equivalent annual annuity (EAA)**. This involves a two-step process:

Step 1: Calculate the NPV of each project for the project's original life.
Step 2: Calculate the annual annuity amount that has the same present value as the project's NPV.

The idea underlying the EAA is that by correctly reflecting the time value of money when each project's NPV is converted to an equivalent annual annuity (EAA) amount, mutually exclusive projects with different lives can be validly ranked and compared by the size of the EAA.

Step 1: Calculate each project's NPV. In Table 12.8 it was determined that the three-year project J had an NPV of $243.43, and the six-year project K had an NPV of $306.58.

Step 2: Calculate the EAA for each project. Using tables, the EAA is determined by dividing each project's NPV by the $PVIFA_{i,n}$, where i is the required rate of return and n is the project's life. This determines the annuity amount that would produce a PV that is the same as the project's NPV. For project J the $PVIFA_{10\%,3}$ is equal to 2.487, whereas the $PVIFA_{10\%,6}$ for project K is equal to 4.355. Dividing each project's NPV by the appropriate $PVIFA_{i,n}$, the EAA is determined for each project:

$$EAA_J = NPV/PVIFA_{i,n}$$
$$= \$243.43/2.487$$
$$= \$97.88$$

$$EAA_K = \$306.58/4.355$$
$$= \$70.38$$

Using a financial calculator, calculate PMT with a present value (*PV*) equal to the NPV of the project, a time (*N*) equal to the life of the project, and an interest rate (*I/Y*) equal to the discount rate of the project.

Project J: 243.43 +/– *PV*, 3 *N*, 10 *I/Y. COMP PMT* = $97.89

Project K: 306.58 +/– *PV*, 6 *N*, 10 *I/Y. COMP PMT* = $70.39

How do we interpret the EAA?

If you had a time value of money of 10% per annum and were offered a choice of $243.43 today or an amount of $97.89 at the end of each of the next three years, which would you prefer? The answer is you would be indifferent because the present value of both annual amounts is $243.43.

Now, if you were offered an annual amount of $97.89 or an annual amount of $70.39, which would you prefer? Clearly, you would prefer the higher amount of $97.89. However, you might recognise that there is a problem with this answer because the $97.89 is only for three years, whereas the $70.39 is for six years. But, as we are comparing mutually exclusive projects assuming a replacement chain we can validly compare the EAA value of each project and conclude that project J is preferable to project K.

To confirm this, we can create a replacement chain comparison by assuming that each project is replaced in infinity—that is, a perpetual replacement. So project J's annual amounts of $97.89 will have a present value in perpetuity of $97.89/0.10 = $978.90 and project K's annual amounts of $70.39 will have a present value in perpetuity of $70.39/0.10 = $703.90. Comparing the present values in perpetuity produces the same conclusion as comparing the EAA—project J is better.

Concept check

12.6   When evaluating two mutually exclusive projects with unequal lives, is the project with the higher NPV better? Why or why not?

12.7   What is the EAA of a project whose NPV is $11 500 over four years with a discount rate of 8%?

For answers go to MyFinanceLab or www.pearson.com.au/9781442539174

ONE STEP FURTHER

FREE CASH FLOW

The process to evaluate an investment project (e.g. NPV, IRR) and determine if it adds value to the firm requires estimating future cash flows in accordance with *Principle 3: Cash—not profits—is king*.

One way analysts can make these estimates is to calculate the *free cash flow*, comprising the amount of cash available from the project for distribution to the creditors and the owners who provide finance for the project. The free cash flow can be calculated from projected accrual accounting financial statements as follows:

Free cash flow = Net Operating Income (Profit) – Taxes + Depreciation Expense
          – Increase in Capital Expenditure (CAPEX) – Increase in Net
          Working Capital

Inflation and capital-budgeting decisions

Inflation is the general increase in prices in an economy over time and is usually reflected as a percentage rate *per annum (p.a.)*. Predictions of the future rate of inflation can be helpful to estimate the future cash-flow amounts of a capital-budgeting project. For example, if the rate of inflation is predicted to be 10% p.a., then an item that has a price of $10 today can be expected to have a price of $10 (1 + 0.10) = $11 in one year's time, a price of $10 (1 + 0.10)^2 = $12.10 in two years time and so on.

Although every project is affected a little differently by inflation, there are at least three general ways in which inflation can impact the capital-budgeting evaluation process:

1. Estimates of future cash inflow and outflow amounts will be affected by changes in the prices of materials purchased, the prices of items for sale, wages, and administrative expenses.
2. The salvage value of the project may be affected by inflation.
3. Inflation will affect the required rate of return on the project. This stems from the Fisher effect, which was referred to in Chapter 9. It states that the nominal required rate of return on a project is approximately given by:[2]

$$R_j = R_j^* + r \qquad\qquad\qquad (12\text{-}1)$$

where R_j is the required rate of return in nominal terms (that is, actual or observed market rates), R_j^* is the required rate of return in real terms (that is, after deducting inflation from the nominal rate), and r is the weighted average anticipated inflation rate over the life of the project.

How should financial managers include inflation in their capital-budgeting decisions? The general answer is by ensuring consistency:

- If inflation is included in estimates of future cash-flow amounts, inflation must be included in the discount rate (i.e. nominal cash-flow amounts evaluated by a nominal discount rate).
- If inflation is *not* included in estimates of future cash-flow amounts, inflation must *not* be included in the discount rate (i.e. real cash-flow amounts evaluated by a real discount rate).

Usually it is preferable to estimate nominal cash-flow amounts that include inflation because the weighted average cost of capital that is used as the discount rate in project evaluation is a nominal value.

Although it can sometimes be easier to estimate real cash-flow amounts that exclude inflation, it is important to ensure that the nominal discount rate is converted to a real rate to evaluate the project's real cash-flow amounts.

EXAMPLE 12.6   Inflation in capital budgeting

A company has a one-year project with an initial outlay of $1 million that is expected to generate sales of 1 million units during the year. Although the company's finance manager has forecast future inflation during the next year to be 3% p.a., she wants to do the NPV evaluation of the project with estimates of real cash-flow amounts. Accordingly, she has determined that as each unit currently sells for $1.80, the real cash-inflow value from sales in year 1 is expected to be 1 million × $1.80 = $1.8 million with the real value of the total cost of sales being $0.6 million. She knows that as the company's weighted average cost of capital of 9.18% p.a. is a nominal rate it will have to be converted to a real rate to be used as the discount rate to correctly evaluate the real cash-flow estimates.

By rearranging equation 12-1 the real discount rate can be approximated as the nominal rate – rate of inflation = 9.18% – 3% = 6.18%.[3] Alternatively, by rearranging equation (9-1) an accurate real rate would be $R = (i - r) / (1 + r) = (0.0918 - 0.03) / (1 + 0.03) = 0.06 = 6\%$ p.a. Given a real discount rate of 6% p.a., the NPV in real dollars of the project is +$132 075 million, given by:

$$NPV = \frac{1\,200\,000}{1 + 0.06} - 1\,000\,000$$

$$= 132\,075$$

The company's managing director has asked the finance manager to evaluate the project using nominal values, assuming that all cash flows and the discount rate are equally affected by the expected inflation of 3% p.a.

The cash-flow estimates would now be:

Outlay	–$1 million
Sales: 1 million x $1.80 (1 + 0.03)	$1.854 million
Less: Costs $0.6 million (1 + 0.03)	0.618 million
Net cash inflow	$1.236 million

The given nominal discount rate of 9.18% p.a. can now be used to calculate the NPV of these nominal cash-flow estimates. Alternatively, by applying equation (9-1), the 6% p.a. real discount rate can be converted to a nominal rate.

$$i = R + r + rR$$

$$= 0.06 + 0.03 + 0.06 \times 0.03$$

$$= 0.918 \text{ or } 9.18\%$$

The NPV in nominal dollars of the project will be +$132 075:

$$NPV = \frac{1\,236\,000}{1 + 0.0918} - 1\,000\,000$$

$$= 132\,075$$

These calculations show that, if all cash flows as well as the discount rate are equally affected by a single expected rate of inflation, the net-present-value amount is the same whether the evaluation uses real or nominal values. However, caution must be exercised in generalising from this specific example. This is because most projects have a range of different cash-flow items that will be affected by different changes in prices in the future. For example, suppose the price of items for sale is expected to increase by 5% p.a., whereas the prices of major inputs such as electricity are forecast to increase by 10% p.a. or more. Accordingly, evaluating estimates of nominal cash-flow amounts that have incorporated different price changes with a nominal discount rate can improve the confidence of using the resultant NPV to decide to accept or reject a project.

Concept check

12.8 Why should inflation be considered in capital-budgeting decisions?

12.9 What would happen to the NPV of a project if inflation was expected to have similar impacts on the cash flows and the discount rate of the project?

For answers go to MyFinanceLab or www.pearson.com.au/9781442539174

GFC

DEFLATION

After the negative impact on the global economy from the rapid increase in oil prices in the mid 1970s, inflation has been a major focus of governments, central banks, businesses and investors. However, since the Global Financial Crisis, the focus has shifted to avoiding deflation and the negative impact that a general fall in prices would have on businesses undertaking capital-investment projects. For example, assets might need to be sold at a value below their original purchase price, and the balance sheet of the firm might contract, thereby altering gearing ratios and capital rationing.

Summary

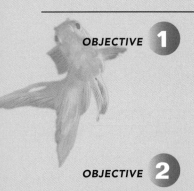

OBJECTIVE 1

This chapter examined the guidelines to measure the cash flows associated with a firm's investment projects. Relying on *Principle 3: Cash—not profits—is king* and *Principle 4: Incremental cash flows—it's only what changes that counts*, the focus was on *incremental* cash flows that occur if the investment is accepted. Beyond this general principle, it is important to consider whether cash flows diverted from existing products need to be included in the evaluation, to look for incidental or synergistic effects on cash flows, to include working-capital requirements, to consider incremental expenses, to ignore sunk costs, to include opportunity costs, to examine overhead costs carefully and, most importantly, to ignore interest payments and financing cash-flow amounts.

OBJECTIVE 2

In general, a project's incremental cash flows occur in one of three time categories: (1) the initial outlay, (2) the annual cash flows, and (3) the terminal cash flow.

To measure a project's incremental cash flows:

Project's incremental cash flows = project's change in operating cash flows –
change in net working capital – change in capital spending

To include the components of a project's change in operating cash flows:

Project's incremental cash flows = change in earnings before interest and taxes –
change in taxes + change in depreciation –
change in net working capital – change in capital spending

OBJECTIVE 3

One typical capital-budgeting project is the asset-replacement decision, with a major incremental cash inflow being the cost saving associated with replacing the old asset with the new asset. In these projects, particular attention needs to be given to the tax treatment of any profit/loss on disposal of the old asset and to the differential depreciation expenses between the old asset and the new asset.

OBJECTIVE 4

Another major type of capital-budgeting project involves the generation of incremental revenue from the introduction of new products or services. There are inherent differences in the determination of incremental cash flows for asset-replacing and revenue-generating projects.

OBJECTIVE 5

Capital rationing can create problems by imposing a limit on the dollar size of the capital budget. Capital rationing is not, in general, consistent with the goal of maximisation of shareholders' wealth because acceptable positive NPV projects are not able to be implemented. However, as it exists in practice in many firms, the profitability index is useful to identify projects that provide the maximum present value of benefits for every dollar of rationed capital.

Mutually exclusive projects occur when alternative investment projects perform essentially the same task and only one of the alternatives can be implemented. In general, to identify the best mutually exclusive projects, it is necessary to rank each project by one of the discounted-cash-flow criteria (NPV, PI, IRR), with the project having the highest ranking being selected. However, conflicting rankings between the various evaluation methods can occur because of the size-disparity problem, the time-disparity problem, and unequal lives. The problem for projects with different lives arises because each alternative needs to be evaluated on a comparative basis. This can be achieved by assuming a chain of replacement of similar projects and calculating the NPV of replacement chain projects with equal lives or calculating an equivalent annual annuity amount from the NPV for each project with a different life.

Key terms

If you are a car manufacturer, you've got to be ready for the next generation of cars. While gas-powered vehicles may be extremely efficient, we could also have a hybrid—gas and electricity powered or even propelled by electricity generated by a hydrogen–oxygen chemical reaction. Given all the uncertainty associated with the future direction of automobiles and how they will be powered, it only makes sense to explore all avenues and make sure you're not left behind. That is, if you want to be a leader in this market and if it does in fact develop, you'll have an early presence in it if you develop and refine your potential product line. That is the whole idea behind an option to expand a product line.

In the fuel-efficient automobile market, the Toyota Prius and the Honda Insight have taken the initial lead, with Ford's Prodigy, GM's Precept and Daimler's ESX3 entering the competition. This is not an inexpensive effort; in fact, it has been estimated that the Toyota Prius, which employs an expensive electric-alone drive for much of its duty cycle, produces a loss per vehicle sold of approximately $10 000. Thinking about the discussion in this chapter dealing with the option to expand a product, why do you think these manufacturers are willing to take on this type of loss-producing project? Does this make sense to you?

Now take a look at some of the different products being developed in this area. Which ones do you think have the highest chance of success? For example, Honda's new FCX car (hondacorporate.com/?onload=fcx) works on fuel cells. Check out how they work at **www.howstuffworks.com/fuel-cell.htm**.

Also, see what Toyota is doing at **www.toyota.com** and check GM's new efforts at **www.chevrolet.com/volt**.

Has your opinion changed on whether or not these are appropriate projects to take on?

12-1 If a project requires additional investment in working capital, how should this be treated in calculating cash flows?

12-2 If depreciation is not a cash-flow expense, does it affect the level of cash flows from a project in any way?

12-3 How do *sunk costs* affect the determination of cash flows associated with an investment proposal?

12-4 What is meant by a project's *opportunity costs*?

12-5 Why must financing costs such as interest be excluded from the project cash flows when determining NPV?

12-6 How is tax payable/receivable on asset disposal determined?

12-7 What are mutually exclusive projects? Why might the existence of mutually exclusive projects cause problems in the implementation of the discounted-cash-flow capital-budgeting criteria?

12-8 What are common reasons for capital rationing? Is capital rationing rational?

12-9 How should managers compare two mutually exclusive projects of unequal size? Would your approach change if capital rationing existed?

12-10 What causes the time-disparity ranking problem? How should capital-budgeting decisions be made in the presence of the time-disparity problem?

12-11 Why might two mutually exclusive projects having unequal lives be incomparable? How should managers deal with this problem?

12-12 Define equivalent annual annuity (EAA). How is EAA calculated?

12-13 In general, how should inflation be incorporated into capital-budgeting evaluations?

12-14 'The wine industry has some unique aspects when it comes to making capital investment decisions.'

    (a) List some of the assets in which a wine producer must invest.
    (b) Explain why capital investment in this industry has some 'unique' or non-typical aspects.

Self-test problems

For answers go to MyFinanceLab
www.pearson.com.au/myfinancelab

ST-1 Howard Enterprises Ltd of Sydney, maker of Hownow electronic components, is considering replacing one of its current hand-operated assembly machines with a new fully automated machine. This replacement would mean the need for one less employee, generating salary and benefits savings. Given the following information, determine the cash flows associated with this replacement. Assume that the company pays its profits as franked dividends and that its shareholders are ordinary Australian residents who are able to make good use of the franking credits.

Existing situation
One full-time machine operator—salary and benefits, $25 000 per year
Cost of maintenance—$2000 per year
Cost of defects—$6000 per year
Original depreciable value of old machine—$50 000
Annual depreciation—$5000 per year
Expected life—10 years
Age—5 years
Expected salvage value in 5 years—$0
Current salvage value—$5000
Company tax rate—30%

Proposed situation
Cost of fully automated machine—$60 000
Installation fee—$3000
Shipping fee—$3000
Cost of maintenance—$3000 per year
Cost of defects—$3000 per year
Expected life—5 years
Salvage value—$20 000
Depreciation method—straight-line over 5 years

    (a) Identify the cash flows associated with this machine-replacement project.
    (b) Given a discount rate of 15%, calculate the payback period, NPV, PI and IRR. Should this project be accepted?

ST-2 The Sun Company, which has a required rate of return of 10% on projects, has decided to invest in a new operation that has an NPV of $10 000. However, the financial manager has been alerted to the fact that working-capital effects were ignored when the NPV was computed. The project will require trade debtors (accounts receivable) balances averaging $50 000 per month to be carried and for inventories of $80 000 to be held so that the project can be implemented. Part of the inventories are being financed by trade creditors (accounts payable), whose monthly balances are estimated to be 40% of inventories.

    (a) Determine how much working capital the company must carry, on average.
    (b) What will happen to this working capital when the project comes to the end of its life?
    (c) If the project has an estimated life of five years, what impact, if any, will allowing for working capital have on the decision to accept the project?

ST-3 The firm of Pirhana Fisheries, which has a required return of 12% on projects, is considering two investments. The expected cash flows for each project are as follows:

YEAR	PROJECT Y	PROJECT Z
0	–$300 000	–$300 000
1	200 000	200 000
2	500 000	200 000
3		200 000
4		300 000
5		100 000

    (a) Is project Y acceptable? Project Z?
    (b) If the projects are mutually exclusive, what would be your recommendation?

12-1 (*Recognition of cash flows*) Following a feasibility study conducted for $400 000 last year, a company is considering investing in a new plant costing $5 million. The plant will occupy unused premises with a market value of $1 million that are already owned by the company. The company headquarters' overheads are currently $3 million per year; these are allocated annually as expenses to new or old projects on the basis of 3% of the plant cost. The plant is expected to generate sales of $4 million per year for its estimated life of eight years (50% of sales are expected to be on credit). The required rate of return is 24%. Cost of sales is expected to be 40% of sales, plus depreciation of the plant to a written-down value of 20% of cost by the end of the project. The company evaluates projects on the basis of after-tax cash flows, and the relevant tax rate is 30%. (Tax is paid in the accounting year to which the profit belongs.) At the end of the project's life, the plant is expected to have a resale value of $2 million. The following table is an itemised list that contains the company accountant's estimate of the cash flows for this project. This list is intended to be used to determine the project's NPV.

For more problems and for answers to problems marked with an asterisk (*) go to MyFinanceLab at www.pearson.com.au/myfinancelab

ITEM		YEAR 0	YEARS 1–8	OTHER
1	Plant cost and feasibility study	−$5 400 000		
2	Sales		$4 000 000	
3	Cost of sales (40%)		−$1 600 000	
4	Depreciation expense			(not a cash flow)
5	Allocation of overheads		−$150 000	
6	Interest expense (24% of plant cost)		−$1 200 000	
7	Annual profit		$1 050 000	
8	Tax on profit (30%)		−$315 000	
9	After-tax profit		$735 000	
10	Profit on sale of plant			$1 000 000 (year 8 only)
11	Tax on profit on sale			−$300 000 (year 8 only)
	Totals:	−$5 400 000	+$735 000 per yr	$700 000 (year 8 only)

(a) Is any item incorrect in the above list? Explain why.

(b) Have any relevant items been omitted from the list? Explain why.

(c) Prepare a cash-flow list that you believe is correct. Use a better format than the one above if appropriate.

12-2 (*Relevant cash flows*) Herbal Ltd is a growing cosmetic company whose products are made solely from botanical ingredients. Due to the rapid expansion, Herbal is considering the introduction of a new facial product called Herbal Softening Cream. This expansion is based on a market study conducted six months ago at a cost of $50 000. The production of this new product will use up floor space which Herbal currently rents out for $60 000 annually. Annual sales revenue is currently $25 million and the introduction of the new product is expected to boost annual sales by $1.5 million a year. Nevertheless, the new product will to some extent overlap existing products' sales, reducing them by 0.5% annually. Currently, the production of each beauty product is overseen by a product manager who is paid $65 000 per year. Cost of sales is 40% of the selling price. Due to the introduction of the new product, the consultants will have to undergo retraining, which will cost the company $10 000 per consultant. In addition, new plant and equipment must be purchased costing $500 000 and requiring maintenance costing $70 000 every second year. An old machine that has a salvage value of $100 000 will be converted to use on the new line as a back-up for times when production of the new cream is struggling to meet capacity. The manager of one of the other product lines will be transferred to the new line, in order to bring experience to the activity. The new product is expected to have a six-year effective life, after which the firm thinks it will have to phase it out or reinvest to give it a new lease of life. In addition to the divisional manager, the introduction of the Herbal Softening Cream will require the employment of seven beauty consultants who are each paid $45 000 p.a., one of whom is currently working for another product line and would otherwise have been made redundant and received a 'payout' of $45 000. The company is owned by the founding family who can use franking credits.

(a) Determine the initial outlay to start up this project (i.e. year 'zero').

(b) What are the annual cash flows in years 1 to 6?

(c) Prepare a time diagram showing the net annual cash flows over the life of the project.

(d) Assume that sales are expected to grow by 5% annually; re-compute the above cash-flow estimates where relevant.

12-3 (*Relevant cash flows—working-capital requirements*) After conducting the cash-flow estimations in problem 12-2, the financial manager of Herbal Ltd has explained to the divisional manager that the analysis is incomplete because working-capital effects were overlooked. The company works to a standard that specifies that each $1000 of annual sales must be backed up by holdings of $200 of inventories, supplied by creditors who require to be paid monthly. In addition, 90% of sales are on credit terms, the resultant accounts receivable being collected monthly.

(a) How much must the company tie up in (i) inventory and (ii) accounts receivable?

(b) What is the effect of the accounts payable?

(c) Re-compute the net annual cash flows.

(d) If the required rate of return is 14%, determine if the project should go ahead.

(e) Assume sales are projected to grow by 5% annually. What effect will this have on the cash flows and the investment decision?

12-4 (*Relevant cash flows*) Revisit Noodles Plus, which was introduced in problem 11-13. We know that the owners of Noodles Plus want to rejuvenate the four existing stores at a cost of $150 000 each. Advertising expense is estimated to be $40 000 for all stores and the rejuvenation of the stores is expected to bring in extra sales of $140 000 per store for the next five years. These figures are original estimates, but recently the project has run into a few complexities which are causing headaches for the owners. The company's accountant is querying the omission of depreciation expense, which amounts to $10 000 per year per store for the estimated five years of the project's life, with no residual value. Also, he has pointed out that Noodles Plus has not yet paid the marketing consultants $15 000 for the report that recommended the new image and logo. One of the store managers, too, has written a brief memo stating that there will be a need for extra soft-drink and food inventory worth about $10 000 per store. In addition, he has pointed out that staff salaries of about $2000 per store will have to be paid during the initial training of those staff, and about the same amount will need to be provided for temporary replacement staff while that training is taking place.

(a) Explain how these issues will be accounted for in the capital-budgeting process.

(b) Recalculate the incremental cash flows for the project.

12-5 (*Relevant cash flows*) Netspec Ltd is a market leader in Australia in the provision of fixed-line broadband services. To compete with other Internet service providers, Netspec is considering investing $20 million in a wireless broadband network in the major Australian capital cities. The money will be spent largely on erecting wireless towers and the associated hardware and software. The company intends to finance the investment through an 8% p.a. loan facility that it has with a local financial institution. A market survey commissioned by Netspec before committing to the investment shows that 40 000 existing fixed-line clients will switch to the wireless service, which costs $10 more than the existing fixed-line service, while there is a potential for 10 000 new clients. The survey was conducted by an independent market research company and cost Netspec $50 000.

Netspec currently offers customers a wide range of products where the subscription price is a function of the download volume. A typical plan that allows 20GB of download per month is offered at $49.95.

(a) What are the expected cash inflows associated with Netspec's investment in wireless broadband?

(b) What is the main concern for Netspec when deciding which cash inflows are relevant to the evaluation of this capital investment?

(c) How should Netspec deal with the cost of the market survey?

(d) How should the cash flows associated with the servicing of debt finance be treated in this capital-budgeting problem?

12-6* (*Taxation and depreciation*) The business of Barney Brothers, operated by two partners each with a marginal tax rate of 47%, is considering selling one of its old assembly machines. The machine, purchased for $50 000 five years ago, had an expected life of 10 years and an expected salvage value of zero. Assume that Barney Brothers uses straight-line depreciation, creating depreciation of $5000 per year, and could sell the old machine for $35 000.

(a) What would be the taxes associated with this sale?

(b) If the old machine was sold for $15 000, what would be the taxes associated with this sale?

(c) If the old machine was sold for $25 000, what would be the taxes associated with this sale?

12-7* (*Size-disparity ranking problem*) Aetna Ltd is considering purchasing one of two X-ray machines for the coming year. The more expensive of the two is the better and will produce a higher cost saving. Assume that these projects are mutually exclusive and that the required rate of return is 10%. The following net cash flows are given:

YEAR	PROJECT A	PROJECT B
0	–$500 000	–$5 000 000
1	700 000	6 000 000

(a) Calculate the net present value.

(b) Calculate the profitability index.

(c) Calculate the internal rate of return.

(d) If there is no capital-rationing constraint, which project should be selected? If there is a capital-rationing constraint, how should the decision be made?

12-8 (*Time-disparity ranking problem*) Novavax Ltd is considering two mutually exclusive projects. The cash flows associated with the projects are as follows:

YEAR	PROJECT A	PROJECT B
0	–$150 000	–$150 000
1	45 000	0
2	45 000	0
3	45 000	0
4	45 000	80 000
5	45 000	200 000

The required rate of return on these projects is 12%.

(a) What is each project's payback period?

(b) What is each project's net present value?

(c) What is each project's internal rate of return?

(d) What has caused the ranking conflict?

(e) Which project should be accepted? Why?

12-9* (*Unequal-lives ranking problem*) O'Bright Ltd, distributors of lighting supplies, are considering two mutually exclusive pieces of equipment that perform the same task. The two alternatives available provide the following set of net cash flows:

YEAR	EQUIPMENT A	EQUIPMENT B
0	–$20 000	–$20 000
1	12 590	6 625
2	12 590	6 625
3	12 590	6 625
4		6 625
5		6 625
6		6 625
7		6 625
8		6 625
9		6 625

Equipment A has an expected life of three years, whereas equipment B has an expected life of nine years. Assume a required rate of return of 15%.

(a) Calculate each project's payback period.

(b) Calculate each project's net present value.

(c) Calculate each project's internal rate of return.

(d) Are these projects comparable?

(e) Compare these projects using replacement chains and EAA. Which project should be selected? Support your recommendation.

12-10 (*EAAs*) Greenberg Trading is considering two mutually exclusive projects, one with a four-year life and one with a nine-year life. The net cash flows from the two projects are as follows:

YEAR	PROJECT A	PROJECT B
0	−$160 000	−$160 000
1	65 000	35 000
2	65 000	35 000
3	65 000	35 000
4	85 000	40 000
5		40 000
6		40 000
7		45 000
8		45 000
9		45 000

(a) Assuming a 10% required rate of return on both projects, calculate each project's EAA. Which project should be selected?

(b) Calculate the present value of an infinite-life replacement chain for each project.

12-11 (*Cash flow calculations—EAA*) Pisces Trading Ltd is a small business owned by Donald and Harry Tang. The Tang brothers are considering the replacement of the ducted heating system in their head office. They were presented with two heating models, the Braemar and the Brivis. The current heating system has been fully depreciated and would have no resale value. The Braemar model will cost $15 000 and last for eight years, while the Brivis costs $21 000 and has a useful life of 10 years. The Brivis is also more energy-efficient and is expected to produce a cost saving in gas bills of $4000 per year, while the cost saving associated with the Braemar model is $2500 a year. Both models would require annual maintenance that would cost $500 a year. Pisces Trading adopts the straight-line depreciation method whereby assets are fully depreciated by the end of their useful life. The company's applicable tax rate is 30% and its discount rate on capital-budgeting projects is 12%.

(a) Calculate the cash flows associated with the two heating models.

(b) What are the NPVs of the two models?

(c) Calculate the EAA for the two models. Which model should be chosen? Why?

12-12* (*Capital rationing*) Southcorp is the largest Australian-owned wine producer and one of the top five wine producers in the world. The firm is considering seven capital-investment proposals, for which the funds available are limited to a maximum of $12 million. The projects are independent and have the following costs and profitability indexes associated with them:

PROJECT	COST	PROFITABILITY INDEX
A	$4 000 000	1.18
B	3 000 000	1.08
C	5 000 000	1.33
D	6 000 000	1.31
E	4 000 000	1.19
F	6 000 000	1.20
G	4 000 000	1.18

(a) Under strict capital rationing, which projects should be selected?

(b) What problems are there with capital rationing?

12-13 (*Asset-replacement project*) Garcia's Truckin' Ltd is considering the purchase of a new production machine for $200 000. The purchase of this machine will result in an increase in earnings before interest and taxes of $50 000 per year. To operate this machine properly, workers would have to go through a brief training session that would cost $5000 after tax. In addition, it would cost $5000 after tax to install the machine properly. Also, because this machine is extremely efficient, its purchase would necessitate an increase in inventory of $20 000. The machine has an expected life of 10 years, after which it will have no salvage value. Finally, to purchase the new machine, it appears that the firm would have to borrow $100 000 at 8% interest from its local bank, resulting in additional interest payments of $8000 per year. Assume straight-line depreciation and that the machine is being depreciated down to zero, a 30% marginal tax rate, and a required rate of return of 10%.

  (a) What is the initial outlay associated with this project?
  (b) What are the annual after-tax cash flows associated with this project for years 1 to 9?
  (c) What is the terminal cash flow in year 10? (What is the annual after-tax cash flow in year 10 plus any additional cash flows associated with termination of the project?)
  (d) What is the NPV of the project? Should it be accepted?

12-14 (*Asset-replacement project*) Sembawang Ltd is one of the largest semi-conductor producers in Asia and it is considering the replacement of a manually operated machine with a fully automated one. Currently, three full-time operators are needed to operate the machine, costing the company a total of $120 000 in salaries annually. The manual machine also requires maintenance amounting to $12 000 per year. The machine was purchased four years ago at a cost of $80 000 and at that time was expected to have a useful life of 20 years after which time it would have to be scrapped. However, if Sembawang were to sell the machine at the current market price, it would get $20 000. The automated machine will cost $200 000, including an installation and shipping cost of $8000. The automated machine costs more to maintain at $18 000 per year but will reduce the cost of defects from $7000 to $2000 per year. The company has a policy of following the straight-line method of depreciation to determine deprecia- tion expense. The automated machine is expected to last for eight years and have zero salvage value. Sembawang Ltd is based in Singapore and therefore does not pay franked dividends, so all capital budgeting has to be done on an after-tax basis. The relevant company tax rate is 30%.

  (a) Determine the cash flows associated with this replacement.
  (b) Given that the required rate of return is 15%, compute the payback period, NPV, PI and IRR. Based on these calculations, advise the firm if the automated machine should be purchased.

12-15* (*Asset-replacement project*) Brookfield is an assembly business run by a sole proprietor whose marginal tax rate is 47%. The owner is considering the purchase of a new, fully automated machine to replace an older, manually operated one. The machine being replaced, now five years old, originally had an expected life of 10 years, and it was being depreciated using the straight-line method from a cost of $20 000 down to zero, and could be sold for $15 000. The old machine was operated by one operator who earned $15 000 per year in salary and $2000 per year in fringe benefits. The annual costs of maintenance and defects associated with the old machine were $7000 and $3000 respectively. The replacement machine being considered has a purchase price of $50 000, a salvage value after five years of $10 000, and would be fully depreciated over five years using the straight-line depreciation method. To get the automated machine in running order, there would be a $3000 shipping fee and a $2000 installation charge. In addition, because the new machine would work faster than the old one, investment in raw materials and goods-in-process inventories would need to be increased by a total of $5000. The annual costs of maintenance and defects on the new machine would be $2000 and $4000 respectively. The new machine also requires maintenance workers to be specially trained; fortunately, a similar machine was purchased three months ago, and at that time the maintenance workers went through the $5000 training program needed to familiarise themselves with the new equipment. The firm's management is uncertain whether to charge half of this $5000 training fee to the new project. Finally, to purchase the new machine, it appears that the firm would have to borrow an additional $20 000 at 10% interest from its local bank, resulting in additional interest payments of $2000 per year. The required rate of return on projects of this kind is 20%.

  (a) What is the project's initial outlay?
  (b) What are the differential cash flows over the project's life?
  (c) What is the terminal cash flow?
  (d) Draw a cash-flow diagram for this project.

(e) If the firm requires a minimum payback period on projects of this type of three years, should this project be accepted?

(f) Calculate the project's AROR.

(g) What is its net present value?

(h) What is its profitability index?

(i) What is its internal rate of return?

(j) Should the project be accepted? Why or why not?

12-16 (*Revenue-generating project*) The Laser Co. Ltd has ordinary, Australian-resident shareholders and the company pays its profits as franked dividends which have a high utilisation factor in the hands of shareholders. The board of directors is considering a major investment to expand its highly technical facilities. The expansion will take a total of four years until it is completed and ready for operation. The following data and assumptions describe the proposed expansion:

(a) To make this expansion feasible, R&D expenditures of $200 000 must be made immediately to ensure that the construction facilities are competitively efficient ($t = 0$).

(b) At the end of the first year the land will be purchased and construction on stage 1 of the facilities will begin, involving a cash outflow of $150 000 for the land and $300 000 for the technical facilities.

(c) Stage 2 of the construction will involve a $300 000 cash outflow at the end of year 2.

(d) At the end of year 3, when production begins, inventory will be increased by $50 000.

(e) The first sales from the operation of the new plant will occur at the end of year 4 and be $800 000 and continue at that level for 10 years (with the final flow from sales occurring at the end of year 13).

(f) Operating costs on these sales consist of $100 000 fixed operating costs per year and variable operating costs equal to 40% of sales.

(g) When the plant is closed, equipment will be sold for $50 000 and the land will be sold for $200 000 ($t = 13$).

The company has a 12% required rate of return. What is the NPV of this project? Should it be accepted?

12-17* (*Asset-replacement project*) Free-Range Eggs is a business that is operated by three partners, each of whom has a marginal tax rate of 47%. The firm is considering replacing a five-year-old carton-making machine that originally cost $50 000, presently has a book value of $25 000, and could be sold for $60 000. This machine is currently being depreciated using the straight-line method down to a terminal value of zero over the next five years, generating depreciation of $5000 per year. The replacement machine would cost $125 000, have a five-year expected life over which it would be depreciated using the straight-line method, and have no salvage value at the end of five years. The new machine would produce savings before depreciation and taxes of $45 000 per year. Assuming a required rate of return of 10%, calculate the NPV of the project and advise if it should be accepted.

12-18 (*Revenue-generating projects*) The Salute Corporation is an Australian-based company with a large proportion of foreign shareholders. Its core business is the production of machinery used in the heavy-industry sector. It has recently completed a $400 000, two-year marketing study on whether to introduce a new machine to the market. Based on the results, Salute has estimated that 10 000 of its new machines can be sold annually over the next six years at a price of $9615 each. Variable costs per machine are $7400 and fixed costs total $12 million a year. Working capital specifically for this project is estimated to be $2 million.

Start-up costs include $40 million to build production facilities and $2.4 million in land. The $40 million investment will be depreciated to zero over the life of the project. At the end of the project, the facilities (including the land) will be sold for an estimated $8.4 million. The market value of the land is not expected to change.

Finally, start-up costs will also entail fully tax-deductible expenses of $1.4 million. These will be deductible at the end of the first year of production. The tax rate applicable to Salute is 30%. The after-tax discount rate is 10%.

Calculate the NPV of the project and advise Salute on whether it should proceed with the project.

12-19 (*Comprehensive cash-flow capital-budgeting calculation*) Hillside Industries is considering the expansion of its operation by introducing a plant extension. The new plant, which has an expected life of 10 years, will cost $1 000 000 to erect and make operational on some existing land owned by

Hillside. The land has an estimated market value of $500 000. Additional spare parts of $100 000 and additional inventory of $400 000 will be required to support the new operation. The plant is expected to have a salvage value of $50 000 at the end of its life. The annual revenue and expenses associated with the project are estimated as follows:

Revenue	$1 500 000
Operating expenses	$950 000
Increased overhead expense	$100 000
Increased interest expense	$75 000
Increased head office expense	$150 000
Allowable depreciation	$100 000

The required rate of return for the project is 15% and the corporate tax rate is 30%. Hillside is not integrated into the imputation tax system and therefore all capital-budgeting projects have to be carried out on an after-tax basis. Calculate the NPV for this project and advise Hillside Industries on an appropriate course of action.

12-20 (*Capital budgeting and inflation*) Due to the group's strong financial performance in the last financial year, Discounted Health Store Ltd is drafting up proposals to open a new store in South Melbourne. According to estimates provided by the company's financial analysts, the cost of setting up a new store, including advertising, is $1 250 000. Of this amount, $250 000 is working capital. The new store's sales in the first year of operation are expected to be $400 000 and the expected growth in sales is 10% p.a. Financial analysts are of the view that the company's average cost of goods sold margin of 40% is appropriate for this new store. Other expenses, including overhead and salary, are approximately 20% of sales. The company is placing a 10-year period on the life of the store. These cash-flow estimates, however, are in real terms and inflation has not been accounted for. Inflation is forecasted to be 3% p.a. for the next five years and 4% p.a. for subsequent years. The real required rate of return for this project is 12% p.a.

    (a) Calculate the nominal cash flows associated with this project.
    (b) What are the nominal discount rates? (Hint: There are two nominal discount rates for this project.)
    (c) Based on your calculations in **(a)** and **(b)**, what is the NPV of the project in nominal terms?

12-21 (*Comprehensive capital budgeting and EAA calculation*) It is the end of the financial year and the management team of Tiger Air, a budget airline that provides short-haul flights in the South-East Asia region, is reviewing the functionality of its aircraft. It has come to the airline's attention that one of its aircraft has experienced a considerable amount of down time and is in need of an overhaul. The overhaul is expected to cost a total of $3 million, including $2 million for engine replacement, $400 000 for safety devices, $200 000 for new carpet and seating, and $200 000 for repainting the aircraft. After the overhaul, it is expected that the aircraft will have a useful life of five years, at which time it can be sold for a salvage value of $300 000. Until the aircraft is scrapped, the annual operating cost, including fuel, will be $1 500 000. It is also agreed that the cost of the overhaul, except for the painting expense, will be recorded as an investment (in the accounting book), to be depreciated using the straight-line method over the remaining useful life of the aircraft. The cost of painting, on the other hand, will be treated as an expense that produces an immediate tax benefit.

    Parallel to the overhaul option, the management team is also considering the purchase of a new aircraft. If a new aircraft is purchased, the existing aircraft will have to be scrapped in the current condition at approximately $750 000. The new aircraft will cost $7 500 000 but will be longer lasting, having an estimated useful life of 10 years. This new aircraft is expected to be more efficient in fuel consumption and therefore the annual operating cost is estimated to be $900 000. The new aircraft will also be depreciated for accounting purposes using the straight-line method down to zero, while management is hoping to fetch a salvage value of $800 000 for the aircraft.

    Tiger Air's existing after-tax cost of capital is 8%, which is deemed to be appropriate for a capital-budgeting decision of this nature. The tax rate that the company faces is 30%. Calculate the equivalent annual cost for the overhaul versus purchase option and advise Tiger Air on the most economically viable course of action.

12-22 (*Comprehensive capital budgeting*) Stan Levan is the sole trader owner of a KeyMan franchise at a local shopping centre that specialises in cutting keys and engraving trophies and jewellery items. Stan, who has a personal marginal tax rate of 40%, is considering the purchase of a new computer-aided engraving machine that costs $30 000. As the new machine will engrave a larger range of trophies than Stan's old machine is able to, he will need to carry a larger range of 'blank' trophies, which he estimates will require an increase of his inventory to about $1000. Over its five-year estimated life (straight-line depreciation to a salvage value of zero), the new engraving machine is expected to generate in its first year of operation extra sales of about $15 000, as well as wastage savings of $1000. Given the recent history, Stan expects inflation for the foreseeable future to average 3% p.a.

The old engraving machine (which has a 10-year expected life) was purchased five years ago for $20 000 and Stan has been depreciating it on a 10% p.a. straight-line basis, down to an expected salvage value of zero. Stan's cousin (who owns a small jewellery store in a country town) has told Stan that he will pay $8000 to buy the old engraving machine if Stan wants to replace it now. During the period for which Stan has been using the old engraving machine he has carried an average inventory amount of $700 worth of trophies.

Stan has just spent $400 on an interstate trip to see a demonstration of the new engraving machine, which he believes he had to spend to make an informed decision to purchase the new machine.

(a) Detail the initial outlay amount that should be included in a capital-budgeting evaluation to purchase the new engraving machine.

(b) Detail the annual incremental cash-flow amounts that should be included in a capital-budgeting evaluation to purchase the new engraving machine.

(c) Detail the terminal cash-flow amounts that should be included in a capital-budgeting evaluation to purchase the new engraving machine.

(d) Assuming a 15% p.a. discount rate, calculate the NPV to evaluate the new engraving machine project and provide a recommendation to Stan.

Case study

You have just been appointed to the newly created financial analyst position with the Australian company, Samphore Pty Ltd, which manufactures an innovative medical diagnostic test for breast cancer. Although the company has its operations in Australia, it was recently sold to a private equity firm based in the United States whose shareholders are unable to utilise the value of Australian dividend franking credits. The new owners of Samphore Pty Ltd have just appointed a recently retired eminent pharmacological researcher to head the company. Yesterday, you received the following memo from this new chief executive officer (CEO).

MEMO
To: Financial Analyst
From: CEO
Subject: New product

The capital projects committee, which I chair, will be meeting soon to consider an investment to produce a new diagnostic test for prostate cancer that has recently been approved by the Australian health authorities. Although the regulatory approval to sell the test is for five years, with an option to seek further approval after that time, the company's experience with other diagnostic tests is that it is likely to be superseded by a new test by the end of the initial five years. The following information has been provided by the accounting division with input from production and marketing.

Cost of new plant and equipment:		$7 900 000
Freight and installation costs:		$100 000
Estimated sales pattern:		

Year	Number of units
1	70 000
2	120 000
3	140 000
4	80 000
5	60 000

Sales price per unit:	$300/unit in years 1 to 4; $260/unit in year 5
Cost of sales:	$180 per unit
Annual fixed costs:	$200 000
Depreciation:	Prime-cost method over five years with no salvage value
Working capital:	There will be an initial requirement of $100 000 just to get the project under way. After that, extra investment will be necessary to bring the total of working capital up to 10% of the year's estimated sales. This means that the total of working capital will decrease from year 4. The final amount of working capital will be liquidated at the end of year 5.

I am also told that the discount rate to evaluate this type of new product is 22% p.a. before tax which, with the government's proposed reduction of the corporate tax rate to 28%, would be 15% p.a. after tax.

Prepare a report for me that addresses the following issues:

1. I have read that accounting profits are not the appropriate measure of project benefits. Therefore, in which way should we measure the annual payoffs from this project?
2. Do annual profits have any role to play in the capital-budgeting process?
3. How should we allow for depreciation in making this capital investment?
4. What is the significance of the Australian tax system for our company when it makes capital-budgeting decisions?
5. What is the amount of the initial outlay?
6. What is the relevant amount of profits and cash flows returned by the project each year?
7. What is the terminal cash flow for this project?
8. Show a cash-flow diagram that summarises the project's outlay and future benefits.
9. Compute the project's NPV and explain what it signifies.
10. Compute the project's IRR and explain what it signifies.
11. Should we invest in this project? Why or why not?

Notes

1. The pre-tax and after-tax examples are not just two different ways of formulating the *same problem* for a *given* decision maker. Rather, it reflects the decision-making objective to maximise the after-tax wealth of the firm's owners. The pre-tax evaluation is appropriate for a taxation category 1 company to correctly include the zero value of company tax savings on shareholder wealth due to the full integration of the Australian dividend imputation system. On the other hand, the after-tax evaluation is appropriate for entities (sole traders, partnerships, companies effectively subject to a classical tax system) because the wealth of the owners is directly affected by the amount of tax paid by the entity.
2. More exactly, $(1 + R_j) = (1 + R_j^*)(1 + r)$; thus $R_j = R_j^* + r + R_j^*r$. However, because R_j^*r is assumed to be extremely small and inconsequential, it is generally dropped from consideration.
3. As observed in note 2, the Fisher effect, as shown in the above equation, is only an approximate relationship. The exact relationship between a real rate of 6% and an expected inflation rate of 3% is that the resultant nominal rate is equal to $(1.06)(1.03) - 1 = 0.0918$, or 9.18%.

After reading this chapter, you should be able to:

1. Explain the importance of risk analysis in the capital-budgeting process.
2. Explain relevant measures of risk in capital budgeting.
3. Determine the acceptability of a new project using both the risk-adjusted discount rate and the certainty-equivalent method of adjusting for risk.
4. Use sensitivity, scenario and simulation analyses and probability trees to investigate the determinants of project cash flows.
5. Describe the different types of real options in capital budgeting.

For a complete eBook go to MyFinanceLab
www.pearson.com.au/myfinancelab

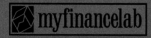

Risk in capital budgeting

CHAPTER PREVIEW

This chapter completes the discussion of decision rules for when to invest in new projects. Chapter 11 introduced the different capital-budgeting decision criteria, and Chapter 12 looked at measuring a project's relevant cash flows. Through all of this discussion of capital-budgeting techniques, it was implicitly assumed that the level of risk associated with each investment was the same. However, these assumptions do not hold in real-life situations. How does a firm estimate the potential worst-case scenarios from taking on an investment project? How does an analyst deal with projects with different levels of risk? What other 'what if' scenarios should the firm consider? These are the types of issues that are addressed in this chapter.

The chapter begins with a discussion of the importance of risk analysis in capital budgeting, followed by an investigation of the different techniques that allow risk to be incorporated into the capital-budgeting decision and the different tools that assist firms in obtaining an understanding of the riskiness of project cash flows. The chapter ends with a discussion of the different types of real options inherent in capital budgeting.

The focus of this chapter is on evaluating risk, which is central to *Principle 1: The risk–return trade-off—we won't take on additional risk unless we expect to be compensated with additional return*. The material in this chapter also relies heavily on *Principle 9: All risk is not equal—some risk can be diversified away, and some cannot*.

The importance of risk analysis

OBJECTIVE 1

Explain the importance of risk analysis in the capital-budgeting process.

In the previous chapter, we calculated the expected cash flows for a potential investment project. We then used the investment criteria we learned in Chapter 11 to perform an NPV analysis of those cash flows to determine whether the investment would add value to the firm. We assumed that the cash flows for different projects all had the same level of risk for the firm. In reality, however, the future cash flows associated with the introduction of a new sales outlet or a new product are estimates of what is expected to happen in the future, not necessarily what will happen in the future. Even the initial outlay may be uncertain. For example, in 1987 the Channel Tunnel's cost was estimated to be $12 billion, but by its opening in 1994 the cost had blown out to around $22 billion. The Sydney Opera House is another example of a project whose cash-flow forecasts were widely off the mark; its costs were much greater than originally estimated.

It is clear that different projects have different levels of risk and, as a result, financial managers need to evaluate the risk of the proposed investment project.

There are two fundamental reasons to perform a project risk analysis before making the final accept/reject decision:

- *Project cash flows are risky.* Our NPV calculation is based on estimates of future cash flows, but the future cash flows that actually occur will almost certainly not be equal to our estimates. So, it is very helpful to explore the nature of the risks the project entails so that we can be better prepared to manage the project if it is accepted.

• *Forecasts are made by humans who can be either too optimistic or too pessimistic when making their cash-flow forecasts.* The fact that the analyst may not be totally objective about the analysis injects a source of bias into the investment decision-making process. Overly optimistic biases can result in the acceptance of investments that fail to produce the optimistic forecasts, while a pessimistic bias can lead to the firm passing up worthwhile projects. Both types of bias are costly to the firm's shareholders. A careful risk analysis of projects can minimise these biases.

Concept check

13.1 What are the reasons for performing a project risk analysis?

13.2 How does the optimism or pessimism of a manager doing a cash-flow forecast influence the cash-flow estimates?

For answers go to MyFinanceLab or www.pearson.com.au/9781442539174

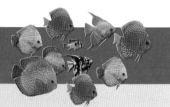

Regardless of your program

PROJECT RISK FOR ENTREPRENEURS

Some day you may want to start your own business. But starting a new business is a very risky investment. About 40% of new businesses shut their doors during their first year, and only about one in five make it longer than five years. In part, this is because, as a group, entrepreneurs tend to be very optimistic and tend to put too little emphasis on evaluating the risks of their new ventures.

But a budding entrepreneur can avoid this mistake by drawing on the principles of financial management. As we will see in this chapter, there are several ways to predict and analyse possible outcomes for a new project under consideration. Assessing risk is so important to the entrepreneur that there's a

whole field dedicated to it: specialists, called decision analysts, study decision making under conditions of uncertainty by modelling the possible outcomes. Decision analysis is taught both in management departments of business schools and in operations research departments in schools of engineering.

Clearly, both marketing and economics play a crucial role in the evaluation of a new business venture since the entrepreneur will need to forecast sales under a variety of scenarios that describe possible future states of the economy. Also, knowledge of cost accounting and operations is important for risk analysis since the entrepreneur will need to carefully calculate the cost of production under various circumstances.

OBJECTIVE **Relevant measures of risk in capital budgeting**

Explain relevant measures of risk in capital budgeting.

project's stand-alone risk
The total risk of a project, ignoring the possibility that part of the risk can be diversified away.

project's contribution-to-firm risk
The risk that remains after part of a project's total risk is diversified away.

systematic risk
The proportion of variations in investment returns that cannot be eliminated through investor diversification. These variations result from factors that affect all shares.

Before beginning the discussion of how to adjust for risk, it is important to determine just what type of risk is to be adjusted for. In capital budgeting, a project's risk can be looked at on three levels. First, there is the **project's stand-alone risk**, which is a project's risk ignoring the fact that much of this risk will be diversified away as the project is combined with the firm's other projects and assets. Second, there is the **project's contribution-to-firm risk**, which is the amount of risk that the project contributes to the firm as a whole; this measure considers the fact that some of the project's risk will be diversified away as the project is combined with the firm's other projects and assets, but it ignores the effects of diversification on the part of the firm's shareholders. Finally, there is **systematic risk**, which is the risk of the project from the viewpoint of a well-diversified shareholder; this measure considers the fact that some of a project's risk will be diversified away as the project is combined with the firm's other projects and, in addition, some of the remaining risk will be diversified away by shareholders as they combine this company's shares with other assets in their portfolios. The notion of systematic risk, as measured by beta, was introduced in Chapter 9, where it was suggested that it is the relevant measure of risk for a diversified investor. Graphically, these three levels of risk are shown in Figure 13.1.

FIGURE 13.1 Looking at three measures of a project's risk

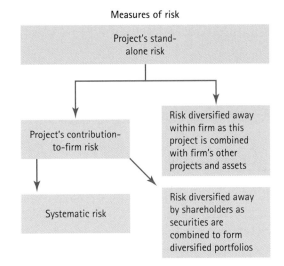

Perspective:

Project standing alone: Ignores diversification within the firm and within the shareholder's portfolio.

Project from the company's perspective: Ignores diversification within the shareholder's portfolio, but allows for diversification within the firm.

Project from the shareholder's perspective: Allows for diversification within the firm and within the shareholder's portfolio.

Should the financial manager be interested in the project's stand-alone risk? The answer is no. Perhaps the easiest way to understand why not is to look at a real-life example. Let us take the case of research and design projects at Johnson & Johnson, makers of products such as Johnson's baby powder. Each year Johnson & Johnson takes on hundreds of new research and development (R&D) projects, knowing that each has only about a 10% probability of being successful. If the projects are successful, the profits can be enormous; if they fail, the investment is lost. If the company had only one project, and it was an R&D project, the company would have a 90% chance of failure. Thus, if these R&D projects were looked at individually and their total project risk measured, they would have to be judged as enormously risky. However, if the effect of the diversification that comes about from taking on several hundred independent R&D projects a year is consolidated, all with a 10% chance of success, it can be seen that each individual project does not add much in the way of risk to Johnson & Johnson. In short, because much of a project's risk is diversified away within the firm, total project risk is an inappropriate measure of the meaningful level of risk of a capital-budgeting project.

Thus, looking at the project from the company's perspective, it is seen that part of the project's stand-alone risk can be diversified away within the firm itself. But should financial managers be interested in the project's contribution-to-firm risk? Once again, the answer is no, provided investors are well diversified and there is no chance of bankruptcy.

If the shareholder is well diversified, the relevant risk is *systematic risk*. From the earlier discussion of risk in Chapter 9 it was seen that, as shareholders, if we combine our security with other securities to form a diversified portfolio, much of the risk of our security would be diversified away. Thus, all that affects the shareholders is the systematic risk of the project, and as such this is all that is theoretically relevant for capital budgeting.

Concept check

13.3 In capital budgeting, a project's risk can be looked at on three levels. What are they and what are the measures of risk?

13.4 Is a project's stand-alone risk the appropriate level of risk for capital budgeting? Why or why not?

13.5 What type of risk affects all shareholders and is theoretically the correct measure of risk for capital budgeting?

For answers go to MyFinanceLab or www.pearson.com.au/9781442539174

Back to the principles

The discussion of capital budgeting and risk is based on **Principle 9: All risk is not equal—some risk can be diversified away, and some cannot**. That principle describes how difficult it is to measure a project's risk as a result of diversification. This is because diversification takes place both within the firm, where the new project is just one of many projects, and in the shareholder's portfolio, where the company's stock is just one of many stocks he or she holds.

MEASURING RISK FOR CAPITAL-BUDGETING PURPOSES AND A DOSE OF REALITY—IS SYSTEMATIC RISK ALL THERE IS?

According to the capital asset pricing model (CAPM), systematic risk, or beta, is the only relevant risk for capital-budgeting purposes. However, reality complicates this somewhat. In many instances a firm will have undiversified shareholders, including owners of small businesses. Because they are not diversified, the relevant measure of risk for those shareholders is the project's contribution-to-firm risk.

The possibility of bankruptcy also affects the view of what measure of risk is relevant. Because the project's contribution-to-firm risk can affect the possibility of bankruptcy, this may be an appropriate measure of risk since there are costs associated with bankruptcy. First, if a firm fails, its assets, in general, cannot be sold for their true economic value. Moreover, the amount of money actually available for distribution to shareholders is further reduced by liquidation and legal fees. Finally, the opportunity cost associated with the delays related to the legal process further reduces the funds available to the shareholder. Therefore, reducing the chance of bankruptcy has a very real value associated with it.

For a firm with a probability of bankruptcy there are indirect 'spillover' costs associated with production, sales, and the quality and efficiency of management. For example, such a firm

Finance at work

GLOBAL STRATEGIES TO REDUCE RISK

In the late 1990s the Australian firm Mildara–Blass wines, now Beringer–Blass, acquired a controlling interest in a German direct-distribution wine club. Why might they have done this instead of setting up their own distribution channels in that country? The answer lies in the reduction of risk. By this strategic acquisition, the company gained instant marketing expertise in a market where it had none. It also gained a large outlet for sales of its own products and a foothold in the wider European Union. This is one example of the use of strategies such as joint ventures, alliances and acquisitions to lessen the risk of international projects.

By the use of such global strategies, firms seek competitive advantages outside their own borders, and can exploit economies of scale. For example, the concept of a 'world car' is attractive to car manufacturers because the design and development costs could be spread across a large market, thus reducing the cost per unit. Firms also spread risk by this means. For example, they can reduce the risk of a blockage of supply of components if they have a diversified sourcing program. Japanese car manufacturers establish manufacturing plants in

Australia not only to service the local market but also to spread risk. One risk is currency risk—a lower value of the Australian dollar may make exports more readily saleable from Australia than from Japan.

To remain successful, companies must think beyond their own countries. R&D programs must concentrate on world's best practice with a view to the wider global market. Access to the large Chinese market is restricted unless companies establish ventures locally. This has motivated companies such as Foster's Brewing and pharmaceutical manufacturer FH Faulding to establish plants in China. As a result, R&D costs and production expertise developed in Australia can be spread across a wider volume of sales than would be possible in the domestic market. This is part of a long-term strategy to defeat the technological risks that would arise if these companies remained content to service just the Australian market. For example, product development costs cannot be justified in many cases where sales potential is small, so opening up the markets provides a means of staying technologically up to date. Nowadays, global thinking is a must rather than an option for many companies.

might have a difficult time recruiting and retaining quality managers because jobs with the firm would be viewed as being insecure. Suppliers would be less willing to sell on credit. Customers may lose confidence in the firm, fearing that it might not be around to honour warranties or to supply spare parts for its products in the future. As a result, the eventual bankruptcy may become self-fulfilling as potential customers and suppliers flee. Thus the project's contribution-to-firm risk is also a relevant risk measure for capital budgeting, because diversification of a firm's projects may decrease the risk of bankruptcy. That is, financial managers should take into account whether a new project will materially impact on the likelihood that a firm will face bankruptcy. If a small business is basically a single-project firm, for example, there is a greater chance that this may be the case. Finally, it is extremely difficult to measure a project's systematic risk. As will be seen later in the chapter, it is much easier to talk about it than it is to measure it.

Given all this, what do financial managers use? The answer is that consideration is given to both measures. In theory, systematic risk is correct. But bankruptcy costs and undiversified shareholders violate the assumptions of the theory, which brings us back to the concept of a project's contribution-to-firm risk. Still, the concept of systematic risk holds value for capital-budgeting decisions, because that is the risk that shareholders are compensated for. Bear in mind that the goal is to maximise shareholders' or owners' wealth. As such, this book will concern itself with both the project's contribution-to-firm risk and the project's systematic risk, and not try to rank them in importance for capital-budgeting purposes.

Incorporating risk into the capital-budgeting process

The past two chapters ignored any risk differences between projects. This assumption enabled the focus to stay on other important issues in capital budgeting without being side-tracked by the additional complexity of risk. However, different investment projects do in fact contain different levels of risk. There are several methods for incorporating risk into the analysis. One method is to incorporate risk into the required rate of return. In this respect, the firm's current, overall required rate of return is called the *cost of capital* and it implicitly measures the required rate of return based on the firm's current risk structure. However, if a new project has a different degree of risk to the firm as it currently stands, it is inappropriate to use the cost of capital. Instead, it is more apt to use a **risk-adjusted discount rate**, which is explicitly based on the notion that investors require higher rates of return on more risky projects. The second method for incorporating risk into the capital budgeting is called the **certainty-equivalent** approach—this approach attempts to incorporate the manager's 'utility function' into the analysis.

RISK-ADJUSTED DISCOUNT RATES

Chapters 11 and 12 introduced the concept of net present value (NPV) as the most reliable capital-budgeting technique, where the NPV is obtained by discounting future expected cash flows back to the present using an appropriate discount rate. However, the chapter did not discuss how to obtain this 'appropriate discount rate'. Generally speaking, a project's discount rate reflects the costs incurred by the firm to raise funds to finance the project, called the cost

OBJECTIVE 3

Determine the acceptability of a new project using both the risk-adjusted discount rate and the certainty-equivalent method of adjusting for risk.

risk-adjusted discount rate
A method for incorporating the project's level of risk into the capital-budgeting process, in which the discount rate is adjusted upward to compensate for higher-than-normal risk or downward to compensate for lower-than-normal risk.

certainty equivalent
The amount of cash a person would require with certainty to make him or her indifferent to the choice between this certain sum and a particular risky or uncertain sum.

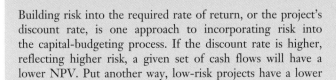

FYI

Building risk into the required rate of return, or the project's discount rate, is one approach to incorporating risk into the capital-budgeting process. If the discount rate is higher, reflecting higher risk, a given set of cash flows will have a lower NPV. Put another way, low-risk projects have a lower discount rate and thus a higher NPV, other things being equal. In this respect, it is easier to accept low-risk projects, which is consistent with the idea of risk: the more risk confronted by the decision maker, the less inclined he or she will be to accept that risk unless the rewards are correspondingly high.

of capital. The rationale behind the use of the project's cost of capital as the discount rate is that, for it to be profitable, the project has to generate a return at least as good as what it costs the company to raise the capital to finance the project. As a result, projects whose returns do not meet the cost of capital should not be undertaken.

The cost of capital can be calculated for the firm at any point in time and can be used as the discount rate in future capital-budgeting projects as long as the project under evaluation has the same level of risk as the firm. For example, the opening of a new retailing outlet is considered to entail the same level of risk as a firm that specialises in retailing. However, if the new project is in a totally different line of business, it is unlikely that the risks will be the same and so in this case the existing cost of capital is unlikely to incorporate the right assessment of risk for the new project. For instance, suppose that the firm is a general retailer and it decides to expand into the fast-food industry. In this case, the risk of the two activities is likely to differ. The distinction between existing risk and new-project risk can be seen even more clearly if we imagine a firm currently diversified across several different markets, such as general retailing, mining and motor-vehicle importing. It is unlikely that the firm's operating risks would be appropriate for a new project confined to the mining side of the firm, let alone to a new project that is in a completely different market (such as agricultural production). In this case the risk-adjusted discount rate has to be employed to account for the differing level of risk associated with the new project.

The use of the risk-adjusted discount rate involves adjusting the discount rate to reflect the risk associated with a certain project. Its usage is based on the concept that investors demand a higher return for more risky projects. In other words, other things being equal, the project with the higher level of risk is obviously less desirable than the one that entails a lower level of risk. This is the basic axiom behind the risk–return trade-off that was examined in Chapter 9.

Back to the principles

All the methods used to compensate for risk in capital budgeting find their roots in fundamental **Principle 1: The risk–return trade-off**. In fact, the risk-adjusted discount method puts this concept directly into play.

The required rate of return on any investment should include compensation for delaying consumption equal to the risk-free rate of return, plus compensation for any risk taken on. If the risk associated with the investment is greater than the risk involved in a typical endeavour, the discount rate is adjusted upward to compensate for this added risk. Once the firm determines the appropriate required rate of return for a project with a given level of risk, the cash flows are discounted back to the present at the risk-adjusted discount rate. Then the normal capital-budgeting criteria are applied, except in the case of the internal rate of return. For the IRR, the hurdle rate with which the project's internal rate of return is compared, now becomes the risk-adjusted discount rate. Expressed mathematically, the net present value using the risk-adjusted discount rate becomes:

$$NPV = \sum_{t=1}^{n} \frac{ACF_t}{(1 + k^*)^t} - IO$$
(13-1)

Where ACF_t = expected annual cash flow in year t
k^* = the risk-adjusted discount rate
IO = the initial outlay or the investment amount
n = the project's expected life

The logic behind the risk-adjusted discount rate stems from the idea that if the project has more risk than a typical project, a higher required rate of return should apply. Otherwise, marginal projects will lower the firm's share price—that is, reduce shareholders' wealth. This will occur as the market raises its required rate of return on the firm to reflect the addition of a more risky project; the incremental cash flows resulting from the acceptance of the new project are not large enough to fully offset this change. By the same logic, if the project has less than normal risk, a reduction in the required rate of return is appropriate. Thus, the risk-adjusted discount method attempts to apply more stringent standards—that is, requires a higher rate of return—to projects that will increase the firm's risk level.

EXAMPLE 13.1 Risk-adjusted discount rate

A toy manufacturer is considering the introduction of a line of fishing equipment with an expected life of five years. In the past, this firm has been quite conservative in its investment in new products, sticking primarily to standard toys. In this context, the introduction of a line of fishing equipment is considered an abnormally risky project. Management thinks that the normal 10% required rate of return for the firm is not sufficient. Instead, the minimally acceptable rate of return on this project should be 15%. The initial outlay would be $110 000, and the expected cash flows from this project are as follows:

YEAR	EXPECTED CASH FLOW
1	$30 000
2	30 000
3	30 000
4	30 000
5	30 000

Discounting this annuity back to the present at 15% yields a present value of the future cash flows of $100 560. Because the initial outlay on this project is $110 000, the net present value becomes –$9440, and the project should be rejected. If the normal required rate of return of 10% had been used inappropriately as the discount rate, the project would have been wrongly accepted with a net present value of $3730.

In practice, when the risk-adjusted discount rate is used, projects are generally grouped according to purpose, or risk class; then the discount rate pre-assigned to that purpose or risk class is used. For example, a firm with a normal required rate of return of 12% (reflecting the average risk for the firm as a whole) might use the rate-of-return categorisation as detailed in Table 13.1.

The purpose of this categorisation of projects is to make their evaluation easier, but it also introduces a sense of arbitrariness into the calculations that makes the evaluation less meaningful. The trade-offs involved in the classification above are obvious; time and effort are minimised, but only at the cost of precision.

TABLE 13.1 Required rate of return for projects with different levels of risk

PROJECT	REQUIRED RATE OF RETURN (%)
Replacement decision	12
Modification or expansion of existing product line	15
Project unrelated to current operations	18
Research and development operations	25

ONE STEP FURTHER

RISK-ADJUSTED RETURN ON CAPITAL

Risk adjustment is not only important in capital-budgeting decisions but also plays an instrumental part in other facets of a business's operations. One common risk-adjusted measure of return used in the banking and insurance industry is the risk-adjusted return on capital (RAROC). RAROC measures the return of a division after adjusting for risk relative to the division's capital. The concept of RAROC was developed in the 1970s and is primarily used as a method to quantify the amount of equity capital required by each business unit to support its operational activities. The RAROC system allocates capital on the basis of two premises: risk management and performance evaluation. For risk management purposes, this process involves measuring the overall risk or volatility of the cash flows associated with each unit's activities and the corresponding contribution to the overall bank risk. Generally speaking, the more risk the unit has, the more equity capital is required to maintain the financial soundness of its activities. As far as performance evaluation is concerned, RAROC provides an indication of how well a particular unit performs in relation to the allocated amount of capital.

CERTAINTY-EQUIVALENT APPROACH

The second method that is commonly used to adjust for risk in capital budgeting is the certainty-equivalent approach, where cash flows as opposed to the discount rate are adjusted according to how risky they are. To give some idea of how this approach works, suppose you are contemplating investing in a fast-food outlet. The payoff in a year's time is expected to be $2.6 million, but this payoff is risky. It is risky because the decision maker cannot know for sure, at the time the investment is made, what the level of sales will be during the year and what amount will be recouped at the end of the year. Reflecting this risk, the decision maker has ascertained that the discount rate should be 20%. However, if the decision maker was asked, 'What risk-free sum of money would you exchange, if it was known with certainty, for the risky payoff of $2.6 million?', and the decision maker answered, 'I would accept a guaranteed sum of $2.2 million', then this $2.2 million is the certainty equivalent of the risky sum of money.

The certainty-equivalent approach involves a direct attempt to allow the decision maker to incorporate his or her utility function into the analysis. In other words, there is a subjective judgement that incorporates the decision maker's assessment of risk and attitude towards risk. Because the decision maker has accepted the two sums, certain versus risky, as equivalent, the financial manager is indifferent to the two sets of cash flows. To a certain extent this process is like a television game show, where contestants are offered a valuable prize or, alternatively, a notional amount of cash to add to their pool of money. If they choose the cash, their chance of winning the game is increased as the winner is the contestant who has the greatest pool of funds by the end of the game. However, accepting the cash is an uncertain outcome, since the winner is not known until later when the show concludes; that is, contestants are trading certain outcomes from the prizes for uncertain outcomes in the form of winning the game. In some cases contestants are willing to make a trade, and in some cases they are not; it all depends on how risk averse they are. The main difference between what the financial manager is doing and what is done in such game shows is that in the game show contestants are in general not indifferent with respect to the certain outcome and the risky outcome, whereas in the certainty-equivalent approach managers are indifferent.

To further illustrate the concept of a certainty equivalent, let us look at a simple coin toss. Assume you can play the game only once and if it comes out heads you win $10 000 and if it comes out tails you win nothing. Obviously, you have a 50% chance of winning $10 000 and a 50% chance of winning nothing, with an expected value of $5000. Thus, $5000 is your uncertain expected value outcome. The certainty equivalent then becomes the certain, or riskless, amount you would demand, to make you indifferent with regard to playing or not playing the game. If you are indifferent with respect to receiving $3000 for certain and not playing the game, then $3000 is the certainty equivalent.

To simplify future calculations and problems, let us define the *certainty-equivalent coefficient* (α_t), which represents the ratio of the certain outcome to the risky outcome, between which the financial manager is indifferent. In equation form, α_t can be represented as follows:

$$\alpha_t = \frac{\text{certain flow in period } t}{\text{risky cash flow in period } t} \qquad \textbf{(13-2)}$$

Equation (13-2) shows that the lower the risk, the higher the certain cash flow and thus the larger the value of alpha. In light of equation (13-2), the NPV of the project can be shown to be:

$$NPV = \sum_{t=1}^{n} \frac{\alpha_t ACF_t}{(1 + k_{rf})^t} - IO \qquad \textbf{(13-3)}$$

Where ACF_t = expected annual cash flow in year t
$\qquad \alpha_t$ = the certainty-equivalent coefficient in year t
$\qquad k_{rf}$ = the risk-free rate of return
$\qquad IO$ = the initial outlay or the investment amount
$\qquad n$ = the project's expected life

Note that by applying the certainty-equivalent coefficient to the risky cash flows, we have effectively transformed the risky cash flows into certain cash flows. As a result, it is appropriate to discount these certain cash flows back to the present using the risk-free rate.

EXAMPLE 13.2   Certainty equivalent

If you were offered a certain sum as opposed to the value of 100 BHP-Billiton shares in a year's time, and you expected the shares to be worth $20 each, you might say you were willing to accept $1700 for sure instead of the chance of receiving $2000. In this case, your certainty equivalent (α) would be $1.700/$2000 = 0.85. On the other hand, if you were offered some shares in a new mining company with highly speculative prospects, you might be willing to accept just $2 for each $10 potential, but very uncertain, share value, thus making your certainty equivalent (α) equal to $2/$10 = 0.2.

It can be seen that the certainty equivalent (α) can vary between 0, in the case of extreme risk, and 1, in the case of certainty. To obtain the value of the equivalent certain cash flow, we need only multiply the risky cash flow by α_t. When this is done, we are indifferent with respect to this certain cash flow and the risky cash flow. In the example of the BHP-Billiton shares, the certainty equivalent coefficient is 0.85, and it is easy to see that multiplying this by the expected but risky cash flow of $2000 gives us the equivalent certain cash flow of $1700. That is:

certain cash flow$_t$ = $\alpha_t \times$ risky cash flow$_t$

Once this risk is taken out of the project's cash flows, those risk-free cash flows are discounted back to the present at the risk-free rate of interest, and the project's net present value or profitability index is determined. If the internal rate of return is calculated, it is then compared with the risk-free rate of interest rather than the firm's cost of capital in determining whether it should be accepted or rejected.

EXAMPLE 13.3 Certainty equivalents in capital budgeting

A firm with a 10% required rate of return is considering building new research facilities with an expected life of five years. The initial outlay associated with this project involves a certain cash outflow of $120 000. The expected cash inflows and certainty-equivalent coefficients are as follows:

YEAR, t	EXPECTED CASH FLOW, ACF_t	CERTAINTY-EQUIVALENT COEFFICIENT, α_t
1	$10 000	0.95
2	20 000	0.90
3	40 000	0.85
4	80 000	0.75
5	80 000	0.65

The risk-free rate of interest is 6%. What is the project's net present value?

To determine the net present value of this project using the certainty-equivalent approach, we must first remove the risk from the future cash flows. This is done by multiplying each expected cash flow by the corresponding certainty-equivalent coefficient, α_t.

EXPECTED CASH FLOW, ACF_t	CERTAINTY-EQUIVALENT COEFFICIENT, α_t	$\alpha_t \times ACF_t$
$10 000	0.95	$9 500
20 000	0.90	18 000
40 000	0.85	34 000
80 000	0.75	60 000
80 000	0.65	52 000

The equivalent riskless cash flows (the right-hand column of the preceding table) are then discounted back to the present at the riskless interest rate, not the firm's cost of capital. The cost of capital would be used if this project had the same level of risk as a typical project for this firm. However, these equivalent cash flows have no risk at all; hence, the appropriate discount rate is the risk-free rate, which is 6%:

YEAR, t	EQUIVALENT RISKLESS CASH FLOW	DISCOUNT FACTOR AT 6%	PRESENT VALUE
1	$9 500	0.943	$8 958.50
2	18 000	0.890	16 020.00
3	34 000	0.840	28 560.00
4	60 000	0.792	47 520.00
5	52 000	0.747	38 844.00
		Total present value of inflows	$139 902.50
		Less: Initial outlay	120 000.00
		Net present value	$19 902.50

Applying the normal capital-budgeting decision criteria, we find that the project should be accepted, as its net present value is greater than zero.

CERTAINTY-EQUIVALENT VERSUS RISK-ADJUSTED DISCOUNT RATE METHODS

The primary difference between the certainty-equivalent approach and the risk-adjusted discount rate approach involves the point at which the adjustment for risk is incorporated into the calculations. The certainty equivalent penalises, or adjusts downward, the value of the expected annual cash flows, ACF_t, which results in a lower net present value for a risky project. The risk-adjusted discount rate, conversely, leaves the cash flows at their expected value and adjusts the required rate of return upward to compensate for added risk, the risk-adjusted rate being denoted k^*. In either case the project's net present value is being adjusted downward to compensate for additional risk. The computational differences are illustrated in Table 13.2.

In addition to the difference in the point of adjustment for risk, the risk-adjusted discount rate makes the implicit assumption that risk becomes greater as we move further out in time. Although this is not necessarily a good or a bad assumption, you should be aware of it and understand it. Let us look at an example in which the risk-adjusted discount rate is used and then determine what certainty-equivalent coefficients, α_t, would be necessary to arrive at the same solution.

TABLE 13.2 Computational steps in certainty-equivalent and risk-adjusted discount rate methods

CERTAINTY EQUIVALENT	RISK-ADJUSTED DISCOUNT RATE
STEP 1:	STEP 1:
Adjust the expected cash flows, ACF_t, downward for risk by multiplying them by the corresponding certainty-equivalent risk coefficient, α_t.	Adjust the discount rate upward for risk.
STEP 2:	STEP 2:
Discount the certainty-equivalent, riskless cash flows back to the present using the risk-free rate of interest, i_F.	Discount the expected cash flows back to the present using the risk-adjusted discount rate, k^*.
STEP 3:	STEP 3:
Apply the normal decision criteria, except in the case of the internal rate of return where the risk-free rate of interest replaces the cost of capital as the hurdle rate.	Apply the normal decision criteria, except in the case of the internal rate of return, where the risk-adjusted discount rate replaces the cost of capital as the hurdle rate.

EXAMPLE 13.4 Certainty equivalents versus risk-adjusted discount rate

Assume that a firm with a required rate of return that is normally 12% is considering introducing a new product. This product has an initial outlay of $800 000, an expected life of 10 years, and cash flows of $100 000 each year during its life. Because of the increased risk associated with this project, management is requiring a 15% rate of return. Let us also assume that the risk-free rate of return is 6%.

If the firm chose to use the certainty-equivalent method, the certainty-equivalent cash flows would be discounted back to the present at 6%, the risk-free rate of interest. The present value of the $100 000 cash flow occurring at the end of the first year discounted back to the present at 15% is $87 000. The present value of this $100 000 flow discounted back to the present at the risk-free rate of 6% is $94 300. Thus, if the certainty-equivalent approach were used, a certainty-equivalent coefficient, α_1, of 0.9226 would be necessary to produce a present value of $87 000 (i.e. $100 000 \times 0.9226/1.06$). In other words, the same results can be obtained in the first year by using the risk-adjusted discount rate and adjusting the discount rate up to 15% or by using the certainty-equivalent approach and adjusting the expected cash flows by a certainty-equivalent coefficient of 0.9226.

Under the risk-adjusted discount rate, the present value of the $100 000 cash flow occurring at the end of the second year becomes $75 600, and to produce an identical present value under the certainty-equivalent approach, a certainty-equivalent coefficient of 0.8494 would be needed. Following this through for the life of the project yields the certainty-equivalent coefficients given in Table 13.3.

TABLE 13.3	Certainty-equivalent coefficients yielding same results as risk-adjusted discount rate of 15%									
YEAR	1	2	3	4	5	6	7	8	9	10
α_t	0.9226	0.8494	0.7833	0.7222	0.6653	0.6128	0.5654	0.5215	0.4797	0.4427

What does the analysis in Example 13.4 suggest? It indicates that, if the risk-adjusted discount rate method is used, we are adjusting downward more severely the value of future cash flows that occur further in the future than earlier cash flows.

FYI

If performed properly, either of the methods to adjust for risk discussed above can do a good job. However, by far the most popular method of risk adjustment is the risk-adjusted discount rate (RADR). The reason for the popularity of the RADR over the certainty-equivalent approach is simply its ease of implementation. Apart from confronting various measurement and implementation problems, it has the advantage that it is free of the decision maker's subjective judgement or utility function.

RISK-ADJUSTED DISCOUNT RATE AND MEASUREMENT OF A PROJECT'S SYSTEMATIC RISK

As has been discussed above, the shareholders' current required rate of return (R_E) is valid for a new project only if the risk of the new project is the same as the existing risk of the firm. To overcome this limitation, it was suggested that a risk-adjusted discount rate (RADR) could be used—the higher the risk of the project, the higher the required rate of return. However, how are the different risks of different projects assessed (particularly if it is thought that they do not carry the same risk as the firm currently does)? One solution to this problem lies in the use of a model first introduced in Chapter 9, namely the capital asset pricing model (CAPM). This model specifies the required rate of return on a project as a function of its systematic risk. Thus, it incorporates an explicit allowance for risk, whereas the dividend-discount model as represented by equation (10-12) does not directly incorporate a risk variable.

It will be recalled that the CAPM states that the required rate of return on an investment, j, is given by equation (9-19):

$$R_j = R_f + \beta_j (R_m - R_f)$$

The advantage of this approach is that if the systematic risk of a project can be assessed the required rate of return can be determined—as simple as that! Well, not quite so simple, because, as will be discussed shortly, the use of systematic risk faces a number of estimation problems and other difficulties. Nevertheless, it puts us on the right track to finding a relationship between the required return on a project and its risk.

When systematic risk, or beta, was initially talked about in Chapter 9, the implication was that it was being measured for the entire firm. Thus, if the systematic risk of a new project differs from that of the existing firm, the existing firm's beta is not appropriate for the new project. As will be seen, estimating the appropriate level of systematic risk for a single project is even more fraught with difficulties. To truly understand what is trying to be done, and the difficulties that will be encountered, let us step back a bit and examine systematic risk and the risk adjustment for a project.

The incentive is to use the CAPM to determine the level of risk and thus the appropriate risk–return trade-off for a particular project. The expected return on this project is then compared with the risk–return trade-off suggested by the CAPM to determine whether or not the project should be accepted. If the project appears to be a typical one for the firm, using the CAPM to determine the appropriate risk–return trade-off and then judging the project against it may be a warranted approach. But if the project is not a typical project, what should be done? Historical data generally do not exist for a new project. In fact, for some capital investments historical data would not have much meaning. What financial managers need to do is make the best out of a bad situation. They can either (1) fake it—that is, use historical accounting data, if available, to substitute for historical price data in estimating systematic risk, or (2) attempt to find a substitute firm in the same industry as the capital-budgeting project and use the substitute firm's estimated systematic risk as a proxy for the project's systematic risk.

BETA ESTIMATION USING ACCOUNTING DATA

When dealing with a project that is identical to the firm's other projects, we need only to estimate the level of systematic risk for the firm and use that estimate as a proxy for the project's risk. Unfortunately, when projects are not typical of the firm, this approach does not work. For example, when a diversified company introduces a new food through its food-product division, the new product probably carries with it a different level of systematic risk than is typical for the company as a whole, because the beta of the diversified firm is likely to be different from that of any of its individual divisions or projects.

The general procedure for finding beta as the slope of the regression line was illustrated in the appendix to Chapter 9, where a regression was run for the relationship between the returns on a company's shares and the returns on the market index. The resultant beta was the beta of the company's equity or shares. To get an approximation of the systematic risk level of, say, one of the food-products divisions of this company, one would need to know the return on the food products and then run a regression of this divisional return against the returns on the market index. However, the only source of data on the return of the food products lies within the firm's accounting records. The rate of return, then, can be approximated by the ratio of net profit of the division to the amount of the assets invested in the division.

How good is the accounting beta technique? It certainly is not as good as a direct calculation of the beta. In fact, the correlation between the accounting beta and the beta calculated on historical share return data is only about 0.6. Better luck has been experienced with multiple regression models used to predict betas, but in many cases there may not be any realistic alternative to the calculation of the accounting beta. Because of the importance of adjusting for a project's risk, the accounting beta method is much preferred to doing nothing.

THE PURE PLAY METHOD FOR ESTIMATING A PROJECT'S BETA

pure play method
A way of estimating a project's beta by identifying firms that are engaged in the same business as the project.

Whereas the accounting beta method attempts to directly estimate a project's or a division's beta, the **pure play method** attempts to identify publicly traded firms that are engaged solely in the same business as the project or division. Once the proxy or pure play firm is identified, its

FYI

When the project's risk differs from the overall risk of the firm, estimating the project's beta is a challenging task. Apart from using accounting data as a proxy to estimate beta for the project, the firm can also attempt to quantify a project's beta by analysing the correlation in the pattern of cash flows between the new project and existing projects whose betas are already known. This approach requires an understanding of the factors that determine beta, such as the business cycle, the proportion of fixed costs versus variable costs, known as the degree of operating leverage, and the firm's capital structure.

systematic risk (beta) is determined and then used as a proxy for the project's or the division's level of systematic risk. What the decision makers are doing is looking for a publicly traded firm on the outside that looks like their project and then using that firm's required rate of return to judge their project.

The firm's decision makers do not necessarily have to compute betas from scratch. This is because the betas of some Australian listed companies are compiled from time to time by services such as the Australian Graduate School of Management and the ASX. However, the relative smallness of the Australian capital market limits the search for a suitable proxy firm.

In using a proxy firm's beta, we are implicitly assuming that the systematic risk and the capital structure of the proxy firm are identical to those of the project. However, when the capital structure of the proxy firm is different from the capital structure that will be used to finance the project, some adjustment must be made for the difference. Thus, if the proxy firm has a different debt–equity ratio, or different 'gearing', the proxy firm's beta can theoretically be 'de-geared' to remove the effect of gearing, thus revealing the pure project risk, then 're-geared' to reflect the level of gearing that will be used to finance the project. Although not a perfect approach, it does provide some insights into the level of systematic risk a project might have.

Concept check

13.6 What is the most commonly used method for incorporating risk into the capital-budgeting decision? How is this technique related to the risk–return trade-off?

13.7 Describe two methods for estimating a project's systematic risk.

For answers go to MyFinanceLab or
www.pearson.com.au/9781442539174

OBJECTIVE **4**

Use sensitivity, scenario and simulation analyses and probability trees to investigate the determinants of project cash flows.

Tools for analysing the risk of project cash flows

We can assume that the actual cash flows an investment produces will almost never equal the expected cash flows we used to estimate the investment's NPV. There are many possible cash-flow outcomes for risky projects, and simply specifying a single expected cash flow can provide a misleading characterisation of the investment. While it is generally impossible to specify all the possible ways in which an investment can perform, an analyst can use some basic tools to better understand the uncertain nature of future cash flows and, consequently, the reliability of the NPV estimate.

The first tool we will consider is *sensitivity analysis*, which is designed to identify the most important forces that ultimately determine the success or failure of an investment. The second tool we will consider is *scenario analysis*, which allows the analyst to consider alternative scenarios in which a number of possible variables differ. Finally, we will consider the use of *simulation*, which allows the analyst to consider very large numbers of possible scenarios.

SENSITIVITY ANALYSIS

sensitivity analysis
A technique for assessing risk—for example, the sensitivity of a project's NPV to changes in one or more of the factors that determine the NPV, such as the discount rate.

Sensitivity analysis involves determining how the distribution of possible net present values or internal rates of return for a particular project is affected by a change in one particular input variable. This is done by changing the value of one input variable while holding all other input variables constant. The distribution of possible net present values or internal rates of return that is generated is then compared with the distribution of possible returns generated before the change was made, to determine the effect of the change. For this reason, sensitivity analysis is commonly called 'what if?' analysis.

For example, a pharmaceutical producer which is considering producing an Alzheimer's drug may wish to determine the effect of a more pessimistic forecast of the anticipated market growth rate. After the more pessimistic forecast replaces the original forecast in the model, the simulation is rerun. The two outputs are then compared to determine how sensitive the results are to the revised estimate of the market growth rate.

By modifying assumptions made about the values and ranges of the input factors and rerunning the simulation, management can determine how sensitive the outcome of the project is to these changes. If the output appears to be highly sensitive to one or two of the input factors, the financial manager may wish to spend additional time refining those input estimates to make sure they are accurate. In particular, sensitivity analysis helps managers to identify which variables have the greatest effect on net present value or the IRR. For example, by successively altering the values of different economic factors, the pharmaceutical producer might find that its share of the market is the single greatest factor impacting on the NPV, and so this will tell the managers to put particular emphasis on market share as the key to ensuring that the project is successful if implemented, as well as to place special emphasis on that variable in the analysis.

Practitioners commonly use sensitivity analysis without probability distributions to look at the effect of variations in the factors that impact on project selection. The popularity of this non-statistical approach to sensitivity analysis has grown with the proliferation of spreadsheet software. The spreadsheet model can be built in such a way that the modeller can easily vary one or more values and instantly see the effect on the final output, such as NPV or IRR. Spreadsheets are widely used in the building of budgetary models for firms. The approach used in capital budgeting is very similar; for example, the factors that combined to produce the cash flows of the gourmet pizza business illustrated in Table 12.4 could be built as a spreadsheet model, from which the decision makers could easily see how *sensitive* the project was to changes in values of the variables, as well as which variables were of critical importance to the project.

Example 13.5 provides an illustration of the application of sensitivity analysis.

EXAMPLE 13.5 Sensitivity analysis

Crainium, Inc. is considering an investment in a new plasma cutting tool to be used in cutting out steel silhouettes that will be sold through the firm's catalogue sales operations. The silhouettes can be cut into any two-dimensional shape such as a state, university mascot, logo, etc. The products are expected to sell for an average price of $25 per unit, and the company analysts expect the firm can sell 200 000 units per year at this price for a period of five years. Launching this service will require the purchase of a $1.5 million plasma-cutter and materials handling system that will have a residual or salvage value in five years of $250 000. In addition, the firm expects to have to invest an additional $500 000 in working capital to support the new business. Other pertinent information concerning the business venture is provided below:

Initial cost of equipment	$1 500 000
Expected life of equipment	5 years
Salvage value of equipment	$250 000
Working capital requirement	$500 000
Depreciation method	Straight line
Annual depreciation expense	$250 000
Variable cost per unit	$20
Fixed cost per year	$400 000
Discount rate	12%
Corporate tax rate	30%

Crainium's analysts have estimated the project's expected or base-case cash flows as well as the NPV and IRR to be the following:

	YEAR 0	YEAR 1	YEAR 2	YEAR 3	YEAR 4	YEAR 5
Revenue		5 000 000	5 000 000	5 000 000	5 000 000	5 000 000
Variable cost		–4 000 000	–4 000 000	–4 000 000	–4 000 000	–4 000 000
Depreciation expense		–250 000	–250 000	–250 000	–250 000	–250 000
Fixed cost		–400 000	–400 000	–400 000	–400 000	–400 000
Net operating income		350 000	350 000	350 000	350 000	350 000
Less: Taxes		–105 000	–105 000	–105 000	–105 000	–105 000
Net profit after tax		245 000	245 000	245 000	245 000	245 000
Add back depreciation		250 000	250 000	250 000	250 000	250 000
Initial cost	–1 500 000					
Salvage value						250 000
Increase in working capital	–500 000					500 000
Net cash flows	–2 000 000	495 000	495 000	495 000	495 000	1 245 000
NPV	$209 934					
IRR	15.59%					

Although the project is expected to have a $209 934 NPV and a 15.59% IRR (which exceeds the project's 10% discount rate), it is risky, so the firm's analysts want to explore the importance of uncertainty in the project cash flows. They therefore decide to perform a sensitivity analysis on this proposed investment. The key input variables are unit sales, price per unit, variable cost per unit, and annual fixed costs. In particular, the following changes are considered in the analysis:

	PESSIMISTIC	EXPECTED FORECAST	OPTIMISTIC
Unit sales	180 000	200 000	220 000
Price per unit	22.5	25	27.5
Variable cost per unit	22	20	18
Annual fixed cost	440 000	400 000	360 000

The pessimistic forecasts for unit sales and price per unit represent a 10% decrease from the expected forecasts while the optimistic forecasts show a 10% increase. Similarly, pessimistic forecasts for the cost variables are 10% higher than the expected level and optimistic forecasts show a 10% reduction in the expected forecasts.

The objective of this analysis is to explore the effects of the prescribed changes in the key input variables on the project's NPV. In this instance, we estimate the project's NPV for pessimistic and optimistic forecasts of each of the variables. The resulting NPVs are then compared to the expected base-case NPV which was shown above to be $209 934. This comparison allows us to determine to which variables the project's NPV is most sensitive.

The following results were obtained when NPV was recalculated for each of the estimates:

	PESSIMISTIC NPV	EXPECTED NPV	OPTIMISTIC NPV
Unit sales	–$42 400	$209 934	$462 269
Price per unit	–$1 051 737	$209 934	$1 471 606
Variable cost per unit	–$799 402	$209 934	$1 219 272
Annual fixed cost	$109 001	$209 934	$310 868

To gauge a better understanding of how the NPV of the project changes as the values of key input variables change, we can work out the percentage change in the NPV in response to changes in the estimates of key variables.

	PESSIMISTIC CHANGE IN NPV (%)	OPTIMISTIC CHANGE IN NPV (%)
Unit sales	–120.20%	120.20%
Price per unit	–600.98%	600.98%
Variable cost per unit	–480.79%	480.79%
Annual fixed cost	–48.08%	48.08%

As is obvious from the sensitivity analysis, pessimistic forecasts of key variables lead to a reduction in the NPVs, while optimistic forecasts of key variables result in higher NPVs. The most critical input variable, however, is price per unit as a 10% change in the unit price leads to 600% change in NPV, followed closely by variable cost per unit.

The results of this analysis suggest two courses of action. First, Crainium's management should make sure that they are as comfortable as possible with their price per unit forecast as well as their estimate of the variable cost per unit. This might entail using additional market research to explore the pricing issue and a careful cost accounting study of unit production costs. Second, should the project be implemented, it would be imperative that the company monitor these two critical factors (price per unit and variable cost per unit) very closely so that they could react quickly should an adverse change in either variable occur.

SCENARIO ANALYSIS

Sensitivity analysis involves changing only one input variable at a time and analysing its effect on the investment NPV. This is very useful when attempting to determine the most critical factor that influences the NPV of a project, but it ignores the fact that some of the variables may move in unison or be correlated. For example, when unit sales are less than expected, it is probably the case that the unit selling price will be less than expected. To consider the effects of multiple changes in key variables, analysts often resort to **scenario analysis**, which allows the financial manager to simultaneously consider the effects of changes in the estimates of multiple variables on the investment opportunity's NPV. Each scenario consists of a different set of estimates for the project input variables.

As an illustration of the application of scenario analysis in analysing risk, we will consider an investment opportunity for Longhorn Enterprises in Example 13.6.

scenario analysis
A technique that allows the financial manager to simultaneously consider the effects of changes in the estimates of multiple input variables on the NPV of an investment project.

EXAMPLE 13.6 *Scenario analysis*

Longhorn Enterprises has the opportunity to manufacture and sell a novelty 'third brake light' for automobiles. The light is mounted in the rear window of an automobile to replace the factory-installed third brake light. The replacement light can be shaped into the logo of your favourite university mascot or other preferred symbol.

Producing the light requires an initial investment of $500 000 in manufacturing equipment, which depreciates over a five-year time period toward a $50 000 salvage value, plus an investment of $20 000 in net operating working capital (increase in receivables and inventory less increase in accounts payable). The discount rate used to analyse the project cash flows is 10%. Additional information in relation to the project is summarised below:

Initial cost of equipment	$500 000
Expected life of equipment	5 years
Salvage value of equipment	$50 000
Working capital requirement	$20 000
Depreciation method	Straight line
Annual depreciation expense	$90 000
Discount rate	10%
Corporate tax rate	30%

Longhorn's management estimates that it can sell 15 000 units per year for the next five years and expects to sell them for $200 each. Longhorn's management team has identified four key input variables for the project: unit sales, price per unit, variable cost per unit, and cash fixed costs (that is, fixed costs other than depreciation) per year. The expected values for the key variables, along with corresponding estimates for best- and worst-case scenarios, are summarised below:

	EXPECTED OR BASE CASE	WORST CASE	BEST CASE
Unit sales	15 000	12 500	18 000
Price per unit	200	190	220
Variable cost per unit	150	160	130
Annual cash fixed cost	285 000	285 000	285 000
Depreciation expense	90 000	90 000	90 000

To consider the worst-case scenario, we analyse the project cash flows and NPV using the worst-case estimates as follows:

	YEAR 0	YEAR 1	YEAR 2	YEAR 3	YEAR 4	YEAR 5
Revenue (12 500 × 190)		2 375 000	2 375 000	2 375 000	2 375 000	2 375 000
Variable cost (12 500 × 160)		−2 000 000	−2 000 000	−2 000 000	−2 000 000	−2 000 000
Depreciation expense		−90 000	−90 000	−90 000	−90 000	−90 000
Fixed cost		−285 000	−285 000	−285 000	−285 000	−285 000
Net operating income		0	0	0	0	0
Taxes		0	0	0	0	0
Net operating profit after tax		0	0	0	0	0
Add back depreciation		90 000	90 000	90 000	90 000	90 000
Initial outlay	−500 000					
Salvage value						50 000
Increase in working capital	−20 000					20 000
Net cash flows	−520 000	90 000	90 000	90 000	90 000	160 000
NPV	−$135 365					
IRR	0.00%					

Since the worst-case scenario has much lower estimates of revenues due to the lower selling price and number of units sold, the resulting cash-flow estimates are much lower. Indeed, when we analyse the investment's NPV, we get a worst-case estimate of −$135 365, which means that in this case the project reduces shareholder wealth. But what is the likelihood that this worst-case scenario will occur? We will leave this question unanswered for the moment, but will return to it shortly when we discuss the use of simulation analysis.

What about the best-case scenario? If this rosy outcome were to occur, then the following cash flows would result:

	YEAR 0	YEAR 1	YEAR 2	YEAR 3	YEAR 4	YEAR 5
Revenue (18 000 × 220)		3 960 000	3 960 000	3 960 000	3 960 000	3 960 000
Variable cost (18 000 × 130)		–2 340 000	–2 340 000	–2 340 000	–2 340 000	–2 340 000
Depreciation expense		–90 000	–90 000	–90 000	–90 000	–90 000
Fixed cost		–285 000	–285 000	–285 000	–285 000	–285 000
Net operating income		1 245 000	1 245 000	1 245 000	1 245 000	1 245 000
Taxes		–373 500	–373 500	–373 500	–373 500	–373 500
Net operating profit after tax		871 500	871 500	871 500	871 500	871 500
Add back depreciation		90 000	90 000	90 000	90 000	90 000
Initial outlay	–500 000					
Salvage value						50 000
Increase in working capital	–20 000					20 000
Net cash flows	–520 000	961 500	961 500	961 500	961 500	1 031 500
NPV	$3 168 306					
IRR	184.04%					

In this case the NPV of the project is $3 168 306 and the IRR is 184.04%!

Combining our analysis of the expected or base-case, worst-case and best-case scenarios indicates a wide range of possible NPVs for the project:

SCENARIO	NPV
Expected or base case	$859 717
Worst case	–$135 365
Best case	$3 168 306

In fact, we have learned that the investment is expected to create value for Longhorn with an expected NPV equal to $859 717. However, this estimate is based on Longhorn's forecast of the expected values for the key variables (unit sales, unit price, variable cost per unit, and cash fixed costs).

In evaluating what Longhorn's management feels are the worst- and best-case estimates of these variables, we have discovered a wide range of possible NPVs depending on what actually happens. What we do not know is the likelihood or probability that the worst-case or best-case scenario will occur. Moreover, we do not know the probability of the project losing money (i.e. have a negative NPV).

Simulation, discussed below, offers the analyst a useful tool for risk analysis that provides us not only with estimates of NPV for many scenarios but also with probabilities for those scenarios.

SIMULATION ANALYSIS

Scenario analysis provides the analyst with a discrete number of estimates of project NPVs for a limited number of cases or scenarios. **Simulation analysis**, on the other hand, provides the analyst with a very powerful tool for generating thousands of estimates of NPV that are built upon thousands of values for each of the investment's key variables. These different values arise out of each variable's individual probability distribution. This may sound confusing if you have not heard the term *probability distribution* in a while, so here is a simple example.

Let's say that the unit selling price for Longhorn's third brake light product can be either $180 or $220 with equal probability of 50%. The expected price then is $200 = (.50 × $180) + (.50 × $220). The probability distribution for unit price in this instance is fully described by the two possible values for price and their corresponding probabilities.

simulation analysis
The process of imitating the performance of an investment project through repeated evaluations, usually using a computer; in the general case, experimentation on a mathematical model that has been designed to capture the critical realities of the decision-making situation.

MANAGING YOUR PERSONAL RISKS

Not unlike in large corporations, risk analysis and management play a vital role in personal financial success. Nevertheless, more often than not, individuals tend to overlook the importance of personal risk management in preserving their wealth. Broadly speaking, personal risk-management strategies are devised to protect your financial health from adverse impacts caused by unforeseeable personal circumstances such as an unexpected job loss. A systematic approach to personal risk management involves determining the financial assets that need protecting, quantifying the potential financial loss and implementing measures to manage the risk such as taking out insurance contracts. Fortunately, a number of products exist in the financial market that can help you insure against unfortunate events that may undermine the achievement of your long-term financial goals. The type and amount of risk insurance that you need largely depend upon your personal financial circumstances and objectives, lifestyle needs, number of dependants and your age. The most common types of risk insurance are life insurance, total and permanent disability (TPD) insurance, income protection, and trauma insurance.

Life insurance provides financial protection in the event of death and the cost of the insurance depends on the type of cover selected. A regular review of your cover is necessary to ensure you are not under or over insured. In determining the most appropriate policy, a balance must be achieved between affordability and the most favourable policy conditions. TPD is an additional cover to death cover and is designed to provide a lump sum should you suffer an illness or injury which totally and permanently incapacitates you and prevents you from working again. Similarly, an income protection policy will pay you an income in the event of being unable to work due to illness or injury. Income protection insurance replaces up to 75% of your monthly income for a specified period. Finally, trauma insurance is a lump-sum payment for those who suffer a specified traumatic event such as diagnosis of cancer, coronary disease, etc. The specific purpose of this insurance is to provide for medical treatment, child care and debt management.

It is never too early to think about managing your personal risk. A well-constructed financial plan, coupled with a suitable risk-management strategy, is the key to financial success.

Let's consider how Longhorn might use simulation analysis to evaluate the NPV of its proposed brake-light project. The simulation process is summarised in the following five-step process:

Step 1. Estimate probability distributions for each of the investment's key input variables (i.e. the variables or factors that determine the project's cash flows). In the Longhorn example, the key factors are those that determine project revenues, which include the number of units that are sold and the price per unit they command, as well as the factors underlying the cost of manufacturing and selling the brake lights (variable and fixed costs).

Step 2. Randomly select one value for each of the key variables from their respective probability distributions.

Step 3. Combine the values selected for each of the key variables to estimate project cash flows for each year of the project's life and calculate the project's NPV.

Step 4. Store or save the calculated value of the NPV and repeat Steps 2 and 3. Simulations are easily carried out using readily available computer software that allows one to easily repeat Steps 2 and 3 thousands of times.

Step 5. Use the stored values of the project NPV to construct a histogram or probability distribution of NPV.

Once you have finished running the simulation, it is time to sit down and interpret the results. Note that in Step 5 we summarise the final set of simulation results in a probability distribution of possible NPVs like the one found in Figure 13.2. So, we can now analyse the distribution of *possible* NPVs to determine the probability for a negative NPV. In Figure 13.2, we see that the probability of achieving an NPV greater than zero is 85%, indicating a 15% probability that the project will produce an NPV that is less than zero. What a simulation does is allow us to analyse all sources of uncertainty simultaneously, and get some idea as to what might happen—before we actually commit to the investment.

FIGURE 13.2 Probability distribution of NPVs for the marketing of Longhorn's brake lights

The final output of the simulation is a probability distribution of the project's NPVs. Having set up and run the simulation experiment, the analyst not only knows the expected NPV but can also make probability statements about the likelihood of achieving any particular value of NPV. For example, in the results that follow, the probability of achieving a positive NPV is 85%.

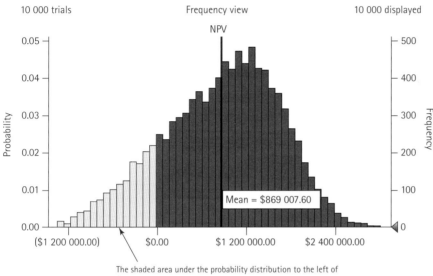

The shaded area under the probability distribution to the left of $0 includes 15% of the area under the probability distribution and indicates that the likelihood the project will produce a negative NPV is 15%!

Finance at work

UNIVERSAL STUDIOS' ISLANDS OF ADVENTURE

A major capital-budgeting decision led Universal Studios to build its *Islands of Adventure* theme park. The purpose of this $2.6 billion investment was to take direct aim at the first crack of the tourist's dollar in Orlando, USA. Although this capital-budgeting decision may, on the surface, seem like a relatively simple decision, forecasting the expected cash flows associated with this theme park would have been quite complicated.

To begin with, Universal was introducing a product that would compete directly with itself. The original Universal Studios featured rides like Back to the Future and Jaws. Would there be enough tourist dollars to support both theme parks, or would the new Islands of Adventure park simply cannibalise ticket sales to the older Universal Studios? In addition, what would happen if Disney countered with a new park of its own?

From Universal's point of view, the objective may have been threefold: to increase its share of the tourist market; to

prevent losing market share as tourists looked for the latest in technological rides and entertainment; and to promote Universal's, and its parent company Seagrams', other brands and products. However, for companies in very competitive markets, the evolution and introduction of new products may serve more to preserve market share than to expand it.

So, how did all this turn out?

It must have turned out reasonably well because Universal followed up this investment by putting another $100 million into new rides based on Universal franchises: the Mummy, Shrek, and Jimmy Neutron. Then in October 2003, Universal's theme parks changed ownership as NBC signed a deal to merge with Universal. The new media conglomerate called NBC Universal now controls NBC, more than a dozen local television stations, several cable networks and five theme parks, all owned by NBC's parent company, General Electric.

PROBABILITY TREES

probability tree
A schematic representation of a problem in which all possible outcomes are graphically displayed.

A **probability tree** is a graphic exposition of the sequence of possible outcomes. It presents the decision maker with a schematic representation of the problem in which all possible outcomes are pictured. Moreover, the computations and results of the computations are shown directly on the tree, so the information can be easily understood.

To illustrate the use of a probability tree, suppose that a firm is considering an investment proposal that requires an initial outlay of $1 million and will yield resultant cash flows for the next two years. During the first year, let us assume that there are three possible outcomes, as shown in Table 13.4. Graphically, each of these three possible alternatives is represented on the probability tree in Figure 13.3 as one of the three possible branches.

TABLE 13.4 Possible investment outcomes in year 1

	PROBABILITY		
	0.5 OUTCOME 1	0.3 OUTCOME 2	0.2 OUTCOME 3
Cash flow	$600000	$700000	$800000

FIGURE 13.3 First stage of a probability-tree diagram

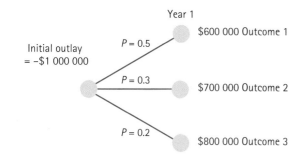

The second step in the probability tree is to continue drawing branches in a similar manner so that each of the possible outcomes during the second year is represented by a new branch. For example, if outcome 1 occurs in year 1, a 20% chance of a $300000 cash flow and an 80% chance of a $600000 cash flow in year 2 have been projected. Two branches would be sent out from the outcome 1 node, reflecting these two possible outcomes. The cash flows that occur if outcome 1 takes place and the probabilities associated with them are called *conditional outcomes* and *conditional probabilities* because they can occur only if outcome 1 occurs during the first year.

Finally, to determine the probability of the sequence of a $600000 flow in year 1 *and* a $300000 outcome in year 2, the probability of the $600000 flow (0.5) is multiplied by the conditional probability of the second flow (0.2), telling us that this sequence has a probability of 0.1, in other words a 10% chance of occurring—this is called its *joint probability*. Letting the values in Table 13.4 represent the conditional outcomes and their respective conditional probabilities, the probability tree can be completed, as shown in Figure 13.4.

By examining the probability tree, the financial manager is provided with the expected internal rate of return for the investment, the range of possible outcomes, and a listing of each possible outcome with the probability associated with it. In this case, the expected internal rate of return is 14.74%, and there is a 10% chance of incurring the worst possible outcome with an internal rate of return of –7.55%. There is a 2% probability of achieving the most favourable outcome, an internal rate of return of 37.98%.

Decision making with probability trees does not mean simply the acceptance of any project with an internal rate of return greater than the firm's required rate of return, because the project's required rate of return has not yet been adjusted for risk. As a result, the financial decision maker must examine the entire distribution of possible internal rates of return and then, based on that examination, decide (given her or his aversion to risk) if enough of this distribution is above the appropriate risk-adjusted required rate of return to warrant acceptance of the project. Thus, the probability tree allows the manager to quickly visualise the possible future events, their probabilities and their outcomes. In addition, the calculation of the expected internal rate of return and enumeration of the distribution should aid the financial manager in determining the risk level of the project.

FIGURE 13.4   A complete probability-tree diagram

Time			(A) Internal rate of return for each branch	(B) Joint probability	(A) × (B)
0 years	1 year	2 years			

			(A) Internal rate of return for each branch	(B) Joint probability	(A) × (B)
$600 000 → P = 0.2	$300 000		−7.55%	0.10	−0.7550
P = 0.8	$600 000		13.07	0.40	5.2280
P = 0.2	$300 000		0.00	0.06	0.0000
P = 0.3	$500 000		13.90	0.09	1.2510
$700 000 P = 0.5	$700 000		25.69	0.15	3.8535
P = 0.2	$400 000		14.83	0.04	0.5932
P = 0.7	$600 000		27.18	0.14	3.8052
$800 000 P = 0.1	$800 000		37.98	0.02	0.7596
				1.00	

−$1 000 000

P = 0.5
P = 0.3
P = 0.2

Expected internal rate of return = 14.7355%

Finally, note that the probability-tree diagram naturally incorporates the situation where the cash flows in one year are dependent on another year's outcome; this means that probability trees must be used to formulate problems where successive outcomes are dependent on each other. For example, to evaluate whether or not to conduct an oil exploration program, the first branches in Figure 13.4 might represent three different types of soil strata, with the next branches from each of the first dealing with the probability of finding oil given the first soil type, as well as with the estimated payoffs from each branch.

Concept check

13.8   What is the difference between scenario and sensitivity analysis?

13.9   Explain how simulation works.

13.10   How can probability trees assist in risk analysis?

For answers go to MyFinanceLab or
www.pearson.com.au/9781442539174

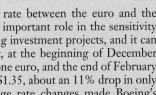

International spotlight

CURRENCY RISK

When multinational firms do their risk analyses, a very important variable that they consider is uncertainty about exchange rates. For example, in 2010 Boeing began deliveries of its 787 Dreamliner aircraft, which competes directly with European manufacturer Airbus. Boeing produces these planes in the United States, paying workers and suppliers in US dollars. Airbus, on the other hand, has costs that are more closely tied to the euro. What this means is that when the dollar is very strong relative to the euro, Airbus has a competitive advantage over Boeing. However, when the euro is strong relative to the dollar, Boeing has a competitive advantage over Airbus.

As a result, the exchange rate between the euro and the US dollar plays a particularly important role in the sensitivity and scenario analysis of Boeing investment projects, and it can fluctuate dramatically. In fact, at the beginning of December 2009 it took US$1.51 to buy one euro, and the end of February 2010 that had dropped to US$1.35, about an 11% drop in only three months. These exchange rate changes made Boeing's Dreamliner more expensive for those buying it with euros, and made the Airbus less expensive for those buying it with US dollars.

OBJECTIVE 5

Describe the different types of real options in capital budgeting.

Real options in capital budgeting

NPV provides the proper tool for evaluating whether a project is expected to add value to the firm. However, NPV is generally calculated using a static set of expected future cash flows that do not reflect the fact that managers are likely to make changes to the operation of the investment over its life in response to changing circumstances that alter the profitability of the investment. For example, if a project that had an expected life of 10 years generated better than expected cash flows, its life may be extended, perhaps to 20 years. However, if its cash flows did not meet expectations, it may be scaled back or shut down earlier than anticipated.

Having the flexibility to alter an investment's scale, scope and timing enhances the value of an investment. All else being equal, we would surely prefer an investment that allows managers substantial flexibility in how it is implemented over an investment with no flexibility. However, traditional estimates of investment NPVs often ignore the implications of this flexibility, and so they tend to understate project values.

Opportunities to alter the project's cash-flow stream after the project has begun are commonly referred to as **real options**. For example, if you own land that can be developed at your discretion, we would say that the ownership of the land includes an option to build.

While there are a number of different categories of real options, the most common real options, or sources of flexibility, that can add value to an investment opportunity include:

real options
Opportunities that allow for the alteration of the project's cash-flow stream while the project is being operated.

- *timing option*—the option to delay a project until estimated future cash flows are more favourable
- *expansion option*—the option to increase the scale and scope of an investment in response to realised demand
- *contract, shut-down and abandonment options*—the options to slow down production, halt production temporarily, or stop production permanently (abandonment).

THE OPTION TO DELAY A PROJECT

There is no question that the estimated cash flows associated with a project can change over time. Let's consider Go-Power Batteries, a company that developed a high-voltage, nickel-metal hydride battery that can be used to power a hybrid automobile. It is still relatively expensive to manufacture the nickel-metal hydride battery, and the market for the hybrid car is still relatively small. As a result, gearing up to manufacture the batteries at the present time provides cash flows that are quite uncertain. However, owning the technology to produce the batteries may be quite valuable, because it is possible that, in the future, the technology may improve and the demand for hybrid automobiles may increase if petrol prices continue to rise. Hence, having the option to delay manufacturing the hydride battery until a time when the profitability of the venture is more certain is extremely valuable.

What is the source of the timing option? Do all projects have this option? Not at all! In some cases the opportunity to make an investment is short-lived, and if one firm passes it up, another will take it up. In the battery example above, the option to delay probably rests on patent protection, which gives the owner the right to develop the new technology over the life of the patent. However, even here there are limits in that a competitor may develop a superior technology that makes the hydride battery obsolete.

THE OPTION TO EXPAND A PROJECT

Just as we saw with the option to delay a project, the estimated cash flows associated with a project can change over time, making it valuable to expand its scale and scope. For example, if the new hydride battery project were launched and petrol prices were to rise, the demand for the battery might increase dramatically. If this indeed happened, having the ability to expand the scale of production of the battery would be quite valuable. Because this expansion option can have significant value, firms try to design their production facilities in ways that allow them to easily expand capacity in response to realised increases in demand.

EXAMPLE 13.7   The option to expand a project

You are considering introducing a new drive-in restaurant called Smooth-Thru, featuring high-protein, vitamin-laced smoothies along with other organic foods. The initial outlay on this new restaurant is $2.4 million and the present value of the free cash flows (excluding the initial outlay) is $2 million, such that the project has a negative expected NPV of –$400 000. Looking more closely, you find that there is a 50% chance that this new restaurant will be well received and will produce annual cash flows of $320 000 per year forever (a perpetuity), while there is a 50% chance of it producing a cash flow of only $80 000 per year forever (a perpetuity) if it isn't received well. The required rate of return you use to discount the project cash flows is 10%. However, if the new restaurant is successful, you will be able to build four more of them and they will have costs and cash flows similar to the successful restaurant's cash flows. If your new restaurant is not received favourably, you will not expand. Ignoring the fact that there would be a time delay in building the additional new restaurants if the project were favourably received, determine the project's NPV.

In analysing this problem, we recognise that if the new restaurant is favourably received, the PV of the perpetual cash flows is 320 000/0.1 = 3 200 000, giving an NPV of 3 200 000 – 2 400 000 = $800 000.

In contrast, if the new restaurant is unfavourably received, the PV of the perpetual cash flows is 80 000/0.1 = 800 000, giving the project an NPV of 800 000 – 2 400 000 = –$1 600 000.

Obviously, if the first restaurant is not a success, you will not build any more restaurants. On the other hand, if the first one proves to be a success, you have an option to build more restaurants.

Graphically, this project can be presented as follows:

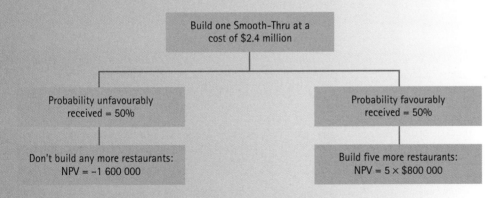

Assuming that you will open five Smooth-Thru restaurants if the first is favourably received and only one if it is not, and that each of these outcomes has a 50% probability, the expected NPV is:

Expected NPV = (0.5 × 5 × 800 000) + (0.5 × 1 × –1 600 000) = $1 200 000

Without the option to expand, you will only have one restaurant (even if that restaurant is a success). As a result, the NPV of the project without the option to expand is:

NPV = (0.5 × 800 000) + (0.5 × –1 600 000) = $400 000

Adding the option to expand allows the firm to take advantage of the increased certainty that the project will be received favourably and expand on it. This partially explains why many large restaurant chains introduce new theme restaurants in the hope that they succeed. If they do, the chain can open additional new restaurants or franchise them.

THE OPTION TO REDUCE THE SCALE AND SCOPE OF A PROJECT

The option to reduce the scale and scope of an investment is the mirror image of the option to expand. In the face of worse than expected performance, it is very valuable to have the option to slow down or contract production, shut it down temporarily until prospects for the investment improve, or abandon the investment altogether.

The existence of this type of flexibility or optionality can greatly reduce the risks associated with the investment and thereby increase the project's value. To illustrate, let's go back to our example of the new hydride battery used in hybrid automobiles and, this time, examine the option to abandon the project. Assume that after a few years of production of the new batteries the cost of petrol falls dramatically, while the cost of producing the batteries remains high. Under these circumstances the manufacturer may decide first to scale back production and then, ultimately, to abandon the project and sell the technology, including all the patent rights it has developed. To the extent that the technology has value in applications other than hybrid automobiles, and to the extent that the manufacturer can realise value from the sale of the technology and patent rights, the original investment risk is minimised.

Concept check

13.11   What are real options and how do they relate to the notion of managerial flexibility?

13.12   Contrast the option to expand with the option to contract. When would you expect the option to contract to be most valuable?

For answers go to MyFinanceLab or
www.pearson.com.au/9781442539174

Summary

OBJECTIVE 1

A project's NPV estimate is simply an estimate. We therefore need to perform a project risk analysis of NPV before making the final accept/reject decision. This is particularly important as project cash flows are risky and forecasts are made by humans and so can be either too optimistic or too pessimistic.

OBJECTIVE 2

A project's risk can be looked at on three different levels: the project's stand-alone risk, the project's contribution-to-firm risk and the project's systematic risk. If the firm has a well-diversified portfolio of projects and the firm's shareholders have a well-diversified portfolio of different stocks, the relevant measure of risk for capital-budgeting purposes is systematic risk.

OBJECTIVE 3

Two commonly used methods for incorporating risk into capital budgeting are (1) the certainty-equivalent method, and (2) risk-adjusted discount rates. The certainty-equivalent approach involves a direct attempt to incorporate the decision maker's utility function into the analysis. Under this method, cash flows are adjusted downward by multiplying them by certainty-equivalent coefficients, α_t's, which transform the risky cash flows into equivalent certain cash flows in terms of desirability. A project's net present value using the certainty-equivalent method for adjusting for risk becomes

$$NPV = \sum_{t=1}^{n} \frac{\alpha_t ACF_t}{(1 + k_{rf})^t} - IO \tag{13-3}$$

The risk-adjusted discount rate involves an upward adjustment of the discount rate to compensate for risk. This method is based on the concept that investors demand higher returns for riskier projects.

OBJECTIVE 4

There are a number of approaches to assist the financial manager in analysing the risk of a project. In sensitivity analysis, the NPV is recalculated assuming a change in a certain input variable. This process allows the analyst to identify the input variable that the project NPV is most sensitive to. With scenario analysis, the analyst develops alternative sets of estimates for each of the input variables that correspond to sets of circumstances that the analyst thinks might occur in order to see how the investment might perform in those circumstances. The simulation and probability-tree methods are used to provide information as to the location and shape of the distribution of possible outcomes. Decisions can be based directly on these methods, or they can be used to determine input into either certainty-equivalent or risk-adjusted discount method approaches.

Opportunities to alter the project's cash-flow stream after the project has begun are commonly referred to as real options and include the flexibility to alter an investment's scale, scope and timing. Three of the most common types of options that can add value to a capital-budgeting project are (1) the option to delay a project until the future cash flows are more favourable—an option that is common when the firm has exclusive rights, perhaps a patent, to a product or technology; (2) the option to expand a project, perhaps in size or even to include new products that would not have otherwise been feasible; and (3) the option to abandon a project if the future cash flows fall short of expectations.

OBJECTIVE 5

Key terms

certainty equivalent	445	risk-adjusted discount rate	445
probability tree	462	scenario analysis	457
project's contribution-to-firm risk	442	sensitivity analysis	454
project's stand-alone risk	442	simulation analysis	459
pure play method	453	systematic risk	442
real options	464		

For a complete flashcard glossary go to MyFinanceLab at www.pearson.com.au/myfinancelab

Web works

You have decided to use the pure play method for estimating a project's beta. Let's assume that your new product is in the pharmaceutical industry. That means the first thing you'll have to do is calculate the beta on a drug company that most closely matches your new product. Let's choose *Pfizer*. To do this use the *MSN Money* site (**http://investing.money.msn.com/investments/company-report**), which is a research site for the Microsoft network. If you have the company's ticker symbol, which is a unique one-to-four place alphabetical 'nickname' (for *Pfizer* the ticker symbol is 'pfe'), you can go to the company report which provides a one-page overview of the company, including its beta.

You can also find the beta on *Yahoo! Finance* by following these steps:
1. From the Yahoo! home page (**www.yahoo.com**), choose 'Yahoo! Finance'.
2. Enter the ticker symbol in the search box and select the company from the automatic drop-down box.
3. On the left-hand side menu click on 'Key Statistics'.
4. The table under the heading 'Trading Information' will contain information about the company's beta.

Just as with *MSN Money*, in order to get the information for a given firm, you need to know its ticker symbol. The *MSN Money* site is a place to find the ticker symbol if you don't know it. Let's look up four companies using both *MSN Money* and *Yahoo! Finance*:
- Hewlett-Packard Company (HPQ)
- Wells Fargo & Company (WFC)
- Walt Disney Co. (DIS)
- Texas Instruments Inc. (TXN)

What do you think the betas would be for these companies? Remember that the beta of the market is 1.0; less risky companies would be less than 1, and more risky ones would be more than 1. Were you close? Are the betas on both sites the same? Why might there be differences in the betas?

Review questions

13-1 What is the objective of project risk analysis and why is it critical to the investment decision-making process?

13-2 The preceding chapter examined the payback-period capital-budgeting criterion. Often this capital-budgeting criterion is used as a risk-screening device. Explain the rationale behind its use.

13-3 What are the similarities in and the differences between the risk-adjusted discount rate method and the certainty-equivalent method for incorporating risk into the capital-budgeting decision?

13-4 Explain why equivalent riskless cash flows, obtained by applying the certainty equivalents, should be discounted at the risk-free rate, not the project's required rate of return.

13-5 When can the firm's beta be used as a measure of a project's systematic risk? If the firm's beta cannot be used, how can a project's beta be measured?

13-6 How do you perform sensitivity analysis and what is its purpose? How is sensitivity analysis different from scenario analysis?

13-7 What is simulation? What is the merit in using a simulation approach?

13-8 Discuss the five-step process used to carry out a simulation analysis of project risk.

13-9 What is the merit of using the probability-tree technique for evaluating capital-budgeting projects?

13-10 'The original NPV of a project may be understated because it overlooks the possibility of delaying, expanding or abandoning the project in the future.' Discuss.

Self-test problems

For answers go to MyFinanceLab
www.pearson.com.au/myfinancelab

ST-1 The United Company is considering two mutually exclusive solar-energy projects to be commenced in 2011. Both require an initial outlay of $25 000 and will operate for five years. The probability distributions associated with each project for years 1 to 5 are given below:

CASH FLOW, YEARS 1–5

PROJECT A		PROJECT B	
PROBABILITY	CASH FLOW	PROBABILITY	CASH FLOW
0.20	$10 000	0.20	$6 000
0.60	15 000	0.60	18 000
0.20	20 000	0.20	30 000

Because project B is the riskier of the two projects, United's management has decided to apply a required rate of return of 18% to its evaluation, but only a 12% required rate of return to project A.

(a) Determine the expected value of each project's cash flows.
(b) Determine each project's risk-adjusted net present value.

ST-2 The firm of Gemmology Ltd is considering two mutually exclusive projects. The expected values for each project's cash flows are as follows:

YEAR	PROJECT A	PROJECT B
0	–$300 000	–$300 000
1	100 000	200 000
2	200 000	200 000
3	200 000	200 000
4	300 000	300 000
5	300 000	400 000

The company has decided to evaluate these projects using the certainty-equivalent method. The certainty-equivalent coefficients for each project's cash flows are:

YEAR	PROJECT A	PROJECT B
0	1.00	1.00
1	0.95	0.90
2	0.90	0.80
3	0.85	0.70
4	0.80	0.60
5	0.75	0.50

Given that this company's normal required rate of return is 15% and the risk-free rate is 8%, which project should be selected?

ST-3 Imperial Properties owns two adjacent four-unit apartment buildings that are both on 5000 square metres of property in Hawthorn, Victoria. One of the properties is in very good condition and the apartments can be rented for $2000 per month. The units in the other property require some refurbishing and in their current condition can only be rented for about $1500 per month.

Recent zoning changes, combined with changes in market demand, suggest that both lots can be redeveloped. If they are redeveloped, the existing units would be torn down and new luxury apartment buildings would be built on the site, each with 10 apartment units. The cost of the 10-unit buildings is estimated to be $1.5 million and each of the 10 units can be rented for $2500 per month under current market conditions. Similar properties that have been refurbished are selling for 10 times their annual rentals. Identify the real options in this example.

Problems

13-1 *(Risk-adjusted NPV)* Denway Motors is evaluating two mutually exclusive projects, both of which require an initial outlay of $400000. Each project has an expected life of six years. The cash flows associated with these projects are uncertain but the management team has been able to determine the probability distribution of cash flows. The probability distributions associated with the annual cash flows from each project are given below:

For more problems and for answers to problems marked with an asterisk (*) go to MyFinanceLab at www.pearson.com.au/myfinancelab

CASH FLOW, YEARS 1–5

	PROJECT A		PROJECT B
PROBABILITY	CASH FLOW	PROBABILITY	CASH FLOW
0.10	$70000	0.10	$40000
0.40	95000	0.20	50000
0.40	80000	0.40	75000
0.10	85000	0.20	80000
		0.10	110000

The normal required rate of return for Denway Motors is 9%, but because these projects are riskier than the average project Denway Motors is requiring a higher-than-normal rate of return on them. On project A it is requiring a 12% rate of return and on project B a 15% rate of return.

  (a) Determine the expected value for each project's cash flows.
  (b) Determine each project's risk-adjusted net present value.
  (c) What other factors might be considered in deciding between these projects?

13-2 (*Certainty equivalents*) The following cash flows are estimates for a project that Nova Construction is considering:

TIME	EXPECTED CASH FLOWS	EQUIVALENT RISK-FREE CASH FLOWS
0	−$4 000 000	−$4 000 000
1	2 500 000	2 200 000
2	2 000 000	1 500 000
3	1 500 000	800 000
4	1 000 000	450 000

Calculate the certainty-equivalent coefficients for these cash flows.

13-3* (*Certainty equivalents*) The firm of Wheelock is considering two mutually exclusive projects. The expected values for each project's cash flows are given below:

YEAR	PROJECT A	PROJECT B
0	−$1 000 000	−$1 000 000
1	500 000	500 000
2	700 000	600 000
3	600 000	700 000
4	500 000	800 000

The management has decided to evaluate these projects using the certainty-equivalent method. The certainty-equivalent coefficients for each project's cash flows are estimated below:

YEAR	PROJECT A	PROJECT B
0	1.00	1.00
1	0.95	0.90
2	0.85	0.75
3	0.80	0.65
4	0.75	0.50

Given that this company's normal required rate of return is 15% and the risk-free rate is 5%, which project should be selected?

13-4 (*Certainty equivalents*) Henderson Land Ltd has decided to use the certainty-equivalent method in determining whether or not a new investment should be made. The expected cash flows associated with this investment and the estimated certainty-equivalent coefficients are as follows:

YEAR	EXPECTED VALUES FOR CASH FLOWS	CERTAINTY-EQUIVALENT COEFFICIENTS
0	−$100 000	1.00
1	30 000	0.95
2	25 000	0.90
3	30 000	0.83
4	20 000	0.75
5	25 000	0.65

Given that Henderson Land's normal required rate of return is 15% and that the risk-free rate is 8%, should this project be accepted?

13-5 (*Certainty equivalents*) Fraser & Neave is considering two mutually exclusive projects. The expected values for each project's cash flows are given below:

YEAR	PROJECT A	PROJECT B
0	–$1 500 000	–$1 500 000
1	800 000	950 000
2	750 000	1 200 000
3	750 000	300 000
4	400 000	200 000

Fraser & Neave has decided to evaluate these projects using the certainty-equivalent method. The certainty-equivalent coefficients for each project's cash flows are as follows:

YEAR	PROJECT A	PROJECT B
0	1.00	1.00
1	0.90	0.95
2	0.90	0.75
3	0.70	0.60
4	0.65	0.50

Given that this company's normal required rate of return is 12% and the risk-free rate is 6%, which project should be selected?

13-6* (*Risk-adjusted discount rates and risk classes*) Artha Securities is examining two capital-budgeting projects with six-year lives. The first, project A, is a replacement project; the second, project B, is a project unrelated to current operations. The company uses the risk-adjusted discount rate method and groups projects according to purpose and then uses a required rate of return or discount rate that has been pre-assigned to that purpose or risk class. The expected cash flows for these projects are given below:

	PROJECT A	PROJECT B
Initial investment	$350 000	$500 000
Cash inflows:		
Year 1	$40 000	$155 000
Year 2	55 000	135 000
Year 3	60 000	140 000
Year 4	95 000	135 000
Year 5	135 000	140 000
Year 6	150 000	135 000

The purpose/risk classes and pre-assigned required rates of return are as follows:

PURPOSE	REQUIRED RATE OF RETURN (%)
Replacement decision	12
Modification or expansion of existing product line	15
Project unrelated to current operations	18
Research and development (R&D) expenditures	20

Determine the projects' risk-adjusted net present values.

13-7 (*Risk-adjusted discount rates and risk classes*) Hathaway Engines is a producer of motor-vehicle components. It is considering two separate projects for implementation. The two projects have the same time lives of six years but are entirely different in nature. Project Red is looking at the viability of replacing an assembly machine, while Project Gold is considering an R&D project for a new type of engine that is more fuel-efficient than existing engines. The cash flows of the two projects have been estimated as follows:

YEAR	PROJECT RED	PROJECT GOLD
0	–$1 000 000	–$5 000 000
1	450 000	0
2	450 000	0
3	350 000	2 000 000
4	350 000	2 000 000
5	250 000	2 500 000
6	250 000	2 500 000

The company's schedule for required rates of return associated with different risk classes is:

PURPOSE	REQUIRED RATE OF RETURN
Replacement decision	10%
Modification or expansion of existing product line	13%
Project unrelated to current operations	18%
Research and development operations	22%

(a) Calculate the NPV for the Red project.
(b) Calculate the NPV for the Gold project.

13-8* (*Risk-adjusted NPV*) Parkway Holdings Ltd is evaluating two mutually exclusive projects, both of which require an initial outlay of $100 000 on food-production equipment. Each project has an expected life of five years. The probability distributions associated with the annual cash flows from each project are given below:

CASH FLOW, YEARS 1–5

PROJECT A		PROJECT B	
PROBABILITY	CASH FLOW	PROBABILITY	CASH FLOW
		0.10	$10 000
0.10	$35 000	0.20	30 000
0.40	40 000	0.40	45 000
0.40	45 000	0.20	60 000
0.10	50 000	0.10	80 000

The normal required rate of return for Parkway Holdings is 10%, but because these projects are riskier than most, they are requiring a higher than normal rate of return on them. On project A they are requiring a 12% rate of return and on project B a 13% rate of return.

(a) Determine the expected value for each project's cash flows.
(b) Determine each project's risk-adjusted net present value.
(c) What other factors might be considered in deciding between these projects?

13-9 (*Risk-adjusted discount rate and certainty equivalents*) Neustal Ltd is considering a new project that is deemed to have a higher level of risk than existing projects. As a result, risk adjustment has to be made in coming up with a decision on whether this project is worth undertaking. The cash flows for the project have been estimated as follows:

TIME	CASH FLOWS
0	–$5 000 000
1	2 000 000
2	2 000 000
3	2 500 000
4	2 500 000
5	1 500 000

The normal required rate of return for Neustal is 12% p.a. However, since this project is deemed to be more risky, the required rate of return on this project has been determined to attract a 4% risk premium. In addition, the following certainty-equivalent coefficient schedule is widely used in the company for capital-budgeting purposes:

YEAR	CERTAINTY-EQUIVALENT COEFFICIENT
0	1
1	0.95
2	0.90
3	0.80
4	0.70
5	0.60

(a) Calculate the NPV of the project using the risk-adjusted method.
(b) Calculate the NPV of the project using the certainty-equivalent approach using a risk-free rate of 6% p.a.

13-10 (*Sensitivity analysis*) Pulse Pharmaceuticals is considering a substantial investment in the research and development of a treatment to slow down the balding process in humans. The treatment will cost $200 000 million to develop and revenue is expected to be $80 million in the first year. Total ongoing expenses are estimated to be 20% of sales. Revenue is expected to grow at the rate of 5% p.a. for five years. The discount rate for the project is 14% p.a.

(a) Calculate the NPV for the project based on the current estimate of 5% growth in sales.
(b) Perform a sensitivity analysis on the NPV of the project using a 10% growth rate and a 0% growth rate.

13-11 (*Scenario analysis*) Botanical Care is a cosmetic company that produces a range of skin-care and hair-care products using botanical ingredients. It aims to add to the existing range a new product called Animal, which is a gel-based product to be used on pets. Financial analysts predict that the product can stay in the market for five years, although at this stage it is uncertain as to whether the product will be favourably received by the market. They have also provided the following annual estimates:

	EXPECTED OR BASE CASE	UNFAVOURABLE	FAVOURABLE
Unit sales	30 000	5 000	50 000
Price per unit ($)	15	10	22
Variable cost per unit ($)	1.5	2	1.1
Annual cash fixed cost ($)	185 000	185 000	185 000

The discount rate is 8%. Perform a scenario analysis for the Animal project.

13-12 (*Scenario analysis*) Family Security is considering introducing tiny GPS trackers that can be inserted in the sole of a child's shoe, which would then allow for the tracking of that child if he or she was ever lost or abducted. The estimates, which might be off by 10% (either above or below), associated with this new product are:

Unit price	$125
Variable costs per unit	$75
Annual fixed costs	$250 000
Expected sales p.a.	10 000

Since this is a new product line, you are not confident in your estimates and would like to know how well you will fare if your estimates on the items listed above are 10% higher or 10% lower than expected. Assume that this new product line will require an initial outlay of $1 million, with no working-capital investment, and will last for 10 years, being depreciated down to zero using straight-line depreciation. In addition, the firm's required rate of return or cost of capital is 10%, while the firm's marginal tax rate is 34%.

Calculate the project's NPV under the 'best-case scenario' (that is, use the high estimates—unit price 10% above expected, variable costs 10% less than expected, fixed costs 10% less than expected, and expected sales 10% more than expected). Similarly, calculate the project's NPV under the 'worst-case scenario'.

13-13 (*Probability trees*) NOL Ltd is evaluating an investment proposal with an expected life of two years. This project will require an initial outlay of $1 500 000. The resultant possible cash flows are given below.

Possible outcomes in year 1:

	PROBABILITY		
	0.6	0.3	0.1
	Outcome 1	Outcome 2	Outcome 3
Cash flow =	$700 000	$850 000	$1 000 000

Conditional outcomes and probabilities for year 2:

If ACF_1 = $700 000		If ACF_1 = $850 000		If ACF_1 = $1 000 000	
ACF_2	Probability	ACF_2	Probability	ACF_2	Probability
$300 000	0.3	$400 000	0.2	$600 000	0.1
700 000	0.5	700 000	0.4	900 000	0.5
1 100 000	0.2	1 000 000	0.2	1 100 000	0.4
		1 300 000	0.2		

(a) Construct a probability tree representing the possible outcomes.
(b) Determine the joint probability of each possible sequence of events taking place.
(c) What is the expected IRR of this project?
(d) What is the range of possible IRRs for this project?

13-14* (*Probability trees*) The Swat Company is considering an investment project in a new type of fly spray, with an expected life of two years. The initial outlay on this project would be $600 000, and the resultant possible cash flows are given below.

Possible outcomes in year 1:

	PROBABILITY		
	0.4	0.4	0.2
	Outcome 1	Outcome 2	Outcome 3
Cash flow =	$300 000	$350 000	$450 000

Conditional outcomes and probabilities for year 2:

If ACF_1 = $300 000		If ACF_1 = $350 000		If ACF_1 = $450 000	
ACF_2	Probability	ACF_2	Probability	ACF_2	Probability
$200 000	0.3	$250 000	0.2	$300 000	0.2
300 000	0.7	450 000	0.5	500 000	0.5
		650 000	0.3	700 000	0.2
				1 000 000	0.1

(a) Construct a probability tree representing the possible outcomes.
(b) Determine the joint probability of each possible sequence of events taking place.
(c) What is the expected IRR of this project?
(d) What is the range of possible IRRs for this project?

13-15 (*Probability trees*) The Concourt Company is considering expanding its operations into computer-based basketball games. The managers feel that there is a three-year life associated with this project, and it will initially involve an investment of $100 000. They also believe that there is a 60% chance of success and a cash flow of $100 000 in year 1, and a 40% chance of failure and a $10 000 cash flow in year 1. If the project fails in year 1, there is a 60% chance that it will produce cash flows of only $10 000 in years 2 and 3. There is also a 40% chance that it will really fail and the company will earn nothing in year 2 and get out of this line of business, with the project terminating and no cash flow occurring in year 3. If, conversely, the project succeeds in the first year, then cash flows in the second year are expected to be $200 000, $175 000 or $150 000, with probabilities of 0.30, 0.50 and 0.20 respectively. Finally, if the project succeeds in the third and final year of operation, the cash flows are expected to be either $30 000 more or $20 000 less than they were in year 2, with an equal chance of occurrence.

(a) Construct a probability tree representing the possible outcomes.
(b) Determine the joint probability of each possible sequence of events.
(c) What is the expected IRR?
(d) What is the range of possible IRRs for this project?

13-16 (*NPV and probabilities*) Norseman is a mining firm based in Western Australia. One of its core activities is to develop minefields. Currently it is considering a project to develop a minefield in the Gibson Desert. The success of this project is largely dependent on the economy of China, where most of Norseman's ores are exported to. According to market research that Norseman has paid $200 000 for, the project will require an investment of $2 000 000 for extraction rights and the necessary equipment. It also shows that the project has a 60% chance of succeeding, in which case Norseman will get an annual net cash flow of $850 000 for 10 years. If the project fails, Norseman will receive only $20 000 in the first two years and nothing after that because of the closure of the mine. Norseman requires a 9% return on projects of this type. What is the NPV of the project?

13-17 (*Comprehensive risk analysis*) Blinkeria is considering introducing a new line of hand scanners that can be used to copy material and then download it into a personal computer. These scanners are expected to sell for an average price of $100 each, and the company analysts performing the analysis expect that the firm can sell 100 000 units per year at this price for a period of five years, after which time they expect demand for the product to end as a result of new technology being introduced. In addition, variable costs are expected to be $20 per unit, while fixed costs, not including depreciation, are forecast to be $1 000 000 per year. To manufacture this product, Blinkeria will need to buy a computerised production machine for $10 million that has no residual or salvage value, and will have an expected life of five years. In addition, the firm expects it will have to invest an additional $300 000 in working capital to support the new business. Other pertinent information concerning the business venture is provided below:

Initial cost of the machine	$10 000 000
Expected life	5 years
Salvage value of the machine	$0
Working capital requirement	$300 000
Depreciation method	Straight line
Depreciation expense	$2 000 000 per year
Cash fixed costs—excluding depreciation	$1 000 000 per year
Variable costs per unit	$20
Required rate of return or cost of capital	10%
Tax rate	34%

(a) Calculate the project's NPV.
(b) Determine the sensitivity of the project's NPV to a 10% decrease in the number of units sold.
(c) Determine the sensitivity of the project's NPV to a 10% decrease in the cost per unit.

(d) Determine the sensitivity of the project's NPV to a 10% increase in the variable costs per unit.

(e) Determine the sensitivity of the project's NPV to a 10% increase in the annual fixed operating costs.

(f) Use scenario analysis to evaluate the project's NPV under worst- and best-case scenarios for the project's value drivers. The values for the expected or base case along with the worst- and best-case scenarios are listed below:

	EXPECTED OR BASE CASE	WORST CASE	BEST CASE
Unit sales	100 000	70 000	130 000
Unit price	$100	$90	$120
Variable costs per unit	$30	$32	$27
Annual fixed costs	$1 000 000	$1 200 000	$900 000
Depreciation expense	$2 000 000	$2 000 000	$2 000 000

13-18 (*Real options and capital budgeting*) You are considering introducing a new Tex-Mex-Thai fusion restaurant. The initial outlay on this new restaurant is $6 million and the present value of the free cash flows (excluding the initial outlay) is $5 million, such that the project has a negative expected NPV of $1 million. Looking more closely, you find that there is a 50% chance that this new restaurant will be well received and will produce annual cash flows of $800 000 per year forever (a perpetuity), while there is a 50% chance of it producing a cash flow of only $200 000 per year forever (a perpetuity) if it isn't received well. The required rate of return you use to discount the project cash flows is 10%. However, if the new restaurant is successful, you will be able to build 10 more of them and they will have costs and cash flows similar to the successful restaurant cash flows.

(a) In spite of the fact that the first restaurant has a negative NPV, should you build it anyway? Why or why not?

(b) What is the expected NPV for this project if only one restaurant is built but isn't well received? What is the expected NPV for this project if 10 more are built after one year and are well received?

13-19 (*Real options and capital budgeting*) Go-Power Batteries has developed a high-voltage, nickel-metal hydride battery that can be used to power a hybrid automobile and it can sell the technology immediately to Toyota for $10 million. Alternatively, Go-Power Batteries can invest $50 million in a plant and produce the batteries itself and sell them. Unfortunately, the present value of the cash flows from such a plant would be only $40 million, such that the plant has a negative expected NPV of –$10 million. The problem, Go-Power executives recognise, is the small size of the market for hybrid cars today. Under what assumptions might Go-Power Batteries decide not to sell the technology to Toyota and delay investment in the new plant?

Case study

It's been four months since you took a position as an assistant financial analyst at Caledonia Products. During that time, you've had a promotion and are now working as a special assistant for capital budgeting to the CEO. Your latest assignment involves the analysis of several risky projects. Because this is your first assignment dealing with risk analysis, you have been asked not only to provide a recommendation on the projects in question but also to respond (in writing) to a number of questions aimed at judging your understanding of risk analysis and capital budgeting:

1. In capital budgeting, risk can be measured from three perspectives. What are those three measures of a project's risk?

2. According to the CAPM, which measurement of a project's risk is relevant? What complications does reality introduce into the CAPM view of risk and what does that mean for our view of the relevant measure of a project's risk?

3. What are the similarities and differences between the risk-adjusted discount rate and certainty-equivalent methods for incorporating risk into the capital-budgeting decision?

4. Why might we use the probability-tree technique for evaluating capital-budgeting projects?

5. Explain how simulation works. What is the value of using a simulation approach?

6. What is sensitivity analysis and what is its purpose?

7. Caledonia Products is using the certainty-equivalent approach to evaluate two mutually exclusive investment proposals with an expected life of four years. The expected net cash flows are as follows:

YEAR	PROJECT A	PROJECT B
0	−$150000	−$200000
1	40000	50000
2	40000	60000
3	40000	60000
4	100000	50000

The certainty-equivalent coefficients for the net cash flows are as follows:

YEAR	PROJECT A	PROJECT B
0	1.00	1.00
1	.90	.95
2	.85	.85
3	.80	.80
4	.70	.75

Which of the two investment proposals should be chosen, given that the after-tax risk-free rate of return is 7%?

8. Caledonia is considering an additional investment project with an expected life of two years and would like some insights on the level of risk this project has, using the probability-tree method. The initial outlay on this project would be $600000, and the resultant possible cash flows are as follows.

Possible outcomes in year 1:

	PROBABILITY		
	.4	.4	.2
	Outcome 1	Outcome 2	Outcome 3
Cash flow =	$300000	$350000	$450000

Conditional outcomes and probabilities for year 2:

If ACF_1 = $300000		If ACF_1 = $350000		If ACF_1 = $450000	
ACF_2	Probability	ACF_2	Probability	ACF_2	Probability
$200000	0.3	$250000	0.2	$300000	0.2
300000	0.7	450000	0.5	500000	0.5
		650000	0.3	700000	0.2
				1000000	0.1

(a) Construct a probability tree representing the possible outcomes.

(b) Determine the joint probability of each possible sequence of events taking place.

(c) What is the expected IRR of this project?

(d) What is the range of possible IRRs for this project?

Learning objectives

After reading this chapter, you should be able to:

1. Understand the basic concepts underlying the cost of capital.
2. Understand the key factors influencing a company's weighted average cost of capital.
3. Describe the assumptions generally required to measure and use the weighted average cost of capital.
4. Calculate the weighted average cost of capital for a company.
5. Calculate a project-specific required rate of return as an alternative to the weighted average cost of capital.

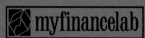

Cost of capital

CHAPTER PREVIEW

In this chapter the concepts behind the cost of capital are considered, as well as the procedures for estimating a company's weighted average cost of capital. For the time being it is assumed that a company finances its investment projects with a constant debt–equity mix. This assumption will be relaxed in Chapter 16 when the relationship between the company's capital structure mix of debt and equity and its cost of capital is considered.

Introduction

Having studied risk and rates of return (Chapter 9), the valuation of financial securities (Chapter 10) and capital budgeting (Chapters 11–13), we are now ready to connect the *investment decision*, concerned with determining which investment projects are acceptable, with the *financing decision*, concerned with determining the proportions of debt and equity finance to be used to fund the initial outlay of the investment projects being evaluated. The cost of capital is the connecting link, as it provides the percentage rate (RRR, i) that the NPV, PI and IRR evaluation methods use to determine whether the incremental cash flows of an investment project will increase shareholder wealth.

This is illustrated by a simple one-year investment project with an initial outlay of $100 000 that is expected to produce a cash inflow of $120 000 in one year's time, as represented by the following time diagram:

```
                          $120 000
            1 year      |
       ┌──────────────────┤
            10%
$100 000
```

All of the $100 000 for the initial outlay is to be provided by an investor who has a specified required rate of return of 10% per annum. For the firm to be able to repay at the end of one year the investor's $100 000 plus pay the 10% rate of return required by the investor ($100 000 × 10% = $10 000), the project has to produce a net cash inflow in a year's time of $110 000. We can therefore say that the cost for the firm to use the investor's $100 000 capital for one year is $10 000, or alternatively $10 000/$100 000 = 10% per annum.

If we use this 10% per annum cost of capital as the discount rate to calculate the project's net present value (NPV), the answer is +$9090:

$$NPV = -\$100\,000 + \frac{\$120\,000}{(1 + 10\%)} = \$9090$$

We can interpret the NPV amount of +$9090 in the following way. As this project is expected to provide a cash inflow of $120 000 in one year's time, there will be a surplus of $10 000 above the $110 000 that is required at the end of year 1 to satisfy the investor. This $10 000 surplus at the end of year 1 has a present value of $9090 when discounted at 10% per annum. Consequently, we can conclude that this project's expected cash flow will be sufficient to repay the investor's $100 000, pay the $10 000 return required by the investor, plus provide a surplus amount that represents the increase in wealth that the project will provide to the owners of the firm.

As this example shows, it is the investor's required rate of return that determines the firm's cost of capital and, by using this rate as the discount rate to evaluate investment projects, we can determine whether the project's expected cash inflows will be sufficient to pay all of the project's operating and financing costs plus add wealth to the owners of the firm. This is reflected in a positive NPV for the project.

FIGURE 14.1 Cost of capital: connecting investment and financing decisions

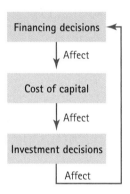

This chapter examines the concepts underlying the cost of capital and details the procedures for estimating a company's weighted average cost of capital. To do this we will assume that the proportions of debt and equity finance used by the company to fund its investment projects are kept constant. Then, in Chapter 16, this assumption will be relaxed and the impact of changing the capital-structure financing mix on the firm's cost of capital will be examined.

This connection between the investment and financing decisions is illustrated in Figure 14.1, which shows how financing decisions that change the source of finance the firm uses to fund its assets affect its cost of capital, which in turn affects which investment projects it will accept (investment decisions). The figure also shows that the riskiness of the investment projects that are selected can affect the firm's cost of capital, which in turn can influence the financing options available to the firm.

Regardless of your program

UNDERSTANDING THE ROLE OF THE COST OF CAPITAL

Imagine for a moment that your best friend comes to you with the news that she has just inherited a significant amount of money and is considering spending $500 000 to purchase a 'Just Snooze' franchise bedroom furniture store in your city. Since you have just studied capital budgeting you are aware of the need to forecast the relevant cash flows for the franchise, discount them back to the present and compare the discounted sum with the $500 000 initial outlay to determine the project's NPV. If the NPV is significantly positive, then you would advise your friend to buy the franchise.

The discount rate that you use to calculate the NPV should reflect the costs of raising the capital needed to finance the investment. As the initial investment in this case will be provided by your friend's inheritance, the cost of capital will be your friend's opportunity cost of the money. As your friend has lots of other opportunities to invest her money, the returns that are likely to be generated by the Just Snooze franchise need to be evaluated relative to those of other opportunities.

For example, she could put the money in the bank and earn a reasonable rate of interest without taking much risk, or she could make a risky investment by buying the listed shares in Just Snooze Limited for an expected return much higher than the interest rate.

Which of these investments would you use as the appropriate cost of capital for discounting the cash flows of the Just Snooze franchise? Quite obviously the risk of buying the Just Snooze franchise is greater than putting the money in the bank, so the expected rate of return from investing in Just Snooze Limited shares would be better to use as the discount rate to calculate the project's NPV. However, the risk from investing in Just Snooze Limited shares will also reflect how the company has financed its investments, which is not likely to be the same as how your friend would finance the Just Snooze franchise, so we need to think about the mix of financing sources used when evaluating the opportunity cost of capital and determining the discount rate to calculate a project's NPV.

The concept of the cost of capital

OBJECTIVE 1

Understand the basic concepts underlying the cost of capital.

The cost of capital can be looked at from two perspectives. When a firm borrows money it has to pay regular amounts of interest to the debt investors. Similarly, when it uses equity funds it has to make profits that can either be paid to the shareholders as dividends or be retained for future investment on behalf of the shareholders. For the firm to grow and prosper in the future, it needs to ensure that it has sufficient cash inflows to pay the costs (interest and profits/dividends) of using the debt and equity capital that investors have provided to it.

This leads to the second perspective, that the amount of the firm's cost of capital is determined by the amount of return that investors require for them to provide debt and equity finance to the firm. Although the investors receive their return from the firm either as interest or as dividend and capital-gains amounts, it is usual for these amounts to be expressed as a proportion of the amount invested, giving a percentage rate of return.

Linking the two perspectives together, it is the rate of return required by investors that determines the firm's cost of capital. Therefore, the cost of capital becomes the minimum rate of return that the firm must earn on its investment projects in order to be able to pay the rate of return investors require to compensate them for the risk their investment in the firm exposes them to.

Evaluating investment projects

The cost of capital is the rate of return that the firm must earn on the capital invested in projects if it wants to keep the investors providing the capital satisfied. The firm can ensure its investment projects are able to do this by using the cost of capital as the discount rate to evaluate investment projects. Projects with a positive NPV have cash flows that are able to repay the capital invested, pay the costs of the capital invested and also provide the firm's owners with some extra value. The NPV is the present value amount of this extra value and represents the increase in the wealth of the firm's owners.

Apart from using the cost of capital as the discount rate to calculate a project's NPV, it can also be used as the required rate of return (RRR) to evaluate investment projects by comparison with the project's internal rate of return (IRR).

If a project's cash flows result in an internal rate of return (IRR) that is exactly equal to RRR (i.e. the project's cost of capital), we can conclude that the project's net cash inflows are just sufficient to only repay the amount of capital invested and to pay the costs of this capital. Consequently, the project would not increase the wealth of the firm's owners which for a company would be reflected in no change in the share price.

However, if the project's internal rate of return (IRR) is different from the cost of capital (i.e. project RRR), we would expect the price of the company's shares to change (increase if IRR > RRR, decrease if IRR < RRR). In Figure 14.2, the internal rates of return for projects A, B and C exceed the company's cost of capital (i.e. RRR), so these projects should be accepted, which would require total capital of $17 million. In contrast, projects D and E should be rejected, because the firm is paying more for the costs of its capital (RRR) than it is earning

FYI

You will find that in this text and often in practice there are a number of different names used to refer to the cost of capital. For example, the *cost of capital* is frequently used interchangeably with the *weighted cost of capital*, the *weighted average cost of* *capital (WACC)*, the *cost of finance*, the *cost of funds*, the *required rate of return of finance*, the *hurdle rate for new investments*, the *discount rate for evaluating a new investment*, and the *opportunity cost of funds*.

(IRR), which would result in a fall in the company' share value. Consequently, we can identify that *the maximum cost of capital for a company will be equal to the rate of return from the investment project that will result in the price of the company's ordinary shares remaining unchanged.* This is why the cost of capital is sometimes called the *hurdle rate*, because unless investment projects can earn a rate of return (i.e. IRR) that can *hurdle* over this cost of capital (i.e. RRR) they should be rejected.

You may have noticed in Figure 14.2 that the line representing the cost of capital is upward sloping; the reasons for this will be discussed in later chapters.

The capital structure of the Salinas Company, detailed in Table 14.1 shows that the company is using three sources of capital—debt, preference shares and ordinary shares—totalling $2 000 000.

The company's management is now considering an investment project that would require an initial outlay of $200 000 and is expected to produce cash inflows that generate an internal rate of return (IRR) of 14% per annum. Assume that the current percent per annum cost of each source of capital (equal to the investors' required rates of return) has been determined to be:

Cost of debt	10%
Cost of preference shares	12%
Cost of ordinary shares	16%

Given this information, should the company make the new investment? The lenders and preference shareholders would probably encourage the company to undertake the project, because it will generate sufficient cash flows (14%) to pay the returns they require (10% and

FIGURE 14.2   Investment and financing schedules

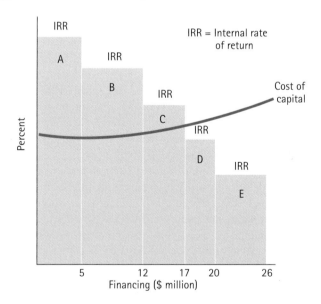

TABLE 14.1   Salinas Company capital structure

	AMOUNT	% OF CAPITAL STRUCTURE
Debt	$600 000	30
Preference shares	200 000	10
Ordinary shares	1 200 000	60
Total liabilities and equity	$2 000 000	100

12%). However, because the 14% internal rate of return on the initial investment is less than the ordinary shareholders' required rate of return of 16%, shareholders might argue that the project should not be accepted. How does the financial manager resolve these differences?

First, the financial manager would need to know what percentage of the project's initial outlay of $200000 is to be provided by each type of investor. If the same capital structure mix (30% debt, 10% preference shares and 60% ordinary shares), as reflected in Table 14.1, is to be maintained, a weighted average cost of capital can be calculated, with the weights equal to the percentage of capital to be provided by each source.

For this example, the weighted average cost of the individual sources of capital, as computed in Table 14.2, is 13.8% per annum.

TABLE 14.2 Salinas Company weighted average cost of capital

	WEIGHT (% OF FINANCING)	COST OF INDIVIDUAL SOURCES	WEIGHTED COST
Debt	30	10%	3.0%
Preference shares	10	12%	1.2%
Ordinary shares	60	16%	9.6%
	100	Weighted cost of capital	13.8%

What does this weighted average cost of capital of 13.8% p.a. mean for investment project evaluation? It means that any investment that produces an internal rate of return (IRR) of at least 13.8% p.a. will be able to pay the proportionate annual costs of each source of finance used to fund the investment's initial outlay. So, for the investment project with a 14% p.a. internal rate of return, we can conclude that it should be implemented because this project's cash inflows will be able to repay the $200000 initial outlay, pay the costs of the debt, preference share and equity capital used to fund the initial outlay, and provide some surplus (= 14% − 13.8%) for the shareholders.

As the IRR evaluation concluded that the project is acceptable, the ordinary shareholders can expect to receive the 16% p.a. return they require for the equity capital they provided *plus* the surplus the project is expected to generate. Consequently, as each share, which gives an entitlement to this surplus, is now more valuable, an increase in the ordinary share price would be expected.

As most companies tend to use both debt and ordinary share capital to finance their investment projects, the *cost of capital* is a shorthand reference to the weighted average cost of capital. Later sections will provide more detail of the calculation of the components that comprise the weighted average cost of capital.

BUT WHAT IF?

Using the weighted average cost of capital as the discount rate to evaluate (NPV, IRR) investment projects may be fine in theory, but what if a company could use cheaper debt for the entire amount needed for the investment project's initial outlay? Is it really necessary to use the weighted average cost of capital, or would it be alright to make the decision based simply on the cost of debt? The answer to this question is NO! The reason is detailed below.

Consider the example of the Aussie Company whose management believes that purchasing $500000 in new equipment could be expected to generate an IRR of 15% p.a. Aussie Company's financial officer has estimated the cost of ordinary equity capital to be 18% p.a. Although the company usually finances its projects with equal amounts of debt and equity, the company's bank is willing to lend the entire $500000 at an interest rate of 12% p.a. Without even having to do any calculations, management knows that the company's earnings per share and share price should increase if the project earns an IRR of 15% p.a., as it exceeds the 12% p.a. cost of the debt capital.

Because the company can finance the project fully by debt, management has decided to proceed and borrows the $500 000 from the bank at 12% p.a. The investment is made, and all seems well.

The following year management has a new investment project costing $500 000 that has an expected internal rate of return of 17% p.a. When management approaches the bank for financing, they find the bank is unwilling to lend any more money as the company has used up all of its *debt capacity*. The only way the company can raise the $500 000 for the new project is to issue new ordinary shares. However, as the new investment project's rate of return of 17% p.a. does not exceed the cost of equity of 18% p.a., management believes that it should not issue new shares to fund the project and decides to reject the project.

What is the moral of the story for Aussie Company? Intuitively, it can be seen that Aussie's management has made a mistake, because using all its debt capacity to proceed with the investment project in the first year has denied it the opportunity to invest in the second year in a project with a higher internal rate of return.

What should the company's management have done? As a general rule, the cost of a single source of debt or equity finance should never be used as the hurdle rate (discount rate) for capital-budgeting decisions. As this example shows, when a company uses debt for a project, it has implicitly used up some of its capacity to raise new debt for future investment projects. Only when the company complements the use of debt capital with equity capital will it be able to continue to use more debt in the future.[1]

Although sometimes it is only practical for a company to fund the initial outlay of a particular project with either all debt or all equity capital, the correct discount rate to evaluate the project is the **weighted average cost of capital** and not the cost of an individual source of capital.

weighted average cost of capital
A composite of the individual costs of financing incurred by each capital source. A firm's weighted average cost of capital is a function of (1) the individual costs of capital, and (2) the capital structure mix.

For answers go to MyFinanceLab or
www.pearson.com.au/9781442539174

Concept check

14.1 Define the concept of an investor's required rate of return.

14.2 How is the investor's required rate of return related to the firm's cost of capital?

14.3 What is meant by the phrase 'a firm's weighted average cost of capital'?

14.4 Why should the weighted average cost of capital be used to evaluate an investment project when only one source of finance (e.g. debt) is used to fund the initial outlay?

OBJECTIVE **2**

Understand the key factors influencing a company's weighted average cost of capital.

Factors determining the weighted average cost of capital

Before examining in detail the calculation of the weighted average cost of capital, we need to consider the elements in the business environment that at a particular time cause the costs of the individual sources of capital to be high or low.

Figure 14.3 identifies four primary factors that influence the cost of individual sources of capital: general economic conditions, the marketability of the firm's securities (market conditions), operating and financing conditions within the firm, and the amount of financing needed for new investments.

As the costs of capital are determined by the required rates of return of investors, we can relate these four variables to the discussion in Chapter 9, where an investor's required rate of return was seen as comprising a risk-free rate plus a risk premium.

The right-hand margin of Figure 14.3 presents an illustration of what determines the cost of capital for a particular source of finance, which could be debt or equity. The starting point is the risk-free rate, determined by the general economic conditions (e.g. 9% p.a.). Owing to the additional risk associated with this source of finance, the firm has to earn an additional return (e.g. 7% p.a.) above the risk-free rate, resulting in the investors' required rate of return of 16%, which is equal to the firm's cost of capital.

Following is a brief look at each of the factors that impact on the risk-free and risk premium components comprising the cost of a particular source of capital.

FIGURE 14.3   Primary factors influencing the cost of particular sources of capital

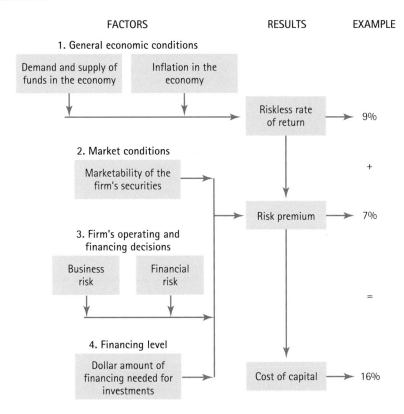

FACTOR 1: GENERAL ECONOMIC CONDITIONS

General economic conditions determine the demand for and supply of capital within the economy, as well as the level of expected inflation. This economic variable is reflected in the interest rate on short-term government securities, which are commonly used as the risk-free rate of return. If, for example, the demand for money in the economy increases without an equivalent increase in supply, lenders will raise their required interest rate. Similarly, if inflation is expected, investors will require a higher rate of return to compensate for the anticipated purchasing power loss.[2]

FACTOR 2: MARKETABILITY CONDITIONS

To invest capital in a firm, investors usually purchase a firm's debt and equity securities. As these investments expose the investors to risk, they will require a return in addition to the risk-free rate. The difference between this higher rate and the risk-free rate is called the **risk premium**.

    If a security is not readily marketable when the investor wants to sell, or even if a continuous demand for the security exists but its price fluctuates significantly, investors will require a relatively higher risk premium. Conversely, a lower risk premium will be required for securities that are readily marketable and have a reasonably stable price.

    As the firm's cost of capital is determined by investors' required rates of return, when investors increase their required rate of return the firm's cost of capital rises simultaneously.

risk premium
The additional return expected for assuming risk.

FACTOR 3: FIRM'S OPERATING AND FINANCING DECISIONS

Decisions made within the firm that affect the variability of cash flows and the returns to investors will affect investor risk. The risk resulting from operating and financing decisions can be divided into two main types: business risk and financial risk.

business risk
The relative dispersion or variability in the firm's expected earnings before interest and taxes (EBIT). The nature of the firm's operations causes its business risk and is affected by the firm's cost structure, product demand characteristics and intra-industry competitive position. In capital-structure theory, business risk is distinguished from financial risk.

financial risk
The added variability in earnings available to the firm's ordinary shareholders and the added chance of insolvency caused by the use in the firm's financial structure of securities bearing a limited rate of return. The use of financial leverage gives rise to financial risk.

cost of capital
The rate that must be earned in order to satisfy the required rate of return of the firm's investors. It may also be defined as the rate of return on investments at which the price of the firm's ordinary shares will remain unchanged. The cost of capital is based on the opportunity cost of funds as determined in the capital markets.

flotation (issue) costs
The underwriter's spread and issuing costs associated with the issuance and marketing of new securities.

Business risk is reflected in the variability of operating cash flows and is partly determined by the extent of fixed operating costs resulting from investment decisions. **Financial risk** is the increased variability in cash flows and returns resulting from the use of debt or preference share finance. Both of these forms of risk are explained in more detail in Chapter 15, but we can conclude that, as business risk and financial risk increase or decrease, investors' required rate of return (and thus the firm's **cost of capital**) will move in the same direction.

FACTOR 4: AMOUNT OF FINANCING

As the amount of financing that the firm requires increases, the costs of sources of capital can increase, for the following reasons.

When more debt and equity securities are issued to raise finance, the **flotation (issue) costs** that are incurred can affect the percentage cost of the funds to the firm.[3]

If a firm approaches the market for large amounts of capital relative to the firm's size, suppliers of capital become hesitant to invest without clear evidence of the firm's ability to manage a large investment and generate sufficient cash flows. As a result of the increased risk that investors face, there is an increase in the rate of return they require.

As the value of an issue of securities increases, there can be greater difficulty in selling the securities to the market without reducing the security price. As will be shown later in the chapter, this reduction in price has the effect of increasing the firm's cost of capital.

GFC

LIQUIDITY

During normal economic conditions financial markets facilitate the transfer of money from investors who have a surplus of funds to entities that have a deficit of funds, with the return/cost of capital being the link between the two. However, at the height of the Global Financial Crisis there was a period when fear among investors that they would lose their money saw the flow of money (liquidity) in the financial markets virtually grind to a halt. This rare and extreme phenomenon meant that even if a business had a viable investment project that could generate cash flows to pay the costs of capital it could not obtain finance from the financial markets. As the GFC has receded, we have gradually witnessed the return to liquidity of the market.

OBJECTIVE 3

Describe the assumptions generally required to measure and use the weighted average cost of capital.

Assumptions of the weighted average cost of capital

Before examining in detail how to determine the costs of debt and equity capital, we need to address some simplifying assumptions that underlie the combination of these costs into the weighted average cost of capital.

CONSTANT BUSINESS RISK

As a general principle, the cost of a particular source of debt or equity capital is determined by the rate of return that investors providing that capital require to compensate them for the risk their investment will expose them to. A component of this risk is the firm's current business risk, which is determined by management's investment policies, particularly the impact of fixed operating costs on the variability of earnings.

This raises the problem that, if the level of the firm's business risk will be altered by an investment decision, investors will respond by changing their required rates of return, which in turn will change the firm's cost of capital, which in turn will change the discount rate that should be used to evaluate the investment project.

In practice, it is difficult to assess the amount of change in the firm's cost of capital that will result from a given increase or decrease in business risk. For this reason, when calculating a firm's weighted average cost of capital we will usually assume that any investment project under consideration will not significantly change the firm's business risk or investors' required rates of return.

Importantly, this means that *the firm's weighted average cost of capital can be used as the appropriate discount rate only for an investment project that has a business risk level similar to the business risk of the firm's existing assets.*

If an investment project will significantly change the firm's business risk, then the financial manager will need to alter (up or down) the weighted cost of capital measure used as the discount rate to evaluate the project. There is no clear guidance as to how much this alteration should be, and in practice it is the result of the application of experience and professional judgement.

CONSTANT FINANCIAL RISK

Financial risk was defined as the increased variability in returns on ordinary shares that results from the increased use of debt and preference share financing.[4] So, if the firm borrows too much debt finance, which requires regular payment of principal and interest amounts, there is the increased risk of financial distress or, in the extreme case, bankruptcy. This increased risk is reflected in an increase in the rates of return required by debt, preference share and ordinary share investors.

For this reason, we will assume that the firm will keep its financial risk constant by funding its investment projects in the same proportions of debt and equity as its existing capital structure. This means that the weighted average cost of capital calculated using the current mix of financing in the firm's capital structure will be the appropriate discount rate at which to evaluate investment projects.

CONSTANT DIVIDEND POLICY

A third assumption underlying the weighted average cost of capital calculation relates to the dividend policy of a company. As will be seen in a later section, we will generally assume that future dividend amounts will increase at a constant annual growth rate. Also, we will assume that this dividend growth rate is a function of the company's earning capabilities and not merely the result of paying out a larger percentage of the company's profits. That is, we will implicitly assume that the company's dividend payout ratio (dividends/net income) will be constant.

Computing the weighted average cost of capital

OBJECTIVE 4

Calculate the weighted average cost of capital for a company.

As a general principle, a firm's weighted average cost of capital is a composite of the costs of each source of finance, weighted by the percentage of finance provided from each source. So, for example, a company that is financed by 40% debt at a 10% p.a. cost and 60% ordinary equity at a cost of 18% p.a. will have a weighted average cost of capital equal to $0.40 \times 10\% + 0.60 \times 18\% = 14.8\%$ p.a.

Therefore, to compute the weighted average cost of capital in practice, there are three major steps:

1. Determine the cost of each source of finance. This cost will be obtained by either observing directly the current interest rate or yield for debt or by using valuation models to estimate the rate of return required by preference and ordinary share investors. Although our examples calculate a single cost for each of debt, preference shares and ordinary shares, in practice a company's cost of debt may comprise the weighted costs of a number of different debt instruments. Similarly, the company may not have issued preference shares, so that its weighted average cost of capital only comprises the cost of debt and cost of ordinary equity.

FIGURE 14.4 Basic steps in computing the weighted average cost of capital

1. Compute the cost of capital for each and every source of financing (i.e. each source of debt, preference shares and ordinary shares).

2. Determine the percentage of debt, preference shares and ordinary shares to be used in the financing of future investments.

3. Calculate the firm's weighted average cost of capital using the percentage of financing as the weights.

2. Determine the percentage of total capital that will be provided by each source of capital in the broad categories of debt, preference shares and ordinary shares.

3. Using the individual costs and the capital-structure percentages in the first two steps, compute an overall or weighted average cost of capital.

This basic approach to calculating the weighted average cost of capital is summarised in Figure 14.4.

In reality, determining some of the components for steps 1 and 2 is not straightforward. One complication involves including in step 1 the effect of taxation on the costs of finance which is discussed next.

TAXATION CONSIDERATIONS

To include the impact of the Australian dividend imputation system on shareholder wealth, Chapters 2 and 11 classified Australian firms into three taxation categories, as summarised below:

- **Taxation category 1** comprises companies where the Australian dividend imputation tax system results in company income tax deductions being of no value to the after-tax wealth of shareholders. As a consequence, it is recommended that these companies evaluate the pre-tax cash flows of capital investment projects by using a pre-tax cost of capital as the discount rate.
- **Taxation category 2** includes two main groups of business entities:
  (a) Non-company firms (sole traders and partnerships), where the owners pay personal taxes on the firm's net income. As the owners of these firms can maximise their after-tax wealth by maximising the firm's tax deductions, it is recommended that the firm evaluate the after-tax cash flows of investment projects by using an after-tax cost of capital as the discount rate, with the relevant tax rate being the marginal personal income-tax rate of the owners.
  (b) Australian companies whose shareholders are unable to use the value of franking (imputation) credits. As these companies are effectively subject to a classical tax system it is recommended that the after-tax cash flows from their investment projects be evaluated by using the company's after-tax cost of capital as the discount rate.
- **Taxation category 3** comprises Australian companies between taxation categories 1 and 2, as they have an *effective tax rate* that lies between zero (category 1) and the statutory company tax rate T (category 2). Capital-budgeting evaluation for these companies requires identification of the project's after-*effective*-tax cash flows that are evaluated with the cost of capital computed on an after-*effective*-tax basis used as the discount rate. A major practical issue for companies in taxation category 3 is to determine their effective tax rate. As this is an issue beyond the scope of this textbook, the following discussion will only examine the impact of taxation on the weighted average cost of capital for taxation category 1 and taxation category 2 entities.

Step 1: Determining individual costs of capital

Although in today's financial markets there are a large variety of instruments that firms can use to obtain finance, this chapter examines just the three major representative types of finance: bond-type debt, preference shares and ordinary shares. Also, as it is only companies that are able to issue preference and ordinary shares, the following discussion focuses predominantly on determining the cost of capital for a large publicly listed company, although it is important to remember that the general cost of capital principles also apply to non-company firms.

As discussed earlier, the reason for calculating the cost of capital is *to determine the rate of return the company must earn on its investments to ensure it can pay the required rates of return of the investors who provide the capital.*

COST OF DEBT

The focus in this section will be on determining the cost of debt finance raised from bond-type instruments (corporate bonds, debentures and notes); other debt instruments such as term loans and leases are discussed in Chapter 18.

Applying the general principle outlined above, the cost of debt will be equal to the *rate of return required by the providers of debt* (also known as *creditors*).

In Chapter 10 we obtained the required rate of return of bond investors by solving for R_b, either by a trial-and-error process or with the use of a financial calculator. Equation (14-1) represents this process, except that we now have replaced the symbol b (bonds) with d (debt) to reflect the focus on the cost of debt.

$$P_0 = \frac{I_1}{(1 + R_d)^1} + \frac{I_2}{(1 + R_d)^2} + \dots + \frac{I_n}{(1 + R_d)^n} + \frac{M}{(1 + R_d)^n}$$ **(14-1)**

$$P_0 = I_t(PVIFA_{R_d,n}) + \$M(PVIF_{R_d,n})$$

where P_0 = the market price of the debt
I_t = the annual dollar interest paid to the investor
M = the maturity value of the debt
R_d = the required rate of return of the debt investor
n = the number of years to maturity

As a starting point, we can take R_d as being the firm's cost of bond-type debt finance. However, before we can use this as the cost of debt in the evaluation of investment projects, we need to consider the implications of the interest paid for debt finance being tax-deductible.

To correctly include these tax implications it is necessary to determine the taxation category of the firm that is intending to raise the debt finance because this will determine whether a before-tax or after-tax cost of debt is required.

Before-tax cost of debt (taxation category 1 companies)

For this category of Australian company, shareholder wealth is not affected by company tax deductions for interest. Consequently, the relevant cost of debt is before-tax which will be equal to the rate of return (R_d) required by the company's debt investors. Example 14.1 illustrates this calculation.

EXAMPLE 14.1   Calculation of before-tax cost of debt

Assume that debt investors are willing to pay $90.83 for debentures issued by Ash Company that have a $100 par value, pay 8% in annual coupons (interest) and mature in 20 years. Using equation (14-1) to solve for R_d the debenture investors' required rate of return is 9% p.a.

$$\$90.83 = \sum_{t=1}^{20} \frac{\$8}{(1 + 0.09)^t} + \frac{\$100}{(1 + 0.09)^{20}}$$

As the company pays the debenture coupon amounts from its before-tax cash flows, the required rate of return (R_d) of 9% p.a. calculated above is the company's before-tax cost of debt ($K_{d,BT}$). This means that for every dollar of debt capital used to finance investment projects, the company must earn at least 9 cents before-tax each year in order to pay the 9% p.a. rate of return that the debt investors require.

Usually when a firm issues new debt there are costs other than interest that it must pay. The effect of issue costs that are normally paid upfront by the company is to reduce the amount of finance it receives from the debt issue, which thereby increases its cost of debt. Consequently, for bond-type instruments, the *net price* after issue costs should be used in place of the market price to solve for the before-cost of debt to the company ($K_{d,BT}$), as shown in equation (14-2).

$$NP_0 = \sum_{t=1}^{n} \frac{I_t}{(1 + K_{d,BT})^t} + \frac{M}{(1 + K_{d,BT})^n} \tag{14-2}$$

where NP_0 represents the net amount received by the company from issuing each unit of debt.

In equation (14-2), $K_{d,BT}$ has been used in place of R_d to reflect the focus on solving for the *before-tax* cost of debt that includes the effect of issue costs. The remaining variables retain their meaning from equation (14-1).

The impact of issue costs is to increase the before-tax cost of debt. For example, if Ash Company only receives $85 per debenture after issue costs, it still has to pay the same amount of coupon interest. Using equation (14-2) to obtain $K_{d,BT}$:

$$\$85 = \sum_{t=1}^{20} \frac{\$8}{(1 + K_{d,BT})^t} + \frac{\$100}{(1 + K_{d,BT})^{20}}$$

$$= \$8(PVIFA_{K_{d,BT},20}) + \$100(PVIF_{K_{d,BT},20})$$

We can solve for $K_{d,BT}$ by trial and error using present-value tables. As the net price of $85 received by the company is below the market price of $90.83 in Example 14.1, the company's before-tax cost of debt must be above 9% due to the inverse relationship between price and yield. Trying 10% gives a present value of $83.01, which is a little lower than the target of $85. On this result we can conclude that the before-tax cost of debt is between 9% and 10%. To be more accurate, we would need to use interpolation, as follows:

RATE	VALUE		DIFFERENCES IN VALUES	
9%	$90.83			
			$5.83	
$K_{d,BT}$	$85.00 net proceeds			$7.82
10%	$83.01			

Solving for $K_{d,BT}$ by interpolation,

$$K_{d,BT} = 9\% + \frac{\$5.83}{\$7.82}(10\% - 9\%) = 9.75\%$$

Solving for $K_{d,BT}$ by using a financial calculator gives 9.73%.
We have now determined that Ash Company's before-tax cost debt from issuing new debentures is 9.73% p.a.[5]

Calculator solution

DATA INPUT		FUNCTION KEY
85		PV
8	+/−	PMT
100	+/−	FV
20		N
FUNCTION KEY		ANSWER
COMP I/Y		9.73(%)

Back to the principles

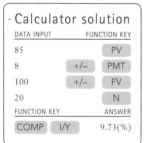

The bond investor's required rate of return is the discount rate that produces a present value of the bond's coupon and principal amounts exactly equal to the bond's current price in the financial markets. In essence, we are valuing the bond, which relies on two basic principles of finance: **Principle 1: The risk–return trade-off**—we won't take on additional risk unless we expect to be compensated with additional return, and **Principle 2: The time value of money**—a dollar received today is worth more than a dollar received in the future.

In addition, the calculation of the bond investor's required rate of return relies on the observed market price of the company's bonds being an accurate reflection of their worth. Buyers and sellers only stop trading when they are convinced that the price properly reflects all available information (**Principle 6: Efficient capital markets—the markets are quick and the prices are right**). This means that investors are ever vigilant and quickly act on information that affects the riskiness and consequently the price of a firm's bonds and other securities.

After-tax cost of debt (taxation category 2 companies)

As the reduction in the tax payable by these firms resulting from the tax deduction of interest increases in after-tax wealth of the firm's owners, the after-tax cash flows expected from investment projects should be evaluated with an after-tax cost of capital. Accordingly, this will require the after-tax cost of debt to be determined as follows.

As every \$1 of interest paid by the firm results in a reduction of the firm's tax liability equal to \$1 times the firm's marginal tax rate, the after-tax cost of debt ($K_{d,AT}$) is equal to:

$$K_{d,AT} = K_{d,BT}(1 - T) \qquad \textbf{(14-3)}$$

where, depending on the firm, T = marginal tax rate for individuals or the statutory company tax rate.

If Ash Company in the previous example were in taxation category 2, with a statutory company tax rate, T, of 30%, its after-tax cost to issue new debt would be:

$$K_{d,AT} = 9.73\% \ (1 - 0.30) = 6.81\% \text{ p.a.}$$

This after-tax cost of debt of 6.81% p.a. means that for every dollar of new debt finance invested in a project Ash Company must earn each year from the project *after-tax* cash flows of at least 6.81 cents, to ensure it can pay all the costs associated with the debt raised by the new debenture issue.

How can the company's after-tax cost of debt of 6.81% p.a. be lower than the 9.73% p.a. rate of return that debt investors require? Because the government by allowing interest payments to be tax-deductible provides the company and its owners with a tax subsidy to use debt finance, whereas payments to owners (e.g. dividends) for the use of equity finance are not tax-deductible. Another way at looking at the effect of this tax subsidy for interest payments is that it enables more of an investment project's return to be available for the owners, which results in an increase in the owners' wealth.

Back to the principles

The tax-deductibility of interest expense makes debt finance less costly to the firm. However, whether this cost saving translates to an increase in the wealth of a company's shareholders depends on the taxation system. This is an example of **Principle 8: Taxes bias business decisions.**

COST OF PREFERENCE SHARES

Determining the cost of raising finance by issuing preference shares follows the same basic principle as for the cost of debt. The objective is to determine the *rate that must be earned by the company to pay the rate of return that preference share investors require.*

In Chapter 10 we saw that the value of an irredeemable preference share, P_0, promising a constant dividend per year, was defined as follows:

$$P_0 = \frac{\text{dividend}}{\text{required rate of return for a preference shareholder}} = \frac{D}{R_p} \qquad \textbf{(14-4)}$$

Rearranging equation (14-4), the required rate of return for a preference shareholder, R_p can be found by:

$$R_p = \frac{\text{dividend}}{\text{market price}} = \frac{D}{P_0} \qquad (14\text{-}5)$$

For example, if Ash Company had previously issued irredeemable preference shares that paid 15 cents in annual dividends and currently sell in the share market for $1.50, the rate of return required by the company's existing preference shareholders would be:

$$R_p = \frac{\$0.15}{\$1.50} = 10\%$$

Because the company pays preference dividends from its after-tax income, the previously calculated R_p of 10% p.a. is the *after-tax* cost of existing preference shares ($R_{p,AT}$).

However, when the company issues new preference shares the *after-tax* cost of preference shares, $R_{p,AT}$ will be higher due to the impact of issue costs.

After-tax cost of issuing new preference shares (taxation category 2 companies)

Ash Company intends to issue new preference shares at a price of $1.50 per share that will pay the same dividend as existing preference shares of $0.15 per share. However, as the company will incur costs of $0.15 per share to issue the new preference shares, it will receive a net amount of $1.35 for each new preference share (designated NP_0), rather than the full $1.50 market price.

Therefore, the after-tax cost of new preference shares, $K_{p,AT}$, will be:

$$K_{p,AT} = \frac{\text{dividend}}{\text{net price}} = \frac{D}{NP_0} \qquad (14\text{-}6)$$

$$K_{p,AT} = \frac{\$0.15}{\$1.35} = 11.11\%$$

This rate of 11.11% p.a. means that, to pay the issue costs and dividend for the new preference shares, the company must generate each year from the investment project earnings after tax of 11.11 cents for every dollar of preference share capital raised.

Sometimes companies issue redeemable preference shares that have a finite life. For these shares, the cost is calculated in the same manner as illustrated earlier for the cost of debt, with the only difference being a finite number of preference divided amounts instead of amounts for coupons and principal.

Before-tax cost of issuing new preference shares (taxation category 1 companies)

A major feature of the Australian dividend imputation system is that preference and ordinary share dividends can have franking (imputation) credits. As taxation category 1 companies have shareholders who can fully utilise the value of imputation credits, the recommendation is to evaluate the before-tax cash flows from investment projects with a before-tax weighted average cost of capital. Therefore, a taxation category 1 company that issues new preference shares will need to determine a before-tax cost of preference shares. This requires grossing up the preference dividend amount to a before-tax value, as illustrated below.

If Ash Company's preference dividend of 15 cents per share is fully franked and shareholders can utilise the value of the franking credits, then if the company tax rate is 30% the company has to generate before-tax earnings of 21.43 cents per share to be able to pay the 15 cents per share preference dividend.

Before-tax income necessary to pay the dividend	21.43 cents
Less: Company tax ($T = 0.30$)	6.43 cents
After-tax dividend	15.00 cents

Alternatively, the grossed-up preference dividend amount can be calculated as:

$$\frac{\$0.15}{1 - 0.3} = 21.43 \text{ cents}$$

To take into account issue costs when the company issues new preference shares, the formula for calculating the before-tax cost of new preference share finance ($K_{p,BT}$) becomes:

$$K_{p,BT} = \frac{D/(1 - T)}{NP_0} \qquad \textbf{(14-7)}$$

For example, if it costs Ash Company 15 cents to issue each new preference share with a market price of $1.50, the before-tax cost of preference shares will be:

$$= \frac{\$0.15/(1 - 0.30)}{\$1.35} = \frac{0.2143}{1.35} = 0.1587$$

This cost of 15.87% p.a. means that the investment project must generate earnings before taxes of 15.87 cents for every dollar of new preference share capital invested in the project.[6]

COST OF ORDINARY EQUITY

We have seen that to raise new capital with bond-type debt or preference shares the company has to sell new securities to investors, which incurs issue costs. However, to raise new equity capital from ordinary shareholders the company has two alternatives. The first is to avoid issue costs by using retained earnings that comprise the earnings (profit) of the company that are not paid to the ordinary shareholders as a dividend. The second is to incur issue costs by selling new shares to investors. As retained earnings have historically represented a major source of equity capital for many companies, the following sections will separately determine (1) the cost of ordinary equity when sourced from retained earnings, and (2) the cost of ordinary equity when raised by an issue of shares.

COST OF ORDINARY EQUITY PROVIDED BY RETAINED EARNINGS

When a company's board of directors decides to retain some or all of a year's profits, they are serving in a *fiduciary* capacity to the shareholders, because they are effectively investing the money that belongs to the shareholders as it has not be paid to them as dividends. If the company's objective is to maximise the wealth of its ordinary shareholders, profits should only be retained if the company can invest the money in projects that can provide a rate of return that is at least as good as the shareholders' next best investment opportunity.[7] If the company's investment projects can't satisfy this requirement, shareholders should demand that all profits be paid to them as dividends so that they have the opportunity to invest this money more profitably themselves.

In reality, it is not feasible for management to know the rates of return that all shareholders require from their alternative investment opportunities. However, we can use the readily available data of ordinary share prices and dividend amounts to infer the rate of return that a company's ordinary shareholders as a whole currently require. This underlying process is the basis of the two alternative approaches (the dividend growth valuation model approach and the CAPM approach) used to measure the required rate of return of existing ordinary shareholders and thus to estimate the cost for a company of obtaining new ordinary equity capital.

(a) Dividend growth valuation model approach

In Chapter 10 the intrinsic value of an ordinary share was defined as being equal to the present value of the expected future dividends, discounted at the ordinary shareholders' *required rate of return*. Since an ordinary share has no maturity date, these dividends were assumed to extend to infinity and were modelled by a perpetuity. For an investor with a required rate of return of R_E, the value of an ordinary share (P_0), promising dividends of D_t in year t, was calculated by:

$$P_0 = \frac{D_1}{(1 + R_E)^1} + \frac{D_2}{(1 + R_E)^2} + \cdots + \frac{D_n}{(1 + R_E)^n} + \frac{D_\infty}{(1 + R_E)^\infty}$$ **(14-8)**

We can observe the current market price of the share (P_0), and if we could estimate all future dividends (D_t) to infinity, equation (14-8) could be rearranged to solve for R_E. However, in reality, trying to estimate the amounts of an infinite stream of dividends is impossible. But, if it is reasonable to assume that all future dividend amounts will increase at a constant annual rate of growth (g) that is less than the shareholder's required rate (R_E), then we can rearrange the constant dividend growth valuation model and estimate R_E as follows:[8]

$$R_E = \frac{\text{dividend in year 1}}{\text{market price}} + \text{annual growth rate in dividends}$$ **(14-9)**

$$= \frac{D_1}{P_0} + g$$

Remember from Chapter 10 that D_1 is the estimate of the dividend amount at the end of future period 1. As the value of the last dividend per share (D_0) paid by the company should be observable, equation (14-10) can be used to estimate the expected rate of return for ordinary shareholders, given the anticipated growth rate of dividends (g) and the current market price of the shares (P_0):

$$R_E = \frac{D_1}{P_0} + g = \frac{D_0 (1 + g)}{P_0} + g$$ **(14-10)**

EXAMPLE 14.2   Calculation of ordinary shareholders' required rate of return using the dividend growth valuation model

Ash Company's ordinary shareholders recently received a dividend (D_0) of 20 cents per share, and they expect dividends to grow (g) at a constant annual rate of 10%. If the current market price of the company's ordinary shares (P_0) is $4.40, the existing ordinary shareholders' required rate of return can be estimated (from 14-10) as:

$$R_E = \frac{\$0.20(1.10)}{\$4.40} + 0.10$$

$$= \frac{\$0.22}{\$4.40} + 0.10$$

$$= 0.15 = 15\%$$

Back to the principles

The dividend growth valuation model for ordinary share valuation relies on three of the fundamental principles of finance. First, share value is equal to the present value of the expected future dividends. This reflects: **Principle 2: The time value of money—a dollar received today is worth more than a dollar received in the future**. Furthermore, dividends represent actual cash receipts to shareholders and are incorporated into the valuation model in a manner that reflects the timing of their receipt. This attribute of the dividend growth valuation model reflects **Principle 3: Cash—not profits—is king**. Finally, the rate used to discount the expected future dividends back to the present reflects the riskiness of dividends. The higher the riskiness of dividend payments, the higher the investor's required rate of return. This reflects **Principle 1: The risk–return trade-off—we won't take on additional risk unless we expect to be compensated with additional return**.

Before-tax cost of retained earnings (taxation category 1 companies)

Under the Australian dividend imputation system, ordinary share dividends can have franking (imputation) credits. For a taxation category 1 company with shareholders who can utilise the value of these franking credits, it is recommended to evaluate the before-tax cash-flow amounts expected from an investment project with a before-tax weighted average cost of capital.

To calculate the *before-tax cost of ordinary equity* ($R_{E,BT}$), the grossed-up (i.e. before-tax) value of ordinary dividends needs to be used in the dividend growth valuation model. If the ordinary dividends are fully franked $R_{E,BT}$ can be easily calculated using equation (14-11):

$$R_{E,BT} = \frac{D_0\,(1 + g)/(1 - T)}{P_0} + g \qquad \textbf{(14-11)}$$

As there are no issue costs with retained earnings, no further adjustment is needed for the ordinary shareholders' before-tax required rate of return ($R_{E,BT}$) to be used as the company's before-tax cost of retained earnings, $K_{RE,BT}$.

EXAMPLE 14.3 **Calculation of before-tax cost of retained earnings using the dividend growth valuation model**

Assume that Ash Company is a taxation category 1 company. The company's ordinary shareholders recently received a fully franked dividend of 20 cents per share, and they expect future fully franked dividend amounts to grow at an annual rate of 10%. If the current market price of each ordinary share is $4.40 and the company tax rate (T) is 30%, the ordinary shareholders' before-tax required rate of return using equation (14-1) would be:

$$K_{RE,BT} = \frac{\$0.20(1.10)/(1 - 0.30)}{\$4.40} + 0.10$$

$$= \frac{\$0.31}{\$4.40} + 0.10$$

$$= 0.17 = 17\%$$

This rate of 17% p.a. means that for each dollar of retained earnings used to fund the investment project, the company will need to generate before-tax net cash flows of 17 cents each year in order to be able to pay the constantly growing future dividend amounts required by ordinary shareholders.

After-tax cost of retained earnings (taxation category 2 companies)

As the Ash Company in Example 14.3 was assumed to be a taxation category 1 company, we needed to estimate the before-tax cost of retained earnings. However, if the company were in taxation category 2 so that its shareholders could not utilise the value of franking credits, an after-tax cost of retained earnings would need to be included in the calculation of the company's after-tax weighted average cost of capital.

The after-tax cost of retained earnings is estimated by equation (14-10) because it uses after-tax dividend amounts. So, the after-tax cost of retained earnings for the Ash Company is 15% p.a. as calculated in Example 14.2.

As many companies *aim* to continually grow the dividend amounts paid to ordinary shareholders, the dividend growth valuation model is useful to estimate the required rate of return of ordinary shareholders. However, the practical difficulty in using this model is estimating what the growth rate for future dividends (g) should be.

(b) CAPM approach

An alternative way to estimate the required rate of return on ordinary equity that avoids having to estimate the dividend growth rate (g) is to use the capital asset pricing model (CAPM) (outlined in Chapters 9 and 13). According to the CAPM, the rate of return that ordinary share investors require (R_E) comprises the risk-free rate (R_f) plus a risk premium $\beta(R_m - R_f)$ appropriate for the level of systematic risk (beta) associated with the investment:

$$R_E = R_f + \beta(R_m - R_f) \tag{14-12}$$

where R_E = the required rate of return of the ordinary shareholders
$\quad\quad R_f$ = the risk-free rate
$\quad\quad \beta$ = beta, or the measure of the share's systematic risk
$\quad\quad R_m$ = the expected rate of return for the market as a whole

---

EXAMPLE 14.4 **Calculation of ordinary shareholders' required rate of return using the CAPM**

Assume that the risk-free rate is 7% p.a. and the average expected rate of return in the market is 17% p.a. If Ash Company's ordinary shares have a beta of 0.74, we can use the CAPM to estimate the required rate of return of the company's ordinary shareholders as:

$$R_E = R_f + \beta(R_m - R_f)$$
$$= 7\% + 0.74\,(17\% - 7\%) = 14.4\%$$

After-tax cost of retained earnings (taxation category 2 companies)

The rate of 14.4% p.a. calculated in Example 14.4 is Ash Company ordinary shareholders' *after-tax* required rate of return because it has been calculated using an estimate of the systematic risk of *after-tax* returns to shareholders (β). So, for a taxation category 2 company, the after-tax cost of retained earnings, $K_{RE,AT}$, will be equal to this CAPM estimate of R_E, as no adjustments are required for issue costs.

Before-tax cost of retained earnings (taxation category 1 companies)

The R_m value that was used in the CAPM calculation in Example 14.4 represents the average rate of return that investors require from the market portfolio. If we look more closely at what comprises this market return, it largely reflects components for the return provided by the dividends and capital gains from a broad portfolio of companies. For example, assume that in Example 14.4 the R_m of 17% comprises a rate of return of 6% from fully franked dividends and a rate of return from capital gains of 11%. However, as dividends are paid from the after-tax profits of companies, this dividend rate of 6% is an after-tax value. Therefore, to determine the before-tax rate of return from fully franked dividends, the 6% after-tax dividend rate needs to be grossed up[9] (6%/[1 − 0.30] = 8.57%). This means that investors currently require a before-tax rate of return of 8.57% from dividends paid by companies comprising the market portfolio. Assuming no taxation adjustment is required to the estimate of the before-tax return from capital gains, the before-tax value for R_m to be used in the CAPM will be equal to 8.57% + 11% = 19.57% p.a.

EXAMPLE 14.5   Calculation of before-tax cost of retained earnings using the CAPM

The before-tax return that shareholders require from investing in the market portfolio, (R_m), has been estimated to be 19.57% p.a. Using the CAPM, Ash Company's before-tax return on ordinary equity and thus the cost of retained earnings would be estimated as:

$K_{RE,BT} = 7\% + 0.74\ (19.57\% - 7\%) = 16.3\%$

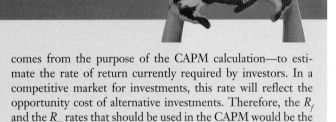

International spotlight

RISK-FREE RATE AND MARKET RETURN

To use the CAPM requires identification of the current yield on government bonds as a proxy for the risk-free rate (R_f) and the historical return on a broad-based share-market index as proxy for the return on the market portfolio (R_m). Adding an international perspective raises the questions of 'the yield on bonds issued by which government?' and 'the return from which share market?', because they will be different for each country. Some guidance to the answer to these questions

comes from the purpose of the CAPM calculation—to estimate the rate of return currently required by investors. In a competitive market for investments, this rate will reflect the opportunity cost of alternative investments. Therefore, the R_f and the R_m rates that should be used in the CAPM would be the risk-free rate and the market-portfolio rate that are competing for the funds of investors. Example 9.8 in Chapter 9 provides further details of how to estimate these rates in practice.

COST OF ORDINARY EQUITY PROVIDED BY A NEW SHARE ISSUE

If retained earnings do not provide all the equity capital needed for investment projects, the company has to issue new ordinary shares to obtain the additional equity capital. As was the case with retained earnings, the company should not raise new equity capital from shareholders unless the expected return from the investment projects being evaluated exceeds the costs of this source of equity capital.

In the previous sections, the required rate of return for ordinary shareholders (estimated via either the dividend growth valuation model or the CAPM) was used as the company's cost of retained earnings. However, to issue new shares to investors, the company incurs issue costs (which can be substantial amounts) that should be included in the calculation of the cost of ordinary equity from issuing new shares.

When a company issues new shares, the investors pay the issue price for each new share (P_0) and expect to receive future dividend amounts (D). However, from the company's perspective the issue costs reduce the amount of money it receives from the sale of the new shares to the net price per share, NP_0. As the company now has a reduced amount available to invest in new projects to generate the future dividend amounts, the effect is to increase the company's cost of ordinary equity. Depending on the tax category of the entity evaluating investment projects, the cost of ordinary equity provided by issuing new shares will need to be either a before-tax rate or an after-tax rate. The calculation of each using the dividend growth valuation model is outlined below.

Before-tax cost of issuing ordinary shares (taxation category 1 companies)

For a taxation category 1 company that pays fully franked dividends, the before-company-tax cost of issuing ordinary shares can be estimated by using the dividend growth valuation model, incorporating the grossed-up amount of the fully franked dividend, the estimated growth rate of fully franked dividends (g) and the net price from the sale of the shares (NP_0):

$$K_{E,BT} = \frac{D_0(1 + g)/(1 - T)}{NP_0} + g \qquad\qquad \textbf{(14-13)}$$

EXAMPLE 14.6 **Calculation of before-tax cost of issuing ordinary shares using the dividend growth valuation model**

Assume that Ash Company is a taxation category 1 company and intends to issue new ordinary shares to investors at a price of $4.40 but will incur issue costs equal to 3.4% of the share price. Accordingly, the share issue will provide the company with a net price per share of $4.25 ($4.40 minus 3.4% of $4.40). The company intends to maintain the same dividend per share and dividend growth rate as for Example 14.3. The before-company-tax cost of issuing new ordinary shares is estimated as:

$$K_{E,BT} = \frac{\$0.20(1.10)/(1 - 0.30)}{\$4.25} + 0.10$$

$$= \frac{\$0.31}{\$4.25} + 0.10$$

$$= 0.1729 = 17.29\%$$

The before-tax cost of issuing ordinary shares of 17.29% p.a. means that the company's investment projects must earn 17.29 cents for every dollar of the net proceeds ($4.25) raised from the new share issue to be able to pay the costs to issue the new shares and to pay the ordinary shareholders' before-tax required rate of return of 17 cents on every dollar they have invested (as determined in Example 14.3).

After-tax cost of issuing ordinary shares (taxation category 2 companies)
To determine an after-tax cost of issuing ordinary shares, the only adjustment to the dividend growth valuation model is to include the net share price (NP_0):

$$K_{E,AT} = \frac{D_0(1 + g)}{NP_0} + g \qquad \qquad \textbf{(14-14)}$$

EXAMPLE 14.7 **Calculation of after-tax cost of issuing ordinary shares using the dividend growth valuation model**

Assume that Ash Company is a taxation category 2 company and intends to issue new shares at a net price of $4.25 and maintain the same amount of dividend per share and dividend growth rate as in Example 14.3. The after-tax cost for the issue of new ordinary shares is estimated as:

$$= \frac{\$0.20(1.10)}{\$4.25} + 0.10$$

$$= \frac{\$0.22}{\$4.25} + 0.10$$

$$= 0.152 = 15.2\%$$

Concept check

14.5 How do you estimate the firm's cost of new debt financing?

14.6 What are the two approaches to estimating a firm's cost of equity financing?

14.7 What are issue (flotation) costs and how do they impact on a firm's cost of capital when it issues new bonds or equity?

For answers go to MyFinanceLab or
www.pearson.com.au/9781442539174

Now that we are able to estimate the costs of each of the major sources of debt and equity capital, the next step in the calculation of the weighted average cost of capital (WACC) is determining the capital structure weights.

Step 2: Determining capital-structure weights

In step 1 the individual costs of each major source of capital were estimated. These costs now have to be combined to calculate a single weighted average cost of capital value. To do this requires determining the proportions, or weights, of each individual type of capital used by the firm.

As a general principle, *the weights for computing the weighted average cost of capital should reflect the firm's financing mix in its current capital structure*. For example, if debt providers normally provide 30% of the company's long-term finance and ordinary shareholders provide the remaining 70%, these same financing-mix proportions should be used to calculate the weighted average cost of capital that will be used as the discount rate to evaluate new investment projects. However, determining the value of these financing weights is not quite so straightforward and there are some issues that need to be considered first.

(1) THE EFFECT OF CHANGING THE FINANCING MIX ON THE FIRM'S FINANCIAL RISK AND COSTS OF CAPITAL

As a general rule, the percentages of the different types of capital used to fund new investment projects should be the same as the percentages of the various sources of finance used to calculate the weighted average cost of capital. This is because, if management alters the percentages of debt and equity finance to fund new projects, the firm's financial risk will change, which in turn will change the return that existing and new debt and equity investors require, and thus change the individual costs of capital to be used to calculate the weighted average cost of capital.

This problem can be resolved if it is reasonable to expect that the firm's debt/equity financing mix is likely to be relatively stable over time. Consequently, the firm's weighted average cost of capital calculated with the current financing-mix proportions will be appropriate to use as the discount rate to evaluate new investment projects that can be expected to be financed with similar proportions of debt and equity.

In reality, though, companies often raise significant amounts of new debt and equity finance to fund new investment projects in amounts that cause the recent financing-mix proportions to change. When this occurs, the assumption of a stable debt–equity financing mix appears not to be appropriate for the calculation of the weighted average cost of capital. However, this may not be a major problem, because many companies have a **target capital structure** that reflects a desired debt–equity financing mix. Even though the company may temporarily depart from its target financing mix, over the longer term it will obtain new debt or equity finance to bring the proportions of debt and equity in its capital structure back to the target. Accordingly, it is this target financing-mix proportions that should be used as the weights to calculate the company's weighted average cost of capital.

target capital structure
A desired composition of fund sources in the firm's financial or capital structure.

EXAMPLE 14.8 Calculation of capital structure weights

Ash Company's current financing mix is shown in Table 14.3. As the company does not want to alter its financial risk, new investment projects will on average be financed with the same mix of funds. Given the assumption of a constant target financing mix, it is appropriate to use the current financing mix percentages as the weights to compute Ash Company's weighted cost of capital.

TABLE 14.3 Ash Company capital structure

	AMOUNT OF FUNDS RAISED	PERCENTAGE OF TOTAL
Debentures	$1 750 000	35
Preference shares	250 000	5
Retained earnings	1 000 000	20
Ordinary shares	2 000 000	40
Total financing	5 000 000	100

(2) MARKET VALUES INSTEAD OF BOOK VALUES TO DETERMINE FINANCING-MIX WEIGHTS

In Example 14.8, dollar values for the various sources of finance were used to determine the percentage weights. These dollar values should be the *current market values* (prices) of the firm's sources of finance and not the accounting or book values. This is because the required rates of return that debt and equity investors currently require are determined by the true risk of their investment. For example, investors would consider an equity investment in the company to be of high risk if debt finance comprised 90% of the company's total market value.

Book values, on the other hand, are a result of the accounting process that uses historical cost and other accounting conventions that are not appropriate for determining the risks and costs of debt and equity capital obtained from investors via the financial markets.

For a large company that has a bond-type debt and equity securities it has issued traded in the financial markets, determining current market values is relatively easy, being equal to the current market price per security (e.g. debenture, preference share or ordinary share) multiplied by the number of securities on issue. Similarly, the total market value of the company is equal to the sum total of the market values of each source of finance.

A problem can arise when the *current* market value weights of debt and equity are significantly different from the *target* capital-structure mix mentioned earlier. If the current market value weights are considered to be a temporary departure from the target capital-structure weights, the weighted average cost of capital should be calculated using weights reflecting the target capital-structure mix. However, the individual costs of capital that are combined with these target-mix weights may need to be adjusted to reflect the impact of the temporary current market values on the risk to investors and therefore the rates of return that they require.

Step 3: Computing and using the weighted average cost of capital

We now have all the components needed to compute the weighted average cost of capital (K_o). This calculation is demonstrated by using the data previously estimated for the Ash Company. In the first instance we will assume Ash Company is a taxation category 1 company, and accordingly we will need to calculate the company's before-tax weighted average cost of capital. To do this, it is assumed that the amounts in Table 14.3 are market values and reflect the company's target financing mix. The estimates of the individual before-tax costs of each source of capital calculated previously are detailed in Table 14.4.

TABLE 14.4 Before-tax cost-of-capital components for Ash Company

FUNDS	COMPONENT COSTS (BEFORE TAX) (%)*
Debentures	9.73
Preference shares	15.87
Retained earnings	17.00
Ordinary shares	17.29

* These have been calculated using methods outlined in the previous sections.

Table 14.5 combines the weights from Table 14.3 and the individual before-tax cost for each finance source from Table 14.4 into the company's before-tax weighted average cost of capital $(K_{0,BT})$.

TABLE 14.5 Before-tax weighted average cost of capital for Ash Company

(1) FUNDS	(2) WEIGHT	(3) INDIVIDUAL COSTS	(4) WEIGHTED COSTS (2 × 3)
Debentures	35%	9.73%	3.41%
Preference shares	5%	15.87%	0.79%
Retained earnings	20%	17.00%	3.40%
Ordinary shares	40%	17.29%	6.92%
		Weighted cost of capital $(K_{0,BT})$:	14.52%

Given that the assumptions of constant business risk, constant financial risk and constant dividend policy are a reasonable reflection of reality, Ash Company's before-tax weighted average cost of capital is 14.52% p.a. This is the minimum rate of return the company needs to earn from the before-tax net cash flows of an investment project with similar business risk to the company as a whole, to be able to pay the costs of finance used to fund the initial outlay of the project. Accordingly, to ensure that the investment project satisfies this requirement, the rate of 14.52% is used as the rate (RRR) to discount estimates of the project's before-tax net cash flows to determine the project's NPV. Alternatively, the RRR of 14.52% can be compared with the IRR calculated from the project's before-tax cash flows.

EXAMPLE 14.9 Use of before-tax weighted average cost of capital to evaluate an investment project

Ash Company is considering an investment project to expand its production capacity. The investment has an initial outlay of $1 million and is estimated to produce before-tax net cash flows of $400 000 for the next four years. As the capital structure detailed in Table 14.3 reflects current market values and is also the company's target financing mix, the finance for this project's initial outlay is assumed to be raised in the same proportions of debt and equity. Also, as the business risk of this project is the same as that of the company's existing business, the before-tax weighted average cost of capital of 14.52% (calculated in Table 14.5) is appropriate to be used to evaluate the project by calculating the project's NPV:

$$NPV = -1\,000\,000 + \frac{400\,000}{(1+0.1452)} + \frac{400\,000}{(1+0.1452)^2} + \frac{400\,000}{(1+0.1452)^3} + \frac{400\,000}{(1+0.1452)^4}$$

$$= \$153\,165$$

As the NPV is +$153 165, the project is acceptable.

This positive NPV amount means that the before-tax net cash flows estimated for the project will be sufficient to:

• repay the initial outlay of $1 million
• pay the before-tax costs of the debt, preference shares and ordinary equity used to finance the initial outlay in their respective proportions
• provide some surplus (represented by the NPV amount of +$153 165) to the company's shareholders.

Because the Ash Company was assumed to be in taxation category 1, the before-tax weighted average cost of capital was calculated in Example 14.9. However, if the company were in taxation category 2, an after-tax weighted average cost of capital should be calculated by combining the individual after-tax costs of capital, as detailed in Example 14.10. This after-tax weighted average cost of capital would then be used to evaluate the after-tax cash flows of the investment project.

EXAMPLE 14.10 **Use of after-tax weighted average cost of capital to evaluate an investment project**

Assume that Ash Company is a taxation category 2 company and is evaluating the same investment project as detailed in Example 14.9. As the company tax rate is 30%, the after-tax net cash flows from the project would be:

Before-tax cash flow	$400 000
– Company tax @ 30%	120 000
After-tax cash flow	280 000

The after-tax weighted average cost of capital combines the individual after-tax costs of capital estimated from the previous sections with the target capital-structure weights:

(1) FUNDS	(2) WEIGHT[a]	(3) INDVIDUAL COSTS[b]	(4) WEIGHTED COSTS (2 × 3)
Debentures	35%	6.81%	2.38%
Preference shares	5%	11.11%	0.56%
Retained earnings	20%	15.00%	3.00%
Ordinary shares	40%	15.20%	6.08%
		Weighted average cost of capital ($K_{0, AT}$):	12.02%

a   Taken from the target financing mix presented in Table 14.3.
b   Taken from the after-tax costs calculated in previous sections.

Evaluating the project using NPV:

$$NPV = -1\,000\,000 + \frac{280\,000}{(1 + 0.1202)} + \frac{280\,000}{(1 + 0.1202)^2} + \frac{280\,000}{(1 + 0.1202)^3} + \frac{280\,000}{(1 + 0.1202)^4}$$

$$= -\$149\,900$$

As the NPV is –$149 900, the project should be rejected.

The negative NPV means that the after-tax net cash flows estimated for the project will not be sufficient to:

- repay the initial outlay of $1 million
- pay the after-tax costs of the debt, preference shares and ordinary equity used to finance the initial outlay in their respective proportions
- provide some surplus to the company's shareholders.

The difference in the project NPVs in Examples 14.9 and 14.10 reflects the impact on the wealth of category 2 company shareholders of the double taxation of company income. As it is subject to a classical tax system, the more Ash Company in Example 14.10 can reduce the income tax it pays on the project cash flows, the greater the likelihood the project will have a positive NPV.

Although the process detailed above to calculate the weighted average cost of capital is relatively straightforward, in practice many of the components can be difficult to measure. This is particularly the case with the cost of equity, which is dependent on either estimates of the growth rate of future dividend amounts (g) or estimates of systematic risk (β) and market returns (R_m). Similarly, to be able to use the calculated weighted average cost of capital as the discount rate to evaluate investment projects, it is necessary for the assumptions about constant business risk and constant financial risk to be a reasonable reflection of reality.

It is therefore important to remember that the calculated weighted average cost of capital is, at best, an approximation of the minimum rate of return required from an investment project. Even so, using this approximation to evaluate investment projects is certainly better than using an arbitrarily selected discount rate. Also, *sensitivity analysis* (discussed in Chapter 13) can assist decision makers to identify the impact of variations in the discount rate on a project's NPV. For example, although Ash Company in Example 14.9 used an estimate of the before-tax cost of capital of 14.5%, it could recalculate the project NPV with discount rates of 15% and 16% to determine if the project NPV was still positive at these higher rates.

ONE STEP FURTHER

COST OF CAPITAL AND RISK

Looking at the costs of the various sources of capital in Table 14.4, debt finance from issuing debentures has the lowest before-tax cost, at 9.73%, with the cost of equity finance from issuing preference shares being significantly higher at 15.87%, followed by retained earnings at 17% and issuing new ordinary shares at 17.29%. These costs primarily reflect the return required by investors to compensate them for the variability (risk) of future cash flows from their investment. Consequently, debenture investors, who are entitled to receive regular coupon amounts and a principal amount at the end of the debenture term, face much less risk (variability of cash flows) than ordinary shareholders, who may receive dividends if the company makes a profit and who face an uncertain share price in the future.

Finance at work

WEIGHTED AVERAGE COST OF CAPITAL

It is rare for a company to publish its weighted average cost of capital. However, from 1999 to 2003 the Australian wine and brewing company, Foster's Ltd, did just that, as shown below.

The company's cost of debt was identified from its annual reports, which enabled estimates of the company's cost of equity to be made. Some observations can be made from the table:

- The cost of debt varied from year to year but was consistently and significantly lower than the cost of equity.

- The proportion of debt finance varied significantly from year to year, and one explanation for the larger percentage of debt used in 2001–2003 was the fall in the cost of debt in those years.

- The weighted average cost of capital varied from year to year, partially reflecting changes in the cost of debt but also reflecting changes in the cost of equity.

Returns on capital and cost of capital for Foster's Ltd, 1999–2003

	1999	2000	2001	2002	2003	AVERAGE
Weighted cost of capital (%)	13.8	12.2	11.1	10.6	9.5	11.4
Cost of debt (%)	4.7	5.1	4.0	3.4	2.8	4.0
Cost of equity (%)	16.6	15.4	16.7	16.6	13.9	15.8
Net debt-to-equity ratio (%)	31	45	79	83	66	61

OBJECTIVE 5

Calculate a project-specific required rate of return as an alternative to the weighted average cost of capital.

Relaxing the assumptions: required rate of return for individual projects

Two major assumptions were made in the preceding sections to facilitate the calculation of the weighted average cost of capital (K_0) and its use as the discount rate (RRR) to evaluate an investment project. First, it was assumed that the business risk of the project was similar to the company's overall business risk. Second, to keep financial risk constant, it was assumed that the same proportions of debt, preference shares and ordinary shares as reflected in the company's current capital structure would be used to finance the investment project.

Sometimes the real situation for a company may be significantly different from these two assumptions. For example, the company may be considering an investment project that has significantly different business risk characteristics from those of its existing operations. Or the company has decided to change its target financing mix and intends to fund a particular project with only one source of finance (e.g. debt) and then use another source (e.g. equity) for the next investment.

Figure 14.5 illustrates the problem that can occur from using a single weighted average cost of capital value as the discount rate to evaluate projects that have different levels of risk.

The horizontal line in Figure 14.5, which represents the company's calculated weighted average cost of capital, K_0, does not allow for varying levels of project risk and therefore is appropriate to use only as the discount rate to evaluate projects that have a level of risk shown at point RL_0. On the other hand, the return–risk line in the figure applies the principle that a higher cost of capital should be used as the discount rate when the level of project risk increases.

Investments A and B in Figure 14.5 illustrate incorrect decisions that can result when a single weighted average cost of capital (K_0) is used as the discount rate to evaluate all investment

FIGURE 14.5   Return–risk relationship

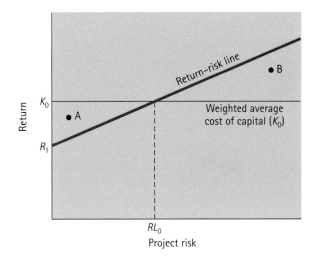

projects. Investment A would be rejected (as its return is less than K_0) even though its risk is below the firm's risk level of RL_0, whereas investment B would be accepted (as its return is more than K_0) even though its business risk exceeds RL_0.

On the other hand, if a discount rate different from K_0, as indicated by the return–risk line, was used to evaluate the projects, investment A should be accepted because, even though the expected return for investment A is below the weighted average cost of capital, the reduction in risk associated with this project justifies accepting the lower expected return. Conversely, investment B should be rejected because its expected return is not sufficient for the increased risk associated with the project. This example confirms the principle that *different costs of capital (required rates of return) should be used for investments having different levels of risk.*

To determine an appropriate discount rate to correctly evaluate an investment project given its level of risk, it is necessary to remember the discussion in Chapter 9 on the types of risk. Risk can be viewed as the total variability in returns for the investment, without any regard to how it relates to the company's other investments. Under this view, *project risk* could be looked at in isolation.

Alternatively, the risk of a project could be viewed in terms of its contribution to the riskiness of the company's portfolio of assets. Taking this approach, risk would be measured as the standard deviation of the returns for all the company's assets taken together, including the new project.

A third option, and the one this section takes, is to consider the *risk to shareholders*. It is reasonable to assume that the company's shareholders hold a diversified portfolio of investments, so the measure of project risk should be the incremental systematic risk (beta, β) that the project adds to the diversified portfolios of shareholders. Given this perspective, the capital asset pricing model (CAPM) can be used to determine the rate of return that shareholders require for the incremental systematic risk a project exposes them to.

Using the CAPM, the required rate of return that shareholders require for the *j*th project (K_j) may be expressed as follows:[10]

$$K_j = R_f + \beta_j(R_m - R_f) \tag{14-15}$$

where β_j (beta) measures the volatility of the *j*th project returns relative to the shareholders' widely diversified portfolios. As in Chapter 9, R_m and R_f represent the expected return for the market portfolio and for a risk-free asset respectively.[11]

EXAMPLE 14.11 Required rate of return for an individual project with risk different from the firm's existing business

Assume that Ash Company is a taxation category 1 company that has no debt and is considering a capital investment project to be funded wholly by retained earnings. The project cash flows are expected to provide a before-tax internal rate of return (IRR) of 18% p.a. The company's management has assessed the riskiness of the project in terms of its contribution to the risk of a diversified share investor's portfolio and has estimated a beta of 1.12 for the project. If the expected before-tax return for a diversified portfolio of assets, R_m, is 19.5%, and the risk-free rate, R_p, is 7%, the before-tax required rate of return for retained earnings to be invested in the project would be:

$$K_j = 0.07 + 1.12(0.195 - 0.07) = 0.21 = 21\%$$

Because the 18% before-tax internal rate of return (IRR) expected from the project is less than the before-tax required rate of return (RRR) of 21%, the investment project should be rejected. Alternatively, we can conclude that the project's before-tax cash flows generating an 18% p.a. return on the funds invested are not sufficient to pay the 21% p.a. before-tax cost of retained earnings.

Although conceptually attractive, the use of the CAPM in this way to calculate a project's required rate of return is difficult because of measurement problems. The primary difficulty lies in measuring the project's beta—that is, the systematic risk of the project. About the only practical way to overcome this problem, as was suggested in Chapter 13, is to use the beta of a 'pure-play' firm as a proxy for the project's beta.

Also, the CAPM maintains that the relevant risk (measured by beta) that should be used to determine the required rate of return is limited to the portion of the risk that the *investor* cannot eliminate through diversification. For this premise to hold, liquidation costs are assumed to be zero if the firm fails, whereas in reality liquidation costs are generally significant. This means that if a project significantly increases the probability of firm failure, the total variability of project returns as measured by the standard deviation would be the appropriate risk measure to use and not incremental systematic risk as measured by beta.

Also note that in Example 14.11 the CAPM estimate of the shareholder's required return was used as the cost of equity because the project was all-equity financed. If debt finance is also to be used, the cost of equity (K_j) is likely to be *higher* as a result of the debt increasing financial risk. Thus, if a project is to be financed by debt as well as equity, a weighted average cost of capital for the project will need to be computed. This will require the financial manager to include the cost of debt, as well as to try to estimate the required rate of return on equity that reflects the increased financial risk arising from the use of debt.

Your money

YOUR COST OF CAPITAL

As we learnt in Chapter 12, your recently deceased uncle left you a bequest of $500 000 and you were trying to decide how to invest it. You have now decided that you want to invest this money in the purchase of a residential property in your neighbourhood which you will rent out for five years and then sell.

You have done some research and you think that for each of the next five years you would be able to receive a fixed annual net rental amount equal to 5.5% of the property's current capital value. Given that your marginal tax rate is 40%, you can expect to receive each year ($500 000 × 0.055) (1 − 0.40) = $16 500 after tax from the rental property.

You have also determined that the historical growth rate of property prices in your area has averaged 7% p.a. and you think it is reasonable to assume that this rate will continue for the next few years. Accordingly, you have estimated that the sale price for the property in five years time will be: 500000 PV, 5N, 7 I/Y, COMP FV, giving $701276. If sold at this price you would have earned a capital gain of $701276 − $500000 = $201276. As 50% of this capital gain would be taxed at your 40% marginal rate, you would have to pay capital gains tax of 201275 × 0.50 × 0.40 = $41455, so that the after-tax proceeds from the sale would be $701276 − $41455 = $659821.

Your estimates of the project's incremental after-tax cash flows are summarised below:

	YEAR 0	YEAR 1	YEAR 2	YEAR 3	YEAR 4	YEAR 5
Purchase of property	−500000					
After-tax net cash flow		16 500	16 500	16 500	16 500	16 500
Sale of property						659 821
NCF	−500000	16 500	16 500	16 500	16 500	676 321

You know that to calculate the NPV to evaluate this investment project you also need a discount rate (RRR). As all of the $500000 to be invested in the property project is your money, the weighted average cost of capital will be equal to the cost of your equity capital. If you purchase the property, you forgo the opportunity to invest the $500000 in an alternative investment. For example, you could earn interest of 5% p.a. from a five-year bank term deposit. But as the property investment is risky, reflecting the uncertainty of the future cash-flow amounts from the project, you think that a risk premium of 4% p.a. above this term-deposit rate is appropriate. As the initial investment of the project is 100% funded by your equity capital, this gives a 9% p.a. after-tax weighted average cost of capital. Using this as the discount rate (RRR), the NPV of the property investment project would be calculated as:

500000 +/− CF_0, 16500 CF_1, 16500 CF_2, 16500 CF_3, 16500 CF_4, 676321 CF_5, 9 I/Y, NPV, COMP giving −6982

Conclusion: As the property investment project has a negative NPV, it should be rejected. This is because the after-tax net cash flows estimated for the project are not sufficient to pay back the $500000 initial investment and pay the 9% p.a. rate of return that you require from your $500000 of equity capital.

Summary

Cost of capital is an important component of financial management. Where a firm uses more than one source of finance, the weighted average cost of capital needs to be calculated by combining the cost of each source of finance in the proportions (weights) of the amount of the total finance that each source provides.

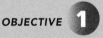

OBJECTIVE 1

For investment project evaluation, the weighted average cost of capital is the minimum rate of return that must be generated by the project's net cash flows in order to satisfy the rate of return that investors who provide the finance for the project require. If a project's net cash flows cannot satisfy this minimum rate of return, the project should be rejected.

To determine whether an investment project should be accepted or rejected, the weighted average cost of capital is used as the discount rate (RRR).

- An investment project that has an internal rate of return (IRR) that exactly equals the weighted average cost of capital (RRR) will produce an NPV = 0. In other words, the project's net cash flows are only just sufficient to repay the initial outlay and pay the costs of each source of finance used to fund the initial outlay. As the project will not produce any surplus net cash flows, there should be no change in the wealth of the firm's owners, which for the shareholders of a company would be reflected by no change in share price.
- If the internal rate of return (IRR) from an investment project is greater than the cost of capital (RRR), the project will have an NPV > 0. The amount of the positive NPV is a present-value measure of the surplus net cash flows generated by the project after the initial outlay and the costs of each source of finance have been paid. This positive NPV represents the increase in the wealth of the firm's owners, which for the shareholders of a company would be reflected by an increase in the company's share price.

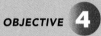**OBJECTIVE 2**

The value of a company's weighted average cost of capital is determined by the return required by debt and equity investors, which will reflect:
- general economic conditions
- the marketability of the company's securities (debt and shares)
- the company's operating and financing decisions
- the amount of finance to be raised by the company.

OBJECTIVE 3

Determining the cost of each source of finance that needs to be combined into the weighted average cost of capital requires identification of:
- the taxation category appropriate for the firm
- the components of a source of finance that represents the return to investors (interest for debt, dividends for equity) and thus the cost of finance to the firm.

To use the company's current weighted average cost of capital as the discount rate (RRR) to evaluate its investment projects assumes that the projects have the same business risk as that of the company's existing business and will be financed in the same proportions of debt and equity as that of the company's current capital structure.

OBJECTIVE 4

For companies in **taxation category 1** it is recommended that the before-tax value of project cash flows be evaluated with a before-tax weighted average cost of capital, which requires determination of:
- before-tax cost of debt: equal to the effective interest rate on new debt adjusted for issue costs
- before-tax cost of preference shares: equal to the grossed-up dividend yield on the net price received for new preference shares
- before-tax cost of ordinary equity:
  - retained earnings: if historical dividend data reasonably reflect the expectations of shareholders, the before-tax cost of retained earnings is equal to the grossed-up ordinary share dividend yield plus the anticipated percentage increase (g) in dividends
  - new share issue: based on the before-tax cost of retained earnings, which includes the effect of flotation (issue) costs on the market price
  - CAPM: the before-tax market return needs to include an average dividend yield grossed up by 1 minus the statutory company tax rate.

For firms in **taxation category 2** (companies subject to a classical tax system and non-company firms) it is recommended that the after-tax value of project cash flows be evaluated with an after-tax weighted average cost of capital, which requires determination of:
- after-tax cost of debt: effective interest rate on new debt reduced by the firm's tax deduction for interest
- after-tax cost of preference shares: equal to the observed dividend yield on net price received by the company for new preference shares
- after-tax cost of ordinary equity:
  - retained earnings: equal to the observed ordinary share dividend yield plus the anticipated percentage increase (g) in dividends
  - new share issue: based on the cost of retained earnings adjusted for flotation (issue) costs
  - CAPM: the after-tax cost of equity can also be computed by using the standard CAPM.

OBJECTIVE 5

A firm's weighted average cost of capital combines the individual costs of financing weighted by the percentage of financing provided by each source. When using the weighted average cost of capital as the discount rate for investment project evaluation, it is usually assumed that the project will have the same business and financial risk as that of the firm's existing business.

If the risk associated with a project is significantly different from that of the firm's existing assets, it is not appropriate to use the firm's weighted average cost of capital as the discount rate (RRR) to evaluate the project. Instead, a project-specific rate of return that reflects the risk of the project to the firm's owners needs to be estimated and used as the discount rate (RRR) to evaluate the project.

business risk	486	risk premium	485
cost of capital	486	target capital structure	499
financial risk	486	weighted average cost of capital	484
flotation (issue) costs	486		

For a complete flashcard glossary
go to MyFinanceLab at
www.pearson.com.au/myfinancelab

Web works

Foster's Group Ltd is a leading Australian alcoholic beverage company.

1. (*Defining Foster's Group's capital structure*). Your first exercise is to assess Foster's Group's capital structure. Begin by going to **www.fostersgroup.com** to obtain the company's most recent annual report. You may assume that the firm's liabilities are trading for prices that are reflected in their book values. Remember, however, that the only liabilities you want to include in the capital structure are permanent (or long-term) indebtedness, the current portion of the firms' long-term debt, and any short-term, interest-bearing notes payable. For the equity component of the capital structure you will need to determine the market value of Foster's Group's shares. To do this, you can multiply the ratio of price-to-book value of common equity by the current book value of the firm's equity. For example, if the price-to-book ratio was 1.5 times and the book value of the company's equity was $10 million, then the market value of the company's common equity would be $15 million.

2. (*Cost of debt*). Assuming Foster's Group's credit rating is AAA, what is the current yield required on new debt with this rating?

3. (*Cost of equity*). Use the capital asset pricing model to estimate the cost of equity capital for Foster's Group Ltd. You can assume an equity market risk premium of 7%. Use **http://finance.ninemsn.com.au** to get an equity beta for Foster's Group Ltd and use the current 20-year treasury bonds to estimate the risk-free rate of interest.

4. (*Weighted average cost of capital*). If Foster's Group's marginal tax rate is 30%, what is its WACC based on your answers to the preceding questions?

Review questions

14-1   Define the term *cost of capital*.

14-2   Why do we calculate a firm's cost of capital?

14-3   In computing the cost of capital, which sources of capital do we consider?

14-4   In general, what factors determine a firm's cost of capital? In answering this question, identify the factors that are within management's control and those that are not.

14-5   What limitations exist in using the firm's cost of capital as an investment hurdle rate?

14-6   (a) How is a firm's cost of capital affected by the tax rate applicable to firms in each of the three taxation categories?
   (b) What is the effect on the cost of capital of the issue costs associated with a new security issue?

14-7   (a) Distinguish between internal equity (retained earnings) and new ordinary shares.
   (b) Why is a cost associated with internal equity?
   (c) Compare approaches that could be used in computing the cost of ordinary equity.

14-8   How can we avoid the limitation of the weighted average cost of capital approach when it requires that we assume that business risk is constant?

14-9   What differences might we expect to see in practice in the relative costs of different sources of capital?

Self-test problems

For answers go to MyFinanceLab
www.pearson.com.au/myfinancelab

ST-1 (*Individual costs of capital*) Compute the cost for the following sources of financing:

(a) A $100 par-value bond with a market price of $97 and a coupon interest rate of 10%. Costs for a new issue would be approximately 5%. The bonds mature in 10 years and the corporate tax rate is 30%. Estimate the cost of debt before tax.

(b) Preference shares selling for $10 with an annual unfranked dividend payment of 80 cents. If the company sells a new issue, the costs will be 90 cents per share.

(c) Internally generated equity totalling $4.8 million. The price of ordinary shares is $7.50 per share, and the dividends per share were 98 cents last year. These dividends are not expected to increase, or to be franked.

(d) New ordinary shares whose most recent dividend was 28 cents. The company's dividends per share should continue to increase at an 8% growth rate into the indefinite future. The market price of the shares is currently $5.30; however, issue costs of 60 cents per share are expected if the new shares are issued. Estimate the after-tax cost of ordinary shares, assuming that dividends are not franked.

(e) Preference shares (see **b**) and ordinary shares (see **d**) for taxation category 1 companies under the imputation system. The company's marginal tax rate is 30%.

ST-2 (*Weighted average cost of capital*) Tania Owens is the new financial manager for Brister Ltd (classed as a taxation category 1 company under the dividend imputation system). She is preparing her recommendations for the company's capital budget and needs to estimate the company's weighted average cost of capital.

The market value of the company's current capital structure consists of $2 million in debt, $500 000 in preference shares and $2.5 million in ordinary equity. This capital mix is to be maintained for future investments.

The cost of debt (before tax) is 7.92%.

The company's preference shares sell for $9.50 and pay a fully franked dividend of 94 cents per share. A new offering of these shares would entail underwriting costs and a price discount of 8% of the present market price.

The ordinary equity portion of the investments will be financed by profits retained within the company of $150 000. Management expects to pay a fully franked dividend at the end of this year of 16.75 cents, and dividends should increase at an annual rate of 9% thereafter. The current price of ordinary shares is $3. The company's marginal tax rate is 30%.

ST-3 (*Individual project—required return*) Scudder Corporation is evaluating three investments that have the expected returns and betas listed below. Managers want to determine the required rates of return of the projects using the capital asset pricing model. The expected before-company-tax return of a diversified portfolio is 15%. The rate on government securities is 8%. Which investments should they make?

INVESTMENT	EXPECTED BEFORE-TAX (%)	BETA RETURN (%)
A	18.8	1.10
B	13.5	0.90
C	15.0	0.80

Problems

For more problems and for answers to problems marked with an asterisk (*) go to MyFinanceLab at
www.pearson.com.au/myfinancelab

14-1* (*Cost of debt*) Belton is issuing a $100 par-value bond that pays 7% annual interest and matures in 15 years. Investors are willing to pay $95.80 for the bond. Issue costs will be 11% of market value. The company pays only 18% in taxes. What will be the firm's after-tax cost of debt on the bond?

14-2 (*Cost of debt*) The Walgren Company is contemplating a new investment to be financed 33% from debt. The firm could sell new $100 par-value bonds at a net price of $95. The coupon interest rate is 13%, and the bonds would mature in 15 years. If the company is taxed at 30%, what is the after-tax cost of capital to Walgren for bonds?

14-3 (*Cost of debt*) Sincere Stationery needs to raise $500 000 to improve its manufacturing plant. It has decided to issue $100 par-value debt with a 14% annual coupon rate and a 10-year maturity. If the investors require a 9% rate of return:

    (a) Compute the market value of the bonds.
    (b) What will the net price be if issue costs are 10.5% of the market price?
    (c) How many debt securities will the firm have to issue to receive the needed funds?
    (d) What is the firm's after-tax cost of debt if its average tax rate is 25% and its marginal tax rate is 30%?

14-4 (*Cost of debt*)

    (a) Rework problem 14-3 assuming a 12% coupon rate. What effect does changing the coupon rate have on the firm's after-tax cost of capital?
    (b) Why is there a change?

14-5* (*Cost of preference shares*) The preference shares of Walter Industries (a taxation category 1 company) sell for $3.60 and pay 25 cents in dividends. The net price of the security after issuance costs is $3.25. What is the cost of capital for the preference shares under dividend imputation if shares are fully franked and Walter's marginal tax rate is 30%?

14-6 (*Cost of preference shares*) Your firm is planning to issue preference shares. The shares sell for $12; however, if new shares are issued, the company will receive only $10.30. The fully franked dividend rate is 13%. What is the before-tax cost of capital for the shares to your firm if the company tax rate is 30%?

14-7* (*Cost of new equity*) Salte Corporation is issuing ordinary shares at a market price of $2.70. Dividends last year were 14.5 cents and are expected to grow at an annual rate of 6% forever. Issue costs will be 6% of market price. What is Salte's after-tax cost of equity? If the dividends were fully franked and the company's tax rate was 30%, what would be the before-tax cost of equity?

14-8 (*Cost of new equity*) The ordinary shares of the Bestsold Company Ltd (a taxation category 1 company) sell for $5.80. If a new issue is made, the issue cost is estimated to be 8%. The company pays 50% of its earnings in dividends, and a 40-cent dividend was recently paid. Earnings per share five years ago were 50 cents. Earnings are expected to continue to grow at the same annual rate in the future as during the past five years. The firm's marginal tax rate is 30%. Calculate the cost of **(a)** internal equity, and **(b)** external equity, each under dividend imputation.

14-9* (*Cost of retained earnings*) Pathos Co.'s ordinary shares are currently selling for $21.50. Fully franked dividends paid last year were 70 cents per share. Costs on issuing shares will be 10% of market price. The dividends and earnings per share are projected to have an annual growth rate of 15%. What is the before-tax cost of retained profits for Pathos if the company tax rate is 30% and it is a taxation category 1 company?

14-10 (*Cost of retained earnings*) The ordinary shares of Oxford Limited are currently selling for $22.50 and the company has just paid last year's dividend amount of $0.80. The costs for the company to issue new shares will be 10% of the market share price. The company's earnings per share and dividends are expected to have an annual growth rate of 16%. Oxford Limited is a taxation category 2 company. Determine the after-tax cost of retained profits if the company tax rate is 30%.

14-11* (*Individual or component costs of capital*) Compute the cost for the following sources of financing. Assume a company tax rate of 30%.

    (a) Debt that has a $100 par value (face value) and a contract or coupon interest rate of 11%. A new issue would have issue costs of 5% of the $112.50 market value. The debt matures in 10 years.
    (b) A new ordinary share issue that paid an 18 cents dividend last year. Earnings per share have grown at a rate of 7% per year. This growth rate is expected to continue into the foreseeable future. The company maintains a constant dividend/earnings ratio of 30%. The price of this share is now $2.75, but 5% issue costs are anticipated. Dividends are fully franked (for a taxation category 1 company).
    (c) Internal equity where the current market price of the ordinary shares is $4.30. The expected dividend this year should be 35 cents, increasing thereafter at a 7% annual growth rate. Dividends are fully franked (for a taxation category 1 company).
    (d) Preference shares for a taxation category 2 company paying an unfranked dividend of 13.5 cents per share. If a new issue is offered, issue costs will be 12% of the current price of $1.75.

(e) A bond selling to yield 12% after issue costs, but prior to adjusting for the marginal corporate tax rate of 30%. In other words, 12% is the rate that equates the net proceeds from the bond with the present value of the future cash flows (principal and interest).

14-12 (*Individual or component costs of capital*) Compute the before-tax cost for the following sources of financing:

(a) A debt issue selling to yield 8% after issue costs. In other words, 8% is the rate that equates the net proceeds from the debt with the present value of the future cash flows (principal and interest). The marginal company tax rate is 30%.

(b) A new ordinary share issue that paid a 10.5-cent dividend last year. The earnings per share have grown at a rate of 5% per year. This growth rate is expected to continue into the foreseeable future. The company maintains a constant dividend/earnings ratio of 40%. The price of this share is now $2.50, but 9% issue costs are anticipated. Calculate $K_{E,BT}$ under full dividend imputation, if the company's marginal tax rate is 30%.

(c) A bond that has a $100 par value and a contract or coupon interest rate of 12%. A new issue would net the company 90% of the $115 market value. The bonds mature in 20 years, and the firm's average tax rate is 20% and its marginal tax rate is 30%. The taxation category 1 company has a policy of paying fully franked dividends.

(d) Preference shares with an unfranked dividend of 7 cents per share. If a new issue is offered, the company can expect to net 85 cents per share although the current price is $1.

(e) Internal equity where the current market price of the ordinary shares is $3.80. The expected franked dividend this forthcoming year should be 30 cents, increasing thereafter at a 4% annual growth rate. This taxation category 1 company's tax rate is 30%.

14-13 (*Individual or component costs of capital*) Compute the after-tax cost for the following sources of financing:

(a) A $1000 par-value bond with a market price of $970 and a coupon interest rate of 10%. The costs to sell a new series of bonds to investors are estimated to be 5% of the bonds' market price. The bonds mature in 10 years and the corporate tax rate is 30%.

(b) A preference share selling for $100 with an annual dividend payment of $8. When the company sells new shares, it will have to pay issue costs of $9 per share.

(c) Retained earnings totalling $4.8 million. Each of the company's ordinary shares has a current price of $53, and paid a dividend of $2.80 last year. It is expected that dividends will grow at 8% p.a. indefinitely.

(d) The issue of new ordinary shares at the current market price of $53, incurring issue costs of $6 per share. A dividend of $2.80 was paid last year and dividends are expected to grow at 8% p.a. indefinitely.

14-14* (*Market value weights*) The most recent (abbreviated) balance sheet for Orion Limited is provided below:

	($ MILLION)
Liabilities	
Debt (debentures)	$20
Equity	
500 000 preference shares	$5
10 million ordinary shares	$15
Total	$40

The company's debentures have a maturity of five years and a total face value of $20 million paying a coupon rate (half-yearly) of 12% p.a. The current yield on company debentures of similar rating is 15% p.a. The current market price for the company's preference shares is $4 and the price for its ordinary shares is $3.90.

(a) Calculate the market values for each of the company's sources of long-term finance.
(b) Calculate the proportions of the company's long-term financing mix, using:
   (i) book values
   (ii) market values

(c) How can you explain the difference between the book value and the market value weights calculated in **(b)**?

14-15 (*Market value weights*) The following data have been obtained for each of the long-term securities issued by Balail Ltd:

	NO. OF SECURITIES ON ISSUE	MARKET PRICE/SECURITY
Corporate bonds	50 million	$95
Preference shares	36 million	$18
Ordinary shares	750 million	$6.75

(a) Calculate the market values for each of the company's sources of long-term finance.

(b) Calculate the market value weights of the company's long-term financing mix.

14-16* (*Weighted average cost of capital*) The capital structure for the Carion Company is provided below. The company plans to maintain its debt structure in the future. The firm has determined the following after-tax costs: 5.5% for bonds, 13.5% for preference shares and 18% for an issue of ordinary equity. Determine the company's after-tax weighted average cost of capital.

CAPITAL STRUCTURE	($'000)
Bonds	1 083
Preference shares	268
Ordinary equity	3 681
	5 032

14-17 (*Weighted average cost of capital*) Orion Limited in problem 14-14 is a taxation category 2 company subject to a 30% corporate tax rate. It has determined its market value weights, and it needs to determine its after-tax weighted average cost of capital. The company's management has gathered the following information additional to that provided in problem 14-14. The preference dividend is $0.60 and the costs to issue new preference shares are estimated to be 10% of the issue price. The company's ordinary shares are estimated to have a beta of 1.8 and retained earnings are expected to be more than sufficient to fund the ordinary equity component of any new investment projects. The risk-free interest rate is currently 7% p.a. and the risk premium for a market portfolio investment is estimated to be 8%.

(a) Calculate the after-tax cost of each of the company's long-term financing sources.

(b) Using the appropriate proportions from problem 14-14, calculate the company's after-tax weighted average cost of capital.

14-18 (*Individual project—required return*) Pellington Company is examining two capital investments. Management wants to analyse the riskiness of the projects in terms of their effect on the riskiness of an investor's diversified portfolio. The beta for project A is 1.10 and 1.25 for B. The expected return for a diversified portfolio is 13%. The risk-free rate is 7%. Project A is expected to return 16.8%; project B, 20.5%. Which investment(s) should the company accept?

14-19* (*Individual project—required return*) Hastings Ltd is analysing several investments. The expected returns and betas of each project are given below. The firm's cost of capital is 16.5%. The current rate on long-term government securities is 8.5%. The expected return for a well-diversified portfolio is 15%. Which investments should the firm accept?

PROJECT	INVESTMENT'S EXPECTED RETURN (%)	BETA
A	18.0	1.2
B	13.8	0.9
C	15.3	1.0
D	11.4	0.7

14-20 (*Integrated problem*) The capital structure for Nealon Ltd (a taxation category 1 company) is provided below. Issue costs would be (a) 15% of market value for a new bond issue, (b) 12 cents per share for ordinary shares, and (c) 20 cents per share for preference shares. The fully franked ordinary share dividends for next year will be 16.75 cents and are projected to have an annual growth rate of 6%. What is the weighted average cost of capital if the firm finances in the proportions shown below? Market prices are $103.50 for bonds, $1.90 for preference shares and $3.50 for ordinary shares. There will be $500 000 of retained profits available. The company tax rate is 30%.

Nealon Ltd, balance sheet:

TYPE OF FINANCING	PERCENTAGE OF FUTURE FINANCING
Bonds (8%, $100 par, 16-year maturity)	38
Preference shares (5000 shares outstanding, 15 cents franked dividend)	15
Ordinary equity	47
Total	100

14-21 (*Integrated problem*) Correlli Ltd, a taxation category 2 company, has done some preliminary evaluation of the following four investment projects, as detailed below.

INVESTMENT	INVESTMENT COST	RATE OF RETURN (%)
A	$200 000	18
B	125 000	16
C	150 000	12
D	275 000	10

The latest balance sheet for the company shows:

	$
Long-term debt	
Bonds: Par $100, annual coupon 16.35%, 5 years to maturity	1 500 000
Equity	
Preference shares (55 000 shares outstanding, 94 cents dividend)	550 000
Ordinary shares (825 000 shares issued)	1 650 000
Total	$3 700 000

The company's bank has advised that the interest rate on any new debt finance provided for the projects would be 8% p.a.

The company's preference shares currently sell for $9.09, and to induce investors to take up a new offering of preference shares the company would have to set the issue price at a discount of 4% off the present market price.

The company's existing shares sell for $3.03 each and management has disclosed that it expects to pay a dividend of 16 cents at the end of the next year. Historically, dividends have increased at an annual rate of 9% p.a. and are expected to continue to do so in the future. The ordinary equity component to finance new projects will require new shares to be sold at a 10% discount from the current $3.03 price, and the costs for undertaking the new issue are estimated to be 30 cents per share. The company tax rate is 30%.

(a) Determine the market value proportions of debt, preference shares and ordinary equity comprising the company's capital structure.
(b) Calculate the after-tax costs of finance for each source of finance.
(c) Determine the after-tax weighted average cost of finance for the company.
(d) Determine which investments should be made.

14-22 (*Integrated problem*) Stamfax Corp. is a company located in a country that has a classical tax system with a company tax rate of 25%. The company's finance manager is considering three capital investment projects that have been proposed by divisional managers who have estimated each project's net cash flows and calculated the following:

PROJECT	INITIAL OUTLAY	IRR (%)
A	$5 000 000	14
B	3 500 000	12
C	7 650 000	9

The company's current capital structure is reflected in the following extract from the latest balance sheet:

	$
Long-term debt	
Bonds: Par $100, semi-annual coupon 8.25%, 7 years to maturity	7 500 000
Debentures: Par $100, quarterly coupon 9.70%, 4 years to maturity	2 000 000
Equity	
Ordinary shares (5 000 000 shares issued)	5 000 000
Total	$14 500 000

The current market price for the company's bonds is $108.55, $110.95 for its debentures and $2.44 for its ordinary shares.

The company has recently paid an ordinary dividend of 22 cents per share. Although this dividend amount has been constant for the last three years, the company's chief executive has publicly stated that she expects ordinary dividends to grow at 4% p.a. next year and into the foreseeable future. The finance manager has estimated that the costs to issue new instruments to the market will be equivalent to a price discount of 5% for bonds, 6% for debentures and 10% for ordinary shares.

(a) Determine the market value weights of the company's current capital structure.
(b) Calculate for each source of finance the current cost to issue new instruments.
(c) Determine the weighted average cost of finance for the company.
(d) Determine which investment projects are acceptable.

Case study

You have just started working in the finance department of Sanderson and Ogilvy Limited. Your first task is to restate the long-term finance component of the following balance-sheet extract to reflect market values:

Bonds ($1000, 8% annual coupon, 30 year maturity)	$150 million
Ordinary shares (100 million issued)	$100 million

Once you have completed this, you have to review the evaluation of a proposal for a major plant and equipment investment project. You have ascertained that the evaluation has been completed using estimates provided by the company's operational staff of the project's incremental cash flows and the directive from the company's managing director that 100% of the funds for this project will be provided by retained earnings. You remember from your job interview that John Sanderson, the company's managing director, told you that 'he knows everything about finance' and that as retained earnings are a costless source of finance he can maximise the NPV of a project by funding all of the initial investment with retained earnings.

1. If the current yield on the company's bonds is 7% p.a. and the current market price of its ordinary shares is $3.50, determine the current market-value weights of the company's capital structure.

2. Why do you need to calculate the market-value weights of long-term debt and equity?
3. Are retained earnings a costless source of ordinary equity finance?
4. Should the weighted average cost of capital be used to evaluate this project?
5. The company is subject to a classical tax system at a marginal tax rate of 28%. Also, the company recently paid an ordinary dividend of 34 cents per share and future dividend amounts are expected to grow at an annual rate of 4% p.a. Calculate the company's after-tax weighted average cost of capital.
6. If the company makes a major change to its long-term debt/equity ratio, what effect will this have on the company's weighted average cost of capital?

Notes

1. The issue of debt capacity will be discussed more fully in Chapter 16.
2. This effect was referred to in Chapter 9 as the Fisher effect.
3. There is an alternative view that flotation or issue costs should be regarded as an addition to the outlay of investment projects rather than be treated as the costs of obtaining new funds. See J. R. Ezzell and R. B. Porter, 'Flotation costs and the weighted average cost of capital', *Journal of Financial and Quantitative Analysis*, 11 September 1976, pp. 403–13.
4. This concept is further explained in Chapter 15.
5. The difference between 9.75% and 9.73% is simply the result of rounding when tables are used.
6. Under the imputation system the preference shareholder will receive a cash dividend of 15 cents but will be taxed on the grossed-up value of 21 cents, with an imputation credit of 6 cents available to offset the personal tax payable.
7. Other factors may justify management not adhering completely to this principle. These issues will be covered in the discussion on dividend policy in Chapter 17.
8. For additional explanation, see Chapter 10.
9. For consistency, the risk-free rate should also, in principle, be adjusted to a pre-company-tax basis. However, this cannot be carried out appropriately unless it is known what part (if any) of the rate should be grossed up. Moreover, at a practical level, this adjustment may (depending on the value of beta) make little difference to the ultimate value of K_{RE}, because we are adding R_f to the right-hand side of the calculation and also subtracting it (multiplied by beta).
10. For further explanation, see Ezra Solomon, 'Measuring a company's cost of capital', *Journal of Business*, October 1955, pp. 95–117; Stewart C. Myers, 'Interactions of corporate financing and investment decisions—implications for capital budgeting', *Journal of Finance*, March 1974, pp. 1–25; Richard S. Bower and Jeffery M. Jenks, 'Divisional screening rates', *Financial Management*, Autumn 1975, pp. 42–49; Donald I. Tuttle and Robert H. Litzenberger, 'Leverage diversification and capital market effects on a risk-adjusted capital budgeting framework', *Journal of Finance*, June 1968, pp. 427–43; John D. Martin and David F. Scott Jr, 'Debt capacity and the capital budgeting decision', *Financial Management*, Summer 1976, pp. 7–14; and R. R. Officer, 'The cost of capital of a company under an imputation tax system', *Accounting and Finance*, May 1994, pp. 1–17.
11. It will be assumed here that the firm finances all its investments with equity. Thus, the problems that arise from having to adjust for different financing mixes can be ignored. This issue is simply beyond the scope of this book; however, to see how it is done, refer to Thomas Conine and Maurry Tamarkin, 'Divisional cost of capital estimation: adjusting for financial leverage', *Financial Management*, Spring 1985, pp. 54–58.

Capital-structure and dividend policy

Part 4

15 Analysis and impact of leverage

16 Capital-structure policy

17 Dividend policy and internal financing

After reading this chapter, you should be able to:

1 Understand and distinguish between business risk and financial risk.
2 Use break-even analysis.
3 Calculate measures of operating leverage, financial leverage and combined leverage.
4 Understand and use EBIT–EPS and comparative leverage ratios to analyse a company's capital structure.

Analysis and impact of leverage

chapter

15

CHAPTER PREVIEW

This chapter examines tools that are useful aids to the financial manager in analysing a company's capital structure. Break-even analysis is examined first as it provides the foundation to the analysis of operating leverage and financial leverage. Two other basic tools of capital-structure management are also examined—EBIT–EPS analysis and comparative leverage ratios.

Regardless of your program

LEVERAGE

The concept of 'leverage' in finance comes from the lever in mechanics. A lever is a bar that by resting on a pivot is able to magnify the ability of a person to lift a heavy object. Accordingly, in finance, which has a major focus on risk, leverage analysis demonstrates how the extent to which the firm's operating and financing costs are fixed magnifies the variability of operating profit (EBIT) and net profit (EPS).

Introduction

Chapters 9 ('Risk and rates of return'), 10 ('Valuation of bonds and shares') and 14 ('Cost of capital') focused on the valuation of financial assets and the measurement of the cost of capital. Figure 15.1 illustrates how the cost of capital provides a direct link between the company's asset structure and its financial structure. The cost of capital when used as the discount rate to evaluate and select capital investment projects impacts on a company's asset structure. In turn, the cost of capital is affected by the company's debt and equity mix—that is, its capital structure.

Business and financial risk

OBJECTIVE **1**

Understand and distinguish between business risk and financial risk.

In the previous chapters our focus was on the evaluation of capital investment projects that expose the company to different degrees of risk due to the variability of the net cash-flow amounts expected from the project. As our attention in this chapter and the next chapters is on financing rather than investment decisions, it is helpful to separate the variability of expected cash-flow amounts into two components—a business risk component that is induced by the firm's investment decisions and a financial risk component that reflects the composition of the firm's capital structure.

Business risk reflects the variability (*relative dispersion*) in expected earnings before interest and taxes (EBIT).[1] This variability is illustrated in Figure 15.2, which shows a subjectively

FIGURE 15.1 Cost of capital as a link between a firm's asset structure and its financial structure

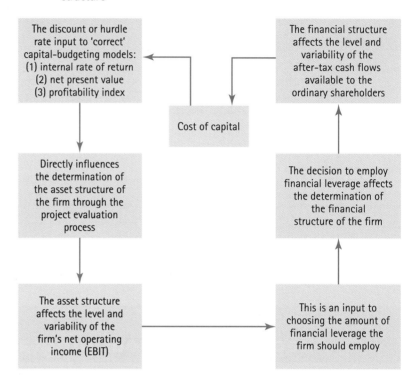

estimated probability distribution of next year's EBIT for the Pierce Grain Company and the same type of projection for Pierce's larger competitor, the Blackburn Seed Company.

The left-hand curve, for Pierce Grain Company, shows an expected value of EBIT of $100 000, with an associated standard deviation of $20 000. The standard deviation is a statistical measure of dispersion, which means that if next year's EBIT for Pierce fell by one standard deviation from the expected EBIT of $100 000, the actual EBIT would be $80 000 (i.e. $100 000 – 20 000).

Looking at the right-hand curve, Blackburn's expected EBIT is $200 000, with an associated standard deviation of $20 000. This means that if next year's EBIT for Blackburn fell by one standard deviation from the expected EBIT of $200 000, the actual EBIT would be $180 000 (i.e. $200 000 – 20 000).

You will notice that, although the expected values of each company's EBIT are different, they both have the same standard deviation value of $20 000. Does this same standard deviation value mean that the two companies have the same business risk? The answer is no. To determine the business risk of the two companies, we need to calculate a relative measure of dispersion, called the coefficient of variation, by dividing the standard deviation by its expected value:

Pierce's coefficient of variation of expected EBIT = $20 000/$100 000 = 0.20
Blackburn's coefficient of variation of expected EBIT = $20 000/$200 000 = 0.10

As the Pierce Grain Company has a larger coefficient of variation of expected EBIT, we can conclude that it has larger relative dispersion and therefore a higher degree of business risk than Blackburn Seed Company.

It is important to note that the relative dispersion in EBIT, measured by expected coefficient of variation, does not *cause* business risk but is the *result* of several influences on the company's operations, such as its operating cost structure, product-demand characteristics and

FIGURE 15.2   Subjective probability distribution of next year's EBIT

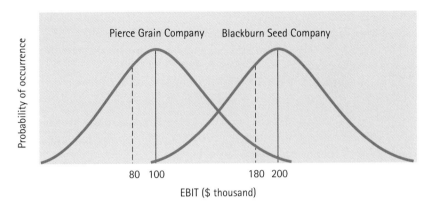

intra-industry competitive position. All of these influences are a direct result of the company's investment decisions.

Financial risk, on the other hand, is a direct result of decisions on how much debt finance should be used relative to equity finance. More specifically, financial risk is due to the impact of financial leverage[2] on the variability in earnings available to the company's ordinary shareholders.

Financial leverage occurs when a portion of the company's assets are financed with securities, such as debt and preference shares, which pay a fixed amount of return to investors. The benefit to the company is that, once it has paid the fixed interest and preference dividend amounts, all of the remaining earnings accrue to the ordinary shareholders. However, the downside of financial leverage is that it exposes ordinary shareholders to a greater degree of variability in the earnings they receive and in the extreme case exposes them to the risk that the company will become insolvent. How this occurs is discussed in detail in the later section, 'Operating leverage and financial leverage'.

Similar to financial leverage is **operating leverage**, which is the proportion of fixed operating costs in the company's cash flows and is reflected in the responsiveness of the company's earnings before interest and taxes to changes in revenue. We will look next at cost–volume–profit analysis, or *break-even analysis*, which focuses on operating leverage.

financial leverage
The use of securities to finance a portion of the firm's assets that pay investors a fixed (limited) rate of return. Financial leverage can arise from the use of either debt or preference-share financing. The use of financial leverage exposes the firm to financial risk.

operating leverage
The responsiveness of the firm's earnings before interest and taxes to changes in revenue. This responsiveness arises from the proportion of the firm's operating costs that are fixed.

> **Concept check**
> 15.1 Explain the concept of 'business risk' within the context of financial-structure management.
> 15.2 Explain the concept of 'financial risk' within the context of financial-structure management.
> 15.3 Distinguish between 'financial leverage' and 'operating leverage'.

For answers go to MyFinanceLab or
www.pearson.com.au/9781442539174

Break-even analysis

The technique of break-even analysis is used in a wide array of large and small businesses, because it is based on straightforward assumptions and it provides information that assists decision making.

OBJECTIVE

Use break-even analysis.

OBJECTIVE AND USES

The objective of the *break-even analysis* we will be conducting is to answer the question 'How far can sales fall before the firm breaks even and earns zero EBIT?' The focus of break-even analysis can be on the break-even *quantity* of sales volume, or on the break-even *value* of sales, corresponding to the break-even quantity of sales volume.

Specifically, the break-even sales volume or value will be the amount that results in an EBIT amount equal to zero. Accordingly, break-even analysis enables the financial manager to (1) determine the quantity or value of sales that must be made in order to cover all operating costs, as distinct from financial costs, and (2) calculate the EBIT that will be achieved at various sales levels. For example, hotels need to know exactly what their break-even occupancy rate is. This break-even occupancy rate can be used in the hotel's advertising strategy: special packages are offered during quiet periods to keep occupancy levels above the break-even point.

Some of the other applications of break-even analysis include:

- *Capital expenditure analysis.* Used as a *complementary* technique to the discounted-cash-flow evaluation of investment projects to identify in a rough way the minimum sales volume needed from a project to be economically viable.
- *Financing decisions.* Analysis of the firm's cost structure reveals the proportion of sales revenue that is used to pay fixed operating costs (i.e. operating leverage). If this proportion is high, the firm might reasonably decide not to add any fixed financing costs on top of the high fixed operating costs.

ASSUMED BEHAVIOUR OF COSTS

As the focus of the break-even model we are using is on sales to EBIT, the operating costs of the firm must be separated into two mutually exclusive categories: fixed costs and variable costs.

A *fixed cost* (also referred to as an indirect cost) does not vary in amount as the sales volume or the quantity of output changes. In a manufacturing setting, fixed operating costs would include administrative salaries, depreciation, insurance, property taxes and rent.

A firm that has determined the total amount of its fixed operating costs will find that, when production or sales volumes increase, the amount of fixed cost per unit of product decreases. This is because the total fixed cost amount is spread over larger and larger quantities of product. Conversely, a decrease in volume will result in an increase in the amount of fixed cost per unit.

On the other hand, a *variable cost* (also referred to as a direct cost) is fixed per unit of output but varies in total as output changes. For a manufacturing operation, variable costs would include direct labour, direct materials, energy costs, packaging and sales commissions. The total variable cost is equal to the variable cost per unit multiplied by the quantity produced or sold. The break-even model assumes proportionality between total variable costs and sales volume. Thus, if the number of units sold rises by 10%, the model assumes that variable costs will rise by 10%.

In reality, many costs do not behave neatly as either fixed or variable. For example, you may recall from your study of economics that in the long run all costs are variable, so classification of fixed and variable costs is essentially a short-run concept. Nor does any law or accounting principle dictate that a certain item of the firm's total costs should always be classified as fixed or variable. For example, energy costs in one firm may be predominantly fixed, whereas in another they may vary with output and be classified as variable.[3]

Furthermore, some costs may be fixed for a while, then rise sharply to a higher level as a higher output is reached, remain fixed, and then rise again with further increases in production. Such costs can be termed **semivariable costs**. An example might be the total amount for salaries paid to production supervisors. Should output increase for a short period, management is not likely to hire new supervisors but will need to do so if the production increase is expected to be sustained. To deal with this complex type of semivariable cost structure, the financial manager needs to (1) identify the most relevant output range for planning purposes, and then (2) approximate the cost effect over this range by segregating a portion to fixed costs and a portion to variable costs.

TOTAL REVENUE AND VOLUME OF OUTPUT

Besides determining the value of fixed and variable costs, the break-even model requires estimates of output volume or sales revenue. The *output volume* is the firm's level of operations

semivariable costs
Charges that behave as variable costs over certain ranges of output and as fixed costs over other ranges of output. Also called 'semi-fixed costs'.

expressed as a unit quantity produced or sold. Consequently, *sales revenue* is equal to the selling price per unit multiplied by the quantity sold.

FINDING THE BREAK-EVEN POINT

The break-even model is a simple adaptation of the firm's income statement expressed in the following analytical format:

sales – (total variable cost + total fixed cost) = operating profit (EBIT) **(15-1)**

The break-even point of units of product sold is the number of units that results in just enough sales revenue being generated to pay for the fixed and variable operating costs. In other words, solving for the units sold in equation (15-2):

sales price per unit × units sold – [variable cost per unit × units sold + total fixed cost] = EBIT = $0 **(15-2)**

The break-even level of units sold can be found by algebraic analysis.

Algebraic analysis

To explain the algebraic method for finding the break-even output level, some notation needs to be adopted. Let:

Q = the number of units sold
Q_B = the break-even level of Q
P = the unit sales price
F = total fixed costs anticipated over the planning period
V = the unit variable cost

Equation (15-2) is repeated below as equation (15-2a) with the model symbols used in place of words.

$$(P \times Q) - [(V \times Q) + F] = \text{EBIT} = \$0 \qquad \textbf{(15-2a)}$$

$$(P \times Q) - (V \times Q) - F = \$0$$

$$Q(P - V) = F$$

$$Q_B = \frac{F}{P - V} \qquad \textbf{(15-3)}$$

Equation (15-3) says: the break-even level of output Q_B can be obtained by dividing total fixed operating costs, F, by price per unit minus variable cost per unit $(P - V)$.

$P - V$ is called the *contribution margin*, because it identifies the amount of sales revenue after variable costs that can contribute to the payment of fixed costs.

Example 15.1 illustrates the calculation of the break-even level of units sold.

EXAMPLE 15.1   Calculation of the break-even level of units sold

Even though the Pierce Grain Company manufactures several different products, it has observed over a lengthy period that its product mix is rather constant. This allows management to use an average sales price per unit and an average variable cost per unit for the company. The average sales price is $10 per unit and the average variable cost is $6 per unit. Total fixed costs for the company are $100 000 per year.

Using equation (15-3), the break-even point in units produced and sold for the company during the coming year would be:

$$Q_B = \frac{F}{P - V} = \frac{\$100\,000}{\$10 - \$6} = 25\,000 \text{ units}$$

The break-even point of 25 000 units is confirmed as follows:

Sales revenue (25 000 × $10)	$250 000
– Variable costs (25 000 × $6)	(150 000)
Contribution margin	100 000
– Fixed costs	(100 000)
Operating profit (EBIT)	0

BREAK-EVEN POINT IN SALES REVENUE

For firms with many products it is often more convenient to compute the break-even point in sales revenue rather than units of output/sales. We can use the simple mathematical relationships on which cost–volume–profit analysis is based to find the break-even point in sales dollars.

Sales – (total variable cost + total fixed cost) = EBIT

Letting total sales = S, total variable cost = VC, and total fixed cost = F, the preceding relationship becomes: $S - (VC + F) = \text{EBIT}$

Because variable cost per unit of output and selling price per unit are *assumed* to be constant over the relevant output range in break-even analysis, the ratio of total sales to total variable cost, $VC : S$, is a constant for any level of sales. This permits us to rewrite the previous expression as:

$$S = \frac{VC}{S} S - F = \text{EBIT}$$

and

$$S\left(1 - \frac{VC}{S}\right) - F = \text{EBIT}$$

At the break-even point, however, EBIT = 0, and the corresponding break-even level of sales can be represented as S^*.

$$S^*\left(1 - \frac{VC}{S}\right) - F = 0$$

or

$$S^*\left(1 - \frac{VC}{S}\right) = F$$

Therefore,

$$S^* = \frac{F}{1 - [(VC)/S]} \qquad \textbf{(15-4)}$$

EXAMPLE 15.2 Calculation of the break-even level of sales revenue

Table 15.1 provides the current cost structure for Pierce Grain Company. This type of financial statement is referred to as an *analytical income* (profit and loss) *statement*, because the costs are classified as variable and fixed instead of the classification used in published income statements.

TABLE 15.1 Pierce Grain Company analytical income statement

Sales	$300000
Less: Total variable costs	180000
Revenue before fixed costs	120000
Less: Total fixed costs	100000
EBIT	$20000

The application of equation (15-4) to Pierce Grain's analytical income statement in Table 15.1 permits the break-even sales level for the firm to be computed as:

$$S^* = \frac{\$100\,000}{1 - (\$180\,000/\$300\,000)}$$

$$= \frac{\$100\,000}{1 - 0.60} \qquad = \$250\,000$$

Back to the principles

The preceding discussion on break-even analysis reinforces the importance of **Principle 3: Cash—not profits—is king**. The use of break-even analysis reminds us that cash is used to pay operating expenses, acquire assets, and distribute earnings in the form of cash dividends. Another way of understanding Principle 3 is: accounting profits are an opinion; cash is reality. Financial asset values are based on the firm's ability to generate cash flows. You cannot be misled over long time periods by cash-flow generation.

LIMITATIONS OF BREAK-EVEN ANALYSIS

Break-even analysis is a useful tool but it has limitations that should be kept in mind. These include the following:

* The relationship between cost, volume and profit is assumed to be linear. This is realistic only over narrow ranges of output.
* Total sales revenue is assumed to increase linearly with the volume of output. This implies that *any* quantity can be sold over the relevant output range at that *single* price. To be more realistic, it may be necessary to compute a different sales revenue curve for each range of output and then to calculate corresponding break-even points at differing prices.
* A constant production and sales mix is assumed. Should the company decide to produce more of one product and less of another, a new break-even point would have to be found. Only if the variable cost-to-sales ratios were identical for the products involved would the new calculation be unnecessary.
* Break-even computations are a static form of analysis. A new break-even point needs to be calculated when there is a change in the firm's cost or price structure. Break-even analysis is more helpful, therefore, in stable industries than in dynamic ones.

For answers go to MyFinanceLab or
www.pearson.com.au/9781442539174

OBJECTIVE 3

Calculate measures of operating leverage, financial leverage and combined leverage.

Operating leverage and financial leverage

Break-even analysis assists in answering the question of how much the firm's sales quantity and revenue will need to be in order to just pay its variable and fixed operating costs and therefore result in zero operating profit (EBIT).

The analysis of operating and financial leverage is related to break-even analysis, but it is more dynamic as its aim is to identify how much operating profit (EBIT) and net profit (earnings per share, EPS) will vary in response to variations in the amount of the firm's sales revenue.

OPERATING LEVERAGE

Operating leverage occurs when the firm has *fixed* operating costs in its cost structure. Fixed operating costs do *not* include interest charges incurred from the firm's use of debt financing, because these are incorporated in the analysis of financial leverage (to be discussed later).

The reason why our focus is on fixed operating costs is because they have a direct impact on the responsiveness of the firm's EBIT to fluctuations in sales revenue. Specifically, a firm with a high proportion of fixed operating costs has a high degree of operating leverage, which results in significant fluctuations in EBIT when sales revenue fluctuates.

The data provided for the Pierce Grain Company in Table 15.2 will be used to illustrate the concept of operating leverage, assuming a financial planning period of one year.

The first column in Table 15.2 shows that currently the company has annual sales revenue of $300 000 (referred to as the base sales level at period *t*), producing EBIT of $20 000. The second column answers the question of how much Pierce Grain's EBIT will be if there is a positive 20% change in sales revenue. The sales value of $360 000 (referred to as the forecast sales level at period *t* + 1) reflects the 20% rise anticipated over the planning period (i.e. $300 000 × 1.2 = $360 000).

Notice from Table 15.2 that the amount of total variable costs increased in direct proportion to the increase in sales revenue (i.e. variable cost-to-sales ratio of 0.6) but the amount of total fixed costs stayed the same at $100 000.

Given this variable and fixed cost structure for Pierce Grain, the 20% increase in sales revenue resulted in an increase in EBIT from $20 000 to $44 000. The responsiveness of EBIT to the change in sales revenue can be measured by calculating the percentage change in EBIT from *t* to *t* + 1, as follows:

$$\text{Percentage change in EBIT} = \frac{\$44\,000 - \$20\,000}{\$20\,000}$$

$$= \frac{\$24\,000}{\$20\,000} \qquad = 120\%$$

TABLE 15.2 Concept of operating leverage: increase in Pierce Grain Company sales

ITEM	BASE SALES LEVEL, *t*	FORECAST SALES LEVEL, *t* + 1
Sales	$300 000	$360 000
Less: Total variable costs	180 000	216 000
Revenue before fixed cost	120 000	144 000
Less: Total fixed costs	100 000	100 000
EBIT	$20 000	$44 000

The *degree of operating leverage* relates the percentage change in EBIT to the percentage change in sales:

Degree of operating leverage from the base sales level(s) = DOL_S

$$= \frac{\text{percentage change in EBIT}}{\text{percentage change in sales}} \qquad \textbf{(15-5)}$$

The degree of operating leverage for Pierce Grain Company is:

$$DOL_{\$300\,000} = \frac{120\%}{20\%} = 6 \text{ times}$$

What does the degree of operating leverage of 6 for Pierce Grain Company mean? It means that we can expect the percentage change in EBIT to be 6 times the percentage change in the amount of sales revenue from the base level. For example, if Pierce Grain Company estimates a 5% rise in sales revenue over the coming period, its EBIT would be expected to rise by:

$$(\text{percentage change in sales}) \times (DOL_{sales}) = \text{percentage change in EBIT}$$
$$(5\%) \times (6) = 30\%$$

What if the direction of the fluctuation in sales revenue is expected to be negative rather than positive? The operating-leverage measures hold in the negative direction as well, as illustrated in Table 15.3.

At the $240\,000 sales level, which represents a 20% decrease from the base level, Pierce Grain Company's EBIT is expected to be minus $4000. The percentage change of EBIT fluctuation is calculated as:[4]

$$\text{Percentage change in EBIT} = \frac{-\$4\,000 - \$20\,000}{\$20\,000_t}$$

$$= \frac{-\$24\,000}{\$20\,000}$$

$$= -120\%$$

The degree of operating leverage is:

$$DOL_{\$300\,000} = \frac{-120\%}{-20\%} = 6 \text{ times}$$

This example illustrates that the degree-of-operating-leverage measure works in the positive or the negative direction. The implication is that a negative percentage change in sales revenue can result in a several-fold magnification of the percentage change in EBIT.

Up to now, to calculate the degree of operating leverage we have needed two analytical income statements: one for the base period and another for the subsequent period that incorporates the possible change in sales revenue.

TABLE 15.3 Concept of operating leverage: decrease in Pierce Grain Company sales

ITEM	BASE SALES LEVEL, t	FORECAST SALES LEVEL, t + 1
Sales	$300 000	$240 000
Less: Total variable costs	180 000	144 000
Revenue before fixed cost	120 000	96 000
Less: Total fixed costs	100 000	100 000
EBIT	$20 000	–$4 000

If unit cost data are available for the base level of sales, the calculation can be simplified as:

$$DOL_{sales} = \frac{Q(P-V)}{Q(P-V)-F}$$ (15-6)

Observe that equation (15-6) uses all the variables that were previously defined in the algebraic analysis of the break-even model. Example 15.3 illustrates this calculation.

EXAMPLE 15.3 **Calculation of degree of operating leverage using cost data**

Pierce Grain Company sells its product at $P = \$10$ per unit, the unit variable cost is $V = \$6$, and total fixed costs over the planning horizon are $F = \$100\,000$. Assuming that Pierce Grain is operating at a $\$300\,000$ sales volume, the base level of output Q will be $\$300\,000/\$10 = 30\,000$ units. The degree of operating leverage can be found by application of equation (15-6):

$$DOL_{\$300\,000} = \frac{30\,000(\$10 - \$6)}{30\,000(\$10 - \$6) - \$100\,000} = \frac{\$120\,000}{\$20\,000}$$

$$= 6 \text{ times}$$

Equation (15-6) requires knowledge of unit cost data to carry out the computations. If these cost data are not available, an analytical income statement for the base period can be used, with the degree of operating leverage equal to:

$$DOL_{sales} = \frac{\text{revenue before fixed costs}}{\text{EBIT}}$$ (15-7)

$$= \frac{S - VC}{S - VC - F}$$

EXAMPLE 15.4 **Calculation of degree of operating leverage using base-period income-statement data**

From the base-period data for Pierce Grain Company shown in either Table 15.2 or Table 15.3, sales revenue $S = \$300\,000$, total variable costs $VC = \$180\,000$, and fixed operating costs $F = \$100\,000$:

$S - VC = \$120\,000$; $S - VC - F = \$20\,000$

Using equation (15-7):

$$DOL_{\$300\,000} = \frac{\$120\,000}{\$20\,000} = 6 \text{ times}$$

As the three versions to calculate the degree of operating leverage all produce the same result, data availability will sometimes dictate which formulation can be applied. The crucial consideration is that financial managers understand what the degree of operating-leverage measurement tells them. For example, the Pierce Grain Company financial managers now know that a 1% change in sales revenue (up or down) will be magnified six times, resulting in a 6% up or down change in EBIT!

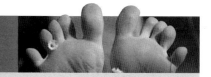

FYI

An interesting question is which type of leverage is more under the control of management? You would be correct if you came to the conclusion that the firm's managers have less control over the variable and fixed components of the operating cost structure and almost complete control over the debt and equity components of the capital structure. What the firm actually does to generate sales revenue (e.g. manufacture a product, provide a service) will determine to a significant degree the division between fixed and variable operating costs. There is more room for substitution among the various sources of debt and equity capital than there is among the labour and other inputs that enable the firm to meet its operating requirements. Thus, you can anticipate more focus by financial managers on decisions that determine the degree of financial leverage than the degree of operating leverage.

Concept check

15.7 If a firm's degree of operating leverage happens to be six times, what precisely does that mean?

15.8 What does the degree-of-operating-leverage concept suggest when a negative shock in production volume and sales revenue occurs?

15.9 When is operating leverage present in the firm's cost structure? What condition is necessary for operating leverage not to be present in the firm's cost structure?

For answers go to MyFinanceLab or
www.pearson.com.au/9781442539174

International spotlight

FIXED OPERATING COSTS

Many businesses in developed countries complain about the high fixed operating costs associated with employing people. Apart from having to pay employees a regular wage, employers incur costs such as holiday pay, sickness and accident insurance, and provision of retirement benefits. To reduce the effect of these fixed operating costs on EBIT and earnings per share, there has been a major transfer of the labour component of businesses from developed countries to countries that not only have low wage rates but also have few or no other employment costs.

FINANCIAL LEVERAGE

Financial leverage reflects the amount of the firm's assets that are financed with securities requiring the firm to pay a fixed rate of return to investors. As we will see below, a major reason why companies use sources of financing that pay fixed amounts to investors is to increase the return that can be provided to its ordinary shareholders. However, financial leverage also determines how much the return to ordinary shareholders will change when EBIT changes, that is the *risk* to ordinary shareholders.

For the analysis of financial leverage we will use earnings per share (EPS) as the measure of the return to ordinary shareholders. This does not mean that earnings per share is the appropriate criterion to analyse all financing decisions, but it enables us to readily identify the effect of financial leverage on the earnings received by shareholders.

To illustrate the effects of financial leverage, let's assume that the Pierce Grain Company is just starting as a business. The company's owners have calculated that $200 000 will be needed to purchase the necessary assets to conduct the business. Three possible financing plans to raise the $200 000 are presented in Table 15.4.

In Plan A, the entire $200 000 is raised by the company selling 200 000 ordinary shares at $1 each. As no finance has been provided by fixed-rate securities like debt, Plan A has no financial leverage. Plan B has a moderate amount of financial leverage, because 25% of the assets

| TABLE 15.4 | Pierce Grain Company possible financial structures |

Plan A: 0% debt

		Total debt	$0
		Ordinary equity[a]	$200 000
Total assets	$200 000	Total liabilities and equity	$200 000

Plan B: 25% debt at 8% interest rate

		Total debt	$50 000
		Ordinary equity[b]	150 000
Total assets	$200 000	Total liabilities and equity	$200 000

Plan C: 40% debt at 8% interest rate

		Total debt	$80 000
		Ordinary equity[c]	120 000
Total assets	$200 000	Total liabilities and equity	$200 000

a 200 000 ordinary shares.
b 150 000 ordinary shares.
c 120 000 ordinary shares.

are financed with a debt issue that pays a fixed 8% annual interest rate. Plan C has the most financial leverage, because 40% of the assets are financed with a debt issue that also pays a fixed rate of interest of 8% per annum.[5]

For each financing plan, Table 15.5 presents the impact of financial leverage on earnings per share associated with different amounts of EBIT. For example, if EBIT should increase by 100% from $20 000 to $40 000, earnings per share under Plan A would rise from $5 to $10 per share, an increase of 100%. However, the same 100% rise in EBIT would result in earnings per share under Plan B increasing by 125%, and by 147% under Plan C.

This example shows that for Plans B and C the 100% increase in EBIT (from $20 000 to $40 000) was magnified to produce a greater than 100% increase in earnings per share.

| TABLE 15.5 | Pierce Grain Company analysis of financial leverage at different EBIT levels |

(1)	(2)	(3) = (1) – (2)	(4) = (3) × 0.5	(5) = (3) – (4)	(6) EARNINGS PER	
EBIT	INTEREST	EBT	TAXES	NET INCOME	SHARE (CENTS)	
Plan A: 0% debt; $200 000 equity; 200 000 shares						
$0	$0	$0	$0	$0	0	
20 000	0	20 000	10 000	10 000	5.00	
40 000	0	40 000	20 000	20 000	10.00	100%
60 000	0	60 000	30 000	30 000	15.00	
80 000	0	80 000	40 000	40 000	20.00	
Plan B: 25% debt; 8% interest rate; $150 000 equity; 150 000 shares						
$0	$4 000	$(4 000)	$(2 000)[a]	$(2 000)	(1.33)	
20 000	4 000	16 000	8 000	8 000	5.33	
40 000	4 000	36 000	18 000	18 000	12.00	125%
60 000	4 000	56 000	28 000	28 000	18.67	
80 000	4 000	76 000	38 000	38 000	25.33	
Plan C: 40% debt; 8% interest rate; $120 000 equity; 120 000 shares						
$0	$6 400	$(6 400)	$(3 200)[a]	$(3 200)	(2.67)	
20 000	6 400	13 600	6 800	6 800	5.67	
40 000	6 400	33 600	16 800	16 800	14.00	147%
60 000	6 400	53 600	26 800	26 800	22.33	
80 000	6 400	73 600	36 800	36 800	30.67	

a The credit arising from carry-back and carry-forward tax provisions.

By employing financial leverage in Plans B and C, the company could increase the returns (EPS) to shareholders. However, financial leverage also exposed the shareholders to financial risk. This is because for the same range of EBIT ($0 to $80 000), the plans with financial leverage produced more variation in EPS. For example, the EPS for Plan C varied from –$2.67 to $30.67. We can say then that a company using financial leverage exposes its owners to financial risk when:

$$\frac{\text{percentage change in EPS}}{\text{percentage change in EBIT}} > 1.00$$

We can follow the same procedures that were used for measuring operating leverage to obtain a measure of the degree of financial leverage that reflects the sensitivity of earnings per share (EPS) to fluctuations in EBIT:

Degree of financial leverage (DFL) from base EBIT level = DFL_{EBIT}

$$= \frac{\text{percentage change in EPS}}{\text{percentage change in EBIT}} \qquad \textbf{(15-8)}$$

EXAMPLE 15.5   Calculation of degree of financial leverage

Using the data for Pierce Grain Company in Table 15.5, the degree of financial leverage for each financing plan from a base level of EBIT of $20 000 is:

Plan A: $DFL_{\$20\,000} = \dfrac{100\%}{100\%} = 1.00$ time

Plan B: $DFL_{\$20\,000} = \dfrac{125\%}{100\%} = 1.25$ times

Plan C: $DFL_{\$20\,000} = \dfrac{147\%}{100\%} = 1.47$ times

Rather than having to compute percentage changes in EBIT and earnings per share, the degree of financial leverage, DFL, can be found directly, as follows:

$$DFL_{EBIT} = \frac{\text{EBIT}}{\text{EBIT} - I} \qquad \textbf{(15-9)}$$

In equation (15-9) the variable, I, represents the sum of all fixed financing costs, comprising both the total interest expense incurred on *all* the firm's contractual debt obligations and the fixed dividend amounts on preference shares.

EXAMPLE 15.6   Alternative calculation of degree of financial leverage

Applying equation (15-9) to each of Pierce Grain Company's financing plans (Table 15.5) at a base EBIT level of $20 000, the degree of financial leverage can be calculated:

Plan A: $DFL_{\$20\,000} = \dfrac{\$20\,000}{\$20\,000 - 0} = 1.00$ time

$$\text{Plan B: } DFL_{\$20\,000} = \frac{\$20\,000}{\$20\,000 - \$4\,000} = 1.25 \text{ times}$$

$$\text{Plan C: } DFL_{\$20\,000} = \frac{\$20\,000}{\$20\,000 - \$6\,400} = 1.47 \text{ times}$$

Like operating leverage, the *degree of financial leverage* concept applies in the negative direction as well as the positive. So, for example, if Pierce Grain Company's EBIT falls by 10%, it can be expected that for Plan C, with a degree of financial leverage of 1.47 times, EPS will fall by 10% × 1.47 = 14.7%.

Back to the principles

The extent of variability on the earnings stream (EPS) available to a company's ordinary shareholders from combining operating and financial leverage can be dramatic. When there is a high degree of both leverage types, a large sales increase will result in a very large rise in earnings per share. However, there is a significant downside, because should the change in sales be negative, the shareholders would face a very large fall in earnings per share. Consequently, a very risky way for a company to do business is to combine a high degree of financial leverage with a high degree of operating leverage.

Importantly, the markets will not be fooled by a company that has significantly increased its earnings per share in the current year because it has combined high degrees of both operating leverage and financial leverage. Recall **Principle 6: Efficient capital markets—the markets are quick and the prices are right**. Chapter 1 stated that efficient markets deal with the speed with which information is impounded into security prices. Should the company become over-levered in the eyes of the markets (say, from an overly large issue of new debt securities), the company's share price would quickly be adjusted downward. The capital markets fully understand the double-edged sword of operating and financial leverage magnifying fluctuations in revenue.

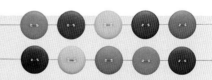

Your money

PERSONAL FINANCIAL LEVERAGE

As sooner or later you are likely to have to borrow a significant amount of money to buy a car or a house, the concepts underlying financial leverage are relevant to your personal financial situation. For example, if you want to buy a house that costs $500 000, one question you have to answer is how much financial leverage is appropriate for you? If you have saved $100 000, then you will have to borrow $400 000, which is a debt to equity ratio of 4:1. Can you afford to make the interest and principal repayments on the debt? A 25-year housing loan charging interest at 0.5% per month will require monthly repayments of 400 000 PV, 25 × 12 = 300 N, 0.5 I/Y, COMP PMT giving $2577.21 per month. If the bank requires your

loan repayments to be no more than 30% of your gross after-tax income, then you would need to earn 2577.21/0.30 = $8590 a month after-tax for the bank to lend you $400 000.

What can you do? One alternative is to reduce your financial leverage by finding a cheaper house. For example, a house costing $400 000 will require you to borrow $300 000 which, with your $100 000, will reduce your financial leverage debt to equity ratio to 3:1. Assuming the same housing loan conditions, your loan repayments would be 300 000 PV, 25 × 12 = 300 N, 0.5 I/Y, COMP PMT giving $1932.90 per month, which would require you to earn a gross after-tax income of 1932.90/0.30 = $6443 a month.

For answers go to MyFinanceLab or
www.pearson.com.au/9781442539174

COMBINATION OF OPERATING LEVERAGE AND FINANCIAL LEVERAGE

We have seen that a company's operating and financial leverage is the result of fixed operating and fixed financial costs respectively and that these fixed costs magnify the effect of changes in sales revenue to changes in EBIT and changes in EPS. The degree of operating leverage is a measure of how much EBIT is likely to change in response to changes in sales revenue and the degree of financial leverage is a measure of how much earnings per share (EPS) is likely to change in response to changes in EBIT. As EBIT is a common component of both operating and financial leverage, the change in EPS in response to a change in sales revenue will reflect the 'combined leverage', as illustrated in Figure 15.3.

A *degree of combined leverage* can also be calculated. To illustrate, let us look at Pierce Grain Company again. Assume that the company's operating cost structure is as detailed in Table 15.1 and that the company has adopted the 25% debt-financing Plan B detailed in Table 15.4. The 'Forecast base sales level, *t*' column in Table 15.6 details these operating and financing amounts and shows that with a forecast sales revenue of $300 000 the company can expect to generate earnings of 5 cents per share.

The second column in Table 15.6 details the amounts associated with an increase of 20% in sales revenues in the next year, which results from an increase in sales volume from 30 000 to 36 000 units. Comparing these amounts with those in the first column, we can identify the following:

- The 20% increase in sales revenue was magnified into a 120% rise in EBIT. From the base sales level of $300 000, this is a degree of operating leverage of 6 times.
- The 120% rise in EBIT resulted in an increase in earnings per share of 150%. This is a degree of financial leverage of 1.25 times.
- Combining operating and financial leverage, the 20% rise in sales revenue has been magnified to a 150% increase in EPS. The degree of combined leverage can be expressed as:

$$\begin{array}{l}\text{degree of combined} \\ \text{leverage from the} \\ \text{base sales level}\end{array} = \text{DCL}_{sales} = \frac{\text{percentage change in EPS}}{\text{percentage change in sales}} \qquad \textbf{(15-10)}$$

$$= 150\%/20\% = 7.5 \text{ times}$$

FIGURE 15.3 Leverage and earnings fluctuations

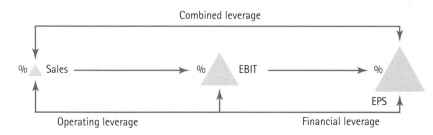

TABLE 15.6 Pierce Grain Company combined leverage analysis

ITEM	FORECAST BASE SALES LEVEL, t	SELECTED SALES LEVEL, t + 1	PERCENTAGE CHANGES
Sales	$300000	$360000	+20%
Less: Total variable costs	180000	216000	
Revenue before fixed costs	$120000	$144000	
Less: Total fixed costs	100000	100000	
EBIT	$20000	$44000	+120%
Less: Interest expense	4000	4000	
Earnings before taxes (EBT)	$16000	$40000	
Less: Taxes at 50%	8000	20000	
Net income	$8000	$20000	+150%
Less: Preference dividends	0	0	
Net earnings	$8000	$20000	+150%
Number of shares	150000	150000	
Earnings per share (EPS)	$0.053	$0.133	

Degree of operating leverage = $DOL_{\$300000} = \dfrac{120\%}{20\%} = 6$ times

Degree of financial leverage = $DFL_{\$20000} = \dfrac{150\%}{120\%} = 1.25$ times

Degree of combined leverage = $DCL_{\$300000} = \dfrac{150\%}{20\%} = 7.50$ times

The degree of combined leverage from the base sales level of $300000 is 7.5 times. This means that Pierce Grain Company's use of both operating and financial leverage will cause EPS to change 7.5 times any percentage change from the base sales revenue level of $300000. So, for example, a 10% fall in sales revenue to $270000 will result in a 75% fall in EPS to 1.25 cents.

The degree of combined leverage is actually the *product* (not the simple sum) of the operating and financial leverage measures as detailed in equation 15-11:

$$DOL_{sales} \times DFL_{EBIT} = DCL_{sales} \qquad \text{(15-11)}$$

So for Pierce Grain Company: $DCL_{\$300000} = 6 \times 1.25 = 7.5$ times

The degree of combined leverage can also be calculated without having to determine any percentage changes or calculating separate degree-of-leverage values, by equation (15-12):[6]

$$DCL_{sales} = \frac{Q(P-V)}{Q(P-V)-F-I} \qquad \text{(15-12)}$$

EXAMPLE 15.7 Calculation of degree of combined leverage

The variable cost definitions (V) in equation (15-12) are the same as used earlier in the chapter. Using equation (15-12) and the data in Table 15.6, the degree of combined leverage for Pierce Grain Company is:

$$DCL_{\$300000} = \frac{30000(\$10 - \$6)}{30000(\$10 - \$6) - \$100000 - \$4000}$$

$$= \frac{\$120000}{\$16000} = 7.5 \text{ times}$$

IMPLICATIONS OF LEVERAGE ANALYSIS

Leverage analysis identifies how a change in sales revenue produces magnified change in EBIT and earnings per share (EPS). Specifically, it shows that it is possible to influence the total exposure of the company's owners to the variability of EPS by influencing the amount of fixed operating costs and fixed financing costs. This requires knowledge of the degree of operating, financial and combined leverage.

For example, if significant variations in sales revenue are inherent in the business the company is in and it has a high degree of operating leverage, then adopting a financing mix with a low degree of financial leverage would minimise any *additional* fluctuations in EPS resulting from changes in EBIT. Conversely, a company that has a low degree of operating leverage might choose to use a high degree of financial leverage, with the aim of increasing EPS significantly if it expects sales revenues to increase.

Back to the principles

Business risk, financial risk and the three measurements of leverage all relate directly to **Principle 1: The risk–return trade-off—we won't take on additional risk unless we expect to be compensated with additional return**. Should a company with a high degree of business risk exposure increase its financial risk by deciding to use a high degree of financial leverage, we would expect the company's weighted average cost of capital to rise and its share price to fall. So, the nature of the company's financing mix is critical for both the financial manager and the shareholders. This central area of financial decision making is explored further in Chapter 16, 'Capital-structure policy'.

EBIT–EPS analysis

OBJECTIVE 4

Understand and use EBIT–EPS and comparative leverage ratios to analyse a company's capital structure.

Understanding the impact of investment and financing decisions on the wealth of the owners of the firm has been a consistent theme of this book. Two of the key variables affecting owner wealth are the amount of earnings (net profit) that the firm expects to generate in the future and the risk (variability) of those earnings. We saw in the previous section that, by increasing the degree of operating and financial leverage, the earnings (EPS) available for the owners of a company would increase significantly when sales revenue increased but they would fall significantly if sales revenue fell. We also saw that management often can not do much about the degree of operating leverage but that its choice of debt and equity finance can affect the degree of financial leverage. One way that a company can examine the impact that alternative capital structures with different degrees of financial leverage will have on EPS is by EBIT–EPS analysis.

Specifically, EBIT–EPS identifies the mix of debt and equity finance (i.e. degree of financial leverage) that will maximise earnings per share for a particular level (or range) of EBIT. Initially we will assume that an increase in EPS is equivalent to an increase in shareholder wealth. However, our analysis of financial leverage tells us that this is only part of the picture, because we also need to recognise the impact that the variability (risk) of these earnings (EPS) has on shareholder wealth.

To illustrate EBIT–EPS analysis, we will return to the example of the Pierce Grain Company and assume that the company's current capital structure is the 25% debt financing mix of Plan B, detailed in Tables 15.4 and 15.5. Furthermore, we will assume that EBIT from existing operations is expected to be $20000 per year. The company is considering a capital investment project that will cost $50000 and increase projected EBIT to $30000 per year. The company can raise the project's initial outlay of $50000 by (1) selling 50000 ordinary shares at $1 each, or (2) selling $50000 of new debt with an interest rate of 8.5%. These capital structures and corresponding EPS amounts are summarised in Table 15.7.

Part A of Table 15.7 details the company's current capital structure and the new capital structure after the addition of either the new share alternative or the new debt alternative. The bottom line of Part B shows the EPS expected to result from the company's projected EBIT. If the new project is rejected and the additional $50000 of finance is not raised, an EPS of 5.3 cents from an EBIT of $20000 would be expected.

Acceptance of the project will result in EBIT increasing to $30000, producing EPS of 6.5 cents if the $50000 investment is financed by new shares and 7.2 cents if new debt financing is used.

Using the criterion of selecting the capital-structure financing mix that will provide the highest EPS, the new debt-financing alternative would be favoured. But what if the company's business risk caused the expected EBIT level to vary over a considerable range? Could we be sure that the debt-financing alternative would *always* produce the higher EPS for shareholders? The answer is no. We can use an EBIT–EPS chart to confirm this answer.

EBIT–EPS CHART

The EBIT–EPS chart illustrates the impact of alternative capital structures on EPS over a range of EBIT levels. As the relationship between EBIT and EPS is assumed to be linear, the chart can be constructed from two EBIT–EPS points for each of the new capital-structure alternatives. Using the Pierce Grain Company example, the first EBIT–EPS point for each alternative can be taken directly from Part B of Table 15.7. If EBIT after the expansion is

TABLE 15.7 Pierce Grain Company analysis of financing choices

PART A: CAPITAL STRUCTURES

EXISTING CAPITAL STRUCTURE		WITH NEW ORDINARY SHARE FINANCING		WITH NEW DEBT FINANCING	
Long-term debt at 8%	$50000	Long-term debt at 8%	$50000	Long-term debt at 8%	$50000
Ordinary shares	150000	Ordinary shares	200000	Long-term debt at 8.5%	50000
				Ordinary shares	150000
Total liabilities & equity	$200000	Total liabilities & equity	$250000	Total liabilities & equity	$250000
Ordinary shares	150000	Ordinary shares	200000	Ordinary shares	150000

PART B: PROJECTED EPS LEVELS

	EXISTING CAPITAL STRUCTURE	WITH NEW SHARE FINANCING	WITH NEW DEBT FINANCING
EBIT	$20000	$30000	$30000
Less: Interest expense	4000	4000	8250
Earnings before taxes (EBT)	$16000	$26000	$21750
Less: Taxes at 50%	8000	13000	10875
Net income	$8000	$13000	$10875
Less: Preference dividends	0	0	0
Net earnings	$8000	$13000	$10875
EPS	$0.053	$0.065	$0.072

Finance at work

THE COCA-COLA COMPANY'S FINANCIAL POLICIES

The fact that the effects of financial leverage can be measured provides management with the opportunity to shape corporate policies around the decision to use or to avoid leverage-inducing debt instruments. The Coca-Cola Company has very specific policies on the use of financial leverage.

The 'primary objective' of the company is to maximise shareholder wealth, which means maximising the price of the company's existing ordinary shares. To achieve this objective, the company has developed a strategy that centres on investment in its core business and 'optimising' its cost of capital through properly designed financial policies.

Determining an appropriate (optimal) financing mix is a crucial activity of financial management. The Coca-Cola Company does not typically raise capital by issuing shares, and uses debt to lower its weighted average cost of capital and increase the return on shareholders' equity. Accordingly, the company searches for a 'prudent' level of debt use that is affected by (1) its projected cash flows, (2) interest coverage ratios, and (3) ratio of long-term debt to total capitalisation. Further, the company is highly concerned about the bond rating that it receives.

Source: The Coca-Cola Company, Annual Report, Form 10-K, 2009, pp. 56–59.

expected to be $30 000, the new share-financing capital-structure plan will result in an EPS of 6.5 cents whereas the new debt-financing capital-structure plan will have an EPS of 7.2 cents.

The second EBIT–EPS point can be determined by answering the following question: for each capital structure alternative what amount of EBIT will result in the EPS being exactly equal to zero? In other words, what is the amount of EBIT that will *just cover* the fixed financing costs? For the capital structure with new share financing, the fixed financing costs are $4000 for the existing interest expense, so an EBIT of $4000 would result in that capital structure producing an EPS of zero. For the capital structure with new debt financing, the fixed interest cost would be $8250, consisting of $4000 for the existing interest expense plus $4250 for the interest from the new debt issue. Thus, an EBIT amount of $8250 would be needed for the EPS with this capital structure to be zero.

The EBIT–EPS analysis chart representing the two alternative capital structures being considered by Pierce Grain Company is shown in Figure 15.4, with EBIT charted on the horizontal axis and EPS on the vertical axis.

The intercepts on the horizontal axis represent the amount of EBIT required for each capital structure to produce an EPS of zero: an EBIT of $4000 for the new share-financing plan and $8250 for the new debt-financing plan. The other points on the chart represent the EPS for each financing plan that would be expected if EBIT was $30 000: an EPS of 6.5 cents for the new share-financing plan and 7.25 cents for the new debt plan. A straight line is then drawn linking the two points for each plan.

From the line for each plan, the EPS amounts that can be expected for different EBIT amounts can be identified. Notice that the line for the new debt plan has a *steeper slope* than the line for the new share plan. This reflects the higher financial leverage of the capital structure with new debt that results in larger changes in EPS from changes in EBIT.

Also note that the lines for each financing plan *intersect*. This intersection is called the **indifference point**. Below the indifference point the EPS expected from the new share plan exceeds that expected from the new debt plan. Above the indifference point the reverse is the case, with the EPS expected from the new debt plan exceeding the EPS expected from the new share plan.

The indifference point, encircled in Figure 15.4, occurs at an EBIT level of $21 000 and produces an EPS of 4.25 cents for each plan. It is called the indifference point because at an EBIT of $21 000 the company would be indifferent between a capital structure with new shares or with new debt because both financing plans result in the same EPS of 4.25 cents.

indifference point
The level of earnings before interest and taxes (EBIT) that will equate earnings per share (EPS) between two financing plans with different degrees of financial leverage.

FIGURE 15.4 EBIT–EPS analysis chart

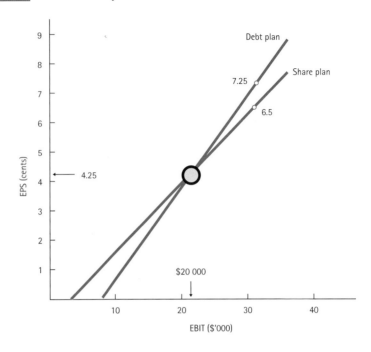

COMPUTING INDIFFERENCE POINTS

The EBIT–EPS indifference point, which identifies the EBIT level at which the EPS will be the same regardless of the financing plan chosen for the new capital structure, is sometimes called the break-even point. As Figure 15.4 showed for Pierce Grain Company, at EBIT amounts in excess of the indifference point the more highly levered debt-financing plan will generate a higher EPS, whereas below the indifference point the share-financing plan with less leverage will generate a higher EPS.

Although the indifference point values can be identified from an accurately drawn EBIT–EPS chart, it is usually easier to use equation (15-13) to solve for the amount of EBIT that produces the same EPS for each financing plan:

$$\underset{\text{EPS: Share plan}}{\frac{(EBIT - I)(1 - T) - PREF}{S_s}} = \underset{\text{EPS: Debt plan}}{\frac{(EBIT - I)(1 - T) - PREF}{S_b}} \qquad \textbf{(15-13)}$$

where I = interest expense
 T = the firm's income-tax rate
 $PREF$ = preference dividends paid
 S_s and S_b = the total number of shares outstanding under the share and debt (i.e. borrowing) plans respectively

If there are no preference shares in the financing plan, PREF is zero. However, if preference shares are part of one of the financing plans, equation (15-13) reflects the fact that preference dividends are not tax-deductible whereas interest (I) is tax-deductible.

EXAMPLE 15.8 Calculating the EBIT indifference point

Using the data for Pierce Grain Company in Table 15.7, the indifference level of EBIT for the new share and new debt-financing plans will be when:

$$\frac{(\text{EBIT} - \$4\,000)(1-0.5)}{200\,000} = \frac{(\text{EBIT} - 8\,250)(1-0.5)}{150\,000}$$

To solve for EBIT requires application of standard algebraic rules. If you are not sure how to do this, below is a suggested step-by-step process.

1. As these problems often have a large number in the denominator, which can make some of the calculations in later steps difficult, the first step is to divide the denominator amount by either 100, 10 000, 100 000, etc. In this example, divide each denominator amount by 10 000, giving:

$$\frac{(\text{EBIT} - 4\,000)(1-0.5)}{20} = \frac{(\text{EBIT} - 8\,250)(1-0.5)}{15}$$

2. For each side of the equation multiply the bracket components in the numerator:

$$\frac{0.5\,\text{EBIT} - 2\,000}{20} = \frac{0.5\,\text{EBIT} - 4\,125}{15}$$

3. For each side of the equation multiply the numerator by the other side's denominator amount:

$$15(0.5\,\text{EBIT} - 2\,000) = 20(0.5\,\text{EBIT} - 4\,125)$$

4. For each side of the equation multiply the bracket components:

$$7.5\,\text{EBIT} - 30\,000 = 10\,\text{EBIT} - 82\,500$$

5. Move the common terms to each side of the equation:

$$82\,500 - 30\,000 = 10\,\text{EBIT} - 7.5\,\text{EBIT}$$

6. Simplify each side of the equation:

$$52\,500 = 2.5\,\text{EBIT}$$

7. Divide both sides of the equation by 2.5:

$$\text{Solution: } 21\,000 = \text{EBIT}$$

For an EBIT of $21 000 the EPS will be 4.25 cents under both plans. This can be confirmed algebraically by replacing EBIT = 21 000 in each side of the original equation:

New share plan: $\dfrac{(21\,000 - 4\,000)(1-0.5)}{200\,000} = 4.25$ cents

New debt plan: $\dfrac{(21\,000 - 8\,250)(1-0.5)}{150\,000} = 4.25$ cents

USING EBIT–EPS CHARTS

The EBIT–EPS chart can be used to indicate which financing plan should be adopted to maximise EPS and therefore shareholder wealth. For example, if the management of Pierce Grain Company is reasonably confident that the amount of EBIT after the investment project is implemented will be close to the estimated $30 000, then the EBIT–EPS graph shows that the company should use the new debt-financing plan because it results in an EPS that is higher than that of the new share-financing plan.

If management is not confident about the expected EBIT amount, the indifference point indicates that EBIT would have to fall to below $21 000 before the EPS from the new share plan would be higher than the debt plan.

However, it is important to note that underlying this type of analysis of EBIT–EPS charts are some assumptions, for example that the amount of EBIT in the future can be reasonably estimated, and that a higher EPS is equivalent to higher shareholder wealth.

WHAT ABOUT RISK?

A major limitation of EBIT–EPS analysis is the assumption that choosing a capital structure that maximises the amount of EPS is equivalent to maximising shareholder wealth. This is because it is not only the amount of EPS that determines shareholder wealth but also the variability (risk) of these earnings (returns).

The conclusion from the EBIT–EPS chart for the Pierce Grain Company was that above the EBIT–EPS indifference point a more highly levered financial plan should be adopted because it produces larger EPS amounts. However, as demonstrated in the earlier section, financial leverage causes a percentage change in EBIT to produce a magnified percentage change in EPS. This means that a more highly levered financing plan will increase the variability (risk) of EPS in response to changes in EBIT.

This raises the question of what the effect on shareholder wealth will be if on the one hand a capital structure with higher financial leverage can produce a larger EPS but on the other it makes these EPS more variable (riskier).

We know that shareholders require a higher return to compensate them for higher risk. Therefore, whether the expected EPS from a capital structure with a certain degree of financial leverage will result in an increase in shareholder wealth will depend on whether the expected EPS will at least equal the amount the shareholders require to compensate them for the risk they face. EBIT–EPS analysis on its own is not able to answer this question.

One way to expand EBIT–EPS analysis to indicate the effect of financial leverage on shareholder wealth is to ascribe a price–earnings ratio to each financing plan. With all other things being equal, it would be expected that the financing plan with lower financial leverage and therefore lower financial risk would have a higher price–earnings ratio than a plan with higher financial leverage.

Assuming the price–earnings ratio for each financing plan can be determined, a notional value to shareholders from each plan can be obtained by multiplying the expected EPS for each plan by its price–earnings ratio. The plan that results in the higher value would be selected, as it would maximise shareholder wealth.

The problem with using price–earnings ratios to incorporate financial risk into EBIT–EPS analysis is determining an appropriate price–earnings ratio for each plan. One possibility is to

Back to the principles

The technique of EBIT–EPS analysis is well known within company financial planning departments. This tool of capital-structure management is best used if related to **Principle 3: Cash—not profits—is king** and **Principle 6: Capital markets—the markets are quick and the prices are right**.

Thus, the cash flows (as opposed to accounting profits) that are available to the firm after a financing choice is made will drive market prices. Recall from Chapter 1 that efficient markets will not be fooled by accounting changes that merely manipulate reported earnings. In the context of using these tools, then, the proper way to think of earnings per share and uncommitted earnings per share is on a cash basis rather than on an accounting accrual basis. The company pays its debt obligations not out of accounting profits but out of cash flows.

use observed price–earnings ratios for sharemarket-listed companies that have similar business risk and financing mix as proxies for the financing plans being analysed.

We must therefore conclude that EBIT–EPS analysis and charts are useful but limited tools to illustrate the impact of different financing plans on EPS and shareholder wealth. As we have seen, the major limitation is that EBIT–EPS analysis doesn't explicitly deal with the variability and valuation of the company's earnings. Other tools such as calculating the degree of leverage and analysing comparative leverage ratios can assist with assessing the risk associated with alternative financing choices.

Comparative leverage ratios

When financial ratio analysis was discussed in Chapter 5, two types of *leverage* ratios were identified.

1. *Balance sheet leverage ratios.* Computed from balance-sheet data to compare the company's use of debt finance and equity finance.
2. *Coverage ratios.* Generally computed from the income (profit and loss) statement, although sometimes balance-sheet data is needed. Coverage ratios provide estimates of the firm's ability to service its fixed-cost financing contracts. Apart from indicating the ability to pay fixed financing obligations, a firm with high coverage ratios implies that it has unused debt capacity.

USE OF LEVERAGE RATIOS

Leverage ratios can be used to analyse financing choices by identifying the effect that each alternative financing plan has on key financial ratios. For example, the financial manager can compare existing ratios calculated from the current capital structure with projected ratios that reflect the contractual commitments of each of the new financing alternatives. Table 15.8 is a sample worksheet for comparing the leverage ratios of different financing plans.

In reality, a number of versions of the coverage ratio section of the worksheet would need to be prepared, as it is likely that EBIT would vary over a considerable range of outcomes. A probability distribution could then be constructed for each coverage ratio over the possible values of EBIT. This would provide the financial manager with some indication of the risk (particularly of financial distress) associated with each financing plan.

INDUSTRY NORMS

The information provided by comparative leverage ratio analysis is enhanced if the company's ratios are compared with some standard. For example, industry ratios are widely used by

TABLE 15.8 Comparative leverage ratios: worksheet for analysing financing plans

RATIO	COMPUTATION METHOD	EXISTING RATIO	RATIO WITH ORDINARY SHARE FINANCING	RATIO WITH NEW DEBT FINANCING
Balance-sheet leverage ratios				
1. Debt ratio	total liabilities / total assets	____ %	____ %	____ %
2. Long-term debt to total capitalisation	long-term debt / (long-term debt + equity)	____ %	____ %	____ %
3. Total liabilities to equity	total liabilities / equity	____ %	____ %	____ %
4. Equity ratio	equity / total assets	____ %	____ %	____ %
Coverage ratios				
1. Times interest earned	EBIT / annual interest expense	____ times	____ times	____ times

corporate financial analysts, investment bankers, bank loan officers and debt-rating agencies as the standard for comparison, even though they may reflect data from companies whose basic business-risk exposure differs. On the whole, however, companies operating in the *same* industry tend to exhibit capital-structure ratios that cluster around a central value, which is called a *norm*.

As business risk varies from industry to industry, leverage (capital-structure) ratios also tend to vary from industry to industry.[7] For example, equity ratios indicate that the major producers in the steel industry use financial leverage to a lesser degree than do large firms in the retail industry.

This is not to say that all companies in the same industry will maintain leverage ratios 'close' to the industry norm. For instance, some very profitable companies in a particular industry may have balance-sheet leverage ratios reflecting their use of a high proportion of debt, whereas moderately profitable companies in the same industry may consider such a capital structure unduly risky and have ratios more in line with the industry norm. This illustrates one of the main uses of industry ratios. It should be possible to identify the reason for a company choosing to deviate in a material manner from the industry norm for the key ratios.

Concept check

For answers go to MyFinanceLab or
www.pearson.com.au/9781442539174

15.15 Explain the meaning of the EBIT–EPS indifference point.

15.16 How are various leverage ratios and industry norms used in capital-structure management?

ONE STEP FURTHER

SALES, CASH FLOW AND LEVERAGE

In earlier chapters, capital-budgeting techniques were used to assist the search by companies for projects that would add to shareholder wealth. Making capital investments in positive NPV projects is important not only for the owners of a business but also for the aggregate economy. This is because high levels of real capital investment over time are associated with high levels of societal wealth. Conversely, the majority of the members of countries that have low levels of real capital investment tend to be poor. So, it follows that national economic policy making needs to focus on the variables that positively affect the spending by firms on capital investment projects.

Two researchers* from the Federal Reserve Bank of Boston studied the investment spending of 396 United States domestic manufacturing companies and found some important relationships among the variables that seemed to influence the size of company capital budgets. They suggest that both capital budgets and the use of financial leverage depend on expected profits. This is close to asserting that a firm's capacity to generate future cash flows from its business operations is a major determinant of its capital-structure financing mix. This is likely to be because the firm's ability to pay the interest on its debt contracts depends on its ability to generate future operating cash flows.

Also, the researchers suggest that general business conditions (i.e. strong or weak) affect not only the size of the firm's capital budget but also management's decision to use more or less financial leverage in the capital budget. Such a logical combination of (1) the state of business conditions, and (2) the expectation of future operating profits (cash flows) means that the underlying nature of the firm's business should be the most important factor affecting its ultimate financing mix. That is, *business risk* and commercial strategy directly affect the firm's decision to use financial leverage.

Perhaps it is not surprising that leverage, liquidity and other variables have little influence on capital spending once the general business climate (represented by sales or cash flow) has been taken into account. Also, as the choice of leverage, like capital spending, depends on the prospect for profit, a good business climate can foster both investment and debt financing. In this economic environment, higher leverage does not deter investment; instead, it may appear to facilitate investment.

If at other times companies increase their leverage while reducing their capital spending, it might appear that higher leverage deters investment. However, this observed behaviour could occur because existing capital is providing a better return when compared with the return expected from new investments. Accordingly, appearances can be deceiving. It seems that investment and leverage decisions jointly depend on business conditions but this dependency entails no consistent relationship between indebtedness and investment.

For government economic policy, the evidence suggests that macroeconomic incentives for investment would be no less effective today than they have been in the past. In particular, the volume of investment spending in the economy would appear to respond to monetary and fiscal policies that result in expectations of increases in sales and profits.

* R. W. Kopcke with M. M. Howrey, 'A panel study of investment: sales, cash flow, the cost of capital, and leverage', *New England Economic Review*, January/February 1994, p. 23.

GFC

DELEVERAGING

Individuals and businesses that had high degrees of financial leverage were hit hard by the economic downturn caused by the Global Financial Crisis. In the extreme case their income fell to such an extent that they were not able to make interest and principal payments on the money they had borrowed and were made bankrupt. For many others their response has been to deleverage and use any spare cash they had available to repay the principal amount outstanding on their borrowings.

Summary

This chapter began by examining a number of tools that can assist the financial manager to choose an appropriate mix of debt and equity finance for the company's capital structure. In previous chapters the risk of an investment project was caused by the uncertainty (variability) of the project's cash flows. In this chapter the focus was on the variability of the company's residual earnings stream (e.g. earnings per share) caused by business and financial risk.

A major component of business risk is the way that fixed operating costs magnify the variability of earnings before interest and tax (EBIT) and for financial risk the way that fixed financing costs magnify the variability of earnings per share (EPS). Given these risks, a major task for financial managers is to analyse the effect of fluctuations of sales volumes and revenues on the variability of operating profit (EBIT) and residual earnings (EPS).

OBJECTIVE 1

OBJECTIVE 2

Break-even analysis identifies the quantity of sales or amount of sales revenue that will result in EBIT being zero. The break-even model can also be used to analyse the impact of price changes, cost-structure changes or volume changes on operating profit (EBIT).

OBJECTIVE 3

Operating leverage reflects the proportion of the firm's operating costs that are fixed and the impact on the responsiveness of EBIT to changes in sales revenues. The extent to which fixed operating costs magnify changes of sales revenue into even greater changes in EBIT is measured by the degree of operating leverage.

A firm has financial leverage when it finances a portion of its assets with securities such as debt and/or preference shares that pay investors a fixed rate of return. The effect of fixed financing costs, such as interest and preference dividends, is to magnify changes in EBIT into larger changes in earnings per share (EPS). The degree of financial leverage measures the sensitivity of EPS to changes in EBIT and is defined as the percentage change in EPS divided by the percentage change in EBIT. All other things being equal, the more fixed-cost finance sources the firm uses the greater its degree of financial leverage.

The combined effect of the firm using varying degrees of operating and financial leverage can be measured by the degree of combined leverage, which is defined as the percentage change in earnings per share divided by the percentage change in sales. The degree of combined leverage measure allows the financial manager to quickly assess the expected impact of changes in sales revenues on earnings per share.

OBJECTIVE 4

EBIT–EPS analysis and charts are useful tools for the financial manager to identify the effect on EPS that alternative financing plans with different degrees of financial leverage have when EBIT changes.

Another component in the assessment of different financing plans is to compare balance-sheet leverage ratios and coverage ratios with the firm's historical ratios and/or industry norms.

Key terms

financial leverage	521	**operating leverage**	521
indifference point	537	**semivariable costs**	522

Web works

Coca-Cola Amatil consistently publishes an outstanding and useful annual report, found at **www.ccamatil.com.au**. Coca-Cola is one of the few firms that we are aware of which actually includes a 'glossary' in its annual report. Many of the entries in its glossary are of a financial nature. Look at (a) return on capital employed, (b) cost of goods sold, and (c) earnings before interest and tax. Then see how their listings compare with those noted in the glossary to this text. You will notice that the resulting definitions are very close in each case.

Hint: These concepts drive the decision-making processes of financial executives. Thus, you want to make such concepts a part of your everyday vocabulary.

Review questions

15-1 Distinguish between business risk and financial risk. What gives rise to, or causes, each type of risk?

15-2 Define the term *financial leverage*. Does the firm use financial leverage if preference shares are present in the capital structure?

15-3 Define the term *operating leverage*. What type of effect occurs when the firm uses operating leverage?

15-4 A manager in your firm decides to employ break-even analysis. Of what shortcomings should this manager be aware?

15-5 What is meant by total risk exposure? How may a firm move to reduce its total risk exposure?

15-6 If a firm has a degree of combined leverage of 3.0 times, what earnings available to the firm's ordinary share investors would be expected from a negative sales revenue fluctuation of 15%?

15-7 Break-even analysis assumes linear revenue and cost functions. In reality, these linear functions over large output and sales levels are not likely to exist. Why?

15-8 What is the primary weakness of EBIT–EPS analysis as a financing decision tool?

Self-test problems

ST-1 (*Break-even point*) You are an analyst for a manufacturing firm that produces a single product and you have determined the following cost-structure information based on an output level of 10 million units. Using this information, find the break-even point in units of output for the firm.

For answers go to MyFinanceLab
www.pearson.com.au/myfinancelab

Return on operating assets	= 30%
Operating asset turnover	= 6 times
Operating assets	= $20 million
Degree of operating leverage	= 4.5 times

ST-2 (*Leverage analysis*) For your company you have prepared an analytical profit and loss statement of the most recent year's operations, which ended yesterday. Your supervisor has just handed you a memorandum that asks for written responses to the questions that follow the statement:

Sales	$20 000 000
Variable costs	12 000 000
Revenue before fixed costs	$8 000 000
Fixed costs	5 000 000
EBIT	$3 000 000
Interest expense	1 000 000
Earnings before taxes	$2 000 000
Taxes (0.50)	1 000 000
Net income	$1 000 000

(a) At this level of output, what is the degree of operating leverage?
(b) What is the degree of financial leverage?
(c) What is the degree of combined leverage?
(d) What is the firm's break-even point in sales dollars?
(e) If sales should increase by 30%, by what percentage would earnings before taxes (and net income) increase?
(f) Prepare an analytical profit and loss statement that verifies the calculations from part **(e)** above.

ST-3 (*Fixed costs and the break-even point*) Bonaventure Manufacturing expects to earn $210 000 next year after taxes from sales of $4 million. The firm manufactures a combined bookshelf and desk unit that sells for $200 and has a variable cost per unit of $150. Bonaventure has a 30% tax rate.

(a) What are the firm's fixed costs expected to be next year?
(b) Calculate the firm's break-even point in both units and dollars.

ST-4 (*EBIT–EPS analysis*) Four engineers from Martin-Bowing Company are leaving the firm in order to form their own company. The new firm will produce and distribute computer software on a national basis. The software will be aimed at scientific markets and at businesses wanting to install

comprehensive information systems. Private investors are willing to finance the new company and two financing plans are being studied. Both of these plans involve the use of some financial leverage, but one is much more highly levered than the other.

Plan A requires the firm to sell $1 million of bonds with an effective interest rate (yield) of 14%. In addition, $5 million would be raised by selling ordinary shares at $5 each.

Plan B also involves raising $6 million. This would be accomplished by selling $3 million of bonds at an effective interest rate of 16%. The other $3 million would come from selling ordinary shares at $5 each.

In both cases the use of financial leverage is considered to be a permanent part of the firm's capital structure, so no fixed maturity date is used in the analysis. The firm considers a 50% tax rate appropriate for planning purposes.

(a) Find the EBIT indifference level associated with the two financing plans, and prepare an EBIT–EPS analysis chart.
(b) Prepare an analytical income statement that demonstrates that EPS will be the same regardless of the plan selected for the EBIT level found in part (a).
(c) A detailed financial analysis of the firm's prospects suggests that long-term EBIT will be above $1 188 000 annually. Taking this into consideration, which plan will generate the higher EPS?
(d) Suppose that long-term EBIT is forecast to be $1 188 000 per year. Under Plan A a price–earnings ratio of 13 would apply, and under Plan B a price–earnings ratio of 11 would apply. If this set of financial relationships does hold, which financing plan would you recommend be implemented?
(e) Again, assume an EBIT level of $1 188 000. What price–earnings ratio applied to the EPS of Plan B would provide the same share price as that projected for Plan A? Refer to your data from part (d).

Problems

For more problems and for answers to problems marked with an asterisk (*) go to MyFinanceLab at
www.pearson.com.au/myfinancelab

15-1 (*Fixed costs and the break-even point*) Cypress Books expects to earn $55 000 next year after taxes. Sales will be $400 000. The store is located near the shopping district surrounding the Eastville University. Its average product sells for $28 a unit. The variable cost per unit is $18. The store experiences a 45% tax rate.

(a) What are the store's fixed costs expected to be next year?
(b) Calculate the store's break-even point in both units and dollars.

15-2* (*Fixed costs and the break-even point*) Albert's Cooling Equipment manufactures small refrigerators and hopes to earn $80 000 next year after taxes from sales of $2 million. The refrigerators sell for $80 per unit and have a variable cost of $56. Albert's experiences a 40% tax rate.

(a) What are the firm's fixed costs expected to be next year?
(b) Calculate the firm's break-even point in both units and dollars.

15-3* (*Fixed costs*) Denton Heat Treating projects that next year its fixed costs will total $120 000. Its only product sells for $12 per unit, of which $7 is a variable cost. The management of Denton is considering the purchase of a new machine that will lower the variable cost per unit to $5. The new machine, however, will add to fixed costs through an increase in depreciation expense. How large can the addition to fixed costs be to keep the firm's break-even point in units produced and sold unchanged?

15-4 (*Break-even point and selling price*) Heritage Chain Company will produce 175 000 units next year. All of this production will be sold as finished goods. Fixed costs will total $335 000 and variable costs are relatively predictable at 80% of sales.

(a) If Heritage Chain wants to achieve an earnings before interest and taxes level of $270 000 next year, at what price per unit must it sell its product?
(b) Based on your answer to part (a), set up an analytical income statement that will verify your solution.

15-5   (*Sales mix and break-even point*) Queensland Components produces four lines of motor-vehicle accessories for major motor-vehicle manufacturers. The lines are known by the code letters A, B, C and D. The current sales mix for Queensland Components and the contribution margin ratio (unit contribution margin divided by unit sales price) for these product lines are as follows:

PRODUCT LINE	PERCENTAGE OF TOTAL SALES	CONTRIBUTION MARGIN RATIO (%)
A	33½	40
B	41⅔	32
C	16⅔	20
D	8⅓	60

Total sales for next year are forecast to be $120 000. Total fixed costs will be $29 400.

   (a) Prepare a table showing (i) sales, (ii) total variable costs, and (iii) the total contribution margin associated with each product line.
   (b) What is the aggregate contribution margin ratio indicative of this sales mix?
   (c) At this sales mix, what is the break-even point in dollars?

15-6*   (*Sales mix and break-even point*) Because of production constraints, Queensland Components (see problem 15-5) may have to adhere to a different sales mix for next year. The alternative plan is below:

PRODUCT LINE	PERCENTAGE OF TOTAL SALES
A	25
B	36⅔
C	33⅓
D	5

   (a) Assuming that all other facts in problem 15-5 remain the same, what effect will this different sales mix have on Queensland Components' break-even point in dollars?
   (b) Which sales mix will Queensland Components' management prefer?

15-7*   (*Operating leverage*) The Country Metals Company manufactures an assortment of wood-burning stoves. The average selling price for the various units is $500. The associated variable cost is $350 per unit and fixed costs for the firm average $180 000 annually.

   (a) What is the break-even point in units for the company?
   (b) What is the dollar sales volume the firm must achieve to reach the break-even point?
   (c) What is the degree of operating leverage for a production and sales level of 5000 units for the firm? (Calculate to three decimal places.)
   (d) What will be the projected effect on earnings before interest and taxes if the firm's sales level increases by 20% from the volume noted in part **(c)**?

15-8*   (*Break-even point and operating leverage*) Some financial data for three firms are given below:

	EASY CHAIRS	SUNLIGHT SKY LIGHTS	JEFFREY WHOLESALERS
Average selling price per unit	$32.00	$875.00	$97.77
Average variable cost per unit	$17.38	$400.00	$87.00
Units sold	18 770	2 800	11 000
Fixed costs	$120 350	$850 000	$89 500

   (a) What is the profit for each company at the indicated sales volume?
   (b) What is the break-even point in units for each company?
   (c) What is the degree of operating leverage for each company at the indicated sales volume?
   (d) If sales were to decline, which firm would suffer the largest relative decline in profitability?

15-9   (*Leverage analysis*) Your firm's accountant supplies you with the following analytical income statement and desires answers to the four questions listed below the statement.

Sales	$10 000 000
Variable costs	8 000 000
Revenue before fixed costs	$2 000 000
Fixed costs	500 000
EBIT	$1 500 000
Interest expense	200 000
Earnings before taxes	$1 300 000
Taxes	650 000
Net income	$650 000

    (a) At this level of output, what is the degree of operating leverage?
    (b) What is the degree of financial leverage?
    (c) What is the degree of combined leverage?
    (d) What is the firm's break-even point in sales dollars?

15-10 (*Leverage analysis*) You have developed the following analytical profit and loss statement for your company. It represents the most recent year's operations, which ended yesterday.

Sales	$45 750 000
Variable costs	22 800 000
Revenue before fixed costs	$22 950 000
Fixed costs	9 200 000
EBIT	13 750 000
Interest expense	1 350 000
Earnings before taxes	$12 400 000
Taxes (0.50)	6 200 000
Net income	$6 200 000

Your supervisor has just handed you a memo asking for written responses to the following questions:

    (a) At this level of output, what is the degree of operating leverage?
    (b) What is the degree of financial leverage?
    (c) What is the degree of combined leverage?
    (d) What is the firm's break-even point in sales dollars?
    (e) If sales increase by 25%, by what percent would earnings before taxes (and net income) increase?

15-11* (*Break-even point*) You are a hard-working analyst in the finance office for a manufacturing firm that produces a single product. You have developed the following cost-structure information for the firm. All of it pertains to an output level of 10 million units. Using this information, find the break-even point in units of output for the firm.

Return on operating assets	= 25%
Operating asset turnover	= 5 times
Operating assets	= $20 million
Degree of operating leverage	= 4 times

15-12* (*EBIT–EPS analysis*) Four recent arts graduates have interested a group of venture capitalists in backing a new business enterprise. The proposed business would consist of a series of retail outlets to distribute and service a full line of revolutionary vacuum cleaners and accessories. Two million dollars is needed to launch the new firm's operations and two financing plans have been proposed by the graduates.

    Plan A is an all-ordinary-share structure. Two million dollars would be raised by selling 160 000 ordinary shares.

Plan B would involve the use of long-term debt financing. One million dollars would be raised by marketing debt with an effective interest rate of 12%. Under this alternative, selling 80 000 ordinary shares would raise another million dollars.

The debt funds raised under Plan B are considered to have no fixed maturity date, in that this portion of financial leverage is thought to be a permanent part of the company's capital structure. The fledgling executives have decided to use a 40% tax rate in their analysis, and they have hired you on a consulting basis to do the following:

(a) Find the EBIT indifference level associated with the two financing proposals.
(b) Prepare an analytical income statement that proves EPS will be the same regardless of the plan chosen at the EBIT level found in part (a).

15-13* (*EBIT–EPS analysis*) A group of retired university professors has decided to form a small manufacturing company to produce a range of traditional office furniture. Two financing plans have been proposed by the investors.

Plan A is an all-ordinary-share alternative, where 5 million shares will be sold to net the firm $4 per share.

Plan B involves the use of financial leverage. A debt issue with a 20-year maturity period will be privately placed. The debt issue will carry an interest rate of 10%, and the principal borrowed will amount to $6 million. The corporate tax rate is 50%.

(a) Prepare an EBIT–EPS analysis chart for this company.
(b) Find the EBIT indifference level associated with the two financing proposals.
(c) If a detailed financial analysis projects that long-term EBIT will always be close to $2.4 million annually, which plan will provide for the higher EPS?

15-14 (*EBIT–EPS analysis*) Three recent computer-science graduates are forming a company to write and distribute software for various personal computers. The company's software products have been tested and displayed at several trade shows and computer fairs and 12 retail outlets have already been identified and are committed to purchasing the software. All that is lacking for the next phase of the company's development is adequate financing. A small group of private investors is interested in providing finance and two financing proposals are being evaluated.

The first (Plan A) is an all-ordinary-share capital structure. Two million dollars would be raised by selling shares at $10 each.

Plan B would involve the use of financial leverage. One million dollars would be raised selling bonds with an effective interest rate of 11% (per annum). Under this second plan, the remaining $1 million would be raised by selling shares at $10 per share. The use of financial leverage is considered to be a permanent part of the firm's capitalisation, so no fixed maturity date is needed for the analysis. A 34% tax rate is appropriate for the analysis.

(a) Find the EBIT indifference level associated with the two financing plans using an EBIT–EPS graph. Check your results algebraically.
(b) A detailed financial analysis of the firm's prospects suggests that the long-term EBIT will be above $300 000 annually. Taking this into consideration, which plan will generate the higher EPS?
(c) Suppose that long-term EBIT is forecast to be $300 000 per year. Under Plan A, a price–earnings ratio of 19 would apply. Under Plan B, a price–earnings ratio of 15 would apply. If this set of financial relationships does hold, which financing plan would you recommend?

15-15 (*EBIT–EPS analysis*) Albany Golf Equipment is analysing three different financing plans for a newly formed subsidiary. The plans are described below:

PLAN A	PLAN B	PLAN C
Ordinary shares:	Bonds at 9%:	Preference shares at 9%:
$100 000	$20 000	$20 000
	Ordinary shares:	Ordinary shares:
	80 000	80 000

In all cases the ordinary shares will be sold to net Albany $10 per share. The subsidiary is expected to generate an average EBIT per year of $22 000. The management of Albany places great emphasis on EPS performance. Income is taxed at a 50% rate.

(a) Where feasible, find the EBIT indifference levels between the alternatives.

(b) Which financing plan do you recommend that Albany pursue?

15-16 (*Break-even point*) Union Wines sells its most popular wine for $30 a bottle, of which 70% is required to pay the variable costs of production and sales. If the company's fixed costs are $360000, how many bottles of wine must the company sell to break even?

15-17 (*Break-even point*) You are employed as a financial analyst for a single-product manufacturing firm. Your supervisor has made the following cost-structure information available to you, all of which pertains to an output level of 1600000 units.

Return on operating assets	= 15%
Operating asset turnover	= 5 times
Operating assets	= $3 million
Degree of operating leverage	= 8 times

Your task is to find the break-even point in units of output for the firm.

15-18 (*Fixed costs*) Marco Computer Games is forecasting fixed costs next year of $300000. The firm's single product wholesales for $20 per unit and incurs a variable cost per unit of $14. The firm may acquire some new computer graphics equipment that would lower variable costs per unit to $12. The new equipment, however, would add to fixed costs through the price of an annual maintenance agreement. How large can this increase in fixed costs be and still keep the firm's present break-even point in units produced and sold unchanged?

15-19 (*Leverage analysis*) You have been supplied with the following analytical income statement and requested to answer the four questions following the statement.

Sales	$12000000
– Variable costs	9000000
Revenue before fixed costs	$3000000
– Fixed costs	2000000
EBIT	$1000000
– Interest expense	200000
Earnings before taxes	$800000
– Taxes	400000
Net income	$400000

(a) At this level of output, what is the degree of operating leverage?

(b) What is the degree of financial leverage?

(c) What is the degree of combined leverage?

(d) What is the firm's break-even point in sales dollars?

15-20 (*Break-even point and selling price*) Lavender Garden Pots will produce 200000 units next year. All of this production will be sold as finished goods. Fixed costs will total $300000 and variable costs are predicted to be 75% of sales.

(a) If Lavender Garden Pots wants to achieve earnings before interest and taxes (EBIT) of $240000 next year, at what price per unit must it sell its product?

(b) Based on your answer to part **(a)**, set up an analytical income statement that will verify your solution.

15-21 (*Fixed costs and break-even point*) Al's Orchids sells pots of orchid plants to supermarkets for $17 a pot and next year expects to earn $38000 after tax from sales of $420002. The variable cost per orchid pot is $9 and the firm is subject to a 35% tax rate.

(a) What are Al's Orchids' fixed costs expected to be next year?

(b) Calculate the firm's break-even point in both units and dollars.

15-22 (*Operating leverage*) The B. H. Williams Company manufactures a range of timber chicken coops that can be easily assembled by the home handyperson. The average selling price for the various coops is $475 and the associated variable cost is $350 per unit. Fixed costs for the firm average $200 000 annually.

   (a) What is the break-even point in units for the company?
   (b) What is the dollar sales volume that the firm must achieve to reach the break-even point?
   (c) What is the degree of operating leverage for a production and sales level of 6000 units for the firm?
   (d) What will be the projected effect on earnings before interest and taxes if the firm's sales level increases by 13% from the volume noted in part **(c)**?

15-23 (*Leverage analysis*) An analytical income statement for your company follows:

Sales	$13 750 000
– Variable costs	9 500 000
Revenue before fixed costs	$4 250 000
– Fixed costs	3 000 000
EBIT	$1 250 000
– Interest expense	250 000
Earnings before taxes	$1 000 000
– Taxes	430 000
Net income	$570 000

   (a) At this level of output, what is the degree of operating leverage?
   (b) What is the degree of financial leverage?
   (c) What is the degree of combined leverage?
   (d) What is the firm's break-even point in sales dollars?

15-24 (*Leverage analysis*) An analytical income statement for last year's operations follows.

Sales	$18 000 000
– Variable costs	7 000 000
Revenue before fixed costs	$11 000 000
– Fixed costs	6 000 000
EBIT	$5 000 000
– Interest expense	1 750 000
Earnings before taxes	$3 250 000
– Taxes	1 250 000
Net income	$2 000 000

   (a) At this level of output, what is the degree of operating leverage?
   (b) What is the degree of financial leverage?
   (c) What is the degree of combined leverage?
   (d) If sales increase by 15%, by what percent would earnings before taxes (and net income) increase?
   (e) What is the firm's break-even point in sales dollars?

15-25 (*Integrative problem*) Imagine that you were hired recently as a financial analyst for a relatively new highly leveraged company that manufactures only one product, a state-of-the-art snow ski. Up to this point the company has been operating without much quantitative knowledge of the business and financial risks that it faces.

   The winter season has just ended, so the CEO of the company has started to focus more on the financial aspects of managing the business. She has set up a meeting for next week to discuss matters such as the business and financial risks faced by the company. You have been asked to prepare an analysis to assist the discussions.

   As a first step, you have compiled the following information regarding the cost structure of the company:

Output level	50 000 units
Operating assets	$2 000 000
Operating asset turnover	7 times
Return on operating assets	35%
Degree of operating leverage	5 times
Interest expense	$400 000
Tax rate	35%

As the next step, you need to *determine the break-even point in units of output* for the company. One of your strong points has been that you always prepare supporting work papers, which show how you arrived at your conclusions, and you expect the CEO will want to review your work papers for this task.

You also have the information to *prepare an analytical income statement* for the company, which you will need in order to answer the following questions.

(a) What is the current degree of financial leverage?
(b) What is the current degree of combined leverage?
(c) What is the firm's break-even point in sales dollars?
(d) If sales increase by 30% (as the CEO expects), by what percent would EBT (earnings before taxes) and net income increase?
(e) Prepare another analytical income statement, this time to verify the calculations from part (d).

15-26 (*Integrative problem*) You are employed by an IT consulting company to provide the owners with financial analysis and advice. You have determined the following information about the current cost structure of the company:

Output level (number of clients)	1250
Operating assets	$1 250 000
Operating asset turnover	1.5 times
Return on operating assets	40%
Degree of operating leverage	2.5 times
Interest expense	$84 000
Tax rate	30%
Number of ordinary shares on issue	100 000

The company's managing director is concerned about the impact of an economic downturn on the company's finances and has asked you to address the following:

(a) What is the break-even number of clients for the company?
(b) Prepare an analytical income statement for the current activity of the company and calculate the earnings per share (EPS).
(c) Prepare an analytical income statement for the break-even level of activity of the company.
(d) What is the current degree of financial leverage?
(e) What is the current degree of combined leverage?
(f) If sales revenue falls by 20%, by what percent would EPS (earnings per share) fall?
(g) Prepare another analytical income statement, this time to verify the calculations from part (f).

15-27 (*Integrative problem*) Onephone Limited is a newly listed telecom company that has prepared the following analytical income statement for the financial year just ended:

Sales: 1.04 m customers x average annual billing per customer $750	$780 000 000
Variable costs	156 000 000
Revenue before fixed costs	$624 000 000
Fixed costs	350 000 000
EBIT	$274 000 000
Interest expense	54 000 000
Earnings before taxes	$220 000 000
Taxes (25%)	55 000 000
Net income	$165 000 000
Number of issued ordinary shares	50 000 000

Your task is to address the following:

    (a) What is the break-even sales value for the company?

    (b) Prepare an analytical income statement for the break-even level of activity of the company.

    (c) What is the current degree of operating leverage?

    (d) What is the current degree of financial leverage?

    (e) What is the current degree of combined leverage?

    (f) If sales revenue rises by 10%, by what percent would EPS (earnings per share) rise?

    (g) Prepare another analytical income statement, this time to verify the calculations from part **(f)**.

Case study

You are employed as the financial manager for Argon Services Limited. Up to this time the company has used only equity finance to fund its investment projects. One reason for this practice has been that the board of directors knows that there is a direct relationship between changes in the company's EBIT and changes in the returns to shareholders as measured by EPS. The company's after-tax profits (at a company income tax rate of 30%) are currently $900 000, but due to the recent closure of a major competitor you expect sales in the foreseeable future to increase significantly and have budgeted for sales to increase by about $300 000 from the current level.

At the recent meeting of the company's board of directors you strongly argued that, if the company changed its capital structure to finance the expected expansion in sales by using debt finance, it could significantly magnify any expected increase in earnings per share. However, the company's chief executive is extremely conservative and is concerned that there will be a downturn in the economy and that next year's sales and EBIT will be less than the expected levels. He is particularly keen to ensure that, if a worst-case scenario of an EBIT downturn of 20% occurs, the after-tax profit available for shareholders will not fall more than 1.3 times as much as this extreme downturn in EBIT. You have been asked to answer the following questions.

    1. Why is there a direct relationship between changes in EBIT and changes in EPS if the company is 100% equity financed?

    2. Why does borrowing money affect the relationship between changes in EBIT and changes in EPS?

    3. If the company decides to include debt in its capital structure, what is the maximum annual amount of interest the company can pay in the future.

Notes

1.   If what the accountants call 'other income' and 'other expenses' are equal to zero, then EBIT is equal to net operating income (NOI). Accordingly, EBIT and NOI are often used interchangeably.
2.   Note that the concept of financial risk used here differs from that used in the examination of cash management and marketable-securities management in Chapter 8.
3.   In greenhouse agriculture, where plant growth is stimulated under strictly controlled temperatures, heat costs will tend to be fixed whether the building is full or only half full of seedlings. However, in a metal stamping operation, where items such as levers are being produced, there is no need to heat the plant to as high a temperature when the machines are stopped and the workers are not there. In the latter case, the energy costs will tend to be variable.
4.   From Table 15.3, the difference between an EBIT amount of +$20000 at t and –4000 at $t + 1$ is –$24000.
5.   In actual practice, moving from a 25% to a 40% debt ratio would probably result in a higher interest rate on the additional debt. That effect is ignored here in order to concentrate on the ramifications of using different proportions of debt in the financial structure.
6.   As was the case with the degree of financial leverage measure, the variable, I, in the combined leverage measure must include any preference-share dividends when preference shares are in the financial structure.
7.   See, for example, Eli Schwartz and J. Richard Aronson, 'Some surrogate evidence in support of the concept of optimal financial structure', *Journal of Finance*, 22, March 1967, pp. 10–18; David F. Scott Jr, 'Evidence on the importance of financial structure', *Financial Management*, 1, Summer 1972, pp. 45–50; and David F. Scott Jr and John D. Martin, 'Industry influence on financial structure', *Financial Management*, 4, Spring 1975, pp. 67–73.

Learning objectives

After reading this chapter, you should be able to:

1   Distinguish between *financial structure* and *capital structure*.
2   Appreciate the main principles in choosing an appropriate capital structure for a company.
3   Understand three theoretical models to explain how a company's capital structure influences the value of its shares.
4   Appreciate that agency costs, free cash flow and dividend imputation can affect capital-structure policy.
5   Appreciate aspects of the actual management of capital structure by companies.

For a complete eBook go to MyFinanceLab
www.pearson.com.au/myfinancelab

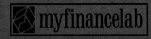

Capital-structure policy

CHAPTER PREVIEW

This chapter examines how firms choose the mix of long-term debt and equity finance to fund their investment projects, a process that is also called 'capital-structure policy'. Some theoretical models are used to identify the major factors that appear to affect this choice, particularly the impact of financial leverage on the risk and cost of equity and whether there is an optimal capital structure that firms should aim to achieve. Finally, what is known of the actual management of capital structure is briefly examined.

Financial structure and capital structure

At the outset a distinction needs to be made between the terms *financial structure* and *capital structure*. A firm's **financial structure** is all the short- and long-term items that appear in the liability and equity section of its balance sheet, whereas **capital structure** only reflects the mix of the *long-term* sources of funds it uses.

Therefore, the difference between financial structure and capital structure is the exclusion of current liabilities from the measurement of capital structure, as illustrated by equation (16-1).

Capital structure = financial structure – current liabilities   **(16-1)**

The major reason a distinction is made between financial structure and capital structure is to focus attention on different aspects of the financing mix. For example, one aspect of prudent **financial-structure design** concerns the maturity composition of the sources of funds as reflected by the question of how the total financing sources should be divided between short- and long-term components.

There are also other questions that focus attention on capital-structure design, such as what proportion of total long-term financing should be provided by long-term debt or equity?

To answer questions such as these, recall the *hedging principle* from Chapters 5 and 7. This principle states that short-lived assets should be financed with short-term sources of finance and long-lived assets should be financed with long-term sources of finance. Applying the hedging principle, a firm should fund its long-lived capital investments, represented primarily by non-current assets on its balance sheet, with long-term sources of finance.

Given the amount of long-term finance that a company requires to fund its investment in long-lived assets, the objective of *capital-structure management* is to determine the mix of long-term debt and equity that will maximise the company's share price and shareholder wealth.

Although this mix can be viewed in terms of the absolute dollar *amounts* of long-term debt, preference shares and ordinary equity to be used by the company, this chapter will predominantly be using relative proportions. For example, should long-term debt provide, say, 30% of the total long-term finance and the other 70% be provided by a combination of preference shares and ordinary equity, or should the proportions be different from these?

To try and answer questions such as this, the next section looks at the theory of capital structure.

OBJECTIVE 1

Distinguish between *financial structure* and *capital structure*.

financial structure
The mix of all the short- and long-term sources of finance that appear on the firm's balance sheet.

capital structure
The mix of long-term sources of debt and equity finance used by the firm.

financial-structure design
The mixture of short-term and long-term permanent financing components to minimise the cost of raising a given amount of funds.

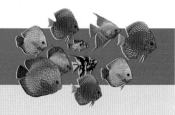

Regardless of your program

CAPITAL-STRUCTURE MATTERS

When an individual or a firm borrows money, the terms of the debt agreement requires the borrower to pay to the lender regular interest amounts and to repay the debt principal. This requirement is backed by the legal system so that if the borrower fails to meet the terms of the agreement the lender can go to the courts to enforce payment and in the extreme case can petition for the bankruptcy of an individual or the liquidation of a company. On the other hand, the providers of equity finance usually have no enforceable agreement to receive regular amounts or the repayment of their investment. So understanding the factors that influence capital-structure policy, particularly how much money you or a firm should borrow, is important.

OBJECTIVE **2**

Appreciate the main principles in choosing an appropriate capital structure for a company.

optimal capital structure
The capital structure which, when raising a given amount of funds, minimises the company's weighted average cost of capital and maximises the company's share price and shareholder wealth.

For answers go to MyFinanceLab or
www.pearson.com.au/9781442539174

A glance at capital-structure theory

From the perspective of maximising the earnings available from ordinary shareholders it makes sense for a company to strive to minimise its operating costs (e.g. materials and wages) and its costs of capital (e.g. interest on debt). We know from earlier chapters that the costs of capital reflect the level of risk faced by the providers of capital and, because of its lower risk, that debt has a lower cost to the company than equity. Consequently, it would not be unreasonable to conclude that a company should have a capital structure that uses as much cheaper long-term debt as possible.

However, in Chapter 15, when discussing the analysis and impact of leverage, we saw that the payment of interest cash flows for the use of debt (i.e. financial leverage) not only increased the company's earnings per share (EPS) but also increased the variability (risk) of those earnings for the ordinary shareholders. Through EBIT–EPS analysis and charts we were able to identify the effect of different capital structures on the amount of EPS, but we found it was difficult to quantify the impact that changes in the variability of EPS had on the company's share price and shareholder wealth.

Given these impacts of financial leverage and assuming that a company's operating revenues and costs are held constant, the question that capital-structure theory attempts to answer is: can a company vary the mix of long-term debt and equity financing sources that it uses into an **optimal capital structure** that minimises its weighted average cost of capital and therefore maximises its share price?

> ## Concept check
> 16.1 What is the objective of capital-structure management?
> 16.2 What is the main attribute of an optimal capital structure?

ANALYTICAL SETTING

To identify the effects of capital-structure decisions on a company's weighted average cost of capital and therefore on its share price, we will use a framework that economists call 'partial equilibrium analysis'. In a partial equilibrium analysis the focus is on the effect that changes in a main factor will have on key items of interest, ignoring the impact of other factors on the key items.

With capital-structure management, there are two key items of interest:

- the company's weighted average cost of capital (K_0)
- the market price of the company's ordinary share (P_0).

The company's financial leverage is the main factor that will be varied; other financial decisions such as the choice of capital investments and the company's dividend policy will be held constant.

There are a number of other assumptions that we also need to make in order to assist the analysis of the company's capital structure:

1. The company's income is not subject to any taxation. The major implication of removing this assumption is discussed later.
2. Capital structures consist only of ordinary equity and long-term debt. Furthermore, the degree of financial leverage used by the company is altered by it issuing ordinary shares and using the proceeds to retire existing debt, or by issuing debt and using the proceeds to repurchase ordinary shares. This permits financial leverage to be varied while maintaining constant the total book value of the company's capital structure.
3. The expected values of all investors' forecasts of the future amounts of the company's net operating income (EBIT) are identical. Also, the company's EBIT is not expected to grow over time, so each year's forecast is the same as for any other year. This is consistent with the assumption below, where the company's dividend stream is not expected to grow.
4. The securities for raising debt (bonds) and equity (ordinary shares) are traded in perfect or efficient financial markets. This means that transaction costs and legal restrictions do not impede any investors' incentives to execute portfolio changes that they expect will increase their wealth. Information is freely available. Moreover, companies and individuals that have equivalent credit risk can borrow money at the same rate of interest.

One of the key items of interest in the analysis of capital structure is the market price of the company's ordinary share (P_0). To facilitate our analysis, we will adopt a *simplified* version of the basic dividend valuation model presented in Chapters 10 and 14. This model is restated below as equation (16-2):

$$P_0 = \sum_{t=1}^{\infty} \frac{D_t}{(1 + K_E)^t} \qquad \textbf{(16-2)}$$

where P_0 = the current price of the firm's ordinary share
D_t = the cash dividend per share expected by investors during period t
K_E = the cost of ordinary equity

Again, to simplify our analysis, we will make the following assumptions concerning the valuation process implicit in equation (16-2):

1. The company retains none of its current earnings. This means that all of each period's earnings per share will be paid to shareholders in the form of cash dividends. In other words, the company's dividend payout ratio is 100%, which means that cash dividends per share in equation (16-2) are equal to earnings per share for the same period.
2. Cash dividends paid will not change over the infinite holding period. Thus, $D_1 = D_2 = D_3 = \ldots = D_\infty$. There is no expected growth by investors in the dividend stream. As this dividend stream is perpetual, and according to the mathematics of perpetuities, equation (16-2) can be reduced to equation (16-3), where E_t represents earnings per share during period t.

$$P_0 = \frac{D_t}{K_E} = \frac{E_t}{K_E} \qquad \textbf{(16-3)}$$

Given this analytical setting, we are ready to examine the relationship between capital structures with different amounts of financial leverage and the company's weighted average cost of capital and its ordinary share price.

What we are going to find, however, is that there is no generally accepted capital-structure theory but a number of differing views.

The first view takes the extreme position that the amount of financial leverage in the capital structure has no effect on the company's weighted average cost of capital and share price. The

FYI

The aim of the discussion, together with illustrations of the two extreme positions, is to highlight the major impacts of different capital structures on share prices and shareholder wealth. This is not to say that financial markets really behave in strict accordance with either position—they don't! The point is to identify how things might work. Then, by relaxing various restrictive assumptions, like in the moderate view, we may have a more useful theory to explain reality.

second view takes the opposing extreme position that with a capital structure of nearly 100% debt finance the company will minimise a company's weighted average cost of capital and maximise its share price. The third view takes a moderate position and proposes that a company's weighted average cost of capital can be minimised, and its share price maximised, by a capital structure that has some financial leverage, but not too much. We will now look at each view in more detail.

OBJECTIVE

Understand three theoretical models to explain how a company's capital structure influences the value of its shares.

Theories of capital structure and shareholder wealth

EXTREME POSITION 1: CAPITAL STRUCTURE HAS NO EFFECT ON WEALTH

Extreme position 1 argues that the company's weighted average cost of capital, K_0, and its ordinary share price, P_0, are both *independent* of the degree of financial leverage.[1] Consequently, no matter how *modest* or *excessive* the proportion of long-term debt financing used by the company in its capital structure, its ordinary share price will not be affected. If this position is correct, then the only factor that determines the company's share price is the amount of its earnings before interest and tax (EBIT) and therefore financial managers should only concentrate on decisions to maximise EBIT and not worry about the debt and equity composition of the company's capital structure.

The following example of Rix Camper Company illustrates how the conclusions from extreme position 1 were derived.

Suppose that Rix Camper Company has the following financial characteristics:

Ordinary shares issued	2 000 000 shares
Ordinary share price, P_0	$10 per share
Expected level of earnings before interest and tax (EBIT)	$2 000 000
Dividend payout ratio	100%

Currently the company's capital structure is unlevered, consisting entirely of ordinary equity and no financial leverage. The company's market value is 2 million ordinary shares × $10 per share = $20 million and its earnings per share (E) and dividends per share (D) are both equal to EBIT $2 000 000/2 000 000 shares = $1.

By rearranging equation (16-3) we can determine the cost of ordinary equity for Rix Camper Company, as follows:

$$K_E = \frac{D_t}{P_0} = \frac{\$1}{\$10} = 10\%$$

As the capital structure only comprises equity, the company's weighted average cost of capital, K_0, is equal to the cost of ordinary equity, K_E, which is 10%.

Now the management of Rix Camper decides to have a capital structure with some financial leverage and sells $8 million worth of long-term debt at an interest rate of 6%. As we are assuming there is no taxation of company income, this 6% interest rate is equal to the company's cost of debt, K_d. The company uses the $8 million raised from the sale of the debt to buy back

TABLE 16.1	Rix Camper Company's financial data reflecting the capital-structure adjustment

Capital-structure information

Ordinary shares issued = 1 200 000

Debt at 6% = $8 000 000

Earnings information

Expected level of earnings before interest and tax (EBIT)	$2 000 000
Less: Interest expense ($8 million × 6%)	480 000
Earnings available to shareholders	$1 520 000
Earnings per share ($1 520 000/1 200 000)	$1.267
Dividends per share	$1.267
Percentage change in both earnings per share and dividends per share relative to the unlevered capital structure	26.7%

$8 000 000/$10 = 800 000 of its issued ordinary shares. This buyback represents 40% of the number (i.e. 800 000/2 000 000) and value (i.e. $8m/$20m) of the originally issued ordinary shares.

After the capital-structure change has been accomplished, Rix Camper has the financial characteristics displayed in Table 16.1.

The earnings information section of Table 16.1 shows that the capital-structure change results in the dividend paid to owners being 26.7% higher than it was when the company used no debt in its capital structure. But does this higher dividend result in a higher ordinary share price and therefore higher shareholder wealth?

According to extreme position 1, the answer is no. This is because the cost of equity used to determine the present value of the 26.7% higher dividends will no longer be 10% but will increase to reflect the increased variability of the company's earnings and dividends caused by financial leverage.

However, when this increased cost of equity is combined with the cheaper cost of debt, the company's weighted average cost of capital will remain constant at 10%. Accordingly, the present value of the company's constant EBIT stream of $2 million when discounted at the company's weighted average cost of capital of 10% will be unchanged.

Therefore, the main proposition of extreme position 1 is that changing the amount of financial leverage in a company's capital structure does not affect the company's EBIT, does not affect its weighted average cost of capital, and does not affect its share price and the wealth of its shareholders. This is why extreme position 1 is called the 'independence hypothesis', as shareholder wealth is independent of capital structure.

To illustrate how extreme position 1 demonstrates that there will be no change in the company's share price, we will continue with the example of the Rix Camper Company.

When Rix Camper Company was all-equity financed, its total market value was 2 million ordinary shares × $10 per share = $20 million. Also, the cost of ordinary equity, K_E, and the weighted average cost of capital, K_0, were both equal to 10%.

If, after introducing debt into its capital structure, the company's weighted average cost of capital, K_0, remains constant at 10%, as extreme position 1 proposes, then the market value of the company's debt and equity securities will be as illustrated below:

Expected level of earnings before interest and tax (EBIT)	$2 000 000
Present value at K_0 = 10%	
= Market value of expected EBIT (2 000 000/0.10)	$20 000 000
– Market value of the new debt	8 000 000
= Market value of the ordinary shares	$12 000 000

After the capital-structure change, 1.2 million shares are now outstanding (2 million – 800 000 bought back), so with a market value of ordinary equity of $12 000 000, we can determine the market price of each ordinary share as $12 million/1.2 million = $10. This is exactly the same market value per share, P_0, that existed *before* the capital-structure change. As the share price hasn't changed, shareholder wealth hasn't changed.

The important question that arises from extreme position 1 is why does the company's weighted average cost of capital (K_0) remain constant at 10% when the capital structure is either all equity or includes debt with an **explicit cost** (K_d) of 6%?

explicit cost of debt
The actual cost incurred by using debt funds.

The answer is that the only way the weighted average cost of capital can stay constant at 10% when the company is using debt is if the cost of ordinary equity, K_E, rises above its previous all-equity level of 10%. Equation (16-3) can be rearranged to solve for the new cost of ordinary equity in a levered capital structure, K_E:

$$K_E = \frac{D_t}{P_0} = \$1.267 / \$10 = 12.67\%$$

This answer shows that after debt was included in the company's capital structure the cost of ordinary equity *rose* from 10% to 12.67% per annum, which is 26.7% higher than before the capital-structure change. Notice from Table 16.1 that this 26.7% increase in the cost of equity is *exactly* equal to the rise in earnings and dividends per share after the capital-structure adjustment to include debt.

There are a number of implications that can be drawn from this relationship:

- Even though a capital structure with a greater degree of financial leverage produces larger earnings and dividends per share, the cost of ordinary equity will rise at exactly the same rate as the earnings and dividends.
- The reason why the cost of equity rises with financial leverage is because the variability (risk) of the higher earnings and dividends that shareholders can expect to receive increases.
- Although shareholders in a capital structure that has financial leverage can expect to receive more dividends, this extra dividend amount is only just sufficient to compensate them for the extra variability (risk) of those dividends. As a result, the company's share price remains constant and shareholder wealth is not affected by changes in capital structure.
- The rise in the cost of equity directly offsets the cost saving from the use of cheaper debt finance, so that the weighted average cost of capital remains constant irrespective of the capital structure's degree of financial leverage.
- As financial leverage does not affect EBIT, discounting EBIT by the constant weighted average cost of capital results in a constant value of the company that is independent of its capital structure.

Figure 16.1 graphically represents these implications. The horizontal axis represents the amount of financial leverage, commencing with a capital structure of zero debt to one with nearly 100% debt. The vertical axis represents the percentage weighted average cost of capital.

The following observations can be made from Figure 16.1:

- A company with an unlevered capital structure of zero debt will have a weighted average cost of capital (K_0) that is equal to the cost of equity (K_E). This cost is represented by point A.
- Because debt investors face lower risk than equity investors, the company's cost of debt (K_d) is lower than its cost of equity (K_E). Under the assumptions detailed earlier, the cost of debt is constant over the whole range of financial leverage, which is reflected in the straight K_d line.
- When debt is substituted for equity in the company's capital structure, the increase in financial leverage causes an increase in the risk to shareholders, resulting in a rise in the company's cost of equity (K_E). This is represented by point B on the upward-sloping K_E line.
- When the increased cost of equity in a capital structure with financial leverage is combined with the cheaper cost of debt, the weighted average cost of capital (K_0) remains constant, as represented by the straight K_0 line.

The effect of a constant cost of capital on the company's share price is illustrated in Figure 16.2, which shows that the share price (P_0) does not change as financial leverage changes. This is why extreme position 1 concludes that shareholder wealth is independent of the company's capital structure.

Figure 16.3 illustrates the extreme position 1 view of capital structure by representing the value of the company as a 'pie'. So:

- The size of the company-value pie will be determined by the company's underlying operating profitability and business risk, because it is these components that determine the amount of the company's EBIT and the amount of the present value of EBIT discounted at the constant weighted average cost of capital.
- The size of the company-value pie does not change if the company changes its capital structure. This is illustrated by the size (value) of the two pies being the same for the different capital structures.
- In perfect markets where investors can personally substitute debt for equity to replicate the debt and equity mix of the company's capital structure, the company cannot create extra value (i.e. size of the pie) by doing something that investors could do for themselves. Consequently, changing the company's capital structure only changes the proportions of the company-value pie that is split between debt and equity investors.

You may have noticed from the discussion above that debt financing has not only an explicit cost, K_d, primarily determined by the interest rate or yield, but also an **implicit cost**. The implicit cost of debt is the change in the cost of ordinary equity caused by the financial risk imposed on shareholders by the company using financial leverage (additional debt). Therefore, the real cost to the company from using debt finance should be the sum of both the explicit and the implicit costs.

If extreme position 1 is a correct view of reality, the main implication for capital-structure policy is that financial managers will be wasting their time searching for a mix of long-term debt and equity that will increase the company's share price and shareholder wealth.

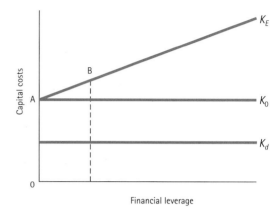

FIGURE 16.1 Capital costs and financial leverage (no taxes): extreme position 1

FIGURE 16.2 Share price and financial leverage (no taxes): extreme position 1

FIGURE 16.3 Constant company value: extreme position 1

Company value   Company value

implicit cost of debt
The change in the cost of ordinary equity brought on by using financial leverage.

EXTREME POSITION 2: CAPITAL STRUCTURE HAS A SIGNIFICANT EFFECT ON WEALTH

Not long after extreme position 1 was published, financial managers and academics questioned its proposition that capital-structure policy was irrelevant to shareholder wealth. This led to extreme position 2, which proposes that share prices and shareholder wealth can be maximised by a company adopting a capital structure with the maximum amount of debt.

The basic proposition of extreme position 2 is that, no matter how much financial leverage in the company's capital structure, both the cost of debt, K_d, and the cost of equity capital, K_E, remain constant. Therefore, because the cost of debt is less than the cost of equity, capital structures with more financial leverage will have a lower weighted average cost of capital (K_0) and thus a higher share price. This is why extreme position 2 is sometimes called the '*dependence* hypothesis', because the weighted average cost of capital and the share price depend on the proportion of debt in a company's capital structure.

How does extreme position 2 reach conclusions that are the opposite of extreme position 1? We will use the same example of the Rix Camper Company where the company changes its capital structure by using the proceeds from selling $8 million of new debt at a 6% interest rate to buy back 800 000 of its ordinary shares. The effects of this capital-structure change as proposed by extreme position 2 are shown below:

Expected level of earnings before interest and tax (EBIT)	$2 000 000
– Interest expense ($8 million × 6%)	480 000
= Earnings available to ordinary shareholders	$1 520 000
(capitalised at constant K_E = 10%)	
= Market value of the shares ($1 520 000/0.10)	$15 200 000
+ Market value of the new debt	8 000 000
= Market value of debt and equity	$23 200 000

You will notice that the expected earnings amount available to the ordinary shareholders ($1 520 000) is the same as for extreme position 1 (detailed earlier in Table 16.1). However, extreme position 2 proposes that the cost of equity (K_E) is not affected by changes in capital structure because the *implicit* costs of financial leverage are included in the *explicit* cost debt. Consequently, in this example the cost of equity remains constant at 10%, resulting in the market value of ordinary shares being $15 200 000. As this levered capital structure has 1.2 million ordinary shares, the share price would be expected to increase to $15.2m/1.2m = $12.67, which is a 26.7% rise on the previous price of $10 per share for the unlevered capital structure. This 26.7% share price change is exactly equal to the percentage change in earnings per share and dividends per share calculated in Table 16.1.

So, by using debt which has a cheaper cost than ordinary equity, and assuming that extreme position 2 is correct and the cost of equity does not increase with leverage, the company can lower its weighted average cost of capital, K_0, and thereby maximise its share price and shareholder wealth.

After the change in the company's capital structure, the market value of Rix Camper Company's ordinary shares of $15.2 million as a percent of the total market value of $23.2 million gives a market-value weight of equity of 0.655. With a market-value weight of the company's debt of 0.345 ($8 million/$23.2 million) and a constant cost of equity (K_E = 10%), the company's weighted average cost of capital becomes:

$$K_0 = (0.345)(6.00\%) + (0.655)(10.00\%) = 8.62\%$$

So, by changing from an unlevered to a levered capital structure, the company has lowered its weighted average cost of capital from 10% to 8.62% and increased its share price from $10 to $12.67 per share.

Figure 16.4 illustrates these essential elements of extreme position 2 where you can see the following:

- The cost of debt and the cost of equity stay the same for capital structures with different amounts of financial leverage, with the cost of debt being lower than the cost of equity.
- If the company has no debt (i.e. zero financial leverage), its weighted average cost of capital (K_0) is the same as its cost of equity (K_E). This is represented by point A.
- When the company substitutes debt for equity, its cost of equity remains constant, as represented by point B. However, the combination of the cheaper explicit cost of debt and the constant cost of equity results in the weighted average cost of capital (K_0) falling.

The effect of the lower weighted cost of capital on the company's share price is illustrated in Figure 16.5, which shows that the share price (P_0) rises as financial leverage increases. This is why extreme position 2 concludes that shareholder wealth is dependent on the company's choice of capital structure.

MODERATE POSITION: CAPITAL STRUCTURE HAS SOME EFFECT ON WEALTH

You may feel that the previous discussion of the two extreme positions is only an academic exercise. For example, many of the assumptions underlying extreme position 1 do not reflect reality and the logical conclusion from extreme position 2 is that a company can maximise its share price and shareholder wealth by having a capital structure comprising 99.9% of debt! However, the reason for examining the two extreme positions is that reality is likely to be somewhere between these two extremes, and understanding the dynamics underlying each extreme position can help to explain the real-world relationship between capital structure and shareholder wealth.

The moderate position lies between the two extreme positions and proposes that when two additional factors are included a company can increase its share price and shareholder wealth by selecting a capital structure that has some debt but not too much. The two additional factors are:

1. Interest payments are tax deductible.
2. Financial distress and liquidation incur costs.

Tax deductibility of interest expense

One of the assumptions underlying the extreme positions is that there is no taxation. The moderate position includes the fact that a company's net operating income is subject to income tax and that the company can claim a tax deduction for the amount of interest paid for the use of debt finance but not for the amount of dividends paid for the use of equity finance. Initially, we will assume that the company is subject to a classical tax system with the company paying income tax on its net income, and that shareholders pay income tax at their personal rate on dividends received from the company.

The tax deductibility of interest in a classical-tax-system environment means that for the same amount of EBIT the company pays less income tax when it uses debt finance instead of equity finance. This is called the **tax shield** on interest and makes the after-tax cost of debt finance ($K_{d,\,AT}$) lower than the explicit cost of debt (K_d) used in the two extreme positions.

Using the example of the Rix Camper Company, we can identify the effect of the tax shield on the total cash flow expected to be paid to the company's debt and ordinary share security holders. For extreme position 1 where there were no taxes, you can see from Table 16.1 that the total dividends paid to ordinary shareholders in the 100% equity capital structure was

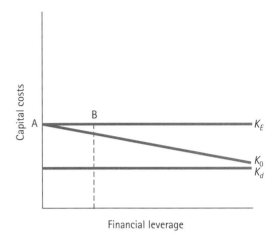

FIGURE 16.4 Capital costs and financial leverage (no taxes): extreme position 2

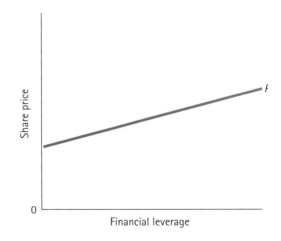

FIGURE 16.5 Share price and financial leverage (no taxes): extreme position 2

tax shield
The reduction in income tax due to the tax deduction allowed to businesses for interest paid on debt capital.

$2 million, and after the capital-structure change the dividends paid to ordinary shareholders ($1.52 million) and interest expense ($480 000) totalled $2 million. The conclusion was that changing the company's capital structure did not affect the total of the cash flows paid by the company to the providers of debt and equity finance.

However, Table 16.2 shows that, when company income is taxed, the total of the cash flows paid to all the security holders after the company pays income tax increases by $240 000 when the company changes from an unlevered (all equity) to a levered capital structure. This increase is the result of the tax-deductible $480 000 interest expense reducing the amount of income tax paid by the company by $240 000. In other words, the amount of the tax shield from the use of debt finance is $240 000 and this is reflected in the expected payment to all (debt and equity) security holders.

TABLE 16.2 Rix Camper Company's cash flows to all investors—the case of taxes

	UNLEVERED CAPITAL STRUCTURE	LEVERED CAPITAL STRUCTURE
Expected level of net operating income	$2 000 000	$2 000 000
Less: Interest expense	0	480 000
Earnings before taxes	$2 000 000	$1 520 000
Less: Taxes (assumed at 50%)	1 000 000	760 000
Earnings available to shareholders	$1 000 000	$760 000
Expected payments to all security holders	$1 000 000	$1 240 000

An alternative way to calculate the annual amount of the tax shield is:

$$\text{Annual amount of the tax shield} = R_d \times M \times T \qquad \text{(16-4)}$$

where R_d = the interest rate paid on the debt
M = is the principal amount of the debt
T = the firm's marginal tax rate

EXAMPLE 16.1 Calculation of annual tax shield amount

The levered capital structure for Rix Camper Company comprises $8 million of debt ($M$) at an interest rate of 6% per annum (R_d). At the company income-tax rate of 50% (T), the annual amount of the tax shield is equal to:

0.06×8 million $\times 0.50 = \$240\,000$

The moderate position therefore proposes that financial leverage increases shareholder wealth because it is the shareholders who get the benefit of the interest tax shield. This is evident if the earnings per share are calculated from the amounts in Table 16.2:

- Unlevered capital structure: $1 million/2 million shares = $0.50 per share
- Levered capital structure: $760 000/1.2 million shares = $0.633 per share

If the annual amount of the interest tax shield continues into perpetuity, then the *value* of the interest tax shield to shareholders will be equal to the present value of the perpetuity of the annual interest tax shield amount. Assuming the current interest rate (R_d) is the appropriate discount rate to use to calculate the present value of this perpetuity, the term R_d in equation (16-4) is cancelled out, leaving:

$$\text{Value of the tax shield} = M \times T \qquad \text{(16-5)}$$

EXAMPLE 16.2   Calculation of the value of the interest tax shield

As the levered capital structure for Rix Camper Company produces an annual tax shield amount of \$240 000, at an interest rate of 6% per annum, the value of the tax shield is equal to:

Present value of annual tax shield amount: \$240 000/0.06 = \$4 000 000

or $M \times T$ = \$8 million $\times$ 0.50 = \$4 000 000

The value of the interest tax shield to shareholder wealth is also reflected in the weighted average cost of capital. Even if we accept that extreme position 1 is totally correct and the cost of equity increases with financial leverage, the interest tax shield associated with debt finance will result in the after-tax cost of debt being lower than indicated by the K_d line in Figure 16.1. The result is that for capital structures with financial leverage any increase in the cost of equity will be less than the savings obtained from using debt that is not only cheaper but also provides the interest tax shield. The overall result will be a fall in the company's weighted average cost of capital (K_0).

The logical conclusion of this version of the moderate position is similar to that for extreme position 2: a capital structure with 99.9% debt will maximise the value of the interest tax shield and thereby minimise the company's weighted average after-tax cost of capital.

But is this conclusion realistic? Can a company continue to lower its weighted average cost of capital and increase shareholder wealth by using more and more financial leverage? Common sense would tell us no. The inclusion of the costs of financial distress and liquidation into the moderate position imposes a limit to financial leverage.

Back to the principles

The preceding section is a compelling example of **Principle 8: Taxes bias business decisions**. The interest paid on debt is tax-deductible, while dividends paid to ordinary shareholders are not. Depending on the impact of other tax laws, like the dividend imputation system, there is the potential for companies to receive a tax incentive to finance investment projects with debt finance rather than with new issues of ordinary shares.

Costs of financial distress and liquidation

The second component of the moderate position is the inclusion of the costs of financial distress and liquidation. As a company uses more debt in its capital structure, there is an increased probability that it will have difficulty paying, or in the extreme case be unable to pay, the principal and interest amounts due on its debt. When a company has difficulty in making these payments, it incurs costs of financial distress that can be explicit, such as an increase in the interest rate charged on its loans, or implicit, such as suppliers refusing to provide further goods until accounts are paid. Also, the company may forgo investing in profitable projects because staff time is consumed in trying to meet the demands for payment and investors may not be willing to provide additional finance.

At some point of financial leverage the costs of financial distress will be large enough to outweigh the tax shield advantage of debt financing.[2] When this happens, the company's weighted average cost of capital will start rising and the share price will start to fall.

In the extreme case that a company cannot pay its debt obligations, liquidation proceedings will commence. There are extensive legal rules and procedures associated with company liquidation and personal bankruptcy; however, for our purposes the main impact of liquidation is the forced sale of the company's assets to pay its debts. As there is a likelihood the assets will be sold for something less than their market values, the debt-holders may suffer some losses and the shareholders may lose up to 100% of their investment in the company.

Moderate view: saucer-shaped weighted average cost of capital curve

The relationship between capital structure and the company's weighted average cost of capital that results from the moderate view under a classical tax system is depicted in Figure 16.6.

The following observations can be made from Figure 16.6:

- As depicted in extreme position 1, the implicit costs of debt cause the cost of equity (K_E) to rise as financial leverage increases. Beyond a certain point of financial leverage (point B) the cost of equity rises at an exponential rate, reflecting the increased risk to shareholders of having to pay the costs of financial distress or ultimately losing all their investment if the company is liquidated.
- Up to moderate amounts of financial leverage (point A) the company can borrow funds at a relatively low cost of debt (K_d), which includes the tax shield. However, at higher amounts of financial leverage (beyond point A) the company exposes itself to the risks and costs of financial distress, which also causes an increase in the cost of debt. At even higher amounts of financial leverage (beyond point B) the increased risk of liquidation significantly increases the risks and cost of debt.
- The outcome of these effects of financial leverage on the costs of debt and equity is a saucer-shaped (or U-shaped) weighted average cost of capital curve (K_0). Up to moderate amounts of financial leverage (point A) the weighted average cost of capital falls, because, even though the cost of equity is rising, it does not rise at a fast enough rate to offset the cost of using cheaper tax-deductible debt. Thus, capital structures with financial leverage between points 0 and A will result in the company increasing its share price.
- The continual reduction in the weighted average cost of capital begins to stop after point A, because the increased risk of financial distress causes the cost of debt to rise and the cost of equity to start rising at a faster rate. However, it is not until point B that the costs of financial distress outweigh the interest tax shield from using more debt. The result is a (relatively) flat weighted average cost of capital between points A and B.
- Point B represents the company's **debt capacity**. Debt capacity is the maximum proportion of debt that the company can include in its capital structure and still maintain its lowest weighted average cost of capital. Beyond point B, additional debt can be raised only at much

debt capacity
The maximum proportion of debt that the firm can include in its capital structure and still maintain its lowest weighted average cost of capital.

FIGURE 16.6 Capital costs and financial leverage: the moderate view, considering taxes and financial distress

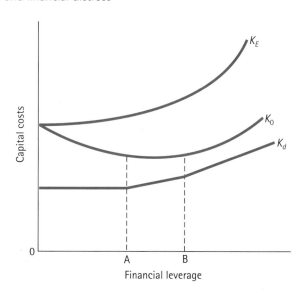

higher interest rates, and at the same time this excessive use of financial leverage causes the company's cost of equity to rise at a much faster rate than previously. The weighted average cost of capital then rises quite rapidly, resulting in a decline in the company's share price.

- The company's **optimal range of financial leverage** lies between points A and B. This is the financing mix that minimises the company's weighted average cost of capital and therefore, by the valuation process, maximises the share price and shareholder wealth.

Other factors affecting capital-structure policy

There are other factors that can modify the conclusions of the moderate position. We will briefly examine three of these—agency costs, free cash flow and dividend imputation.

AGENCY COSTS

The separation of the ownership and management of companies that was mentioned in Chapter 1 means that company managers can be thought of as agents for the shareholders.[3] This imposes *agency costs* on shareholders to ensure that managers act in the shareholders' best interests, such as having to provide managers with appropriate incentives and having to pay to monitor managers' decisions and actions.

Incentives usually take the form of executive compensation plans and perquisites. Perquisites are benefits in addition to normal compensation, such as providing personal staff, sporting-club memberships or luxurious company cars. To monitor management decisions and actions, shareholders ultimately bear the costs for lawyers to prepare appropriate contracts of employment and for accountants to audit the company's financial statements.

The natural conflict of interest between shareholders and debt-holders also results in agency costs. For example, acting in the shareholders' best interests might cause management to invest in riskier projects, but this change in the risk structure of the company's assets could lead to a downward revision of its credit rating, which in turn would lower the current market value of debt issued by the company. Existing debt-holders would be unhappy with this result, as value would be transferred from them to shareholders.

To reduce this conflict of interest, the creditors (debt-holders) may require protective covenants to be included in debt contracts. These covenants are discussed in more detail in Chapter 18, but essentially they impose restrictions on future management decisions. For example, covenants could restrict the future payment by the company of cash dividends on ordinary shares, limit the company's acquisition or sale of assets, or limit further the amount of debt finance the company could raise. To ensure that the company complies with the protective covenants, monitoring costs have to be incurred, which are borne by ordinary shareholders.

As with many costs, the agency costs of debt involve a number of trade-offs. Figure 16.7 details some of the trade-offs involved with the use of protective debt covenants.

The left-hand panel of Figure 16.7 shows that if the company can raise debt finance that carries no protective covenants it will have low monitoring costs and not lose operating flexibility and efficiencies. However, the trade-off will be having to pay high interest rates, because lenders will not have covenants that protect their position.

Conversely, including many protective covenants in its debt contracts should reduce the interest rate the company has to pay for its debt. However, the trade-off will be incurring significant monitoring costs and losing some operating efficiencies (which also translates into higher costs).

Impact of agency costs on capital structure

When a company has a capital structure with low financial leverage, indicated by a low debt-to-equity ratio, the risk of it not paying its debt obligations

OBJECTIVE 4

Appreciate that agency costs, free cash flow and dividend imputation can affect capital-structure policy.

optimal range of financial leverage
The range of various capital-structure combinations that yield the lowest overall weighted average cost of capital for the firm.

FIGURE 16.7 Agency costs and debt: trade-offs

NO PROTECTIVE DEBT COVENANTS	MANY PROTECTIVE DEBT COVENANTS
High interest rates	Low interest rates
Low monitoring costs	High monitoring costs
No lost operating efficiencies	Many lost operating efficiencies

is low. Consequently, the interest rate the company will be required to pay for debt finance will be low and there will be little need for its creditors to insist on a long list of protective covenants. However, when the debt-to-equity ratio is high and there is a greater risk that the company will have difficulty paying its debt obligations, it is logical for lenders to charge a higher interest rate, demand more monitoring and require many protective covenants to be included in the debt contracts.

Just as the likelihood of firm failure (financial distress) raises a company's weighted average cost of capital (K_0), so do agency costs. Consequently, higher agency costs will result in a *lower* market value of the company's shares.

By combining the value of the tax shield from debt, the costs associated with financial distress and agency costs, the moderate position proposes:

Market value of levered firm = market value of unlevered firm +
present value of tax shield –
present value of financial distress costs –
present value of agency costs   **(16-5)**

This relationship between firm value and financial leverage is presented graphically in Figure 16.8. It shows that for capital structures with moderate amounts of financial leverage up to point A, the tax-shield effect dominates and actual market value of the firm rises. Capital structures with financial leverage between points A and B expose the firm to some likelihood of financial distress, and these costs, together with agency costs, cause a slowing of the rise in the actual market value of the firm. At point B the firm's actual market value is maximised because it is beyond that point that financial distress and agency costs start to outweigh the value of the tax shield causing the actual market value of the firm to fall.

The conclusion from Figure 16.8 is that the *objective* for the financial manager is to identify the capital structure that is represented by point B. However, there is a practical problem in implementing this conclusion, because the costs of financial distress and monitoring can only be estimated by subjective means. So, beyond the broad principles identified by the moderate

FIGURE 16.8 Firm value considering taxes, financial distress costs and agency costs

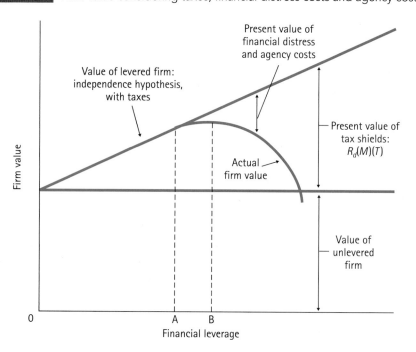

position, adopting a capital structure that maximises shareholder wealth will require a degree of management judgement.

FREE CASH FLOW

In 1986 Professor Michael C. Jensen extended the concept of agency costs in capital-structure management by focusing on 'free cash flow', which he defined as follows:[4]

> Free cash flow is cash flow in excess of that required to fund all projects that have positive net present values when discounted at the relevant cost of capital.

Jensen argued that a company with substantial free cash flow is likely to experience misbehaviour by managers and poor decisions that are *not* in the best interests of ordinary shareholders. This is because managers are more likely to spend any free cash flow on things (such as company jets) that benefit them rather than to pay it out as higher dividends to the benefit of shareholders.

But all is not lost for shareholders, because Jensen identified the 'control hypothesis' for debt creation. He argued that shareholders would benefit from the company using higher financial leverage because there would be increased external control over the management team. For example, if the company issued new debt and used the proceeds to purchase outstanding shares, not only would management have to satisfy the external lenders that there was sufficient cash to service the debt but the amount of free cash flow that management could spend on themselves would be less.

Another explanation of the benefit to shareholders from the company using financial leverage is the 'threat hypothesis'. This hypothesis argues that managers work under the threat of losing their job if the company's financial performance is poor. Thus, it is in the shareholders' interests for the company to adopt a capital structure with more financial leverage, because this will force the company's managers to work more efficiently to avoid financial failure. The result should be a reduction in the agency costs associated with free cash flow, which should therefore produce an increase in the market price of the company's ordinary shares.

Although this *free cash flow theory of capital structure* adds to the factors that appear to influence the relationship between capital structure and shareholder wealth, it does not provide a theoretical solution to the question of how much financial leverage is enough. Nor does it identify how much leverage is too much leverage. Its main contribution is to assist thinking about how shareholders and their boards of directors might use debt to control management behaviour and decisions.

Back to the principles

The discussion on agency costs, free cash flow and control hypothesis for debt creation reminds us of **Principle 7: The agency problem— managers won't work for owners unless it's in their best interest**. The control hypothesis put forth by Jensen suggests that managers will work harder for shareholder interests when they have to 'sweat it out' to meet contractual interest payments on debt. But we also learned that conflict between managers and debt investors can lead to agency costs associated with the firm using debt capital. Thus, the theoretical benefits that flow from minimising the agency costs of free cash flow by using more debt will cease when the rising agency costs of debt exactly offset those benefits. You can see how difficult it is, then, for financial managers to precisely identify the firm's true optimal capital structure.

DIVIDEND IMPUTATION

In the previous discussion of the moderate position, a classical tax system was assumed. This is the system that applies in many countries such as the United States, and is used in most of the academic finance literature examining capital-structure policy. Although the classical tax system in Australia was replaced in the mid 1980s with the dividend imputation system we identified in Chapter 2, it is still possible for some Australian companies to be effectively taxed as if they were under a classical tax system. Accordingly, in Chapter 2 three taxation categories of Australian firms were specified to reflect the different impact of dividend imputation on shareholder wealth. We will use these same categories to briefly examine the impact of dividend imputation on the capital-structure policy of Australian firms.

Taxation category 1

Taxation category 1 comprises Australian companies that are well integrated by the dividend imputation tax system as the value of company tax savings from deductions for expenses like interest have little or no value for the company's shareholders. Consequently, as there is no effective tax benefit from capital structures using debt finance, the company's weighted average cost of capital curve labelled $K_{0(1)}$ in Figure 16.9 is much flatter and above the taxation category 2 company curve, $K_{0(2)}$. In addition, the optimum capital structure for taxation category 1 companies will tend to start to the left, as shown by the point A(1).

Taxation category 2

Taxation category 2 comprises Australian companies that are not integrated by the dividend imputation system. As shareholders receive the full value of company tax savings from interest paid by the company, taxation category 2 companies are effectively subject to a classical tax system and the 'moderate position' of capital structure applies, as depicted by the weighted average cost of capital curve, $K_{0(2)}$, in Figure 16.9. This results in an optimum capital structure represented by the shaded region from A(2) to B(2).

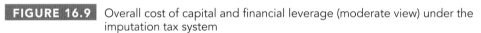

FIGURE 16.9 Overall cost of capital and financial leverage (moderate view) under the imputation tax system

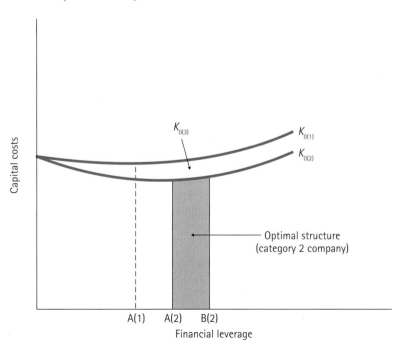

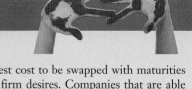

International spotlight

FINANCING MIX AND GLOBAL FINANCIAL MARKETS

One outcome of global financial markets is the ability of businesses not only to obtain finance in their home currency but also to raise debt and equity funds in foreign currencies. Another outcome is the availability of interest-rate and currency swaps, which enables funds that are raised with maturities and currencies with the lowest cost to be swapped with maturities and currencies that the firm desires. Companies that are able to access a large number of financial markets have the potential to ensure a continuous supply of finance and to reduce their weighted average cost of capital.

Taxation category 3

Taxation category 3 comprises companies that are only partially integrated by the imputation tax system so that the value of company tax deductions to shareholders depends on the company's *effective* tax rate (defined in Chapter 2). For shareholders in companies with an effective company tax rate close to the corporate tax rate, the tax shield on debt has a value similar to that of taxation category 2 firms. On the other hand, shareholders of companies with a low effective tax rate will be similar to shareholders of taxation category 1 companies. Consequently, the impact of financial leverage on the weighted average cost of capital for category 3 companies is represented by the region in Figure 16.9 labelled $K_{0(3)}$, which lies between the $K_{0(1)}$ curve and the $K_{0(2)}$ curve.

IMPACT ON CAPITAL-STRUCTURE POLICY

Common sense tells us that the composition of a company's assets will largely determine shareholder wealth, because the assets reflect the extent to which the company has implemented successful investment projects that produce free cash flows that can either be paid to shareholders as higher dividends or retained to increase assets such as cash or other investments.

So, what conclusions can we draw from our examination of capital-structure policy? It would appear that a company's share price can be affected by its capital-structure decisions.[5] As a general principle, if the company can lower its weighted average cost of capital by changing the mix of debt and equity funds in its capital structure, assuming other things being equal (e.g. constant EBIT), the present value of the company's operating cash flows (EBIT) will be greater and therefore the company's share price and shareholder wealth will rise.

The problem with this general principle is that in reality other things are seldom equal. As we have seen, financial leverage increases the volatility (risk) of the earnings (EPS/dividends) available for shareholders. Also we have seen that too much financial leverage causes costs of financial distress and in the extreme case the chance of company liquidation.

A further component of the trade-off of the costs and risks between debt and equity finance is the tax-deductibility of interest. This is particularly relevant under a classical tax system where the value of the tax shield from the deductibility of interest lowers the cost of debt, so that the judicious use of debt can lower the company's weighted average cost of capital. Conversely, for some Australian companies the dividend imputation system has the potential to reduce or remove this tax advantage of debt over equity finance.

Concept check
16.3 What is the enduring controversy with capital-structure theory?
16.4 Explain the extreme position 1 as it relates to capital-structure policy.
16.5 Explain the moderate view of the relationship between a company's capital structure and its weighted average cost of capital.
16.6 How do agency costs and free cash flow relate to capital-structure policy?

For answers go to MyFinanceLab or www.pearson.com.au/9781442539174

ONE STEP FURTHER

A TAXONOMY OF BONDS

Bonds can be a major source of debt finance in the capital structure of large organisations. As most bond issues are not secured, investors have to rely on the 'quality' of the issuer in judging whether it will be able to make future coupon and principal payments. This is why the majority of bond issues are made by government bodies and by corporations that have substantial financial resources and good credit ratings. Even so, there is an almost bewildering range of variants of the bond.

In Australia, the name *treasury bonds* refers to bonds issued by the federal government. In addition to conventional coupon bonds, the treasury has made issues of *indexed bonds*, which make coupon payments at a real interest rate along with an indexation component that varies in line with the rate of inflation.

Corporate bonds in Australia are not as widespread as in countries such as the United States, in part because there are relatively few Australian companies with the necessary financial standing. A recent variation is *income bonds*, which pay a coupon indefinitely and therefore (like preference shares) do not have a maturity date.

Australian organisations can also issue bonds overseas to raise funds in either Australian dollars or a foreign currency. A *eurobond* is the name given to a bond issued in a country that differs from the country of the currency in which the bond is issued. A *kangaroo bond* is a name given to Australian-dollar bonds issued by foreign organisations.

In addition to the basic types of local and international bonds, there are many other special types of bonds. For example, *zero coupon bonds* pay no coupon interest, and so return only the principal amount at maturity. *Junk bonds* is the name given to bonds that are rated as having a high probability that the issuer will not be able to pay the coupons and principal amounts when they fall due. Unlike the typical bond, they are issued by organisations that have a low credit rating, and to compensate investors for the high risk of default they offer investors a high yield. *Mortgage-backed bonds*, unlike most bonds, offer security, which takes the form of a pool of mortgage-secured housing loans.

Appreciate aspects of the actual management of capital structure by companies.

A glance at actual capital-structure management

Now that you have an appreciation of the theoretical identification of the major factors influencing capital-structure policy, we will briefly examine the opinions and practices of financial executives who decide the proportions of debt and equity for the company's capital structure.

Listed Australian companies were surveyed in 1983 and 1987–88 regarding their capital-structure policies and practices.[6] In the 1983 survey an overwhelming majority of companies agreed with the concept of an optimal capital structure, with the amount of debt finance used in a company's capital structure affecting its weighted average cost of capital. Eighty-seven percent of companies believed that the weighted average cost of capital could be lowered by a judicious use of financial leverage, and 88% believed that excess debt could adversely affect the company's share price.

In both surveys[7], three-quarters of the companies indicated that they had target debt–equity ratios, with internal management being reported in 1983 as the dominant influence on the setting of the capital-structure ratios. Other influences were investment bankers, commercial bankers and, to a much lesser extent, trade creditors, external security analysts and comparative industry ratios.

The 1987–88 survey was concerned with how companies analysed their financial risk and from the answers shown in Table 16.3 it is clear that cash-flow-based estimates of the ability to service and repay debt dominated the other methods.

In a recent survey[8], 392 Chief Financial Officers (CFOs) of US companies were asked to rate the importance of 14 factors in determining their company's capital structure. The highest rating influencing the decision to use debt finance for over 59% of respondents was maintaining the company's financial flexibility, with an important consideration being not to limit the company's ability to issue either debt or equity by pushing the firm's capital structure to the limits of the company's debt capacity.

The next important factor for the CFOs was not increasing the proportion of debt finance beyond the point that would trigger a downgrade of the company's credit rating and signal to the markets a greater risk of the company facing financial distress and possible bankruptcy. The third major factor influencing capital-structure choice for slightly less than 50% of the CFOs was the tax benefits from debt finance. In summary, the opinions of these US CFOs support the moderate theory of capital-structure policy.

CAPITAL-STRUCTURE POLICIES OVER TIME

Looking at ratios like debt–equity over time, it is evident that capital-structure policy is not static but changes in response to economic and financial market conditions. For example, in Australia during the 1980s, particularly during the resources boom of 1980–81 and following the deregulation of financial markets from 1984 to 1988, many companies significantly increased the proportion of long-term debt in their capital structure. However, in the early 1990s, when interest rates rose significantly, followed by a major economic recession, a number of these highly levered companies collapsed, causing significant losses for both debt and equity investors. For those companies that survived this period the focus of capital-structure policy was then to reduce the proportion of long-term debt to what managers and the markets considered to be more acceptable levels.

The latter period of the 1990s and most of the 2000s comprised low rates of inflation, low inflationary expectations, low nominal interest rates, growing GDP and rising company profits. During this period Australian companies found it relatively easy to raise both debt and equity finance, with the latter supported by the dividend imputation system, enabling companies to issue shares to replace cash dividends (discussed further in Chapter 17).

The surveys of CFOs indicate that, in practice, capital-structure decisions are more complex than indicated by the moderate position. For example, companies tend to use less debt than expected and maintain a large cushion of spare borrowing (debt capacity). Also, financial-market conditions can affect the timing of when a company is able to make new issues of equity and debt.

TABLE 16.3 Methods of assessing exposure to financial risk

METHOD USED BY COMPANIES	PERCENTAGE OF COMPANIES
Interest cover	12.5
Cash flow projections/ability to repay debt	45.8
Asset value	2.1
Gearing ratio	4.1
All the above	16.7
Not disclosed	18.8

Source: David E. Allen, 'The determinants of the capital structure of listed Australian companies: The financial manager's perspective', *Australian Journal of Management*, 16, December 1991, p. 112. Reprinted with the permission of the Australian Graduate School of Management, publisher of the *Australian Journal of Management*.

CHANGING CAPITAL STRUCTURES

In response to the relatively low nominal interest rates during the early to mid 2000s many companies increased the proportion of debt finance in their capital structures and, while economic activity was strong, they were able to generate sufficient cash flows from their operations to pay the interest and principal amounts. However, the severe economic downturn associated with the Global Financial Crisis caused many highly levered companies throughout the world to experience significant financial distress, with some defaulting on their debt obligations and being liquidated.

Similar to the experience of recent decades, the observable response of companies that survived the GFC was to adopt a more conservative capital-structure policy to reduce and limit the proportion of long-term debt finance used. However, as the GFC had a major negative impact on the operations of both debt and equity markets globally, the major way companies were able to reduce their debt–equity ratio was to increase retained earnings by reducing the proportion of profits paid out as dividends to shareholders.

It is not uncommon for the managers of companies to be reluctant to issue new shares when they believe the company's share price is too low. If more shares have to be issued to raise the required amount of funds, then not only will there be a negative impact on earnings per share (EPS) but also a greater likelihood of diluting the ownership share of the company's existing shareholders. For these reasons companies often prefer to raise external capital with debt rather than equity.

This preference for raising external debt is compounded by the fact that investors tend be sceptical of the motives of companies that issue new shares. As a result, when companies do issue shares it is often greeted as a signal that the companies' shares are overpriced. Indeed, when companies announce their intention to issue equity, their share price generally falls.

PECKING ORDER THEORY OF CAPITAL STRUCTURE

US finance professor Stewart C. Myers[9] suggested that because of the information issues that arise when a company issues equity, capital-structure policy tends to adhere to the following pecking order:

1. The investment opportunities of companies tend to drive their dividend policies. This is close to the residual dividend theory (see Chapter 17), which holds that companies use profits first to fund investment projects and then pay the residual amount to shareholders as a dividend.
2. Internally generated funds (e.g. retained earnings) tend to be used first to finance investment opportunities, and external finance is sought only if more funds are needed.
3. When external financing is necessary, the company will choose first to issue debt securities, and will raise new equity as the last option.
4. As more external funds are sought to fund acceptable projects (with positive net present values), this financing pecking order will be followed: more risky debt, then convertible securities, and last raising new equity.

The implication of the pecking-order theory is that, if companies carry out the hierarchy of financing preferences suggested, they do not have an optimal capital structure with defined-target financial-leverage ratios. The financial-leverage ratios that are observed merely reflect the cumulative financing needs of companies over time.

MANAGERIAL IMPLICATIONS

It is evident from this chapter that as yet there is no single theory that is able to explain and predict capital-structure policy. However, from our examination of the various theories of capital-structure and actual capital-structure management, we are able to identify some of the effects of financial leverage on the company and its owners—for example, the impact of debt on the variability of earnings, the value of the interest tax shield from debt, the risks and costs of financial distress and liquidation, debt capacity, agency costs, free cash flow, and information issues.

The difficult task for financial managers is to incorporate all of these factors when deciding on a capital structure. In addition, this text has consistently stated that the test of good capital-structure policy is the effect on the wealth of the owners of the business. Therefore, although capital-structure theory is unable to identify a single debt–equity that will maximise owner wealth, the theory can help financial managers to identify capital structures that have a reasonable probability of being beneficial or detrimental to share prices.

Concept check

16.7 What factors do you think will influence target debt ratios in actual business practice?

16.8 How do you think executives can make the concept of debt capacity operational?

For answers go to MyFinanceLab or www.pearson.com.au/9781442539174

WHY DOES CAPITAL STRUCTURE MATTER TO YOU?

When a company borrows money it is legally obligated to pay interest and repay the debt principal. If a company uses more debt than it can afford to service it faces the risk of defaulting on its debt and being forced into liquidation. Not only will this have very costly implications for the company's lenders but also for its creditors, shareholders and employees. If you were a lender or other creditor to the company you might be lucky to recover a few cents for every dollar you loaned. If you were a shareholder you would be likely to lose all the money you had invested in the company's shares. If you were

an employee and the company were liquidated you would lose your job. Even if you were not an employee of the company, some of your superannuation/retirement fund might have been invested in the company's shares that are now worthless.

So, although you may not be working as a financial manager for a company, you need to understand some basic facts about the different ways companies raise finance and how these capital-structure choices affect the company's earnings, risk and its ability to invest in the future.

Summary

OBJECTIVE 1

This chapter began by making a distinction between financial structure, which reflects all the company's short- and long-term financing sources, and capital structure, which consists of the company's long-term sources of finance.

OBJECTIVE 2

The focus of this chapter is capital-structure policy, particularly choosing the mix of long-term sources of finance. Consistent with other topics in this book, the maximisation of shareholder wealth was the objective underlying an examination of how companies should decide on the mix of long-term debt and equity finance.

Given this objective, it is necessary to consider the question of whether capital structure has an effect on shareholder wealth. More specifically, does the mix of long-term debt and equity finance used by a company have an impact on its weighted average cost of capital, its share price and therefore the wealth of its shareholders?

OBJECTIVE 3

Capital-structure theory attempts to answer this question by focusing on the impact of varying the proportion of debt finance (financial leverage) on the company's weighted average cost of capital. Two extreme positions of this impact were initially examined. The first extreme position demonstrated that, in a perfect market world with no taxes, a company's weighted average cost of capital would be unaffected by the amount of financial leverage in its capital structure, and therefore its share price would not change. The second extreme position concluded that, in a world with taxes where interest payments were tax-deductible, a company could maximise its share price by maximising its financial leverage.

As these two extreme positions depend on a number of theoretical assumptions that do not reflect reality, a third 'moderate' position was examined. The moderate position adds the risk and costs of financial distress to the conclusions from the two extreme positions. The result is an optimal capital structure with a mix of debt and equity that minimises the company's weighted average cost of capital and therefore maximises its share price and shareholder wealth.

OBJECTIVE 4

Complicating the identification of an optimal capital structure are agency costs. An example of the agency costs of debt is lenders requiring protective covenants to be included in debt contracts that prevent management from adopting a capital structure with a level of financial leverage that is beneficial to shareholders.

Another type of agency cost occurs when managers have an incentive not to pay free cash flow out to shareholders as higher cash-dividend payments but to use it for their own benefit. One way this conflict between managers and shareholders can be reduced is by the company adopting a capital structure with higher amounts of financial leverage. The free cash-flow theory proposes that shareholders should benefit from the higher payments to service the debt, restricting the amount of free cash flow that management can spend on themselves, as well as from the increased external oversight of management behaviour by debt-holders.

As a key component of the moderate position assumes a classical tax system where the value of the interest tax shield reduces the cost of debt capital, the impact of the Australian dividend imputation system on capital-structure policy was examined. Applying the classifications outlined in Chapter 2, taxation category 1 companies with an effective zero value of the interest tax shield would adopt capital structures with lower proportions of debt than taxation category 2 companies.

OBJECTIVE 5

Surveys of the views of financial managers from large companies indicate that most agree with the concept of an optimal capital structure and try to identify a target debt ratio. However, the focus of these targets is not so much on minimising the company's weighted average cost of capital but on the company's ability to service the fixed financing costs associated with debt.

Historical surveys in Australia and overseas show that company capital structures change in significant ways over time, indicating that the issues considered by managers in deciding the firm's financing mix are more complex than suggested by the moderate view of capital structure as reflected in the following pecking order:

- There is a significant preference for the use of retained earnings to finance investments.
- Companies maintain a large cushion of spare borrowing capacity.
- Issuing securities to raise either debt or equity finance is timed to coincide with favourable market conditions.

capital structure	555	implicit cost of debt	561	For a complete flashcard glossary go to MyFinanceLab at www.pearson.com.au/myfinancelab
debt capacity	566	optimal capital structure	556	
explicit cost of debt	560	optimal range of financial leverage	567	
financial structure	555	tax shield	563	
financial-structure design	555			

Review questions

16-1 Define the following terms:

(a) financial structure
(b) capital structure
(c) optimal capital structure
(d) debt capacity

16-2 What is the objective of capital-structure management?

16-3 Why might firms whose sales levels change drastically over time choose to use debt only sparingly in their capital structures?

16-4 What condition would cause capital-structure management to be a meaningless activity?

16-5 What does the term *independence hypothesis* mean as it applies to capital-structure theory?

16-6 Who have been the foremost advocates of the independence hypothesis?

16-7 A financial manager might say that the firm's weighted average cost of capital is saucer-shaped or U-shaped. What does this mean?

16-8 Why should the financial manager be familiar with the business cycle?

16-9 In almost every instance, what funds source do managers use first in the financing of their capital budgets?

16-10 You believe that your company is subject to the *fully integrated dividend imputation system*:

(a) What does this mean?
(b) Should you accept the moderate position regarding optimal capital structure for your company? Explain.

16-11 Contrast the extent to which taxation category 1, 2 and 3 firms should use the tax-shield advantage of financial leverage.

Self-test problems

ST-1 (*Capital-structure theory*) Deep End Supplies has a capital structure of 100% ordinary equity. Some financial data for the company are shown below:

For answers go to MyFinanceLab
www.pearson.com.au/myfinancelab

Number of ordinary shares issued	= 9 million
Current share price, P_0	= $3
Expected level of EBIT	= $5 400 000
Dividend payout ratio	= 100%

In answering the following questions, assume that corporate income is not taxed.

(a) Under the present capital structure, what is the total value of the company?
(b) What is the cost of ordinary equity capital, K_E? What is the weighted average cost of capital, K_0?

(c) Now, suppose that Deep End sells $1.5 million of long-term debt with an interest rate of 8%, and the proceeds are used to retire the outstanding shares. According to extreme position 1:

   (i)   What will be the dividend per share flowing to the company's ordinary shareholders?
   (ii) By what percentage has the dividend per share changed owing to the capital-structure change?
   (iii) What will be the company's cost of ordinary equity after the capital-structure change?
   (iv) By what percentage has the cost of ordinary equity changed as a result of the capital-structure change?
   (v)   What will be the weighted average cost of capital after the capital-structure change?

ST-2 (*Value of tax shield*) Dataflex Ltd is currently all-equity financed and has estimated its cost of equity at 16%. As the company's current EBIT of $4.5 million is expected to continue into the foreseeable future, its management considers that there is virtually no risk of financial distress if it borrows $5 million at an interest rate of 9% p.a. to repurchase some of its issued shares. As most of the company's shareholders cannot utilise the value of imputation credits, the company is considered to fall into taxation category 2 and the current corporate tax rate is 30%.

   (a) What is the value of the company with an all-equity capital structure?
   (b) What is the value of the company if it borrows the money and uses the proceeds to repurchase shares?

ST-3 (*Debt and financing mix*) Some financial data and the industry norm for three companies are shown in the following table:

MEASURE	COMPANY X	COMPANY Y	COMPANY Z	INDUSTRY NORM
Total debt to total assets	20%	30%	10%	30%
Times interest and preference dividend coverage	8 times	16 times	19 times	8 times
Price–earnings ratio	9 times	11 times	9 times	9 times

   (a) Which company appears to be employing debt to the most appropriate degree in its financing mix?
   (b) In this situation, which 'effects' of debt in the financing mix appear to dominate the market valuation process?

Problems

For more problems and for answers to problems marked with an asterisk (*) go to MyFinanceLab at www.pearson.com.au/myfinancelab

16-1 (*Capital-structure theory*) Southbend Automotive Ltd has an all-ordinary-share capital structure. Selected financial data for the company are shown below:

Ordinary shares outstanding	= 4 000 000
Ordinary share price, P_0	= $5 per share
Expected level of EBIT	= $2 000 000
Dividend payout ratio	= 100%

In answering the following questions, assume that company income is not taxed.

   (a) Under the present capital structure, what is the total value of the company?
   (b) What is the cost of ordinary share capital, K_E? What is the weighted average cost of capital, K_0?
   (c) Now, suppose that Southbend Automotive Ltd sells $2 million of long-term debt with an interest rate of 5% p.a., and the proceeds are used to retire the ordinary shares. According to extreme position 1, what will be the company's cost of ordinary equity *after* the capital-structure change?

(i) What will be the dividend per share flowing to the company's ordinary shareholders?

(ii) By what percentage has the dividend per share changed as a result of the capital-structure change?

(iii) By what percentage has the cost of ordinary equity changed as a result of the capital-structure change?

(iv) What will be the weighted average cost of capital after the capital-structure change?

16-2* (*Capital-structure theory*) South Bend Auto Parts has an all-ordinary-share capital structure. Some financial data for the company are shown below:

Ordinary shares outstanding	= 6 000 000
Ordinary share price, P_0	= $4 per share
Expected level of EBIT	= $4 200 000
Dividend payout ratio	= 100%

In answering the following questions, assume that company income is not taxed.

(a) Under the present capital structure, what is the total value of the company?

(b) What is the cost of ordinary capital, K_E? What is the weighted average cost of capital, K_0?

(c) Now, suppose that South Bend sells $1 million of long-term debt with an interest rate of 10%, and the proceeds are used to retire the ordinary shares. According to extreme position 1, what will be the company's cost of ordinary equity after the capital-structure change?

(i) What will be the dividend per share flowing to the company's shareholders?

(ii) By what percentage has the dividend per share changed as a result of the capital-structure change?

(iii) By what percentage has the cost of ordinary capital changed as a result of the capital-structure change?

(iv) What will be the weighted average cost of capital after the capital-structure change?

16-3 (*Capital-structure theory*) Sanpore Ltd has an ordinary-share capital structure. Relevant financial characteristics for the company are shown below:

Ordinary shares outstanding	= 2 000 000
Share price, P_0	= $11 per share
Expected level of EBIT	= $4 750 000
Dividend payout ratio	= 100%

Assume in answering this question that company income is not taxed.

(a) Under the present capital structure, what is the total value of the company?

(b) What is the cost of equity capital, K_E? What is the weighted average cost of capital, K_0?

(c) Now, suppose that Sanpore sells $1 million of long-term debt with an interest rate of 9%. p.a., and the proceeds are used to retire ordinary shares. According to extreme position 1, what will be the company's cost of ordinary equity after the capital-structure change?

(i) What will be the dividend per share flowing to the company's ordinary shareholders?

(ii) By what percentage has the dividend per share changed as a result of the capital-structure change?

(iii) By what percentage has the cost of equity changed as a result of the capital-structure change?

(iv) What will be the weighted average cost of capital after the capital structure change?

16-4* (*Value of tax shield*) The management of Bywater Co. considers the company's current EBIT of $2 million will continue into the foreseeable future. As the company is currently all-equity financed with a cost of equity at 12%, the management is considering borrowing $1 500 000 at an interest rate of 8% to repurchase some of the issued shares. The company is located in the United States and is subject to a classical tax system with a corporate tax rate of 35%.

(a) What is the value of the company with an all-equity capital structure?

(b) What is the value of the company if it borrows the money and uses the proceeds to repurchase shares?

16-5 (*Value of tax shield*) Although the Australian company Xeon Mining Ltd consistently generates EBIT of $3 million and pays income tax at the rate of 30%, its shareholders cannot utilise the franking credits that they receive with dividends from the company. The company is currently all-equity financed with a cost of equity at 15%, and its management is considering issuing $6 000 000 of bonds at an interest rate of 10% to repurchase some of the issued shares.

(a) What is the value of the company with an all-equity capital structure?
(b) What is the value of the company if it borrows the money and uses the proceeds to repurchase shares?

16-6* (*Risk of financial distress*) ITC Ltd is an Australian company with a majority of shareholders that are not integrated by the dividend imputation system. The company pays income tax at a rate of 30% on all its annual EBIT. The company's current EBIT is $1 million but historically it has varied by as much as 50% around this amount. Up until now the company has been 100% financed by equity at a cost of 16% and its management has heard about the value of the tax shield and is considering borrowing $4 million at an interest rate of 12% to buy back most of the issued shares.

(a) What is the value of the company with an all-equity capital structure?
(b) What is the value of the company if it borrows the money and uses the proceeds to repurchase shares?
(c) What is the risk of financial distress for the company?

16-7 (*Risk of financial distress*) Tarrango Developments is a Singapore-based company subject to a classical tax system with a tax rate of 20%. Historically the company has been very successful with its property developments and is currently generating EBIT of $6 million, but due to increased competition in its markets many of its tenants are shifting to newer developments. All of the company's finance has come from shares issued at a cost of 17%. Due to a boardroom dispute, the company is proposing to buy all the shares from the disaffected shareholders by borrowing $25 million at an interest rate of 14%.

(a) What is the value of the company with an all-equity capital structure?
(b) What is the value of the company if it borrows the money and uses the proceeds to repurchase shares?
(c) What is the risk of financial distress for the company?

16-8* (*Debt and financing mix*) Some financial data for three companies and the industry norm are displayed below:

MEASURE	COMPANY A	COMPANY B	COMPANY C	INDUSTRY NORM
Debt ratio	20%	15%	35%	25%
Times interest covered	11 times	9 times	6 times	9 times
Price–earnings ratio	12 times	10 times	5 times	10 times

(a) Which company appears to be using too much debt in its financing mix?
(b) Which company appears to be employing debt to the most appropriate degree?
(c) What explanation can you provide for the higher price–earnings ratio enjoyed by company B as compared with company A?

16-9 (*Debt and financing mix*) Some financial data and the appropriate industry norm are shown in the following table:

MEASURE	XERXES LTD	YABSCO LTD	ZOFTAN LTD	INDUSTRY NORM
Total debt to total assets	35%	10%	30%	35%
Times interest and preference dividend covered	7 times	16 times	14 times	7 times
Price–earnings ratio	8 times	8 times	10 times	8 times

(a) Which company appears to be using debt in its financing mix to the most appropriate degree?
(b) In this situation, which 'effect' of debt appears to dominate the market's valuation process?

16-10 (*Capital-structure theory*) Paragon Hardware Ltd has an all-ordinary-share capital structure. Some financial data for the company are as follows:

Ordinary shares outstanding	= 900 000
Ordinary share price, P_0	= $30 per share
Expected level of EBIT	= $6 300 000
Dividend payout ratio	= 100%

In answering the following questions, assume that company income is not taxed.

(a) Under the present capital structure, what is the total value of the company?

(b) What is the cost of ordinary share capital, K_E? What is the weighted average cost of capital, K_0?

(c) Now, suppose that Paragon sells $2.25 million of long-term debt with an interest rate of 9%, and that the proceeds are used to retire the ordinary shares. According to extreme position 1, what will be the company's cost of ordinary equity *after* the capital-structure change?

    (i) What will be the dividend per share flowing to the company's ordinary shareholders?

    (ii) By what percentage has the dividend per share changed as a result of the capital-structure change?

    (iii) By what percentage has the cost of ordinary equity changed as a result of the capital-structure change?

    (iv) What will be the weighted average cost of capital after the capital-structure change?

16-11 (*Capital-structure theory*) Fernando Hotels has an all-ordinary-share capital structure. Selected financial data for the company are shown below:

Ordinary shares outstanding	= 575 000
Ordinary share price, P_0	= $38 per share
Expected level of EBIT	= $4 500 000
Dividend payout ratio	= 100%

In answering the following questions, assume that company income is not taxed.

(a) Under the present capital structure, what is the total value of the company?

(b) What is the cost of ordinary share capital, K_E? What is the weighted average cost of capital, K_0?

(c) Now, suppose that Fernando sells $1.5 million of long-term debt with an interest rate of 11%, and that the proceeds are used to retire the ordinary shares. According to extreme position 1, what will be the company's cost of ordinary equity *after* the capital-structure change?

    (i) What will be the dividend per share flowing to the company's ordinary shareholders?

    (ii) By what percentage has the dividend per share changed as a result of the capital-structure change?

    (iii) By what percentage has the cost of ordinary equity changed as a result of the capital-structure change?

    (iv) What will be the weighted average cost of capital after the capital-structure change?

16-12 (*Debt and financing mix*) Some financial data for three companies are as follows:

MEASURE	COMPANY A	COMPANY B	COMPANY C	INDUSTRY NORM
Debt ratio	20%	25%	40%	20%
Times interest covered	8 times	10 times	7 times	9 times
Price–earnings ratio	9 times	11 times	6 times	10 times

(a) Which company appears to be excessively levered?

(b) Which company appears to be employing financial leverage to the most appropriate degree?

(c) What explanation can you provide for the higher price–earnings ratio enjoyed by company B as compared with company A?

16-13 (*Debt and financing mix*) Some financial data for three companies are displayed below:

MEASURE	AMPAC LTD	BRISKER CO	CROSBY LTD	INDUSTRY NORM
Debt ratio	40%	35%	10%	35%
Times interest covered	8 times	13 times	16 times	7 times
Price–earnings ratio	8 times	11 times	8 times	8 times

(a) Which company appears to be using too much debt in its financing mix?

(b) In this situation, which 'financial leverage effect' appears to dominate the market's valuation process?

16-14 (*Value of tax shield*) The management of DDP Inc. considers the company's current EBIT of $250 million will continue into the foreseeable future. As the company is currently all-equity financed with a cost of equity at 16% p.a., management is considering borrowing $150 000 000 at an interest rate of 8% to repurchase some of the company's issued shares. The company is subject to a classical tax system with a corporate tax rate of 28%.

(a) What is the value of the company with an all-equity capital structure?

(b) What is the value of the company if it borrows the money and uses the proceeds to repurchase shares?

16-15 (*Risk of financial distress*) Amori Corp. is a company subject to a classical tax system with a tax rate of 25%. All of the company's finance has come from shares issued at a cost of 14% p.a. and the company is currently generating EBIT of $16 million p.a. which is expected to remain constant in the foreseeable future. After a review of its capital structure, the company is proposing to borrow $25 million at an interest rate of 8% to buy back some of the issued shares.

(a) What is the value of the company with an all-equity capital structure?

(b) What is the value of the company if it borrows the money and uses the proceeds to repurchase shares?

(c) What is the risk of financial distress for the company?

Case study

The management of Eldine Ltd is considering an increase in its use of financial leverage. The proposal is to sell $6 million of bonds that would mature in 20 years and have a coupon rate of 12% that is paid annually to investors. To ensure that it can repay the bonds when they mature, the company will establish a sinking fund account into which it will pay one-twentieth of the bond's face value each year. Although in recent years business conditions have been very poor, many economists are forecasting an improvement in the coming year that will affect the entire economy. Eldine's management has been saying, 'If we made it through this recession, we can make it through anything.'

The company has a policy of maintaining an operating cash balance at all times of $750 000. Cash collections next year are estimated to be $3 million from sales and $400 000 from miscellaneous asset sales. Next year's cash payments have been forecast to comprise $700 000 for raw materials, $1 200 000 for wages and salaries and $1 200 000 for non-discretionary items including all tax payments. The company is subject to a 30% tax rate.

1. At present, Eldine Ltd is all-equity financed. If the company makes the bond issue, determine the total fixed cash flows the company must pay next year for this new debt finance.
2. If the company issues the bonds, determine your forecast of the company's expected cash balance at the end of next year.
3. As Eldine's financial consultant, do you recommend that it issue the bonds?
4. What would you expect to happen to the company's cost of equity capital?
5. What would you expect to happen to the market price of the company's ordinary shares?

Notes

1. David Durand, 'Costs of debt and equity funds for business: Trends and problems of measurement', Conference on Research in Business Finance, National Bureau of Economic Research, New York, 1952, reprinted in Ezra Solomon (ed.), *The Management of Corporate Capital*, Free Press, New York, 1959, pp. 91–116. Nobel Prize winning Professors Modigliani and Miller were leading proponents of the independence hypothesis in its various forms. See Franco Modigliani and Merton M. Miller, 'The cost of capital, corporation finance and the theory of investment', *American Economic Review*, 48, June 1958, pp. 261–97; Franco Modigliani and Merton H. Miller, 'Corporate income taxes and the cost of capital: A correction', *American Economic Review*, 53, June 1963, pp. 433–43; and Merton H. Miller, 'Debt and taxes', *Journal of Finance*, 32, May 1977, pp. 261–75.
2. Even this argument that the trade-off between liquidation costs and the tax-shield benefit of debt financing can lead to an optimal structure has its detractors. See Robert Haugen and Lemma W. Senbet, 'The insignificance of bankruptcy costs to the theory of optimal capital structure', *Journal of Finance*, 33, May 1978, pp. 383–93.
3. Economists have studied the problems associated with control of the corporation for decades. An early classic work on this topic was A. A. Berle Jr and G. C. Means, *The Modern Corporation and Private Property*, Macmillan, New York, 1932. The recent emphasis in corporate finance and financial economics stems from the important contribution of Michael C. Jensen and William H. Meckling, 'Theory of the firm: Managerial behavior, agency costs and ownership structure', *Journal of Financial Economics*, 3, October 1967, pp. 305–60. Professors Jensen and Smith have analysed the bondholder–shareholder conflict in a very clear style. See Michael C. Jensen and Clifford W. Smith Jr, 'Stockholder, manager, and creditor interests: Applications of agency theory', in Edward I. Altman and Marti G. Subrahmanyam (eds), *Recent Advances in Corporate Finance*, Richard D. Irwin, Homewood, IL, 1985, pp. 93–131. An entire volume dealing with agency problems, including those of capital-structure management, is Amir Barnea, Robert A. Haugen and Lemma W. Senbet, *Agency Problems and Financial Contracting*, Prentice Hall, Englewood Cliffs, NJ, 1985.
4. Michael Jensen, 'Agency costs of free cash flow, corporate finance, and takeovers', *American Economic Review*, 76, May 1986, pp. 323–29.
5. The relationship between capital structure and enterprise valuation by the marketplace continues to stimulate considerable research output. The complexity of the topic is reviewed in Stewart C. Myers, 'The capital structure puzzle', *Journal of Finance*, 39, July 1984, pp. 575–92. Ten useful papers are contained in Benjamin M. Friedman (ed.), *Corporate Capital Structures in the United States*, National Bureau of Economic Research and University of Chicago Press, Chicago, 1985. Also see Stewart C. Myers, 'Still searching for optimal capital structure', *Journal of Applied Corporate Finance*, Spring 1993, pp. 4–14.
6. Ray Anderson, 'Financial management: Financial policies and practices of Australian companies', in R. W. Peacock (ed.), *Business Finance in Australia: Selected Readings*, rev. edn, SA Institute of Technology, Adelaide, 1990, pp. 140–46; David E. Allen, 'The determinants of the capital structure of listed Australian companies: The financial manager's perspective', *Australian Journal of Management*, 16, December 1991, pp. 103–26.
7. In the 1987 survey respondents were not specifically asked if they accepted the concept of an optimal capital structure.
8. John Graham and Campbell Harvey, 'The theory and practice of corporate finance: Evidence from the field', *Journal of Financial Economics*, 60, 2001.
9. Stewart C. Myers, 'The capital structure puzzle', *Journal of Finance*, 39, July 1984, pp. 574–92; Stewart C. Myers, 'Still searching for optimal capital structure', *Journal of Applied Corporate Finance*, Spring 1993, pp. 4–14.

Learning objectives

After reading this chapter, you should be able to:

1 Understand the terminology used in relation to a company's dividend policy.
2 Understand rival theories of the relationship between dividend policy and share price.
3 Distinguish between the types of dividend policies used by companies in practice.
4 Appreciate the implications of dividend imputation and capital-gains tax for a company's dividend policy.
5 Appreciate the procedures that a company follows in the payment of dividends.
6 Understand the use of bonus shares, share splits and share buybacks by companies.

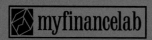

Dividend policy and internal financing

Chapter **17**

CHAPTER PREVIEW

The consistent theme of this book has been applying the objective of maximising the wealth of the firm's owners to financial decision making. Previous chapters examined how investment decisions (Chapters 11–13) and financing decisions (Chapters 15 and 16) affect owner wealth, with the link between the two being the cost of capital (Chapter 14). In these previous chapters the focus was on ordinary shareholders who obtain their wealth as the owners of the company from dividends and the value (price) of the company's ordinary shares. In this chapter the *dividend and internal* financing policies of companies are examined. It aims to answer the question: can management influence the price of the company's shares and therefore shareholder wealth through its dividend policies? The chapter also identifies the key procedures a company must follow to pay dividends to its shareholders.

Terminology

Before examining the particular issues relating to dividend policy, several key terms and inter-relationships need to be understood.

The dividend policy of a company includes two basic components. The first component is the **dividend payout ratio**, which is the amount of the company's current-year earnings (profit) paid to shareholders as dividends. For example, if the company pays a dividend per share of 20 cents from earnings per share of 40 cents, the dividend payout ratio is 50% ($0.20/$0.40).

The second component is the *stability* of the dividend amount over time. As will be seen later in the chapter, a dividend that is a stable amount from year to year may be almost as important to shareholders as the amount of the dividend received each year.

In formulating its dividend policy, the company's management and board of directors face a number of trade-offs. For example, if management has decided the amount of finance it needs for new investment projects and has chosen its debt–equity mix to fund these investments, a decision to pay a large proportion of earnings as a dividend means simultaneously deciding to have little, if any, retained earnings. Low retained earnings in turn results in a greater reliance on raising external equity finance and incurring significant issue costs. Conversely, given the company's investment and financing decisions, a low dividend payout will provide the company with large retained earnings, which will mean less need to raise external equity funds. These trade-offs are illustrated in Figure 17.1.

OBJECTIVE 1

Understand the terminology used in relation to a company's dividend policy.

dividend payout ratio
The amount of dividends relative to the company's net income or earnings per share.

Concept check

17.1 What is the dividend payout ratio?
17.2 How does the company's dividend policy affect its need for externally generated finance?

For answers go to MyFinanceLab or
www.pearson.com.au/9781442539174

FIGURE 17.1 Dividend–retention–financing trade-offs

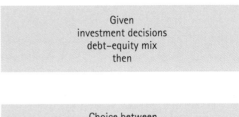

Given
investment decisions
debt–equity mix
then

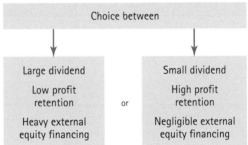

Choice between

Large dividend	or	Small dividend
Low profit retention		High profit retention
Heavy external equity financing		Negligible external equity financing

Regardless of your program

CHANGING A COMPANY'S DIVIDEND

The decision to initiate, increase or decrease a company's cash dividend is an important decision that is made by the company's board of directors. The board, in turn, relies on the input of the company's management team to make the right decision. When the board is considering an increase in the company's dividend payout, a prime consideration is whether payment of the increased dividend amount can be sustained in the future.

They do not want to increase dividends today if it is likely that they will have to cut dividends in the future. Accordingly, the company's board will seek advice from the marketing department on future sales and from people in operations to get a better understanding of the factors likely to affect the company's cost structure in the future.

OBJECTIVE **2**

Understand rival theories of the relationship between dividend policy and share price.

Does dividend policy affect share price?

The fundamental question is this: *does a policy to adopt a high dividend payout ratio cause the company's share price to decrease, increase, or have no impact?*

At first glance it would be reasonable to conclude that the amount of a company's dividend must have an impact on its share price, because in Chapter 10 the value of a share was calculated as being equal to the present value of future dividends. Also, you can observe from the financial press that many pages are devoted to company dividend announcements, so dividends must be regarded as important news to investors.

So why do some people argue that the amount of a company's net profit that is paid out as dividends has no effect on shareholder wealth? This is why the dividend question has been a controversial issue for well over three decades and has even been called the 'dividend puzzle'.[1]

Three basic views of dividend policy

Similar to the analysis of capital-structure policy in Chapter 16, this section details three basic views regarding the impact of dividend policy on share price. The first view argues that the amount of a company's net profit that is paid out to shareholders as a dividend has no effect on share price and therefore dividend policy is irrelevant to shareholder wealth. The second view contends that a high dividend payout will result in a high share price, while the third view proposes that a low dividend payout can have a positive effect on share price. We will briefly examine each of these three views in turn.

VIEW 1: DIVIDEND POLICY IS IRRELEVANT TO SHARE PRICE

Much of the controversy about the relationship between dividend policy and share price reflects disagreements between the academic community and the professional community. Experienced company managers report that they believe that dividend payout decisions can result in changes in share price and therefore are important to shareholder wealth. On the other hand, some academics propose that the amount of net profit paid out as dividends does not affect share prices. They argue that the identification by managers of a relationship between dividends and share price may be an illusion.[2]

The position that a company's dividend policy has no impact on its share prices rests on two preconditions. First, it is assumed that the company has made its investment and capital-structure decisions and that these decisions will not be altered by the amount of any dividend payments. Second, it is assumed that 'perfect' capital markets exist, which means that (1) investors can buy and sell shares without incurring any transaction costs (such as brokerage), (2) companies can issue shares without any cost of doing so, (3) there are no company or personal taxes, (4) complete information about the company is readily available, (5) there are no conflicts of interest between management and shareholders, and (6) financial distress and liquidation costs are nonexistent.

The first assumption—that the investment and capital-structure decisions have already been made—removes the impact of these decisions so that only the effect of dividend payout decisions on share prices are identified. The second assumption, that of perfect markets, also allows the effect of dividend policy to be studied in isolation, much as a physicist studies motion in a vacuum to avoid the influence of friction.

Given these assumptions, there is no relationship between dividend payout and share price. This is because investors are only concerned with the amount of the *total* returns resulting from the company's investment decisions, and as there is a perfect market they will be indifferent to receiving these returns as dividends now or later as capital gains. Therefore, as it is the investment decisions that determine the share price, one dividend policy is as good as another.

Also, investors recognise that once the company has selected its investment projects, the dividend payout decision is really just a choice of the equity finance component of the projects being provided by either:

1. issuing new shares so that the net profit can be used to pay high dividends, or
2. retaining net profit (retained earnings) by paying low dividends so that new shares don't have to be issued.

In the first case, shareholders receive high dividends now, whereas in the second case the value of their shares should increase to reflect the amount of retained earnings, providing shareholders with capital gains. The only difference between the two cases is the nature of the return (dividend or capital gain), as total returns should be about the same. Thus, to argue that a high dividend payout can make shareholders better off is to argue that paying out cash (as dividends) with one hand and taking it back with the other hand (issuing shares) will have a positive effect on share prices.

The company's dividend payout decision could affect its share price if shareholders have no way other than dividends to receive a regular income from their shareholding. However, if it is assumed that capital markets are relatively efficient, a shareholder who needs current income could always sell some shares. Similarly, if the company pays a dividend, shareholders could convert any dividend received, in whole or in part, to purchase shares. Therefore, shareholders can personally create any desired income stream, no matter what dividend policy is employed by the company. This is illustrated in the following example.

Example of dividend irrelevance

Dowell Venture Ltd is a newly created joint-venture company that has a two-year lease to mine sand. The company has just commenced its business and will operate for only two years (year 1 and year 2), after which time it will be liquidated. The company is financed by ordinary shares only.

Table 17.1 presents Dowell Venture Ltd's balance sheet at the time of its formation, as well as the projected cash flows for years 1 and 2. The anticipated cash flows are based on an expected return on sand-mining projects of 20% per annum, which is exactly the same rate that shareholders require on their investment in the company's shares.

At the end of year 1 an additional investment of $300 000 will be required, which may be financed by either (1) retaining $300 000 of the year 1 profits, or (2) issuing new shares, or (3) some combination of both.

The company is considering two dividend plans for the payout of the year 1 profits of $400 000:

- Plan 1: pay $100 000 in dividends and retain the balance ($300 000) for reinvestment.
- Plan 2: pay $250 000 in dividends and retain the balance ($150 000) for reinvestment. As the retained earnings of $150 000 fall short of the $300 000 needed for reinvestment, the company would need to issue $150 000 in new shares to make up the shortfall.

Table 17.2 depicts these two dividend plans and the corresponding new share issue.

To answer the question of which dividend plan is preferable to the investors, three steps must be taken: (1) calculate the amount and timing of the dividend stream for the *original* investors; (2) determine the present value of the dividend stream for each dividend plan; (3) select the dividend alternative that provides the higher value to the investors.

Step 1: Computing the dividend streams

The first step in this process is presented in Table 17.3.

Looking first at line 1 of Table 17.3, you can see the year 1 dividend amounts for the two plans are the same as detailed in Table 17.2.

TABLE 17.1   Dowell Venture Ltd, financial data

	START OF YEAR 1	
Total assets	$2 000 000	
Ordinary shares (100 000 shares)	$2 000 000	

	YEAR 1	YEAR 2
Projected cash available from operations for paying dividends or for reinvesting[a]	$400 000	$460 000

a Year 1: 2 000 000 × 0.20 = $400 000; Year 2: 2 300 000 × 0.20 = $460 000.

TABLE 17.2   Dowell Venture Ltd, year 1 proposed dividend plans

	PLAN 1	PLAN 2
Internally generated cash flow	$400 000	$400 000
Dividend for year 1	100 000	250 000
Cash available for reinvestment	$300 000	$150 000
Amount of investment in year 1	300 000	300 000
Additional external financing required	0	$150 000

TABLE 17.3 Dowell Venture Ltd, Step 1: Measurement of proposed dividend streams

	PLAN 1		PLAN 2	
	TOTAL AMOUNT	AMOUNT PER SHARE[a]	TOTAL AMOUNT	AMOUNT PER SHARE[a]
Year 1				
(1) Dividend	$100 000	$1.00	$250 000	$2.50
Year 2				
Total dividend consisting of:				
(2) Original investment:				
(a) old investors	$2 000 000		$2 000 000	
(b) new investors	0		150 000	
(3) Retained earnings from year 1	300 000		150 000	
(4) Profits for year 2	460 000		460 000	
(5) Total dividend to all investors in year 2	$2 760 000		$2 760 000	
(6) Less dividends to new investors:				
(a) original investment	0		(150 000)	
(b) profits for new investors (20% of $150,000 investment)	0		(30 000)	
(7) Liquidating dividends available to original investors in year 2	$2 760 000	$27.60	$2 580 000	$25.80

a Number of original shares outstanding equals 100 000.

Now the amount of the dividend to be paid at the end of year 2 to the original shareholders has to be calculated. To do this calculation, it is assumed that these shareholders receive:

- the amount of their original investment in the company when it is liquidated at the end of year 2 (line 2, Table 17.3)
- any funds retained within the business in year 1 (line 3)
- the profits for year 2 (line 4).

In addition, with plan 2 the dividends to be paid to the new investors must be subtracted from the total available dividends (line 6). The remaining dividends (line 7) represent the amount that original shareholders will receive at the end of year 2.

The amounts of the dividends received by the original company shareholders can therefore be summarised as follows:

DIVIDEND PLAN	YEAR 1	YEAR 2
1	$1.00	$27.60
2	$2.50	$25.80

Step 2: Determining the present value of the cash-flow streams
Using the basic dividend valuation model from Chapter 10, the share price for each of the dividend payment plans can be calculated:

$$\text{Share price (plan 1)} = \frac{\$1.00}{(1+0.20)} + \frac{\$27.60}{(1+0.20)^2} = \$20$$

$$\text{Share price (plan 2)} = \frac{\$2.50}{(1+0.20)} + \frac{\$25.80}{(1+0.20)^2} = \$20$$

Therefore, the two dividend plans result in the same shareholder wealth because the market price of the company's shares is $20 regardless of the dividend policy.

Step 3: Select the best dividend plan

The conclusion from this example is that the company's dividend policy is irrelevant to the share price and therefore shareholder wealth. Also, this example shows that a policy to shift dividend payments between years does not affect the value of the company's shares. Therefore, the only way the company can increase the price of its shares and the wealth of its shareholders is to undertake investment projects that have expected returns exceeding the required return of 20%.

VIEW 2: HIGH DIVIDEND PAYOUT INCREASES SHARE PRICE

The previous view that a company's dividend policy is irrelevant to shareholder wealth implicitly assumes that shareholders would use the same required rate of return for income from the company that they received either as dividends or through capital gains.

However, the second view argues that the cash flow shareholders receive from dividends is more predictable than converting capital gains to income. This is because the company's management can control the amount of dividends paid to shareholders but it cannot dictate the price of the company's shares. Consequently, shareholders are less certain of the amount they will receive from capital gains than from dividends.

The incremental risk associated with capital gains relative to dividend income implies that shareholders would require a higher rate of return to discount capital gains than to discount dividends. In other words, shareholders would value a dollar of expected dividends more highly than a dollar of expected capital gains. They might, for example, require a rate of 14% for a share that pays out its entire earnings as dividends, but require a 20% return for a high-growth share that pays no dividends and retains all its earnings. The effect of these differential required rates of return is that shareholders would give a higher value to dividend income than to future capital gains. This view, which says that dividends are more certain than capital gains, and therefore more valuable, has been called the 'bird-in-the-hand' theory.

The view that dividends are less risky than capital gains, and should therefore be more highly valued, has its critics. The critics argue that, if a company's investment and capital-structure decisions are set before the dividend policy decision, the company's operating cash flows, both in expected amount and variability, will be unaffected by the amount of dividend payout.

This means that increasing or decreasing a company's dividend payout ratio does not change the basic riskiness of the share. Rather, if an increased dividend payout requires management to issue new shares, there is only a transfer of risk *and* ownership from the current shareholders to the new shareholders. Even though the current shareholders who receive the higher dividend have traded an uncertain capital gain for a 'safe' asset (the cash dividend), if risk reduction was their only goal they could have kept the money in the bank and not bought the shares in the first place.

Back to the principles

The bird-in-the-hand theory proposing a relationship between a company's dividend policy and its share price relates directly to **Principle 2: The time value of money—a dollar received today is worth more than a dollar received in the future**. The bird-in-the-hand theory suggests that a dollar of dividends received today should be valued more highly than an uncertain capital gain that might be received in the future. The fundamental premise of this position is that the cash dividend in your hand (placed there today by the company's dividend policy) is more certain (less risky) than a possible capital gain. Many practitioners adhere to this theory; but many also adhere to the theory that is advanced in the next section. If nothing else, dividend policy is important to the company and its shareholders because it is controversial.

Although the arguments of the critics of the bird-in-the-hand theory have some logic, there is still a strong perception among many investors and professional investment advisers that dividend policy does affect share prices. They frequently argue their case based on their own personal experience. As expressed by one investment adviser:

> In advising companies on dividend policy, we're absolutely sure on one side that the investors in large public companies want dividends. We're absolutely sure on the other side that ... the high-technology companies should have no dividends. For the high earners—the ones that have a high rate of return like 20%, or more than their cost of capital—we think they should have a low payout ratio. We think a typical industrial company which earns its cost of capital—just earns its cost of capital—probably should be in the average (dividend payout) range of 40 to 50%.[3]

VIEW 3: LOW DIVIDEND PAYOUT INCREASES SHARE PRICE

The third view of dividend policy proposes that high dividend payouts have a negative effect on share prices largely due to differences in the tax treatment of dividend income and capital gains. Because most investors pay income taxes, their objective is to maximise the after-tax return they receive from an investment relative to the risk assumed. This objective is realised by investors *minimising* their effective tax rate and, whenever possible, *deferring* the payment of taxes.

In 1985 capital-gains tax was introduced in Australia, and applies to the gains from the sale of shares. Under Australian income-tax law the shareholder's marginal tax rate is applied to both dividend income and capital gains. However, the law provides a concession to capital gains vis-a-vis dividend income, because for most investors only half the capital gain is taxed (see Chapter 2). Also, taxes on dividend income are paid when the dividend is received, while taxes on price appreciation (capital gains) are deferred until the shares are actually sold.

Thus, when it comes to tax considerations, many shareholders may prefer a company to retain its earnings and provide them with capital gains as opposed to cash dividends. Therefore, shares that allow tax deferral (pay low dividends and have high capital gains) will possibly sell at a higher price relative to shares that require current taxation (pay high dividends and have low capital gains).

This suggests that a policy of low dividend payout and high retention will result in a higher share price. Note that this tax-induced preference for a low dividend payout and high capital gain applies to a classical tax system (refer to Chapters 2, 11, 14 and 16) and has not included the impact of the Australian *dividend imputation system*, which will be discussed in a later section.

What is the correct view of the relationship between dividend policy and share price?

If there was a world where the perfect-market assumptions applied, the view that dividend policy doesn't affect the share price and therefore is irrelevant to shareholder wealth would be difficult to refute. However, as many of these perfect-market assumptions do not apply in reality, this view does not answer the dividend policy question. Similarly, criticism can be levelled at the high-dividend payout view that assumes that shareholder risk and return are affected by how the company's earnings are split between dividends and retained earnings.

This leaves the third view, which is essentially a tax argument against high dividend payouts. If this view is correct and a low dividend payout policy increases the company's share price, why do we observe companies continuing to pay out significant amounts of their net profit as dividends? There must be some missing elements of the 'dividend puzzle' that these three views have ignored.

Scholars and practitioners have identified several plausible extensions to the three views. Some of the more popular additions include (1) the residual-dividend theory, (2) the clientele effect, (3) the information effect, (4) agency costs, and (5) expectations theory. Each of these is now briefly examined.

THE RESIDUAL-DIVIDEND THEORY

When it raises external finance for investment projects by issuing new securities, the company incurs significant issue costs. To pay for these issue costs, the company has to issue more securities than would be needed just to finance the initial outlay for the investments. For example, if the equity finance component to fund new investment projects is $30 000 000 and it costs $1 000 000 to issue new shares, the company will have to issue 31 000 000 one-dollar shares to raise a total of $31 000 000. If the projects are expected to produce incremental net profit of $4 000 000 per annum, the return on equity from the projects will be $4 000 000 / $31 000 000 = 0.129 (12.9% per annum). On the other hand, if the $30 000 000 can be funded from retained earnings, which have no issue costs, the return on equity from the projects will be $4 000 000 / $30 000 000 = 0.1333 (13.33%). Thus, in this example, the cost of issuing new shares is reflected in the reduction in the return on equity.

As the absence of issue costs make retained earnings a cheaper form of equity finance than issuing new shares, it would be expected that shareholders would benefit from the company retaining as much of its earnings as possible for investment projects. Consequently, dividends should only be paid when there are 'residual earnings' remaining after the financing of new investments. This is why this dividend policy is called the **residual-dividend theory**.[4]

Under the residual-dividend theory, the company's policy would be:

1. All investment projects should be financed in accordance with the optimum debt–equity ratio that minimises the weighted average cost of capital.
2. An investment project is acceptable if its net present value is positive—that is, the expected return exceeds the weighted average cost of capital.
3. The equity portion of new investments should be financed *first* by retained earnings. Only after retained earnings are fully utilised should the company issue new ordinary shares.
4. The residual amount of earnings remaining after the equity component of all investments has been funded can be paid as dividends to shareholders. However, if all earnings are needed for the equity finance portion, then no dividend should be paid.

Example 17.1 illustrates the residual-dividend policy.

residual-dividend theory
A theory asserting that the dividends to be paid should equal the equity capital left over after the financing of profitable investments.

EXAMPLE 17.1   Illustration of residual-dividend policy

Krista Ltd has determined its optimal capital structure and finances 40% of its investments with debt and the remaining 60% with ordinary equity. Two million dollars of earnings (net profit) have been generated from its operations that can be used to either finance the ordinary-equity portion of new investments or pay dividends.

The company's management is considering five investment opportunities and Figure 17.2 graphs the expected rate of return for these investments, along with the company's weighted average cost of capital.

Projects A, B and C should be accepted because the internal rate of return of each is above the company's weighted average cost of capital. As these three projects will require $2.5 million in total financing, the company will need to raise $1 million in new debt (40% of $2.5 million) and $1.5 million (60% of $2.5 million) would need to be provided by equity.

Under the residual-dividend theory, the company is able to fund all of the $1.5 million of equity from the $2 million retained earnings and therefore it is able to pay the residual amount of $500 000 as dividends.

What would be the dividend decision if project D had also been acceptable? If this investment costing $1.5 million were added to the other proposed capital expenditures, $4 million in new financing would be needed. Of this amount, new debt finance would provide $1.6 million (40% × $4 million) and equity would need to provide $2.4 million (60% × $4 million). As there is only $2 million of equity available from retained earnings, the $400 000 shortfall would have to be raised by issuing new shares. Also, there would be zero residual earnings available for dividends, so no dividend would be paid to shareholders.

FIGURE 17.2   Krista Ltd investment schedule

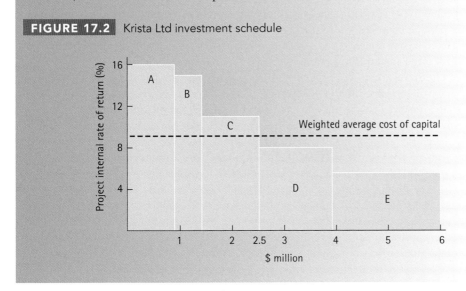

As the dividend payout under the residual-dividend theory is determined by (1) the acceptable investment projects, (2) the capital-structure mix, and (3) the availability of internally generated capital, a residual-dividend policy should have no direct influence on the market price of the company's ordinary shares.

THE CLIENTELE EFFECT

In the earlier example of Dowell Venture Ltd (Tables 17.1, 17.2 and 17.3), shareholders should be indifferent to the two dividend policies because they both resulted in the same share price.

However, what if for some reason a group of the company's shareholders thought that the dividend plan that Dowel Venture management had decided to adopt was paying them too little or too much dividend income? No problem. These shareholders could simply satisfy their personal income preferences by purchasing or selling the company's shares. Shareholders who did not consider the amount of the dividend received in any given year to be sufficient could sell a portion of their shares and 'create a dividend'. Conversely, if the dividend payment was larger than the shareholders desired, they could purchase shares with the 'excess cash' created by the dividend.

However, such adjustments in share ownership are not cost free. When a shareholder buys or sells shares, brokerage fees and government levies are incurred. Even more costly for shareholders who are subject to a classical tax system is that they will have to buy shares with the after-tax cash amount of dividends received. Also, when shares are bought or sold, shareholders need to determine whether the current share price is fair, too high or too low. To do this requires acquiring information that can be time consuming and costly.

Finally, aside from the cost of buying or selling shares, some institutional investors such as superannuation funds may be restricted on the extent to which they can sell shares and 'spend' the proceeds, whereas there are no restrictions on the use of income received from dividends, interest or rent.

After taking these factors into consideration, some investors would not want to buy the shares of companies that have a dividend policy that requires them to create an 'equivalent dividend' income. Consequently, investors will group into those who have a preference for either dividend income or for capital gains, and will want to purchase the shares of companies that have a dividend policy that is consistent with their preference. The result is that the dividend policy of a company can be expected to attract a clientele (group) of shareholders who consider the company's dividend payout policy satisfies their preferences.

For example, the clientele comprising individuals and institutions that want current income would be expected to purchase the shares of companies that have a high dividend payout policy. On the other hand, a clientele whose preference is to defer taxes (such as wealthy individuals) would be expected to buy the shares of companies that have no (or a small) dividend payout and the potential for large capital gains.

A positive **clientele effect** will occur when a company adopts a particular dividend policy that is so attractive to a clientele of investors that the increase in demand to purchase the company's shares results in a rise in the share price. A negative clientele effect could occur if the company changed its dividend policy and a large number of its clientele decided to sell their shares.

It can be argued, however, that unless there is a greater aggregate demand by a particular shareholder clientele for a particular dividend policy that companies in the market cannot satisfy, then for any company one dividend policy is as good as the other. This is because, although some shareholders may want to sell their shares in response to a change in a company's dividend policy, other investors will want to buy the shares because the new dividend policy meets their preferences.

The general opinion of the clientele effect is that, although a company's dividend policy is unlikely to have a persistent effect on its share price, the company needs to be aware that major changes in its dividend policy can cause its existing shareholder clientele to shift to another company, which can have a temporary effect on the share price.

clientele effect
The belief that individuals and institutions that need current income will invest in companies that have high dividend payouts. Other investors prefer to hold securities that offer only small dividend income but large capital gains. Thus, there is a 'clientele' of investors.

THE INFORMATION EFFECT

From previous chapters we know that a company's share price and the wealth of its shareholders are primarily determined by its investment decisions and perhaps to some extent by its capital-structure decisions. So far our examination of the impact of dividend policy on shareholder wealth has produced no clear conclusion.

To further add to this situation, shareholders know from experience that a large unexpected change in the dividend amount paid by a company can have a significant impact on its share price. When this occurs, how can it be suggested that a company's dividend policy does not have an effect on its share price and shareholder wealth?

One explanation of why a major change in the share price may not be directly caused by a change in the dividend amount is because there may be some other factors that are associated with the dividend change that investors are responding to. For example, it may be that investors are using the unexpected change in dividend as a *signal* about the company's financial condition, especially its future earnings.

In this way, an unexpected dividend decrease, or even a less than expected increase, might signal to investors that management is forecasting less favourable earnings in the future. Conversely, a dividend increase that is larger than expected might signal to investors that management expects significantly higher earnings in the future.

The argument in support of this view is that management frequently has information about the company that it cannot or does not want to make available to investors. This results in **information asymmetry**, where management and investors have different (asymmetrical = not the same) accessibility to information about the company. Consequently, investors are constantly trying to obtain up-to-date and accurate information about the current and future performance of companies, and any information that becomes available has to be interpreted.

So, investors may interpret a company that announces an unexpected increase in dividends as a signal that the company's management considers that these dividend payments can be maintained in the foreseeable future. Conversely, an announcement of an unexpected fall in dividends may be interpreted as the company experiencing financial difficulties and making no commitment to future dividend payments.

Consequently, the amount of a dividend may not itself directly affect the company's share

information asymmetry
The difference in accessibility to information between managers and investors, which may result in a lower share price than would be the case under conditions of certainty.

price but the dividend announcement may be useful as a way for the company to communicate with investors and inform investors about future earnings.

Back to the principles

Principle 7: The agency problem—managers won't work for owners unless it's in their best interest warned us that, especially in large companies, there can be conflict between management and owners, especially since managers' objective should be to make financial decisions that maximise the wealth of the ordinary shareholders. As we will see in the next section, dividend policy may be one way to reduce this problem.

AGENCY COSTS

The discussion of dividend policy so far has avoided the issue of the potential for conflict between the interests of the company's shareholders and its managers. A major characteristic of listed public companies is that the managers and major shareholders are typically not the same people. One effect of the separation of management and ownership is information asymmetry due to the two groups not having the same access to information about the company. Even so, the general principle adopted throughout this book is that management should make investment and financing decisions that maximise shareholder wealth. If this principle is applied by managers, then the market value of a listed company with separate owners and managers would not be any different from the value of the same business if it was managed and owned by the same person.

In a competitive economy, there at least two factors that encourage company managers to make decisions to maximise shareholder wealth:

1. Low share prices may attract takeover bids. If management does not make decisions to maximise the company's share price, then new investors can buy the underpriced shares, take control of the company and replace the management.
2. A competitive labour market should enable shareholders to easily replace underperforming managers.

If these two market mechanisms worked perfectly without any cost, the potential for conflict between the interests of managers and shareholders would be nonexistent. In reality, however, conflicts may still exist, resulting in the company's share price not being maximised. As this difference in share price is a cost to shareholders for having to engage managers as their agents, it has been given the name *agency cost*.[5]

Companies, either independently or as required by regulatory authorities, can minimise the agency costs associated with the separation of ownership and management by having the company's financial statements audited by independent accountants, assigning supervisory functions to the company's board of directors, creating covenants in lending agreements that restrict management's powers, and providing incentive plans for management that encourage decisions that benefit shareholders.

A company's dividend policy can also be perceived by shareholders as one of the ways to minimise agency costs. For example, if the payment of a dividend requires the company to issue shares to fund its investment projects, management will have to provide convincing information to investors that the equity finance will be used profitably. In this way the payment of dividends indirectly results in a closer monitoring of management's investment activities, and therefore dividends may have a positive impact on the company's share price.

EXPECTATIONS THEORY

The word *expected* is a common thread throughout much of the discussion of dividend policy because how a company's share price responds to the announcement of the dividend payout is determined not only by the decision itself but also by investors' prior expectations of the decision.

As the time approaches for the company to announce the amount of its next dividend, investors form expectations as to how much that dividend will be. These expectations are based on their assessment of available information of several company factors, such as past dividend decisions, current and expected earnings, identifiable investment strategies and financing decisions. Investors also consider such things as the condition of the general economy, the strength or weakness of the industry, and possible changes in government policies.

When the dividend decision is announced, investors compare the actual dividend amount with their expectations. If the amount is as expected, even if it represents an increase from prior years, the price of the shares will remain unchanged. However, if the dividend amount is higher or lower than expected, investors will need to reassess their perceptions about the company and try to interpret the meaning of the *unexpected* change in the dividend amount. They may consider that the unexpected dividend change is providing information about the management's view of the company's future earnings and future dividend amounts.

In short, dividend policy may have no effect on the company's share price unless the announced net profit and dividend payout departs from investors' expectations.

EMPIRICAL EVIDENCE

Our search for an answer to the question of whether a company's dividend policy can affect its share price and shareholder wealth has so far been less than conclusive. Maybe analysis of empirical data will help.

One way is to empirically test for a relationship between a company's dividend yield (dividend/share price) and the total return received by shareholders. Although this type of test has been conducted with the use of highly sophisticated statistical techniques, the results to date have been mixed. For example, a 1979 Australian study found that dividend yields were positively related to share returns, but when data over long periods were further examined it was found that shares paying lower dividends tended to have higher prices and thereby provided investors with higher returns. The researchers conceded that their methodology was not perfect and one explanation of the mixed results may have been the random sampling error associated with the statistical methods.[6]

This study also highlighted the problem of trying to disentangle the effect of dividend policy from other influences on share prices and returns. For example, because share prices primarily reflect the valuation of future cash flows, it would be necessary to know the amount of dividends investors *expected* to receive. However, these expectations cannot be observed, so researchers are restricted to using historical data only, which may or may not be a correct reflection of current expectations of future dividends.

Also, most of the empirical studies of dividend policy that have been conducted assume that there is a linear relationship between dividend payments and share prices. It may be that the actual relationship is nonlinear or possibly even discontinuous.

As the empirical studies examining dividends and share prices have not provided any conclusive evidence, an alternative is to ask financial managers and market professionals what they believe to be the relevance of dividend policy to shareholder wealth. A study of financial executives at 318 firms listed on the New York Stock Exchange in 1983 found some evidence that favours the relevance of dividend policy, but this was not overwhelming. For the most part, managers were divided between believing that dividends were important and having no opinion on the matter.[7]

A 1992 Australian study focused on the institutional ownership (insurance companies, superannuation funds and other financial institutions) of listed shares in Australia, because the share-trading activity of these entities has a significant influence on share prices.[8]

The investment managers of the institutional entities were surveyed for their views on the relevance of dividends and dividend policy to investors. The results favoured the relevance of dividend policy, with approximately 88% of respondents agreeing with the statement that 'an increased dividend increases a firm's share price' and only 12% responding that dividend policy was irrelevant to share prices.

As to investor preferences for either dividends or capital gains, the evidence from this Australian survey was mixed. About one-third of respondents preferred capital gains, one-third ranked capital gains equally with dividends, and the final third preferred dividends.

The investment managers were also asked to respond to a number of other closed-end statements. There was significant agreement with statements relating to the information contribution of dividends. In particular, the managers believed that investors were very sensitive to the effect of changes of dividend policy on share prices, and that shareholders were attracted to companies that had dividend policies appropriate to the shareholders' particular tax profiles. The managers were equally divided on the view that a company's industry was a determinant of its payout ratio. Finally, nearly 80% of the managers felt that companies responded to the dividend preferences of their shareholders—that is, that there is a clientele effect.

WHAT ARE WE TO CONCLUDE?

We have now looked at a number of attempts to identify a relationship (if any) between a company's dividend policy and its share price and we have not been able to reach a definitive conclusion. Nevertheless, as managers must develop a dividend policy for their company, the following recommendations based on the available knowledge can be made:

1. As a company's investment opportunities increase, the dividend payout ratio should decrease to enable as much retained earnings as possible to be used for the equity component of the investments, thereby avoiding the costs associated with issuing new shares.
2. A company's dividend policy appears to affect its share price, not because of the amount of the current dividend, but because the policy informs the market of management's view of the company's *expected* earning power and the riskiness of those earnings. It seems that management's actions in setting the current dividend can carry greater weight with investors than a statement by management that earnings will be increasing.
3. If there is an influence of dividends on share price, it is probably due to the desire of investors to minimise and defer their taxes (under the classical tax system), and to the role of dividends in minimising agency costs.
4. As the expectations of investors seem to be an important component in determining share prices, management should avoid making dividend decisions that give investors a negative surprise.
5. A company's dividend policy might effectively be treated as a *long-term residual*. Rather than projecting investment requirements for a single year, management should anticipate financing needs for several years. Then, given the company's debt–equity mix, dividends should be paid from the period's net earnings that are expected to remain after the necessary equity financing has been provided by retained earnings. However, the planned dividend stream should distribute the residual net earnings evenly over the planning period. Conversely, if over the long term all of the internally generated net earnings are needed for reinvestment, the company should adopt a policy of paying no dividends.

Dividend policy in practice

OBJECTIVE **3**

Distinguish between the types of dividend policies used by companies in practice.

In addition to setting a company's dividend policy in a constantly changing and competitive environment, there are other practical considerations associated with the payment of dividends that financial managers need to be aware of.

LEGAL ASPECTS

Two categories of legal restrictions can limit the amount of dividends a company may pay to its shareholders. The first are *statutory restrictions*. For example, Australian corporations law used to only allow companies to pay dividends from profits (including past retained profits) and not out of capital. However, in June 2010 the corporations law was changed[9] so that a company can only pay a dividend if each of the following two tests are satisfied:

1. Fairness to shareholders: the payment of the dividend is fair and reasonable to the company's shareholders as a whole.
2. No material prejudice to creditors: the payment of the dividend does not materially prejudice the company's ability to pay its creditors.

The second type of legal restriction is unique to each company and comes from 'restrictive covenants' that may be included in its debt and preference-share contracts with investors. These are discussed further in Chapter 18 and may include the provision that the company cannot declare a dividend prior to debt being repaid, or the company may be required to maintain a given amount of working capital. Similarly, preference shares may stipulate that ordinary dividends may not be paid when any preference dividend amounts are outstanding.

LIQUIDITY POSITION

Contrary to common opinion, the fact that a company shows a large amount of retained earnings in the balance sheet does not mean that the company has the cash available to pay dividends. This is because the retained profits are likely to have been invested in long-term assets and not liquid assets such as cash.

Generally, a company with sizeable retained earnings that have been invested in long-term assets will generate cash from those investments. However, this cash is typically either reinvested in the company within a short period or used to pay maturing debt. Therefore, although a company may be extremely profitable, it may have limited liquidity and be *cash poor*. So, the company's liquidity position will have a direct bearing on its ability to pay cash dividends.

ABSENCE OR LACK OF OTHER SOURCES OF FINANCING

To fund the equity component of investment projects, a company can choose to either (1) retain profits, or (2) pay out the profits as dividends and issue new equity securities. For many small or new companies, this second option is not available because they do not have access to the capital markets. Therefore they must rely more heavily on retained profits and will adopt a low dividend payout policy.

EARNINGS PREDICTABILITY

The setting by management of the company's dividend payout ratio will depend to some extent on the predictability of net profit over time. If net profit is expected to fluctuate significantly in the future, management may not be able to rely on a constant dividend payout ratio providing sufficient retained earnings for future investment needs. Consequently, in good net profit years, a low dividend payout ratio may be applied, so a large amount of the net profit is retained for future investment. Conversely, a company that expects a stable net profit over time will be less concerned about generating sufficient retained earnings to meet future capital requirements, and so it will be able to pay out a larger portion of its current-year net profits as a dividend.

OWNERSHIP CONTROL

Often for large companies there are no shareholders that own a sufficient number of shares to control the management decisions of the company. However, for many small and medium-sized companies, a high priority for the shareholders that own a majority of the company's shares is to maintain voting and management control. If these dominant shareholders do not have the funds available to purchase more shares, they will not support proposals by the company's management to raise equity finance by a new share offer because the issuing of new shares to other investors and not them will result in a dilution of their control. Accordingly, they will prefer management to finance new investments by using debt and retained earnings rather than by issuing new shares. This can constrain the company's growth to the amount of debt capital available and to the company's ability to generate profits.

INFLATION

Ideally, the depreciation amount representing the wear and tear of a company's physical assets will be reflected in retained earnings that can be used to finance replacement assets. However, in a period of inflation the cost of equivalent equipment increases significantly more than the amount of retained earnings associated with depreciation. Therefore, to be able to fund the acquisition of new assets the company will require a greater retention of net profit with a consequent adverse effect on the dividend amount that can be paid.

ALTERNATIVE ANNUAL DIVIDEND PAYMENT POLICIES

Given the factors detailed above, most companies can be identified as adopting one of the following year-to-year dividend payment policies:

1. *Constant dividend payout ratio.* In this policy, the percentage of net profit paid out in dividends is held constant. As the dividend-to-net-profit ratio is stable, the dollar amount of the dividend naturally fluctuates from year to year as net profit varies.
2. *Stable dollar dividend per share.* This policy maintains a relatively stable dollar dividend amount over time. An increase in the dollar dividend amount usually does not occur until management is convinced that the higher dividend amount can be maintained in the future. Management also will not reduce the dollar dividend amount until it feels sure that a continuation of the present dividend amount cannot be supported by future profits.
3. *Small, regular dividend plus a year-end extra.* A company following this policy pays a small regular dollar dividend amount plus a year-end *extra dividend* in prosperous years. The extra dividend is declared towards the end of the fiscal year, when the company's net profit for the period can be accurately estimated. The objective of this policy is to avoid the expectation that a high dividend amount will be paid permanently. However, this purpose may be defeated if the extra dividend amount tends to *recur* and investors come to expect that it will continue to be paid in the future.

Of the three annual dividend policies, the stable dollar dividend is by far the most common. This is illustrated in Figure 17.3, which graphs over 20 years the general tendency of companies to pay stable, but increasing, dividend amounts, even though the profits fluctuate significantly.

FIGURE 17.3   Company earnings and dividends

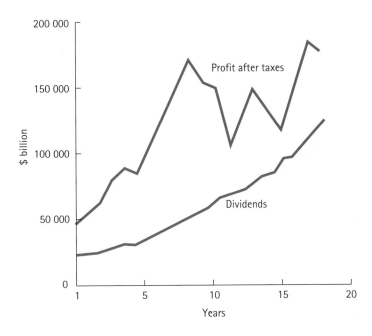

International spotlight

BENEFITS OF LOW DIVIDEND PAYMENTS

During periods of strong economic activity, financially strong companies tend to focus their business strategy on growth. Because retained earnings with no issue costs are a lower cost way to finance the equity component of this growth, companies may decide to pay less dividends to shareholders. Although this has the effect of reducing company dividend yields (cash dividend divided by current price of ordinary shares), there is not likely to be a negative effect on share prices because during buoyant market conditions the majority of investors focus on capital gains.

For these growth companies, capital-budgeting decisions are given greater importance than the dividend decision. In extreme cases, this would be reflected by the company adopting a residual-dividend policy. To find high net present value projects, many growth companies have to look internationally, which is likely to impose on the companies' additional risks (e.g. uncertain exchange rates) and different taxation systems. However, these international investments can provide the benefits of diversification by spreading risk geographically, as well as providing the company with lower cost operations.

GFC

CUTTING DIVIDEND PAYMENTS

The severe economic downturn associated with the Global Financial Crisis significantly reduced net profits. As there was also considerable uncertainty as to how long the negative effects of the crisis would last, the response of many companies was to significantly reduce the amount of dividends they paid per share. In addition to directly reducing the dividend income of share investors, this reduction also had a negative impact on the valuation of shares.

Dividend imputation

OBJECTIVE 4

Appreciate the implications of dividend imputation and capital-gains tax for a company's dividend policy.

The discussion of dividend policy has so far ignored the impact of the Australian dividend imputation system and capital-gains tax. In Chapter 2, discussing the Australian dividend imputation system, a distinction was made between:

- companies with shareholders that are able to fully utilise the value of dividend imputation (franking) credits (taxation category 1)
- companies with shareholders that are not able to utilise any value of dividend imputation (franking) credits (taxation category 2) and
- other companies with shareholders that are able to partially utilise the value of dividend imputation (franking) credits (taxation category 3).

The focus in this section is on taxation category 1 companies that have individual Australian shareholders who are able to fully utilise the value of dividend imputation (franking) credits. For these shareholders, the dividend imputation system results in some or all of the personal income tax levied on the dividend amounts they receive being effectively prepaid by the company.

Whether an individual shareholder has to pay any income tax on the franked dividends they receive will depend on whether their marginal personal income tax rate, T_p, is more or less than the company tax rate, T_c:

- When T_c exceeds T_p, shareholders will pay no tax on the dividends received and can apply any surplus franking credits against tax levied on any other taxable income they may have, or if this is not possible they can claim a refund of the surplus franking credit.

- When T_c is less than T_p, the shareholder will have to pay the shortfall between the personal tax levied on the grossed-up dividend value and the value of the franking credits.

If the company decides to *retain* some of its after-tax earnings, the company's share price should increase to reflect the value of the retained earnings. However, shareholders who sell their shares at the higher price would be liable to capital-gains tax. Under the current Australian capital-gains tax law, individual shareholders are taxed on only 50% of the realised capital-gain amount. Alternatively, shareholders can defer the capital-gains tax liability by delaying selling the shares.

Combining the impact of dividend imputation and capital-gains tax, it would be expected that individual shareholders with a marginal personal income-tax rate (T_p) that is lower than the corporate income-tax rate (T_c) would prefer to receive dividends with surplus franking credits rather than capital gains.

For those shareholders whose marginal personal income-tax rate (T_p) is more than the corporate income-tax rate (T_c), we cannot be sure of their preferences. This is because we do not know the size of any capital gains to be taxed, and how long any capital-gains tax could be delayed by deferring sale of the shares. However, unless capital gains are very large and are delayed for a long time, these shareholders may also prefer to receive fully franked dividends rather than have the company retain profits.

DIVIDEND POLICY AND DIVIDEND IMPUTATION

Although Australian listed companies may have some shareholders (e.g. foreign) who are not able to fully utilise the value of imputation (franking) credits, the focus of dividend policy should be to maximise the after-tax wealth of the majority of shareholders by paying a dividend that provides shareholders with as many franking credits as possible.

Consequently, there is evidence[10] that many Australian companies changed their dividend policy. Figure 17.4 shows that in 1987, following the start of dividend imputation, only about 13% of companies paid fully franked dividends, but by 1992 that proportion had increased to a peak of about 60%, before falling back to 47% by 1998. Also, from 1996 about 35% of companies paid unfranked dividends, which means that 65% of companies paid either fully or partly franked dividends.

FIGURE 17.4 Company dividends paid

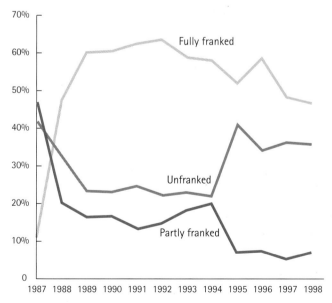

Source: M. Kenny, *The Australian Dividend Handbook 1998–99*, ANZ Securities Ltd, Sydney, 1998, p. 9.

From 1 July 2000 changes were made in Australia (see Chapter 2) to the taxation of capital gains. On the one hand, these changes encourage companies to retain a greater proportion of profits, which should result in an increase in the company's share price and provide capital gains for shareholders. On the other hand, the taxation benefit of franking credits to shareholders encourages companies to have high dividend payouts.

DIVIDEND REINVESTMENT PLANS

dividend reinvestment plan (DRP)

A plan arranged by a company under which shareholders forgo cash dividends in exchange for the purchase of fully paid shares in the company, usually at a discount below the market price.

A problem for Australian companies that increase their dividend payouts to provide franking credits to shareholders is how to provide equity finance for investment projects. As will be seen in Chapter 19, the common ways for a company to raise external equity are by rights issues to existing shareholders or by private issues (placements). As rights issues are costly and private issues are limited in the amount of funds that can be raised in any one year, an alternative way a company can obtain equity finance is by a **dividend reinvestment plan (DRP)**.

Under a DRP the company declares a dividend and shareholders can choose to forgo receiving the dividend as cash and instead use the dividend amount to purchase new shares in the company at a discount below the market price.

The advantage to the company of a DRP is that it is able to provide franking credits to shareholders as a dividend is notionally paid, but does not have to pay out the cash that would normally occur with dividends. Accordingly, the company can satisfy shareholder demands for franking credits and at the same time keep internal equity finance available for investment.

When a shareholder elects to participate in a DRP, the company effectively uses the shareholder's dividend amount as payment for new fully paid ordinary shares issued at a price that can be between 2.5% and 10% below the market price. In addition, the new shares are issued to shareholders free of costs such as brokerage and stamp duty.

As the shareholders are considered to have received a dividend (although not paid in cash but in shares), the dividend amount is taxable to the shareholder, but the associated franking credits can be used to offset any personal income-tax liability. Capital-gains tax will apply when the new shares issued under the DRP are subsequently sold through the share market.

Although DRPs can allow companies to lift their dividend payouts substantially, they have the disadvantage of potentially diluting the company's earnings per share if large numbers of shareholders elect to receive new shares. For this reason, some Australian companies have suspended the offering of a DRP and only pay dividends in cash. Other companies have continued with a DRP but have reduced the price discount, and some companies have completely removed the price discount.

OBJECTIVE 5

Appreciate the procedures that a company follows in the payment of dividends.

Dividend payment procedures

Once a company has decided on its dividend policy, there are a number of procedural questions that need to be answered. For example, how frequently are dividend payments to be made and on what date should shareholder entitlement to dividends be determined? To answer these questions it is necessary to have an understanding of dividend payment procedures.

Companies usually pay dividends twice a year. The *final dividend* is often paid after the annual general meeting (AGM) and an *interim dividend* is paid at the discretion of directors approximately six months before the final dividend. For example, the board of directors of XYZ Limited announced on 17 June their recommendation that for the financial year just ended the company would pay a fully franked dividend (DPS) of 17.5 cents per share. Of this amount, 8.5 cents had already been paid as an interim dividend on 3 January, and the final dividend of 9 cents would be paid after 6 August, the date of the company's AGM.

date of record

Date at which company books are to be closed for determining the investors to receive the next dividend payment. See also **ex-dividend**.

An additional procedural requirement is the setting of the **date of record** (say, 5 pm on 2 July). This means that the final dividend will be paid only to the shareholders who are recorded on the company's Register of Members at 5 pm on 2 July.

A problem could arise if a shareholder in XYZ Limited sold his or her shares on 1 July, one day prior to the date of record, as there would not be sufficient time for the new shareholders to be recorded on the company's Register of Members by the 2 July date. To avoid this problem, the stock exchange applies the rule that only shareholders who buy shares prior to the fifth working day before the date of record will be entitled to the final dividend. This prior date (25 June) is known as the **ex-dividend** date. Therefore, any purchaser of the company's shares on or after 25 June would not be entitled to receive the final dividend of 9 cents; instead, the dividend would be paid to the previous shareholder who had sold the shares.

This gives rise to the identification of shareholders who own shares **cum-dividend** and are entitled to the next dividend payment, and shareholders who buy ex-dividend shares and do not have entitlement to the next dividend payment. Generally, the price of the company's shares will fall on the day they are quoted by the stock exchange as ex-dividend, because buyers will not be entitled to the next dividend payment.

Finally, on the **payment date**, which is shortly after the AGM, the company mails dividend cheques to all the investors.

For XYZ Limited, the events surrounding the payment of dividends are illustrated in Figure 17.5.

ex-dividend
Indicates that a share carries no right to a recently declared dividend. See also **cum-dividend**.

cum-dividend
Indicates that the price paid for the purchase of a share includes the entitlement to receive a dividend declared by the company.

payment date
The date on which the company mails dividend cheques to all investors.

FIGURE 17.5 Dividend payment procedures

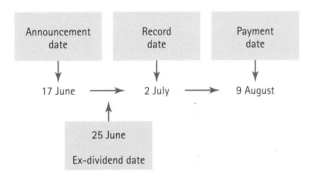

As most of the return from share investment is usually provided by capital gains, and only a relatively minor component comes from the dividend yield (dividend/share price), the major focus of many shareholders is on the company's share price, not on its dividend policy. However, during periods of low interest rates, dividend yields can make shares more attractive than bonds, especially for retirees who need a steady stream of income from their investments to fund their day-to-day living expenses. Also, a reliable stream of dividend cheques from a portfolio of high-dividend-yield shares can help to offset any short-term price volatility in share prices. For Australian investors, the **franking (imputation) credits** can make dividends more attractive compared with interest.

For individuals in the Australian workforce, the legislative requirement for employers to contribute a minimum percentage to a super-annuation fund has significantly increased retirement savings. Recent changes to the Australian superannuation regulations now allow individuals to choose the fund their superannuation contributions are paid to. One outcome of this change has been an increased examination of the performance of the superannuation funds. Other changes to the Australian superannuation laws allow the establishment of self-managed superan-nuation funds, where individuals can invest their superannuation contributions themselves instead of relying on an institution to do it for them.

franking (imputation) credits
An amount of income tax paid by the company that is credited to shareholders when they receive company dividends and which can be used by the shareholders to offset income tax levied on the grossed-up dividend amount imputed to them.

OBJECTIVE 6

Understand the use of
bonus shares, share splits
and share buybacks by
companies.

bonus shares and **share
splits**
Shares issued free to
shareholders in proportion to
existing holdings.

Bonus shares and share splits

An associated part of a company's dividend policy is the decision to issue **bonus shares** (share dividends) or to use **share splits**.

Both bonus shares and share splits involve the company issuing new 'free' shares on a pro-rata basis to all the current shareholders, while the company's assets, earnings, risk and shareholders' percentage of ownership in the company remain unchanged. The only *definite* result from either is the increase in the number of shares outstanding.

To illustrate the effect of a bonus share issue, we will use the following example of a company with the following characteristics:

- The company has issued 1 million fully paid ordinary shares.
- The company's after-tax profit is $500 000, so its earnings per share (EPS) are $500 000/ 1 million = 50 cents.
- The company's shares are currently selling at a price–earnings multiple of 10, so the current share price is 50 cents × 10 = $5 per share.

The company's management is planning to announce a 1-for-5 bonus issue. This means that a shareholder owning 10 shares will receive two additional shares, which would seem to increase his or her personal worth by 2 shares × $5 = $10. But this conclusion is not correct for the following reason.

Under the 1-for-5 bonus issue the company will be issuing 200 000 new shares (1 000 000/5). But since the $500 000 in after-tax profits does not change, the EPS will become $500 000/ 1 200 000 shares = 41.67 cents. If the company's price–earnings multiple remains at 10, the market price of each share after the bonus issue should fall to 41.67 cents EPS × 10 = $4.17.

After the bonus issue the shareholder owns 12 shares worth $4.17 each, which is a total value of $50, exactly the same as before the bonus issue. Thus, theoretically shareholders should not be better off or worse off than before the bonus issue. In this example, the $4.17 price is called a *theoretical price*, because in reality it is not possible to predict the actual share price after the bonus issue.

Another way in which the company can provide 'free' shares to shareholders is to use a share split. If, for example, the company decided to use a 1-for-1 share split, a shareholder owning 10 shares would receive 10 new shares.

Using the same logic as for the bonus share issue, the company would have 2 million issued shares after the share split, so its EPS would be $500 000/2 million shares = 25 cents per share and the theoretical share price would fall to $2.50 per share (25 cents EPS × 10). This means that the shareholder who now has 20 shares worth $2.50 will own $50 total value, which is the same position as before the share split.

These examples may make you wonder why a company would use a bonus issue or a share split, since both represent only a proportionate distribution of additional shares to the present shareholders.[11]

RATIONALE FOR A BONUS ISSUE OR SHARE SPLIT

Although bonus issues and share splits occur far less frequently than *cash* dividends, how do companies justify these distributions of new shares?

Proponents of bonus issues and share splits frequently maintain that shareholders receive a financial benefit because the price of the company's shares does not fall precisely in proportion to the increase in the number of shares. For example, with the 1-for-5 bonus issue the price of the shares might not decrease to the theoretical price of $4.17, resulting in the total value of the shareholders' holding being greater than before the bonus issue.

Two reasons have been advanced as to why the company's share price will not fall as much as theoretically predicted.

First, many financial executives believe that an optimal price range exists for a company's shares. When the share price exceeds this range, it is perceived to be too expensive for many small investors and this restraint in the demand for the shares puts downward pressure on the share price. For example, the way a share price of $20 is perceived is different from the way a share price of $10 after a 1-for-1 share split is perceived.

The second reason argues for *information content* of the announcement of bonus shares or share splits. For example, a bonus issue may be interpreted as indicating that the company's management is confident it can continue to achieve profits that will allow it to pay dividends on the expanded share base. Consequently, the company's shares are perceived by investors to be more valuable than before the bonus issue announcement.

Although bonus issues and share splits are often considered to be associated with companies with growing earnings and their announcement signals favourable news to investors, the empirical evidence fails to clearly identify a positive price effect.

Most studies indicate that investors are perceptive in identifying the true meaning of a share distribution. For example, if the bonus issue or share split is not accompanied by a positive trend in earnings and increases in cash dividends, share price increases surrounding the announcement tend to be insignificant.[12] Therefore, the assertion that bonus issues or share splits can help increase shareholder wealth should be treated with suspicion.

Share buybacks

In a number of countries, including Australia, the United Kingdom, Canada and the United States, companies can buy back ordinary shares that have previously been issued to shareholders. There are many claimed benefits from share buybacks:

- They are a way of providing an internal investment opportunity—the company buys back its shares which are trading below their asset-backing value. After the buyback, the share price is expected to rise because the asset value will be divided by a lower number of shares.
- They are an approach for modifying the company's capital structure. For example, a company could raise debt and purchase its shares in order to increase its financial leverage.
- They can have a favourable impact on earnings per share (EPS). Given no change in total earnings, a reduction in the number of shares will increase EPS. The test is whether the share price is improved as a result.
- They can eliminate a minority-ownership group of shareholders, dissident or apathetic shareholders, or odd-lot shareholdings.
- They can reduce the firm's servicing costs of small shareholders.
- They can be a takeover defence by buying out shareholders who would be likely to sell to a bidder.
- They can help retain the balance of power when, say, a major shareholder in a small or family company dies or retires and his or her shares are purchased by the company.
- They provide possible taxation advantages to shareholders.

There are legislative[13] and stock exchange rules to ensure that the following potential disadvantages of share buybacks are minimised:

- The reduction of issued capital could increase the risk of failure of the company and prejudice the interests of the remaining creditors and shareholders.
- Management could use the procedure to maintain or gain control over a company.
- There could be improper discrimination between shareholders.
- Share prices could be manipulated, for example by placing a 'floor' price under the current market price.

DO SHAREHOLDERS PREFER DIVIDENDS OR SHARE BUYBACKS?

If given the choice between a dividend payment and a share buyback, which would a shareholder prefer? In perfect markets, where there are no taxes, no commissions to be paid when buying and selling shares, and no informational content associated with a dividend, the shareholder would be indifferent to the choice. This is because the share price after a buyback will increase and shareholders can always create a dividend stream by selling the higher priced shares when income is needed.

However, if market imperfections exist, there are a number of reasons why shareholders may have a preference to either receive cash from the company via a dividend or via a share buyback.

First, the company may have to pay too high a price to buy back the shares, which will be to the detriment of the remaining shareholders. Also, if a relatively large number of shares are being bought back, the share price in the market may be bid up too high, only to fall after the buyback has occurred. Second, as a result of the buyback, the market may perceive the riskiness of the company as increasing, which would lower the price–earnings ratio and thus the price of the shares. Third, dividends and share buybacks may have different tax advantages or disadvantages for shareholders.

SHARE BUYBACKS AS FINANCING OR INVESTMENT DECISIONS

Although buying back shares when the company has excess cash has been regarded as a dividend decision, a share buyback can also be a financing decision. For example, by issuing debt and then buying back shares, a company can immediately alter its capital structure towards a higher proportion of debt.

A share buyback can also be regarded as an investment decision. For example, management may view the company's shares as being materially undervalued in the market and consider buying back shares to be a good investment opportunity for the company. However, this decision cannot and should not be viewed as an investment decision because buying its own shares does not provide the company with future returns as other investments do. No company can survive, much less prosper, by investing only in its own shares.

SHARE BUYBACK PROCEDURE IN AUSTRALIA

The Australian corporations law specifies five types of buyback procedures for ordinary shares that companies are permitted to use:

1. *Minimum holding.* This is the repurchase of a parcel of shares containing fewer shares than a 'marketable parcel' as defined by the stock exchange rules.
2. *Employee-share scheme.* This is the buyback of shares from employees (or past employees), which have been issued to them under an employee share purchase scheme.
3. *On-market purchase.* This is the purchase by a company of its own shares in the ordinary course of share-market trading.
4. *Selective purchase.* This is the purchase by a company of some of its shares from one or more specific shareholders (other than holders of employee shares).
5. *Equal-access purchase.* This is an offer made to all the holders of one class of ordinary shares for the company to purchase the same proportion of their holdings.

There are a number of corporations law conditions that are designed to protect creditors and shareholders when a company buys back its shares, and these conditions can vary with the type of buyback used. One of the major conditions is that in any 12-month period a public company can buy back up to 10% of its issued capital without the approval of its shareholders. A buyback can go over the 10% limit in 12 months with the passing of an ordinary resolution by a simple majority vote of shareholders. There are also specific stock exchange rules that listed companies must follow for an on-market buyback.

In general, Australian companies that use buybacks purchase between 5% and 10% of their issued shares. Off-market buybacks have been most commonly used, because on-market buybacks do not allow for distribution of franking credits to shareholders. This is because, when selling through an on-market buyback, a shareholder is selling to a broker, so the sale price is regarded for tax purposes as a full return of capital.

The last question to ask is whether share buybacks maximise the wealth of ordinary shareholders.

THE INFORMATION SIGNALS OF SHARE BUYBACKS

Research findings in the United Kingdom and the United States have found significant increases in company share prices following announcements of share buybacks.

An Australian study examining 64 listed companies that completed share buybacks between 1989 and 1997 found that share prices increased on average above what would normally have been expected in the market. The resultant positive 'abnormal' returns began to occur over the five days leading up to the public announcement of the buyback and amounted to a cumulative abnormal return of 3.8%. As the share price continued to rise after the announcement, average cumulative positive abnormal returns of 4.1% over 10 days resulted.

This study indicated that the positive link between share buybacks and share prices was stronger after 1995 when changes were made to Australian corporations law, which reduced the regulation and company costs involved in a share buyback.

The positive abnormal returns found in the study occurred with on-market buybacks where companies purchased their shares in the ordinary course of share-market trading. However, these abnormal returns did not occur where the buybacks were undertaken as employee-share purchases, equal-access purchases or selective purchases.

These findings can be explained by the finance theory that share buybacks are providing an information signal to investors that the company's management considers that either the current share price is undervalued by the share market or that its future EPS will be above market expectations.

However, according to Gary Wingrove, a director of KPMG Corporate Finance, although share prices may increase immediately after a buyback announcement, over the long term 'it doesn't last unless management remains active in promoting the business or actively doing other things'.

Sources: M. Davis, 'A profitable message in share buybacks', *The Australian Financial Review*, 25 October 1999, p. 23; and J. McCallum, 'The buyback makes a comeback', *Business Review Weekly*, 31 March 2000, pp. 80–81.

Summary

The key issue in the determination of a company's dividend policy is the dividend payout ratio, which measures the percentage of a year's earnings (net profit) paid out in dividends. As the amount of net profit paid out as dividends impacts on the amount of retained earnings, the dividend payout decision has an immediate impact on the equity component of the company's capital structure. In particular, if the dividend payout is increased, less retained earnings will be available to internally finance investments.

OBJECTIVE 1

To understand the effect of a company's dividend policy on its share price, we started with the assumption of a perfect market world, and demonstrated that the amount of a company's net profit that is paid out as a dividend has no impact on the company's share price. However, in the real world the cost of issuing shares creates a preference for a company to adopt a low dividend payout policy to provide as much retained earnings as possible for its investment projects. There are also other market imperfections that may cause a company's dividend policy to affect its share price, including (1) differential tax levied on dividend income and capital gains received by shareholders, (2) agency costs, (3) clientele effect, (4) information content of a given dividend policy.

OBJECTIVE 2

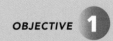

Given the interaction between the dividend payout and retained earnings, and the objective of financial management to maximise the wealth of shareholders, the following points can be made about dividend policy.

OBJECTIVE 3

1. As the future value of the company primarily comes from investment projects, the company should decide on a dividend payment that is the *residual* amount of net profit remaining after the equity portion of investment projects is funded.
2. Other factors need to be considered, including the company's liquidity position, the accessibility to capital markets, inflation, legal restrictions on the payment of dividends, the stability of earnings, and the desire of investors to maintain control of the company.
3. Even given imperfections in the market and the primacy of funding investment projects to generate wealth for shareholders, annual dividend payments need to be made so as to avoid large and unexpected changes in the amount of dividend per share.

OBJECTIVE 4

The response of many Australian companies to the dividend imputation system has been high payouts of franked dividends. For these companies the dividend payment can no longer be determined as a residual amount of profits, because a dominant factor of dividend policy is the provision of franking credits to shareholders.

OBJECTIVE 5

A company's dividend policy is determined and implemented by its board of directors in accordance with the following procedures:

- Declaration date: the date when the dividend amount is formally declared by the board of directors
- Date of record: the date when the company's share transfer books are to be closed, to determine who is entitled to receive the dividend
- Ex-dividend date: after this date, the right to receive the dividend is not transferred with the sale of the company's shares
- Payment date: the date the dividend is paid to the shareholders.

To replace the funds lost by high dividend payouts, some Australian companies have implemented dividend reinvestment plans.

OBJECTIVE 6

Bonus issues and share splits can be used by companies either in lieu of cash dividends or to supplement them. Although at present, no empirical evidence identifies a relationship between bonus issues and share splits and the market price of shares, a bonus issue or a share split could conceivably be used to keep the share price within an optimal trading range. If investors perceived that a bonus issue provided favourable information about the company's future, an increase in share price could result.

As an alternative to paying a dividend, companies can buy back shares. However, Australian shareholders may still prefer dividends to a share buyback due to the value of franking credits that can only be received with dividends.

Key terms

For a complete flashcard glossary go to MyFinanceLab at www.pearson.com.au/myfinancelab

Web works

Share buyback plans, as discussed in this chapter, have become a rather common financial policy activity within corporate Australia and indeed worldwide. In 2005 the Motorola Board of Directors authorised a share buyback scheme. You can review management's discussion of the Motorola share buyback in the company's annual report for 2006 at **www.nyse.com**. Various pages of that report will give you details, for example, on how much Motorola spent on common stock repurchases in 2006, and how many fewer shares were left outstanding over the year due to the repurchase program.

17-1 What is meant by the term *dividend payout ratio*?

17-2 Explain the trade-off between retaining internally generated funds and paying cash dividends.

17-3 **(a)** What are the assumptions of a perfect market?
(b) What effect does dividend policy have on the share price in a perfect market?

17-4 What is the impact of issue costs on the financing decision?

17-5 **(a)** What is the *residual-dividend theory*?
(b) Why is this theory operational only in the long term?

17-6 Why might investors prefer capital gains to the same amount of dividend income?

17-7 What legal restrictions may limit the amount of dividends to be paid?

17-8 How does a company's liquidity position affect the payment of dividends?

17-9 How can ownership control constrain the growth of a firm?

17-10 **(a)** Why is a stable dollar dividend policy popular from the viewpoint of the company?
(b) Is it also popular with investors? Why?

17-11 **(a)** Should Australian companies maximise franked dividends?
(b) Does the residual-dividend theory apply to a company that maximises franked dividends?

17-12 Why do many companies adopt a dividend reinvestment scheme? What are the differences between a DRP and a BSP?

17-13 Explain *declaration date*, *date of record*, and *ex-dividend date*.

17-14 What are the advantages of a bonus issue or a share split over a cash dividend?

17-15 Why would a firm repurchase its own shares? Explain any disadvantages of such buybacks.

ST-1 (*Dividend growth rate*) Schulz Ltd maintains a constant dividend payout ratio of 35%. Earnings per share last year were 82 cents and are expected to grow indefinitely at a rate of 12%. What will be the dividend per share this year? In five years?

For answers go to MyFinanceLab
www.pearson.com.au/myfinancelab

ST-2 (*Residual-dividend theory*) The Britton Company is considering four investment opportunities. The required investment outlays and expected rates of return for these investments are shown below. The firm's cost of capital is 14%. The investments are to be financed by 40% debt and 60% ordinary shares. Internally generated funds totalling $750000 are available for reinvestment.

(a) Which investments should be accepted? According to the residual-dividend theory, what amount should be paid out in dividends?
(b) How would your answer change if the cost of capital were 10%?

INVESTMENT	INVESTMENT COST	INTERNAL RATES OF RETURN (%)
A	$275000	17.50
B	325000	15.72
C	550000	14.25
D	400000	11.65

ST-3 (*Dividend reinvestment plans*) The ABC Company has declared a fully franked dividend per share of 5 cents, requiring a payment to shareholders of $50000. However, the company is anxious to retain funds for investment projects.

(a) A DRP is designed and shareholders are to be offered new shares in the company for $5 each (10% below the current market price). Restate the shareholders' equity section of the balance sheet below if all shareholders accept the offer.

Shareholders' equity	
Paid-up capital (1 000 000 ordinary shares)	$1 400 000
Dividend account	50 000
Retained earnings	850 000
	$2 300 000

(b) Jenny Brown owns 10 000 ABC shares which she purchased in 20X1. Her taxable income is about $20 000. The company's tax rate is 30%. Discuss whether she should take the cash dividend or join the DRP.

Problems

For more problems and for answers to problems marked with an asterisk (*) go to MyFinanceLab at www.pearson.com.au/myfinancelab

17-1* (*Residual-dividend theory*) Terra Cotta finances new investments by 40% debt and 60% equity. The firm needs $640 000 for financing new investments. If retained earnings available for reinvestment equal $400 000, how much money will be available for dividends in accordance with the residual-dividend theory?

17-2 (*Long-term residual-dividend policy*) The Akubra Manufacturing Company, operating under the classical tax system, has projected its investment opportunities over a five-year planning horizon. The cost of each year's investment and the amount of internal funds available for reinvestment for that year are given below. The firm's debt–equity mix is 35% debt and 65% equity. There are currently 100 000 paid-up ordinary shares.

(a) What would be the dividend each year if the residual-dividend theory were used on a year-to-year basis?

(b) What target stable dividend can Akubra establish by using the long-term residual-dividend theory over the future planning horizon?

(c) Why might a residual-dividend policy applied to the five years as opposed to individual years be preferable?

(d) If Akubra operated under the dividend imputation system, why might a residual-dividend policy not be a good policy?

YEAR	COST OF INVESTMENTS	INTERNAL FUNDS AVAILABLE FOR REINVESTMENT OR FOR DIVIDENDS
1	$350 000	$250 000
2	475 000	450 000
3	200 000	600 000
4	980 000	650 000
5	600 000	390 000

17-3 (*Dividends in perfect markets*) The management of Harris Ltd is considering two dividend policies for the years 20X5 and 20X6, one and two years away. In 20X7 the management is planning to liquidate the firm. One plan would pay a dividend of 25 cents in 20X5 and 20X6 and a liquidating dividend of $4.57 in 20X7. The alternative would be to pay out 42.5 cents in dividends in 20X5, 47.5 cents in dividends in 20X6, and a final dividend of $4.07 in 20X7. The required rate of return for the ordinary shareholders is 18%. Management is concerned about the effect of the two dividend streams on the value of the ordinary shares.

(a) Assuming perfect markets, what would be the effect?

(b) What factors in the real world might change the conclusion you reached in part **(a)**?

17-4* (*Issue costs and issue size*) Your firm needs to raise $10 million. Assuming that issue costs are expected to be $1.50 per share and that the market price of the shares is $12, how many shares would have to be issued? What is the dollar size of the issue?

17-5 (*Issue costs and issue size*) If issue costs for a share issue are 14%, how large must the issue be so that the firm will net $6 100 000? If the shares sell for $7.60, how many shares must be issued?

17-6 (*Dividend policies*)

    (a) The earnings for the Crystal Cargo Company have been predicted for the next five years and are listed below. There are 1 million shares outstanding. Determine the yearly dividend per share to be paid if the following policies are enacted:

        (i) Constant dividend payout ratio of 40%

        (ii) Stable dollar dividend targeted at 50% of the total earnings over the five-year period

        (iii) Each year, 80% of profits after taxes to be issued as fully franked dividends

    (b) Discuss how Crystal could pay out the high dividends under **(iii)** and still fund its investment projects without too many rights issues or private placements to obtain new equity.

YEAR	PROFITS AFTER TAXES
1	$1 400 000
2	2 000 000
3	1 860 000
4	900 000
5	2 800 000

17-7* (*Dividend policies*)

    (a) The earnings for Masgron Limited have been predicted for the next four years and are listed below. There are 240 million shares outstanding. Determine the yearly dividend per share to be paid if the following policies are enacted:

        (i) Constant dividend payout ratio of 60%

        (ii) Stable dollar dividend targeted at 60% of the total earnings over the five-year period

        (iii) Each year, 90% of profits after taxes to be issued as fully franked dividends

    (b) If you were an Australian individual investor who had recently retired from the workforce, which dividend policy would you prefer?

YEAR	PROFITS AFTER TAXES
1	$145 000 000
2	165 000 000
3	185 000 000
4	200 000 000

17-8 (*Bonus issue*) Abca Ltd has issued 2.5 million ordinary shares. Net income is $600 000, and the price–earnings ratio for the shares is 10. Management is planning a 1-for-4 bonus issue.

    (a) What will be the price of the shares after the bonus issue?

    (b) If you owned 150 shares before the issue, would the total value of your shares change? Explain.

    (c) What would be your position financially after the bonus issue, relative to now? Assume a proportionate reduction in the share price.

17-9* (*Bonus issue*) You own 20% of Rainy Corp, which recently sold for $8.60 before a planned 1-for-2 bonus issue announcement. Before the bonus issue there were 800 000 paid-up ordinary shares.

    (a) What is your financial position before the issue, and what will it be after the issue? (Assume that the share price falls proportionately.) You purchased the shares in 1985.

    (b) Your sharebroker believes that the market will react positively to the bonus issue and that the price will fall only 20% after the issue. If she is correct, what will your net gain be?

17-10 (*Bonus issue*) Coca-Cola Amatil has announced a 1-for-4 bonus issue to shareholders. In addition, the DPS was increased from 14 cents to 18 cents. Assume that the share price prior to the announcement was $10, and you owned 5000 shares in the group prior to the bonus issue.

    (a) Calculate your change in shareholder wealth if the share price ex-bonus was 5% greater than the theoretical price.

    (b) Why do you think the group did not simply increase its dividend rate without making the bonus issue?

17-11* (*Share split*) You own 5% of the Trexco Company's ordinary shares, which most recently sold for $98 prior to a planned two-for-one share-split announcement. Before the split there were 25 000 ordinary shares.

  (a) Relative to now, what will your financial position be after the share split? (Assume that the share price falls proportionately.)

  (b) The financial manager believes that the price will fall only 40% after the split because she feels that the price is above the optimal price range. If she is correct, what will your net gain be?

17-12 (*Share buyback*) The Aeronaut Company Ltd is planning to pay dividends of $500 000. There are 5 000 000 paid-up ordinary shares, with an EPS of 25 cents. The shares should sell for $4 after the ex-dividend date. If, instead of paying a dividend, management decides to repurchase shares:

  (a) What should the buyback price be?

  (b) How many shares should be repurchased, and what would the new EPS be?

  (c) If you own 10 000 shares, would you prefer that the company pays the dividend or repurchases the shares? Would you seek further information to help you decide this?

17-13 (*Share buyback*) You need to reduce the size of your share portfolio. In the portfolio is a parcel of 1000 ordinary shares in Massive Engineering Ltd, which you purchased three years ago for $7 per share. These could be sold now in the share market for $8 per share. However, Massive has just announced an off-market offer to buy back its shares for $8 each, comprising $2 franked dividend and $6 return of capital.

  (a) Your present taxation rate is 47.5%. Should you sell the shares on the market or accept the buyback offer? Show your workings.

  (b) You plan to retire soon and your taxation rate will fall to 17%. Recalculate the two possibilities at the new tax rate. Show your workings.

17-14 (*Dividend policies*) The earnings for Carlson Cargo have been predicted for the next five years and are listed below. There are 1 million shares outstanding. Determine the yearly dividend per share to be paid if the following policies are enacted:

  (a) Constant dividend payout ratio of 40%

  (b) Stable dollar dividend targeted at 40% of the earnings over the five-year period

  (c) Small, regular dividend of $0.50 per share plus a year-end extra when the profits in any year exceed $1 500 000. The year-end extra dividend will equal 50% of profits exceeding $1 500 000.

YEAR	PROFITS AFTER TAX
1	$1 500 000
2	2 000 000
3	1 750 000
4	950 000
5	2 500 000

17-15 (*Dividend policies*) The earnings for Harmony Pianos Ltd have been predicted for the next five years and are listed below. There are 1 million shares outstanding. Determine the yearly dividend per share to be paid if the following policies are enacted:

  (a) Constant dividend payout ratio of 40%

  (b) Stable dollar dividend targeted at 40% of the earnings over the five-year period

  (c) Small, regular dividend of $0.50 per share plus a year-end extra when the profits in any year exceed $1 500 000. The year-end extra dividend will equal 50% of profits exceeding $1 500 000.

YEAR	PROFITS AFTER TAX
1	$1 000 000
2	2 000 000
3	1 600 000
4	900 000
5	3 000 000

17-16 (*Issue costs and issue size*) If issue costs for a share issue are 18%, how large must the issue be so that the firm will net $5 800 000? If the shares sell for $85, how many shares must be issued?

17-17 (*Bonus issue*) RCB Ltd has issued 2 million ordinary shares. Net income is $550 000, and the price–earnings ratio for the shares is 10. Management is planning a 1-for-5 bonus issue.

    (a) What will be the price of the shares after the bonus issue?

    (b) If you owned 100 shares before the issue, would the total value of your shares change? Explain.

    (c) What would be your position financially after the bonus issue, relative to now? Assume a proportionate reduction in the share price.

17-18 (*Residual-dividend theory*) Sevmill Ltd finances new investments by 35% debt and 65% equity. The company needs $650 000 for financing new investments. If retained earnings available for reinvestment equal $375 000, how much money will be available for dividends in accordance with the residual-dividend theory?

17-19 (*Dividends in perfect markets*) The management of Montford Ltd is considering two dividend policies for the years 20X7 and 20X8, one and two years away. In 20X9 the management is planning to liquidate the firm. One plan would pay a dividend of $2.55 in 20X7 and 20X8 and a liquidating dividend of $45.60 in 20X9. The alternative would be to pay out $4.35 in dividends in 20X7, $4.70 in dividends in 20X8, and a final dividend of $40.62 in 20X9. The required rate of return for the ordinary shareholders is 17%. Management is concerned about the effect of the two dividend streams on the value of the ordinary shares.

    (a) Assuming perfect markets, what would be the effect?

    (b) What factors in the real world might change the conclusion you reached in **(a)**?

17-20 (*Long-term residual-dividend policy*) Wellington Company, operating under the classical tax system, has projected its investment opportunities over a five-year planning horizon. The cost of each year's investment and the amount of internal funds available for reinvestment for that year are given below. The firm's debt–equity mix is 40% debt and 60% equity. There are currently 125 000 paid-up ordinary shares.

    (a) What would be the dividend each year if the residual-dividend theory were used on a year-to-year basis?

    (b) What target stable dividend can Wellington establish by using the long-term residual-dividend theory over the future planning horizon?

    (c) Why might a residual-dividend policy applied to the five years as opposed to individual years be preferable?

    (d) If Wellington operated under the dividend imputation system, why might a residual-dividend policy not be a good policy?

YEAR	COST OF INVESTMENTS	INTERNAL FUNDS AVAILABLE FOR REINVESTMENT OR FOR DIVIDENDS
1	$360 000	$225 000
2	450 000	440 000
3	230 000	600 000
4	890 000	650 000
5	600 000	400 000

17-21 (*Share buyback*) Phyllis Ltd is planning to pay dividends of $550 000. There are 275 000 paid-up ordinary shares, with an EPS of $6. The shares should sell for $45 after the ex-dividend date. If, instead of paying a dividend, management decides to repurchase shares:

    (a) What should the buyback price be?

    (b) How many shares should be repurchased, and what would the new EPS be?

    (c) If you owned 100 shares, would you prefer that the company pays the dividend or repurchases the shares? Would you seek further information to help you decide this?

Case study

Karuna Ltd is an Australian public company with 25 individual shareholders who are the descendants of the company's founder. In recent years the company has experienced significant growth in its sales in both Australia and the countries that it exports to. The company has reached the stage that the only way it can maintain its recent growth rate is to establish subsidiaries in its major overseas markets. As this will require a significant capital investment, the company's directors are investigating obtaining equity funding by floating the company on the Australian Securities Exchange. One of the issues the directors have to consider with the float is whether influential new investors will be alienated by the company's long-established dividend policy. Since the introduction of the Australian dividend imputation system the company has paid out virtually all its annual net profits as a fully franked dividend.

1. What reason can you give for Karuna Ltd's current dividend policy?
2. What are the financing implications for the company if it has a high dividend payout ratio?
3. What can the company do to maintain its high dividend payout, with the associated franking credits, and avoid having to issue new shares to raise the equity finance needed for investment projects?
4. Why is alienating influential investors a concern for the company's board of directors?

Notes

1. Donald H. Chew Jr (ed.), 'Do dividends matter? A discussion of corporate dividend policy', in *Six Roundtable Discussions of Corporate Finance with Joel Stern*, Quorum Books, New York, 1986, pp. 67–101; Joel M. Stern and Donald H. Chew Jr, *The Revolution in Corporate Finance*, Basil Blackwell, New York, 1986; Fischer Black, 'The dividend puzzle', *Journal of Portfolio Management*, 2, Winter 1976, pp. 5–8; and Robert E. G. Nicol, 'The dividend puzzle: An Australian solution?', *Australian Accounting Review*, 1, no. 4, 1992, pp. 42–45.
2. Merton Miller, 'Can management use dividends to influence the value of the firm?', in Joel M. Stern and Donald H. Chew Jr (eds), *The Revolution in Corporate Finance*, Basil Blackwell, New York, 1986, pp. 299–305.
3. From a discussion by John Childs, an investment adviser at Kidder Peabody, in Donald H. Chew Jr (ed.), 'Do dividends matter? A discussion of corporate dividend policy', op. cit., pp. 83–84.
4. The residual-dividend theory is consistent with the 'pecking order' theory of finance as described by Stewart Myers, 'The capital structure puzzle', *Journal of Finance*, July 1984, pp. 575–92.
5. See M. C. Jensen and W. H. Meckling, 'Theory of the firm: Managerial behavior, agency costs, and ownership structure', *Journal of Financial Economics*, October 1976, pp. 305–60.
6. R. Ball, P. Brown, F. Finn and R. Officer, 'Dividends and the value of the firm: Evidence from the Australian equity market', *Australian Journal of Management*, April 1979, pp. 13–25. Also see F. Black and M. Scholes, 'The effects of dividend yield and dividend policy on common stock prices and returns', *Journal of Financial Economics*, 1, May 1974, pp. 1–22; P. Hess, 'The ex-dividend behavior of stock returns: Further evidence on tax effects', *Journal of Finance*, 32, May 1982, pp. 445–56; R. H. Litzenberger and K. Ramaswamy, 'The effect of personal taxes and dividends on capital asset prices: Theory and empirical evidence', *Journal of Financial Economics*, 7, June 1979, pp. 163–95; M. H. Miller and M. Scholes, 'Dividends and taxes: Some empirical evidence', *Journal of Political Economy*, 90, 1982, pp. 1118–41; and P. Hess, 'The dividend debate: 20 years of discussion', in Joel M. Stern and Donald H. Chew Jr (eds), *The Revolution in Corporate Finance*, Basil Blackwell, New York, 1986, pp. 310–19.
7. Kent Baker, Gail E. Farrelly and Richard B. Edelman, 'A survey of management views on dividend policy', *Financial Management*, Autumn 1985, pp. 78–84.
8. R. H. Anderson, 'The managers' dilemma: Dividends or growth', *JASSA*, December 1993, pp. 2–5.
9. *The Corporations Amendment (Corporate Reporting Reform) Act 2010*.
10. The following Australian references are prior to the changes to capital gains in Australia in 2000: R. G. Graham and Z. P. Matolcsy, 'Tax changes, dividend imputation and the optimum dividend policy', *JASSA*, July 1987, pp. 27–29; G. Walker, 'Imputation: The real differences—why company behaviour is changing', *JASSA*, September 1989, pp. 14–18; B. Rosser and P. Calvert, 'Dividend policy and taxation', *The Australian Corporate Treasurer*, October 1989, pp. 6–8; R. R. Officer, 'The change from a classical to a full imputation system of company taxation in Australia: Implications for dividend and financing policies of companies', Working Paper no. 29, Graduate School of Management, University of Melbourne, November 1989; D. Hamson and P. Ziegler, 'The impact of dividend imputation on firms' financial decisions', *Accounting and Finance*, November 1990, pp. 29–53; T. Stolarek, 'Corporate dividend policy in a lower inflation environment', *The Australian Corporate Treasurer*, February 1991, pp. 9–11; P. F Howard and R. L. Brown, 'Dividend policy and capital structure under the imputation tax system: Some clarifying comments', *Accounting and Finance*, May 1992, pp. 51–61; R. E. G. Nicol, 'The dividend puzzle: An Australian solution?', *Australian Accounting Review*, 4, 1992, pp. 42–55; D. Bellamy, 'Evidence of imputation clienteles in the Australian equity market', *Asia Pacific Journal of Management*, October 1994, pp. 275–87; P. H. Monkhouse, 'The valuation of projects under the dividend imputation tax system', *Accounting and Finance*, 36, 1996, pp. 185–212.
11. Both bonus shares and new shares resulting from share splits can receive franked dividends and both can be liable for capital-gains tax on sale. Bonus shares can be subject to income tax if deemed by the Australian Tax Office to have been 'paid' out of company profits. Companies therefore tend to ensure that this does not happen. Following the *Company Law Review Act 1998* par value was abolished for ordinary shares. Prior to this, the issue of bonus shares required an accounting entry to transfer the dollar amount of a bonus issue from share premium reserves to paid-up capital accounts in company balance sheets. Because such entries were not required for share splits, a basis for distinguishing between the issue of bonus shares and share splits could be made based on the accounting treatment. Such a basis no longer exists. In the United States, the New York Stock Exchange requires that a free issue of shares exceeding 25% of shares currently outstanding be called a share split. The American Institute of Certified Public Accountants states that a free share issue exceeding 20% to 25% of outstanding shares is for all practical purposes a share split.
12. James A. Millar and Bruce D. Fielitz, 'Stock split and stock-dividend decisions', *Financial Management*, Winter 1973, pp. 35–45; Eugene Fama, Lawrence Fisher, Michael Jensen and Richard Roll, 'The adjustment of stock prices to new information', *International Economic Review*, February 1969, pp. 1–21; T. Copeland, 'The evidence against stock splits', in Joel M. Stern and Donald H. Chew Jr (eds), *The Revolution in Corporate Finance*, Basil Blackwell, New York, 1986, pp. 12–16; and P. M. Healy and K. G. Palepu, 'How investors interpret changes in corporate financial policy', *Journal of Applied Corporate Finance*, 1989, pp. 59–64.
13. Australian *Corporations Act 2001*.

Long-term financing

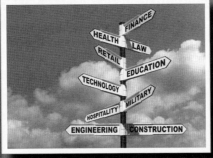

18 Long-term debt finance

19 Shares and convertible securities

Learning objectives

After reading this chapter, you should be able to:

1 Understand the role of bonds in corporate finance.
2 Determine the cost of bond finance.
3 Appreciate the importance of term loans in business finance.
4 Understand how to amortise a term loan.
5 Determine the effect of non-interest charges on the cost of a loan.
6 Understand the interest-rate risk exposure of borrowing money.
7 Describe other forms of debt, such as leases and 'hire-purchase'.
8 Evaluate lease versus loan finance (via the Appendix to the chapter).

For a complete eBook go to MyFinanceLab
www.pearson.com.au/myfinancelab

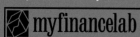

Long-term debt finance

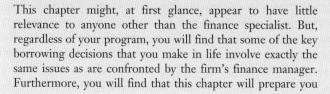

Chapter 18

CHAPTER PREVIEW

There is a host of medium- to long-term debt instruments available in the capital market. This chapter emphasises two representative types of debt, *bonds* and *term loans*, and it also discusses lease finance. The characteristics and workings of these instruments are explained, along with their significance in the capital market. The chapter is strongly tied to *Principle 2: The time value of money—a dollar received today is worth more than a dollar received in the future*. The time value of money is directly reflected in the interest rate paid for debt funds, and, other things being equal, the firm should aim to raise debt at the least cost. However, the cost of funds must also be related to *Principle 1: The risk–return trade-off—we won't take on additional risk unless we expect to be compensated with additional return*. In the context of debt finance, this principle means that the higher the firm's risk as perceived by lenders (or investors), the higher the interest rate that the firm will have to pay for borrowed money.

Regardless of your program

This chapter might, at first glance, appear to have little relevance to anyone other than the finance specialist. But, regardless of your program, you will find that some of the key borrowing decisions that you make in life involve exactly the same issues as are confronted by the firm's finance manager. Furthermore, you will find that this chapter will prepare you for a better understanding of much of the daily reporting in the media of some of the 'big issues' in finance and economics, such as the meaning of corporate and government 'credit ratings' and how these relate to interest rates and economic events such as the GFC.

Bonds

OBJECTIVE 1

Understand the role of bonds in corporate finance.

Some of the characteristics of bond-type instruments were introduced in Chapter 4 (where financial mathematics was applied to the task of 'pricing' bonds and where it was shown how the price varies inversely to changes in market interest rates). Chapter 10 discussed in more detail how to value bonds and how to infer the investors' current required rate of return from the market price of the bond. As we saw in Chapter 14, this rate plays a role in determining the cost of capital.

The typical (or conventional) bond of the type discussed so far in this book has been around for at least several centuries. Bond-type financing grew in importance in the Industrial Revolution that achieved prominence in England in the 18th and 19th centuries. Like shares in a joint-stock company (see Chapter 1), bonds were designed to be issued in units so that some investors could invest a small sum whereas others could invest large sums. That way, a bond issue could pool together a large volume of funds, in keeping with the debt-financing needs of increasingly industrialised societies and increasingly large companies.

The present-day bond market is dominated by large firms and governments. The global bond market has grown to the point that it rivals the total capitalisation of the world's stock markets.[1] This may seem surprising in view of the relatively low profile of bonds (in contrast, just about everyone in developed countries knows at least something about the stock market, whose fortunes are followed avidly by innumerable investors, both large and small).

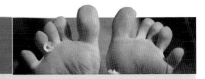

FYI

Like large companies, governments rely substantially on bonds to finance their capital-expenditure programs. This is in line with a philosophy of public finance which holds that long-term assets (notably government infrastructure such as roads, bridges, power stations, schools, hospitals and so on) should be financed by long-term borrowings (such as bonds). This is viewed as more equitable than if such assets were financed solely out of current government revenues, because it means that the repayment burden is shared with future generations of citizen taxpayers, who also share the benefits from these long-life community assets.

CORPORATE BONDS

Corporate bonds are not a major feature of the Australian financial landscape, where term loans are much more prominent as a source of long-term business finance, as indicated in Table 18.1. One reason for this is that the majority of local companies are not large by world standards and lack the financial standing to attract large-scale investors, such as managed funds, which hold significant quantities of bonds in their portfolios. The lack of a significant secondary market, too, discourages both bond issuers and investors (bond buyers). However, in 2010 the Federal Budget announced plans to widen the scope of the corporate bond market so that investing in such bonds will become accessible to the ordinary investor and, at the same time, make long-term debt funding potentially cheaper for companies that are presently excluded from the bond market (see the *Finance at Work* feature, 'Plans to increase access to the bond market').

Bond issues are made directly to primary investors, thus bypassing financial intermediaries such as banks. Often, the bonds are 'placed' with an investment fund or, in the case of a very large bond issue, with a syndicate of such funds. The issuing company may be assisted in the placement process by a bond dealer or an adviser such as a broker or a merchant bank, who will be paid a fee for this service. In contrast, loans from financial intermediaries are usually secured by some of the firm's assets, which increases the readiness of institutional lenders to make the loan. Furthermore, loans can readily be made in small or large amounts and are suitable for small or big firms. These are further reasons why term loans are more widely available for long-term debt in Australian financial markets.

However, moves to widen access to bond finance should prove popular with suitable Australian companies and thus increase the relative usage of bond finance. This is largely because bonds are potentially cheaper than borrowing term loans from intermediaries such as banks. The reason for this is that bank borrowing means that the firm is also paying the costs of the banks' operations plus its profit margin (as indicated in the bottom half of Figure 18.1),

TABLE 18.1 Use of bonds and term loans for business finance (amounts borrowed domestically, year ended 30 June 2009

BONDS[a]	TERM LOANS[b]
$40 billion[c]	$250 billion

a Approximation; excludes bonds issued by financial institutions
b Commitments (i.e. this amount shows loans approved but not yet advanced and so the actual volume of lending is likely to be overstated somewhat)
c In addition, similar amounts were issued offshore

Finance at work

10 10 10 10

PLANS TO INCREASE ACCESS TO THE BOND MARKET

In the 2010 Federal Budget, plans were announced to create a workable mechanism for ASX-listed Australian companies wanting to issue bonds. This is to be accomplished by allowing 'listed companies with a sound history of continuous disclosure'[a] to make issues of at least $50 million under simplified disclosure requirements.[b]

One of the aims of this reform is to give Australian companies an alternative source of debt funds, which will have the added benefit of putting downward pressure on interest rates charged to businesses by banks. At the same time, new investment opportunities will be available to retail investors, with bond investment becoming a viable avenue of investment for those seeking safer income-generating assets than ordinary

shares, with the added benefit that they will earn the same yields as wholesale investors.

Opening up bond listings in this way is intended to create a deep, liquid corporate bond market which will also appeal to fund managers wishing to create managed corporate bond funds. An added benefit of a viable corporate bond market is to provide an alternative to the government bond market, as the federal government's own bond issues are planned to diminish as the Budget moves to surplus in coming years.

a 'Reins loosened for bonds', *The Australian Financial Review*, 12 May 2010.
b The simplified disclosure requirements, for initial offerings, include a short prospectus that focuses on the terms of the offer and the ability of the issuer to fulfil repayment obligations. Subsequent issues can be made by updating the initial disclosure information.

FIGURE 18.1 Borrowing by (a) issuing bonds (b) intermediated finance

(a) Issuing bonds—the firm issues bonds to borrow directly from investors

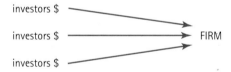

(b) Term loan—the firm borrows via a financial intermediary such as a bank

whereas bonds are sold directly by the firm to investors (as shown in the top half of Figure 18.1) and thus avoid the costs of financial intermediation.

For a company (or government organisation, for that matter), access to bond finance is presently heavily dependent on having a particular formalised type of credit rating known as a *bond rating*, a topic to which we now turn.

BOND RATINGS

Internationally, there are thousands of individual bonds. Potentially, this range would make it difficult for prospective bond buyers (investors) to separate 'good' (relatively safe) bonds from those that are less safe. This has led to the development of **bond ratings**, which are assessments of the creditworthiness of the bond issuers. In the main, the bond rating is an assessment of the likelihood or otherwise that the bond issuer might default. (*Bond default* refers to the issuer failing to make, or being late in making, the scheduled coupon interest payments and/or the maturity value).

bond rating
An assessment, carried out by an organisation called a *ratings agency*, of the likelihood of default by the issuer of the bond.

Bond ratings are assigned by organisations called *ratings agencies*. The two most prominent such agencies are Standard & Poors (S&P) and Moody's. Bonds that are relatively safe are termed *investment grade*. Less distinguished bonds are called *speculative* or *highly speculative*. (Colloquially, speculative bonds are sometimes called *junk bonds*). Table 18.2 describes the main categories of bond ratings for S&P and Moody's.

Ratings are important in the functioning of both the primary market and the secondary market. In the first instance, an issuer needs a rating to maximise the potential pool of bond buyers. Ratings are equally important in supporting marketability in the secondary market, which is itself an attraction to buyers of initial offerings (who know that having a suitable rating means that a given bond is more likely to be marketable than if it does not have such a rating). Furthermore, changes in ratings may be made during the life of the bond issue, which signals important information to the market concerning changes in the financial standing of the issuer. (A case in point is the bankruptcy of General Motors in the mid 2000s—its bonds had been assigned a 'junk' rating well before it underwent formal bankruptcy proceedings.) Furthermore, AAA-rated bonds have had an historical error rate of only 0.02% (meaning two in 10 000 AAA-rated bond issuers actually defaulted). However, despite their success at rating conventional bonds, the ratings agencies failed the test of the GFC, which saw the demise of many highly rated MBS (mortgage-backed securities).

The first bond ratings date back to the United States in 1909. Since that time, the rating agencies—notably Moody's and Standard & Poor's—have emerged as the main providers of ratings on corporate bonds, and these agencies have spread their operations globally to countries such as Australia. However, companies or governments are not automatically entitled to have a rating. A rating comes at a cost in the form of a fee payable to the ratings agency. To obtain the rating, the organisation must 'open its books' fully to the agency, which assesses the ability of the bond issuer to meet future obligations to pay interest coupons and the principal at maturity. Although these assessments deal with expectations about future prospects of servicing debt, several historical factors seem to play a significant role in the determination of the rating. Bond ratings are favourably affected by (1) a greater reliance on equity as opposed to debt in financing the firm, (2) profitable operations, (3) low variability in past earnings, (4) large firm size, and (5) little use of subordinated debt.

TABLE 18.2 Interpreting bond-rating classifications

Ratings are intended to reflect the likelihood of future default by the issuing firm.

BOND RATING CATEGORY	STANDARD & POOR'S	MOODY'S	DESCRIPTION
Investment grade			
Prime or strongest	AAA	Aaa	Highest quality, extremely strong capacity to pay
High quality	AA	Aa	Very strong capacity to pay
Upper medium	A	A-1, A	Upper medium quality, strong capacity to pay
Medium	BBB	Baa-1, Baa	Lower medium quality, changing circumstances could impact the firm's ability to pay
Not investment grade			
Speculative	BB	Ba	Speculative elements, faces uncertainties
Highly speculative	B, CCC, CC	B, Caa, Ca	Extremely speculative and highly vulnerable to nonpayment
Default	D	C	Doesn't pay interest

Note: S&P ratings from AA to CCC may carry a suffix in the form of a + or – sign, which indicates a slightly higher or slightly lower rating than the primary alphabetic grade.

YIELD SPREADS

The organisation's bond rating affects the rate of return demanded by bond investors. This rate of return is known as the yield. The poorer the bond rating of the issuer, the higher the yield demanded in the capital markets. This is consistent with Principle 1: *The risk–return trade-off—we won't take on additional risk unless we expect to be compensated with additional return.*

The other side of the coin is that the investor's yield is the starting point in determining the bond issuer's overall cost of raising new funds, and so the bond rating is very significant to the firm's finance manager. It is important, too, for other reasons, such as the symbolic value of a high rating, which raises the credibility of the issuer in the eyes of the financial markets and the community in general.

The relationship between bond ratings and yields can be portrayed in terms of *yield spreads*. The *spread* refers to the interest rate (yield) premium that is observed in the financial markets for a low-rated bond over a high-rated bond. For instance, in Australia the highest rating bonds are presently those issued by the federal government, which carry a top rating (AAA from S&P; Aaa from Moody's). Other, lower rated bonds have spreads, such as those indicated in Table 18.3.

Spreads vary in line with economic conditions. In the aftermath of the sub-prime crisis, following a loss of confidence and trust in debt markets, along with a liquidity squeeze, spreads were considerably greater than those in Table 18.3. For instance, spreads on A-rated bonds were almost 4% per annum in 2009, a year earlier than the data in Table 18.3.

TABLE 18.3   Yield spreads on Australian bonds

Premium[a] (spread) required above federal government (AAA-rated) bonds, June 2010

BOND RATING	SPREAD ABOVE AAA RATING[b]
AA	1.5%
A	2.0%
BBB	2.6%

a Rounded to nearest single decimal point
b Weighted average spread of corporate bonds above federal government securities of average maturity 1 to 5 years

Source: Reserve Bank of Australia

Concept check

18.1 What general types of Australian companies are presently able to issue corporate bonds?

18.2 What is the importance of having a bond rating? Would an AA bond's spread be higher or lower than that of a BB bond?

For answers go to MyFinanceLab or www.pearson.com.au/9781442539174

Back to the principles

Because bonds are usually unsecured, ratings fulfil an important service in providing investors with an independent assessment of the 'quality' of the bond issuer. The lower the rating—in other words, the riskier the bond issuer—the greater the rate of return demanded by investors. Thus, bond ratings are an application of **Principle 1: The risk–return trade-off—we won't take on additional risk unless we expect to be compensated with additional return.**

Determine the cost of bond finance.

The cost of bond finance

As indicated above, a bond's *rating* is typically the starting point for the determination of the cost of bonds, because it determines the investor's required *yield*. From a technical point of view, Chapters 4 and 10 outlined the mathematical features of how bonds operate, as is now reviewed in Example 18.1.

EXAMPLE 18.1 Review of the characteristics of a bond

Coen Company Ltd plans to raise long-term finance by issuing a $25 000 000 par bond in units of $100 (i.e. a total of 250 000 units will be issued at a face (par) value of $100 each). Being a *par* bond, the price is identical to the face value, that is $100. The issue is for a three-year term with coupon interest at 10% per annum paid half-yearly. This represents total coupon interest of $10 per year and thus coupon payments of $5 per half-year. With the par bond being sold at face value, we know (from earlier chapters) that the investor's yield will be the same as the coupon rate, that is 10% per annum. It is customary to 'quote' financial data related to a bond-type security on the basis of a unit of $100. Accordingly, the relevant financial information for Coen Company Ltd is summarised below, using the symbols introduced in Chapter 10:

Subscription value (price), V_b	$100
Maturity/redemption/face value, M	$100
Half-yearly coupon amounts, equal to annual interest ($I = $10) divided by 2	$5
Term, equal to the number of years, n (3), multiplied by the number of interest payments per year (2)	6 half-years
Annual yield, equal to the half-yearly interest rate (5%) multiplied by 2, giving the annual yield, R_b	10%

It will be recalled that these cash flows are linked (for a bond with half-yearly coupon payments) by equation (10-3):

$$V_b = \sum_{t=1}^{2n} \frac{\$I/2}{(1 + R_b/2)^t} + \frac{\$M}{(1 + R_b/2)^{2n}}$$

If the present-value tables are used, V_b is calculated via the equivalent formula, equation (10-3a), as:

$$V_b = \frac{\$I}{2}(PVIFA_{R_b/2,2n}) + \$M(PVIF_{R_b/2,2n})$$

Substituting in equation (10-3a) confirms that the price is equal to the present value of the future cash flows:

$$V_b = \$5(PVIFA_{5\%,6}) + \$100(PVIF_{5\%,6})$$
$$= \$5(5.076) + \$100(0.746)$$
$$= \$25.38 + \$74.60$$
$$= \$99.98 \approx \$100.00$$

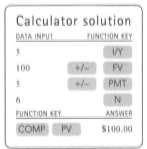

Calculator solution

DATA INPUT		FUNCTION KEY
5		I/Y
100	+/−	FV
5	+/−	PMT
6		N
FUNCTION KEY		ANSWER
COMP PV		$100.00

This example confirms what we first saw in Chapter 4—if a bond is issued at par, or face value, and so the yield R_b equals the annual coupon rate, then the price V_b is equal to the maturity value M (i.e. $100).

THE COST OF ISSUING A BOND

If a company is contemplating the issue of a bond-type security, the firm's financial manager will seek the most favourable borrowing terms. A public offering may be at a lower yield than a private placement, because of the greater marketability of a public issue (which arises from the fact that investors have the ability to re-sell their bond holdings on the secondary market). However, a private placement is likely to be easier to arrange and it will avoid some of the issue costs (or *flotation costs*) associated with a public offering. These issue costs may include advisers' fees, legal fees, accounting fees and underwriting costs. In addition, the issuer may have to pay another firm (such as an investment bank) to sell the issue to investors. All in all, the various issue and marketing costs may total up to 10% of the face value of the bond. Example 18.2 builds on Example 18.1 by illustrating the potential difference between the costs of a public issue and the costs of a private placement.

EXAMPLE 18.2 Determining the costs of issuing a bond

Suppose that the debt issue outlined in Example 18.1 represents a private placement. It is assumed that there are no issue costs, so the interest cost to Coen Ltd will be equal to the yield of 10% per year. As an alternative, Coen is considering a public offering. This is expected to be successful at a coupon rate of 9% per year (as opposed to 10% for the private placement). However, we must now take into account the issue costs, which are estimated to total $1 845 000 (an average of $7.38 per $100 unit) for a public issue. The effect of these fees is to reduce the proceeds of the issue, so the net subscription amount actually received by Coen will be reduced from $100 per unit to $92.62. Making this adjustment to the cash flows in Example 18.1 enables us to re-solve the present-value equation in order to find the 'true' interest rate that incorporates the effect of the issue costs:

Net subscription proceeds per unit, V_b	$92.62
Maturity/redemption value, M	$100
Half-yearly coupon amounts (9% × $100 × 0.5)	$4.50
Term	6 half-years
'True' interest rate	?%

To determine the interest rate, again substitute in equation (10-3a):

$$\$92.62 = \$4.50(PVIFA_{i\%,6}) + \$100(PVIF_{i\%,6})$$

To solve this equation for i, the most convenient method is by financial calculator, which shows that the half-yearly rate is very close to 6%, representing a nominal annual interest rate of 12%. Using financial tables to identify i, it is necessary to proceed by trial and error:

$$\$92.62 = \$4.50(PVIFA_{i\%,6}) + \$100(PVIF_{i\%,6})$$

Trying $i = 6\%$ gives a present value of: $4.50(4.917) + $100(0.705)

= $22.13 + $70.50

= $92.63 (which means that the half-yearly rate is almost exactly 6%, or 12% p.a.)

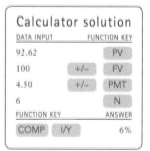

Calculator solution

DATA INPUT		FUNCTION KEY
92.62		PV
100	+/−	FV
4.50	+/−	PMT
6		N
FUNCTION KEY		**ANSWER**
COMP I/Y		6%

BOND PRICES AND THEIR USE BY THE FINANCIAL MANAGER

It was seen in Chapter 4 that the price of a bond changes during its life as market interest rates change. The financial manager can make use of this information to assess the current interest rate that the firm will have to offer on a new issue of securities, as is shown in Example 18.3.

EXAMPLE 18.3 Using the current market yield of a bond to estimate the cost of a new issue

Suppose that Coen Ltd has previously made a public issue of the bond outlined in Example 18.1. One year later, the company's financial manager is contemplating a new issue with a two-year maturity. The market price of the former 10% issue is currently $103.65. As is shown in the following computation, this means that investors in Coen Ltd are currently receiving a yield of 8% for debt that has two years remaining until maturity. Thus, if Coen were to make a *new* issue of two-year debt, it can be inferred that it would have to offer investors a rate of 8% per annum. (Note that the cost to the company may be greater than the investors' yield of 8%, owing to the effect of issue costs, as discussed above.)

Current market price, V_b	$103.65
Maturity/redemption value, M	$100
Half-yearly coupon amounts	$5
Remaining term	4 half-years
Interest rate	?%

To show that the interest rate is 4% per half-year (or 8% per year), we again substitute in equation (10-3a):

$$103.65 = \$5.00(PVIFA_{i\%,4}) + \$100.00(PVIF_{i\%,4})$$

Trying $i = 4\%$ gives a present value of $5(3.630) + $100(0.855)

$$= \$18.15 + \$85.50$$
$$= \$103.65$$

Calculator solution

DATA INPUT		FUNCTION KEY
4		N
100	+/–	FV
5	+/–	PMT
103.65		PV
FUNCTION KEY		ANSWER
COMP I/Y		3.99%

It should be noted in passing that the bond market in Australia is somewhat 'thin', meaning that trading volumes are low, so financial managers relying on reported trades should be alert to the possibility of anomalous data. Relying on the market price as the best estimate of the true value of a security is based on the concept of market efficiency (discussed in Chapters 1 and 9), which assumes that there are a large number of competing buyers and sellers whose collective actions ensure a 'fair' price.

For example, Coen Ltd might want an estimate of the yield it would need to offer investors on five-year bonds. If there is no reliable information on trading in Coen bonds with a five-year maturity (or no such maturities are on issue by Coen), the company could look at five-year yields on a company with a comparable bond rating. Alternatively, the finance manager could start with the current yield on federal government (AAA) bonds and then add a suitable spread. Suppose, in this regard, that Coen's bonds carry an A rating from S&P and the applicable spread above AAA is 2% per annum. Thus, if the yield on five-year federal government bonds is currently 7%, adding a 2% spread indicates Coen would have to offer investors a yield of about 9%.

Concept check

18.3 What factors affect the cost of a new bond issue?

18.4 How does the finance manager make use of current bond prices?

For answers go to MyFinanceLab or
www.pearson.com.au/9781442539174

GFC

SECURITISATION AND 'ENGINEERED' DEBT SECURITIES

Bonds outlined in this chapter and in previous chapters are known as *conventional bonds*. These are bonds issued predominantly by large companies and governments, as one of their major forms of long-term debt finance. The investor receives the promise to be paid coupon interest at specific intervals during the life of the bond, with the face value repaid at maturity. These payments are made from the issuer's own financial resources and so the bond rating depends on the financial standing of the issuer.

In contrast, the bond-type instruments at the heart of the GFC were 'engineered' by a process known as *securitisation*, which was mentioned briefly in earlier chapters. Through this process a pool of housing loan repayments are ultimately transferred to investors—along with the related loan risks.

The basic securitisation process

Securitisation can be defined as the process of converting an asset to a debt security. Assets that have been securitised include housing loans, credit card receivables and motor-vehicle finance. Of these, housing loans are the most significant in volume and also the most prominent because of their role in the sub-prime crisis (SPC) that triggered the GFC. Globally, annual securitisation activity grew from about US$0.5 trillion in 2000 to a peak of US$2.5 trillion in 2006, before falling dramatically following the SPC. The US accounted for the major part of this activity.

In the context of the sub-prime crisis, securitisation was carried out by housing finance institutions, notably commercial banks, many of which in effect sold substantial amounts of their housing loan assets. This was accomplished, in the first instance, by the lender pooling together the loan repayments of a large group of individual borrowers (for example, a pool of term loans with principal totalling $500 million might be created by aggregating 2000 loans with an average balance of $250 000). The total payments receivable on this pool would be sold, further down the line, to investors. In this way, housing loan assets ultimately were converted to bond-type instruments known as mortgage-backed securities (MBS), although herein we will use the wider term of *asset-backed securities* (*ABS*).

In the securitisation process, the original lenders are known as *originators*. They continue to administer the loans and deal face to face with the individual borrowers, in return for a management fee from the buyers of the cash flows. The originators also transfer the risks to the buyers of the cash flows, and the loans are shifted 'off balance sheet' of the originators.

The initial buyer of the pool of cash flows is a specifically created legal entity known as a *special purpose vehicle* (SPV). This entity is established for the sole purpose of acquiring the loan cash flows; it holds no other assets and its operations terminate when the loan receivables have been amortised. The SPV also inherits the loan risks (such as defaults by borrowers). The following diagram summarises the funds flow, so far, in this process of securitisation:

Asset-backed securities

The SPV is typically established by the originator or a *hedge fund*.[2] The SPV agrees to pay the originator a lump sum representing the present value of the mortgage-payment receivables. In order to pay this sum to the originator, the SPV issues securities of an equivalent amount. For example, the above-mentioned $500 million pool of mortgages would be financed by issuing $500 million of bond-type securities. These are known generally as *asset-backed securities* (*ABS*), the backing assets being the mortgage loans. The SPV expects to earn a profit margin from the fact that the interest rate it earns on the loan receivables is greater than the average of the interest rates paid to the buyers of the issued securities.

Typically, the SPV 'slices up' its cash-flow receivables by creating and issuing three classes of ABS—these are known as *tranches* (pronounced 'tronsh') after the French word for 'slice'. Each tranche occupies a different risk category, based primarily on the degree of exposure to defaults by the originators' loan borrowers. The exposure arises because securitisation passes on the risks to the ultimate investors who buy the tranches.

According to Hull[3], either the originator or the hedge fund would establish the SPV by buying the riskiest tranche of the cash flows from the loan receivables. Notably, this tranche is the first to bear borrowers' defaults (being the primary bearer of risk, this has become known as the *equity tranche*). Next to bear risk is the middle or *mezzanine tranche*. Finally, least risky is the so-called *senior tranche*. The funds flow from the SPV to buyers of these tranches is summarised in the following diagram. In the diagram, the prefix '*ABS*' is attached to each security slice to indicate that the security is backed by the actual loan assets that generated the original cash flows:

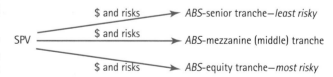

The relationship between these tranches and risk can be examined numerically. Suppose the above-mentioned $500 million of asset-backed securities comprise a $400 million *ABS*-senior tranche, a $75 million *ABS*-mezzanine tranche and, finally, a $25 million *ABS*-equity tranche. Thus, if asset-derived losses were, say, $25 million, all of the equity tranche would be wiped out. Alternatively, if total losses were, say, $150 million, the two lower tranches would be wiped out and the senior tranche would suffer a $50 million loss.

The senior tranche would aim for an AAA rating, which would be necessary to make the securities readily marketable. This would be enhanced by insuring that tranche against default. The insurance would be carried out through a financial instrument known as a *credit default swap*. The mezzanine tranche, being uninsured and in a higher risk category, would attract a rating such as BBB.

The collateralised debt obligation

As remarked by Hull, with a rating as high as AAA, it was 'usually not difficult'[4] to find investors who were willing to buy the *ABS*-senior tranches, particularly as they offered higher yields than conventional AAA-rated bonds. However, selling the BBB tranche was more difficult. This led to the development of the *collateralised debt obligation* (*CDO*), whereby a vehicle (legal entity) would be established to purchase the *ABS*-mezzanine tranche and pay for it by creating and selling a further group of (*CDO*) securities as indicated in this diagram:

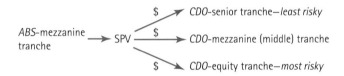

The main distinction between the two types of securities is that *ABS* cash flows are backed by the original assets (such as the housing loans), whereas the *CDO* cash flows are merely backed by other securities, namely the *ABS*. The result is that the *CDO* securities are more risky than the *ABS*. For example, suppose the purchase of the above-mentioned $75 million *ABS*-mezzanine is financed by issuing the following tranches: $50 million *CDO*-senior, $18 million *CDO*-mezzanine and $7 million *CDO*-equity. It can therefore be seen that total losses of $100 million in the original asset pool (only 20% of its $500 million total value) would wipe out the $75 million *ABS*-mezzanine tranche and so in turn would wipe out the entire *CDO*-senior tranche and the other *CDO* tranches.

In effect, therefore, the creation of the *CDO* magnifies the loss exposure of the underlying asset-backed securities. As implied by the preceding numerical examples, a 20% loss in the original asset pool would not have impacted at all on the *ABS*-senior securities but it would have totally wiped out the *CDO*-senior securities. This is despite the fact that the *CDO*-senior tranche typically carried the same AAA-rating as the *ABS*-senior tranche. It might be thought that the insurer (such as American International Group) would make good these losses, but the losses induced by the sub-prime crisis were so large that they were unable to be covered.

The paradox here is that the *CDO*-senior tranche is 'engineered' from an underlying *ABS*-mezzanine that has only a BBB rating, a fact that has not been lost on critics of financial engineering and 'structured' debt such as the *CDO*. Hull points out that, on average, AAA-rated *CDO* tranches had 'lost about 80% of their value by the end of 2007 and were essentially worthless by

mid-2009'.[5] It is no surprise, therefore, to see the use of the phrase 'toxic debt' to describe the *CDO*. The same critics might wonder, too, how top-quality (AAA-rated) securities could have been 'engineered' from low-quality *sub-prime* loans. In this respect, the systemic nature of the sub-prime crisis caused losses on a large scale that had never been envisaged by the ratings agencies. Reflecting the ultimate failure of the *CDO* model, annual *CDO* issues had declined to virtually zero by 2009 from a peak of about US$500 billion in 2006.

Securities' investors and other institutions

The preceding discussion has suggested a complex risk relationship between securities such as the *ABS* and the *CDO*, which is matched by convoluted arrangements between SPVs, banks and hedge funds. Many iconic financial institutions such as Citigroup and UBS suffered big losses. Of the large investment banks, Lehman Brothers went bust, while other prominent Wall Street players were in effect rescued by takeovers or by restructuring. Insurance companies, too, were unable to meet all of the default losses that they had covered. Most notoriously, the world's largest insurer, American International Group (AIG), was subsequently rescued by the US government on the grounds that the company was 'too big to fail'. In total, the US Financial Crisis Inquiry Commission reported that 12 of the country's top 13 financial institutions had been at risk of failure.[6]

End investors that bought *CDO*s included banks, insurance companies, pension schemes and managed investment funds. Those buyers with legitimate investment motives were attracted by the yields that were higher than comparably rated conventional bonds. In some cases, the *CDO* purchases were 'leveraged' (that is, financed by borrowed funds in a way that was made possible by the higher yield spreads on the *CDO*s). Among such leveraged investors, some commentators have singled out the role of *structured investment vehicles* (SIVs). Whereas SPVs are 'one-off' entities, SIVs were established to have a continuing existence as portfolio managers, investing in long-term securities (including *CDO*s). The SIV business model was 'borrowing short and lending long'[7]—that is, issuing short-term *commercial paper*[8], at low interest rates, in order to buy the longer term, higher yielding *CDO*s. In other words, the purpose was to profit from the *maturity spread* between low-yielding short-term debt and high-yielding long-term securities. However, the arrival of the sub-prime crisis saw the SIV's *CDO* assets becoming rapidly worthless, with the result that lenders failed to renew ('roll over') the short-term funding. Therefore, to raise cash the SIVs had to 'sell [CDO] assets at a loss'[9] and banks then had to step in 'with emergency liquidity'[10] because they had given funding guarantees to the SIVs in order to make their business model more acceptable to the buyers of the commercial paper. As a result, the banks were sometimes forced to take possession of the (devalued) *CDO* assets and bring them back onto their own books. In this way, the wheel turned full circle—banks had initially used securitisation[11] to shift loans off their balance sheets and now they were bringing them back.

Although the sub-prime crisis was essentially a US event, it spread globally, largely through the financial markets. In this way, the sub-prime crisis evolved into what became known as the

Global Financial Crisis. Internationally, many non-US financial institutions shared in the exposure to the sub-prime crisis, partly through involvement in the structured vehicles and hedge funds. In addition, many of the end investors were from other countries. Further damage was done by the attendant liquidity crisis[12], which impacted on firms in the real economy, as did the recessionary effects of the sub-prime crisis.

According to *The Australian*[13], 'there is never one easy explanation of greed and corruption', but members of the 2011 Financial Crisis Inquiry Commission variously attributed blame, for the crisis, mainly to the commercial and investment banks for poor practices and to the US central bank (the Federal Reserve) for inadequate regulation, which led up to the 'bubble' whose collapse precipitated the SPC.[14] The wider consequences and global reach of the sub-prime crisis receive elaboration in Chapter 20.

Term loans

OBJECTIVE **3**

Appreciate the importance of term loans in business finance.

As indicated in Table 18.1, Australian firms rely on loans from financial intermediaries for a great proportion of their debt funding. This table shows that lending in the form of term loans is far greater than debt funds provided via corporate bonds. Banks are by far the major providers of loan funds, with more than 70% of the market for this type of commercial finance. The main uses of such funds are the construction or purchase of property, the purchase of plant and equipment, and the refinancing of former loans. Typically, this type of borrowing is for a maturity of around two to five years, although it may range from one to ten years or longer for real estate. Often the maturity matches the economic life of the asset that is financed by the loan. For example, a motor vehicle would be financed typically by a four- or five-year loan or lease. This form of loan has a specific maturity (or 'term'), which gives rise to the name *term loan*. In contrast, financing such as a bank overdraft (see Chapter 7) is a form of 'revolving credit' which has no specific term.

CHARACTERISTICS OF TERM LOANS

The borrower of a term loan contracts with the lender to repay the loan over a specified period or term. The sum borrowed (known as the *principal*) may be at a fixed interest rate, in which case the repayments will be fixed for the term. Alternatively, the loan may be at a variable rate, which means that the lender can vary the rate during the course of the loan. Often, variable-rate loans are more aptly called *floating-rate loans*, meaning that the rate 'floats' at some margin above an agreed base rate or indicator rate (e.g. at 1% per year above the rate on 90-day bank bills). The rate is varied at intervals, such as every three months or six months (the *reset interval*), in accordance with the lending contract.

Initial negotiation for a loan may take place directly between the applicant and the financier or it may occur via a finance broker. If the application is for a relatively small loan, approval may be rapid. This is particularly so if the applicant is well known to the financier—for example, if the financier is the applicant's existing bank. If the loan is for a relatively large sum, the application is likely to be subject to more scrutiny. Even then, however, if the applicant is well known to the lender and if the business is known to be profitable and to have modest levels of existing debt, approval may be relatively straightforward. On the other hand, if the loan is for a sum that is large enough to represent a substantial potential risk to the financier, it will be subject to detailed evaluation. A loan for a project whose success or failure would materially affect the future well-being of the applicant's organisation represents such a potential risk.

A loan application that is to be scrutinised intensely will have to be accompanied by a substantial amount of supporting information. The financier will evaluate the strategic strengths and weaknesses of the applicant's existing business as well as the quality and 'track record' of its senior managers and directors. Financial statements will be analysed for potential trouble spots. Attention will be paid to profitability ratios, to the ability to service debt, to efficiency ratios, and to gearing. The financier will ask the applicant to submit forecasts in the form of pro-forma financial statements over the term of the loan. These statements will be analysed independently by the lender, in order to form an opinion about their validity in light of the firm's products or services (or its project) and prospective economic conditions. The emphasis will be on trying to judge the adequacy of future cash flows and profitability, for these are key determinants of the ability to repay the debt. Attention will also be paid to potential security for the loan, both in terms of the net asset position and in terms of specific collateral. Ultimately, the lender may want to take specific security and to impose other constraints or covenants on the borrower's business, in order to protect against loss in the event of default.

THE LOAN CONTRACT

The loan is supported by a legal agreement that specifies the amount borrowed, the basis of repayments and interest calculation, and any fees. In addition, there is likely to be a number of other loan conditions, most of which are aimed at protecting the lender in the event of default by the borrower during the course of the loan. These conditions are also likely to be determinants of loan pricing; for example, a secured loan (one with collateral) will be priced lower than an unsecured loan, other things being equal. Some of these loan conditions are now discussed.

Collateral

Term loans are generally backed by some form of collateral or security. Short- to medium-term loans may be secured by a *chattel mortgage*, which is a legal contract that specifies an asset, such as machinery or equipment, as collateral for the loan.

Longer term loans may be secured by real-estate mortgages. In some cases, particularly for smaller businesses, collateral will be extended to a firm's owners or directors—for example by requiring personal guarantees from those persons and by taking security over their personal assets (such as real estate).

Restrictive covenants

In addition to requiring collateral, the lender often places restrictions on the borrower that, if violated, make the loan due and payable immediately. These restrictive covenants are designed to prohibit the borrower from engaging in activities that would have the spill-over effect of increasing the likelihood of default and losses to the lender. Some common restrictions are:

- *Working-capital requirement.* This restriction requires the borrower to maintain a minimum amount of working capital. As seen in Part 2 of this book, adequate working capital is necessary to enable a firm to meet its current financial obligations. Very often, this restriction specifies a minimum current ratio, such as 2 to 1 or 3 to 1, or a minimum dollar value of working capital. The actual requirement would reflect the norm for the borrower's industry, as well as the lender's particular desires.
- *Additional borrowing.* This type of restriction requires that the lender's approval must be given before further debt issues or borrowings can take place.
- *Periodic financial statements.* Many loan agreements require the borrower to supply the lender with financial statements on a regular basis, such as quarterly or half-yearly. These typically include profit and loss statements and balance sheets.

One type of covenant is the *negative pledge*. This type of unsecured lending involves the borrower agreeing ('pledging') *not* to do specified things that would weaken the lender's position. Thus, the effectiveness of the covenant, from the lender's perspective, depends on the goodwill of the borrower in complying with the terms of the pledge. Also, there are problems of enforceability if the pledge is broken, since this type of lending is unsecured.

The presence of lending covenants has an indirect effect on the cost of funds. For example, if a borrower is highly restricted by covenants of the above kind, it may be more difficult in future to raise necessary funds and their cost might be higher than would otherwise be the case. In addition, it might be difficult to manage the business freely in the presence of some of the asset restrictions imposed by the covenants.

LOAN PRICING

Loan 'pricing' refers to the interest rate and any other fees charged by the lender. The starting point is the lender's cost of raising funds. This varies over time with interest-rate movements. The lender adds a margin to the cost of funds. The margin reflects the lender's desired profit level, and it takes into account other factors, such as (1) the borrower's access to alternative sources of funds, (2) the borrower's credit standing and the risk of the loan, and (3) the relationship between lender and customer.

Access to alternative sources of funds

Some borrowers (notably large companies with good bond ratings) have direct access to local or overseas financial markets. Thus, a bank will have to price loans competitively in order to attract their business. However, many firms do not have direct access to financial markets, so they must rely on borrowing from an intermediary. In these cases, the lender will endeavour to negotiate a rate that it believes the borrower is willing to pay. The lender's bargaining position will be strongest if the borrower has limited alternatives.

Borrower's credit standing and the risk of the loan

Often, a bank or other financier has established knowledge of the borrower's business, as the bank and the borrower may have had a banking relationship for a number of years. This means that the lender has a degree of 'inside' knowledge that would not be held by others and thus the lender is potentially in a good position to assess the borrower's creditworthiness and to appraise the risk associated with a loan. The higher the perceived risk, the higher the interest rate. If the loan is for a specific project, the riskiness of the project will also be taken into account when pricing the loan.

Relationship between lender and customer

The total 'relationship' with the customer will have a bearing on loan pricing. From a bank's viewpoint, the profitability of the customer's business overall with the bank is what counts. The bank earns revenue from the customer's loan interest, together with fees charged on loans and for other services. On the other hand, the bank incurs expenses in the form of its cost of funds, the costs of providing services to the customer, and the interest paid on the customer's deposits. Furthermore, the bank will assess the desirability of doing business with a potential borrower in light of the prospective opportunity to 'cross-sell' other financial products and services (for instance to sell EFTPOS/credit-card processing services, cash-management services, insurance products, superannuation products, and so on). Thus, a bank might 'bend' the interest rate on a loan to make it look more attractive, knowing that other sources of revenue from the customer will compensate.

Back to the principles

The interest rate on debt finance is a direct outcome of **Principle 2: The time value of money—a dollar received today is worth more than a dollar received in the future**. If a firm borrows a million dollars today, it can expect to pay back more than a million dollars in the future. The difference is the cost of borrowing money, most appropriately measured as an interest rate. However, the 'price' of finance is not always clear, as there may be other non-interest (dollar) charges as well as non-financial costs. Correctly evaluating the cost of debt is therefore not always an easy matter and the firm's finance manager must be alert to all of the 'tricks of the trade' used by lenders to increase their return and therefore the true rate paid by the borrower.

Concept check

18.5 What is *collateral*, a *chattel mortgage* and a *restrictive covenant*?

18.6 What factors affect the price that a business pays for loan finance?

For answers go to MyFinanceLab or
www.pearson.com.au/9781442539174

OBJECTIVE **4**

Understand how to
amortise a term loan.

Amortisation of term loans

Having negotiated the interest rate, the term of the loan and the principal amount loaned, the repayments can be calculated. These factors are related by the equation for the present value of an annuity (see Chapter 4), as shown in Example 18.4.

EXAMPLE 18.4 Determining the repayments on a term loan

A firm has negotiated to borrow $15000 from its bank. The loan is to be repaid by equal instalments at the end of each of five years, at an interest rate of 8% per year. The relationship between the sum borrowed (which is a present value) and the repayments is given by equation (4-16):

$$PV = PMT(PVIFA_{i,n})$$

For this loan, i is 8% and n is 5, so (from Appendix D at the back of the book) $PVIFA_{8\%,5}$ is 3.993. Thus, the present value being $15000, we have:

$$\$15\,000 \approx PMT(3.993)$$

Therefore:

$$PMT \approx \$15\,000/3.993 \approx \$3756.57$$

Calculator solution

DATA INPUT	FUNCTION KEY
15 000	PV
8	I/Y
5	N

FUNCTION KEY	ANSWER
COMP PMT	–3756.85

To check that the repayments do, in fact, repay the debt as well as interest at a rate of 8%, look at Table 18.4. This table is called an *amortisation schedule*—a schedule that shows the behaviour of a debt over its term, until it is extinguished or 'amortised'. It is a characteristic of term loans that the repayments include an interest component as well as a component that reduces the outstanding principal balance to zero by the end of the loan term. (In contrast, the principal sum raised via a bond-type instrument is repaid at maturity, with coupon interest being the only payments in the meantime.)

Although the above loan has been amortised on an annual basis, a similar procedure is followed for amortising a loan with a different payment frequency. For example, if a loan has

---

TABLE 18.4 Amortisation schedule for the term loan in Example 18.4

(1) YEAR	(2) OPENING BALANCE	(3) INTEREST[a]	(4) REPAYMENT	(5) REDUCTION OF BALANCE[b]	(6) CLOSING BALANCE[c]
1	$15000.00	$1200.00	$3756.85	$2556.85	$12443.15
2	12443.15	995.45	3756.85	2761.40	9681.75
3	9681.75	774.54	3756.85	2982.31	6699.44
4	6699.44	535.96	3756.85	3220.89	3478.55
5	3478.55	278.30[d]	3756.85	3478.55	0.00

a Interest equals column (2) × 0.08 (8%).
b Reduction of balance equals the repayment (4) minus the interest (3).
c Closing balance equals column (2) minus column (5).
d Adjusted slightly so that final closing balance equals zero.

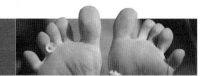

FYI

It was explained in Chapter 4 that, where an interest rate is compounded more than once per year, the effective annual interest rate differs from the nominal annual rate. Equation (4-9a) showed that, if the nominal annual interest rate is j, and if this is compounded m times per year, the effective annual rate, EAR, is given by:

$$EAR = (1 + j/m)^m - 1$$

This means that, to portray the 'true' cost of debt borrowing, the nominal annual rate as stated by the lender must be converted to an effective annual rate. For instance, the bond in Example 18.2 was shown to have a cost of 12% per annum. But this annual rate is in fact payable or compounded twice a year, so in equation (4-9a) $m = 2$ and $j = 12\%$ (0.12 as a decimal). Therefore, the effective annual rate is given by:

$$EAR = (1 + j/m)^m - 1 = (1 + 0.12/2)^2 - 1 = (1.06)^2 - 1$$
$$= 0.1236 \ (12.36\%)$$

In contrast, the loan in Example 18.4 has annual payments and thus annual compounding of interest. This means, as explained in Chapter 4, that the disclosed nominal annual interest rate of 8% is in this case identical to the effective rate.

---

monthly repayments, you need to know the applicable monthly interest rate (one-twelfth of the nominal annual interest rate or APR) in order to be able to complete an amortisation schedule on a month-by-month basis.

VARIANTS OF THE TERM LOAN

Interest-only loan

Borrowers may be able to negotiate a variety of ways of repaying the loan. For example, an *interest-only loan* has repayments that cover the cost of interest but do not amortise the principal. Thus, payments are kept to a minimum. This type of loan would suit someone such as a builder or property developer who needs funds to finance a development, but who intends to discharge the debt, on completion of the project, out of the cash flows arising at that time. For example, suppose that a developer wants $1 million 'bridging finance' for 12 months. An interest-only loan at a nominal rate of 12% per year, compounded and payable monthly, would thus be at a rate of 1% per month, requiring repayments of $10 000 each month. In contrast, a term loan with repayments of the principal and interest would have monthly instalments of $88 849 ($PMT = PV/PVIFA_{1\%,12} = \$1\,000\,000/11.255 = \$88\,849$).

Balloon payment

Lenders often are willing to structure the debt's cash flows to suit the needs of the borrower. Another way of accomplishing this is to have relatively low repayments during the term of the debt, sufficient to repay part of the principal but leaving a balance outstanding that is paid off as a lump sum at the end of the loan term. Such a lump sum is often known as a **balloon payment**. This type of loan would suit a firm that wishes to conserve cash flow by reducing debt-servicing commitments, as outlined in Example 18.5. The 'catch' with this type of loan is that the borrower needs to find the amount of the balloon payment at the end of the loan term, or refinance the debt to repay the sum over an extended time period.

balloon payment
A final lump-sum payment to discharge a debt, such as the residual value of a finance lease.

EXAMPLE 18.5   Term loan with a 'balloon' payment

Suppose that Led Printers has installed a new printing press costing $150 000. The rate of usage of this press is expected to increase progressively over a few years before it reaches capacity. Thus, Led has asked its bank to match the cash flows from the use of the press by structuring a loan with lower initial payments, over a term of five years. On a normal (fully amortised) type

PART 5 Long-term financing

of term loan at 8% annually, the yearly repayments would be $37 569. (Obviously the payment amount is 10 times the $15 000 loan in Example 18.4.)

However, with a $50 000 balloon payment, the annual payments would each be reduced to $29 046.

As is the case with any other debt, the amount borrowed on a loan with a balloon payment is the present value of all the subsequent repayments. If the balloon payment is denoted by the symbol B, its present value is therefore equal to $B(PVIF_{i,n})$. If the regular instalments payable at the end of each period are represented by the amount PMT, their present value is equal to $PMT(PVIFA_{i,n})$. Thus, the total present value is given by:

$$PV = PMT(PVIFA_{i,n}) + B(PVIF_{i,n})$$

$$PMT = \frac{PV - B(PVIF_{i,n})}{(PVIFA_{i,n})}$$

Therefore, for a five-year, $150 000 loan at 8%, with a balloon payment of $50 000, the annual instalment amount is given by:

$$PMT = \frac{\$150\,000 - \$50\,000(PVIF_{8\%,5yr})}{(PVIFA_{8\%,5yr})}$$

$$\approx \frac{\$150\,000 - \$50\,000(0.681)}{3.993}$$

$$\approx \frac{\$150\,000 - \$34\,050}{3.993}$$

$$\approx \$29\,038$$

If you were to prepare an amortisation schedule for this debt, the format in Table 18.4 would be followed. The difference is that the final entry in the 'closing-balance' column would equal the amount then to be paid as the balloon payment. The calculator solution for this payment involves the input of the balloon payment as an FV amount, along with PV, n and i, then simply compute PMT.

DATA INPUT		FUNCTION KEY
5		N
8		I/Y
150 000		PV
50 000	+/–	FV
FUNCTION KEY		**ANSWER**
COMP PMT		–29 045.65

Concept check

18.7 What is meant by 'loan amortisation'? How does a term loan differ from a bond in this respect?

18.8 What is an interest-only loan?

18.9 What is a balloon payment?

For answers go to MyFinanceLab or www.pearson.com.au/9781442539174

OBJECTIVE 5

Determine the effect of non-interest charges on the cost of a loan.

The effect of non-interest fees on the loan cost

It was seen previously that the basic rate charged on a loan is subject to a number of factors that may be negotiated between lender and borrower, and depends on the borrower's credit-worthiness, bargaining position and relationship with the lender. But the basic rate expressed in the loan contract is not the end of the story. Lenders use other means, such as charging fees, to increase their returns on loans. Thus, in order not to be misled about the *true* cost of the funds, the borrower must understand how to account for such fees.

The basic problem of the non-interest fees is that they are expressed in dollars, whereas the cost of finance is expressed as an interest rate. This problem can be overcome by incorporating the dollar fees into the interest rate, as will now be shown.

UPFRONT FEES

Upfront fees are—as the name implies—fees that are charged at the time of taking out a loan. Typically they are given names such as *application fee*, *establishment fee*, *origination fee* or *initiation fee*. In effect, this type of fee reduces the initial loan proceeds received by the borrower and thus increases the 'true' interest rate in much the same way as the flotation or issue costs of a bond.

EXAMPLE 18.6   Effect of upfront fees

Suppose that the borrower of the $15 000, 8% term loan in Example 18.4 is charged an establishment fee that is expressed as 2% of the loan amount. This fee would therefore amount to $300. In effect, this would reduce the net proceeds of the loan, from the borrower's viewpoint, to a cash inflow of $14 700 ($15 000 received from the lender, less $300 paid to the lender). The consequence is that the interest rate paid by the borrower is really greater than 8%. To work out the effect on the interest rate, $14 700 will be used as the present value of the Example 18.4 loan, whose annual payment remains $3756.85:

$$\$14\,700 = \$3756.85 \,(PVIFA_{i,5})$$

Thus, $PVIFA_{i,5}$ is equal to $14 700/$3756.85, an amount of 3.9128. Reading across the row for five periods in Appendix D, a value of 3.9128 lies between the table entries for 8% (a value of 3.9927) and 9% (a value of 3.8897); where it lies corresponds to an interest rate of about 8.8%.

One conclusion from this example is that the borrower, if shopping around between lenders, would be better off paying up to about 8.7% on a loan of $15 000 if that loan was free of fees of the above amount ($300). This is despite the claimed interest rate being 8%.

Calculator solution		
DATA INPUT		FUNCTION KEY
5		N
14 700		PV
3756.85	+/−	PMT
FUNCTION KEY		ANSWER
COMP I/Y		8.77(%)

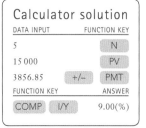

Loan fees are expressed in dollars, whereas the cost of interest is expressed as a percentage. Because these two types of loan cost are on different scales, they cannot be directly compared.

This dilemma is overcome by incorporating the dollar fees into the interest rate.

ONGOING FEES

In addition to, or instead of, fees charged at the time the loan is advanced, other fees might be imposed during the term of the loan. These ongoing fees are given names such as 'account processing fee', 'administration fee' or 'handling fee'. For instance, if the lender charged an administration fee of $10 every month, the effect would be to add $10 to the monthly repayments. Again, this would have the consequence of increasing the true interest rate. Suppose that the borrower in Example 18.6 is now subject to an annual fee of $100. This would, in effect, increase the annual repayment amount to $3856.85, which in turn increases the annual nominal interest rate to 9% per annum, as shown in the calculator solution opposite. If this $100 annual fee is now combined with the $300 establishment fee, the joint effect is to increase the cost of borrowing to nearly 9.8%.

Calculator solution		
DATA INPUT		FUNCTION KEY
5		N
15 000		PV
3856.85	+/−	PMT
FUNCTION KEY		ANSWER
COMP I/Y		9.00(%)

Your money

THE CONSUMER FINANCE JUNGLE

Just as term loans provide the bulk of business finance in Australia, this type of loan underlies almost all housing and consumer finance from banks, credit unions and other institutional lenders. And, when we borrow personally, we face the same problems with non-interest fees and charges as do business borrowers. Different lenders use different names and charge different amounts; some charge one type of fee, others different types. Some (rarely) charge none at all, while others might charge a wide range of fees. Some of these amounts represent charges imposed by government bodies, which the lender collects from the borrower and then remits to the relevant body. However, the majority of fees are simply a means by which the lender boosts the income from the loans.

At the time a loan is taken out, there are various *upfront* fees and charges. These charges may be given names such as 'application fees', 'establishment fees', 'membership fees' and the like. In essence, they reduce the net proceeds of the loan and so increase its cost.

Subsequently, there are *ongoing* charges that are payable during the life of the loan (often at the same time as the regular instalment amounts), such as 'processing fees' or 'account-keeping fees'. These charges in effect add to the regular repayments and so also increase the cost of the loan.

Additionally, there are *termination fees* payable when the loan is discharged. However, if the loan is 'prepaid', that is prematurely repaid in full (before its scheduled term), the borrower may face an additional *exit fee* payable at that time.

The effect of such fees can be incorporated into the interest rate by making appropriate adjustments to the loan's cash-flow schedule. However, the situation is confused by the fact that different loans offer different bundles of 'features' (such as the ability to 'redraw' sums of money that have previously been repaid voluntarily in excess of the minimum instalment specified in the lending contract). In marketing jargon, the lender is endeavouring to 'add value' to the basic loan product, in the hope that borrowers will choose their loans above competitors' loans, and often some extra price is payable by the borrower for this added value. However, it is difficult to ascribe a monetary value to these features.

The loan-choice problem is exacerbated by the fact that most long-term loans, such as housing loans, are at a variable interest rate that can be reset by the lender as market interest rates shift over time, with the consequence that repayments, too, are reset. This creates *repayment risk* for borrowers, who face uncertainty about their future commitments and so may face budgetary stress in times of rising interest rates. An additional problem is that there is no guarantee that a lender whose loan is the least expensive today will always be so.

Thus, uninformed borrowers may face a bewildering range of issues (many of which they are not even consciously aware). However, perhaps the biggest countervailing force in favour of the consumer is that increased competition can put downwards pressure on the base loan rate. In this respect, one of the many consequences of the GFC is that securitisation has virtually come to a halt, which in turn has starved some non-bank lenders of cash (such as Aussie Home Loans), with the result that their share of the housing loan market has more than halved from its pre-GFC level of 20% or so. In response, there have been some government-inspired moves to boost funding of the non-bank lending sector, which does appear to be capable of regaining at least some of the ground that it has lost.

OPPORTUNITY COSTS

Trying to determine the 'true' cost of a new loan may be difficult if the loan is borrowed from the borrower's existing bank. This is because, in many cases, the bank takes account of its profit on the total banking relationship with the customer, in ways discussed previously. For example, if the bank were to require the customer to place funds of, say, $5000 on deposit as a condition of the loan (such deposits are known as 'compensating balances'), the opportunity cost of this arrangement should be evaluated. It might, for instance, mean a reduction of 1% per annum in the deposit rate that could otherwise be earned elsewhere, in which case the borrower needs to include this effect when determining the overall cost of the loan. In this situation, an extra cash outflow of $50 (1% of $5000), representing the annual amount of interest forgone on the deposit, could be added to the annual loan instalment, increasing it to $3806.85, thus enabling revision of the true interest rate on the loan. The effect on the loan in Example 18.6 would be to increase the nominal annual interest rate from 8% to 8.5% per annum, as shown in the relevant calculator solution opposite.

Calculator solution

DATA INPUT		FUNCTION KEY
5		N
14 700		PV
3856.85	+/–	PMT
FUNCTION KEY		**ANSWER**
COMP	I/Y	9.79(%)

Calculator solution

DATA INPUT		FUNCTION KEY
5		N
15 000		PV
3806.85	+/–	PMT
FUNCTION KEY		**ANSWER**
COMP	I/Y	8.50(%)

For answers go to MyFinanceLab or www.pearson.com.au/9781442539174

Concept check

18.10 What are some examples of the different names that lenders give to *upfront fees* and *ongoing fees*?

18.11 Why is it necessary to incorporate non-interest costs into the loan interest rate?

Interest-rate exposure of loans

OBJECTIVE **6**

Understand the interest-
rate risk exposure of
borrowing money.

In the context of bonds—specifically bonds with a fixed coupon rate—interest-rate risk was seen in Chapter 4 as the responsiveness of the bond price to changes in interest rates. For example, if rates rise, an investor suffers from the fall in the bond price. However, from the bond issuer's (borrower's) viewpoint, the exposure is the opposite—a rise in rates is beneficial, in an *opportunity cost* sense, because the issuer has a fixed coupon rate and need not pay a higher interest rate during the life of the bond.

BORROWING AT A FIXED INTEREST RATE

The loan in Example 18.4 is at a fixed rate. The main advantage of this form of debt is that the borrower knows the future commitments and may avoid the consequence of subsequent increases in interest rates. However, a fixed-rate loan has the disadvantage that, if current market rates move down during the term of the loan, the borrower suffers an opportunity cost in the form of missing the opportunity to take advantage of the lower rate.

BORROWING AT A VARIABLE INTEREST RATE

Much long-term lending in Australia is at a variable or floating rate. As noted above, this allows the lender to change the rate from time to time. The main disadvantage of floating-rate debt is that borrowers do not know their future commitments. The interest-rate climate in the first decade of the new millennium has featured low and relatively stable rates apart from the period after the sub-prime crisis. Thus for quite a long period borrowers may not have seen interest-rate volatility as a problem. However, in the late 1980s, for example, interest rates changed frequently upwards, with the consequence that many borrowers faced a large increase in their debt-servicing costs. This coincided with an economic downturn, with the result that sales, profits and cash flows fell, thus diminishing the ability to service debt. These circumstances were cited as the major cause of a large number of the business bankruptcies that occurred in the late 1980s and early 1990s. Thus it is vital for firms to incorporate interest-rate volatility into their budgets when they assess their debt capacity.

The usual effect of increasing the interest rate during the course of a variable-rate loan is to increase the amount of the remaining instalments so that the debt will be amortised by the original date. This is illustrated in Example 18.7.

EXAMPLE 18.7   **Effect of increasing the rate on a variable-rate loan**

Assume that the Example 18.4 loan had been advanced at a variable rate, initially 8% per annum, and that this rate remained stable for the first two years. Table 18.4 shows that the balance at the end of the second year is $9681.75. If the interest rate at that time was increased to 9% per annum, the lender would increase the required annual repayment to $3824.82 for the remaining three years, in order to amortise the balance of the debt over its remaining term, as shown in the calculator solution. (Alternatively, the borrower could negotiate with the lender to extend the term, leaving the former instalment unchanged.)

Calculator solution	
DATA INPUT	FUNCTION KEY
3	N
9681.75	PV
9	I/Y
FUNCTION KEY	ANSWER
COMP PMT	−3824.82

Although the use of a fixed-rate loan can avoid rising rates in the future, it suffers from the problem that the borrower cannot benefit from falling rates. Once the rate is locked in, or fixed, the borrower is bound by that rate. In order to 'unwind' a fixed-rate contract, a borrower must pay a fee, the amount of which may seem quite punitive. However, the lender would argue that the fee merely represents the loss of earnings that it would suffer if it allowed the borrower to withdraw from a fixed-rate agreement. The interest-rate risk that arises from uncertainty about future rates and associated commitments can, to some extent, be managed by the use of *derivative* financial instruments as discussed in Chapter 21.

For answers go to MyFinanceLab or
www.pearson.com.au/9781442539174

OBJECTIVE **7**

Describe other forms of debt, such as leases and 'hire-purchase'.

Other forms of long-term debt

There is no doubt that term loans, particularly from banks, are the dominant form of long-term debt for Australian business firms. Term loans are often asset-specific and secured, although they may be used as a general component of the long-term debt of a company. From a legal position, the borrower is the legal owner of any asset(s) financed by the term loan, although the asset(s) may be used as collateral for the debt via means such as a chattel mortgage or a real-estate mortgage. From a taxation perspective, deductions are allowed for the periodic loan interest.

FINANCE LEASES

A finance lease is explicitly asset-specific, for the simple reason that the business that 'borrows' the lease and uses the asset is not the legal owner. Rather, the legal owner (called the *lessor*) allows the user (called the *lessee*) to use the asset for the term of the lease, in return for the lessee making the agreed payments to the lessor. Usually a finance lease covers 100% of the cost of the asset and, at the end of the lease term, the lessee (user) may make an offer to purchase the asset in return for a final payment, called the *residual value*. The existence of this residual value means that the regular lease repayments (instalments) do not fully amortise the debt. Another difference from term loans is that lease instalments are made at the beginning of each period (an annuity due), so in effect the first instalment acts like a deposit or a down-payment.

Lease financing grew from negligible beginnings in the years after World War II to a position of quite extensive usage in Australia's financial markets. However, as indicated in Table 18.5, in the past decade or so lease financing has been declining and has not exceeded around $6 billion per year, whereas term loans have increased more than two-fold over the same period and bonds have increased even more so.

The main reason for the relative decline in popularity of lease financing is the introduction of the goods and services tax (GST) in July 2000, as discussed in Chapter 2. For purposes of the GST, a lease is regarded as 'provision of a service' by the lessor (the legal owner of the leased asset) and so the GST is added to the lease payment. Although the GST component may subsequently be claimed back by registered businesses, leasing suffers the competitive disadvantage that repayments on term loans are GST-free.

Australian companies may raise leases under contracts written in overseas jurisdictions that are free of the GST. The Appendix to this chapter discusses leases in more detail, with emphasis on the financial evaluation of a lease compared with a loan (which is called the 'lease or buy decision').

TABLE 18.5 Lease finance advanced[a]

2001	2004	2007	2010
$6.4 billion	$6.2 billion	$6.3 billion	$4.6 billion

a Commitments, that is, this amount shows leases approved but not yet advanced and so the actual volume of lending is likely to be overstated somewhat.

Source: Copyright © Commonwealth of Australia, Australian Bureau of Statistics, *Lending Finance, Australia*, cat. no. 5671.0.

HIRE-PURCHASE FINANCING

Like leasing, hire-purchase is asset-specific. However, the user is called the hirer (or purchaser) of the goods, which are financed/provided by the financier. Another similarity is that the cash-flow pattern may be much the same: (1) regular instalments at the beginning of each period and (2) a balloon or residual payment at the end of the term. However, at the end of the term of the hire-purchase agreement, ownership of the goods or property passes automatically to the hirer (unlike a lease, where ownership passes only if the lessee makes an offer to acquire the goods and the lessor accepts this offer).

From a taxation perspective, the distinguishing feature of a hire-purchase agreement is that the hirer is treated from the outset as the owner of the goods. Thus, the hirer can claim tax deductions for interest expense as well as depreciation of the asset. These deductions are therefore the same as for a term loan that finances a specific asset. In contrast (see this chapter's Appendix), the lessee can claim only the lease instalments as a tax deduction. Also, for the purposes of the Australian GST, hire-purchase is treated like the buying of an asset, and so, unlike leasing, hire-purchase instalments do not attract a GST component.

The procedure for evaluating a hire-purchase agreement can be based on the same methodology as lease evaluation (see the Appendix). However, because the taxation treatment of hire-purchase is the same as if the asset had been financed with a term loan, the choice between a hire-purchase agreement and a term loan can be based solely on the interest rate, as shown in Example 18.8.

EXAMPLE 18.8   Hire-purchase evaluation based on the interest rate

Assume that a firm can arrange a hire-purchase agreement for an asset worth $15 000, featuring five annual payments of $2618.19 (at the beginning of each year), followed by a balloon payment of $6000 at the end of the fifth year. The hirer wants to know the interest rate for comparison with other forms of borrowing.

The present value of the regular hire-purchase instalments is given by Chapter 4's equation (4-20) for the present value of an annuity due:

$$PV_{due} = PMT\left\{1 + \frac{[1-(1+i)^{-(n-1)}]}{i}\right\} \qquad \textbf{(4-20)}$$

$$= \$2618.19\left\{1 + \frac{[1-(1+i)^{-(5-1)}]}{i}\right\}$$

In addition, the PV of the $6000 balloon payment is given by use of equation (4-5a):

$$PV = FV_n(1+i)^{-n} \qquad \textbf{(4-5a)}$$

$$= \$6000(1+i)^{-5}$$

Thus, the total PV of all the lease payments is given by:

$$\$15\,000 = 2618.19\left\{1 + \frac{[1-(1+i)^{-4}]}{i}\right\} + \$6000(1+i)^{-5}$$

Solving for i by trial and error gives $i = 9\%$. Since payments are annual, this means that the nominal annual interest rate is 9% per annum.

See calculator solution opposite.

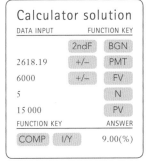

Calculator solution

DATA INPUT		FUNCTION KEY
	2ndF	BGN
2618.19	+/−	PMT
6000	+/−	FV
5		N
15 000		PV
FUNCTION KEY		ANSWER
COMP I/Y		9.00(%)

Using Chapter 4's equation (4-21), the present value of the five regular instalments is given by:

$$PV_{due} = PMT(1 + PVIFA_{i,n-1}) \tag{4-21}$$
$$= \$2618.19(1 + PVIFA_{i,4})$$

In addition, the present value of the balloon payment is given by $\$6000(PVIF_{i,5})$. Thus, the total present value of $\$15\,000$ is given by:

$$\$15\,000 = \$2618.19(1 + PVIFA_{i,4}) + \$6000(PVIF_{i,5}).$$

If you have the patience to try out various combinations of *PVIFA* (Appendix D) and *PVIF* (Appendix B), you will find that the relevant interest rate is 9%.

The interest rate of 9% in Example 18.8 is greater than the rate of 8% on the otherwise comparable term loan in Example 18.4. This raises the question as to why a financier would price a loan differently from hire-purchase. In this case, the lower rate on the term loan might reflect the fact that the lender has secured the loan with more than adequate collateral, giving superior protection in the event of default by the borrower. In other circumstances, however, the financier might see less risk in advancing funds via a hire-purchase agreement, because legal title to the goods does not pass until the final hire-purchase instalment is made. All in all, if the risks are similar, it is quite likely that the 'prices', too, will be similar.

The amortisation schedule for the hire-purchase agreement in Example 18.8 is shown in Table 18.6.

TABLE 18.6 Hire-purchase amortisation schedule

(1) YEAR	(2) OPENING BALANCE $	(3) REPAYMENT $	(4) INTEREST[a] $	(5) CLOSING BALANCE[b] $
1	15 000.00	2618.19	1 114.36	13 496.17
2	13 496.17	2618.19	979.02	11 857.00
3	11 857.00	2618.19	831.49	10 070.30
4	10 070.30	2618.19	670.69	8 122.80
5	8 122.80	2618.19	495.39[c]	6 000.00[d]

a   Interest equals column (2) minus column (3), multiplied by 0.09 (9%).
b   Closing balance equals column (2) minus (3) plus (4).
c   Adjusted so that closing balance equals 6 000.00.
d   Balloon value at end of year 5, repaid at that time.

Concept check

For answers go to MyFinanceLab or
www.pearson.com.au/9781442539174

18.13   What is the main difference between a lease contract and a hire-purchase contract?

Back to the principles

If the interest rate on a term loan from a given lender is higher than the rate on a hire-purchase agreement from that same lender, the higher rate might simply reflect the higher risk from the lender's perspective. This is an example of **Principle 1: The risk–return trade-off—We won't take on additional risk unless we expect to be compensated with additional return.**

International spotlight

BANKS TAP OVERSEAS BOND MARKETS TO FUND AUSTRALIAN BUSINESSES

The requirement that a company have a suitable bond rating becomes even more important if it wishes to borrow in overseas markets. We have seen in Chapter 3 that a significant amount of Australia's financing needs are supplied from overseas. Ironically, some of these overseas funds are borrowed by the banking sector to provide Australian dollar term loans to Australian households and businesses. According to *The Australian Financial Review*[15], Australia's big four banks (the ANZ, the Commonwealth Bank, the National Australia Bank and Westpac) sought a total of $120 billion in 2010, putting each among the top 12 global borrowers. It is estimated that about a quarter of these banks' annual funding needs to come from this source.

The banks subsequently on-lend these overseas funds to business borrowers and households in Australia. This reinforces the fact that firms which cannot access bond markets directly will tend to pay more for funds via term loans, because the banks add their operating costs and profit margin to the cost that they pay for funds raised offshore.

The main reasons that Australian banks borrow offshore are lower overseas interest rates and access to amounts of finance that the Australian financial markets are not able to provide. As indicated in Table 18.1, offshore corporate bond issues by Australian non-financial institutions were about $40 billion in 2009. This figure is overshadowed by that of banks and other financial institutions, whose offshore capital raisings may be as high as three times the corporate bonds issued by non-financial corporations.

Summary

In Australia, bonds are the traditional instrument for government bodies to raise long-term debt finance. In a business context, corporate bonds have also gained popularity in recent years, but their use is restricted to large firms with a high financial standing as evidenced by a good bond rating. The cost of issuing a bond may include various issue costs that can be incorporated into the interest rate.

OBJECTIVE 1

OBJECTIVE 2

Term loans are the dominant form of debt finance for Australian businesses, largely because the Australian corporate bond market is not well developed and the majority of Australian companies do not have a bond rating. Term loans are obtained from lenders such as banks and finance companies. Variants of the loan include a 'balloon' payment at the end of the term, or the loan might be on an 'interest-only' basis. In order to protect the lender, restrictive covenants may be placed on the borrower and security or collateral may be taken.

OBJECTIVE 3

The process of repaying a term loan is known as 'amortisation'. The periodic repayments include an interest component and a component that progressively reduces the loan balance to zero by the end of the loan term. The cost of a term loan is not only the interest rate but also the spill-over effects of such covenants, which may, however, be difficult to quantify.

OBJECTIVE 4

The cost of a term loan is also affected by the presence of non-interest fees and charges on the loan, along with other elements of the bank–customer relationship.

OBJECTIVE 5

Loans and other forms of debt can be on a variable interest-rate basis, with an adverse exposure to rising interest rates (which lead to increased repayments) or on a fixed-rate basis which has the opposite exposure.

OBJECTIVE 6

In addition to term loans and bonds, finance leases are common in many countries, but their use in Australia has been curtailed by the introduction of the GST. Hire-purchase agreements can be structured in exactly the same way as leases, but they differ in legal form and in taxation treatment and they avoid the GST.

OBJECTIVE 7

OBJECTIVE 8 Finance leases and their evaluation are discussed in the Appendix to this chapter, which shows how to determine whether a lease or a loan is worth more to the firm as a form of debt finance.

Key term

For a complete flashcard glossary
go to MyFinanceLab at
www.pearson.com.au/myfinancelab

balloon payment	**631**
bond rating	**619**

Review questions

18-1 Why might a large company prefer to raise long-term debt through a corporate bond issue? Why might the company prefer a private placement to a public issue? Why are such bond issues not accessible to all Australian companies?

18-2 Briefly discuss some of the costs that a bond issuer could incur when making a new issue. What effect do these costs have on the issuer's interest rate?

18-3 Use your answer to 18-2 to explain why the investor's current yield might differ from the cost to the company of issuing bonds.

18-4 Other things being equal, why is a bond issue more likely to be cheaper than a term loan? Why, then, do not more Australian firms issue bonds?

18-5 What is a yield spread? How can the finance manager use this to help determine the prospective cost of a new bond issue?

18-6 What characteristics distinguish term loans from other forms of debt such as bonds?

18-7 Briefly explain the nature of *securitisation*. What role does an SPV play in the securitisation process?

18-8 Distinguish between an *asset-backed security* (*ABS*) and a *collateralised debt obligation* (*CDO*). Why is an *ABS* likely to be more risky than a conventional bond with a similar debt rating? Why, in turn, is a *CDO* more risky than an *ABS*?

18-9 List and discuss the major types of restrictions usually found in the covenants of loan agreements.

18-10 What is the basic problem in trying to compare a variable-rate loan with a fixed-rate loan? What are the risk exposures of each?

18-11 Explain why investment projects should be evaluated by discounting cash flows at the cost of capital, even if the assets for the project can be financed 100% by debt.

18-12 What factors are likely to affect the 'price' that a firm pays for its borrowings?

18-13 'There may be a difference between the interest rate disclosed by the lender and the 'true' cost to the borrower.' Explain.

18-14 Briefly explain some of the reasons why the big banks borrow funds from overseas and how the use to which they put these funds provides evidence of the potential cost disadvantage to firms (the banks' customers) who borrow via term loans.

18-15 Why is it necessary to incorporate non-interest fees into the interest rate when comparing two or more loans?

18-16 What are some of the circumstances under which a borrower might want to make use of (i) an interest-only loan or (ii) a loan with a balloon payment?

ST-1 (*Bond analysis*) Megacorp Ltd is a very large company with a AAA debt rating. It is contemplating a bond issue of $100 million for a term of five years, with coupon interest to be paid half-yearly. The company's treasurer has observed that AAA-rated company debentures with about five years until maturity have a yield of 7.5% per year. A merchant bank has advised Megacorp that, for a fee of $1 million, it can place the debt privately with an investment fund. The investment fund will, however, require a premium of 0.25% above the current yield to compensate for the lack of marketability. What will be the interest rate that Megacorp will effectively have to pay for these funds if it proceeds with the deal?

For answers go to MyFinanceLab
www.pearson.com.au/myfinancelab

ST-2 (*Analysing a term loan*) Calculate the annual instalment payment and the principal and interest components of a five-year loan carrying a 10% rate of interest. The amount borrowed is $50 000. What is the answer if the loan is for two and a half years, with interest compounded (charged) half-yearly at a rate of 20% p.a.? Payments are at the end of each period.

ST-3 (*Analysing a term loan*) Southern Pacific Ltd is contemplating the purchase of a new machine. The total cost of the machine is $120 000 and the firm plans to pay a deposit of $20 000. The firm's bank has offered two alternative repayment plans, both at a rate of 14%. Plan A involves equal instalments payable at the end of each of the next five years. Plan B requires five equal annual payments at the end of each year plus a balloon payment of $20 000 at the end of year 5.

    (a) Compute the annual payment on plan A.
    (b) Determine the principal and interest components of the loan in plan A.
    (c) Compute the annual instalment on plan B.
    (d) Determine the principal and interest components of the loan in plan B.

ST-4 (*Cost of term loan finance*) For plan B in ST-3, the lender wants an 'establishment fee' of $5000 before the loan will be granted, and for plan A the lender wants an annual fee of $704 payable at the same time as each regular instalment. Which loan plan would Southern Pacific prefer?

See Chapters 4 and 10 for additional bond problems.

Note: In problems that call for computation of an effective annual interest rate, it will be recalled that the effective rate p.a. is given by equation (4-9a), $EAR = (1 + j/m)^m - 1$ (where j = the nominal rate p.a., and m = the number of times the rate j is compounded within a year).

For more problems and for answers to problems marked with an asterisk (*) go to MyFinanceLab at
www.pearson.com.au/myfinancelab

18-1 (*Bond spreads and costs*) Federal government bonds with five-year maturity and half-yearly coupons are trading at a yield of 5.9%.

    (a) What would be the yield on five-year Axpro Ltd bonds, according to Table 18.2, if they are rated BBB?
    (b) If the bond in **(a)** faces issue costs totalling $5.79 per $100 face value, what is the overall percentage cost of the issue?

18-2 (*Bond yields and prices*) Nanocorporation Limited, which presently has an A rating for its bonds, last made a bond issue five years ago. The issue was for a 10-year maturity, with a coupon rate of 12% p.a. (paid half-yearly). Now the company is contemplating a new five-year bond issue. Government bonds (AAA rated), whose yield differs by 0.5% p.a. from that of AA bonds (which in turn differ by 0.5% from A-rated bonds), are currently trading on the following basis:

1-year maturity	6.4%
2-year maturity	6.6%
3-year maturity	6.7%
4-year maturity	6.8%
5-year maturity	7%
10-year maturity	8%

    (a) What yield would Nanocorp need to offer investors in order to attract them to buy its new bond issue?
    (b) What is the current price of Nanocorp's bonds (per $100 face value)?

18-3 (*Bond analysis*) Assume that Megacorp Ltd (see problem ST-1) can float a five-year, $100 million debt issue in the eurobond market. The current yield in that market for top-rated debt is 7.5% per year, a little lower than in the Australian market. An international merchant bank has offered to underwrite the issue and meet all other costs for a total fee of $9.65 million. Would you recommend that the company proceed with the private placement (ST-1) or accept the offer from the merchant bank?

18-4 (*Bond analysis—advanced*) Multico Ltd has two alternatives for a new bond issue of $50 million. The issue will be for 10 years with coupons paid half-yearly. The company can make a public issue or a private placement. A public issue would be able to attract funds at a yield of 8% per year. It would be offered at par. Multico prefers to have the issue underwritten, which the Macco Merchant Bank is willing to undertake for a fee of $300 000 plus 5% of the face value. In addition, the cost of preparing a prospectus and other fees are expected to amount to $200 000. The company's trading bank, Whobank, is encouraging the firm to make a private placement, which they say can be done quickly and with minimum fuss, owing to Multico's strong A+ rating. A private issue would be sold at a discount of 4% of face value and, in addition, the bank would charge an upfront placement fee of $500 000. Furthermore, the bank would levy a service fee of 0.2% of the face value, payable at the end of each half-year for the life of the bond. Should Multico arrange for the public issue or the private placement?

18-5 (*Securitisation, ABS and CDO*) OZloans has a parcel of housing loans worth $200 million that it wants to 'sell' in order to raise funds for new lending. To pay this sum to OZloans, the SPV will issue three 'slices' of *ABS*: equity tranche, 5%, mezzanine tranche, 25%, and senior tranche, 70%. Assuming that the *ABS*-mezzanine tranche is purchased by another vehicle, draw a funds-flow diagram from the originator through to the *CDO* securities, showing the dollar amounts of each of the *ABS* and *CDO* securities issued (for the three *CDO* tranches, the percentages of equity, mezzanine and senior are 5%, 20% and 75% respectively).

18-6 (*Securitisation losses*) With reference to problem 18-5, draw a table to show the losses that would be suffered by (i) the *ABS* tranches and (ii) the *CDO* tranches, if the amount of OZloans' original loan default losses was 10%, 20%, 30% and 40%, respectively, of the total balance of the loans.

18-7* (*Loan instalments*) Compute the annual instalments for a five-year term loan of $100 000 carrying an 18% p.a. rate of interest, with payments at the end of each year.

18-8* (*Term loan with non-annual payments*) Compute the amount of each half-yearly instalment on a $100 000 term loan with payments at the end of each period, over two and a half years, with interest charged on the half-yearly balance at a rate of 18% p.a., compounded half-yearly. Prepare an amortisation schedule for this loan.

18-9 (*Loan instalments and analysis*) Compare the loan in problem 18-7 with an alternative $100 000 five-year loan that has the same stated annual interest rate but has half-yearly repayments. Which loan is preferable and why?

18-10 (*Amortisation of a term loan*) Determine the respective yearly/half-yearly principal and interest components of the loans in problems 18-7 and 18-9.

18-11* (*Variable-rate loan analysis*) Your firm has taken out a $100 000 loan over two and a half years with interest initially at 9% per half-year, and payments due at the end of each period. Immediately after the second instalment was paid, you were notified that the lender had increased the rate by 0.5% per half-year period.

   (a) What is the annual interest rate effectively levied on this loan?
   (b) How does this annual rate change as a result of the lender's decision to change the half-yearly rate outlined above?
   (c) Compute the new payment after the interest-rate change and prepare an amortisation schedule for the remainder of the loan term.

18-12 (*Variable-rate loan analysis*) Assume that the loan in problem 18-7 was originally advanced on a variable interest rate basis, and that the relevant market interest rate dropped by 2% p.a. right at the beginning of the second year.

   (a) What is the revised annual instalment for the remainder of the loan term?
   (b) Prepare an amortisation schedule for the remainder of the loan term.

18-13* (*Cost of loan funds*) The ProCess Company needs $250 000 to purchase a new computer system. The computer supplier has offered to finance the system with a $50 000 deposit followed by five annual instalments 'in arrears' (that is, at the end of each period) of $59 663.11. Alternatively, the firm's bank has offered to lend the firm $250 000 to be repaid in five annual instalments at the end of each year, based on an interest rate of 16%. Finally, the firm can arrange to obtain the needed $250 000 through a finance broker, which requires a lump-sum payment of $385 080 in five years.

    (a) What is the annual interest rate on the loan from the computer firm?
    (b) What will the annual payments to the bank be?
    (c) What is the interest rate on the loan from the broker?
    (d) Based on cost considerations only, from whom should the money be borrowed?

18-14 (*Cost of a term loan*) Temple Freight Forwarding Company needs $300 000 to finance the construction of several prefabricated metal warehouses. The firm that manufactures the warehouses has offered to finance the purchase with a $50 000 down-payment followed by five annual instalments of $69 000 each. Alternatively, Temple's bank has offered to lend the firm $300 000 to be repaid in 10 half-yearly instalments based on a nominal annual rate of interest of 16%. Finally, the firm could finance the needed $300 000 through a loan from a finance broker requiring a single lump-sum payment of $425 000 in five years.

    (a) What is the effective annual rate of interest on the loan from the warehouse manufacturer?
    (b) What will the annual payments on the bank loan be?
    (c) What is the annual rate of interest for the term loan from the finance broker?
    (d) Based on cost considerations only, which source of financing should Temple select?

18-15* (*Cost of loan funds*) Diamond Jewellers is planning to install a $400 000 burglar alarm system for its large shop in the centre of the city. The firm's bank has offered to lend the full $400 000, in the form of an 'interest only' loan, secured by a chattel mortgage over the alarm system, with interest payments due at the end of each year. The rate quoted by the bank is 14% p.a., the last interest instalment being payable along with the principal in four years time, at which time the bank will require a fee of 1% of the principal in order to discharge the mortgage. Alternatively, the bank can arrange a long-term bill facility, interest and principal being payable in four years time, at a rate of 6.85% per half-year (i.e. 13.7% annually, compounded half-yearly). This would involve the bank arranging to find a provider of the funds, with the bank guaranteeing repayment, in return for which the bank would levy an arrangement fee of $5000 payable at the time the loan was arranged. Finally, the alarm manufacturer can provide finance at a rate of 14.25% p.a., by means of a term-loan with principal and interest payments at the end of each of the four years.

    (a) What is the repayment pattern on each of the loan alternatives?
    (b) Based only on the cost of finance, which loan would you recommend?
    (c) What other factors might be relevant to your decision?

18-16 (*Loan analysis including non-interest fees*) Your business intends to borrow a $20 million term loan from GB bank, to finance some new construction equipment. The business can afford repayments of $900 000 at the end of each month for two years, and the interest rate is 9% p.a. compounded monthly. When your boss checks the loan figures on her new financial calculator, she finds that there seems to be 'something wrong' with the figures, but she is not sure what is happening.

    (a) Explain in which way(s) the figures might not make sense to your boss, who does not know much about financial mathematics. (Assume that the interest rate is fixed and cannot be altered.)
    (b) If the company could afford to pay more than $900 000 per month, what would be the monthly payment for two years?
    (c) Assume that the bank charges a $200 000 'settlement fee' at the time of advancing the loan and also a monthly 'processing fee' of $2000. What effect do these fees have on the cost of the loan finance? (Assume that the monthly loan repayments are the figures that you worked out in **(b)**.)

18-17 (*Loan analysis including non-interest costs*) You work for Redrock Resorts (RR), a new five-star complex located near Alice Springs in Australia's Northern Territory. RR is seeking a $6 million term-loan repayable over five years. Northern Territory United Service Bank (NOTUS) has offered the loan at an interest rate of 12% *APR*, repayable at the end of each quarter. A.S. International Finance Group (ASIF) has quoted a $133 467 repayment per month (payable at the end of each period).

    (a) Explain, with supporting computations, whether or not one of the above loans is preferable to the other on financial grounds.

(b) Assume you have just discovered that NOTUS requires a $180 000 'application fee' before it will approve the loan. What effect, if any, will this have on your loan choice? (*Show all supporting computations.*)

(c) Suppose that ASIF also wants a fee—a 'transaction fee' of $3000 per month, payable at the same time as the regular monthly instalment amount. Would this change your loan choice? (*Show all supporting computations.*)

18-18 (*Comprehensive cost of finance, including non-interest fees*) You have decided to upgrade your television viewing at home. Astracorp has been advertising a two-year satellite-TV contract for $200 per month, payable at the end of each month. In addition, there is a 'special' $720 price, payable upfront, for installing the antenna and the wiring. Alternatively, Kabelworld will provide a cable-TV subscription for $240 per month payable at the end of each month, and, if you sign a two-year contract, they will include free wiring and connection. Both companies offer the same range of TV channels and both companies offer these 'special' prices only if you agree to pay by direct monthly debit from your credit card account, on which interest is charged at a nominal annual interest rate of 12%.

(a) Should you accept the Astracorp contract or the Kabelworld contract? (Hint: base your decision on the PV of cash flows.)

(b) If Astracorp allows you to pay the installation fee in 24 equal monthly payments of $30, at the end of each month, does this change your decision in **(a)**?

(c) Assume that Astracorp has just advised you that you have to pay a $240 fee to check and align the satellite dish (antenna) in 12 months time. Will this change your decision?

18-19 (*Hire-purchase analysis and decision*) LHP Ltd is a company whose shareholders are unable to enjoy imputation tax credits. The company can buy a new $100 000 piece of equipment with an estimated life of four years, with depreciation on a straight-line basis and an estimated disposal value of $10 000. The company's bank is willing to finance the asset with a loan at 8% p.a. As an alternative to the bank loan, the equipment manufacturer can arrange a hire-purchase agreement with instalments of $24 306 at the beginning of each year for four years, followed by a balloon payment of 20% of the asset value at the end of the fourth year. Should LHP buy the asset with the help of the bank loan or take the hire-purchase agreement?

Case study

Working in the corporate advisory division of Truss Loan/Finance Consultants (TLC), you have been asked to brief your boss about a client, AstarCorp, which is seeking to raise $50 million finance for a five-year term. In the past, Astar has relied mainly on its bank for debt finance, but you figure that the company would satisfy the listing requirements under the new government rules for corporate bond issues. Although Astar does not have a bond rating, TLC's bond division estimates that the company would be able to succeed if it offered a 2.2% p.a. yield premium above the relevant yield on federal government bonds (see the AAA rating table, below). In this respect, the manager of the bond division estimates that issue costs for a bond 'float' would cost $1 503 000 plus any underwriting fees. Your firm is willing to act as underwriter for a fee of 1% of the face value (which is based on the standard amount it charges for a bond issue of this size).

MATURITY	AAA YIELD*
1 year	5.1%
3 years	5.2%
5 years	5.3%
10 years	6%

* Expressed as a nominal annual interest rate.

Astar's bankers, WhoBank, had previously been approached directly by the company about obtaining a new loan. At the time, they quoted an *APR* of 9%. On the company's behalf, you have since re-contacted the bank and (knowing that they now have potential competition) they have offered to drop the rate to 8.5%. You have told them that this offer might be accepted, as long as the bank agrees to an 'interest-only' loan with half-yearly interest payments (that is, the principal is paid in full at maturity, just like a bond).

1. Your boss has now asked you to prepare some data to be incorporated into a PowerPoint presentation that he will use to advise Astar of TLC's recommendations. In this regard, you have decided to prepare the following three sets of data:

   (a) Two timelines, showing all the cash flows for the two alternatives: (i) a bond issue, and (ii) a bank loan (in relation to this loan, you have just received a disclosure statement from the bank which advises that WhoBank charges an 'application and documentation' fee of $989 000 payable at the time of loan settlement).

   (b) An analysis of the expected cost of the bond issue. (In this regard, your firm's bond department has recommended underwriting because the market's reaction to Astar is untested.)

   (c) An analysis of the cost of the loan.

2. It is quite possible that Astar could see a potential conflict of interest for your firm. Why is this so? How could your boss propose to overcome any fears that Astar might have in this regard?

Notes

1. Professor Niall Ferguson, 'Human Bondage', episode 2, *The Ascent of Money*, BBC Worldwide Limited, 2009.
2. A simplified description of a hedge fund is that it is an investment mechanism that combines investors' funds with borrowed money to take a position in assets such as securities or commodities.
3. John C. Hull, *Fundamentals of Futures and Options Markets*, 7th edn, Pearson, Boston, 2011, p. 192.
4. ibid., p. 196.
5. ibid., p. 192.
6. *The Weekend Australian*, 29–30 January 2011.
7. *The Role of Structured Investment Vehicles in the Recent Financial Crisis*, www.economistsview.typepad.com/...2007/09/the-role-of-str.html (accessed 11 September 2010).
8. As discussed previously in Chapter 7, *commercial paper* is the US-derived term for what is traditionally called a *promissory note* in Australia.
9. *So What is a Structured Investment Vehicle (SIV) Anyway?*, http://hubpages.com/hub/So-What-Is-a-Structured-Investment-Vehicle-Anyway (accessed 15 September 2010).
10. *The Role of Structured Investment Vehicles in the Recent Financial Crisis*, op. cit.
11. One of the main motives for the development of securitisation was that it enabled banks to shift loan assets 'off balance sheet' by selling the cash flows (and attendant risks) to the SPVs, the latter not being subject to the same stringent regulatory rules as banks. In particular (simplifying the picture somewhat), banks were required to underpin assets with 8% 'capital', which included equity and was costlier than debt funds. In contrast, putting the loans in an SPV did not have to satisfy any regulatory requirements (although the banks needed to contribute some funds to provide the equity tranche, this amount was less than the required on-balance-sheet capital).
12. With sub-prime loss exposures being widespread among banks and other financial institutions, but such losses not being in the public domain, there was a loss of trust, as a result of which one institution would be unwilling to lend to another. This was one part of the global liquidity squeeze. In addition, bank guarantees of SIV liquidity reputedly put further strains on cash markets.
13. Editorial, *The Weekend Australian*, 29–30 January 2011.
14. ibid.
15. 'Acquiring funds gets even harder', *The Australian Financial Review*, 8–9 May 2010.

Appendix

OBJECTIVE **8**

Evaluate lease versus loan finance.

Introduction to lease finance

In financial markets where leasing is a significant form of finance, it is used to acquire the use of a large variety of assets, ranging from a humble photocopier to a fleet of jet aircraft. Motor cars and trucks dominate the leasing scene. Other important categories of leasing include construction equipment, manufacturing equipment, agricultural machinery, computing equipment, and shop and office fittings and equipment.

The user of leased goods or property is known as the *lessee*. The lessee enters into an agreement to make lease payments or rentals to the *lessor*, in return for which the lessor allows the lessee to use the leased property. The lessor is thus both financier and legal owner of the property. In contrast, under a term loan the borrower is the owner and the lender's rights to the property may extend only to its use as collateral. Significant industry groups of lessees include property services, transport, manufacturing, retailing, construction and agriculture. A lease may be negotiated directly with a lessor, such as a bank or finance company, or a finance broker may bring together the lessor and the lessee.

Lease payments are generally payable 'in advance', that is, at the beginning of each period, whereas term loan payments are generally payable at the end of each period. There are other points of departure, too. A lease is for a specific asset or group of assets, whereas a term loan may be used to finance a particular asset or it may be used for general purposes. Often a lease will finance 100% of the cost of the asset. This is not necessarily the case for a term loan.

The following sections distinguish between the different types of lease, briefly review the history and accounting treatment of leases, and explain how they work.

TYPES OF LEASE ARRANGEMENTS

It is customary to distinguish between *finance leases* and *operating leases*. A **finance lease** (also known as a *capital lease*) is an agreement in which the lessee incurs most of the risks and enjoys most of the benefits of ownership. The lease is non-cancellable and the lessee is often responsible for maintenance. The sum of the repayments exceeds the value of the leased property (just as a term loan's total repayments exceed the sum borrowed), which means that there is an interest charge. In this form, the lease is essentially another form of lending by the lessor and a clear substitute for some other debt borrowing on the part of the lessee. In contrast, an **operating lease** is generally cancellable on giving of specified notice and so is often regarded as short term or temporary in nature. This appendix is concerned mainly with finance leases.

FINANCE LEASES

As mentioned above, a finance lease is in many cases a clear substitute for loan borrowing to finance an asset, since the lessee faces an interest cost that arises from the fact that the sum of the repayments exceeds the value of the leased property. Usually, finance leases are at a fixed interest rate and thus have fixed repayments. Also, customarily the regular periodic instalments on a lease are payable at the beginning of each period rather than at the end (as is the case with a term loan). It will be recalled from Chapter 4 that an annuity payable at the beginning of each period is called an *annuity due*. The workings of an annuity due are reviewed in Example 18.A1, which also shows how to determine the interest rate. As is also shown in Example 18.A1, a finance lease typically includes a lump-sum balloon payment at the end of the lease term, known as the **residual value**. On payment of this residual value, it is often the case that the lessor will accept the lessee's offer for transfer of ownership of the asset. Determining the interest rate on a lease contract is outlined in Example 18.A1.

---

finance lease
A non-cancellable contractual commitment on the part of the firm leasing the asset (the lessee) to make a series of payments to the firm that actually owns the asset (the lessor) for the use of the asset.

operating lease
A contractual commitment on the part of the firm leasing the asset (the lessee) to make a series of payments to the firm that actually owns the asset (the lessor) for the use of the asset. An operating lease differs from a financial lease in that it can be cancelled at any time after proper notice has been given to the lessor.

residual value
The final lump-sum or balloon payment on a lease.

EXAMPLE 18.A1   Determining the interest rate on a finance lease

Let us suppose that there is an asset worth $15 000 that has been financed by means of a finance lease. The lessor requires the lessee to make instalments of $2618.19 at the beginning of each of five years (thus forming an *annuity due*). These annual instalments are followed by a *residual value* of $6000 at the end of the fifth year. This pattern of cash flows is identical to that of the hire-purchase agreement outlined in Example 18.8 (except that the balloon payment is called 'residual value' in the case of a lease), and thus the interest rate is 9% per annum, as determined in Example 18.8. Similarly, the figures in the relevant *lease amortisation schedule* are identical to the figures in Table 18.6.

LEASE PAYMENTS AND THE GST

At the time of the introduction of the Australian goods and services tax (GST), *The Australian Financial Review* (4 June 1999) remarked that 'there appears to be a clear bias in favour of hire-purchase or borrowing over leasing'. This belief was based on the fact that lease instalments attract the GST. In contrast, payments on a term loan or a bond or hire-purchase are free of the GST. This is because, under the GST legislation, they are classified as 'financial services', which are exempt from the GST. However, lease instalments are classified as a 'supply' and so the GST is applicable to them. The way this works is that a 10% GST component is added to the net amount of the instalments. For example, the lessee of the Example 18.A1 lease would actually pay the lessor annual instalments of $2880.01, consisting of the following components:

Net amount of lease instalment	$2618.19
Plus GST (10%)	261.82
Total payment to lessor	$2880.01

However, business enterprises that are registered for GST purposes can claim a refund of the GST component of relevant lease instalments. In such a case, the Example 18.A1 lessee would pay $2880.01 upfront and then subsequently claim a refund of the $261.82 GST component, meaning that the net amount of the lease payment would be $2618.19. Consequently, apart from a small timing difference between paying the GST as a component of a lease instalment and subsequently claiming the refund (which typically will be three or more months later), the GST can be ignored for decision-making purposes. Nevertheless, the fact that other forms of debt do not involve payment of the GST has made leasing an unattractive proposition in Australia.

ACCOUNTING FOR LEASES

The accounting treatment of leases is governed by Australian accounting standards, which are incorporated into legislative reporting requirements by the Accounting Standards Review Board (ASRB). Among other things, lessees are required to bring finance leases into the balance sheet, reporting both a *lease asset* (in the form of the goods or property used) and a *lease liability* (in the form of the debt obligation to the lessor).

To be classified as a *finance lease*, the primary test is that the lease effectively transfers from the lessor to the lessee substantially all the risks and benefits incident to ownership of the leased property. Such an effective transfer of ownership is deemed to occur if:

(a) the lease is non-cancellable, and
(b) either of the following tests is met:
  (i) the lease term is for 75% or more of the useful life of the leased property
  (ii) the present value, at the beginning of the lease term, of the minimum lease payments equals or exceeds 90% of the fair value of the leased property to the lessor at the inception of the lease.

As mentioned above, a finance lease will implicitly pass the test in (b)(ii) because it incorporates an interest element. Any lease that does not meet the finance lease test is automatically classified as an *operating lease*.

The lessee's reporting of a leased asset is matched, at the time the lease is taken out, by an equal but opposite lease liability. Subsequently, the debt owing on the lease liability is reported at the end of each accounting period (as shown in the relevant amortisation schedule) and the lease asset is 'depreciated' in the manner that would be appropriate to that asset if it was owned legally by the lessee.

THE LEASE OR BUY DECISION

The primary decision to acquire or invest in an asset will be based on criteria discussed in Chapters 11 and 12. If an investment has a positive net present value (NPV), estimated by discounting its net cash flows at the cost of capital, it is worth acquiring the asset. However, this does not, in itself, tell us whether it is better to finance the use of the asset by means of a lease or by buying the asset using some other borrowing.

How, then, is it possible to determine whether to lease or to borrow (buy)? One approach is to estimate, in present-value dollars, the consequences for wealth. Suppose that, by agreeing to repay $110 000 at the end of a year, you are offered a kind of 'lease' that enables you to obtain the use of goods worth $100 000. So, the value obtained now—your present value of leasing (*PVL*)—is $100 000. Alternatively, if you offer an identical repayment amount of $110 000 to a lender, the lender will advance a loan of $98 000 for one year, enabling you to purchase goods of that value. This amount of $98 000 is the present value of borrowing (*PVB*). Clearly, in this case you appear to be $2000 better off by leasing. To you, the net advantage of this lease is $2000. More generally, the net advantage of leasing (*NAL*) is defined as follows:

$$NAL = PVL - PVB$$

DETERMINING THE NET ADVANTAGE OF LEASING (NAL)

In order to determine the *NAL*, it is necessary to identify the *PVL* and the *PVB*. From the previous example, it is relatively easy to identify the *PVL*; it is simply equal to the present value of the future lease cash flows. It is the upfront value that the lessor delivers to you when you undertake the lease. In the above case, since the lessor provides an upfront value of $100 000 in return for you agreeing to make the future lease payment, the *PVL* is $100 000.

What about the *PVB*? As shown when term loans were discussed earlier in this chapter, the amount that you can borrow on any loan is just the present value of the future payments. So, if you discount the future *lease* cash flows at the interest rate that you would otherwise have to pay on a *loan*, this tells you how much the lender would be willing to lend you if your future *loan* cash-flow commitments (payments) were identical to those on an alternative lease.

For example, suppose that a lender charges 12.24% on loans. This means that if you agree to repay $110 000 in a year's time the lender will lend you $98 000, which is the present value of that $110 000:

$$\$110\,000/(1 + i) = \$110\,000/(1.1224) = \$98\,000$$

This sum of $98 000 therefore represents the *present value of borrowing* (*PVB*)—the amount that could be *borrowed* in return for future payments identical to those required on the lease. Thus, as previously identified:

$$NAL = PVL - PVB = \$100\,000 - \$98\,000 = \$2000$$

It might seem that this is a convoluted way of going about a simple task. But we will soon see that it is necessary to have a clear understanding of how to measure the *PVL* and the *PVB* in order to identify the *NAL*.

The relevance of the firm's taxation position

The way of going about lease evaluation depends on the firm's taxation position. In previous chapters, starting in Chapter 2, the general argument was developed that financial decision making falls into three main taxation categories. A summary of these categories, for capital-budgeting purposes, is found in Chapter 11 and that summary should be revisited for more detail. Briefly, the three taxation categories (which are also relevant to lease evaluation) are:

- *Taxation category 1: Companies that are well-integrated with the dividend imputation tax system.* Lease evaluation should be on the basis of pre-tax cash flows.
- *Taxation category 2: Companies that are not integrated with the dividend imputation tax system, as well as non-company businesses such as sole traders and partnerships.* Lease-evaluation should be on the basis of after-tax cash flows (using the statutory tax rate for a company, or using the business owner(s) marginal tax rate for a sole trader or partnership).
- *Taxation category 3: Companies that are partially integrated with the dividend imputation tax system.* Evaluation should be on the basis of after-effective-tax cash flows.

Following are more comprehensive examples of lease evaluation, first on the basis of pre-tax cash flows, and then on the basis of after-tax cash flows.

Lease evaluation for a taxation category 1 firm (based on pre-tax cash flows)

The immediate objective is to determine the *NAL*, which is equal to *PVL – PVB*. It will be recalled that measurement of *PVL* and *PVB* involves the following procedures:

PVL = present value of future lease cash flows = upfront value of the lease
PVB = present value of lease payments, discounted at the *loan* interest rate

In the following examples of lease evaluation, the analysis is simplified by showing the lease payments net of GST (i.e. the payments are shown at the amount of $2618.19, which excludes the GST component). An illustration of lease evaluation is given in Example 18.A2.

EXAMPLE 18.A2   Net advantage of leasing—pre-tax cash flows

Assume that a firm in taxation category 1 wants to choose between the lease first shown in Example 18.A1 (whose amortisation is shown in Table 18.6) and the loan first shown in the main body of this chapter as Example 18.4 (and amortised in Table 18.4).

The *PVL* is represented by the upfront value of the lease, in other words the value of the leased property, which is $15 000.

To determine the *PVB*, the lease payments need to be discounted at the *loan* interest rate. These lease payments are set out on the following timeline:

Year 1	Year 2	Year 3	Year 4	Year 5	
$2618.19	$2618.19	$2618.19	$2618.19	$2618.19	$6000

Using equation (4-20) plus equation (4-5), the total present value of the *annuity-due* lease payments plus the residual value, when discounted at the loan interest rate of 8%, is given by:

$$2618.19\left\{1 + \frac{[1 - (1.08)^{-4}]}{.08}\right\} + \$6000(1.08)^{-5}$$

$$= \$15\,373.50 = PVB$$

From the above timeline, the total present value of the lease payments can be split into two components:

1. *Present value of the lease instalments.* This is represented by equation (4-21) as $2618.19(1 + PVIFA_{8\%,4})$
2. *Present value of the residual payment.* This is represented by equation (4-6) as $6000(PVIF_{8\%,5})$.

Adding together these two components gives the *PVB*. That is,

$$PVB = \$2618.19(1 + PVIFA_{8\%,4}) + \$6000(PVIF_{8\%,5})$$

Using the end-of-book Appendixes D and B respectively, the total present value therefore equals:

$$\$2618.19(1 + 3.312) + \$6000(0.681) = \$11\,289.64 + \$4083.60$$

$$= \$15\,373.24 = PVB$$

From the calculator solution opposite, the *PVB* is 15 373.47.

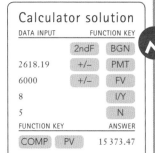

Calculator solution

DATA INPUT		FUNCTION KEY
	2ndF	BGN
2618.19	+/−	PMT
6000	+/−	FV
8		I/Y
5		N
FUNCTION KEY		ANSWER
COMP	PV	15 373.47

Therefore, the net advantage to leasing, *NAL*, is given by:

$$NAL = PVL - PVB = \$15\,000 - \$15\,373.50 = -\$373.50$$

The fact that *NAL* is *negative* in Example 18.A2 indicates that the loan is preferable to the lease. That is, a loan with future repayments identical to the lease payments would enable you to borrow $373.50 more than the proceeds of the lease.

It is worth observing that, in this case, you would obtain the same decision based on the respective interest rates—the loan's interest rate is 8%, whereas that of the lease is 9%. What the *NAL* identifies, however, is *how much* better off (or worse off, in this case) you are by leasing as opposed to borrowing.

The effect of non-interest costs on lease evaluation
Lease evaluation may be affected by other *non-interest* costs. For instance, suppose that the Example 18.4 loan, from earlier in this chapter, involved a $400 establishment fee that did not apply to the lease. Other things being equal, this would negate the advantage of borrowing; its advantage of +$373.50 would become −$26.50. Allowance also needs to be made for any other non-interest costs that differ between leasing and purchasing. For example, it is customary to require the lessee to pay maintenance under a finance lease; but, if the lessor agreed to pay it, this would have to be incorporated into the evaluation. For instance, if the lessor in Example 18.A2 agreed to pay maintenance of $40 per annum, this would in effect reduce each annual lease instalment to $2578.19, so reducing the *PVB* to $15 200.98.[1]

Lease evaluation for a taxation category 2 firm
(based on the firm's after-tax cash flows)
A company that is not integrated with the imputation tax system falls into taxation category 2 and so it is appropriate to base the lease evaluation on the company's *after-tax* cash flows. This is true also of a non-company business such as a sole trader or a partnership. The above $15 000 lease and loan will again be used as the basis for comparison. The objective, as before, will be

to determine the value of the cash flows associated with the lease, but this time on an after-tax basis. To determine the present value of borrowing (*PVB*), Example 18.A3 will again discount the lease cash flows at the interest rate on the loan, but this time an after-tax loan interest rate must be used for consistency with the after-tax cash flows.[2]

EXAMPLE 18.A3   Net advantage of leasing—after-tax cash flows

Assume that a firm in taxation category 2 wants to choose between the lease first shown in Example 18.A1 (whose amortisation is shown in Table 18.6) and the loan first shown in Example 18.4 (and amortised in Table 18.4). In order to make the analysis more realistic in an after-tax context, the following assumptions will be made:

- The firm is not a company, and its profits are taxed at the owner's personal tax rate of 47 cents in the dollar. (If the firm was organised as a company, the evaluation would be exactly the same as is shown here, except that the statutory company tax rate, *T*, would be substituted for the rate of 47% used in this example.)
- The leased asset is depreciated by the straight-line (prime-cost) method down to a book value of $1500 at the end of the lease term, with an estimated disposal value of $9000.
- The lessee makes an offer to take ownership of the asset at the end of the lease term, and the lessor accepts this offer in return for receipt of the final lease payment (the residual value).

To assist in the development of a methodology for lease evaluation on an after-tax basis, a five-step process for determining the *NAL* is presented.

Step 1: Identify the direct lease cash flows
'Direct lease cash flows' are defined here as the cash flows that arise directly from taking out and repaying the lease (as well as their tax consequences), along with the effects of disposing of the leased asset if the lessee takes ownership of the asset at the end of the lease term. These cash flows are listed as items 1 to 4 in Table 18.A1.

Before proceeding, when interpreting Table 18.A1 it should be noted that most lease cash flows occur at the beginning of the relevant period. For example, the second lease instalment is at the beginning of year 2; this time is essentially the same as the end of period 1. Therefore the cash flow at the beginning of year 2 is shown at *t* = 1, because this cash flow needs to be discounted back only one period to find its present value.

TABLE 18.A1   Lease cash flows, after tax

	t = 0 BEGINNING YEAR 1 $	t = 1 BEGINNING YEAR 2 $	t = 2 BEGINNING YEAR 3 $	t = 3 BEGINNING YEAR 4 $	t = 4 BEGINNING YEAR 5 $	t = 5 END YEAR 5 $	t = 6 END YEAR 6 $
Direct lease cash flows:							
1. Proceeds of lease	+15000.00						
2. Lease payments	−2618.19	−2618.19	−2618.19	−2618.19	−2618.19	−6000.00	
3. Tax benefits from payments		+1230.55	+1230.55	+1230.55	+1230.55	+1230.55	
4. Tax payable on disposal of leased asset at profit							−1410.00
Indirect cash flows:							
5. Depreciation tax benefits forgone		−1269.00	−1269.00	−1269.00	−1269.00	−1269.00	
6. Tax avoided on disposal of depreciated asset at profit							+3525.00
Upfront benefit (PVL)	+12381.81						
Future cash flows		−2656.64	−2656.64	−2656.64	−2656.64	−6038.45	+2115.00

Note: The end of one year is identical mathematically to the beginning of the following year.

The first numbered item shown in Table 18.A1 is the gross proceeds of the lease—the cash 'inflow' of $15 000 that represents the value of the leased asset.

The second item is the lease payments, $2618.19 per year at the beginning of each of five years (i.e. the first payment is due when the lease is taken out). These regular payments are followed by the residual value of $6000 payable at the end of year 5.

The third item is the tax benefit arising from the lease payments. A lessee may claim the amount of any lease instalments or rentals (excluding the residual) as a tax deduction. Thus, each lease instalment represents a tax deduction of $2618.19, so tax payable will be reduced by $1230.55 per year (47% of $2618.19). The benefits of tax deductions have been treated as occurring a year after the relevant item to which they relate. This is somewhat debatable, but it will suffice as a simplifying assumption. (The timing of tax payments was discussed in Chapter 2.)

The fourth item relates to the tax consequences of selling the leased asset. This asset was acquired by making the residual payment of $6000. If the asset is sold for $9000, there is therefore a taxable gain of $3000. Assuming for simplicity that this gain is taxed at the owner's full tax rate, $3000 taxable gain will increase the amount of tax payable by $1410 (47% of $3000).

Step 2: Identify the indirect lease cash flows
It was argued in Chapters 11 and 12 that financial evaluation must include allowance for *opportunity costs*.[3] In the same way, there may be opportunity costs associated with leasing, because leasing means that the lessee is forgoing the benefits and costs of ownership. The opportunity costs that arise from the above lease are listed in Table 18.A1 as items 5 and 6, explained below:

The fifth item is depreciation tax benefits forgone. The asset cost $15 000 and is depreciated down to $1500 after five years, so annual depreciation is $2700 ($13 500/5). This depreciation is a tax deduction, the benefit of which is to reduce the tax payable by $1269 per year (47% of $2700). However, the lessee is not the owner, and therefore forgoes this tax benefit. This is an opportunity cost of leasing and so it is shown as a lease cash outflow (i.e. a cash flow of –$1269 per year).

The sixth item is tax avoided on the sale of the depreciated asset. If the asset had been purchased rather than leased, and was sold for its estimated disposal value of $9000, there would have been a taxable gain of $7500 ($9000 minus the book value of $1500). This would have added $3525 to the owner's tax payable (47% of $7500). However, the lessee avoids having to make this payment, so it is an 'opportunity benefit' of leasing and is thus shown as a lease cash inflow (+$3525).

Note: You might also expect to see the $9000 cash proceeds of disposal of the asset listed in Table 18.A1. This could be done, but the amount of $9000 is common to both the lease alternative and the purchase alternative, so this cash flow is not incremental. (Remember from Chapters 11 and 12 that only incremental cash flows are relevant to financial evaluation.) And you might expect to see the forgone loan payments and their tax effects listed as an indirect effect of leasing; however, the effects of the loan are incorporated into the after-tax loan interest rate that is used to compute the *PVB*, which is dealt with in step 4.

Step 3: Determine the present value of leasing (PVL)
The *PVL* is the upfront value received by the lessee. This is the net cash flow at $t = 0$. As shown in the second-last line of Table 18.A1, this amount is $12 381.81. Note that this is not actually the same as the value of the leased equipment ($15 000). The reason for this is clear: at $t = 0$ the first instalment on the lease, which is a cash outflow of $2618.19, occurs at the same time as the value of $15 000 is received, so the net cash inflow at that time is +$12 381.81.

Step 4: Determine the present value of borrowing (PVB)
To determine the *PVB*, the *future* net cash flows of the lease need to be discounted at the loan interest rate. These future cash flows, after tax, are shown in the final line of Table 18.A1. For

consistency, the loan interest rate, too, must be expressed on an after-tax basis. The pre-tax loan interest rate is 8% (as shown in Example 18.4), so the after-tax rate is 4.24% (which equals 8%(1 – 0.47)). The calculation of the *PVB* now follows. (Note that in this computation the intention is to show the initial cash value that would be received via the loan, so algebraic cash-flow signs from the final line of Table 18.A1 have been reversed in such a way that the *PVB* amount emerges as a positive cash flow.)

$$PVB = \frac{\$2656.64}{(1.0424)} + \frac{\$2656.64}{(1.0424)^2} + \frac{\$2656.64}{(1.0424)^3} + \frac{\$2656.64}{(1.0424)^4} + \frac{\$6038.45}{(1.0424)^5} - \frac{\$2115.00}{(1.0424)^6}$$

$$= \$12\,846.76$$

Step 5: Compute the net advantage of leasing (NAL)

$$NAL = PVL - PVB = \$12\,381.81 - \$12\,846.76 = -\$464.95$$

The amount of the *PVL* is –$464.95. This means that, on an after-tax basis, there is an advantage to purchasing of $464.95. Put another way, the firm could borrow an extra $464.95 via a term loan if the firm outlaid the same after-tax future cash flows as are required to service the lease. So the loan appears to be the better alternative.

Concluding note concerning the tax rate
The lease evaluation in Table 18.A1 is for a taxation category 2 firm that is not organised as a company, so the tax computations in the table are based on the assumed 47% marginal personal tax rate of the firm's owner(s). However, if the firm had instead been a company that was not integrated with the dividend imputation tax system, the relevant tax rate would have been the company's statutory tax rate, T (at the time of writing, 30%).

Calculator solution		
DATA INPUT		FUNCTION KEY
Reset to NORMAL mode, then:		
	CFi 2ndF	CA
0		ENT
2656.64		ENT
2656.64		ENT
2656.64		ENT
2656.64		ENT
6038.45		ENT
2115.00	+/–	ENT
	2ndF	CASH
RATE (I/Y) = 4.24		ENT
		▼
FUNCTION KEY		ANSWER
NPV_PV = COMP		12 846.76

Lease evaluation for a taxation category 3 firm (based on the effective company tax rate)

If a company is only partially integrated with the dividend imputation tax system, it falls into taxation category 3. In this case, lease evaluation should be based on the firm's cash flows after *effective* tax. For example, if the firm conducting the evaluation in Table 18.A1 was a company with an effective tax rate, T_{eff}, of, say, 20% (as opposed to the statutory tax rate, T, of 30%), this effective tax rate would be used for all the tax computations in the table.

INTERACTION BETWEEN LEASING AND INVESTMENT DECISION

The decision to acquire an asset is based on its net present value, obtained by discounting the expected cash flows at the cost of capital, as discussed in Chapters 11 to 14. However, it is possible that the decision to reject an asset investment may be reversed if the *NAL* is sufficiently great. For example, assume that an asset's NPV of purchasing, *NPV(P)*, is –$5000, indicating that the investment is not warranted. However, suppose now that the *NAL* is +$12 000. This suggests that, if the asset is leased, its acquisition is now warranted because the combined amount of the *NAL* plus the *NPV(P)* is greater than zero, namely +$7000. Drawing on this notion, the flowchart in Figure 18.A1 can be used to perform lease–purchase analysis.

Tracing the left-hand branch of Figure 18.A1, if the *NPV(P)* is positive, the asset should be acquired and it should then be leased only if *NAL* is also positive; otherwise, it should be bought outright.

The right-hand branch deals with the initial *NAL* being negative, in which case the decision to reject the investment is not altered. However, if *NAL* is positive, it should be added to the (negative) *NPV(P)*, and if the combined amount is positive the asset should be acquired by leasing; otherwise it should be rejected.

FIGURE 18.A1 Lease–purchase analysis

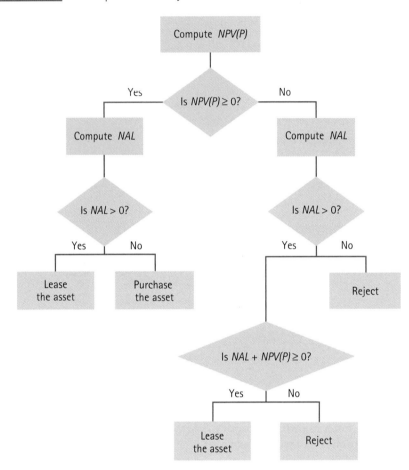

LEASING DISPLACES DEBT

The above approach to lease evaluation is based on the assumption that the firm maintains a target capital structure. Accordingly, if a lease is arranged, it is necessary to displace an equivalent amount of debt so as to preserve the target capital structure. For example, suppose that a company has $10 million of debt and $10 million of equity, representing a debt–equity ratio of 1:1. If it took out a $1 million lease, it would have to sacrifice $1 million other debt in order to maintain its 1:1 debt–equity ratio.

The necessity to compare like with like

In order to validly conclude that the *NAL* represents the financial advantage or disadvantage of leasing, it must be assumed that the lease cash flows are of similar risk to the loan cash flows. Otherwise, the *apparent* advantage may simply reflect different risks. For example, assume that the amount of the residual payment on the lease was not guaranteed by the lessee under the lease contract, but was instead based on the value of the leased asset at the end of the lease term. In that event, the financier would be comparing a fixed cash-flow stream for the loan (whose contractual repayments are specified in the loan contract) with an uncertain cash-flow stream for the lease (the amount of the lease residual payment being based on an uncertain future asset value).

Another aspect of the need to compare like with like is that the lease must have similar debt characteristics to the loan. For example, they must be of the same term and both must have a fixed interest rate (or both a variable or floating rate with a similar 'base'). If this was not the case, there would be spill-over effects that would limit the validity of the apparent *NAL*. For instance, how could you validly compare a variable-rate loan with a fixed-rate lease?

POTENTIAL BENEFITS FROM LEASING

The competitive situation is likely to ensure that the 'price' of leasing and loans is similar in financial markets where leasing is significant. Otherwise, there would be little demand for the uncompetitive form of financing. An exception might arise if the lessor (as legal owner) could take advantage of tax benefits that were denied to the lessee (e.g. because the lessee had a low tax rate relative to the lessor). In such a case, the lessor could in effect split these tax benefits with the lessee by lowering the 'price' of the lease.

In the example of cash flows presented in Table 18.A1 there appears to be an advantage in favour of borrowing. That is, the *NAL* is negative. The main reason for this is that the loan was priced more cheaply—its pre-tax interest rate of 8% was 1% less than the lease rate of 9%. Why would the lease be priced differently from the loan, thus appearing to give the loan a financial advantage in the form of a negative *NAL*? The different price might reflect different risk perceptions by the financier. For instance, the leased asset might be of a specialised nature that makes it of little use to anyone other than the current lessee, and the financier might believe that the funds could be better secured by loan covenants and collateral rather than a lease (where the asset is often the only security). Accordingly, the financier is indeed likely to price the lease higher. The problem here is that the *apparent* financial advantage of the loan might simply reflect this risk differential—the borrower can have 'cheaper' loan finance, but at the 'cost' of accepting covenants and assets tied up as security.

Although lease evaluation might become more difficult as a result of such factors, there might be objective grounds for an advantage to leasing. For example, a leasing company might have specific skills and expertise in managing a particular type of asset, backed up by high-quality management systems. This lessor might also be able to gain economies of scale from high-volume purchases of the asset. A case in point is motor vehicle *fleet management*, where the lessor not only claims special skills in managing fleets but can also purchase vehicles in volume, at a lower unit price than could an individual purchaser. (Some reports suggest that fleet purchasers can obtain discounts of about $3000 on popular makes of six-cylinder vehicles, representing about 10% of the vehicle cost.) The upshot is that the lessor may have genuine advantages that it can pass on to the lessee in the form of favourable lease payments. In any event, it is the lessee's *perception* of the advantage of leasing that counts, even if the financial benefits are not obvious or are difficult to isolate and quantify. Fleet management firms emphasise the services that they provide. The selling point is: 'All you have to do is fill the car with petrol.'

There are many other, non-financial, reasons that have been advanced in favour of leasing. When reading about them in the following sections, bear in mind that a lessee acquires the use of an asset via an *intermediary*, the lessor. In a sense, the lessee is appointing the lessor to act as an agent to acquire the asset on behalf of the lessee. The basic question that arises from this is: 'Why does adding another financial intermediary (the lessor) save the lessee money?' Remember that, for the lease to be 'cheaper' than owning, the lessor must be able to perform the functions of ownership at a lower cost than the lessee could perform them, and be willing to pass these savings on to the lessee in the form of lower rental rates or to provide other services that have genuine value to the lessee.

Flexibility and convenience

It is argued that leasing is more *flexible* and easier to arrange than borrowing. Leasing is suited to the piecemeal acquisition of relatively small assets, which can be acquired quickly and with less documentation than is required for a loan. Another argument is that a divisional manager may be able to arrange a lease without the time-consuming process of preparing a formal asset-acquisition proposal and submitting it to someone higher in the organisational hierarchy. A third argument is that lease payments may be structured to coincide with the revenues

generated by the asset. For example, an asset with a relatively long period of low productivity could be financed by a lease with low instalments and a relatively large residual value.

Arguments in favour of the *convenience* of leasing take many forms, too. Such arguments relate, for example, to the way leasing avoids the documentation associated with ownership and the need to prepare records such as depreciation schedules. Also, the lessor may arrange to service and maintain the asset without the necessity for this to be initiated by the lessee. This line of reasoning is that the firm's managers can better spend their time running the firm, leaving the lessor to attend to the chores of ownership. In contemporary business language, the managers can be left free to concentrate on the 'core business' of the firm.

It is difficult to generalise about the validity of the above arguments. For some firms there may be particular benefits from leasing that do not apply to other firms. The benefits and costs of aspects such as documentation will vary from one situation to another. Leasing may have a comparative advantage in situations such as those discussed above, where economies of scale and special skills prevail, or where there are other benefits that the lessee perceives to be of value. On the other hand, some arguments for leasing are countered by the availability of the same benefits on loans—for example, lenders would probably be willing to structure loan-servicing cash flows to suit a firm's revenue pattern if the lessor were willing to do so for a lease.

Lack of restrictions

Unlike loan contracts, leases do not generally contain restrictive covenants. The relevance of this depends on the way the lender perceives the risk, since absence of such protective covenants may mean that the lessor will price the lease higher than a loan. In this case, the lessee must somehow try to evaluate the benefits of a cheaper loan against the costs of the covenants, as discussed above.

Avoidance of risk of obsolescence

This argument may be true of operating leases, which the lessee can cancel. However, it is not valid in the case of finance leases, for the cost of the asset is fully amortised by the lease payments.

A related argument is that a lessor, as owner of the equipment, will maintain it well and keep it in top working condition. Again, this is more likely to be true of operating leases, where the lessor will want to be able to readily re-lease the equipment to another firm if the original lessee cancels the contract. Under most finance leases, the lessee is responsible for the maintenance and servicing of the leased goods.

100% financing

Another alleged benefit of leasing is that it provides a firm with 100% financing; it is pointed out that the borrow-and-buy alternative generally involves a down-payment or deposit, whereas leasing does not. This argument falls down because, in theory, the firm could borrow the down-payment to make up the difference. More fundamentally, given that investors and creditors are reasonably intelligent, it is sensible to conclude that they would consider that similar amounts of lease and debt financing would add equivalent amounts of risk to the firm's capital structure.

Ease of obtaining credit

It is sometimes argued that firms with a poor credit rating can obtain a lease (which depends less on having a 'relationship' with a lender such as a banker) more easily than they can obtain a loan. The validity of this depends on the efficiency with which financiers assess credit risk. A lessor who recognises a lessee's lower credit standing will accordingly increase the price of the lease.

Tax savings

The relevance of tax deductions generated by leasing versus borrowing is restricted to firms where business tax deductions are valued by owners or shareholders, as discussed previously.

In any event, the value of these deductions is a matter that needs to be considered on a case-by-case basis and to be integrated into the overall lease evaluation.

Conservation of working capital

One of the oldest and most widely used arguments in favour of leasing is the assertion that a lease conserves the firm's working capital. The argument is essentially that acquisition of an asset via leasing does not require outlay of the full amount of cash, and so funds are retained in the business. The flaw in this assertion is that borrowings can fund the purchase of the asset, thus 'conserving' cash in any case. A related assertion is that, since leasing often has lower periodic instalments than other forms of debt (arising from the presence of the residual balloon payment), working capital is conserved.

As pointed out above, the lessee's *perception* of the advantages or disadvantages of one form of finance over another may sway the borrowing decision and influence the way in which lessors promote their lease products.

WHY DO FIRMS LEASE?

The decision of a firm to lease or purchase will depend on its *perception* of the merits of one way of acquiring the use of assets over the other. In the case of operating leases (which have been mentioned only briefly above), there may be no argument in favour of purchasing; for example, an asset may be wanted for only a very short time and so a cancellable, operating lease will be preferred. For finance leases, the firm's decision may be based on its size and status as a borrower. For example, in a US study[4], it was found that smaller and financially weaker firms tended to justify the use of lease financing on qualitative grounds such as flexibility, the conservation of working capital, financing restrictions and transferring the risks of obsolescence. On the other hand, larger and financially stronger firms tended to use more formal comparisons of the cost of leasing versus other forms of borrowing. The survey found that lessees based their decisions on the following factors, in decreasing order of importance:

- Implied interest rate
- Threat of obsolescence
- Income taxes
- Flexibility
- Conservation of working capital
- Less restrictive financing.

Summary

In the markets where leasing is significant, this type of finance comes largely from banks and finance companies. The appendix focused on the finance lease, which typically includes an interest element that makes it readily comparable with borrowing. However, lease evaluation is made more complex by factors that are difficult to quantify, such as perceived ownership risks and services that the lessor may perform in lieu of the lessee, thus providing convenience and time-saving benefits to the lessee. Although lease evaluation was presented in a quantifiable way, other factors will affect the lessee's perception of the worth or otherwise of the lease arrangement.

Many of the non-financial benefits ascribed to leasing are fallacious, despite the fact that the lessee may perceive that they have value. Although the lease evaluation may be complex, part of the evaluation should be a financial assessment that estimates the net advantage to leasing (*NAL*). The *NAL* is found by listing all the *direct* lease cash flows (including their tax effect where relevant), as well as the *indirect* cash flows (on an incremental basis, allowing for opportunity costs). These indirect cash flows may include lost depreciation benefits that are only obtained by a purchaser, as well as the effects of any profit on disposal of the asset. The net future cash flows from servicing the lease are discounted at the cost of loan borrowing, giving rise to the present value of borrowing (*PVB*). The net proceeds of the lease are called the present value of leasing (*PVL*). The net advantage to leasing, then, is given by:

$$NAL = PVL - PVB$$

If the *NAL* is positive, it means that leasing is worth more than borrowing. If it is negative, then borrowing is preferred to leasing.

Lease evaluation should be conducted on a pre-tax basis for organisations that do not pay tax and for companies (in taxation category 1) that are well integrated with the dividend imputation tax system. However, evaluation should be on the basis of the company's after-tax cash flows (computed at the nominal or statutory tax rate, T) for taxation category 2 companies that are not integrated with the dividend imputation tax system. (Similarly, lease evaluation should be based on after-tax cash flows, computed at the owners' marginal personal tax rates, for firms that are not organised on a company basis, if their owners pay tax on the firm's profits.) Finally, for category 3 companies that are partially integrated with the imputation tax system, evaluation should be on the basis of after-*effective*-company-tax cash flows, the relevant tax rate being the effective company tax rate, T_{eff}. When estimating the lease cash flows on an after-tax basis, it is necessary to ensure that the tax rate that is used to compute the benefits of tax deductions is consistent with the rate used to compute the after-tax cost of borrowing and the *PVB*.

Key terms

For a complete flashcard glossary go to MyFinanceLab at www.pearson.com.au/myfinancelab

finance lease	**646**
operating lease	**646**
residual value	**646**

Review questions

18-A1 Define each of the following:

(a) Finance lease

(b) Operating lease

18-A2 Is it true that leases are a form of 'off-balance-sheet finance'? How are finance leases disclosed in the financial statements of lessee firms?

18-A3 Discuss the main similarities and differences between hire-purchase and a lease as ways of financing a firm's assets.

ST-A1 (*Analysing a finance lease*) The partnership of Jensen Transport is considering the possibility of leasing a $100 000 truck-servicing facility. This newly developed piece of equipment facilitates the cleaning and servicing of diesel prime-movers used on long-haul trips. A finance company has approached Jensen with an offer to structure a finance lease with a rental charge of $23 982 at the beginning of each of the next five years, with no residual payment.

For answers go to MyFinanceLab
www.pearson.com.au/myfinancelab

  (a) What is the interest rate implicit in this lease?
  (b) Prepare an amortisation schedule.
  (c) Assume that the lease payments are restructured to allow for a residual payment of 20% of the value of the equipment. What would be the annual instalment, assuming that the interest rate is the same as in **(a)**?
  (d) Determine the interest and principal components of the lease in **(c)**.
  (e) What would be the effect on the cost of the lease in **(a)** if the lessor charged a $500 'arrangement fee' for providing the finance?

ST-A2 (*Lease versus purchase analysis*) The partners of Jensen Transport have been offered a loan at an interest rate of 12% p.a., as an alternative to the lease analysed in ST-A1 **(a)**. In addition, the lessors have done a 'fleet purchase' deal with the truck suppliers and, as a result of their bulk-buying savings, they are willing to pass on some benefits by including insurance and maintenance (worth $4000 annually, payable 'in advance') as an incentive to take out the lease. The partners have approached you for advice as to whether they should lease or borrow, given the following additional information (assume that tax savings are realised at the time the underlying transaction occurs):

Useful life of equipment	5 years
Salvage value (estimated)	$0
Depreciation method	straight-line
Marginal tax rate of partners	47%
Cost of capital (based on target debt/total-asset ratio of 30%)	16%

  (a) Determine the net advantage of leasing the equipment. Where does most of this advantage come from?
  (b) Should Jensen lease the equipment?
  (c) Assume that Jensen is a company that pays its profits as franked dividends, with ordinary Australian residents as shareholders. What is the *NAL*?

18-A1 (*Lease analysis*) Newlife Gymnasium wishes to arrange finance for a new set of equipment that will cost $280 000 fully installed. The lease interest rate quoted by a finance company is 12% p.a. for a term of four years, with payments at the beginning of each year, and with a residual value of 35% of the cost payable at the end of the term.

For more problems and for answers to problems marked with an asterisk (*) go to MyFinanceLab at
www.pearson.com.au/myfinancelab

  (a) What will be the payment pattern on this lease?
  (b) Determine the annual interest and principal components of the lease.
  (c) If the finance company is willing to pay the annual service cost for the equipment, valued at $1438 annually (at the beginning of each year), what effect will this have on the interest cost of the lease in **(a)**?

18-A2* (*Lease analysis*) Hacme Leasing Company is willing to arrange a lease on behalf of Myponga Abattoir for its new $1 million meat-packing equipment that is necessary to enable it to fill an export contract. A finance lease can be arranged for a term of four years, with half-yearly payments of $127 407 each, starting at the time the lease contract is signed, followed by a residual payment of $200 000 at the end of the lease term.

  (a) What is the effective interest rate on the lease?
  (b) Determine the half-yearly interest and principal components of the lease payments.

(c) Assume that Hacme has to pay $10 000 in government duties for registration of the lease. This would not have to be paid on alternative borrowings. What is the effect on the cost of the lease?

18-A3 (*Lease versus buy evaluation*) Mountain Springs, a partnership operated by the Von Trapp family, is contemplating the purchase of a new computer and software to help prepare delivery schedules and accounts-receivable billing for its deliveries of spring water to customers. The total cost of the system is $80 000 and it will last four years, at which time its estimated disposal value is $20 000. The firm uses the straight-line depreciation method and it plans to depreciate the system to its expected disposal value. The partners think that the computer will save $30 000 annually in operating expenses (excluding depreciation and taxes). The firm has been offered a four-year lease contract, with annual payments of $21 000 beginning when the contract comes into effect, and with a residual value of $20 000. The lessor has offered to absorb all insurance and maintenance expenses (worth $3000 per year, payable in advance). All the partners have a marginal tax rate of 47%.

(a) Estimate the net advantage of leasing (*NAL*) given that loan finance is otherwise available at 13% p.a.
(b) Should the firm lease the system?
(c) If Mountain Springs were to be organised as a company that pays franked dividends and has ordinary Australian residents as its shareholders (who can well use franking credits), what would your decision be?

18-A4 (*Lease versus buy*) XS Removals is operated by a sole proprietor, Xavier Smith. The firm wishes to consider purchasing a new truck to haul its large rubbish-removal skips. The firm is presently financed by a mix of 70% owner's equity and 30% debt, the after-tax cost of capital being 12%. Pertinent details are given below:

Acquisition price of the truck	$20 000
Useful life	4 years
Salvage value (estimated)	$4000
Depreciation method, down to zero book value	straight-line
Annual cash-savings from the truck, before tax and depreciation	$6000
Rate of interest on a 4-year term loan	10%
Marginal tax rate	47%
Annual finance-lease rentals (4 years) payable at the beginning of each year	$6000
Residual	$7000
Annual operating expenses paid by the lessor	$1000

(a) Evaluate whether the truck acquisition is justified as an investment project.
(b) Should XS Removals lease the truck? (Assume that losses on disposal of an asset are tax-deductible.)

18-A5* (*Lease versus buy evaluation*) XS Ltd is a rubbish-removal firm which pays its profits as franked dividends that are able to be well used by its ordinary Australian-resident shareholders. It has been offered the same investment opportunity as outlined in problem 18-A4.

(a) Should the company invest in the truck? Its pre-tax cost of capital is 16%.
(b) Should the company lease the truck?

18-A6 (*Lease analysis*) Arsson Fire Fighting Equipment Ltd is an Australian company whose shareholders enjoy the full benefit of imputation tax credits. The company has been offered a lease on some new equipment worth $500 000, requiring payments of $96 223 for a term of five years plus a residual value of 25%. The equipment is expected to have no disposal value, as it is highly specialised. Alternatively, the company's bank can arrange a five-year loan of $500 000 with an equal payment of $125 228 at the end of each year. Should Arsson Ltd accept the loan or the lease?

1. Using $2578.19 as the payment and $6000 as the residual (future value), with *n* equal to 5 and *i* equal to 8%, the present value is computed as $15 200.98.
2. An alternative way to evaluate the lease on an after-tax basis is to incorporate the tax benefits (from the debt interest) that are forgone by leasing into the table of cash flows (as a negative flow) and then use the pre-tax rate of interest on the debt as the discount rate when computing the *PVB*. The equivalence of this method with the approach used in the text (discounting after-tax cash flows at the after-tax cost of debt) is summarised in Thomas E. Copeland and J. Fred Weston, *Financial Policy and Corporate Theory*, 3rd edn, Addison-Wesley, Reading, MA, 1987, p. 623.
3. For example, if excess factory space is rented out, and then the factory owner makes the decision to expand and so takes possession of the space, rent is forgone. So this becomes an opportunity cost of the decision to expand the firm's activities.
4. W. L. Ferrara, J. B. Thies and M. W. Dirsmith, 'The lease–purchase decision', National Association of Accountants, 1980. Cited in 'Leasing—a review of the empirical studies', *Managerial Finance*, 15, nos 1 & 2, 1989, pp. 13–20.

Learning objectives

After reading this chapter, you should be able to:

1. Understand the distinction between equity, debt and hybrid capital.
2. Explain the basic features and terminology of ordinary shares.
3. Understand secondary issues and be able to calculate the value of rights.
4. Explain the basic features and terminology of preference shares.
5. Explain the basic features and terminology of convertible securities.

Shares and convertible securities

Chapter

19

CHAPTER PREVIEW

This chapter examines three major sources of long-term finance: ordinary shares, preference shares and convertible securities. Chapters 10 and 16 considered the valuation of and the theory behind the use of ordinary and preference shares in a company's capital structure. In this chapter, the focus is on the terminology, the basic features, the similarities and differences, and the advantages and disadvantages of ordinary shares, preference shares and convertible securities as sources of long-term finance.

Equity and other classes of finance

OBJECTIVE 1

Understand the distinction between equity, debt and hybrid capital.

The sources of long-term finance for companies are debt and equity. Chapter 18 examined the typical instruments used by a company to raise long-term debt finance. This chapter examines three non-debt financial instruments—ordinary shares, preference shares and convertible securities—that companies can issue to raise long-term finance.

Before a company raises new long-term finance, its management has to decide on the extent to which it will use debt, equity or hybrid instruments. Each of these forms of finance has different characteristics, which are briefly outlined below.

Debt involves contractual commitments by the company to pay interest and principal amounts to lenders, who become creditors of the company. Although debt instruments do not entitle the debt providers to ownership of the company, they can influence the management of the company through protective covenants, and if the company defaults on its borrowing obligations the legal system will assist recovery of any amounts owing.

Ordinary shareholders purchase an ownership interest in the company in return for dividends and/or capital gains. Although, as a group, ordinary shareholders are the ultimate owners of the company, the extent of control that can be exercised by an individual shareholder is limited to the proportion of shares owned in the company. From the company's perspective,

Regardless of your program

GETTING YOUR FAIR SHARE

If you are interested in starting your own business, you will be sharing your dream with many other students who are completing almost every conceivable degree program. If you start a company, you, and maybe your friends and family, will become shareholders and will need to understand the characteristics of ordinary shares. If your company grows, then you will also need to be familiar with other types of financial instruments that can be used to raise debt and equity finance.

the amount of ordinary dividends paid to shareholders is at the discretion of the board of directors, so equity finance does not impose fixed financial claims on the company.

Hybrid finance is provided by a range of securities that have characteristics of both debt and equity. The most popular hybrid securities are preference shares and convertible notes. Preference shares are classified as a hybrid security because the fixed preference dividend amount imposes a debt-like fixed financial claim on the company.

Care is needed in analysing company balance sheets that contain hybrid securities, because they are not identifiable as a separate accounting category and will be classified as either debt or equity. For example, a hybrid security like preference shares, which has more characteristics of equity than debt, is classified as part of shareholders' equity. An additional complication with hybrid securities is the taxation treatment of the amounts paid by the company and received by investors. For example, the taxation law may allow the interest component of convertible notes to be a tax deduction to the company only if the notes satisfy specified conditions.

In the next section we will examine equity financing with ordinary shares, and hybrid securities will be examined later in the chapter.

hybrid finance
Finance provided by securities issued by companies that have characteristics of both debt and equity. They comprise preference shares and convertible securities.

Back to the principles

The focus of this chapter is on companies that issue various forms of equity instruments in the financial markets. Australia, like many other developed countries around the world, has a complex and competitive system of financial markets that allows for the quick transfer of savings from economic units with a surplus to economic units with a savings deficit. Such a system of highly developed financial markets allows new projects to be financed and increases the overall wealth of the economy. A major aspect of the financial system is **Principle 6: Efficient capital markets—the markets are quick and the prices are right**. If the markets are 'efficient', prices will quickly and accurately reflect all available information about the value of underlying securities. Another implication of efficient markets is that expected risks and expected cash flows matter more to market participants than do accounting changes and the pattern of the past price changes. With security prices and returns competitively determined in the financial markets, more financial managers will participate in the markets, which in turn helps to ensure the basic concept of market efficiency.

OBJECTIVE **2**

Explain the basic features and terminology of ordinary shares.

Ordinary shares

Ordinary shares have a number of distinctive characteristics:

- They entitle the holder to ownership of the company, whereas under normal circumstances debt-holders and preference shareholders can be viewed as creditors of the company.
- They do not have a maturity date and therefore exist as long as the company does.
- There is no limit on the amount of dividends paid to the holders of ordinary shares as long as the company law requirements (detailed in Chapter 17) are met.
- The dividend amount per ordinary share is determined by the company's board of directors.
- In the event of the winding up of the company, the ordinary shareholders, as owners of the company, cannot exercise their claim on the company's assets until the debt-holders and preference shareholders have been satisfied.

In examining ordinary shares, we will first look at their features or characteristics and then focus on the process for a company to raise equity finance through initial flotation, rights offerings and private placements. Finally, the advantages and disadvantages of the use of ordinary shares will be examined.

FEATURES OF ORDINARY SHARES

This initial section examines ordinary share claims on the company's income and assets, shareholder voting rights, and the meaning and importance of the limited-liability and pre-emptive right features.

Claim on income

As the owners of the company, the ordinary shareholders have the right to the company's residual income (net profit) after debt-holders and preference shareholders have been paid. This residual income may be paid directly to the shareholders in the form of dividends or it may be retained and reinvested.

Although ordinary shareholders benefit immediately from the distribution of net income in the form of dividends, they also benefit from the reinvestment of this net income. This is because retained earnings can be used to provide finance for new investment projects, which should increase future profits that can be paid out as higher dividend amounts. The end result of retained earnings should be an increase in the price of the company's ordinary shares. In effect, then, shareholders will benefit from the company's residual income being either directly distributed to them in the form of dividends or indirectly in the form of capital gains.

The right to claim the company's residual income has both advantages and disadvantages for ordinary shareholders. The major advantage is that the potential return from owning shares is limitless, because once the claims of debt and preference shares have been paid, any residual income flows to the ordinary shareholders in the form of dividends or capital gains. The major disadvantage of ordinary shares is that, if the payments the company is required to make to debt-holders and preference shareholders totally absorb all the company's income so no profit is earned, ordinary shareholders will receive nothing.

Claims on assets

Just as ordinary shares have the residual claim on the company's net income, they also have a residual claim on the company's assets in the case of its liquidation. However, in liquidation the claims of ordinary shareholders are considered only after the amounts owing to debt-holders and preference shareholders have been satisfied. Therefore, when a company is liquidated because of financial difficulties, it is likely that all of its assets will be used to pay debt-holders, so the claims of the ordinary shareholders will be unsatisfied. This uncertainty of shareholders' residual claim on assets adds to the risk of owning ordinary shares, so, while ordinary shares can provide investors with a large return, they also expose investors to large risks.

Voting rights

The ownership of ordinary shares entitles the holder to elect the company's board of directors and to vote on resolutions at company general meetings. In addition, ordinary shareholders must approve any change in the constitution and the renounceable rules of the company.

The voting for directors and major changes to the company's constitution and rules normally occurs at the company's annual general meeting. Although shareholders may attend the meeting and vote in person, most shareholders of large companies vote by **proxy**, whereby they give a designated party the temporary power of attorney to vote for them at the company meeting. Generally, shareholders appoint the company's directors as their proxy; however, in times of financial distress or when company takeovers are threatened, *proxy fights* can occur as rival groups battle to be given the proxy votes of shareholders.

proxy
A means of voting in which a designated party is provided with the temporary power of attorney to vote for the signer at the firm's annual meeting.

Limited liability

Although ordinary shareholders are the owners of the company, their liability to the company's creditors in the case of the company's liquidation is limited to the amount of equity finance provided to the company with each share. The advantage of limited liability is that it assists in the raising of equity funds, because investors who might not otherwise invest their funds in the company are willing to do so.

Pre-emptive rights

pre-emptive right
The right entitling the ordinary shareholder to maintain his or her proportionate share of ownership in the firm.

Pre-emptive rights are a legal characteristic of ordinary shares that entitles each ordinary shareholder to maintain his or her proportionate share of ownership in the company. This means that, when new shares are to be issued by the company, ordinary shareholders have the first right of refusal to purchase the shares. For example, a shareholder who owns 25% of the company's shares should be entitled to purchase 25% of any new share issue. If they choose not to subscribe to all of the new shares, their proportional share of ownership will fall.

Back to the principles

In theory, the shareholders elect the company's board of directors, generally through proxy voting, and the board of directors in turn picks the company's management. However, in reality the system frequently works the other way around. Management nominates individuals for the board of directors and distributes ballots to shareholders. The shareholders can either cast their own vote or appoint selected directors as their proxy to vote on their behalf. When the majority of shareholders use proxies, the end result is that management effectively selects the directors, who can have more allegiance to the managers than to the shareholders. **Principle 7: The agency problem—managers won't work for owners unless it's in their best interest** creates problems and costs for shareholders when there is a divergence of interests between managers and shareholders and the board of directors does not ensure that managers act on behalf of the shareholders.

FLOTATION

In examining equity finance, the major focus here is with large *public companies*. These companies have their ordinary shares listed on a stock market, like the Australian Securities Exchange (ASX), which enables their shares to be readily traded by investors.

flotation
The first public issue of shares and/or debt by a company. Can be contrasted with secondary or subsequent issues.

Flotation is the name given to the process by which a company uses the stock market for the first time to issue its ordinary shares to the public and have those shares listed on a stock exchange for trading. For this process to occur, there are considerable stock-exchange listing and company law requirements that the company must satisfy.

For example, to ensure that listed companies have sufficient shares to be traded, the ASX Listing Rules require a limited liability company to have a minimum number of shareholders owning a parcel of the main class of ordinary shares with a minimum value. A listing fee is also payable to the ASX on a sliding scale according to the value of the issued securities, and annual fees are also payable.

Similarly, before a public company can offer shares to investors, the corporations law usually requires the company to provide investors with a prospectus in which the company is required to disclose all the information that investors would reasonably need in order to make an informed assessment of the future operating and financial performance of the company. Any forecast income statement provided by directors that is included in a prospectus must be reviewed by an investigating accountant. All those involved with the preparation and issue of the prospectus can be held liable if the law is broken.

underwriting
The purchase and subsequent resale by an underwriter of new securities that have been taken up by the public by the closing date of the issue.

To ensure that the company being floated on the stock market raises the required amount of funds by selling its shares to a wide spread of investors, the majority of floats are *underwritten* by a sharebroking firm or merchant bank. For a fee, the underwriter guarantees to purchase any shares that are not purchased by investors. The fees for **underwriting** are set at a percentage of the funds raised by the share issue, and can range from 1% to 7%, with the average being around 4%.

In contemplating flotation, the company's management needs to consider two aspects:

1. *The overall costs.* There are substantial costs involved in a flotation, including underwriting fees, commissions paid to brokers to market the shares, costs of preparing and issuing prospectuses, and stock-exchange listing fees. The overall costs for small-cap industrial company floats (less than $100 million raised) can be as high as 10% of the funds raised. For large-cap industrial company floats (more than $100 million raised) the costs can be as low as 4.5% of the funds raised.[1] This difference primarily occurs because the overall costs tend to be proportionately higher for smaller issues, as many flotation requirements are fixed costs and underwriting fees tend to be higher for smaller, more risky companies.

2. *The issue price.* An important management decision with flotation is the price at which the company's shares will be offered to the public. The issue price has to satisfy the existing shareholders of the company, who are selling all or part of their business to the public, and it should ideally be the same as the 'true price' when the shares first trade in the share market.

   The problem for management is that there is no existing benchmark by which to determine this 'true price'. The issue price has to be estimated to reflect the activities of the company, its historical performance and its potential to generate future profits in relation to its industry and the general share market.

   It is an acknowledged phenomenon that the flotation issue price tends to be too low, because it is common for the newly issued shares to sell on the market on the first day of listing at a premium above the issue price. There is no agreement among researchers as to why this is so.[2] Such underpricing, especially in a buoyant share market, provides gains for **stags**—investors who purchase new shares through a prospectus and sell the shares at a profit on the first day of listing.

stags
Investors who purchase new shares through a prospectus and sell on the first day that the shares are quoted by the stock exchange, in an attempt to make a profit.

There are a number of downsides to flotation that also need to be considered. One major downside is the significant amount of time, effort and expenditure that the listing process entails. Also, the managers and shareholders of a company that goes public will need to come to terms with learning to get on with a whole new set of stakeholders. As well as running the company, the CEO has to satisfy analysts, sharebrokers, regulators and the media. Media attention and the scrutiny by investors requiring short-term results may make it hard for the listed company to take risks or to restructure.

Concept check

19.1 What costs are incurred with flotation?

19.2 Do you think the costs for a new bond issue would be more or less than for a flotation issue of ordinary shares?

For answers go to MyFinanceLab or www.pearson.com.au/9781442539174

GFC

WHEN TO FLOAT?

The number of flotations in any year is generally affected by the peaks and troughs of the share-market cycle. When the market is buoyant and share prices are high and rising, a new issue of shares will be sought by investors, so many companies choose to float and be listed on the stock exchange. The reverse is true when prices are low and falling.[3]

This can be seen from the following statistics of the listing of new companies on the Australian Securities Exchange from 2006 to 2010. Of particular note is the impact in 2009 of the Global Financial Crisis, which resulted in a significant fall in the number of new listings and the initial capital raised.

YEAR	NUMBER OF NEW LISTINGS	INITIAL CAPITAL RAISED (A$m)
2006	227	23 108
2007	284	19 694
2008	236	11 206
2009	45	1 885
2010	93	11 460

Source: ASX Limited 2010 Annual Report, reproduced with permission. Copyright © ASX Limited ABN 98008624691 (ASX) 2011. All rights reserved.

OBJECTIVE 3

Understand secondary issues and be able to calculate the value of rights.

dilution
Any action of a company that results in a reduction of ordinary shareholder interests. For example, if new shares are issued by a company but are not made available to current shareholders, their proportionate ownership of the company will be reduced or diluted.

rights issue
An issue of rights to existing shareholders.

For answers go to MyFinanceLab or
www.pearson.com.au/9781442539174

SECONDARY ISSUES

A secondary issue is the name given to any share issue made by a company after its flotation. One of the overriding considerations with secondary issues is *pre-emptive rights*, which are a legal characteristic of ordinary shares that entitles existing ordinary shareholders to maintain their proportionate share of ownership and value in the company.

So, when a company wants to raise equity finance by a secondary share issue, it has to do so in a way to avoid the **dilution** of interests of the existing shareholders. The major way in which this is achieved is through a **rights issue**. Under a rights issue, all existing shareholders are entitled to take up the new shares in proportion to their present holdings and shareholders who subscribe to the issue retain their proportionate voting power.

An alternative secondary-issue method is private placement. Because under this method new shares are offered only to select shareholders, the proportionate holdings of most current shareholders will be diluted. To minimise this dilution, companies with shares listed on the ASX are restricted from privately placing more than 10% of their total issued ordinary shares in any 12-month period without the approval of all shareholders.

Concept check

19.3 What are the differences between flotation and secondary issues?
19.4 What role does the stock exchange play in equity capital raising?

RIGHTS ISSUES

To raise new equity finance under a rights issue, the company offers existing shareholders the right to purchase a specified number of new shares proportionate to their existing shareholding. The significant features of rights issues are:

1. Most rights issues are *renounceable*. This means that shareholders can choose not to subscribe to the issue and can sell their entitlements to purchase new shares (their 'rights') in the share market during a stated period. A consideration for small shareholders who do not wish to purchase the new shares is the transaction costs that they would incur to sell the rights through the share market. As a service to these shareholders, some companies arrange to sell unexercised rights and pay the net proceeds to the shareholders.

   If the rights issue is *non-renounceable*, the right to purchase new shares cannot be sold, and shareholders are only able to decide whether to purchase the new shares or not.

2. For every rights issue there is a rights trading period (usually 30 to 60 days) during which shareholders can sell their existing shares ex-rights (see below) as well as the rights themselves. After this period the existing and newly issued shares of the company are traded normally.

3. In a similar manner to a flotation, a prospectus is required for a rights issue, with its accompanying disclosure and due diligence requirements.

4. A rights issue will tend to be underwritten if:
   • the issue is non-renounceable, or
   • the issue is a large one and/or the issuing company is little known, or
   • the subscription price is not at a substantial discount to the market price. Market experience has shown that shareholders are more attracted to an issue when its subscription price is below the market value. New shares under a rights issue are generally offered at a discount of 15–20% below market value.

5. It has become the norm for companies to at least maintain the current dividend per share on the expanded number of shares after a rights issue. This increase should be regarded as a cost of a rights issue to the company.

Dates surrounding a rights issue

There are a number of dates that are associated with a rights issue. Following are the dates for a hypothetical company. On 1 March the company announces that all 'holders of record' (shareholders registered in the company books) as at 6 April will be issued rights, which will expire on 30 May and will be mailed to them on 25 April.

In this example, 1 March is the *announcement date*, 6 April the *holder-of-record date*, and 30 May the *expiration date*. While this seems rather straightforward, it is complicated by the fact that, if a shareholder sells his or her shares a day or two before the holder-of-record date (6 April), the company may not have time to record the transaction and replace the old owner's name with that of the new owner. To deal with the problem that the rights might then be sent to the wrong shareholder, an additional date has been created, the *ex-rights date*. The ex-rights date occurs four trading days before the holder-of-record date.

On or after the ex-rights date the company's existing shares are bought and sold without the rights. Therefore, whoever owns the shares on the day prior to the ex-rights date will receive the rights. Thus, with the holder-of-record date of 6 April, the ex-rights date is set four trading days earlier, 2 April. This means that anyone purchasing the company's shares on or before 1 April will receive the rights to purchase new shares, whereas anyone purchasing the shares on or after 2 April will not.

The price at which the existing shares are traded prior to the ex-rights date is referred to as the **cum-rights price**, whereas the price on or after the ex-rights date is the **ex-rights price**. The timing of this process and the terminology are shown in Table 19.1.

There are three questions and theoretical relationships that need to be explained about rights issues. First, how many existing shares must a shareholder own in order to have the right to purchase a new share? Second, what is the theoretical value of a right? Finally, what effect do rights issues have on the value of a company's ordinary share? Each of these questions will be looked at in turn.

cum-rights price
The price paid for the purchase of an ordinary share which includes the right to subscribe for an announced new share issue.

ex-rights price
The price paid for the purchase of an ordinary share which excludes the right to subscribe to a new share issue that has recently closed.

NUMBER OF RIGHTS

Let us continue with the example of our hypothetical company and assume that it has 6 million issued shares that are currently selling for $10 per share. To finance the equity component of its new projects, the company needs to raise an additional $10.5 million, and wishes to do so with a rights issue. To ensure that all of the new shares under the rights issue will be purchased, the company's management has set the rights issue subscription price at $7 per share. Compared to the current $10 market price for the company's issued shares this is a discount of $3/$10 = 30%. The number of new shares that must be sold under the rights issue at $7 per share to raise the desired amount of $10.5 million is equal to:

$$\text{New shares to be sold} = \frac{\text{desired funds to be raised}}{\text{subscription price}}$$

$$= \frac{\$10\,500\,000}{\$7}$$

$$= 1\,500\,000 \text{ shares}$$

TABLE 19.1 Illustration of timing of a rights issue

Share sells cum-rights	1 March	Announcement date		
	1 April	The owner of the share at this date receives the rights		
	2 April	Ex-rights date	}	four trading days
Share sells ex-rights	6 April	Holder-of-record date		
	25 April	Mailing date		
	30 May	Expiration date		

To issue 1.5 million shares, the company would have to issue 1.5 million rights. Given that there are 6 million shares already on issue, a shareholder will be entitled to receive one right for every four shares held (6 million ÷ 1.5 million = 4). Therefore, under this 1-for-4 rights issue, the holder of four existing shares receives one right, which entitles them to purchase one new share for $7.

Theoretical value of a right

Because the subscription price to a new share (e.g. $7) under the rights issue is below the current market price (e.g. $10), there is some value to the right. The theoretical value of the right will depend on (1) the relationship between the subscription price and the market price of the shares, and (2) the number of rights to be issued.

To determine the theoretical value of a right, we first need to determine the market value of the company. Originally, as the company had 6 million shares outstanding, selling at $10 each, it had a total market value of $60 million.

Assuming that the market value of the company goes up by exactly the amount of $10.5 million raised by the rights issue, the new market value of the company will be $70.5 million. Dividing this new market value of $70.5 million by the new total number of issued shares, 7.5 million (6 million plus 1.5 million), the new theoretical market value (TMV) for the shares will be $9.40 each. That is, after the rights issue, the *ex-rights* market value (price) of the company's shares will fall to $9.40 per share.

From the perspective of a shareholder who owns four existing shares and under the rights issue is entitled to subscribe for one new share at $7, the *theoretical value of the right* is the difference between the new market price (the ex-rights price) of $9.40 and the subscription price of $7 = $2.40.

Theoretical value of one right = market price of share ex-rights − subscription price

$$R = P_{ex} - S \qquad\qquad \textbf{(19-1)}$$

$$R = \$9.40 - \$7 = \$2.40$$

where R = value of one right
P_{ex} = ex-rights price of the share
S = subscription price

Alternatively, the theoretical value of a right can be determined using the cum-rights share price (e.g. $10) and the number of shares an existing shareholder has to own (e.g. 4 shares) to be entitled to one right.

4 shares × cum-rights share price ($10)	$40.00
Add subscription price of 1 right	7.00
	47.00
Divide by 5 (the increased number of shares held)	
TMV of shares ex-rights	9.40
Less rights issue subscription price	7.00
Theoretical value of right	$2.40

The theoretical value of a right can also be determined from the following equation:

$$R = \frac{N(P_{on} - S)}{N + 1} \qquad\qquad \textbf{(19-2)}$$

$$R = \frac{4(\$10 - \$7)}{4 + 1}$$

$$= \$2.40$$

where R = value of one right
  P_{on} = cum-rights price of the share
  N = number of shares required by a shareholder to own one right
  S = subscription price

The previous calculations of the theoretical value of a right show that existing shareholders who purchase new shares under the rights issue do not benefit or lose from the rights issue. They do receive something of value, the right worth \$2.40, but they lose exactly that amount in the form of a decline in the price of their old shares (4 shares × \$0.60 = \$2.40). Of course, existing shareholders will lose value if they do not exercise or sell their rights. Examining the behaviour of shareholders shows that only a small percentage neglect to exercise or sell their rights.

A major concern for the company's management is to set a rights issue subscription price that is low enough so that the price of existing shares traded in the market during the period of the rights issue will not fall below it. For example, if the subscription price is set at \$9 and the price of existing shares in the market falls from \$10 to \$8, then existing shareholders could increase their shareholding by paying \$8 per share instead of subscribing to a new share via the rights issue for \$9.

Actual value of a right

After the ex-rights date, the right to subscribe to new shares is separated from the existing shares, and as the right is able to be bought and sold separately the stock exchange separately records the market price of each right. It is possible for the market price of the right to be different from the theoretical value calculated earlier.

One reason is that transactions costs to buy and sell shares and rights can limit investor arbitrage, which would push the market price of the right to its theoretical value. Another reason is that speculation and the irregular sale of rights over the subscription period may cause shifts in supply that push the market price of the right above or below its theoretical value.

PLACEMENTS

A **placement** occurs when a company issues shares only to a specific party or parties without the shares being offered to all existing shareholders. At least 95% of placements are made to institutional investors such as investment funds, superannuation funds and life offices.

For the company, a placement is a *cheaper* and *quicker* means of raising equity finance than a rights issue, for the following reasons:

placement
The offer of financial securities directly to selected potential purchasers, in contrast to a public offering.

- Under Australian company legislation and stock-exchange regulations, no *prospectus* is required if the issue is classified as an 'excluded offer'. A number of conditions are required to satisfy this provision, including a limit on the number of investors that can participate in the placement and a minimum dollar amount required to be raised per placement.
- *Underwriting* can usually be avoided, because there is little risk that the shares will not be purchased and the required funds obtained. Companies tend to engage a sharebroking firm or a merchant bank for a fee to market the shares with institutions on a 'best efforts' basis. This means that, although there is a chance that some institutions will decide not to purchase the shares, a determined effort will be made to raise the funds at the issue price.
- Whereas shares under a rights issue usually have to be offered at a price that is at a substantial discount from the current market price, placements can be made at the market price or at a much smaller discount because they are being offered only to institutional investors. This means that the company needs to issue fewer shares with a placement to raise a given amount of funds. This in turn reduces the servicing costs of the shares, and the reduction in earnings per share is less than for a rights issue.
- A rights issue may require up to 40 days to organise and conduct, whereas a placement can be arranged quickly with institutional investors.

Other advantages that placements provide to issuing companies are:

- Although stock exchange rules restrict placements within any 12-month period to a maximum percentage of issued capital, it is possible for companies to exceed this limit if shareholders formally ratify the decision.
- Management can make placements for strategic purposes—for example to defend against a takeover offer, to provide part ownership to specific parties such as suppliers, customers or major lenders, or to increase or decrease the ownership of overseas shareholders.

The major criticism of placements comes from existing shareholders who are not given the opportunity to subscribe to the new issue and therefore cannot prevent dilution of their ownership rights. If the placement price is below the current market price for the company's shares, there is a transfer of wealth from the existing shareholders to the new investors.

Irrespective of this criticism of placements, large Australian companies use placements to raise new equity finance, due to their relative cheapness and the speed with which they can be allocated to institutions.

> ## Concept check
> 19.5 What is the difference between a rights issue and a private placement?
> 19.6 What are the advantages and disadvantages of private placements?

For answers go to MyFinanceLab or
www.pearson.com.au/9781442539174

ADVANTAGES AND DISADVANTAGES OF ORDINARY SHARES

The raising of finance by a company selling ordinary shares has several advantages and disadvantages in comparison with the company issuing new debt and preference shares.

Advantages
1. The company is not legally required to pay dividends to the holders of ordinary shares, whereas the legal system can be used by debt investors to enforce the payment of interest and principal payments on debt. Thus, in times of financial distress the company can conserve cash by stopping payment of ordinary dividends, but it cannot do this with debt.
2. Because ordinary shares have no maturity date, there is no redemption cash outflow as there is with debt. It is possible, if the company desires, to buy back its shares but there is no legal obligation for the company to do so.
3. By issuing ordinary shares the company increases its financial resources as well as its future borrowing capacity. Conversely, issuing debt increases the company's financial resources but also reduces its borrowing capacity. If the company's capital structure already has a high proportion of debt, investors may be unwilling to provide new debt finance until the existing equity base is enlarged. Thus, financing with ordinary shares increases the company's future financing flexibility.

Disadvantages
1. Depending on the tax status of the company, the tax-shield resulting from the tax deduction for interest payments can provide a financial benefit to shareholders. This advantage will be lost if the company issues new ordinary shares rather than raising new debt finance.
2. The costs to raise finance by issuing ordinary shares tend to be larger than for issuing new debt.
3. Issuing new ordinary shares may result in a change in the ownership and control of the company. This will occur with a share placement, and, although under a rights issue shareholders have a pre-emptive right to retain their proportionate control, they may not have the funds to subscribe to the new shares. If this is the case, the original shareholders may see their control diluted by the issuance of new ordinary shares.

BUSINESS ANGELS TO THE RESCUE

Before you can start your own business you will need to obtain finance. Usually equity will be provided by your savings and money invested by your family and friends and you may be able to borrow some money from the bank. If your business is successful, a major problem will be how to obtain sufficient equity capital to finance future growth when your business is not large enough to have shares listed on the stock exchange. An important source of informal venture capital to small and medium-sized businesses (SMEs) is from 'business angels'.

Historically, a business angel was a cash-rich individual with the strange mix of being a philanthropist to the arts and an entrepreneur who was the last-minute investor in Broadway and West End stage productions that had run into financial difficulties before the opening night.

Since that time, the following definition of a business angel is generally accepted around the world:

An individual who invests equity capital directly into a business, usually a small or medium-sized business. These investors

often also work in some capacity with the business, alongside the original owners, and often become a director of the company. However, neither of these features is considered essential for an investor to be classed as a business angel. Business angels may provide loan finance and other assistance in addition to equity investment.[4]

Linking the business owner with a business-angel investor can involve a large amount of time and frustration, particularly as small business owners can be unprepared and unable to provide sufficient information for investors.

One solution to this problem is the development of venture-capital broking or 'introduction agencies', which through databases, bulletins, investment journals, investment forums and the Internet facilitate the matching of potential business angel investors to small and medium-sized businesses in need of capital.

Preference shares

OBJECTIVE

Explain the basic features and terminology of preference shares.

Subject to company legislation and stock-exchange requirements, a company has the ability to create different classes of shares with different rights for shareholders. One major example is preference shares, which give preference shareholders a preferential right to the payment of dividends before other classes of shares, and often a preferential return of capital on the winding-up of a company.

Preference shares emerged at the end of the 19th century to provide a means for companies to raise capital from investors who wanted more security than they would have received as ordinary shareholders. Although legally preference shares are classified as equity, they can be considered a hybrid form of finance, because they contain elements of both debt (e.g. a constant preference dividend cash flow) and equity (e.g. entitlement to assets when the company is liquidated).

FEATURES OF PREFERENCE SHARES

As modern preference shares can have a diversity of rights attached to them, each preference-share issue is unique. The following sections examine some of the features of preference shares and their advantages and disadvantages as a source of finance for a company.

Multiple classes

If a company desires, it can issue more than one series or class of preference shares, and each class can have different characteristics. For example, one class may give the shareholders priority to receive dividend payments and repayment capital on the winding up of the company over a second class of preference shares.

Dividends

A company can pay preference dividends from its income once the interest on its debt has been paid and before the payment of dividends to ordinary shareholders. In addition, preference dividends are not normally deductible for tax purposes, in contrast to the interest paid on debt finance.

Most preference shares are *non-participating*, which means that the preference shareholders are not entitled to dividends in excess of the stated dividend amount or rate that applies to that preference share class. If preference shares are *participating*, the preference shareholders may also be entitled to be paid some of the net profits that are available to ordinary shareholders.

Most preference shares are *cumulative*, which requires the company to pay any unpaid preference dividend amounts from previous periods before any ordinary dividends are declared. The purpose of this feature is to provide the preference shareholder with some degree of protection to receive their preference dividend entitlement.

Australian companies can gain additional flexibility with preference-share issues, by paying *franked* or *unfranked* preference dividends.

Redemption

As the Australian company and taxation law imposes strict rules on the redemption of preference shares, most preference shares issued by Australian companies are irredeemable and therefore, like ordinary shares, are valued as a perpetuity.

Claims on assets and income

Many preference shares have a priority claim over ordinary shares to the assets of the company in the case of its winding up (i.e. liquidation). However, this claim is only effected once the company has paid all the amounts owing to its debt holders.

Preference shares also have a priority claim over ordinary shares for the company to pay preference dividends before ordinary dividends are paid. Therefore, from an investor's perspective, preference shares are a riskier investment than debt, because preference dividends can only be paid after debt interest has been paid, but preference shares are less risky than ordinary shares because of their prior claims on the company's assets and net income.

Protective provisions

Holders of preference shares are not entitled to the same general voting rights as ordinary shareholders, but they can have limited voting rights if dividends are in arrears or if circumstances threaten the nature of their security. In addition, they may be given the right to approve the issue of further preference shares that rank with or ahead of them.

Convertibility

Since the 1990s many Australian preference-share issues have the feature of being convertible into a predetermined number of ordinary shares.[5] As many investors are attracted to preference shares with this convertibility feature, the increased demand for and price of the preference shares reduces the cost of the issue to the company. Convertible (and converting) preference shares will be discussed in more detail later in this chapter.

Concept check

19.7 What features of a preference share are different from those of bonds?

19.8 What provisions are available to protect a preference shareholder?

19.9 What preference-share cash-flow amounts are needed to determine the intrinsic value of a preference share?

For answers go to MyFinanceLab or www.pearson.com.au/9781442539174

ADVANTAGES AND DISADVANTAGES

In contrast to debt and ordinary shares, preference shares are not a major source of finance for companies. Instead they tend to be used as a 'special purpose' method of financing where one or more of the equity and debt features can be used to the advantage of the issuing company. Therefore, the characteristics of each class of preference-share issue will depend on the needs and standing of the company, on legal and taxation aspects, and on trends in the capital market.

Advantages[6]

1. Unlike interest on debt, non-payment of preference dividends does not force a company into liquidation. Also, no repayment is required with non-redeemable preference shares.
2. Apart from the rarely issued participating preference shares, the dividends paid to preference shareholders are limited to a fixed amount. Also, unlike debt issues where interest must be paid, preference dividends can be avoided, or paid later if the preference shares are cumulative.
3. There is no dilution of the ownership control of ordinary shareholders from a preference-share issue.
4. Because preference shares provide less security for investors than debt issues, it may be expected that issuing companies would have to pay a higher preference dividend than the interest rate on debt. However, this difference in rate can be reduced if preference dividends have franking credits that Australian shareholders are able to use.
5. Even though preference shares are legally regarded as equity, the fixed dividend amount has a leverage effect on earnings per share. This can be an advantage to a company that is restricted from issuing more fixed-interest debt because of constraints imposed by existing debt commitments.
6. It is often claimed that by issuing preference shares a company can increase its equity base, which enables it to issue more debt in the future. This claim will not be correct if, in an efficient capital market, professional investors recognise that the fixed preference dividend has a similar effect on financial leverage as fixed interest payments on debt. Therefore, investors who are aware of the actual leverage and debt capacity of the company will price its debt and equity securities accordingly.

Disadvantages

1. Debt interest is tax-deductible, but normally preference dividends are not. This provides a disadvantage to companies that are subject to a classical tax system if they issue preference shares.
2. The non-payment of a preference-share dividend can provide a negative signal to investors about the company's profitability, which can result in a fall in the company's ordinary share price. Usually, it is only in response to the most adverse profitability circumstances that companies do not pay preference dividends.

International spotlight

GLOBAL SHARE MARKETS

Historically, stock exchanges were established on a geographical basis to serve the share market for a particular region. For example, each state in Australia had its own stock exchange servicing companies and investors in that state. From the 1970s the development of communication technologies facilitated the state-based stock exchanges to merge to form one major stock exchange for Australia—the ASX.

What of the future? The advent of Internet trading, where investors can potentially buy and sell shares quickly and cheaply from any market in the world, is a major pressure for national stock markets to become more integrated and even to merge. This pressure is reinforced by global companies that want ready access to a large pool of investors who are not limited by national boundaries and who can supply large amounts of equity finance.

For answers go to MyFinanceLab or
www.pearson.com.au/9781442539174

OBJECTIVE **5**

Explain the basic features
and terminology of
convertible securities.

convertible securities
Debt or preference shares that
can be converted to ordinary
shares by the holder subject to
specified conditions.

Convertible securities

A **convertible security** is a preference share or a debt instrument (e.g. a bond) that enables the holder to convert the security to (i.e. exchange it for) a specified number of ordinary shares. This convertibility feature is essentially giving the holder a call option on the company's ordinary shares and this option has value. This combination of features is the reason that convertible securities are called 'hybrid securities'.

A major attraction of convertible securities to investors is that they provide a stable income from either preference dividends or debt interest, in addition to the possibility of capital gains if converted to ordinary shares.

When a convertible security is initially issued, the company receives an amount equal to the issue price of the security minus issue costs. Depending on whether the underlying security of the convertible is a preference share or debt, the company will treat the convertible as if it were a normal issue of preference shares or debt with the regular payment of dividends or interest.

In accordance with the terms and conditions that were specified when the convertible security was originally issued, the holder of the convertible can choose to exchange the underlying security for ordinary shares. Once the holder exchanges the convertible for ordinary shares, he or she is treated by the company as an ordinary shareholder and henceforth will receive only ordinary dividends.

Although convertibility can be added to any form of debt, the *convertible note* has been commonly issued in Australia. The following sections discuss the characteristics and features of convertible notes, how to value them, and the reasons that companies use them. We will then look at convertible (and converting) preference shares.

CONVERTIBLE NOTES

The underlying security of a convertible note is an *unsecured* bond-type instrument that pays the holder a regular coupon (interest) amount and a face value amount at the end of a specified term. The distinguishing feature of a convertible note is that it also provides the holder with an option to convert the face value of the note to ordinary shares. In the event of the company being liquidated before conversion, unsecured notes rank behind debentures and other secured debt instruments for payment from the company's assets. However, unsecured notes can provide some protection to holders if they have a trust deed that contains protective covenants restricting the amount of borrowing and the operations of the issuing company.

The major features of a convertible note issue are detailed below:

1. *Coupon (interest) rate.*
2. *Par (face) value.*
3. *Conversion price.* The conversion price is the amount of the note's par value that is required to obtain one ordinary share on conversion.
4. *Conversion ratio.* The conversion ratio is the number of shares that can be received for each note and is equal to the par value divided by the conversion price. Note-holders will tend to convert when the share price on the market exceeds the conversion price.

As with preference shares, more than one class of convertible note can be issued by a company. For example, one class of notes can be subordinated to rank behind all other liabilities in the event of the winding up of the company.

As a convertible-note-holder could be prejudiced if the issuing company made new equity issues in which the note-holder did not participate, most convertible-note issues provide that note-holders can participate in ordinary-share rights issues, and also in bonus issues if notes are converted.

VALUATION OF CONVERTIBLE NOTES

The valuation of a convertible note depends primarily on (1) the security value of the unsecured note, and (2) the conversion value.

Security value

The **security value** (SV) of a convertible note is the price the underlying unsecured note would sell for in the absence of the conversion feature. In other words, the convertible note is valued on the assumption that conversion does *not* take place at maturity, which means that it is valued as if it were just a bond-like debt security.

> **security value**
> The term applied to a convertible security for the price it would sell for in the absence of its conversion feature. In the case of a convertible unsecured note, this would be the value of a similar non-convertible unsecured note.

The holder of the note is entitled to receive coupon interest until the conversion date, plus the face value of the note at maturity. Therefore, the security value is equal to the present value of the coupon (interest) payments plus the present value of the maturity value (also known as the 'principal' or 'par' or 'face' value of the note).

The security value for a note with half-yearly coupon payments can be found by solving for SV in equation (19-3):

$$SV = \sum_{t=1}^{2n} \frac{IP/2}{\left(1 + \frac{i}{2}\right)^t} + \frac{P}{\left(1 + \frac{i}{2}\right)^{2n}} \qquad \textbf{(19-3)}$$

Example 19.1 illustrates the calculation of the security value of a convertible note.

EXAMPLE 19.1 Calculation of the security value of a convertible note

Northern Limited issued convertible notes with 10 years to maturity with a par of $4.40, paying half-yearly interest at a coupon rate of 9.5% per annum and a conversion feature that entitles holders to exchange one convertible note for one ordinary share. It is known that the current yield on 10-year corporate bonds that have a similar debt rating to Northern Limited is 11% per annum. This yield can therefore be used as a proxy to value the debt security component of Northern Limited's convertible notes with the following data:

I = coupon interest rate = 9.5% per year
P = par (face) value of the note = $4.40
i = yield (required rate of return) = 11% per year
n = number of years to maturity = 10 years

The security value is equal to the present value of the coupon payments of $4.40 × 0.095/2 = $0.2090 per half-year, for t = 20 half-years, discounted at 0.11/2 = 0.055 (5.5%) per half-year plus the present value of the $4.40 par value.

Substituting in equation (19-3):

$$SV = \sum_{t=1}^{20} \frac{\$0.2090}{(1 + 0.055)^t} + \frac{\$4.40}{(1 + 0.055)^{20}}$$

$$= \$0.2090 \, PVIFA_{20,5.5\%} + \$4.40 \, PVIF_{20,5.5\%}$$

$$= \$.2090 \, (11.9504) + \$4.40 \, (0.3427)$$

$$= \$2.4976 + \$1.5079$$

$$= \$4.01$$

Calculator solution	
DATA INPUT	FUNCTION KEY
20	N
5.5	I/Y
0.209	PMT
4.40	FV
FUNCTION KEY	ANSWER
COMP PV	−4.01

The security value (*SV*) of $4.01 calculated in Example 19.1 is the *minimum* value of one convertible note, and reflects the current value to note-holders who decide not to convert to shares their entitlement to receive the regular coupon amounts plus the $4.40 par value on maturity of the notes. However, as the convertible note-holders also have the right to choose to convert the notes to ordinary shares, the *conversion value* also needs to be estimated.

Conversion value

conversion value
The value of the shares for which a convertible security can be exchanged.

The **conversion value** of a convertible note is the current market value of the ordinary shares for which each note can be exchanged and is equal to the conversion ratio × the current share price. In the case of the Northern Limited issue, with a conversion ratio of 1, the conversion value would be equal to the current market price of one ordinary share.

Complicating the valuation of convertible notes is the fact that investors are in general willing to pay a premium for the right to be able to choose to convert the notes to shares, which gives them a hedge against uncertain future share prices.

conversion premium
The price paid by purchasers of a convertible security for the option to convert to shares.

The **conversion premium** is the difference between the current market price of the convertible and the higher of its security value and its conversion value.

Continuing from Example 19.1, as the current security value (*SV*) of Northern Limited's convertible notes is $4.01, regardless of what happens to the price of the company's ordinary shares, the lowest value on the market for the convertible notes (assuming the yield stays constant) would be $4.01.

If the current market price for the company's ordinary shares is, say, $3.95 (conversion value = $.05 × 1 = $3.95), the convertible note would be worth more to the note-holder as straight debt ($4.01) than if it were converted to an ordinary share with a current value of $3.95.

On the other hand, if the current market price for the company's ordinary shares is, say, $4.20, the convertible note would be worth more to the note-holder if converted to an ordinary share that is currently worth $4.20 than as straight debt with a current value of $4.01.

Consequently, if there is the opportunity for investors to make capital gains by being able to convert the notes in the future to higher priced shares, they will be willing to pay a conversion premium in addition to the security or conversion value.

In summary, as convertible notes offer investors stable income from debt—and thus less risk of price decline due to adverse share conditions—while retaining the possibility of capital gains from share price rises, *the convertible note is valued as a note when the price of the ordinary shares is low and as an ordinary share when the ordinary share price rises*.

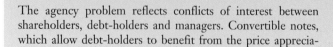

FYI

The agency problem reflects conflicts of interest between shareholders, debt-holders and managers. Convertible notes, which allow debt-holders to benefit from the price appreciation of equity, can help to align the interests of shareholders and debt-holders and reduce the agency problem.

REASONS FOR ISSUING CONVERTIBLE NOTES

As with preference shares, convertible notes are a 'special purpose' source of finance, when compared with the use of straight debt and ordinary equity finance. Following are some of the reasons why companies might consider issuing convertible notes.

1. They provide *development* or *venture* capital for new companies with high growth potential or for major development projects within large companies. As the development phase involves heavy initial cash outflows, and if the project is successful resultant high cash inflows, a convertible note allows the use of cheaper debt finance during the early stages,

and later, when high profits are generated, producing high share prices, note-holders will be encouraged to convert to shares.

The reason that convertible notes can provide cheaper debt finance than comparable straight debt finance comes from the conversion premium. Because convertible-note-holders can benefit from upward movements in the share price by conversion, they are willing to accept less coupon interest during the period of the note than for comparable non-convertible debt. This occurred in the example of Northern Limited, whose convertible-note-holders were willing to accept a coupon interest rate of 9.5% per annum whereas the current yield for comparable 'straight' debt was 11% per annum.

2. While exposure to higher risk and uncertainty results in straight debt having to provide investors with a higher coupon interest rate, this is not necessarily the case with convertibles. Viewing a convertible note as comprising a straight debt component and an option component to purchase ordinary shares, any increase in risk and uncertainty should raise the cost of the straight-debt component of the convertible. However, the option component benefits from the effect of this increase in risk and uncertainty on share-price volatility as there is greater likelihood that the option will be of value at some point before the expiration date. Thus, the negative effect of an increase in risk and uncertainty on the straight-debt portion of a convertible note can be more than offset by the positive effect of the conversion feature.

3. Although convertible notes can provide a cheaper source of debt, the taking up of the conversion option component when the company's share price exceeds the conversion price will result in some dilution in the total market value of the company's ordinary shares.

CONVERTIBLE PREFERENCE SHARES

A convertible preference share consists of a preference share that gives the holder an option to convert to ordinary shares. The conditions for conversion will be specified when the convertible preference shares are created. For example, the convertible preference shares may be issued for a specific period (such as five years) and if the option to convert is not exercised by the holder the preference shares will be redeemed on the maturity date.

Alternatively, the holder may have the option to convert to ordinary shares after a minimum stated period, or otherwise automatic conversion occurs at the end of the specified period. As there is ultimately conversion to ordinary shares, there is no redemption by the issuing company.

Finance at work

DECISIONS

The financial managers of companies are constantly balancing the demand for finance against the company's supply of retained earnings and the costs of raising external funds. In order to obtain sufficient finance for favourable investment projects, the financial manager may have to choose between issuing new ordinary shares, preference shares or hybrid securities. Further, it may be necessary to decide whether to raise the external capital via a public offering or via a private placement to a limited number of potential investors. An important component in making this decision is an awareness of securities markets regulations and taxation requirements. Also, it will often be necessary to obtain specialised advice from investment bankers, sharebrokers and accountants.

Summary

OBJECTIVE 1

The holders of a company's debt and preference shares can be viewed as creditors of the company, whereas the ordinary shareholders are the owners of the company. Ordinary shares do not have a maturity date or a limit on the dividend amount that the company can pay to the ordinary shareholders. On the other hand, the dividends for a preference share and the coupons for a bond are fixed. Hybrid instruments have some of the characteristics of both debt and equity.

OBJECTIVE 2

The funds raised by issuing ordinary shares are a key source of the equity finance for a company. For ordinary shares to be listed and freely traded on the stock exchange, a company must have a flotation of its shares to the public. Although the ordinary shareholders are the true owners of the company, they cannot exercise a claim on company assets in the event of the winding up of the company until the debt-holders and preference shareholders have been satisfied. However, ordinary shareholders have the right to elect the board of directors and to maintain their proportionate share in the firm, called the pre-emptive right.

OBJECTIVE 3

A company can raise new equity funds through a rights issue, which allows ordinary shareholders to purchase new shares issued by the company and maintain their proportionate ownership. A company can also raise ordinary share finance through private placements to selected shareholders, although company law and stock-exchange listing requirements restrict the amount of new shares that can be issued via a private placement.

OBJECTIVE 4

Preference shares are called a 'hybrid' security because they possess many characteristics of both ordinary shares and debt. The debt characteristic comes from the payment of a fixed dividend amount to the preference shareholders, which takes priority over dividend payments to ordinary shareholders. In addition, the priority of preference shareholders to company assets in the event of the winding up of the company ranks behind debt-holders and before ordinary shareholders. In the past many issues of preference shares were redeemable, but new issues of preference shares tend to be irredeemable and convertible to ordinary shares.

OBJECTIVE 5

Convertible securities are debt instruments or preference shares that the investor can exchange for a specified number of ordinary shares. The characteristics of convertible securities are constantly evolving to reflect changes in tax legislation and financial market conditions.

The valuation of a convertible note is a function of the value of the straight debt component plus the value of the component that entitles conversion into ordinary shares. Because convertible notes provide investors with the security of debt and the capital-gains potential of ordinary shares, they generally sell for a premium above the higher of the security value or the conversion value. This premium reflects the value of the convertible-note-holder's option to convert to ordinary shares.

Key terms

For a complete flashcard glossary go to MyFinanceLab at www.pearson.com.au/myfinancelab

You can find information on mutual funds at **http://finance.yahoo.com**. Click on 'Investing' and follow the 'Mutual Funds' link to find the 'Top Performers'. What is the highest return for the three-month, one-year, three-year and five-year funds?

Review questions

19-1 Explain the statement that 'debt and equity have different characteristics that need to be considered in financing decisions'.

19-2 What is hybrid finance?

19-3 What are the advantages and disadvantages of the ordinary shareholder's residual claim on income from the point of view of the investor?

19-4 Explain the relevance of the following for an initial share flotation:

(a) prospectus
(b) underwriting
(c) issue price

19-5 What is meant by 'dilution' and 'pre-emptive right'? Are these terms related? How?

19-6 Since a rights issue allows ordinary shareholders to purchase shares at a price below the current market price, why is it not of value to the ordinary shareholder?

19-7 What are the advantages to a company of private ordinary-share placements? Why are some shareholders critical of such placements?

19-8 Why are preference shares referred to as hybrid securities?

19-9 Why does a convertible note sell at a premium above its value as a note or ordinary share?

19-10 Convertible notes are said to provide the capital-gains potential of ordinary shares and the security of straight debt. Explain this statement.

19-11 What are some reasons for a company to issue convertible securities?

19-12 Browse the ASX website, **www.asx.com.au**.

(a) ASX-listed companies: select three companies of your choice. Explain their industry class and principal activities. Browse their web pages (see Internet address) and indicate any recent major changes in business operations that may affect profitability and the share price.
(b) Upcoming floats on ASX: how many companies are planning to float? Name one that could be attractive for stags and explain why.

Self-test problems

ST-1 (*Rights issue*) A company is considering a rights issue to raise $30 million. Currently this company has 30 million shares outstanding, selling for $6 per share. The subscription price of the new shares would be $4 per share.

For answers go to MyFinanceLab
www.pearson.com.au/myfinancelab

(a) How many shares must be sold to raise the desired funds?
(b) How many shares must a shareholder own in order to have one right?
(c) Calculate the theoretical ex-rights price.
(d) What is the value of one right?

ST-2 (*Convertible terminology*) Aquarius Limited has just issued 9.4 million 11.5% convertible notes to raise $11.3 million. The notes are for a 10-year term and interest is payable each June and December. Holders can convert each note to one ordinary share after the first five years of the notes up to the maturity date. A straight unsecured note for a company with a similar credit rating to Aquarius was yielding 14% on a date shortly after the issue. Also, at that time the company's ordinary shares were selling for $1.10 and the market price of a convertible note was $1.30. Determine the following:

(a) Issue price
(b) Conversion price
(c) Conversion value
(d) Security value
(e) Conversion premium

Problems

For more problems and for answers to problems marked with an asterisk (*) go to MyFinanceLab at www.pearson.com.au/myfinancelab

19-1* (*Rights issue*) The L. Turner Company is considering raising $12 million through a rights issue. It has 10 million ordinary shares outstanding, currently selling for $8.40 each. The subscription price on the new shares will be $6 per share.

(a) How many shares must be sold to raise the desired funds?
(b) How many shares must a shareholder own in order to have one right?
(c) What is the theoretical value of the shares ex-rights?
(d) What is the value of one right?

19-2 (*Rights issue*) Mawson Manufacturing Ltd is considering a rights issue to raise $70 million to finance new projects. Its paid-up capital is 40 million ordinary shares, and the current share price is $10. The issue price for the rights offering would be $7 per share.

(a) How many shares must be taken up in order to raise the desired funds?
(b) How many shares must a shareholder own in order to have one right?
(c) What is the theoretical ex-rights price?
(d) What is the value of one right?

19-3* (*Rights issue*) The B. Fuller Corporation is in the process of selling ordinary shares through a rights issue. Prior to the new issue, the firm had 5 million ordinary shares outstanding. Through the rights issue, it plans to issue an additional 1 million shares at a subscription price of $3. After the shares went ex-rights, the market price was $4. What was the price of the Fuller ordinary shares just prior to the rights issue?

19-4 (*Convertible terminology*) In 2003 the Andyfield Company issued some $100 par value, 6% convertible unsecured notes due in 2013. The conversion price on these convertibles is $4 per share. The price of the ordinary shares is now $2.72. The convertibles have a BB rating, and straight BB unsecured notes are now yielding 9%. The market price of the convertibles is now $84.02. Determine the following (assuming that note interest payments are made annually):

(a) Conversion ratio
(b) Conversion value
(c) Security value
(d) Conversion premium

19-5* (*Convertible terminology*) The Padis Company had made an issue of 5% convertible preference shares. The conversion price is $2.70 per share to 30 September 20X7. The price of the company's ordinary shares is now $1.32 and the convertibles are selling for $1.78. The par value of the convertibles is $2.50. Similar quality preference shares without the conversion option are currently yielding 8%. Determine the following:

(a) Conversion ratio
(b) Conversion value
(c) Conversion premium

19-6 (*Convertible terminology*) The Ecotosleptics Company has an issue of 6% non-redeemable convertible preference shares outstanding. The conversion price on these securities is $28 per share. The price of the ordinary shares is now $14. The preference shares are selling for $20. The par value of the preference shares is $25 per share. Similar quality preference shares without the conversion feature are currently yielding 8%. Determine the following:

(a) Conversion ratio
(b) Conversion value
(c) Value as preference shares
(d) Conversion premium

19-7 (*Capital management*) Twotel Company Ltd is a growing large company and the current year's net profit after tax is expected to be $6.25 billion. It has issued ordinary capital of 500 million ordinary shares, which are selling on the share market for $14.

Plans are in hand to raise $300 million from an issue of 7% preference shares ($100 face value) and to use the proceeds to buy back ordinary shares.

(a) Estimate the change in the EPS of the ordinary shares after the buyback.
(b) If everything else remained constant, would you expect the company's strategy to increase or reduce its weighted average cost of capital? Explain.

19-8 (*Convertible terminology*) In 2004 Waldron Limited issued $1000 par value, 10% semi-annual convertible notes that mature in 2024. The conversion price on these convertibles is $16.75 per share. The company's ordinary shares were selling for $14.77 on a given date shortly after these convertibles were issued. These convertibles have a B rating, and straight B unsecured notes were yielding 14% on that date. The market price of the convertible was $970 on that date. Determine the following:

(a) Conversion ratio
(b) Conversion value
(c) Security value
(d) Conversion premium

19-9 (*Convertible terminology*) In 2008 Mauney Limited issued $1000 par value, 7% convertible notes due in 2028. The conversion price on these convertibles is $45 per share. The price of the company's ordinary shares is now $26 per share. These convertibles have a BBB rating, and straight BB unsecured notes are now yielding 9%. The market price of the convertibles is now $840.25. Determine the following (assuming that note interest payments are made annually):

(a) Conversion ratio
(b) Conversion value
(c) Security value
(d) Conversion premium

19-10 (*Capital management*) The current year net profit after tax for Arelia Ltd is expected to be $102 million. The company has issued 20 million ordinary shares selling on the share market for $3.50 and intends to use the $30 million raised from a new issue of preference shares to buy back some of its issued ordinary shares. The preference shares will have a $10 face value and pay a preference dividend of 60 cents per share.

(a) Estimate the change in the EPS of the ordinary shares after the buyback.
(b) If everything else remained constant, would you expect the company's strategy to increase or reduce its weighted average cost of capital? Explain.

19-11 (*Capital management*) Apax Computers Ltd is a growing company and the current year's net profit after tax is expected to be $125 million. It has 70 million ordinary shares selling on the share market for $7.

The company plans to raise $200 million from an issue of 8% preference shares ($100 face value) and to use the proceeds to buy back ordinary shares.

(a) Estimate the change in the EPS of the ordinary shares after the buyback.
(b) If everything else remained constant, would you expect the company's strategy to increase or reduce its weighted average cost of capital? Explain.

Case study

For your job as the business reporter for a local newspaper, you are given the task of putting together a series of articles on companies raising equity capital through the share market. Much recent local press coverage has been given to the number of company flotations and the large premiums when the new shares are first listed on the stock exchange.

Your editor would like you to address the following specific issues in your articles.

1. What opportunities does the share market offer the financial manager to raise equity capital?
2. What factors does a company have to consider before flotation?
3. What factors does a company have to consider before having a rights issue?
4. Why would a company consider issuing convertible notes?

Notes

1. Price Waterhouse, Annual Survey of Sharemarket Floats January–December 1997, Price Waterhouse, 1998.
2. K. Rock, 'Why new issues are underpriced', *Journal of Financial Economics*, 1986, pp. 187–212; F. J. Finn and R. Higham, 'The performance of unseasoned new equity issues-cum-stock-exchange listings in Australia', *Journal of Business and Finance*, September 1988, pp. 333–51; I. Welch, 'Seasoned offerings, initiation costs and the underpricing of initial public offerings', *Journal of Finance*, June 1989, pp. 421–49; R. Ibbotson, J. Sindelar and J. Ritter, 'The market's problems with the pricing of initial public offerings', *Journal of Applied Corporate Finance*, Spring 1994, pp. 66–74; J. How, H. Izan and G. Monroe, 'Differential information and the underpricing of initial public offerings: Australian evidence', *Accounting and Finance*, May 1995, pp. 87–105.
3. D. E. Allen, 'The determinants of the capital structure of listed Australian companies: The financial manager's perspective', *Australian Journal of Management*, 16, December 1991, pp. 103–26.
4. Industry Commission, *Informal Equity Investment: Small Business Research Program*, information paper, AGPS, Canberra, 1997, copyright Commonwealth of Australia.
5. In response to Australian income tax changes in 1989, these convertible preference shares have tended to be non-redeemable.
6. G. Donaldson, 'In defence of preferred stock', *Harvard Business Review*, July–August 1962, pp. 123–36.

Special topics in finance

Part 6

20 International business finance   **21 Corporate risk management**

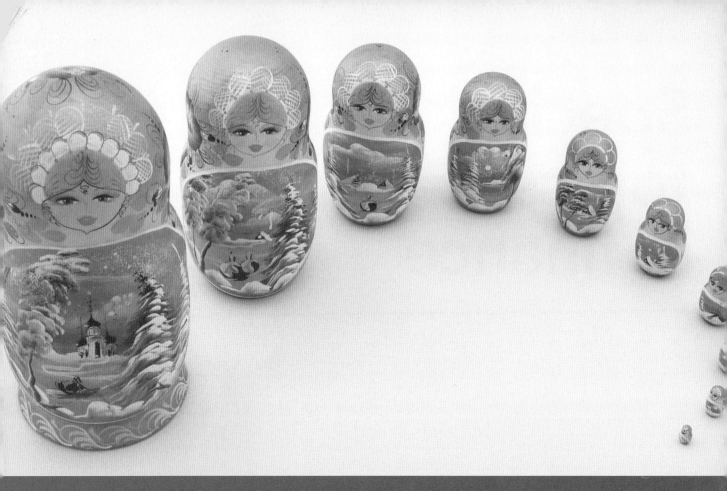

Learning objectives

After reading this chapter, you should be able to:

1 Discuss the internationalisation of business.
2 Understand the nature and importance of the foreign exchange market and exchange-rate quotations.
3 Describe interest-rate and purchasing-power parity.
4 Explain exchange-rate risk and the different techniques used to manage exchange-rate risk.
5 Discuss the risks that are unique to the capital-budgeting analysis of direct foreign investments.

For a complete eBook go to MyFinanceLab
www.pearson.com.au/myfinancelab

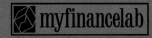

myfinancelab

International business finance

chapter 20

CHAPTER PREVIEW

This chapter highlights the complications that an international business faces when it deals in multiple currencies. The chapter begins with a discussion of the foreign exchange market on which foreign currencies are traded on a daily basis. Business dealings in foreign currencies give rise to what is known as exchange-rate risk. This is the risk that the firm's revenues, cash flows and bottom line will be affected by fluctuations in the exchange rate. The chapter therefore continues with a description of different types of exchange-rate risk and effective strategies to manage these risks. For the international firm, direct foreign investment is a capital-budgeting decision—with some additional complexities. A discussion of the risks that are unique to capital-budgeting analysis of foreign direct investments closes the chapter.

As you study this chapter, you will be reminded of two of the principles that tie this entire text together: *Principle 1: The risk–return trade-off—we won't take on additional risk unless we expect to be compensated with additional return*, and *Principle 3: Cash—not profits—is king.* Look for the principles as you work through the discussions.

The globalisation of product and financial markets

OBJECTIVE 1

Discuss the internationalisation of business.

Financial decision making has never been as global as it is today. Defined as the integration of national economies and their firms across the globe, globalisation is a source of growth for many companies. The trend of globalisation is most evident through the growth in world trade as a percentage of world aggregate output measured by the global gross national product (GNP). In the early 1960s global exports and imports made up about one-fifth of the aggregate global output, whereas today they make up more than one-third and are likely to grow even further.

In addition to the significant increase in world trade in recent years, there has also been a rise in the global level of international direct and portfolio investment. *Direct investment* refers to investment by a company in an overseas business over which it has control, such as when it builds an offshore manufacturing facility or purchases the majority of the shares in an overseas company. *Portfolio investment*, on the other hand, involves investment overseas in financial assets with maturities greater than one year, such as foreign shares and bonds, where the investor does not have control over the management of the investments. The motivation for portfolio investment is twofold: to obtain returns higher than those obtainable in the domestic capital markets, and to reduce portfolio risk through international diversification.

The increase in world trade and investment activity is also reflected in the globalisation of financial markets. For example, the globally integrated foreign exchange markets have grown rapidly in the last 20 years measured by the increased daily dollar volume of foreign currency transactions. An important point for financial management is that even a purely domestic firm that buys all its inputs and sells all its output in its home country is not immune to globalisation, nor can it totally ignore the workings of the international financial markets. The globalisation of the purely domestic firm's competitors will affect its competitiveness in the market.

> ## Concept check
> 20.1 What is globalisation? How does globalisation manifest?
> 20.2 What are the main reasons underlying portfolio investment?

GFC

ASIA IN THE FINANCIAL TURMOIL OF THE GFC

The Global Financial Crisis was a clear manifestation of the high degree of globalisation in financial markets. From what appeared to be a home-grown problem for the US, the sub-prime loan crisis spread to all corners of the world. Asia was no exception. It was hit hard by a financial tsunami which was not of its own making. Unlike the Asian financial crisis of 1997, which was caused by poor macroeconomic policies and weak financial systems in the region, this time most Asian countries were affected despite strong macro-economic fundamentals and sound banks and corporations.

The impact of the crisis was such that regional growth declined by as much as 2%, hurting many businesses and millions of people, who found themselves again impoverished after losing their jobs. The ramifications of the GFC in Asia showed how easily even the healthiest of banking sectors could be dragged into the international turmoil, despite having very little exposure to the toxic debt known as mortgage-backed securities. For example, South Korean banks had a mere $70 million exposure to risky mortgage-backed securities, and nonperforming loans were at an all-time low. Still, South Korea was exposed to the global crisis because its banks relied more on foreign financing

than banks in other countries in Asia. In addition, as confidence slowly dissipated in the region's financial markets, banks became nervous about parting with funds, credit tightened and stock markets plunged.

In the wake of the GFC, global leaders have attempted to introduce new regulatory measures to make the financial sector safer. Concrete proposals include revised accounting standards, closer supervision of credit rating agencies and hedge funds, an early warning system of potential risks and a central role for the International Monetary Fund (IMF) in the global financial architecture. At their June 2010 meeting, G-20 leaders, comprising finance ministers and central bank governors of 20 industrialised nations, further called for higher bank capital to help avert another financial crisis. In particular, the G-20 called for banks to increase common equity as a percentage of their so-called Tier 1 capital to allow them to withstand a shock of the magnitude of the recent financial crisis without significant government support. This proposed move will certainly make banks safer. But is it enough to prevent another global financial crisis? Only time will tell.

Regardless of your program

WORKING IN A FLAT WORLD

The world has become an increasingly international place in which to live and work. Thomas Friedman expounds on this theme in his book, *The World Is Flat*, which looks closely at how global boundaries have collapsed, flattening the playing field for all firms worldwide.[1] It no longer matters whether you major in accounting, engineering, economics, marketing, management or finance—you will be competing with individuals from

around the world with the same training. As Thomas Friedman explains in his book, the convergence of technology and events has allowed India, China and many other countries to become part of the global supply chain for services and manufacturing. Let there be no doubt, there is no going back—not in terms of business or your personal life. The playing field you will be on for the rest of your life is an international one.

Exchange rates and the foreign exchange market

OBJECTIVE 2

Understand the nature and importance of the foreign exchange market and exchange-rate quotations.

The **foreign exchange market** facilitates the exchange of currencies of different countries. Short-term financial assets, such as bank deposits, are also exchanged in the foreign exchange market. The **exchange rate** between two currencies that is quoted on the foreign exchange market provides a mechanism for the transfer of purchasing power from one currency to the other. An interesting feature of the foreign exchange market is that it is not located in one physical place. Rather, it comprises an international network of electronic connections such as telephone, fax, telex, computer and data display screens between foreign exchange dealers, brokers and customers. In Australia, foreign exchange dealers, comprising banks and other finance organisations, are licensed to buy and sell foreign currencies. The Reserve Bank of Australia was the licensing authority until March 2002 when the role was transferred to the Australian Securities and Investments Commission (ASIC). Foreign exchange brokers are other organisations that act as intermediaries between the other market participants.

foreign exchange market
The market in which the currencies of various countries are traded.

exchange rate
The rate at which one currency can be exchanged (bought/sold) for another.

The foreign exchange market is the largest market on earth as measured by the daily dollar volume of transactions. According to the triennial survey conducted by the Bank for International Settlements in April 2010, the daily turnover in the foreign exchange market rose to approximately US$4.0 trillion, representing an increase of 20% from 2007 based on current exchange rates. In Australia, the daily turnover stands at US$192.1 billion, showing a 12.34% growth from the 2007 daily turnover. The foreign exchange market is also said to be the most perfect market of all. It is characterised by a large number of buyers and sellers, a relatively free flow of information and homogenous product. Product homogeneity means that, no matter where you buy the currency, it is very likely that the notes or coins that you get will be identical. The foreign exchange market is also a 24-hour market. At any point in time there are foreign exchange transactions taking place in some region of the globe.

The foreign exchange market operates simultaneously at two levels. At the first level, customers buy and sell small amounts of foreign exchange through banks or dealers. This is called the retail segment of the foreign exchange market. At the second level, dealers buy and sell foreign exchange from other dealers in the same country, from dealers in foreign exchange markets located in other countries, or from their large corporate clients. This is called the inter-bank or wholesale segment of the foreign exchange market. Inter-bank transactions account for the vast majority of all foreign exchange transactions.

Because currency markets provide transactions in a continuous manner for a very large volume of sales and purchases, the markets are efficient in the sense that it is difficult to make a profit by shopping around from one dealer to another. Minute differences in the exchange-rate quotes from different dealers are quickly eliminated by a mechanism known as arbitrage, which

FYI

The Australian dollar (AUD) was introduced in 1966 to replace the Australian pound that had been in circulation in Australia since 1929. Shortly after its introduction, the AUD, like most other currencies in the world at that time, was fixed against the US dollar at the parity rate of 1.12 per one US dollar. In 1971 the peg against the US dollar was removed and replaced by a peg against a basket of currencies known as the 'trade-weighted index'. The selected currencies in the basket reflected the relative strength of those countries as Australia's major trading partners.

In 1983, as part of the deregulation of the Australian financial system, the AUD was 'floated', allowing its value to be determined by the demand and supply of the currency. As with any other currency, the value of the AUD is determined by the relative strength of the Australian economy, its level of exports and imports, the level of monetary activity and the deficits or surpluses in its balance of payments. Since it was floated, the value of the AUD has varied. In 2001, at its lowest point, one AUD could buy only US$0.46, while in early November 2010, the AUD rose sharply following the RBA decision to add 25 basis points to the cash rate and traded close to parity with the US dollar.

will be discussed later in this chapter. Thus, simultaneous quotes by different dealers in Sydney, Singapore and London are likely to be the same.

EXCHANGE-RATE QUOTATION

Unlike other markets, where money is being exchanged for a different commodity, in the foreign exchange market money is being exchanged for money. Remember that the exchange rate is the price of one currency in terms of another, but which one is which?

A **direct exchange rate** quotes the price of one unit of foreign currency in terms of the home currency. Most countries follow a direct quotation system against the US dollar (USD), so the exchange rate is represented as the amount of the home currency required to buy 1 USD. For example, an exchange rate quote of 1.30 between the USD and the Singapore dollar (SGD) would be interpreted as 1 USD is worth 1.30 SGD. In practice, the currency in the unit of 1 is displayed first. For example, in this case the USD is in the unit of 1 so the quotation would be USD/SGD 1.30.

In contrast to a direct quote, an **indirect exchange-rate** quotation states the price of one unit of home currency in terms of the foreign currency. Many countries belonging to the Commonwealth, such as England, Australia and New Zealand, tend to adopt an indirect quotation system. This is a tradition dating back to the time before England adopted the decimal currency system. Understandably, the old English currency system, which was not divisible by 10, made it difficult for calculations to be done in pounds. From 1971 the pound's coinage system was changed to the decimal system, but the tradition of quoting in one unit of the home currency, which in the case of England is the pound, continues. In the case of Australia, the exchange rate is quoted as AUD/USD 0.98, which is read as 1 AUD is worth 0.98 USD. It is quite straightforward to convert a direct quote into an indirect quote and vice versa. Generally speaking, an indirect quote is calculated as the *reciprocal* of the direct quote, as illustrated in Example 20.1.

direct exchange-rate rate
The exchange rate that indicates the number of units of the home currency required to buy one unit of a foreign currency.

indirect exchange-rate rate
The exchange rate that indicates the number of units of the foreign currency required to buy one unit of home currency.

EXAMPLE 20.1 Exchange-rate quotation

You are about to travel to both the United States and the United Kingdom for two months and you want to obtain USD2000 and GBP1000 before you go. The exchange rates are quoted as follows:

AUD/USD 0.9889
AUD/GBP 0.6266

You will need to convert these quotes into direct quotes and calculate the amount of AUD you need to purchase your desired amount of the foreign currencies.

The quotes are indirect as they give the amount of foreign currency for one unit of the home currency (being the AUD). Hence the direct quotes are:

$$USD/AUD = \frac{1}{\text{indirect quote}} = \frac{1}{0.9889} = 1.0112$$

$$GBP/AUD = \frac{1}{\text{indirect quote}} = \frac{1}{0.6266} = 1.5959$$

To buy 2000 USD you will need $2000 \times 1.0112 = 2022.40$ AUD
To buy 1000 GBP you will need $1000 \times 1.5959 = 1595.9$ AUD

TYPES OF FOREIGN EXCHANGE TRANSACTIONS

There are two major types of exchange-rate transactions: spot transactions and forward transactions. The spot exchange rate applies to spot transactions, while the forward rate is applicable to forward exchange contracts.

Spot transactions

Spot transactions are those taking place at the effective spot exchange rates. By definition, spot transactions encompass both those that result in an immediate exchange of currency and inter-bank transactions that result in settlement two business days later. *Spot exchange rates* are quoted by foreign exchange dealers to apply to spot transactions with their customers, and they comprise two figures. The first is the rate at which the dealer is prepared to *buy* one currency in exchange for another and the second is the rate at which the dealer is prepared to *sell* one currency in exchange for another. The price at which the dealer is willing to buy foreign currency is the *bid* price and the price at which they are willing to sell is the *ask* price. The *ask rate* is also known as the selling rate or the offer rate. As the dealer aims to make a profit on a round transaction to compensate for the risk inherent in the business, the ask price is always greater than the bid price. The difference between these two prices is known as the **bid–ask spread**. The spread exists as a margin to compensate the dealers for holding the risky foreign currency and for providing the service of exchanging currencies.

When there is a large volume of transactions exchanging two currencies and the trading is continuous, the bid–ask spread is small and can be less than 0.5% of the spot rate for the major currencies. The spread is much higher for infrequently traded currencies. For example, looking at the rates quoted in Table 20.1, we can see that for the AUD/USD rate the spread is equal to 0.9920 – 0.9887 = 0.0033, which is approximately 0.33% of the bid rate, whereas for

spot transaction
A transaction where delivery will occur immediately. For foreign exchange, this delivery is, by convention, two business days after the transaction is agreed to.

bid–ask spread
The difference between the ask quote and the bid quote.

TABLE 20.1 Australian dollar exchange rates correct as of 12 November 2010

	ASK	BID
American dollar	0.9887	0.9920
British pound	0.6143	0.6189
Canadian dollar	0.9943	1.0029
Chinese yuan	6.5325	6.605
Danish krone	5.4334	5.4356
Euro	0.7293	0.7298
Hong Kong dollar	7.8359	7.8381
Indian rupee	43.62	44.03
Japanese yen	81.310	82.11
Malaysian ringgit	3.0498	3.05
Mexican peso	12.1143	12.2265
New Zealand dollar	1.2691	1.2801
Norwegian kroner	5.869	5.9305
Singapore dollar	1.2764	1.2898
South African rand	6.8504	6.9137
South Korean won	1097.95	1114.67
Sri Lankan rupee	110.05	111.13
Swedish krona	6.7642	6.8351
Swiss franc	0.9637	0.9732
Taiwan dollar	29.61	30.06
Thai baht	29.46	29.73

Source: www.ozforex.com.au

the South Korean won the spread is 1114.67 – 1097.95 = 16.72, which is approximately 1.52% of the bid rate.

Because every foreign exchange transaction will involve two currencies, we need to know which currency is being bought and sold and for how much of the other currency. Generally, in a direct quotation system the bid and ask exchange rate applies to the foreign currency that is denominated in the unit of 1. For example, the bid (ask) exchange rate is the exchange rate at which dealers are willing to buy (sell) one unit of foreign currency. However, due to the indirect quotation system in the foreign exchange market in Australia, the exchange rate involving the Australian dollar that is quoted to *retail* customers indicates the number of units of the foreign currency the dealer is prepared to buy and sell in exchange for one unit of the AUD.

Looking at the *retail market* exchange rates in Table 20.1, we can see that the bank is prepared to *buy* USD0.9920 from a customer in exchange for AUD1 and is prepared to *sell* USD0.9887 to a customer in exchange for AUD1. Similarly, the exchange rate quoted between the British pound (GBP) and the AUD is the rate at which the bank is prepared to *buy* GBP0.6189 from a customer in exchange for AUD1 and is prepared to *sell* GPB0.6143 to a customer in exchange for AUD1. In general, the bid price in Table 20.1 is the rate at which the bank is willing to buy foreign currency for 1 AUD and the ask price is the rate at which the bank is prepared to sell foreign currency for 1 AUD. Note that, because Australia follows an indirect quotation system, the 'buy' quote is greater than the 'sell' quote, as 'buy' and 'sell' refer to buying and selling foreign currencies.

EXAMPLE 20.2 Exchange-rate quotation

An Australian business must pay 1000 euros (EUR) to a German firm. How many dollars (AUD) will be required for this transaction using the rates in Table 20.1?

As the business wants to buy euro, the bank will have to sell euro. The rate at which the dealer/bank is selling euro is 0.7293 EUR for 1 AUD. As a result, to buy 1000 euro the business will need to pay 1000/0.7293 = AUD1371.18.

Concept check

20.3 What is the difference between a direct quote and an indirect quote?
20.4 What is a spot exchange rate?

For answers go to MyFinanceLab or www.pearson.com.au/9781442539174

Forward transactions

forward exchange contract
A contract that requires the delivery of one currency at a specified future date for a specified amount of another currency.

A **forward exchange contract** is an agreement between two parties that requires delivery, at a specified future date, of one currency for a specified amount of another currency. The exchange rate for the forward transaction is called the *forward exchange rate* and is agreed today; however, the actual payment of one currency and the receipt of the other currency take place at the future date specified in the contract. The two most important features of forward contracts are that the transaction will not take place until some time in the future but the applicable exchange rate, the forward rate, is determined today. For example, a 30-day forward contract entered into on 1 March will require delivery of the currencies on 31 March. Note that the forward rate quoted today is not likely to be the same as the spot rate that will apply in the future when the transaction takes place, as that spot rate will depend on the market conditions at that time and it may be more or less than today's forward rate.

Assume that you are going to receive a payment denominated in pounds from a British customer in 30 days. If you wait for 30 days and exchange the pounds at the spot rate, you will receive a dollar amount reflecting the exchange rate in 30 days (that is, the future spot rate). As of today, you have no way of knowing the exact dollar value of your future pound receipts.

Consequently, you cannot make precise plans about the use of these dollars. If, conversely, you buy a forward contract, then you know the exact dollar value of your future receipts, and you can make precise plans concerning their use. The forward contract, therefore, can reduce your uncertainty about the future, and the major advantage of the forward market is that of risk reduction. Forward contracts are therefore primarily used to reduce **exchange-rate risk**.

Forward contracts are usually quoted for periods of 30, 90 and 180 days. A contract for any intermediate date can be obtained, usually with the payment of a small premium. Forward contracts for periods longer than 180 days can be obtained by special negotiations with banks. Contracts for periods greater than one year can be costly.

A forward rate can be quoted outright, in which case it is similar to a spot rate quotation, where the bid price indicates the price at which dealers are willing to buy the foreign currency forward and the ask price indicates the price at which dealers are willing to sell the foreign currency forward. Forward rates, however, are more commonly quoted as forward points, or a margin to be added or subtracted from the spot rates. In a direct quote, if the forward rates are greater than the spot rates, it is said that the foreign currency is trading at a *forward premium*. In this case, the forward points are increasing and the forward rates are obtained by adding the forward points to the spot rates. In the opposite case, where the foreign currency is trading at a discount, the forward points are decreasing and the forward rates are obtained by subtracting the forward points from the spot rates. Example 20.3 details the calculations of forward rates.

> **exchange-rate risk**
> The variability of future cash flows caused by variations in exchange rates.

EXAMPLE 20.3 Forward-rate quotation

The following quotes are provided by the foreign-exchange dealer:

1 AUD =	1.2855 – 1.2865 SGD
3-month forward	50 – 70
6-month forward	120 – 90

What are the three-month and six-month forward rates?

The three-month forward points are increasing (from 50 to 70) so they need to be added to the current spot rates (1.2855 + 0.0050 and 1.2865 + 0.0070). Note that the forward points are the value of the fourth decimal place, so 1 point = 0.0001. The three-month forward rate is therefore:

1 AUD = 1.2905 – 1.2935 SGD

The six-month forward points are decreasing (from 120 to 90) so they need to be subtracted from the current spot rates (1.2855 – 0.0120 and 1.2865 – 0.0090). The six-month spot rate is therefore:

1 AUD = 1.2735 – 1.2775 SGD

Note that in Example 20.3 the quote is indirect from an Australian perspective. Therefore, the home currency is trading at a three-month forward premium and a six-month forward discount. In direct quotes, the forward margins give an indication of whether the foreign currency is trading at a forward discount or premium. In short, the currency in the unit of 1 is the one that is trading at a forward discount or premium, as indicated by the forward margins. This premium or discount is also called the **forward spot differential** and is calculated as the difference between the forward rate and the spot rate.

We can also calculate the annual percentage amount of the forward discount or premium of the home currency (in an indirect quote) or the foreign currency (in a direct quote) in relation to another currency from the respective spot rates (S) and forward rates (F), as follows:

> **forward spot differential**
> A premium or discount calculated as the difference between the forward rate and the spot rate.

$$P \text{ (or } D) = \frac{F - S}{S} \times \frac{12}{n} \times 100$$

(20-1)

where n = number of months in the forward contract

P = the annualised percentage premium, if $F > S$

D = the annualised percentage discount if $F < S$

Example 20.4 gives a calculation of a forward premium.

EXAMPLE 20.4 Calculation of the forward premium

The 30-day (1-month) forward euro is selling at EUR0.7280 per AUD1, whereas the current spot rate is EUR0.7299 per AUD1. This difference represents a forward discount percent per annum for AUD of:

$$\frac{0.7280 - 0.7299}{0.7280} \times \frac{12}{1} \times 100 = -3.13\%$$

That is, 1 AUD is worth 3.13% fewer euros forward than currently at spot.

FYI

Although declining in importance, the US dollar is still the most traded currency in the world. According to statistics published by the Bank of International Settlement in 2010, the US dollar was involved in 42.45% of all foreign exchange transactions, followed by the euro, which accounted for approximately 19.55% of all transactions. Despite an increase in the percentage of transactions involving the Australian dollar, from 3.3% to 3.8% in the 2007–2010 period, the Australian dollar remains the fifth most traded currency in the world. Apart from the US dollar, the euro and the Australian dollar, the Japanese yen and the pound sterling round up the top five.

EXCHANGE RATES AND ARBITRAGE

The foreign exchange market is international, with dealers around the world linked electronically with each other. Therefore, at any point in time the exchange rate quoted in different countries for the same currencies should be the same. If the exchange-rate quotations were *out of line*, then an enterprising trader could make a profit by buying in the market where the currency was cheaper and selling it in another. Such a buy-and-sell strategy would involve a zero net investment of funds with no risk, yet would provide a sure profit. A person who undertakes such activity is called an **arbitrageur**, and the process of buying and selling in more than one market to make a riskless profit is called *arbitrage*. Spot exchange markets are said to be efficient in the sense that arbitrage opportunities do not persist for any length of time. That is, the exchange rates between currencies quoted in two different markets are quickly brought *in line*, aided by the arbitrage process. The process of buying the currency where it is cheap will push up the price of that currency, while the action of selling the currency in the market where it is more expensive will drive down the price. If this process continues, the price between the two markets will be in equilibrium and no more arbitrage will be possible. **Simple arbitrage** eliminates exchange-rate differentials across the markets for a single currency. **Triangular arbitrage** does the same across the markets for all currencies. Covered interest arbitrage eliminates differentials across currency and interest-rate markets.

arbitrageur
A person involved in the process of buying and selling in more than one market to make riskless profits.

simple arbitrage
Buying and selling in more than one market to make a riskless profit in a single currency.

triangular arbitrage
Arbitrage across the markets for all currencies.

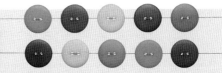

Your money

INTERNATIONAL INVESTING

Today, trading in stocks, bonds and other investments takes place around the clock and around the world. Indeed, there are a number of multinational companies, such as Sony and Toyota, that trade on exchanges in more than one country. So, why would you want to invest internationally? The main advantage is that, because stock and bond prices in different countries don't always move together, international investments diversify your portfolio. When the stock or bond market in one country is weak, the market in another country may be strong. As a result, by investing in different markets, you can potentially reduce your investment risk without having to compromise too much return. For example, in 2009, the Australian stock markets rebounded and produced average returns of 33%, but the stock market in Norway earned 89%.

Another important reason underlying personal international investment is the small size of the Australian financial market. The market capitalisation of the Australian stock market is merely 2% of the global stock-market capitalisation. As a result, by investing exclusively in the Australian financial markets, you are limiting yourself to a very small number of available investments. The fast-growing emerging markets such as China and India also provide excellent opportunities for Australian investors with an appetite for risk to share in their enormous growth potential.

The concepts of interest-rate and purchasing-power parity provide the basis for understanding how prices and rates of interest across different countries are related to one another.

OBJECTIVE 3

Describe interest-rate and purchasing-power parity.

Interest-rate parity theory

Forward rates generally entail a premium or a discount relative to current spot rates. However, these forward premiums and discounts differ between currencies and maturities. These differences depend solely on the difference in the level of interest rates between the two countries, called the *interest-rate differential*. The value of the premium or discount can be theoretically computed from the **interest-rate parity (IRP) theory**. This theory, which aims to link exchange-rate differential to interest-rate differential, states that, except for the effects of small transaction costs, the forward premium or discount should be equal and opposite in size to the difference in the national interest rates for securities of the same maturity. Mathematically, the forward premium or discount, expressed as a percentage, has to satisfy the following relationship:

$$P = \frac{i^* - i}{1 + i} \qquad \textbf{(20-2)}$$

where P = the forward premium or discount in percentage
i^* = the interest rate in the foreign country
i = the interest rate in the home currency

interest-rate parity (IRP) theory
Proposes that (except for the effect of small transaction costs) the difference between the current spot rate and the forward exchange rate should reflect the differences in the national interest rates for securities of the same maturity.

COVERED INTEREST ARBITRAGE

The rationale for IRP is provided by the **covered interest arbitrage** argument. This argument states that, if the premiums (or discounts) reflected in current forward rates are not exactly equal to the current interest-rate differential, then arbitrage or riskless profits can be made.

This arbitrage would be accomplished by *simultaneously borrowing* in the currency with the lower interest rate, *investing* in the currency with the higher interest rate, and *covering* the exchange position in the forward-exchange market by entering into a forward contract to sell foreign currency at the time the investment matures. The entire process is known as 'covered interest arbitrage'. This arbitrage is 'covered' because there is no exchange-rate risk.

To illustrate the process of covered interest-rate arbitrage, assume that an investor starts with one unit of home currency. If this amount is invested domestically at the domestic interest rate, the end of the period return would be *1+ i* where *i* is the domestic interest rate. As an

covered interest arbitrage
Arbitrage designed to eliminate differentials across currency and interest-rate markets.

alternative to investing domestically, the investor can choose to invest in a foreign currency, which necessitates the conversion of the home currency into the foreign currency. Under a direct quote, one unit of home currency is equivalent to $1/S$ unit of foreign currency where S is the exchange rate. This amount is invested at the foreign interest to yield $1/S(1 + i^*)$ at the end of the period, where i^* is the foreign interest rate. This investor can eliminate the exchange-rate risk arising from this transaction by entering into a forward contract to sell foreign currency at the inception of the investment. Effectively, the investor locks in an exchange rate at which he or she converts the foreign-currency-denominated investment back into domestic currency. Hence, the home-currency value of the investment is $1/S(1 + i^*)F$. To eliminate the opportunity for arbitrage to take place, the return from a domestic investment has to be exactly the same as the return from a foreign investment. Hence:

$$1 + i = \frac{1}{S} \times (1 + i^*) \times F$$

Rearranging gives:

$$F = S \times \frac{1 + i}{1 + i^*} \qquad\qquad \textbf{(20-3)}$$

Note that equation (20-3) applies to direct exchange-rate quotation. With indirect exchange-rate quotation, the relationship becomes:

$$F = S \times \frac{1 + i^*}{1 + i} \qquad\qquad \textbf{(20-4)}$$

Equations (20-3) and (20-4) indicate that the forward exchange rate is determined by the spot exchange rate and the respective interest rates in the domestic and foreign markets. Therefore, if the forward contract rate quoted in the foreign exchange market is different from the computed price, there is the potential to make arbitrage profits using the covered-interest-arbitrage routine. The forward markets are *efficient* in the sense that the quotes in the market represent the 'correct' price of the contract. The markets' efficiency also implies that no profit can be made by computing the prices at every instant and buying/selling forward when they appear incorrect. Some minor deviations from the computed correct price may exist for short periods. These deviations, however, are such that after the transactions costs have been recognised no net profit can be made. Numerous empirical studies attest to the efficiency of the forward markets.

Example 20.5 demonstrates how to calculate the forward rate.

EXAMPLE 20.5   Calculation of the forward rate

The USD/AUD spot rate is 0.8870. Interest rate in Australia is 6.5% per annum, while interest rate in the United States is 5.6% per annum. According to the covered interest arbitrage, what is the three-month forward rate?

The three-month forward rate can be calculated by applying equation (20-4):

$$F = S \times \frac{1 + i^*}{1 + i} = 0.8870 \times \frac{1 + 0.056 \times \frac{3}{12}}{1 + 0.065 \times \frac{3}{12}} = 0.8850$$

The result shows that, to prevent arbitrage, the currency with the higher interest rate will have a forward discount, while the currency with the lower interest rate will have a forward premium.

UNCOVERED INTEREST ARBITRAGE

Uncovered interest arbitrage is a deviation from covered interest arbitrage whereby the proceeds of the foreign currency investment are not protected by a forward contract but rather are converted back to the local currency at the prevailing spot rate. The arbitrage is therefore uncovered, as the foreign currency position is left 'uncovered' and so is exposed to foreign exchange-rate risk. As opposed to covered interest arbitrage, where a forward exchange rate is used to convert the foreign currency investment to the home currency, in an uncovered interest arbitrage the foreign currency investment is converted to home currency using the spot rate at the time of conversion. The uncovered interest parity that is maintained by uncovered interest arbitrage can be written as:

$$E(S) = S \times \frac{1 + i}{1 + i^*}$$ **(20-5)**

where $E(S)$ is the expected spot rate at the maturity of the investment.

While covered interest arbitrage and uncovered interest arbitrage are sound in theory, there are significant deviations from both parity conditions in reality. There are many reasons for these deviations, including transactions costs, political risk and tax differentials.

Concept check
20.5 In simple terms, what does the interest-rate parity theory mean?
20.6 What is the difference between covered interest-rate parity and uncovered interest-rate parity?

For answers go to MyFinanceLab or www.pearson.com.au/9781442539174

Purchasing-power parity

Purchasing-power parity (PPP) is the parity relationship that links exchange rates to inflation differentials between two countries. There are two versions of PPP, absolute PPP and relative PPP, which are examined below.

THE LAW OF ONE PRICE AND ABSOLUTE PPP

Underlying the PPP relationship is the **law of one price**. The law of one price is a proposition that, in competitive markets where there are no transportation costs or barriers to trade, the same good sold in different countries sells for the same price if all the different prices are expressed in terms of the same currency. The idea is that the 'worth' in terms of marginal utility of a good does not depend on where it is bought or sold. *The Economist* magazine maintains a Big Mac index, where prices of a Big Mac hamburger are compared across countries. If the law of one price holds, the price of a Big Mac should be the same no matter where it is sold. In actual fact, there is significant deviation from the law of one price, as it seems that Big Macs are sold at different prices in different countries, after taking into account exchange-rate differences. Trade impediments such as transportation costs, tariffs, taxes, existence of non-traded goods and so on are the main reasons for these deviations.

Absolute PPP maintains that if the law of one price holds for a single good it should apply to a basket of goods. Symbolically:

$$P = SP^*$$ **(20-6)**

where P is the price of a basket of domestic goods or the domestic price level, P^* is the price of an equivalent basket of foreign goods or the foreign price level, and S is the exchange rate.

RELATIVE PPP

Relative PPP overcomes the weaknesses of absolute PPP by maintaining that, although at one point in time the price of a basket of domestic goods would not be the same as the price of a

purchasing-power parity (PPP) theory
In the long run, exchange rates adjust so that the purchasing power of each currency tends to remain the same. Thus, exchange-rate changes tend to reflect international differences in inflation rates. Countries with high rates of inflation tend to experience declines in the value of their currency.

law of one price
The proposition that in competitive markets the same goods should sell for the same price where prices are stated in terms of a single currency.

basket of foreign goods, over time the change in the exchange rate should be determined by the changes in the price levels between two countries, more commonly known as inflation.

The derivation of the relative PPP condition is based on the absolute PPP.

At time t, absolute PPP gives $\qquad P_t = S_t P^*_t$

At time $t + 1$, absolute PPP gives $\qquad P_{t+1} = S_{t+1} P^*_{t+1}$

Dividing the second line by the first one gives:

$$\frac{P_{t+1}}{P_t} = \frac{S_{t+1}}{S_t} \times \frac{P^*_{t+1}}{P^*_t}$$

Since the change in price levels represents inflation, the above equation can be written as:

$$1 + \Delta P = (1 + \Delta S) \times (1 + \Delta P^*) \qquad\qquad\qquad \textbf{(20-7)}$$

where ΔP is the domestic rate of inflation, ΔS is the percentage change in exchange rate, and ΔP^* is the foreign inflation rate.

Equation (20-7) is the equation for relative PPP. However, a more commonly used approximation of relative PPP is:

$$\Delta S = \Delta P - \Delta P^* \qquad\qquad\qquad\qquad\qquad\qquad \textbf{(20-8)}$$

Relative PPP suggests that long-run changes in spot exchange rates are influenced by international differences in inflation rates. More specifically, the foreign exchange value of the currency of countries with high rates of inflation will tend to decline. Thus, if the United Kingdom experiences a 4% rate of inflation in a year when Europe experiences only a 2% rate, the GBP would be expected to decline in value by approximately 2% (4% − 2%) against the euro. As a result, if the beginning value of the euro was GBP0.80/EUR1, a 2% inflation rate in Europe and a 4% inflation rate in the United Kingdom would mean that to purchase the same goods in 12 months would require either GBP0.832, that is, 0.0 × (1 + 0.04), or EUR1.02, that is, 1 × (1 + 0.02). According to the PPP, this would result in the expected spot exchange rate of the euro at the end of that year (S_t + 1) being GBP0.80 × (1.04/1.02), or GBP0.816. This is the rate that will convert GBP0.832 to EUR1.02 and thereby preserve the purchasing power of the two currencies.

Empirical tests of PPP theory have shown that the parity condition tends to hold better in the long run and in emerging countries that experience high rates of inflation.

Finance at work

THE BIG MAC INDEX

The Economist's Big Mac index is based on the theory of purchasing-power parity (PPP), according to which exchange rates should adjust to equalise the price of a basket of goods and services around the world. The basket in this case is a hamburger: a McDonald's Big Mac.

The latest Big Mac index was published in March 2010 and showed by how much, in Big Mac PPP terms, selected currencies were overvalued or undervalued. The price of the Big Mac was collected in various countries, based on which a PPP exchange rate between two countries was calculated. This PPP exchange rate was then compared with the actual exchange rate to determine the extent to which a currency was overvalued

or undervalued in PPP terms. As it turned out, the most over-valued currency was the Norwegian kroner: the exchange rate that would equalise the price of an Icelandic Big Mac with an American one was 12.1 kroner to the dollar; the actual rate was 6.25, making the kroner 93% too dear. The most undervalued currency was the Chinese yuan, at 48% below its PPP rate.

The index is supposed to give a guide to the direction in which currencies should, in theory, head in the long run. It is only a rough guide, because its price reflects non-tradeable elements—such as rent and labour. For that reason, it is probably least rough when comparing countries at approximately the same stage of development.

International Fisher effect

According to the domestic Fisher effect (FE), the nominal interest rates (i) that are observed in the financial markets reflect the expected inflation rate (r) and a real rate of return (R):

$$1 + i = (1 + R)(1 + r) \qquad\qquad\qquad \textbf{(20-9)}$$

and

$$i = R + r + rR$$

While there is mixed empirical support for the Fisher effect internationally (IFE), it is widely thought that, for the major industrial countries, the real rate, R, is about 3% per annum when a long-term period is considered. In such a case, with the previous assumption regarding inflation rates, the annual nominal interest rate in the United Kingdom would be 7.12% $[(1 + 0.03)(1 + 0.04) - 1]$ and Germany, which uses the euro currency, would be 5.06% $[(1 + 0.03)(1 + 0.02) - 1]$.

In addition, according to interest-rate parity (IRP), and equation (20-2), the expected premium for the euro forward rate should be 1.96% $[(0.0712 - 0.0506)/1.0506]$. Starting with a current spot rate value of GBP0.40/1EUR gives us a one-year forward rate of GBP0.40(1.0196) = GBP0.408/EUR. As you may notice, this one-year forward rate is exactly the same as the PPP expected spot rate one year from today. In other words, if the real rate (R) is the same in both Germany and the United Kingdom, and expectations regarding inflation rates hold true, today's one-year forward rate is likely to be the same as the future spot rate one year from now.

Thus, in *efficient markets*, with rational expectations, the forward rate is an unbiased (not necessarily accurate) forecast of the future spot rate (unbiased forecast rate, or UFR). The relationships between inflation and interest rates, and spot and forward rates, are depicted in Figure 20.1.

Concept check

20.7 What does the law of one price say?

20.8 What is the international Fisher effect?

For answers go to MyFinanceLab or
www.pearson.com.au/9781442539174

FIGURE 20.1 Efficient foreign exchange market relationships

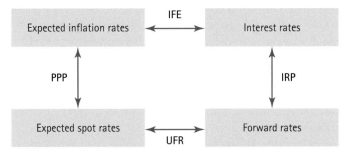

UFR = unbiased forward rate; IFE = international Fisher effect;
IRP = interest-rate parity; PPP = purchasing-power parity.

ONE STEP FURTHER

FORECASTING EXCHANGE RATES

Forecasting a financial price is an extremely useful but difficult task, and forecasting an exchange rate is no exception. According to the unbiased forward rate theory, the forward rate should be an unbiased predictor of the future spot rate. Unfortunately, empirical evidence has shown that the forward rate is a very poor predictor of the future spot rate. In practice, there are two main approaches to forecasting exchange rates: fundamental analysis and technical analysis.

In the fundamental approach, an exchange rate is believed to be determined by a range of *fundamental* factors, such as GDP, interest rate, inflation rate, trade balance, unemployment, productivity indexes and so on. These statistics will then be modelled to come up with an equilibrium exchange rate, a theoretically correct exchange rate given the values of the fundamental variables. However, forecasting models vary according to data characteristics and the experience of forecasters. The reliability of these forecasting models therefore largely depends on the model specification.

The technical approach, on the other hand, focuses on only a small subset of the data—price information. Technical analysts aim to predict future exchange rates based on extrapolation of previous exchange-rate data, not on fundamental economic indicators. Technical analysis is mainly concerned with identifying patterns of exchange-rate movements and assumes that those patterns will repeat themselves in the future. Many economists voice their doubts regarding the validity of technical forecast models. The basis for their argument is the concept of efficient markets, where today's prices are independent of historical prices, hence it is not possible to forecast future prices based on historical price behaviours. Practitioners, on the other hand, believe that technical analysis is valuable, especially in forecasting short-term exchange rates. There is some evidence that trading strategies based on signals provided by technical analyses return a marginally higher return than a buy-and-hold strategy. Nevertheless, it is arguable if this profit can be exploited in the long run and on a repeated basis.

There is no denying that forecasting exchange rates is an extremely challenging task. After all, the future is not ours to see!

OBJECTIVE **4**

Explain exchange-rate risk and the different techniques used to manage exchange-rate risk.

Exposure to exchange-rate risk

Assets or cash flows valued or denominated in a foreign currency will have different domestic currency values whenever the exchange rate changes. As a result, when a firm has assets or cash flows denominated in a foreign currency, it is said to have exposure to exchange-rate risk. The typical scenarios that give rise to exchange-rate exposure are:

- *International trade contracts.* When companies enter into international trade contracts that obligate them to receive or make payments in foreign currencies in the future, they are exposed to exchange rate risks as the value of the contract in the local currency is dependent on exchange rate movements.
- *Foreign portfolio investments.* When companies and individuals invest in financial assets that are denominated in foreign currencies, they face exchange-rate risk as changes in exchange rates affect their effective return expressed in the local currency.

- *Direct foreign investment.* When a parent company invests in assets denominated in a foreign currency, resulting in foreign currency denominated balance sheets and income statements, the parent company receives the repatriated profit stream in dollars. Thus, the exchange-rate risk concept applies to fluctuations in the dollar value of the assets located abroad.

Back to the principles

In international transactions, just as in domestic transactions, the key to value is the timing and amounts of cash spent and received. However, economic transactions across international borders add an element of risk because cash flows are denominated in the currency of the country in which business is being transacted. Consequently, the dollar value of the cash flows will depend on the exchange rate that exists at the time the cash changes hands. The fact remains, however, that it is cash spent and received that matters. This is the point of **Principle 3: Cash—not profits—is king**.

FYI

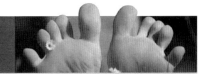

In July 2002 the national currencies of 11 countries of the European Union, often referred to as Euroland (Germany, France, Italy, Spain, Portugal, Belgium, the Netherlands, Luxembourg, Ireland, Finland and Austria), were replaced with the euro. Without question, Germany and France are the big players, accounting for over 50% of Euroland's output.

The European Union went for a single currency for several reasons. First, it made it easier for goods, people and services to travel across national borders. As a result, the economies of the European Union flourished. A common currency eliminated the exchange costs that occur when trading, for example, German marks for French francs. More importantly, it eliminated the uncertainty associated with exchange-rate fluctuations and hence reduced the costs associated with the management of exchange-rate risks within the euro zone. It also helped to eliminate cost differences for goods in different countries. For example, just before the euro was introduced, the 'Classic' Swatch watch was selling for 39.2 euros in Belgium and only 25.7 euros in Italy. The introduction of the euro made it easier to compare prices and eliminate the discrepancies.

Exchange rate exposures can be broadly classified as translation, transaction and economic exposures.

TRANSLATION EXPOSURE

Translation exposure arises because the foreign operation of a domestic business has its accounting statements denominated in the currency of the country in which the operation is located. Foreign-currency assets and liabilities are considered exposed if their foreign-currency value is to be translated into the parent company currency at a future date using the exchange rate current at the time of translation, that is, the spot exchange rate in effect at the balance-sheet date. This is because the domestic-currency value of these foreign-currency assets and liabilities will change from one balance-sheet date to another if the current spot exchange rate is used for the translation changes. These changes in domestic-currency value will be reported as exchange gains and losses in the domestic-currency financial statements.

Asset, liability and equity amounts that are translated at the historic exchange rate—that is, the rate that applied when these items were first recognised in the company's accounts—are not considered to be exposed. This is because the domestic-currency values of these amounts will not change as a result of spot exchange-rate changes. The rate (current or historic) used to translate various accounts depends on the translation procedure used and will be specified by accounting standards.

translation exposure
Arises because the foreign operation of a domestic business has its accounting statements denominated in the currency of the country in which the operation is located.

Any translation exchange-rate gains and losses that are reported in the domestic-currency accounts are *unrealised*, as the underlying foreign-currency value has not changed, only its domestic-currency translated value. Thus, if financial markets are efficient and managerial goals are consistent with owner wealth maximisation (and if agency and signalling costs are negligible so that investors recognise that the gains and losses are a product of accounting procedures and not cash flows), a firm should not have to use real resources for hedging against possible unrealised losses caused by translation exposure. However, if there are significant agency or information costs, or if markets are not efficient (that is, if translation losses and gains raise information costs for investors, or if they endanger the firm's ability to satisfy debt or other covenants, or if the evaluation of the firm's managers depends on translated accounting data), a firm may indeed find it economical to hedge against translation losses or gains.

TRANSACTION EXPOSURE

Foreign-currency accounts receivable, foreign-currency accounts payable, foreign-currency fixed-price sales and foreign-currency purchase contracts are examples of transactions where the foreign-currency value is fixed at a time that is different from the time when the transactions produce foreign-currency cash flows. Therefore, at the time these contracts are entered into there is uncertainty (due to uncertain future spot rates) as to what the domestic-currency value of the resulting foreign-currency cash flows will be.

transaction exposure
The net contracted foreign-currency transactions for which the settlement amounts are subject to changing exchange rates.

Transaction exposure identifies the amount of net contracted foreign currency for which the settlement domestic currency cash-flow amounts will vary due to changing exchange rates. Normally, a company must set up an additional reporting system to track transactions exposure, because several of these amounts are not recognised in the accounting books of the firm.

Translation and transaction exposure may be neutralised or hedged by a change in the asset and liability position in the foreign currency. For example, an exposed asset position such as an account receivable can be *hedged* or *covered* by creating a liability of the same amount and maturity denominated in the foreign currency, such as a forward contract to *sell* the foreign currency. An exposed liability position such as an account payable can be covered by acquiring assets of the same amount and maturity in the foreign currency, for example a forward contract to *buy* the foreign currency. The objective is to have a zero net-asset position in the foreign currency. This eliminates exchange risk, since the loss (gain) in the value of the liability (asset) is exactly offset by the gain (loss) in the value of the asset (liability) when the spot rate changes. Two popular forms of hedge are the money-market hedge and the forward-market hedge. In both types of hedge the *amount* and the *duration* of the asset (liability) positions are *matched*.

Money-market hedge

In a money-market hedge, the exposed foreign currency amount is offset by borrowing or lending in the money market. For example, consider the case of an Australian firm with a net foreign currency liability position of 3000 Malaysian ringgit (MYR). The firm knows the exact amount of its ringgit liability in 30 days, but it does not know the liability in Australian dollars. Assume that the money-market rates in both Australia and Malaysia are 1% for lending and 1.5% for borrowing for 30 days and that the current spot rate is MYR1.8695/AUD1. The Australian business can take the following steps to hedge:

Step 1: Calculate the present value of the foreign currency liability (MYR3000) that is due in 30 days using the money-market rate applicable for the foreign country (1% in Malaysia). The present value of MYR3000 is MYR3000/(1 + 0.01) = 2970.30.

Step 2: Exchange dollars on today's spot market to obtain MYR2970.30. The dollar amount needed today is AUD1588.82 (2970.30/1.8695).

Step 3: Invest MYR2970.30 in a Malaysian one-month money-market instrument at 1%. This investment will compound to exactly MYR3000 in one month. Thus, the future liability of MYR3000 is covered by the MYR2970.30 investment made today.[2]

Note that if the Australian business did not own today the AUD required in step 2, it could borrow AUD1588.82 from the Australian money market at the going rate of 1.5%. In 30 days the Australian business would need to repay AUD1612.65 [that is, AUD1588.82 × (1 + 0.015)].

Assuming that the Australian business borrows the money, its management may base its decisions on the knowledge that the Malaysian goods will cost it A$1612.65 in 30 days to pay the Malaysian business 3000 ringgit. Thus, the Australian business need not wait for the future spot exchange rate to be revealed. On today's date, the future dollar payment of AUD1612.65 for MYR3000 is known with certainty. This certainty helps the Australian business in making its pricing and financing decisions.

Many large businesses hedge in the money market. To do so, the firm needs to borrow (creating a liability) in one market, lend or invest in the other money market, and use the spot exchange market on today's date. The mechanics of covering a *net-asset position* in the foreign currency are the exact *reverse* of the mechanics of covering the *liability position*. A net-asset position in ringgit would require the Australian business to (1) borrow in the Malaysian money market in ringgit, (2) convert to dollars on the spot exchange market, (3) invest in the Australian money market, and (4) when the net assets are converted into ringgit (i.e. when the firm receives what it is owed), pay off the ringgit loan and the interest. The cost of a money-market hedge is the cost of doing business in three different markets. Information about the three markets is needed, and analytical calculations of the type indicated here must be made.

Small businesses and infrequent traders find the cost of the money-market hedge prohibitive, owing especially to the need for information about the money market. These firms instead use the forward-market hedge provided by the foreign exchange market, which has very similar hedging benefits to the money-market hedge.

The forward-market hedge

The forward market provides a second possible hedging mechanism. A net asset (liability) position is covered by a liability (asset) in the forward market. Consider again the case of the Australian firm with a liability of 3000 ringgit that must be paid in 30 days. The firm may take the following steps to cover its liability position.

Step 1: Enter into a forward contract today with a foreign exchange bank to purchase MYR3000 in 30 days. The 30-day forward rate quoted by the bank is MYR/AUD = 1.8587.

Step 2: On the 30th day pay the bank A$1614.03 (3000/MYR1.8587) and collect MYR3000. Pay these ringgit to the Malaysian supplier. By the use of the forward contract the Australian business knows the exact value of the future payment in dollars (AUD1614.03). The exchange risk in ringgit is totally eliminated by the net-asset position in the forward ringgit. In the case of a net-asset exposure, the steps open to the Australian firm would be the exact opposite: sell the ringgit forward, and on the future day receive and deliver the ringgit to collect the agreed-on Australian dollar amount.

The use of the forward market as a hedge against exchange risk is simple and direct. The firm directs its banker that it needs to buy or sell a foreign currency on a future date, and the banker gives a forward quote.

The forward-market hedge and the money-market hedge give an identical future dollar payment (or receipt) if the forward contracts are priced according to the interest-rate-parity theory. You may have noticed that the dollar payments in the examples of the money-market hedge and the forward-market hedge were, respectively, AUD1612.65 and AUD1614.04. Recall from our previous discussion that in efficient markets the forward contract rate does indeed conform to IRP theory and the cost of a money-market hedge should be the same as the cost of a forward hedge after taking into account transaction costs. Nevertheless, in reality, forward quotes are not available on many long-term transactions, especially those that involve a thinly traded currency.

Hedging with currency options

The forward-market hedge is not adequate for some types of exposure. For example, the foreign-currency asset or liability position may not be known with certainty so the forward hedge cannot be accomplished. In addition to forward-market and money-market hedges, a company can also hedge its exposure by entering into a foreign-currency option contract. These contracts give the holder the right to *choose* at or before a specified future date to buy or sell a foreign currency at an exchange rate which is set at the time the option contract is entered into. In compensation for being given this right to choose, the option-holder pays an amount at the time of entering into the option contract called the *option premium*. The advantage of an option over a money-market or forward-market hedge is that the option-holder can choose to exercise the option if it is to the holder's advantage to do so, and can choose not to exercise the option if so desired. As a result, if the foreign-currency payments or revenues do not eventuate, the company loses only the premium that has been paid for the option.

ECONOMIC EXPOSURE

The economic value of a firm can be defined as the present value of its future cash flows and this value may vary in response to exchange-rate changes. This change in value may be caused by a rate-change-induced decline in the level of expected cash flows and/or by an increase in the riskiness of these cash flows. **Economic exposure** refers to the overall impact of exchange-rate changes on the value of the firm and includes not only the strategic impact of changes in competitive relationships that arise from exchange-rate changes but also the economic impact of transactions exposure and, if any, translation exposure.

Economic exposure to exchange-rate changes depends on the competitive structure of the markets for a firm's inputs and its outputs, and on how these markets are influenced by changes in exchange rates. This influence, in turn, depends on several economic factors, including price elasticity of the products, the degree of competition from foreign markets, as well as the direct (through prices) and indirect (through incomes) impact of exchange-rate changes on these markets. Assessing the economic exposure faced by a particular firm thus depends on the ability to understand and model the structure of the markets for its major inputs (purchases) and outputs (sales).

A company need not engage in any overseas business activity to be exposed to the economic effects of exchange-rate changes, because product markets and financial markets in most countries are related and influenced to a large extent by the same global forces. The output of a company engaged in business activity within only one country may be competing with imported products, or it may be competing for its inputs with other domestic and foreign purchasers. For example, an Australian chemical company that does no international business may nevertheless find that its profit margins depend directly on the USD/AUD exchange rate. This is because the company uses oil as an input in its production process, and the Australian domestic price of oil is heavily influenced by the international price of oil, which is denominated in USD.

In summary, although translation exposure need not be managed, it might be useful for a firm to manage its transaction and economic exposures because they affect firm value directly. In most companies, transaction exposure is generally tracked and managed by using a variety of financial hedges that involve currency forwards and options. Economic exposure is long term and much more difficult to define in operating terms, and very few companies manage it actively. Managing economic exposure usually involves restructuring the operation process, pricing strategies, costing and sale locations. Therefore, in most companies, economic exposure is generally considered part of the strategic planning process, rather than a finance function.

economic exposure
Long-term changes in the value of the firm as a result of exchange-rate fluctuations.

Concept check

20.9 What is exchange-rate exposure?

20.10 Differentiate between translation exposure, transaction exposure and economic exposure.

For answers go to MyFinanceLab or
www.pearson.com.au/9781442539174

Direct foreign investment

OBJECTIVE **5**

Discuss the risks that are unique to the capital-budgeting analysis of direct foreign investments.

Direct foreign investment occurs when a company from one country makes a physical investment, such as building a factory, in another country. A **multinational corporation (MNC)** is the corporation that has control over this investment. The decision process for this type of investment is very similar to the capital-budgeting decision in the domestic context—with some additional considerations. Most real-world capital-budgeting decisions are made with uncertain future outcomes. Recall that a capital-budgeting decision has three major components: the estimation of the future cash flows (including the initial cost of the proposed investment), the estimation of the risk of these cash flows, and the choice of the proper discount rate to reflect the risk. We will assume that the NPV criterion is appropriate as we examine (1) the risks associated with direct foreign investment, and (2) factors to be considered in making the investment decision that may be unique to the international scene.

direct foreign investment
A physical investment, such as an investment in a building or factory, which a company makes in a foreign country.

multinational corporation (MNC)
A corporation with holdings and/or operations in one or more countries.

Back to the principles

The major reason for direct foreign investment by US companies is the prospect of higher rates of return from these investments—as you know from **Principle 1: The risk–return trade-off—we won't take on additional risk unless we expect to be compensated with additional return**. While there may be higher expected rates of return with many foreign investments, many of them also come with increased risk. During the last decade, many European and Japanese firms have been increasing their sales and setting up production facilities abroad, especially in the United States.

When corporations invest abroad they generally set up a subsidiary in the country in which they are investing. Funds then are transferred back, or repatriated, to the parent firm in its home country through dividends, royalties and management fees, with both the dividends and royalties subject to taxation in both the foreign and the home country. Moreover, many countries restrict the flow of funds back to the home country. As a result, there is often a difference between the cash flows that a project produces and the cash flows that can be repatriated to the parent country. To evaluate these investment projects, firms *discount the cash flows that are expected to be repatriated to the parent firm*. In most cases, the timing is crucial. If a project generates cash flows in 2012 that cannot be repatriated until 2015, the cash flows must be discounted from the 2015 date when the cash will actually be received.

Once the cash flows are estimated, they must be discounted back to present at the appropriate discount rate or required rate of return, with both the discount rate or the required rate of return and the cash flows being measured in the same currency. Thus, if the discount rate is based on dollar-based interest rates, the cash flows must also be measured in dollars (see Example 20.6).

EXAMPLE 20.6   International capital budgeting

You are working for a company based in Melbourne that is looking at a new project that will produce the following cash flows, which are expected to be repatriated to the parent company and are measured in South African rand (SAR).

YEAR	0	1	2	3	4
Cash flows (in millions of SAR)	−8	4	4	5	6

In addition, the risk-free rate in Australia is 4% and this project is riskier than most; as such, the firm has determined that it requires a 9% premium over the risk-free rate. Thus, the appropriate discount rate for this project is 13%. In addition, let's assume that the current AUD/SAR spot exchange rate is 6.88 (1 AUD = 6.88 SAR) and the one-year AUD/SAR forward exchange rate is 6.62.

You will need to calculate the expected cash flows for this project in Australian dollars, and then use these cash flows to calculate the project's NPV.

Conceptually, to calculate the project's NPV you must first convert the South African rand (SAR) into Australian dollars. Unfortunately, the futures markets only provide exchange rates for the SAR for about a year forward. However, with equation (20-3) you can use the one-year forward rate and the spot rate to calculate the interest rate differential in the two countries. You can then use the forward exchange rate to convert the cash flows measured in SARs into Australian dollars. From there, you simply calculate the project's NPV in Australian dollars using a 13% required rate of return.

Using equation (20-3) gives you:

$$F = S \times \frac{1+i}{1+i^*} \text{ hence}$$

$$\frac{1+i}{1+i^*} = \frac{F}{S} = \frac{6.62}{6.88} = 0.9622$$

The above calculation suggests that the interest differential between Australia and South Africa is 0.9622. Using this interest rate differential, you can work out the implied forward exchange rate for year 2, year 3 and year 4 as follows:

YEAR	SPOT RATE	×	(INTEREST RATE DIFFERENTIAL)^n	=	FORWARD RATE FOR YEAR n
0	6.88			=	6.88
1	6.88	×	0.9622	=	6.62
2	6.88	×	$(0.9622)^2$	=	6.37
3	6.88	×	$(0.9622)^3$	=	6.13
4	6.88	×	$(0.9622)^4$	=	5.90

You can now use these forward exchange rates to convert the cash flows measured in SARs to Australian dollars as follows:

YEAR	CASH FLOWS (MIL OF SAR)	÷	IMPLIED FORWARD RATE	=	CASH FLOWS (MIL OF AUD)
0	−8	÷	6.88	=	−1.16
1	4	÷	6.62	=	0.60
2	4	÷	6.37	=	0.63
3	5	÷	6.13	=	0.82
4	6	÷	5.90	=	1.02

At a 13% discount rate, the NPV of the project in Australian dollars is:

YEAR	CASH FLOWS (MIL OF AUD)	×	DISCOUNT FACTOR	=	PRESENT VALUE
0	−1.16	×	1	=	−1.16
1	0.60	×	$1/(1+0.13)$	=	0.53
2	0.63	×	$1/(1+0.13)^2$	=	0.49
3	0.82	×	$1/(1+0.13)^3$	=	0.57
4	1.02	×	$1/(1+0.13)^4$	=	0.62
			Net present value		1.05

The NPV of the project in this case is $1.05 million. It is important to remember that the only cash flows that are relevant are those that are expected to be repatriated back to the home country. In addition, it is important to keep in mind that you use a required rate of return from investing in the same currency that the cash flows are measured in. Here, the required rate of return was in Australian dollars, so we converted the cash flows into Australian dollars to maintain consistency.

RISKS IN DIRECT FOREIGN INVESTMENTS

Risks in domestic capital budgeting arise from two sources: business risk and financial risk. The international capital-budgeting problem incorporates these risks as well as political risk and exchange risk.

Business risk and financial risk

International business risk arises from the uncertainty of economic conditions in the foreign country. Thus, the Australian MNC needs to be aware of the business climate in both Australia and the foreign country. Additional business risk is due to competition from other MNCs, local businesses and imported goods. Financial risk refers to the risks introduced into the profit stream by the firm's capital structure. The financial risks of foreign operations are not very different from those of domestic operations.

Political risk

Political risk arises because the foreign subsidiary conducts its business in a political system different from that of the home country. For example, many foreign governments are less stable than the Australian government. A change in a country's political set-up frequently brings a change in policies with respect to businesses—and especially with respect to foreign businesses. An extreme change in policy might involve nationalisation or even outright expropriation of certain businesses. These are the political risks of conducting business abroad. A business with no investment in plant and equipment is less susceptible to these risks, as it can more easily move its operations elsewhere.

Some examples of political risk are:

- expropriation of plant and equipment without compensation
- expropriation with minimal compensation that is below actual market value
- non-convertibility of the subsidiary's foreign earnings into the parent's currency—the problem of *blocked funds*
- substantial changes in the laws governing taxation
- governmental controls in the foreign country regarding the sale price of the products, wages and compensation to personnel, hiring of personnel, making of transfer payments to the parent, and local borrowing
- requirement of certain amounts of local equity participation in the business. Some governments require that the majority of the equity participation belong to their country.

All these controls and governmental actions introduce risks to the cash flows of the investment to the parent company. These risks must be considered before making a foreign-investment decision. The MNC may decide against investing in countries with risks of expropriation. Other risks can be borne, provided that the returns from the foreign investments are high enough to compensate for them. Insurance against some types of political risks may be purchased from private insurance companies or from the Australian government Export Finance and Investment Corporation (EFIC).

Exchange risk

The exposure of the firm's assets is best measured by the effects of exchange-rate changes on the firm's future-earnings stream—that being *economic* exposure rather than *translation* exposure. For instance, changes in the exchange rate may adversely affect sales by making competing imported goods cheaper. Changes in the cost of goods sold may result if some components are imported and their price in the foreign currency changes because of exchange-rate fluctuations. The thrust of these examples is that the effect of exchange-rate changes on income-statement items should be properly measured to evaluate exchange risk. Finally, exchange risk affects the dollar-denominated profit stream of the parent company, whether or not it affects the foreign-currency profits.

If the foreign sales volume was expected to be low, the MNC might consider setting up a *sales office* in the foreign country. The product would be exported to the foreign country from production facilities in the home country or from some other foreign subsidiary. An NPV calculation would then be employed, and the acceptance of this scheme would be ensured because no direct capital investment would be needed. If the estimated sales levels were high enough that the establishment of a plant in the foreign country appeared to be profitable (owing to the potential savings in transportation costs), yet the NPV of the direct foreign investment was negative, the MNC might consider a *licensing* or an *affiliate* arrangement with a local company. The MNC would provide the technology, and the interested domestic firm would finance and set up the plant. In this case, the MNC would not bear the risks of a direct foreign investment, but instead would receive a royalty payment from the sales of the affiliate company.

Concept check

For answers go to MyFinanceLab or
www.pearson.com.au/9781442539174

20.11   What are some of the risks associated with direct foreign investments?

Summary

OBJECTIVE 1

The growth of our global economy, the increasing number of multinational corporations and the increase in foreign trade itself underscore the importance of the study of international finance.

OBJECTIVE 2

The foreign exchange market is where one currency is traded for another and exchange-rate quotations provide the price of one currency in terms of another. Depending on whether you buy or sell foreign currency, the relevant exchange rate is either the bid rate or the ask rate. There are two major types of foreign exchange transactions: spot transactions where settlement takes place within two working days and forward transactions where settlement takes place in the future. Forward contracts are widely used as a tool to manage exchange-rate risk exposure.

OBJECTIVE 3

Interest-rate parity (IRP) theory argues that the forward exchange rate is influenced by the interest rate differential between the two countries and, in particular, that the currency of the country with the higher interest rate should appreciate. Similarly, purchasing-power parity (PPP) proposes that the inflation differential between two countries has a bearing on the forward exchange rate in such a way that the country with higher inflation will have a depreciating currency. In rational and efficient markets, forward rates are unbiased forecasts of future spot rates that are consistent with the IRP and PPP.

OBJECTIVE 4

Exchange-rate risk exists because the exact spot rate that will prevail on a future date is not known with certainty today. The concept of exchange-rate risk is applicable to a wide variety of businesses, including export–import firms and firms involved in making direct foreign investments or international investments in securities. Exchange exposure is a measure of exchange-rate risk. Different strategies are open to businesses to counter the exposure to this risk, including the money-market hedge, the forward-market hedge, futures contracts and options. Each strategy involves different costs.

The complexities encountered in the direct foreign investment decision include the usual sources of risk—business and financial—and additional risks associated with fluctuating exchange rates and political factors. Political risk is due to differences in political climates, institutions and processes between the home country and abroad.

Under these conditions, the estimation of future cash flows and the choice of the proper discount rates are more complicated than for the domestic investment situation.

OBJECTIVE **5**

Key terms

Review questions

20-1 What additional factors are encountered in international financial management as compared with domestic financial management? Discuss each factor briefly.

20-2 What different types of businesses operate in the international environment? Why are the techniques and strategies available to these firms different?

20-3 What is meant by arbitrage profits?

20-4 What are the markets and mechanics involved in generating covered interest arbitrage profits?

20-5 The exchange rate given by a foreign exchange dealer is HKD/AUD 6.95. Is this a direct quote or an indirect quote from an Australian perspective?

20-6 Briefly explain the law of one price. What are some of the reasons that account for deviations from the law of one price?

20-7 How do the purchasing-power parity, the interest-rate parity and the Fisher effect explain the relationships between the current spot rate, the future spot rate and the forward rate?

20-8 What is meant by (a) exchange risk, (b) political risk?

20-9 How can exchange risk be measured?

20-10 What are the differences between transaction, translation and economic exposures? Should all of them be ideally reduced to zero?

20-11 What steps can a firm take to reduce exchange risk? Indicate at least two different techniques.

20-12 What are the major differences between a money-market hedge and a forward-market hedge?

20-13 Compare and contrast the use of forward-contract and foreign-currency options as the two hedging methods. Under what circumstances would options be preferable?

20-14 Assume that in the Australian foreign exchange market the forward rate for the Indian currency, the rupee, is not quoted. If you were exposed to exchange risk in rupees, how could you cover your position?

20-15 What risks are associated with direct foreign investment? How do these risks differ from those encountered in domestic investment?

20-16 How is the direct foreign-investment decision made? What are the inputs to this decision process? Are these inputs more complicated than those for the domestic-investment decision? If so, why?

20-17 A corporation desires to enter a particular foreign market. The analysis indicates that a direct investment in the plant in the foreign country will not be profitable. What other course of action can the company take to enter the foreign market? What are the important considerations?

Self-test problems

For answers go to MyFinanceLab
www.pearson.com.au/myfinancelab

Use the data below for self-test problems ST-1 and ST-2.

A foreign exchange dealer in Sydney currently quotes buying/selling euro (EUR):

CONTRACT	EUR/AUD
Spot	0.691 – 0.695
30-day	0.684 – 0.689
90-day	0.705 – 0.725

ST-1 (*Foreign exchange arbitrage*) In Tokyo the exchange rate between EUR/AUD at the same time is 0.696–0.699. Is there any opportunity for arbitrage? Devise a strategy that results in a profit, assuming that you start with AUD10 000.

ST-2 (*Calculating forward rates*) What is the bid–ask spread for a 30-day forward rate? A 90-day forward rate? Explain the difference.

ST-3 (*Covered interest parity*) If the interest rates on 30-day money-market instruments in Australia and Europe are 8% and 5% (annualised) respectively, what is the price of the 30-day forward euro according to covered interest parity?

Problems

For more problems and for answers to
problems marked with an asterisk (*)
go to MyFinanceLab at
www.pearson.com.au/myfinancelab

Use the data below for the following problems.

The following quotes are obtained from a dealer in Sydney. The bid and ask quotes refer to the rate at which the dealer buys and sells foreign currencies for 1 AUD:

COUNTRY (CURRENCY)	CONTRACT	FOREIGN CURRENCY (AUD)
Canada (CAD)	Spot	1.1043/1.1030
	30-day	1.1023/1.1008
	90-day	1.0980/1.0963
Japan (JPY)	Spot	73.78/72.48
	30-day	73.41/72.06
	90-day	72.58/71.23
Switzerland (CHF)	Spot	0.9542/0.9370
	30-day	0.9579/0.9402
	90-day	0.9640/0.9461

20-1 (*Converting currencies*) An Australian business needs to pay in two business days (a) 10 000 Canadian dollars, (b) 2 million yen, and (c) 50 000 Swiss francs to businesses abroad. What are the dollar payments required to obtain the foreign currencies?

20-2 (*Converting currencies*) An Australian business pays $10 000, $15 000 and $20 000 to suppliers in, respectively, Japan, Switzerland and Canada. How much, in local currencies, do the suppliers receive in two business days time?

20-3 (*Indirect quotes*) Compute the AUD equivalent for the spot Canadian dollar, yen and Swiss franc exchange rates.

20-4 (*Foreign exchange arbitrage*) You own AUD10 000. The spot exchange rate quoted in Tokyo is JPY75.20/73.90 per AUD. Are arbitrage profits possible? Set up an arbitrage scheme with your capital. What is the gain (loss) in dollars?

20-5 (*Spot and forward rates*) Compute the percent-per-annum premium (discount) on the 30-day and 90-day yen, Swiss franc and Canadian dollar buying quotes.

20-6 (*Covered interest parity*) Assume that the interest rate on the Australian 30-day treasury bill is 15% (annualised). The corresponding Canadian rate is 18%. Can an Australian trader make arbitrage profits? If the trader had AUD100 000 to invest, indicate the steps he or she would take. What would be the net profit? (Ignore transactions and other costs.)

20-7 (*Covered interest parity*) If the interest rates on the 30-day instruments in Australia and Japan are 15% and 12% p.a. respectively, what should be the correct price of the 30-day forward selling yen rate? Use the spot rate from the table.

20-8 (*Covered interest parity*) The 30-day treasury-bill rate in Australia is 15% p.a. Using the 30-day forward selling quotes, compute the 30-day interest rates in Canada, Switzerland and Japan implied by the forward rates.

20-9 (*Purchasing-power parity*) The expected inflation rate in Australia for the coming year is 4% p.a., while the expected rate of inflation in Canada is 6% p.a. According to the relative PPP theory, what would be the expected change in the exchange rate?

20-10 (*International capital budgeting*) Assume you are working for a firm based in Australia that is considering a new project in China. This new project will produce the following cash flows measured in Chinese yuan (CNY), which are expected to be repatriated to the parent company in Australia:

YEAR	CASH FLOWS (MILLIONS OF CNY)
0	−120
1	40
2	45
3	60
4	60

In addition, assume the risk-free rate in Australia is 5%, and that this project is riskier than most, and as such, the firm has determined that it requires a 12% premium over the risk-free rate. Thus, the appropriate discount rate for this project is 17%. In addition, the current spot exchange rate is CNY/AUD 6.48 and the one-year forward exchange rate is 6.72.

What is the project's NPV?

20-11 (*International capital budgeting*) Rapid Software, a Melbourne-based firm, is considering a new project in the south of India. This new project will produce the following cash flows measured in Indian rupees (INR) which are expected to be repatriated to the parent company in Australia.

YEAR	CASH FLOWS (MILLIONS OF INR)
0	−50
1	15
2	28
3	32
4	35

The current risk-free rate in Australia is 4.75%. Rapid Software determines that this project is risky and requires a 14% premium over the risk-free rate.

Thus, the appropriate discount rate for this project is 18.75%. The bank has provided Rapid Software with the following exchange rate quotes:

- Spot INR/AUD 44.14
- One year forward INR/AUD 43.95

What is the project's NPV?

Case study

For your job as the business reporter for a local newspaper, you are given the assignment of putting together a series of articles on the multinational finance market and the international currency market for your readers. Much recent local press coverage has been given to losses in the foreign exchange markets by JGAR, a local firm that is a subsidiary of Daedlufetarg, a large German manufacturing firm. Your editor would like you to address several specific questions dealing with multinational finance. Prepare a response to the following memorandum from your editor:

To: Business reporter
From: Perry White, Editor, *Daily Planet*
Re: Series on multinational finance

In your upcoming series on multinational finance, I would like you to make sure that you cover several specific points. In addition, before you begin this assignment, I want to make sure we are all reading from the same script, as accuracy has always been the cornerstone of the *Daily Planet*. I'd like a response to the following questions before we proceed.

1. What new problems and factors have been encountered in international as opposed to domestic financial management?
2. What does the term 'arbitrage profits' mean?
3. What can a firm do to reduce exchange risk?
4. What are the differences between a forward contract, a futures contract and options?

Use the following data in your response to the remaining questions:

Selling quotes for foreign currencies in Sydney

COUNTRY (CURRENCY)	CONTRACT	FOREIGN CURRENCY (AUD)
Canada (CAD)	Spot	0.8450
	30-day	0.8415
	90-day	0.8390
Japan (JPY)	Spot	90.28
	30-day	90.50
	90-day	90.90
Switzerland (CHF)	Spot	0.8150
	30-day	0.8182
	90-day	0.8328

5. An Australian business needs to pay (a) 15 000 CAD, (b) 1.5 million JPY, and (c) 55 000 CHF to businesses abroad. What are the dollar payments to the respective countries?
6. An Australian business pays AUD20 000, AUD5000 and AUD15 000 to suppliers in, respectively, Japan, Switzerland and Canada. How much, in local currencies, do the suppliers receive?
7. Compute the direct quote for the spot and forward Canadian-dollar contract.

Notes

1.   Thomas L. Friedman, *The World Is Flat: A Brief History of the 21st Century*, Farrar, Strous and Giroux, New York, 2007.
2.   Observe that 2970.30 MYR × (1 + 0.01) = 3000 MYR.

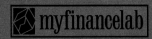

Corporate risk management

chapter 21

CHAPTER PREVIEW

This chapter deals with another important area of corporate policies—risk management. In previous chapters, financial decision making in the presence of risk has been discussed, but we have ignored the possibility that the firm can take actions to alter the risk. In this chapter, we learn that a lot of the risks that a firm is exposed to are at least partially controllable.

The process of analysing a firm's risk measures and determining how best to handle its risk exposure is the focus of risk management, which is a specialised area of finance. A number of techniques are available to the financial manager for managing risk. One common risk-management technique is through the use of financial instruments known as derivatives. These financial products are so named because their value or price is determined by, or 'derived' from, the price of another asset. It will be demonstrated in this chapter how the use of financial derivatives can help the firm manage risk exposure rather effectively.

The chapter emphasises *Principle 1: The risk–return trade-off—we won't take on additional risk unless we expect to be compensated with additional return.* Be on the lookout for this concept.

Five-step corporate risk-management process

OBJECTIVE 1

Define corporate risk management in the context of the five-step risk management process.

Corporations have spent considerable effort in recent years devising strategies for assessing and managing the risks that they are exposed to in doing business. Any risk-management approach generally starts with a procedure for identifying the various risks the firm faces and ends with guidelines for dealing with those risks. The following five-step process illustrates how some of the best-run companies manage risk.

Step 1: Identify and understand the firm's major risks
As it is not possible to manage risks that have not been identified and understood, the first step in any risk-management program is to develop a full understanding of the types of risks the firm faces. These risks relate to the factors that drive the firm's cash-flow volatility. The most common sources include the following:

- *Demand risk.* This involves fluctuations in product or service demand driven by competitive forces and the effects of the state of the economy in general. Some of this risk is strictly focused on the firm, for example product quality, on-time delivery, etc. External competition, as well as the status of the regional and national economy, also influence a firm's demand for its goods and services.
- *Commodity risk.* Price fluctuations in commodities that are essential to a firm's core business can wreak havoc on the firm's cash flow. For example, the dramatic price increase in the cost of fuel that occurred in 2007–08 produced huge losses for airline companies as it drove up their cost of operations substantially.
- *Country or political risk.* Where the firm does business can create problems related to maintaining operations in the face of political unrest or unfavourable governmental interference

in the firm's operations. The political unrest in Thailand in early 2010 is a good example of how the political climate represents a source of risk for companies conducting businesses in Bangkok. Loss of business has led to the closure of many companies, especially smaller ones.

- *Operational risk.* Cost overruns related to the firm's operations is another source of volatility in corporate cash flow.
- *Foreign-exchange risk.* Unfavourable shifts in the exchange rate between Australia and the foreign countries in which a firm does business can lead to dramatic decreases in corporate cash flow.

Of the risk factors outlined above, four of the five sources of risk are external to the firm. Only operational risk is largely under the direct control of the firm's management. Thus, risk management generally focuses on factors that influence a firm's cash-flow volatility that come from outside the firm. This is not to say that operational risks cannot be shifted or managed. They can, for example, be spread out or diffused through outsourcing some of the firm's business functions such as manufacturing, assembly or information technology.

Step 2: Decide which types of risks to keep and which to transfer

This is perhaps the most critical step in the risk-management process. Deciding which risks the firm should retain and which risks the firm should mitigate by passing them along to an outside party is at the very heart of risk management. For example, oil and gas exploration and production firms have historically chosen to assume the risk of fluctuations in the price of oil and gas. Because oil and gas price fluctuations are a central part of their business, their investors expect to be exposed to this risk when they buy their stock. However, many of these firms have recently decided that their real business is oil and gas exploration and production, not energy price speculation. These firms believe that they can operate more efficiently if they mitigate future price fluctuations.

Step 3: Decide how much risk to assume

Figure 21.1 illustrates the concept of a firm's 'appetite' for assuming risk, or its risk profile. The figure provides three distributions of cash flows that correspond to three different approaches to risk management. The High Risk cash-flow distribution represents a scenario where the firm's management does no risk mitigation or transfer. In this case, the firm's cash flows can be as high as $120 million or as low as $15 million, and the expected cash flow is $66.81 million. The Medium Risk scenario involves some risk reductions that pass along risk at the cost of a slight reduction in the expected cash flow to $61 million, but with a minimum cash flow of $30 million. Finally, the Low Risk scenario offers an expected cash flow of $58.34 million, but has a minimum cash flow of only $50 million. If the firm has principal and interest payments totalling $30 million, dividends of $10 million and planned capital expenditures of $8 million, then the risk that the firm's cash flow will not be sufficient to cover all $48 million of the planned expenditures varies from one scenario to another. For example, in the Low Risk scenario, there is a zero probability that the firm's cash flows will be insufficient to cover the planned expenditures, but in the Medium Risk scenario there is an 11.46% probability that the firm will not have enough cash to do all that it plans. For the High Risk scenario, the risk increases further, such that there is a 16.53% probability that the firm will not generate the needed $48 million in cash flow.

In Step 3, management is faced with the question of which risk-management scenario it prefers. Unfortunately, there is no formula like the NPV formula that we can use to make this decision. Such a choice is more like the capital-structure choice, where there is a trade-off between the cost of financial distress, which is more likely to arise in the higher risk scenario, and the cost associated with limiting the firm's risk.

FIGURE 21.1 Cash flow distributions for alternative risk-management strategies

Each of the three probability distributions corresponds to a different approach to managing firm risk. The High Risk strategy can be interpreted as the 'does nothing to transfer risk' strategy. The Medium Risk strategy involves transferring some of the firm's risk to outside parties using the tools of risk management discussed later. Finally, the Low Risk strategy represents the cash flow distribution that results when the firm engages in a risk management strategy whereby it offloads all the risks that it possibly can.

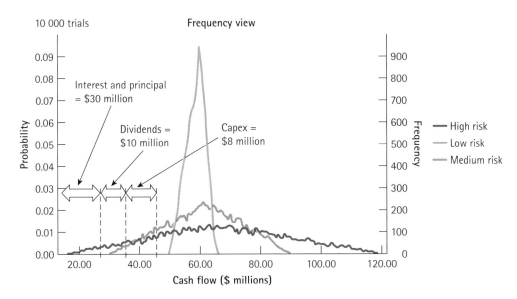

Legend:

RISK SCENARIO	EXPECTED CASH FLOW	STANDARD DEVIATION IN CASH FLOW	PROBABILITY OF NOT BEING ABLE TO MEET CAPEX, DIVIDEND, AND PRINCIPAL AND INTEREST REQUIREMENTS
Low risk	$58.34 million	$3.14 million	0.00%
Medium risk	$61 million	$12.33 million	11.46%
High risk	$66.81 million	$21.44 million	16.53%

Step 4: Incorporate risk into all the firm's decisions and processes

Once the firm decides on those risks that it will keep and those it will transfer, it is time to implement a system for controlling the firm's risk exposures. This means that every major investment, operating and financing decision the firm makes must take into consideration the impact on overall firm risk. For those risks that will be transferred, the firm's management must determine an appropriate means of transferring the risk. In some instances this may involve the purchase of insurance. For example, if the firm is located along the Florida Gulf Coast, it may want to purchase storm-damage insurance to reimburse the firm for any storm damage it might incur during the hurricane season. The point here is that once the firm has determined that it wants to transfer the risks associated with a facet of its operations, it must then select a cost-effective method for making the transfer. This critical element of the risk-management process is the prime focus of this chapter.

Step 5: Monitor and manage the risks the firm assumes

To assure that the firm's day-to-day decisions are consistent with its chosen risk profile, it is necessary that it put in place an effective monitoring system. Typically, this means that the firm centralises the responsibility for monitoring the firm's risk exposure with a chief risk officer who reports directly to the company CEO and also presents regularly to the firm's board of directors.

All five steps of the risk management process are essential to implementing and sustaining a risk-management program. In the balance of this chapter we will review the alternative approaches that can be taken to managing a firm's risk exposure.

> **Concept check**
> 21.1 What are the five steps in the risk-management process?
> 21.2 Describe the primary types of risk that a firm might face.

For answers go to MyFinanceLab or www.pearson.com.au/9781442539174

Regardless of your program

WELCOME TO A RISKY WORLD

The focus of corporate risk management is on managing the factors that determine the risk to a firm's cash flows. Very simply, this risk can be thought of as coming both from forces outside the control of the firm, such as competition from firms selling similar products or the overall health of the economy in general, and from factors that are under the control of the firm's management. With respect to the latter, the biggest source of risk comes from uncertainty about the firm's revenues, which are determined to a large extent by the successes and failures of the firm's marketing efforts. Another important contributor to the risk of a firm's cash flows is the firm's production costs. For example, production cost overruns are a major source of risk that can be controlled to some extent through the use of well-designed and maintained accounting systems that are used by the firm's operating managers to monitor and control the firm's operations. So, even though you may not be directly involved in the risk management of your firm, your actions contribute to the underlying risk of the firm's cash flows.

OBJECTIVE

Understand the difference between forward and futures contracts and how they can be used to manage risk.

Forward contracts

A forward contract is a contract wherein a price is agreed upon today for an asset to be sold in the future. Forward contracts are broadly defined as a derivative product as the value of these contracts depends on the value of the asset that is being bought and sold in the future. These contracts are usually privately negotiated between the buyer and the seller so the specific terms of the contracts can be tailor made to meet the specific needs of the users. The key feature of a forward contract is the fact that the price determination is made at the time of the contract but the actual purchase and sale do not occur until the maturity of the contract in the future. Whenever you lock in a price today on a transaction that will occur in the future, you have entered into a forward contract.

Since forward contracts allow buyers and sellers to agree upon a price to be paid in the future, these agreements can be used to offset the risk of adverse fluctuations in future prices. Consequently, the risk of such an adverse price movement is transferred to the other party to the forward contract. Let's see how this works by considering the risk of fluctuating fuel costs and airline fuel costs.

hedging
A strategy designed to minimise exposure to unwanted risk by taking a position in one market that offsets exposure to price fluctuations in an opposite position in another market.

HEDGING COMMODITY PRICE RISK USING FORWARD CONTRACTS

The term **hedging** refers to a strategy designed to offset the exposure to price risk. To illustrate how forward contracts can be used to hedge a firm's exposure to risk, consider the problem faced by Pacific Airlines. In six months the firm will need to purchase jet fuel that is currently selling for $100 per barrel and it does not want to suffer the risks associated with future price fluctuations in the cost of fuel. For simplicity, we will assume that the firm needs just one barrel of fuel. You can multiply the results by any number of barrels to adjust the outcome for Pacific Airlines' actual fuel needs.

The firm can enter into a forward contract today with a delivery price equal to the current price of fuel of $100, which will have the payoffs found in Panel A of Figure 21.2. The firm that owns this position is said to have taken a long position in the forward contract. Note that if the actual price of jet fuel rises to $130, then the forward contract is worth $30 per barrel to Pacific Airlines. Thus, in six months the effective cost of fuel remains at $100 for Pacific Airlines because the market price of fuel in six months is $130, but Pacific Airlines gets a payoff of $30 from the long position in the forward contract.

To further illustrate the use of forward contracts for hedging purposes, let us consider the situation faced by the Pilot Refining Company, which anticipates that it will have jet fuel refined and ready for sale in six months. However, the price it can realise from the sale of the jet fuel is subject to market fluctuations. To eliminate the risk of a drop in the price, Pilot can sell a forward contract (i.e. take a short position) for the delivery in six months at a delivery price of $100. The payoff to this contract is found in Panel B of Figure 21.2. For example, if the price

FIGURE 21.2 Delivery-date profits or losses (payoffs) from a forward contract to hedge currency risk

The term **long position** is often used to refer to the ownership of a security, contract or commodity. That is, if you purchase a share of stock you are said to be 'long' the stock, such that when the price of the stock goes up the holder of the long position benefits or profits. Correspondingly, a **short position** is the opposite of a long position and involves the sale of a security, contract or commodity. This means that the payoff to a short position is simply the negative of the payoff to a long position. If you would make money with a long position this means you would lose money with a short position, and vice versa.

(Panel A) Long position in forward contract

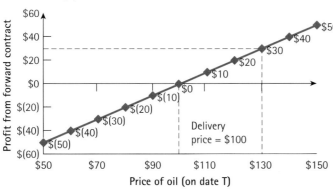

(Panel B) Short position in forward contract

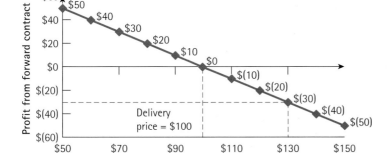

of jet fuel rises to $130 on the delivery date, then Pilot can sell its jet fuel for this price but the firm will suffer a loss of $30 on the forward contract, such that the net price received per barrel will be $100. As a general rule, while forward contracts can be used to eliminate the uncertainty relating to cash flows of a business, the act of entering into a forward contract can produce a loss to the company, depending on the movement of the underlying asset price. When you buy a forward contract, you will gain when the underlying asset price increases and lose otherwise.

Forward contracts can also be used to hedge currency risk. To illustrate, consider the currency risks faced by Rio Tinto, which generates revenues from the sale of a wide range of metals and minerals all over the world. The majority of these commodities are priced in US dollars. For illustration purposes, assume that Rio Tinto expects to receive US$50 million from its North American operation in three months and another US$50 million in six months. Rio Tinto would like to lock in the exchange rate on these two cash flows and thereby eliminate any risk of an unfavourable move in exchange rates.

To hedge the first cash flow, to be received in three months, Rio Tinto uses a forward-market hedge arranged with its investment banker. The investment banker indicates that the three-month forward AUD/USD rate is 0.9560. To hedge its exchange-rate risk Rio Tinto uses the following two-step procedure:

Step 1: Enter into a three-month forward contract, which requires Rio Tinto to sell US$50 million three months from now at a rate of 0.9560.

Step 2: Three months from now Rio Tinto takes its cash flow of US$50 million and converts it at the contracted rate, providing Rio Tinto with US$50/0.9560 = 52.3 million Australian dollars.

The effect of entering into the hedge to sell the US dollar forward is that Rio Tinto locks in this exchange rate with the forward-market hedge transaction. No matter what happens to the exchange rate over the next three months, Rio Tinto will receive the same dollar amount for the US$50 million as agreed to in the forward contract.

The risk of currency fluctuation on the second cash flow of US$50 million can be similarly eliminated with a six-month forward contract. In this case the quoted six-month forward AUD/USD rate is 0.9420 which means that Rio Tinto locks in revenues of 50/0.9420 = 53.08 million Australian dollars.

EXAMPLE 21.1 Hedging crude oil price risk for forward contracts

Progressive Refining Inc. operates a specialty refining company that refines crude oil and sells the refined by-products to the cosmetic and plastic industries. The firm is currently planning for its refining needs one year ahead. The firm's analysts estimate that Progressive will need to purchase 1 million barrels of crude oil at the end of the current year to provide the feedstock for its refining needs for the coming year. The 1 million barrels of crude will be converted into by-products at an average cost of $30 per barrel. Progressive will then sell the by-products for $165 per barrel. The current spot price of oil is $125 per barrel, and Progressive has been offered a forward contract by its investment banker to purchase the needed oil for a delivery price in one year of $130 per barrel. Ignoring taxes, if oil prices in one year are as low as $110 or as high as $140, what will be Progressive's profits assuming the firm does not enter into the forward contract? If the firm were to enter into the forward contract to purchase oil for $130 per barrel, demonstrate how this would effectively lock in the firm's cost of fuel today, thus hedging the risk that fluctuating crude oil prices pose for the firm's profits for the next year.

If Progressive does not enter into the forward contract, its profits will be influenced by the market price of oil. The following table details the profits of the company corresponding to different oil prices. As can be seen from the table, at the current oil price level, if the company leaves the oil price unhedged, the annual profit is expected to be $10 million.

OIL PRICE	OIL COST (OIL PRICE × 1 MILLION)	REFINING COST ($30 × 1 MILLION)	REVENUE ($165 × 1 MILLION)	ANNUAL PROFITS
110	110 000 000	30 000 000	165 000 000	25 000 000
115	115 000 000	30 000 000	165 000 000	20 000 000
120	120 000 000	30 000 000	165 000 000	15 000 000
125	125 000 000	30 000 000	165 000 000	10 000 000
130	130 000 000	30 000 000	165 000 000	5 000 000
135	135 000 000	30 000 000	165 000 000	–
140	140 000 000	30 000 000	165 000 000	–5 000 000

If the company is concerned about oil price risk, it can hedge this risk by entering into a forward contract. By purchasing a forward contract for crude oil at a fixed delivery price of $130 in this case, the firm can lock in its cost of crude oil. The expected hedged annual profits for the company are therefore:

$$\text{Annual Profits} = \text{Revenue} - (\text{Oil cost} + \text{Refining cost})$$
$$= 165 \times 1\,000\,000 - (130 \times 1\,000\,000 + 30 \times 1\,000\,000)$$
$$= \$5\,000\,000$$

By hedging oil price risk, Progressive effectively eliminates the uncertainty of future profits as a result of fluctuations in the price of crude oil. The expected hedged profit is therefore a certain $5 million.

LIMITATIONS OF FORWARD CONTRACTS

Generally, forward contracts are negotiated contracts between the firm managing its risk exposure and a financial intermediary such as an investment bank. The primary advantage of this type of bilateral arrangement is that the contract can be tailored to the specific needs of the firm that is engaging in risk management. However, there are some potentially serious limitations of this approach:

1. *Credit risk exposure.* Both parties to the contract are exposed to credit or default risk. This is the risk that the other party to the transaction might default on their obligation. Using bilateral negotiated contracts to manage price risk also exposes the firm to credit or default risk of the person or institution on the other side of the transaction.

FINANCIAL DERIVATIVES IN YOUR DAILY LIFE

Not only does risk management play an important role in your professional life, it should play an important role in your personal life as well. As an example, in the not-too-distant future you are likely to purchase your first house. You are also likely to finance the purchase with a mortgage. Prior to the settlement, mortgage providers usually offer borrowers the choice to lock in the mortgage interest rate. For instance, you have the choice between locking in the mortgage rate of 6.5% today or waiting to take the interest rate on the day when you actually settle the purchase. If you choose to lock in the rate, you will eliminate the risk of having to pay a higher rate of interest should rates increase before you close on the home purchase. If you do this, you will have entered into a forward contract with your financial institution. In effect, you have agreed upon a price which in this case is the interest rate for a transaction that will take place on a future date. After your purchase, you will continue to make risk-management choices. However, individuals typically manage the risk of their house losing value due to fire, theft or natural disasters like earthquakes and floods by taking out insurance policies as opposed to purchasing financial derivatives.

2. *Sharing of strategic information.* Since the two parties to a forward contract know who the other party is, they learn about the specific risks that are being hedged. If the parties to the agreement were anonymous, as would be the case if exchange-traded contracts were used, then no such sharing of information would occur.

3. *Market values of negotiated contracts not being easily determined.* Without a market value for the negotiated forward contract, it is difficult to assess the gains and losses the firm has experienced at any point in time.

The limitations noted can be addressed through the use of exchange-traded contracts. Specifically, exchange-traded futures, which will be discussed in the next section, provide alternative means for managing corporate risk that do not suffer from the limitations of bilateral negotiated forward contracts.

Futures

futures contract
Legally binding agreement to buy or sell a stated commodity or financial instrument at a specified price at some future specified time on an organised exchange.

commodity futures
A contract to buy or sell a stated commodity such as wheat, corn or metals at a specified price and at a specified future date on an organised exchange.

financial futures
A contract to buy or sell a financial asset such as treasury securities, certificates of deposit, foreign currencies or stock indices at a specified price at a specified future time on an organised exchange.

A future, or **futures contract**, is a contract to buy or sell a stated commodity such as soybeans or corn or a financial claim such as treasury bonds at a specified price at some future specified time. Similarly to forward contracts, the assets that are being bought and sold as specified in the futures contract are known as the 'underlying asset'. There are two basic categories of futures contracts that are traded on futures exchanges or markets: **commodity futures** and **financial futures**. Commodity futures are traded on agricultural products, such as wheat and corn, as well as metals, wood products and fibres. Financial futures come in a number of different forms, including futures on treasury bills, notes and bonds, certificates of deposit, eurodollars, foreign currencies and stock indices.

As with the case of forward contracts, for each futures contract, there is a buyer and a seller. The buyer of the futures contract is said to have a *long position* in the futures contract, whereas the seller has a *short position*. It is worthy to note here that this is a contract that *requires* its holder to buy or sell the asset, regardless of what happens to its value during the interim. Although both forward and futures contracts allow for a transaction in the future at a price set today, they differ significantly in their arrangements. Specifically, forward contracts are negotiated between two parties so their terms and conditions are rather flexible. Futures contracts, on the other hand, are traded on an organised exchange, such as the ASX in Australia. As a result, futures have a number of defining characteristics that are absent from forward contracts.

To develop a further understanding of futures contracts and futures markets, let us examine several features of futures contracts. A futures contract is distinguished by (1) an organised exchange, (2) a standardised contract with limited price changes and margin requirements, (3) a clearinghouse in each futures market, and (4) daily resettlement of contracts. Remember, a futures contract is legally binding. That means you must buy or sell a commodity in the future as specified by the contract.

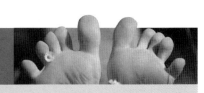

FYI

The futures markets originated in mediaeval times. In fact, England, France and Japan all developed futures markets of their own. In the United States, several futures markets sprang up in the early years, but it was not until the establishment of the Chicago Board of Trade (CBT) in 1848 that the futures markets were provided with their true roots. Although this market has been in operation for 150 years, it was not until the early 1970s—when the futures markets expanded from agricultural commodities to financial futures—that financial managers began to regularly venture into this market. In Australia, futures contracts were primarily traded on the Sydney Futures Exchange (SFE), which commenced operations in 1960 with the trading of wool futures. Recently the SFE merged with the Australian Stock Exchange to create the Australian Securities Exchange (ASX). The new ASX provides a uniform trading platform for all types of derivatives.

The organised exchange

The importance of having organised exchanges associated with a futures market such as the ASX is that they provide a central trading place. If there were no central trading place, there would be no potential to generate the depth of trading necessary to support a secondary market; in a very circular way, the existence of a secondary market encourages more traders to enter the market and in turn provides additional liquidity.

An organised exchange also encourages confidence in the futures market by allowing for the effective regulation of trading. The various exchanges set and enforce rules and collect and disseminate information on trading activity and the commodities being traded. Together, the liquidity generated by having a central trading place, effective regulation and the flow of information through the organised exchanges have effectively fostered their development.

Standardised contracts

To develop a strong secondary market in any security, there must be many identical securities—or, in this case, futures contracts—outstanding. In effect, standardisation of contracts leads to more frequent trades on that contract, leading to greater liquidity in the secondary market for that contract, which in turn draws more traders into the market. Futures contracts are highly standardised and very specific with respect to the description of the goods to be delivered and the time and place of delivery. More specifically, a futures contract is standardised with respect to the size of the contract, the maturity date and the daily price-movement limit. For example, the contract specification for a 10-year T-bond contract that is traded on the ASX is detailed in Table 21.1.

Through this standardisation of contracts, trading has built up in enough identical contracts to allow for the development of a strong and highly liquid secondary market. To encourage investors to participate in the futures market, daily price limits are set on most futures contracts. Without these limits, it is thought that there would be more price volatility on most futures contracts than many investors would be willing to accept. These daily price limits are set to protect investors, to maintain order on the futures exchanges and to encourage the level of trading volume necessary to develop a strong secondary market. This limit protects against runaway price movements. These daily price limits do not halt trading once the limit has been reached, but they do provide a boundary within which trading must occur. The price of an oats

TABLE 21.1 Contract specification for a futures contract on 10-year T-bonds traded on the ASX

Contract unit	Commonwealth Government treasury bonds with a face value of $100000, a coupon rate of 6% per annum and a term to maturity of 10 years, no tax rebate allowed.
Contract month	March/June/September/December up to two quarter-months ahead.
Commodity code	XT
Listing date	16/03/2001
Minimum price movement	Prices are quoted in yield percent per annum in multiples of 0.005%. For quotation purposes, the yield is deducted from an index of 100. The minimum fluctuation of 0.005% equals approximately $40 per contract, varying with the level of interest rates.
Last trading day	The fifteenth day of the contract month (or the next succeeding business day where the fifteenth day is not a business day). Trading ceases at 12 noon.
Settlement day	The business day following the last permitted day of trading.
Trading hours	5.10 pm – 7.00 am and 8.30 am – 4.30 pm (during US daylight-saving time). 5.10 pm – 7.30 am and 8.30 am – 4.30 pm (during US non-daylight-saving time).
Settlement method	The arithmetic mean, taken at 9.45 am, 10.30 am and 11.15 am on the last day of trading by 10 dealers, randomly selected for each time, at which they would buy and sell a series of bonds previously declared by SFE for that contract month, excluding the two highest and two lowest buying quotations and the two highest and two lowest selling quotations for each bond. All bought and sold contracts in existence as at the close of trading in the contract month shall be settled by the clearinghouse at the cash settlement price.

contract may rise 10 cents very early in the trading day—'up the limit', in futures jargon. This will not stop trading; it only means that no trade can take place above that level. As a result, any dramatic shifts in the market price of a futures contract must take place over a number of days, with the price of the contract going 'up the limit' each day.

Futures clearinghouse

The main purpose of the futures clearinghouse is to guarantee that all trades will be honoured. In other words, the existence of the clearinghouse reduces the risk of default associated with the trading of futures. This is done by having the clearinghouse interpose itself as the buyer to every seller and the seller to every buyer. Because of this substitution of parties, it is not necessary for the original seller (or buyer) to find the original buyer (or seller) when he or she decides to clear his or her position. As a result, all an individual has to do is make an equal and opposite transaction that will provide a net zero position with the clearinghouse and cancel out that individual's obligation.

Because no trades occur directly between individuals but between individuals and the clearinghouse, buyers and sellers realising gains in the market are assured that they will be paid. Because futures contracts are traded with minimal 'good faith' money, as we will see in the next section, it is necessary to provide some security to traders so that when money is made it will be paid. There are other important benefits of a clearinghouse, including providing a mechanism for the delivery of commodities and the settlement of disputed trades, but these benefits also serve to encourage trading in the futures markets and thereby create a highly liquid secondary market.

Margin requirements and marking to market

Another safeguard of the futures market is a margin requirement. Although margin requirements on futures resemble stock margin requirements in that there is an initial margin and a maintenance margin that comes into play when the value of the contract declines, similarities between futures and stock margins end there.

Before exploring margin requirements on futures, there needs to be an understanding of the meaning of a margin on futures. The concept of a margin on futures contracts has a meaning that is totally different from its usage in reference to common stocks. The margin on common stocks refers to the amount of equity the investor has invested in the stocks. With a futures contract, no equity has been invested, because nothing has been bought. All that has happened is that a contract has been signed obligating the two parties to a future transaction and defining the terms of that transaction. This is the important point: there is no actual buying or selling occurring with a futures contract; it is merely an agreement to buy or sell some commodity in the future. As a result, the term **futures margin** refers to 'good faith' money that both parties to the futures contract to put down to ensure that the contract will be carried out.

futures margin
'Good faith' money the parties to a futures contract put down to ensure that the contract will be carried out.

The *initial margin* required for commodities deposited by both buyer and seller is much lower than the margin required for common stock, generally amounting to only 3% to 10% of the value of the contract. For example, if September oats contracts were selling at $1.65 per bushel, then one contract for 5000 bushels would be selling for $1.65 × 5000 = $8250. The initial margin on oats is $400 per contract, which represents only about 4.85% of the contract price. Needless to say, the leverage associated with futures trading is tremendous—on both the upside and the downside. Small changes in the price of the underlying commodity result in very large changes in the value of the futures contract, because very little has to be put down to 'own' a contract. Moreover, for many futures contracts, if the financial manager can satisfy the broker that he or she is not engaged in trading as a speculator but as a hedger, the manager can qualify for reduced initial margins. Because of the low level of the initial margin, there is also a *maintenance* or *variation margin* requirement that forces the investor or financial manager to replenish the margin account to a level specified by the exchange after any market loss. When the balance of the account falls below the maintenance margin, a margin call will be made to the investor asking him or her to replenish the account. If the payment is not made by the due date, the futures position will be closed out in two working days.

One additional point deserves mention. The initial margin requirement can be fulfilled by supplying treasury bills instead of cash. These treasury bills are valued at 90% of their value for margin purposes, so it takes $100 000 worth of treasury bills to provide a $90 000 margin. The advantage of using treasury bills as margin is that the investor earns money on them, whereas brokerage firms do not pay interest on funds in commodity cash accounts. Moreover, if the financial manager is going to carry treasury bills anyway, he or she can just deposit the bills with the broker and purchase the futures contracts with no additional cash outlay.

Suppose you are a financial manager and you want to hedge against an increase in the price of oats. Currently, a September 2011 futures contract for the delivery of oats has a price of $1.65 per bushel. You need oats in September 2011 and feel that this is an exceptional price— oats will probably be selling for more than that per bushel in September. Thus, you want to lock in this price, and to do this you purchase one contract for 5000 bushels at 165 cents or $1.65 per bushel. On purchasing the September 2011 oats contract, the only cash you will have to put up will be the initial margin of $400. Let's further assume that the price of oats futures then falls to a level of 161 cents per bushel the day after you make your purchase. In effect, you have incurred a loss of 4 cents per bushel on 5000 bushels—a total loss on your investment of $200.

At this point, the concept of daily resettlement comes into play. What this means is that all futures positions are brought to the market at the end of each trading day and all gains and losses, in this case a loss, are then settled. This process is known as **marking to market**. You have lost $200, which is then subtracted from your margin account, lowering it to $200 ($400 initially, less the $200 loss). Because the margin account has fallen below the maintenance margin on oats, which is $250, you would have to replenish the account back to its initial level of $400. If on the following day the price of September oats contracts fell another cent to 160 cents per bushel, you would have lost another 1 cent on 5000 bushels—a loss of $50. This would then be subtracted from your margin account during the daily resettlement at the end of the trading day, leaving $350 in the account. Because your margin account would not be below the maintenance margin requirement of $250, you would not have to add any additional funds to the account. Let's carry our example one day further, this time to the upbeat side, and put some profits in. Let's assume that on the third day the price of September oats contracts is up 5 cents per bushel. This means that you have made 5 cents on 5000 bushels—a total profit of $250. This brings your margin account up from $350 to $600, which is $200 above the initial margin of $400. You can then withdraw this $200 from your margin account.

An example of marking to market is shown in Example 21.2.

marking to market
The process of calculating and settling gains or losses on a futures position on a daily basis.

EXAMPLE 21.2 Marking to market

On 21 July 2010 you bought a December 2011 gold futures contract at the price of AUD1415 per ounce. Each contract is for delivery of 10 ounces of gold. The initial margin is AUD1000 and the maintenance margin is AUD800. The next day the price of the December 2011 futures contract fell to AUD1397 per ounce and on 23 July the price increased to AUD1423 per ounce. Mark your position to market on each of the days and indicate if you have to deposit more money into your account.

On 22 July the price of the December futures contract fell to AUD1397 per ounce. As a buyer of the contract, you incurred a loss of $10 \times (1397 - 1415) = -AUD180$. Hence your margin balance is $1000 - 180 = AUD820$. Since this balance is more than the maintenance margin of AUD800, you do not need to top up your account.

On 23 July the price of the December futures contract increased to AUD1423. Hence you made a profit of $10 \times (1423 - 1397) = AUD260$. Your margin balance is $820 + 260 = AUD1080$, which is greater than the maintenance margin and therefore you do not have to top up your account.

Obviously, the purpose of margin requirements is to provide some measure of safety for futures traders and, despite the very small level of margin requirements imposed, they do a reasonable job. They are set in accordance with the historical price volatility of the underlying commodity in such a way that it is extremely unlikely that a trader will ever lose more than is in his or her margin account in any one day.

HEDGING WITH FUTURES

The golden rule of hedging with derivatives is to create a derivative position that offsets the position that you are trying to hedge. Effectively, hedgers want to have a derivative position such that if they lose money in their direct holdings as a result of fluctuations in market prices then the derivative position will return a profit to offset the losses in their physical position. As an example, if a company is a gold producer and wants to hedge against a falling gold price, it will enter into a derivative position that will profit if the gold price falls. With futures contracts, this can be achieved by selling gold futures. Since futures contracts effectively lock in the price of gold, a fall in the price of gold will benefit the seller, as it can sell the gold at the higher predetermined price of gold as opposed to the current market price. Example 21.3 shows how hedging with futures is done.

EXAMPLE 21.3 Hedging with futures

You are the financial manager of a wool cooperative. The next load of 5000 kilograms of wool should be available to the market by December 2011. Since wool prices in December 2011 are uncertain, you would like to hedge against a possible decline in wool prices by using a futures contract. Currently the December 2011 futures contract on fine wool in the ASX has a price of 1217 cents.

First, it is important to understand the price quotation. According to the contract specification provided by the ASX, the futures price of fine wool contracts is in cents per kilogram of wool and each contract covers 2500 kilograms of wool. To hedge your exposure, you will need to sell a futures contract because you want to sell wool in December 2011. The price of wool that you are effectively locking in is 1217 cents or $12.17 per kilogram. In addition, each contract covers only 2500 kilograms of wool and your expected production is 5000 kilograms, so you will need to sell two futures contracts.

Let us assume that in December 2011 the price of wool indeed falls, as you expected, to $10.15 per kilogram. Since you have locked in a price of $12.17 by selling futures contracts, you effectively make $12.17 − $10.15 = $2.02 per kilogram, making an overall profit on the futures position of 5000 × 2.02 = $10 100. The gain on the futures position should help ease the declining revenue as the result of the fall in price.

In practice, hedging with futures contracts is almost never as neat and tidy as the hypothetical examples we present here. Since futures contracts are only available for a subset of all assets and for a limited set of maturities, it is often not possible to form a perfect hedge. Restrictions on available futures contracts and maturities give rise to the following practical problems:

- It may not be possible to find a futures contract on the exact asset that is the source of risk.
- The hedging firm may not know the exact date when the hedged asset will be bought or sold.
- The maturity of the futures contract may not match the period that the underlying asset is to be held or must be acquired, in which case the hedge may have to be shut down before the futures contract expiration date.

Failure of the hedge for any of the above reasons leads to what is known as **basis risk**. Basis risk arises any time the asset underlying the futures contract is not identical to the asset that underlies the firm's risk exposure. That is, basis risk occurs whenever the price of the asset that underlies the futures contract is not perfectly correlated with the price risk the firm is trying to hedge. As a consequence, where the basis is non-zero, the firm does not have a perfect hedge.

In the hypothetical hedges we have described thus far, we have assumed that the asset underlying the futures contract is exactly the same as the one on which the futures contract is written. Where this is the case, the firm can combine its position in the underlying asset with a futures contract of equal value on a similar product, such that the basis risk is zero at the expiration of the contract, and the hedge works.

If futures contracts are not available for every commodity and maturity, then the financial analyst must choose a contract (underlying asset) and a maturity that best fits his or her needs. For example, since there are no active futures contracts for jet fuel, airlines sometimes hedge their jet fuel risk exposure using the heating oil futures contracts. The common sense guide to choosing a contract in this circumstance involves examining the relationship between the price changes of the commodities that are traded and the commodity risk that needs to be hedged. In general, when the correlation is higher, the hedge will be better.

The choice of a contract expiration date would seem rather simple. Select a futures contract that most nearly matches the maturity of the firm's risk exposure. For example, if the firm's risk exposure ends at the end of the month, it seems only reasonable that we hedge its returns using a futures contract that expires as close as possible to the end of the month. In theory, this is the appropriate solution to the problem; however, in practice, firms often select a futures contract with a slightly longer maturity date. The rationale here is that futures contract prices often behave erratically in the month in which they expire. In addition, if the hedger has a long position in the futures contract and the contract expires before the date when the asset risk exposure is resolved, the hedging firm runs the risk of having to take delivery of the commodity underlying the futures contract.

Overall, the standardisation of futures contracts makes hedging with futures 'imperfect'. Most of the time, hedgers find it difficult to find futures contracts with the underlying asset and maturity dates that perfectly match their hedging needs. In addition, the practice of cross-hedging is certainly not foolproof. Although the correlation of price movements between the hedged asset and the underlying asset is high, there is no guarantee that the correlation will hold over time. For these reasons, forward contracts offer better alternatives to the hedgers. Similar to futures contracts, forward contracts carry an obligation for the purchase and sale of a particular asset at a specified time at a predetermined price. However, unlike futures contracts, forward contracts are not standardised and can be negotiated between the two parties. Forward contracts, therefore, can be specifically tailored to your hedging needs. Unfortunately, forward contracts have their own drawbacks, which include high credit risk and low liquidity.

basis risk
Risk associated with imperfect hedging that arises because the asset underlying the futures contract is not identical to the asset that underlies the firm's risk exposure.

Back to the principles

The area of risk management has grown rapidly over the last decade. In response to the volatile interest rates, commodity prices and exchange rates from the late 1970s to the 1990s, financial managers turned to the futures, options and swap markets for relief. Once again, the financial markets demonstrated their dynamic and adaptive nature by finding new ways of reducing risk without affecting return. The inspiration for such behaviour, of course, finds its roots in **Principle 1: The risk–return trade-off—we won't take on additional risk unless we expect to be compensated with additional return.**

OBJECTIVE 3

Understand options and
how they can be used to
manage risk.

option contract
Agreement that gives the holder
the right, but not the obligation,
to buy (or sell) a commodity
or financial instrument at a
specified price on or before
a specified date.

call option
A contract that gives its holder
the right to purchase an asset
at a specified price over a given
time period.

put option
A contract that gives its holder
the right to sell an asset at a
specified price over a given
time period.

option writing
The process of selling put and/or
call options.

striking or exercise price
The price at which the asset may
be purchased from the option
writer in the case of a call or sold
to the option writer in the case
of a put.

option premium
The cost of the option.

Options

There are many situations where firms would like to guarantee a minimum revenue but they do not need to absolutely fix their revenue. For example, an oil company may need to sell oil next year for at least $40 per barrel to meet their payroll and interest obligations, but they may still want a share of the upside if oil prices increase substantially. They can accomplish this if they hedge with options rather than with forward or futures contracts.

An option, or **option contract**, gives its owner the right to buy or sell an asset at a specified price over a limited time period. There are two basic types of options: calls and puts. A **call option** gives its owner the right, but not the obligation, to purchase a given number of shares of stock or an asset at a specified price over a given period. Note that a key difference between an option contract and a futures contract is that the option owner does *not* have to exercise the option. If the price of the underlying common stock or asset on which the option is written goes up, the owner of a call option makes money. You have the option to buy something, for example shares, at a set price even though the market price of the stock has risen above the fixed exercise price.

A **put option**, on the other hand, gives its owner the right, but not the obligation, to sell an asset at a specified price within a given period. The owner of a put makes money when the price of the underlying common stock or asset on which the put is written drops in value. Just as with a call, a put option gives its owner the *right* to sell the common stock or asset at a set price, but it is not a promise to sell.

Because there is no underlying security, a purchaser of an option can be viewed as betting against the seller or *writer* of the option. For this reason, the options markets are often referred to as a *zero sum game*. If someone makes money, then someone must lose money; if profits and losses were added up, the total for all options would equal zero. If commissions are considered, the total becomes negative, and we have a 'negative sum' game. As we will see, the options markets are quite complicated and risky. Some experts refer to them as legalised institutions for transferring wealth from the unsophisticated to the sophisticated. However, for the financial manager they can be tools for eliminating risk.

When an option is purchased, it is nothing more than a contract that allows the purchaser to either buy in the case of a call or sell in the case of a put the underlying stock or asset at a predetermined price. That is, no asset has changed hands, but the price has been set for a future transaction that will occur *only if and when* the option purchaser wants it to. In this section, the process of selling puts and calls will be referred to as **option writing**. In addition, selling options is referred to as *shorting* or *taking a short position* in those options, whereas buying an option is referred to as *taking a long position*.

The option **striking or exercise price** is the price at which the stock or asset may be purchased from the writer in the case of a call or sold to the writer in the case of a put.

The **option premium** is merely the price of the option. It is generally stated in terms of dollars per share rather than per option contract, which covers 100 shares. Thus, if a call option premium is $2, an option contract would cost $200 and allow the purchase of 100 shares of stock at the exercise price.

The option expiration date is the date on which the option contract expires. An American option is one that can be exercised at any time up to the expiration date. A European option can be exercised only on the expiration date. Apart from American options and European options, there are also Bermudan options. Obviously, these names have nothing to do with where these options come from; rather they refer to the time-frame over which the options can be exercised. While American options can be exercised at any time before the expiry date and European options only on expiry date, Bermudan options can be exercised for a period of time prior to the expiry date but not for the entire life of the option.

The value of an option lies in the fact that it presents the holder with a choice to exercise the option when doing so is profitable and to do nothing otherwise. Whether an option is exercised or not depends on the price movement of the asset. A call will provide a positive payoff to its holder when the market price of the asset is higher than the exercise price. Effectively, this is the situation when the holder of the option can buy an asset at a price which is less than the market price, giving rise to a profit equal to the difference between the two prices. When an option can be exercised profitably, the option is said to be in the money. Similarly, an option is said to be out of the money when exercising will give rise to a loss and therefore it does not make sense to exercise. If the market price of the asset is the same as the exercise price, the option is said to be selling at the money. For example, if ANZ's common stock was selling for $28 per share, a call on ANZ with an exercise price of $25 would be in the money, whereas a call on ANZ with an exercise price of $30 would be out of the money. In other words, an in-the-money option will result in a gain if exercised immediately, while an out-of-the-money option will result in a loss to the holders. Since options holders have the choice, not an obligation, to exercise the options, out-of-the-money options are never to be exercised.

The option premium mentioned earlier is made of up the **intrinsic value** and the **time value**. The intrinsic value refers to the amount by which the stock is in the money. Thus, for a call the intrinsic value is the amount by which the stock price exceeds the exercise price. If the call is out of the money—that is, the exercise price is above the stock price—then its intrinsic value is zero. Intrinsic values can never be negative as the holder of an option never has to exercise an option. For a put, the intrinsic value is again the minimum value the put can sell for, which is the exercise price less the stock price. For example, a BHP-Billiton April 20 put—that is, a put on BHP-Billiton stock with an exercise price of $45 that expires in April—when BHP-Billiton's common stock was selling for $42 per share would have an intrinsic value of $45 – $42 = $3. If the put was selling for anything less than $3, investors would buy puts and sell the stock until all profits from this strategy had been exhausted. Arbitrage, this process of buying and selling like assets for different prices, keeps the price of options at or above their intrinsic value. If an option is selling for its intrinsic value, it is said to be selling at parity. This usually occurs at the expiry date of the option.

The time value of an option is the amount by which the option premium exceeds the intrinsic value of the option. The time value represents the amount above the intrinsic value of an option that an investor is willing to pay to participate in capital gains from investing in the option. At expiration, the time value of the option falls to zero and the option sells for its intrinsic value, because the chance for future capital gains has been exhausted. These relationships are as follows:

Call intrinsic value = stock price – exercise price
Put intrinsic value = exercise price – stock price
Call time value = call premium – (stock price – exercise price)
Put time value = put premium – (exercise price – stock price)

Example 21.4 demonstrates the use of options.

intrinsic value of an option
The payoff of an option to its holder if exercised immediately.

time value of an option
The extent to which the option premium exceeds the intrinsic value.

EXAMPLE 21.4 Understanding options

On 4 December 2010 you bought a call option on Rio Tinto's common stock for $10 with an exercise price of $75. The option expires in March 2011. The current Rio Tinto's stock price is $83. What is the intrinsic value of your option? What is its time value? If, at the expiry date of the option, the stock price of Rio Tinto was $88, would you exercise the option? Why or why not?

The intrinsic value of an option is the profit that you will make if you exercise the option immediately, hence the intrinsic value of the option is $83 – $75 = $8 per share. The time value of the option is therefore $10 – $8 = $2 per share. When the option expires, the market price of the stock is higher than the exercise price, suggesting that you can buy Rio Tinto stocks at a price lower than the current market price. As a result, you exercise the option. The rule for a call option is that if the market price is greater than the exercise price, you should exercise the option. The payoff to you in this case is $88 – $75 = $13 per share.

From the viewpoint of the financial manager, options have some attractive features that help explain their popularity. There are three reasons for this popularity:

1. *Leverage.* Calls offer the financial manager the chance for unlimited capital gains with a very small investment. Because a call is only an option to buy, the most a financial manager can lose is what was invested, which is usually a very small percentage of what it would cost to buy the stock itself, whereas the potential for gain is unlimited. As we will see, when a financial manager owns a call, he or she controls or benefits directly from any price increases in the stock. The idea of magnifying the potential return is an example of leverage. It is similar to the concept of leverage in physics, where a small amount of force can lift a heavy load. Here, a small investment is doing the work of a much larger investment. Unfortunately, leverage is a double-edged sword. Small price increases can produce a large percentage profit, but small price decreases can produce large percentage losses. With an option, the maximum loss is limited to the amount invested.
2. *Financial insurance.* For the financial manager, this is the most attractive feature of options. A put can be looked on as an insurance policy, with the premium paid for the put being the cost of the policy. The transactions costs associated with exercising the put can then be looked on as the deductibles. When a put with an exercise price equal to the current stock price is purchased, it insures the holder against any declines in the stock price over the life of the put. Through the use of a put, a pension fund manager can reduce the risk exposure in a portfolio with little in cost and little change to the portfolio. One dissimilarity between a put and an insurance policy is that with a put an investor does not need to own the asset, in this case the stock, before buying the insurance. A call, because it has limited potential losses associated with it, can also be viewed as an investment insurance policy. With a call, the investor's potential losses are limited to the price of the call, which is quite a bit below the price of the stock itself.
3. *Investment alternative expansion.* From the viewpoint of the investor, the use of puts, calls and combinations of them can materially increase the set of possible investment alternatives available.

GRAPHING OPTION-PRICING RELATIONSHIPS

Perhaps the easiest way to gain an understanding of the pricing of options is to look at them graphically. Figure 21.3 is a profit and loss graph for the purchase of a call on Commonwealth Bank (CBA) stock with an exercise price of $55 that is bought for $6.25. This is termed a 'CBA 55 call'. In Figure 21.3 and all other profit and loss graphs, the vertical axis represents the profits or losses realised on the option's expiration date, and the horizontal axis represents the stock price on the expiration date. Remember that, because we are viewing the value of the option at expiration, the option has no time value and therefore it sells for exactly its intrinsic value. To keep things simple, any transaction costs are ignored.

For the CBA 55 call shown in Figure 21.3, the call will be worthless at expiration if the value of the stock is less than the exercise or striking price. This is because it would make no sense

FIGURE 21.3 Purchase a call on CBA stock with an exercise price of $55 for a premium of $6.25

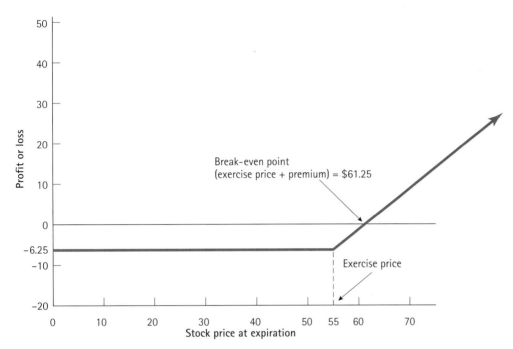

for an individual to exercise the call option to purchase CBA stock for $55 per share if he or she could buy the same stock from a broker at a price less than $55. Although the option will be worthless at expiration, if the stock price is below the exercise price, the most that an investor can lose is the option premium—that is, how much he or she paid for the option, which in this case was $6.25. While this may be the entire investment in the option, it is also generally only a fraction of the stock's price. Once the stock price climbs above the exercise price, the call option takes on a positive value and increases in a linear one-to-one basis as the stock price increases. Moreover, there is no limit on how high the profits can climb. In the case of the CBA 55 call, once the price of stock rises above $55, the call begins taking on value, and once it hits $55 + 6.25 = $61.25, the investor breaks even. The investor has earned enough in the way of profits to cover the $6.25 premium he or she paid for the option in the first place.

To the call writer, the profit and loss graph is the mirror image of the call purchaser's graph. As noted earlier, the options market is a zero sum game in which one individual gains at the expense of another. Figure 21.4 shows the profits and losses at expiration associated with writing a call option. Once again, we will look at the profits and losses at expiration, because at that point in time options have no time value. The maximum profit to the call writer is the premium, or how much the writer received when the option was sold, whereas the maximum loss is unlimited.

Looking at the profit and loss graph presented in Figure 21.5 for the purchase of a CBA 55 put that is bought for $3, we see that the lower the price of the CBA stock, the more the put is worth. Here the put begins to take on value only once the price of the stock drops below the exercise price, which in this case is $55. Then, for every dollar that the price of the stock drops, the put increases in value by one dollar. Once the stock drops to $52 per share, the put purchaser breaks even by making $3 on the put, which exactly offsets what was initially paid for the put. Here, as with the purchase of a call option, the most an investor can lose is the premium, which, although small in dollar value relative to the potential gains, still represents 100% of the investment. The maximum gain associated with the purchase of a put is limited only by the fact that the lowest a stock's price can fall to is zero.

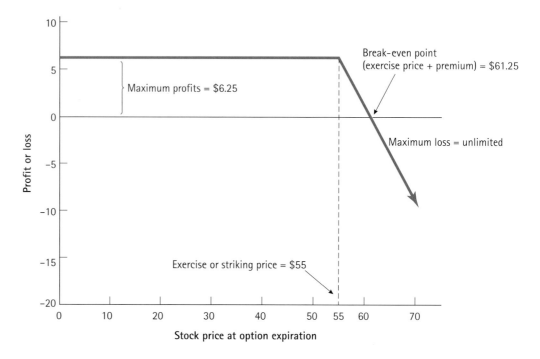

FIGURE 21.4 Write a call on CBA stock with an exercise price of $55 for a premium of $6.25

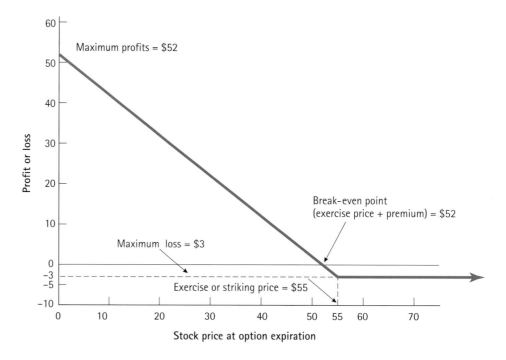

FIGURE 21.5 Purchase a put on CBA stock with an exercise price of $55 for a premium of $3

To a put writer, the profit and loss graph is the mirror image of the put purchaser's graph. This is shown in Figure 21.6. Here the most a put writer can earn is the premium, or amount for which the put was sold. The potential losses for the put writer are limited only by the fact that the stock price cannot fall below zero.

FIGURE 21.6 Write a put on CBA stock with an exercise price of $55 for a premium of $3

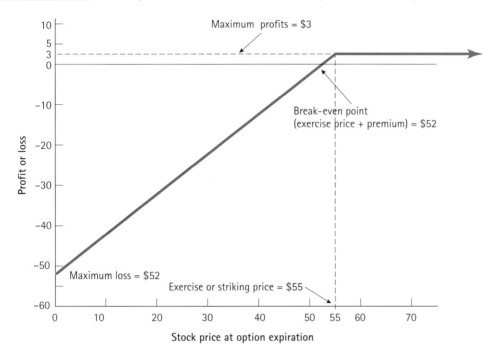

All of our graphs have shown the price of the option at expiration. When we re-examine these relationships at a time before expiration, we find that the options now take on some time value. In other words, investors are willing to pay more than the intrinsic value for an option because of the uncertainty of the future stock price. That is, although the stock price may fluctuate, the possible losses on the option are limited, whereas the possible gains are almost unlimited. The most you can ever lose when you purchase a put or call option is the premium, or what you paid for it. Although this may seem rather small relative to the price of the stock, it is still 100% of your investment.

ONE STEP FURTHER

EXOTIC OPTIONS

The modern financial system is characterised by market sophistication and product innovation. Apart from calls and puts, which are termed 'plain vanilla' options, the market also trades options with complicated structures and payoffs. These options are known as 'exotic options' or simply 'exotics'. The most common type of exotic option is a barrier option, which comes into existence or out of existence if the price of the underlying asset hits a certain level, called the 'barrier'. Knocked-in barrier options come into existence only if the underlying asset reaches the pre-set barrier. The buyers of knocked-in barrier options would not have the option if the barrier was not reached. Knocked-out barrier options, on the other hand, cease to exist if the underlying asset hits the barrier. Barrier options are generally much riskier than plain vanilla options as, despite the paid premium, there is a possibility that the options will not be knocked in or they will be knocked out. Another type of exotic option is the shout option, whose holders have the right to lock in, or shout, the payoff at any point in time prior to the expiry of the option while retaining the right to benefit further from future market movement. The final payoff is the greater of the payoff at expiration or the payoff at the point of 'shouting'. By shouting, the holder of shout options essentially locks in the minimum profit that he or she will receive. And if you cannot make up your mind if you want a call option or a put option, the 'chooser' option is for you. Chooser options allow you to make the choice of whether you want the option to be a call or a put after you have purchased the option but before the expiry date. Chooser options are particularly appropriate if you believe there will be a significant swing in the price of the underlying asset but you are unsure of the direction of the swing. The list of exotics goes on, but these examples illustrate how innovative and responsive financial markets are to users' needs.

HEDGING WITH OPTIONS

Like forward and future contracts, options can be used to hedge a range of financial risks that are not within the control of the firm such as interest rate, foreign currency and commodity price risks. Options allow the financial manager to obtain a minimum selling price or a maximum buying price, with the added flexibility of not undertaking the transaction when to do so is not in the company's favour. Remember that both calls and puts are options to buy and sell assets at a specified price. The worst that can happen is that the options become worthless and the firm loses the premium paid for the options. The obvious advantage of options over futures and forward contracts is that they allow the firm to alleviate the downside risk associated with price fluctuations but at the same time let the holders enjoy any upside potential. In other words, when you hold an option, you cannot incur a negative payoff, whereas futures and forward contracts obligate participants to undertake the transaction and can lead to a negative payoff. If options did not cost anything, everyone would be opting for options to hedge their financial risks. Unfortunately, options come at a cost, while futures and forward contracts do not cost anything to enter. As a result, in structuring the risk-management program, financial managers need to carefully consider the advantages and disadvantages of different derivative products.

Hedgers always take a long position on calls and puts, while option writers are speculators who are willing to take on the risk in exchange for a return in the form of the option premium. As a general rule, if you have a long exposure in the underlying asset market, which is the situation when you want to buy the underlying asset in the future and need to hedge against an increase in the price of the asset, you will buy a call option. On the other hand, if you have a short exposure in the underlying asset market, you will want to hedge against a fall in the asset price and thus buy a put option. Options on a broad range of financial assets are available including stock indices, interest rate, foreign currency and treasury bond futures.

Let's look at an example of how foreign-currency options might be used. As firms trade more and more internationally, the need to protect sales against undesirable currency fluctuations becomes increasingly important. For example, Rio Tinto might use currency options to protect sales of its aluminium to Chinese customers. Because aluminium is produced in Australia and sold abroad, its costs in labour and materials are based on the dollar. However, as the dollar fluctuates relative to the Chinese yuan, so must the sale price in Chinese yuan for Rio Tinto to receive the same amount of dollars in China.

Problems surface when the value of the Chinese yuan falls relative to that of the dollar. For each sale to bring the same amount of dollars back to Rio Tinto, the selling price in Chinese yuan would have to be *increased*. Unfortunately, increasing prices might lead to lost sales. To guard against this situation, Rio Tinto might purchase *put options* on the Chinese yuan to cover the anticipated sales. These puts would give Rio Tinto the option to sell or convert

Finance at work

THE NATIONAL AUSTRALIA BANK'S FOREIGN-CURRENCY OPTION TRADING SCANDAL

On 14 January 2004, the financial market in Australia was shocked at the news of the National Australia Bank (NAB) losing $180 million in unauthorised currency trading conducted by four members of the trading desk—Luke Duffy, David Bullen, Vince Vicarra and Gianni Gray. Despite the alleged loss of only $180 million before tax, within minutes a billion dollars were wiped off the value of the company as market participants reacted negatively to the news. As events unfolded, it was revealed that the unauthorised transactions were made in order to try and cover initial losses incurred in October 2003. These 30-something dealers speculated that the super-heated Australian dollar would remain stable or fall against the US dollar over the summer and accordingly wrote options on this pair of currencies. As the Australian dollar steadily rose in value, making it the best performing currency of the year, the loss snowballed to $180 million as first reported. Nevertheless, subsequent investigations into the trading scandal suggested that it could cost NAB up to $600 million. In the process of writing unauthorised currency options, these traders, three of whom were based in Melbourne, also engaged in phantom trades, pretending that they had entered into offsetting trades to stop the loss created by the original trade. These trades never took place. It was later revealed that the dealers were motivated to cover the initial loss to safeguard their six-digit bonuses for the year. Prior to the scandal blow-out, Luke Duffy received a $250 000 bonus and David Bullen $200 000.

The NAB scandal bore a close resemblance to the loss suffered by Barings Bank, which subsequently bankrupted it, in the early 1990s as a result of unauthorised derivatives trading by one single employee, the rogue trader Nick Leeson. As was the case with the NAB situation, the options Leeson was buying could be purchased relatively cheaply, but the money at risk was many times their face value. Leeson was able to disguise his losses only because he had authority over Barings' back office. The salutary lesson learned from the Barings collapse was the need for complete separation between the trading room and the back office. Despite NAB supposedly having an ironclad separation in place, the four traders had been dealing outside their 'value at risk' (VaR) for some time. Most worrying for NAB were allegations by David Bullen that his bosses were aware of these breaches and tolerated them while the team racked up profits of $6 million to $8 million a month. The trading scandal cost both the CEO, Frank Cicutto, and the chairman, Charles Allen, their jobs, and is another reminder of how risky derivatives can be and how important it is to have an adequate supervision system in place.

Source: Based on S. Kemp, 'Secretive clique felt it was untouchable', *Sydney Morning Herald*, 21 January 2004.

Chinese yuan into dollars at a preset price. If, after the put options were purchased, the Chinese yuan fell, Rio Tinto could keep its selling prices constant in terms of the Chinese yuan and make up for the loss in the currency exchange with the profits on the puts. Conversely, if the value of the Chinese yuan rose relative to the value of the dollar, Rio Tinto could lower its price in Chinese yuan, sell more aluminium, and still bring home the same dollars per sale—all that would be lost would be the price paid for the put options.

Concept check

21.7 What is an option? Name and explain two basic types of options.
21.8 What is the premium of an option?
21.9 If you exercise a call option on ANZ's shares with an exercise price of $26, what exactly do you do?

For answers go to MyFinanceLab or www.pearson.com.au/9781442539174

ONE STEP FURTHER

OPTION PRICING

Option pricing, or the calculation of the premium payable on options, is an extremely interesting but complex area in finance. Generally speaking, the value of an option is determined by how likely the option is to end up in the money. Accordingly, a number of factors have been identified as having a bearing on the price of an option, including the current price of the underlying asset, the exercise price, the time to expiry, the volatility of the asset price, the interest rate and, in the case of options on financial assets, whether the assets pay any income (such as dividends in the case of a stock). Despite the identification of these factors, the formulation of a systematic model to calculate the price of an option is a challenging task.

In a seminal paper published in 1973, Fischer Black and Myron Scholes presented a framework for the valuation of call and put options. In particular, they showed that the price of a call or a put option could be calculated using a model that incorporated factors that influenced the value of an option (as specified above). However, it was Robert Merton, an economist from the Massachusetts Institute of Technology, expanding on the work of Black and Scholes, who provided a mathematical understanding of option pricing, producing what he called the 'Black–Scholes option pricing model'. For their pioneering work in modern option pricing theory, Robert Merton and Myron Scholes, together with the late Fischer Black, were awarded the prestigious Nobel Prize in economics in 1997.

Shortly after the Black–Scholes option pricing model was published in 1979, Cox, Ross and Rubinstein advanced the binominal option pricing model. This model works on the premise that the underlying asset price follows a simple, stationary binomial process. That is, at any given point in time the underlying asset price can only go up or down by a given percentage in the next period. Despite the computational burden associated with pricing a multi-stage option, the binominal option pricing model has been shown to be powerful in pricing American options, options on dividend-paying stocks and exotic options whose payoffs are complex and unconventional.

Swaps

OBJECTIVE **4**

Understand interest-rate and currency swaps and how they can be used to manage risk.

interest-rate swap
Derivative instrument in which one party agrees to pay or receive a variable-rate interest stream and the other party agrees to a fixed-rate stream.

Swaps are essentially contracts between two parties that specify the terms and conditions relating to a stream of cash-flow exchanges over a period of time. Unlike futures and options, which can be traded on an organised exchange such as the ASX, swaps are OTC contracts that are negotiated between the two parties. In Australia, commercial banks are the major providers of swap contracts. The most popular swap is an **interest-rate swap**, which accounts for a majority of the transactions in interest-rate derivatives. Interest-rate swaps allow financial managers to control interest-rate risk, whereas another popular swap, the currency swap, provides a facility to manage exchange-rate risks.

An interest-rate swap in an agreement between two parties to swap a stream of cash flows at a certain payment frequency, for example every three months, over a period of time. In an interest-rate swap, one party will pay a fixed interest rate, also known as the *swap rate*, on an agreed notional amount, while the other party pays a variable or floating interest rate, also calculated on the same notional amount. The notional amount is not exchanged but it needs to be specified for the purpose of calculating the cash-flow payment for each party. The fixed interest rate, as the name suggests, is fixed at the time of the swap initiation and does not change over the life of the swap. The floating rate, on the other hand, is based on a reference rate that changes over time. In Australia the most popular reference rate used in swap contracts is the bank-bill swap rate (BBSW). By entering into an interest-rate swap, the financial manager can effectively transform the nature of the firm's existing liability. For example, if the firm currently pays a fixed interest rate on its borrowing, by entering into a swap that pays a floating rate and receives a fixed rate, the firm effectively transforms its fixed-rate borrowings into floating-rate borrowings. Similarly to futures contracts, there are no costs associated with a swap at inception.

Example 21.5 demonstrates the use of interest-rate swaps.

EXAMPLE 21.5   Interest-rate swaps

Bluestone Ltd currently has a three-year roll-over commercial bill facility that allows it to borrow $5 000 000 for three months. At each roll-over date, the interest rate is reset. In other words, Bluestone pays a variable interest rate on its commercial bill borrowings. There have been indications in the market that interest rates will go up in the near future. As a result, Bluestone would like to manage this possible increase in interest rates by negotiating a swap with Westpac. In this swap, Bluestone will pay Westpac a stream of cash flows based on a fixed interest rate in exchange for a stream of cash flows based on a reference interest rate, known as the BBSW. Since Bluestone has a $5 000 000 liability, it will need to set the notional amount of the swap at $5 000 000. In addition, if Bluestone wants to hedge interest-rate risk for the remaining life of the commercial bill facility, it will need to organise a swap that lasts three years. The final terms of the swap provided by Westpac are as follows:

- Term of the swap: 3 years
- Frequency of payment: 3 months
- Swap rate: 6% per annum
- Variable rate: BBSW + 0.1%
- Notional amount: $5 000 000.

The swap can be graphically presented as follows:

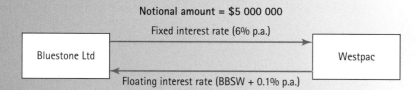

Assuming that Bluestone is currently paying BBSW + 0.5% on its commercial bill facility, its net interest payment is:

Interest payable on commercial bills:	BBSW + 0.5%
Interest payable on swap	6%
Interest receivable on swap	BBSW + 0.1%
Net interest payable	6.4%

As a result, if interest goes up, Bluestone will not be affected, as it is now paying 6.4% per annum on its commercial bill facility regardless of what the variable interest rate is.

The other popular swap that can be used to control exchange-rate risk is the **currency swap**. Whereas options and futures contracts generally have a fairly short duration, a currency swap provides the financial manager with the ability to hedge away exchange-rate risk over long periods. It is for this reason that currency swaps have gained in popularity. A currency swap is simply an exchange of debt obligations in different currencies. Actually, a currency swap can be quite simple, with two firms agreeing to pay each other's debt obligation. For example, an Australian company might agree to an interest rate of 6% in Australian dollars in exchange for an interest rate of 4.5% in US dollars over a period of time.

How does this serve to eliminate exchange-rate risk? If an Australian firm has much of its income coming from sales in England, it might enter into a currency-swap arrangement with an English firm. If the value of the British pound depreciates from, say, 2.60 dollars to the pound

currency swap
An exchange of debt obligations in different currencies.

FYI

Although interest-rate swaps provide financial managers with a great facility to manage interest-rate risk, most interest-rate swaps are entered into in order to reduce the cost of borrowing rather than to hedge an existing interest-rate exposure. The cost-savings associated with an interest-rate swap arise from the fact that, if each company borrows in the market that it has the comparative advantage in, regardless of their borrowing requirement, and swap that borrowing with another company, both companies will be better off than approaching the market directly. Assume that Company A has a comparative advantage in borrowing fixed-rate loans and Company B has a comparative advantage in borrowing variable-rate loans. If Company A wants a fixed-rate loan and Company B wants a variable-rate loan, they should borrow directly in the market. On the other hand, if Company A wants a variable-rate loan and Company B wants a fixed-rate loan, they should not borrow directly in the market as they do not have the comparative advantage in the market in which they want to borrow. In this case, Company A should borrow fixed and Company B should borrow variable. They can then swap these borrowings with each other. The interest-rate swap, therefore, helps both companies achieve a lower cost of borrowing.

Finance at work

In 2002 the Australian government made the headlines for allegedly losing up to $4.8 billion in currency swaps. This is how it happened. Prior to 2002 the Australian government ran a budget deficit and to finance this deficit it borrowed from the international financial markets to take advantage of the lower interest rates overseas. However, instead of approaching the international markets directly, the government borrowed in Australian dollars and swapped these Australian-dollar-denominated borrowings paying Australian interest rates for US-dollar-denominated borrowings paying US interest rates. It worked out to be cheaper to do this than to borrow US dollars directly. The benefit for Australian taxpayers was to be delivered in the lower interest rates paid on the US-dollar borrowings, an outcome that depended on Australian interest rates remaining higher than those in the United States, and the Australian dollar not losing its value. Unfortunately, from 2000 onwards the Australian dollar gradually lost its value, hitting an all-time low in 2002. The tumbling Australian dollar made the US-dollar-denominated debt more expensive, causing enormous losses on the currency-swap portfolio. On top of the tumbling dollar, the interest gap between Australia and the United States also lessened, raising concerns about the rationale behind the currency swaps in the first place. This experience, together with many other derivative scandals worldwide, highlights the risk associated with derivatives and the need for prudential supervision of their use.

to 2.40 dollars to the pound, then each dollar of sales in England will bring fewer dollars back to the company in Australia. This would be offset by the effects of the currency swap, because it would cost the Australian firm fewer dollars to fulfil the English firm's interest obligations. That is, pounds cost less to purchase, and the interest payments owed are in pounds. The nice thing about a currency swap is that it allows the firm to engage in long-term exchange-rate risk hedging, because the debt obligation covers a relatively long time period.

Needless to say, there are many variations of the currency swap. One of the more popular is the interest-rate currency swap, where the principal is not included in the swap; that is, only interest-payment obligations in the different currencies are swapped. The key to controlling risk is to get an accurate estimate of the net exposure level to which the firm is subjected. Then the firm must decide whether it feels it is prudent to subject itself to the risk associated with possible exchange-rate fluctuations.

These swaps look like a great idea—enter into a contract that reduces risk—but, just as with the other derivative securities, they are dangerous if used by those who don't understand the risks associated with them.

GFC

AIG TORN APART BY THE GFC AND CREDIT DEFAULT SWAPS

Since their debut in the early 1990s, credit default swaps (CDS) have been touted by many as the innovation of the decade. Perhaps it was so until the recent collapse of American International Group (AIG), the world's largest insurer, in which the CDS was believed to be the culprit. In a CDS, the buyer makes a periodic payment to the seller in exchange for a payout if a 'credit event' takes place. The credit event is specified in the contract, but generally includes credit downgrades and bankruptcies. The CDS essentially protects the buyer from the risk of default from a bond issue. Being the world's largest insurer, AIG sold a lot of credit default swaps to many financial institutions which wished to seek credit-risk protection. For a long time, selling credit default swaps was a great source of profit for AIG as bond issuers traditionally almost never went bankrupt, so what it meant for AIG was that they collected the payments without having to do anything. Many of the credit default swaps that AIG sold offered protection against default of mortgage-backed bonds, those bonds whose interest and principal payments are sourced from a pool of mortgage repayments.

Then the sub-prime crisis hit. A large number of mortgage-backed bonds were defaulted upon, calling for a huge payout that AIG had to foot. Making a payout to a contract holder was not something new to AIG. After all, that's what it does. However, what makes a CDS different from a car insurance policy is the fact that CDS bond defaults are highly co-related whereas road accidents are not. While a car accident sustained by one policy-holder does not make others more accident prone, one bond default makes others more likely. The company lost more than $10 billion in 2007 and $14.7 billion in the first six months of 2008. As AIG was struggling to meet its CDS-related financial commitments, Moody's and S&P downgraded the company's ratings. This credit downgrade was the last straw for AIG: it had to put up $13 billion worth of collateral to guarantee its ability to pay, an amount of money that it simply did not have. AIG was officially bankrupt. The failure of a company the size of AIG, however, was deemed to be detrimental to the soundness of the financial system, and the US government subsequently bailed out the company, making it the largest bailout of a private company in US history.

Concept check

21.10 What is the swap rate?
21.11 How can an interest-rate swap be used to manage interest-rate risk?
21.12 What is a currency swap?

For answers go to MyFinanceLab or www.pearson.com.au/9781442539174

International spotlight

FUTURES AND OPTIONS AND THE GLOBAL CORPORATION

Over the past 10 years, the use of futures and options by corporations has exploded. The primary way they are used is to hedge away risk in commodity markets, foreign-exchange rates and interest rates. How might you become involved with them? Maybe your first job will be working for McDonald's. To say the least, McDonald's, with operations in 91 countries, gets much of its income from its overseas operations. As a result, currency fluctuations can have a dramatic effect on its profits. With profits from abroad coming in currencies such as the baht (Thailand), the won (Korea) and the ringgit (Malaysia), things got pretty scary in late 1997, when all of these currencies collapsed. How does a company such as McDonald's protect itself and take some of the risk out of its international operations? The answer is: by using futures and options to hedge away the interest-rate risk.

Given the risks that globalisation brings, futures and options are a great tool to use in reducing those risks. It is important to keep in mind that they can also be used by smaller firms. For example, if you have a small specialty bakery with customers in England, France and Germany, you could easily eliminate your exchange-rate risk with currency options. In addition, you could lock in the future price of your raw materials in the futures markets.

Summary

OBJECTIVE 1

The process of analysing a firm's exposure to different kinds of risks and determining how best to handle that risk exposure is called risk management. The five-step risk-management process includes the following: (1) Identify and understand the firm's major risks; (2) Decide which types of risks to keep and which to transfer; (3) Decide how much risk to assume; (4) Incorporate risk into all the firm's decisions and processes; and (5) Monitor and manage the risks the firm assumes.

OBJECTIVE 2

Forward and futures contracts are similar in that they are contracts to buy or sell a stated commodity (such as soybeans or corn) or a financial claim (such as treasury bonds) at a specified price at some future specified time. The contract requires its holder to buy or sell the asset regardless of what happens to its value during the interim. The importance of forward and futures contracts is that they can be used by financial managers to lock in the price of a commodity or an interest rate and thereby eliminate one source of risk. A futures contract is a specialised form of a forward contract distinguished by (1) an organised exchange, (2) a standardised contract with limited price changes and margin requirements, (3) a clearinghouse in each futures market, and (4) daily resettlement of contracts.

OBJECTIVE 3

Options are contracts that give the holder the right but not an obligation to buy or sell a certain asset in the future at a price specified in the contract. There are two major types of options: call options, which give the owner the right to purchase assets, and put options, which give the owner the right to sell assets at a specified price over a given period. A call purchaser expects the price of the asset to increase, while a put purchaser is betting that the price of the underlying asset will drop. The cost of options is known as a premium and the premium is made up of the intrinsic value and the time value of the option.

OBJECTIVE 4

An interest-rate swap is an agreement between two parties to swap a stream of cash flows based on a fixed and a floating interest rate. Interest-rate swaps can be used by financial managers to manage interest-rate risk. A currency swap, on the other hand, is an exchange of debt obligations in different currencies. Exchange-rate variations are offset by the effects of the swap. One major advantage of a currency swap is that it allows for the hedging of exchange-rate risk over a long period of time.

Key terms

For a complete flashcard glossary go to MyFinanceLab at www.pearson.com.au/myfinancelab

basis risk	727	intrinsic value of an option	729
call option	728	marking to market	725
commodity futures	722	option contract	728
currency swap	737	option premium	728
financial futures	722	option writing	728
futures contract	722	put option	728
futures margin	724	striking or exercise price	728
hedging	718	time value of an option	729
interest-rate swap	736		

Web works

If you ever need to convert money from one currency to another, the Web is the place to go. There are a number of different currency converters available that are easy to use.

First, take a look at the *FX Converter* at **www.oanda.com/convert/classic**. Use it to convert 100 Fiji dollars into Australian dollars. How much are the 100 Fiji dollars worth in Australian dollars?

Now use the *Bank of Canada* currency converter at **www.bankofcanada.ca/en/exchform.html** to convert 100 Croatian kunas to Australian dollars. How much are they worth?

Next try the *Yahoo! Finance* currency calculator at **finance.yahoo.com/m3?u** to convert 100 Australian dollars into euros. How many euros would you get for $100?

Use whichever currency calculator you prefer to change 100 Australian dollars to euros, convert those euros to Japanese yen, and then convert those Japanese yen into Australian dollars. How many Australian dollars do you have?

21-1 Define the term *risk management*.

21-2 A firm's cash flows are risky for a number of reasons. Identify and discuss five sources of risk or volatility in firm cash flows.

21-3 What is a forward contract and how does it typically differ from an exchange-traded futures contract?

21-4 What are the limitations of the use of forward contracts to construct a hedge against price risk? How does an organised futures exchange control for these limitations?

21-5 What is the difference between a commodity future and a financial future? Give an example of each.

21-6 Describe the essential aim of a hedge using interest-rate futures contracts. In your answer, distinguish between the aims of a long position and the aims of a short position.

21-7 Why is it said that futures are a 'two-edged sword'?

21-8 What are the issues relating to the use of futures as a hedging tool?

21-9 Explain the role of the clearinghouse in a futures contract.

21-10 What is meant by *marking to market* and what is the purpose of marking to market?

21-11 Distinguish between a call option and a put option. Comment on the differences between the strategies for buying a call and writing a put.

21-12 What is the difference between American options and European options? Other things being equal, would you be prepared to pay more for the American options or the European options?

21-13 Describe the situation in which an option-holder would exercise her option?

21-14 What is the basic nature of an interest-rate swap? What is meant by 'notional amount'?

21-15 Outline some of the ways in which currency swaps can be used for hedging.

ST-1 (*Hedging commodity price risk using forward contracts*) CCP Refining Inc. operates a specialty refining company that refines crude oil and sells the refined by-products to fertiliser plants throughout Australia. The firm is currently planning for its refining needs for one year hence. The firm's analysts estimate that it will need to purchase 1 million barrels of crude oil at the end of the current year to provide the feedstock for its refining needs for the coming year. The 1 million barrels of crude will be converted into by-products at an average cost of $25 per barrel, which CCP expects to sell for $100 million, or $100 per barrel of crude used. The current spot price of oil is $50 per barrel, and CCP has been offered a forward contract by its investment banker to purchase the needed oil for a delivery price in one year of $55 per barrel.

For answers go to MyFinanceLab
www.pearson.com.au/myfinancelab

    (a) Ignoring taxes, if oil prices in one year were as low as $40 or as high as $70, what would CCP's profits be (assuming the firm did not enter into the forward contract)?

    (b) If the firm were to enter into the forward contract, demonstrate how this would effectively lock in the firm's cost of fuel today, thus hedging the risk fluctuating crude oil prices pose for the firm's profits for the next year.

ST-2 (*Call options*) In relation to Figure 21.3, state the break-even point, the maximum loss and the maximum profit if the strike price was $60 and the premium was $6. What would be the outcome at expiry date if the share was then priced at $69? What if the price was $48?

ST-3 (*Call options*) For the option in ST-2, state the maximum profit, the break-even point and the maximum loss from the perspective of the option writer.

Problems

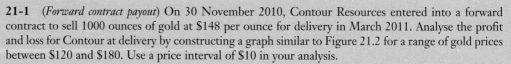

For more problems and for answers to problems marked with an asterisk (*) go to MyFinanceLab at www.pearson.com.au/myfinancelab

21-1 (*Forward contract payout*) On 30 November 2010, Contour Resources entered into a forward contract to sell 1000 ounces of gold at $148 per ounce for delivery in March 2011. Analyse the profit and loss for Contour at delivery by constructing a graph similar to Figure 21.2 for a range of gold prices between $120 and $180. Use a price interval of $10 in your analysis.

21-2 (*Forward contract payout*) Repeat problem 21-1, but this time draw the profit or loss graph from the perspective of the party who bought the forward contract.

21-3 (*Futures*) On 16 June 2010 you buy a December 2010 silver futures contract at a price of $26 per ounce. Each futures contract covers 1000 ounces of silver. Assume that the price movements of the silver futures contract in the next five trading days are as follows:

DATE	FUTURES PRICE
17 June	26.24
18 June	26.12
19 June	25.43
20 June	25.93
23 June	26.14

The initial margin is $500. Mark the futures to market for the above dates and calculate the balance of the margin.

21-4 (*Hedging with futures*) Pinnacles Ltd is a major producer of copper and is based in Western Australia. Due to the nature of its business, Pinnacles is exposed to commodity price risk, particularly copper price risk. Recently, Pinnacles signed a 10-year contract with a Chinese company to supply them with copper priced at the time of delivery. The next delivery of 2000 tonnes takes place in March 2011 and Pinnacles wants to hedge the commodity price risk associated with this delivery. The following copper futures contracts are available. The price quoted is per tonne.

CONTRACT	PRICE
December 2010	$6615
March 2011	$6690
June 2011	$6620

(a) Which of these futures contracts should Pinnacles use to hedge its exposure? Does the company long or short the futures contract?

(b) Each futures contract covers 10 tonnes of copper. How many contracts does Pinnacles need to hedge its exposure?

(c) What is Pinnacles' revenue from the sale, given that it uses a futures contract to hedge the price risk?

(d) Assume that, when Pinnacles delivers the copper to its Chinese partner, the price of copper is $6650 per tonne. What is the gain or loss from its futures position?

21-5 (*Call options*) Draw a profit or loss graph, similar to Figure 21.3, for the purchase of a call with an exercise price of $65 for which a $9 premium is paid. Identify the break-even point, the maximum profit and the maximum loss. Now draw the profit or loss graph assuming an exercise price of $70 and a $6 premium.

21-6 (*Call options*) Repeat problem 21-5, but this time draw the profit or loss graph (similar to Figure 21.4) for the call writer.

21-7 (*Put options*) Draw a profit or loss graph (similar to Figure 21.5) for the purchase of a put contract with an exercise price of $45 for which a premium of $5 is paid. Identify the break-even point, the maximum profit and the maximum loss.

21-8 (*Put options*) Repeat problem 21-7, but this time draw the profit or loss graph (similar to Figure 21.6) for the seller of the put contract.

21-9 (*Interest-rate swaps*) Kum Tong Ltd has a $2 000 000 investment in a bond portfolio that pays a variable interest rate. Returns from the bond portfolio are received semi-annually. In the last senior management meeting, the CFO suggested that interest rates were likely to fall, causing a loss of return on the bond portfolio. As a result, he wants the treasury department to use an interest-rate swap contract to hedge this possible fall in interest rates in the next two years.

(a) Design an interest-rate swap to achieve this objective. Clearly indicate which party is paying a fixed interest rate and which party is paying a variable interest rate.
(b) Your local bank quotes the following swap rate in exchange for the bank-bill swap rate (BBSW):
6% if bank pays fixed
6.2% if counter-party pays fixed

Assume that the BBSW for the next four quarters turns out to be 6.1%, 6.02%, 5.98% and 5.8%. Calculate the amount payable by each party at each payment date in the next four quarters.

21-10 (*Interest-rate swap*) The Prince Racket Company manufactures a line of tennis and racket-ball equipment. The firm recently entered into a loan agreement for $20 million that carries a floating rate of interest equal to BBSW plus 100 basis points (1%). The loan has a five-year maturity and requires the firm to make semi-annual payments. At the time the loan was being negotiated, the company was approached by their banker with a suggestion as to how the firm might lock in the rate of interest on the loan at 8% using a fixed-for-floating interest-rate swap. Under the agreement the company would make a cash payment to the swap counter party equal to the fixed-rate coupon payment and receive in return a coupon payment reflecting the floating rate.

(a) Calculate the swap cash flows over the next five years based on the following set of hypothetical BBSW rates:

YEAR	SIX-MONTH BBSW
0	6.80%
0.5	7.20%
1	8.00%
1.5	7.40%
2	7.80%
2.5	8.60%
3	9.00%
3.5	9.20%
4	8.40%
4.5	7.60%
5	–

(b) What would motivate a firm's management to enter into such a swap contract?

Case study

For your job as the business reporter for a local newspaper, you are given the task of putting together a series of articles on the derivatives markets. Much recent local press coverage has been given to the dangers of those markets and the losses that some firms have experienced. Your editor would like you to address several specific questions, in addition to demonstrating the use of futures contracts and options and applying them to several problems. Prepare a response to the following memorandum from your editor:

To: Business reporter
From: Perry White, Editor, *Daily Planet*
Re: Series on the derivative securities market

In your upcoming series on the derivatives markets, I would like to make sure you cover several specific points. In addition, before you begin this assignment, I want to make sure we are all reading from the same script, as accuracy has always been the cornerstone of the *Daily Planet*. As such, I'd like a response to the following questions before we proceed:

1. What opportunities do the derivative securities markets (i.e. futures and options markets) provide to the financial manager?
2. When might a firm become interested in purchasing interest-rate futures? Foreign-exchange futures? Stock-index futures?
3. What can a firm do to reduce exchange-rate risk?
4. How do treasury bond futures and options on treasury bonds differ?
5. What is an option on a futures contract? Give an example of one and explain why it exists.
6. Draw a profit or loss graph for the purchase of a call option with an exercise price of $25 for which a $6 premium is paid. Identify the break-even point, the maximum profit and the maximum loss.
7. Repeat question 6, but draw the profit or loss graph for the call *writer*.
8. What is a currency swap and who might use one?
9. What is the main difference between an interest-rate swap and a currency swap?

Compound sum of $1

n	1%	2%	3%	4%	5%	6%	7%	8%	9%	10%
1	1.010	1.020	1.030	1.040	1.050	1.060	1.070	1.080	1.090	1.100
2	1.020	1.040	1.061	1.082	1.102	1.124	1.145	1.166	1.188	1.210
3	1.030	1.061	1.093	1.125	1.158	1.191	1.225	1.260	1.295	1.331
4	1.041	1.082	1.126	1.170	1.216	1.262	1.311	1.360	1.412	1.464
5	1.051	1.104	1.159	1.217	1.276	1.338	1.403	1.469	1.539	1.611
6	1.062	1.126	1.194	1.265	1.340	1.419	1.501	1.587	1.677	1.772
7	1.072	1.149	1.230	1.316	1.407	1.504	1.606	1.714	1.828	1.949
8	1.083	1.172	1.267	1.369	1.477	1.594	1.718	1.851	1.993	2.144
9	1.094	1.195	1.305	1.423	1.551	1.689	1.838	1.999	2.172	2.358
10	1.105	1.219	1.344	1.480	1.629	1.791	1.967	2.159	2.367	2.594
11	1.116	1.243	1.384	1.539	1.710	1.898	2.105	2.332	2.580	2.853
12	1.127	1.268	1.426	1.601	1.796	2.012	2.252	2.518	2.813	3.138
13	1.138	1.294	1.469	1.665	1.886	2.133	2.410	2.720	3.066	3.452
14	1.149	1.319	1.513	1.732	1.980	2.261	2.579	2.937	3.342	3.797
15	1.161	1.346	1.558	1.801	2.079	2.397	2.759	3.172	3.642	4.177
16	1.173	1.373	1.605	1.873	2.183	2.540	2.952	3.426	3.970	4.595
17	1.184	1.400	1.653	1.948	2.292	2.693	3.159	3.700	4.328	5.054
18	1.196	1.428	1.702	2.026	2.407	2.854	3.380	3.996	4.717	5.560
19	1.208	1.457	1.753	2.107	2.527	3.026	3.616	4.316	5.142	6.116
20	1.220	1.486	1.806	2.191	2.653	3.207	3.870	4.661	5.604	6.727
21	1.232	1.516	1.860	2.279	2.786	3.399	4.140	5.034	6.109	7.400
22	1.245	1.546	1.916	2.370	2.925	3.603	4.430	5.436	6.658	8.140
23	1.257	1.577	1.974	2.465	3.071	3.820	4.740	5.871	7.258	8.954
24	1.270	1.608	2.033	2.563	3.225	4.049	5.072	6.341	7.911	9.850
25	1.282	1.641	2.094	2.666	3.386	4.292	5.427	6.848	8.623	10.834
30	1.348	1.811	2.427	3.243	4.322	5.743	7.612	10.062	13.267	17.449
40	1.489	2.208	3.262	4.801	7.040	10.285	14.974	21.724	31.408	45.258
50	1.645	2.691	4.384	7.106	11.467	18.419	29.456	46.900	74.354	117.386

n	11%	12%	13%	14%	15%	16%	17%	18%	19%	20%
1	1.110	1.120	1.130	1.140	1.150	1.160	1.170	1.180	1.190	1.200
2	1.232	1.254	1.277	1.300	1.322	1.346	1.369	1.392	1.416	1.440
3	1.368	1.405	1.443	1.482	1.521	1.561	1.602	1.643	1.685	1.728
4	1.518	1.574	1.630	1.689	1.749	1.811	1.874	1.939	2.005	2.074
5	1.685	1.762	1.842	1.925	2.011	2.100	2.192	2.288	2.386	2.488
6	1.870	1.974	2.082	2.195	2.313	2.436	2.565	2.700	2.840	2.986
7	2.076	2.211	2.353	2.502	2.660	2.826	3.001	3.185	3.379	3.583
8	2.305	2.476	2.658	2.853	3.059	3.278	3.511	3.759	4.021	4.300
9	2.558	2.773	3.004	3.252	3.518	3.803	4.108	4.435	4.785	5.160
10	2.839	3.106	3.395	3.707	4.046	4.411	4.807	5.234	5.695	6.192
11	3.152	3.479	3.836	4.226	4.652	5.117	5.624	6.176	6.777	7.430
12	3.498	3.896	4.334	4.818	5.350	5.936	6.580	7.288	8.064	8.916
13	3.883	4.363	4.898	5.492	6.153	6.886	7.699	8.599	9.596	10.699
14	4.310	4.887	5.535	6.261	7.076	7.987	9.007	10.147	11.420	12.839
15	4.785	5.474	6.254	7.138	8.137	9.265	10.539	11.974	13.589	15.407
16	5.311	6.130	7.067	8.137	9.358	10.748	12.330	14.129	16.171	18.488
17	5.895	6.866	7.986	9.276	10.761	12.468	14.426	16.672	19.244	22.186
18	6.543	7.690	9.024	10.575	12.375	14.462	16.879	19.673	22.900	26.623
19	7.263	8.613	10.197	12.055	14.232	16.776	19.748	23.214	27.251	31.948
20	8.062	9.646	11.523	13.743	16.366	19.461	23.105	27.393	32.429	38.337
21	8.949	10.804	13.021	15.667	18.821	22.574	27.033	32.323	38.591	46.005
22	9.933	12.100	14.713	17.861	21.644	26.186	31.629	38.141	45.923	55.205
23	11.026	13.552	16.626	20.361	24.891	30.376	37.005	45.007	54.648	66.247
24	12.239	15.178	18.788	23.212	28.625	35.236	43.296	53.108	65.031	79.496
25	13.585	17.000	21.230	26.461	32.918	40.874	50.656	62.667	77.387	95.395
30	22.892	29.960	39.115	50.949	66.210	85.849	111.061	143.367	184.672	237.373
40	64.999	93.049	132.776	188.876	267.856	378.715	533.846	750.353	1051.642	1469.740
50	184.559	288.996	450.711	700.197	1083.619	1670.669	2566.080	3927.189	5988.730	9100.191

n	21%	22%	23%	24%	25%	26%	27%	28%	29%	30%
1	1.210	1.220	1.230	1.240	1.250	1.260	1.270	1.280	1.290	1.300
2	1.464	1.488	1.513	1.538	1.562	1.588	1.613	1.638	1.664	1.690
3	1.772	1.816	1.861	1.907	1.953	2.000	2.048	2.097	2.147	2.197
4	2.144	2.215	2.289	2.364	2.441	2.520	2.601	2.684	2.769	2.856
5	2.594	2.703	2.815	2.932	3.052	3.176	3.304	3.436	3.572	3.713
6	3.138	3.297	3.463	3.635	3.815	4.001	4.196	4.398	4.608	4.827
7	3.797	4.023	4.259	4.508	4.768	5.042	5.329	5.629	5.945	6.275
8	4.595	4.908	5.239	5.589	5.960	6.353	6.767	7.206	7.669	8.157
9	5.560	5.987	6.444	6.931	7.451	8.004	8.595	9.223	9.893	10.604
10	6.727	7.305	7.926	8.594	9.313	10.086	10.915	11.806	12.761	13.786
11	8.140	8.912	9.749	10.657	11.642	12.708	13.862	15.112	16.462	17.921
12	9.850	10.872	11.991	13.215	14.552	16.012	17.605	19.343	21.236	23.298
13	11.918	13.264	14.749	16.386	18.190	20.175	22.359	24.759	27.395	30.287
14	14.421	16.182	18.141	20.319	22.737	25.420	28.395	31.691	35.339	39.373
15	17.449	19.742	22.314	25.195	28.422	32.030	36.062	40.565	45.587	51.185
16	21.113	24.085	27.446	31.242	35.527	40.357	45.799	51.923	58.808	66.541
17	25.547	29.384	33.758	38.740	44.409	50.850	58.165	66.461	75.862	86.503
18	30.912	35.848	41.523	48.038	55.511	64.071	73.869	85.070	97.862	112.454
19	37.404	43.735	51.073	59.567	69.389	80.730	93.813	108.890	126.242	146.190
20	45.258	53.357	62.820	73.863	86.736	101.720	119.143	139.379	162.852	190.047
21	54.762	65.095	77.268	91.591	108.420	128.167	151.312	178.405	210.079	247.061
22	66.262	79.416	95.040	113.572	135.525	161.490	192.165	228.358	271.002	321.178
23	80.178	96.887	116.899	140.829	169.407	203.477	244.050	292.298	349.592	417.531
24	97.015	118.203	143.786	174.628	211.758	256.381	309.943	374.141	450.974	542.791
25	117.388	144.207	176.857	216.539	264.698	323.040	393.628	478.901	581.756	705.627
30	304.471	389.748	497.904	634.810	807.793	1025.904	1300.477	1645.488	2078.208	2619.936
40	2048.309	2846.941	3946.340	5455.797	7523.156	10346.879	14195.051	19426.418	26520.723	36117.754
50	13779.844	20795.680	31278.301	46889.207	70064.812	104354.562	154942.687	229345.875	338440.000	497910.125

n	31%	32%	33%	34%	35%	36%	37%	38%	39%	40%
1	1.310	1.320	1.330	1.340	1.350	1.360	1.370	1.380	1.390	1.400
2	1.716	1.742	1.769	1.796	1.822	1.850	1.877	1.904	1.932	1.960
3	2.248	2.300	2.353	2.406	2.460	2.515	2.571	2.628	2.686	2.744
4	2.945	3.036	3.129	3.224	3.321	3.421	3.523	3.627	3.733	3.842
5	3.858	4.007	4.162	4.320	4.484	4.653	4.826	5.005	5.189	5.378
6	5.054	5.290	5.535	5.789	6.053	6.328	6.612	6.907	7.213	7.530
7	6.621	6.983	7.361	7.758	8.172	8.605	9.058	9.531	10.025	10.541
8	8.673	9.217	9.791	10.395	11.032	11.703	12.410	13.153	13.935	14.758
9	11.362	12.166	13.022	13.930	14.894	15.917	17.001	18.151	19.370	20.661
10	14.884	16.060	17.319	18.666	20.106	21.646	23.292	25.049	26.924	28.925
11	19.498	21.199	23.034	25.012	27.144	29.439	31.910	34.567	37.425	40.495
12	25.542	27.982	30.635	33.516	36.644	40.037	43.716	47.703	52.020	56.694
13	33.460	36.937	40.745	44.912	49.469	54.451	59.892	65.830	72.308	79.371
14	43.832	49.756	54.190	60.181	66.784	74.053	82.051	90.845	100.509	111.190
15	57.420	64.358	72.073	80.643	90.158	100.712	112.410	125.366	139.707	155.567
16	75.220	84.953	95.857	108.061	121.713	136.968	154.002	173.005	194.192	217.793
17	98.539	112.138	127.490	144.802	164.312	186.277	210.983	238.747	269.927	304.911
18	129.086	148.022	169.561	194.035	221.822	253.337	289.046	329.471	375.198	426.875
19	169.102	195.389	225.517	260.006	299.459	344.537	395.993	454.669	521.525	597.625
20	221.523	257.913	299.937	348.408	404.270	468.571	542.511	627.443	724.919	836.674
21	290.196	340.446	398.916	466.867	545.764	637.256	743.240	865.871	1007.637	1171.343
22	380.156	449.388	530.558	625.601	736.781	865.668	1018.238	1194.900	1400.615	1639.878
23	498.004	593.192	705.642	838.305	994.653	1178.668	1394.986	1648.961	1946.854	2295.829
24	652.385	783.013	938.504	1123.328	1342.781	1602.988	1911.129	2275.564	2706.125	3214.158
25	854.623	1033.577	1248.210	1505.258	1812.754	2180.063	2618.245	3140.275	3761.511	4499.816
30	3297.081	4142.008	5194.516	6503.285	8128.426	10142.914	12636.086	15716.703	19517.969	24201.043
40	49072.621	66519.313	89962.188	121388.437	163433.875	219558.625	294317.937	393684.687	525508.312	700022.688

Present value of $1

n	1%	2%	3%	4%	5%	6%	7%	8%	9%	10%
1	0.990	0.980	0.971	0.962	0.952	0.943	0.935	0.926	0.917	0.909
2	0.980	0.961	0.943	0.925	0.907	0.890	0.873	0.857	0.842	0.826
3	0.971	0.942	0.915	0.889	0.864	0.840	0.816	0.794	0.772	0.751
4	0.961	0.924	0.888	0.855	0.823	0.792	0.763	0.735	0.708	0.683
5	0.951	0.906	0.863	0.822	0.784	0.747	0.713	0.681	0.650	0.621
6	0.942	0.888	0.837	0.790	0.746	0.705	0.666	0.630	0.596	0.564
7	0.933	0.871	0.813	0.760	0.711	0.665	0.623	0.583	0.547	0.513
8	0.923	0.853	0.789	0.731	0.677	0.627	0.582	0.540	0.502	0.467
9	0.914	0.837	0.766	0.703	0.645	0.592	0.544	0.500	0.460	0.424
10	0.905	0.820	0.744	0.676	0.614	0.558	0.508	0.463	0.422	0.386
11	0.896	0.804	0.722	0.650	0.585	0.527	0.475	0.429	0.388	0.350
12	0.887	0.789	0.701	0.625	0.557	0.497	0.444	0.397	0.356	0.319
13	0.879	0.773	0.681	0.601	0.530	0.469	0.415	0.368	0.326	0.290
14	0.870	0.758	0.661	0.577	0.505	0.442	0.388	0.340	0.299	0.263
15	0.861	0.743	0.642	0.555	0.481	0.417	0.362	0.315	0.275	0.239
16	0.853	0.728	0.623	0.534	0.458	0.394	0.339	0.292	0.252	0.218
17	0.844	0.714	0.605	0.513	0.436	0.371	0.317	0.270	0.231	0.198
18	0.836	0.700	0.587	0.494	0.416	0.350	0.296	0.250	0.212	0.180
19	0.828	0.686	0.570	0.475	0.396	0.331	0.277	0.232	0.194	0.164
20	0.820	0.673	0.554	0.456	0.377	0.312	0.258	0.215	0.178	0.149
21	0.811	0.660	0.538	0.439	0.359	0.294	0.242	0.199	0.164	0.135
22	0.803	0.647	0.522	0.422	0.342	0.278	0.226	0.184	0.150	0.123
23	0.795	0.634	0.507	0.406	0.326	0.262	0.211	0.170	0.138	0.112
24	0.788	0.622	0.492	0.390	0.310	0.247	0.197	0.158	0.126	0.102
25	0.780	0.610	0.478	0.375	0.295	0.233	0.184	0.146	0.116	0.092
30	0.742	0.552	0.412	0.308	0.231	0.174	0.131	0.099	0.075	0.057
40	0.672	0.453	0.307	0.208	0.142	0.097	0.067	0.046	0.032	0.022
50	0.608	0.372	0.228	0.141	0.087	0.054	0.034	0.021	0.013	0.009

n	11%	12%	13%	14%	15%	16%	17%	18%	19%	20%
1	0.901	0.893	0.885	0.877	0.870	0.862	0.855	0.847	0.840	0.833
2	0.812	0.797	0.783	0.769	0.756	0.743	0.731	0.718	0.706	0.694
3	0.731	0.712	0.693	0.675	0.658	0.641	0.624	0.609	0.593	0.579
4	0.659	0.636	0.613	0.592	0.572	0.552	0.534	0.516	0.499	0.482
5	0.593	0.567	0.543	0.519	0.497	0.476	0.456	0.437	0.419	0.402
6	0.535	0.507	0.480	0.456	0.432	0.410	0.390	0.370	0.352	0.335
7	0.482	0.452	0.425	0.400	0.376	0.354	0.333	0.314	0.296	0.279
8	0.434	0.404	0.376	0.351	0.327	0.305	0.285	0.266	0.249	0.233
9	0.391	0.361	0.333	0.308	0.284	0.263	0.243	0.225	0.209	0.194
10	0.352	0.322	0.295	0.270	0.247	0.227	0.208	0.191	0.176	0.162
11	0.317	0.287	0.261	0.237	0.215	0.195	0.178	0.162	0.148	0.135
12	0.286	0.257	0.231	0.208	0.187	0.168	0.152	0.137	0.124	0.112
13	0.258	0.229	0.204	0.182	0.163	0.145	0.130	0.116	0.104	0.093
14	0.232	0.205	0.181	0.160	0.141	0.125	0.111	0.099	0.088	0.078
15	0.209	0.183	0.160	0.140	0.123	0.108	0.095	0.084	0.074	0.065
16	0.188	0.163	0.141	0.123	0.107	0.093	0.081	0.071	0.062	0.054
17	0.170	0.146	0.125	0.108	0.093	0.080	0.069	0.060	0.052	0.045
18	0.153	0.130	0.111	0.095	0.081	0.069	0.059	0.051	0.044	0.038
19	0.138	0.116	0.098	0.083	0.070	0.060	0.051	0.043	0.037	0.031
20	0.124	0.104	0.087	0.073	0.061	0.051	0.043	0.037	0.031	0.026
21	0.112	0.093	0.077	0.064	0.053	0.044	0.037	0.031	0.026	0.022
22	0.101	0.083	0.068	0.056	0.046	0.038	0.032	0.026	0.022	0.018
23	0.091	0.074	0.060	0.049	0.040	0.033	0.027	0.022	0.018	0.015
24	0.082	0.066	0.053	0.043	0.035	0.028	0.023	0.019	0.015	0.013
25	0.074	0.059	0.047	0.038	0.030	0.024	0.020	0.016	0.013	0.010
30	0.044	0.033	0.026	0.020	0.015	0.012	0.009	0.007	0.005	0.004
40	0.015	0.011	0.008	0.005	0.004	0.003	0.002	0.001	0.001	0.001
50	0.005	0.003	0.002	0.001	0.001	0.001	0.000	0.000	0.000	0.000

n	21%	22%	23%	24%	25%	26%	27%	28%	29%	30%
1	0.826	0.820	0.813	0.806	0.800	0.794	0.787	0.781	0.775	0.769
2	0.683	0.672	0.661	0.650	0.640	0.630	0.620	0.610	0.601	0.592
3	0.564	0.551	0.537	0.524	0.512	0.500	0.488	0.477	0.466	0.455
4	0.467	0.451	0.437	0.423	0.410	0.397	0.384	0.373	0.361	0.350
5	0.386	0.370	0.355	0.341	0.328	0.315	0.303	0.291	0.280	0.269
6	0.319	0.303	0.289	0.275	0.262	0.250	0.238	0.227	0.217	0.207
7	0.263	0.249	0.235	0.222	0.210	0.198	0.188	0.178	0.168	0.159
8	0.218	0.204	0.191	0.179	0.168	0.157	0.148	0.139	0.130	0.123
9	0.180	0.167	0.155	0.144	0.134	0.125	0.116	0.108	0.101	0.094
10	0.149	0.137	0.126	0.116	0.107	0.099	0.092	0.085	0.078	0.073
11	0.123	0.112	0.103	0.094	0.086	0.079	0.072	0.066	0.061	0.056
12	0.102	0.092	0.083	0.076	0.069	0.062	0.057	0.052	0.047	0.043
13	0.084	0.075	0.068	0.061	0.055	0.050	0.045	0.040	0.037	0.033
14	0.069	0.062	0.055	0.049	0.044	0.039	0.035	0.032	0.028	0.025
15	0.057	0.051	0.045	0.040	0.035	0.031	0.028	0.025	0.022	0.020
16	0.047	0.042	0.036	0.032	0.028	0.025	0.022	0.019	0.017	0.015
17	0.039	0.034	0.030	0.026	0.023	0.020	0.017	0.015	0.013	0.012
18	0.032	0.028	0.024	0.021	0.018	0.016	0.014	0.012	0.010	0.009
19	0.027	0.023	0.020	0.017	0.014	0.012	0.011	0.009	0.008	0.007
20	0.022	0.019	0.016	0.014	0.012	0.010	0.008	0.007	0.006	0.005
21	0.018	0.015	0.013	0.011	0.009	0.008	0.007	0.006	0.005	0.004
22	0.015	0.013	0.011	0.009	0.007	0.006	0.005	0.004	0.004	0.003
23	0.012	0.010	0.009	0.007	0.006	0.005	0.004	0.003	0.003	0.002
24	0.010	0.008	0.007	0.006	0.005	0.004	0.003	0.003	0.002	0.002
25	0.009	0.007	0.006	0.005	0.004	0.003	0.003	0.002	0.002	0.001
30	0.003	0.003	0.002	0.002	0.001	0.001	0.001	0.001	0.000	0.000
40	0.000	0.000	0.000	0.000	0.000	0.000	0.000	0.000	0.000	0.000
50	0.000	0.000	0.000	0.000	0.000	0.000	0.000	0.000	0.000	0.000

n	31%	32%	33%	34%	35%	36%	37%	38%	39%	40%
1	0.763	0.758	0.752	0.746	0.741	0.735	0.730	0.725	0.719	0.714
2	0.583	0.574	0.565	0.557	0.549	0.541	0.533	0.525	0.518	0.510
3	0.445	0.435	0.425	0.416	0.406	0.398	0.389	0.381	0.372	0.364
4	0.340	0.329	0.320	0.310	0.301	0.292	0.284	0.276	0.268	0.260
5	0.259	0.250	0.240	0.231	0.223	0.215	0.207	0.200	0.193	0.186
6	0.198	0.189	0.181	0.173	0.165	0.158	0.151	0.145	0.139	0.133
7	0.151	0.143	0.136	0.129	0.122	0.116	0.110	0.105	0.100	0.095
8	0.115	0.108	0.102	0.096	0.091	0.085	0.081	0.076	0.072	0.068
9	0.088	0.082	0.077	0.072	0.067	0.063	0.059	0.055	0.052	0.048
10	0.067	0.062	0.058	0.054	0.050	0.046	0.043	0.040	0.037	0.035
11	0.051	0.047	0.043	0.040	0.037	0.034	0.031	0.029	0.027	0.025
12	0.039	0.036	0.033	0.030	0.027	0.025	0.023	0.021	0.019	0.018
13	0.030	0.027	0.025	0.022	0.020	0.018	0.017	0.015	0.014	0.013
14	0.023	0.021	0.018	0.017	0.015	0.014	0.012	0.011	0.010	0.009
15	0.017	0.016	0.014	0.012	0.011	0.010	0.009	0.008	0.007	0.006
16	0.013	0.012	0.010	0.009	0.008	0.007	0.006	0.006	0.005	0.005
17	0.010	0.009	0.008	0.007	0.006	0.005	0.005	0.004	0.004	0.003
18	0.008	0.007	0.006	0.005	0.005	0.004	0.003	0.003	0.003	0.002
19	0.006	0.005	0.004	0.004	0.003	0.003	0.003	0.002	0.002	0.002
20	0.005	0.004	0.003	0.003	0.002	0.002	0.002	0.002	0.001	0.001
21	0.003	0.003	0.003	0.002	0.002	0.002	0.001	0.001	0.001	0.001
22	0.003	0.002	0.002	0.002	0.001	0.001	0.001	0.001	0.001	0.001
23	0.002	0.002	0.001	0.001	0.001	0.001	0.001	0.001	0.001	0.000
24	0.002	0.001	0.001	0.001	0.001	0.001	0.001	0.000	0.000	0.000
25	0.001	0.001	0.001	0.001	0.001	0.000	0.000	0.000	0.000	0.000
30	0.000	0.000	0.000	0.000	0.000	0.000	0.000	0.000	0.000	0.000
40	0.000	0.000	0.000	0.000	0.000	0.000	0.000	0.000	0.000	0.000

Sum of an annuity of $1 for *n* periods

n	1%	2%	3%	4%	5%	6%	7%	8%	9%	10%
1	1.000	1.000	1.000	1.000	1.000	1.000	1.000	1.000	1.000	1.000
2	2.010	2.020	2.030	2.040	2.050	2.060	2.070	2.080	2.090	2.100
3	3.030	3.060	3.091	3.122	3.152	3.184	3.215	3.246	3.278	3.310
4	4.060	4.122	4.184	4.246	4.310	4.375	4.440	4.506	4.573	4.641
5	5.101	5.204	5.309	5.416	5.526	5.637	5.751	5.867	5.985	6.105
6	6.152	6.308	6.468	6.633	6.802	6.975	7.153	7.336	7.523	7.716
7	7.214	7.434	7.662	7.898	8.142	8.394	8.654	8.923	9.200	9.487
8	8.286	8.583	8.892	9.214	9.549	9.897	10.260	10.637	11.028	11.436
9	9.368	9.755	10.159	10.583	11.027	11.491	11.978	12.488	13.021	13.579
10	10.462	10.950	11.464	12.006	12.578	13.181	13.816	14.487	15.193	15.937
11	11.567	12.169	12.808	13.486	14.207	14.972	15.784	16.645	17.560	18.531
12	12.682	13.412	14.192	15.026	15.917	16.870	17.888	18.977	20.141	21.384
13	13.809	14.680	15.618	16.627	17.713	18.882	20.141	21.495	22.953	24.523
14	14.947	15.974	17.086	18.292	19.598	21.015	22.550	24.215	26.019	27.975
15	16.097	17.293	18.599	20.023	21.578	23.276	25.129	27.152	29.361	31.772
16	17.258	18.639	20.157	21.824	23.657	25.672	27.888	30.324	33.003	35.949
17	18.430	20.012	21.761	23.697	25.840	28.213	30.840	33.750	36.973	40.544
18	19.614	21.412	23.414	25.645	28.132	30.905	33.999	37.450	41.301	45.599
19	20.811	22.840	25.117	27.671	30.539	33.760	37.379	41.446	46.018	51.158
20	22.019	24.297	26.870	29.778	33.066	36.785	40.995	45.762	51.159	57.274
21	23.239	25.783	28.676	31.969	35.719	39.992	44.865	50.422	56.764	64.002
22	24.471	27.299	30.536	34.248	38.505	43.392	49.005	55.456	62.872	71.402
23	25.716	28.845	32.452	36.618	41.430	46.995	53.435	60.893	69.531	79.542
24	26.973	30.421	34.426	39.082	44.501	50.815	58.176	66.764	76.789	88.496
25	28.243	32.030	36.459	41.645	47.726	54.864	63.248	73.105	84.699	98.346
30	34.784	40.567	47.575	56.084	66.438	79.057	94.459	113.282	136.305	164.491
40	48.885	60.401	75.400	95.024	120.797	154.758	199.630	295.052	337.872	442.580
50	64.461	84.577	112.794	152.664	209.341	290.325	406.516	573.756	815.051	1163.865

n	11%	12%	13%	14%	15%	16%	17%	18%	19%	20%
1	1.000	1.000	1.000	1.000	1.000	1.000	1.000	1.000	1.000	1.000
2	2.110	2.120	2.130	2.140	2.150	2.160	2.170	2.180	2.190	2.200
3	3.342	3.374	3.407	3.440	3.472	3.506	3.539	3.572	3.606	3.640
4	4.710	4.779	4.850	4.921	4.993	5.066	5.141	5.215	5.291	5.368
5	6.228	6.353	6.480	6.610	6.742	6.877	7.014	7.154	7.297	7.442
6	7.913	8.115	8.323	8.535	8.754	8.977	9.207	9.442	9.683	9.930
7	9.783	10.089	10.405	10.730	11.067	11.414	11.772	12.141	12.523	12.916
8	11.859	12.300	12.757	13.233	13.727	14.240	14.773	15.327	15.902	16.499
9	14.164	14.776	15.416	16.085	16.786	17.518	18.285	19.086	19.923	20.799
10	16.722	17.549	18.420	19.337	20.304	21.321	22.393	23.521	24.709	25.959
11	19.561	20.655	21.814	23.044	24.349	25.733	27.200	28.755	30.403	32.150
12	22.713	24.133	25.650	27.271	29.001	30.850	32.824	34.931	37.180	39.580
13	26.211	28.029	29.984	32.088	34.352	36.786	39.404	42.218	45.244	48.496
14	30.095	32.392	34.882	37.581	40.504	43.672	47.102	50.818	54.841	59.196
15	34.405	37.280	40.417	43.842	47.580	51.659	56.109	60.965	66.260	72.035
16	39.190	42.753	46.671	50.980	55.717	60.925	66.648	72.938	79.850	87.442
17	44.500	48.883	53.738	59.117	65.075	71.673	78.978	87.067	96.021	105.930
18	50.396	55.749	61.724	68.393	75.836	84.140	93.404	103.739	115.265	128.116
19	56.939	63.439	70.748	78.968	88.211	98.603	110.283	123.412	138.165	154.739
20	64.202	72.052	80.946	91.024	102.443	115.379	130.031	146.626	165.417	186.687
21	72.264	81.698	92.468	104.767	118.809	134.840	153.136	174.019	197.846	225.024
22	81.213	92.502	105.489	120.434	137.630	157.414	180.169	206.342	236.436	271.028
23	91.147	104.602	120.203	138.295	159.274	183.600	211.798	244.483	282.359	326.234
24	102.173	118.154	136.829	158.656	184.166	213.976	248.803	289.490	337.007	392.480
25	114.412	133.333	155.616	181.867	212.790	249.212	292.099	342.598	402.038	471.976
30	199.018	241.330	293.192	356.778	434.738	530.306	647.423	790.932	966.698	1181.865
40	581.812	767.080	1013.667	341.979	1779.048	2360.724	3134.412	4163.094	5529.711	7343.715
50	1668.723	2399.975	3459.344	4994.301	7217.488	10435.449	15088.805	21812.273	31514.492	45496.094

n	21%	22%	23%	24%	25%	26%	27%	28%	29%	30%
1	1.000	1.000	1.000	1.000	1.000	1.000	1.000	1.000	1.000	1.000
2	2.210	2.220	2.230	2.240	2.250	2.260	2.270	2.280	2.290	2.300
3	3.674	3.708	3.743	3.778	3.813	3.848	3.883	3.918	3.954	3.990
4	5.446	5.524	5.604	5.684	5.766	5.848	5.931	6.016	6.101	6.187
5	7.589	7.740	7.893	8.048	8.207	8.368	8.533	8.700	8.870	9.043
6	10.183	10.442	10.708	10.980	11.259	11.544	11.837	12.136	12.442	12.756
7	13.321	13.740	14.171	14.615	15.073	15.546	16.032	16.534	17.051	17.583
8	17.119	17.762	18.430	19.123	19.842	20.588	21.361	22.163	22.995	23.858
9	21.714	22.670	23.669	24.712	25.802	26.940	28.129	29.369	30.664	32.015
10	27.274	28.657	20.113	31.643	33.253	34.945	36.723	38.592	40.556	42.619
11	34.001	35.962	38.039	40.238	42.566	45.030	47.639	50.398	53.318	56.405
12	42.141	44.873	47.787	50.895	54.208	57.738	61.501	65.510	69.780	74.326
13	51.991	55.745	59.778	64.109	68.760	73.750	79.106	84.853	91.016	97.624
14	63.909	69.009	74.528	80.496	86.949	93.925	101.465	109.611	118.411	127.912
15	78.330	85.191	92.669	100.815	109.687	119.346	129.860	141.302	153.750	167.285
16	95.779	104.933	114.983	126.010	138.109	151.375	165.922	181.867	199.337	218.470
17	116.892	129.019	142.428	157.252	173.636	191.733	211.721	233.790	258.145	285.011
18	142.439	158.403	176.187	195.993	218.045	242.583	269.885	300.250	334.006	371.514
19	173.351	194.251	217.710	244.031	273.556	306.654	343.754	385.321	431.868	483.968
20	210.755	237.986	268.783	303.598	342.945	387.384	437.568	494.210	558.110	630.157
21	256.013	291.343	331.603	377.461	429.681	489.104	556.710	633.589	720.962	820.204
22	310.775	356.438	408.871	469.052	538.101	617.270	708.022	811.993	931.040	1067.265
23	377.038	435.854	503.911	582.624	673.626	778.760	900.187	1040.351	1202.042	1388.443
24	457.215	532.741	620.810	723.453	843.032	982.237	1144.237	1332.649	1551.634	1805.975
25	554.230	650.944	764.596	898.082	1054.791	1238.617	1454.180	1706.790	2002.608	2348.765
30	1445.111	1767.044	2160.459	2640.881	3227.172	3941.953	4812.891	5873.172	7162.785	8729.805
40	9749.141	12936.141	17153.691	22728.367	30088.621	39791.957	52570.707	69376.562	91447.375	120389.375

n	31%	32%	33%	34%	35%	36%	37%	38%	39%	40%
1	1.000	1.000	1.000	1.000	1.000	1.000	1.000	1.000	1.000	1.000
2	2.310	2.320	2.330	2.340	2.350	2.360	2.370	2.380	2.390	2.400
3	4.026	4.062	4.099	4.136	4.172	4.210	4.247	4.284	4.322	4.360
4	6.274	6.362	6.452	6.542	6.633	6.725	6.818	6.912	7.008	7.104
5	9.219	9.398	9.581	9.766	9.954	10.146	10.341	10.539	10.741	10.946
6	13.077	13.406	13.742	14.086	14.438	14.799	15.167	15.544	15.930	16.324
7	18.131	18.696	19.277	19.876	20.492	21.126	21.779	22.451	23.142	23.853
8	24.752	25.678	26.638	27.633	28.664	29.732	30.837	31.982	33.167	34.395
9	33.425	34.895	36.429	38.028	39.696	41.435	43.247	45.135	47.103	49.152
10	44.786	47.062	49.451	51.958	54.590	57.351	60.248	63.287	66.473	69.813
11	59.670	63.121	66.769	70.624	74.696	78.998	83.540	88.335	93.397	98.739
12	79.167	84.320	89.803	95.636	101.840	108.437	115.450	122.903	130.822	139.234
13	104.709	112.302	120.438	129.152	138.484	148.474	159.166	170.606	182.842	195.928
14	138.169	149.239	161.183	174.063	187.953	202.925	219.058	236.435	255.151	275.299
15	182.001	197.996	215.373	234.245	254.737	276.978	301.109	327.281	355.659	386.418
16	239.421	262.354	287.446	314.888	344.895	377.690	413.520	452.647	495.366	541.985
17	314.642	347.307	383.303	422.949	466.608	514.658	567.521	625.652	689.558	759.778
18	413.180	459.445	510.792	567.751	630.920	700.935	778.504	864.399	959.485	1064.689
19	542.266	607.467	680.354	761.786	852.741	954.271	1067.551	1193.870	1334.683	1491.563
20	711.368	802.856	905.870	1021.792	1152.200	1298.809	1463.544	1648.539	1856.208	2089.188
21	932.891	1060.769	1205.807	1370.201	1556.470	1767.380	2006.055	2275.982	2581.128	2925.862
22	1223.087	1401.215	1604.724	1837.068	2102.234	2404.636	2749.294	3141.852	3588.765	4097.203
23	1603.243	1850.603	2135.282	2462.669	2839.014	3271.304	3767.532	4336.750	4989.379	5737.078
24	2101.247	2443.795	2840.924	3300.974	3833.667	4449.969	5162.516	5985.711	6936.230	8032.906
25	2753.631	3226.808	3779.428	4424.301	5176.445	6052.957	7073.645	8261.273	9642.352	11247.062
30	10632.543	12940.672	15737.945	19124.434	23221.258	28172.016	34148.906	41357.227	50043.625	60500.207

Present value of an annuity of $1 for *n* periods

n	1%	2%	3%	4%	5%	6%	7%	8%	9%	10%
1	0.990	0.980	0.971	0.962	0.952	0.943	0.935	0.926	0.917	0.909
2	1.970	1.942	1.913	1.886	1.859	1.833	1.808	1.783	1.759	1.736
3	2.941	2.884	2.829	2.775	2.723	2.673	2.624	2.577	2.531	2.487
4	3.902	3.808	3.717	3.630	3.546	3.465	3.387	3.312	3.240	3.170
5	4.853	4.713	4.580	4.452	4.329	4.212	4.100	3.993	3.890	3.791
6	5.795	5.601	5.417	5.242	5.076	4.917	4.767	4.623	4.486	4.355
7	6.728	6.472	6.230	6.002	5.786	5.582	5.389	5.206	5.033	4.868
8	7.652	7.326	7.020	6.733	6.463	6.210	5.971	5.747	5.535	5.335
9	8.566	8.162	7.786	7.435	7.108	6.802	6.515	6.247	5.995	5.759
10	9.471	8.983	8.530	8.111	7.722	7.360	7.024	6.710	6.418	6.145
11	10.368	9.787	9.253	8.760	8.306	7.887	7.499	7.139	6.805	6.495
12	11.255	10.575	9.954	9.385	8.863	8.384	7.943	7.536	7.161	6.814
13	12.134	11.348	10.635	9.986	9.394	8.853	8.358	7.904	7.487	7.103
14	13.004	12.106	11.296	10.563	9.899	9.295	8.746	8.244	7.786	7.367
15	13.865	12.849	11.938	11.118	10.380	9.712	9.108	8.560	8.061	7.606
16	14.718	13.578	12.561	11.652	10.838	10.106	9.447	8.851	8.313	7.824
17	15.562	14.292	13.166	12.166	11.274	10.477	9.763	9.122	8.544	8.022
18	16.398	14.992	13.754	12.659	11.690	10.828	10.059	9.372	8.756	8.201
19	17.226	15.679	14.324	13.134	12.085	11.158	10.336	9.604	8.950	8.365
20	18.046	16.352	14.878	13.590	12.462	11.470	10.594	9.818	9.129	8.514
21	18.857	17.011	15.415	14.029	12.821	11.764	10.836	10.017	9.292	8.649
22	19.661	17.658	15.937	14.451	13.163	12.042	11.061	10.201	9.442	8.772
23	20.456	18.292	16.444	14.857	13.489	12.303	11.272	10.371	9.580	8.883
24	21.244	18.914	16.936	15.247	13.799	12.550	11.469	10.529	9.707	8.985
25	22.023	19.524	17.413	15.622	14.094	12.783	11.654	10.675	9.823	9.077
30	25.808	22.397	19.601	17.292	15.373	13.765	12.409	11.258	10.274	9.427
40	32.835	27.356	23.115	19.793	17.159	15.046	13.332	11.925	10.757	9.779
50	39.197	31.424	25.730	21.482	18.256	15.762	13.801	12.234	10.962	9.915

n	11%	12%	13%	14%	15%	16%	17%	18%	19%	20%
1	0.901	0.893	0.885	0.877	0.870	0.862	0.855	0.847	0.840	0.833
2	1.713	1.690	1.668	1.647	1.626	1.605	1.585	1.566	1.547	1.528
3	2.444	2.402	2.361	2.322	2.283	2.246	2.210	2.174	2.140	2.106
4	3.102	3.037	2.974	2.914	2.855	2.798	2.743	2.690	2.639	2.589
5	3.696	3.605	3.517	3.433	3.352	3.274	3.199	3.127	3.058	2.991
6	4.231	4.111	3.998	3.889	3.784	3.685	3.589	3.498	3.410	3.326
7	4.712	4.564	4.423	4.288	4.160	4.039	3.922	3.812	3.706	3.605
8	5.146	4.968	4.799	4.639	4.487	4.344	4.207	4.078	3.954	3.837
9	5.537	5.328	5.132	4.946	4.772	4.607	4.451	4.303	4.163	4.031
10	5.889	5.650	5.426	5.216	5.019	4.833	4.659	4.494	4.339	4.192
11	6.207	5.938	5.687	5.453	5.234	5.029	4.836	4.656	4.487	4.327
12	6.492	6.194	5.918	5.660	5.421	5.197	4.988	4.793	4.611	4.439
13	6.750	6.424	6.122	5.842	5.583	5.342	5.118	4.910	4.715	4.533
14	6.982	6.628	6.303	6.002	5.724	5.468	5.229	5.008	4.802	4.611
15	7.191	6.811	6.462	6.142	5.847	5.575	5.324	5.092	4.876	4.675
16	7.379	6.974	6.604	6.265	5.954	5.669	5.405	5.162	4.938	4.730
17	7.549	7.120	6.729	6.373	6.047	5.749	5.475	5.222	4.990	4.775
18	7.702	7.250	6.840	6.467	6.128	5.818	5.534	5.273	5.033	4.812
19	7.839	7.366	6.938	6.550	6.198	5.877	5.585	5.316	5.070	4.843
20	7.963	7.469	7.025	6.623	6.259	5.929	5.628	5.353	5.101	4.870
21	8.075	7.562	7.102	6.687	6.312	5.973	5.665	5.384	5.127	4.891
22	8.176	7.645	7.170	6.743	6.359	6.011	5.696	5.410	5.149	4.909
23	8.266	7.718	7.230	6.792	6.399	6.044	5.723	5.432	5.167	4.925
24	8.348	7.784	7.283	6.835	6.434	6.073	5.747	5.451	5.182	4.937
25	8.442	7.843	7.330	6.873	6.464	6.097	5.766	5.467	5.195	4.948
30	8.694	8.055	7.496	7.003	6.566	6.177	5.829	5.517	5.235	4.979
40	8.951	8.244	7.634	7.105	6.642	6.233	5.871	5.548	5.258	4.997
50	9.042	8.305	7.675	7.133	6.661	6.246	5.880	5.554	5.262	4.999

APPENDIX D   Present value of an annuity of $1 for *n* periods

n	21%	22%	23%	24%	25%	26%	27%	28%	29%	30%
1	0.826	0.820	0.813	0.806	0.800	0.794	0.787	0.781	0.775	0.769
2	1.509	1.492	1.474	1.457	1.440	1.424	1.407	1.392	1.376	1.361
3	2.074	2.042	2.011	1.981	1.952	1.923	1.896	1.868	1.842	1.816
4	2.540	2.494	2.448	2.404	2.362	2.320	2.280	2.241	2.203	2.166
5	2.926	2.864	2.803	2.745	2.689	2.635	2.583	2.532	2.483	2.436
6	3.245	3.167	3.092	3.020	2.951	2.885	2.821	2.759	2.700	2.643
7	3.508	3.416	3.327	3.242	3.161	3.083	3.009	2.937	2.868	2.802
8	3.726	3.619	3.518	3.421	3.329	3.241	3.156	3.076	2.999	2.925
9	3.905	3.786	3.673	3.566	3.463	3.366	3.273	3.184	3.100	3.019
10	4.054	3.923	3.799	3.682	3.570	3.465	3.364	3.269	3.178	3.092
11	4.177	4.035	3.902	3.776	3.656	3.544	3.437	3.335	3.239	3.147
12	4.278	4.127	3.985	3.851	3.725	3.606	3.493	3.387	3.286	3.190
13	4.362	4.203	4.053	3.912	3.780	3.656	3.538	3.427	3.322	3.223
14	4.432	4.265	4.108	3.962	3.824	3.695	3.573	3.459	3.351	3.249
15	4.489	4.315	4.153	4.001	3.859	3.726	3.601	3.483	3.373	3.268
16	4.536	4.357	4.189	4.033	3.887	3.751	3.623	3.503	3.390	3.283
17	4.576	4.391	4.219	4.059	3.910	3.771	3.640	3.518	3.403	3.295
18	4.608	4.419	4.243	4.080	3.928	3.786	3.654	3.529	3.413	3.304
19	4.635	4.442	4.263	4.097	3.942	3.799	3.664	3.539	3.421	3.311
20	4.657	4.460	4.279	4.110	3.954	3.808	3.673	3.546	3.427	3.316
21	4.675	4.476	4.292	4.121	3.963	3.816	3.679	3.551	3.432	3.320
22	4.690	4.488	4.302	4.130	3.970	3.822	3.684	3.556	3.436	3.323
23	4.703	4.499	4.311	4.137	3.976	3.827	3.689	3.559	3.438	3.325
24	4.713	4.507	4.318	4.143	3.981	3.831	3.692	3.562	3.441	3.327
25	4.721	4.514	4.323	4.147	3.985	3.834	3.694	3.564	3.442	3.329
30	4.746	4.534	4.339	4.160	3.995	3.842	3.701	3.569	3.447	3.332
40	4.760	4.544	4.347	4.166	3.999	3.846	3.703	3.571	3.448	3.333
50	4.762	4.545	4.348	4.167	4.000	3.846	3.704	3.571	3.448	3.333

n	31%	32%	33%	34%	35%	36%	37%	38%	39%	40%
1	0.763	0.758	0.752	0.746	0.741	0.735	0.730	0.725	0.719	0.714
2	1.346	1.331	1.317	1.303	1.289	1.276	1.263	1.250	1.237	1.224
3	1.791	1.766	1.742	1.719	1.696	1.673	1.652	1.630	1.609	1.589
4	2.130	2.096	2.062	2.029	1.997	1.966	1.935	1.906	1.877	1.849
5	2.390	2.345	2.302	2.260	2.220	2.181	2.143	2.106	2.070	2.035
6	2.588	2.534	2.483	2.433	2.385	2.339	2.294	2.251	2.209	2.168
7	2.739	2.677	2.619	2.562	2.508	2.455	2.404	2.355	2.308	2.263
8	2.854	2.786	2.721	2.658	2.598	2.540	2.485	2.432	2.380	2.331
9	2.942	2.868	2.798	2.730	2.665	2.603	2.544	2.487	2.432	2.379
10	3.009	2.930	2.855	2.784	2.715	2.649	2.587	2.527	2.469	2.414
11	3.060	2.978	2.899	2.824	2.752	2.683	2.618	2.555	2.496	2.438
12	3.100	3.013	2.931	2.853	2.779	2.708	2.641	2.576	2.515	2.456
13	3.129	3.040	2.956	2.876	2.799	2.727	2.658	2.592	2.529	2.469
14	3.152	3.061	2.974	2.892	2.814	2.740	2.670	2.603	2.539	2.477
15	3.170	3.076	2.988	2.905	2.825	2.750	2.679	2.611	2.546	2.484
16	3.183	3.088	2.999	2.914	2.834	2.757	2.685	2.616	2.551	2.489
17	3.193	3.097	3.007	2.921	2.840	2.763	2.690	2.621	2.555	2.492
18	3.201	3.104	3.012	2.926	2.844	2.767	2.693	2.624	2.557	2.494
19	3.207	3.109	3.017	2.930	2.848	2.770	2.696	2.626	2.559	2.496
20	3.211	3.113	3.020	2.933	2.850	2.772	2.698	2.627	2.561	2.497
21	3.215	3.116	3.023	2.935	2.852	2.773	2.699	2.629	2.562	2.498
22	3.217	3.118	3.025	2.936	2.853	2.775	2.700	2.629	2.562	2.498
23	3.219	3.120	3.026	2.938	2.854	2.775	2.701	2.630	2.563	2.499
24	3.221	3.121	3.027	2.939	2.855	2.776	2.701	2.630	2.563	2.499
25	3.222	3.122	3.028	2.939	2.856	2.776	2.702	2.631	2.563	2.499
30	3.225	2.124	3.030	2.941	2.857	2.777	2.702	2.631	2.564	2.500
40	3.226	3.125	3.030	2.941	2.857	2.778	2.703	2.632	2.564	2.500
50	3.226	3.125	3.030	2.941	2.857	2.778	2.703	2.632	2.564	2.500

accounting rate of return (AROR) A capital-budgeting criterion that relates the returns generated by the project, as measured by average accounting profits, to the average dollar size of the investment required.

acid-test ratio (current assets minus inventories) divided by current liabilities; also known as a 'quick ratio'.

acquisition See **takeover**.

agency costs The costs, such as a reduced share price, associated with potential conflict between managers and investors when these two groups are not the same.

agency problem Problem resulting from conflicts of interest between the manager (the shareholder's agent) and the shareholders.

All Ordinaries Index An index number representing the average value of shares on the Australian Securities Exchange. The change in the index number between two dates represents the average rate of return during that time interval (excluding dividends, the effect of which is incorporated into the All Ordinaries Accumulation Index).

annuity A series of equal dollar payments for a specified number of periods.

annuity due An annuity where payments are made at the beginning of each period.

appraisal value The worth of a company as determined by an independent appraiser. Appraisers use a variety of methods to determine the value of a firm; however, replacement value of the firm's assets is often the basis for the appraisal value.

arbitrageur A person involved in the process of buying and selling in more than one market to make riskless profits.

asset allocation Identifying and selecting the asset classes appropriate for a specific investment portfolio and determining the proportions of these assets within the given portfolio.

average-collection-period ratio Provides a basis for determining how rapidly the firm's accounts are being collected; alternatively, the 'accounts receivable turnover ratio'.

balance-sheet leverage ratios Financial ratios used to measure the extent of a firm's use of borrowed funds, calculated using information found in the firm's balance sheet.

balloon payment A final lump-sum payment to discharge a debt, such as the residual value of a finance lease.

bank bill A commercial bill that has been either accepted or endorsed by a bank.

bank overdraft A form of bank lending where the bank allows a customer to borrow money by making payments in excess of the amount that the customer has on deposit in the account.

basis risk Risk associated with imperfect hedging that arises because the asset underlying the futures contract is not identical to the asset that underlies the firm's risk exposure.

beta The relationship between an investment's returns and the market returns. This is a relative measure of the investment's non-diversifiable risk.

bid–ask spread The difference between the ask quote and the bid quote.

bill of exchange A short-term financial instrument requiring the face value to be repaid on demand or at a specified date.

bond A long-term debt security issued by the borrower, promising to pay the owner of the security a predetermined amount of interest each year. Examples include debentures and unsecured notes.

bond rating An assessment, carried out by an organisation called a *ratings agency*, of the likelihood of default by the issuer of the bond.

bonus share issue A distribution of bonus shares.

bonus share plan A plan arranged by a company under which shareholders forgo cash dividends in exchange for fully paid bonus shares in the company, usually at a discount below the market price of the company's shares.

bonus shares Shares issued free to shareholders in proportion to existing holdings.

book value The value of an item in a firm's balance sheet. For a non-current asset, this is the depreciated value of a company's assets (original cost less accumulated depreciation).

break-even analysis An analytical technique used to determine the quantity of output or sales that results in a zero level of earnings before interest and taxes (EBIT). Also, the relationships between the firm's cost structure, volume of output and EBIT are studied.

budget A written forecast of future events designed as an aid to planning and controlling operations and/or financial management.

building societies and credit unions Authorised deposit-taking institutions that provide banking services to their members.

business risk The relative dispersion or variability in the firm's expected earnings before interest and taxes (EBIT). The nature of the firm's operations causes its business risk. This type of risk is affected by the firm's cost structure, product demand characteristics and intra-industry competitive position. In capital-structure theory, business risk is distinguished from financial risk. See also **financial risk**.

call option A contract that gives its holder the right to purchase an asset at a specified price over a given time period.

capital asset pricing model (CAPM) An equation stating that the expected rate of return on an investment is a function of (1) the risk-free rate, (2) the investment's systematic risk, and (3) the expected risk premium in the market.

capital budgeting The decision-making process with respect to investment in fixed assets. Specifically it involves measuring the incremental cash flows associated with investment proposals and evaluating the worth of these cash flows.

capital-expenditure budget Detailed plans by a firm for acquiring plant and equipment over a five-year, 10-year or even longer period. See also **budget**.

capital gain A capital gain occurs when the sale price minus the purchase price is positive.

capital loss A capital loss occurs when the sale price minus the purchase price is negative.

capital market All institutions and procedures that facilitate transactions in long-term financial instruments.

capital rationing The placing of a limit by the firm on the amount of money for its capital budget, or the tightening of restrictions on the capital budget of the firm by placing limits on the amount of money for investment or by raising the required hurdle rate of return.

capital structure The mix of long-term sources of debt and equity finance used by the firm.

cash The currency and coin the firm has on hand in petty cash, cash registers or cheque accounts.

cash break-even analysis Another version of break-even analysis that includes only the cash costs of production within the cost components. This means that non-cash expenses, such as depreciation, are omitted in the analysis.

cash budget A detailed plan of future cash flows. This budget is composed of four elements: cash receipts, cash disbursements, net change in cash for the period, and new financing needed. See also **budget**.

certainty equivalent The amount of cash a person would require with certainty to make him or her indifferent to the choice between this certain sum and a particular risky or uncertain sum.

characteristic line The line of 'best fit' through a series of returns for a firm's shares relative to the market returns. The slope of the line, frequently called beta, represents the average movement of the firm's share returns in response to a movement in the market's returns.

chop-shop or break-up value Estimated by determining the value of the different business segments of the firm. Segment value is computed by applying average valuation ratios of pure play companies to the various business segments of the firm. Firm value is then calculated as the sum of the segment values.

classical tax system A tax system applying to companies and their shareholders, where the net income of the company is taxed twice—first at the company level and then again when dividends are received by the shareholders.

clientele effect The belief that individuals and institutions that need current income will invest in companies that have high dividend payouts. Other investors prefer to hold securities that offer only small dividend income but large capital gains. Thus, there is a 'clientele' of investors.

commercial banks Financial institutions that accept deposits, make loans and provide other financial services to the public.

commodity futures A contract to buy or sell a stated commodity such as wheat, corn or metals at a specified price and at a specified future date on an organised exchange.

common-size financial statements Financial statements that have been converted to a percentage of either sales in the case of the income statement or total assets in the case of the balance sheet. The information within the common-size statements is standardised and consequently can be used to compare firms of very different sizes.

company An entity that *legally* functions separately and apart from its owners.

company-unique risk The risk component that can be eliminated by diversification. Company-unique risk is also known as 'firm-specific' or 'diversifiable' or 'unsystematic' risk.

compound interest The situation in which interest paid on the investment during the first period is added to the principal,

and during the second period interest is earned on the original principal plus the interest earned during the first period.

constant dividend payout ratio A dividend payment policy in which the percentage of earnings paid out in dividends is held constant. The dollar amount fluctuates from year to year as profits vary.

contractual interest rate See **coupon interest rate**.

contribution margin The difference between a product's selling price and its unit variable costs. It is usually measured on a per-unit basis.

conversion premium The price paid by purchasers of a convertible security for the option to convert to shares. See also **security value** and **conversion value**.

conversion value The value of the shares for which a convertible security can be exchanged. See **security value** and **conversion premium**.

convertible securities Debt or preference shares that can be converted to ordinary shares by the holder subject to specified conditions.

correlation coefficient A standardised measure of covariance. While covariance can theoretically take on any value, the correlation coefficient takes on values between –1 and 1.

cost budgets Budgets prepared for every major expense category of the firm, such as production cost, selling cost, administrative cost, financing cost, and research and development cost.

cost of capital The rate that must be earned in order to satisfy the required rate of return of the firm's investors. It may also be defined as the rate of return on investments at which the price of the firm's ordinary shares will remain unchanged. The cost of capital is based on the opportunity cost of funds as determined in the capital markets.

cost of debt The rate that has to be received from an investment in order to achieve the required rate of return for the creditors. The cost is based on the debt-holders' opportunity cost of debt in the capital markets.

cost of ordinary shares The rate of return the firm must earn in order for the ordinary shareholders to receive their required rate of return. The rate is based on the opportunity costs of funds for the ordinary shareholders in the capital markets.

cost of preference shares The rate of return that must be earned on the preference shareholders' investment to satisfy their required rate of return. The cost is based on the preference shareholders' opportunity cost of preference shares in the capital markets.

coupon interest rate The cash flow to be regularly paid to the bondholder as coupon interest payments, expressed as a percentage of par value.

covariance The statistical measure of the degree of co-movement between two asset returns. It essentially measures the tendency of the two stocks to 'co-vary'. A positive covariance between two stock returns suggests that as one return goes up the other tends to go up as well, and vice versa.

coverage ratios A group of ratios that measure a firm's ability to meet its recurring fixed-charge obligations, such as interest on long-term debt, lease payments and/or preference-share dividends.

covered interest arbitrage Arbitrage designed to eliminate differentials across currency and interest-rate markets.

credit scoring The numerical evaluation of credit applicants, where the score is evaluated relative to a predetermined standard.

credit unions See **building societies and credit unions**.

cum-dividend Indicates that the price paid for the purchase of a share includes the entitlement to receive a dividend declared by the company. See also **ex-dividend**.

cum-rights price The price paid for the purchase of an ordinary share which includes the right to subscribe for an announced new share issue. See also **right**.

cumulative feature A requirement that all past unpaid preference-share dividends can be paid before any ordinary-share dividends are declared.

currency swap An exchange of debt obligations in different currencies.

current assets All the assets the firm expects to convert into cash within 12 months.

current liabilities All the liabilities the firm expects to pay within 12 months.

current ratio Current assets divided by current liabilities; a ratio that indicates a firm's degree of liquidity by comparing its current assets with its current liabilities.

date of record Date at which company books are to be closed for determining the investors to receive the next dividend payment. See also **ex-dividend date**.

debt capacity The maximum proportion of debt that the firm can include in its capital structure and still maintain its lowest weighted average cost of capital.

debt ratio Total liabilities divided by total assets; a ratio that measures the extent to which a firm has been financed with debt.

default risk The possibility that the borrower will not repay a debt in the future.

degree of combined leverage The percentage change in earnings per share caused by a percentage change in sales. It is the product of the degree of operating leverage and the degree of financial leverage.

delivery-time stock The inventory needed between the order date and the receipt of the inventory ordered.

depreciation The means by which an asset's cost is expensed over its useful life.

derivative A financial instrument that is derived from or based on the value of an underlying asset.

differential cash flows See **incremental cash flows**.

dilution Any action of a company that results in a reduction of ordinary shareholder interests. For example, if new shares are issued by a company but are not made available to current shareholders, their proportionate ownership of the company will be reduced or diluted.

direct exchange-rate rate The exchange rate that indicates the number of units of the home currency required to buy one unit of a foreign currency.

direct foreign investment A physical investment, such as an investment in a building or factory, which a company makes in a foreign country.

direct investment Investment directly in plant and equipment.

discount factor The quantity that converts a particular future sum of money to its present value.

discount rate The interest rate that converts a future value to the present value.

discounted-cash-flow criteria Capital-budgeting decision-making criteria that are based on the time value of money. See also **internal rate of return**, **net present value**, **profitability index**.

discounted payback period An estimate of the time required for the discounted future cash flows of a project to recoup the initial outlay.

discounting The process of converting a future value to its present value.

discretionary sources of financing The sources of financing that require an explicit decision on the part of the firm's management every time funds are raised.

disposal value See **liquidation value**.

dividend franking account A company account required under tax legislation to record dividend franking credits and debits made by the company. It does not form part of the company's accounting system.

dividend imputation system A tax system applying to companies and their shareholders, where the net income of the company is imputed to the shareholders and taxed at their marginal rate. Although company income is taxed twice—first at the company level and then again when dividends are received by the shareholders—the shareholders receive a credit for the income tax paid by the company.

dividend payout ratio The amount of dividends relative to the company's net income or earnings per share.

dividend reinvestment plan (DRP) A plan arranged by a company under which shareholders forgo cash dividends in exchange for the purchase of fully paid shares in the company, usually at a discount below the market price.

dividend yield The dividend per share divided by the price of the security.

earnings per share (EPS) Earnings per share are equal to net profit (after tax) divided by the number of ordinary shares.

EBIT Common financial notation for 'earnings before interest and taxes'.

EBIT–EPS indifference point The level of earnings before interest and taxes (EBIT) that will equate earnings per share (EPS) between two different financing plans.

economic exposure Long-term changes in the value of the firm as a result of exchange-rate fluctuations.

economies of scale Economies achieved by spreading fixed costs over a larger volume of output, thus reducing the average cost per unit.

effective annual interest rate The effective annual rate, Eff, is the rate obtained by compounding a nominal rate i, m times per year.

efficiency ratio Ratio that provides a basis for assessing how effectively a firm is using its resources to generate sales.

efficient market A market in which the values of all assets and securities at any instant in time fully reflect all available information.

efficient markets hypothesis (EMH) The EMH states that securities prices accurately reflect future expected cash flows and are based on all information available to investors.

efficient portfolios Portfolios with a higher level of return for the same level of risk, or a lower level of risk for the same level of return.

EPS Typical financial notation for 'earnings per share'.

equivalent annual annuity (EAA) An annual annuity amount that yields the same present value as the project's NPV. The annual annuity amount is calculated by dividing the project's NPV by the appropriate $PVIFA_{i\%, n\,yr}$, or by solving for PMT.

equivalent interest rates Interest rates that have the same effective annual rate.

eurobond A bond issued in a country other than the country of the bond's currency.

eurocurrency Currency deposited in or borrowed from a financial market outside the country of the currency's origin.

euromarkets Financial markets involving currencies that are held outside their country of origin.

exchange rate The rate at which one currency can be exchanged (bought/sold) for another.

exchange-rate risk The variability of future cash flows caused by variations in exchange rates.

exchange-traded fund An investment vehicle traded on stock exchanges much like a share or stock. The entity holds investments in assets that meet the investment objective of the entity.

exchange-traded instruments Financial instruments that are bought and sold through an organised exchange.

ex-dividend Indicates that a share carries no right to a recently declared dividend. See also **cum-dividend**.

expectations theory The belief that the market price of ordinary shares is affected by investors' expectations about management decisions.

expected rate of return The arithmetic mean or average of all possible outcomes where each outcome is weighted by its probability.

expected rate of return (bondholder) The discount rate that equates the present value of the future cash flows with the current market price of the bond.

explicit cost of debt The actual cost incurred by using debt funds.

ex-rights date The date on or after which the share sells without rights.

ex-rights price The price paid for the purchase of an ordinary share which excludes the right to subscribe to a new share issue that has recently closed.

external funds Funds raised from outside sources, such as from a bond issue or an equity issue.

factoring accounts receivable The outright sale of a firm's accounts receivable to another party (the factor) who in turn bears the risk of collection.

family issue Offer of new securities to the firm's existing security holders.

finance lease A non-cancellable contractual commitment on the part of the firm leasing the asset (the lessee) to make a series of payments to the firm that actually owns the asset (the lessor) for the use of the asset.

financial analysis The assessment of a firm's financial condition or well-being. Its objectives are to determine the firm's financial strengths and to identify its weaknesses. The primary tool of financial analysis is the financial ratio.

financial asset A non-tangible asset that entitles the holders to receive a set of cash flows in the future.

financial futures A contract to buy or sell a financial asset such as treasury securities, certificates of deposit, foreign currencies or stock indices at a specified price at a specified future time on an organised exchange.

financial intermediary An institution whose business is to bring together individuals and institutions with money to invest or lend with other firms or individuals that need money.

financial leverage The use of securities to finance a portion of the firm's assets that pay investors a fixed (limited) rate of return. Financial leverage can arise from the use of either debt or preference-share financing. The use of financial leverage exposes the firm to financial risk.

financial markets Institutions and procedures that facilitate the transfer of funds between financial and non-financial institutions and businesses.

financial risk The added variability in earnings available to the firm's ordinary shareholders and the added chance of insolvency caused by the use in the firm's financial structure of securities bearing a limited rate of return. The use of financial leverage gives rise to financial risk.

financial structure The mix of all the short- and long-term sources of finance that appear on the firm's balance sheet.

financial-structure design The mixture of short-term and long-term permanent financing components to minimise the cost of raising a given amount of funds.

fixed-asset turnover ratio Sales divided by fixed assets; a ratio indicating how effectively a firm is using its fixed assets to generate sales.

fixed budget Future budget estimates based on a single level of production or sales/revenue. See also **budget**.

fixed costs Charges that do *not* vary in total amount as sales volume or the quantity of output changes over some relevant range of output. Also referred to as 'indirect costs'.

flexible budget Various future budget estimates based on a range of levels of production or sales/revenue. See also **budget**.

float See **flotation**.

floating charge Legal agreement for the general assets of the borrower to be used as security for a loan.

flotation The first public issue of shares and/or debt by a company. Can be contrasted with secondary or subsequent issues.

flotation (issue) costs The underwriter's spread and issuing costs associated with the issuance and marketing of new securities.

foreign exchange market The market in which the currencies of various countries are traded.

formal control Control vested in the shareholders having the majority of the voting ordinary shares.

forward exchange contract A contract that requires the delivery of one currency at a specified future date for a specified amount of another currency.

forward spot differential A premium or discount calculated as the difference between the forward rate and the spot rate.

franking balance The balance in the dividend franking account which determines the extent to which the company's dividends can be franked.

franking debits Reductions made in a company's dividend franking account when franked dividends are paid, and by other items.

franking (imputation) credits An amount of income tax paid by the company that is credited to shareholders when they receive company dividends and which can be used by the shareholders to offset income tax levied on the grossed-up dividend amount imputed to them.

functional control Control exercised by the corporate officers in conducting the daily operations.

funds statement A basic accounting statement identifying how the firm acquired its funds for the period and what it did with those funds; also known as the 'statement of changes in financial position'.

future value interest factor The factor $FVIF_{i,n}$ that converts \$1 to its future value in n periods time at $i\%$ compound interest per period. To determine the future value of, say, \$100, the factor is multiplied by 100.

future value interest factor for an annuity The factor $FVIFA_{i,n}$ that converts a payment of \$1 per period (at the end of the period) to its future value in n periods of time at $i\%$ compound interest per period. To determine the future value of a payment of, say, \$100, the factor is multiplied by 100.

futures contract Legally binding agreement to buy or sell a stated commodity or financial instrument at a specified price at some future specified time on an organised exchange.

futures margin 'Good faith' money the parties to a futures contract put down to ensure that the contract will be carried out.

general annuity An annuity that features a payment frequency that differs from the interest-compounding frequency.

general purpose financial reports The income statement (profit and loss statement), balance sheet and statement of cash flows required to be published under Australian accounting standards.

going-concern value The amount realised if the entire firm is sold as a going concern rather than on the basis of liquidating its assets.

gross profit margin Gross profit divided by net sales; a ratio denoting the gross profit of the firm as a percentage of net sales.

hedge fund An investment fund which is open to a limited range of investors and which can undertake a wider range of investment and trading activities than a mutual fund.

hedging A strategy designed to minimise exposure to unwanted risk by taking a position in one market that offsets exposure to price fluctuations in an opposite position in another market.

hedging principle A working-capital management policy which states that the cash-flow-generating characteristics of a firm's investments should be matched with the cash-flow

requirements of the firm's sources of financing. Very simply, short-lived assets should be financed with short-term sources of financing, while long-lived assets should be financed with long-term sources of financing.

historical return The observed return earned on an investment in the past.

holding-period return The return an investor would receive from holding a security for a designated period of time. For example, a monthly holding-period return would be the return for holding a security during a particular month.

hybrid finance Finance provided by securities issued by companies that have characteristics of both debt and equity. They comprise preference shares andconvertible securities.

implicit cost of debt The change in the cost of ordinary equity brought on by using financial leverage.

incremental cash flows The cash flows that occur only from the acceptance of a capital-budgeting project. The test to determine if a cash flow is *not* incremental is that it will exist both if a project goes ahead and if it does not go ahead (the 'with/without test').

indifference point The level of earnings before interest and taxes (EBIT) that will equate earnings per share (EPS) between two financing plans with different degrees of financial leverage.

indirect exchange-rate rate The exchange rate that indicates the number of units of the foreign currency required to buy one unit of home currency.

information asymmetry The difference in accessibility to information between managers and investors, which may result in a lower share price than would be the case under conditions of certainty.

initial outlay Any cash-flow amount that occurs at or very near to the start of the first period of the project.

initial public offering (IPO) The first time the company's stock is sold to the public.

insolvency The situation in which a firm is unable to meet its maturing liabilities on time.

interest-rate parity theory Proposes that (except for the effect of small transaction costs) the difference between the current spot rate and the forward exchange rate should reflect the differences in the national interest rates for securities of the same maturity.

interest-rate risk The uncertainty surrounding expected returns on a security, brought about by changes in interest rates.

interest-rate swap Derivative instrument in which one party agrees to pay or receive a variable-rate interest stream and the other party agrees to a fixed-rate stream.

internal funds Funds generated within the company through retaining profits.

internal growth A firm's growth rate in earnings resulting from reinvesting company profits rather than distributing the earnings in the form of dividends. The growth rate is a function of the amount retained and the return earned on the retained funds.

internal rate of return (IRR) A capital-budgeting technique that reflects the rate of return a project earns. Mathematically it is the discount rate that equates the present value of the inflows with the present value of the outflows.

intrinsic value The present value of the investment's expected future cash flows, discounted at the investor's required rate of return.

intrinsic value of an option The payoff of an option to its holder if exercised immediately.

inventory loans Loans secured by inventory.

inventory management Involves the control of the assets that are produced to be sold in the normal course of the firm's operations.

inventory-turnover ratio Cost of goods sold divided by inventory; a ratio that measures the number of times a firm's inventories are sold and replaced during the year. This ratio reflects the relative liquidity of inventories.

law of one price The proposition that in competitive markets the same goods should sell for the same price where prices are stated in terms of a single currency.

leverage buyout funds Private equity funds that raise capital from investors and use those funds, along with significant amounts of debt, to acquire controlling interests in operating companies.

leverage ratios Ratios that provide a basis for determining how a firm finances its assets and the ability of the firm to pay for the non-owner-supplied funds.

limited liability Ordinarily, company shareholders are not liable for the debts of the company.

limited liability company (LLC) An organisational form that is a cross between a partnership and a corporation.

liquid assets Cash and marketable securities.

liquidation value The amount that could be realised if an asset were sold independently of the going concern.

liquidity A firm's ability to pay its bills on time. Liquidity is related to the ease and quickness with which a firm can convert its non-cash assets into cash, as well as the size of the firm's investment in non-cash assets vis-a-vis its short-term liabilities.

liquidity (of a security) Liquidity is related to the ease and quickness with which a firm can convert its marketable securities.

liquidity ratios Financial ratios used to assess the ability of a firm to pay its bills on time and to convert its accounts receivable and inventory into cash. Examples of liquidity ratios include the current ratio and the acid-test ratio.

loan amortisation schedule A breakdown of the interest and principal payments on an amortised loan.

long-term debt to total capitalisation ratio Long-term liabilities divided by the sum of all the permanent sources of finance used by a firm; indicates the extent to which a firm has used long-term debt in its permanent financing.

marginal cost of capital The cost of capital that represents the weighted cost of each additional dollar of financing from all sources—debt, preference shares and ordinary shares.

market risk The risk component that cannot be diversified away by holding more than one security in the portfolio. Market risk is also known as systematic risk or non-diversifiable risk and is measured by a factor labelled as *beta*.

market-traded Financial instruments that are bought and sold through an organised market.

market value The value observed in the marketplace, where buyers and sellers negotiate a mutually acceptable price for the asset.

market-value weights The percentage of financing provided by different capital sources, measured by the current market prices of the firm's securities.

marketable securities Security investments that the firm can quickly convert into cash balances.

marking to market The process of calculating and settling gains or losses on a futures position on a daily basis.

maturity date The date on which a borrower is to repay a loan.

merger Occurs when two firms combine to form a single entity.

money market All institutions and procedures that facilitate transactions in short-term financial instruments.

mortgage Legal agreement for a specified property to be security for a loan.

multinational corporation (MNC) A corporation with holdings and/or operations in one or more countries.

mutual fund A professionally managed investment company that pools the investments of many individuals and invests them in financial assets such as stocks, bonds and other types of securities.

mutually exclusive projects A menu of projects that perform essentially the same task, so that acceptance of one will necessarily mean rejection of the others.

negative pledge An agreement that the borrower will not undertake certain activities (e.g. incur any additional debt) which would reduce the unsecured lender's chance of being repaid.

net asset value The difference between the current market value of a fund's assets and the value of its liabilities.

net income (NI) approach to valuation The theory that both the firm's composite cost of capital and its ordinary share price are affected by the firm's degree of financial leverage. Also called the 'dependence hypothesis'.

net income available to ordinary equity Net income less preference dividends available to ordinary shareholders.

net operating income (NOI) approach to valuation The theory that the firm's composite cost of capital and ordinary share price are both independent of a firm's degree of financial leverage. Also called the 'independence hypothesis'.

net present value (NPV) A capital-budgeting concept defined as the present value of the project's annual net cash flows less the project's initial outlay.

net profit margin Net income divided by sales; a ratio that measures the net income of the firm as a percentage of sales.

net working capital The difference between the firm's current assets and its current liabilities.

nominal annual rate of interest The nominal annual rate j is a way of representing how interest is paid (or charged). If the rate j is paid m times per annum, the periodic rate paid is j/m. Alternatively, if a periodic rate i is paid m times per annum, the nominal annual rate is j. A nominal rate is sometimes known as the annual percentage rate (*APR*).

nominal interest rate The interest rate paid on debt securities without an adjustment for loss in purchasing power.

non-current-asset turnover ratio Sales divided by non-current assets; a ratio indicating how effectively a firm is using its non-current assets to generate sales.

official money market The segment of the short-term money market comprising dealers authorised to trade exclusively with the Reserve Bank.

operating income return on investment Ratio that reflects the rate of return on the firm's total investment before interest and taxes.

operating lease A contractual commitment on the part of the firm leasing the asset (the lessee) to make a series of payments to the firm that actually owns the asset (the lessor) for the use of the asset. An operating lease differs from a financial lease in that it can be cancelled at any time after proper notice has been given to the lessor.

operating leverage The responsiveness of the firm's earnings before interest and taxes to changes in revenue. This responsiveness arises from the proportion of the firm's operating costs that are fixed.

operating profit margin Net operating income divided by sales. This ratio serves as an overall measure of operating effectiveness.

opportunity cost of funds The next best rate of return available to the investor for a given level of risk.

optimal capital structure The range of various capital-structure combinations that yield the lowest overall weighted average cost of capital for the firm.

optimal range of financial leverage The range of various financial-structure combinations that generate the lowest composite cost of capital for the firm.

option contract Agreement that gives the holder the right, but not the obligation, to buy (or sell) a commodity or financial instrument at a specified price on or before a specified date. **option premium** The cost of the option.

option writing The process of selling put and/or call options.

ordinary annuity An annuity whose payments are made at the end of each period.

overdraft limit The maximum amount that a customer can borrow with a bank overdraft facility.

over-the-counter instruments Financial instruments that are privately arranged between two parties.

par value The face value of a debt security; the amount that the company is required to repay (redeem) at the end of the loan.

partnership An association of two or more individuals joining together as co-owners to operate a business for profit.

payback period A capital-budgeting criterion defined as the number of years required to recover the initial cash investment.

payment date The date on which the company mails dividend cheques to all investors.

percent-of-sales method A method of financial forecasting that involves estimating the amount of an expense, an asset or a liability for a future period as a percentage of the sales forecast.

permanent investments in assets These assets will not be liquidated or replaced within 12 months; in other words, they will be held for more than one year. Contrast with **temporary investments in assets**.

perpetuity An annuity with an infinite life.

physical budgets Budgets for unit sales, personnel, unit production, inventories and physical facilities. These budgets are used as the basis for generating cost and profit budgets.

placement See **private placement**.

pledging A loan that uses the firm's accounts receivable as collateral.

pooled development funds (PDFs) Investment companies formed subject to federal legislation to provide equity for small and medium-size companies with total assets of less than $50 million.

portfolio investment Investment in financial assets such as shares and bonds.

pre-emptive right The right entitling the ordinary shareholder to maintain his or her proportionate share of ownership in the firm.

preference shares Shares issued by companies which can be distinguished from ordinary shares by their characteristics such as a preferential right to the payment of dividends before other classes of shares including ordinary shares. Often they may have a preferential return of capital on the winding-up of a company.

preferred stock An equity security that holds preference over common stock in terms of the right to the distribution of dividends and the right to the distribution of proceeds in the event of the liquidation and sale of the issuing firm.

premium bond A bond selling at a price above (premium) par value.

present value The value in today's dollars of a future payment discounted back to the present at the required rate of return.

present value interest factor The factor $PVIF_{i,n}$ that converts (discounts) a future value to its present value, at a discount rate of i per period compound interest for n periods. For example, the present value of $200 is equal to the $PVIF_{i,n}$ factor multiplied by 200.

present value interest factor for an annuity The factor $PVIFA_{i,n}$ that converts an annuity payment of $1 per period for n periods to its present value, at i% compound interest per period. For example, the present value of an annuity of $160 per period is equal to the factor multiplied by 160.

price–earnings ratio (PE) The price the market places on $1 of a firm's earnings. For example, if a firm has an earnings per share of $2 and a share price of $30, its PE ratio is 15 ($30 ÷ 2).

primary market The segment of the financial markets in which securities are offered for sale for the first time.

private issue Offer of new securities to a select group of potential investors.

private placement The offer of financial securities directly to selected potential purchasers, in contrast to a public offering.

probability tree A schematic representation of a problem in which all possible outcomes are graphically displayed.

profit budget A budget of forecasted profits based on information gleaned from the cost and sales budgets. See also **budget**.

profit margins Financial ratios (sometimes referred to simply as margins) that reflect the level of a firm's profits relative to sales. Examples include the gross profit margin (gross profit divided by sales), operating profit margin (operating earnings divided by sales), and the net profit margin (net profit divided by sales).

profitability index (PI) A capital-budgeting criterion defined as the ratio of the present value of the future net cash flows to the initial outlay.

profitability ratios Ratios that provide a basis for determining how much of each sales dollar results in profits and how much profit is earned from the firm's assets.

pro-forma financial statements Statements of planned profit or loss, balance-sheet items or cash-flow items.

project's contribution-to-firm risk The risk that remains after part of a project's total risk is diversified away.

project's stand-alone risk The total risk of a project, ignoring the possibility that part of the risk can be diversified away.

promissory note A short-term financial instrument whereby the borrower (drawer) promises to repay the face value, at maturity, to the holder. Also known as **one-name paper** or, in some countries, **commercial paper**.

prospectus A document providing details by a company of a proposed new issue of shares or debt to the public. It requires approval by the Australian Securities and Investments Commission.

proxy A means of voting in which a designated party is provided with the temporary power of attorney to vote for the signer at the firm's annual meeting.

public offering or **issue** Offer of new securities to the public.

purchasing-power parity (PPP) theory In the long run, exchange rates adjust so that the purchasing power of each currency tends to remain the same. Thus, exchange-rate changes tend to reflect international differences in inflation rates. Countries with high rates of inflation tend to experience declines in the value of their currency.

pure play method A way of estimating a project's beta by identifying firms that are engaged in the same business as the project.

put option A contract that gives its holder the right to sell an asset at a specified price over a given time period.

quick ratio See **acid-test ratio**.

real assets Tangible assets such as houses, equipment and inventories. Real assets are distinguished from financial assets.

real interest rate The nominal rate of interest less any loss in purchasing power during the time of the investment.

real options Opportunities that allow for the alteration of the project's cash-flow stream while the project is being operated.

required rate of return (RRR) The minimum rate of return necessary to attract an investor to purchase or hold a security. (It is also the discount rate that equates the present value of the cash flows with the value of the security.)

residual-dividend theory A theory asserting that the dividends

to be paid should equal the equity capital left over after the financing of profitable investments.

residual net present value A modification of the conventional weighted cost-of-capital estimate. Rather than computing the present value of the expected cash flows of a project using the weighted cost of capital, the cash that will flow to the project owners after all debt-holders and preference shareholders have been paid is estimated. These residual flows are then discounted at the owners' required rate of return. Suited to the closely-held company.

residual value The final lump-sum or balloon payment on a finance lease.

restrictive covenants Provisions in the loan agreement that place restrictions on the borrower and make the loan immediately payable and due when violated. These restrictive covenants are designed to maintain the borrower's financial condition on a par with that which existed at the time the loan was made.

return-on-ordinary-equity ratio Net income available to the ordinary shareholders; a ratio relating income to the ordinary shareholder's investment.

return-on-total-assets ratio Net income divided by total assets. This ratio determines the yield on the firm's assets by relating net income to total assets; also called 'return-on-investment ratio'.

right An entitlement of an ordinary shareholder to purchase new ordinary shares in proportion to his or her present holding.

rights issue An issue of rights to existing shareholders.

risk The potential variability in future cash flows. It may be measured by the standard deviation of the expected return.

risk-adjusted discount rate A method for incorporating the project's level of risk into the capital-budgeting process, in which the discount rate is adjusted upward to compensate for higher-than-normal risk or downward to compensate for lower-than-normal risk.

risk aversion The tendency to avoid risk. Risk-averse investors like return but dislike risk.

risk premium The additional return expected for assuming risk.

safety stock The inventory held to accommodate any unusually large and unexpected usage during delivery time.

sale and leaseback arrangement An arrangement arising when a firm sells land, buildings or equipment that it already owns and simultaneously enters into an agreement to lease the property back for a specified period, under specific terms.

salvage value The value of an asset or investment project at the end of its useable life.

scenario analysis A technique that allows the financial manager to simultaneously consider the effects of changes in the estimates of multiple input variables on the NPV of an investment project.

secondary issue An issues of shares and/or debt by a company other than its first issue or flotation.

secondary market The segment of the financial markets in which existing securities are bought and sold.

security Agreement that gives the lender legal access to specific assets of the borrower if the borrower defaults on the loan payments.

security market line A graph of the capital asset pricing model; the return line that reflects the attitudes of investors regarding the minimal acceptable return for a given level of systematic risk (beta).

security value The term applied to a convertible security for the price it would sell for in the absence of its conversion feature. In the case of a convertible unsecured note, this would be the value of a similar non-convertible unsecured note. See also **conversion value** and **conversion premium**.

semivariable costs Charges that behave as variable costs over certain ranges of output and as fixed costs over other ranges of output. Also called 'semi-fixed costs'.

sensitivity analysis A technique for assessing risk—for example, the sensitivity of a project's NPV to changes in one or more of the factors that determine the NPV, such as the discount rate.

share buyback The repurchase by a company of a proportion of its ordinary shares from its present shareholders.

share-market value See **market value**.

share splits A reduction in the value of the existing shares of a company resulting in the distribution of free shares to current shareholders in proportion to their present holdings.

simple arbitrage Buying and selling in more than one market to make a riskless profit in a single currency.

simulation analysis The process of imitating the performance of an investment project through repeated evaluations, usually using a computer; in the general case, experimentation on a mathematical model that has been designed to capture the critical realities of the decision-making situation.

sinking fund A required annual payment that allows for the periodic retirement of debt.

size-disparity problem Occurs when projects of equal cash-flow timing patterns over the lives of the projects, but of unequal size, are evaluated.

skewed distribution A distribution that has a longer 'tail' to the right or left.

sole proprietorship A business owned by a single individual.

solvency declaration A signed statement by company directors that the company is solvent at a specified date (e.g. the date of a share buyback).

spontaneous sources of financing The trade credit and other accounts payable that arise 'spontaneously' in the firm's day-to-day operations.

spot transaction A transaction where delivery will occur immediately. For foreign exchange, this delivery is, by convention, two business days after the spot transaction is agreed to.

stable dollar dividend per share A dividend policy that maintains a relatively stable dollar dividend per share over time.

stags Investors who purchase new shares through a prospectus and sell on the first day that the shares are quoted by the stock exchange, in an attempt to make a profit.

standard deviation A statistical measure of the spread of a probability distribution. It can be used to give a measure of the riskiness of the possible returns from an investment in the future.

statement of changes in financial position See **funds statement**.

striking or exercise price The price at which the asset may be purchased from the option writer in the case of a call or sold to the option writer in the case of a put.

subscription price The price for which the security may be purchased in a rights offering.

sunk cost A past cash outflow or cost that is not incremental to a particular project.

systematic risk The proportion of variations in investment returns that cannot be eliminated through investor diversification. These variations result from factors that affect all shares. Systematic risk is also known as 'non-diversifiable risk' or 'market risk'.

takeover Occurs when one company acquires control of another company.

target capital structure A desired composition of fund sources in the firm's financial or capital structure.

tax savings A reduction in the amount of tax that is associated with a particular decision or action. A negative tax saving occurs when a particular decision or action results in an increase in the amount of tax.

tax shield The reduction in income tax due to the tax deduction allowed to businesses for interest paid on debt capital.

temporary investments in assets Investments in assets that the firm plans to sell (liquidate) within a period no longer than one year. Although temporary investments can be made in fixed assets, this is not the usual case. Temporary investments generally are made in inventories and receivables.

term loans Loans that often have maturities of one to ten years and are repaid in periodic instalments over the life of the loan. Term loans are usually secured by a chattel mortgage on equipment or a mortgage on real property.

term structure of interest rates The relationship between interest rates and the term to maturity, where the risk of default is held constant.

terminal cash flow Any cash flow amount that occurs only at or very near to the final period of the project.

terms of sale Identifies the possible discount for early payment of an account together with the discount period and the total credit period.

time-disparity problem Arises when two projects of equal size have significantly different cash-flow timing patterns over their lives.

time matching concept. See **hedging principle**.

time value of an option The extent to which the option premium exceeds the intrinsic value.

times-interest-earned ratio Earnings before interest and taxes (EBIT) divided by interest expense; a ratio that measures the firm's ability to meet its interest payments from its annual operating earnings.

total-asset turnover ratio Sales divided by total tangible assets; an overall measure of the relation between the firm's tangible assets and the sales they generate.

'total resources' concept A concept of funds, meaning cash and cash equivalents (credit or barter), arising from or used in a firm's transactions with external parties.

trade credit Credit made available by a firm's suppliers in connection with the acquisition of materials. Trade credit appears on the balance sheet as accounts payable.

transaction exposure The net contracted foreign-currency transactions for which the settlement amounts are subject to changing exchange rates.

transfer price The price used within a firm to value the transfer of goods and services between subdivisions.

translation exposure Arises because the foreign operation of a domestic business has its accounting statements denominated in the currency of the country in which the operation is located.

trend analysis An analysis of a firm's financial ratios over time.

triangular arbitrage Arbitrage across the markets for all currencies.

trust deed A document that sets out the rights and responsibilities of the parties to a trust.

underwriting The purchase and subsequent resale by an underwriter of new securities that have not been taken up by the public by the closing date of the issue.

undiversifiable risk The portion of the variation in investment returns that cannot be eliminated through investor diversification.

unofficial money market The segment of the short-term money market comprising all dealers who are not authorised dealers.

unsystematic risk (firm-specific risk or unique risk) The portion of the variation in investment returns that can be eliminated through investor diversification. These variations result from factors that are unique to the particular firm.

value of a bond The present value of the interest payments I in period t, plus the present value of the redemption or par value of the indebtedness, M, at the maturity date.

value of a security The present value of all future cash inflows expected to be received by the investor owning the security.

variable costs Costs that vary in total as sales volume or quantity of output changes. Also known as 'direct costs'.

venture capital Public or private funds from sources other than the official share market provided to actual or possible high-growth projects or firms with risky but potentially high-reward possibilities.

weighted average cost of capital A composite of the individual costs of financing incurred by each capital source. A firm's weighted cost of capital is a function of (1) the individual costs of capital, and (2) the capital-structure mix.

weighted marginal cost of capital The composite cost for each additional dollar of financing. The marginal cost of capital represents the appropriate criterion for making investment decisions.

working capital A concept traditionally defined as a firm's investment in current assets.

yield curve A graphical representation of the term structure of interest rates.

yield to maturity The annual rate of return the investor will earn if a bond is held to maturity.